DICTIONARY OF
NURSING

second edition

A & C Black • London

First edition published in 2003 by
Bloomsbury Publishing Plc.

This second edition published 2007 by
A&C Black Publishers Ltd
38 Soho Square, London W1D 3HB

A CIP record for this book is available from the British Library

ISBN: 978 0 7136 8287 8

Text Production and Proofreading
Joel Adams, Sandra Anderson, Heather Bateman, Emma Djonokusumo,
Ruth Hillmore, Daisy Jackson, Irene Lakhani, Sarah Lusznat,
Katy McAdam, Howard Sargeant

This book is produced using paper that is made from wood grown in
managed, sustainable forests. It is natural, renewable and recyclable. The
logging and manufacturing processes conform to the environmental
regulations of the country of origin.

Text processed and typeset by A&C Black
Printed in Spain by GraphyCems

Preface

This fully-updated dictionary provides the user with a complete guide to the vocabulary in current use by nurses and other health care professionals.

Over 11,000 terms are explained in clear, straightforward English. Areas covered include diseases and conditions, instruments, drugs, treatments and patient care, as well as medical specialisations such as surgery, psychiatry and physiotherapy. Many informal and everyday terms used by patients in describing their condition are also included.

A useful supplement also contains a guide to anatomical terms, illustrated with clear and simple diagrams.

Thanks are due to Glenda Cornwell, Rosemary Cook, Stephen Curtis, Fiona McIntosh, Lynn Davy and Dinah Jackson for their advice on the first edition of this text, and to Kathryn Jones for her helpful comments during the production of this second edition.

Publishers' Note:

While every effort has been made to be as accurate as possible, the author, advisors, editors and publishers of this book cannot be held liable for any errors and omissions, or actions that may be taken as a consequence of using it.

Pronunciation

The following symbols have been used to show the pronunciation of the main words in the dictionary.

Stress is indicated by a main stress mark (') and a secondary stress mark (ˌ). Note that these are only guides, as the stress of the word changes according to its position in the sentence.

Vowels		*Consonants*	
æ	back	b	buck
ɑː	harm	d	dead
ɒ	stop	ð	other
aɪ	type	dʒ	jump
aʊ	how	f	fare
aɪə	hire	g	gold
aʊə	hour	h	head
ɔː	course	j	yellow
ɔɪ	annoy	k	cab
e	head	l	leave
eə	fair	m	mix
eɪ	make	n	nil
eʊ	go	ŋ	sing
ɜː	word	p	print
iː	keep	r	rest
i	happy	s	save
ə	about	ʃ	shop
ɪ	fit	t	take
ɪə	near	tʃ	change
u	annual	θ	theft
uː	pool	v	value
ʊ	book	w	work
ʊə	tour	x	loch
ʌ	shut	ʒ	measure
		z	zone

A

AA *abbreviation* Alcoholics Anonymous

A & E /ˌeɪ ənd ˈiː/, **A & E department** /ˌeɪ ənd ˈiː dɪˌpɑːtmənt/ *noun* same as **accident and emergency department**

A & E medicine /ˌeɪ ənd ˈiː ˌmed(ə)sɪn/ *noun* the medical procedures used in A & E departments

ab- /æb/ *prefix* away from

ABC /ˌeɪ biː ˈsiː/ *noun* the basic initial checks of a casualty's condition. Full form **airway, breathing and circulation**

abdomen /ˈæbdəmən/ *noun* a space inside the body below the diaphragm, above the pelvis and in front of the spine, containing the stomach, intestines, liver and other vital organs ○ *pain in the abdomen* (NOTE: For other terms referring to the abdomen, see words beginning with **coeli-, coelio-**.)

abdomin- /æbdɒmɪn/ *prefix* same as **abdomino-** (*used before vowels*)

abdominal /æbˈdɒmɪn(ə)l/ *adjective* located in the abdomen, or relating to the abdomen

abdominal aorta /æbˌdɒmɪn(ə)l eɪˈɔːtə/ *noun* the part of the aorta which lies between the diaphragm and the point where the aorta divides into the iliac arteries. See illustration at **KIDNEY** in Supplement

abdominal cavity /æbˌdɒmɪn(ə)l ˈkævɪti/ *noun* the space in the body below the chest

abdominal pain /æbˈdɒmɪn(ə)l peɪn/ *noun* pain in the abdomen caused by indigestion or more serious disorders

abdominal viscera /æbˌdɒmɪn(ə)l ˈvɪsərə/ *plural noun* the organs which are contained in the abdomen, e.g. the stomach, liver and intestines

abdominal wall /æbˈdɒmɪn(ə)l wɔːl/ *noun* muscular tissue which surrounds the abdomen

abdomino- /æbdɒmɪnəʊ/ *prefix* referring to the abdomen

abdominopelvic /æbˌdɒmɪnəʊˈpelvɪk/ *adjective* referring to the abdomen and pelvis

abdominoperineal /æbˌdɒmɪnəʊperɪˈniːəl/ *adjective* referring to the abdomen and perineum

abdominoperineal excision /æbˌdɒmɪnəʊperɪˌniːəl ɪkˈsɪʒ(ə)n/ *noun* a surgical operation that involves cutting out tissue in both the abdomen and the perineum

abdominoposterior /æbˌdɒmɪnəʊpɒˈstɪəriə/ *adjective* referring to a position of a fetus in the uterus, where the fetus's abdomen is facing the mother's back

abdominoscopy /æbˌdɒmɪˈnɒskəpi/ *noun* an internal examination of the abdomen, usually with an endoscope

abdominothoracic /æbˌdɒmɪnəʊθɔːˈræsɪk/ *adjective* referring to the abdomen and thorax

abduce /æbˈdjuːs/ *verb* same as **abduct**

abducens nerve /æbˈdjuːs(ə)nz ˌnɜːv/ *noun* the sixth cranial nerve, which controls the muscle which makes the eyeball turn outwards

abducent /æbˈdjuːs(ə)nt/ *adjective* referring to a muscle which brings parts of the body away from each other or moves them away from the central line of the body or a limb. Compare **adducent**

abduct /æbˈdʌkt/ *verb* (*of a muscle*) to pull a leg or arm in a direction which is away from the centre line of the body, or to pull a toe or finger away from the central line of a leg or arm. Compare **adduct**

abduction /æbˈdʌkʃən/ *noun* the movement of a part of the body away from the centre line of the body or away from a neighbouring part. Opposite **adduction**. See illustration at **ANATOMICAL TERMS** in Supplement

abductor /æbˈdʌktə/, **abductor muscle** /æb ˈdʌktə ˌmʌs(ə)l/ *noun* a muscle which pulls a part of the body away from the centre line of the body or away from a neighbouring part. Opposite **adductor**

aberrant /æˈberənt/ *adjective* not usual or expected

aberration /ˌæbəˈreɪʃ(ə)n/ *noun* an action or growth which is not usual or expected

ablation /əˈbleɪʃ(ə)n/ *noun* the removal of an organ or of a part of the body by surgery

abnormal /æbˈnɔːm(ə)l/ *adjective* not usual ○ *abnormal behaviour* ○ *an abnormal movement*

abnormality /ˌæbnɔːˈmælɪti/ *noun* a form or condition which is not usual (NOTE: For other terms referring to abnormality, see words beginning with **terat-, terato-**.)

abocclusion /ˌæbɒˈkluːʒ(ə)n/ *noun* a condition in which the teeth in the top and bottom jaws do not touch

abort /əˈbɔːt/ *verb* to eject an embryo or fetus, or to cause an embryo or fetus to be ejected, and so end a pregnancy before the fetus is fully developed

abortifacient /əˌbɔːtɪˈfeɪʃ(ə)nt/ *noun* a drug or instrument which provokes an abortion

abortion /əˈbɔːʃ(ə)n/ *noun* a situation where a fetus leaves the uterus before it is fully developed, especially during the first 28 weeks of pregnancy, or a procedure which causes this to happen

abortive /əˈbɔːtɪv/ *adjective* not successful ○ *an abortive attempt*

abortus /əˈbɔːtəs/ *noun* a fetus which is expelled during an abortion or miscarriage

abortus fever /əˈbɔːtəs ˌfiːvə/ *noun* same as **brucellosis**

ABO system /ˌeɪ biː ˈəʊ ˌsɪstəm/ *noun* a system of classifying blood groups. ◊ **blood group**

abrasion /əˈbreɪʒ(ə)n/ *noun* a condition in which the surface of the skin has been rubbed off by a rough surface and bleeds

abreaction /ˌæbriˈækʃən/ *noun* the treatment of a person with a neurosis by making him or her think again about past bad experiences

abruptio placentae /əˌbrʌptiəʊ pləˈsentiː/ *noun* an occasion when the placenta suddenly comes away from the uterus earlier than it should, often causing shock and bleeding

abscess /ˈæbses/ *noun* a painful swollen area where pus forms ○ *She had an abscess under a tooth.* ○ *The doctor decided to lance the abscess.* (NOTE: The formation of an abscess is often accompanied by a high temperature. The plural is **abscesses**.)

absorbable suture /əbˌzɔːbəb(ə)l ˈsuːtʃə/ *noun* a suture which will eventually be absorbed into the body, and does not need to be removed

absorbent cotton /əbˌzɔːbənt ˈkɒt(ə)n/ *noun* a soft white material used as a dressing to put on wounds

absorption /əbˈzɔːpʃən/ *noun* the process by which a liquid is taken into a solid

abstinence /ˈæbstɪnəns/ *noun* a deliberate act of not doing something over a period of time, especially not eating or drinking ○ *abstinence from alcohol*

abulia /əˈbuːliə/ *noun* a lack of willpower

abuse *noun* /əˈbjuːs/ **1.** the act of using something wrongly ○ *the abuse of a privilege* **2.** the illegal use of a drug or overuse of alcohol ○ *substance abuse* **3.** same as **child abuse 4.** bad treatment of a person ○ *physical abuse* ○ *sexual abuse* ■ *verb* /əˈbjuːz/ **1.** to use something

wrongly ○ *Heroin and cocaine are drugs which are commonly abused.* **2.** to treat someone badly ○ *sexually abused children* ○ *He had physically abused his wife and child.*

a.c. *adverb* (*used on prescriptions*) before food. Full form **ante cibum**

acanthosis /əˌkænˈθəʊsɪs/ *noun* a disease of the prickle cell layer of the skin, where warts appear on the skin or inside the mouth

acapnia /eɪˈkæpniə/ *noun* the condition of not having enough carbon dioxide in the blood and tissues

acaricide /əˈkærɪsaɪd/ *noun* a substance which kills mites or ticks

acatalasia /eɪˌkætəˈleɪziə/ *noun* an inherited condition which results in a lack of catalase in all tissue

accessory /əkˈsesəri/ *noun* something which helps something else to happen or operate, but may not be very important in itself ■ *adjective* helping something else to happen or operate

accident /ˈæksɪd(ə)nt/ *noun* **1.** an unpleasant event which happens suddenly and harms someone's health ○ *She had an accident in the kitchen and had to go to hospital.* ○ *Three people were killed in the accident on the motorway.* **2.** chance, or something which happens by chance ○ *I met her by accident at the bus stop.*

accidental injury /ˌæksɪdent(ə)l ˈɪndʒəri/ *noun* an injury that happens to someone in an accident

accident and emergency department /ˌæksɪd(ə)nt ənd ɪˈmɜːdʒənsi dɪˌpɑːtmənt/ *noun* the part of a hospital which deals with people who need urgent treatment because they have had accidents or are in sudden serious pain. Abbreviation **A & E**

accident form /ˈæksɪd(ə)nt fɔːm/, **accident report form** /ˌæksɪd(ə)nt rɪˈpɔːt fɔːm/ *noun* a form to be filled in with details of an accident

accident prevention /ˌæksɪd(ə)nt prɪˈvenʃən/ *noun* the work of taking action or changing procedures to prevent accidents from happening

accident ward /ˈæksɪd(ə)nt wɔːd/ *noun* a ward for urgent accident victims. Also called **casualty ward**

accommodation /əˌkɒməˈdeɪʃ(ə)n/, **accommodation reflex** /əˌkɒməˈdeɪʃ(ə)n ˌriːfleks/ *noun* (*of the lens of the eye*) the ability to focus on objects at different distances, using the ciliary muscle

accommodative squint /əˌkɒmədeɪtɪv ˈskwɪnt/ *noun* a squint when the eye is trying to focus on an object which is very close

accouchement /əˈkuːʃmɒŋ/ *noun* the time when a woman is being looked after because her baby is being born, or has just been born

accountability /əˌkaʊntəˈbɪlɪti/ *noun* the state of being responsible to someone else for an action ○ *developing and maintaining standards of accountability*

accountable /əˈkaʊntəb(ə)l/ *adjective* responsible to someone for an action ○ *accountable to the public*

accretion /əˈkriːʃ(ə)n/ *noun* a gradual increase in size, as through growth or external addition ○ *an accretion of calcium around the joint*

acebutolol /ˌæsɪˈbjuːtəlɒl/ *noun* a drug which reduces both the heart rate and how strongly the heart muscles contract, used in the treatment of high blood pressure and irregular heart rhythms

ACE inhibitor /ˈeɪs ɪnˌhɪbɪtə/ *noun* same as **angiotensin-converting enzyme inhibitor**

acephalus /eɪˈsefələs/ *noun* a fetus born without a head

acetabuloplasty /ˌæsɪˈtæbjʊləʊˌplæsti/ *noun* a surgical operation to repair or rebuild the acetabulum

acetabulum /ˌæsɪˈtæbjʊləm/ *noun* the part of the pelvic bone, shaped like a cup, into which the head of the femur fits to form the hip joint. Also called **cotyloid cavity** (NOTE: The plural is **acetabula**.)

acetaminophen /əˌsiːtəˈmɪnəfən/ *noun* US same as **paracetamol**

acetazolamide /əˌsiːtəˈzɒləmaɪd/ *noun* a drug which helps a person to produce more urine, used in the treatment of oedema, glaucoma and epilepsy

acetonaemia /əˌsiːtəʊˈniːmiə/ same as **ketonaemia**

acetone /ˈæsɪtəʊn/ *noun* a colourless volatile substance formed in the body after vomiting or during diabetes. ◊ **ketone**

acetonuria /əˌsiːtəʊˈnjuːriə/ *noun* the presence of acetone in the urine, shown by the fact that the urine gives off a sweet smell

acetylcholine /ˌæsɪtaɪlˈkəʊliːn/ *noun* a substance released from nerve endings, which allows nerve impulses to move from one nerve to another or from a nerve to the organ it controls

COMMENT: Acetylcholine receptors are of two types, muscarinic, found in parasympathetic post-ganglionic nerve junctions, and nicotinic, found at neuromuscular junctions and in autonomic ganglia. Acetylcholine acts on both types of receptors, but other drugs act on one or the other.

acetylcoenzyme A /ˌæsɪtaɪlkəʊˌenzaɪm ˈeɪ/ *noun* a compound produced in the metabolism of carbohydrates, fatty acids and amino acids

acetylsalicylic acid /ˌæsɪtaɪlˌsæləsɪlɪk ˈæsɪd/ *noun* ♦ **aspirin**

achalasia /ˌækəˈleɪziə/ *noun* the condition of being unable to relax the muscles

ache /eɪk/ *noun* a pain which goes on for a time, but is not very severe ○ *He complained of various aches and pains.* ■ *verb* to have a pain in part of the body ○ *His tooth ached so much he went to the dentist.*

Achilles tendon /əˌkɪliːz ˈtendən/ *noun* a tendon at the back of the ankle which connects the calf muscles to the heel and which acts to pull up the heel when the calf muscle is contracted

achillorrhaphy /ˌækɪˈlɔːrəfi/ *noun* a surgical operation to stitch a torn Achilles tendon

achillotomy /ˌækɪˈlɒtəmi/ *noun* a surgical operation to divide the Achilles tendon

achlorhydria /ˌeɪklɔːˈhaɪdriə/ *noun* a condition in which the gastric juices do not contain hydrochloric acid, a symptom of stomach cancer or pernicious anaemia

acholia /eɪˈkəʊliə/ *noun* the absence or failure of the secretion of bile

acholuria /ˌeɪkɒˈluːriə/ *noun* the absence of bile colouring in the urine

acholuric jaundice /ˌeɪkəluːrɪk ˈdʒɔːndɪs/ *noun* a disease where unusually round red blood cells form, leading to anaemia, an enlarged spleen and the formation of gallstones. Also called **hereditary spherocytosis**

achondroplasia /ˌeɪkɒndrəˈpleɪziə/ *noun* an inherited condition in which the long bones in the arms and legs do not grow fully while the rest of the bones in the body grow as usual, resulting in dwarfism

achromatopsia /ˌeɪkrəʊməˈtɒpsiə/ *noun* a rare condition in which a person cannot see any colours, but only black, white and shades of grey

achy /ˈeɪki/ *adjective* feeling aches all over the body (*informal*)

aciclovir /eɪˈsaɪkləʊvɪə/ *noun* a drug that is effective against herpesviruses. Also called **acyclovir**

acidaemia /ˌæsɪˈdiːmiə/ *noun* a state in which the blood has too much acid in it. It is a feature of untreated severe diabetes.

acid–base balance /ˌæsɪd ˈbeɪs ˌbæləns/ *noun* the balance between acid and base, i.e. the pH level, in plasma

acidity /əˈsɪdɪti/ *noun* **1.** the level of acid in a liquid ○ *The alkaline solution may help to reduce acidity.* **2.** same as **hyperacidity**

acidosis /ˌæsɪˈdəʊsɪs/ *noun* **1.** a condition when there are more acid waste products such as urea than usual in the blood because of a lack of alkali **2.** same as **acidity**

acidotic /ˌæsɪˈdɒtɪk/ *adjective* relating to acidosis

acid reflux /ˌæsɪd ˈriːflʌks/ *noun* a condition caused by a faulty muscle in the oesophagus allowing the acid in the stomach to pass into the oesophagus

acid stomach /ˌæsɪd ˈstʌmək/ *noun* same as **hyperacidity**

acinus /ˈæsɪnəs/ *noun* **1.** a tiny sac which forms part of a gland **2.** part of a lobule in the lung (NOTE: The plural is **acini**.)

acne /ˈækni/ *noun* an inflammation of the sebaceous glands during puberty which makes blackheads appear on the skin, usually on the face, neck and shoulders. These blackheads often then become infected. ○ *She is using a cream to clear up her acne.*

acne rosacea /ˌækni rəʊˈzeɪʃə/ *noun* same as **rosacea**

acne vulgaris /ˌækni vʊlˈgɑːrɪs/ *noun* same as **acne**

acoustic /əˈkuːstɪk/ *adjective* relating to sound or hearing

acoustic nerve /əˈkuːstɪk nɜːv/ *noun* the eighth cranial nerve which governs hearing and balance

acquired /əˈkwaɪəd/ *adjective* referring to a condition which is neither congenital nor hereditary and which a person develops after birth in reaction to his or her environment

acquired immunity /əˌkwaɪəd ɪˈmjuːnɪti/ *noun* an immunity which a body acquires from having caught a disease or from immunisation, not one which is congenital

acquired immunodeficiency syndrome /əˌkwaɪəd ˌɪmjʊnəʊdɪˈfɪʃ(ə)nsi ˌsɪndrəʊm/, **acquired immune deficiency syndrome** /əˌkwaɪəd ɪmˌjuːn dɪˈfɪʃ(ə)nsi ˌsɪndrəʊm/ *noun* a viral infection which breaks down the body's immune system. Abbreviation **AIDS**. ◊ **HIV**

acrivastine /əˈkrɪvə stiːn/ *noun* a drug which reduces the amount of histamine produced by the body. It is used in the treatment of rhinitis, urticaria and eczema.

acro- /ˈækrəʊ/ *prefix* referring to a point or tip

acrocephalia /ˌækrəʊsəˈfeɪliə/ *noun* same as **oxycephaly**

acrocyanosis /ˌækrəʊsaɪəˈnəʊsɪs/ *noun* a blue coloration of the extremities, i.e. the fingers, toes, ears and nose, which is due to poor circulation

acrodynia /ˌækrəʊˈdɪniə/ *noun* a children's disease, caused by an allergy to mercury, where the child's hands, feet and face swell and become pink, and the child is also affected with fever and loss of appetite. Also called **erythroedema**, **pink disease**

acromegaly /ˌækrəʊˈmegəli/ *noun* a disease caused by excessive quantities of growth hormone produced by the pituitary gland, causing a slow enlargement of the hands, feet and jaws in adults

acromioclavicular /ˌækrəʊmaɪəʊkləˈvɪkjʊlə/ *adjective* relating to the acromion and the clavicle

acromion /əˈkrəʊmiən/ *noun* the pointed top of the scapula, which forms the tip of the shoulder

acronyx /ˈækrɒnɪks, ˈeɪkrɒnɪks/ *noun* a condition in which a nail grows into the flesh

acroparaesthesia /ˌækrəʊpærɪsˈθiːziə/ *noun* a condition in which the patient experiences sharp pains in the arms and numbness in the fingers after sleep

acrophobia /ˌækrəˈfəʊbiə/ *noun* a fear of heights

acrosclerosis /ˌækrəʊskləˈrəʊsɪs/ *noun* sclerosis which affects the extremities

ACTH *abbreviation* adrenocorticotrophic hormone

actinomycin /ˌæktɪnəʊˈmaɪsɪn/ *noun* an antibiotic used in the treatment of children with cancer

actinomycosis /ˌæktɪnəʊmaɪˈkəʊsɪs/ *noun* a fungal disease transmitted to humans from cattle, causing abscesses in the mouth and lungs (**pulmonary actinomycosis**) or in the ileum (**intestinal actinomycosis**)

action potential /ˈækʃən pəˌtenʃəl/ *noun* a temporary change in electrical potential which occurs between the inside and the outside of a nerve or muscle fibre when a nerve impulse is sent

active immunity /ˌæktɪv ɪˈmjuːnɪti/ *noun* immunity which is acquired by catching and surviving an infectious disease or by vaccination with a weakened form of the disease, which makes the body form antibodies

activities of daily living /æk,tɪvɪtiz əv ˌdeɪli ˈlɪvɪŋ/ *noun* a scale used by geriatricians and occupational therapists to assess the capacity of elderly or disabled people to live independently. Abbreviation **ADLs**

activity /ækˈtɪvɪti/ *noun* **1.** what someone does ○ *difficulty with activities such as walking and dressing* **2.** the characteristic behaviour of a chemical ○ *The drug's activity only lasts a few hours.* □ **antibacterial activity** effective action against bacteria

acuity /əˈkjuːɪti/ *noun* keenness of sight, hearing or intellect

acupressure /ˈækjʊpreʃə/ *noun* a treatment which is based on the same principle as acupuncture in which, instead of needles, fingers are used on specific points on the body, called pressure points

acupuncture /ˈækjʊpʌŋktʃə/ *noun* a treatment based on needles being inserted through the skin into nerve centres in order to relieve pain or treat a disorder

acute /əˈkjuːt/ *adjective* referring to a disease or condition which develops rapidly and can be dangerous ○ *an acute abscess* Opposite **chronic**

acute abdomen /ə,kjuːt ˈæbdəmən/ *noun* any serious condition of the abdomen which requires surgery

acute bed /əˈkjuːt bed/ *noun* a hospital bed reserved for people requiring immediate treatment

acute care /əˈkjuːt keə/ *noun* medical or surgical treatment in a hospital, usually for a short period, for a patient with a sudden severe illness or injury

acute disseminated encephalomyelitis /ə ,kjuːt dɪ,semɪneɪtɪd en,kefələʊmaɪəˈlaɪtɪs/ *noun* an encephalomyelitis or myelitis believed to result from an autoimmune attack on the myelin of the central nervous system

acute glaucoma /ə,kjuːt ɡlɔːˈkəʊmə/ *noun* same as **angle-closure glaucoma**

acute hospital /əˈkjuːt ˌhɒspɪt(ə)l/ *noun* a hospital where people go for major surgery or intensive care of medical or surgical conditions

acutely /əˈkjuːtli/ *adverb* **1.** having or causing a suddenly developing medical condition ○ *acutely ill patients* ○ *acutely toxic chemicals* **2.** extremely (*informal*)

acute respiratory distress syndrome /ə ,kjuːt rɪ,spɪrət(ə)ri dɪˈstres ,sɪndrəʊm/ *noun* an infection of the lungs, often following injury, which prevents them functioning properly. Abbreviation **ARDS**

acute rheumatism /ə,kjuːt ˈruːmətɪz(ə)m/ *noun* same as **rheumatic fever**

acute rhinitis /ə,kjuːt raɪˈnaɪtɪs/ *noun* a virus infection which causes inflammation of the mucous membrane in the nose and throat

acute suppurative arthritis /ə,kjuːt ˌsʌpjʊrətɪv ɑːθˈraɪtɪs/ *noun* same as **pyarthrosis**

acute toxicity /ə,kjuːt tɒkˈsɪsɪti/ *noun* a level of concentration of a toxic substance which makes people seriously ill or can cause death

acyclovir /eɪˈsaɪkləʊvɪə/ *noun* same as **aciclovir**

acystia /eɪˈsɪstiə/ *noun* a condition in which a baby is born without a bladder

Adam's apple /ˌædəmz ˈæp(ə)l/ *noun* a part of the thyroid cartilage which projects from the neck below the chin in a man. Also called **laryngeal prominence**

adapt /əˈdæpt/ *verb* **1.** to change one's ideas or behaviour to fit into a new situation ○ *She has adapted very well to her new job in the children's hospital.* **2.** to change something to make it more useful ○ *The brace has to be adapted to fit the patient.*

adaptation /ˌædæpˈteɪʃ(ə)n/ *noun* **1.** a change which has been or can be made to something **2.** the act of changing something so that it fits a new situation

ADD *abbreviation* attention deficit disorder

Addison's anaemia /ˌædɪs(ə)nz əˈniːmiə/ same as **pernicious anaemia** [Described 1849. After Thomas Addison (1793–1860), from Northumberland, founder of the science of endocrinology.]

Addison's disease /ˈædɪs(ə)nz dɪ,ziːz/ *noun* a disease of the adrenal glands, causing a change in skin colour to yellow and then to dark brown and resulting in general weakness, anaemia, low blood pressure and wasting away. Treatment is with corticosteroid injections. [Described 1849. After Thomas Addison (1793–1860), from Northumberland, founder of the science of endocrinology.]

adducent /əˈdjuːs(ə)nt/ *adjective* referring to a muscle which brings parts of the body together or moves them towards the central line of the body or a limb. Compare **abducent**

adduct /əˈdʌkt/ *verb* (*of a muscle*) to pull a leg or arm towards the central line of the body, or to pull a toe or finger towards the central line of a leg or arm. Opposite **abduct**

adducted /əˈdʌktɪd/ *adjective* referring to a body part brought towards the middle of the body

adduction /əˈdʌkʃən/ *noun* the movement of a part of the body towards the midline or towards a neighbouring part. Compare **abduction**. See illustration at **ANATOMICAL TERMS** in Supplement

adductor /əˈdʌktə/, **adductor muscle** /ə ˈdʌktə ,mʌs(ə)l/ *noun* a muscle which pulls a part of the body towards the central line of the body. Opposite **abductor**

aden- /ædɪn/ *prefix* same as **adeno-** (*used before vowels*)

adenectomy /ˌædɪˈnektəmi/ *noun* the surgical removal of a gland

adenine /ˈædəniːn/ *noun* one of the four basic chemicals in DNA

adenitis /ˌædɪˈnaɪtɪs/ *noun* inflammation of a gland or lymph node. ◊ **lymphadenitis**

adeno- /ædɪnəʊ/ *prefix* referring to glands

adenocarcinoma /ˌædɪnəʊkɑːsɪˈnəʊmə/ *noun* a malignant tumour of a gland

adenohypophysis /ˌædɪnəʊhaɪˈpɒfɪsɪs/ *noun* the front lobe of the pituitary gland which secretes most of the pituitary hormones

adenoid /ˈædɪnɔɪd/ *adjective* like a gland

adenoidal /ˌædɪˈnɔɪd(ə)l/ *adjective* referring to the adenoids

adenoidal tissue /ˌædɪnɔɪd(ə)l ˈtɪʃuː/ *noun* same as **adenoids**

adenoidectomy /ˌædɪnɔɪˈdektəmi/ *noun* the surgical removal of the adenoids

adenoids /ˈædɪnɔɪdz/ *plural noun* a mass of tissue at the back of the nose and throat that can restrict breathing if enlarged. Also called **pharyngeal tonsils**

adenoid vegetation /ˌædɪnɔɪd ˌvedʒə ˈteɪʃ(ə)n/ *noun* a condition in children where the adenoidal tissue is covered with growths and can block the nasal passages or the Eustachian tubes

adenolymphoma /ˌædɪnəʊlɪmˈfəʊmə/ *noun* a benign tumour of the salivary glands

adenoma /ˌædɪˈnəʊmə/ *noun* a benign tumour of a gland

adenomyoma /ˌædɪnəʊmaɪˈəʊmə/ *noun* a benign tumour made up of glands and muscle

adenopathy /ˌædɪˈnɒpəθi/ *noun* a disease of a gland

adenosclerosis /ˌædɪnəʊskləˈrəʊsɪs/ *noun* the hardening of a gland

adenosine /əˈdenəʊsiːn/ *noun* a drug used to treat an irregular heartbeat

adenosine diphosphate /əˌdenəʊsiːn daɪ ˈfɒsfeɪt/ *noun* a chemical compound which provides energy for processes to take place within living cells, formed when adenosine triphosphate reacts with water. Abbreviation **ADP**

adenosine triphosphate /əˌdenəʊsiːn traɪ ˈfɒsfeɪt/ *noun* a chemical which occurs in all cells, but mainly in muscle, where it forms the energy reserve. Abbreviation **ATP**

adenosis /ˌædɪˈnəʊsɪs/ *noun* any disease or disorder of the glands

adenovirus /ˈædɪnəʊˌvaɪrəs/ *noun* a virus which produces upper respiratory infections and sore throats and can cause fatal pneumonia in infants

ADH *abbreviation* antidiuretic hormone

ADHD *abbreviation* attention deficit hyperactivity disorder

adhesion /ədˈhiːʒ(ə)n/ *noun* a stable connection between two parts in the body, either in a healing process or between parts which are not usually connected

adhesive dressing /ədˌhiːsɪv ˈdresɪŋ/ *noun* a dressing with a sticky substance on the back so that it can stick to the skin

adipose /ˈædɪpəʊs/ *adjective* containing fat, or made of fat

adipose degeneration /ˌædɪpəʊs dɪˌdʒenə ˈreɪʃ(ə)n/ *noun* an accumulation of fat in the cells of an organ such as the heart or liver, which makes the organ less able to perform its proper function. Also called **fatty degeneration**

adiposis /ˌædɪˈpəʊsɪs/ *noun* a state where too much fat is accumulated in the body

adiposis dolorosa /ædɪˌpəʊsɪs ˌdɒləˈrəʊsə/ *noun* a disease of middle-aged women in which painful lumps of fatty substance form in the body. Also called **Dercum's disease**

adiposogenitalis /ˌædɪˌpəʊsəʊˌdʒenɪˈteɪlɪs/ *noun* same as **Fröhlich's syndrome**

adiposuria /ədɪpsəʊˈjuːriə/ *noun* the presence of fat in the urine

adiposus /ˌædɪˈpəʊsəs/ ♦ **panniculus adiposus**

aditus /ˈædɪtəs/ *noun* an opening or entrance to a passage

adjustment /əˈdʒʌstmənt/ *noun* a specific directional high-speed movement of a joint performed by a chiropractor

adjuvant /ˈædʒʊvənt/ *adjective* referring to treatment by drugs or radiation therapy after surgery for cancer ■ *noun* a substance added to a drug to enhance the effect of the main ingredient

adjuvant therapy /ˈædʒʊvənt ˌθerəpi/ *noun* therapy using drugs or radiation after cancer surgery

ADLs *abbreviation* activities of daily living

administer /ədˈmɪnɪstə/ *verb* to give someone medicine or a treatment □ **to administer orally** to give a medicine by mouth

admission /ədˈmɪʃ(ə)n/ *noun* the act of being registered as a hospital patient

adnexa /ædˈneksə/ *plural noun* structures attached to an organ

adolescence /ˌædəˈles(ə)ns/ *noun* the period of life when a child is developing into an adult

adolescent /ˌædəˈles(ə)nt/ *noun* a person who is at the stage of life when he or she is developing into an adult ■ *adjective* developing into an adult, or occurring at that stage of life ○ *adolescent boys and girls* ○ *adolescent fantasies*

adoptive immunotherapy /əˌdɒptɪv ɪmjʊnəʊˈθerəpi/ *noun* a treatment for cancer in which the patient's own white blood cells are used to attack cancer cells

ADP *abbreviation* adenosine diphosphate

adrenal /əˈdriːn(ə)l/ *adjective* situated near the kidney ■ *noun* same as **adrenal gland**

adrenalectomy /əˌdriːnəˈlektəmi/ *noun* the surgical removal of one of the adrenal glands

adrenal gland /əˈdriːn(ə)l glænd/ *noun* one of two endocrine glands at the top of the kidneys which secrete cortisone, adrenaline and other hormones. Also called **adrenal body, adrenal**. See illustration at **KIDNEY** in Supplement

adrenaline /əˈdrenəlɪn/ *noun* a hormone secreted by the medulla of the adrenal glands which has an effect similar to stimulation of the sympathetic nervous system

adrenal medulla /əˌdriːn(ə)l meˈdʌlə/ *noun* the inner part of the adrenal gland which secretes adrenaline and noradrenaline. Also called **suprarenal medulla**

adrenergic /ˌædrəˈnɜːdʒɪk/ *adjective* referring to a neurone or receptor which is stimulated by adrenaline. ◊ **beta blocker**

adrenergic receptor /ˌædrənɜːdʒɪk rɪ ˈseptə/ *noun* same as **adrenoceptor**

COMMENT: Three types of adrenergic receptor act in different ways when stimulated by adrenaline. Alpha receptors constrict the bronchi, beta 1 receptors speed up the heartbeat and beta 2 receptors dilate the bronchi.

adrenoceptor /ə,drenəʊ'septə/ *noun* a cell or neurone which is stimulated by adrenaline. Also called **adrenoreceptor, adrenergic receptor**

adrenocortical /ə,driːnəʊ'kɔːtɪk(ə)l/ *adjective* relating to the cortex of the adrenal glands

adrenocorticotrophic hormone /ə,driːnəʊ ,kɔːtəkəʊtrɒfɪk 'hɔːməʊn/ *noun* a hormone secreted by the pituitary gland, which makes the cortex of the adrenal glands produce corticosteroids. Abbreviation **ACTH**. Also called **corticotrophin**

adrenocorticotrophin /ə,driːnəʊkɔːtəkəʊ 'trəʊfɪn/ *noun* adrenaline extracted from animals' adrenal glands and used to prevent haemorrhages or to help asthmatic conditions

adrenogenital syndrome /ə,driːnəʊ 'dʒenɪt(ə)l ,sɪndrəʊm/ *noun* a condition caused by overproduction of male sex hormones, where boys show rapid sexual development and females develop male characteristics

adrenolytic /ədriːnəʊ'lɪtɪk/ *adjective* acting against the secretion of adrenaline

adrenoreceptor /ə,drenəʊrɪ'septə/ *noun* same as **adrenoceptor**

adsorbent /æd'sɔːbənt/ *adjective* being capable of adsorption

adsorption /æd'sɔːpʃ(ə)n/ *noun* the attachment of one substance to another, often the bonding of a liquid with a gas or vapour which touches its surface

adult /'ædʌlt/ *adjective* grown-up ○ *Adolescents reach the adult stage about the age of eighteen or twenty.* ■ *noun* someone who is no longer a child

adult coeliac disease /,ædʌlt 'siːliæk dɪ ,ziːz/ *noun* a condition in adults where the villi in the intestine become smaller and so reduce the surface which can absorb nutrients

adult dentition /,ædʌlt den'tɪʃ(ə)n/ *noun* the 32 teeth which an adult has

adulteration /ə,dʌltə'reɪʃ(ə)n/ *noun* the act of making something less pure by adding another substance

adult respiratory distress syndrome /,ædʌlt rɪ,spɪrət(ə)ri dɪ'stres ,sɪndrəʊm/ *noun* a description of various lung infections which reduce the lungs' efficiency. Abbreviation **ARDS**

advanced trauma life support /əd,vɑːnst ,trɔːma 'laɪf sə,pɔːt/ *noun* the management of a trauma patient during the critical first hour after injury. Abbreviation **ATLS**

adventitious /,ædvən'tɪʃəs/ *adjective* on the outside or in an unusual place

adventitious bursa /,ædvəntɪʃəs 'bɜːsə/ *noun* a bursa which develops as a result of continued pressure or rubbing

adverse /'ædvɜːs/ *adjective* harmful or unfavourable

adverse occurrence /,ædvɜːs ə'kʌrəns/ *noun* a harmful event which occurs during treatment

advocacy /'ædvəkəsi/ *noun* active support for something, especially in order to help people who would have difficulty in gaining attention without your help

adynamic ileus /eɪ,daɪnæmɪk 'ɪliəs/ *noun* same as **paralytic ileus**

aegophony /iː'gɒfəni/ *noun* a high sound of the voice heard through a stethoscope, where there is fluid in the pleural cavity

aer- /eə/ *prefix* same as **aero-** (*used before vowels*)

aeration /eə'reɪʃ(ə)n/ *noun* the adding of air or oxygen to a liquid

aero- /eərəʊ/ *prefix* referring to air

aeroba /eə'rəʊbə/, **aerobe** /'eərəʊb/ *noun* a tiny organism which needs oxygen to survive

aerobic /eə'rəʊbɪk/ *adjective* needing oxygen to live, or taking place in the presence of oxygen

aerogenous /eə'rɒdʒənəs/ *adjective* referring to a bacterium which produces gas

aerophagia /,eərə'feɪdʒə/, **aerophagy** /eə 'rɒfədʒi/ *noun* the habit of swallowing air when suffering from indigestion, so making the stomach pains worse

aerosol /'eərəsɒl/ *noun* tiny particles of a liquid such as a drug or disinfectant suspended in a gas under pressure in a container and used as a spray

aetiology /,iːti'ɒlədʒi/ *noun* **1.** the cause or origin of a disease **2.** the study of the causes and origins of diseases

AfC *abbreviation* Agenda for Change

afebrile /eɪ'fiːbraɪl/ *adjective* with no fever

affect /ə'fekt/ *verb* to make something or someone change, especially to have a bad effect on something or someone ○ *Some organs are rapidly affected if the patient lacks oxygen for even a short time.* ■ *noun* same as **affection**

affection /ə'fekʃ(ə)n/, **affect** /ə'fekt/ *noun* the general state of a person's emotions

affective /ə'fektɪv/ *adjective* relating to a person's moods or feelings

affective disorder /ə'fektɪv dɪs,ɔːdə/ *noun* a condition which changes someone's mood, making him or her depressed or excited

afferent /'æf(ə)rənt/ *adjective* conducting liquid or electrical impulses towards the inside. Opposite **efferent**

afferent nerve /'æf(ə)rənt ,nɜːv/ *noun* same as **sensory nerve**

afferent vessel /ˈæf(ə)rənt ˌves(ə)l/ *noun* a tube which brings lymph to a gland

affinity /əˈfɪnɪti/ *noun* an attraction between two substances

aflatoxin /ˌæfləˈtɒksɪn/ *noun* a poison produced by some moulds in some crops such as peanuts

African trypanosomiasis /ˌæfrɪkən ˌtrɪpənəʊsəʊˈmaɪəsɪs/ *noun* same as **sleeping sickness**

afterbirth /ˈɑːftəbɜːθ/ *noun* the tissues, including the placenta and umbilical cord, which are present in the uterus during pregnancy and are expelled after the birth of a baby

aftercare /ˈɑːftəkeə/ *noun* **1.** the care of a person who has had an operation. Aftercare treatment involves changing dressings and helping people to look after themselves again. **2.** the care of a mother who has just given birth

after-effect /ˈɑːftər ɪˌfekt/ *noun* a change which appears only some time after the cause ○ *The operation had some unpleasant after-effects.*

after-image /ˈɑːftər ˌɪmɪdʒ/ *noun* an image of an object which remains in a person's sight after the object itself has gone

afterpains /ˈɑːftəpeɪnz/ *plural noun* regular pains in the uterus which are sometimes experienced after childbirth

afunctional /eɪ ˈfʌŋkʃən(ə)l/ *adjective* which does not function properly

agalactia /ˌeɪɡəˈlæktiə/ *noun* a condition in which a mother is unable to produce milk after childbirth

agammaglobulinaemia /eɪˌɡæməɡlɒbjʊlɪˈniːmiə/ *noun* a deficiency or absence of immunoglobulins in the blood, which results in a reduced ability to provide immune responses

agar /ˈeɪɡɑː/, **agar agar** /ˌeɪɡə ˈeɪɡə/ *noun* a culture medium based on an extract of seaweed used for growing microorganisms in laboratories

age /eɪdʒ/ *noun* the number of years which a person has lived ○ *What's your age on your next birthday?* ○ *He was sixty years of age.* ○ *The size varies according to age.* ■ *verb* to grow old

age group /ˈeɪdʒ ɡruːp/ *noun* all the people of a particular age or within a particular set of ages ○ *the age group 20–25*

agency /ˈeɪdʒənsi/ *noun* **1.** an organisation which carries out work on behalf of another organisation, e.g. one which recruits and employs nurses and supplies them to hospitals temporarily when full-time nursing staff are unavailable **2.** the act of causing something to happen ○ *The disease develops through the agency of bacteria present in the bloodstream.*

Agenda for Change /əˌdʒendə fə ˈtʃeɪndʒ/ *noun* a pay and reform package designed to ensure that all directly employed NHS staff are paid on the basis of equal pay for work of equal value, implemented in December 2004. Abbreviation **AfC**

agenesis /eɪˈdʒenəsɪs/ *noun* the absence of an organ, resulting from a failure in embryonic development

agent /ˈeɪdʒənt/ *noun* **1.** a chemical substance which makes another substance react **2.** a substance or organism which causes a disease or condition **3.** a person who acts as a representative of another person or carries out some kinds of work on his or her behalf

agglutination /əˌɡluːtɪˈneɪʃ(ə)n/ *noun* the act of coming together or sticking to one another to form a clump, as of bacteria cells in the presence of serum, or blood cells when blood of different types is mixed

agglutinin /əˈɡluːtɪnɪn/ *noun* a factor in a serum which makes cells stick together in clumps

agglutinogen /ˌæɡluːˈtɪnədʒən/ *noun* a factor in red blood cells which reacts with a specific agglutinin in serum

agitation /ˌædʒɪˈteɪʃ(ə)n/ *noun* a state of being very nervous and anxious

aglossia /eɪˈɡlɒsiə/ *noun* the condition of not having a tongue from birth

agnosia /æɡˈnəʊziə/ *noun* a brain disorder in which a person fails to recognise places, people, tastes or smells which they used to know well

agonist /ˈæɡənɪst/ *noun* **1.** a muscle which causes part of the body to move and another muscle to relax when it contracts. Also called **prime mover 2.** a substance which produces an observable physiological effect by acting through specific receptors. ◊ **antagonist**

agony /ˈæɡəni/ *noun* a very severe physical or emotional pain ○ *He lay in agony on the floor.* ○ *She suffered the agony of waiting for weeks until her condition was diagnosed.*

agoraphobia /ˌæɡ(ə)rəˈfəʊbiə/ *noun* a fear of being in open spaces. Compare **claustrophobia**

agoraphobic /ˌæɡ(ə)rəˈfəʊbɪk/ *adjective* afraid of being in open spaces. Compare **claustrophobic**

agranulocytosis /əˌɡrænjʊləʊsaɪˈtəʊsɪs/ *noun* a usually fatal disease where the number of granulocytes, a type of white blood cell, falls sharply because of a bone marrow condition

agraphia /eɪˈɡræfiə/ *noun* the condition of being unable to put ideas into writing

AHF *abbreviation* antihaemophilic factor

aid /eɪd/ *noun* **1.** help **2.** a machine, tool or drug which helps someone do something ○ *He uses a walking frame as an aid to exercising his legs.* ■ *verb* to help someone or something ○ *The procedure is designed to aid the repair of tissues after surgery.*

AID /ˌeɪ aɪ ˈdiː/ *noun* full form **artificial insemination by donor**. Now called **DI**

AIDS /eɪdz/, **Aids** *noun* a viral infection which breaks down the body's immune system. Full form **acquired immunodeficiency syndrome, acquired immune deficiency syndrome**

AIDS dementia /ˌeɪdz dɪ'menʃə/ *noun* a form of mental degeneration resulting from infection with HIV

AIDS-related complex /ˌeɪdz rɪˌleɪtɪd 'kɒmpleks/, **AIDS-related condition** /ˌeɪdz rɪ ˌleɪtɪd kən'dɪʃ(ə)n/ *noun* early symptoms shown by someone infected with the HIV virus, e.g. weight loss, fever and herpes zoster. Abbreviation **ARC**

AIH *abbreviation* artificial insemination by husband

ailment /'eɪlmənt/ *noun* an illness, though not generally a very serious one ○ *Chickenpox is one of the common childhood ailments.*

air bed /'eə bed/ *noun* a mattress which is filled with air, used to prevent the formation of bed-sores. ◊ **conduction**

airborne infection /ˌeəbɔːn ɪn'fekʃən/ *noun* an infection which is carried in the air

air conduction /'eə kənˌdʌkʃən/ *noun* the process by which sounds pass from the outside to the inner ear through the auditory meatus

air embolism /'eər ˌembəlɪz(ə)m/ *noun* a blockage caused by bubbles of air, that stops the flow of blood in vessels

air passage /'eə ˌpæsɪdʒ/ *noun* any tube which takes air to the lungs, e.g. the nostrils, pharynx, larynx, trachea and bronchi

airsickness /'eəsɪknəs/ *noun* a queasy feeling, usually leading to vomiting, caused by the movement of an aircraft

airway /'eəweɪ/ *noun* a passage through which air passes, especially the trachea

akathisia /ˌeɪkə'θɪsiə/ *noun* restlessness

akinesia /ˌeɪkɪ'niːziə/ *noun* a lack of voluntary movement, as in Parkinson's disease

akinetic /ˌeɪkɪ'netɪk/ *adjective* without movement

alacrima /eɪ'lækrɪmə/ *noun* same as **xerosis**

alactasia /ˌeɪlæk'teɪziə/ *noun* a condition in which there is a deficiency of lactase in the intestine, making the patient incapable of digesting lactose, the sugar in milk

alalia /eɪ'leɪliə/ *noun* a condition in which a person completely loses the ability to speak

alanine /'æləniːn/ *noun* an amino acid

alanine aminotransferase /ˌæləniːn ə ˌmiːnəʊ'trænsfəreɪz/ *noun* an enzyme which is found in the liver and can be monitored as an indicator of liver damage. Abbreviation **ALT**

alar cartilage /ˌeɪlə 'kɑːtɪlɪdʒ/ *noun* cartilage in the nose

Albee's operation /'ɔːlbiːz ɒpəˌreɪʃ(ə)n/ *noun* a surgical operation to fuse two or more vertebrae [After Frederick Houdlett Albee (1876–1945), US surgeon.]

albinism /'ælbɪnɪz(ə)m/ *noun* a condition in which a person lacks the pigment melanin and so has pink skin and eyes and white hair. It is hereditary and cannot be treated. ◊ **vitiligo**

albino /æl'biːnəʊ/ *noun* a person who is deficient in melanin and has little or no pigmentation in the skin, hair or eyes

albuginea oculi /ˌælbjʊdʒɪniə 'ɒkjʊlaɪ/ *noun* same as **sclera**

albumin /'ælbjʊmɪn/ *noun* a common protein, which is soluble in water, found in plant and animal tissue and digested in the intestine

albuminuria /ˌælbjʊmɪ'njʊəriə/ *noun* a condition in which albumin is found in the urine, usually a sign of kidney disease, but also sometimes of heart failure

albumose /'ælbjʊməʊz/ *noun* an intermediate product in the digestion of protein

alcohol /'ælkəhɒl/ *noun* a pure colourless liquid which is formed by the action of yeast on sugar solutions and forms part of drinks such as wine and whisky

alcohol abuse /'ælkəhɒl əˌbjuːs/ *noun* the excessive use of alcohol adversely affecting a person's health

alcohol addiction /'ælkəhɒl əˌdɪkʃən/ *noun* a condition in which a person is dependent on the use of alcohol

alcohol-fast /'ælkəhɒl fɑːst/ *adjective* referring to an organ stained for testing which is not discoloured by alcohol

alcoholic /ˌælkə'hɒlɪk/ *adjective* containing alcohol ■ *noun* a person who is addicted to drinking alcohol and shows changes in behaviour and personality

alcoholic cirrhosis /ˌælkəhɒlɪk sɪ'rəʊsɪs/ *noun* cirrhosis of the liver caused by alcoholism

Alcoholics Anonymous /ˌælkəhɒlɪks ə 'nɒnɪməs/ *noun* an organisation of former alcoholics which helps people to overcome their dependence on alcohol by encouraging them to talk about their problems in group therapy. Abbreviation **AA**

alcoholism /'ælkəhɒlɪz(ə)m/ *noun* excessive drinking of alcohol which becomes addictive

alcohol poisoning /'ælkəhɒl ˌpɔɪz(ə)nɪŋ/ *noun* poisoning and disease caused by excessive drinking of alcohol

alcoholuria /ˌælkəhɒl'jʊəriə/ *noun* a condition in which alcohol is present in the urine (NOTE: The level of alcohol in the urine is used as a test for drivers who are suspected of driving while drunk.)

aldosterone /æl'dɒstərəʊn/ *noun* a hormone secreted by the cortex of the adrenal gland, which regulates the balance of sodium and potassium in the body and the amount of body fluid

aldosteronism /æl'dɒst(ə)rənɪz(ə)m/ *noun* a condition in which a person produces too much aldosterone, so that there is too much salt in the blood. This causes high blood pressure and the need to drink a lot of liquids.

aleukaemic /ˌeɪluːˈkiːmɪk/ *adjective* referring to a state where leukaemia is not present

Alexander technique /ˌælɪgˈzɑːndə tek ˌniːk/ *noun* a method of improving the way a person stands and moves, by making them much more aware of how muscles behave

alexia /eɪˈleksiə/ *noun* a condition in which the patient cannot understand printed words. Also called **word blindness**

alfacalcidol /ˌælfəˈkælsɪdɒl/ *noun* a substance related to vitamin D, used by the body to maintain the right levels of calcium and phosphate, and also as a drug to help people who do not have enough vitamin D

algesimeter /ˌældʒɪˈsɪmɪtə/ *noun* an instrument to measure the sensitivity of the skin to pain

-algia /ˈældʒiə/ *suffix* a word ending that indicates a painful condition

algid /ˈældʒɪd/ *adjective* referring to a stage in a disease that causes fever during which the body becomes cold

alienation /ˌeɪliəˈneɪʃ(ə)n/ *noun* a psychological condition in which a person develops the feeling of not being part of the everyday world, and as a result often becomes hostile to other people

alignment /əˈlaɪnmənt/ *noun* the arrangement of something in a straight line, or in the correct position in relation to something else

alimentary /ˌælɪˈment(ə)ri/ *adjective* providing food, or relating to food or nutrition

alimentary canal /ˌælɪˌment(ə)ri kəˈnæl/ *noun* a tube in the body going from the mouth to the anus and including the throat, stomach and intestine, through which food passes and is digested

COMMENT: The alimentary canal is formed of the mouth, throat, oesophagus stomach and small and large intestines. Food is broken down by digestive juices in the mouth, stomach and small intestine, water is removed in the large intestine, and the remaining matter is passed out of the body as faeces.

alimentation /ˌælɪmenˈteɪʃ(ə)n/ *noun* the act of providing food or nourishment

aliquot /ˈælɪkwɒt/ *noun* a part of a larger thing, especially a sample of something which is taken to be examined

alkalaemia /ˌælkəˈliːmiə/ *noun* an excess of alkali in the blood

alkali /ˈælkəlaɪ/ *noun* one of many substances which neutralise acids and form salts (NOTE: The plural is **alkalis**.)

alkaline /ˈælkəlaɪn/ *adjective* containing more alkali than acid

alkalinity /ˌælkəˈlɪnɪti/ *noun* the level of alkali in a body ○ *Hyperventilation causes fluctuating carbon dioxide levels in the blood, resulting in an increase of blood alkalinity.*

alkaloid /ˈælkəlɔɪd/ *noun* one of many poisonous substances found in plants and used as medicines, e.g. atropine, morphine or quinine

alkalosis /ˌælkəˈləʊsɪs/ *noun* a condition in which the alkali level in the body tissue is high, producing cramps

alkaptonuria /ˌælkæptəˈnjʊəriə/ *noun* a hereditary condition where dark pigment is present in the urine

allantois /əˈlæntəʊɪs/ *noun* one of the membranes in the embryo, shaped like a sac, which grows out of the embryonic hindgut

allele /əˈliːl/ *noun* one of two or more alternative forms of a gene, situated in the same area on each of a pair of chromosomes and each producing a different effect

allergen /ˈælədʒən/ *noun* a substance which produces hypersensitivity

allergenic agent /ˌælədʒenɪk ˈeɪdʒənt/ *noun* a substance which produces an allergy

allergic /əˈlɜːdʒɪk/ *adjective* having an allergy to something ○ *She is allergic to cats.* ○ *I'm allergic to penicillin.*

allergy /ˈælədʒi/ *noun* an unusual sensitivity to some substances such as pollen or dust, which cause a physical reaction such as sneezing or a rash in someone who comes into contact with them ○ *She has an allergy to household dust.* ○ *He has a penicillin allergy.* (NOTE: You **have an allergy** or you **are allergic to** something.)

allergy bracelet /ˈælədʒi ˌbreɪslət/ *noun* ♦ **medical alert bracelet**

allied health professional /ˌælaɪd ˈhelθ prə ˌfeʃ(ə)n(ə)l/ *noun* a professional working in medicine who is not a doctor or nurse, e.g. a physiotherapist or paramedic

allo- /æləʊ/ *prefix* different

allocation /ˌæləˈkeɪʃ(ə)n/ *noun* the way an amount of something is divided among the various departments of an organisation, or the amount which is received by a particular department

allodynia /ˌæləˈdɪniə/ *noun* pain of the skin caused by something such as clothing which usually does not cause pain

allograft /ˈæləʊɡrɑːft/ *noun* same as **homograft**

allopathy /əˈlɒpəθi/ *noun* the treatment of a condition using drugs which produce opposite symptoms to those of the condition. Compare **homeopathy**

allopurinol /ˌæləʊˈpjʊərɪnɒl/ *noun* a drug which helps to stop the body producing uric acid, used in the treatment of gout

all or none law /ˌɔːl ɔː 'nʌn lɔː/ *noun* the rule that the heart muscle either contracts fully or does not contract at all

allylestrenol /ˌælaɪl'estrənɒl/ *noun* a steroid used to encourage pregnancy

alopecia /ˌælə'piːʃə/ *noun* a condition in which hair is lost. Compare **hypotrichosis**

alopecia areata /ˌælɒpiːʃə ˌæri'eɪtə/ *noun* a condition in which the hair falls out in patches

alpha /'ælfə/ *noun* the first letter of the Greek alphabet

alpha-adrenoceptor antagonist /ˌælfə ə ˌdriːnəʊrɪ'septə ænˌtægənɪst/, **alpha-adrenoceptor blocker** /'ælfə ˌblɒkə/ *noun* a drug which can relax smooth muscle, used to treat urinary retention and hypertension. Also called **alpha blocker**

alpha-fetoprotein /ˌælfə ˌfiːtəʊ'prəʊtiːn/ *noun* a protein produced by the liver of the human fetus, which accumulates in the amniotic fluid. A high or low concentration is tested for by amniocentesis in the antenatal diagnosis of spina bifida or Down's syndrome, respectively.

Alport's syndrome /'ɔːlpɔːts ˌsɪndrəʊm/ *noun* a genetic disease of the kidneys which sometimes causes a person to lose his or her hearing and sight

alprostadil /æl'prɒstədɪl/ *noun* a drug which makes blood vessels wider, used to treat impotence, prevent coagulation, and maintain babies with congenital heart conditions

ALT *abbreviation* alanine aminotransferase

alternative medicine /ɔːlˌtɜːnətɪv 'med(ə)sɪn/ *noun* the treatment of illness using therapies such as homoeopathy or naturopathy which are not considered part of conventional Western medicine. ◊ **complementary medicine**

altitude sickness /'æltɪtjuːd ˌsɪknəs/ *noun* a condition caused by reduced oxygen in the air above altitudes of 7000 to 8000 feet (3600 metres). Symptoms include headaches, breathlessness, fatigue, nausea and swelling of the face, hands and feet. Also called **high-altitude sickness, mountain sickness**

aluminium hydroxide /ˌæləˌmɪniəm haɪ 'drɒksaɪd/ *noun* a chemical substance used as an antacid to treat indigestion. Formula: Al(OH)$_3$ or Al$_2$O$_3$.3H$_2$O.

alveolar /ˌælvɪ'əʊlə, æl'viːələ/ *adjective* referring to the alveoli

alveolar duct /ˌælvɪ'əʊlə dʌkt/ *noun* a duct in the lung which leads from the respiratory bronchioles to the alveoli. See illustration at **LUNGS** in Supplement

alveolitis /ˌælvɪə'laɪtɪs/ *noun* inflammation of an alveolus in the lungs or the socket of a tooth

alveolus /ˌælvɪ'əʊləs, æl'viːələs/ *noun* a small cavity, e.g. an air sac in the lungs or the socket

into which a tooth fits. See illustration at **LUNGS** in Supplement (NOTE: The plural is **alveoli**.)

Alzheimer plaque /'æltshaɪmə plæk/ *noun* a disc-shaped plaque of amyloid found in the brain in people who have Alzheimer's disease

Alzheimer's disease /'æltshaɪməz dɪˌziːz/ *noun* a disease where a person experiences progressive dementia due to nerve cell loss in specific brain areas, resulting in loss of mental faculties including memory [Described 1906. After Alois Alzheimer (1864–1915), Bavarian physician.]

amalgam /ə'mælgəm/ *noun* a mixture of metals, based on mercury and tin, used by dentists to fill holes in teeth

amaurosis /ˌæmɔː'rəʊsɪs/ *noun* blindness caused by disease of the optic nerve

amaurotic familial idiocy /ˌæmɔːrɒtɪk fə ˌmɪliəl 'ɪdiəsi/, **amaurotic family idiocy** /ˌæmɔːrɒtɪk ˌfæm(ə)li 'ɪdiəsi/ *noun* same as **Tay-Sachs disease**

amb- /æmb/ *prefix* same as **ambi-** (*used before vowels*)

ambi- /æmbi/ *prefix* both

ambidextrous /ˌæmbɪ'dekstrəs/ *adjective* referring to a person who can use both hands equally well and who is not right- or left-handed

ambisexual /ˌæmbɪ'sekʃuəl/ *adjective, noun* same as **bisexual**

amblyopia /ˌæmbli'əʊpiə/ *noun* a lack of normal vision without a structural cause. A common example is squint and other forms may be caused by the cyanide in tobacco smoke or by drinking methylated spirits.

amblyopic /ˌæmbli'ɒpɪk/ *adjective* affected by amblyopia

amblyoscope /'æmbliəʊskəʊp/ *noun* an instrument for measuring the angle of a squint and how effectively someone uses both their eyes together. Also called **orthoptoscope**

ambulatory /ˌæmbju'leɪt(ə)ri/ *adjective* referring to a patient who is not confined to bed but is able to walk

ambulatory care /ˌæmbjuˌleɪt(ə)ri 'keə/ *noun* treatment of a patient which does not involve staying in hospital during the night

amelia /ə'miːliə/ *noun* the absence of a limb from birth, or a condition in which a limb is short from birth

amelioration /əˌmiːliə'reɪʃ(ə)n/ *noun* the process of getting better

ameloblastoma /ˌæmɪləʊblæ'stəʊmə/ *noun* a tumour in the jaw, usually in the lower jaw

amenorrhoea /ˌeɪmenə'riːə/ *noun* the absence of one or more menstrual periods, usual during pregnancy and after the menopause

amentia /eɪ'menʃə/ *noun* the fact of being mentally underdeveloped

ametropia /ˌæmɪ'trəʊpiə/ *noun* a condition in which the eye cannot focus light correctly onto the retina, as in astigmatism, hypermetropia and myopia. Compare **emmetropia**

amfetamine /æm'fetəmiːn/ *noun* an addictive drug, similar to adrenaline, used to give a feeling of wellbeing and wakefulness. Also called **amphetamine**

amikacin /ˌæmɪ'keɪsɪn/ *noun* a type of antibiotic used to treat infections caused by aerobic bacteria

amiloride /ə'mɪləraɪd/ *noun* a drug which helps to increase the production of urine and preserve the body's supply of potassium

amino acid /əˌmiːnəʊ 'æsɪd/ *noun* a chemical compound which is broken down from proteins in the digestive system and then used by the body to form its own protein

aminobutyric acid /əˌmiːnəʊbjuːtɪrɪk 'æsɪd/ *noun* ♦ gamma aminobutyric acid

aminoglycoside /əˌmiːnəʊ'glaɪkəsaɪd/ *noun* a drug used to treat many Gram-negative and some Gram-positive bacterial infections (NOTE: Aminoglycosides include drugs with names ending in **-cin**: **gentamicin**.)

aminophylline /ˌæmɪ'nɒfɪliːn/ *noun* a drug that makes the bronchial tubes wider, used in the treatment of asthma

amiodarone /ˌæmɪ'ɒdərəʊn/ *noun* a drug that makes the blood vessels wider, used in the treatment of irregular heartbeat

amitosis /ˌæmɪ'təʊsɪs/ *noun* the multiplication of a cell by splitting of the nucleus

amitriptyline /ˌæmɪ'trɪptɪliːn/ *noun* a sedative drug used to treat depression and persistent pain

amlodipine /æm'lɒdɪpiːn/ *noun* a drug that helps to control the movement of calcium ions through cell membranes. It is used to treat hypertension and angina.

ammonia /ə'məʊniə/ *noun* a gas with a strong smell, a compound of nitrogen and hydrogen, which is a usual product of human metabolism

amnesia /æm'niːziə/ *noun* loss of memory

amnihook /'æmnihʊk/ *noun* a hooked instrument used to induce labour by pulling on the amniotic sac

amniocentesis /ˌæmniəʊsen'tiːsɪs/ *noun* a procedure which involves taking a test sample of the amniotic fluid during pregnancy using a hollow needle and syringe

amnion /'æmniən/ *noun* the thin sac containing the amniotic fluid which covers an unborn baby in the uterus. Also called **amniotic sac**

amnioscope /'æmniəskəʊp/ *noun* an instrument used to examine a fetus through the cervical channel, before the amniotic sac is broken

amnioscopy /ˌæmni'ɒskəpi/ *noun* an examination of the amniotic fluid during pregnancy

amniotic /ˌæmni'ɒtɪk/ *adjective* relating to the amnion

amniotic fluid /ˌæmniɒtɪk 'fluːɪd/ *noun* the fluid contained in the amnion which surrounds an unborn baby

amniotomy /ˌæmni'ɒtəmi/ *noun* a puncture of the amnion to help induce labour

amoeba /ə'miːbə/ *noun* a form of animal life, made up of a single cell (NOTE: The plural is **amoebae**.)

amoebiasis /ˌæmiː'baɪəsɪs/ *noun* an infection caused by amoebae which can result in amoebic dysentery in the large intestine (**intestinal amoebiasis**) and sometimes affects the lungs (**pulmonary amoebiasis**)

amoebic /ə'miːbɪk/ *adjective* relating to or caused by amoebae

amorphous /ə'mɔːfəs/ *adjective* with no regular shape

amoxicillin /əˌmɒksɪsɪlɪn/ *noun* an antibiotic

Amoxil /ə'mɒksɪl/ a trade name for amoxicillin

amphetamine /æm'fetəmiːn/ *noun* same as **amfetamine**

amphiarthrosis /ˌæmfiɑː'θrəʊsɪs/ *noun* a joint which only has limited movement, e.g. one of the joints in the spine

amphotericin /ˌæmfəʊ'terɪsɪn/ *noun* an antifungal agent, used against *Candida*

ampicillin /ˌæmpɪ'sɪlɪn/ *noun* a type of penicillin, used as an antibiotic

ampoule /'æmpuːl/, **ampule** /'æmpjuːl/ *noun* a small glass container, closed at the neck, used to contain sterile drugs for use in injections

ampulla /æm'pʊlə/ *noun* a swelling of a canal or duct, shaped like a bottle (NOTE: The plural is **ampullae**.)

amputation /ˌæmpjʊ'teɪʃ(ə)n/ *noun* the surgical removal of a limb or part of a limb

amputee /ˌæmpjʊ'tiː/ *noun* someone who has had a limb or part of a limb removed in a surgical operation

amygdala /ə'mɪgdələ/ *noun* an almond-shaped body in the brain, at the end of the caudate nucleus of the thalamus. Also called **amygdaloid body**

amygdaloid body /ə'mɪgdələɪd ˌbɒdi/ *noun* same as **amygdala**

amyl- /æm(ə)l/ *prefix* referring to starch

amylase /'æmɪleɪz/ *noun* an enzyme which converts starch into maltose

amyl nitrate /ˌæm(ə)l 'naɪtreɪt/ *noun* a drug used to reduce blood pressure (NOTE: Amyl nitrate is also used as a recreational drug.)

amyloid /'æmɪlɔɪd/ *noun* a waxy protein that forms in some tissues during the development of various diseases, e.g. forming disc-shaped plaques in the brain in Alzheimer's disease

amyloid disease /ˈæmɪlɔɪd dɪˌziːz/ *noun* same as **amyloidosis**

amyloidosis /ˌæmɪlɔɪˈdəʊsɪs/ *noun* a disease of the kidneys and liver, where amyloid develops in the tissues. Also called **amyloid disease**

amylopsin /ˌæmɪˈlɒpsɪn/ *noun* an enzyme which converts starch into maltose

amylose /ˈæmɪləʊz/ *noun* a carbohydrate of starch

amyotonia /ˌeɪmaɪəˈtəʊniə/ *noun* a lack of muscle tone

amyotonia congenita /ˌeɪmaɪətəʊniə kən ˈdʒenɪtə/ *noun* a congenital disease of children in which the muscles lack tone. Also called **floppy baby syndrome**

amyotrophia /eɪˌmaɪəˈtrəʊfiə/ *noun* a condition in which a muscle wastes away

amyotrophic lateral sclerosis /eɪ ˌmaɪətrɒfɪk ˌlætər(ə)l sklɪəˈrəʊsɪs/ *noun* a motor neurone disease in which the limbs twitch and the muscles gradually waste away. Also called **Gehrig's disease**. Abbreviation **ALS**

amyotrophy /eɪˌmaɪˈɒtrəfi/ same as **amyotrophia**

an- /æn/ *prefix* same as **ana-** (*used before vowels*)

ana- /ænə/ *prefix* without or lacking

anabolic /ˌænəˈbɒlɪk/ *adjective* referring to a substance which synthesises protein

anabolic steroid /ænəˌbɒlɪk ˈstɪərɔɪd/ *noun* a drug which encourages the synthesis of new living tissue, especially muscle, from nutrients

anabolism /æˈnæbəlɪz(ə)m/ *noun* the process of building up complex chemical substances on the basis of simpler ones

anacrotism /əˈnækrətɪz(ə)m/ *noun* a second stroke in the pulse

anaemia /əˈniːmiə/ *noun* a condition in which the level of red blood cells is less than usual or where the haemoglobin is less, making it more difficult for the blood to carry oxygen. The symptoms are tiredness and pale colour, especially pale lips, nails and the inside of the eyelids. The condition can be fatal if not treated.

anaemic /əˈniːmɪk/ *adjective* having anaemia

anaerobe /ˈænərəʊb, ænˈeərəʊb/ *noun* a microorganism which lives without oxygen, e.g. the tetanus bacillus

anaerobic /ˌænəˈrəʊbɪk/ *adjective* **1.** not needing oxygen for metabolism ○ *anaerobic bacteria* **2.** without oxygen ○ *anaerobic conditions*

anaesthesia /ˌænəsˈθiːziə/ *noun* **1.** a state, deliberately produced in a patient by a medical procedure, in which he or she can feel no pain, either in a part or in the whole of the body **2.** a loss of feeling caused by damage to nerves (NOTE: The US spelling is **anesthesia**.)

anaesthetic /ˌænəsˈθetɪk/ *adjective* inducing loss of feeling ■ *noun* a substance given to someone to remove feeling, so that he or she can undergo an operation without pain

anaesthetic induction /ˌænəsθetɪk ɪn ˈdʌkʃən/ *noun* a method of inducing anaesthesia in a patient

anaesthetic risk /ˌænəsθetɪk ˈrɪsk/ *noun* the risk that an anaesthetic may cause serious unwanted side effects

anaesthetise /əˈniːsθətaɪz/, **anaesthetize** *verb* to produce a loss of feeling in a person or in part of the person's body

anaesthetist /əˈniːsθətɪst/ *noun* a specialist who administers anaesthetics

anal /ˈeɪn(ə)l/ *adjective* relating to the anus

analeptic /ˌænəˈleptɪk/ *noun* a drug used to make someone regain consciousness or to stimulate a patient

analgesia /ˌæn(ə)lˈdʒiːziə/ *noun* a reduction of the feeling of pain without loss of consciousness

analgesic /ˌæn(ə)lˈdʒiːzɪk/ *adjective* relating to analgesia ■ *noun* a painkilling drug which produces analgesia and reduces pyrexia

anally /ˈeɪn(ə)li/ *adverb* through the anus ○ *The patient is not able to pass faeces anally.*

analyse /ˈænəlaɪz/ *verb* to examine something in detail ○ *The laboratory is analysing the blood samples.* ○ *When the food was analysed it was found to contain traces of bacteria.*

analysis /əˈnæləsɪs/ *noun* an examination of a substance to find out what it is made of (NOTE: The plural is **analyses**.)

analyst /ˈænəlɪst/ *noun* a person who examines samples of substances or tissue, to find out what they are made of

anaphase /ˈænəfeɪz/ *noun* a stage in cell division, after the metaphase and before the telophase

anaphylactic /ˌænəfɪˈlæktɪk/ *adjective* relating to or caused by extreme sensitivity to a substance

anaphylactic shock /ˌænəfɪlæktɪk ˈʃɒk/ *noun* a sudden severe reaction, which can be fatal, to something such as an injected substance or a bee sting

anaphylaxis /ˌænəfɪˈlæksɪs/ *noun* **1.** extreme sensitivity to a substance introduced into the body **2.** same as **anaphylactic shock**

anaplasia /ˌænəˈpleɪsiə/ *noun* the loss of a cell's typical characteristics, caused by cancer

anaplastic /ˌænəˈplæstɪk/ *adjective* referring to anaplasia

anarthria /ænˈɑːθriə/ *noun* the loss of the ability to speak words properly

anasarca /ˌænəˈsɑːkə/ *noun* the presence of fluid in the body tissues. ◊ **oedema**

anastomose /əˈnæstəməʊz/ *verb* to join two blood vessels or tubular structures together

anastomosis /ə,næstə'məʊsɪs/ *noun* a connection made between two blood vessels or tubular structures, either naturally or by surgery

anatomical /,ænə'tɒmɪk(ə)l/ *adjective* relating to the anatomy ○ *the anatomical features of a fetus*

anatomy /ə'nætəmi/ *noun* **1.** the structure, especially the internal structure, of the body **2.** the branch of science that studies the structure of the bodies of humans, animals and plants ○ *They are studying anatomy.*

ancillary worker /æn'sɪləri ,wɜːkə/ *noun* someone who does a job for patients such cooking or cleaning which is supplementary to medical care

anconeus /æŋ'kəʊniəs/ *noun* a small triangular muscle at the back of the elbow

Ancylostoma /,ænsɪlə'stəʊmə/ *noun* a parasitic worm in the intestine which holds onto the wall of the intestine with its teeth and lives on the blood and protein of the carrier

ancylostomiasis /,ænsɪləʊstə'maɪəsɪs/ *noun* a disease of which the symptoms are weakness and anaemia, caused by a hookworm which lives on the blood of the carrier. In severe cases the person may die.

androgen /'ændrədʒən/ *noun* a male sex hormone, testosterone or androsterone, which increases the male characteristics of the body

androgenic /,ændrə'dʒenɪk/ *adjective* producing male characteristics

andrology /æn'drɒlədʒi/ *noun* the study of male sexual characteristics and subjects such as impotence, infertility and the male menopause

androsterone /æn'drɒstərəʊn/ *noun* one of the male sex hormones

anencephalous /,ænen'kefələs/ *adjective* having no brain

anencephaly /,ænen'kefəli/ *noun* the absence of a brain, which causes a fetus to die a few hours after birth

anergy /'ænədʒi/ *noun* a state of severe weakness and lack of energy

aneurine /ə'njʊərɪn/ *noun* same as **Vitamin B₁**

aneurysm /'ænjərɪz(ə)m/ *noun* a swelling caused by the weakening of the wall of a blood vessel

angi- /ændʒi/ *prefix* same as **angio-** (*used before vowels*)

angiectasis /,ændʒi'ektəsɪs/ *noun* a swelling of the blood vessels

angiitis /,ændʒi'aɪtɪs/ *noun* an inflammation of a blood vessel

angina /æn'dʒaɪnə/ *noun* a pain in the chest following exercise or eating, which is caused by an inadequate supply of blood to the heart muscles because of narrowing of the arteries. It is commonly treated with nitrates or calcium channel blocker drugs.

angina pectoris /æn,dʒaɪnə 'pektərɪs/ *noun* same as **angina**

angio- /ændʒiəʊ/ *prefix* referring to a blood vessel

angiocardiogram /,ændʒiəʊ'kɑːdiəgræm/ *noun* a series of pictures resulting from angiocardiography

angiocardiography /,ændʒiəʊkɑːdi'ɒgrəfi/ *noun* an X-ray examination of the cardiac system after injection with an opaque dye so that the organs show up clearly on the film

angiodysplasia /,ændʒiəʊdɪs'pleɪziə/ *noun* a condition where the blood vessels in the colon dilate, resulting in loss of blood

angiogenesis /,ændʒiəʊ'dʒenəsɪs/ *noun* the formation of new blood vessels, e.g. in an embryo or as a result of a tumour

angiogram /'ændʒiəʊgræm/ *noun* an X-ray picture of blood vessels

angiography /,ændʒi'ɒgrəfi/ *noun* an X-ray examination of blood vessels after injection with an opaque dye so that they show up clearly on the film

angiology /,ændʒi'ɒlədʒi/ *noun* the branch of medicine which deals with blood vessels and the lymphatic system

angioma /,ændʒi'əʊmə/ *noun* a benign tumour formed of blood vessels, e.g. a naevus

angioneurotic oedema /,ændʒiəʊnjʊ,rɒtɪk ɪ'diːmə/ *noun* a sudden accumulation of liquid under the skin, similar to nettle rash

angiopathy /,ændʒi'ɒpəθi/ *noun* a disease of vessels such as blood and lymphatic vessels

angioplasty /'ændʒiəʊ,plæsti/ *noun* plastic surgery to repair a blood vessel, e.g. a narrowed coronary artery

angiosarcoma /,ændʒiəʊsɑː'kəʊmə/ *noun* a malignant tumour in a blood vessel

angiospasm /'ændʒiəʊspæz(ə)m/ *noun* a spasm which constricts blood vessels

angiotensin /'ændʒiəʊtensɪn/ *noun* a polypeptide which affects blood pressure by causing vasoconstriction and increasing extracellular volume

angiotensin-converting enzyme inhibitor /,ændʒiəʊtensɪn kən,vɜːtɪŋ 'enzaɪm ɪn,hɪbɪtə/ *noun* a drug which inhibits the conversion of angiotensin I to angiotensin II, which constricts arteries, used in the treatment of hypertension and heart failure. Also called **ACE inhibitor** (NOTE: ACE inhibitors have names ending in **-pril: captopril.**)

angle-closure glaucoma /,æŋgəl ,kləʊʒə glɔː'kəʊmə/ *noun* an unusually high pressure of fluid inside the eyeball caused by pressure of the iris against the lens, trapping the aqueous humour. Also called **acute glaucoma**

angular vein /ˈæŋɡjʊlə veɪn/ *noun* a vein which continues the facial vein at the side of the nose

anhedonia /ˌænhɪˈdəʊniə/ *noun* a psychological condition in which a person is unable to enjoy all the experiences that most people enjoy

anhidrosis /ˌænhɪˈdrəʊsɪs/ *noun* a condition in which sweating by the body is reduced or stops completely

anhidrotic /ˌænhɪˈdrɒtɪk/ *adjective* referring to a drug which reduces sweating

anhydraemia /ˌænhaɪˈdriːmiə/ *noun* a lack of sufficient fluid in the blood

anhydrous /ænˈhaɪdrəs/ *adjective* referring to compounds or crystals that contain no water

anidrosis /ˌænɪˈdrəʊsɪs/ *noun* same as **anhidrosis**

aniridia /ˌænɪˈrɪdiə/ *noun* a congenital absence of the iris

anisocytosis /ˌænaɪsəʊsaɪˈtəʊsɪs/ *noun* a variation in size of red blood cells

anisomelia /ˌænaɪsəʊˈmiːliə/ *noun* a difference in length of the legs

anisometropia /ˌænaɪsəʊməˈtrəʊpiə/ *noun* a state where the refraction in the two eyes is different

ankle /ˈæŋkəl/ *noun* the part of the body where the foot is connected to the leg

ankyloblepharon /ˌæŋkɪləʊˈblefərɒn/ *noun* a state where the edges of the eyelids are stuck together

ankylosing spondylitis /ˌæŋkɪləʊzɪŋ spɒndɪˈlaɪtɪs/ *noun* a condition occurring more frequently in young men, in which the vertebrae and sacroiliac joints are inflamed and become stiff

ankylosis /ˌæŋkɪˈləʊsɪs/ *noun* a condition in which the bones of a joint fuse together

Ankylostoma /ˌæŋkɪlˈstəʊmə/ *noun* same as **Ancylostoma**

ankylostomiasis /ˌæŋkɪləʊstəˈmaɪəsɪs/ *noun* same as **ancylostomiasis**

annular /ˈænjʊlə/ *adjective* shaped like a ring

annulus /ˈænjʊləs/ *noun* a structure shaped like a ring

ano- /ænəʊ/ *prefix* referring to the anus

anodyne /ˈænədaɪn/ *noun* a drug which reduces pain, e.g. aspirin or codeine ■ *adjective* referring to drugs that bring relief from pain or discomfort

anomalous /əˈnɒmələs/ *adjective* different from what is usual

anomaly /əˈnɒməli/ *noun* something which is different from the usual

anomie /ˈænəmi/ *noun* a psychological condition in which a person develops the feeling of not being part of the everyday world, and behaves as though they do not have any supporting social or moral framework

anonychia /ˌænəˈnɪkiə/ *noun* a congenital absence of one or more nails

anopheles /əˈnɒfəliːz/ *noun* a mosquito which carries the malaria parasite

anoplasty /ˈeɪnəʊplæsti/ *noun* surgery to repair the anus, as in treating haemorrhoids

anorchism /ænˈɔːkɪz(ə)m/ *noun* a congenital absence of testicles

anorectal /ˌeɪnəʊˈrekt(ə)l/ *adjective* referring to both the anus and rectum

anorexia /ˌænəˈreksiə/ *noun* loss of appetite

anorexia nervosa /ˌænəreksiə nɜːˈvəʊsə/ *noun* a psychological condition, usually found in girls and young women, in which a person refuses to eat because of a fear of becoming fat

anosmia /ænˈɒzmiə/ *noun* the lack of the sense of smell

anovular /ænˈɒvjʊlə/ *adjective* without an ovum

anovular bleeding /æn,ɒvjʊlə ˈbliːdɪŋ/ *noun* bleeding from the uterus when ovulation has not taken place

anovulation /æn,ɒvjʊˈleɪʃ(ə)n/ *noun* a condition in which a women does not ovulate and is therefore infertile

anoxaemia /ˌænɒkˈsiːmiə/ *noun* a reduction of the amount of oxygen in the blood

anoxia /æˈnɒksiə/ *noun* a lack of oxygen in body tissue

anoxic /ænˈɒksɪk/ *adjective* referring to anoxia or lacking oxygen

antacid /æntˈæsɪd/ *adjective* preventing too much acid forming in the stomach or altering the amount of acid in the stomach ■ *noun* a substance that stops too much acid forming in the stomach, used in the treatment of gastro-intestinal conditions such as ulcers, e.g. calcium carbonate or magnesium trisilicate

antagonist /ænˈtæɡənɪst/ *adjective* **1.** referring to a muscle which opposes another muscle in a movement **2.** referring to a substance which opposes another substance ■ *noun* a substance which acts through specific receptors to block the action of another substance, but which has no observable physiological effect itself ○ *Atropine is a cholinergic antagonist and blocks the effects of acetylcholine.*

ante- /ænti/ *prefix* before

ante cibum /ˌænti ˈtʃɪbəm, ˌænti ˈsiːbəm/ *adverb* full form of **a.c.**

anteflexion /ˌæntiˈflekʃən/ *noun* the curving forward of an organ, e.g. the usual curvature of the uterus

antemortem /ˌænti'mɔːtəm/ *noun* the period before death

antenatal /ˌænti'neɪt(ə)l/ *adjective* during the period between conception and childbirth

antenatal clinic /ˌænti'neɪt(ə)l ˌklɪnɪk/ *noun* a clinic where expectant mothers are taught how to look after babies, do exercises and have medical checkups. Also called **maternity clinic**

antenatal diagnosis /ˌæntiˌneɪt(ə)l ˌdaɪəg'nəʊsɪs/ *noun* a medical examination of a pregnant woman to see if the fetus is developing in the usual way. Also called **prenatal diagnosis**

antepartum /ˌænti'pɑːtəm/ *noun* the period of three months before childbirth ■ *adjective* referring to the three months before childbirth

antepartum haemorrhage /ˌæntipɑːtəm 'hemərɪdʒ/ *noun* bleeding from the vagina before labour. Abbreviation **APH**

anterior /æn'tɪəriə/ *adjective* in front. Opposite **posterior**

anterior aspect /ænˌtɪəriə 'æspekt/ *noun* a view of the front of the body, or of the front of part of the body. See illustration at **ANATOMICAL TERMS** in Supplement

anterior fontanelle /ænˌtɪəriə fɒntə'nel/ *noun* the cartilage at the top of the head where the frontal bone joins the two parietals

anterior nares /ænˌtɪəriə 'neəriːz/ *plural noun* the two nostrils. Also called **external nares**

anterograde amnesia /ˌæntərəʊgreɪd æm'niːziə/ *noun* a brain condition in which the person cannot remember things which happened recently

anteversion /ˌænti'vɜːʃ(ə)n/ *noun* the tilting forward of an organ, whether usual, as of the uterus, or unusual

anthelmintic /ˌænθel'mɪntɪk/ *noun* a substance which removes worms from the intestine ■ *adjective* removing worms from the intestine

anthracosis /ˌænθrə'kəʊsɪs/ *noun* a lung disease caused by breathing coal dust

anthrax /'ænθræks/ *noun* a disease of cattle and sheep which can be transmitted to humans

anthrop- /ænθrəp/ *prefix* referring to human beings

anthropology /ˌænθrə'pɒlədʒi/ *noun* the study of human beings as a species, especially their culture or development. It differs from sociology in taking a more historical and comparative approach.

anthropometry /ˌænθrə'pɒmətri/ *noun* the study of human body measurements (NOTE: The uses of anthropometry include the design of ergonomic furniture and the examination and comparison of populations.)

anti- /ænti/ *prefix* against

antiarrhythmic /ˌæntieɪ'rɪðmɪk/ *adjective* referring to a drug which corrects an irregular heartbeat

antiasthmatic /ˌæntiæs'mætɪk/ *adjective* referring to a drug that is used to treat asthma

antibacterial /ˌæntibæk'tɪəriəl/ *adjective* destroying bacteria

antibiotic /ˌæntibaɪ'ɒtɪk/ *adjective* stopping the spread of bacteria ■ *noun* a drug which is developed from living substances and which stops the spread of bacteria, e.g. penicillin ○ *He was given a course of antibiotics.* ○ *Antibiotics have no effect against viral diseases.*

antibody /'æntibɒdi/ *noun* a protein that is stimulated by the body to produce foreign substances such as bacteria, as part of an immune reaction ○ *Tests showed that he had antibodies in his blood.*

antibody-negative /ˌæntibɒdi 'negətɪv/ *adjective* showing none of a particular antibody in the blood ○ *The donor tested antibody-negative.*

antibody-positive /ˌæntibɒdi 'pɒzitɪv/ *adjective* showing the presence of particular antibodies in the blood ○ *The patient is HIV antibody-positive.*

anticholinergic /ˌæntikəʊlɪ'nɜːdʒɪk/ *adjective* blocking nerve impulses which are part of the stress response ■ *noun* one of a group of drugs which are used to control stress

anticholinesterase /ˌæntikəʊlɪn'estəreɪz/ *noun* a substance which blocks nerve impulses by reducing the activity of the enzyme cholinesterase

anticoagulant /ˌæntikəʊ'ægjʊlənt/ *adjective* slowing or stopping the clotting of blood ■ *noun* a drug which slows down or stops the clotting of blood, used to prevent the formation of a thrombus (NOTE: Anticoagulants have names ending in **-parin**: **heparin**.)

anticonvulsant /ˌæntikən'vʌls(ə)nt/ *adjective* acting to control convulsions ■ *noun* a drug used to control convulsions, as in the treatment of epilepsy, e.g. carbamazepine

anti-D /ˌænti 'diː/, **anti-D gamma-globulin** /ˌænti ˌdiː ˌgæmə 'glɒbjʊlɪn/ *noun* Rh D immunoglobulin, used to treat pregnant women who develop antibodies when the mother is Rh-negative and the fetus is Rh-positive

antidepressant /ˌæntidɪ'pres(ə)nt/ *adjective* acting to relieve depression ■ *noun* a drug used to relieve depression by stimulating the mood of a depressed person. Examples are tricyclic antidepressants, selective serotonin reuptake inhibitors and monoamine oxidase inhibitors.

anti-D immunoglobulin /ˌænti ˌdiː ɪmjʊnəʊ 'glɒbjʊlɪn/ *noun* immunoglobulin administered to Rh-negative mothers after the birth of an Rh-positive baby, to prevent haemolytic disease of the newborn in the next pregnancy

antidiuretic /ˌæntidaɪjʊ'retɪk/ *noun* a substance which stops the production of excessive amounts of urine ○ *hormones which have an antidiuretic effect on the kidneys* ■ *adjective* preventing the excessive production of urine

antidote /'æntɪdəʊt/ *noun* a substance which counteracts the effect of a poison ○ *There is no satisfactory antidote to cyanide.*

antiembolic /ˌæntiem'bɒlɪk/ *adjective* preventing embolism

antiemetic /ˌæntiɪ'metɪk/ *noun* a drug which prevents vomiting ■ *adjective* acting to prevent vomiting

antiepileptic drug /ˌæntiepɪ'leptɪk drʌg/ *noun* a drug used in the treatment of epilepsy and convulsions, e.g. carbamazepine

antifibrinolytic /ˌæntifaɪbrɪnə'lɪtɪk/ *adjective* acting to reduce fibrosis

antifungal /ˌænti'fʌŋgəl/ *adjective* referring to a substance which kills or controls fungal and yeast infections, e.g. candida and ringworm (NOTE: Antifungal drugs have names ending in **-conazole**: **fluconazole**.)

antigen /'æntɪdʒən/ *noun* a substance that stimulates the body to produce antibodies, e.g. a protein on the surface of a cell or microorganism

antigenic /ˌæntɪ'dʒenɪk/ *adjective* referring to a substance which stimulates the formation of antibodies

antihaemophilic factor /ˌæntihiːmə'fɪlɪk ˌfæktə/ *noun* factor VIII, used to encourage blood-clotting in haemophiliacs. Abbreviation **AHF**

antihelminthic /ˌæntihel'mɪnθɪk/ *noun* a drug used in the treatment of worm infections such as threadworm, hookworm or roundworm

antihistamine /ˌænti'hɪstəmiːn/ *noun* a drug used to control the effects of an allergy which releases histamine, or reduces gastric acid in the stomach for the treatment of gastric ulcers (NOTE: Antihistamines have names ending in **-tidine**: **loratidine** for allergies, **cimetidine** for gastric ulcers.)

antihypertensive /ˌæntihaɪpə'tensɪv/ *adjective* acting to reduce blood pressure ■ *noun* a drug used to reduce high blood pressure

anti-inflammatory /ˌænti ɪn'flæmət(ə)ri/ *adjective* referring to a drug which reduces inflammation

antilymphocytic serum /ˌæntilɪmfəʊ'sɪtɪk ˌsɪərəm/ *noun* a serum used to produce immunosuppression in people undergoing transplant operations. Abbreviation **ALS**

antimalarial /ˌæntimə'leəriəl/ *noun* a drug used to treat malaria and in malarial prophylaxis ■ *adjective* treating or preventing malaria

antimetabolite /ˌæntimə'tæbəlaɪt/ *noun* a substance which can replace a cell metabolism, but which is not active

antimicrobial /ˌæntimaɪ'krəʊbiəl/ *adjective* acting against microorganisms that cause disease

antimigraine /ˌænti'maɪgreɪn/ *noun* a drug used in the treatment of migraine

antimitotic /ˌæntimaɪ'tɒtɪk/ *adjective* preventing the division of a cell by mitosis

antimuscarinic /ˌæntimʌskə'rɪnɪk/ *adjective* referring to a drug which blocks acetylcholine receptors found on smooth muscle in the gut and eye

antimycotic /ˌæntimaɪ'kɒtɪk/ *adjective* destroying fungi

antinauseant /ˌænti'nɔːziənt/ *adjective* referring to a drug which helps to suppress nausea

antioxidant /ˌænti'ɒksɪd(ə)nt/ *noun* a substance which makes oxygen less damaging, e.g. in the body or in foods or plastics ○ *antioxidant vitamins*

antiperistalsis /ˌæntiperɪ'stælsɪs/ *noun* a movement in the oesophagus or intestine which causes their contents to move in the opposite direction to usual peristalsis, so leading to vomiting

antiperspirant /ˌænti'pɜːsp(ə)rənt/ *noun* a substance which prevents sweating ■ *adjective* preventing sweating

antipruritic /ˌæntiprʊ'rɪtɪk/ *noun* a substance which prevents itching ■ *adjective* preventing itching

antipsychotic /ˌæntisaɪ'kɒtɪk/ *noun* a neuroleptic or major tranquilliser drug which calms disturbed people without causing sedation or confusion by blocking dopamine receptors in the brain

antipyretic /ˌæntipaɪ'retɪk/ *noun* a drug which helps to reduce a fever ■ *adjective* reducing fever

anti-Rh body /ˌænti ɑːr 'eɪtʃ ˌbɒdi/ *noun* an antibody formed in a mother's blood in reaction to a Rhesus antigen in the blood of the fetus

antisepsis /ˌæntɪ'sepsɪs/ *noun* a procedure intended to prevent sepsis

antiseptic /ˌæntɪ'septɪk/ *adjective* preventing harmful microorganisms from spreading ○ *She gargled with an antiseptic mouthwash.* ■ *noun* a substance which prevents germs growing or spreading ○ *The nurse painted the wound with antiseptic.*

antiserum /ˌænti'sɪərəm/ *noun* ♦ **serum** (NOTE: The plural is **antisera**.)

antisocial /ˌænti'səʊʃ(ə)l/ *adjective* referring to behaviour which is harmful to other people

antispasmodic /ˌæntispæz'mɒdɪk/ *noun* a drug used to prevent spasms

antitetanus serum /ˌænti'tetənəs ˌsɪərəm/ *noun* a serum which protects a patient against tetanus. Abbreviation **ATS**

antithrombin /ˌæntiˈθrɒmbɪn/ *noun* a substance present in the blood which prevents clotting

antitoxic serum /ˌæntitɒksɪk ˈsɪərəm/ *noun* an immunising agent, formed of serum taken from an animal which has developed antibodies to a disease, used to protect a person from that disease

antitoxin /ˌæntiˈtɒksɪn/ *noun* an antibody produced by the body to counteract a poison in the body

antitragus /ˌæntiˈtreɪgəs/ *noun* a small projection on the outer ear opposite the tragus

antitussive /ˌæntiˈtʌsɪv/ *noun* a drug used to reduce coughing

antivenin /ˌæntiˈvenɪn/, **antivenom** /ˌænti ˈvenəm/, **antivenene** /ˌæntivəˈniːn/ *noun* a substance which helps the body to fight the effects of a particular venom from a snake or insect bite

antiviral /ˌæntiˈvaɪrəl/ *adjective* referring to a drug or treatment which stops or reduces the damage caused by a virus ■ *noun* same as **antiviral drug**

antiviral drug /ˌæntiˈvaɪrəl drʌg/ *noun* a drug which is effective against a virus (NOTE: Antiviral drugs have names ending in **-ciclovir**.)

antral /ˈæntrəl/ *adjective* referring to an antrum

antrectomy /ænˈtrektəmi/ *noun* the surgical removal of an antrum in the stomach to prevent gastrin being formed

antroscopy /ænˈtrɒskəpi/ *noun* an examination of an antrum

antrostomy /ænˈtrɒstəmi/ *noun* a surgical operation to make an opening in the maxillary sinus to drain an antrum

antrum /ˈæntrəm/ *noun* any cavity inside the body, especially one in bone (NOTE: The plural is **antra**.)

anuria /ænˈjʊəriə/ *noun* a condition in which the patient does not make urine, either because of a deficiency in the kidneys or because the urinary tract is blocked

anus /ˈeɪnəs/ *noun* a short passage after the rectum at the end of the alimentary canal, leading outside the body between the buttocks and through which faeces are passed. See illustration at DIGESTIVE SYSTEM in Supplement, UROGENITAL SYSTEM (MALE) in Supplement (NOTE: For other terms referring to the anus, see **anal** and words beginning with **ano-**.)

anvil /ˈænvɪl/ *noun* same as **incus**

anxiety /æŋˈzaɪəti/ *noun* the state of being very worried and afraid

anxiety disorder /æŋˈzaɪəti dɪsˌɔːdə/ *noun* a mental disorder where someone is very worried and afraid, e.g. a phobia

anxiety neurosis /æŋˈzaɪəti njʊˌrəʊsɪs/ *noun* a neurotic condition where the patient is anxious and has morbid fears

anxiolytic /ˌæŋksiəˈlɪtɪk/ *noun* a drug used in the treatment of anxiety ■ *adjective* treating anxiety

aorta /eɪˈɔːtə/ *noun* the main artery in the body, which sends blood containing oxygen from the heart to other blood vessels around the body. See illustration at HEART in Supplement

aortic /eɪˈɔːtɪk/ *adjective* relating to the aorta

aortic aneurysm /eɪˌɔːtɪk ˌænjəˈrɪz(ə)m/ *noun* a serious aneurysm of the aorta, associated with atherosclerosis

aortitis /ˌeɪɔːˈtaɪtɪs/ *noun* inflammation of the aorta

aortography /ˌeɪɔːˈtɒgrəfi/ *noun* an X-ray examination of the aorta after an opaque substance has been injected into it

apathetic /ˌæpəˈθetɪk/ *adjective* referring to a person who takes no interest in anything

apathy /ˈæpəθi/ *noun* the condition of not being interested in anything, or of not wanting to do anything

aperient /əˈpɪəriənt/ *noun* a substance which causes a bowel movement, e.g. a laxative or purgative ■ *adjective* causing a bowel movement

aperistalsis /ˌeɪperɪˈstælsɪs/ *noun* a lack of the peristaltic movement in the bowel

Apert's syndrome /ˈæpɜːts ˌsɪndrəʊm/ *noun* a condition in which the skull grows tall and the lower part of the face is underdeveloped

aperture /ˈæpətʃə/ *noun* a hole

apex /ˈeɪpeks/ *noun* **1.** the top of the heart or lung **2.** the end of the root of a tooth

Apgar score /ˈæpgɑː skɔː/ *noun* a method of judging the condition of a newborn baby in which the baby is given a maximum of two points on each of five criteria: colour of the skin, heartbeat, breathing, muscle tone and reaction to stimuli [Described 1952. After Virginia Apgar (1909–74), US anaesthesiologist.]

APH *abbreviation* antepartum haemorrhage

aphagia /eɪˈfeɪdʒiə/ *noun* a condition in which a person is unable to swallow

aphakia /eɪˈfeɪkiə/ *noun* the absence of the crystalline lens in the eye

aphakic /eɪˈfeɪkɪk/ *adjective* referring to aphakia

aphasia /eɪˈfeɪziə/ *noun* a condition in which a person is unable to speak or write, or to understand speech or writing because of damage to the brain centres controlling speech

aphonia /eɪˈfəʊniə/ *noun* a condition in which a person is unable to make sounds

aphrodisiac /ˌæfrəˈdɪziæk/ *noun* a substance which increases sexual urges ■ *adjective* increasing sexual desire

aphtha /'æfθə/ *noun* a small white ulcer which appears in groups in the mouth in people who have the fungal condition thrush (NOTE: The plural is **apthae**.)

aphthous stomatitis /,æfθəs ,stəʊmə'taɪtɪs/ *noun* canker sores which affect the mucous membrane in the mouth

apical /'æpɪk(ə)l/ *adjective* situated at the top or tip of something

apical abscess /,æpɪk(ə)l 'æbses/ *noun* an abscess in the socket around the root of a tooth

apicectomy /,æpɪ'sektəmi/ *noun* the surgical removal of the root of a tooth

aplasia /eɪ'pleɪziə/ *noun* a lack of growth of tissue

aplastic /eɪ'plæstɪk/ *adjective* unable to develop new cells or tissue

aplastic anaemia /eɪ,plæstɪk ə'niːmiə/ *noun* anaemia caused by the bone marrow failing to form red blood cells

apnea /æp'niːə/ *noun* US same as **apnoea**

apnoea /æp'niːə/ *noun* the stopping of breathing (NOTE: The US spelling is **apnea**.)

apnoeic /æp'niːɪk/ *adjective* where breathing has stopped

apocrine /'æpəkraɪn/ *adjective* referring to apocrine glands

apocrine gland /'æpəkraɪn glænd/ *noun* a gland producing body odour where parts of the gland's cells break off with the secretions, e.g. a sweat gland

apocrinitis /,æpəkrɪ'naɪtɪs/ *noun* the formation of abscesses in the sweat glands

apomorphine /,æpəʊ'mɔːfiːn/ *noun* a substance that comes from morphine, used to make a person cough, sleep or be sick (NOTE: It is administered under the skin and is used to treat drug overdose, accidental poisoning and Parkinson's disease.)

aponeurosis /,æpəʊnjʊ'rəʊsɪs/ *noun* a band of tissue which attaches muscles to each other

apophyseal /æpə'fɪziəl/ *adjective* referring to apophysis

apophysis /ə'pɒfəsɪs/ *noun* a growth of bone, not at a joint

apophysitis /æpəfɪ'saɪtɪs/ *noun* inflammation of an apophysis

apoplexy /'æpəpleksi/ *noun* same as **cerebrovascular accident** (*dated*)

apoptosis /ə'pɒptəsɪs/ *noun* a form of cell death that is necessary both to make room for new cells and to remove cells whose DNA has been damaged and which may become cancerous

appendage /ə'pendɪdʒ/ *noun* a part of the body or piece of tissue which hangs down from another part

appendiceal /,æpən'dɪsiəl/ *adjective* relating to the appendix ○ *There is a risk of appendiceal infection.*

appendicectomy /ə,pendɪ'sektəmi/ *noun* the surgical removal of an appendix

appendicitis /ə,pendɪ'saɪtɪs/ *noun* inflammation of the vermiform appendix

appendicular /,æpən'dɪkjʊlə/ *adjective* **1.** referring to body parts which are associated with the arms and legs **2.** relating to the appendix

appendicular skeleton /,æpen,dɪkjʊlə 'skelɪt(ə)n/ *noun* part of the skeleton, formed of the pelvic girdle, pectoral girdle and the bones of the arms and legs. Compare **axial skeleton**

appendix /ə'pendɪks/ *noun* **1.** a small tube attached to the caecum which serves no function but can become infected, causing appendicitis. Also called **vermiform appendix**. See illustration at DIGESTIVE SYSTEM in Supplement **2.** any small tube or sac hanging from an organ

apperception /,æpə'sepʃ(ə)n/ *noun* the conscious recognition of a stimulus

appetite /'æpɪtaɪt/ *noun* the feeling of wanting food

applanation tonometry /æplə,neɪʃ(ə)n tə'nɒmətri/ *noun* the measuring of the thickness of the cornea

appliance /ə'plaɪəns/ *noun* a piece of apparatus used on the body ○ *He was wearing a surgical appliance to support his neck.*

applicator /'æplɪkeɪtə/ *noun* an instrument for applying a substance

apposition /,æpə'zɪʃ(ə)n/ *noun* **1.** the relative positioning of two things **2.** cell growth in which layers of new material are deposited on existing ones

appraisal /ə'preɪz(ə)l/ *noun* a judgment or opinion on something or somebody, especially one which decides how effective or useful they are

apprehension /,æprɪ'henʃ(ə)n/ *noun* a feeling of anxiety or fear that something bad or unpleasant will happen

apraxia /eɪ'præksiə/ *noun* a condition in which someone is unable to make proper movements

apyrexia /,eɪpaɪ'reksiə/ *noun* the absence of fever

apyrexial /,eɪpaɪ'reksiəl/ *adjective* no longer having any fever

aqua /'ækwə/ *noun* water

aqueduct /'ækwɪdʌkt/ *noun* a tube which carries fluid from one part of the body to another

aqueous /'eɪkwiəs, 'ækwiəs/ *adjective* referring to a solution made with water ■ *noun* a fluid in the eye between the lens and the cornea

aqueous humour /,eɪkwiəs 'hjuːmə/ *noun* same as **aqueous**. See illustration at EYE in Supplement

AR *abbreviation* attributable risk

arachidonic acid /ə,rækɪdɒnɪk 'æsɪd/ *noun* an essential fatty acid

arachnodactyly /ə,ræknəʊ'dæktɪli/ *noun* a congenital condition in which the fingers and toes are long and thin

arachnoid /ə'ræknɔɪd/ *noun* the middle of th three membranes covering the brain. ◊ **dura mater**

arachnoiditis /ə,ræknɔɪ'daɪtɪs/ *noun* inflammation of the arachnoid

arachnoid mater /ə,ræknɔɪd 'meɪtə/, **arachnoid membrane** /ə'ræknɔɪd ,membreɪn/ *noun* same as **arachnoid**

arachnoid villi /ə,ræknɔɪd 'vɪlaɪ/ *plural noun* villi in the arachnoid which absorb cerebrospinal fluid

arborisation /,ɑːbəraɪ'zeɪʃ(ə)n/, **arborization** *noun* the branching ends of some nerve fibres, of a motor nerve in muscle fibre or of venules, capillaries and arterioles

arbovirus /'ɑːbəvaɪrəs/ *noun* a virus transmitted by blood-sucking insects

arc /ɑːk/ *noun* a nerve pathway

ARC *abbreviation* AIDS-related complex *or* AIDS-related condition

arch /ɑːtʃ/ *noun* a curved part of the body, especially under the foot

arch- /ɑːtʃ/ *prefix* chief, most important

arcuate /'ɑːkjuət/ *adjective* arched

arcuate artery /'ɑːkjuət ,ɑːtəri/ *noun* a curved artery in the foot or kidney

arcuate ligaments /'ɑːkjuət ,ɑːtəri/ *plural noun* three ligaments forming a fibrous arch to which the diaphragm is attached

arcus /'ɑːkəs/ *noun* an arch

arcus senilis /,ɑːkəs sə'naɪlɪs/ *noun* an opaque circle around the cornea of the eye which can develop in old age

ARDS /ɑːdz/ *abbreviation* adult respiratory distress syndrome

areola /ə'riːələ/ *noun* the coloured part round a nipple

areolar tissue /ə'riːələ ,tɪʃuː/ *noun* a type of connective tissue

arginine /'ɑːdʒɪniːn/ *noun* an amino acid which helps the liver form urea

Argyll Robertson pupil /ɑː,gaɪl 'rɒbətsən ,pjuːp(ə)l/ *noun* a condition of the eye, in which the lens is able to focus but the pupil does not react to light. It is a symptom of tertiary syphilis or of locomotor ataxia.

ariboflavinosis /eɪ,raɪbəʊfleɪvɪ'nəʊsɪs/ *noun* a condition caused by not having enough vitamin B_2. The symptoms are very oily skin and hair and small cuts in the mouth.

Arnold-Chiari malformation /,ɑːnəld kiˈɛəri mælfɔː,meɪʃ(ə)n/ *noun* a congenital condition in which the base of the skull is malformed, allowing parts of the cerebellum into the spinal canal [Described 1894. After Julius A. Arnold (1835–1915), Professor of Pathological Anatomy at Heidelberg, Germany, and Hans von Chiari (1851–1916), Professor of Pathological Anatomy at Strasbourg and later at Prague, Czech Republic.]

aromatherapy /ə,rəʊmə'θerəpi/ *noun* treatment to relieve tension and promote wellbeing in which fragrant oils and creams containing plant extracts are massaged into the skin

arousal /ə'raʊz(ə)l/ *noun* **1.** feelings and physical signs of sexual desire **2.** the act of waking up from sleep, unconsciousness or a drowsy state

arrector pili /ə,rektə 'paɪlaɪ ,mʌs(ə)l/ *noun* a small muscle which contracts and makes the hair on the skin stand up when someone is cold or afraid

arrest /ə'rest/ *noun* the stopping of a bodily function. ◊ **cardiac arrest**

arrhythmia /ə'rɪðmiə/ *noun* a variation in the rhythm of the heartbeat

arsenic /'ɑːsnɪk/ *noun* a chemical element which forms poisonous compounds such as arsenic trioxide and which was formerly used in some medicines (NOTE: The chemical symbol is **As**.)

artefact /'ɑːtɪfækt/ *noun* something which is made or introduced artificially

arter- /ɑːtə/ *prefix* same as **arterio-** (*used before vowels*)

arterial /ɑː'tɪəriəl/ *adjective* relating to arteries

arterial haemorrhage /ɑː,tɪəriəl 'hem(ə)rɪdʒ/ *noun* a haemorrhage of bright red blood from an artery

arteriectomy /ɑː,tɪəri'ektəmi/ *noun* the surgical removal of an artery or part of an artery

arterio- /ɑːtɪəriəʊ/ *prefix* referring to arteries

arteriogram /ɑː'tɪəriəʊgræm/ *noun* an X-ray photograph of an artery, taken after injection with an opaque dye

arteriography /ɑː,tɪəri'ɒgrəfi/ *noun* the work of taking X-ray photographs of arteries after injection with an opaque dye

arteriole /ɑː'tɪəriəʊl/ *noun* a very small artery

arteriopathy /ɑː,tɪəri'ɒpəθi/ *noun* a disease of an artery

arterioplasty /ɑː'tɪəriəʊplæsti/ *noun* plastic surgery to make good a damaged or blocked artery

arteriorrhaphy /ɑː,tɪəri'ɔːrəfi/ *noun* the act of stitching an artery

arteriosclerosis /ɑː,tɪəriəʊsklə'rəʊsɪs/ *noun* the arterial disease atherosclerosis (*dated*)

arteriotomy /ɑː,tɪəri'ɒtəmi/ *noun* a puncture made in the wall of an artery

arteriovenous /ɑː,tɪəriəʊ'viːnəs/ *adjective* referring to both an artery and a vein

arteritis /,ɑːtə'raɪtɪs/ *noun* inflammation of the walls of an artery

artery /'ɑːtəri/ *noun* a blood vessel taking blood from the heart to the tissues of the body

arthr- /ɑːθr/ *prefix* same as **arthro-** (*used before vowels*)

arthralgia /ɑː'θrældʒə/ *noun* pain in a joint

arthrectomy /ɑː'θrektəmi/ *noun* the surgical removal of a joint

arthritic /ɑː'θrɪtɪk/ *adjective* affected by or relating to arthritis ○ *She has an arthritic hip.* ■ *noun* a person suffering from arthritis

arthritis /ɑː'θraɪtɪs/ *noun* a painful inflammation of a joint. ◊ **osteoarthritis, rheumatoid arthritis**

arthro- /ɑːθrəʊ/ *prefix* referring to a joint

arthroclasia /,ɑːθrəʊ'kleɪʒə/ *noun* removal of ankylosis in a joint

arthrodesis /,ɑːθrəʊ'diːsɪs/ *noun* a surgical operation in which a joint is fused in position, so preventing pain from movement

arthrodynia /,ɑːθrəʊ'dɪniə/ *noun* pain in a joint

arthrography /ɑː'θrɒɡrəfi/ *noun* X-ray photography of a joint

arthrogryposis /,ɑːθrəʊɡrɪ'pəʊsɪs/ *noun* a group of disorders in which movement becomes progressively restricted

arthropathy /ɑː'θrɒpəθi/ *noun* a disease in a joint

arthroplasty /'ɑːθrəʊplæsti/ *noun* a surgical operation to repair or replace a joint

arthroscope /'ɑːθrəʊskəʊp/ *noun* an instrument which is inserted into the cavity of a joint to inspect it

arthroscopy /ɑː'θrɒskəpi/ *noun* a procedure to examine the inside of a joint by means of an arthroscope

arthrosis /ɑː'θrəʊsɪs/ *noun* the degeneration of a joint

arthrotomy /ɑː'θrɒtəmi/ *noun* a procedure that involves cutting into a joint to drain pus

articular /ɑː'tɪkjʊlə/ *adjective* referring to joints

articular cartilage /ɑː,tɪkjʊlə 'kɑːtəlɪdʒ/ *noun* a layer of cartilage at the end of a bone where it forms a joint with another bone. See illustration at BONE STRUCTURE in Supplement, SYNOVIAL JOINT in Supplement

articulate /ɑː'tɪkjʊleɪt/ *verb* to be linked with another bone in a joint

articulation /ɑː,tɪkjʊ'leɪʃ(ə)n/ *noun* a joint or series of joints

artificial /,ɑːtɪ'fɪʃ(ə)l/ *adjective* **1.** made by humans and not a natural part of the body ○ *artificial cartilage* ○ *artificial kidney* ○ *artificial leg* **2.** happening not as a natural process but through action by a doctor or another person or a machine ○ *artificial feeding*

artificial insemination /,ɑːtɪfɪʃ(ə)l ɪn,semɪ 'neɪʃ(ə)n/ *noun* the introduction of semen into a woman's uterus by artificial means

artificial insemination by donor /,ɑːtɪfɪʃ(ə)l ɪnsemɪ,neɪʃ(ə)n baɪ 'dəʊnə/ *noun* same as **donor insemination**. Abbreviation **AID**

artificial insemination by husband /,ɑːtɪfɪʃ(ə)l ɪnsemɪ,neɪʃ(ə)n baɪ 'hʌzbənd/ *noun* artificial insemination using the semen of the husband. Abbreviation **AIH**

artificial lung /,ɑːtɪfɪʃ(ə)l 'lʌŋ/ *noun* a machine through which a person's deoxygenated blood is passed to absorb oxygen to take back to the bloodstream

artificial respiration /,ɑːtɪfɪʃ(ə)l ,respɪ 'reɪʃ(ə)n/ *noun* a way of reviving someone who has stopped breathing, e.g. mouth-to-mouth resuscitation

artificial rupture of membranes /,ɑːtɪfɪʃ(ə)l ,rʌptʃər əv 'membreɪnz/ *noun* the breaking of the amniotic sac with an amnihook, so releasing the amniotic fluid

arytenoid /,ærɪ'tiːnɔɪd/ *adjective* located at the back of the larynx

arytenoid cartilage /ærɪ'tiːnɔɪd ,kɑːtɪlɪdʒ/ *noun* a small cartilage at the back of the larynx

arytenoidectomy /,ærɪ,tiːnɔɪd'ektəmi/ *noun* an operation to remove the arytenoid cartilage

asbestosis /,æsbe'stəʊsɪs/ *noun* a disease of the lungs caused by inhaling asbestos dust

ascariasis /,æskə'raɪəsɪs/ *noun* a disease of the intestine and sometimes the lungs, caused by infestation with *Ascaris lumbricoides*

Ascaris lumbricoides /,æskərɪs lʌmbrɪ 'kɔɪdiːz/ *noun* a type of large roundworm which is a parasite in the human intestine

ascending aorta /ə,sendɪŋ eɪ'ɔːtə/ *noun* the first section of the aorta as it leaves the heart and turns upwards. Compare **descending aorta**

ascending colon /ə,sendɪŋ 'kəʊlɒn/ *noun* the first part of the colon which goes up the right side of the body from the caecum. Compare **descending colon**. See illustration at DIGESTIVE SYSTEM in Supplement

Aschoff nodules /'æʃɒf ,nɒdjuːlz/, **Aschoff's nodules** /'æʃɒfs ,nɒdjuːlz/ *plural noun* nodules which are formed mainly in or near the heart in rheumatic fever

ascites /ə'saɪtiːz/ *noun* an unusual accumulation of fluid from the blood in the peritoneal cavity, occurring in heart and kidney failure or as a result of malignancy

ascorbic acid /ə,skɔːbɪk 'æsɪd/ *noun* same as Vitamin C

ASD *abbreviation* autistic spectrum disorders

-ase /eɪz, eɪs/ *suffix* enzyme

asepsis /eɪ'sepsɪs/ *noun* the absence of microorganisms which cause infection, usually achieved by sterilisation

aseptic /eɪ'septɪk/ *adjective* sterilised, or involving sterilisation, and therefore without infection

aseptic technique /eɪ,septɪk tek'niːks/ *noun* a method of doing something using sterilised equipment

asexual /eɪ'sekʃuəl/ *adjective* not sexual, not involving sexual intercourse

Asian flu /,eɪʒ(ə)n 'fluː/ *noun* ♦ flu

-asis /əsɪs/ ♦ -iasis

asparagine /ə'spærədʒiːn/ *noun* an amino acid

aspartame /ə'spɑːteɪm/ *noun* a protein produced from aspartic acid, used to make substances sweeter

aspartate aminotransferase /ə,spɑːteɪt ə ,miːnəʊ'trænsfəreɪz/ *noun* an enzyme found in heart muscle, liver cells, skeletal muscle cells and some other tissues. It is used in the diagnosis of liver disease and heart attacks.

aspartic acid /ə,spɑːtɪk 'æsɪd/ *noun* an amino acid

aspect /'æspekt/ *noun* a direction from which the body is viewed, e.g. the view from above is the 'superior aspect'

Asperger's syndrome /'æspɜːdʒəz ,sɪndrəʊm/ *noun* a developmental disorder characterised by difficulty in social interaction and a restricted range of interests, more common in boys than girls [Described 1944. After Hans Asperger (1906–80), Austrian psychiatrist.]

aspergillosis /,æspɜːdʒɪ'ləʊsɪs/ *noun* infection of the lungs with the fungus *Aspergillus*

aspermia /eɪ'spɜːmiə/ *noun* the absence of sperm in semen

asphyxia /æs'fɪksiə/ *noun* a condition in which someone is prevented from breathing, e.g. by strangulation or breathing poisonous gas, and therefore cannot take oxygen into the bloodstream

asphyxiation /əs,fɪksi'eɪʃ(ə)n/ *noun* the state of being prevented from breathing, or the act of preventing someone from breathing. ◊ **suffocation**

aspiration /,æspɪ'reɪʃ(ə)n/ *noun* **1.** the act of removing fluid from a cavity in the body, often using a hollow needle **2.** same as **vacuum suction**

aspirator /'æspɪreɪtə/ *noun* an instrument used to suck fluid out of a cavity such as the mouth or the site of an operation

aspirin /'æsprɪn/ *noun* a common pain-killing drug, or a tablet containing this drug. Also called **acetylsalicylic acid**

assay /'æseɪ, ə'seɪ/ *noun* the testing of a substance. ◊ **bioassay, immunoassay**

assessment /ə'sesmənt/ *noun* **1.** a judgment about something ○ *Further treatment will be based on your doctor's assessment of your condition.* **2.** a method of deciding whether a student is learning and progressing well ○ *continuous assessment*

assimilation /ə,sɪmɪ'leɪʃ(ə)n/ *noun* the action of assimilating food substances

assisted suicide /ə,sɪstɪd 'suːɪsaɪd/ *noun* the suicide of someone who is terminally ill with the help of a doctor or friend at the request of the person who is dying

associate /ə'səʊsieɪt/ *verb* to be related to or connected with something ○ *side effects which may be associated with the drug* ○ *The condition is often associated with diabetes.*

associate nurse /ə,səʊsiət 'nɜːs/ *noun* a nurse who assists a primary nurse by carrying out agreed care for someone based on a plan designed by a primary nurse

asthenia /æs'θiːniə/ *noun* a condition in which someone is weak and does not have any strength

asthenic /æs'θenɪk/ *adjective* referring to a general condition in which someone has no strength and no interest in things

asthenopia /,æsθɪ'nəʊpiə/ *noun* same as **eye-strain**

asthma /'æsmə/ *noun* a lung condition characterised by narrowing of the bronchial tubes, in which the muscles go into spasm and the person has difficulty breathing. ◊ **cardiac asthma**

asthmatic /æs'mætɪk/ *adjective* having the lung disease asthma, or relating to asthma ○ *He has an asthmatic attack every spring.* ■ *noun* a person who has asthma

asthmaticus /æs'mætɪkəs/ *adjective* ♦ **status asthmaticus**

astigmatism /ə'stɪgmətɪz(ə)m/ *noun* a condition in which the eye cannot focus vertical and horizontal lines simultaneously, leading to blurring of vision

astringent /ə'strɪndʒənt/ *noun* a substance which makes the skin tissues contract and harden ■ *adjective* referring to an astringent

astrocyte /'æstrəsaɪt/ *noun* a star-shaped cell of the connective tissue of the nervous system

astrocytoma /,æstrəsaɪ'təʊmə/ *noun* a type of brain tumour which develops slowly in the connective tissue of the nervous system

asymmetric /,æsɪ'metrɪk/ *adjective* shaped or arranged so that the two sides do not match or balance each other

asymmetry /æ'sɪmətri/ *noun* a state in which the two sides of the body or of an organ do not resemble each other

asymptomatic /,eɪsɪmptə'mætɪk/ *adjective* not showing any symptoms of disease

asynclitism /æ'sɪŋklɪtɪz(ə)m/ *noun* in childbirth, a situation in which the head of the baby enters the vagina at an angle

asynergia /,æsɪ'nɜːdʒə/, **asynergy** /æ'sɪnədʒi/ *noun* awkward movements and bad coordination, caused by a disorder of the cerebellum. Also called **dyssynergia**

asystole /eɪ'sɪstəli/ *noun* a state in which the heart has stopped beating

ataractic /,ætə'ræktɪk/ *noun* a drug which has a calming effect ■ *adjective* calming

ataraxia /,ætə'ræksiə/, **ataraxis** /,ætə'ræksɪs/ *noun* the state of being calm and not worrying

ataraxic /,ætə'ræksɪk/ *noun, adjective* same as **ataractic**

ataxia /ə'tæksiə/ *noun* a failure of the brain to control movements

ataxic /ə'tæksɪk/ *adjective* having ataxia, or relating to ataxia

ataxic gait /ə,tæksɪk 'geɪt/ *noun* a way of walking in which the person walks unsteadily due to a disorder of the nervous system

ataxy /ə'tæksi/ *noun* same as **ataxia**

atelectasis /,ætə'lektəsɪs/ *noun* the failure of a lung to expand properly

atenolol /ə'tenəlɒl/ *noun* a drug used in controlling blood pressure and angina

ateriovenous malformation /ɑː,tɪəriəʊ ,viːnəs mælfɔː'meɪʃ(ə)n/ *noun* a condition in which the arteries and veins in the brain are not properly formed, leading to strokes or epilepsy. Abbreviation **AVM**

atherogenic /,æθərəʊ'dʒenɪk/ *adjective* referring to something which may produce atheroma

atheroma /,æθə'rəʊmə/ *noun* thickening of the walls of an artery by deposits of a fatty substance such as cholesterol

atheromatous /,æθə'rɒmətəs/ *adjective* referring to atheroma

atherosclerosis /,æθərəʊsklə'rəʊsɪs/ *noun* a condition in which deposits of fats and minerals form on the walls of an artery, especially the aorta or one of the coronary or cerebral arteries, and prevent blood from flowing easily

atherosclerotic /,æθərəʊsklə'rɒtɪk/ *adjective* referring to atherosclerosis

athetosis /,æθə'təʊsɪs/ *noun* repeated slow movements of the limbs, caused by a brain disorder such as cerebral palsy

athlete's foot /,æθliːts 'fʊt/ *noun* an infectious skin disorder between the toes, caused by a fungus. Also called **tinea pedis**

atlas /'ætləs/ *noun* the top vertebra in the spine, which supports the skull and pivots on the axis or second vertebra

atom /'ætəm/ *noun* the smallest part into which an element can be divided and still keep its properties. It consists of a dense, positively charged nucleus surrounded by a system of electrons.

atomiser /'ætəmaɪzə/ *noun* an instrument which sprays liquid in the form of very small drops like mist. Also called **nebuliser**

atony /'ætəni/ *noun* a lack of tone or tension in the muscles

atopen /'ætəpen/ *noun* an allergen which causes an atopy

atopic eczema /eɪ,tɒpɪk 'eksɪmə/, **atopic dermatitis** /eɪ,tɒpɪk dɜːmə'taɪtɪs/ *noun* a type of eczema often caused by a hereditary allergy

atopy /'ætəpi/ *noun* a hereditary allergic reaction

ATP *abbreviation* adenosine triphosphate

atracurium /,ætrə'kjʊəriəm/ *noun* a drug used as a relaxant

atresia /ə'triːziə/ *noun* an unusual closing or absence of a tube in the body

atretic /ə'tretɪk/ *adjective* referring to atresia

atri- /eɪtri/ *prefix* referring to an atrium

atrial /'eɪtriəl/ *adjective* referring to one or both of the atria of the heart

atrial fibrillation /,eɪtriəl faɪbrɪ'leɪʃ(ə)n/ *noun* a rapid uncoordinated fluttering of the atria of the heart, which causes an irregular heartbeat

atrioventricular /,eɪtriəʊven'trɪkjʊlə/ *adjective* referring to the atria and ventricles

atrioventricular bundle /,eɪtriəʊven ,trɪkjʊlə 'bʌnd(ə)l/ *noun* a bundle of modified cardiac muscle which conducts impulses from the atrioventricular node to the septum and then divides to connect with the ventricles. Also called **AV bundle, bundle of His**

atrioventricular node /,eɪtriəʊven'trɪkjʊlə ,nəʊd/ *noun* a mass of conducting tissue in the right atrium of the heart, which continues as the atrioventricular bundle and passes impulses from the atria to the ventricles. Also called **AV node**

at-risk /ət 'rɪsk/ *adjective* exposed to danger or harm of some kind ○ *at-risk children*

atrium /'eɪtriəm/ *noun* one of the two upper chambers in the heart. See illustration at **HEART** in Supplement

atrophic cirrhosis /æ,trɒfɪk sɪ'rəʊsɪs/ *noun* advanced portal cirrhosis in which the liver has become considerably smaller and clumps of new cells are formed on the surface of the liver where fibrous tissue has replaced damaged liver cells. Also called **hobnail liver**

atrophy /'ætrəfi/ *noun* the wasting of an organ or part of the body ■ *verb* (*of an organ or part of the body*) to waste away

atropine /ˈætrəpiːn/ *noun* an alkaloid substance derived from the poisonous plant belladonna and used, among other things, to enlarge the pupil of the eye, to reduce salivary and bronchial secretions during anaesthesia and as a muscarinic antagonist

ATS *abbreviation* antitetanus serum

attack /əˈtæk/ *noun* a sudden occurrence of an illness ○ *He had an attack of fever.* ○ *She had two attacks of laryngitis during the winter.*

attention deficit disorder /əˌtenʃən ˈdefɪsɪt dɪsˌɔːdə/ *noun* a condition in which a person is unable to concentrate, does things without considering their actions properly and has little confidence. It occurs mainly in children. Abbreviation **ADD**

attention deficit hyperactivity disorder /əˌtenʃən ˌdefɪsɪt ˌhaɪpərækˈtɪvɪti dɪsˌɔːdə/ *noun* a condition in which a child has an inability to concentrate and shows disruptive behaviour. Abbreviation **ADHD**

attention deficit syndrome /əˌtenʃən ˈdefɪsɪt ˌsɪndrəʊm/ *noun* same as **attention deficit disorder**

attenuation /əˌtenjuˈeɪʃ(ə)n/ *noun* a reduction in the effect or strength of something such as a virus, either because of environmental conditions or as a result of a laboratory procedure

atticotomy /ˌætɪˈkɒtəmi/ *noun* the removal of the wall in the inner ear. Also called **cortical mastoidectomy**

attitude /ˈætɪtjuːd/ *noun* **1.** an opinion or general feeling about something ○ *a positive attitude towards the operation* **2.** a way of standing or sitting

attributable risk /əˌtrɪbjʊtəb(ə)l ˈrɪsk/ *noun* a measure of the excess risk of disease due to exposure to a particular risk. The excess risk of bacteriuria in oral contraceptive users attributable to the use of oral contraceptives is 1,566 per 100,000. Abbreviation **AR**

atypical /eɪˈtɪpɪk(ə)l/ *adjective* not usual or expected ○ *an atypical renal cyst*

audio- /ɔːdiəʊ/ *prefix* referring to hearing or sound

audiogram /ˈɔːdiəgræm/ *noun* a graph drawn by an audiometer

audiologist /ˌɔːdiˈɒlədʒɪst/ *noun* a specialist who deals in the treatment of hearing disorders

audiology /ˌɔːdiˈɒlədʒi/ *noun* the scientific study of hearing, especially for diagnosing and treating hearing loss

audiometer /ˌɔːdiˈɒmɪtə/ *noun* an apparatus for testing hearing, especially for testing the range of sounds that the human ear can detect

audiometry /ˌɔːdiˈɒmətri/ *noun* the science of testing hearing

audit /ˈɔːdɪt/ *noun* a check on figures, scientific data or procedures ○ *a medical audit regarding the outpatient appointment system*

audit commission /ˈɔːdɪt kəˌmɪʃ(ə)n/ *noun* a government body which examines the accounts of public bodies such as hospital trusts to ensure that public money is being spent wisely

audit cycle /ˈɔːdɪt ˌsaɪk(ə)l/ *noun* the cycle in which medical topics are selected for review, observation and comparison with agreed standards and changes are decided on

auditory /ˈɔːdɪt(ə)ri/ *adjective* relating to hearing

auditory acuity /ˌɔːdɪt(ə)ri əˈkjuːɪti/ *noun* the ability to hear sounds clearly

auditory canals /ˌɔːdɪt(ə)ri kəˈnælz/ *plural noun* the external and internal passages of the ear

auditory nerve /ˈɔːdɪt(ə)ri nɜːv/ *noun* the eighth cranial nerve which governs hearing and balance. See illustration at **EAR** in Supplement. Also called **vestibulocochlear nerve**

auditory ossicles /ˌɔːdɪt(ə)ri ˈɒsɪk(ə)lz/ *plural noun* the three little bones, the malleus, incus and stapes, in the middle ear

Auerbach's plexus /ˌaʊəbɑːks ˈpleksəs/ *noun* a group of nerve fibres in the intestine wall [Described 1862. After Leopold Auerbach (1828–97), Professor of Neuropathology at Breslau, now in Poland.]

aura /ˈɔːrə/ *noun* a warning sensation which is experienced before an attack of epilepsy, migraine or asthma

aural /ˈɔːrəl/ *adjective* referring to the ear

auricle /ˈɔːrɪk(ə)l/ *noun* the tip of each atrium in the heart

auricular /ɔːˈrɪkjʊlə/ *adjective* referring to the ear

auricular vein /ɔːˈrɪkjʊlə veɪn/ *noun* a vein which leads into the posterior facial vein

auriscope /ˈɔːrɪskəʊp/ *noun* an instrument for examining the ear and eardrum. Also called **otoscope**

auscultation /ˌɔːskəlˈteɪʃ(ə)n/ *noun* the act of listening to the sounds of the body using a stethoscope

auscultatory /ɔːˈskʌltət(ə)ri/ *adjective* referring to auscultation

Australia antigen /ɔːˈstreɪliə ˌæntɪdʒən/ *noun* an antigen produced on the surface of liver cells infected with the hepatitis B virus

autism /ˈɔːtɪz(ə)m/ *noun* a condition developing in childhood, characterised by difficulty in social interaction, language and communication problems, learning difficulties and obsessional repetitive behaviour (NOTE: Autism is more common in boys than in girls.)

autistic /ɔːˈtɪstɪk/ *adjective* affected by, or relating to, autism

autistic spectrum disorders /ɔː,tɪstɪk ,spektrəm dɪs'ɔːdəz/ *plural noun* autism in all its different forms and degrees of severity. Abbreviation **ASD**

auto- /ɔːtəʊ/ *prefix* self

autoantibody /,ɔːtəʊ'æntɪbɒdi/ *noun* an antibody formed to attack antigens in the body's own cells

autoclave /'ɔːtəʊkleɪv/ *noun* equipment for sterilising surgical instruments using heat under high pressure ■ *verb* to sterilise equipment using heat under high pressure ○ *Autoclaving is the best method of sterilisation.*

autogenous /ɔː'tɒdʒənəs/, **autogenic** /,ɔːtəʊ'dʒenɪk/ *adjective* produced either in the person's body, or using tissue from the person's own body ○ *an autogenous vein graft*

autograft /'ɔːtəɡrɑːft/ *noun* a transplant made using parts of the person's own body

autoimmune /,ɔːtɔɪ'mjuːn/ *adjective* referring to an immune reaction in a person against antigens in their own cells

autoimmune disease /,ɔːtɔɪ,mjuːn dɪ'ziːz/ *noun* a disease in which the person's own cells are attacked by autoantibodies ○ *Rheumatoid arthritis is thought to be an autoimmune disease.*

autoimmunisation /,ɔːtəʊ,ɪmjʊnaɪ'zeɪʃ(ə)n/, **autoimmunization** *noun* the process leading to an immune reaction in a person to antigens produced in their own body

autoimmunity /,ɔːtɔɪ'mjuːnɪti/ *noun* a condition in which a person's own cells are attacked by autoantibodies

autoinfection /,ɔːtəʊɪn'fekʃ(ə)n/ *noun* an infection by a microorganism already in the body, or infection of one part of the body by another part

autointoxication /,ɔːtəʊɪntɒksɪ'keɪʃ(ə)n/ *noun* the poisoning of the body by toxins produced in the body itself

autologous /ɔː'tɒləɡəs/ *adjective* referring to a graft or other material coming from the same source

autolysis /ɔː'tɒləsɪs/ *noun* a situation in which cells destroy themselves with their own enzymes

automatism /ɔː'tɒmətɪz(ə)m/ *noun* a state in which a person acts without consciously knowing that he or she is acting

autonomic /,ɔːtə'nɒmɪk/ *adjective* governing itself independently

autonomic nervous system /,ɔːtənɒmɪk 'nɜːvəs ,sɪstəm/ *noun* the nervous system formed of ganglia linked to the spinal column. It regulates the automatic functioning of the main organs such as the heart and lungs and works when a person is asleep or even unconscious. ◊

parasympathetic nervous system, sympathetic nervous system

autonomy /ɔː'tɒnəmi/ *noun* the state of being free to act as one wishes

autoplasty /'ɔːtəʊplæsti/ *noun* the repair of someone's body using tissue taken from another part of their body

autopsy /'ɔːtɒpsi/ *noun* the examination of a dead body by a pathologist to find out the cause of death ○ *The autopsy showed that he had been poisoned.* Also called **post mortem**

autosomal /,ɔːtəʊ'səʊm(ə)l/ *adjective* referring to an autosome

autosome /'ɔːtəʊsəʊm/ *noun* a chromosome that is not a sex chromosome

autotransfusion /,ɔːtəʊtræns'fjuːʒ(ə)n/ *noun* an infusion into a person of their own blood

avascular /eɪ'væskjʊlə/ *adjective* with no blood vessels, or with a deficient blood supply

AV bundle /,eɪ 'viː 'bʌnd(ə)l/ *noun* same as **atrioventricular bundle**

aversion therapy /ə'vɜːʃ(ə)n ,θerəpi/ *noun* a treatment by which someone is cured of a type of behaviour by making him or her develop a great dislike for it

avitaminosis /eɪ,vɪtəmɪ'nəʊsɪs/ *noun* a disorder caused by a lack of vitamins

AVM *abbreviation* arteriovenous malformation

AV node /,eɪ 'viː nəʊd/ *noun* same as **atrioventricular node**

AVPU /,eɪ viː piː 'juː/ *noun* a method of rating if a person is conscious: A = alert; V = verbal, responding to verbal commands; P = pain, responding to pain; U = unconscious

avulsion /ə'vʌlʃən/ *noun* an act of pulling away tissue or a body part by force

avulsion fracture /ə,vʌlʃ(ə)n 'fræktʃə/ *noun* a fracture in which a tendon pulls away part of the bone to which it is attached

axial /'æksiəl/ *adjective* referring to an axis

axial skeleton /,æksiəl 'skelɪt(ə)n/ *noun* the bones that make up the vertebral column and the skull. Compare **appendicular skeleton**

axillary /æk'sɪləri/ *adjective* referring to the armpit

axis /'æksɪs/ *noun* **1.** an imaginary line through the centre of the body **2.** a central vessel which divides into other vessels **3.** the second vertebra on which the atlas sits (NOTE: The plural is **axes**.)

axon /'æksɒn/ *noun* a nerve fibre which sends impulses from one neurone to another, linking with the dendrites of the other neurone. See illustration at **NEURONE** in Supplement

azathioprine /,eɪzə'θaɪəpriːn/ *noun* a drug which suppresses the immune response, used after transplant surgery to prevent rejection

-azepam /æzɪpæm/ *suffix* used in names of benzodiazepines ○ *diazepam*

azidothymidine /ˌeɪzɪdəʊˈθaɪmɪdiːn/ *noun* a drug used in the treatment of AIDS. Abbreviation **AZT**. Also called **zidovudine**

azo- /eɪzəʊ/ *prefix* containing a nitrogen group

azoospermia /eɪzəʊəˈspɜːmiə/ *noun* the absence of sperm

azoturia /ˌeɪzəʊˈtjʊəriə/ *noun* the presence of urea or other nitrogen compounds in the urine caused by kidney disease

AZT *abbreviation* azidothymidine

azygous /ˈæzɪgəs/ *adjective* single, not one of a pair

azygous vein /ˈæzɪgəs veɪn/ *noun* a vein which brings blood back into the vena cava from the abdomen

B

Babinski reflex /bə,bɪnski 'riːfleks/, **Babinski's reflex** /bə,bɪnskiz 'riːfleks/ *noun* an unusual curling upwards of the big toe when a finger is lightly run across the sole of the foot, while the others turn down and spread out, a sign of hemiplegia and pyramidal tract disease. Compare **plantar reflex** [Described 1896. After Joseph François Felix Babinski (1857–1932), French-born son of Polish refugees. A pupil of Charcot, he was head of the Neurological clinic at Hôpital de la Pitié, 1890–1927.]

Babinski test /bə'bɪnski test/ *noun* a test for a Babinski reflex

baby /'beɪbi/ *noun* a very young child who is not yet old enough to talk or walk ○ *Babies start to walk when they are about 12 months old.* (NOTE: If you do not know the sex of a baby you can refer to the child as **it**: *The baby was sucking its thumb*)

baby blues /'beɪbi bluːz/ *plural noun* same as **postnatal depression** (*informal*)

bacillaemia /,bæsɪ'liːmiə/ *noun* an infection of the blood by bacilli

bacillary /bə'sɪləri/ *adjective* referring to bacilli

bacille Calmette-Guérin /bæ,siːl ,kælmet 'geræn/ *noun* full form of **BCG** [After A. Calmette (1863–1933) and C. Guérin (1872–1961), French bacteriologists.]

bacilluria /,bæsɪ'ljʊəriə/ *noun* the presence of bacilli in the urine

bacillus /bə'sɪləs/ *noun* a bacterium shaped like a rod (NOTE: The plural is **bacilli**.)

back /bæk/ *noun* **1.** the part of the body from the neck downwards to the waist, which is made up of the spine and the bones attached to it (NOTE: For other terms referring to the back, see **dorsal** and words beginning with **dorsi-, dorso-**.) **2.** the other side from the front ○ *She has a swelling on the back of her hand.* ◊ **dorsum**

backache /'bækeɪk/ *noun* pain in the back, often without a specific cause

backbone /'bækbəʊn/ *noun* a series of bones, the vertebrae, linked together to form a flexible column running from the pelvis to the skull. Also called **rachis, spine**

background carboxyhaemoglobin level /,bækgraʊnd kɑː,bɒksi hiːmə'gləʊbɪn ,lev(ə)l/ *noun* the level of carboxyhaemoglobin in the blood of a person who is not exposed to high levels of carbon monoxide

back pain /'bæk peɪn/ *noun* pain in the back, especially long-lasting or severe pain

backside /'bæksaɪd/ *noun* someone's buttocks (*informal*)

back strain /'bæk streɪn/ *noun* a condition in which the muscles or ligaments in the back have been strained

bacteraemia /,bæktə'riːmiə/ *noun* the fact of having bacteria in the blood. Bacteraemia is not necessarily a serious condition. Compare **septicaemia**

bacteria /bæk'tɪəriə/ plural of **bacterium**

bacterial /bæk'tɪəriəl/ *adjective* relating to bacteria or caused by bacteria ○ *Children with sickle-cell anaemia are susceptible to bacterial infection.*

bacterial plaque /bæk'tɪəriəl ,plæk/ *noun* a hard smooth bacterial deposit on teeth

bactericidal /bæk,tɪəri'saɪdəl/ *adjective* referring to a substance which destroys bacteria

bactericide /bæk'tɪərisaɪd/ *noun* a substance which destroys bacteria

bacteriological /bæktɪəriə'lɒdʒɪk(ə)l/ *adjective* referring to bacteriology

bacteriologist /bæk,tɪəri'ɒlədʒɪst/ *noun* a doctor who specialises in the study of bacteria

bacteriology /bæk,tɪəri'ɒlədʒi/ *noun* the scientific study of bacteria

bacteriolysin /bæk,tɪəri'ɒlɪsɪn/ *noun* a protein, usually an immunoglobulin, which destroys bacterial cells

bacteriolysis /bæk,tɪəri'ɒlɪsɪs/ *noun* the destruction of bacterial cells

bacteriolytic /bæk,tɪəriə'lɪtɪk/ *adjective* referring to a substance which can destroy bacteria

bacteriophage /bæk'tɪəriəfeɪdʒ/ *noun* a virus which affects bacteria

bacteriostatic /bæk‚tɪərɪəʊ'stætɪk/ *adjective* referring to a substance which does not kill bacteria but stops them from multiplying

bacterium /bæk'tɪərɪəm/ *noun* a microscopic organism. Some types are permanently present in the gut and can break down food tissue, but many can cause disease. (NOTE: The plural is **bacteria**.)

COMMENT: Bacteria can be shaped like rods (bacilli), like balls (cocci) or have a spiral form (spirochaetes). Bacteria, especially bacilli and spirochaetes, can move and reproduce very rapidly.

bacteriuria /bæk‚tɪərɪ'jʊərɪə/ *noun* a condition in which bacteria are present in the urine

Bactrim /'bæktrɪm/ a trade name for co-trimoxazole

Baghdad boil /‚bægdæd 'bɔɪl/, **Baghdad sore** /‚bægdæd 'sɔː/ *noun* a skin disease of tropical countries caused by the parasite *Leishmania*. Also called **Oriental sore**

BAHA *abbreviation* bone anchored hearing aid

Baker's cyst /‚beɪkəz 'sɪst/ *noun* a swelling filled with synovial fluid, at the back of the knee, caused by weakness of the joint membrane [Described 1877. After William Morrant Baker (1838–96), member of staff at St Bartholomew's Hospital, London, UK]

baker's itch /‚beɪkəz 'ɪtʃ/, **baker's dermatitis** /'beɪkəz dɜːmə'taɪtɪs/ *noun* an irritation of the skin caused by handling yeast

BAL *abbreviation* British anti-lewisite

balanced diet /‚bælənst 'daɪət/ *noun* a diet which provides all the nutrients needed in the correct proportions

balanitis /‚bælə'naɪtɪs/ *noun* inflammation of the glans of the penis

balanoposthitis /‚bælənəʊpɒs'θaɪtɪs/ *noun* inflammation of the foreskin and the end of the penis

balantidiasis /‚bæləntɪ'daɪəsɪs/ *noun* an infestation of the large intestine by a parasite *Balantidium coli*, which causes ulceration of the wall of the intestine, leading to diarrhoea and finally dysentery

balanus /'bælənəs/ *noun* the round end of the penis. ◊ **glans**

bald /bɔːld/ *adjective* with no hair, especially on the head

baldness /'bɔːldnəs/ *noun* the state of not having any hair

COMMENT: Baldness in men is hereditary; it can also occur in both men and women as a reaction to an illness or to a drug.

Balkan frame /‚bɔːlkən 'freɪm/, **Balkan beam** /‚bɔːlkən 'biːm/ *noun* a frame fitted above a bed to which a leg in plaster can be attached. ◊ **Pearson bed**

ball and cage valve /‚bɔːl ən 'keɪdʒ vælv/ *noun* an artificial heart valve, formed of a silicon ball which moves inside a metal cage to open and shut the valve

ball and socket joint /‚bɔːl ənd 'sɒkɪt dʒɔɪnt/ *noun* a joint where the round end of a long bone is attached to a cup-shaped hollow in another bone in such a way that the long bone can move in almost any direction. Compare **ginglymus**

balloon /bə'luːn/ *noun* a bag of light material inflated with air or a gas, used to unblock arteries

balloon angioplasty /bə‚luːn ‚ændʒiə 'plæsti/ *noun* same as **percutaneous angioplasty**

ballottement /bə'lɒtmənt/ *noun* a method of examining the body by tapping or moving a part, especially during pregnancy

balneotherapy /‚bælniəʊ'θerəpi/ *noun* the treatment of diseases by bathing in hot water or water containing beneficial natural chemicals

balsam /'bɔːls(ə)m/ *noun* a mixture of resin and oil, used to rub on sore joints or to put in hot water and use as an inhalant. ◊ **friar's balsam**

ban /bæn/ *verb* to say that something is not permitted ○ *Smoking is banned throughout the building.* ○ *Use of this drug has been banned.*

bandage /'bændɪdʒ/ *noun* a piece of cloth which is wrapped around a wound or an injured limb ○ *His head was covered with bandages.* ■ *verb* to wrap a piece of cloth around a wound ○ *She bandaged his leg.* ○ *His arm is bandaged up.*

Bandl's ring /'bænd(ə)lz rɪŋ/ same as **retraction ring** [After Ludwig Bandl (1842–92), German obstetrician.]

Bankart's operation /'bæŋkɑːts ɒpə‚reɪʃ(ə)n/ *noun* an operation to repair a recurrent dislocation of the shoulder [First performed 1923. After Arthur Sydney Blundell Bankart (1879–1951), first orthopaedic surgeon at the Middlesex Hospital, London, UK]

Banti's syndrome /'bæntiz ‚sɪndrəʊm/, **Banti's disease** /'bæntiz dɪ‚ziːz/ *noun* same as **splenic anaemia** [Described 1882. After Guido Banti (1852–1925), Florentine pathologist and physician.]

Barbados leg /bɑː‚beɪdɒs 'leg/ *noun* a form of elephantiasis, a large swelling of the leg due to a Filaria worm

barber's itch /‚bɑːbəz 'ɪtʃ/, **barber's rash** /‚bɑːbəz 'ræʃ/ *noun* same as **sycosis barbae**

barbiturate /bɑː'bɪtʃʊrət/ *noun* a sedative drug

barbotage /‚bɑːbə'tɑːʒ/ *noun* a method of spinal analgesia by which cerebrospinal fluid is withdrawn and then injected back

barium /'beərɪəm/ *noun* a chemical element, forming poisonous compounds, used as a contrast medium when taking X-ray photographs of soft tissue (NOTE: The chemical symbol is **Ba**.)

barium enema /ˌbeəriəm 'enɪmə/ *noun* a liquid solution containing barium sulphate which is put into the rectum to increase the contrast of an X-ray of the lower intestine

barium meal /ˌbeəriəm 'miːl/, **barium solution** /ˌbeəriəm səˈluːʃ(ə)n/ *noun* a liquid solution containing barium sulphate which someone drinks to increase the contrast of an X-ray of the alimentary tract

Barlow's disease /'buːləʊz dɪˌziːz/ *noun* scurvy in children, caused by a lack of vitamin C [Described 1882. After Sir Thomas Barlow (1845–1945), physician at various London hospitals and to Queen Victoria, King Edward VII and King George V.]

Barlow's sign /'buːləʊz saɪn/ *noun* a test for congenital dislocation of the hip, in which a sudden movement is felt and sometimes a sound is heard when the joint is manipulated

baroreceptor /ˌbærəʊrɪ'septə/ *noun* one of a group of nerves near the carotid artery and aortic arch, which senses changes in blood pressure

barotrauma /ˌbærəʊ'trɔːmə/ *noun* an injury caused by a sharp increase in pressure

Barr body /'buː ˌbɒdi/ *noun* a dense clump of chromatin found only in female cells, which can be used to identify the sex of a baby before birth [Described 1949. After Murray Llewellyn Barr (1908–95), head of the Department of Anatomy at the University of Western Ontario, Canada.]

Barré-Guillain syndrome /ˌbæreɪ 'giː jæn ˌsɪndrəʊm/ *noun* ♦ **Guillain-Barré syndrome**

barrel chest /ˌbærəl 'tʃest/ *noun* a chest formed like a barrel, caused by asthma or emphysema

barrier cream /'bæriə kriːm/ *noun* a cream put on the skin to prevent the skin coming into contact with irritating substances

barrier nursing /'bæriə ˌnɜːsɪŋ/ *noun* the nursing of someone who has an infectious disease. It involves keeping them away from other patients and making sure that faeces and soiled bedclothes do not carry the infection to other patients.

bartholinitis /ˌbuːθəlɪ'naɪtɪs/ *noun* inflammation of the Bartholin's glands

Bartholin's glands /'buːθəlɪnz glændz/ *plural noun* two glands at the side of the vagina and between it and the vulva, which secrete a lubricating substance. Also called **greater vestibular glands** [After Caspar Bartholin (1655–1748), Danish anatomist.]

basal /'beɪs(ə)l/ *adjective* located at the bottom of something, or forming its base

basal metabolic rate /ˌbeɪsɪk metə'bɒlɪk reɪt/ *noun* the amount of energy used by the body in exchanging oxygen and carbon dioxide when at rest. It was formerly used as a way of testing thyroid gland activity. Abbreviation **BMR**

base /beɪs/ *noun* **1.** the bottom part ○ *the base of the spine* **2.** the main ingredient of an ointment, as opposed to the active ingredient **3.** a substance which reacts with an acid to form a salt ■ *verb* to use something as a base

Basedow's disease /'bæzɪdəʊz dɪˌziːz/ *noun* a form of hyperthyroidism [Described 1840. After Carl Adolph Basedow (1799–1854), general practitioner in Mersburg, Germany.]

basement membrane /ˌbeɪsmənt ˌmem 'breɪn/ *noun* a membrane at the base of an epithelium

basilar /'bæzɪlə/ *adjective* referring to a base

basilic vein /bə,zɪlɪk 'veɪn/ *noun* a large vein running along the inside of the arm

basophil /'beɪsəfɪl/ *noun* a type of white blood cell which has granules in its cytoplasm and contains histamine and heparin

basophilia /ˌbeɪsə'fɪliə/ *noun* an increase in the number of basophils in the blood

basophilic granulocyte /ˌbeɪsəfɪlɪk 'grænjʊləsaɪt/ *noun* same as **basophil**

Batten's disease /'bæt(ə)nz dɪˌziːz/ *noun* a hereditary disease which affects the enzymes of the brain, causing cells in the brain and eye to die

battered baby syndrome /'bætəd ˌbeɪbi ˌsɪndrəʊm/, **battered child syndrome** /'bætəd 'tʃaɪld 'sɪndrəʊm/ *noun* a condition in which a baby or small child is frequently beaten, usually by one or both of its parents, sustaining injuries such as multiple fractures

battledore placenta /'bæt(ə)ldɔː plə,sentə/ *noun* a placenta where the umbilical cord is attached at the edge and not at the centre

Bazin's disease /'beɪzɪnz dɪˌziːz/ *noun* same as **erythema induratum** [Described 1861. After Pierre Antoine Ernest Bazin (1807–78), dermatologist at Hôpital St Louis, Paris, France. He was an expert in parasitology associated with skin conditions.]

BC *abbreviation* bone conduction

BCC *abbreviation* Breast Cancer Campaign

B cell /'biː sel/ *noun* same as **beta cell**

BCG /ˌbiː siː 'dʒiː ˌvæksiːn/, **BCG vaccine** *noun* a vaccine which immunises against tuberculosis. Full form **bacille Calmette-Guérin**

BCh *abbreviation* Bachelor of Surgery

BDA *abbreviation* British Dental Association

bearing down /ˌbeərɪŋ 'daʊn/ *noun* a stage in childbirth when the woman starts to push out the baby from the uterus

bearing-down pain /ˌbeərɪŋ 'daʊn ˌpeɪn/ *noun* pain felt in the uterus during the second stage of labour (NOTE: Bearing-down pain is also associated with uterine prolapse.)

Beck inventory of depression /ˌbek ˌɪnvənt(ə)ri əv dɪ'preʃ(ə)n/ *noun* one of the rating scales for depression, in which a series of 21 questions refers to attitudes frequently shown by people suffering from depression

beclomethasone /ˌbeklə'meθəsəʊn/ *noun* a steroid drug usually used in an inhaler to treat asthma or hay fever

becquerel /'bekərel/ *noun* an SI unit of measurement of radiation. Abbreviation **Bq** (NOTE: Now used in place of the **curie**.)

bed bath /'bed bɑːθ/ *noun* an act of washing the whole body of someone who is unable to get up to wash. Also called **blanket bath**

bed blocking /'bed ˌblɒkɪŋ/ *noun* the fact of people being kept in hospital because other forms of care are not available, which means that other people cannot be treated

bedbug /'bedbʌg/ *noun* a small insect which lives in dirty bedclothes and sucks blood

bed occupancy /'bed ˌɒkjʊpənsi/ *noun* the percentage of beds in a hospital which are occupied

bedpan /'bedpæn/ *noun* a dish into which someone can urinate or defecate without getting out of bed

bed rest /'bed rest/ *noun* a period of time spent in bed in order to rest and recover from an illness

bedridden /'bedˌrɪd(ə)n/ *adjective* referring to someone who has been too ill to get out of bed over a long period of time

bedside manner /ˌbedsaɪd 'mænə/ *noun* the way in which a doctor behaves towards a patient, especially a patient who is in bed □ **a good bedside manner** the ability to make patients feel comforted and reassured

bedsore /'bedsɔː/ *noun* an inflamed patch of skin on a bony part of the body, which develops into an ulcer, caused by pressure of the part on the mattress after lying for some time in one position. Special beds such as air beds, ripple beds and water beds are used to try to prevent the formation of bedsores. Also called **pressure sore**, **decubitus ulcer**

bedstate /'bedsteɪt/ *noun* a record of the current level of occupancy of beds in a hospital or care unit, updated as admissions and discharges occur

bedwetting /'bedwetɪŋ/ *noun* same as **nocturnal enuresis** (NOTE: This term is used mainly about children.)

Beer's knife /'bɪəz naɪf/ *noun* a knife with a triangular blade, used in eye operations [After George Joseph Beer (1763–1821), German ophthalmologist.]

behaviour /bɪ'heɪvjə/ *noun* a way of acting ○ *His behaviour was very aggressive.*

behavioural /bɪ'heɪvjərəl/ *adjective* relating to behaviour

behaviourism /bɪ'heɪvjərɪz(ə)m/ *noun* a psychological theory proposing that only someone's

behaviour should be studied to discover their psychological problems

behaviourist /bɪ'heɪvjərɪst/ *noun* a psychologist who follows behaviourism

behaviour therapy /bɪˌheɪvjə 'θerəpi/ *noun* a form of psychiatric treatment in which someone learns how to improve their condition

Behçet's syndrome /'beɪsets ˌsɪndrəʊm/ *noun* a chronic condition of the immune system with no known cause, experienced as a series of attacks of inflammation of small blood vessels accompanied by mouth ulcers and sometimes genital ulcers, skin lesions and inflamed eyes [Described 1937. After Halushi Behçet (1889–1948), Turkish dermatologist.]

behind /bɪ'haɪnd/ *noun* same as **buttock** (*informal*)

bejel /'bedʒəl/ *noun* a non-venereal form of syphilis which is endemic among children in some areas of the Middle East and elsewhere and is caused by a spirochaete strain of bacteria

belch /beltʃ/ *noun* the action of allowing air in the stomach to come up through the mouth ■ *verb* to allow air in the stomach to come up through the mouth

belching /'beltʃɪŋ/ *noun* the action of allowing air in the stomach to come up through the mouth. Also called **eructation**

belladonna /ˌbelə'dɒnə/ *noun* **1.** a poisonous plant with berries containing atropine. Also called **deadly nightshade 2.** a form of atropine extracted from the belladonna plant

belle indifférence /ˌbel æn'dɪferɑːns/ *noun* an excessively calm state in a person, in a situation which would usually produce a show of emotion

Bellocq's cannula /beˌlɒks 'kænjʊlə/, **Bellocq's sound** /beˌlɒks 'saʊnd/ *noun* an instrument used to control a nosebleed [After Jean Jacques Bellocq (1732–1807), French surgeon.]

Bell's mania /ˌbelz 'meɪniə/ *noun* a form of acute mania with delirium [After Luther Vose Bell (1806–62), American physiologist.]

Bell's palsy /ˌbelz 'pɔːlzi/ *noun* paralysis of the facial nerve on one side of the face, preventing one eye being closed. Also called **facial paralysis** [Described 1821. After Sir Charles Bell (1774–1842), Scottish surgeon. He ran anatomy schools, first in Edinburgh and then in London. Professor of Anatomy at the Royal Academy.]

belly /'beli/ *noun* **1.** same as **abdomen 2.** the fatter central part of a muscle

Bence Jones protein /ˌbens 'dʒəʊnz ˌprəʊtiːn/ *noun* a protein found in the urine of people who have myelomatosis, lymphoma, leukaemia and some other cancers [Described 1848. After Henry Bence Jones (1814–73), physician at St George's Hospital, London, UK]

bends /bendz/ *plural noun* □ **the bends** ♦ caisson disease

Benedict's solution /ˈbenɪdɪkts səˌluːʃ(ə)n/ *noun* a solution used to carry out Benedict's test

Benedict's test /ˈbenɪdɪkts test/ *noun* a test to see if sugar is present in the urine [Described 1915. After Stanley Rossiter Benedict (1884–1936), physiological chemist at Cornell University, New York, USA.]

benign /bəˈnaɪn/ *adjective* generally harmless

benign growth /bəˈnaɪn grəʊθ/ *noun* same as benign tumour

benign pancreatic disease /bəˌnaɪn ˌpæŋkriˈætɪk dɪˌziːz/ *noun* chronic pancreatitis

benign prostatic hypertrophy /bɪˌnaɪn prɒˌstætɪk haɪˈpɜːtrəfi/ *noun* a nonmalignant enlargement of the prostate. Abbreviation **BPH**

benign tumour /bəˌnaɪn ˈtjuːmə/ *noun* a tumour which will not grow again or spread to other parts of the body if it is removed surgically, but which can be fatal if not treated. Also called **benign growth**. Opposite **malignant tumour**

Bennett's fracture /ˌbenɪts ˈfræktʃə/ *noun* a fracture of the first metacarpal, the bone between the thumb and the wrist [Described 1886. After Edward Halloran Bennett (1837–1907), Irish anatomist, later Professor of Surgery at Trinity College, Dublin, Ireland.]

benzocaine /ˈbenzəkeɪn/ *noun* a drug with anaesthetic properties used in some throat lozenges and skin creams

benzodiazepine /ˌbenzəʊdaɪˈæzəpiːn/ *noun* a drug which acts on receptors in the central nervous system to relieve symptoms of anxiety and insomnia, although prolonged use is to be avoided (NOTE: Benzodiazepines have names ending in **-azepam: diazepam**.)

benzoin /ˈbenzəʊɪn/ *noun* a resin used to make friar's balsam

benzyl benzoate /ˌbenzɪl ˈbenzəʊeɪt/ *noun* a colourless oily liquid which occurs naturally in balsams, used in medicines and perfumes

bereavement /bɪˈriːvmənt/ *noun* the loss of someone, especially a close relative or friend, through death

beriberi /ˌberiˈberi/ *noun* a disease of the nervous system caused by lack of vitamin B_1

berylliosis /bəˌrɪliˈəʊsɪs/ *noun* poisoning caused by breathing in particles of the poisonous chemical compound beryllium oxide

Besnier's prurigo /ˌbenieɪz prʊˈraɪgəʊ/ *noun* an itchy skin rash on the backs of the knees and the insides of the elbows [After Ernest Besnier (1831–1909), French dermatologist.]

beta /ˈbiːtə/ *noun* the second letter of the Greek alphabet

beta-adrenergic receptor /ˌbiːtə ˌædrəˈnɜːdʒɪk/ *noun* one of two types of nerve endings that respond to adrenaline by speeding up the heart rate or dilating the bronchi

beta blocker /ˈbiːtə ˌblɒkə/ *noun* a drug which reduces the activity of the heart (NOTE: Beta blockers have names ending in **-olol: atenolol, propranolol hydrochloride**.)

beta cell /ˈbiːtə sel/ *noun* a type of cell found in the islets of Langerhans, in the pancreas, which produces insulin. Also called **B cell**

Betadine /ˈbiːtədiːn/ *noun* a trade name for a form of iodine

betamethasone /ˌbiːtəˈmeθəsəʊn/ *noun* a very strong corticosteroid drug

betaxolol /bɪˈtæksəlɒl/ *noun* a beta blocker drug used in the treatment of high blood pressure and glaucoma

bethanechol /beˈθænɪkɒl/ *noun* an agonist drug used to increase muscle tone after surgery

Betnovate /ˈbetnəveɪt/ *noun* a trade name for an ointment containing betamethasone

bi- /baɪ/ *prefix* two or twice

bias /ˈbaɪəs/ *noun* a systematic error in the design or conduct of a study which could explain the results

bicarbonate of soda /baɪˌkɑːbənət əv ˈsəʊdə/ *noun* same as **sodium bicarbonate**

bicellular /baɪˈseljʊlə/ *adjective* having two cells

biceps /ˈbaɪseps/ *noun* any muscle formed of two parts joined to form one tendon, especially the muscles in the front of the upper arm (**biceps brachii**) and the back of the thigh (**biceps femoris**). ◊ **triceps** (NOTE: The plural is **biceps**.)

bicipital /baɪˈsɪpɪt(ə)l/ *adjective* referring to a biceps muscle

biconcave /baɪˈkɒŋkeɪv/ *adjective* referring to a lens which is concave on both sides

biconvex /baɪˈkɒnveks/ *adjective* referring to a lens which is convex on both sides

bicornuate /baɪˈkɔːnjuət/ *adjective* divided into two parts (NOTE: The word is sometimes applied to a malformation of the uterus.)

bicuspid /baɪˈkʌspɪd/ *adjective* with two points ■ *noun* a premolar tooth

bicuspid valve /ˌbaɪˈkʌspɪd ˌvælv/ *noun* same as **mitral valve**. See illustration at **HEART** in Supplement

b.i.d. *adverb* (*used on prescriptions*) twice daily. Full form **bis in die**

bidet /ˈbiːdeɪ/ *noun* an object for washing the genital and anal areas. It looks like a low toilet.

bifid /ˈbaɪfɪd/ *adjective* in two parts

bifocal /baɪˈfəʊk(ə)l/ *adjective* referring to lenses made with two sections which have different focal lengths, one for looking at things which are near, the other for looking at things which are far away

bifocal glasses /baɪˌfəʊk(ə)l ˈɡlɑːsɪz/, **bifocal lenses** /baɪˈfəʊk(ə)l ˈlenzɪz/, **bifocals** /baɪˈfəʊk(ə)lz/ *plural noun* spectacles with lenses which have two types of lens combined in the same piece of glass, the top part being used for seeing at a distance and the lower part for reading

bifurcate *adjective* /baɪˈfɜːkeɪt/ separating or branching off into two parts ■ *verb* /ˈbaɪfəkeɪt/ to split or branch off into two parts

bifurcation /ˌbaɪfəˈkeɪʃ(ə)n/ *noun* a place where something divides into two parts

bigeminy /baɪˈdʒemɪni/ *noun* same as **pulsus bigeminus**

big toe /ˌbɪɡ ˈtəʊ/ *noun* the largest of the five toes, on the inside of the foot. Also called **great toe**

biguanide /baɪˈɡwɑːnaɪd/ *noun* a drug which lowers blood sugar, used in the treatment of Type II diabetes

bilateral /baɪˈlæt(ə)rəl/ *adjective* affecting both sides

bilateral pneumonia /baɪˌlæt(ə)rəl njuːˈməʊniə/ *noun* pneumonia affecting both lungs

bile /baɪl/ *noun* a thick bitter brownish yellow fluid produced by the liver, stored in the gall bladder and used to digest fatty substances and neutralise acids (NOTE: For other terms referring to bile, see words beginning with **chol-**.)

bilharzia /bɪlˈhɑːtsiə/ *noun* **1.** a fluke which enters the bloodstream and causes bilharziasis. Also called **Schistosoma 2.** same as **bilharziasis** (NOTE: Although strictly speaking, **bilharzia** is the name of the fluke, it is also generally used for the name of the disease: *bilharzia patients*; *six cases of bilharzia*.)

bilharziasis /ˌbɪlhɑːˈtsaɪəsɪs/ *noun* a tropical disease caused by flukes in the intestine or bladder. Also called **bilharzia**, **schistosomiasis**

bili- /bɪli/ *prefix* referring to bile (NOTE: For other terms referring to bile, see words beginning with **chol-**, **chole-**.)

biliary /ˈbɪliəri/ *adjective* referring to bile

biliary colic /ˌbɪliəri ˈkɒlɪk/ *noun* pain in the abdomen caused by gallstones in the bile duct or by inflammation of the gall bladder

bilious /ˈbɪliəs/ *adjective* **1.** referring to bile **2.** referring to nausea (*informal*)

biliousness /ˈbɪliəsnəs/ *noun* a feeling of indigestion and nausea (*informal*)

bilirubin /ˌbɪliˈruːbɪn/ *noun* a red pigment in bile

bilirubinaemia /ˌbɪliruːbɪˈniːmiə/ *noun* an excess of bilirubin in the blood

biliuria /ˌbɪliˈjʊəriə/ *noun* the presence of bile in the urine. Also called **choluria**

biliverdin /ˌbɪliˈvɜːdɪn/ *noun* a green pigment in bile, produced by oxidation of bilirubin

Billings method /ˈbɪlɪŋz ˌmeθəd/ *noun* a method of birth control which uses the colour and consistency of the cervical mucus as guides to whether ovulation is taking place

Billroth's operations /ˈbɪlrɒθs ɒpəˌreɪʃ(ə)nz/ *plural noun* surgical operations in which the lower part of the stomach is removed and the part which is left is linked to the duodenum (**Billroth I**) or jejunum (**Billroth II**) [Described 1881. After Christian Albert Theodore Billroth (1829–94), Prussian surgeon.]

bimanual /baɪˈmænjuəl/ *adjective* done with two hands, or needing both hands to be done

binary /ˈbaɪnəri/ *adjective* made of two parts

binary fission /ˌbaɪnəri ˈfɪʃ(ə)n/ *noun* the process of splitting into two parts in some types of cell division

binaural /baɪnˈɔːrəl/ *adjective* using, or relating to, both ears

binder /ˈbaɪndə/ *noun* a bandage which is wrapped round a limb to support it

Binet's test /ˈbɪneɪz test/ *noun* an intelligence test for children [Originally described 1905 but later modified at Stanford University, California, USA. After Alfred Binet (1857–1911), French psychologist and physiologist.]

binocular /bɪˈnɒkjʊlə/ *adjective* referring to the two eyes

binovular /bɪˈnɒvjʊlə/ *adjective* referring to twins who develop from two different ova

bio- /baɪəʊ/ *prefix* referring to living organisms

bioassay /ˌbaɪəʊəˈseɪ/ *noun* a test of the strength of a drug, hormone, vitamin or serum, by examining the effect it has on living animals or tissue

bioavailability /ˌbaɪəʊəveɪləˈbɪlɪti/ *noun* the extent to which a nutrient or medicine can be taken up by the body

biochemistry /ˌbaɪəʊˈkemɪstri/ *noun* the chemistry of living tissues

biocide /ˈbaɪəʊsaɪd/ *noun* a substance which kills living organisms

biodegradable /ˌbaɪəʊdɪˈɡreɪdəb(ə)l/ *adjective* easily decomposed by organisms such as bacteria or by the effect of sunlight, the sea, etc.

biofeedback /ˌbaɪəʊˈfiːdbæk/ *noun* the control of the autonomic nervous system by someone's conscious thought, as he or she sees the results of tests or scans

biohazard /ˈbaɪəʊˌhæzəd/ *noun* a danger to human beings or their environment, especially one from a poisonous or infectious agent

biological /ˌbaɪəˈlɒdʒɪk(ə)l/ *adjective* referring to biology

biological parent /ˌbaɪəˌlɒdʒɪk(ə)l ˈpeərənt/ *noun* a parent who was physically involved in producing a child

biologist /baɪˈɒlədʒɪst/ *noun* a scientist who specialises in biology

biology /baɪˈɒlədʒi/ *noun* the study of living organisms

biomaterial /ˌbaɪəʊməˈtɪəriəl/ *noun* a synthetic material which can be used as an implant in living tissue

biometry /baɪˈɒmətri/ *noun* the science which applies statistics to the study of living things □ **biometry of a fetus** the measurement of the key parameters of growth of a fetus by ultrasound

bionic ear /baɪˌɒnɪk ˈɪə/ *noun* a cochlear implant (*informal*)

bionics /baɪˈɒnɪks/ *noun* the process of applying knowledge of biological systems to mechanical and electronic devices

biophysical profile /ˌbaɪəʊfɪzɪk(ə)l ˈprəʊfaɪl/ *noun* a profile of a fetus, based on such things as its breathing movement and body movement

biopsy /ˈbaɪɒpsi/ *noun* the process of taking a small piece of living tissue for examination and diagnosis ○ *The biopsy of the tissue from the growth showed that it was benign.*

biorhythm /ˈbaɪəʊrɪð(ə)m/ *noun* a regular process of change which takes place within living organisms, e.g. sleeping, waking or the reproductive cycle (NOTE: Some people believe that biorhythms affect behaviour and mood.)

biostatistics /ˌbaɪəʊstəˈtɪstɪks/ *plural noun* statistics used in medicine and the study of disease

biotechnology /ˌbaɪəʊtekˈnɒlədʒi/ *noun* **1.** the use of biological processes in industrial production, e.g. in the production of drugs **2.** same as **genetic modification**

biotin /ˈbaɪətɪn/ *noun* a type of vitamin B found in egg yolks, liver and yeast

BiPAP /ˈbaɪpæp/ *noun* a breathing apparatus that allows air delivered through a mask to be set at one pressure for inhaling and another for exhaling, maximising breathing efficiency and minimising natural muscular effort. Full form **bi-level positive airway pressure**

biparietal /ˌbaɪpəˈraɪət(ə)l/ *adjective* referring to the two parietal bones

biparous /ˈbɪpərəs/ *adjective* producing twins

bipennate /baɪˈpeneɪt/ *adjective* referring to a muscle with fibres which rise from either side of the tendon

bipolar /baɪˈpəʊlə/ *adjective* with two poles. See illustration at **NEURONE** in Supplement

bipolar disorder /ˌbaɪpəʊlə dɪsˈɔːdə/ *noun* a psychological condition in which someone moves between mania and depression and experiences delusion. Also called **manic-depressive illness, manic depression**

bipolar neurone /baɪˌpəʊlə ˈnjʊərəʊn/ *noun* a nerve cell with two processes, a dendrite and an axon, found in the retina. See illustration at **NEURONE** in Supplement. Compare **multipolar neurone, unipolar neurone**

birth /bɜːθ/ *noun* the act of being born

birth canal /ˈbɜːθ kəˌnæl/ *noun* the uterus, vagina and vulva

birth control /ˈbɜːθ kənˌtrəʊl/ *noun* same as **contraception**

birth control pill /ˈbɜːθ kənˌtrəʊl pɪl/ *noun* same as **oral contraceptive**

birthing chair /ˈbɜːθɪŋ tʃeə/ *noun* a special chair in which a woman sits to give birth

birthing pool /ˈbɜːθɪŋ puːl/ *noun* a special large bath in which pregnant women can relax before and when giving birth

birthmark /ˈbɜːθmɑːk/ *noun* an unusual coloured or raised area on the skin which someone has from birth. Also called **naevus**

birth mother /ˈbɜːθ ˌmʌðə/ *noun* the woman who gave birth to a child

birth parent /ˈbɜːθ ˌpeərənt/ *noun* one of the parents that physically produced a child

birth plan /ˈbɜːθ plæn/ *noun* a list of a pregnant woman's wishes about how the birth of her baby should take place, e.g. whether she wants a natural birth and what pain relief she should be given

birth rate /ˈbɜːθ reɪt/ *noun* the number of births per year, shown per thousand of the population ○ *a birth rate of 15 per thousand* ○ *There has been a severe decline in the birth rate.*

birth trauma /ˈbɜːθ ˌtrɔːmə/ *noun* an injury caused to a baby during delivery

birth weight /ˈbɜːθ weɪt/ *noun* the weight of a baby at birth

bisacodyl /ˌbaɪsəˈkəʊdɪl/ *noun* a laxative drug

bisexual /baɪˈsekʃuəl/ *adjective* referring to a person who is sexually attracted to both males and females

bisexuality /ˌbaɪsekʃuˈælɪti/ *noun* the state of being sexually attracted to both males and females

bis in die /ˌbɪs ɪn ˈdiːeɪ/ *adverb* full form of **b.i.d.**

bismuth /ˈbɪzməθ/ *noun* a chemical element (NOTE: The chemical symbol is **Bi**.)

bistoury /ˈbɪstəri/ *noun* a sharp thin surgical knife

bite /baɪt/ *verb* **1.** to cut into something with the teeth ○ *He bit a piece out of the apple.* **2.** (*of an insect*) to puncture someone's skin ■ *noun* **1.** the action of biting or of being bitten **2.** a place or mark where someone has been bitten ○ *a dog bite* ○ *an insect bite*

bite wing /ˈbaɪt wɪŋ/ *noun* a holder for dental X-ray film, which a person clenches between the teeth, so allowing an X-ray of both upper and lower teeth to be taken

Bitot's spots /ˌbiːtəʊz ˈspɒts/ *plural noun* small white spots on the conjunctiva, caused by vitamin A deficiency [Described 1863. After Pierre A. Bitot (1822–88), French physician.]

bivalve /ˈbaɪvælv/ *noun* an organ which has two valves ■ *adjective* referring to a bivalve organ

black eye /ˌblæk ˈaɪ/ *noun* bruising and swelling of the tissues round an eye, usually caused by a blow

blackhead /ˈblækhed/ *noun* same as **comedo** (*informal*)

black heel /ˈblæk ˌhiːl/ *noun* a haemorrhage inside the heel, characterised by black spots

black out /ˈblæk aʊt/ *verb* to have sudden loss of consciousness ○ *I suddenly blacked out and I can't remember anything more*

blackout /ˈblækaʊt/ *noun* a sudden loss of consciousness (*informal*) ○ *She must have had a blackout while driving.* Also called **fainting fit**

blackwater fever /ˈblækwɔːtə ˌfiːvə/ *noun* a form of malaria where haemoglobin from red blood cells is released into plasma and makes the urine dark

bladder /ˈblædə/ *noun* any sac in the body, especially the sac where the urine collects before being passed out of the body ○ *He is suffering from bladder trouble.* ○ *She is taking antibiotics for a bladder infection.*

Blalock's operation /ˈbleɪlɒks ɒpəˌreɪʃ(ə)n/, **Blalock-Taussig operation** /ˌbleɪlɒk ˈtɔːsɪɡ ɒpəˌreɪʃ(ə)n/ *noun* a surgical operation to connect the pulmonary artery to the subclavian artery, in order to increase blood flow to the lungs of someone who has tetralogy of Fallot

bland /blænd/ *adjective* referring to food which is not spicy, irritating or acid

blanket bath /ˈblæŋkɪt bɑːθ/ *noun* same as **bed bath**

blast /blɑːst/ *noun* **1.** a wave of air pressure from an explosion which can cause concussion **2.** an immature form of a cell before distinctive characteristics develop

-blast /blæst/ *suffix* referring to a very early stage in the development of a cell

blasto- /blæstəʊ/ *prefix* referring to a germ cell

blastocoele /ˈblæstəʊsiːl/ *noun* a cavity filled with fluid in a morula

blastocyst /ˈblæstəʊsɪst/ *noun* an early stage in the development of an embryo

Blastomyces /ˌblæstəʊˈmaɪsiːz/ *noun* a type of parasitic fungus which affects the skin

blastomycosis /ˌblæstəʊmaɪˈkəʊsɪs/ *noun* an infection caused by *Blastomyces*

blastula /ˈblæstjʊlə/ *noun* the first stage of the development of an embryo in animals

bleb /bleb/ *noun* a blister. Compare **bulla**

bleeder /ˈbliːdə/ *noun* **1.** a blood vessel which bleeds during surgery **2.** a person who has haemophilia (*informal*)

bleeding /ˈbliːdɪŋ/ *noun* an unusual loss of blood from the body through the skin, through an orifice or internally

bleeding time /ˈbliːdɪŋ taɪm/ *noun* a test of the clotting ability of someone's blood, by timing the length of time it takes for the blood to congeal

blennorrhagia /ˌblenəʊˈreɪdʒə/ *noun* the discharge of mucus

blennorrhoea /ˌblenəˈriːə/ *noun* the discharge of watery mucus

bleomycin /ˌbliːəʊˈmaɪsɪn/ *noun* an antibiotic used to treat forms of cancer such as Hodgkin's disease

blephar- /blefər/ *prefix* same as **blepharo-** (*used before vowels*)

blepharitis /ˌblefəˈraɪtɪs/ *noun* inflammation of the eyelid

blepharo- /blefərəʊ/ *prefix* referring to the eyelid

blepharoconjunctivitis /ˌblefərəʊkənˌdʒʌŋktɪˈvaɪtɪs/ *noun* inflammation of the conjunctiva of the eyelids

blepharon /ˈblefərɒn/ *noun* an eyelid

blepharospasm /ˈblefərəʊspæz(ə)m/ *noun* a sudden contraction of the eyelid, as when a tiny piece of dust gets in the eye

blepharotosis /ˌblefərəʊˈtəʊsɪs/ *noun* a condition in which the upper eyelid is half closed because of paralysis of the muscle or nerve

blind /blaɪnd/ *adjective* not able to see

blind loop syndrome /ˌblaɪnd ˈluːp ˌsɪndrəʊm/ *noun* a condition which occurs in cases of diverticulosis or of Crohn's disease, with steatorrhoea, abdominal pain and megaloblastic anaemia

blindness /ˈblaɪndnəs/ *noun* the fact of not being able to see

blind spot /ˈblaɪnd spɒt/ *noun* the point in the retina where the optic nerve joins it, which does not register light

blind study /ˌblaɪnd ˈstʌdi/ *noun* an investigation to test an intervention such as giving a drug, in which a person does not know if he or she has taken the active medicine or the placebo

blister /ˈblɪstə/ *noun* a swelling on the skin containing serum from the blood, caused by rubbing, burning or a disease such as chickenpox ■ *verb* to produce blisters

bloated /ˈbləʊtɪd/ *adjective* experiencing the uncomfortable sensation of a very full stomach

block /blɒk/ *noun* **1.** the stopping of a function **2.** a large piece of something ○ *A block of wood fell on his foot.* **3.** a period of time ○ *The training is in two three-hour blocks.* ■ *verb* to fill the space in something and stop other things passing through it ○ *The artery was blocked by a clot.* ○ *He swallowed a piece of plastic which blocked his oesophagus.*

blocking /'blɒkɪŋ/ *noun* a psychiatric disorder, in which someone suddenly stops one train of thought and switches to another

blood /blʌd/ *noun* a red liquid moved around the body by the pumping action of the heart (NOTE: For other terms referring to blood, see words beginning with **haem-, haemo-, haemato-**.)

blood bank /'blʌd bæŋk/ *noun* a section of a hospital or a special centre where blood given by donors is stored for use in transfusions

blood blister /'blʌd ˌblɪstə/ *noun* a swelling on the skin with blood inside, caused by nipping flesh

blood-borne virus /ˌblʌd bɔːn 'vaɪrəs/ *noun* a virus carried by the blood

blood-brain barrier /ˌblʌd breɪn 'bæriə/ *noun* the process by which some substances, which in other parts of the body will diffuse from capillaries, are held back by the endothelium of cerebral capillaries, preventing them from coming into contact with the fluids round the brain

blood clot /'blʌd klɒt/ *noun* a soft mass of coagulated blood in a vein or an artery. Also called **thrombus**

blood count /'blʌd kaʊnt/ *noun* a test to count the number and types of different blood cells in a sample of blood, in order to give an indication of the condition of the person's blood as a whole

blood donor /'blʌd ˌdəʊnə/ *noun* a person who gives blood which is then used in transfusions to other people

blood dyscrasia /ˌblʌd dɪs'kreɪziə/ *noun* any unusual blood condition such as a low cell count or platelet count

blood gas /'blʌd gæs/ *noun* oxygen and carbon dioxide that are naturally present in blood, an imbalance of which may indicate a respiratory disorder

blood-glucose level /ˌblʌd 'gluːkəʊz ˌlev(ə)l/ *noun* the amount of glucose present in the blood. The usual blood-glucose level is about 60–100 mg of glucose per 100 ml of blood.

blood group /'blʌd gruːp/ *noun* one of the different groups into which human blood is classified. Also called **blood type**

COMMENT: Blood is classified in various ways. The most common classifications are by the agglutinogens (factors A and B) in red blood cells and by the Rhesus factor. Blood can therefore have either factor (Group A and Group B) or both factors (Group AB) or neither (Group O) and each of these groups can be Rhesus negative or positive.

blood grouping /'blʌd ˌgruːpɪŋ/ *noun* the process of classifying people according to their blood groups

blood-letting /'blʌd ˌletɪŋ/ *noun* same as **phlebotomy**

blood loss /'blʌd lɒs/ *noun* loss of blood from the body by bleeding

blood pigment /'blʌd ˌpɪgmənt/ *noun* same as **haemoglobin**

blood pressure /'blʌd ˌpreʃə/ *noun* the pressure, measured in millimetres of mercury, at which the blood is pumped round the body by the heart

blood relationship /ˌblʌd rɪ'leɪʃ(ə)nʃɪp/ *noun* a relationship between people who come from the same family and have the same parents, grandparents or ancestors, as opposed to a relationship by marriage

blood sample /'blʌd ˌsɑːmpəl/ *noun* a sample of blood, taken for testing

bloodshot /'blʌdʃɒt/ *adjective* referring to an eye with small specks of blood in it from a small damaged blood vessel

blood sugar /ˌblʌd 'ʃʊgə/ *noun* glucose present in the blood

blood sugar level /ˌblʌd 'ʃʊgə ˌlev(ə)l/ *noun* the amount of glucose in the blood, which is higher after meals and in people with diabetes

blood test /'blʌd test/ *noun* a laboratory test of a blood sample to analyse its chemical composition ○ *The patient will have to have a blood test.*

blood transfusion /'blʌd trænsˌfjuːʒ(ə)n/ *noun* a procedure in which blood given by another person or taken from the patient at an earlier stage is transferred into the patient's vein

blood type /'blʌd taɪp/ *noun* same as **blood group**

blood typing /'blʌd ˌtaɪpɪŋ/ *noun* the analysis of blood for transfusion factors and blood group

blood vessel /'blʌd ˌves(ə)l/ *noun* any tube which carries blood round the body, e.g. an artery, vein or capillary (NOTE: For other terms referring to blood vessels, see words beginning with **angi-, angio-**.)

blood volume /'blʌd ˌvɒljuːm/ *noun* the total amount of blood in the body

blot test /'blɒt test/ *noun* ♦ **Rorschach test**

blue baby /ˌbluː 'beɪbi/ *noun* a baby who has congenital cyanosis, born either with a congenital heart condition or with a collapsed lung, which prevents an adequate supply of oxygen reaching the tissues, giving the baby's skin a slight blue colour (*informal*)

blue litmus /ˌbluː 'lɪtməs/ *noun* treated paper which indicates the presence of acid by turning red

blurred vision /ˌblɜːd 'vɪʒ(ə)n/ *noun* a condition in which someone does not see objects clearly

blush /blʌʃ/ *noun* a rush of red colour to the skin of the face, caused by emotion ■ *verb* to go red in the face because of emotion

BM *abbreviation* Bachelor of Medicine

BMA *abbreviation* British Medical Association

BMI *abbreviation* body mass index

BMR *abbreviation* basal metabolic rate

BNF *abbreviation* British National Formulary

body fluid /ˈbɒdi ˌfluːɪd/ *noun* a liquid in the body, e.g. water, blood or semen

body image /ˌbɒdi ˈɪmɪdʒ/ *noun* the mental image which a person has of their own body. Also called **body schema**

body language /ˈbɒdi ˌlæŋɡwɪdʒ/ *noun* the expression on your face, or the way you hold your body, interpreted by other people as unconsciously revealing your feelings

body odour /ˌbɒdi ˈəʊdə/ *noun* an unpleasant smell caused by perspiration

body scan /ˈbɒdi skæn/ *noun* an examination of the whole of the body using ultrasound or other scanning techniques

body schema /ˌbɒdi ˈskiːmə/ *noun* same as **body image**

body substance isolation /ˈbɒdi ˌsʌbstəns aɪsəˌleɪʃ(ə)n/ *noun* making sure that a trauma victim is kept isolated from the possibility of infection from moist body substances

body temperature /ˈbɒdi ˌtemprɪtʃə/ *noun* the internal temperature of the human body, usually about 37°C

Boeck's disease /ˈbeks dɪˌziːz/, **Boeck's sarcoid** /ˈbeks ˌsɑːkɔɪd/ *noun* same as **sarcoidosis** [Described 1899. After Caesar Peter Moeller Boeck (1845–1913), Professor of Dermatology at Oslo, Norway.]

Bohn's nodules /ˌbɔːnz ˈnɒdjuːlz/, **Bohn's epithelial pearls** /ˌbɔːnz epɪˌθiːliəl ˈpɜːlz/ *plural noun* tiny cysts found in the mouths of healthy infants

boil /bɔɪl/ *noun* a tender raised mass of infected tissue and skin, usually caused by infection of a hair follicle by the bacterium *Staphylococcus aureus*. Also called **furuncle**

bolus /ˈbəʊləs/ *noun* **1.** a mass of food which has been chewed and is ready to be swallowed **2.** a mass of food passing along the intestine

bonding /ˈbɒndɪŋ/ *noun* the process by which a psychological link is formed between a baby and its mother ○ *In autistic children bonding is difficult.*

bone /bəʊn/ *noun* **1.** calcified connective tissue **2.** one of the calcified pieces of connective tissue which make the skeleton ○ *There are several small bones in the human ear.* See illustration at SYNOVIAL JOINT in Supplement

bone-anchored hearing aid /ˌbəʊn ˌæŋkəd ˈhɪərɪŋ eɪd/ *noun* a hearing aid that is fitted surgically into the skull, usually behind the ear. Abbreviation **BAHA**

bone marrow /ˈbəʊn ˌmærəʊ/ *noun* soft tissue in cancellous bone (NOTE: For other terms referring to bone marrow, see words beginning with **myel-, myelo-**.)

bone marrow transplant /ˌbəʊn ˈmærəʊ ˌtrænsplɑːnt/ *noun* the transplant of marrow from a donor to a recipient

bone scan /ˈbəʊn skæn/ *noun* a scan which tracks a radioactive substance injected into the body to find areas where a bone is breaking down or repairing itself

Bonney's blue /ˌbɒniz ˈbluː/ *noun* a blue dye used as a disinfectant [After William Francis Victor Bonney (1872–1953), British gynaecologist.]

bony /ˈbəʊni/ *adjective* relating to bones, or made of bone

bony labyrinth /ˌbəʊni ˈlæbərɪnθ/ *noun* a hard part of the temporal bone surrounding the membranous labyrinth in the inner ear. Also called **osseous labyrinth**

boob /buːb/ *noun* a woman's breast (*informal*)

booster /ˈbuːstər ɪnˌdʒekʃ(ə)n/, **booster injection** *noun* a repeat injection of vaccine given some time after the first injection to maintain the immunising effect

boracic acid /bəˌræsɪk ˈæsɪd/ *noun* a soluble white powder used as a general disinfectant. Also called **boric acid**

borax /ˈbɔːræks/ *noun* a white powder used as a household cleaner and disinfectant

borborygmus /ˌbɔːbəˈrɪɡməs/ *noun* a rumbling noise in the abdomen, caused by gas in the intestine (NOTE: The plural is **borborygmi**.)

borderline /ˈbɔːdəlaɪn/ *adjective* **1.** not clearly belonging to either one of two categories ○ *a borderline case* **2.** referring to a medical condition likely to develop in someone unless an effort is made to prevent it **3.** characterised by emotional instability and self-destructive behaviour ○ *a borderline personality*

Bordetella /ˌbɔːdəˈtelə/ *noun* a bacterium of the family *Brucellaceae* (NOTE: *Bordetella pertussis* causes whooping cough.)

boric acid /ˌbɔːrɪk ˈæsɪd/ *noun* same as **boracic acid**

boron /ˈbɔːrɒn/ *noun* a chemical element which is present in borax, and essential for healthy plant growth (NOTE: The chemical symbol is **B**.)

bosom /ˈbʊz(ə)m/ *noun* a woman's chest or breasts

bottom /ˈbɒtəm/ *noun* **1.** the part of the body on which you sit. ◊ **buttock 2.** the anus (*informal*)

bottom shuffling /ˈbɒtəm ˌʃʌf(ə)lɪŋ/ *noun* the process by which a baby who cannot yet walk moves around by moving itself along on its hands and buttocks

botulinum toxin /ˌbɒtjʊˈlaɪnəm ˌtɒksɪn/ *noun* a poison produced by the bacterium *Clostridium botulinum* and used, in small doses, to treat muscular cramps and spasms

botulism /ˈbɒtʃʊlɪz(ə)m/ *noun* a type of food poisoning, often fatal, caused by a toxin of *Clostridium botulinum* in badly canned or preserved food. Symptoms include paralysis of the muscles, vomiting and hallucinations.

bougie /ˈbuːʒiː/ *noun* a thin tube which can be inserted into passages in the body such as the oesophagus or rectum, either to allow liquid to be introduced or to dilate the passage

bovine spongiform encephalopathy /ˌbəʊvaɪn ˌspʌndʒɪfɔːm enˌkefəˈlɒpəθi/ *noun* a fatal brain disease of cattle. Abbreviation **BSE**. ◊ **Creutzfeldt-Jakob disease**. Also called **mad cow disease**

bowel /ˈbaʊəl/ *noun* the intestine, especially the large intestine (NOTE: **Bowel** is often used in the plural in everyday language.)

bowel movement /ˈbaʊəl ˌmuːvmənt/ *noun* **1.** an act of passing faeces out of the body through the anus ○ *The patient had a bowel movement this morning.* Also called **motion**. ◊ **defecation 2.** the amount of faeces passed through the anus

bowels /ˈbaʊəlz/ *plural noun* same as **bowel**

Bowen's disease /ˈbəʊɪnz dɪˌziːz/ *noun* a form of carcinoma, appearing as red plaques on the skin

bow legs /ˌbəʊ ˈlegz/ *noun* a state where the ankles touch and the knees are apart when a person is standing straight. Also called **genu varum**

Bowman's capsule /ˌbəʊmənz ˈkæpsjuːl/ *noun* the expanded end of a renal tubule, surrounding a glomerular tuft in the kidney, which filters plasma in order to reabsorb useful foodstuffs and eliminate waste. Also called **Malpighian glomerulus**, **glomerular capsule** [Described 1842. After Sir William Paget Bowman (1816–92), surgeon in Birmingham and later in London, who was a pioneer in work on the kidney and in ophthalmology.]

BP *abbreviation* **1.** blood pressure **2.** British Pharmacopoeia

BPH *abbreviation* benign prostatic hypertrophy

Bq *symbol* becquerel

brace /breɪs/ *noun* any type of splint or appliance worn for support, e.g. a metal support used on children's legs to make the bones straight or on teeth which are forming badly ○ *She wore a brace on her front teeth.*

brachi- /breɪki/ *prefix* same as **brachio-** (*used before vowels*)

brachial /ˈbreɪkiəl/ *adjective* referring to the arm, especially the upper arm

brachialis muscle /ˌbreɪkiˈeɪlɪs ˌmʌs(ə)l/ *noun* a muscle that causes the elbow to bend

brachio- /ˈbreɪkiəʊ/ *prefix* referring to the arm

brachiocephalic artery /ˌbreɪkiəʊsəˌfælɪk ˈɑːtəri/ *noun* the largest branch of the arch of the aorta, which continues as the right common carotid and right subclavian arteries

brachiocephalic vein /ˌbreɪkiəʊsəˌfælɪk ˈveɪn/ *noun* one of a pair of large veins on opposite sides of the neck that join to form the superior vena cava. Also called **innominate vein**

brachium /ˈbreɪkiəm/ *noun* an arm, especially the upper arm between the elbow and the shoulder (NOTE: The plural is **brachia**.)

brachy- /bræki/ *prefix* short

brachycephaly /ˌbrækiˈsefəli/ *noun* a condition in which the skull is shorter than usual

brachytherapy /ˌbrækiˈθerəpi/ *noun* a radioactive treatment in which the radioactive material actually touches the tissue being treated

Bradford's frame /ˈbrædfədz freɪm/ *noun* a frame of metal and cloth, used to support a patient [After Edward Hickling Bradford (1848–1926), US orthopaedic surgeon.]

brady- /brædɪ/ *prefix* slow

bradycardia /ˌbrædɪˈkɑːdiə/ *noun* a slow rate of heart contraction, shown by a slow pulse rate of less than 70 beats per minute

bradykinesia /ˌbrædɪkaɪˈniːziə/ *noun* a condition in which the someone walks slowly and makes slow movements because of disease

bradykinin /ˌbrædɪˈkaɪnɪn/ *noun* a chemical produced in the blood when tissues are injured, that plays a role in inflammation. ◊ **kinin**

bradypnoea /ˌbrædɪpˈniːə/ *noun* unusually slow breathing

Braille /breɪl/ *noun* a system of writing using raised dots on the paper to indicate letters which a blind person can read by passing their fingers over the page ○ *The book has been published in Braille.* [Introduced 1829–30. After Louis Braille (1809–52), blind Frenchman and teacher of the blind; he introduced the system which had originally been proposed by Charles Barbier in 1820.]

brain /breɪn/ *noun* the part of the central nervous system situated inside the skull. Also called **encephalon**. See illustration at **BRAIN** in Supplement

brain damage /ˈbreɪn ˌdæmɪdʒ/ *noun* damage caused to the brain as a result of oxygen and sugar deprivation, e.g. after a haemorrhage, accident, or though disease

brain death /ˈbreɪn deθ/ *noun* a condition in which the nerves in the brain stem have died, and the person can be certified as dead, although the heart may not have stopped beating

brain haemorrhage /breɪn ˈhem(ə)rɪdʒ/ *noun* same as **cerebral haemorrhage**

brain scan /ˈbreɪn skæn/ *noun* an examination of the inside of the brain, made by passing X-rays through the head, using a scanner, and reconstituting the images on a computer monitor

brain stem /'breɪn stem/ *noun* the lower narrow part of the brain which connects the brain to the spinal cord

brain tumour /'breɪn ˌtjuːmə/ *noun* a tumour which grows in the brain

bran /bræn/ *noun* the outside covering of the wheat seed, removed when making white flour, but an important source of roughage in the diet

branchia /'bræŋkiə/ *noun* a breathing organ similar to the gill of a fish found in human embryos in the early stages of development (NOTE: The plural is **branchiae**.)

branchial /'bræŋkiəl/ *adjective* referring to the branchiae

branchial cyst /ˌbræŋkiəl 'sɪst/ *noun* a cyst on the side of the neck of an embryo

branchial pouch /ˌbræŋkiəl 'paʊtʃ/ *noun* a pouch on the side of the neck of an embryo

Braun's frame /ˌbraʊnz 'freɪm/, **Braun's splint** /ˌbraʊnz 'splɪnt/ *noun* a metal splint and frame to which pulleys are attached, used for holding up a fractured leg while the person is lying in bed [After Heinrich Friedrich Wilhelm Braun (1862–1934), German surgeon.]

Braxton-Hicks contractions /ˌbrækstən 'hɪks kənˌtrækʃənz/ *plural noun* contractions of the uterus which occur throughout a pregnancy and become more frequent and stronger towards the end [After Dr Braxton-Hicks, 19th century British physician.]

breakbone fever /'breɪkbəʊn ˌfiːvə/ *noun* same as **dengue**

break down /ˌbreɪk 'daʊn/ *verb* **1.** to experience a sudden physical or psychological illness (*informal*) ○ *After she lost her husband, her health broke down.* **2.** to start to cry and become upset (*informal*) ○ *She broke down as she described the symptoms to the doctor.* **3.** to split or cause to split into smaller chemical components, as in the digestion of food

breast /brest/ *noun* one of two glands in a woman which secrete milk. Also called **mamma** (NOTE: For other terms referring to breasts, see words beginning with **mamm-, mammo-, mast-, masto-**.)

breastbone /'brestbəʊn/ *noun* a bone which is in the centre of the front of the thorax and to which the ribs are connected. Also called **sternum**

breast cancer /'brest ˌkænsə/ *noun* a malignant tumour in a breast

breast-fed /'brest fed/ *adjective* referring to a baby which is fed from the mother's breasts ○ *She was breast-fed for the first two months.*

breast implant /'brest ˌɪmplɑːnt/ *noun* a sac containing silicone, implanted to improve the appearance of a breast

breast milk /'brest mɪlk/ *noun* the milk produced by a woman who has recently had a baby

breast palpation /'brest pælˌpeɪʃ(ə)n/ *noun* feeling a breast to see if a lump is present which might indicate breast cancer

breast pump /'brest pʌmp/ *noun* an instrument for taking milk from a breast

breast reconstruction /'brest riːkənˌstrʌkʃ(ə)n/ *noun* the construction of a new breast for a woman who has had a breast removed because of cancer

breath /breθ/ *noun* air which goes in and out of the body when you breathe ○ *He ran so fast he was out of breath.* ○ *Stop for a moment to get your breath back.* ○ *She took a deep breath and dived into the water.*

breathe /briːð/ *verb* to take air in and blow air out through the nose or mouth ○ *The patient has begun to breathe normally.*

breath-holding attack /'breθ ˌhəʊldɪŋ əˌtæk/ *noun* a period when a young child stops breathing, usually because he or she is angry

breathing /'briːðɪŋ/ *noun* same as **respiration** ○ *If breathing is difficult or has stopped, begin artificial ventilation immediately.* (NOTE: For other terms referring to breathing see words beginning with **pneum-, pneumo-, pneumat-, pneumato-**.)

breathlessness /'breθləsnəs/ *noun* difficulty in breathing enough air

breech /briːtʃ/ *noun* the buttocks, especially of a baby ■ *adjective* describes a birth in which the baby is delivered buttocks first, not in the normal head first position, or describes a buttocks-first presentation

breech birth /'briːtʃ ˌbɜːθ/, **breech delivery** /'briːtʃ dɪˌlɪv(ə)ri/ *noun* a birth in which the baby's buttocks appear first rather than its head

breech presentation /'briːtʃ ˌprez(ə)n'teɪʃ(ə)n/ *noun* a position of the baby in the uterus in which the buttocks will appear first during childbirth

bregma /'bregmə/ *noun* the point at the top of the head where the soft gap between the bones of a baby's skull hardens

bretylium tosylate /brəˌtɪliəm 'tɒsɪleɪt/ *noun* an agent used to block adrenergic transmitter release

bridge /brɪdʒ/ *noun* **1.** the top part of the nose where it joins the forehead **2.** an artificial tooth or set of teeth which is joined to natural teeth which hold it in place **3.** a part joining two or more other parts

Bright's disease /'braɪts dɪˌziːz/ *noun* inflammation of the kidneys, characterised by albuminuria and high blood pressure. Also called **glomerulonephritis** [Described 1836. After Richard Bright (1789–1858), physician at Guy's Hospital, London, UK]

British anti-lewisite /ˌbrɪtɪʃ ˌænti'luːɪsaɪt/ *noun* an antidote for gases which cause blistering, also used to treat cases of poisoning such as mercury poisoning. Abbreviation **BAL**

British Dental Association /ˌbrɪtɪʃ 'dent(ə)l əsəʊsi,eɪʃ(ə)n/ *noun* in the UK, a professional association of dentists. Abbreviation **BDA**

British Medical Association /ˌbrɪtɪʃ 'medɪk(ə)l əsəʊsi,eɪʃ(ə)n/ *noun* in the UK, a professional association of doctors. Abbreviation **BMA**

British National Formulary /ˌbrɪtɪʃ ˌnæʃ(ə)nəl 'fɔːmjʊləri/ *noun* a book listing key information on the prescribing, dispensing and administration of prescription drugs used in the UK. Abbreviation **BNF**

British Pharmacopoeia /ˌbrɪtɪʃ ˌfɑːməkə'piːə/ *noun* a book listing drugs approved in the UK and their dosages. Abbreviation **BP**

brittle bone disease /ˌbrɪt(ə)l 'bəʊn dɪˌziːz/ *noun* **1.** same as **osteogenesis imperfecta 2.** same as **osteoporosis**

broad /brɔːd/ *adjective* wide in relation to length

Broadbent's sign /'brɔːdbents saɪn/ *noun* a movement of someone's left side near the lower ribs at each beat of the heart, indicating adhesion between the diaphragm and pericardium in cases of pericarditis [After Sir William Henry Broadbent (1835–1907), British physician.]

broad-spectrum antibiotic /ˌbrɔːd ˌspektrəm ˌæntibaɪ'ɒtɪk/ *noun* an antibiotic used to control many types of microorganism

Broca's aphasia /ˌbrəʊkəz ə'feɪziə/ *noun* a condition in which someone is unable to speak or write, as a result of damage to Broca's area

Broca's area /'brəʊkəz ˌeəriə/ *noun* an area on the left side of the brain which governs the motor aspects of speaking [Described 1861. After Pierre Henri Paul Broca (1824–80), French surgeon and anthropologist. A pioneer of neurosurgery, he also invented various instruments, described muscular dystrophy before Duchenne, and recognised rickets as a nutritional disorder before Virchow.]

Brodie's abscess /ˌbrəʊdiz 'æbses/ *noun* an abscess of a bone, caused by staphylococcal osteomyelitis [Described 1832. After Sir Benjamin Collins Brodie (1783–1862), British surgeon.]

bromhidrosis /ˌbrɒmhɪ'drəʊsɪs/ *noun* a condition in which body sweat has an unpleasant smell

bromide /'brəʊmaɪd/ *noun* a bromine salt (NOTE: Bromides are used as sedatives.)

bromine /'brəʊmiːn/ *noun* a chemical element (NOTE: The chemical symbol is **Br**.)

bromism /'brəʊmɪz(ə)m/ *noun* chronic ill health caused by excessive use of bromides

bromocriptine /ˌbrəʊməʊ'krɪptiːn/ *noun* a drug which functions like dopamine, used to treat excessive lactation, breast pain, some forms of infertility, growth disorder and Parkinson's disease

bronch- /brɒŋk/, **bronchi-** /brɒŋki/ *prefix* same as **broncho-** (*used before vowels*)

bronchi /'brɒŋkaɪ/ plural of **bronchus**

bronchial /'brɒŋkiəl/ *adjective* referring to the bronchi

bronchial breath sounds /ˌbrɒŋkiəl 'breθ ˌsaʊndz/ *plural noun* distinctive breath sounds from the lungs which help diagnosis

bronchiectasis /ˌbrɒŋki'ektəsɪs/ *noun* a disorder of the bronchi which become wide, infected and filled with pus (NOTE: Bronchiectasis can lead to pneumonia.)

bronchio- /brɒŋkiəʊ/ *prefix* referring to the bronchioles

bronchiolar /ˌbrɒŋki'əʊlə/ *adjective* referring to the bronchioles

bronchiole /'brɒŋkiəʊl/ *noun* a very small air tube in the lungs leading from a bronchus to the alveoli. See illustration at **LUNGS** in Supplement

bronchiolitis /ˌbrɒŋkiəʊ'laɪtɪs/ *noun* inflammation of the bronchioles, usually in small children

bronchitic /brɒŋ'kɪtɪk/ *adjective* referring to bronchitis

bronchitis /brɒŋ'kaɪtɪs/ *noun* inflammation of the mucous membrane of the bronchi

broncho- /brɒŋkəʊ/ *prefix* referring to a windpipe

bronchoconstrictor /ˌbrɒŋkəʊkən'strɪktə/ *noun* a drug which narrows the bronchi

bronchodilator /ˌbrɒŋkəʊdaɪ'leɪtə/ *noun* a drug which makes the bronchi wider, used in the treatment of asthma and allergy (NOTE: Bronchodilators usually have names ending in **-terol**; however, the most common bronchodilator is **salbutamol**.)

bronchography /brɒŋ'kɒgrəfi/ *noun* an X-ray examination of the lungs after an opaque substance has been put into the bronchi

bronchomediastinal trunk /ˌbrɒŋkəʊ miːdiəˌstaɪn(ə)l 'trʌŋk/ *noun* the set of lymph nodes draining part of the chest

bronchomycosis /ˌbrɒŋkəʊmaɪ'kəʊsɪs/ *noun* an infection of the bronchi by a fungus

bronchophony /brɒŋ'kɒfəni/ *noun* vibrations of the voice heard over the lungs, indicating solidification in the lungs

bronchopleural /ˌbrɒŋkəʊ'plʊərəl/ *adjective* referring to a bronchus and the pleura

bronchopneumonia /ˌbrɒŋkəʊnjuː'məʊniə/ *noun* an infectious inflammation of the bronchioles, which may lead to general infection of the lungs

bronchopulmonary /ˌbrɒŋkəʊˈpʌlmən(ə)ri/ *adjective* referring to the bronchi and the lungs

bronchorrhoea /ˌbrɒŋkəʊˈriːə/ *noun* the secretion of mucus by the bronchi

bronchoscope /ˈbrɒŋkəʊskəʊp/ *noun* an instrument which is passed down the trachea into the lungs, which a doctor can use to inspect the inside passages of the lungs

bronchoscopy /brɒŋˈkɒskəpi/ *noun* an examination of a person's bronchi using a bronchoscope

bronchospasm /ˈbrɒŋkəʊspæz(ə)m/ *noun* a tightening of the bronchial muscles which causes the tubes to contract, as in asthma

bronchospirometry /ˌbrɒŋkəʊspaɪˈrɒmɪtri/ *noun* a procedure for measuring the volume of the lungs

bronchostenosis /ˌbrɒŋkəʊsteˈnəʊsɪs/ *noun* an unusual constriction of the bronchial tubes

bronchotracheal /ˌbrɒŋkəʊtrəˈkiːəl/ *adjective* referring to the bronchi and the trachea

bronchus /ˈbrɒŋkəs/ *noun* one of the two air passages leading from the trachea into the lungs, where they split into many bronchioles. See illustration at **LUNGS** in Supplement (NOTE: The plural is **bronchi**.)

bronze diabetes /ˌbrɒnz daɪəˈbiːtiːz/ *noun* same as **haemochromatosis**

Broviac catheter /ˈbrəʊviæk ˌkæθɪtə/ *noun* a type of thin catheter used to insert into a vein

brow /braʊ/ *noun* same as **eyebrow**

brown fat /ˌbraʊn ˈfæt/ *noun* dark-coloured body fat that can easily be converted to energy and helps to control body temperature

Brown-Séquard syndrome /ˌbraʊn ˈseɪkɑː ˌsɪndrəʊm/ *noun* a condition in which the spinal cord has been partly severed or compressed, with the result that the lower half of the body is paralysed on one side and loses feeling in the other side [Described 1851. After Charles Edouard Brown-Séquard (1817–94), French physiologist.]

brucellosis /ˌbruːsɪˈləʊsɪs/ *noun* a disease which can be caught from cattle or goats or from drinking infected milk, spread by a species of the bacterium *Brucella*. The symptoms include tiredness, arthritis, headache, sweating, irritability and swelling of the spleen. Also called **abortus fever, Malta fever, mountain fever, undulant fever**

bruise /bruːz/ *noun* a dark painful area on the skin, where blood has escaped under the skin following a blow. ◊ **black eye** ■ *verb* to cause a bruise on part of the body ○ *She bruised her knee on the corner of the table.* □ **she bruises easily** even a soft blow will give her a bruise

bruised /bruːzd/ *adjective* painful after a blow or showing the marks of a bruise ○ *a badly bruised leg*

bruising /ˈbruːzɪŋ/ *noun* an area of bruises ○ *The baby has bruising on the back and legs.*

bruit /bruːt/ *noun* an unusual noise heard through a stethoscope

Brunner's glands /ˈbrʊnəz ˌglændz/ *plural noun* glands in the duodenum and jejunum [Described 1687. After Johann Konrad Brunner (1653–1727), Swiss anatomist at Heidelberg, then at Strasbourg.]

bruxism /ˈbrʌksɪz(ə)m/ *noun* the action of grinding the teeth, as a habit

BSE *abbreviation* bovine spongiform encephalopathy

bubo /ˈbjuːbəʊ/ *noun* a swelling of a lymph node in the groin or armpit

bubonic plague /bjuːˌbɒnɪk ˈpleɪg/ *noun* a usually fatal infectious disease caused by *Yersinia pestis* in the lymph system, transmitted to humans by fleas from rats

buccal /ˈbʌk(ə)l/ *adjective* referring to the cheek or mouth

buccinator /ˈbʌksɪneɪtə/ *noun* a cheek muscle which helps the jaw to move when chewing

Budd–Chiari syndrome /ˌbʌd kɪˈeəri ˌsɪndrəʊm/ *noun* a disease of the liver, where thrombosis has occurred in the hepatic veins [Described 1845. After George Budd (1808–82), Professor of Medicine at King's College Hospital, London; Hans von Chiari (1851–1916), Viennese pathologist who was Professor of Pathological Anatomy at Strasbourg and later at Prague.]

budesonide /bjuːˈdesənaɪd/ *noun* a corticosteroid drug taken by inhalation or in tablets, used in the treatment of hay fever and nasal polyps

Buerger's disease /ˈbɜːgəz dɪˌziːz/ *noun* same as **thromboangiitis obliterans** [Described 1908. After Leo Buerger (1879–1943), New York physician of Viennese origin.]

buffer /ˈbʌfə/ *noun* a substance that keeps a constant balance between acid and alkali ■ *verb* to prevent a solution from becoming acid

buffer action /ˈbʌfər ˌækʃən/ *noun* the balancing process between acid and alkali

buffered /ˈbʌfəd/ *adjective* prevented from becoming acid ○ *buffered aspirin*

bug /bʌg/ *noun* an infectious disease (*informal*) ○ *He caught a bug on holiday.* ○ *Half the staff have got a stomach bug.*

bulb /bʌlb/ *noun* a round part at the end of an organ or bone

bulbar /ˈbʌlbə/ *adjective* **1.** referring to a bulb **2.** referring to the medulla oblongata

bulbospongiosus muscle /ˌbʌlbəʊspʌndʒi
ˈəʊsəs ˌmʌsəl/ *noun* a muscle in the perineum
behind the penis

bulbourethral gland /ˌbʌlbəʊjuˈriːθrəl
ˌglænd/ *noun* one of two glands at the base of the
penis which secrete into the urethra. ◊ **gland**

bulimia /buˈlɪmiə/, **bulimia nervosa** /buˌlɪmiə
nəˈvəʊsə/ *noun* a psychological condition in
which a person eats too much and is incapable of
controlling his or her eating. The eating is followed by behaviour designed to prevent weight
gain, e.g. vomiting, use of laxatives or excessive
exercise.

bulla /ˈbʊlə/ *noun* a large blister (NOTE: The plural is **bullae**.)

bumetanide /bjuːˈmetənaɪd/ *noun* a drug
which helps a patient to produce urine, used in the
treatment of swelling caused by fluid accumulating in the tissues

bumper fracture /ˈbʌmpə ˌfræktʃə/ *noun* a
fracture in the upper part of the tibia (NOTE: It has
this name because it can be caused by a blow
from the bumper of a car.)

bundle branch block /ˈbʌnd(ə)l brɑːntʃ
ˌblɒk/ *noun* an unusual condition of the heart's
conduction tissue

bundle of His /ˌbʌnd(ə)l əv ˈhɪs/ *noun* same as
atrioventricular bundle [Described 1893. After
Ludwig His (1863–1934), Professor of Anatomy
successively at Leipzig, Basle, Göttingen and
Berlin.]

bunion /ˈbʌnjən/ *noun* an inflammation and
swelling of the big toe, caused by tight shoes
which force the toe sideways so that a callus
develops over the joint between the toe and the
metatarsal

buphthalmos /bʌfˈθælməs/ *noun* a type of
congenital glaucoma occurring in infants

bupivacaine /bjuːˈpɪvəkeɪn/ *noun* a powerful
local anaesthetic, used in epidural anaesthesia

buprenorphine /bjuːˈprenəfiːn/ *noun* an opiate drug used in the relief of moderate to severe
pain, and as an opioid substitute in treating drug
addiction

Burkitt's tumour /ˌbɜːkɪts ˈtjuːmə/, **Burkitt's
lymphoma** /ˌbɜːkɪts lɪmˈfəʊmə/ *noun* a malignant tumour, usually on the maxilla, found especially in children in Africa [Described 1957.
After Denis Parsons Burkitt (1911–93), formerly
Senior Surgeon, Kampala, Uganda; later a
member of the Medical Research Council (UK).]

burn /bɜːn/ *noun* an injury to skin and tissue
caused by light, heat, radiation, electricity or
chemicals ■ *verb* to harm or destroy something
by fire ○ *She burnt her hand on the hot frying
pan.* ○ *Most of his hair or his skin was burnt off.*
(NOTE: **burning – burnt** or **burned**)

burning /ˈbɜːnɪŋ/ *adjective* referring to a feeling similar to that of being hurt by fire ○ *She had
a burning pain* or *in her chest.*

burr /bɜː/ *noun* a bit used with a drill to make
holes in a bone such as the cranium or in a tooth

bursa /ˈbɜːsə/ *noun* a sac containing fluid, forming part of the usual structure of a joint such as the
knee and elbow, where it protects against frequent
pressure and rubbing (NOTE: The plural is **bur-
sae**.)

bursitis /bɜːˈsaɪtɪs/ *noun* the inflammation of a
bursa, especially in the shoulder

Buscopan /ˈbʌskəpæn/ a trade name for a
form of hyoscine

butobarbitone /ˌbjuːtəʊˈbɑːbɪtəʊn/ *noun* a
barbiturate drug used as a sedative and hypnotic

buttock /ˈbʌtək/ *noun* one of the two fleshy
parts below the back, on which a person sits,
made up mainly of the gluteal muscles. Also
called **nates**

buttonhole surgery /ˈbʌt(ə)nhəʊl ˌsɜːdʒəri/
noun a surgical operation through a small hole in
the body, using an endoscope

bypass /ˈbaɪpɑːs/ *noun* **1.** a surgical operation
to redirect the blood, usually using a grafted
blood vessel and usually performed when one of
the person's own blood vessels is blocked **2.** a
new route for the blood created by a bypass operation

byssinosis /ˌbɪsɪˈnəʊsɪs/ *noun* a lung disease
which is a form of pneumoconiosis caused by
inhaling cotton dust

C

c *symbol* centi-

C *symbol* Celsius

CABG *abbreviation* coronary artery bypass graft

cachet /'kæʃeɪ/ *noun* a quantity of a drug wrapped in paper, to be swallowed

cachexia /kæ'keksɪə/ *noun* a state of ill health characterised by wasting and general weakness

cadaver /kə'dævə/ *noun* a dead body, especially one used for dissection

cadaveric /kə'dævərɪk/, **cadaverous** /kə'dæv(ə)rəs/ *adjective* referring to a person who is thin or wasting away

caecal /'siːk(ə)l/ *adjective* referring to the caecum

caecosigmoidostomy /ˌsiːkəʊˌsɪgmɔɪ'dɒstəmi/ *noun* an operation to open up a connection between the caecum and the sigmoid colon

caecostomy /siː'kɒstəmi/ *noun* a surgical operation to make an opening between the caecum and the abdominal wall to allow faeces to be passed without going through the rectum and anus

caecum /'siːkəm/ *noun* the wider part of the large intestine in the lower right-hand side of the abdomen at the point where the small intestine joins it and which has the appendix attached to it. See illustration at **DIGESTIVE SYSTEM** in Supplement. Also called **cecum** (NOTE: The plural is **caeca**.)

caesarean /sɪ'zeəriən/, **caesarean section** /sɪ'zeəriən ˌsekʃən/ *noun* a surgical operation to deliver a baby by cutting through the abdominal wall into the uterus. Compare **vaginal delivery**

caesium /'siːziəm/ *noun* a radioactive element, used in treatment by radiation (NOTE: The chemical symbol is **Cs**.)

caesium-137 /ˌsiːziəm wʌn θriː 'sev(ə)n/ *noun* a radioactive substance used in radiology

café au lait spots /ˌkæfeɪ əʊ 'leɪ spɒts/ *plural noun* brown spots on the skin, which are an indication of von Recklinghausen's disease

caffeine /'kæfiːn/ *noun* an alkaloid found in coffee, tea and chocolate, which acts as a stimulant

caisson disease /'keɪs(ə)n dɪˌziːz/ *noun* a condition in which a person experiences pains in the joints and stomach, and dizziness caused by nitrogen in the blood. Also called **the bends**, **compressed air sickness**, **decompression sickness**

calamine /'kæləmaɪn/, **calamine lotion** /'kæləmaɪn ˌləʊʃ(ə)n/ *noun* a lotion, based on zinc oxide, which helps relieve skin irritation, caused e.g. by sunburn or chickenpox

calc- /kælk/ *prefix* same as **calci-** (*used before vowels*)

calcaemia /kæl'siːmiə/ *noun* a condition in which the blood contains an unusually large amount of calcium

calcaneal /kæl'keɪniəl/ *adjective* referring to the calcaneus

calcaneus /kæl'keɪniəs/, **calcaneum** /kæl'keɪniəm/ *noun* the heel bone, situated underneath the talus. See illustration at **FOOT** in Supplement

calcareous degeneration /kælˌkeəriəs dɪˌdʒenə'reɪʃ(ə)n/ *noun* the formation of calcium on bones or at joints in old age

calci- /kælsɪ/ *prefix* referring to calcium

calcification /ˌkælsɪfɪ'keɪʃ(ə)n/ *noun* a process of hardening caused by the formation of deposits of calcium salts

calcified /'kælsɪfaɪd/ *adjective* made hard ○ *Bone is calcified connective tissue.*

calcinosis /ˌkælsɪ'nəʊsɪs/ *noun* a medical condition where deposits of calcium salts form in joints, muscles and organs

calcitonin /ˌkælsɪ'təʊnɪn/ *noun* a hormone produced by the thyroid gland, which is believed to regulate the level of calcium in the blood. Also called **thyrocalcitonin**

calcium /'kælsiəm/ *noun* a metallic chemical element which is a major component of bones and teeth and which is essential for various bodily processes such as blood clotting (NOTE: The chemical symbol is **Ca**.)

calcium antagonist /'kælsiəm ænˌtægənɪst/ *noun* a drug which makes the arteries wider and slows the heart rate. It is used in the treatment of angina.

calcium channel blocker /ˈkælsiəm ˌtʃæn(ə)l ˌblɒkə/, **calcium blocker** /ˈkælsiəm ˌblɒkə/ *noun* a drug which affects the smooth muscle of the cardiovascular system, used in the treatment of angina and hypertension (NOTE: Calcium channel blockers have names ending in **-dipine: nifedipine**. Not to be used in heart failure as they reduce cardiac function further.)

calculosis /ˌkælkjuˈləʊsɪs/ *noun* a condition in which calculi exist in an organ

calculus /ˈkælkjʊləs/ *noun* a hard mass like a little piece of stone, which forms inside the body. Also called **stone** (NOTE: The plural is **calculi**.)

Caldwell–Luc operation /ˌkɔːldwel ˈluːk ɒpəˌreɪʃ(ə)n/ *noun* a surgical operation to drain the maxillary sinus by making an incision above the canine tooth [Described 1893. After George Walter Caldwell (1834–1918), US physician; Henri Luc (1855–1925), French laryngologist.]

calibrator /ˈkælɪbreɪtə/ *noun* an instrument used to enlarge a tube or passage

caliectasis /ˌkeɪliˈektəsɪs/ *noun* swelling of the calyces

callisthenic /ˌkælɪsˈθenɪk/ *adjective* relating to callisthenics

callisthenics /ˌkælɪsˈθenɪks/ *plural noun* energetic physical exercises for improving fitness and muscle tone, including push-ups, sit-ups and star jumps

callosity /kəˈlɒsɪti/ *noun* a hard patch on the skin, e.g. a corn, resulting from frequent pressure or rubbing. Also called **callus**

callus /ˈkæləs/ *noun* **1.** same as **callosity 2.** tissue which forms round a broken bone as it starts to mend, leading to consolidation ○ *Callus formation is more rapid in children and young adults than in elderly people.*

calor /ˈkælə/ *noun* heat

caloric /kəˈlɒrɪk/ *adjective* referring to calories or to heat

calorie /ˈkæləri/ *noun* **1.** a unit of measurement of heat or energy, equivalent to the amount of heat needed to raise the temperature of 1g of water by 1°C. Now called **joule 2.** *also* **Calorie** a unit of measurement of energy in food (*informal*) ○ *a low-calorie diet* Now called **joule** □ **to count calories** to be careful about how much you eat

calvaria /kælˈveəriə/, **calvarium** /kælˈveəriəm/ *noun* the top part of the skull

calyx /ˈkeɪlɪks/ *noun* a part of the body shaped like a cup especially the tube leading to a renal pyramid. See illustration at **KIDNEY** in Supplement (NOTE: The plural is **calyces**.)

CAM /ˌsiː eɪ ˈem/ *abbreviation* complementary and alternative medicine

camphor /ˈkæmfə/ *noun* white crystals with a strong smell, made from a tropical tree, used to keep insects away or as a liniment

Campylobacter /ˈkæmpɪləʊˌbæktə/ *noun* a bacterium which is a common cause of food poisoning in humans and of spontaneous abortion in farm animals

canal /kəˈnæl/ *noun* a tube along which something flows

canaliculitis /ˌkænəlɪkjʊˈlaɪtɪs/ *noun* inflammation of the tear duct canal

canaliculus /ˌkænəˈlɪkjʊləs/ *noun* a little canal, e.g. a canal leading to the Haversian systems in compact bone, or a canal leading to the lacrimal duct (NOTE: The plural is **canaliculi**.)

cancellous bone /ˈkænsələs ˌbəʊn/ *noun* a light spongy bone tissue which forms the inner core of a bone and also the ends of long bones. See illustration at **BONE STRUCTURE** in Supplement

cancer /ˈkænsə/ *noun* a malignant growth or tumour which develops in tissue and destroys it, which can spread by metastasis to other parts of the body and which cannot be controlled by the body itself ○ *Cancer cells developed in the lymph.* ○ *She has been diagnosed as having lung cancer* or *as having cancer of the lung.* (NOTE: For other terms referring to cancer, see words beginning with **carcin-**.)

cancerophobia /ˌkænsərəʊˈfəʊbiə/ *noun* a fear of cancer

cancer phobia /ˈkænsə ˌfəʊbiə/ *noun* same as **cancerophobia**

cancrum oris /ˌkæŋkrəm ˈɔːrɪs/ *noun* severe ulcers in the mouth, leading to gangrene. Also called **noma**

candidiasis /ˌkændɪˈdaɪəsɪs/, **candidosis** /ˌkændɪˈdəʊsɪs/ *noun* infection with a species of the fungus Candida

canicola fever /kəˈnɪkələ ˌfiːvə/ *noun* a form of leptospirosis, giving high fever and jaundice

canine /ˈkeɪnaɪn/, **canine tooth** /ˈkeɪnaɪn ˌtuːθ/ *noun* a pointed tooth next to an incisor. See illustration at **TEETH** in Supplement

canities /kəˈnɪʃiiːz/ *noun* a loss of pigments, which makes the hair turn white

cannabis /ˈkænəbɪs/ *noun* a drug made from the dried leaves or flowers of the Indian hemp plant. Recreational use of cannabis is illegal and its use to relieve the pain associated with conditions such as multiple sclerosis is controversial. Also called **hashish, marijuana**

cannula /ˈkænjʊlə/ *noun* a tube with a trocar or blunt needle inside, inserted into the body to introduce fluids

canthal /ˈkænθəl/ *adjective* referring to the corner of the eye

cantholysis /kænˈθɒləsɪs/ *noun* same as **cantholysis**

canthoplasty /ˈkænθəplæsti/ *noun* **1.** an operation to repair the canthus of the eye **2.** an operation to cut through the canthus to enlarge the groove in the eyelid

canthus /'kænθəs/ *noun* a corner of the eye

cap /kæp/ *noun* **1.** a covering which protects something **2.** an artificial hard covering for a damaged or broken tooth

CAPD *abbreviation* continuous ambulatory peritoneal dialysis

capeline bandage /'kæpəlaɪn ,bændɪdʒ/ *noun* a bandage shaped like a cap, either for the head, or to cover a stump after amputation

capillary /kə'pɪləri/ *noun* a tiny blood vessel between the arterioles and the venules, which carries blood and nutrients into the tissues

capita /'kæpɪtə/ plural of **caput**

capitate /'kæpɪteɪt/, **capitate bone** /'kæpɪteɪt ,bəʊn/ *noun* the largest of the eight small carpal bones in the wrist. See illustration at **HAND** in Supplement

capitellum /,kæpɪ'teləm/ *noun* a rounded enlarged part at the end of a bone, especially this part of the upper arm bone, the humerus, that forms the elbow joint with one of the lower bones, the radius. Also called **capitulum of humerus** (NOTE: The plural is **capitella**.)

capitulum /kə'pɪtjʊləm/ *noun* the rounded end of a bone which articulates with another bone, e.g. the distal end of the humerus (NOTE: The plural is **capitula**.)

capitulum of humerus /kə,pɪtjʊləm əv 'hjuːmərəs/ *noun* same as **capitellum**

caplet /'kæplət/ *noun* a small oblong tablet with a covering that dissolves easily and which usually cannot be broken in two

capsular /'kæpsjʊlə/ *adjective* referring to a capsule

capsule /'kæpsjuːl/ *noun* **1.** a membrane round an organ or joint **2.** a small hollow digestible case filled with a drug that is taken by swallowing ○ *She swallowed three capsules of painkiller.* ○ *The doctor prescribed the drug in capsule form.*

capsulectomy /,kæpsjʊ'lektəmi/ *noun* the surgical removal of the capsule round a joint

capsulitis /,kæpsjʊ'laɪtɪs/ *noun* inflammation of a capsule

capsulotomy /,kæpsjʊ'lɒtəmi/ *noun* a surgical procedure involving cutting into the capsule around a body part, e.g. cutting into the lens of the eye during the removal of a cataract

captopril /'kæptəprɪl/ *noun* a drug which helps to prevent the arteries from being made narrower by an angiotensin. It is used to control high blood pressure.

caput /'kæpət/ *noun* the head (NOTE: The plural is **capita**.)

carbamazepine /,kɑːbə'mæzəpiːn/ *noun* a drug which reduces pain and helps to prevent convulsions. It is used in the treatment of epilepsy, pain and bipolar disorder.

carbenoxolone /,kɑːbə'nɒksələʊn/ *noun* a liquorice agent, used to treat stomach ulcers

carbidopa /,kɑːbɪ'dəʊpə/ *noun* an inhibitor used to enable levodopa to enter the brain in larger quantities in the treatment of Parkinson's disease

carbimazole /kɑː'bɪməzəʊl/ *noun* a drug which helps to prevent the formation of thyroid hormones, used in the management of hyperthyroidism

carbohydrate /,kɑːbəʊ'haɪdreɪt/ *noun* **1.** a biological compound containing carbon, hydrogen and oxygen. Carbohydrates derive from sugar and are an important source of food and energy. **2.** food containing carbohydrates ○ *high carbohydrate drinks*

carbolic acid /kɑː,bɒlɪk 'æsɪd/ *noun* same as **phenol**

carbon /'kɑːbən/ *noun* one of the common nonmetallic elements, an essential component of living matter and organic chemical compounds (NOTE: The chemical symbol is **C**.)

carbon dioxide /,kɑːbən daɪ'ɒksaɪd/ *noun* a colourless gas produced by the body's metabolism as the tissues burn carbon, and breathed out by the lungs as waste (NOTE: The chemical symbol is CO_2.)

carbon dioxide snow /,kɑːbən daɪ,ɒksaɪd 'snəʊ/ *noun* solid carbon dioxide, used in treating skin growths such as warts, or to preserve tissue samples

carbonic anhydrase /kɑː,bɒnɪk æn 'haɪdreɪz/ *noun* an enzyme which acts as a buffer and regulates the body's water balance, including gastric acid secretion and aqueous humour production

carbon monoxide /,kɑːbən mə'nɒksaɪd/ *noun* a poisonous gas found in fumes from car engines, from burning gas and cigarette smoke (NOTE: The chemical symbol is **CO**.)

carboxyhaemoglobin /kɑː,bɒksihiːmə 'gləʊbɪn/ *noun* a compound of carbon monoxide and haemoglobin formed when a person breathes in carbon monoxide from tobacco smoke or car exhaust fumes

carboxyhaemoglobinaemia /kɑː ,bɒksihiːmə,gləʊbɪ'niːmiə/ *noun* the presence of carboxyhaemoglobin in the blood

carbuncle /'kɑːbʌŋkəl/ *noun* a localised staphylococcal infection, which goes deep into the tissue

carcin- /kɑːsɪn/ *prefix* same as **carcino-** (*used before vowels*)

carcino- /kɑːsɪnə/ *prefix* referring to carcinoma or cancer

carcinogen /kɑː'sɪnədʒən/ *noun* a substance which produces a carcinoma or cancer

carcinogenesis /ˌkɑːsɪnəˈdʒenəsɪs/ *noun* the process of forming a carcinoma in tissue

carcinogenic /ˌkɑːsɪnəˈdʒenɪk/ *adjective* causing a carcinoma or cancer

carcinoid /ˈkɑːsɪnɔɪd/, **carcinoid tumour** /ˈkɑːsɪnɔɪd ˌtjuːmə/ *noun* an intestinal tumour, especially in the appendix, which causes diarrhoea

carcinoma /ˌkɑːsɪˈnəʊmə/ *noun* a cancer of the epithelium or glands

carcinomatosis /ˌkɑːsɪnəʊməˈtəʊsɪs/ *noun* a carcinoma which has spread to many sites in the body

carcinomatous /ˌkɑːsɪˈnɒmətəs/ *adjective* referring to carcinoma

carcinosarcoma /ˌkɑːsɪnəʊsɑːˈkəʊmə/ *noun* a malignant tumour containing elements of both a carcinoma and a sarcoma

cardia /ˈkɑːdiə/ *noun* an opening at the top of the stomach which joins it to the gullet

cardiac /ˈkɑːdiæk/ *adjective* referring to the heart

cardiac achalasia /ˌkɑːdiæk ˌækəˈleɪziə/ *noun* a condition in which the patient is unable to relax the cardia, the muscle at the entrance to the stomach, with the result that food cannot enter the stomach. ◊ **cardiomyotomy**

cardiac arrest /ˌkɑːdiæk əˈrest/ *noun* a condition in which the heart muscle stops beating

cardiac asthma /ˌkɑːdiæk ˈæsmə/ *noun* difficulty in breathing caused by heart failure

cardiac catheter /ˌkɑːdiæk ˈkæθɪtə/ *noun* a catheter passed through a vein into the heart, to take blood samples, to record pressure or to examine the interior of the heart before surgery

cardiac catheterisation /ˌkɑːdiæk ˌkæθɪtəraɪˈzeɪʃ(ə)n/ *noun* a procedure which involves passing a catheter into the heart

cardiac cirrhosis /ˌkɑːdiæk sɪˈrəʊsɪs/ *noun* cirrhosis of the liver caused by heart disease

cardiac compression /ˌkɑːdiæk kəmˈpreʃ(ə)n/ *noun* the compression of the heart by fluid in the pericardium

cardiac conducting system /ˌkɑːdiæk kənˈdʌktɪŋ ˌsɪstəm/ *noun* the nerve system in the heart which links an atrium to a ventricle, so that the two beat at the same rate

cardiac cycle /ˌkɑːdiæk ˈsaɪk(ə)l/ *noun* the repeated beating of the heart, formed of the diastole and systole

cardiac decompression /ˌkɑːdiæk ˌdiːkəmˈpreʃ(ə)n/ *noun* the removal of a haematoma or constriction of the heart

cardiac failure /ˌkɑːdiæk ˈfeɪljə/ *noun* same as **heart failure**

cardiac glycoside /ˌkɑːdiæk ˈglaɪkəsaɪd/ *noun* a drug used in the treatment of tachycardia and atrial fibrillation, e.g. digoxin

cardiac index /ˌkɑːdiæk ˈɪndeks/ *noun* the cardiac output per square metre of body surface, usually between 3.1 and 3.8l/min/m² (litres per minute per square metre)

cardiac infarction *noun* same as **myocardial infarction**

cardiac monitor /ˌkɑːdiæk ˈmɒnɪtə/ *noun* same as **electrocardiograph**

cardiac murmur /ˌkɑːdiæk ˈmɜːmə/ *noun* same as **heart murmur**

cardiac muscle /ˈkɑːdiæk ˌmʌs(ə)l/ *noun* a muscle in the heart which makes the heart beat

cardiac neurosis /ˌkɑːdiæk njʊˈrəʊsɪs/ *noun* same as **disordered action of the heart**

cardiac notch /ˌkɑːdiæk ˈnɒtʃ/ *noun* **1.** a point in the left lung, where the right inside wall is bent. See illustration at LUNGS in Supplement **2.** a notch at the point where the oesophagus joins the greater curvature of the stomach

cardiac orifice /ˌkɑːdiæk ˈɒrɪfɪs/ *noun* an opening where the oesophagus joins the stomach

cardiac output /ˌkɑːdiæk ˈaʊtpʊt/ *noun* the volume of blood expelled by each ventricle in a specific time, usually between 4.8 and 5.3l/min (litres per minute)

cardiac pacemaker /ˌkɑːdiæk ˈpeɪsmeɪkə/ *noun* an electronic device implanted on a patient's heart, or which a patient wears attached to the chest, which stimulates and regulates the heartbeat

cardiac reflex /ˌkɑːdiæk ˈriːfleks/ *noun* the reflex which controls the heartbeat automatically

cardiac surgery /ˌkɑːdiæk ˈsɜːdʒəri/ *noun* surgery to the heart

cardiac tamponade /ˌkɑːdiæk ˌtæmpəˈneɪd/ *noun* pressure on the heart when the pericardial cavity fills with blood. Also called **heart tamponade**

cardiac vein /ˈkɑːdiæk veɪn/ *noun* one of the veins which lead from the myocardium to the right atrium

cardinal /ˈkɑːdɪn(ə)l ˈnʌmbə/ *adjective* most important

cardinal ligaments /ˌkɑːdɪn(ə)l ˈlɪgəmənts/ *plural noun* ligaments forming a band of connective tissue that extends from the uterine cervix and vagina to the pelvic walls. Also called **Mackenrodt's ligaments**

cardio- /ˈkɑːdiəʊ/ *prefix* referring to the heart

cardiogenic /ˌkɑːdiəˈdʒenɪk/ *adjective* resulting from activity or disease of the heart

cardiogram /ˈkɑːdiəgræm/ *noun* a graph showing the heartbeat, produced by a cardiograph

cardiograph /ˈkɑːdiəgrɑːf/ *noun* an instrument which records the heartbeat

cardiography /ˌkɑːdiˈɒgrəfi/ *noun* the action of recording the heartbeat

cardiologist /ˌkɑːdiˈɒlədʒɪst/ *noun* a doctor who specialises in the study of the heart

cardiology /ˌkɑːdiˈɒlədʒi/ *noun* the study of the heart, its diseases and functions

cardiomegaly /ˌkɑːdiəʊˈmegəli/ *noun* an enlarged heart

cardiomyopathy /ˌkɑːdiəʊmaɪˈɒpəθi/ *noun* a disease of the heart muscle

cardiomyoplasty /ˌkɑːdiəʊˈmaɪəʊˌplæsti/ *noun* an operation to improve the functioning of the heart, by using the latissimus dorsi as a stimulant

cardiomyotomy /ˌkɑːdiəʊmaɪˈɒtəmi/ *noun* an operation to treat cardiac achalasia by splitting the ring of muscles where the oesophagus joins the stomach. Also called **Heller's operation**

cardiopathy /ˌkɑːdiˈɒpəθi/ *noun* any kind of heart disease

cardiophone /ˈkɑːdiəfəʊn/ *noun* a microphone attached to a patient to record sounds, usually used to record the heart of an unborn baby

cardioplegia /ˌkɑːdiəʊˈpliːdʒiə/ *noun* the stopping of a patient's heart, by chilling it or using drugs, so that heart surgery can be performed

cardiopulmonary /ˌkɑːdiəʊˈpʌlmən(ə)ri/ *adjective* relating to both the heart and the lungs

cardiopulmonary bypass /ˌkɑːdiəʊ ˌpʌlmən(ə)ri ˈbaɪpɑːs/ *noun* a machine or method for artificially circulating the patient's blood during open-heart surgery. The heart and lungs are cut off from the circulation and replaced by a pump.

cardiopulmonary resuscitation /ˌkɑːdiəʊ ˌpʌlmən(ə)ri rɪˌsʌsɪˈteɪʃ(ə)n/ *noun* an emergency technique to make a person's heart start beating again. It involves clearing the airways and then alternately pressing on the chest and breathing into the mouth. Abbreviation **CPR**

cardiopulmonary system /ˌkɑːdiəʊ ˈpʌlmən(ə)ri ˌsɪstəm/ *noun* the heart and lungs considered together as a functional unit

cardioscope /ˈkɑːdiəskəʊp/ *noun* an instrument formed of a tube with a light at the end, used to inspect the inside of the heart

cardiospasm /ˈkɑːdiəʊspæz(ə)m/ *noun* same as **cardiac achalasia**

cardiothoracic /ˌkɑːdiəʊθɒˈræsɪk/ *adjective* referring to the heart and the chest region ○ *a cardiothoracic surgeon*

cardiotocography /ˌkɑːdiəʊtɒˈkɒɡrəfi/ *noun* the recording of the heartbeat of a fetus

cardiotomy /ˌkɑːdiˈɒtəmi/ *noun* an operation that involves cutting the wall of the heart

cardiotomy syndrome /ˌkɑːdiˈɒtəmi ˌsɪndrəʊm/ *noun* fluid in the membranes round the heart after cardiotomy

cardiotoxic /ˌkɑːdiəʊˈtɒksɪk/ *adjective* which is toxic to the heart

cardiovascular /ˌkɑːdiəʊˈvæskjʊlə/ *adjective* referring to the heart and the blood circulation system

cardiovascular disease /ˌkɑːdiəʊˈvæskjʊlə dɪˌziːz/ *noun* any disease which affects the circulatory system, e.g. hypertension

cardiovascular system /ˌkɑːdiəʊˈvæskjʊlə ˌsɪstəm/ *noun* the system of organs and blood vessels by means of which the blood circulates round the body and which includes the heart, arteries and veins

cardioversion /ˌkɑːdiəʊˈvɜːʃ(ə)n/ *noun* a procedure to correct an irregular heartbeat by applying an electrical impulse to the chest wall. ◊ **defibrillation**

carditis /kɑːˈdaɪtɪs/ *noun* inflammation of the connective tissue of the heart

care pathway /ˈkeə ˌpɑːθweɪ/ *noun* the entire process of diagnosis, treatment and care that a patient goes through

care plan /ˈkeə plæn/ *noun* a plan drawn up by the nursing staff for the treatment of an individual patient

caries /ˈkeəriːz/ *noun* decay in a tooth or bone

carina /kəˈriːnə/ *noun* a structure shaped like the bottom of a boat, e.g. the cartilage at the point where the trachea branches into the bronchi

cariogenic /ˌkeəriəʊˈdʒenɪk/ *adjective* referring to a substance which causes caries

carminative /ˈkɑːmɪnətɪv/ *noun* a substance which relieves colic or indigestion ■ *adjective* relieving colic or indigestion

carneous mole /ˌkɑːniəs ˈməʊl/ *noun* matter in the uterus after the death of a fetus

carotenaemia /ˌkærətɪˈniːmiə/ *noun* an excessive amount of carotene in the blood, usually as a result of eating too many carrots or tomatoes, which gives the skin a yellow colour. Also called **xanthaemia**

carotene /ˈkærətiːn/ *noun* an orange or red pigment in carrots, egg yolk and some oils, which is converted by the liver into vitamin A

carotid /kəˈrɒtɪd/, **carotid artery** /kəˌrɒtɪd ˈɑːtəri/ *noun* either of the two large arteries in the neck which supply blood to the head

carotid artery thrombosis /kəˌrɒtɪd ˌɑːtəri θrɒmˈbəʊsɪs/ *noun* the formation of a blood clot in the carotid artery

carp- /kɑːp/ *prefix* same as **carpo-** (*used before vowels*)

carpal /ˈkɑːp(ə)l/ *adjective* referring to the wrist

carpal bones /ˈkɑːp(ə)l bəʊnz/, **carpals** /ˈkɑːp(ə)lz/ *plural noun* the eight bones which make up the carpus or wrist. See illustration at HAND in Supplement

carpal tunnel release /ˌkɑːp(ə)l ˈtʌn(ə)l rɪˌliːs/ *noun* an operation to relieve the compression of the median nerve

carpal tunnel syndrome /ˌkɑːp(ə)l ˈtʌn(ə)l ˌsɪndrəʊm/ *noun* a condition, usually affecting women, in which the fingers tingle and hurt at night. It is caused by compression of the median nerve.

carphology /kɑːˈfɒlədʒi/ *noun* the action of pulling at the bedclothes, a sign of delirium in typhoid and other fevers. Also called **floccitation**

carpo- /kɑːpəʊ/ *prefix* referring to the wrist

carpometacarpal joint /ˌkɑːpəʊmetə ˈkɑːp(ə)l dʒɔɪnt/ *noun* one of the joints between the carpals and metacarpals. Also called **CM joint**

carpopedal spasm /ˌkɑːpəʊpiːd(ə)l ˈspæz(ə)m/ *noun* a spasm in the hands and feet caused by lack of calcium

carpus /ˈkɑːpəs/ *noun* the bones by which the lower arm is connected to the hand. Also called **wrist**. See illustration at **HAND** in Supplement (NOTE: The plural is **carpi**.)

carrier /ˈkæriə/ *noun* **1.** a person who carries bacteria of a disease in his or her body and who can transmit the disease to others without showing any signs of being infected with it ○ *Ten per cent of the population are believed to be unwitting carriers of the bacteria.* **2.** an insect which carries disease and infects humans **3.** a healthy person who carries a chromosome variation that gives rise to a hereditary disease such as haemophilia or Duchenne muscular dystrophy

cartilage /ˈkɑːtɪlɪdʒ/ *noun* thick connective tissue which lines and cushions the joints and which forms part of the structure of an organ. Cartilage in small children is the first stage in the formation of bones.

cartilaginous /ˌkɑːtɪˈlædʒɪnəs/ *adjective* made of cartilage

cartilaginous joint /ˌkɑːtɪˈlædʒɪnəs dʒɔɪnt/ *noun* **1. primary cartilaginous joint** same as **synchondrosis 2. secondary cartilaginous joint** same as **symphysis**

caruncle /kəˈrʌŋkəl/ *noun* a small swelling

cascara /kæˈskɑːrə/, **cascara sagrada** /kæ ˌskɑːrə səˈɡrɑːdə/ *noun* a laxative made from the bark of a tropical tree

case /keɪs/ *noun* a single occurrence of a disease ○ *There were two hundred cases of cholera in the recent outbreak.*

caseation /ˌkeɪsiˈeɪʃ(ə)n/ *noun* the process by which dead tissue decays into a firm and dry mass. It is characteristic of tuberculosis.

case control study /keɪs kənˈtrəʊl ˌstʌdi/ *noun* an investigation in which a group of patients with a disease are compared with a group without the disease in order to study possible causes

case history /ˈkeɪs ˌhɪst(ə)ri/ *noun* details of what has happened to a patient undergoing treatment

casein /ˈkeɪsiɪn/ *noun* one of the proteins found in milk

caseinogen /ˌkeɪsiˈɪnədʒən/ *noun* the main protein in milk, from which casein is formed

Casey's model /ˈkeɪsiz ˌmɒd(ə)l/ *noun* a model for the care of child patients, where the parents are involved in the treatment

castor oil /ˌkɑːstər ˈɔɪl/ *noun* a plant oil which acts as a laxative

castration /kæˈstreɪʃ(ə)n/ *noun* the surgical removal of the sexual organs, usually the testicles, in males

casualty /ˈkæʒuəlti/ *noun* **1.** a person who has had an accident or who is suddenly ill ○ *The fire caused several casualties.* ○ *The casualties were taken by ambulance to the nearest hospital.* **2.** *also* **casualty department** same as **accident and emergency department** ○ *The accident victim was rushed to casualty.*

casualty ward /ˈkæʒuəlti wɔːd/ *noun* same as **accident ward**

CAT /kæt/ *noun* same as **computerised axial tomography**

cata- /kætə/ *prefix* downwards

catabolic /ˌkætəˈbɒlɪk/ *adjective* referring to catabolism

catabolism /kəˈtæbəlɪz(ə)m/ *noun* the process of breaking down complex chemicals into simple chemicals

catalase /ˈkætəleɪz/ *noun* an enzyme present in the blood and liver which catalyses the breakdown of hydrogen peroxide into water and oxygen

catalepsy /ˈkætəlepsi/ *noun* a condition often associated with schizophrenia, where a person becomes incapable of sensation, the body is rigid and he or she does not move for long periods

catalyse /ˈkætəlaɪz/ *verb* to act as a catalyst and help make a chemical reaction take place (NOTE: The US spelling is **catalyze**.)

catalyst /ˈkætəlɪst/ *noun* a substance which produces or helps a chemical reaction without itself changing ○ *an enzyme which acts as a catalyst in the digestive process*

catalytic /ˌkætəˈlɪtɪk/ *adjective* referring to catalysis

catamenia /ˌkætəˈmiːniə/ *noun* menstruation (*technical*)

cataplexy /ˈkætəpleksi/ *noun* a condition in which a person's muscles become suddenly rigid and he or she falls without losing consciousness, possibly caused by a shock

cataract /ˈkætərækt/ *noun* a condition in which the lens of the eye gradually becomes hard and opaque

cataractous lens /ˌkætəˈræktəs ˌlenz/ *noun* a lens on which a cataract has formed

catarrh /kəˈtɑː/ *noun* inflammation of the mucous membranes in the nose and throat, creating an excessive amount of mucus

catatonia /ˌkætəˈtəʊniə/ *noun* a condition in which a psychiatric patient is either motionless or shows violent reactions to stimulation

catatonic /ˌkætəˈtɒnɪk/ *adjective* referring to behaviour in which a person is either motionless or extremely violent

catchment area /ˈkætʃmənt ˌeəriə/ *noun* an area around a hospital which is served by that hospital

catecholamines /kætəˈkɒliːnz/ *plural noun* the hormones adrenaline and noradrenaline which are released by the adrenal glands

catgut /ˈkætɡʌt/ *noun* a thread made from part of the intestines of sheep, now usually artificially hardened, used to sew up cuts made during surgery

catharsis /kəˈθɑːsɪs/ *noun* purgation of the bowels

cathartic /kəˈθɑːtɪk/ *adjective* laxative or purgative

catheter /ˈkæθɪtə/ *noun* a tube passed into the body along one of the passages in the body

catheterisation /ˌkæθɪtəraɪˈzeɪʃ(ə)n/, **catheterization** *noun* the act of putting a catheter into a patient's body

CAT scan /ˈkæt skæn/, **CT scan** /ˌsiː ˈtiː skæn/ *noun* same as **CT scan**

cat-scratch disease /ˈkæt skrætʃ dɪˌziːz/, **cat-scratch fever** /ˈkæt skrætʃ ˌfiːvə/ *noun* an illness in which the patient has a fever and swollen lymph glands, thought to be caused by a bacterium transmitted to humans by the scratch of a cat. It may also result from scratching with other sharp points.

cauda equina /ˌkɔːdə ɪˈkwaɪnə/ *noun* a group of nerves which go from the spinal cord to the lumbar region and the coccyx

caudal /ˈkɔːd(ə)l/ *adjective* (*in humans*) referring to the cauda equina

caudal anaesthetic /ˌkɔːd(ə)l ˌænəsˈθetɪk/ *noun* an anaesthetic, injected into the base of the spine to remove feeling in the lower part of the body. It is often used in childbirth.

caudal analgesia /ˌkɔːd(ə)l ˌæn(ə)lˈdʒiːziə/ *noun* a method of pain relief that involves injecting an anaesthetic into the base of the spine to remove feeling in the lower part of the body

caul /kɔːl/ *noun* **1.** a membrane which sometimes covers a baby's head at birth **2.** same as **omentum**

causalgia /kɔːˈzældʒə/ *noun* burning pain in a limb, caused by a damaged nerve

causal organism /ˌkɔːz(ə)l ˈɔːɡənɪz(ə)m/ *noun* an organism that causes a particular disease

caustic /ˈkɔːstɪk/ *noun* a chemical substance that destroys tissues that it touches ■ *adjective* corrosive and destructive

cauterisation /ˌkɔːtəraɪˈzeɪʃ(ə)n/, **cauterization** *noun* the act of cauterising ○ *The growth was removed by cauterisation.*

cauterise /ˈkɔːtəraɪz/, **cauterize** *verb* to use burning, radiation or laser beams to remove tissue or to stop bleeding

cautery /ˈkɔːtəri/ *noun* a surgical instrument used to cauterise a wound

cavernous /ˈkævənəs/ *adjective* hollow

cavitation /ˌkævɪˈteɪʃ(ə)n/ *noun* the forming of a cavity

cavity /ˈkævɪti/ *noun* a hole or space inside the body

cc *abbreviation* cubic centimetre

CCU *abbreviation* coronary care unit

CD4 /ˌsiː diː ˈfɔː/ *noun* a compound consisting of a protein combined with a carbohydrate which is found in some cells and helps to protect the body against infection □ **CD4 count** a test used to monitor how many CD4 cells have been destroyed in people with HIV

CDH *abbreviation* congenital dislocation of the hip

cefaclor /ˈsefəklɔː/ *noun* an antibacterial drug used to treat septicaemia

cefotaxime /ˌsefəˈtæksiːm/ *noun* a synthetic cephalosporin used to treat bacterial infection by pseudomonads

-cele /siːl/ *suffix* referring to a swelling

cell /sel/ *noun* a tiny unit of matter which is the base of all plant and animal tissue (NOTE: For other terms referring to cells, see words beginning with **cyt-, cyto-**.)

cellular /ˈseljʊlə/ *adjective* **1.** referring to cells, or formed of cells **2.** made of many similar parts connected together

cellulite /ˈseljʊlaɪt/ *noun* lumpy deposits of subcutaneous fat, especially in the thighs and buttocks

cellulitis /ˌseljʊˈlaɪtɪs/ *noun* a usually bacterial inflammation of connective tissue or of the subcutaneous tissue

cellulose /ˈseljʊləʊs/ *noun* a carbohydrate which makes up a large percentage of plant matter

Celsius /ˈselsiəs/ *noun* a metric scale of temperature on which 0° is the point at which water freezes and 100° is the point at which water boils under average atmospheric conditions. Also called **centigrade**. ◊ **Fahrenheit** (NOTE: It is usually written as a **C** after the degree sign: **52°C** (say: 'fifty-two degrees Celsius').) [Described 1742. After Anders Celsius (1701–44), Swedish astronomer and scientist.]

Celsius temperature /ˈselsiəs ˌtemprɪtʃə/ *noun* temperature as measured on the Celsius scale

CEMACH /ˈsiːmæʃ/ *noun* a UK research project investigating the causes of infant deaths and still-

questions refers to attitudes frequently shown by people suffering from depression

beclomethasone /ˌbeklə'meθəsəʊn/ *noun* a steroid drug usually used in an inhaler to treat asthma or hay fever

becquerel /'bekərel/ *noun* an SI unit of measurement of radiation. Abbreviation **Bq** (NOTE: Now used in place of the **curie**.)

bed bath /'bed bɑːθ/ *noun* an act of washing the whole body of someone who is unable to get up to wash. Also called **blanket bath**

bed blocking /'bed ˌblɒkɪŋ/ *noun* the fact of people being kept in hospital because other forms of care are not available, which means that other people cannot be treated

bedbug /'bedbʌg/ *noun* a small insect which lives in dirty bedclothes and sucks blood

bed occupancy /'bed ˌɒkjʊpənsi/ *noun* the percentage of beds in a hospital which are occupied

bedpan /'bedpæn/ *noun* a dish into which someone can urinate or defecate without getting out of bed

bed rest /'bed rest/ *noun* a period of time spent in bed in order to rest and recover from an illness

bedridden /'bedˌrɪd(ə)n/ *adjective* referring to someone who has been too ill to get out of bed over a long period of time

bedside manner /ˌbedsaɪd 'mænə/ *noun* the way in which a doctor behaves towards a patient, especially a patient who is in bed □ **a good bedside manner** the ability to make patients feel comforted and reassured

bedsore /'bedsɔː/ *noun* an inflamed patch of skin on a bony part of the body, which develops into an ulcer, caused by pressure of the part on the mattress after lying for some time in one position. Special beds such as air beds, ripple beds and water beds are used to try to prevent the formation of bedsores. Also called **pressure sore**, **decubitus ulcer**

bedstate /'bedsteɪt/ *noun* a record of the current level of occupancy of beds in a hospital or care unit, updated as admissions and discharges occur

bedwetting /'bedwetɪŋ/ *noun* same as **nocturnal enuresis** (NOTE: This term is used mainly about children.)

Beer's knife /'bɪəz naɪf/ *noun* a knife with a triangular blade, used in eye operations [After George Joseph Beer (1763–1821), German ophthalmologist.]

behaviour /bɪ'heɪvjə/ *noun* a way of acting ○ *His behaviour was very aggressive.*

behavioural /bɪ'heɪvjərəl/ *adjective* relating to behaviour

behaviourism /bɪ'heɪvjərɪz(ə)m/ *noun* a psychological theory proposing that only someone's

behaviour should be studied to discover their psychological problems

behaviourist /bɪ'heɪvjərɪst/ *noun* a psychologist who follows behaviourism

behaviour therapy /bɪ,heɪvjə 'θerəpi/ *noun* a form of psychiatric treatment in which someone learns how to improve their condition

Behçet's syndrome /'beɪsets ,sɪndrəʊm/ *noun* a chronic condition of the immune system with no known cause, experienced as a series of attacks of inflammation of small blood vessels accompanied by mouth ulcers and sometimes genital ulcers, skin lesions and inflamed eyes [Described 1937. After Halushi Behçet (1889–1948), Turkish dermatologist.]

behind /bɪ'haɪnd/ *noun* same as **buttock** (*informal*)

bejel /'bedʒəl/ *noun* a non-venereal form of syphilis which is endemic among children in some areas of the Middle East and elsewhere and is caused by a spirochaete strain of bacteria

belch /beltʃ/ *noun* the action of allowing air in the stomach to come up through the mouth ■ *verb* to allow air in the stomach to come up through the mouth

belching /'beltʃɪŋ/ *noun* the action of allowing air in the stomach to come up through the mouth. Also called **eructation**

belladonna /ˌbelə'dɒnə/ *noun* **1.** a poisonous plant with berries containing atropine. Also called **deadly nightshade 2.** a form of atropine extracted from the belladonna plant

belle indifférence /ˌbel æn'dɪferɑːns/ *noun* an excessively calm state in a person, in a situation which would usually produce a show of emotion

Bellocq's cannula /be,lɒks 'kænjʊlə/, **Bellocq's sound** /be,lɒks 'saʊnd/ *noun* an instrument used to control a nosebleed [After Jean Jacques Bellocq (1732–1807), French surgeon.]

Bell's mania /ˌbelz 'meɪniə/ *noun* a form of acute mania with delirium [After Luther Vose Bell (1806–62), American physiologist.]

Bell's palsy /ˌbelz 'pɔːlzi/ *noun* paralysis of the facial nerve on one side of the face, preventing one eye being closed. Also called **facial paralysis** [Described 1821. After Sir Charles Bell (1774–1842), Scottish surgeon. He ran anatomy schools, first in Edinburgh and then in London. Professor of Anatomy at the Royal Academy.]

belly /'beli/ *noun* **1.** same as **abdomen 2.** the fatter central part of a muscle

Bence Jones protein /ˌbens 'dʒəʊnz ,prəʊtiːn/ *noun* a protein found in the urine of people who have myelomatosis, lymphoma, leukaemia and some other cancers [Described 1848. After Henry Bence Jones (1814–73), physician at St George's Hospital, London, UK]

barium enema /ˌbeəriəm 'enimə/ *noun* a liquid solution containing barium sulphate which is put into the rectum to increase the contrast of an X-ray of the lower intestine

barium meal /ˌbeəriəm 'miːl/, **barium solution** /ˌbeəriəm səˈluːʃ(ə)n/ *noun* a liquid solution containing barium sulphate which someone drinks to increase the contrast of an X-ray of the alimentary tract

Barlow's disease /'bɑːləʊz dɪˌziːz/ *noun* scurvy in children, caused by a lack of vitamin C [Described 1882. After Sir Thomas Barlow (1845–1945), physician at various London hospitals and to Queen Victoria, King Edward VII and King George V.]

Barlow's sign /'bɑːləʊz saɪn/ *noun* a test for congenital dislocation of the hip, in which a sudden movement is felt and sometimes a sound is heard when the joint is manipulated

baroreceptor /ˌbærəʊrɪ'septə/ *noun* one of a group of nerves near the carotid artery and aortic arch, which senses changes in blood pressure

barotrauma /ˌbærəʊ'trɔːmə/ *noun* an injury caused by a sharp increase in pressure

Barr body /'bɑː ˌbɒdi/ *noun* a dense clump of chromatin found only in female cells, which can be used to identify the sex of a baby before birth [Described 1949. After Murray Llewellyn Barr (1908–95), head of the Department of Anatomy at the University of Western Ontario, Canada.]

Barré-Guillain syndrome /ˌbæreɪ 'giː jæn ˌsɪndrəʊm/ *noun* ♦ **Guillain-Barré syndrome**

barrel chest /ˌbærəl 'tʃest/ *noun* a chest formed like a barrel, caused by asthma or emphysema

barrier cream /'bæriə kriːm/ *noun* a cream put on the skin to prevent the skin coming into contact with irritating substances

barrier nursing /'bæriə ˌnɜːsɪŋ/ *noun* the nursing of someone who has an infectious disease. It involves keeping them away from other patients and making sure that faeces and soiled bedclothes do not carry the infection to other patients.

bartholinitis /ˌbɑːθɒlɪ'naɪtɪs/ *noun* inflammation of the Bartholin's glands

Bartholin's glands /'bɑːθəlɪnz glændz/ *plural noun* two glands at the side of the vagina and between it and the vulva, which secrete a lubricating substance. Also called **greater vestibular glands** [After Caspar Bartholin (1655–1748), Danish anatomist.]

basal /'beɪs(ə)l/ *adjective* located at the bottom of something, or forming its base

basal metabolic rate /ˌbeɪsɪk metə'bɒlɪk reɪt/ *noun* the amount of energy used by the body in exchanging oxygen and carbon dioxide when at rest. It was formerly used as a way of testing thyroid gland activity. Abbreviation **BMR**

base /beɪs/ *noun* **1.** the bottom part ○ *the base of the spine* **2.** the main ingredient of an ointment, as opposed to the active ingredient **3.** a substance which reacts with an acid to form a salt ■ *verb* to use something as a base

Basedow's disease /'bæzɪdəʊz dɪˌziːz/ *noun* a form of hyperthyroidism [Described 1840. After Carl Adolph Basedow (1799–1854), general practitioner in Mersburg, Germany.]

basement membrane /ˌbeɪsmənt ˌmem'breɪn/ *noun* a membrane at the base of an epithelium

basilar /'bæzɪlə/ *adjective* referring to a base

basilic vein /bəˌzɪlɪk 'veɪn/ *noun* a large vein running along the inside of the arm

basophil /'beɪsəfɪl/ *noun* a type of white blood cell which has granules in its cytoplasm and contains histamine and heparin

basophilia /ˌbeɪsə'fɪliə/ *noun* an increase in the number of basophils in the blood

basophilic granulocyte /ˌbeɪsəfɪlɪk 'grænjʊləsaɪt/ *noun* same as **basophil**

Batten's disease /'bæt(ə)nz dɪˌziːz/ *noun* a hereditary disease which affects the enzymes of the brain, causing cells in the brain and eye to die

battered baby syndrome /'bætəd ˌbeɪbi ˌsɪndrəʊm/, **battered child syndrome** /'bætəd 'tʃaɪld 'sɪndrəʊm/ *noun* a condition in which a baby or small child is frequently beaten, usually by one or both of its parents, sustaining injuries such as multiple fractures

battledore placenta /'bæt(ə)ldɔː plə,sentə/ *noun* a placenta where the umbilical cord is attached at the edge and not at the centre

Bazin's disease /'beɪzɪnz dɪˌziːz/ *noun* same as **erythema induratum** [Described 1861. After Pierre Antoine Ernest Bazin (1807–78), dermatologist at Hôpital St Louis, Paris, France. He was an expert in parasitology associated with skin conditions.]

BC *abbreviation* bone conduction

BCC *abbreviation* Breast Cancer Campaign

B cell /'biː sel/ *noun* same as **beta cell**

BCG /ˌbiː siː 'dʒiː/, **BCG vaccine** *noun* a vaccine which immunises against tuberculosis. Full form **bacille Calmette-Guérin**

BCh *abbreviation* Bachelor of Surgery

BDA *abbreviation* British Dental Association

bearing down /ˌbeərɪŋ 'daʊn/ *noun* a stage in childbirth when the woman starts to push out the baby from the uterus

bearing-down pain /ˌbeərɪŋ 'daʊn ˌpeɪn/ *noun* pain felt in the uterus during the second stage of labour (NOTE: Bearing-down pain is also associated with uterine prolapse.)

Beck inventory of depression /ˌbek ˌɪnvənt(ə)ri əv dɪ'preʃ(ə)n/ *noun* one of the rating scales for depression, in which a series of 21

chlorine /'klɔːriːn/ *noun* a powerful greenish gas, used to sterilise water (NOTE: The chemical symbol is **Cl**.)

chlormethiazole /ˌklɔːmeˈθaɪəzəʊl/ *noun* a sedative used in the treatment of people with alcoholism

chloro- /klɔːrəʊ/ *prefix* referring to chlorine

chloroform /'klɒrəfɔːm/ *noun* a powerful drug formerly used as an anaesthetic

chloroma /klɒ'rəʊmə/ *noun* a bone tumour associated with acute leukaemia

chlorosis /klɒ'rəʊsɪs/ *noun* a type of severe anaemia due to iron deficiency, affecting mainly young girls

chlorothiazide /ˌklɔːrəʊ'θaɪəzaɪd/ *noun* a drug which helps the body to produce more urine, used in the treatment of high blood pressure, swelling and heart failure

chloroxylenol /ˌklɔːrəʊ'zaɪlənɒl/ *noun* a chemical used as an antimicrobial agent in skin creams and in disinfectants

chlorpheniramine /ˌklɔːfen'aɪrəmiːn/, **chlorpheniramine maleate** /ˌklɔːfenaɪrəmiːn 'mælieɪt/ *noun* an antihistamine drug

chlorpromazine hydrochloride /klɔːˌprəʊməziːn ˌhaɪdrəʊ'klɔːraɪd/ *noun* a drug used to treat schizophrenia and other psychoses

chlorpropamide /klɔː'prəʊpəmaɪd/ *noun* a drug which lowers blood sugar, used in the treatment of diabetes

chlorthalidone /klɔː'θælɪdəʊn/ *noun* a diuretic

choana /'kəʊənə/ *noun* any opening shaped like a funnel, especially the one leading from the nasal cavity to the pharynx (NOTE: The plural is **choanae**.)

chocolate cyst /ˌtʃɒklət 'sɪst/ *noun* an ovarian cyst containing old brown blood

chol- /kɒl/ *prefix* same as **chole-** (*used before vowels*)

cholaemia /kə'liːmiə/ *noun* the presence of an unusual amount of bile in the blood

cholagogue /'kɒləgɒg/ *noun* a drug which encourages the production of bile

cholangiocarcinoma /kəˌlændʒiəʊˌkɑːsɪ 'nəʊmə/ *noun* a rare cancer of the cells of the bile ducts

cholangiography /kəˌlændʒɪ'ɒgrəfi/ *noun* an X-ray examination of the bile ducts and gall bladder

cholangiolitis /kəˌlændʒiəʊ'laɪtɪs/ *noun* inflammation of the small bile ducts

cholangiopancreatography /kəˌlændʒiəʊ ˌpæŋkriə'tɒgrəfi/ *noun* an X-ray examination of the bile ducts and pancreas

cholangitis /ˌkəʊlæn'dʒaɪtɪs/ *noun* inflammation of the bile ducts

chole- /kɒli/ *prefix* referring to bile

cholecalciferol /ˌkɒlɪkæl'sɪfərɒl/ *noun* a form of vitamin D found naturally in fish-liver oils and egg yolks

cholecystectomy /ˌkɒlɪsɪ'stektəmi/ *noun* the surgical removal of the gall bladder

cholecystitis /ˌkɒlɪsɪ'staɪtɪs/ *noun* inflammation of the gall bladder

cholecystoduodenostomy /ˌkɒlɪsɪstəˌdjuːədɪ'nɒstəmi/ *noun* a surgical operation to join the gall bladder to the duodenum to allow bile to pass into the intestine when the main bile duct is blocked

cholecystography /ˌkɒlɪsɪ'stɒgrəfi/ *noun* an X-ray examination of the gall bladder

cholecystokinin /ˌkɒlɪsɪstəʊ'kaɪnɪn/ *noun* a hormone released by cells at the top of the small intestine. It stimulates the gall bladder, making it contract and release bile.

cholecystotomy /ˌkɒlɪsɪ'stɒtəmi/ *noun* a surgical operation to make a cut in the gall bladder, usually to remove gallstones

choledoch- /kəledək/ *prefix* referring to the common bile duct

choledocholithiasis /kəˌledəkəlɪ'θaɪəsɪs/ *noun* same as **cholelithiasis**

choledocholithotomy /kəˌledɪkəʊlɪ 'θɒtəmi/ *noun* a surgical operation to remove a gallstone by cutting into the bile duct

choledochostomy /kəˌledə'kɒstəmi/ *noun* a surgical operation to make an opening in a bile duct

choledochotomy /kəledə'kɒtəmi/ *noun* a surgical operation to make a cut in the common bile duct to remove gallstones

cholelithiasis /ˌkɒlɪlɪ'θaɪəsɪs/ *noun* a condition in which gallstones form in the gall bladder or bile ducts. Also called **choledocholithiasis**

cholelithotomy /ˌkɒlɪlɪ'θɒtəmi/ *noun* the surgical removal of gallstones by cutting into the gall bladder

cholera /'kɒlərə/ *noun* a serious bacterial disease spread through food or water which has been infected by *Vibrio cholerae* ○ *A cholera epidemic broke out after the flood.*

choleresis /kə'lɪərəsɪs/ *noun* the production of bile by the liver

choleretic /ˌkɒlɪ'retɪk/ *adjective* referring to a substance which increases the production and flow of bile

cholestasis /ˌkɒlɪ'steɪsɪs/ *noun* a condition in which all bile does not pass into the intestine but some remains in the liver and causes jaundice

cholesteatoma /kəˌlestiə'təʊmə/ *noun* a cyst containing some cholesterol found in the middle ear and also in the brain

cholesterol /kə'lestərɒl/ *noun* a fatty substance found in fats and oils, also produced by the liver and forming an essential part of all cells

cholesterolaemia /kəˌlestərəˈleɪmiə/ *noun* a high level of cholesterol in the blood

cholesterosis /kəˌlestəˈrəʊsɪs/ *noun* inflammation of the gall bladder with deposits of cholesterol

cholic acid /ˌkəʊlɪk ˈæsɪd/ *noun* one of the bile acids

choline /ˈkəʊliːn/ *noun* a compound involved in fat metabolism and the precursor for acetylcholine

cholinergic /ˌkəʊlɪˈnɜːdʒɪk/ *adjective* referring to a neurone or receptor which responds to acetylcholine

cholinesterase /ˌkəʊlɪˈnestəreɪz/ *noun* an enzyme which breaks down a choline ester

choluria /kəʊˈljʊəriə/ *noun* same as **biliuria**

chondr- /kɒndr/ *prefix* referring to cartilage

chondritis /kɒnˈdraɪtɪs/ *noun* inflammation of a cartilage

chondroblast /ˈkɒndrəʊblæst/ *noun* a cell from which cartilage develops in an embryo

chondrocalcinosis /ˌkɒndrəʊˌkælsɪˈnəʊsɪs/ *noun* a condition in which deposits of calcium phosphate are found in articular cartilage

chondrocyte /ˈkɒndrəʊsaɪt/ *noun* a mature cartilage cell

chondrodysplasia /ˌkɒndrəʊdɪsˈpleɪziə/ *noun* a hereditary disorder of cartilage which is linked to dwarfism

chondrodystrophy /ˌkɒndrəʊˈdɪstrəfi/ *noun* any disorder of cartilage

chondroma /kɒnˈdrəʊmə/ *noun* a tumour formed of cartilaginous tissue

chondromalacia /ˌkɒndrəʊməˈleɪʃə/ *noun* degeneration of the cartilage of a joint

chondrosarcoma /ˌkɒndrəʊsɑːˈkəʊmə/ *noun* a malignant, rapidly growing tumour involving cartilage cells

chorda /ˈkɔːdə/ *noun* a cord or tendon (NOTE: The plural is **chordae**.)

chordee /ˈkɔːdiː/ *noun* a painful condition where the erect penis is curved, a complication of gonorrhoea

chorditis /kɔːˈdaɪtɪs/ *noun* inflammation of the vocal cords

chordotomy /kɔːˈdɒtəmi/ *noun* a surgical operation to cut a cord such as a nerve pathway in the spinal cord in order to relieve intractable pain

chorea /kɔːˈriːə/ *noun* a sudden severe twitching, usually of the face and shoulders, which is a symptom of disease of the nervous system

chorion /ˈkɔːriən/ *noun* a membrane covering the fertilised ovum

chorionic /ˌkɔːriˈɒnɪk/ *adjective* referring to the chorion

chorionic gonadotrophin /ˌkɔːriˌɒnɪk ˌɡəʊnədəʊˈtrəʊfɪn/ *noun* ♦ **human chorionic gonadotrophin**

chorionic villi /ˌkɔːriˌɒnɪk ˈvɪlaɪ/ *plural noun* tiny finger-like folds in the chorion

chorionic villus sampling /ˌkɔːriˌɒnɪk ˈvɪləs ˌsɑːmplɪŋ/ *noun* an antenatal screening test carried out by examining cells from the chorionic villi of the outer membrane surrounding an embryo, which have the same DNA as the fetus

choroid /ˈkɔːrɔɪd/ *noun* the middle layer of tissue which forms the eyeball, between the sclera and the retina. See illustration at **EYE** in Supplement

choroiditis /ˌkɔːrɔɪˈdaɪtɪs/ *noun* inflammation of the choroid in the eyeball

choroidocyclitis /kɔːˌrɔɪdəʊsaɪˈklaɪtɪs/ *noun* inflammation of the choroids and ciliary body

Christmas disease /ˈkrɪsməs dɪˌziːz/ *noun* same as **haemophilia B** [After Mr Christmas, the person in whom the disease was first studied in detail.]

Christmas factor /ˈkrɪsməs ˌfæktə/ *noun* same as **Factor IX**

chrom- /krəʊm/ *prefix* same as **chromo-** (*used before vowels*)

-chromasia /krəmeɪziə/ *suffix* referring to colour

chromatid /ˈkrəʊmətɪd/ *noun* one of two parallel filaments making up a chromosome

chromatin /ˈkrəʊmətɪn/ *noun* a network which forms the nucleus of a cell and can be stained with basic dyes

chromatography /ˌkrəʊməˈtɒɡrəfi/ *noun* a method of separating chemicals through a porous medium, used in analysing compounds and mixtures

chromatophore /krəʊˈmætəfɔː/ *noun* any pigment-bearing cell in the eyes, hair and skin

chromic acid /ˌkrəʊmɪk ˈæsɪd/ *noun* an unstable acid existing only in solution or in the form of a salt, sometimes used in the removal of warts

chromicised catgut /ˌkrəʊmɪsaɪzd ˈkætɡʌt/ *noun* catgut which is hardened with chromium to make it slower to dissolve in the body

chromium /ˈkrəʊmiəm/ *noun* a metallic trace element (NOTE: The chemical symbol is **Cr**.)

chromo- /krəʊməʊ/ *prefix* referring to colour

chromosomal /ˌkrəʊməˈsəʊm(ə)l/ *adjective* referring to chromosomes

chromosome /ˈkrəʊməsəʊm/ *noun* a rod-shaped structure in the nucleus of a cell, formed of DNA, which carries the genes

chromosome mapping /ˈkrəʊməsəʊm ˌmæpɪŋ/ *noun* a procedure by which the position of genes on a chromosome is established

chronic /'krɒnɪk/ *adjective* **1.** referring to a disease or condition which lasts for a long time ○ *He has a chronic chest complaint.* Opposite **acute 2.** referring to serious pain (*informal*)

chronic abscess /ˌkrɒnɪk 'æbses/ *noun* an abscess which develops slowly over a period of time

chronic appendicitis /ˌkrɒnɪk əˌpendɪ'saɪtɪs/ *noun* a condition in which the vermiform appendix is always slightly inflamed. ◊ **grumbling appendix**

chronic catarrhal rhinitis /ˌkrɒnɪk kəˌtɑːrəl raɪ'naɪtɪs/ *noun* a persistent form of inflammation of the nose where excess mucus is secreted by the mucous membrane

chronic fatigue syndrome /ˌkrɒnɪk fə'tiːɡ ˌsɪndrəʊm/ *noun* same as **myalgic encephalomyelitis**

chronic granulomatous disease /ˌkrɒnɪk ˌɡrænjʊ'ləʊmətəs dɪˌziːz/ *noun* a type of inflammation where macrophages are converted into epithelial-like cells as a result of infection, as in tuberculosis or sarcoidosis

chronic obstructive airways disease /ˌkrɒnɪk əbˌstrʌktɪv 'eəweɪz dɪˌziːz/ *noun* abbreviation **COAD**. Now called **chronic obstructive pulmonary disease**

chronic obstructive pulmonary disease /ˌkrɒnɪk əbˌstrʌktɪv 'pʌlmən(ə)ri dɪˌziːz/ *noun* any of a group of progressive respiratory disorders where someone experiences loss of lung function and shows little or no response to steroid or bronchodilator drug treatments, e.g. emphysema and chronic bronchitis. Abbreviation **COPD**

chronic pancreatitis /ˌkrɒnɪk pæŋkriə'taɪtɪs/ *noun* a persistent inflammation occurring after repeated attacks of acute pancreatitis, where the gland becomes calcified

chronic periarthritis /ˌkrɒnɪk periɑː'θraɪtɪs/ *noun* inflammation of tissues round the shoulder joint. Also called **scapulohumeral arthritis**

chronic pericarditis /ˌkrɒnɪk perikɑː'daɪtɪs/ *noun* a condition in which the pericardium becomes thickened and prevents the heart from functioning normally. Also called **constrictive pericarditis**

Chronic Sick and Disabled Persons Act 1970 /ˌkrɒnɪk ˌsɪk ən dɪsˌeɪb(ə)ld 'pɜːs(ə)nz ækt/ *noun* an Act of Parliament in the UK which provides benefits such as alterations to their homes for people with long-term conditions

chronic toxicity /ˌkrɒnɪk tɒk'sɪsɪti/ *noun* exposure to harmful levels of a toxic substance over a period of time

chrysotherapy /ˌkraɪsəʊ'θerəpi/ *noun* treatment which involves gold injections

Chvostek's sign /tʃə'vɒsteks saɪn/ *noun* an indication of tetany, where a spasm is produced if the facial muscles are tapped

chyle /kaɪl/ *noun* a fluid in the lymph vessels in the intestine, which contains fat, especially after a meal

chylomicron /ˌkaɪləʊ'maɪkrɒn/ *noun* a particle of chyle present in the blood

chyluria /kaɪ'ljʊəriə/ *noun* the presence of chyle in the urine

chyme /kaɪm/ *noun* a semi-liquid mass of food and gastric juices, which passes from the stomach to the intestine

chymotrypsin /ˌkaɪməʊ'trɪpsɪn/ *noun* an enzyme which digests protein

Ci *abbreviation* curie

cicatrix /'sɪkətrɪks/ *noun* same as **scar**

-ciclovir /sɪkləvɪə/ *suffix* used in the names of antiviral drugs

-cide /saɪd/ *suffix* referring to killing

cilia /'sɪliə/ plural of **cilium**

ciliary /'sɪliəri/ *adjective* referring to cilia

ciliary body /'sɪliəri ˌbɒdi/ *noun* the part of the eye which connects the iris to the choroid. See illustration at **EYE** in Supplement

ciliary ganglion /ˌsɪliəri 'ɡæŋɡliən/ *noun* a parasympathetic ganglion in the orbit of the eye, supplying the intrinsic eye muscles

ciliary muscle /'sɪliəri ˌmʌs(ə)l/ *noun* a muscle which makes the lens of the eye change its shape to focus on objects at different distances. See illustration at **EYE** in Supplement

ciliary processes /ˌsɪliəri 'prəʊsesɪz/ *plural noun* the ridges behind the iris to which the lens of the eye is attached

ciliated epithelium /ˌsɪlieɪtɪd epɪ'θiːliəm/ *noun* simple epithelium where the cells have tiny hairs or cilia

cilium /'sɪliəm/ *noun* **1.** an eyelash **2.** one of many tiny hair-like processes which line cells in passages in the body and by moving backwards and forwards drive particles or fluid along the passage (NOTE: The plural is **cilia**.)

-cillin /sɪlɪn/ *suffix* used in the names of penicillin drugs ○ *amoxycillin*

cimetidine /sɪ'metɪdiːn/ *noun* a drug which reduces the production of stomach acid, used in peptic ulcer treatment

cimex /'saɪmeks/ *noun* a bedbug or related insect which feeds on birds, humans and other mammals (NOTE: The plural is **cimices**.)

CIN *abbreviation* cervical intraepithelial neoplasia

-cin /sɪn/ *suffix* referring to aminoglycosides ○ *gentamicin*

cinematics /ˌsɪnɪ'mætɪks/ *noun* the science of movement, especially of body movements

cineplasty /'sɪnɪplæsti/ *noun* an amputation where the muscles of the stump of the amputated limb are used to operate an artificial limb

cineradiography /ˌsɪnɪreɪdi'ɒɡrəfi/ *noun* the practice of taking a series of X-ray photographs for diagnosis, or to show how something moves or develops in the body

cinesiology /sɪˌniːsi'ɒlədʒi/ *noun* the study of muscle movements, particularly in relation to treatment

cinnarizine /'sɪnərəziːn/ *noun* an antihistaminic used to treat Ménière's disease

ciprofloxacin /ˌsaɪprəʊ'flɒksəsɪn/ *noun* a powerful antibiotic used in eye drops to treat corneal ulcers and surface infections of the eye, and in the treatment of anthrax in humans

circadian /sɜː'keɪdiən/ *adjective* referring to a pattern which is repeated approximately every 24 hours

circle of Willis /ˌsɜːk(ə)l əv 'wɪlɪs/ *noun* a circle of branching arteries at the base of the brain formed by the basilar artery, the anterior and posterior cerebral arteries, the anterior and posterior communicating arteries and the internal carotid arteries [Described 1664. After Thomas Willis (1621–75), English physician and anatomist.]

circulatory system /ˌsɜːkjʊ'leɪt(ə)ri ˌsɪstəm/ *noun* a system of arteries and veins, together with the heart, which makes the blood circulate around the body

circum- /sɜːkəm/ *prefix* around

circumcision /ˌsɜːkəm'sɪʒ(ə)n/ *noun* the surgical removal of the foreskin of the penis

circumduction /ˌsɜːkəm'dʌkʃən/ *noun* the action of moving a limb so that the end of it makes a circular motion

circumflex /'sɜːkəmfleks/ *adjective* bent or curved

circumoral /ˌsɜːkəm'ɔːrəl/ *adjective* referring to rashes surrounding the lips

circumvallate papillae /sɜːkəmˌvæleɪt pə'pɪliː/ *plural noun* large papillae at the base of the tongue, which have taste buds

cirrhosis /sə'rəʊsɪs/ *noun* a progressive disease of the liver, often associated with alcoholism, in which healthy cells are replaced by scar tissue

cirrhotic /sɪ'rɒtɪk/ *adjective* referring to cirrhosis ○ *The patient had a cirrhotic liver.*

cirs- /sɜːs/ *prefix* referring to dilation

cirsoid /'sɜːsɔɪd/ *adjective* referring to a varicose vein which is dilated

cisplatin /sɪs'pleɪtɪn/ *noun* a chemical substance which may help fight cancer by binding to DNA. It is used in the treatment of ovarian and testicular cancer.

cistern /'sɪstən/, **cisterna** /sɪ'stɜːnə/ *noun* a space containing fluid

citric acid /ˌsɪtrɪk 'æsɪd/ *noun* an acid found in fruit such as oranges, lemons and grapefruit

citric acid cycle /ˌsɪtrɪk 'æsɪd ˌsaɪk(ə)l/ *noun* an important series of events concerning amino

acid metabolism, which takes place in the mitochondria in the cell. Also called **Krebs cycle**

citrulline /'sɪtrʊliːn, 'sɪtrʊlaɪn/ *noun* an amino acid

CJD *abbreviation* Creutzfeldt-Jakob disease

cl *abbreviation* centilitre

clamp /klæmp/ *noun* a surgical instrument to hold something tightly, e.g. a blood vessel during an operation ■ *verb* to hold something tightly

clap /klæp/ *noun* same as **gonorrhoea** (*slang*)

classification /ˌklæsɪfɪ'keɪʃ(ə)n/ *noun* the work of putting references or components into order so as to be able to refer to them again and identify them easily ○ *the ABO classification of blood*

claudication /ˌklɔːdɪ'keɪʃ(ə)n/ *noun* the fact of limping or being lame

claustrophobia /ˌklɔːstrə'fəʊbiə/ *noun* a fear of enclosed spaces or crowded rooms. Compare **agoraphobia**

claustrophobic /ˌklɔːstrə'fəʊbɪk/ *adjective* afraid of being in enclosed spaces or crowded rooms. Compare **agoraphobic**

clavicle /'klævɪk(ə)l/ *noun* same as **collarbone**

clavicular /klə'vɪkjʊlə/ *adjective* referring to the clavicle

clavus /'kleɪvəs/ *noun* **1.** a corn on the foot **2.** severe pain in the head, like a nail being driven in

claw foot /ˌklɔː 'fʊt/ *noun* a deformed foot with the toes curved towards the instep and with a very high arch. Also called **pes cavus**

claw hand /ˌklɔː 'hænd/ *noun* a deformed hand with the fingers, especially the ring finger and little finger, bent towards the palm, caused by paralysis of the muscles

clean /kliːn/ *adjective* **1.** free from dirt, waste products or unwanted substances **2.** sterile or free from infection ○ *a clean dressing* ○ *a clean wound* **3.** not using recreational drugs

cleavage /'kliːvɪdʒ/ *noun* the repeated division of cells in an embryo

cleavage lines /'kliːvɪdʒ ˌlaɪnz/ *plural noun* same as **Langer's lines**

cleft /kleft/ *noun* a small opening or hollow place in a surface or body part ■ *adjective* referring to a surface or body part which has separated into two or more sections

cleft foot /ˌkleft 'fʊt/ *noun* same as **talipes**

cleft lip /ˌkleft 'lɪp/ *noun* a congenital condition in which the upper lip fails to form in the usual way during fetal development. Also called **harelip**

cleft palate /ˌkleft 'pælət/ *noun* a congenital condition in which the palate does not fuse during fetal development, causing a gap between the mouth and nasal cavity in severe cases

cleido- /klaɪdəʊ/ *prefix* referring to the clavicle

cleidocranial dysostosis /ˌklaɪdəʊkreɪniəl ˌdɪsɒsˈtəʊsɪs/ *noun* a hereditary bone malformation, with protruding jaw, lack of collarbone and malformed teeth

client /ˈklaɪənt/ *noun* a person visited by a health visitor or social worker

climacteric /klaɪˈmæktərɪk/ *noun* a period of diminished sexual activity in a man who reaches middle age

climax /ˈklaɪmæks/ *noun* **1.** an orgasm **2.** the point where a disease is at its worst ■ *verb* to have an orgasm

clindamycin /ˌklɪndəˈmaɪsɪn/ *noun* a powerful antibiotic used to treat severe infections and acne

clinic /ˈklɪnɪk/ *noun* **1.** a small hospital or a department in a large hospital which deals only with out-patients or which specialises in the treatment of particular medical conditions ○ *He is being treated in a private clinic.* ○ *She was referred to an antenatal clinic.* **2.** a group of students under a doctor or surgeon who examine patients and discuss their treatment

clinical /ˈklɪnɪk(ə)l/ *adjective* **1.** referring to the physical assessment and treatment of patients by doctors, as opposed to a surgical operation, a laboratory test or experiment **2.** referring to instruction given to students at the bedside of patients as opposed to class instruction with no patient present **3.** referring to a clinic

clinical audit /ˌklɪnɪk(ə)l ˈɔːdɪt/ *noun* an evaluation of the standard of clinical care

clinical care /ˌklɪnɪk(ə)l ˈkeə/ *noun* the care and treatment of patients in hospital wards or in doctors' surgeries

clinical effectiveness /ˌklɪnɪk(ə)l ɪˈfektɪvnəs/ *noun* the ability of a procedure or treatment to achieve the desired result

clinical governance /ˌklɪnɪk(ə)l ˈɡʌv(ə)nəns/ *noun* the responsibility given to doctors to coordinate audit, research, education, use of guidelines and risk management to develop a strategy to raise the quality of medical care

Clinical Management Plan /ˌklɪnɪk(ə)l ˈmænɪdʒmənt ˌplæn/ *noun* a comprehensive statement of a patient's condition that details what medicines and treatments may be used in ongoing care, forming part of the patient's records

clinical medicine /ˌklɪnɪk(ə)l ˈmed(ə)s(ə)n/ *noun* the study and treatment of patients in a hospital ward or in the doctor's surgery, as opposed to in the operating theatre or laboratory

clinical nurse manager /ˌklɪnɪk(ə)l ˈnɜːs ˌmænɪdʒə/ *noun* the administrative manager of the clinical nursing staff of a hospital

clinical nurse specialist /ˌklɪnɪk(ə)l nɜːs ˈspeʃ(ə)lɪst/ *noun* a nurse who specialises in a particular branch of clinical care

clinical pathology /ˌklɪnɪk(ə)l pəˈθɒlədʒi/ *noun* the study of disease as applied to the treatment of patients

clinical psychologist /ˌklɪnɪk(ə)l saɪˈkɒlədʒɪst/ *noun* a psychologist who studies and treats sick patients in hospital

clinical trial /ˌklɪnɪk(ə)l ˈtraɪəl/ *noun* a trial carried out in a medical laboratory on a person or on tissue from a person

clinician /klɪˈnɪʃ(ə)n/ *noun* a doctor, usually not a surgeon, who has considerable experience in treating patients

clinodactyly /ˌklaɪnəʊˈdæktɪli/ *noun* the permanent bending of a finger to one side

clip /klɪp/ *noun* a piece of metal with a spring, used to attach things together

clitoris /ˈklɪtərɪs/ *noun* a small erectile female sex organ, situated at the anterior angle of the vulva, which can be excited by sexual activity. See illustration at UROGENITAL SYSTEM (FEMALE) in Supplement

cloaca /kləʊˈeɪkə/ *noun* the end part of the hindgut in an embryo

clomipramine /kləʊˈmɪprəmiːn/ *noun* a drug used to treat depression, phobias and obsessive-compulsive disorder

clonazepam /kləʊˈnæzɪpæm/ *noun* a drug used to treat epilepsy

clone /kləʊn/ *noun* a group of cells derived from a single cell by asexual reproduction and so identical to the first cell ■ *verb* to reproduce an individual organism by asexual means

clonic /ˈklɒnɪk/ *adjective* referring to clonus

clonic spasms /ˌklɒnɪk ˈspæz(ə)mz/ *plural noun* spasms which recur regularly

clonidine /ˈklɒnɪdiːn/ *noun* a drug which relaxes and widens the arteries, used in the treatment of hypertension, migraine headaches and heart failure

clonus /ˈkləʊnəs/ *noun* the rhythmic contraction and relaxation of a muscle, usually a sign of upper motor neurone lesions

closed fracture /ˌkləʊzd ˈfræktʃə/ *noun* same as **simple fracture**

Clostridium /klɒˈstrɪdiəm/ *noun* a type of bacteria

clot /klɒt/ *noun* a soft mass of coagulated blood in a vein or an artery ○ *The doctor diagnosed a blood clot in the brain.* ○ *Blood clots occur in thrombosis.* ■ *verb* to change from a liquid to a semi-solid state, or to cause a liquid to do this ○ *His blood does not clot easily.* (NOTE: **clotting – clotted**)

clotrimazole /klɒˈtrɪməzəʊl/ *noun* a drug used to treat yeast and fungal infections

clotting /ˈklɒtɪŋ/ *noun* the action of coagulating

clotting factors /ˌklɒtɪŋ ˈfæktəz/ *plural noun* substances in plasma, called Factor I, Factor II, and so on, which act one after the other to make the blood coagulate when a blood vessel is damaged

COMMENT: Deficiency in one or more of the clotting factors results in haemophilia.

clubbing /'klʌbɪŋ/ *noun* a thickening of the ends of the fingers and toes, a sign of many different diseases

club foot /ˌklʌb 'fʊt/ *noun* same as **talipes**

cluster headache /'klʌstə ˌhedeɪk/ *noun* a headache which occurs behind one eye for a short period

Clutton's joint /'klʌt(ə)nz ˌdʒɔɪnt/ *noun* a swollen knee joint occurring in congenital syphilis [Described 1886. After Henry Hugh Clutton (1850–1909), surgeon at St Thomas's Hospital, London, UK]

cm *abbreviation* centimetre

CMHN *abbreviation* community mental health nurse

CM joint /ˌsi: 'em dʒɔɪnt/ *noun* same as **carpometacarpal joint**

CMO *abbreviation* Chief Medical Officer

CMV *abbreviation* cytomegalovirus

C/N *abbreviation* charge nurse

CNS *abbreviation* central nervous system

coagulant /kəʊ'ægjʊlənt/ *noun* a substance which can make blood clot

coagulase /kəʊ'ægjʊleɪz/ *noun* an enzyme produced by a staphylococcal bacteria which makes blood plasma clot

coagulate /kəʊ'ægjʊleɪt/ *verb* to change from liquid to semi-solid, or cause a liquid to do this ○ *His blood does not coagulate easily.* ◊ **clot**

coagulation /kəʊˌægjʊ'leɪʃ(ə)n/ *noun* the action of clotting

coagulum /kəʊ'ægjʊləm/ *noun* same as **blood clot** (NOTE: The plural is **coagula.**)

coalesce /ˌkəʊə'les/ *verb* to combine, or to cause things to combine, into a single body or group

coalescence /ˌkəʊə'les(ə)ns/ *noun* the process by which wound edges come together when healing

coarctation /ˌkəʊɑ:k'teɪʃ(ə)n/ *noun* the process of narrowing

coat /kəʊt/ *noun* a layer of material covering an organ or a cavity ■ *verb* to cover something with something else

coated tongue /ˌkəʊtɪd 'tʌŋ/ *noun* same as **furred tongue**

cobalt /'kəʊbɔ:lt/ *noun* a metallic element (NOTE: The chemical symbol is **Co.**)

cocaine /kəʊ'keɪn/ *noun* a narcotic drug not generally used in medicine because its use leads to addiction, but sometimes used as a surface anaesthetic

cocci /'kɒki/ plural of **coccus**

coccus /'kɒkəs/ *noun* a bacterium shaped like a ball (NOTE: The plural is **cocci.**)

coccy- /kɒksi/ *prefix* referring to the coccyx

coccydynia /ˌkɒksi'dɪniə/ *noun* a sharp pain in the coccyx, usually caused by a blow. Also called **coccygodynia**

coccygeal vertebrae /kɒkˌsɪdʒiəl 'vɜ:tɪbreɪ/ *plural noun* the fused bones in the coccyx

coccyges /kɒk'saɪdʒi:z/ plural of **coccyx**

coccygodynia /ˌkɒksigəʊ'dɪniə/ *noun* same as **coccydynia**

coccyx /'kɒksɪks/ *noun* the lowest bone in the backbone (NOTE: The plural is **coccyges.**)

cochlea /'kɒkliə/ *noun* a spiral tube inside the inner ear, which is the essential organ of hearing. See illustration at **EAR** in Supplement (NOTE: The plural is **cochleae.**)

cochlear /'kɒkliə/ *adjective* referring to the cochlea

cochlear implant /ˌkɒkliə 'ɪmplɑ:nt/ *noun* a type of hearing aid for profound hearing loss

Cochrane database /ˌkɒkrən 'deɪtəbeɪs/ *noun* a database of regular reviews carried out on research

code /kəʊd/ *noun* **1.** a system of numbers, letters or symbols used to represent language or information **2.** same as **genetic code** ■ *verb* **1.** to convert instructions or data into another form **2.** (*of a codon or gene*) to provide the genetic information which causes a specific amino acid to be produced ○ *Genes are sections of DNA that code for a specific protein sequence.*

codeine /'kəʊdi:n/, **codeine phosphate** /ˌkəʊdi:n 'fɒsfeɪt/ *noun* a common painkilling drug that can also be used to suppress coughing and in the treatment of diarrhoea

code of conduct /ˌkəʊd əv 'kɒndʌkt/ *noun* a set of general rules showing how a group of people such as doctors or nurses should work

cod liver oil /ˌkɒd lɪvər 'ɔɪl/ *noun* a fish oil which is rich in calories and vitamins A and D

-coele /si:l/ *suffix* referring to a hollow (NOTE: The US spelling is usually **-cele.**)

coeli- /si:li/ *prefix* same as **coelio-** (*used before vowels*) (NOTE: The US spelling is usually **celi-.**)

coeliac /'si:liæk/ *adjective* referring to the abdomen

coeliac artery /ˌsi:liæk 'ɑ:təri/, **coeliac axis** /ˌsi:liæk 'æksɪs/ *noun* the main artery in the abdomen leading from the abdominal aorta and dividing into the left gastric, hepatic and splenic arteries. Also called **coeliac trunk**

coeliac disease /ˌsi:liæk dɪ'zi:z/ *noun* same as **gluten-induced enteropathy**

coeliac ganglion /ˌsiːliæk ˈgæŋgliən/ *noun* a ganglion on each side of the origins of the diaphragm, connected with the coeliac plexus

coeliac trunk /ˌsiːliæk ˈtrʌŋk/ *noun* same as **coeliac artery**

coelio- /siːliəʊ/ *prefix* referring to a hollow, usually the abdomen

coelioscopy /ˌsiːliˈɒskəpi/ *noun* an examination of the peritoneal cavity by inflating the abdomen with sterile air and passing an endoscope through the abdominal wall (NOTE: The plural is **coelioscopies**.)

coffee ground vomit /ˈkɒfi graʊnd ˌvɒmɪt/ *noun* vomit containing dark pieces of blood, indicating that the person is bleeding from the stomach or upper intestine

cognition /kɒgˈnɪʃ(ə)n/ *noun* the mental action or process of gaining knowledge by using your mind or your senses, or knowledge gained in this way

cognitive /ˈkɒgnɪtɪv/ *adjective* referring to the mental processes of perception, memory, judgment and reasoning ○ *a cognitive impairment*

cognitive disorder /ˌkɒgnɪtɪv dɪsˈɔːdə/ *noun* impairment of any of the mental processes of perception, memory, judgment and reasoning

cognitive therapy /ˌkɒgnɪtɪv ˈθerəpi/ *noun* a treatment of psychiatric disorders such as anxiety or depression which encourages people to deal with their negative ways of thinking

cohort /ˈkəʊhɔːt/ *noun* a group of people sharing a particular characteristic such as age or gender who are studied in a scientific or medical investigation

cohort study /ˈkəʊhɔːt ˌstʌdi/ *noun* an investigation in which a group of people are classified according to their exposure to various risks and studied over a period of time to see if they develop a specific disease, in order to evaluate the links between risk and disease

coil /kɔɪl/ *noun* a device fitted into a woman's uterus as a contraceptive

cold /kəʊld/ *adjective* not warm or hot ■ *noun* an illness, with inflammation of the nasal passages, in which someone sneezes and coughs and has a blocked and running nose ○ *She had a heavy cold.* Also called **common cold**, **coryza**

cold burn /ˈkəʊld bɜːn/ *noun* an injury to the skin caused by exposure to extreme cold or by touching a very cold surface

cold cautery /ˌkəʊld ˈkɔːtəri/ *noun* the removal of a skin growth using carbon dioxide snow

cold pack /ˈkəʊld pæk/ *noun* a cloth or a pad filled with gel or clay which is chilled and put on the body to reduce or increase the temperature

cold sore /ˈkəʊld sɔː/ *noun* a painful blister, usually on the lips or nose, caused by herpes simplex Type I

colectomy /kəˈlektəmi/ *noun* a surgical operation to remove the whole or part of the colon (NOTE: The plural is **colectomies**.)

colic /ˈkɒlɪk/ *noun* **1.** pain in any part of the intestinal tract. Also called **enteralgia**, **tormina 2.** crying and irritability in babies, especially from stomach pains

coliform bacterium /ˌkəʊlifɔːm bækˈtɪəriəm/ *plural noun* any bacterium which is similar to *Escherichia coli*

colistin /kɒˈlɪstɪn/ *noun* an antibiotic which is effective against a wide range of organisms and is used to treat gastrointestinal infections

colitis /kəˈlaɪtɪs/ *noun* inflammation of the colon. Also called **colonitis**

collaborative care /kəˌlæb(ə)rətɪv ˈkeə/ *noun* treatment that involves collaboration between different medical departments or agencies, or involves active medical collaboration between the patient and the providers of treatment

collagen /ˈkɒlədʒən/ *noun* a thick protein fibre forming bundles, which make up the connective tissue, bone and cartilage

collapse /kəˈlæps/ *noun* **1.** a condition in which someone is extremely exhausted or semi-conscious ○ *She was found in a state of collapse.* **2.** a condition in which an organ becomes flat or loses air ○ *lung collapse* ■ *verb* **1.** to fall down in a semi-conscious state ○ *After running to catch his train he collapsed.* **2.** to become flat, or lose air

collapsed lung /kəˌlæpst ˈlʌŋ/ *noun* same as **pneumothorax**

collarbone /ˈkɒləbəʊn/ *noun* one of two long thin bones which join the shoulder blades to the breastbone. Also called **clavicle** (NOTE: Collarbone fracture is one of the most frequent fractures in the body.)

collateral /kəˈlæt(ə)rəl/ *adjective* secondary or less important

Colles' fracture /ˈkɒlɪs(ɪz) ˌfræktʃə/ *noun* a fracture of the lower end of the radius with displacement of the wrist backwards, usually when someone has stretched out a hand to try to break a fall [After Abraham Colles (1773–1843), Irish surgeon.]

colliculus /kəˈlɪkjʊləs/ *noun* one of four small projections (**superior colliculi** and **inferior colliculi**) in the midbrain. See illustration at BRAIN in Supplement (NOTE: The plural is **colliculi**.)

collodion /kəˈləʊdiən/ *noun* a liquid used for painting on a clean wound, where it dries to form a flexible covering

colloid /ˈkɒlɔɪd/ *noun* **1.** a mass of tiny particles of one substance dispersed in another substance **2.** the particles which are suspended in a colloid solution **3.** a thick jelly-like substance which stores hormones, produced in the thyroid gland ■

adjective relating to or resembling a colloid ○ *colloid acne*

collyrium /kə'lɪriəm/ *noun* a solution used to bathe the eyes (NOTE: The plural is **collyria**.)

colo- /kɒləʊ/ *prefix* referring to the colon

coloboma /ˌkɒləʊ'bəʊmə/ *noun* a condition in which part of the eye, especially part of the iris, is missing

colon /'kəʊlɒn/ *noun* the main part of the large intestine, running from the caecum at the end of the small intestine to the rectum

colonic /kə'lɒnɪk/ *adjective* referring to the colon

colonic irrigation /kəˌlɒnɪk ɪrɪ'geɪʃ(ə)n/ *noun* the washing out of the contents of the large intestine using a tube inserted in the anus

colonoscope /kə'lɒnəskəʊp/ *noun* a surgical instrument for examining the interior of the colon

colonoscopy /ˌkɒlə'nɒskəpi/ *noun* an examination of the inside of the colon, using a colonoscope passed through the rectum (NOTE: The plural is **colonoscopies**.)

colony /'kɒləni/ *noun* a group or culture of microorganisms

colostomy /kə'lɒstəmi/ *noun* a surgical operation to make an opening between the colon and the abdominal wall to allow faeces to be passed out without going through the rectum (NOTE: The plural is **colostomies**.)

colostomy bag /kə'lɒstəmi bæg/ *noun* a bag attached to the opening made by a colostomy, to collect faeces as they are passed out of the body

colostrum /kə'lɒstrəm/ *noun* a fluid rich in antibodies and low in fat, secreted by the mother's breasts at the birth of a baby, before the true milk starts to flow

colour blindness /'kʌlə ˌblaɪndnəs/ *noun* a condition of being unable to tell the difference between specific colours

colour index /'kʌlər ˌɪndeks/ *noun* the ratio between the amount of haemoglobin and the number of red blood cells in a specific amount of blood

colp- /kɒlp/ *prefix* same as **colpo-** (*used before vowels*)

colpo- /kɒlpəʊ/ *prefix* referring to the vagina

colpocystitis /ˌkɒlpəʊsɪ'staɪtɪs/ *noun* inflammation of both the vagina and the urinary bladder

colpohysterectomy /ˌkɒlpəʊhɪstə'rektəmi/ *noun* a surgical operation in which the womb is removed through the vagina (NOTE: The plural is **colpohysterectomies**.)

colpopexy /'kɒlpəpeksi/ *noun* a surgical operation to fix a prolapsed vagina to the abdominal wall (NOTE: The plural is **colpopexies**.)

colpoplasty /'kɒlpəplæsti/ *noun* a surgical operation to repair a damaged vagina (NOTE: The plural is **colpoplasties**.)

colporrhaphy /kɒl'pɒrəfi/ *noun* a surgical operation to stitch a prolapsed vagina (NOTE: The plural is **colporraphies**.)

colposcope /'kɒlpəʊskəʊp/ *noun* a surgical instrument used to examine the inside of the vagina. Also called **vaginoscope**

colposcopy /kɒl'pɒskəpi/ *noun* an examination of the inside of the vagina (NOTE: The plural is **colposcopies**.)

colposuspension /ˌkɒlpəʊsə'spenʃən/ *noun* a surgical operation to strengthen the pelvic floor muscles to prevent incontinence

colpotomy /kɒl'pɒtəmi/ *noun* a surgical operation to make a cut in the vagina (NOTE: The plural is **colpotomies**.)

column /'kɒləm/ *noun* ♦ **vertebral column**

coma /'kəʊmə/ *noun* a state of unconsciousness from which a person cannot be awakened by external stimuli

comatose /'kəʊmətəʊs/ *adjective* unconscious or in a coma

combined therapy /kəmˌbaɪnd 'θerəpi/ *noun* the use of two or more treatments at the same time

comedo /'kɒmɪdəʊ/ *noun* a small point of dark, hard matter in a sebaceous follicle, often found associated with acne on the skin of adolescents (NOTE: The plural is **comedones**.)

comforter /'kʌmfətə/ *noun* **1.** someone who helps to make another person less anxious or unhappy **2.** a baby's dummy

commando operation /kə'mɑːndəʊ ˌɒpəreɪʃ(ə)n/, **commando procedure** /kə'mɑːndəʊ prəˌsiːdʒə/ *noun* a major operation to combat cancer of the face and neck. It involves the removal of facial features, which are later rebuilt.

commensal /kə'mensəl/ *noun* an animal or plant which lives on another animal or plant but does not harm it in any way. Both may benefit from the association. ○ *Candida is a commensal in the mouths of 50% of healthy adults.* (NOTE: If a commensal causes harm, it is a **parasite**.) ■ *adjective* living on another animal or plant

comminuted /'kɒmɪnjuːtɪd/ *adjective* referring to a fracture where the bone is broken in several places

comminuted fracture /ˌkɒmɪnjuːtɪd 'fræktʃə/ *noun* a fracture where the bone is broken in several places

Commission for Health Improvement /kəˌmɪʃ(ə)n fə 'helθ ɪmˌpruːvmənt/ in the UK, the independent inspection body for the National Health Service, with the role of helping to raise standards of patient care. It aims to identify where improvement is required and share good practice. Abbreviation **CHI**

commissure /'kɒmɪsjʊə/ *noun* a structure which joins two similar tissues, e.g. a group of nerves which crosses from one part of the central nervous system to another. ◊ **corpus callosum**, **grey commissure**

Committee on Safety of Medicines /kə ˌmɪti ɒn ˌseɪfti əv 'med(ə)sɪnz/ *noun* the official body which advises the British Government on the safety and quality of medicines

commode /kə'məʊd/ *noun* a special chair with a removable basin used as a toilet by people with limited mobility

common bile duct /ˌkɒmən 'baɪl dʌkt/ *noun* a duct leading to the duodenum, formed of the hepatic and cystic ducts

common carotid artery /ˌkɒmən kə'rɒtɪd ˌɑːtəri/ *noun* the main artery running up each side of the lower part of the neck. Also called **carotid**

common cold /ˌkɒmən 'kəʊld/ *noun* same as **cold**

common hepatic duct /ˌkɒmən hɪ'pætɪk dʌkt/ *noun* a duct from the liver formed when the right and left hepatic ducts join

common iliac artery /ˌkɒmən 'ɪliæk ˌɑːtəri/ *noun* one of two arteries which branch from the aorta in the abdomen and in turn divide into the internal iliac artery, leading to the pelvis, and the external iliac artery, leading to the leg

communicable disease /kəˌmjuːnɪkəb(ə)l dɪ'ziːz/ *noun* a disease which can be passed from one person to another or from an animal to a person. ◊ **contagious disease**, **infectious disease**

communicating artery /kə'mjuːnɪkeɪtɪŋ ˌɑːtəri/ *noun* one of the arteries which connect the blood supply from each side of the brain, forming part of the circle of Willis

community /kə'mjuːnɪti/ *noun* a group of people who live and work in a district ○ *The health services serve the local community.*

community care /kəˌmjuːnɪti 'keə/ *noun* the providing of help to people such as those who are elderly or mentally ill in order to allow them to stay in their own homes, rather than requiring them to be cared for in hospitals or care homes

community health /kəˌmjuːnɪti 'helθ/ *noun* the health of a local community, or provision of services for a local community

community health council /kəˌmjuːnɪti 'helθ ˌkaʊnsəl/ *noun* a statutory body of interested people from outside the medical professions charged with putting forward the patients' point of view on local health issues. Abbreviation **CHC**

community hospital /kə'mjuːnɪti ˌhɒspɪt(ə)l/ *noun* a hospital serving a local community

community midwife /kəˌmjuːnɪti 'mɪdwaɪf/ *noun* a midwife who works in a community as part of a primary health care team

community nurse /kəˌmjuːnɪti 'nɜːs/ *noun* a nurse who treats people in a local community

community paediatrician /kəˌmjuːnɪti piːdiə'trɪʃ(ə)n/ *noun* a paediatrician serving a local community

community pharmacist /kəˌmjuːnɪti 'fɑːməsɪst/, **retail pharmacist** /ˌriːteɪl 'fɑːməsɪst/ *noun* a person who makes medicines and sells them in a chemist's shop

community psychiatric nurse /kəˌmjuːnɪti ˌsaɪki'ætrɪk/ *noun*. Also called **community mental health nurse**. Abbreviation **CPN**

community trust /kəˌmjuːnɪti 'trʌst/ *noun* an independent non-profit-making body set up to represent an area of public concern

compact bone /ˌkɒmpækt 'bəʊn/ *noun* a type of bone tissue which forms the hard outer layer of a bone. See illustration at **BONE STRUCTURE** in Supplement

compartment /kəm'pɑːtmənt/ *noun* one of the areas into which an enclosed space is divided

compatibility /kəmˌpætɪ'bɪlɪti/ *noun* the ability of two drugs not to interfere with each other when administered together

compatible /kəm'pætɪb(ə)l/ *adjective* able to function together without being rejected ○ *The surgeons are trying to find a compatible donor* or *a donor with a compatible blood group.*

compensate /'kɒmpənseɪt/ *verb* **1.** to give someone an amount of money or something else to pay for loss or damage **2.** (*of an organ*) to make good the failure of an organ by making another organ, or the undamaged parts of the same organ, function at a higher level ○ *The heart has to beat more strongly to compensate for the narrowing of the arteries.* **3.** to emphasise a particular ability or personality characteristic in order to make the lack of another one seem less bad

compensation /ˌkɒmpən'seɪʃ(ə)n/ *noun* **1.** something which makes something else seem less bad or less serious **2.** an amount of money or something else given to pay for loss or damage ○ *The drugs caused him to develop breathing problems, so he thinks he's entitled to medical compensation.* **3.** the act of giving money to pay for loss or damage ○ *compensation for loss of a limb* **4.** a situation where the body helps to correct a problem in a particular organ by making another organ, or the undamaged parts of the same organ, function at a higher level **5.** behaviour that emphasises a particular ability or personality characteristic in order to make the lack of another one seem less bad

competence /'kɒmpɪt(ə)ns/ *noun* the ability to do something well, measured against a standard, especially ability which you get through experience or training ○ *encouraging the development of professional competence in the delivery of care to patients*

competency /'kɒmpɪt(ə)nsi/ *noun* a guideline, usually one of several, for the medical treatment that is to be given in particular circumstances

complaint /kəm'pleɪnt/ noun 1. an expression of dissatisfaction about something or someone ○ *The hospital administrator wouldn't listen to the complaints of the consultants.* 2. an illness ○ *a chest complaint* ○ *a nervous complaint*

complement noun /'kɒmplɪmənt/ a substance which forms part of blood plasma and is essential to the work of antibodies and antigens ■ *verb* /'kɒmplɪment/ to complete something by providing useful or pleasing qualities which it does not itself have

complementary /ˌkɒmplɪ'ment(ə)ri/ *adjective* 1. combining with or adding to something else ○ *Ultrasound and CT provide complementary information.* 2. used in or using complementary medicine ○ *complementary therapies* 3. referring to genes which are necessary to each other and produce their effect only when they are present together

complementary   medicine /ˌkɒmplɪment(ə)ri 'med(ə)sɪn/ noun the forms of alternative medicine which are now accepted by practitioners of conventional Western medicine, e.g. acupuncture and osteopathy

complete abortion /kəmˌpliːt ə'bɔːʃ(ə)n/ noun an abortion where the whole contents of the uterus are expelled

complete blood count /kəmˌpliːt 'blʌd kaʊnt/ noun a test to find the exact numbers of each type of blood cell in a sample of blood. Abbreviation **CBC**

complicated fracture /ˌkɒmplɪkeɪtɪd 'fræktʃə/ noun a fracture with an associated injury of tissue, as when a bone has punctured an artery

complication /ˌkɒmplɪ'keɪʃ(ə)n/ noun 1. a condition in which two or more conditions exist in someone, whether or not they are connected ○ *He was admitted to hospital suffering from pneumonia with complications.* 2. a situation in which someone develops a second condition which changes the course of treatment for the first ○ *She appeared to be improving, but complications set in and she died in a few hours.*

compos mentis /ˌkɒmpɒs 'mentɪs/ *adjective* not affected by a mental disorder (NOTE: The phrase is from Latin and means 'of sound mind'.)

compound fracture /ˌkɒmpaʊnd 'fræktʃə/ noun a fracture where the skin surface is damaged or where the broken bone penetrates the surface of the skin. Also called **open fracture**

compress noun /'kɒmpres/ a wad of cloth soaked in hot or cold liquid and applied to the skin to relieve pain or swelling, or to force pus out of an infected wound ■ *verb* /kəm'pres/ to squeeze or press something

compressed air sickness /kəmˌprest 'eə ˌsɪknəs/ noun same as **caisson disease**

compression /kəm'preʃ(ə)n/ noun 1. the act of squeezing or pressing ○ *The first-aider applied compression to the chest of the casualty.* 2. a serious condition in which the brain is compressed by blood or cerebrospinal fluid accumulating in it or by a fractured skull

compression stocking /kəmˌpreʃ(ə)n 'stɒkɪŋ/ noun a strong elastic stocking worn to support a weak joint in the knee or to hold varicose veins tightly

compulsion /kəm'pʌlʃ(ə)n/ noun 1. an act of forcing someone to do something, or the fact of being forced to do something ○ *You are under no compulsion to treat a violent patient.* 2. a strong psychological force which makes someone do something, often unwillingly ○ *She felt a sudden compulsion to wash her hands again.*

compulsive /kəm'pʌlsɪv/ *adjective* referring to a feeling which cannot be stopped ○ *She has a compulsive desire to steal.*

compulsive–obsessive disorder /kəm ˌpʌlsɪv əb'sesɪv dɪsˌɔːdə/ noun same as **obsessive–compulsive disorder**

compulsory admission /kəmˌpʌlsəri əd 'mɪʃ(ə)n/ noun the process of admitting someone who is mentally ill to hospital for treatment whether or not they consent

computed tomography /kəmˌpjuːtɪd tə 'mɒɡrəfi/ noun same as **computerised axial tomography**. Abbreviation **CT**

computerised axial tomography /kəm ˌpjuːtəraɪzd ˌæksiəl tə'mɒɡrəfi/ noun a system of examining the body in which a narrow X-ray beam, guided by a computer, photographs a thin section of the body or of an organ from several angles, using the computer to build up an image of the section. Abbreviation **CAT**. Also called **computed tomography**

-conazole /kɒnəzəʊl/ *suffix* used in the names of antifungal drugs ○ *fluconazole*

concave /'kɒnkeɪv/ *adjective* curving towards the inside ○ *a concave lens*

concept /'kɒnsept/ noun a thought or idea, or something which someone might be able to imagine

conception /kən'sepʃən/ noun the point at which a woman becomes pregnant and the development of a baby starts

conceptual framework /kənˌseptʃuəl 'freɪmwɜːk/ noun the theoretical basis on which something is formed

conceptus /kən'septəs/ noun an embryo or fetus together with all the tissues that surround it during pregnancy (NOTE: The plural is **conceptuses**.)

concha /'kɒŋkə/ noun a part of the body shaped like a shell (NOTE: The plural is **conchae**.)

concordance /kən'kɔːd(ə)ns/ noun 1. a state in which two or more things are in the correct or expected relationship to each other. For example, the atrioventricular concordance is the relationship between the atria and the ventricles in the heart. **2.** the fact of two related people sharing the same genetic characteristic ○ *the concordance of schizophrenia in identical twins* **3.** an agreement between a professional and a patient on a course of treatment, especially related to use of medicines

concretion /kən'kriːʃ(ə)n/ *noun* a mass of hard material which forms in the body, e.g. a gallstone or deposits on bone in arthritis

concussion /kən'kʌʃ(ə)n/ *noun* **1.** the act of applying force to any part of the body **2.** loss of consciousness for a short period, caused by a blow to the head

condition /kən'dɪʃ(ə)n/ *noun* **1.** the particular state of someone or something ○ *in poor condition* ○ *Her condition is getting worse.* ○ *The conditions in the hospital are very good.* **2.** a particular illness, injury or disorder ○ *He is being treated for a heart condition.*

conditioned reflex /kən,dɪʃ(ə)nd 'riːfleks/ *noun* an automatic reaction by a person to a stimulus, or an expected reaction to a stimulus which comes from past experience

conditioned response /kən,dɪʃ(ə)nd rɪ'spɒns/ *noun* a response to a stimulus as a result of associating it with an earlier stimulus

COMMENT: The classic example of a conditioned response is Pavlov's experiment with dogs in which they produced saliva, ready to eat their food, when a bell rang, because on previous occasions they had been fed when the bell was rung.

condom /'kɒndɒm/ *noun* a rubber sheath worn on the penis during intercourse as a contraceptive and also as a protection against sexually transmitted disease

conducting system /kən'dʌktɪŋ ,sɪstəm/ *noun* the nerve system in the heart which links an atrium to a ventricle, so that the two beat at the same rate

conduction /kən'dʌkʃən/ *noun* the process of passing heat, sound or nervous impulses from one part of the body to another

conductive deafness /kən,dʌktɪv 'defnəs/, **conductive hearing loss** /kən,dʌktɪv 'hɪərɪŋ ,lɒs/ *noun* deafness caused by inadequate conduction of sound into the inner ear

conductor /kən'dʌktə/ *noun* **1.** a substance or object which allows heat, electricity, light or sound to pass along it or through it **2.** a tube with a groove in it along which a knife is slid to cut open a sinus

condyle /'kɒndaɪl/ *noun* a rounded end of a bone which articulates with another

condyloid process /'kɒndɪlɔɪd ,prəʊses/ *noun* a projecting part at each end of the lower jaw which forms the head of the jaw, joining the jaw to the skull

condyloma /,kɒndɪ'ləʊmə/ *noun* a growth usually found on the vulva (NOTE: The plural is **condylomas** or **condylomata**.)

cone /kəʊn/ *noun* **1.** a shape with a circular base or top and a part that tapers to a point, or an object with this shape **2.** one of two types of cell in the retina of the eye which is sensitive to light, used especially in the perception of bright light and colour. ◊ **rod** ■ *verb* to show a rapid change for the worse in neurological condition due to herniation of the midbrain through the foramen magnum in the skull, caused by raised pressure inside the brain (NOTE: **cones – coning – coned**)

cone biopsy /'kəʊn baɪ,ɒpsi/ *noun* the removing of a cone of tissue from the cervix for examination

confabulation /kən,fæbjʊ'leɪʃ(ə)n/ *noun* the act of making up plausible stories to cover up loss of memory

confidentiality /,kɒnfɪdenʃi'ælɪti/ *noun* an obligation not to reveal professional information about a person or organisation

confounding factor /kən'faʊndɪŋ ,fæktə/ *noun* a factor which has an association with both a disease and a risk factor and thus complicates the nature of the relationship between them

confused /kən'fjuːzd/ *adjective* unable to think clearly or act rationally ○ *Many severely confused patients do not respond to spoken communication.*

confusion /kən'fjuːʒ(ə)n/ *noun* the state of being confused

congenital /kən'dʒenɪt(ə)l/ *adjective* existing at or before birth

congenital aneurysm /kən,dʒenɪt(ə)l 'ænjərɪz(ə)m/ *noun* a weakening of the arteries at the base of the brain, present at birth

congenital cataract /kən,dʒenɪt(ə)l 'kætərækt/ *noun* a cataract which is present at birth

congenital dislocation of the hip /kən,dʒenɪt(ə)l dɪslə,keɪʃ(ə)n əv ðə 'hɪp/ *noun* a condition in which a person is born with weak ligaments in the hip, so that the femur does not stay in position in the pelvis

congenital heart disease /kən,dʒenɪt(ə)l 'hɑːt dɪ,ziːz/, **congenital heart defect** /kən,dʒenɪt(ə)l 'hɑːt ,diːfekt/ *noun* a heart condition existing at birth

congenital hyperthyroidism /kən,dʒenɪt(ə)l ,haɪpə'θaɪrɔɪdɪz(ə)m/ *noun* a disease caused by a malfunction of the thyroid before birth or in early life

congenital malformation /kən,dʒenɪt(ə)l ,mælfɔː'meɪʃ(ə)n/ *noun* a malformation which is present at birth, e.g. a cleft palate

congenital syphilis /kən͵dʒenɪt(ə)l ˈsɪfɪlɪs/ *noun* syphilis which is passed on from a mother to her unborn child

congenital toxoplasmosis /kən͵dʒenɪt(ə)l ͵tɒksəʊplæzˈməʊsɪs/ *noun* a condition in which a baby has been infected with toxoplasmosis by its mother while still in the uterus

congestion /kənˈdʒestʃən/ *noun* an accumulation of blood in an organ. ◊ **nasal congestion**

congestive /kənˈdʒestɪv/ *adjective* referring to congestion

conisation /͵kɒnaɪˈzeɪʃ(ə)n/, **conization** *noun* the surgical removal of a cone-shaped piece of tissue

conjoined twins /kən͵dʒɔɪnd ˈtwɪnz/ *plural noun* twins who are joined together at birth. Also called **Siamese twins**

COMMENT: Conjoined twins are always identical and can be joined at the head, chest or hip. In some cases they can be separated by surgery, but this is not possible if they share a single important organ such as the heart.

conjugate /ˈkɒndʒʊɡeɪt/, **conjugate diameter** /͵kɒndʒʊɡət daɪˈæmɪtə/ *noun* a measurement of space in a woman's pelvis, used to calculate if it is large enough for a child to be delivered

conjunctiva /͵kɒndʒʌŋkˈtaɪvə/ *noun* a membrane which covers the front of the eyeball and the inside of the eyelids. See illustration at **EYE** in Supplement (NOTE: The plural is **conjunctivas** or **conjunctivae**.)

conjunctival /͵kɒndʒʌŋkˈtaɪv(ə)l/ *adjective* referring to the conjunctiva

conjunctivitis /kən͵dʒʌŋktɪˈvaɪtɪs/ *noun* inflammation of the conjunctiva from a range of causes

connective tissue /kə͵nektɪv ˈtɪʃuː/ *noun* tissue which forms the main part of bones and cartilage, ligaments and tendons, in which a large proportion of fibrous material surrounds the tissue cells

Conn's syndrome /ˈkɒnz ͵sɪndrəʊm/ *noun* a condition in which excessive production of the hormone aldosterone causes fluid retention and high blood pressure

consanguinity /͵kɒnsæŋˈgwɪnɪti/ *noun* a blood relationship between people

conscious /ˈkɒnʃəs/ *adjective* 1. awake and aware of what is happening ○ *He became conscious in the recovery room two hours after the operation.* 2. deliberate and intended ○ *a conscious choice*

-conscious /ˈkɒnʃəs/ *suffix* giving importance to ○ *health-conscious* ○ *safety-conscious*

consciousness /ˈkɒnʃəsnəs/ *noun* the state of being mentally alert and knowing what is happening

consensus management /kənˈsensəs ͵mænɪdʒmənt/ *noun* a form of management which aims to get everyone to agree on what actions should be taken

consent /kənˈsent/ *noun* agreement to allow someone to do something ○ *The parents gave their consent for their son's heart to be used in the transplant operation.*

consent form /kənˈsent fɔːm/ *noun* a form which a patient signs to show that he or she agrees to have a particular operation

conservative treatment /kən͵sɜːvətɪv ˈtriːtmənt/ *noun* medical or surgical treatment which is limited to conventional measures rather than more extreme or risky procedures ○ *Symptoms usually resolve with conservative treatment.*

consolidation /kən͵sɒlɪˈdeɪʃ(ə)n/ *noun* a stage in mending a broken bone in which the callus formed at the break changes into bone

constipation /͵kɒnstɪˈpeɪʃ(ə)n/ *noun* difficulty in passing faeces

constrictive pericarditis /kən͵strɪktɪv ͵perɪkɑːˈdaɪtɪs/ *noun* same as **chronic pericarditis**

constrictor /kənˈstrɪktə/ *noun* a muscle which squeezes an organ or which makes an organ contract

consultant /kənˈsʌltənt/ *noun* 1. a doctor who is a senior specialist in a particular branch of medicine and who is consulted by GPs ○ *She was referred to a consultant at the orthopaedic hospital.* 2. a senior specialised doctor in a hospital

consumption /kənˈsʌmpʃ(ə)n/ *noun* 1. the act of taking food or liquid into the body ○ *the patient's increased consumption of alcohol* 2. a former name for pulmonary tuberculosis

contact dermatitis /͵kɒntækt ͵dɜːməˈtaɪtɪs/ *noun* inflammation of the skin caused by touch, e.g. by touching some types of plant, soap or chemical. Also called **irritant dermatitis**

contact lens /ˈkɒntækt lenz/ *noun* a tiny plastic lens which fits over the eyeball and is worn instead of spectacles to improve eyesight

contact tracing /ˈkɒntækt ͵treɪsɪŋ/ *noun* the process of tracing people with whom someone with an infectious disease has been in contact

contagious /kənˈteɪdʒəs/ *adjective* able to be transmitted by touching an infected person or objects which an infected person has touched

contagious disease /kən͵teɪdʒəs dɪˈziːz/ *noun* a disease which can be transmitted by touching an infected person or objects which an infected person has touched. ◊ **communicable disease, infectious disease**

containment /kənˈteɪnmənt/ *noun* 1. action taken to restrict the spread of something undesirable or dangerous such as a disease ○ *government policy of containment of the SARS virus* 2. the eradication of a global disease such as smallpox by removing it region by region

contaminate /kən'tæmɪneɪt/ *verb* **1.** to make something impure by touching it or by adding something to it ○ *Supplies of drinking water were contaminated by refuse from the factories.* ○ *The whole group of tourists fell ill after eating contaminated food.* **2.** to spread infection to someone or something

continence /'kɒntɪnəns/ *noun* **1.** the ability to control the discharge of urine and faeces **2.** self-restraint

continent /'kɒntɪnənt/ *adjective* able to exercise control over the discharge of urine and faeces

continuing education /kən,tɪnjuɪŋ ,edjʊ 'keɪʃ(ə)n/ *noun* regular courses or training designed to bring professional people up to date with the latest developments in their particular field

continuous ambulatory peritoneal dialysis /kən,tɪnjuəs ,æmbjʊlət(ə)ri perɪtə,niːəl daɪ'æləsɪs/ *noun* a method of dialysis of people while they are walking about. Abbreviation **CAPD**

continuous positive airways pressure /kən,tɪnjuəs ,pɒzɪtɪv 'eəweɪz ,preʃə/ *noun* a method used in intensive care which forces air into the lungs of someone with lung collapse. Abbreviation **CPAP**

contra- /kɒntrə/ *prefix* against, opposite, contrasting

contraception /,kɒntrə'sepʃən/ *noun* the prevention of pregnancy, e.g. by using devices such as a condom or an IUD, or drugs in the form of contraceptive pills or injections at regular intervals. Also called **birth control**

contraceptive /,kɒntrə'septɪv/ *adjective* preventing conception ○ *a contraceptive device* or *drug* ■ *noun* a drug or device which prevents pregnancy

contraceptive sheath /,kɒntrə'septɪv ʃiːθ/ *noun* same as **condom**

contraceptive sponge /,kɒntrə'septɪv spʌndʒ/ *noun* a piece of synthetic sponge impregnated with spermicide, which is inserted into the vagina before intercourse

contractibility /'kɒntræktɪbɪlɪti/ *noun* the capacity to contract

contraction /kən'trækʃən/ *noun* **1.** the act of making something smaller or of becoming smaller ○ *the contraction of dental services* **2.** a tightening movement which makes a muscle shorter, which makes the pupil of the eye smaller or which makes the skin wrinkle

contracture /kən'træktʃə/ *noun* a permanent tightening of a muscle caused by fibrosis

contraindication /,kɒntrəɪndɪ'keɪʃ(ə)n/ *noun* something which suggests that someone should not be treated with a specific drug or not continue with a specific treatment because circumstances make that treatment unsuitable

contralateral /,kɒntrə'lætərəl/ *adjective* located on or affecting the opposite side of the body. Opposite **ipsilateral**

contrast medium /'kɒntrɑːst ,miːdiəm/ *noun* a radio-opaque dye, or sometimes gas, put into an organ or part of the body so that it will show clearly in an X-ray photograph ○ *In an MRI scan no contrast medium is required; in a CAT scan iodine-based contrast media are often required.*

contrecoup /'kɒntrəkuː/ *noun* an injury to one point of an organ such as the brain, caused by a blow received on an opposite point of the organ

control /kən'trəʊl/ *verb* **1.** to have the ability or authority to direct someone or something ○ *Sometimes we need help to control people who think they have waited too long.* **2.** to limit or restrain something ○ *administered drugs to control the pain* ■ *noun* **1.** the ability or authority to control something ○ *After her stroke she had no control over her left arm.* ○ *The administrators are in control of the admissions policy.* **2.** a person or group whose test data are used as a comparison in a study **3.** a comparison in a study

controlled drug /kən,trəʊld 'drʌg/ *noun* a drug which is not freely available, which is restricted by law and classified as A, B, or C and of which possession may be an offence. Also called **controlled substance**

controlled substance /kən,trəʊld 'sʌbstəns/ *noun* same as **controlled drug**

controlled trial /kən,trəʊld 'traɪəl/ *noun* a trial in which members of one group are treated with a test substance and those of another group are treated with a placebo as a control

controls assurance /kən'trəʊlz ə,ʃʊərəns/ *noun* a process designed to provide evidence that NHS organisations are doing their best to manage themselves both in order to meet their objectives and to protect patients, staff and the public against risks of all kinds

contused wound /kən,tjuːzd 'wuːnd/ *noun* a wound caused by a blow where the skin is bruised as well as torn and bleeding

contusion /kən'tjuːʒ(ə)n/ *noun* same as **bruise**

convalescence /,kɒnvə'les(ə)ns/ *noun* a period of time when someone is convalescing

convergent strabismus /kən,vɜːdʒənt strə 'bɪzməs/, **convergent squint** /kən,vɜːdʒənt 'skwɪnt/ *noun* a condition in which one or both of a person's eyes look towards the nose. Also called **cross eye**

conversion /kən'vɜːʃ(ə)n/ *noun* the process of changing one thing into another ○ *the conversion of nutrients into tissue*

convex /'kɒnveks/ *adjective* curving towards the outside ○ *a convex lens*

convoluted /ˈkɒnvəluːtɪd/ *adjective* folded and twisted

convolution /ˌkɒnvəˈluːʃ(ə)n/ *noun* a twisted shape ○ *the convolutions of the surface of the cerebrum*

convulsion /kənˈvʌlʃən/ *noun* the rapid involuntary contracting and relaxing of the muscles in several parts of the body ○ *The child had convulsions.* ◊ **fit** (NOTE: Often used in the plural.)

Cooley's anaemia /ˈkuːliz əˌniːmiə/ *noun* same as **thalassaemia** [Described 1927. After Thomas Benton Cooley (1871–1945), Professor of Paediatrics at Wayne College of Medicine, Detroit, USA.]

Coombs' test /ˈkuːmz test/ *noun* a test for antibodies in red blood cells, used as a test for erythroblastosis fetalis and other haemolytic syndromes [Described 1945. After Robin Royston Amos Coombs (1921–2006), Quick Professor of Biology, and Fellow of Corpus Christi College, Cambridge, UK]

coordination /kəʊˌɔːdɪˈneɪʃ(ə)n/ *noun* **1.** the combining of two or more things as an effective unit, or the way things combine effectively ○ *requires coordination between nursing staff and doctors* **2.** the ability to use two or more parts of the body at the same time to carry out a movement or task ○ *The patient showed lack of coordination between eyes and hands.*

COPD *abbreviation* chronic obstructive pulmonary disease

coping mechanism /ˈkəʊpɪŋ ˌmekənɪz(ə)m/ *noun* a method of dealing with situations which cause psychological stress

copper /ˈkɒpə/ *noun* a metallic trace element (NOTE: The chemical symbol is **Cu**.)

copr- /kɒpr/ *prefix* faeces

coprolith /ˈkɒprəlɪθ/ *noun* a lump of hard faeces in the bowel

cor /kɔː/ *noun* the heart

coraco-acromial /ˌkɒrəkəʊ əˈkrəʊmiəl/ *adjective* referring to the coracoid process and the acromion

coracoid process /ˈkɒrəkɔɪd ˌprəʊses/ *noun* a projecting part on the shoulder blade

cord /kɔːd/ *noun* a long flexible structure in the body like a thread

cordectomy /kɔːˈdektəmi/ *noun* a surgical operation to remove a vocal cord (NOTE: The plural is **cordectomies**.)

cordotomy /kɔːˈdɒtəmi/ *noun* another spelling of **chordotomy**

corium /ˈkɔːriəm/ *noun* same as **dermis**

corn /kɔːn/ *noun* a hard painful lump of skin usually on a foot, where something such as a tight shoe has rubbed or pressed on the skin. Also called **heloma**

cornea /ˈkɔːniə/ *noun* a transparent part of the front of the eyeball. See illustration at EYE in Supplement (NOTE: The plural is **corneae**. For other terms referring to the cornea, see words beginning with **kerat-, kerato-**.)

corneal /ˈkɔːniəl/ *adjective* relating to a cornea

corneal graft /ˌkɔːniəl ˈɡrɑːft/ *noun* **1.** a surgical operation to graft corneal tissue from a donor or from a dead person to replace diseased tissue. Also called **corneal transplant**, **keratoplasty** **2.** a piece of corneal tissue used in a graft

corneal reflex /ˌkɔːniəl ˈriːfleks/ *noun* a reflex from touching or hitting the cornea which makes the eyelid close

corneal transplant /ˈkɔːniəl ˌtrænsplɑːnt/ *noun* same as **corneal graft**

cornification /ˌkɔːnɪfɪˈkeɪʃ(ə)n/ *noun* same as **keratinisation**

cornu /ˈkɔːnjuː/ *noun* a structure in the body which is shaped like a horn

corona /kəˈrəʊnə/ *noun* a structure in the body which is shaped like a crown

coronal /ˈkɒrən(ə)l, kəˈrəʊn(ə)l/ *adjective* referring to a corona

coronal plane /ˌkɒrən(ə)l ˈpleɪn/ *noun* a plane at right angles to the median plane, dividing the body into dorsal and ventral halves. See illustration at ANATOMICAL TERMS in Supplement

coronal suture /ˌkɒrən(ə)l ˈsuːtʃə/ *noun* a horizontal joint across the top of the skull between the parietal and frontal bones

coronary /ˈkɒrən(ə)ri/ *noun* same as **coronary thrombosis** (*informal*) ■ *adjective* referring to any structure shaped like a crown, but especially to the arteries which supply blood to the heart muscles

coronary artery /ˈkɒrən(ə)ri ˌɑːtəri/ *noun* one of the two arteries which supply blood to the heart muscles

coronary artery bypass graft /ˌkɒrən(ə)ri ˌɑːtəri ˈbaɪpɑːs ɡrɑːft/, **coronary artery bypass** /ˌkɒrən(ə)ri ˌɑːtəri ˈbaɪpɑːs/ *noun* a surgical operation to treat angina by grafting pieces of vein around the diseased part of a coronary artery

coronary care unit /ˌkɒrən(ə)ri ˈkeə ˌjuːnɪt/ *noun* the section of a hospital caring for people who have heart disorders or who have had heart surgery. Abbreviation **CCU**

coronary heart disease /ˌkɒrən(ə)ri ˈhɑːt dɪˌziːz/ *noun* any disease affecting the coronary arteries, which can lead to strain on the heart or a heart attack. Abbreviation **CHD**

coronary sinus /ˌkɒrən(ə)ri ˈsaɪnəs/ *noun* a vein which takes most of the venous blood from the heart muscles to the right atrium

coronary thrombosis /ˌkɒrən(ə)ri θrɒm ˈbəʊsɪs/ *noun* a blood clot which blocks the coronary arteries, leading to a heart attack. Also called **coronary**

coronavirus /kə'rəunə,vaɪrəs/ *noun* a type of virus which has been identified in people who have the common cold

coroner /'kɒrənə/ *noun* a public official, either a doctor or a lawyer, who investigates sudden or violent deaths

coronoid process /'kɒrənɔɪd ,prəuses/ *noun* a projecting piece of bone on the ulna

corpora plural of **corpus**

corpse /kɔːps/ *noun* the body of a dead person

corpus /'kɔːpəs/ *noun* any mass of tissue (NOTE: The plural is **corpora**.)

corpus callosum /,kɔːpəs kə'ləusəm/ *noun* the thick band of nerve fibres that connects the two hemispheres of the brain and allows them to communicate. See illustration at **BRAIN** in Supplement (NOTE: The plural is **corpora callosa**.)

corpus cavernosum /,kɔːpəs ,kævə'nəusəm/ *noun* a part of the erectile tissue in the penis and clitoris. See illustration at **UROGENITAL SYSTEM (MALE)** in Supplement (NOTE: The plural is **corpora cavernosa**.)

corpuscle /'kɔːpʌs(ə)l/ *noun* **1.** a small round mass **2.** a cell in blood or lymph

corpus luteum /,kɔːpəs 'luːtiəm/ *noun* a body which forms in each ovary after a Graafian follicle has ruptured. The corpus luteum secretes the hormone progesterone to prepare the uterus for implantation of the fertilised ovum. (NOTE: The plural is **corpora lutea**.)

corpus spongiosum /,kɔːpəs ,spʌnʒɪ'əusəm/ *noun* the part of the penis round the urethra, forming the glans. See illustration at **UROGENITAL SYSTEM (MALE)** in Supplement (NOTE: The plural is **corpora spongiosa**.)

corrective /kə'rektɪv/ *adjective* intended to correct an irregularity or problem ○ *corrective lenses* ■ *noun* a drug which changes the harmful effect of another drug

Corrigan's pulse /,kɒrɪgənz 'pʌls/ *noun* a condition occurring in the arterial pulse in the neck in which there is a visible rise in pressure followed by a sudden collapse, caused by aortic regurgitation. Also called **water-hammer pulse**

corrugator muscle /'kɒrəgeɪtə ,mʌs(ə)l/ *noun* one of the muscles which produce vertical wrinkles on the forehead when someone frowns

cortex /'kɔːteks/ *noun* the outer layer of an organ, as opposed to the soft inner medulla (NOTE: The plural is **cortices** or **cortexes**.)

Corti /'kɔːti/ ♦ **organ of Corti**

cortical mastoidectomy /,kɔːtɪk(ə)l ,mæstɔɪ'dektəmi/ *noun* same as **atticotomy**

cortices plural of **cortex**

corticospinal /,kɔːtɪkəu'spaɪn(ə)l/ *adjective* referring to both the cerebral cortex and the spinal cord

corticosteroid /,kɔːtɪkəu'stɪərɔɪd/ *noun* **1.** any steroid hormone produced by the cortex of the adrenal glands **2.** a drug which reduces inflammation, used in asthma, gastro-intestinal disease and in adrenocortical insufficiency

corticotrophin /,kɔːtɪkəu'trəufɪn/ *noun* same as **adrenocorticotrophic hormone**

cortisol /'kɔːtɪsɒl/ *noun* same as **hydrocortisone**

cortisone /'kɔːtɪzəun/ *noun* a hormone secreted in small quantities by the adrenal cortex ○ *The doctor gave her a cortisone injection in the ankle.*

Corynebacterium /kəu,raɪnibæk'tɪəriəm/ *noun* a genus of bacteria which includes the bacterium which causes diphtheria

coryza /kə'raɪzə/ *noun* an illness, with inflammation of the nasal passages, in which someone sneezes and coughs and has a blocked and running nose (*technical*) Also called **cold**, **common cold**

cosmetic surgery /kɒz,metɪk 'sɜːdʒəri/ *noun* a surgical operation to improve a person's appearance

cost- /kɒst/ *prefix* same as **costo-** (*used before vowels*)

costal /'kɒst(ə)l/ *adjective* referring to the ribs

costive /'kɒstɪv/ *noun* a drug which causes constipation

costo- /kɒstəu/ *prefix* referring to the ribs

cot death /'kɒt deθ/ *noun* ♦ **sudden infant death syndrome**

co-trimoxazole /,kəu traɪ'mɒksəzəul/ *noun* a drug used to combat bacteria in the urinary tract

cotyledon /,kɒtɪ'liːd(ə)n/ *noun* one of the divisions of a placenta

cotyloid cavity /'kɒtɪlɔɪd ,kævɪti/ *noun* same as **acetabulum**

couching /'kautʃɪŋ/ *noun* a surgical operation to displace the opaque lens of an eye as a treatment for cataracts

cough /kɒf/ *noun* a reflex action, caused by irritation in the throat, when the glottis is opened and air is sent out of the lungs suddenly ■ an infection that causes coughing ○ *She has a bad cough and cannot make the speech.* ■ *verb* to send air out of the lungs suddenly because the throat is irritated ○ *The smoke made him cough.* ○ *She has a cold and keeps on coughing and sneezing.*

cough medicine /'kɒf ,med(ə)sɪn/, **cough linctus** /'kɒf ,lɪŋktəs/, **cough mixture** /'kɒf ,mɪkstʃə/ *noun* a liquid taken to soothe the irritation which causes a cough

counselling /'kaunsəlɪŋ/ *noun* a method of treating especially psychiatric disorders in which a specialist talks with a person about his or her condition and how to deal with it

counterextension /ˌkaʊntərɪk'stenʃən/ *noun* an orthopaedic treatment in which the upper part of a limb is kept fixed and traction is applied to the lower part of it

counterirritant /ˌkaʊntər'ɪrɪt(ə)nt/ *noun* a substance which alleviates the pain in an internal organ by irritating an area of skin whose sensory nerves are close to those of the organ in the spinal cord

coupling /'kʌplɪŋ/ *noun* **1.** an act of joining together or linking two people, things or processes **2.** something which joins two things, especially a device for connecting two pieces of pipe, hose or tube

couvade /kuː'vɑːd/ *noun* an act of copying the actions of having a baby while a woman is actually giving birth, done by the father in some Native South American societies

Cowper's glands /'kuːpəz glændz/ *plural noun* two glands at the base of the penis which secrete into the urethra. Also called **bulbourethral glands** [Described 1700. After William Cowper (1666–1709), English surgeon.]

cowpox /'kaʊppks/ *noun* an infectious viral disease of cattle which can be transmitted to humans. It was used as a constituent of the first vaccines for smallpox.

cox- /kpks/ *prefix* the hip joint

coxa /'kpksə/ *noun* the hip joint (NOTE: The plural is **coxae**.)

coxalgia /kpk'sældʒə/ *noun* pain in the hip joint

coxa vara /ˌkpksə 'veərə/ *noun* an unusual development of the hip bone, making the legs bow

Coxsackie virus /kpk'sæki ˌvaɪrəs/ *noun* one of a group of enteroviruses which enter the cells of the intestines and can cause diseases such as aseptic meningitis and Bornholm disease [After Coxsackie, New York, where the virus was first identified.]

CPAP *abbreviation* continuous positive airways pressure

CPN *abbreviation* community psychiatric nurse

CPR *abbreviation* cardiopulmonary resuscitation

crab /kræb/, **crab louse** /'kræb laʊs/ *noun* a louse, *Phthirius pubis*, which infests the pubic region and other parts of the body with coarse hair. Also called **pubic louse**

crack /kræk/ *noun* a thin break ○ *There's a crack in one of the bones in the skull.* ■ *verb* to make a thin break in something, or become split ○ *She cracked a bone in her leg.*

cradle /'kreɪd(ə)l/ *noun* a metal frame put over a person in bed to keep the weight of the bedclothes off the body ■ *verb* to carry a child with

one arm under the thigh and the other under the upper back

cradle cap /'kreɪd(ə)l kæp/ *noun* a yellow deposit on the scalp of babies, caused by seborrhoea

cramp /kræmp/ *noun* a painful involuntary spasm in the muscles, in which the muscle may stay contracted for some time

crani- /kreɪni/ *prefix* same as **cranio-** (*used before vowels*)

crania plural of **cranium**

cranial /'kreɪniəl/ *adjective* referring to the skull

cranio- /kreɪniəʊ/ *prefix* the skull

craniometry /ˌkreɪni'ɒmɪtri/ *noun* the process of measuring skulls to find differences in size and shape

craniopharyngioma /ˌkreɪniəʊfəˌrɪndʒi'əʊmə/ *noun* a tumour in the brain originating in the hypophyseal duct (NOTE: The plural is **craniopharyngiomas** or **craniopharyngiomata**.)

craniostenosis /ˌkreɪniəʊstе'nəʊsɪs/, **craniosynostosis** /ˌkreɪniəʊˌsɪnəʊ'stəʊsɪs/ *noun* the early closing of the bones in a baby's skull, so making the skull contract

craniotabes /ˌkreɪniəʊ'teɪbiːz/ *noun* thinness of the bones in the occipital region of a child's skull, caused by rickets, marasmus or syphilis

craniotomy /ˌkreɪni'ɒtəmi/ *noun* a surgical operation on the skull, especially one cutting away part of the skull (NOTE: The plural is **craniotomies**.)

cranium /'kreɪniəm/ *noun* same as **skull** (NOTE: The plural is **craniums** or **crania**.)

CRB check /ˌsiː ɑː 'biː tʃek/ *noun* a check with the Criminal Records Bureau to establish whether a candidate has any convictions that disallow him or her from working with children or other vulnerable members of society. Also called **disclosure check**

creatine /'kriːtiːn/ *noun* a compound of nitrogen found in the muscles, produced by protein metabolism and excreted as creatinine

creatinine /kri'ætɪniːn/ *noun* a substance which is the form in which creatine is excreted

creatinuria /kriˌætɪ'njʊəriə/ *noun* excess creatine in the urine

creatorrhoea /ˌkriːətə'riːə/ *noun* the presence of undigested muscle fibre in the faeces, occurring in some pancreatic diseases

Credé's method /kre'deɪz ˌmeθəd/ *noun* **1.** a method of extracting a placenta by massaging the uterus through the abdomen **2.** the putting of silver nitrate solution into the eyes of a baby born to a mother who has gonorrhoea, in order to prevent gonococcal conjunctivitis [Described 1860. After Karl Sigmund Franz Credé (1819–92), German gynaecologist.]

creeping eruption /ˌkriːpɪŋ ɪˈrʌpʃən/ *noun* an itching skin complaint, caused by larvae of various parasites which creep under the skin

crepitation /ˌkrepɪˈteɪʃ(ə)n/ *noun* an unusual soft crackling sound heard in the lungs through a stethoscope. Also called **rale**

crepitus /ˈkrepɪtəs/ *noun* a harsh crackling sound heard through a stethoscope in a person with inflammation of the lungs

crest /krest/ *noun* a long raised part on a bone

crest of ilium /ˌkrest əv ˈɪliəm/ *noun* same as **iliac crest**

Creutzfeldt-Jakob disease /ˌkrɔɪtsfelt ˈjækɒb dɪˌziːz/ *noun* a disease of the nervous system caused by a slow-acting prion which eventually affects the brain. It may be linked to BSE in cows. Abbreviation **CJD**. ◊ **variant CJD** [Described 1920 by H.G. Creutzfeldt (1885–1964); 1921 by A.M. Jakob (1884–1931), German psychiatrists]

cribriform /ˈkrɪbrɪfɔːm/ *adjective* having small holes like a sieve

cribriform plate /ˈkrɪbrɪfɔːm pleɪt/ *noun* the top part of the ethmoid bone which forms the roof of the nasal cavity and part of the roof of the eye sockets

cricoid /ˈkraɪkɔɪd/ *adjective* relating to the lowest part of the cartilage of the larynx

cricoid cartilage /ˌkraɪkɔɪd ˈkɑːtəlɪdʒ/ *noun* ring-shaped cartilage in the lower part of the larynx. See illustration at LUNGS in Supplement

cri-du-chat syndrome /ˌkriː djuː ˈʃɑː ˌsɪndrəʊm/ *noun* a congenital condition, caused by loss of part of chromosome 5, which is characterised in babies by a cry suggestive of that of a cat

Crigler-Najjar syndrome /ˌkrɪglə ˈnædʒɑː ˌsɪndrəʊm/ *noun* a genetically controlled condition in which bilirubin cannot be formed, leading to jaundice or even brain damage

crista /ˈkrɪstə/ *noun* **1.** a ridge, e.g. the border of a bone **2.** a fold in the inner membrane of a mitrochondrion (NOTE: The plural is **cristae**.)

crista galli /ˌkrɪstə ˈɡælaɪ/ *noun* a projection from the ethmoid bone

criterion /kraɪˈtɪəriən/ *noun* an accepted standard used in making a decision or judgment about something (NOTE: The plural is **criteria**.)

critical care /ˌkrɪtɪk(ə)l ˈkeə/ *noun* specialist nursing and medical treatment given to patients who are critically ill

critical list /ˈkrɪtɪk(ə)l lɪst/ *noun* the list of patients in a hospital whose condition is medically life-threatening

CRNA *abbreviation* certified registered nurse anaesthetist

Crohn's disease /ˈkrəʊnz dɪˌziːz/ *noun* a persistent inflammatory disease, usually of the lower intestinal tract, characterised by thickening and scarring of the intestinal wall and obstruction [Described 1932. After Burrill Bernard Crohn (1884–1983), New York physician.]

COMMENT: No certain cause has been found for Crohn's disease, where only one section of the intestine becomes inflamed and can be blocked.

cromolyn sodium /ˌkrəʊməlɪn ˈsəʊdiəm/ *noun* a drug that helps to prevent the release of histamine and other substances which cause many of the symptoms of asthma and hay fever

cross-dresser /ˌkrɒs ˈdresə/ *noun* someone who wears clothes usually worn by people of the opposite sex, e.g. a transvestite

cross-dressing /ˌkrɒs ˈdresɪŋ/ *noun* the practice of wearing clothes usually worn by people of the opposite sex, e.g. by transvestites

cross-infection /ˌkrɒs ɪnˈfekʃən/ *noun* an infection passed from one patient to another in hospital, either directly or from nurses, visitors or equipment

crossmatch /krɒsˈmætʃ/ *verb* (*in transplant surgery*) to match a donor to a recipient as closely as possible to avoid tissue rejection. ◊ **blood group**

crossmatching /krɒsˈmætʃɪŋ/ *noun* the process of matching a transplant donor to a recipient as closely as possible to avoid tissue rejection

cross-resistance /ˌkrɒs rɪˈzɪstəns/ *noun* the development by a disease agent of resistance to a number of similar drugs or chemicals of the same class

crotamiton /krəˈtæmɪt(ə)n/ *noun* a chemical that kills mites, used to treat scabies

crotch /krɒtʃ/ *noun* the point where the legs meet the body, where the genitals are. Also called **crutch**

croup /kruːp/ *noun* acute infection of the upper respiratory passages which blocks the larynx, affecting children

crown /kraʊn/ *noun* the top part of a tooth above the level of the gums ■ *verb* to put an artificial crown on a tooth

crowning /ˈkraʊnɪŋ/ *noun* **1.** the act of putting an artificial crown on a tooth **2.** a stage in childbirth in which the top of the baby's head becomes visible

cruciate /ˈkruːʃiət/ *adjective* shaped like a cross

cruciate ligament /ˌkruːʃiət ˈlɪɡəmənt/ *noun* any ligament shaped like a cross, especially either of two ligaments behind the knee which prevent the knee from bending forwards

crude death rate /ˌkruːd ˈdeθ ˌreɪt/ *noun* the number of deaths in a year, divided by the total population

crura plural of **crus**

crural /'kruərəl/ *adjective* referring to the thigh, leg or shin

crura of the diaphragm /,kruərə əv ðə 'daɪəfræm/ *plural noun* the long muscle fibres joining the diaphragm to the lumbar vertebrae

crus /krʌs/ *noun* a long projecting part (NOTE: The plural is **crura**.)

crus cerebri /,krʌs 'serɪbraɪ/ *noun* each of the nerve tracts between the cerebrum and the medulla oblongata (NOTE: The plural is **crura cerebri**.)

crush fracture /'krʌʃ ,fræktʃə/ *noun* a fracture by compression of the bone

crush syndrome /'krʌʃ ,sɪndrəum/ *noun* a condition in which a limb has been crushed, as in an accident, causing kidney failure and shock

crutch /krʌtʃ/ *noun* **1.** a strong support for someone with an injured leg, formed of a stick with a T-bar which fits under the armpit, especially formerly, or a holding bar and elbow clasp **2.** same as **crotch**

cry- /kraɪ/ *prefix* same as **cryo-** (*used before vowels*)

cryaesthesia /,kraɪiːs'θiːziə/ *noun* the fact of being sensitive to cold

cryo- /kraɪəu/ *prefix* cold

cryobank /'kraɪəubæŋk/ *noun* a place where biological material such as semen and body tissue can be stored at extremely low temperatures

cryoprecipitate /,kraɪəuprɪ'sɪpɪtət/ *noun* a precipitate such as from blood plasma, which separates out on freezing and thawing

cryoprobe /'kraɪəuprəub/ *noun* an instrument used in cryosurgery with a tip that is kept very cold to destroy tissue

cryosurgery /,kraɪəu'sɜːdʒəri/ *noun* surgery which uses extremely cold instruments to destroy tissue

cryotherapy /,kraɪəu'θerəpi/ *noun* treatment using extreme cold, as in removing a wart with dry ice

crypt /krɪpt/ *noun* a small cavity in the body

crypto- /krɪptəu/ *prefix* hidden

cryptococcal meningitis /,krɪptəkɒk(ə)l menɪn'dʒaɪtɪs/ *noun* a form of meningitis that is a feature of cryptococcosis

cryptococcosis /,krɪptəukə'kəusɪs/ *noun* an infection mainly affecting the brain or nervous system, caused by the fungus *Cryptococcus neoformans*. It occurs most often in people with HIV infection.

cryptomenorrhoea /,krɪptəumenə'riːə/ *noun* the retention of menstrual flow, usually caused by an obstruction

cryptorchidism /krɪp'tɔːkɪdɪz(ə)m/, **cryptorchism** /krɪp'tɔːkɪz(ə)m/ *noun* a condition in a young male in which the testicles do not move down into the scrotum

cryptosporidia /,krɪptəuspə'rɪdiə/ plural of **cryptosporidium**

cryptosporidiosis /,krɪptəuspə,rɪdi'əusɪs/ *noun* an infectious condition of humans and domestic animals, spread by an intestinal parasite *Cryptosporidium parvum*. Its symptoms are fever, diarrhoea and stomach cramps.

cryptosporidium /,krɪptəuspə'rɪdiəm/ *noun* a parasite which contaminates drinking water supplies, causing intestinal infection (NOTE: The plural is **cryptosporidia**.)

crypts of Lieberkühn /,krɪpts əv 'liːbəkuːn/ *plural noun* tubular glands found in the mucous membrane of the small and large intestine, especially those between the bases of the villi in the small intestine. Also called **Lieberkühn's glands** [Described 1745. After Johann Nathaniel Lieberkuhn (1711–56), Berlin anatomist and physician.]

CSF *abbreviation* cerebrospinal fluid

CT *abbreviation* computed tomography

CT scan /,si: 'ti: skæn/ *noun* a computer picture of a slice of the body or an organ produced by a CT scanner. Also called **CAT scan**

cubital /'kjuːbɪt(ə)l/ *adjective* referring to the ulna

cubitus /'kjuːbɪtəs/ *noun* same as **ulna**

cuboid /'kjuːbɔɪd/, **cuboid bone** /'kjuːbɔɪd bəun/ *noun* one of the tarsal bones in the foot. See illustration at **FOOT** in Supplement

cuff /kʌf/ *noun* an inflatable ring put round the arm and inflated when blood pressure is being measured

cuirass respirator /kwɪ,ræs 'respɪreɪtə/ *noun* a type of artificial respirator which surrounds only the chest

culdoscope /'kʌldəuskəup/ *noun* an instrument used to inspect the interior of a woman's pelvis, introduced through the vagina

culdoscopy /kʌl'dɒskəpi/ *noun* an examination of the interior of a woman's pelvis using a culdoscope

culture /'kʌltʃə/ *noun* **1.** the shared values and behaviour of a group **2.** microorganisms or tissues grown in a culture medium in a laboratory ■ *verb* to grow microorganisms or tissues in a culture medium

cumulative /'kjuːmjʊlətɪv/ *adjective* growing by adding

cuneiform /'kjuːnɪfɔːm bəunz/, **cuneiform bone** /'kjuːnɪfɔːm/ *noun* one of the three tarsal bones in the foot. See illustration at **FOOT** in Supplement

cupola /'kjuːpələ/ *noun* a dome-shaped structure

curare /kjʊ'rɑːri/ *noun* a drug derived from South American plants, antagonist to acetylcholine and used surgically to paralyse muscles during operations without causing unconsciousness (NOTE: Curare is the poison used to make poison arrows.)

curettage /ˌkjʊəˈretɪdʒ/ *noun* the procedure of scraping the inside of a hollow organ, often the uterus, to remove a growth or tissue for examination. Also called **curettement**

curette /kjʊəˈret/ *noun* a surgical instrument like a long thin spoon, used for scraping the inside of an organ ■ *verb* to scrape an organ with a curette (NOTE: **curettes – curetting – curetted**.)

curettement /kjʊəˈretmənt/ same as **curettage**

curie /ˈkjʊəri/ *noun* a former unit of measurement of radioactivity, replaced by the becquerel. Symbol **Ci**

Curling's ulcer /ˌkɜːlɪŋz ˈʌlsə/ *noun* an ulcer of the duodenum following severe injury to the body

curvature /ˈkɜːvətʃə/ *noun* the way in which something bends from a straight line ○ *greater* or *lesser curvature of the stomach*

cushingoid /ˈkʊʃɪŋɔɪd/ *adjective* showing symptoms of Cushing's disease

Cushing's disease /ˈkʊʃɪŋz dɪˌziːz/, **Cushing's syndrome** /ˈkʊʃɪŋz ˌsɪndrəʊm/ *noun* a condition in which the adrenal cortex produces too many corticosteroids [Described 1932. After Harvey Williams Cushing (1869–1939), surgeon, Boston, USA.]

cusp /kʌsp/ *noun* **1.** the pointed tip of a tooth **2.** a flap of membrane forming a valve in the heart

cuspid /ˈkʌspɪd/ *noun* same as **canine**

cut /kʌt/ *noun* **1.** a reduction in the number or amount of something. **2.** a place where the skin has been penetrated by a sharp instrument ○ *She had a bad cut on her left leg.* ○ *The nurse will put a bandage on your cut.* ■ *verb* **1.** to make an opening in something using a knife, scissors or other sharp thing ○ *The surgeon cut the diseased tissue away with a scalpel.* ○ *She cut her finger on the broken glass.* **2.** to reduce the number or amount of something ○ *Accidents have been cut by 10%.* (NOTE: **cutting – cut**)

cut- /kjuːt/ *prefix* referring to the skin

cutaneous /kjuːˈteɪniəs/ *adjective* referring to the skin

cutaneous leishmaniasis /kjuːˌteɪniəs liːʃməˈnaɪəsɪs/ *noun* a form of skin disease caused by the tropical parasite *Leishmania*. Also called **Delhi boil**

cutdown /ˈkʌtdaʊn/ *noun* the procedure of cutting a vein to insert a cannula or administer an intravenous drug

cuticle /ˈkjuːtɪk(ə)l/ *noun* same as **epidermis**

cutis /ˈkjuːtɪs/ *noun* the skin

cutis anserina /ˌkjuːtɪs ˈænseraɪnə/ *noun* a reaction of the skin when someone is cold or frightened, the skin being raised into many little bumps by the action of the arrector pili muscles. Also called **goose bumps**

CVA *abbreviation* cerebrovascular accident

cyan- /saɪən/ *prefix* same as **cyano-** (*used before vowels*)

cyanide /ˈsaɪənaɪd/ *noun* a poison which kills very rapidly when drunk or inhaled

cyano- /saɪənəʊ/ *prefix* blue

cyanocobalamin /ˌsaɪənəʊkəʊˈbæləmɪn/ same as **Vitamin B₁₂**

cyanosed /ˈsaɪənəʊst/ *adjective* with blue skin ○ *The patient was cyanosed round the lips.*

cyanosis /ˌsaɪəˈnəʊsɪs/ *noun* a condition characterised by a blue colour of the peripheral skin and mucous membranes, a symptom of lack of oxygen in the blood, e.g. in heart or lung disease

cyanotic /ˌsaɪəˈnɒtɪk/ *adjective* referring to or having cyanosis

cycle /ˈsaɪk(ə)l/ *noun* a series of events which recur regularly

cyclic /ˈsɪklɪk, ˈsaɪklɪk/ *adjective* **1.** occurring or repeated in cycles **2.** referring to organic compounds composed of a closed ring of atoms

cyclical /ˈsɪklɪk(ə)l/ *adjective* referring to cycles

-cycline /saɪklɪn/ *suffix* used in names of antibiotics ○ *tetracycline*

cyclitis /sɪˈklaɪtɪs/ *noun* inflammation of the ciliary body in the eye

cyclo- /saɪkləʊ/ *prefix* cycles

cyclodialysis /ˌsaɪkləʊdaɪˈæləsɪs/ *noun* a surgical operation to connect the anterior chamber of the eye and the choroid, as a treatment of glaucoma

cyclopentolate /ˌsaɪkləʊˈpentəleɪt/ *noun* a drug used to paralyse the ciliary muscle

cyclophosphamide /ˌsaɪkləʊˈfɒsfəmaɪd/ *noun* a drug which suppresses immunity, used in the treatment of leukaemia, lymphoma, Hodgkin's disease and tumours

cycloplegia /ˌsaɪkləʊˈpliːdʒə/ *noun* paralysis of the ciliary muscle which makes it impossible for the eye to focus properly

cyclopropane /ˌsaɪkləʊˈprəʊpeɪn/ *noun* a flammable hydrocarbon gas used as a general anaesthetic and in organic synthesis

cyclothymia /ˌsaɪkləʊˈθaɪmiə/ *noun* a mild form of bipolar disorder in which the person experiences alternating depression and excitement

cyclotomy /saɪˈklɒtəmi/ *noun* a surgical operation to make a cut in the ciliary body (NOTE: The plural is **cyclotomies**.)

-cyclovir /saɪkləʊvɪə/ *suffix* used in the names of antiviral drugs

cyesis /saɪˈiːsɪs/ *noun* same as **pregnancy** (*technical*)

cyst /sɪst/ *noun* an unusual growth in the body shaped like a pouch, containing liquid or semi-liquid substances

cyst- /sɪst/ *prefix* the bladder

cystadenoma /ˌsɪstədɪˈnəʊmə/ *noun* an adenoma in which fluid-filled cysts form (NOTE: The plural is **cystadonomas** or **cystadonomata**.)

cystalgia /sɪˈstældʒə/ *noun* pain in the urinary bladder

cystectomy /sɪˈstektəmi/ *noun* a surgical operation to remove all or part of the urinary bladder (NOTE: The plural is **cystectomies**.)

cystic /ˈsɪstɪk/ *adjective* **1.** referring to cysts **2.** referring to a bladder

cysticercosis /ˌsɪstɪsɜːˈkəʊsɪs/ *noun* a disease caused by infestation of tapeworm larvae from pork

cystic fibrosis /ˌsɪstɪk faɪˈbrəʊsɪs/ *noun* a hereditary disease in which there is malfunction of the exocrine glands such as the pancreas, in particular those which secrete mucus, causing respiratory difficulties, male infertility and malabsorption of food from the gastrointestinal tract. Also called **fibrocystic disease**, **mucoviscidosis**

cystine /ˈsɪstiːn/ *noun* an amino acid. It can cause stones to form in the urinary system of people who have a rare inherited metabolic disorder.

cystinosis /ˌsɪstɪˈnəʊsɪs/ *noun* a disorder affecting the absorption of amino acids, resulting in excessive amounts of cystine accumulating in the kidneys

cystinuria /ˌsɪstɪˈnjʊəriə/ *noun* cystine in the urine

cystitis /sɪˈstaɪtɪs/ *noun* inflammation of the urinary bladder, which makes someone pass water often and with a burning sensation

cystocele /ˈsɪstəsiːl/ *noun* a hernia of the urinary bladder into the vagina

cystogram /ˈsɪstəgræm/ *noun* an X-ray photograph of the urinary bladder

cystography /sɪˈstɒgrəfi/ *noun* an examination of the urinary bladder by X-rays after radio-opaque dye has been introduced

cystolithiasis /ˌsɪstəlɪˈθaɪəsɪs/ *noun* a condition in which stones are formed in the urinary bladder

cystometer /sɪˈstɒmɪtə/ *noun* an apparatus which measures the pressure in the bladder

cystometry /sɪˈstɒmɪtri/ *noun* measurement of the pressure in the bladder

cystopexy /sɪˈstɒpeksi/ *noun* a surgical operation to fix the bladder in a different position. Also

called **vesicofixation** (NOTE: The plural is **cystopexies**.)

cystoplasty /ˈsɪstəˌplæsti/ *noun* a surgical operation on the bladder (NOTE: The plural is **cystoplasties**.)

cystoscope /ˈsɪstəskəʊp/ *noun* an instrument made of a long tube with a light at the end, used to inspect the inside of the bladder

cystoscopy /sɪˈstɒskəpi/ *noun* an examination of the bladder using a cystoscope (NOTE: The plural is **cystoscopies**.)

cystostomy /sɪˈstɒstəmi/, **cystotomy** /sɪˈstɒtəmi/ *noun* a surgical operation to make an opening between the bladder and the abdominal wall to allow urine to pass without going through the urethra. Also called **vesicostomy** (NOTE: The plurals are **cystostomies** and **cystotomies**.)

cystourethrography /ˌsɪstəʊˌjʊərɪˈθrɒgrəfi/ *noun* X-ray examination of the bladder and urethra

cystourethroscope /ˌsɪstəʊjʊˈriːθrəskəʊp/ *noun* an instrument used to inspect the bladder and urethra

cyt- /saɪt/ *prefix* same as **cyto-** (*used before vowels*)

cyto- /saɪtəʊ/ *prefix* cell

cytochemistry /ˌsaɪtəʊˈkemɪstri/ *noun* the study of the chemical activity of cells

cytogenetics /ˌsaɪtəʊdʒəˈnetɪks/ *noun* a branch of genetics which studies the function of cells, especially chromosomes, in heredity

cytokine /ˈsaɪtəʊkaɪn/ *noun* a protein secreted by cells of the lymph system which is involved in controlling response to inflammation

cytokinesis /ˌsaɪtəʊkaɪˈniːsɪs/ *noun* changes in the cytoplasm of a cell during division

cytological smear /ˌsaɪtəlɒdʒɪk(ə)l ˈsmɪə/ *noun* a sample of tissue taken for examination under a microscope

cytology /saɪˈtɒlədʒi/ *noun* the study of the structure and function of cells

cytolysis /saɪˈtɒlɪsɪs/ *noun* the breaking down of cells

cytomegalovirus /ˌsaɪtəʊˈmegələʊˌvaɪrəs/ *noun* one of the herpesviruses which can cause serious congenital disorders in a fetus if it infects the pregnant mother. Abbreviation **CMV**

cytometer /saɪˈtɒmɪtə/ *noun* an instrument attached to a microscope, used for measuring and counting the number of cells in a specimen

cytopenia /ˌsaɪtəʊˈpiːniə/ *noun* a deficiency of cellular elements in blood or tissue

cytoplasm /ˈsaɪtəʊplæz(ə)m/ *noun* a substance inside the cell membrane which surrounds the nucleus of a cell

cytoplasmic /ˌsaɪtəʊˈplæzmɪk/ *adjective* referring to the cytoplasm of a cell

cytosine /'saɪtəʊsiːn/ *noun* one of the four basic chemicals in DNA

cytosome /'saɪtəʊsəʊm/ *noun* the body of a cell, not including the nucleus

cytotoxic /ˌsaɪtəʊ'tɒksɪk/ *adjective* **1.** referring to a drug or agent which prevents cell divi-sion **2.** referring to cells in the immune system which destroy other cells

cytotoxic drug /ˌsaɪtəʊtɒksɪk 'drʌg/ *noun* a drug which reduces the reproduction of cells, used to treat cancer

cytotoxin /ˌsaɪtəʊ'tɒksɪn/ *noun* a substance which has a toxic effect on cells

D

d *symbol* deci-

da *symbol* deca-

da Costa's syndrome /dɑː 'kɒstəz ˌsɪndrəʊm/ *noun* same as **disordered action of the heart** [Described 1871. After Jacob Mendes da Costa (1833–1900), Philadelphia surgeon, who described this condition in soldiers in the American Civil War.]

dacryo- /dækriəʊ/ *prefix* tears

dacryoadenitis /ˌdækriəʊædɪ'naɪtɪs/ *noun* inflammation of the lacrimal gland

dacryocystitis /ˌdækriəʊsɪ'staɪtɪs/ *noun* inflammation of the lacrimal sac when the tear duct, which drains into the nose, becomes blocked

dacryocystography /ˌdækriəʊsɪ'stɒɡrəfi/ *noun* contrast radiography to determine the site of an obstruction in the tear ducts

dacryocystorhinostomy /ˌdækriəʊˌsɪstəʊraɪ'nɒstəmi/ *noun* a surgical operation to bypass a blockage from the tear duct which takes tears into the nose. Abbreviation **DCR** (NOTE: The plural is **dacryocystorhinostomies**.)

dacryolith /'dækriəʊlɪθ/ *noun* a stone in the lacrimal sac

dacryoma /ˌdækri'əʊmə/ *noun* a benign swelling in one of the tear ducts (NOTE: The plural is **dacryomas** or **dacryomata**.)

dactyl /'dæktɪl/ *noun* a finger or toe

dactyl- /dæktɪl/ *prefix* same as **dactylo-** (*used before vowels*)

dactylitis /ˌdæktɪ'laɪtɪs/ *noun* inflammation of the fingers or toes, caused by bone infection or rheumatic disease

dactylo- /dæktɪləʊ/ *prefix* referring to the fingers or toes

dactylology /ˌdæktɪ'lɒlədʒi/ *noun* signs made with the fingers in place of words when talking to a person who is unable to hear, or when a person who is unable to hear or speak wants to communicate

dactylomegaly /ˌdæktɪləʊ'meɡəli/ *noun* a condition in which a person has longer fingers than usual

DAH *abbreviation* disordered action of the heart

Daltonism /'dɔːltənɪz(ə)m/ *noun* the commonest form of colour blindness, in which someone cannot see the difference between red and green. Also called **protanopia** [Described 1794. After John Dalton (1766–1844), English chemist and physician. Founder of the atomic theory, he himself was colour-blind.]

D & C /diː ən/ *abbreviation* dilatation and curettage

dander /'dændə/ *noun* very small fragments that fall from the feathers, hair or skin of animals or people

dandruff /'dændrəf/ *noun* pieces of dead skin from the scalp which fall out when the hair is combed. Also called **pityriasis capitis**, **scurf**

D and V /ˌdiː ən 'viː/ *abbreviation* diarrhoea and vomiting

Dandy-Walker syndrome /ˌdændi 'wɔːkə ˌsɪndrəʊm/ *noun* a congenital condition in which there is no Magendie's foramen in the brain

dark adaptation /dɑːk ˌædæp'teɪʃ(ə)n/ *noun* the reflex changes which enable the eye to continue to see in dim light. For example, the pupil becomes larger and the rods in the retina become more active than the cones.

data /'deɪtə/ *plural noun* information in words or figures about a particular subject, especially information which is available on computer (NOTE: In scientific usage, **data** is used with a plural verb: *The data are accurate*. In everyday language, **data** is often used with a singular verb: *The recent data supports our case*.)

data bank /'deɪtə bæŋk/ *noun* a store of information in a computer ○ *The hospital keeps a data bank of information about possible kidney donors*.

database /'deɪtəbeɪs/ *noun* a structured collection of information in a computer that can be automatically retrieved and manipulated

Data Protection Act /ˌdeɪtə prə'tekʃ(ə)n ˌækt/ *noun* a parliamentary act intended to protect information about individuals that is held on computers. It ensures that all information is stored securely and allows people to have access to their entries.

daughter /'dɔːtə/ *noun* a female child of a parent ○ *They have two sons and one daughter*.

day blindness /ˈdeɪ ˌblaɪndnəs/ *noun* same as **hemeralopia**

day care /ˈdeɪ keə/ *noun* supervised recreation or medical care provided during the day for people who need special help, e.g. some elderly people or small children

day case /ˈdeɪ keɪs/ *noun* same as **day patient**

day case surgery /ˈdeɪ keɪs ˌsɜːdʒəri/ *noun* same as **day surgery**

day centre /ˈdeɪ ˌsentə/ *noun* a place providing day care

day nursery /ˈdeɪ ˌnɜːs(ə)ri/ *noun* a place where small children can be looked after during the daytime while their parents or guardians are at work

day patient /ˈdeɪ ˌpeɪʃ(ə)nt/ *noun* a patient who is in hospital for treatment for a day and does not stay overnight. Also called **day case**

day patient care /ˈdeɪ ˌpeɪʃ(ə)nt ˌkeə/ *noun* care for patients who are resident in a hospital during the daytime only

day recovery ward /ˌdeɪ rɪˈkʌv(ə)ri ˌwɔːd/ *noun* a ward where day patients who have had minor operations can recover before going home

day surgery /ˈdeɪ ˌsɜːdʒəri/ *noun* a surgical operation which does not require the patient to stay overnight in hospital. Also called **day case surgery**

dB *abbreviation* decibel

DCR *abbreviation* dacryocystorhinostomy

DDS *abbreviation US* doctor of dental surgery

DDT *abbreviation* dichlorodiphenyltrichloroethane

de- /diː/ *prefix* removal or loss

dead fingers /ˌded ˈfɪŋgəz/, **dead man's fingers** /ˌded mænz ˈfɪŋgəz/ *noun* same as **Raynaud's disease**

dead space /ded speɪs/ *noun* a breath in the last part of the process of breathing in air which does not get further than the bronchial tubes

deaf /def/ *adjective* not able to hear in circumstances where most people would. ◊ **hearing-impaired**

deaf and dumb /ˌdef ən ˈdʌm/ *noun* not able to hear or to speak (NOTE: This term is regarded as offensive.)

deafness /ˈdefnəs/ *noun* the fact of being unable to hear in circumstances where most people would

deamination /diːˌæmɪˈneɪʃ(ə)n/ *noun* the process by which amino acids are broken down in the liver and urea is formed

death /deθ/ *noun* the permanent end of all natural functions

death rate /ˈdeθ reɪt/ *noun* the number of deaths per year per thousand of population ○ *The death rate from cancer of the liver has remained stable.*

debility /dɪˈbɪlɪti/ *noun* general weakness

debridement /dɪˈbriːdmənt/ *noun* the removal of dirt or dead tissue from a wound to help healing

deca- /dekə/ *prefix* ten. Symbol **da**

Decadron /ˈdekədrɒn/ a trade name for dexamethasone

decalcification /diːˌkælsɪfɪˈkeɪʃ(ə)n/ *noun* the loss of calcium salts from teeth and bones

decannulation /diːˌkænjʊˈleɪʃ(ə)n/ *noun* the removal of a tracheostomy tube

decapitation /dɪˌkæpɪˈteɪʃ(ə)n/ *noun* the act or process of cutting off the head of a person or animal

decapsulation /diːˌkæpsjʊˈleɪʃ(ə)n/ *noun* a surgical operation to remove a capsule from an organ, especially from a kidney

decay /dɪˈkeɪ/ *noun* **1.** the process by which tissues become rotten, caused by the action of microorganisms and oxygen **2.** damage caused to tissue or a tooth by the action of microorganisms, especially bacteria ■ *verb (of tissue)* to rot ○ *The surgeon removed decayed matter from the wound.*

deci- /desi/ *prefix* one tenth (10^{-1}) ○ *decigram* Symbol **d**

decibel /ˈdesɪbel/ *noun* a unit of measurement of the loudness of sound, used to compare different levels of sound. Symbol **dB**

decidua /dɪˈsɪdjuə/ *noun* a membrane which lines the uterus after fertilisation (NOTE: The plural is **deciduas** or **deciduae**.)

COMMENT: The decidua is divided into several parts: the **decidua basalis**, where the embryo is attached, the **decidua capsularis**, which covers the embryo and the **decidua vera** which is the rest of the decidua not touching the embryo. It is expelled after the birth of the baby.

decidual /dɪˈsɪdjuəl/ *adjective* referring to the decidua

deciduoma /dɪˌsɪdjuˈəʊmə/ *noun* a mass of decidual tissue remaining in the uterus after birth (NOTE: The plural is **deciduomas** or **deciduomata**.)

deciduous /dɪˈsɪdjuəs/ *adjective* referring to teeth discarded at a later stage of development

deciduous dentition /dɪˌsɪdjuəs denˈtɪʃ(ə)n/ *noun* the set of twenty teeth which are gradually replaced by the permanent teeth as a child grows older

deciduous tooth /dɪˈsɪdjuəs tuːθ/ *noun* same as **primary tooth**

decilitre /ˈdesɪliːtə/ *noun* a unit of measurement of liquid equal to one tenth of a litre. Symbol **dl** (NOTE: The US spelling is **deciliter**.)

decimetre /ˈdesɪmiːtə/ *noun* a unit of measurement of length equal to one tenth of a metre. Symbol **dm** (NOTE: The US spelling is **decimeter**.)

decompensation /ˌdiːˌkɒmpən'seɪʃ(ə)n/ *noun* a condition in which an organ such as the heart cannot cope with extra stress placed on it and so is unable to perform its function properly

decomposition /ˌdiːkɒmpə'zɪʃ(ə)n/ *noun* the process where dead matter is rotted by the action of bacteria or fungi

decompression /ˌdiːkəm'preʃ(ə)n/ *noun* **1.** reduction of pressure **2.** a controlled reduction of atmospheric pressure which occurs as a diver returns to the surface

decompression sickness /ˌdiːkəm ˌpreʃ(ə)n 'sɪknəs/ *noun* same as **caisson disease**

decongestant /ˌdiːkən'dʒestənt/ *adjective* reducing congestion and swelling ■ *noun* a drug which reduces congestion and swelling, sometimes used to unblock the nasal passages

decontamination /ˌdiːkəntæmɪ'neɪʃ(ə)n/ *noun* the removal of a contaminating substance such as radioactive material

decortication /ˌdiːkɔːtɪ'keɪʃ(ə)n/ *noun* the surgical removal of the cortex of an organ

decrudescence /ˌdiːkruː'des(ə)ns/ *noun* a reduction in the symptoms of a disease

decubitus /dɪ'kjuːbɪtəs/ *noun* the position of a person who is lying down

decubitus ulcer /dɪˌkjuːbɪtəs 'ʌlsə/ *noun* same as **bedsore**

decussation /ˌdiːkʌ'seɪʃ(ə)n/ *noun* the crossing of nerve fibres in the central nervous system. Also called **chiasm**

deep /diːp/ *adjective* located, coming from or reaching relatively far inside the body. Opposite **superficial**

deep cervical vein /ˌdiːp 'sɜːvɪk(ə)l ˌveɪn/ *noun* a vein in the neck which drains into the vertebral vein

deep dermal burn /ˌdiːp 'dɜːm(ə)l ˌbɜːn/ *noun* a burn which is so severe that a graft will be necessary to repair the skin damage. Also called **full thickness burn**

deep facial vein /ˌdiːp 'feɪʃ(ə)l ˌveɪn/ *noun* a small vein which drains from the pterygoid process behind the cheek into the facial vein

deep plantar arch /ˌdiːp 'plæntər ˌɑːtʃ/ *noun* a curved artery crossing the sole of the foot

deep vein /ˌdiːp 'veɪn/ *noun* a vein which is inside the body near a bone, as opposed to a superficial vein near the skin

deep-vein thrombosis /ˌdiːp veɪn θrɒm 'bəʊsɪs/ *noun* a condition arising when a thrombus formed in the deep veins of a leg or the pelvis travels to a lung where it may cause death. The condition may affect anyone who is inactive for long periods. Also called **phlebothrombosis**. Abbreviation **DVT**

defecation /ˌdefə'keɪʃ(ə)n/, **defaecation** *noun* the act of passing out faeces from the bowels

defence /dɪ'fens/ *noun* resistance against an attack of a disease

defence mechanism /dɪ'fens ˌmekənɪz(ə)m/ *noun* a subconscious reflex by which a person prevents himself or herself from showing emotion

deferent /'defərənt/ *adjective* going away from the centre

defervescence /ˌdefə'ves(ə)ns/ *noun* a period during which a fever is subsiding

defibrillation /diːˌfɪbrɪ'leɪʃ(ə)n/ *noun* a procedure to correct an irregular heartbeat by applying a large electrical impulse to the chest wall, especially in potentially life-threatening circumstances. Also called **cardioversion**

defibrillator /diː'fɪbrɪleɪtə/ *noun* an apparatus used to apply an electric impulse to the heart to make it beat regularly

defibrination /diːˌfaɪbrɪ'neɪʃ(ə)n/ *noun* the removal of fibrin from a blood sample to prevent clotting

deficiency /dɪ'fɪʃ(ə)nsi/ *noun* a lack of something necessary

deficit /'defɪsɪt/ *noun* the amount by which something is less than it should be

defloration /ˌdiːflɔː'reɪʃ(ə)n/ *noun* the act of breaking the hymen of a virgin, usually at the first sexual intercourse

deflorescence /ˌdiːflɔː'res(ə)ns/ *noun* the disappearance of a rash

deformans /diː'fɔːmænz/ ♦ **osteitis deformans**

deformity /dɪ'fɔːmɪti/ *noun* an unusual shape of part of the body

degeneration /dɪˌdʒenə'reɪʃ(ə)n/ *noun* a change in the structure of a cell or organ so that it no longer works properly

degenerative disease /dɪˌdʒen(ə)rətɪv dɪ 'ziːz/, **degenerative disorder** /dɪˌdʒen(ə)rətɪv dɪs'ɔːdə/ *noun* a disease or disorder in which there is progressive loss of function of a part of the body, or in which a part of the body fails to repair itself

deglutition /ˌdiːgluː'tɪʃ(ə)n/ *noun* the action of passing food or liquid, and sometimes also air, from the mouth into the oesophagus (*technical*) Also called **swallowing**

dehiscence /dɪ'hɪs(ə)ns/ *noun* the act of opening wide

dehydration /ˌdiːhaɪ'dreɪʃ(ə)n/ *noun* a dangerous lack of water in the body resulting from inadequate intake of fluids or excessive loss through sweating, vomiting or diarrhoea

dehydrogenase /ˌdiːhaɪˈdrɒdʒəneɪz/ *noun* an enzyme that transfers hydrogen between chemical compounds

déjà vu /ˌdeɪʒɑ ˈvuː/ *noun* an illusion that a new situation is a previous one being repeated, usually caused by a disease of the brain

deleterious /ˌdeliˈtɪəriəs/ *adjective* damaging or harmful

Delhi boil /ˌdeli ˈbɔɪl/ *noun* same as **cutaneous leishmaniasis**

delirium /dɪˈlɪriəm/ *noun* a mental state in which someone is confused, excited and restless and has hallucinations

delirium alcoholicum /dɪˌlɪriəm ˌælkə ˈhɒlɪkəm/ *noun* ♦ **delirium tremens**

delirium tremens /dɪˌlɪriəm ˈtriːmenz/, **delirium alcoholicum** /dɪˌlɪriəm ˌælkə ˈhɒlɪkəm/ *noun* a state of mental illness usually found in long-term alcoholics who attempt to give up alcohol consumption. It includes hallucinations about insects, trembling and excitement. Abbreviation **DTs**

delivery /dɪˈlɪv(ə)ri/ *noun* the birth of a child

delta /ˈdeltə/ *noun* the fourth letter of the Greek alphabet

deltoid /ˈdeltɔɪd/, **deltoid muscle** /ˈdeltɔɪd ˌmʌs(ə)l/ *noun* a big triangular muscle covering the shoulder joint and attached to the humerus, which lifts the arm sideways

delusion /dɪˈluːʒ(ə)n/ *noun* a false belief which a person holds which cannot be changed by reason ○ *He suffered from the delusion that he was wanted by the police.*

dementia /dɪˈmenʃə/ *noun* the loss of mental ability and memory due to organic disease of the brain, causing disorientation and personality changes

demi- /demi/ *prefix* half

demography /dɪˈmɒgrəfi/ *noun* the study of populations and environments or changes affecting populations

demulcent /dɪˈmʌlsənt/ *noun* a soothing substance which relieves irritation in the stomach

demyelinating /diːˈmaɪəlɪneɪtɪŋ/ *adjective* relating to the destruction of the myelin sheath round nerve fibres

demyelination /diːˌmaɪəlɪˈneɪʃ(ə)n/ *noun* the destruction of the myelin sheath round nerve fibres, caused, e.g. by injury to the head, or as the main result of multiple sclerosis

dendrite /ˈdendraɪt/ *noun* a branched structure growing out from a nerve cell, which receives impulses from the nerve endings of other nerve cells at synapses. See illustration at **NEURONE** in Supplement. Also called **dendron**

dendritic /denˈdrɪtɪk/ *adjective* referring to a dendrite

dendron /ˈdendrɒn/ *noun* same as **dendrite**

denervation /ˌdiːnəˈveɪʃ(ə)n/ *noun* the stopping or cutting of the nerve supply to a part of the body

dengue /ˈdeŋgi/ *noun* a tropical disease caused by an arbovirus transmitted by mosquitoes, characterised by high fever, pains in the joints, headache and rash. Also called **breakbone fever**

denial /dɪˈnaɪəl/ *noun* a person's refusal to accept that he or she has a serious medical problem

Denis Browne splint /ˌdenɪs braʊn ˈsplɪnt/ *noun* a metal splint used to correct a club foot [Described 1934. After Sir Denis John Wolko Browne (1892–1967), Australian orthopaedic and general surgeon working in Britain.]

dens /denz/ *noun* a tooth, or something shaped like a tooth

dent- /dent/ *prefix* referring to a tooth or teeth

dental /ˈdent(ə)l/ *adjective* referring to teeth or to the treatment of teeth ○ *dental caries* ○ *dental surgeon*

dental hygiene /ˌdent(ə)l ˈhaɪdʒiːn/ *noun* procedures to keep the teeth clean and healthy

dental impaction /ˌdent(ə)l ɪmˈpækʃ(ə)n/ *noun* a condition in which a tooth is closely pressed against other teeth and cannot grow normally

dental plate /ˈdent(ə)l pleɪt/ *noun* a prosthesis made to the shape of the mouth, which holds artificial teeth

dental prosthesis /ˌdent(ə)l prɒsˈθiːsɪs/ *noun* one or more false teeth

dentine /ˈdentiːn/ *noun* a hard substance which surrounds the pulp of teeth, beneath the enamel

dentistry /ˈdentɪstri/ *noun* the profession of a dentist, or the branch of medicine dealing with teeth and gums

dentition /denˈtɪʃ(ə)n/ *noun* the number, arrangement and special characteristics of all the teeth in a person's jaws

COMMENT: Children have incisors, canines and molars, which are replaced over a period of years by the permanent teeth: eight incisors, four canines, eight premolars and twelve molars, the last four molars being called the wisdom teeth.

dentoid /ˈdentɔɪd/ *adjective* shaped like a tooth

denture /ˈdentʃə/ *noun* a set of false teeth, fixed to a device which fits inside the mouth

deodorant /diːˈəʊd(ə)rənt/ *noun* a substance which hides or prevents unpleasant smells ■ *adjective* hiding or preventing odours

deontology /ˌdiːɒnˈtɒlədʒi/ *noun* the ethics of duty and of what is morally right or wrong

deoxygenate /diːˈɒksɪdʒəneɪt/ *verb* to remove oxygen from something

deoxygenated blood /diːˌɒksɪdʒəneɪt ˈblʌd/ *noun* blood from which most of the oxygen has been removed by the tissues. It is darker than arterial oxygenated blood. Also called **venous blood**. Compare **deoxygenated blood**

deoxyribonucleic acid /diːˌɒksiraɪbəʊnjuːˌkleɪɪk ˈæsɪd/ *noun* full form of **DNA. ♦ RNA**

Department of Health /dɪˌpɑːtmənt əv ˈhelθ/ *noun* in the UK, the government department in charge of health services. Abbreviation **DH**

dependant /dɪˈpendənt/ *noun* a person who is looked after or supported by someone else ○ *He has to support a family of six children and several dependants.*

dependence /dɪˈpendəns/, **dependency** /dɪˈpendənsi/ *noun* the fact of needing the suuport of something or someone such as a carer, nurse or doctor, or of being addicted to a drug

dependent /dɪˈpendənt/ *adjective* 1. needing the support of someone or something 2. addicted to a drug 3. referring to a part of the body which is hanging down

dependent relative /dɪˌpendənt ˈrelətɪv/ *noun* a person who is looked after by another member of the family

depersonalisation /diːˌpɜːs(ə)n(ə)laɪˈzeɪʃ(ə)n/, **depersonalization** *noun* a psychiatric state in which someone does not believe he or she is real

depilation /ˌdepɪˈleɪʃ(ə)n/ *noun* the removal of hair

depilatory /dɪˈpɪlət(ə)ri/ *noun* a substance which removes hair ■ *adjective* removing hair

Depo-Provera a trademark for a progesterone derivative used in birth control and the treatment of endometriosis which is administered by three-monthly injection

depressant /dɪˈpres(ə)nt/ *noun* a drug which reduces the activity of part of the body, e.g. a tranquilliser

depressed /dɪˈprest/ *adjective* 1. experiencing a mental condition that prevents someone from carrying out the normal activities of life in the usual way □ **clinically depressed** Same as **depressed** 2. feeling miserable and worried (*informal*) ○ *He was depressed after his exam results.* 3. referring to something such as a metabolic rate which is below the usual level

depressed fracture /dɪˌprest ˈfræktʃə/ *noun* a fracture of a flat bone such as those in the skull where part of the bone has been pushed down lower than the surrounding parts

depression /dɪˈpreʃ(ə)n/ *noun* 1. a mental condition that prevents someone from carrying out the normal activities of life in the usual way 2. a hollow on the surface of a part of the body

depressor /dɪˈpresə/ *noun* a muscle which pulls part of the body downwards

deprivation /ˌdeprɪˈveɪʃ(ə)n/ *noun* 1. the fact of not being able to have something that you need

or want ○ *sleep deprivation* 2. the lack of basic necessities of life

deradenitis /dɪˌrædɪˈnaɪtɪs/ *noun* inflammation of the lymph nodes in the neck

Dercum's disease /ˈdɜːkəmz dɪˌziːz/ *noun* same as **adiposis dolorosa** [Described 1888. After François Xavier Dercum (1856–1931), Professor of Neurology at Jefferson Medical College, Philadelphia, USA.]

derealisation /diːˌrɪəlaɪˈzeɪʃ(ə)n/, **derealization** *noun* a psychological state in which someone feels the world around him or her is not real

derm- /dɜːm/ *prefix* same as **derma-** (*used before vowels*)

-derm /dɜːm/ *suffix* skin

derma- /dɜːmə/ *prefix* skin

dermal /ˈdɜːm(ə)l/ *adjective* referring to the skin

dermatitis /ˌdɜːməˈtaɪtɪs/ *noun* inflammation of the skin

dermato- /dɜːmətəʊ/ *prefix* referring to the skin

dermatochalasis /ˌdɜːmətəʊkəˈlæsɪs/ *noun* a condition where a fold of skin moves down over the eyelid, common in older people

dermatological /ˌdɜːmətəˈlɒdʒɪk(ə)l/ *adjective* referring to dermatology

dermatologist /ˌdɜːməˈtɒlədʒɪst/ *noun* a doctor who specialises in the study and treatment of the skin and its diseases

dermatology /ˌdɜːməˈtɒlədʒi/ *noun* the study and treatment of the skin and its diseases

dermatome /ˈdɜːmətəʊm/ *noun* 1. a special knife used for cutting thin sections of skin for grafting 2. an area of skin supplied by one spinal nerve

dermatomycosis /ˌdɜːmətəʊmaɪˈkəʊsɪs/ *noun* a skin infection caused by a fungus that is not a dermatophyte

dermatomyositis /ˌdɜːmətəʊmaɪəʊˈsaɪtɪs/ *noun* a collagen disease with a wasting inflammation of the skin and muscles

dermatophyte /ˈdɜːmətəʊfaɪt/ *noun* a fungus belonging to one of three genera which affect the skin or hair, causing tinea

dermatophytosis /ˌdɜːmətəʊfaɪˈtəʊsɪs/ *noun* a fungal infection of the skin caused by a *dermatophyte*

dermatoplasty /ˈdɜːmətəʊplæsti/ *noun* a skin graft, replacing damaged skin by skin taken from another part of the body or from a donor

dermatosis /ˌdɜːməˈtəʊsɪs/ *noun* a disease of the skin

dermis /ˈdɜːmɪs/ *noun* a thick layer of living skin beneath the epidermis. Also called **corium**

dermo- /dɜːməʊ/ *prefix* same as **derma-**

dermoid /ˈdɜːmɔɪd/ *adjective* 1. referring to the skin 2. like skin

Descemet's membrane /deʃə'mets ˌmembreɪn/ *noun* one of the deep layers of the cornea [Described 1785. After Jean Descemet (1732–1810), French physician; Professor of Anatomy and Surgery in Paris.]

descending aorta /dɪˌsendɪŋ eɪ'ɔːtə/ *noun* the second section of the aorta, which turns downwards. Compare **ascending aorta**

descending colon /dɪˌsendɪŋ 'kəʊlɒn/ *noun* the third section of the colon which goes down the left side of the body. Compare **ascending colon**. See illustration at DIGESTIVE SYSTEM in Supplement

desensitisation /diːˌsensɪtaɪ'zeɪʃ(ə)n/, **desensitization** *noun* the act of making someone or something no longer sensitive to something such as an allergen

designer drug /dɪ'zaɪnə drʌg/ *noun* a drug that has been modified to enhance its properties (*informal*)

desogestrel /ˌdesə'dʒestrəl/ *noun* a hormone used as an oral contraceptive

desquamation /ˌdeskwə'meɪʃ(ə)n/ *noun* the continual process of losing the outer layer of dead skin

detached retina /dɪˌtætʃt 'retɪnə/ *noun* a condition in which the retina becomes partially separated from the eyeball, causing loss of vision. Also called **retinal detachment**

COMMENT: A detached retina can be caused by a blow to the eye, or simply is a condition occurring in old age. If left untreated the eye will become blind. A detached retina can sometimes be attached to the choroid again using lasers.

detergent /dɪ'tɜːdʒənt/ *noun* a cleaning substance which removes grease and bacteria

deterioration /dɪˌtɪəriə'reɪʃ(ə)n/ *noun* the fact of becoming worse ○ *The nurses were worried by the deterioration in the patient's reactions.*

detox /'diːtɒks/ *noun* same as **detoxication** (*informal*)

detoxication /diːˌtɒksɪ'keɪʃ(ə)n/, **detoxification** /diːˌtɒksɪfɪ'keɪʃ(ə)n/ *noun* the removal of toxic substances to make a poisonous substance harmless

detrition /dɪ'trɪʃ(ə)n/ *noun* the fact of wearing away by rubbing or use

detritus /dɪ'traɪtəs/ *noun* rubbish produced when something disintegrates

detrusor muscle /dɪ'truːzə ˌmʌs(ə)l/ *noun* the muscular coat of the urinary bladder

detumescence /ˌdiːtjuː'mes(ə)ns/ *noun* **1.** (*of the penis or clitoris after an erection or orgasm*) the process of becoming limp **2.** (*of a swelling*) the process of disappearing

deuteranopia /ˌdjuːtərə'nəʊpiə/ *noun* a form of colour blindness in which someone cannot see green

develop /dɪ'veləp/ *verb* **1.** to become larger and stronger, or more complex ○ *The embryo is developing normally.* ○ *A swelling developed under the armpit.* ○ *The sore throat developed into an attack of meningitis.* **2.** to make something start to happen ○ *We're developing a new system for dealing with admission to A & E.* **3.** to make something start to grow or become larger, stronger or more complex ○ *He does exercises to develop his muscles.* **4.** to start to have an illness ○ *The baby may be developing a cold.*

development /dɪ'veləpmənt/ *noun* **1.** the process of growing, or of becoming larger and stronger, or more complex ○ *The development of the embryo takes place in the uterus.* **2.** something which happens and causes a change in a situation ○ *Report any developments to me at once.*

developmental delay /dɪˌveləpmənt(ə)l dɪ ˌleɪ/ *noun* the fact of being later than usual in developing, either physically or psychologically

deviance /'diːviəns/ *noun* sexual behaviour which is considered unusual

deviated nasal septum /ˌdiːvieɪtɪd ˌneɪz(ə)l 'septəm/, **deviated septum** /ˌdiːvieɪtɪd 'septəm/ *noun* an unusual position of the septum of the nose which may block the nose and cause nosebleeds

deviation /ˌdiːvi'eɪʃ(ə)n/ *noun* **1.** the fact of being different from what is usual or expected or something which is different from what is usual or expected **2.** an unusual position of a joint or of the eye, as in strabismus

dexamethasone /ˌdeksə'meθəsəʊn/ *noun* a synthetic steroid drug that is used to treat inflammation and hormonal imbalances

Dexa scan /'deksə skæn/ *noun* a technique to assess changes in someone's bone density, as in osteoporosis or in Paget's disease. Full form **Dual Energy X-Ray Absorptiometry**

dextro- /dekstrəʊ/ *prefix* referring to the right, or the right side of the body

dextromoramide /ˌdekstrə'mɔːrəmaɪd/ *noun* an opioid drug used to reduce pain

dextrose /'dekstrəʊz/ *noun* same as **glucose**

DH *abbreviation* Department of Health

DI *abbreviation* donor insemination

di- /daɪ/ *prefix* two, double

dia- /daɪə/ *prefix* **1.** through or throughout **2.** across **3.** in different or opposite directions **4.** apart

diabetes /ˌdaɪə'biːtiːz/ *noun* **1.** one of a group of diseases which cause the body to produce large amounts of urine. ◊ **gestational diabetes 2.** same as **diabetes mellitus**

diabetes insipidus /daɪəˌbiːtiːz ɪn'sɪpɪdəs/ *noun* a rare disorder of the pituitary gland causing an inadequate amount of the hormone vasopressin, which controls urine production, to be produced, leading to excessive passing of urine and extreme thirst

diabetes mellitus /ˌdaɪəˌbiːtiːz ˈmelɪtəs/ *noun* a disease where the body cannot control sugar absorption because the pancreas does not secrete enough insulin

COMMENT: Diabetes mellitus has two forms: Type I may have a viral trigger caused by an infection which affects the cells in the pancreas which produce insulin; Type II is caused by a lower sensitivity to insulin, is common in older people, and is associated with obesity. Symptoms of diabetes mellitus are tiredness, unusual thirst, frequent passing of water and sweet-smelling urine. Blood and urine tests show high levels of sugar. Treatment for Type II diabetes involves keeping to a strict diet and reducing weight, and sometimes the use of oral hypoglycaemic drugs such as glibenclamide. Type I diabetes is treated with regular injections of insulin.

diabetic cataract /ˌdaɪəbetɪk ˈkætərækt/ *noun* a cataract which develops in people who have diabetes

diabetic coma /ˌdaɪəbetɪk ˈkəʊmə/ *noun* a state of unconsciousness caused by untreated diabetes

diabetic retinopathy /ˌdaɪəbetɪk retɪˈnɒpəθi/ *noun* a disease of the retina, caused by diabetes

diabetogenic /ˌdaɪəbetəˈdʒenɪk/ *adjective* which causes diabetes

diabetologist /ˌdaɪəbeˈtɒlədʒɪst/ *noun* a doctor specialising in the treatment of diabetes mellitus

diaclasia /ˌdaɪəˈkleɪziə/ *noun* a fracture made by a surgeon to repair an earlier fracture which has set badly, or to correct a deformity

diadochokinesis /daɪˌædəkəʊkaɪˈniːsɪs/ *noun* the natural ability to make muscles move limbs in opposite directions

diagnosis /ˌdaɪəgˈnəʊsɪs/ *noun* the act of diagnosing a condition or illness ○ *The doctor's diagnosis was a viral infection, but the child's parents asked for a second opinion.* ○ *They found it difficult to make a diagnosis.* Compare **prognosis** (NOTE: The plural is **diagnoses**.)

diagnostic /ˌdaɪəgˈnɒstɪk/ *adjective* referring to diagnosis

diagnostic and treatment centre /ˌdaɪəgnɒstɪk ən ˈtriːtmənt ˌsentə/ *noun* a facility mainly for day surgery or short-term stay, where a range of planned operations such as joint replacements, hernia repair and cataract removal can be undertaken. Abbreviation **DTC**

diagnostic radiographer /daɪəgˌnɒstɪk ˌreɪdiˈɒgrəfə/ *noun* ♦ **radiographer**

dialysate /daɪˈælɪsət/ *noun* material which is subjected to dialysis

dialyser /ˈdaɪəlaɪzə/ *noun* an apparatus which uses a membrane to separate solids from liquids, e.g. a kidney machine

dialysis /daɪˈæləsɪs/ *noun* **1.** a procedure in which a membrane is used as a filter to separate soluble waste substances from the blood **2.** same as **renal dialysis**

diapedesis /ˌdaɪəpɪˈdiːsɪs/ *noun* the movement of white blood cells through the walls of the capillaries into tissues in the development of inflammation

diaphoresis /ˌdaɪəfəˈriːsɪs/ *noun* excessive perspiration

diaphoretic /ˌdaɪəfəˈretɪk/ *noun* a drug which causes sweating ■ *adjective* causing sweating

diaphragm /ˈdaɪəfræm/ *noun* **1.** a thin layer of tissue stretched across an opening, especially the flexible sheet of muscle and fibre which separates the chest from the abdomen and moves to pull air into the lungs in respiration **2.** same as **vaginal diaphragm**

diaphragmatic /ˌdaɪəfrægˈmætɪk/ *adjective* referring to a diaphragm, or like a diaphragm

diaphyseal /ˌdaɪəˈfɪziəl/ *adjective* referring to a diaphysis

diaphysis /daɪˈæfəsɪs/ *noun* the long central part of a long bone. Also called **shaft**. See illustration at BONE MARROW in Supplement

diaphysitis /ˌdaɪəfəˈsaɪtɪs/ *noun* inflammation of the diaphysis, often associated with rheumatic disease

diarrhoea /ˌdaɪəˈriːə/ *noun* a condition in which someone frequently passes liquid faeces ○ *attack of diarrhoea* ○ *mild/severe diarrhoea*

diarthrosis /ˌdaɪɑːˈθrəʊsɪs/ *noun* same as **synovial joint**

diastase /ˈdaɪəsteɪz/ *noun* an enzyme which breaks down starch and converts it into sugar

diastasis /ˌdaɪəˈsteɪsɪs/ *noun* a condition in which a bone separates into parts

diastema /ˌdaɪəˈstiːmə/ *noun* **1.** an unusually wide space between adjacent teeth **2.** an unusual gap in any body part or organ

diastolic /ˌdaɪəˈstɒlɪk/ *adjective* relating to the diastole

diastolic pressure /ˌdaɪəstɒlɪk ˈpreʃə/ *noun* blood pressure taken at the diastole (NOTE: Diastolic pressure is always lower than systolic.)

diathermy /ˌdaɪəˈθɜːmi/ *noun* the use of high-frequency electric current to produce heat in body tissue

diathermy needle /daɪəˌθɜːmi ˈniːd(ə)l/ *noun* a needle used in surgical diathermy

diathermy snare /ˌdaɪəˈθɜːmi sneə/ *noun* a snare which is heated by electrodes and burns away tissue

diathesis /daɪ'æθəsɪs/ *noun* the general inherited constitution of a person in relation to their susceptibility to specific diseases or allergies

diazepam /daɪ'æzəpæm/ *noun* a tranquilliser used in the short term to treat anxiety and as a muscle relaxant. In the long term it is potentially addictive.

diazoxide /ˌdaɪə'zɒksaɪd/ *noun* a drug used as a vasodilator, to reduce hypertension

DIC *abbreviation* disseminated intravascular coagulation

dicephalus /daɪ'sefələs/ *noun* a fetus with two heads

dichlorphenamide /ˌdaɪklɔː'fenəmaɪd/ *noun* a drug used to treat glaucoma

dichromatism /ˌdaɪkrəʊ'mætɪz(ə)m/ *noun* colour blindness in which only two of the three primary colours can be seen. Compare **monochromatism**, **trichromatism**

diclofenac sodium /ˌdaɪkləʊfenæk 'səʊdiəm/ *noun* an anti-inflammatory drug used to treat rheumatic disease

dicrotism /'daɪkrətɪz(ə)m/ *noun* a condition in which the pulse occurs twice with each heartbeat

die /daɪ/ *verb* to stop living ○ *His father died last year.* ○ *She died in a car crash.* (NOTE: **dying – died**)

diet /'daɪət/ *noun* the amount and type of food eaten ○ *a balanced diet* ■ *verb* to reduce the quantity of food you eat, or to change the type of food you eat, in order to become thinner or healthier ○ *He is dieting to try to lose weight.*

dietary /'daɪət(ə)ri/ *noun* a system of nutrition and energy ○ *The nutritionist supervised the dietaries for the patients.* ■ *adjective* referring to a diet

dietary fibre /'daɪət(ə)ri ˌfaɪbə/ *noun* fibrous matter in food, which cannot be digested. Also called **roughage**

COMMENT: Dietary fibre is found in cereals, nuts, fruit and some green vegetables. There are two types of fibre in food: insoluble fibre, e.g. in bread and cereals, which is not digested, and soluble fibre, e.g. in vegetables and pulses. Foods with the highest proportion of fibre include wholemeal bread, beans and dried apricots. Fibre is thought to be necessary to help digestion and avoid developing constipation, obesity and appendicitis.

dietetic /ˌdaɪə'tetɪk/ *adjective* referring to diets

dietetics /ˌdaɪə'tetɪks/ *noun* the study of food, nutrition and health, especially when applied to people's food intake

dietitian /ˌdaɪə'tɪʃ(ə)n/ *noun* someone who specialises in the study of diet, especially someone in a hospital who supervises dietaries as part of the medical treatment of patients

Dietl's crisis /'diːt(ə)lz ˌkraɪsɪs/ *noun* a painful blockage of the ureter, causing back pressure on the kidney which fills with urine and swells [After Joseph Dietl (1804–78), Polish physician.]

diet sheet /'daɪət ʃiːt/ *noun* a list of suggestions for quantities and types of food given to someone to follow

differential /ˌdɪfə'renʃəl/ *adjective* referring to a difference

differential diagnosis /ˌdɪfəˌrenʃ(ə)l ˌdaɪəg 'nəʊsɪs/ *noun* the identification of one disease from a number of other similar diseases by comparing the range of symptoms of each

differentiation /ˌdɪfərenʃi'eɪʃ(ə)n/ *noun* the development of specialised cells during the early embryo stage

diffuse /dɪ'fjuːs/ *verb* /dɪ'fjuːz/ /dɪ'fjuːs/; /dɪ 'fjuːz/ to spread through tissue, or cause something to spread ○ *Some substances easily diffuse through the walls of capillaries.* ■ *adjective* referring to a disease which is widespread in the body, or which affects many organs or cells

diffusion /dɪ'fjuːʒ(ə)n/ *noun* the process of mixing a liquid with another liquid, or a gas with another gas

digest /daɪ'dʒest/ *verb* to break down food in the alimentary canal and convert it into components which are absorbed into the body

digestion /daɪ'dʒestʃən/ *noun* the process by which food is broken down in the alimentary canal into components which can be absorbed by the body

digestive /daɪ'dʒestɪv/ *adjective* relating to digestion

digestive juice /daɪ'dʒestɪv juːs/ *noun* ♦ **gastric juice** (*usually plural*)

digestive system /daɪ'dʒestɪv ˌsɪstəm/ *noun* the set of organs such as the stomach, liver and pancreas which are associated with the digestion of food. Also called **alimentary system**

digestive tract /daɪ'dʒestɪv trækt/ *noun* same as **alimentary canal**

digit /'dɪdʒɪt/ *noun* **1.** a finger or a toe **2.** a number

digitalin /ˌdɪdʒɪ'teɪlɪn/, **digitalis** /ˌdɪdʒɪ 'teɪlɪs/ *noun* a drug derived from foxglove leaves, used in small doses to treat heart conditions

digitalise /'dɪdʒɪtəlaɪz/, **digitalize** *verb* to treat someone who has heart failure with digoxin

digital palpation /ˌdɪdʒɪt(ə)l pæl'peɪʃ(ə)n/ *noun* an examination of part of the body by feeling it with the fingers

digitoxin /ˌdɪdʒɪ'tɒksɪn/ *noun* an extract of foxglove leaves, used as a drug to stimulate the heart in cases of heart failure or irregular heartbeat

digoxin /daɪˈdʒɒksɪn/ *noun* an extract of fox-glove leaves, which acts more rapidly than digi-toxin when used as a heart stimulant

dihydrocodeine tartrate /daɪˌhaɪdrəʊ ˌkəʊdiːn ˈtɑːtreɪt/ *noun* an analgesic used to treat severe pain

dilatation /ˌdaɪleɪˈteɪʃ(ə)n/, **dilation** /daɪ ˈleɪʃ(ə)n/ *noun* the act of making a hollow organ or a passage in the body bigger or wider ○ *dilata-tion of the cervix during labour*

dilatation and curettage /daɪleɪˌteɪʃ(ə)n ən kjʊəˈretɪdʒ/ *noun* a surgical operation to scrape the interior of the uterus to obtain a tissue sample or to remove products of miscarriage. Abbrevia-tion **D & C**

dilate /daɪˈleɪt/ *verb* to become wider or larger, or make something become wider or larger ○ *to dilate the pupil of the eye*

dilator /daɪˈleɪtə/ *noun* an instrument used to widen the entrance to a cavity

dilator pupillae muscle /daɪˌleɪtə pjuːˈpɪliː ˌmʌs(ə)l/ *noun* a muscle in the iris which pulls the iris back and so makes the pupil expand

diltiazem hydrochloride /dɪlˌtaɪəzəm ˌhaɪdrəˈklɔːraɪd/ *noun* a calcium channel blocker used to treat hypertension

diluent /ˈdɪljuənt/ *noun* a substance which is used to dilute a liquid, e.g. water

dilute /daɪˈluːt/ *adjective* with water added ■ *verb* to add water to a liquid to make it less con-centrated ○ *Dilute the disinfectant in four parts of water.*

dimenhydrinate /ˌdaɪmenˈhaɪdrəneɪt/ *noun* an antihistamine drug that relieves travel sickness

dimetria /daɪˈmiːtriə/ *noun* a condition in which a woman has a double uterus

dioptre /daɪˈɒptə/ *noun* a unit of measurement of the refraction of a lens

DIP *abbreviation* distal interphalangeal joint

diphenoxalate /ˌdaɪfenˈɒksɪleɪt/ *noun* a drug related to pethidine that is used to treat diarrhoea, sometimes mixed with a little atropine in com-mercial preparations

diphtheria /dɪfˈθɪəriə/ *noun* a serious infec-tious disease of children, caused by the bacillus *Corynebacterium diphtheriae*, characterised by fever and the formation of a fibrous growth like a membrane in the throat which restricts breathing

diphtheroid /ˈdɪfθərɔɪd/ *adjective* referring to a bacterium similar to the diphtheria bacterium

-dipine /dɪpɪn/ *suffix* used in the names of cal-cium channel blockers ○ *nifedipine*

dipl- /dɪpl/ *prefix* same as **diplo-** (*used before vowels*)

diplacusis /ˌdɪpləˈkjuːsɪs/ *noun* a disorder of the cochlea in which a person hears one sound as two sounds of different pitch

diplegia /daɪˈpliːdʒə/ *noun* paralysis of a simi-lar part on both sides of the body, e.g. paralysis of both arms. Compare **hemiplegia**

diplegic /daɪˈpliːdʒɪk/ *adjective* referring to diplegia

diplo- /dɪpləʊ/ *prefix* double

diploe /ˈdɪpləʊiː/ *noun* a layer of spongy bone tissue filled with red bone marrow, between the inner and outer layers of the skull

diploid /ˈdɪplɔɪd/ *adjective* referring to a cell where there are two copies of each chromosome, except the sex chromosome. In humans the dip-loid number of chromosomes is 46.

diplopia /dɪˈpləʊpiə/ *noun* a condition in which someone sees single objects as double. Also called **double vision**

direct contact /daɪˌrekt ˈkɒntækt/ *noun* a sit-uation where someone or something physically touches an infected person or object

director /daɪˈrektə/ *noun* an instrument used to limit the incision made with a surgical knife

dis- /dɪs/ *prefix* **1.** undoing or reversal **2.** removal from **3.** lacking or deprived of

disability /ˌdɪsəˈbɪlɪti/ *noun* a condition in which part of the body does not function in the usual way and makes some activities difficult or impossible. ◊ **learning disability**

Disabled Living Foundation /dɪsˌeɪb(ə)ld ˈlɪvɪŋ faʊnˌdeɪʃ(ə)n/ *noun* a charity which aims to help disabled people live independently

disarticulation /ˌdɪsɑːtɪkjʊˈleɪʃ(ə)n/ *noun* the amputation of a limb at a joint, which does not involve dividing a bone

disc /dɪsk/ *noun* a flat round structure. ◊ **intervertebral disc**

discharge /dɪsˈtʃɑːdʒ/ *noun* /ˈdɪstʃɑːdʒ/ **1.** the secretion of liquid from an opening **2.** the process of sending a patient away from a hospital because the treatment has ended ■ *verb* **1.** to secrete liquid out of an opening ○ *The wound dis-charged a thin stream of pus.* **2.** to send a patient away from hospital because the treatment has ended ○ *He was discharged from hospital last week.*

discharge planning /ˈdɪstʃɑːdʒ ˌplænɪŋ/ *noun* the work of making a plan for when a patient leaves hospital to live at home

disclosure check /dɪsˈkləʊʒə tʃek/ *noun* same as **CRB check**

discomfort /dɪsˈkʌmfət/ *noun* a feeling of mild pain ○ *You may experience some discomfort after the operation.*

discrete /dɪˈskriːt/ *adjective* separate, not joined together

disease /dɪˈziːz/ *noun* a condition that stops the body from functioning in the usual way ○ *an infectious disease* ○ *She is suffering from a very serious disease of the kidneys* or *from a serious* *kidney disease.* ○ *He is a specialist in occupational diseases.* (NOTE: The term **disease** is applied to all physical and mental reactions which make a person ill. Diseases with distinct characteristics have individual names. For other terms referring to disease, see words beginning with **path-, patho-**.)

disfigure /dɪs'fɪgə/ *verb* to change someone's appearance so as to make it less pleasant to look at ○ *Her legs were disfigured by scars.*

disinfect /ˌdɪsɪn'fekt/ *verb* to make the surface of something or somewhere free from microorganisms ○ *She disinfected the skin with surgical spirit.* ○ *All the patient's clothes have to be disinfected.*

disinfectant /ˌdɪsɪn'fektənt/ *noun* a substance used to kill microorganisms on the surface of something

disinfection /ˌdɪsɪn'fekʃən/ *noun* the removal of microorganisms on the surface of something

COMMENT: The words **disinfect, disinfectant**, and **disinfection** are used for substances which destroy microorganisms on instruments, objects or the skin. Substances used to kill microorganisms inside infected people are **antibiotics**.

disinfestation /ˌdɪsɪnfe'steɪʃ(ə)n/ *noun* the removal of insects or other pests from a place, person or animal

dislocate /'dɪsləkeɪt/ *verb* to displace a bone from its usual position at a joint, or to become displaced ○ *He fell and dislocated his elbow.* ○ *The shoulder joint dislocates easily.*

dislocation /ˌdɪslə'keɪʃ(ə)n/ *noun* a condition in which a bone is displaced from its usual position at a joint. Also called **luxation**

dismember /dɪs'membə/ *verb* to cut off or pull off someone's arms or legs, often violently or in an accident

dismemberment /dɪs'membəmənt/ *noun* the state of being dismembered

disordered action of the heart /dɪsˌɔːdəd ˌækʃən əv ðə 'hɑːt/ *noun* a condition in which someone has palpitations, breathlessness and dizziness, caused by effort or worry. Also called **da Costa's syndrome, cardiac neurosis**. Abbreviation **DAH**

disorientation /ˌdɪsɔːriən'teɪʃ(ə)n/ *noun* a condition in which someone is confused and does not know where he or she is

dispensary /dɪ'spensəri/ *noun* a place where drugs are prepared or mixed and given out according to a doctor's prescription, e.g. part of a chemist's shop or a department in a hospital

dispensing optician /dɪˈspensɪŋ ɒpˌtɪʃ(ə)n/ *noun* a person who fits and sells glasses but does not test eyes

dispensing practice /dɪ'spensɪŋ ˌpræktɪs/ *noun* a doctor's practice which dispenses prescribed medicines to its patients

displace /dɪs'pleɪs/ *verb* to put something out of its usual place

displacement /dɪs'pleɪsmənt/ *noun* the fact of being moved out of the usual position ○ *fracture of the radius together with displacement of the wrist*

disposition /ˌdɪspə'zɪʃ(ə)n/ *noun* a person's general character or tendency to act in a particular way

dissect /daɪ'sekt/ *verb* to cut and separate tissues in a body to examine them

dissection /daɪ'sekʃən/ *noun* the action of cutting and separating parts of a body or an organ as part of a surgical operation, an autopsy or a course of study

disseminated /dɪ'semɪneɪtɪd/ *adjective* occurring in every part of an organ or in the whole body

disseminated intravascular coagulation /dɪˌsemɪneɪtɪd ˌɪntrəˌvæskʊlə kəʊˌægjʊ'leɪʃ(ə)n/ *noun* a disorder that causes extensive clot formation in the blood vessels, followed by severe bleeding. Abbreviation **DIC**

disseminated sclerosis /dɪˌsemɪneɪtd sklə'rəʊsɪs/ *noun* same as **multiple sclerosis**

dissemination /dɪˌsemɪ'neɪʃ(ə)n/ *noun* the fact of being widespread throughout the body

dissociation /dɪˌsəʊʃi'eɪʃ(ə)n/ *noun* **1.** the separation of parts or functions **2.** (*in psychiatry*) a condition in which part of the consciousness becomes separated from the rest and becomes independent

dissociative disorder /dɪ'səʊsiətɪv dɪsˌɔːdə/ *noun* a type of hysteria in which someone shows psychological changes such as a split personality or amnesia rather than physical ones

distal /'dɪst(ə)l/ *adjective* further away from the centre of a body

Distalgesic /ˌdɪst(ə)l'dʒiːzɪk/ a trade name for the analgesic co-proxamol

distally /'dɪst(ə)li/ *adverb* placed further away from the centre or point of attachment. Opposite **proximally**. See illustration at **ANATOMICAL TERMS** in Supplement

distension /dɪs'tenʃən/ *noun* a condition in which something is swollen ○ *Distension of the veins in the abdomen is a sign of blocking of the portal vein.*

distichiasis /ˌdɪstɪ'kaɪəsɪs/ *noun* the presence of extra eyelashes, sometimes growing on the meibomian glands

distraction /dɪ'strækʃən/ *noun* **1.** something that takes a person's attention away from something else **2.** a state where someone is very emotionally and mentally troubled

district general hospital /ˌdɪstrɪkt ˌdʒen(ə)rəl 'hɒspɪt(ə)l/ *noun* a hospital which serves the needs of the population of a specific district

district nurse /ˌdɪstrɪkt 'nɜːs/ *noun* a nurse who visits and treats people in their homes

disturbed /dɪ'stɜːbd/ *adjective* affected by a psychiatric disorder ○ *severely disturbed children*

disulfiram /daɪ'sʌlfɪræm/ *noun* a drug used to treat alcoholism by causing severe nausea if alcohol is consumed with it

dithranol /'dɪθrənɒl/ *noun* an anti-inflammatory drug used to treat dermatitis and psoriasis

diuresis /ˌdaɪjʊ'riːsɪs/ *noun* an increase in the production of urine

diuretic /ˌdaɪjʊ'retɪk/ *adjective* causing the kidneys to produce more urine ■ *noun* a substance which makes the kidneys produce more urine and, in the treatment of oedema and hypertension

diurnal /daɪ'ɜːn(ə)l/ *adjective* **1.** happening in the daytime **2.** happening every day

divarication /daɪˌværɪ'keɪʃ(ə)n/ *noun* **1.** separation into widely spread branches **2.** the point at which a structure forks or divides

divergence /daɪ'vɜːdʒəns/ *noun* **1.** a condition in which one eye points directly at the object of interest but the other does not **2.** the process of moving apart to follow different courses **3.** the amount of difference between two quantities, especially where the difference is unexpected **4.** a deviation from a typical behaviour pattern or expressed wish

divergent strabismus /daɪˌvɜːdʒənt strə'bɪzməs/, **divergent squint** /daɪˌvɜːdʒənt 'skwɪnt/ *noun* a condition in which a person's eyes both look away from the nose. Opposite **convergent strabismus**

diverticula /ˌdaɪvə'tɪkjʊlə/ *plural noun* plural of **diverticulum**

diverticular disease /ˌdaɪvə'tɪkjʊlə dɪˌziːz/ *noun* a disease of the large intestine, where the colon thickens and diverticula form in the walls, causing pain in the lower abdomen

diverticulitis /ˌdaɪvətɪkjʊ'laɪtɪs/ *noun* inflammation of diverticula formed in the wall of the colon

diverticulosis /ˌdaɪvətɪkjʊ'ləʊsɪs/ *noun* a condition in which diverticula form in the intestine but are not inflamed. In the small intestine, this can lead to blind loop syndrome.

diverticulum /ˌdaɪvə'tɪkjʊləm/ *noun* a little sac or pouch which develops in the wall of the intestine or another organ (NOTE: The plural is **diverticula**.)

division /dɪ'vɪʒ(ə)n/ *noun* the action of cutting or splitting into parts

divulsor /dɪ'vʌlsə/ *noun* a surgical instrument used to expand a passage in the body

dizygotic /ˌdaɪzaɪ'gɒtɪk/ *adjective* developed from two separately fertilised eggs

dizygotic twins /ˌdaɪzaɪgɒtɪk 'twɪnz/ *plural noun* twins who are not identical and not always of the same sex because they come from two different ova fertilised at the same time. Also called **fraternal twins**

dizziness /'dɪzinəs/ *noun* the feeling that everything is going round because the sense of balance has been affected

dl *abbreviation* decilitre

DLE *abbreviation* disseminated lupus erythematosus

dm *abbreviation* decimetre

DNA *noun* one of the nucleic acids, the basic genetic material present in the nucleus of each cel. Full form **deoxyribonucleic acid**. ◊ **RNA**

DNA fingerprint /ˌdiː en eɪ 'fɪŋgəprɪnt/ *noun* same as **genetic fingerprint**

DNA fingerprinting /ˌdiː en ˌeɪ 'fɪŋgəprɪntɪŋ/ *noun* same as **genetic fingerprinting**

DOA *abbreviation* dead on arrival

dobutamine /dəʊ'bjuːtəmiːn/ *noun* a drug used to stimulate the heart

doctor /'dɒktə/ *noun* a person who has trained in medicine and is qualified to examine people when they are ill to find out what is wrong with them and to prescribe a course of treatment

COMMENT: In the UK surgeons are traditionally not called 'Doctor', but are addressed as 'Mr', 'Mrs', etc. The title 'doctor' is also applied to persons who have a higher degree from a university in a non-medical subject. So 'Dr Jones' may have a degree in music, or in any other subject without a connection with medicine.

Döderlein's bacillus /'dɜːdələɪnz bəˌsɪlʌs/ *noun* a bacterium usually found in the vagina [After Albert Siegmund Gustav Döderlein (1860–1941), German obstetrician and gynaecologist.]

dolicho- /dɒlɪkəʊ/ *prefix* long

dolichocephalic /ˌdɒlɪkəʊse'fælɪk/ *adjective* referring to a person with an unusually long skull

dolichocephaly /ˌdɒlɪkəʊ'sefəli/ *noun* a condition of a person who has a skull which is longer than usual, the measurement across the skull being less than 75% of the length of the head from front to back

dolor /'dɒlə/ *noun* pain

dolorimetry /ˌdɒlə'rɪmətri/ *noun* the measurement of pain

domiciliary /ˌdɒmɪ'sɪliəri/ *adjective* at home or in the home

dominance /'dɒmɪnəns/ *noun* the characteristic of a gene form (**allele**) that leads to the trait which it controls being shown in any individual carrying it

dominant /'dɒmɪnənt/ *adjective* important or powerful ∎ *noun* (*of an allele*) having the characteristic that leads to the trait which it controls being shown in any individual carrying it. Compare **recessive**

domino booking /'dɒmɪnəʊ ˌbʊkɪŋ/ *noun* an arrangement for the delivery of a baby, where the baby is delivered in hospital by a midwife and the mother and child return home soon afterwards

Donald-Fothergill operation /ˌdɒnəld 'fɒðəɡɪl ɒpəˌreɪʃ(ə)n/ *noun* an operation to close the neck of the vagina

donor /'dəʊnə/ *noun* a person who gives blood, tissue, organs or reproductive material to be used to treat another person

donor card /'dəʊnə kɑːd/ *noun* a card carried by people stating that they give permission for their organs to be transplanted into other people after they have died

donor insemination /ˌdəʊnə ɪnsemɪ 'neɪʃ(ə)n/ *noun* artificial insemination using the sperm of an anonymous donor. Abbreviation **DI**

dopa /'dəʊpə/ *noun* a chemical related to adrenaline and dopamine. It occurs naturally in the body and in the form levodopa is used to treat Parkinson's disease.

dopamine /'dəʊpəmiːn/ *noun* a substance found in the medulla of the adrenal glands, which also acts as a neurotransmitter. Lack of dopamine is associated with Parkinson's disease.

dopaminergic /ˌdəʊpəmɪ'nɜːdʒɪk/ *adjective* referring to a neurone or receptor stimulated by dopamine

Doppler transducer /'dɒplə trænzˌdjuːsə/ *noun* a device to measure blood flow, commonly used to monitor fetal heart rate

Doppler ultrasound /ˌdɒplə 'ʌltrəsaʊnd/ *noun* the use of the Doppler effect in ultrasound to detect red blood cells

Doppler ultrasound flowmeter /ˌdɒplə ˌʌltrəsaʊnd 'fləʊmiːtə/ *noun* a device which measures the flow of blood and detects steady or irregular flow, allowing abnormalities or blockages to be detected

dorsa /'dɔːsə/ *plural of* **dorsum**

dorsal /'dɔːs(ə)l/ *adjective* referring to the back. Opposite **ventral**

dorsal vertebrae /ˌdɔːs(ə)l 'vɜːtɪbreɪ/ *plural noun* the twelve vertebrae in the back between the cervical vertebrae and the lumbar vertebrae

dorsi- /'dɔːsi/ *prefix* referring to the back

dorsiflexion /ˌdɔːsɪ'flekʃən/ *noun* flexion towards the back of part of the body, e.g. raising the foot at the ankle. Compare **plantar flexion**

dorso- /dɔːsəʊ/ *prefix* same as **dorsi-**

dorsoventral /ˌdɔːsəʊ'ventrəl/ *adjective* referring to both the front and the back of the body

dorsum /'dɔːsəm/ *noun* the back of any part of the body (NOTE: The plural is **dorsa**.)

dosage /'dəʊsɪdʒ/ *noun* a measured quantity of a drug calculated to be necessary for someone ○ *a low dosage* ○ *The doctor decided to increase the dosage of antibiotics.* ○ *The dosage for children is half that for adults.*

dose /dəʊs/ *noun* **1.** a measured quantity of a drug or radiation which is to be given to someone at one time ○ *It is dangerous to exceed the prescribed dose.* **2.** a short period of experiencing a minor illness (*informal*) ○ *a dose of flu* **3.** an infection with a sexually transmitted disease (*informal*) ∎ *verb* to provide someone with medication (*informal*) ○ *She has been dosing herself with laxatives.*

dosimeter /dəʊ'sɪmɪtə/ *noun* an instrument which measures the amount of X-rays or other radiation received

dosimetry /dəʊ'sɪmətri/ *noun* the act of measuring the amount of X-rays or radiation received, using a dosimeter

double-blind randomised controlled trial /ˌdʌb(ə)l blaɪnd ˌrændəmaɪzd kənˌtrəʊld 'traɪəl/ *noun* a trial used to test new treatments in which patients are randomly placed in either the treatment or the control group without either the patient or doctor knowing which group any particular patient is in

double pneumonia /ˌdʌb(ə)l njuː'məʊniə/ *noun* same as **bilateral pneumonia**

double uterus /ˌdʌb(ə)l 'juːt(ə)rəs/ *noun* a condition in which the uterus is divided into two sections by a membrane. Also called **uterus didelphys**. ◊ **dimetria**

double vision /ˌdʌb(ə)l 'vɪʒ(ə)n/ *noun* same as **diplopia** (*informal*)

douche /duːʃ/ *noun* a liquid forced into the body to wash out a cavity, or a device used for washing out a cavity

down below /ˌdaʊn bɪ'ləʊ/ *adverb* used to refer politely to the genital area (*informal*)

Down's syndrome /'daʊnz ˌsɪndrəʊm/ *noun* a condition due to the existence of an extra copy of chromosome 21, in which a baby is born with slanting eyes, a wide face, speech difficulties and usually some degree of learning difficulty [Described 1866. After John Langdon Haydon Down (1828–96), British physician at Normansfield Hospital, Teddington, UK]

downstairs /daʊn'steəz/ *adverb* used to refer politely to the genital area (*informal*)

down there /ˌdaʊn 'ðeə/ *adverb* used to refer politely to the genital area (*informal*)

doxepin /'dɒksɪpɪn/ *noun* a drug used as a sedative and antidepressant

doxycycline /ˌdɒksiˈsaɪkliːn/ *noun* a widely used antibiotic derived from tetracycline

DPT *abbreviation* diphtheria, whooping cough, tetanus

DPT vaccine /ˌdiː piː ˈtiː ˌvæksiːn/, **DPT immunisation** /ˌdiː piː ˈtiː ɪmjʊnaɪˌzeɪʃ(ə)n/ *noun* a combined vaccine or immunisation against the three diseases, diphtheria, whooping cough and tetanus

Dr *abbreviation* doctor (NOTE: used when writing someone's name: *Dr Smith*)

drachm /dræm/ *noun* a measure used in pharmacy, equal to 3.8g dry weight or 3.7ml liquid measure

dracontiasis /ˌdrækɒnˈtaɪəsɪs/, **dracunculiasis** /drəˌkʌŋkjʊˈlaɪəsɪs/ *noun* a tropical disease caused by the guinea worm *Dracunculus medinensis* which enters the body from infected drinking water and forms blisters on the skin, frequently leading to secondary arthritis, fibrosis and cellulitis

Dracunculus /drəˈkʌŋkjʊləs/ *noun* a parasitic worm which enters the body and rises to the skin to form a blister. The infection frequently leads to secondary arthritis, fibrosis and cellulitis. Also called **guinea worm**

dragee /dræˈʒeɪ/ *noun* a sugar-coated tablet or pill

drain /dreɪn/ *noun* a tube to remove liquid from the body ■ *verb* to remove liquid from the body ○ *an operation to drain the sinus* ○ *They drained the pus from the abscess.*

drainage /ˈdreɪnɪdʒ/ *noun* the removal of liquid from the site of an operation or pus from an abscess by means of a tube or wick left in the body for a time

drape /dreɪp/ *noun* a thin material used to place over someone about to undergo surgery, leaving the operation site uncovered

drawn /drɔːn/ *adjective* appearing tired and careworn, usually as a result of anxiety, grief or illness

draw-sheet /ˈdrɔː ʃiːt/ *noun* a sheet under a person in bed, folded so that it can be pulled out as it becomes soiled

drepanocyte /ˈdrepənəʊsaɪt/ *noun* same as **sickle cell**

drepanocytosis /ˌdrepənəʊsaɪˈtəʊsɪs/ *noun* same as **sickle-cell anaemia**

dressing /ˈdresɪŋ/ *noun* a covering or bandage applied to a wound to protect it ○ *The patient's dressings need to be changed regularly.*

drill /drɪl/ *noun* a tool which rotates very rapidly to make a hole, especially a surgical instrument used in dentistry to remove caries ■ *verb* to make a hole with a drill ○ *A small hole is drilled in the skull.* ○ *The dentist drilled one of her molars.*

Drinker respirator /ˈdrɪŋkə ˌrespɪreɪtə/ *noun* a machine which encloses the whole of the body

except the head, and in which air pressure is increased and decreased, so forcing the person to breathe in and out. Also called **iron lung**

drip /drɪp/ *noun* a system for introducing liquid slowly and continuously into the body, by which a bottle of liquid is held above a person and the fluid flows slowly down a tube into a needle in a vein or into the stomach ○ *After her operation, the patient was put on a drip.*

drip feed /ˈdrɪp fiːd/ *noun* a drip containing nutrients

drop /drɒp/ *noun* **1.** a small quantity of liquid **2.** a sudden reduction or fall in the quantity of something ○ *a drop in pressure* ■ *plural noun* **drops** liquid medicine for the eye, nose, or ear administered with a dropper ■ *verb* **1.** to fall or let something fall ○ *Pressure in the artery dropped suddenly.* **2.** to reduce suddenly

drop attack /ˈdrɒp əˌtæk/ *noun* a condition in which a person suddenly falls down, though he or she is not unconscious, caused by sudden weakness of the spine

droperidol /drɒˈperɪdɒl/ *noun* a drug used to keep someone in a calm state before an operation

drop foot /ˈdrɒp fʊt/ *noun* a condition, caused by a muscular disorder, in which the ankle is not strong and the foot hangs limp

droplet /ˈdrɒplət/ *noun* a very small quantity of liquid

droplet infection /ˈdrɒplət ɪnˌfekʃən/ *noun* an infection developed by inhaling droplets containing a virus, e.g. from a sneeze

dropper /ˈdrɒpə/ *noun* a small glass or plastic tube with a rubber bulb at one end, used to suck up and expel liquid in drops

dropsy /ˈdrɒpsi/ *noun* same as **oedema** (*dated*)

drop wrist /ˌdrɒp ˈrɪst/ *noun* a condition caused by a muscular disorder, in which the wrist is not strong and the hand hangs limp

drug /drʌg/ *noun* **1.** a natural or synthetic chemical substance which is used in medicine and affects the way in which organs or tissues function **2.** a substance taken by choice which produces a strong effect on a person's feelings and state of mind ○ *recreational drug* ○ *controlled drugs*

drug addict /ˈdrʌg ˌædɪkt/ *noun* a person who is physically and mentally dependent on taking a particular drug regularly ○ *a heroin addict* ○ *a morphine addict*

drug addiction /ˈdrʌg əˌdɪkʃən/ *noun* the fact of being mentally and physically dependent on taking a particular drug regularly. Also called **drug dependence**

drug allergy /ˈdrʌg ˌælədʒi/ *noun* a reaction to a particular drug

drug tolerance /ˈdrʌg ˌtɒlərəns/ *noun* a condition in which a drug has been given to someone for so long that his or her body no longer reacts to it, and the dosage has to be increased

dry /draɪ/ *adjective* **1.** not wet ○ *The surface of the wound should be kept dry.* **2.** containing only a small amount of moisture ○ *She uses a cream to soften her dry skin.* (NOTE: **drier – driest**) ■ *verb* to remove moisture from something (NOTE: **dries – drying – dried**)

dry beriberi /ˌdraɪ ˌberiˈberi/ *noun* beriberi associated with loss of feeling and paralysis

dry-eye syndrome /ˌdraɪ ˈaɪ ˌsɪndrəʊm/ *noun* same as **xerosis**

dry out /ˌdraɪ ˈaʊt/ *verb* **1.** same as **dry 2. to** treat someone for alcoholism, or undergo treatment for alcoholism (*informal*)

dry socket /ˌdraɪ ˈsɒkɪt/ *noun* inflammation of the socket of a tooth which has just been removed

DTC *abbreviation* diagnostic and treatment centre

DTs *abbreviation* delirium tremens

Duchenne muscular dystrophy /duːˌʃen ˌmʌskjʊlə ˈdɪstrəfi/, **Duchenne's muscular dystrophy** /duːˌʃenz ˌmʌskjʊlə ˈdɪstrəfi/, **Duchenne** /duːˈʃen/ *noun* an inherited form of muscular dystrophy that weakens the muscles of the upper respiratory and pelvic areas. It usually affects boys and causes early death. [Described 1849. After Guillaume Benjamin Arnaud Duchenne (1806–75), French neurologist.]

Ducrey's bacillus /duːˌkreɪz bəˈsɪləs/ *noun* a type of bacterium found in the lungs, causing chancroid. [Described 1889. After Augusto Ducrey (1860–1940), Professor of Dermatology in Pisa, then Rome, Italy.]

duct /dʌkt/ *noun* a tube which carries liquids, especially one which carries secretions

ductless /ˈdʌktləs/ *adjective* without a duct

ductless gland /ˌdʌktləs ˈɡlænd/ *noun* same as **endocrine gland**

ductule /ˈdʌktjuːl/ *noun* a very small duct

ductus /ˈdʌktəs/ *noun* same as **duct**

ductus deferens /ˌdʌktəs ˈdefərənz/ *noun* one of two tubes along which sperm pass from the epididymus to the seminal vesicles near the prostate gland. Also called **vas deferens**. See illustration at **UROGENITAL SYSTEM (MALE)** in Supplement

dull /dʌl/ *adjective* referring to pain which is not strong but which is continuously present ○ *She complained of a dull throbbing pain in her head.* ○ *He felt a dull pain in the chest.* ■ *verb* to make a sensation or awareness of a sensation less sharp ○ *The treatment dulled the pain for a while.* ○ *The drug had dulled her senses.*

dumbness /ˈdʌmnəs/ *noun* same as **mutism**

dumping syndrome /ˈdʌmpɪŋ ˌsɪndrəʊm/ *noun* same as **postgastrectomy syndrome**

duo- /djuːəʊ/ *prefix* two

duoden- /djuːəʊdiːn/ *prefix* referring to the duodenum

duodenal /ˌdjuːəʊˈdiːn(ə)l/ *adjective* referring to the duodenum

duodenal papillae /djuːəʊˌdiːn(ə)l pəˈpɪliː/ *plural noun* small projecting parts in the duodenum where the bile duct and pancreatic duct open

duodenal ulcer /djuːəʊˌdiːn(ə)l ˈʌlsə/ *noun* an ulcer in the duodenum

duodenoscope /ˌdjuːəʊˈdiːnəʊskəʊp/ *noun* an instrument used to examine the inside of the duodenum

duodenostomy /ˌdjuːəʊdɪˈnɒstəmi/ *noun* a permanent opening made between the duodenum and the abdominal wall

duodenum /ˌdjuːəˈdiːnəm/ *noun* the first part of the small intestine, going from the stomach to the jejunum. See illustration at **DIGESTIVE SYSTEM** in Supplement

duplex imaging /ˌdjuːpleks ˈɪmɪdʒɪŋ/ *noun* a type of ultrasonic imaging where the speed of the flow of blood is measured

Dupuytren's contracture /duːˌpwiːtrənz kənˈtræktʃə/ *noun* a condition in which the palmar fascia becomes thicker, causing the fingers, usually the middle and fourth fingers, to bend forwards [Described 1831. After Baron Guillaume Dupuytren (1775–1835), French surgeon.]

dura /ˈdjʊərə/ *noun* same as **dura mater**

dural /ˈdjʊər(ə)l/ *adjective* referring to the dura mater

dura mater /ˌdjʊərə ˈmeɪtə/ *noun* the thicker outer membrane of the three covering the brain. Also called **dura**, **pachymeninx**. ◊ **arachnoid**

duty /ˈdjuːti/ *noun* the activities which a person has to do as part of their job ○ *What are the duties of a night sister?* (NOTE: The plural is **duties**.) □ **to be on duty** to be working ○ *She's on duty from 2 p.m. till 10 p.m.* □ **a duty of care** the requirement to treat a patient in an appropriate way, as part of the work of being a health professional

d.v.t., DVT *abbreviation* deep-vein thrombosis

dwarfism /ˈdwɔːfɪz(ə)m/ *noun* a condition in which the growth of a person has stopped, leaving him or her much smaller than average

dynamic splint /daɪˌnæmɪk ˈsplɪnt/ *noun* a splint which uses springs to help the person move

dynamometer /ˌdaɪnəˈmɒmɪtə/ *noun* an instrument for measuring the force of muscular contraction

-dynia /dɪniə/ *suffix* pain

dys- /dɪs/ *prefix* difficult or impaired

dysaesthesia /ˌdɪsiːsˈθiːziə/ *noun* the impairment of a sense, in particular the sense of touch

dysarthria /dɪsˈɑːθriə/, **dysarthrosis** /ˌdɪsɑːˈθrəʊsɪs/ *noun* difficulty in speaking words clearly, caused by damage to the central nervous system

dysbasia /dɪsˈbeɪziə/ *noun* difficulty in walking, especially when caused by a lesion to a nerve

dyschezia /dɪsˈkiːziə/ *noun* difficulty in passing faeces

dyschondroplasia /ˌdɪskɒndrəʊˈpleɪziə/ *noun* a condition in which the long bones are shorter than usual

dyschromatopsia /ˌdɪskrəʊməˈtɒpsiə/ *noun* a condition where someone cannot distinguish colours

dyscoria /dɪsˈkɔːriə/ *noun* an unusually shaped pupil of the eye

dyscrasia /dɪsˈkreɪziə/ *noun* any unusual body condition (*dated*)

dysdiadochokinesia /ˌdɪsdaɪˌædəkəʊkaɪˈniːsiə/, **dysdiadochokinesis** /ˌdɪsdaɪˌædəkəʊkaɪˈniːsɪs/ *noun* the inability to carry out rapid movements, caused by a disorder or lesion of the cerebellum

dysentery /ˈdɪs(ə)ntri/ *noun* an infection and inflammation of the colon, causing bleeding and diarrhoea

dysfunction /dɪsˈfʌŋkʃən/ *noun* an unusual functioning of an organ

dysfunctional /dɪsˈfʌŋkʃən(ə)l/ *adjective* **1.** not working properly **2.** unable to relate to other people emotionally or socially

dysfunctional uterine bleeding /dɪs ˌfʌŋkʃən(ə)l ˌjuːtəraɪn ˈbliːdɪŋ/ *noun* bleeding in the uterus not caused by a menstrual period

dysgenesis /dɪsˈdʒenəsɪs/ *noun* unusual development

dysgerminoma /dɪsˌdʒɜːmɪˈnəʊmə/ *noun* a malignant tumour of the ovary or testicle

dysgraphia /dɪsˈɡræfiə/ *noun* difficulty in writing caused by a brain lesion

dyskariosis /dɪsˌkæriˈəʊsɪs/ *noun* the fact of becoming mature in an unusual way

dyskinesia /ˌdɪskaɪˈniːziə/ *noun* the inability to control voluntary movements

dyslalia /dɪsˈleɪliə/ *noun* a disorder of speech, caused by an unusual development of the tongue

dyslexia /dɪsˈleksiə/ *noun* a disorder of development, where a person is unable to read or write properly and confuses letters

dyslogia /dɪsˈləʊdʒə/ *noun* difficulty in putting ideas into words

dysmaturity /ˌdɪsməˈtʃʊərɪti/ *noun* a condition affecting newborn babies, shown by wrinkled skin, long fingernails and toenails and relatively little body fat

dysmenorrhoea /ˌdɪsmenəˈriːə/ *noun* pain experienced at menstruation

dysostosis /ˌdɪsɒsˈtəʊsɪs/ *noun* unusual formation of bones

dyspareunia /ˌdɪspæˈruːniə/ *noun* difficult or painful sexual intercourse in a woman

dyspepsia /dɪsˈpepsiə/ *noun* a condition in which a person feels pains or discomfort in the stomach, caused by indigestion

dysphagia /dɪsˈfeɪdʒiə/ *noun* difficulty in swallowing

dysphasia /dɪsˈfeɪziə/ *noun* difficulty in speaking and putting words into the correct order

dysphemia /dɪsˈfiːmiə/ *noun* same as **stammering**

dysphonia /dɪsˈfəʊniə/ *noun* difficulty in speaking caused by impairment of the vocal cords, or by laryngitis

dysplasia /dɪsˈpleɪziə/ *noun* an unusual development of tissue

dyspnoea /dɪspˈniːə/ *noun* difficulty or pain in breathing

dyspnoeic /dɪspˈniːɪk/ *adjective* difficult or painful when breathing

dyspraxia /dɪsˈpræksiə/ *noun* difficulty in carrying out coordinated movements

dysrhythmia /dɪsˈrɪðmiə/ *noun* an unusual rhythm, either in speaking or in electrical impulses in the brain

dyssocial /dɪsˈsəʊʃ(ə)l/ *adjective* same as **antisocial**

dyssynergia /ˌdɪsɪˈnɜːdʒiə/ *noun* same as **asynergia**

dystaxia /dɪsˈtæksiə/ *noun* an inability to coordinate the muscles

dystocia /dɪsˈtəʊsiə/ *noun* difficult childbirth

dystonia /dɪsˈtəʊniə/ *noun* disordered muscle tone, causing involuntary contractions which make the limbs deformed

dystrophia /dɪsˈtrəʊfiə/ *noun* the wasting of an organ, muscle or tissue due to lack of nutrients in that part of the body. Also called **dystrophy**

dystrophia adiposogenitalis /dɪsˌtrəʊfiə ædɪˌpəʊsəʊdʒenɪˈteɪlɪs/ *noun* same as **Fröhlich's syndrome**

dystrophy /ˈdɪstrəfi/ *noun* same as **dystrophia**

dysuria /dɪsˈjʊəriə/ *noun* difficulty in passing urine

E

ear /ɪə/ *noun* an organ on the side of the head which is used for hearing (NOTE: For other terms referring to ears, see **auricular** and words beginning with **ot-, oto-**.)

Ear, Nose & Throat /ˌɪə ˌnəʊz ən ˈθrəʊt/ *noun* the study of the ear, nose and throat. Abbreviation **ENT**. Also called **otorhinolarngology**

earache /ˈɪəreɪk/ *noun* pain in the ear. Also called **otalgia**

ear canal /ˈɪə kəˌnæl/ *noun* one of several passages in or connected to the ear, especially the external auditory meatus, the passage from the outer ear to the eardrum

eardrum /ˈɪədrʌm/ *noun* the membrane at the end of the external auditory meatus leading from the outer ear, which vibrates with sound and passes the vibrations on to the ossicles in the middle ear. Also called **myringa, tympanum** (NOTE: For other terms referring to the eardrum, see words beginning with **tympan-, tympano-**.)

early onset pre-eclampsia /ˌɜːli ˌɒnset ˌpriː ɪˈklæmpsiə/ *noun* pre-eclampsia which appears earlier than the 37th week of the pregnancy

earwax /ˈɪəwæks/ *noun* same as **cerumen**

Ebola virus /ɪˈbəʊlə ˌvaɪrəs/ *noun* a highly contagious virus found in West Africa. Patients who are affected with it vomit, have bloody diarrhoea and blood seeps through their skin.

eburnation /ˌiːbəˈneɪʃ(ə)n/ *noun* the conversion of cartilage into a hard mass with a shiny surface like bone

ecbolic /ekˈbɒlɪk/ *noun* a substance which produces contraction of the uterus and so induces childbirth or abortion ■ *adjective* causing contraction of the uterus

ecchymosis /ˌekɪˈməʊsɪs/ *noun* a dark area on the skin made by blood which has escaped into the tissues after a blow. Also called **bruise, contusion**

eccrine /ˈekrɪn/ *adjective* referring to a gland, especially a sweat gland, which does not disintegrate and remains intact during secretion. Also called **merocrine**

eccyesis /ˌeksaɪˈiːsɪs/ *noun* same as **ectopic pregnancy**

ECG *abbreviation* electrocardiogram

echo- /ekəʊ/ *prefix* referring to sound

echocardiogram /ˌekəʊˈkɑːdiəgræm/ *noun* a record of heart movements made using ultrasound

echocardiography /ˌekəʊkɑːdiˈɒgrəfi/ *noun* the use of ultrasound to examine the heart

echoencephalography /ˌekəʊenˌkefəˈlɒgrəfi/ *noun* the use of ultrasound to examine the brain

echography /eˈkɒgrəfi/ *noun* same as **ultrasonography**

echovirus /ˈekəʊˌvaɪrəs/ *noun* one of a group of viruses which can be isolated from the intestine and which can cause serious illnesses such as aseptic meningitis, gastroenteritis and respiratory infection in small children. Compare **reovirus**

eclampsia /ɪˈklæmpsiə/ *noun* a serious condition of pregnant women at the end of pregnancy, caused by toxaemia, in which the woman has high blood pressure and may go into a coma. ◊ **pre-eclampsia**

ecmnesia /ekˈniːziə/ *noun* a condition in which someone is not able to remember recent events, while remembering clearly events which happened some time ago

E. coli /ˌiː ˈkəʊlaɪ/ *noun* same as **Escherichia coli**

economy class syndrome /ɪˈkɒnəmi klɑːs ˌsɪndrəʊm/ *noun* same as **deep-vein thrombosis**

écraseur /ˌeɪkrɑːˈzɜː/ *noun* a surgical instrument, usually with a wire loop, used to cut a part or a growth off at its base

ECT *abbreviation* electroconvulsive therapy

ect- /ekt/ *prefix* same as **ecto-** (*used before vowels*)

ecto- /ektəʊ/ *prefix* outside

-ectomy /ektəmi/ *suffix* referring to the removal of a part by surgical operation

ectoparasite /ˌektəʊˈpærəsaɪt/ *noun* a parasite which lives on the skin. Compare **endoparasite**

ectopia /ekˈtəʊpiə/ *noun* a condition in which an organ or part of the body is not in its usual position

ectopic /ek'tɒpɪk/ *adjective* not in the usual position. Opposite **entopic**

ectopic heartbeat /ek,tɒpɪk 'hɑːtbiːt/ *noun* an unusual extra beat of the heart which originates from a point other than the sinoatrial node. Also called **extrasystole, premature beat**

ectopic pacemaker /ek,tɒpɪk 'peɪsmeɪkə/ *noun* an unusual focus of the heart muscle which takes the place of the sinoatrial node

ectopic pregnancy /ek,tɒpɪk 'pregnənsi/ *noun* a pregnancy where the fetus develops outside the uterus, often in one of the Fallopian tubes. Also called **extrauterine pregnancy, eccyesis**

ectro- /ektrəʊ/ *prefix* referring to a usually congenital absence or lack of something

ectrodactyly /,ektrəʊ'dæktɪli/ *noun* a congenital absence of all or part of a finger

ectromelia /,ektrəʊ'miːliə/ *noun* a congenital absence of one or more limbs

ectropion /ek'trəʊpiən/ *noun* a turning of the edge of an eyelid outwards. ◊ **eversion**

eczema /'eksɪmə/ *noun* a non-contagious inflammation of the skin, with an itchy rash and blisters

eczematous /ek'semətəs/ *adjective* referring to eczema

eczematous dermatitis /ek,semətəs ,dɜːmə'taɪtɪs/ *noun* an itchy inflammation or irritation of the skin due to an allergic reaction to a substance which a person has touched or absorbed

EDD *abbreviation* expected date of delivery

edentulous /ɪ'dentjʊləs/ *adjective* having lost all teeth

EDTA /,i: di: ti: 'eɪ/ *noun* a colourless chemical that can bind to heavy metals to remove them from the bloodstream. Full form **ethylene diamine tetra-acetate**

Edwards' syndrome /'edwədz ,sɪndrəʊm/ *noun* a severe genetic disorder that results in malformations of the brain, kidney, heart, hands and feet. It is caused by an extra copy of chromosome 18 and those people who have it usually die within six months.

EEG *abbreviation* electroencephalogram

EFA *abbreviation* essential fatty acid

effacement /ɪ'feɪsmənt/ *noun* the thinning of the cervix before it dilates in childbirth

effective dose /ɪ,fektɪv 'dəʊs/ *noun* a size of dose which will produce the effect required

effector /ɪ'fektə/ *noun* a nerve ending in muscles or glands which is activated to produce contraction or secretion

efferent /'efərənt/ *adjective* carrying something away from part of the body or from the centre. Opposite **afferent**

efferent nerve /'efərənt nɜːv/ *noun* same as **motor nerve**

effleurage /,eflɜː'rɑːʒ/ *noun* a form of massage where the skin is stroked in one direction to increase blood flow

effort syndrome /'efət ,sɪndrəʊm/ *noun* same as **disordered action of the heart**

effusion /ɪ'fjuːʒ(ə)n/ *noun* a discharge of blood, fluid or pus into or out of an internal cavity

egg /eg/ *noun* a reproductive cell produced in the female body by an ovary, and which, if fertilised by the male sperm, becomes an embryo

ego /'iːgəʊ/ *noun* (*in psychology*) the part of the mind which is consciously in contact with the outside world and is influenced by experiences of the world

EHO *abbreviation* Environmental Health Officer

EIA *abbreviation* exercise-induced asthma

Eisenmenger syndrome /'aɪzənmeŋə ,sɪndrəʊm/ *noun* heart disease caused by a septal defect between the ventricles, with pulmonary hypertension [Described 1897. After Victor Eisenmenger (1864–1932), German physician.]

ejaculate /ɪ'dʒækjʊleɪt/ *verb* to send out semen from the penis

ejaculation /ɪ,dʒækjʊ'leɪʃ(ə)n/ *noun* the sending out of semen from the penis

ejaculatio praecox /ɪdʒækjʊ,leɪʃiəʊ 'priːkɒks/ *noun* a situation where a man ejaculates too early during sexual intercourse

ejaculatory duct /ɪ'dʒækjʊlətri dʌkt/ *noun* one of two ducts leading from the seminal vesicles through the prostate gland to the urethra. See illustration at **UROGENITAL SYSTEM (MALE)** in Supplement

elastic cartilage /ɪ,læstɪk 'kɑːtəlɪdʒ/ *noun* flexible cartilage, e.g. in the ear and epiglottis

elastic fibre /ɪ,læstɪk 'faɪbə/ *noun* fibre which can expand easily and is found in elastic cartilage, the skin and the walls of arteries and the lungs. Also called **yellow fibre**

elastic tissue /ɪ,læstɪk 'tɪʃuː/ *noun* connective tissue which contains elastic fibres, e.g. in the walls of arteries or of the alveoli in the lungs

elastin /ɪ'læstɪn/ *noun* a protein which occurs in elastic fibres

elation /ɪ'leɪʃ(ə)n/ *noun* the state of being happy, stimulated and excited

elbow /'elbəʊ/ *noun* a hinged joint where the upper arm bone (**humerus**) joins the forearm bones (**radius** and **ulna**)

elbow crutch /'elbəʊ krʌtʃ/ *noun* a crutch which surrounds the arms at the elbows and has a handle to hold lower down the shaft

elective care /ɪ,lektɪv 'keə/ *noun* hospital care which is planned in advance, rather than a response to an emergency

elective surgery /ɪ,lektɪv 'sɜːdʒəri/, **elective treatment** /ɪ,lektɪv 'triːtmənt/ *noun* surgery or treatment which a patient can choose to have but is not urgently necessary to save his or her life

electro- /ɪˈlektrəʊ/ *prefix* referring to electricity

electrocardiogram /ɪˌlektrəʊˈkɑːdiəgræm/ *noun* a chart which records the electrical impulses in the heart muscle. Abbreviation **ECG, EKG**

electrocardiograph /ɪˌlektrəʊˈkɑːdiəgrɑːf/ *noun* an apparatus for measuring and recording the electrical impulses of the muscles of the heart as it beats

electrocardiography /ɪˌlektrəʊkɑːdɪˈɒgrəfi/ *noun* the process of recording the electrical impulses of the heart

electrocardiophonography /ɪˌlektrəʊkɑːdiəfəˈnɒgrəfi/ *noun* the process of electrically recording the sounds of the heartbeats

electrocautery /ɪˌlektrəʊˈkɔːtəri/ *noun* same as **galvanocautery**

electroconvulsive therapy /ɪˌlektrəʊkən ˌvʌlsɪv ˈθerəpi/ *noun* the treatment of severe depression and some mental disorders by giving someone who has been anaesthetised small electric shocks in the brain to make him or her have convulsions. Abbreviation **ECT**. Also called **electroplexy**

electrode /ɪˈlektrəʊd/ *noun* the conductor of an electrical apparatus which touches the body and carries an electric shock

electroencephalogram /ɪˌlektrəʊɪnˈsefələgræm/ *noun* a chart on which the electrical impulses in the brain are recorded. Abbreviation **EEG**

electroencephalograph /ɪˌlektrəʊɪnˈsefələgrɑːf/ *noun* an apparatus which records the electrical impulses in the brain

electroencephalography /ɪˌlektrəʊɪnsefəˈlɒgrəfi/ *noun* the process of recording the electrical impulses in the brain

electrolysis /ɪlekˈtrɒləsɪs/ *noun* the destruction of tissue such as unwanted hair by applying an electric current

electrophoresis /ɪˌlektrəʊfəˈriːsɪs/ *noun* the analysis of a substance by the movement of charged particles towards an electrode in a solution

electroplexy /ɪˈlektrəʊpleksi/ *noun* same as **electroconvulsive therapy**

electroretinogram /ɪˌkektrəʊˈretɪnəgræm/ *noun* the printed result of electroretinography. Abbreviation **ERG**

electroretinography /ɪˌlektrəʊretɪˈnɒgrəfi/ *noun* the process of recording electrical changes in the retina when stimulated by light

electrosurgery /ɪˌlektrəʊˈsɜːdʒəri/ *noun* an operation in which the surgeon uses an electrical current to cut or cauterise tissue

electrotherapy /ɪˌlektrəʊˈθerəpi/ *noun* the treatment of a disorder such as some forms of

paralysis by using low-frequency electric current to try to revive the muscles

element /ˈelɪmənt/ *noun* a basic simple chemical substance which cannot be broken down into simpler substances. ◊ **trace element**

elephantiasis /ˌelɪfənˈtaɪəsɪs/ *noun* a condition in which parts of the body swell and the skin becomes hardened, frequently caused by infestation with various species of the parasitic worm *Filaria*

elevate /ˈelɪveɪt/ *verb* to raise something or to lift something up ○ *To control bleeding, apply pressure and elevate the part.*

elevation sling /ˌelɪˈveɪʃ(ə)n slɪŋ/ *noun* a sling tied round the neck, used to hold an injured hand or arm in a high position to control bleeding

elevator /ˈelɪveɪtə/ *noun* **1.** a muscle which raises part of the body **2.** a surgical instrument used to lift part of a broken bone

elimination /ɪˌlɪmɪˈneɪʃ(ə)n/ *noun* the removal of waste matter from the body

elimination diet /ɪˌlɪmɪˈneɪʃ(ə)n ˌdaɪət/ *noun* a structured diet where different foods are eliminated one at a time in order to see the effect on symptoms, used in conditions such as allergies and attention deficit hyperactivity disorder

ELISA /ɪˈlaɪzə/ *noun* a process in which an enzyme binds to an antibody or antigen and causes a colour change that shows the presence or amount of protein in a sample of biological material. Full form **enzyme-linked immunosorbent assay**

elixir /ɪˈlɪksə/ *noun* a sweet liquid which hides the unpleasant taste of a drug

elliptocytosis /ɪˌlɪptəʊsaɪˈtəʊsɪs/ *noun* a condition in which unusual oval-shaped red cells appear in the blood

emaciation /ɪˌmeɪsiˈeɪʃ(ə)n/ *noun* **1.** the fact of being extremely thin and underweight **2.** the loss of body tissue

emasculation /ɪˌmæskjʊˈleɪʃ(ə)n/ *noun* the removal of the penis

embalm /ɪmˈbɑːm/ *verb* to preserve a dead body by using special antiseptic chemicals to prevent decay

embolectomy /ˌembəˈlektəmi/ *noun* a surgical operation to remove a blood clot

emboli /ˈembəli/ *plural of* **embolus**

embolisation /ˌembəlaɪˈzeɪʃ(ə)n/, **embolization** *noun* the use of emboli inserted down a catheter into a blood vessel to treat internal bleeding

embolism /ˈembəlɪz(ə)m/ *noun* the blocking of an artery by a mass of material, usually a blood clot, preventing the flow of blood

embolus /ˈembələs/ *noun* **1.** a mass of material which blocks a blood vessel, e.g. a blood clot, air bubble or fat globule **2.** material inserted into a blood vessel down a catheter to treat internal bleeding (NOTE: The plural is **emboli**.)

embryo /'embriəʊ/ *noun* an unborn baby during the first eight weeks after conception (NOTE: After eight weeks, the embryo is called a **fetus**.)

embryological /ˌembriə'lɒdʒɪk(ə)l/ *adjective* referring to embryology

embryology /ˌembri'ɒlədʒi/ *noun* the study of the early stages of the development of an embryo

embryonic /ˌembri'ɒnɪk/ *adjective* referring to an embryo

embryonic membrane /ˌembriɒnɪk 'membreɪn/ *noun* one of the two layers around an embryo providing protection and food supply, i.e. the **amnion** and the **chorion**

emergency /ɪ'mɜːdʒənsi/ *noun* a situation where urgent immediate action has to be taken

emesis /'eməsɪs/ *noun* same as **vomiting**

emetic /ɪ'metɪk/ *noun* a substance which causes vomiting ■ *adjective* causing vomiting

eminence /'emɪnəns/ *noun* something which protrudes from a surface, e.g. a lump on a bone or swelling on the skin

emissary vein /'emɪsəri ˌveɪn/ *noun* a vein through the skull which connects the venous sinuses with the scalp veins

emission /ɪ'mɪʃ(ə)n/ *noun* a discharge or release of fluid

emmetropia /emɪ'trəʊpiə/ *noun* the correct focusing of light rays by the eye onto the retina giving normal vision. Compare **ametropia**

emollient /ɪ'mɒliənt/ *noun* a substance which soothes or smooths the skin, e.g. to prevent the development of eczema ■ *adjective* smoothening

emotion /ɪ'məʊʃ(ə)n/ *noun* a strong feeling

empathy /'empəθi/ *noun* the ability to understand the problems and feelings of another person

emphysema /ˌemfɪ'siːmə/ *noun* a condition in which the walls of the alveoli of the lungs break down, reducing the surface available for gas exchange and resulting in a lower oxygen level in the blood and shortness of breath. It can be caused by smoking, living in a polluted environment, old age, asthma or whooping cough.

empirical treatment /ɪmˌpɪrɪk(ə)l 'triːtmənt/ *noun* treatment which is based on symptoms and clinical experience rather than on a thorough knowledge of the cause of the disorder

empowerment /ɪm'paʊəmənt/ *noun* the act of giving someone authority and power to make decisions that will affect them

empyema /ˌempaɪ'iːmə/ *noun* the collection of pus in a cavity, especially in the pleural cavity. Also called **pyothorax**

emulsion /ɪ'mʌlʃən/ *noun* a combination of liquids such as oil and water which do not usually mix

EN *abbreviation* enrolled nurse

en- /en, ɪn/ *prefix* **1.** in, into **2.** to provide with **3.** to cause to be **4.** to put into or cover with **5.** to go into

enalapril /e'næləprɪl/ *noun* a drug used for the short-term management of high blood pressure

enamel /ɪ'næm(ə)l/ *noun* the hard white shiny outer covering of the crown of a tooth

enarthrosis /ˌenɑː'θrəʊsɪs/ *noun* a ball and socket joint, e.g. the hip joint

encapsulated /ɪn'kæpsjʊleɪtɪd/ *adjective* enclosed in a capsule or in a sheath of tissue

encefalin /en'kefəlɪn/ *noun* another spelling of **encephalin**

encephal- /enkɪfæl/ *prefix* same as **encephalo-** (*used before vowels*)

encephala /en'kefələ/ plural of **encephalon**

encephalin /en'kefəlɪn/ *noun* a peptide produced in the brain which acts as a natural painkiller. ◊ **endorphin**

encephalitis /ˌen.kefə'laɪtɪs, enˌsefə'laɪtɪs/ *noun* inflammation of the brain

encephalo- /enkefələ/ *prefix* referring to the brain

encephalocele /en'kefələʊsiːl/ *noun* a condition in which the brain protrudes through a congenital or traumatic gap in the skull bones

encephalogram /en'kefələgræm/, **encephalograph** /en'kefələgrɑːf/ *noun* an X-ray photograph of the ventricles and spaces of the brain taken after air has been injected into the cerebrospinal fluid by lumbar puncture

encephaloma /enˌkefə'ləʊmə/ *noun* a tumour of the brain

encephalomyelitis /enˌkefələʊmaɪə'laɪtɪs/ *noun* a group of diseases which cause inflammation of the brain and the spinal cord

encephalomyelopathy /enˌkefələʊmaɪə'lɒpəθi/ *noun* any condition where the brain and spinal cord are diseased

encephalon /en'kefəlɒn/ *noun* same as **brain** (NOTE: The plural is **encephala**.)

encephalopathy /enˌkefə'lɒpəθi/ *noun* any disease of the brain

enchondroma /ˌenkɒn'drəʊmə/ *noun* a tumour formed of cartilage growing inside a bone

encopresis /ˌenkəʊ'priːsɪs/ *noun* faecal incontinence not associated with a physical condition or disease

encysted /en'sɪstɪd/ *adjective* enclosed in a capsule like a cyst

end- /end/ *prefix* same as **endo-** (*used before vowels*)

endarterectomy /ˌendɑːtə'rektəmi/ *noun* the surgical removal of the lining of a blocked artery. Also called **rebore**

endarteritis /ˌendɑːtə'raɪtɪs/ *noun* inflammation of the inner lining of an artery

endarteritis obliterans /ˌendɑːtˌraɪtɪs ə 'blɪtərənz/ *noun* a condition where inflammation in an artery is so severe that it blocks the artery

endaural /end'ɔːrəl/ *adjective* inside the ear

endemic /en'demɪk/ *adjective* referring to any disease which is very common in specific places ○ *This disease is endemic to Mediterranean countries.*

endo- /endəʊ/ *prefix* inside

endobronchial /ˌendəʊ'brɒŋkiəl/ *adjective* inside the bronchi

endocardial /ˌendəʊ'kɑːdiəl/ *adjective* referring to the endocardium

endocardial pacemaker /ˌendəʊkɑːdiəl 'peɪsmeɪkə/ *noun* a pacemaker attached to the lining of the heart

endocarditis /ˌendəʊkɑː'daɪtɪs/ *noun* inflammation of the membrane lining of the heart

endocardium /ˌendəʊ'kɑːdiəm/ *noun* a membrane which lines the heart. See illustration at HEART in Supplement

endocervicitis /ˌendəʊsɜːvɪ'saɪtɪs/ *noun* inflammation of the membrane in the neck of the uterus

endocervix /ˌendəʊ'sɜːvɪks/ *noun* a membrane which lines the neck of the uterus

endochondral /ˌendəʊ'kɒndrəl/ *adjective* inside a cartilage

endocrine /'endəʊkraɪn/ *adjective* relating to the endocrine glands or the hormones they secrete

endocrine gland /'endəʊkraɪn glænd/ *noun* a gland without a duct which produces hormones which are introduced directly into the bloodstream, e.g. the pituitary gland, thyroid gland, the adrenal gland and the gonads. Also called **ductless gland**. Compare **exocrine gland**

endocrine system /'endəʊkraɪn ˌsɪstəm/ *noun* a system of related ductless glands

endocrinologist /ˌendəʊkrɪ'nɒlədʒɪst/ *noun* a doctor who specialises in the study of endocrinology

endocrinology /ˌendəʊkrɪ'nɒlədʒi/ *noun* the study of the endocrine system, its function and effects

endoderm /'endəʊdɜːm/ *noun* the inner of three layers surrounding an embryo. Also called **entoderm**

endodermal /ˌendəʊ'dɜːm(ə)l/ *adjective* referring to the endoderm. Also called **entodermal**

endogenous /en'dɒdʒənəs/ *adjective* developing or being caused by something inside an organism. Compare **exogenous**

endogenous depression /en,dɒdʒənəs dɪ 'preʃ(ə)n/ *noun* depression caused by no obvious external factor

endogenous eczema /en,dɒdʒənəs 'eksɪmə/ *noun* eczema which is caused by no obvious external factor

endolymph /'endəʊlɪmf/ *noun* a fluid inside the membranous labyrinth in the inner ear

endometrial /ˌendəʊ'miːtriəl/ *adjective* referring to the endometrium

endometrial laser ablation /ˌendəʊmiːtriəl 'leɪzə əb,leɪʃ(ə)n/ *noun* a gynaecological surgical procedure using a laser to treat fibroids or other causes of thickening of the lining of the uterus

endometriosis /ˌendəʊmiːtri'əʊsɪs/ *noun* a condition affecting women, in which tissue similar to the tissue of the uterus is found in other parts of the body

endometritis /ˌendəʊmɪ'traɪtɪs/ *noun* inflammation of the lining of the uterus

endometrium /ˌendəʊ'miːtriəm/ *noun* the mucous membrane lining the uterus, part of which is shed at each menstruation (NOTE: The plural is **endometria**.)

endomyocarditis /ˌendəʊmaɪəʊkɑː'daɪtɪs/ *noun* inflammation of the muscle and inner membrane of the heart

endomysium /ˌendəʊ'mɪsiəm/ *noun* connective tissue around and between muscle fibres

endoneurium /ˌendəʊ'njʊəriəm/ *noun* fibrous tissue between the individual fibres in a nerve

endoparasite /ˌendəʊ'pærəsaɪt/ *noun* a parasite which lives inside its host, e.g. in the intestines. Compare **ectoparasite**

endophthalmitis /ˌendɒfθæl'maɪtɪs/ *noun* inflammation of the interior of the eyeball

endorphin /en'dɔːfɪn/ *noun* a peptide produced by the brain which acts as a natural painkiller. ◊ **encephalin**

endoscope /'endəskəʊp/ *noun* an instrument used to examine the inside of the body, made of a thin tube which is passed into the body down a passage. The tube has a fibre optic light, and may have small surgical instruments attached.

endoscopic retrograde cholangiopancreatography /ˌendəʊskɒpɪk ,retrəgreɪd kə 'lændʒiəʊpæŋkriə'tɒgrəfi/ *noun* a method used to examine the pancreatic duct and bile duct for possible obstructions. Abbreviation **ERCP**

endoscopy /en'dɒskəpi/ *noun* an examination of the inside of the body using an endoscope

endoskeleton /'endəʊ,skelɪt(ə)n/ *noun* the inner structure of bones and cartilage in an animal

endosteum /en'dɒstiəm/ *noun* a membrane lining the bone marrow cavity inside a long bone

endothelial /ˌendəʊ'θiːliəl/ *adjective* referring to the endothelium

endothelioma /ˌendəʊθiːliˈəʊmə/ *noun* a malignant tumour originating inside the endothelium

endothelium /ˌendəʊˈθiːliəm/ *noun* a membrane of special cells which lines the heart, the lymph vessels, the blood vessels and various body cavities. Compare **epithelium**, **mesothelium**

endotoxin /ˌendəʊˈtɒksɪn/ *noun* a toxic substance released after the death of some bacterial cells

endotracheal /ˌendəʊˈtreɪkiəl/ *adjective* same as **intratracheal**

endotracheal tube /ˌendəʊˈtreɪkiəl ˌtjuːb/ *noun* a tube passed down the trachea, through either the nose or mouth, in anaesthesia or to help a person breathe

end plate /ˈend pleɪt/ *noun* the end of a motor nerve, where it joins muscle fibre

end stage renal disease /ˌend steɪdʒ ˈriːn(ə)l dɪˌziːz/ *noun* the stage of kidney disease at which uraemia occurs and dialysis needs to start. Abbreviation **ESRD**

enema /ˈenɪmə/ *noun* a liquid substance put into the rectum to introduce a drug into the body, to wash out the colon before an operation or for diagnosis

energy /ˈenədʒi/ *noun* the force or strength to carry out activities ○ *You need to eat certain types of food to give you energy.*

enervation /ˌenəˈveɪʃ(ə)n/ *noun* **1.** general nervous weakness **2.** a surgical operation to remove a nerve

engagement /ɪnˈɡeɪdʒmənt/ *noun* (*in obstetrics*) the moment where part of the fetus, usually the head, enters the pelvis at the beginning of labour

engorged /ɪnˈɡɔːdʒd/ *adjective* excessively filled with liquid, usually blood

engorgement /ɪnˈɡɔːdʒmənt/ *noun* the excessive filling of a vessel, usually with blood

enkephalin /enˈkefəlɪn/ *noun* US another spelling of **encephalin**

enophthalmos /ˌenɒfˈθælməs/ *noun* a condition in which the eyes are very deep in their sockets

Enrolled Nurse /ɪnˌrəʊld ˈnɜːs/ *noun* ♦ **second-level nurse**

ensiform cartilage /ˌensɪfɔːm ˈkɑːtəlɪdʒ/ *noun* same as **xiphoid process**

ENT *abbreviation* Ear, Nose & Throat

ENT department /ˌiː en ˈtiː dɪˌpɑːtmənt/ *noun* a department of otorhinolaryngology

enter- /entə/ *prefix* same as **entero-** (*used before vowels*)

enteral /ˈentərəl/ *adjective* referring to the intestine. Compare **parenteral**

enteral feeding /ˌentərəl ˈfiːdɪŋ/ *noun* the feeding of a person by a nasogastric tube or by the

infusion of liquid food directly into the intestine. Also called **enteral nutrition**

enteralgia /ˌentərˈældʒə/ *noun* same as **colic**

enterally /ˈentərəli/ *adverb* referring to a method of feeding a person by nasogastric tube or directly into the intestine

enteral nutrition /ˌentərəl njuːˈtrɪʃ(ə)n/ *noun* same as **enteral feeding**

enteric /enˈterɪk/ *adjective* referring to the intestine

enteric-coated /en,terɪk ˈkəʊtɪd/ *adjective* referring to a capsule with a coating which prevents it from being digested and releasing the drug until it reaches the intestine

enteritis /ˌentəˈraɪtɪs/ *noun* inflammation of the mucous membrane of the intestine

entero- /entərəʊ/ *prefix* referring to the intestine

Enterobacteria /ˌentərəʊbækˈtɪəriə/ *noun* a family of Gram-negative bacteria, including Salmonella, Shigella, Escherichia and Klebsiella

enterobiasis /ˌentərəʊˈbaɪəsɪs/ *noun* a common children's disease, caused by threadworms in the large intestine which cause itching round the anus. Also called **oxyuriasis**

Enterobius /ˌentəˈrəʊbiəs/ *noun* a small thin nematode worm, one species of which, *Enterobius vermicularis*, infests the large intestine and causes itching round the anus. Also called **threadworm**, **pinworm**

enterocele /ˈentərəʊsiːl/, **enterocoele** /ˈentərəʊsiːl/ *noun* a hernia of the intestine

enterocolitis /ˌentərəʊkəˈlaɪtɪs/ *noun* inflammation of the colon and small intestine

enterolith /ˈentərəʊlɪθ/ *noun* a stone in the intestine

enteron /ˈentərɒn/ *noun* the whole intestinal tract

enteropathy /ˌentəˈrɒpəθi/ *noun* any disorder of the intestine. ♦ **gluten-induced enteropathy**

enteroscope /ˈentərəskəʊp/ *noun* an instrument for inspecting the inside of the intestine

enterostomy /ˌentəˈrɒstəmi/ *noun* a surgical operation to make an opening between the small intestine and the abdominal wall

enterotomy /ˌentəˈrɒtəmi/ *noun* a surgical incision in the intestine

enterotoxin /ˌentərəʊˈtɒksɪn/ *noun* a bacterial exotoxin which particularly affects the intestine

enterovirus /ˌentərəʊˈvaɪrəs/ *noun* a virus which prefers to live in the intestine. Enteroviruses include poliomyelitis virus, Coxsackie viruses and the echoviruses.

entoderm /ˈentəʊdɜːm/ *noun* same as **endoderm**

entodermal /ˌentəʊˈdɜːm(ə)l/ *adjective* same as **endodermal**

Entonox /ˈentənɒks/ *noun* a gas consisting of 50% oxygen and 50% nitrous oxide that is used as a painkiller during childbirth

entopic /ɪnˈtɒpɪk/ *adjective* located or taking place in the usual position. Opposite **ectopic**

entropion /ɪnˈtrəʊpiən/ *noun* a turning of the edge of the eyelid towards the inside

enucleation /ɪˌnjuːkliˈeɪʃ(ə)n/ *noun* the surgical removal of all of a tumour

enuresis /ˌenjʊˈriːsɪs/ *noun* the involuntary passing of urine

enuretic /ˌenjʊˈretɪk/ *adjective* referring to enuresis, or causing enuresis

environment /ɪnˈvaɪrənmənt/ *noun* the conditions and influences under which an organism lives

environmental /ɪnˌvaɪrənˈment(ə)l/ *adjective* referring to the environment

Environmental Health Officer /ɪnˌvaɪrənment(ə)l ˈhelθ ˌɒfɪsə/ *noun* an official of a local authority who examines the environment and tests for air pollution, bad sanitation, noise pollution and similar threats to public health. Abbreviation **EHO**

enzyme /ˈenzaɪm/ *noun* a protein substance produced by living cells which aids a biochemical reaction in the body (NOTE: The names of enzymes mostly end with the suffix **-ase**.)

enzyme-linked immunosorbent assay /ˌenzaɪm lɪŋkt ˌɪmjʊnəʊˌsɔːbənt ˈæseɪ/ *noun* full form of **ELISA**

eonism /ˈiːənɪz(ə)m/ *noun* cross-dressing, when a male wears female dress

eosin /ˈiːəʊsɪn/ *noun* a red crystalline solid used as a biological staining dye

eosinopenia /ˌiːəʊsɪnəˈpiːniə/ *noun* a reduction in the number of eosinophils in the blood

eosinophil /ˌiːəʊˈsɪnəfɪl/ *noun* a type of cell that can be stained with eosin

eosinophilia /ˌiːəʊsɪnəˈfɪliə/ *noun* an excess of eosinophils in the blood

ependyma /ɪˈpendɪmə/ *noun* a thin membrane which lines the ventricles of the brain and the central canal of the spinal cord

ependymal /ɪˈpendɪm(ə)l/ *adjective* referring to the ependyma

ependymal cell /ɪˈpendɪm(ə)l sel/ *noun* one of the cells which form the ependyma

ependymoma /ɪˌpendɪˈməʊmə/ *noun* a tumour in the brain originating in the ependyma

ephedrine /ˈefɪdriːn/ *noun* a drug that relieves asthma and blocked noses by causing the air passages to widen

ephidrosis /ˌefɪˈdrəʊsɪs/ *noun* an unusual amount of sweat

epi- /epɪ/ *prefix* on or over

epiblepharon /ˌepɪˈblefərɒn/ *noun* an unusual fold of skin over the eyelid, which may press the eyelashes against the eyeball

epicanthus /ˌepɪˈkænθəs/, **epicanthic fold** /ˌepɪkænθɪk ˈfəʊld/ *noun* a large fold of skin in the inner corner of the eye, common in babies and also found in adults of some groups such as the Chinese

epicardial /ˌepɪˈkɑːdiəl/ *adjective* referring to the epicardium

epicardial pacemaker /ˌepɪkɑːdiəl ˈpeɪsmeɪkə/ *noun* a pacemaker attached to the surface of the ventricle

epicardium /ˌepɪˈkɑːdiəm/ *noun* the inner layer of the pericardium which lines the walls of the heart, outside the myocardium. See illustration at **HEART** in Supplement

epicondyle /ˌepɪˈkɒndaɪl/ *noun* a projecting part of the round end of a bone above the condyle

epicondylitis /ˌepɪkɒndɪˈlaɪtɪs/ *noun* same as **tennis elbow**

epicranium /ˌepɪˈkreɪniəm/ *noun* the five layers of the scalp, the skin and hair on the head covering the skull

epicritic /ˌepɪˈkrɪtɪk/ *adjective* referring to the nerves which govern the fine senses of touch and temperature

epidemic /ˌepɪˈdemɪk/ *adjective* spreading quickly through a large part of the population ○ *The disease rapidly reached epidemic proportions.* ■ *noun* an outbreak of an infectious disease which spreads very quickly and affects a large number of people

epidemiologist /ˌepɪˌdiːmɪˈɒlədʒɪst/ *noun* a person who specialises in the study of diseases in groups of people

epidemiology /ˌepɪˌdiːmiˈɒlədʒi/ *noun* the study of diseases in the community, in particular how they spread and how they can be controlled

epidermal /ˌepɪˈdɜːm(ə)l/ *adjective* referring to the epidermis

epidermis /ˌepɪˈdɜːmɪs/ *noun* the outer layer of the skin, including the dead skin on the surface. Also called **cuticle**

epidermoid cyst /ˌepɪdɜːmɔɪd ˈsɪst/ *noun* same as **sebaceous cyst**

epidermolysis /ˌepɪdɜːˈmɒləsɪs/ *noun* separation of the epidermis from the tissue underneath, usually forming a blister

epidermolysis bullosa /ˌepɪdɜːˌmɒləsɪs bʊˈləʊsə/ *noun* a group of disorders where blisters form on the skin

Epidermophyton /ˌepɪdɜːˈmɒfɪtən/ *noun* a fungus which grows on the skin and causes athlete's foot, among other disorders

epididymal /ˌepɪˈdɪdɪm(ə)l/ *adjective* referring to the epididymis

epididymectomy /ˌepɪdɪdɪˈmektəmi/ *noun* the removal of the epididymis

epididymis /ˌepɪˈdɪdɪmɪs/ *noun* a long twisting thin tube at the back of the testis, which forms part of the efferent duct of the testis, and in which spermatozoa are stored before ejaculation. See illustration at **UROGENITAL SYSTEM (MALE)** in Supplement

epididymitis /ˌepɪdɪdɪˈmaɪtɪs/ *noun* inflammation of the epididymis

epididymo-orchitis /epɪˌdɪdɪməʊ ɔːˈkaɪtɪs/ *noun* inflammation of the epididymis and the testes

epidural /ˌepɪˈdjʊərəl/ *adjective* on the outside of the dura mater. Also called **extradural** ■ *noun* same as **epidural anaesthesia**

epidural anaesthesia /epɪˌdjʊərəl ˌænəsˈθiːziə/ *noun* a local anaesthesia in which anaesthetic is injected into the space between the vertebral canal and the dura mater

epidural block /ˌepɪdjʊərəl ˈblɒk/ *noun* analgesia produced by injecting an analgesic solution into the space between the vertebral canal and the dura mater

epidural space /ˌepɪdjʊərəl ˈspeɪs/ *noun* a space in the spinal cord between the vertebral canal and the dura mater

epigastric /ˌepɪˈɡæstrɪk/ *adjective* referring to the upper abdomen ○ *The patient complained of pains in the epigastric area.*

epigastrium /ˌepɪˈɡæstriəm/ *noun* the part of the upper abdomen between the ribcage and the navel. Also called **the pit of the stomach**

epiglottis /ˌepɪˈɡlɒtɪs/ *noun* a flap of cartilage at the root of the tongue which moves to block the windpipe when food is swallowed, so that the food does not go down the trachea

epiglottitis /ˌepɪɡlɒˈtaɪtɪs/ *noun* inflammation and swelling of the epiglottis

epilation /ˌepɪˈleɪʃ(ə)n/ *noun* the process of removing hair by destroying the hair follicles

epilepsy /ˈepɪlepsi/ *noun* a disorder of the nervous system in which there are convulsions and loss of consciousness due to a disordered discharge of cerebral neurones

epileptic /ˌepɪˈleptɪk/ *adjective* having epilepsy, or relating to epilepsy ■ *noun* a person with epilepsy (NOTE: The word 'epileptic' to describe a person is now avoided.)

epileptic fit /ˌepɪleptɪk ˈfɪt/ *noun* an attack of convulsions, and sometimes unconsciousness, due to epilepsy

epileptiform /ˌepɪˈleptɪfɔːm/ *adjective* being similar to epilepsy

epiloia /ˌepɪˈlɔɪə/ *noun* a hereditary disease of the brain associated with learning disabilities, epilepsy and tumours on the kidney and heart. Also called **tuberose sclerosis**

epimenorrhagia /ˌepɪmenəˈreɪdʒə/ *noun* very heavy bleeding during menstruation occurring at very short intervals

epimenorrhoea /ˌepɪmenəˈriːə/ *noun* menstruation at shorter intervals than twenty-eight days

epiphora /eˈpɪfərə/ *noun* a condition in which the eye fills with tears either because the lacrimal duct is blocked or because excessive tears are being secreted

epiphyseal /ˌepɪˈfɪziəl/ *adjective* referring to an epiphysis

epiphysis /eˈpɪfəsɪs/ *noun* the area of growth in a bone which is separated from the main part of the bone by cartilage until bone growth stops. See illustration at **BONE STRUCTURE** in Supplement. Compare **diaphysis**, **metaphysis**

epiplo- /epɪpləʊ/ *prefix* referring to the omentum

epiploon /eˈpɪpləʊɒn/ *noun* same as **omentum**

episclera /ˈepɪsklɪərə/ *noun* the outer surface of the sclera of the eyeball

episcleritis /ˌepɪskləˈraɪtɪs/ *noun* inflammation of the outer surface of the sclera in the eyeball

episi- /əpɪzi/, **episio-** /əpɪziəʊ/ *prefix* referring to the vulva

episiorrhaphy /əˌpɪziˈɔːrəfi/ *noun* a procedure for stitching torn labia majora

episiotomy /əˌpɪziˈɒtəmi/ *noun* a surgical cut of the perineum near the vagina to prevent tearing during childbirth

episodic /ˌepɪˈsɒdɪk/ *adjective* happening in separate but related incidents, e.g. asthma which occurs in separate attacks

epispadias /ˌepɪˈspeɪdiəs/ *noun* a congenital condition where the urethra opens on the top of the penis and not at the end. Compare **hypospadias**

epistaxis /ˌepɪˈstæksɪs/ *noun* same as **nosebleed**

epithelial /ˌepɪˈθiːliəl/ *adjective* referring to the epithelium

epithelialisation /ˌepɪˌθiːliəlaɪˈzeɪʃ(ə)n/, **epithelialization** *noun* the growth of skin over a wound

epithelioma /epɪθiːliˈəʊmə/ *noun* a tumour arising from epithelial cells

epithelium /ˌepɪˈθiːliəm/ *noun* the layer or layers of cells covering an organ, including the skin and the lining of all hollow cavities except blood vessels, lymphatics and serous cavities. Compare **endothelium**, **mesothelium**

Epstein–Barr virus /ˌepstaɪn ˈbɑː ˌvaɪrəs/ *noun* a virus which probably causes glandular fever. Also called **EB virus** [Isolated and described 1964. After Michael Anthony Epstein (b. 1921), Bristol pathologist; Murray Llewellyn

Barr (1908–95), Canadian anatomist and cytologist, head of the Department of Anatomy at the University of Western Ontario, Canada.]

epulis /ɪˈpjuːlɪs/ *noun* a small fibrous swelling on a gum

equi- /iːkwɪ, ekwɪ/ *prefix* equal

equilibrium /ˌiːkwɪˈlɪbriəm/ *noun* a state of balance

ER *abbreviation* **1.** *US* emergency room **2.** endoplasmic reticulum

Erb's palsy /ˌɜːbz ˈpɔːlzi/, **Erb's paralysis** /ˌɜːbz pəˈræləsɪs/ *noun* a condition in which an arm is paralysed because of birth injuries to the brachial plexus. ◊ **Bell's palsy**

ERCP *abbreviation* endoscopic retrograde cholangiopancreatography

erectile /ɪˈrektaɪl/ *adjective* able to become erect

erectile dysfunction /ɪˌrektaɪl dɪsˈfʌŋkʃən/ *noun* a condition in which a man finds it difficult or impossible to have or maintain an erection during intercourse

erection /ɪˈrekʃən/ *noun* a state where a body part such as the penis becomes swollen because of engorgement with blood

erector /ɪˈrektə/ *noun* a small muscle which raises a body part

erector spinae /ɪˌrektə ˈspaɪniː/ *noun* a large muscle starting at the base of the spine, and dividing as it runs up the spine

ERG *abbreviation* electroretinogram

ergonomics /ˌɜːɡəˈnɒmɪks/ *noun* the study of humans at work

ergot /ˈɜːɡət/ *noun* a disease of rye caused by the fungus *Clariceps purpurea*

ergotamine /ɜːˈɡɒtəmiːn/ *noun* a drug that causes narrowing of blood vessels and alleviates migraine, derived from the ergot fungus

ergotism /ˈɜːɡətɪz(ə)m/ *noun* poisoning caused by eating rye which has been contaminated with the ergot fungus

erogenous /ɪˈrɒdʒənəs/ *adjective* producing sexual excitement

erogenous zone /ɪˈrɒdʒənəs zəʊn/ *noun* a part of the body which, if stimulated, produces sexual arousal, e.g. the penis, clitoris or nipples

erotic /ɪˈrɒtɪk/ *adjective* relating to or arousing the feeling of sexual desire

ERPC *abbreviation* evacuation of retained products of conception

eructation /ˌiːrʌkˈteɪʃ(ə)n/ *noun* same as **belching**

eruption /ɪˈrʌpʃən/ *noun* something which breaks through the skin, e.g. a rash or pimple

ery- /erɪ/ *prefix* same as **erythro-**

erythema /ˌerɪˈθiːmə/ *noun* redness on the skin, caused by hyperaemia of the blood vessels near the surface

erythema ab igne /ˌerɪθiːmə æb ˈɪɡneɪ/ *noun* a pattern of red lines on the skin caused by exposure to heat

erythema induratum /ˌerɪθiːmə ˌɪndjʊ ˈreɪtəm/ *noun* a tubercular disease where ulcerating nodules appear on the legs of young women. Also called **Bazin's disease**

erythema multiforme /ˌerɪθiːmə ˈmʌltɪfɔːmi/ *noun* the sudden appearance of inflammatory red patches and sometimes blisters on the skin

erythema nodosum /ˌerɪθiːmə nəʊˈdəʊsəm/ *noun* an inflammatory disease where red swellings appear on the front of the legs

erythema pernio /ˌerɪθiːmə ˈpɜːniəʊ/ *noun* same as **chilblain**

erythematous /ˌerɪˈθiːmətəs/ *adjective* referring to erythema

erythr- /erɪθr/ *prefix* same as **erythro-** (*used before vowels*)

erythrasma /ˌerɪˈθræzmə/ *noun* a persistent bacterial skin infection occurring in a fold in the skin or where two skin surfaces touch, such as between the toes. It is caused by *Corynebacterium*.

erythro- /ɪrɪθrəʊ/ *prefix* red

erythroblast /ɪˈrɪθrəblæst/ *noun* a cell which forms an erythrocyte or red blood cell

erythroblastosis /ɪˌrɪθrəʊblæˈstəʊsɪs/ *noun* the presence of erythroblasts in the blood, usually found in haemolytic anaemia

erythroblastosis fetalis /ɪˌrɪθrəʊblæ ˌstəʊsɪs fiːˈtɑːlɪs/ *noun* a blood disease affecting newborn babies, caused by a reaction between the rhesus factor of the mother and the fetus

erythrocyte /ɪˈrɪθrəsaɪt/ *noun* a mature red blood cell

erythrocyte sedimentation rate /ɪ ˌrɪθrəsaɪt sedɪmenˈteɪʃ(ə)n reɪt/ *noun* a test that measures how fast erythrocytes settle in a sample of blood plasma, used to confirm whether various blood conditions are present. Abbreviation **ESR**

erythrocytosis /ɪˌrɪθrəsaɪˈtəʊsɪs/ *noun* an increase in the number of red blood cells in the blood

erythroderma /ɪˌrɪθrəˈdɜːmə/ *noun* a condition in which the skin becomes red and flakes off

erythroedema /ɪˌrɪθrɔːˈdiːmə/ *noun* same as **acrodynia**

erythrogenesis /ɪˌrɪθrəˈdʒenəsɪs/, **erythropoiesis** /ɪˌrɪθrəpɔːˈiːsɪs/ *noun* the formation of red blood cells in red bone marrow

erythropenia /ɪˌrɪθrəˈpiːniə/ *noun* a condition in which a person has a low number of erythrocytes in their blood

erythroplasia /ɪˌrɪθrəˈpleɪziə/ *noun* the formation of lesions on the mucous membrane

erythropoiesis /ɪˌrɪθrəpɔɪˈiːsɪs/ *noun* same as **erythrogenesis**

erythropoietin /ɪˌrɪθrəˈpɔɪətɪn/ *noun* a hormone which regulates the production of red blood cells

erythropsia /ˌerɪˈθrɒpsiə/ *noun* a condition in which someone sees things as if coloured red

eschar /ˈeskɑː/ *noun* a dry scab, e.g. one forming on a burn

Escherichia /ˌeʃəˈrɪkiə/ *noun* a bacterium commonly found in faeces

Escherichia coli /eʃəˌrɪkiə ˈkəʊlaɪ/ *noun* a Gram-negative bacterium associated with acute gastroenteritis. Also called **E. coli**

Esmarch's bandage /ˈesmɑːks ˌbændɪdʒ/ *noun* a rubber band wrapped round a limb as a tourniquet before a surgical operation and left in place during the operation so as to keep the site free of blood [Described 1869. After Johann Friedrich August von Esmarch (1823–1908), Professor of Surgery at Kiel, Germany.]

esotropia /esəˈtrəʊpiə/ *noun* a type of squint, where the eyes both look towards the nose. Also called **convergent strabismus**

ESR *abbreviation* erythrocyte sedimentation rate

ESRD *abbreviation* end-stage renal disease

essence /ˈes(ə)ns/ *noun* a concentrated oil from a plant, used in cosmetics, and sometimes as analgesics or antiseptics

essential amino acid /ɪˌsenʃəl əˌmiːnəʊ ˈæsɪd/ *noun* an amino acid which is necessary for growth but which cannot be synthesised in the body and has to be obtained from the food supply

COMMENT: The essential amino acids are: isoleucine, leucine, lysine, methionine, phenylalanine, threonine, tryptophan and valine.

essential element /ɪˌsenʃəl ˈelɪmənt/ *noun* a chemical element which is necessary to the body's growth or function, e.g. carbon, oxygen, hydrogen and nitrogen

essential fatty acid /ɪˌsenʃəl ˌfæti ˈæsɪd/ *noun* an unsaturated fatty acid which is necessary for growth and health. Abbreviation **EFA**

COMMENT: The essential fatty acids are linoleic acid, linolenic acid and arachidonic acid.

essential hypertension /ɪˌsenʃəl ˈhaɪpəˌtenʃən/ *noun* high blood pressure without any obvious cause

essential oil /ɪˌsenʃəl ˈɔɪl/ *noun* a medicinal or fragrant oil distilled from some part of a plant

essential tremor /ɪˌsenʃəl ˈtremə/ *noun* an involuntary slow trembling movement of the hands often seen in elderly people

essential uterine haemorrhage /ɪˌsenʃəl ˌjuːtəraɪn ˈhem(ə)rɪdʒ/ *noun* heavy uterine bleeding for which there is no obvious cause

ethambutol /ɪˈθæmbjʊtɒl/ *noun* a drug that is part of the treatment for bacterial infections such as tuberculosis

ethanol /ˈeθənɒl/ *noun* a colourless liquid, present in alcoholic drinks such as whisky, gin and vodka, and also used in medicines and as a disinfectant. Also called **ethyl alcohol**

ethene /ˈiːθiːn/ *noun* same as **ethylene**

ether /ˈiːθə/ *noun* an anaesthetic substance, now rarely used

ethical /ˈeθɪk(ə)l/ *adjective* concerning ethics

ethical committee /ˈeθɪk(ə)l kəˌmɪti/ *noun* a group of specialists who monitor experiments involving human beings or who regulate the way in which members of the medical profession conduct themselves

ethics /ˈeθɪks/ *noun* ♦ **medical ethics**

ethinyloestradiol /ˌeθɪn(ə)lˌiːstrəˈdaɪɒl/ *noun* an artificial hormone related to oestrogen that is effective in small doses. It forms part of hormone replacement therapy.

ethmoid /eθˈmɔɪd/, **ethmoidal** /eθˈmɔɪd(ə)l/ *adjective* referring to the ethmoid bone or near to the ethmoid bone

ethmoidal sinuses /eθˌmɔɪd(ə)l ˈsaɪnəsɪz/ *plural noun* air cells inside the ethmoid bone

ethmoid bone /ˈeθmɔɪd bəʊn/ *noun* a bone which forms the top of the nasal cavity and part of the orbits

ethmoidectomy /ˌeθmɔɪˈdektəmi/ *noun* an operation to remove the lining between the sinuses

ethmoiditis /ˌeθmɔɪˈdaɪtɪs/ *noun* inflammation of the ethmoid bone or of the ethmoidal sinuses

ethnic /ˈeθnɪk/ *adjective* relating to a culturally or racially distinctive group of people

ethyl alcohol /ˌiːθaɪl ˈælkəhɒl/ *noun* same as **ethanol**

ethylene /ˈeθəliːn/ *noun* a gas used as an anaesthetic

ethylestrenol /ˌeθ(ə)lˈestrənɒl/ *noun* an anabolic steroid

etiology /ˌiːtiˈɒlədʒi/ *noun US* same as **aetiology**

eucalyptus /ˌjuːkəˈlɪptəs/ *noun* a genus of tree growing mainly in Australia, from which a strongly smelling oil is distilled

eucalyptus oil /ˌjuːkəˈlɪptəs ɔɪl/ *noun* an aromatic medicinal oil distilled from the leaves of various species of tree in the genus *Eucalyptus*

eugenics /juːˈdʒenɪks/ *noun* the study of how to improve the human race by genetic selection

eunuch /ˈjuːnək/ *noun* a castrated male

euphoria /juːˈfɔːriə/ *noun* a feeling of extreme happiness

Eustachian canal /juːˈsteɪʃ(ə)n kəˌnæl/ *noun* a passage through the porous bone forming the outside part of the Eustachian tube

Eustachian tube /juːˈsteɪʃ(ə)n tjuːb/ *noun* the tube which connects the pharynx to the middle ear. See illustration at **EAR** in Supplement [Described 1562, but actually named after Eustachio by Valsalva a century later. Bartolomeo Eustachio (1520–74), physician to the Pope and Professor of Anatomy in Rome.]

euthanasia /ˌjuːθəˈneɪziə/ *noun* the painless killing of an incurably ill person or someone in a permanent coma in order to end their distress. Also called **mercy killing** (NOTE: This practice is illegal in most countries.)

euthyroid /juːˈθaɪrɔɪd/ *noun* a condition where the thyroid is functioning normally

evacuant /ɪˈvækjuənt/ *noun* a medicine which makes a person have a bowel movement

evacuation /ɪˌvækjuˈeɪʃ(ə)n/ *noun* the act of removing the contents of something, especially discharging faeces from the bowel

evacuation of retained products of conception /ɪvækjuˌeɪʃ(ə)n əv rɪˌteɪnd ˌprɒdʌkts əv kənˈsepʃən/ *noun* a D & C operation performed after an abortion or miscarriage to ensure the uterus is left empty. Abbreviation **ERPC**

evaluation /ɪˌvæljuˈeɪʃ(ə)n/ *noun* the act of examining and calculating the quantity or level of something ○ *In further evaluation of these patients no side-effects of the treatment were noted.*

eventration /ˌiːvenˈtreɪʃ(ə)n/ *noun* the pushing of the intestine through the wall of the abdomen

eversion /ɪˈvɜːʃ(ə)n/ *noun* the act of turning towards the outside or turning inside out. See illustration at **ANATOMICAL TERMS** in Supplement

evertor /ɪˈvɜːtə/ *noun* a muscle which makes a limb turn outwards

evidence-based /ˈevɪd(ə)ns beɪst/ *adjective* based on the results of well-designed trials of specific types of treatment for specific conditions ○ *evidence-based practice*

evidence-based medicine /ˈevɪd(ə)ns beɪst ˌmed(ə)sɪn/ *noun* medical practice where findings from research are used as the basis for decisions

evisceration /ɪˌvɪsəˈreɪʃ(ə)n/ *noun* the surgical removal of the abdominal viscera. Also called **exenteration**

evolution /ˌiːvəˈluːʃ(ə)n/ *noun* a process of change in organisms which takes place over a very long period involving many generations

evulsion /ɪˈvʌlʃən/ *noun* the act of extracting something by force

Ewing's tumour /ˈjuːɪŋz ˈtjuːmə/, **Ewing's sarcoma** /ˌjuːɪŋz sɑːˈkəʊmə/ *noun* a malignant tumour in the marrow of a long bone [Described 1922. After James Ewing (1866–1943), Professor of Pathology at Cornell University, New York, USA.]

EWS /ˌiː ˌdʌb(ə)ljuː ˈes/ *noun* an 'early warning system' designed to alert healthcare professionals to new developments in technologies, pharmaceuticals and treatments

ex- /eks/ *prefix* same as **exo-** (*used before vowels*)

exacerbation /ɪgˌzæsəˈbeɪʃ(ə)n/ *noun* **1.** the fact of making a condition worse **2.** a period when a condition becomes worse

exanthem /ɪgˈzænθəm/ *noun* a skin rash found with infectious diseases like measles or chickenpox

exanthematous /ˌeksænˈθemətəs/ *adjective* referring to an exanthem or like an exanthem

exception /ɪkˈsepʃən/ *noun* **1.** something that does not fit into or is excluded from a general rule or pattern **2.** the act or condition of being excluded

exchange transfusion /ɪksˌtʃeɪndʒ trænsˈfjuːʒ(ə)n/ *noun* a method of treating leukaemia or erythroblastosis in newborn babies, where almost all the blood is removed from the body and replaced with healthy blood

excise /ɪkˈsaɪz/ *verb* to cut something out

excision /ɪkˈsɪʒ(ə)n/ *noun* an operation by a surgeon to cut and remove part of the body such as a growth. Compare **incision**

excitation /ˌeksɪˈteɪʃ(ə)n/ *noun* the state of being mentally or physically aroused

excite /ɪkˈsaɪt/ *verb* **1.** to stimulate someone or something **2.** to give an impulse to a nerve or muscle

excoriation /ɪksˌkɔːriˈeɪʃ(ə)n/ *noun* a raw skin surface or mucous membrane after rubbing or burning

excrement /ˈekskrɪmənt/ *noun* same as **faeces**

excrescence /ɪkˈskres(ə)ns/ *noun* a growth on the skin

excreta /ɪkˈskriːtə/ *plural noun* waste material from the body, especially faeces

excretion /ɪkˈskriːʃ(ə)n/ *noun* the act of passing waste matter, e.g. faeces, urine or sweat, out of the body

excruciating /ɪkˈskruːʃieɪtɪŋ/ *adjective* extremely painful ○ *He had excruciating pains in his head.*

exenteration /ekˌsentəˈreɪʃ(ə)n/ *noun* same as **evisceration**

exercise /'eksəsaɪz/ *noun* **1.** physical or mental activity, especially the active use of the muscles as a way of keeping fit, correcting a deformity or strengthening a part ○ *Regular exercise is good for your heart.* ○ *He doesn't do or take enough exercise.* **2.** a particular movement or action designed to use and strengthen the muscles ■ *verb* to take exercise, or exert part of the body in exercise ○ *He exercises twice a day to keep fit.*

exercise-induced asthma /ˌeksəsaɪz ɪn ˌdjuːst 'æsmə/ *noun* asthma which is caused by exercise such as running or cycling. Abbreviation **EIA**

exfoliation /eksˌfəʊli'eɪʃ(ə)n/ *noun* the loss of layers of tissue such as sunburnt skin

exfoliative /eks'fəʊlieɪtɪv/ *adjective* referring to exfoliation

exfoliative dermatitis /eksˌfəʊliətɪv ˌdɜːmə 'taɪtɪs/ *noun* a typical form of dermatitis where the skin becomes red and comes off in flakes

exhalation /ˌekshə'leɪʃ(ə)n/ *noun* the act of breathing out. Opposite **inhalation**

exhale /eks'heɪl/ *verb* to breathe out. Opposite **inhale**

exhibitionism /ˌeksɪ'bɪʃ(ə)nɪz(ə)m/ *noun* a desire to show the genitals to a person of the opposite sex

exo- /eksəʊ/ *prefix* out of, outside

exocrine gland /'eksəkraɪn glænd/ *noun* a gland with ducts which channel secretions to particular parts of the body such as the liver, the sweat glands, the pancreas and the salivary glands. Compare **endocrine gland**

exogenous /ek'sɒdʒənəs/ *adjective* developing or caused by something outside the organism. Compare **endogenous**

exomphalos /ek'sɒmfələs/ *noun* same as **umbilical hernia**

exophthalmic goitre /ˌeksɒfθælmɪk 'ɡɔɪtə/ *noun* a form of hyperthyroidism, in which the neck swells and the eyes protrude. Also called **Graves' disease**

exophthalmos /ˌeksɒf'θælməs/ *noun* protruding eyeballs

exostosis /ˌeksə'stəʊsɪs/ *noun* a benign growth on the surface of a bone

exotic /ɪɡ'zɒtɪk/ *adjective* referring to a disease which occurs in a foreign country

exotoxin /ˌeksəʊ'tɒksɪn/ *noun* a poison, produced by bacteria, which affects parts of the body away from the place of infection, e.g. the toxins which cause botulism or tetanus

exotropia /ˌeksəʊ'trəʊpiə/ *noun* same as **divergent strabismus**

expectant mother /ɪkˌspektənt 'mʌðə/ *noun* a pregnant woman

expectorant /ɪk'spekt(ə)rənt/ *noun* a drug which helps someone to cough up phlegm

expectoration /ɪkˌspektə'reɪʃ(ə)n/ *noun* the act of coughing up fluid or phlegm from the respiratory tract

experiential learning /ɪkˌspɪərienʃəl 'lɜːnɪŋ/ *noun* the process of learning from experience

expert patient /ˌekspɜːt 'peɪʃ(ə)nt/ *noun* a patient with a long-term illness who has been taught how to manage his or her own medical care

expiration /ˌekspə'reɪʃ(ə)n/ *noun* **1.** the act of breathing out, or pushing air out of the lungs ○ *Expiration takes place when the chest muscles relax and the lungs become smaller.* Opposite **inspiration 2.** death

expire /ɪk'spaɪə/ *verb* **1.** to breathe out **2.** to die

exploration /ˌeksplə'reɪʃ(ə)n/ *noun* a procedure or surgical operation where the aim is to discover the cause of symptoms or the nature and extent of an illness

exploratory surgery /ɪkˌsplɒrət(ə)ri 'sɜːdʒəri/ *noun* a surgical operation in which the aim is to discover the cause of a person's symptoms or the nature and extent of an illness

expression /ɪk'spreʃ(ə)n/ *noun* **1.** the look on a person's face which shows what he or she thinks and feels ○ *His expression showed that he was annoyed.* **2.** the act of pushing something out of the body ○ *the expression of the fetus and placenta during childbirth*

exsanguinate /ɪk'sæŋɡwɪneɪt/ *verb* to drain blood from the body

exsanguination /ɪkˌsæŋɡwɪ'neɪʃ(ə)n/ *noun* the removal of blood from the body

extension /ɪk'stenʃən/ *noun* **1.** the stretching or straightening out of a joint **2.** the stretching of a joint by traction

extensor /ɪk'stensə/, **extensor muscle** /ɪk 'stensə ˌmʌs(ə)l/ *noun* a muscle which makes a joint become straight. Compare **flexor**

exterior /ɪk'stɪəriə/ *noun* the outside of something

externa /ɪk'stɜːnə/ ♦ **otitis**

external cardiac massage /ɪkˌstɜːn(ə)l ˌkɑːdiæk 'mæsɑːʒ/ *noun* a method of making someone's heart start beating again by rhythmic pressing on the breastbone

external ear /ɪkˌstɜːn(ə)l 'ɪə/ *noun* same as **outer ear**

external haemorrhoids /ɪkˌstɜːn(ə)l 'hemərɔɪdz/ *plural noun* haemorrhoids in the skin just outside the anus

external iliac artery /ɪkˌstɜːn(ə)l 'ɪliæk ˌɑːtəri/ *noun* an artery which branches from the aorta in the abdomen and leads to the leg

external jugular /ɪkˌstɜːn(ə)l 'dʒʌɡjʊlə/ *noun* the main jugular vein in the neck, leading from the temporal vein

external nares /ɪkˌstɜːn(ə)l 'neəriːz/ *plural noun* same as **anterior nares**

external otitis /ɪkˌstɜːn(ə)l əˈtaɪtɪs/ *noun* same as **otitis externa**

external respiration /ɪkˌstɜːn(ə)l ˌrespɪˈreɪʃ(ə)n/ *noun* the part of respiration concerned with oxygen in the air being exchanged in the lungs for carbon dioxide from the blood

exteroceptor /ˈekstərəʊseptə/ *noun* a sensory nerve which is affected by stimuli from outside the body, e.g. in the eye or ear

extinction /ɪkˈstɪŋkʃən/ *noun* **1.** the destruction or stopping of something **2.** the lessening or stopping of a conditioned behavioural response through lack of reinforcement

extirpation /ˌekstɜːˈpeɪʃ(ə)n/ *noun* the total removal of a structure, an organ or growth by surgery

extra- /ekstrə/ *prefix* outside

extracapsular /ˌekstrəˈkæpsjʊlə/ *adjective* outside a capsule

extracapsular fracture /ˌekstrəˌkæpsjʊlə ˈfræktʃə/ *noun* a fracture of the upper part of the femur, which does not involve the capsule round the hip joint

extracellular /ˌekstrəˈseljʊlə/ *adjective* outside cells

extracellular fluid /ˌekstrəseljʊlə ˈfluːɪd/ *noun* a fluid which surrounds cells

extract *noun* /ˈekstrækt/ a preparation made by removing water or alcohol from a substance, leaving only the essence ■ *verb* /ɪkˈstrækt/ to take out something ○ *Adrenaline extracted from the animal's adrenal glands is used in the treatment of asthma.*

extraction /ɪkˈstrækʃən/ *noun* the removal of part of the body, especially a tooth

extradural /ˌekstrəˈdjʊərəl/ *adjective* same as **epidural**

extradural haematoma /ˌekstrəˌdjʊərəl ˌhiːməˈtəʊmə/ *noun* a blood clot which forms in the head outside the dura mater, caused by a blow

extradural haemorrhage /ˌekstrəˌdjʊərəl ˈhem(ə)rɪdʒ/ *noun* a serious condition where bleeding occurs between the dura mater and the skull

extraembryonic membranes /ˌekstrə embriˌɒnɪk ˈmembreɪnz/ *plural noun* membranes which are not part of the embryo

extrapleural /ˌekstrəˈplʊərəl/ *adjective* outside the pleural cavity

extrapyramidal /ˌekstrəpɪˈræmɪd(ə)l/ *adjective* outside the pyramidal tracts

extrapyramidal system /ˌekstrəpɪˌræmɪd(ə)l ˈsɪstəm/ *noun* a motor system which carries motor nerves outside the pyramidal system

extrapyramidal tracts /ˌekstrəpɪˌræmɪd(ə)l ˈtrækts/ *plural noun* same as **extrapyramidal system**

extrasensory /ˌekstrəˈsensəri/ *adjective* involving perception by means other than the usual five senses

extrasystole /ˌekstrəˈsɪstəli/ *noun* same as **ectopic heartbeat**

extrauterine /ˌekstrəˈjuːtəraɪn/ *adjective* occurring or developing outside the uterus

extrauterine pregnancy /ˌekstrəjuːtəraɪn ˈpregnənsi/ *noun* same as **ectopic pregnancy**

extravasation /ekˌstrævəˈseɪʃ(ə)n/ *noun* a situation where a bodily fluid, such as blood or secretions, escapes into tissue

extraversion /ˌekstrəˈvɜːʃ(ə)n/ *noun* same as **extroversion**

extravert /ˈekstrəvɜːt/ *noun* same as **extrovert**

extremities /ɪkˈstremətiz/ *plural noun* the parts of the body at the ends of limbs, e.g. the fingers, toes, nose and ears

extremity /ɪkˈstremɪti/ *noun* **1.** a limb **2.** the part of a limb farthest away from the body, especially the hand or foot **3.** a situation or state of great distress or danger **4.** the greatest intensity of something

extrinsic /eksˈtrɪnsɪk/ *adjective* external, originating outside a structure

extrinsic factor /eksˌtrɪnsɪk ˈfæktə/ *noun* a former term for vitamin B_{12}, which is necessary for the production of red blood cells

extrinsic muscle /eksˌtrɪnsɪk ˈmʌs(ə)l/ *noun* a muscle which is some way away from the part of the body which it operates

extroversion /ekstrəˈvɜːʃ(ə)n/ *noun* **1.** (*in psychology*) a condition in which a person is interested in people and things other than themselves **2.** a congenital turning of an organ inside out

extrovert /ˈekstrəvɜːt/ *noun* a person who is interested in people and things in the external world

extubation /ˌekstjuːˈbeɪʃ(ə)n/ *noun* the removal of a tube after intubation

eye /aɪ/ *noun* the part of the body with which a person sees (NOTE: For other terms referring to the eye, see **ocular**, **optic** and words beginning with **oculo-**, **ophth-**, **ophthalm-**, **ophthalmo-**.)

eyeball /ˈaɪbɔːl/ *noun* the round ball of tissue through which light passes, located in the eye socket and controlled by various muscles

eyebrow /ˈaɪbraʊ/ *noun* an arch of skin with a line of hair above the eye

eye drops /ˈaɪ drɒps/ *plural noun* medicine in liquid form which is put into the eye in small amounts

eyelash /ˈaɪlæʃ/ *noun* a small hair which grows out from the edge of the eyelid

eyelid /ˈaɪlɪd/ *noun* a piece of skin which covers the eye. Also called **blepharon**, **palpebra**

(NOTE: For other terms referring to the eyelids, see words beginning with **blephar-, blepharo-**.)

eye socket /'aɪ ˌsɒkɪt/ *noun* same as **orbit**

eyestrain /'aɪstreɪn/ *noun* tiredness in the muscles of the eye with a headache, which may be caused by an activity such as reading in bad light or working on a computer screen. Also called **asthenopia**

eyetooth /'aɪtuːθ/ *noun* a canine tooth, one of two pairs of pointed teeth next to the incisors (NOTE: The plural is **eyeteeth**.)

F

F *abbreviation* Fahrenheit

face /feɪs/ *noun* the front part of the head, where the eyes, nose and mouth are placed ■ *verb* to have your face towards or to look towards something ○ *Please face the screen.*

face delivery /ˈfeɪs dɪˌlɪv(ə)ri/ *noun* a birth where the baby's face appears first

face lift /ˈfeɪs lɪft/, **face-lifting operation** /ˈfeɪs ˌlɪftɪŋ ɒpəˌreɪʃ(ə)n/ *noun* a surgical operation to remove wrinkles on the face and neck

face presentation /ˈfeɪs prez(ə)n,teɪʃ(ə)n/ *noun* a position of a baby in the uterus where the face will appear first at birth

facet /ˈfæsɪt/ *noun* a flat surface on a bone

facet syndrome /ˈfæsɪt ˌsɪndrəʊm/ *noun* a condition in which a joint in the vertebrae becomes dislocated

facial /ˈfeɪʃ(ə)l/ *adjective* relating to, or appearing on, the face ○ *The psychiatrist examined the patient's facial expression.*

facial bone /ˈfeɪʃ(ə)l bəʊn/ *noun* one of the fourteen bones which form the face

COMMENT: The bones which make up the face are: two maxillae forming the upper jaw; two nasal bones forming the top part of the nose; two lacrimal bones on the inside of the orbit near the nose; two zygomatic or malar bones forming the sides of the cheeks; two palatine bones forming the back part of the top of the mouth; two nasal conchae or turbinate bones which form the sides of the nasal cavity; the mandible or lower jaw; and the vomer in the centre of the nasal septum.

facial paralysis /ˈfeɪʃ(ə)l pəˌræləsɪs/ *noun* same as **Bell's palsy**

facies /ˈfeɪʃiiːz/ *noun* someone's facial appearance, used as a guide to diagnosis

factor /ˈfæktə/ *noun* **1.** something which has an influence or which makes something else take place **2.** a substance, variously numbered, e.g. Factor I, Factor II, in the plasma, which makes the blood coagulate when a blood vessel is injured

Factor II /ˌfæktə ˈtuː/ *noun* same as **prothrombin**

Factor IX /ˌfæktə ˈnaɪn/ *noun* a protein in plasma which promotes the clotting of blood and is lacking in people with haemophilia B. Also called **Christmas factor**

Factor VIII /ˌfæktər ˈeɪt/ *noun* a protein in plasma which promotes the clotting of blood and is lacking in people with haemophilia A

Factor XI /ˌfæktər ɪˈlev(ə)n/ *noun* a protein in plasma which promotes the clotting of blood and is lacking in people with haemophilia C

Factor XII /ˌfæktə ˈtwelv/ *noun* a protein in plasma which promotes the clotting of blood and is lacking in some people with haemophilia. Also called **Hageman factor**

fade away /ˌfeɪd əˈweɪ/ *verb* to be in the process of dying (*informal*)

faecal /ˈfiːk(ə)l/ *adjective* referring to faeces

faecal impaction /ˌfiːkl(ə)l ɪmˈpækʃən/ *noun* a condition in which a hardened mass of faeces stays in the rectum

faecal incontinence /ˌfiːk(ə)l ɪnˈkɒntɪnəns/ *noun* an inability to control the bowel movements

faecalith /ˈfiːkəlɪθ/ *noun* same as **coprolith**

faecal matter /ˈfiːk(ə)l ˌmætə/ *noun* solid waste matter from the bowels

faeces /ˈfiːsiːz/ *plural noun* solid waste matter passed from the bowels through the anus. Also called **stools**, **bowel movement** (NOTE: For other terms referring to faeces, see words beginning with **sterco-**.)

Fahrenheit /ˈfærənhaɪt/, **Fahrenheit scale** /ˈfærənhaɪt skeɪl/ *noun* a scale of temperatures where the freezing and boiling points of water are 32° and 212° under standard atmospheric pressure (NOTE: Used in the US, but less common in the UK. Usually written as an **F** after the degree sign: **32°F** (say: 'thirty-two degrees Fahrenheit').)

fail /feɪl/ *verb* **1.** not to be successful in doing something ○ *The doctor failed to see the symptoms.* ○ *She has failed her pharmacy exams.* ○ *He failed his medical and was rejected by the police force.* **2.** to become weaker and less likely to recover

failure to thrive /ˌfeɪljə tə ˈθraɪv/ *noun* same as **marasmus**

faint /feɪnt/ *verb* to stop being conscious for a short time and, usually, fall down ■ *noun* a loss of consciousness for a short period, caused by a temporary reduction in the blood flow to the brain

fainting fit /ˈfeɪntɪŋ fɪt/, **fainting spell** /ˈfeɪntɪŋ spel/ *noun* same as **syncope** ○ *She often had fainting fits when she was dieting.*

Fairbanks' splint /ˈfeəbæŋks splɪnt/ *noun* a special splint used for correcting Erb's palsy

faith healing /ˈfeɪθ ˌhiːlɪŋ/ *noun* the treatment of pain or illness by a person who prays and may also lay his or her hands on the patient

falciform /ˈfælsɪfɔːm/ *adjective* in the shape of a sickle

falciform ligament /ˌfælsɪfɔːm ˈlɪɡəmənt/ *noun* a piece of tissue which separates the two lobes of the liver and attaches it to the diaphragm

fallen arches /ˌfɔːlən ˈɑːtʃɪz/ *plural noun* a condition in which the arches in the sole of the foot are not high

Fallopian tube /fəˈləʊpiən tjuːb/ *noun* one of two tubes which connect the ovaries to the uterus. See illustration at **UROGENITAL SYSTEM (FEMALE)** in Supplement. Also called **oviduct**, **salpinx** (NOTE: For other terms referring to Fallopian tubes, see words beginning with **salping-**, **salpingo-**.) [Described 1561. After Gabriele Fallopio (1523–63), Italian man of medicine. He was Professor of Surgery and Anatomy at Padua, where he was also Professor of Botany.]

Fallot's tetralogy /ˌfæləʊz teˈtrælədʒi/ *noun* same as **tetralogy of Fallot**

false rib /ˌfɔːls ˈrɪb/ *noun* one of the bottom five ribs on each side which are not directly attached to the breastbone

familial /fəˈmɪliəl/ *adjective* referring to a family

familial adenomatous polyposis /fəˌmɪliəl ædəˌnɒmətəs ˌpɒlɪˈpəʊsɪs/ *noun* a hereditary disorder where polyps develop in the small intestine. Abbreviation **FAP**

familial disorder /fəˌmɪliəl dɪsˈɔːdə/ *noun* a hereditary disorder which affects several members of the same family

family /ˈfæm(ə)li/ *noun* a group of people who are related to each other, especially mother, father and children

family doctor /ˌfæm(ə)li ˈdɒktə/ *noun* a general practitioner

family planning /ˌfæm(ə)li ˈplænɪŋ/ *noun* the use of contraception to control the number of children in a family

family planning clinic /ˌfæm(ə)li ˈplænɪŋ ˌklɪnɪk/ *noun* a clinic which gives advice on contraception

family therapy /ˌfæm(ə)li ˈθerəpi/ *noun* a type of psychotherapy where members of the family of a person with a disorder meet a therapist to discuss the condition and try to come to terms with it

famotidine /fəˈmɒtɪdiːn/ *noun* a histamine which reduces the secretion of gastric acid and is used to treat ulcers

Fanconi syndrome /fænˈkəʊni ˌsɪndrəʊm/ *noun* a kidney disorder where amino acids are present in the urine [Described 1927. After Guido Fanconi (1892–1979), Professor of Paediatrics at the University of Zurich, Switzerland.]

fantasy /ˈfæntəsi/ *noun* a series of imaginary events which someone believes really took place

FAP *abbreviation* familial adenomatous polyposis

farcy /ˈfɑːsi/ *noun* a form of glanders which affects the lymph nodes

farmer's lung /ˌfɑːməz ˈlʌŋ/ *noun* a type of asthma caused by an allergy to rotting hay

fascia /ˈfeɪʃə/ *noun* fibrous tissue covering a muscle or an organ (NOTE: The plural is **fasciae**.)

fasciculation /fəˌsɪkjʊˈleɪʃ(ə)n/ *noun* small muscle movements which appear as trembling skin

fasciculus /fəˈsɪkjʊləs/ *noun* a bundle of nerve fibres (NOTE: The plural is **fasciculi**.)

fasciitis /ˌfæʃiˈaɪtɪs/ *noun* an inflammation of the connective tissue between muscles or around organs

fastigium /fæˈstɪdʒiəm/ *noun* the highest temperature during a bout of fever

fat /fæt/ *adjective* big and round in the body ○ *You ought to eat less – you're getting too fat.* (NOTE: **fatter – fattest**) ■ *noun* **1.** a white oily substance in the body, which stores energy and protects the body against cold **2.** a type of food which supplies protein and Vitamins A and D, especially that part of meat which is white, and solid substances like lard or butter produced from animals and used for cooking, or liquid substances like oil ○ *If you don't like the fat on the meat, cut it off.* ○ *Fry the eggs in some fat.* (NOTE: **Fat** has no plural when it means the substance; the plural **fats** is used to mean different types of fat. For other terms referring to fats, see **lipid** and words beginning with **steato-**.)

fatigue /fəˈtiːɡ/ *noun* very great tiredness

fatigue fracture /fəˈtiːɡ ˌfræktʃə/ *noun* ♦ **stress fracture**

fatty /ˈfæti/ *adjective* containing fat

fatty acid /ˌfæti ˈæsɪd/ *noun* an organic acid belonging to a group that occurs naturally as fats, oils and waxes. ◊ **essential fatty acid**

fatty degeneration /ˌfæti dɪˌdʒenəˈreɪʃ(ə)n/ *noun* same as **adipose degeneration**

fauces /ˈfɔːsiːz/ *noun* an opening between the tonsils at the back of the throat, leading to the pharynx

FDA *abbreviation* US Food and Drug Administration

fear /fɪə/ *noun* a state where a person is afraid of something ○ *fear of flying*

febricula /fe'brɪkjʊlə/ *noun* a low fever

febrifuge /'febrɪfjuːdʒ/ *noun* a drug which prevents or lowers a fever, e.g. aspirin ■ *adjective* preventing or lowering fever

febrile /'fiːbraɪl/ *adjective* referring to a fever, or caused by a fever

febrile convulsion /ˌfiːbraɪl kən'vʌlʃ(ə)n/ *noun* a convulsion in a child, lasting a short time, associated with a fever

febrile disease /'fiːbraɪl dɪˌziːz/ *noun* a disease which is accompanied by fever

fecundation /ˌfekən'deɪʃ(ə)n/ *noun* the act of bringing male and female reproductive matter together. Also called **fertilisation**

feedback /'fiːdbæk/ *noun* **1.** information or comments about something which has been done ○ *The initial feedback from patients on the new service was encouraging.* **2.** the linking of the result of an action back to the action itself

Fehling's solution /'feɪlɪŋz səˌluːʃ(ə)n/ *noun* a solution used in Fehling's test to detect sugar in urine [Described 1848. After Hermann Christian von Fehling (1812–85), Professor of Chemistry at Stuttgart, Germany.]

Fehling's test /'feɪlɪŋz test/ *noun* a test for the presence of aldehydes and sugars in a biological sample by means of Fehling's solution

felon /'felən/ *noun* same as **whitlow**

Felty's syndrome /'feltiːz ˌsɪndrəʊm/ *noun* a condition, associated with rheumatoid arthritis, in which the spleen is enlarged and the number of white blood cells increases [Described 1924. After Augustus Roi Felty (1895–1963), physician at Hartford Hospital, Connecticut, USA.]

female condom /ˌfiːmeɪl 'kɒndɒm/ *noun* a rubber sheath inserted into the vagina before intercourse, covering the walls of the vagina and the cervix

female sex hormone /ˌfiːmeɪl 'seks ˌhɔːməʊn/ *noun* same as **oestrogen**

feminisation /ˌfemɪnaɪ'zeɪʃ(ə)n/, **feminization** *noun* the development of female characteristics in a male

femoral /'femərəl/ *adjective* referring to the femur or to the thigh

femoral artery /ˌfemərəl 'ɑːtəri/ *noun* a continuation of the external iliac artery, which runs down the front of the thigh and then crosses to the back of the thigh

femoral canal /ˌfemərəl kə'næl/ *noun* the inner tube of the sheath surrounding the femoral artery and vein

femoral head /ˌfemərəl 'hed/ *noun* the head of the femur, the rounded projecting end part of the thigh bone which joins the acetabulum at the hip

femoral hernia /ˌfemərəl 'hɜːniə/ *noun* a hernia of the bowel at the top of the thigh

femoral neck /ˌfemərəl 'nek/ *noun* the narrow part between the head and the diaphysis of the femur. Also called **neck of the femur**

femoral nerve /'femərəl nɜːv/ *noun* a nerve which governs the muscle at the front of the thigh

femoral pulse /ˌfemərəl 'pʌls/ *noun* a pulse taken in the groin

femoral triangle /ˌfemərəl 'traɪæŋgəl/ *noun* a slight hollow in the groin which contains the femoral vessels and nerve. Also called **Scarpa's triangle**

femoral vein /'femərəl veɪn/ *noun* a vein running up the upper leg, a continuation of the popliteal vein

femur /'fiːmə/ *noun* the bone in the top part of the leg which joins the acetabulum at the hip and the tibia at the knee. Also called **thighbone**. See illustration at PELVIS in Supplement (NOTE: The plural is **femora**.)

-fen /fen/ *suffix* used in names of non-steroidal anti-inflammatory drugs ○ *ibuprofen*

fenestra /fə'nestrə/ *noun* a small opening in the ear

fenestra ovalis /fəˌnestrə əʊ'vɑːlɪs/ *noun* same as **oval window**

fenestra rotunda /fəˌnestrə rəʊ'tʌndə/ *noun* same as **round window**

fenestration /ˌfenə'streɪʃ(ə)n/ *noun* a surgical operation to relieve deafness by making a small opening in the inner ear

fenoprofen /ˌfenəʊ'prəʊfen/ *noun* a non-steroidal, anti-inflammatory drug that is used to manage the pain of arthritis

fentanyl /'fentənɪl/ *noun* a narcotic drug that is a powerful painkiller

fermentation /ˌfɜːmen'teɪʃ(ə)n/ *noun* a process where carbohydrates are broken down by enzymes from yeast and produce alcohol. Also called **zymosis**

ferric /'ferɪk/ *adjective* containing iron with a valency of three

ferritin /'ferɪtɪn/ *noun* a protein found in the liver that binds reversibly to iron and stores it for later use in making haemoglobin in red blood cells

ferrous /'ferəs/ *adjective* containing iron with a valency of two

ferrous sulphate /ˌferəs 'sʌlfeɪt/ *noun* a white or pale green iron salt that is used in the treatment of iron-deficient anaemia

ferrule /'feruːl/ *noun* a metal or rubber cap or ring that strengthens and protects the lower end of a crutch or walking stick ■ *verb* to fit a ferrule onto a crutch or walking stick

fertile /'fɜːtaɪl/ *adjective* able to produce children. Opposite **sterile**

fertilisation /ˌfɜːtɪlaɪˈzeɪʃ(ə)n/, **fertilization** *noun* the joining of an ovum and a sperm to form a zygote and so start the development of an embryo

fertility /fɜːˈtɪlɪti/ *noun* the fact of being fertile. Opposite **sterility**

fertility rate /fɜːˈtɪlɪti reɪt/ *noun* the number of births per year calculated per 1000 females aged between 15 and 44

FESS *abbreviation* functional endoscopic sinus surgery

fester /ˈfestə/ *verb* (*of an infected wound*) to become inflamed and produce pus ○ *His legs were covered with festering sores.*

festination /ˌfestɪˈneɪʃ(ə)n/ *noun* a way of walking in which a person takes short steps, seen in people who have Parkinson's disease

fetal /ˈfiːt(ə)l/ *adjective* referring to a fetus

fetal alcohol syndrome /ˌfiːt(ə)l ˈælkəˈhɒl ˌsɪndrəʊm/ *noun* damage caused to the fetus by alcohol in the blood of the mother, which affects the growth of the embryo, including its facial and brain development. Abbreviation **FAS**

fetal dystocia /ˌfiːt(ə)l dɪsˈtəʊsiə/ *noun* a difficult childbirth caused by a malformation or malpresentation of the fetus

fetal heart /ˌfiːt(ə)l ˈhɑːt/ *noun* the heart of the fetus

fetal monitor /ˌfiːt(ə)l ˈmɒnɪtə/ *noun* an electronic device which monitors the fetus in the uterus

fetal position /ˈfiːt(ə)l pəˌzɪʃ(ə)n/ *noun* a position where a person lies curled up on his or her side, like a fetus in the uterus

fetishism /ˈfetɪʃɪz(ə)m/, **fetichism** *noun* a psychological disorder in which someone gets sexual satisfaction from touching objects

feto- /ˈfiːtəʊ/ *prefix* fetus

fetoprotein /ˌfiːtəʊˈprəʊtiːn/ *noun* ♦ **alpha-fetoprotein**

fetor /ˈfiːtə/ *noun* a bad smell

fetoscope /ˈfiːtəskəʊp/ *noun* a stethoscope used in fetoscopy

fetoscopy /fɪˈtɒskəpi/ *noun* an examination of a fetus inside the uterus, taking blood samples to diagnose blood disorders

fetus /ˈfiːtəs/ *noun* an unborn baby from two months after conception until birth, before which it is called an embryo

FEV *abbreviation* forced expiratory volume

fever /ˈfiːvə/ *noun* **1.** a rise in body temperature ○ *She is running a slight fever.* ○ *You must stay in bed until the fever has gone down.* **2.** a condition when the temperature of the body is higher than usual ▶ also called **pyrexia**

fever blister /ˈfiːvə ˌblɪstə/ *noun* same as **fever sore**

fever sore /ˈfiːvə sɔː/ *noun* a cold sore or burning sore, usually on the lips

fiber /ˈfaɪbə/ *noun US* same as **fibre**

fibr- /faɪbr/ *prefix* referring to fibres, fibrous (*used before vowels*)

-fibrate /faɪbreɪt/ *suffix* used in names of lipid-lowering drugs

fibre /ˈfaɪbə/ *noun* **1.** a structure in the body shaped like a thread **2.** same as **dietary fibre**

fibre optics /ˌfaɪbər ˈɒptɪks/, **fibreoptics** /ˌfaɪbərˈɒptɪks/ *noun* the use of thin fibres which conduct light and images to examine internal organs

fibrescope /ˈfaɪbəskəʊp/ *noun* a device made of bundles of optical fibres which is passed into the body, used for examining internal organs

fibrillation /ˌfaɪbrɪˈleɪʃ(ə)n/ *noun* the fluttering of a muscle

fibrin /ˈfɪbrɪn/ *noun* a protein produced by fibrinogen, which helps make blood coagulate

fibrin foam /ˈfɪbrɪn fəʊm/ *noun* a white material made artificially from fibrinogen, used to prevent bleeding

fibrinogen /fɪˈbrɪnədʒən/ *noun* a substance in blood plasma which produces fibrin when activated by thrombin

fibrinolysin /ˌfɪbrɪˈnɒləsɪn/ *noun* an enzyme which digests fibrin. Also called **plasmin**

fibrinolysis /ˌfɪbrɪˈnɒləsɪs/ *noun* the removal of blood clots from the system by the action of fibrinolysin on fibrin. Also called **thrombolysis**

fibrinolytic /ˌfɪbrɪnəˈlɪtɪk/ *adjective* referring to fibrinolysis ○ *fibrinolytic drugs* Also called **thrombolytic**

fibro- /faɪbrəʊ/ *prefix* referring to fibres

fibroadenoma /ˌfaɪbrəʊˌædɪˈnəʊmə/ *noun* a benign tumour formed of fibrous and glandular tissue

fibroblast /ˈfaɪbrəʊblæst/ *noun* a long flat cell found in connective tissue, which develops into collagen

fibrocartilage /ˌfaɪbrəʊˈkɑːtəlɪdʒ/ *noun* cartilage and fibrous tissue combined

fibrochondritis /ˌfaɪbrəʊkɒnˈdraɪtɪs/ *noun* inflammation of the fibrocartilage

fibrocyst /ˈfaɪbrəʊsɪst/ *noun* a benign tumour of fibrous tissue

fibrocystic /ˌfaɪbrəʊˈsɪstɪk/ *adjective* referring to a fibrocyst

fibrocystic disease /ˌfaɪbrəʊˈsɪstɪk dɪˌziːz/, **fibrocystic disease of the pancreas** /ˌfaɪbrəʊ ˌsɪstɪk dɪˌziːz əv ðə ˈpæŋkriəs/ *noun* same as **cystic fibrosis**

fibrocyte /ˈfaɪbrəʊsaɪt/ *noun* a cell which derives from a fibroblast and is found in connective tissue

fibroid /ˈfaɪbrɔɪd/ *adjective* like fibre

fibroid tumour /ˌfaɪbrɔɪd ˈtjuːmə/ *noun* a benign tumour in the muscle fibres of the uterus. Also called **uterine fibroid, fibromyoma**

fibroma /faɪˈbrəʊmə/ *noun* a small benign tumour formed in connective tissue

fibromyoma /ˌfaɪbrəʊmaɪˈəʊmə/ *noun* same as **fibroid tumour**

fibroplasia /ˌfaɪbrəʊˈpleɪziə/ *noun* ♦ **retrolental fibroplasia**

fibrosarcoma /ˌfaɪbrəʊsɑːˈkəʊmə/ *noun* a malignant tumour of the connective tissue, most common in the legs

fibrosis /faɪˈbrəʊsɪs/ *noun* the process of replacing damaged tissue by scar tissue

fibrositis /ˌfaɪbrəˈsaɪtɪs/ *noun* a painful inflammation of the fibrous tissue which surrounds muscles and joints, especially the muscles of the back

fibrous /ˈfaɪbrəs/ *adjective* made of fibres, or like fibre

fibrous capsule /ˌfaɪbrəs ˈkæpsjuːl/ *noun* fibrous tissue surrounding a kidney. Also called **renal capsule**

fibrous joint /ˈfaɪbrəs dʒɔɪnt/ *noun* a joint where fibrous tissue holds two bones together so that they cannot move, as in the bones of the skull

fibrous pericardium /ˌfaɪbrəs periˈkɑːdiəm/ *noun* the outer part of the pericardium which surrounds the heart, and is attached to the main blood vessels

fibrous tissue /ˌfaɪbrəs ˈtɪʃuː/ *noun* strong white tissue which makes tendons and ligaments and also scar tissue

fibula /ˈfɪbjʊlə/ *noun* the thinner of the two bones in the lower leg between the knee and the ankle. Compare **tibia** (NOTE: The plural is **fibulae**.)

fibular /ˈfɪbjʊlə/ *adjective* referring to the fibula

field of vision /ˌfiːld əv ˈvɪʒ(ə)n/ *noun* same as **visual field**

fight or flight reaction /ˌfaɪt ɔː ˈflaɪt ri ˌækʃən/ *noun* the theory that an organism which is faced with a threat reacts either by preparing to fight or to escape

fil- /fɪl/ *prefix* referring to a thread

filament /ˈfɪləmənt/ *noun* a long thin structure like a thread

filamentous /ˌfɪləˈmentəs/ *adjective* like a thread

Filaria /fɪˈleəriə/ *noun* a thin parasitic worm which is found especially in the lymph system, and is passed to humans by mosquitoes (NOTE: The plural is **Filariae**.)

filariasis /ˌfɪləˈraɪəsɪs/ *noun* a tropical disease caused by parasitic threadworms in the lymph system, transmitted by mosquito bites

filiform /ˈfɪlɪfɔːm/ *adjective* shaped like a thread

filiform papillae /ˌfɪlɪfɔːm pəˈpɪliː/ *plural noun* papillae on the tongue which are shaped like threads, and have no taste buds

filipuncture /ˈfɪlɪpʌŋktʃə/ *noun* the procedure of putting a wire into an aneurysm to cause blood clotting

filling /ˈfɪlɪŋ/ *noun* a surgical operation carried out by a dentist to fill a hole in a tooth with amalgam

filter /ˈfɪltə/ *noun* a piece of paper or cloth through which a liquid is passed to remove any solid substances in it ■ *verb* to pass a liquid through a membrane, piece of paper or cloth to remove solid substances ○ *Impurities are filtered from the blood by the kidneys.*

FIM *abbreviation* functional independence measure

fimbria /ˈfɪmbriə/ *noun* a fringe, especially the fringe of hair-like processes at the end of a Fallopian tube near the ovaries (NOTE: The plural is **fimbriae**.)

finger /ˈfɪŋgə/ *noun* one of the five parts at the end of the hand, but usually not including the thumb (NOTE: The names of the fingers are: **little finger, third finger** or **ring finger, middle finger, forefinger** or **index finger**.)

finger-nose test /ˌfɪŋgə ˈnəʊz ˌtest/ *noun* a test of coordination, where the person is asked to close their eyes, stretch out their arm and then touch their nose with their index finger

fingerprint /ˈfɪŋgəprɪnt/ *noun* a mark left by a finger when something is touched. ◊ **genetic fingerprint**

firm /fɜːm/ *noun* a group of doctors and consultants in a hospital, especially one to which a trainee doctor is attached during clinical studies (*informal*)

first aid /ˌfɜːst ˈeɪd/ *noun* help given by a non-medical person to someone who is suddenly ill or injured before full-scale medical treatment can be given ○ *She gave him first aid in the street until the ambulance arrived.*

first-aid kit /ˌfɜːst ˈeɪd ˌkɪt/ *noun* a box with bandages and dressings kept ready to be used in an emergency

first-aid post /ˌfɜːst ˈeɪd ˌpəʊst/, **first-aid station** /ˌfɜːst ˈeɪd ˌsteɪʃ(ə)n/ *noun* a place where injured people can be taken for immediate care

first-degree burn /ˌfɜːst dɪˌgriː ˈbɜːn/ *noun* a former classification of the severity of a burn, where the skin turns red

first-degree haemorrhoids /ˌfɜːst dɪˌgriː ˈhemərɔɪdz/ *plural noun* haemorrhoids which remain in the rectum

first-degree relative /ˌfɜːst dɪˌgriː ˈrelətɪv/ *noun* a relative with whom an individual shares 50% of their genes, e.g. a father, mother, sibling or child

first intention /ˌfɜːst ɪnˈtenʃən/ *noun* the healing of a clean wound where the tissue forms again rapidly and no prominent scar is left

first-level nurse /ˌfɜːst ˌlev(ə)l ˈnɜːs/, **first-level Registered Nurse** /ˌfɜːst ˌlev(ə)l ˌredʒɪstəd ˈnɜːs/ *noun* a nurse who has passed qualifying examinations, is registered as such with the Nursing and Midwifery Council and can act in an independent decision-making role. Compare **second-level nurse**

fission /ˈfɪʃ(ə)n/ *noun* the act of dividing into two or more parts

fissure /ˈfɪʃə/ *noun* a crack or groove in the skin, tissue or an organ

fistula /ˈfɪstjʊlə/ *noun* a passage or opening which has been made unusually between two organs, often near the rectum or anus

fit /fɪt/ *adjective* strong and physically healthy ○ *She exercises every day to keep fit.* ○ *The doctors decided the patient was not fit for surgery.* (NOTE: **fitter – fittest**) ■ *noun* a sudden attack of a disorder, especially convulsions and epilepsy ○ *She had a fit of coughing.* ○ *He had an epileptic fit.* ○ *The baby had a series of fits.* ■ *verb* **1.** to provide a piece of equipment for someone to wear ○ *She was fitted with temporary support.* **2.** to have convulsions ○ *The patient has fitted twice.* (NOTE: **fitting – fitted**. Note also: you fit someone **with** an appliance.)

fitness /ˈfɪtnəs/ *noun* the fact of being strong and healthy ○ *Being in the football team demands a high level of physical fitness.* ○ *He had to pass a fitness test to join the police force.*

5-hydroxy-tryptamine /ˌfaɪv haɪˌdrɒksi ˈtrɪptəmiːn/ *noun* a compound which exists in blood platelets and is released after tissue is injured, and is a neurotransmitter important in sleep, mood and vasoconstriction. Also called **serotonin**

fixated /fɪkˈseɪtɪd/ *adjective* referring to a person who has too close an attachment to another person, often to a parent

fixator /fɪkˈseɪtə/ *noun* a metal rod placed through a bone to keep a part of the body rigid

flaccid /ˈflæksɪd, ˈflæsɪd/ *adjective* soft or flabby

flaccidity /flækˈsɪdɪti, flæˈsɪdɪti/ *noun* the state of being flaccid

Flagyl /ˈflædʒaɪl/ a trade name for metronidazole

flail /fleɪl/ *verb* to thrash around with uncontrollable or violent movements, particularly of the arms

flail chest /ˈfleɪl tʃest/ *noun* a condition in which the chest is not stable, because several ribs have been broken

flap /flæp/ *noun* a flat piece attached to something, especially a piece of skin or tissue still attached to the body at one side and used in grafts

flare /fleə/ *noun* red colouring of the skin at an infected spot or in urticaria

flashback /ˈflæʃbæk/ *noun* a repeated and very vivid memory of a traumatic event

flat foot /ˌflæt ˈfʊt/, **flat feet** /ˌflæt ˈfiːt/ *noun* a condition in which the soles of the feet lie flat on the ground instead of being arched as usual. Also called **pes planus**

flatulence /ˈflætjʊləns/ *noun* gas or air which collects in the stomach or intestines causing discomfort

COMMENT: Flatulence is generally caused by indigestion, but can be made worse if the person swallows air (**aerophagy**).

flatulent /ˈflætjʊlənt/ *adjective* having flatulence, or caused by flatulence

flatus /ˈfleɪtəs/ *noun* air and gas which collects in the intestines and is painful

flea /fliː/ *noun* a tiny insect which sucks blood and is a parasite on animals and humans

flecainide /fleˈkeɪnaɪd/ *noun* a drug that helps to correct an irregular heartbeat

flex /fleks/ *verb* to bend something

flexibilitas cerea /fleksɪˌbɪlɪtəs ˈsɪəriə/ *noun* a condition in which, if someone's arms or legs are moved, they remain in that set position for some time

flexion /ˈflekʃən/ *noun* the act of bending a joint

Flexner's bacillus /ˌfleksnəz bəˈsɪləs/ *noun* a bacterium which causes bacillary dysentery

flexor /ˈfleksə/, **flexor muscle** /ˈfleksə ˌmʌs(ə)l/ *noun* a muscle which makes a joint bend. Compare **extensor**

flexure /ˈflekʃə/ *noun* **1.** a bend in an organ **2.** a fold in the skin

floaters /ˈfləʊtəz/ *plural noun* same as **muscae volitantes**

floating kidney /ˌfləʊtɪŋ ˈkɪdni/ *noun* same as **nephroptosis**

floating rib /ˌfləʊtɪŋ ˈrɪb/ *noun* one of the two lowest ribs on each side, which are not attached to the breastbone

flooding /ˈflʌdɪŋ/ *noun* same as **menorrhagia**

floppy baby syndrome /ˌflɒpi ˈbeɪbi ˌsɪndrəʊm/ *noun* same as **amyotonia congenita**

flora /ˈflɔːrə/ *noun* bacteria which exist in a particular part of the body

florid /ˈflɒrɪd/ *adjective* with an unhealthily glowing pink or red complexion

flowmeter /ˈfləʊmiːtə/ *noun* a meter attached to a pipe, e.g. as in anaesthetic equipment, to measure the speed at which a liquid or gas moves in the pipe

flu /fluː/ *noun* **1.** same as **influenza 2.** a very bad cold (*informal*) (NOTE: Sometimes written '**flu** to show it is a short form of **influenza**.)

flucloxacillin /fluːˈklɒksəsɪlɪn/ *noun* a drug related to penicillin and effective against streptococcal infections and pneumonia

fluconazole /fluːˈkɒnəzəʊl/ *noun* a drug used to treat fungal infections such as candidiasis

fluctuation /ˌflʌktʃuˈeɪʃ(ə)n/ *noun* the feeling of movement of liquid inside part of the body or inside a cyst when pressed by the fingers

fluid /ˈfluːɪd/ *noun* 1. a liquid 2. any gas, liquid or powder which flows

fluid balance /ˈfluːɪd ˌbæləns/ *noun* the maintenance of the balance of fluids in the body during dialysis or other treatment

fluke /fluːk/ *noun* a parasitic flatworm which settles inside the liver, in the bloodstream and in other parts of the body

flunitrazepam /ˌfluːnaɪˈtræzɪpæm/ *noun* a tranquilliser that, because of its association with 'date rape' cases, is a controlled drug in the UK

fluorescence /fluəˈres(ə)ns/ *noun* the sending out of light from a substance which is receiving radiation

fluorescent /fluəˈres(ə)nt/ *adjective* referring to a substance which sends out light

fluoride /ˈfluəraɪd/ *noun* a chemical compound of fluorine and sodium, potassium or tin ○ *fluoride toothpaste*

fluorine /ˈfluəriːn/ *noun* a chemical element found in bones and teeth (NOTE: The chemical symbol is **F**.)

fluoroscope /ˈfluərəskəʊp/ *noun* an apparatus which projects an X-ray image of a part of the body onto a screen, so that the part of the body can be examined as it moves

fluoroscopy /fluəˈrɒskəpi/ *noun* an examination of the body using X-rays projected onto a screen

fluoxetine /fluːˈɒksətiːn/ *noun* a drug that increases serotonin in the brain and is used to treat anxiety and depression

flush /flʌʃ/ *noun* a red colour in the skin ■ *verb* 1. to wash a wound with liquid 2. (*of person*) to turn red

flutter /ˈflʌtə/, **fluttering** /ˈflʌtərɪŋ/ *noun* a rapid movement, especially of the atria of the heart, which is not controlled by impulses from the sinoatrial node

flux /flʌks/ *noun* an excessive production of liquid from the body

focal /ˈfəʊk(ə)l/ *adjective* referring to a focus

focal distance /ˌfəʊk(ə)l ˈdɪstəns/, **focal length** /ˈfəʊk(ə)l leŋθ/ *noun* the distance between the lens of the eye and the point behind the lens where light is focused

focal epilepsy /ˌfəʊk(ə)l ˈepɪlepsi/ *noun* epilepsy arising from a localised area of the brain

focus /ˈfəʊkəs/ *noun* 1. the point where light rays converge through a lens 2. the centre of an infection (NOTE: The plural is **foci**.) ■ *verb* 1. to adjust a lens until an image is clear and sharp 2. to see clearly ○ *He has difficulty in focusing on the object.*

focus group /ˈfəʊkəs gruːp/ *noun* a discussion group of lay people brought together under professional guidance to discuss issues such as care

foetal /ˈfiːt(ə)l/ *adjective* another spelling of **fetal** (NOTE: The spelling **foetal** is common in general use in British English, but the spelling **fetal** is the accepted international spelling for technical use.)

foetoscope /ˈfiːtəskəʊp/ *noun* another spelling of **fetoscope**

foetoscopy /fɪˈtɒskəpi/ *noun* another spelling of **fetoscopy**

foetus /ˈfiːtəs/ *noun* another spelling of **fetus** (NOTE: The spelling **foetus** is common in general use in British English, but the spelling **fetus** is the accepted international spelling for technical use.)

folacin /ˈfəʊləsɪn/ *noun* same as **folic acid**

folic acid /ˌfəʊlɪk ˈæsɪd/ *noun* a vitamin in the Vitamin B complex found in milk, liver, yeast and green vegetables such as spinach, which is essential for creating new blood cells

follicle /ˈfɒlɪk(ə)l/ *noun* a tiny hole or sac in the body

follicle-stimulating hormone /ˌfɒlɪk(ə)l ˌstɪmjʊleɪtɪŋ ˈhɔːməʊn/ *noun* a hormone produced by the pituitary gland which stimulates ova in the ovaries and sperm in the testes. Abbreviation FSH

follicular /fəˈlɪkjʊlə/, **folliculate** /fəˈlɪkjʊlət/ *adjective* referring to follicles

folliculitis /fəˌlɪkjʊˈlaɪtɪs/ *noun* inflammation of the hair follicles, especially where hair has been shaved

fomentation /ˌfəʊmenˈteɪʃ(ə)n/ *noun* same as **poultice**

fomites /ˈfəʊmɪtiːz/ *plural noun* objects touched by someone with a communicable disease which can then be the means of passing on the disease to others

fontanelle /ˌfɒntəˈnel/ *noun* the soft cartilage between the bony sections of a baby's skull

food allergen /ˈfuːd ˌælədʒen/ *noun* a substance in food which produces an allergy

food allergy /ˈfuːd ˌælədʒi/ *noun* an allergy to a specific food such as nuts, which causes a severe reaction that may lead to life-threatening anaphylactic shock

food canal /ˈfuːd kəˌnæl/ *noun* the passage from the mouth to the rectum through which food passes and is digested

food intolerance /ˈfuːd ɪnˌtɒlərəns/ *noun* an adverse reaction to some foods such as oranges, eggs, tomatoes and strawberries

food poisoning /ˈfuːd ˌpɔɪz(ə)nɪŋ/ *noun* an illness caused by eating food which is contaminated with bacteria

foot /fʊt/ *noun* the end part of the leg on which a person stands

foramen /fəˈreɪmən/ *noun* a natural opening inside the body, e.g. the opening in a bone through which veins or nerves pass (NOTE: The plural is **foramina**.)

foramen magnum /fəˌreɪmən ˈmæɡnəm/ *noun* the hole at the bottom of the skull where the brain is joined to the spinal cord

foramen ovale /fəˌreɪmən əʊˈvɑːleɪ/ *noun* an opening between the two parts of the heart in a fetus

COMMENT: The foramen ovale usually closes at birth, but if it stays open the blood from the veins can mix with the blood going to the arteries, causing cyanosis.

forced expiratory volume /ˌfɔːst ek ˈspɪrət(ə)ri ˌvɒljuːm/ *noun* the maximum amount of air that can be expelled in a given time. Abbreviation **FEV**

forceps /ˈfɔːseps/ *noun* a surgical instrument with handles like a pair of scissors, made in different sizes and with differently shaped ends, used for holding and pulling

forceps delivery /ˈfɔːseps dɪˌlɪv(ə)ri/ *noun* childbirth where the doctor uses forceps to help the baby out of the mother's uterus

fore- /fɔː/ *prefix* in front

forearm /ˈfɔːrɑːm/ *noun* the lower part of the arm from the elbow to the wrist

forebrain /ˈfɔːbreɪn/ *noun* the front part of the brain in an embryo

forefinger /ˈfɔːfɪŋɡə/ *noun* the first finger on the hand, next to the thumb

foregut /ˈfɔːɡʌt/ *noun* the front part of the gut in an embryo

foreign /ˈfɒrɪn/ *adjective* **1.** not belonging to your own country ○ *foreign visitors* ○ *a foreign language* **2.** referring to something that is found where it does not naturally belong, especially something found in the human body that comes from a source outside the body ○ *a foreign object* ○ *foreign matter*

foreign body /ˌfɒrɪn ˈbɒdi/ *noun* a piece of material which is not part of the surrounding tissue and should not be there, e.g. sand in a cut, dust in the eye or a pin which has been swallowed ○ *The X-ray showed the presence of a foreign body.*

forensic /fəˈrensɪk/ *adjective* relating to the use of science in solving criminal investigations or settling legal cases

forensic medicine /fəˌrensɪk ˈmed(ə)s(ə)n/ *noun* the branch of medical science concerned with finding solutions to crimes against people and which involves procedures such as conduct-

ing autopsies on murdered people or taking blood samples from clothes

foreskin /ˈfɔːskɪn/ *noun* the skin covering the top of the penis, which can be removed by circumcision. Also called **prepuce**

forewaters /ˈfɔːwɔːtəz/ *plural noun* fluid which comes out of the vagina at the beginning of childbirth when the amnion bursts

formaldehyde /fɔːˈmældɪhaɪd/ *noun* a gas with an unpleasant smell that is a strong disinfectant. When dissolved in water to make **formalin**, it is also used to preserve medical specimens.

formalin /ˈfɔːməlɪn/ *noun* a solution of formaldehyde in water, used to preserve medical specimens

formication /ˌfɔːmɪˈkeɪʃ(ə)n/ *noun* an itching feeling where the skin feels as if it were covered with insects

formula /ˈfɔːmjʊlə/ *noun* **1.** a way of indicating a chemical compound using letters and numbers, e.g. H_2SO_4 **2.** instructions on how to prepare a drug

formulary /ˈfɔːmjʊləri/ *noun* a book that lists medicines together with their formulae

fornix /ˈfɔːnɪks/ *noun* an arch (NOTE: The plural is **fornices**.)

fornix cerebri /ˌfɔːnɪks ˈserɪbraɪ/ *noun* a section of white matter in the brain between the hippocampus and the hypothalamus. See illustration at **BRAIN** in Supplement

foscarnet /fɒsˈkɑːnət/ *noun* an antiviral drug administered by intravenous injection that is effective against herpesviruses that are resistant to acyclovir. It is especially used for people with AIDS.

fossa /ˈfɒsə/ *noun* a shallow hollow in a bone or the skin

foster children /ˈfɒstə ˌtʃɪldrən/ *plural noun* children brought up by people who are not their own parents

foster parent /ˈfɒstə ˌpeərənt/ *noun* a woman or man who brings up a child born to other parents

Fothergill's operation /ˈfɒðəɡɪlz ɒpəˌreɪʃ(ə)n/ *noun* a surgical operation to correct prolapse of the uterus [After W. E. Fothergill (1865–1926), British gynaecologist.]

foundation hospital /faʊnˈdeɪʃ(ə)n ˌhɒspɪt(ə)l/ *noun* in the UK, a type of hospital that is independent of its Local Health Authority in financial matters

fourchette /fʊəˈʃet/ *noun* a fold of skin at the back of the vulva

fovea /ˈfəʊviə/, **fovea centralis** /ˌfəʊviə sen ˈtrɑːlɪs/ *noun* a depression in the retina which is the point where the eye sees most clearly. See illustration at **EYE** in Supplement

FP10 /ˌef piː ˈten/ *noun* in the UK, an NHS prescription from a GP

fracture /'fræktʃə/ *verb* **1.** (*of bone*) to break ○ *The tibia fractured in two places.* **2.** to break a bone ○ *He fractured his wrist.* ■ *noun* a break in a bone ○ *rib fracture* or *fracture of a rib*

fragile-X syndrome /ˌfrædʒaɪl 'eks ˌsɪndrəʊm/ *noun* a hereditary condition in which part of an X chromosome is constricted, causing mental impairment

fragilitas ossium /frəˌdʒɪlɪtəs 'ɒsiəm/ *noun* a hereditary condition where the bones are brittle and break easily, similar to osteogenesis imperfecta

frame /freɪm/ *noun* **1.** the particular size and shape of someone's body **2.** the main part of a building, ship or bicycle, etc., which holds it together ○ *the bicycle has a very light frame* ○ *I've broken the frame of my glasses* **3.** a solid support for something. ♢ **walking frame, Zimmer frame**

framycetin /fræ'maɪsətɪn/ *noun* an antibiotic

fraternal twins /frəˌtɜːn(ə)l 'twɪnz/ *plural noun* same as **dizygotic twins**

freckle /'frek(ə)l/ *noun* a harmless small brownish patch on the skin that becomes more noticeable after exposure to the sun. Freckles are often found in people with fair hair. Also called **lentigo** ■ *verb* to mark something, or become marked with freckles

freeze /friːz/ *verb* to anaesthetise part of the body (*informal*) ○ *They froze my big toe to remove the nail.*

Freiberg's disease /'fraɪbɜːgz dɪˌziːz/ *noun* osteochondritis of the head of the second metatarsus [Described 1914. After Albert Henry Freiberg (1869–1940), US surgeon.]

fremitus /'fremɪtəs/ *noun* vibrations or trembling in part of someone's body, felt by the doctor's hand or heard through a stethoscope

frenectomy /frə'nektəmi/ *noun* an operation to remove a frenum

frenotomy /frə'nɒtəmi/ *noun* an operation to split a frenum

frenum /'friːnəm/**, frenulum** /'frenjʊləm/ *noun* a fold of mucous membrane under the tongue or by the clitoris

frequency /'friːkwənsi/ *noun* **1.** the number of times something takes place in a given time ○ *the frequency of micturition* **2.** the rate of vibration in oscillations

Freudian /'frɔɪdiən/ *adjective* understandable in terms of Freud's theories, especially with regard to human sexuality ■ *noun* someone who is influenced by or follows Freud's theories or methods of psychoanalysis

friable /'fraɪəb(ə)l/ *adjective* easily broken up into small pieces

friar's balsam /ˌfraɪəz 'bɔːlsəm/ *noun* a mixture of various plant oils, including benzoin and balsam, which can be inhaled as a vapour to relieve bronchitis or congestion

friction /'frɪkʃ(ə)n/ *noun* the rubbing together of two surfaces

friction fremitus /ˌfrɪkʃən 'fremɪtəs/ *noun* a scratching sensation felt when the hand is placed on the chest of someone who has pericarditis

friction murmur /ˌfrɪkʃən 'mɜːmə/ *noun* the sound of two serous membranes rubbing together, heard with a stethoscope in someone who has pericarditis or pleurisy

Friedländer's bacillus /'friːdlendəz bə ˌsɪləs/ *noun* the bacterium *Klebsiella pneumoniae* which can cause pneumonia [Described 1882. After Carl Friedländer (1847–87), pathologist at the Friedrichshain Hospital, Berlin, Germany.]

Friedman's test /'friːdmənz test/ *noun* a test for pregnancy [After Maurice H. Friedman (1903–91), US physician.]

Friedreich's ataxia /ˌfriːdraɪks ə'tæksiə/ *noun* an inherited nervous disease which affects the spinal cord and is associated with club foot, an unsteady walk and speech difficulties. Also called **dystrophia adiposogenitalis** [Described 1863. After Nicholaus Friedreich (1825–82), Professor of Pathological Anatomy at Würzburg, later Professor of Pathology and Therapy at Heidelberg, Germany.]

frigidity /frɪ'dʒɪdɪti/ *noun* the fact of being unable to experience orgasm, sexual pleasure or sexual desire

fringe medicine /'frɪndʒ ˌmed(ə)sɪn/ *noun* types of medical practice which are not usually taught in medical schools, e.g. homeopathy or acupuncture (*informal*)

frog plaster /'frɒg ˌplɑːstə/ *noun* a plaster cast made to keep the legs in an open position after an operation to correct a dislocated hip

Fröhlich's syndrome /'frɜːlɪks ˌsɪndrəʊm/ *noun* a condition in which someone becomes obese and the genital system does not develop, caused by an adenoma of the pituitary gland [Described 1901. After Alfred Fröhlich (1871–1953), Professor of Pharmacology at the University of Vienna, Austria.]

frontal /'frʌnt(ə)l/ *adjective* referring to the forehead or to the front of the head. Opposite **occipital**

frontal bone /'frʌnt(ə)l bəʊn/ *noun* a bone forming the front of the upper part of the skull behind the forehead

frontal lobe /'frʌnt(ə)l ləʊb/ *noun* the front lobe of each cerebral hemisphere

frontal lobotomy /ˌfrʌnt(ə)l ləʊ'bɒtəmi/ *noun* formerly, a surgical operation on the brain to treat mental illness by removing part of the frontal lobe

frontal sinus /ˌfrʌnt(ə)l ˈsaɪnəs/ *noun* one of two sinuses in the front of the face above the eyes and near the nose

front passage /ˌfrʌnt ˈpæsɪdʒ/ (*informal*) **1.** same as **urethra 2.** same as **vagina**

frostbite /ˈfrɒstbaɪt/ *noun* an injury caused by very severe cold which freezes tissue

frozen shoulder /ˌfrəʊz(ə)n ˈʃəʊldə/ *noun* stiffness and pain in the shoulder, caused by inflammation of the membranes of the shoulder joint after injury or a period of immobility, when deposits may form in the tendons

frozen watchfulness /ˌfrəʊz(ə)n ˈwɒtʃfəlnəs/ *noun* an expression of petrified fear on a child's face, especially in children who have been abused

fructose /ˈfrʌktəʊs/ *noun* fruit sugar found in honey and some fruit, which together with glucose forms sucrose

frusemide /ˈfruːsəmaɪd/ *noun* same as **furosemide**

FSH *abbreviation* follicle-stimulating hormone

-fuge /fjuːdʒ/ *suffix* driving away

fulguration /ˌfʌlɡəˈreɪʃ(ə)n/ *noun* the removal of a growth such as a wart by burning with an electric needle. Also called **electrodesiccation**

full thickness burn /ˌfʊl ˌθɪknəs ˈbɜːn/ *noun* same as **deep dermal burn**

fulminant /ˈfʊlmɪnənt/, **fulminating** /ˈfʊlmɪneɪtɪŋ/ *adjective* referring to a dangerous disease which develops very rapidly

fumigation /ˌfjuːmɪˈɡeɪʃ(ə)n/ *noun* the process of killing insects in an area with gas or smoke

function /ˈfʌŋkʃən/ *noun* the particular work done by an organ ○ *What is the function of the pancreas?* ○ *The function of an ovary is to form ova.* ■ *verb* to work in a particular way ○ *The heart and lungs were functioning normally.* ○ *His kidneys suddenly stopped functioning.*

functional /ˈfʌŋkʃən(ə)l/ *adjective* referring to a disorder or illness which does not have a physical cause and may have a psychological cause, as opposed to an organic disorder

functional endoscopic sinus surgery /ˌfʌŋkʃən(ə)l ˌendəskɒpɪk ˈsaɪnəs ˌsɜːdʒəri/ *noun* the removal of soft tissue in the sinuses using an endoscope. Abbreviation **FESS**

functional enuresis /ˌfʌŋkʃən(ə)l ˌenjʊˈriːsɪs/ *noun* bedwetting which has a psychological cause

functional independence measure /ˌfʌŋkʃən(ə)l ˌɪndɪˈpendəns ˌmeʒə/ *noun* a measure of disability. Abbreviation **FIM**

fundoplication /ˌfʌndəʊplɪˈkeɪʃ(ə)n/ *noun* the process of wrapping the fundus of the stomach round the lower end of the oesophagus

fundus /ˈfʌndəs/ *noun* the bottom of a hollow organ such as the uterus

fungal /ˈfʌŋɡəl/ *adjective* relating to, or caused by, fungi ○ *a fungal skin infection*

fungate /ˈfʌŋɡeɪt/ *verb* (*of some skin cancers*) to increase rapidly at a late stage of tumour formation

fungicide /ˈfʌŋɡɪsaɪd/ *noun* a substance used to kill fungi

fungiform papillae /ˌfʌŋɡɪfɔːm pəˈpɪliː/ *noun* rounded papillae on the tip and sides of the tongue, which have taste buds

fungoid /ˈfʌŋɡɔɪd/ *adjective* like a fungus

fungus /ˈfʌŋɡəs/ *noun* an organism such as yeast or mould, some of which cause disease (NOTE: The plural is **fungi**. For other terms referring to fungi, see words beginning with **myc-, myco-**.)

funiculitis /fjuːˌnɪkjʊˈlaɪtɪs/ *noun* inflammation of the spermatic cord

funiculus /fjuːˈnɪkjʊləs/ *noun* one of the three parts of the white matter in the spinal cord ○ *The three parts are called the lateral, anterior and posterior funiculus.*

funis /ˈfjuːnɪs/ *noun* an umbilical cord

funnel chest /ˌfʌn(ə)l ˈtʃest/ *noun* same as **pectus excavatum**

funny bone /ˈfʌni bəʊn/ *noun* same as **olecranon** (*informal*)

furfuraceous /ˌfɜːfjəˈreɪʃəs/ *adjective* referring to skin which is scaly

furor /ˈfjʊərɔː/ *noun* an attack of wild violence, especially in someone who is mentally unwell

furosemide /fjʊˈrɒsəmaɪd/ *noun* a drug which causes an increase in urine production, used to relieve water retention in the body. Also called **frusemide**

furred tongue /ˌfɜːd ˈtʌŋ/ *noun* a condition when the papillae of the tongue are covered with a whitish coating. Also called **coated tongue**

furuncle /ˈfjʊərʌŋkəl/ *noun* same as **boil**

furunculosis /fjʊəˌrʌŋkjʊˈləʊsɪs/ *noun* a condition in which several boils appear at the same time

fusidic acid /fjuːˌsɪdɪk ˈæsɪd/ *noun* an antibiotic used to prevent protein synthesis

fusiform /ˈfjuːzɪfɔːm/ *adjective* referring to muscles which are shaped like a spindle, with a wider middle section which becomes narrower at each end

fusion /ˈfjuːʒ(ə)n/ *noun* the act of joining, especially a surgical operation to relieve pain in the joint by joining the bones at the joint permanently so that they cannot move

Fybogel /ˈfaɪbəʊdʒel/ a trade name for ispaghula

G

g *abbreviation* gram

GABA /'gæbə/ *abbreviation* gamma aminobutyric acid

gag /gæg/ *noun* an instrument placed between the teeth to stop the mouth from closing ■ *verb* to experience a reaction similar to that of vomiting ○ *Every time the doctor tries to examine her throat, she gags.* ○ *He started gagging on the endotracheal tube.*

gait /geɪt/ *noun* a way of walking

galacto- /gəlæktəʊ/ *prefix* referring to milk

galactocele /gə'læktəsiːl/ *noun* a breast tumour which contains milk

galactorrhoea /gə,læktə'rɪə/ *noun* the excessive production of milk

galactosaemia /gə,læktə'siːmiə/ *noun* a congenital condition where the liver is incapable of converting galactose into glucose, with the result that a baby's development may be affected (NOTE: The treatment is to remove galactose from the diet.)

galactose /gə'læktəʊs/ *noun* a sugar which forms part of milk, and is converted into glucose by the liver

galea /'geɪliə/ *noun* any part of the body shaped like a helmet, especially the loose band of tissue in the scalp (NOTE: The plural is **galeae**.)

gall /gɔːl/ *noun* same as **bile**

gall bladder /'gɔːl ˌblædə/ *noun* a sac situated underneath the liver, in which bile produced by the liver is stored. See illustration at DIGESTIVE SYSTEM in Supplement

Gallie's operation /'gæliz ɒpə,reɪʃ(ə)n/ *noun* a surgical operation where tissues from the thigh are used to hold a hernia in place [Described 1921. After William Edward Gallie (1882–1959), Professor of Surgery at the University of Toronto, Canada.]

gallipot /'gælipɒt/ *noun* a little container for ointment

gallium /'gæliəm/ *noun* a metallic element a radioisotope of which is used to detect tumours or other tissue disorders (NOTE: The chemical symbol is **Ga**.)

gallop rhythm /'gæləp ˌrɪð(ə)m/ *noun* the rhythm of heart sounds, three to each cycle, when someone is experiencing tachycardia

gallstone /'gɔːlstəʊn/ *noun* a small stone formed from insoluble deposits from bile in the gall bladder. ◊ **calculus**

galvanism /'gælvənɪz(ə)m/ *noun* a treatment using low voltage electricity

galvanocautery /,gælvənəʊ'kɔːtəri/ *noun* the removal of diseased tissue using an electrically heated needle or loop of wire. Also called **electrocautery**

gamete /'gæmiːt/ *noun* a sex cell, either a spermatozoon or an ovum

gamete intrafallopian transfer /,gæmiːt ɪntrəfə,ləʊpiən 'trænsfɜː/ *noun* a technique to combine eggs and sperm outside the body and then insert them into the Fallopian tubes. Abbreviation GIFT

gametocyte /gə'miːtəʊsaɪt/ *noun* a cell which is developing into a gamete

gametogenesis /gə,miːtəʊ'dʒenəsɪs/ *noun* the process by which a gamete is formed

gamgee tissue /'gæmdʒiː ˌtɪʃuː/ *noun* a surgical dressing, formed of a layer of cotton wool between two pieces of gauze

gamma aminobutyric acid /,gæmə ə ,miːnəʊbjuː,tɪrɪk 'æsɪd/ *noun* an amino acid neurotransmitter. Abbreviation GABA

gamma camera /'gæmə ˌkæm(ə)rə/ *noun* a camera for taking photographs of parts of the body into which radioactive isotopes have been introduced

gamma globulin /,gæmə 'glɒbjʊlɪn/ *noun* a protein found in plasma, forming antibodies as protection against infection

gamma ray /'gæmə reɪ/ *noun* a ray which is shorter than an X-ray and is given off by radioactive substances

gangli- /gæŋgli/ *prefix* referring to ganglia

ganglion /'gæŋgliən/ *noun* **1.** a mass of nerve cell bodies and synapses usually covered in connective tissue, found along the peripheral nerves with the exception of the basal ganglia **2.** a cyst of a tendon sheath or joint capsule, usually at the wrist, which results in a painless swelling containing fluid (NOTE: [all senses] The plural is **ganglia**.)

ganglionectomy /ˌgæŋgliəˈnektəmi/ *noun* the surgical removal of a ganglion

gangrene /ˈgæŋgriːn/ *noun* a condition in which tissues die and decay, as a result of bacterial action, because the blood supply has been lost through injury or disease of the artery ○ *After she had frostbite, gangrene set in and her toes had to be amputated.*

gangrenous /ˈgæŋgrɪnəs/ *adjective* referring to, or affected by, gangrene

gargle /ˈgɑːg(ə)l/ *noun* a mildly antiseptic solution used to clean the mouth ■ *verb* to put some antiseptic liquid solution into the back of the mouth and then breathe out air through it

gargoylism /ˈgɑːgɔɪlɪz(ə)m/ *noun* a congenital condition of the metabolism which causes polysaccharides and fat cells to accumulate in the body, resulting in mental impairment, swollen liver and coarse features. Also called **Hurler's syndrome**

gas /gæs/ *noun* **1.** a substance such as nitrogen, carbon dioxide or air, which is neither solid nor fluid at ordinary temperatures and can expand infinitely (NOTE: The plural **gases** is used only when referring to different types of gas.) **2.** gas which accumulates in the stomach or alimentary canal and causes pain

gas and air analgesia /ˌgæs ənd ˈeər æn(ə)lˌdʒiːziə/ *noun* a form of analgesia used when giving birth, in which a mixture of air and gas is given

gas exchange /ˈgæs ɪksˌtʃeɪndʒ/ *noun* the process by which oxygen in the air is exchanged in the lungs for waste carbon dioxide carried by the blood

gas gangrene /ˌgæs ˈgæŋgriːn/ *noun* a complication of severe wounds in which the bacterium *Clostridium welchii* breeds in the wound and then spreads to healthy tissue which is rapidly decomposed with the formation of gas

gash /gæʃ/ *noun* a long deep cut made accidentally by something sharp ○ *She had to have three stitches in the gash in her thigh.* ■ *verb* to make a long deep cut in something accidentally ○ *She gashed her hand on the broken glass.*

gasp /gɑːsp/ *noun* a short breath taken with difficulty ○ *His breath came in short gasps.* ■ *verb* to breathe with difficulty taking quick breaths ○ *She was gasping for breath.*

gas pain /ˈgæs peɪn/ *noun* a pain caused by excessive formation of gas in the stomach or intestine. ◊ **flatus**

gastr- /gæstr/ *prefix* same as **gastro-** (*used before vowels*)

gastrectomy /gæˈstrektəmi/ *noun* the surgical removal of the stomach

gastric /ˈgæstrɪk/ *adjective* referring to the stomach

gastric acid /ˌgæstrɪk ˈæsɪd/ *noun* hydrochloric acid secreted into the stomach by acid-forming cells

gastric flu /ˌgæstrɪk ˈfluː/ *noun* any mild stomach disorder (*informal*)

gastric juice /ˌgæstrɪk dʒuːs/ *noun* the mixture of hydrochloric acid, pepsin, intrinsic factor and mucus secreted by the cells of the lining membrane of the stomach to help the digestion of food (NOTE: Often used in the plural.)

gastric lavage /ˌgæstrɪk ˈlævɪdʒ/ *noun* a lavage of the stomach, usually to remove a poisonous substance which has been absorbed. Also called **stomach washout**

gastric pit /ˌgæstrɪk ˈpɪt/ *noun* a deep hollow in the mucous membrane forming the walls of the stomach

gastric ulcer /ˌgæstrɪk ˈʌlsə/ *noun* an ulcer in the stomach. Abbreviation **GU**

gastrin /ˈgæstrɪn/ *noun* a hormone which is released into the bloodstream from cells in the lower end of the stomach, stimulated by the presence of protein, and which in turn stimulates the flow of acid from the upper part of the stomach

gastrinoma /ˌgæstrɪˈnəʊmə/ *noun* a tumour of the islet cells, leading to excessive gastric acid

gastritis /gæˈstraɪtɪs/ *noun* inflammation of the stomach

gastro- /gæstrəʊ/ *prefix* referring to the stomach

gastrocele /ˈgæstrəʊsiːl/ *noun* a condition in which part of the stomach wall becomes weak and bulges out. Also called **stomach hernia**

gastrocnemius /ˌgæstrɒkˈniːmiəs/ *noun* a large calf muscle

gastrocolic /ˌgæstrəʊˈkɒlɪk/ *adjective* referring to the stomach and colon

gastrocolic reflex /ˌgæstrəʊkɒlɪk ˈriːfleks/ *noun* a sudden peristalsis of the colon produced when food is taken into an empty stomach

gastroduodenal /ˌgæstrəʊˌdjuːəʊˈdiːn(ə)l/ *adjective* referring to the stomach and duodenum

gastroduodenoscopy /ˌgæstrəʊˌdjuːəʊdɪˈnɒskəpi/ *noun* an examination of the stomach and duodenum

gastroduodenostomy /ˌgæstrəʊˌdjuːəʊdɪˈnɒstəmi/ *noun* a surgical operation to join the duodenum to the stomach so as to bypass a blockage in the pylorus

gastroenteritis /ˌgæstrəʊentəˈraɪtɪs/ *noun* inflammation of the membrane lining the intestines and the stomach, caused by a viral infection and resulting in diarrhoea and vomiting

gastroenterology /ˌgæstrəʊentəˈrɒlədʒi/ *noun* the study of the digestive system and its disorders

gastroenterostomy /ˌgæstrəʊentəˈrɒstəmi/ *noun* a surgical operation to join the small intestine directly to the stomach so as to bypass a peptic ulcer

gastroepiploic /ˌgæstrəʊepɪˈplɔɪk/ *adjective* referring to the stomach and greater omentum

gastroepiploic artery /ˌgæstrəʊepɪˌplɔɪk ˈɑːtəri/ *noun* an artery linking the gastroduodenal artery to the splenic artery

Gastrografin /ˌgæstrəʊˈgræfɪn/ a trade name for an enema used in bowel X-rays

gastroileac reflex /ˌgæstrəʊˌɪliæk ˈriːfleks/ *noun* automatic relaxation of the ileocaecal valve when food is present in the stomach

gastrointestinal /ˌgæstrəʊɪnˈtestɪn(ə)l/ *adjective* referring to the stomach and intestine ○ *gastrointestinal bleeding.* Abbreviation **GI**

gastrojejunostomy /ˌgæstrəʊdʒɪdʒuːˈnɒstəmi/ *noun* a surgical operation to join the jejunum to the stomach

gastrolith /ˈgæstrəʊlɪθ/ *noun* a calculus in the stomach

gastro-oesophageal reflux /ˌgæstrəʊ ɪˌsɒfədʒiəl ˈriːflʌks/, **gastro-oesophageal reflux disease** /ˌgæstrəʊ ɪˌsɒfədʒiəl ˈriːflʌks dɪˌziːz/ *noun* the return of bitter-tasting, partly digested food from the stomach to the oesophagus

gastropexy /ˈgæstrəʊpeksi/ *noun* a surgical operation to attach the stomach to the wall of the abdomen

gastroplasty /ˈgæstrəʊplæsti/ *noun* surgery to correct a deformed stomach

gastrorrhoea /ˌgæstrəˈrɪə/ *noun* an excessive flow of gastric juices

gastroschisis /ˌgæstrəʊˈsaɪsɪs/ *noun* a split in the wall of the abdomen, with viscera passing through it

gastroscope /ˈgæstrəskəʊp/ *noun* an instrument formed of a tube or bundle of glass fibres with a lens attached, which a doctor can pass down into the stomach through the mouth to examine the inside of the stomach

gastroscopy /gæˈstrɒskəpi/ *noun* an examination of the stomach using a gastroscope

gastrostomy /gæˈstrɒstəmi/ *noun* a surgical operation to create an opening into the stomach from the wall of the abdomen, so that food can be introduced without passing through the mouth and throat

gastrotomy /gæˈstrɒtəmi/ *noun* a surgical operation to open up the stomach

Gaucher's disease /ˈgəʊʃeɪz dɪˌziːz/ *noun* an enzyme disease where fatty substances accumulate in the lymph glands, spleen and liver, causing anaemia, a swollen spleen and darkening of the skin. The disease can be fatal in children. [Described 1882. After Philippe Charles Ernest Gaucher (1854–1918), French physician and dermatologist.]

gauze /gɔːz/ *noun* a thin light material used to make dressings

gauze dressing /ˈgɔːz ˌdresɪŋ/ *noun* a dressing of thin light material

gavage /gæˈvɑːʒ/ *noun* the forced feeding of someone who cannot eat or who refuses to eat

gay /geɪ/ *adjective* relating to sexual activity among people of the same sex

GDC *abbreviation* General Dental Council

Gehrig's disease /ˈgeɪrɪgz dɪˌziːz/ *noun* same as **amyotrophic lateral sclerosis**

Geiger counter /ˈgaɪgə ˌkaʊntə/ *noun* an instrument for the detection and measurement of radiation [Described 1908. After Hans Geiger (1882–1945), German physicist who worked with Rutherford at Manchester University, UK]

gel /dʒel/ *noun* a suspension that sets into a jelly-like solid

gelatin /ˈdʒelətɪn/ *noun* a protein found in collagen which is soluble in water, used to make capsules for medicines

gelatinous /dʒəˈlætɪnəs/ *adjective* referring to gelatin or something with a texture like jelly

gemellus /dʒɪˈmeləs/ *noun* either of the two muscles arising from the ischium. Also called **gemellus superior muscle, gemellus inferior muscle**

gender /ˈdʒendə/ *noun* the fact of being of the male or female sex

gender reassignment surgery /ˌdʒendə riːəˈsaɪnmənt ˌsɜːdʒəri/ *noun* surgery to change someone's sex

gender reorientation /ˌdʒendə riːˌɔːriənˈteɪʃ(ə)n/ *noun* the alteration of a person's sex through surgical and drug treatment

gene /dʒiːn/ *noun* a unit of DNA on a chromosome which governs the synthesis of a protein sequence and determines a particular characteristic

general amnesia /ˌdʒen(ə)rəl æmˈniːziə/ *noun* a sudden and complete loss of memory, to the extent that a person does not even remember who he or she is

general anaesthesia /ˌdʒen(ə)rəl ˌænəsˈθiːziə/ *noun* loss of feeling and loss of sensation throughout the body, after being given an anaesthetic

general anaesthetic /ˌdʒen(ə)rəl ænəsˈθetɪk/ *noun* a substance given to make someone lose consciousness so that a major surgical operation can be carried out

General Dental Council /ˌdʒen(ə)rəl ˈdent(ə)l ˌkaʊnsəl/ *noun* in the UK, the official body that registers and supervises dentists. Abbreviation **GDC**

general hospital /ˌdʒen(ə)rəl ˈhɒspɪt(ə)l/ *noun* a hospital which does not specialise in particular types of illness or particular age groups

General Household Survey /ˌdʒen(ə)rəl ˌhaʊshəʊld ˈsɜːveɪ/ *noun* a survey of households carried out continuously by the Office for National Statistics

generalised /ˈdʒen(ə)rəlaɪzd/, **generalized** *adjective* **1.** spreading throughout the body. Opposite **localised 2.** not having a specific cause

generalised anxiety disorder /ˌdʒen(ə)rəlaɪzd æŋˈzaɪəti dɪsˌɔːdə/ *noun* a state of continual anxiety for which there is no specific cause

General Medical Council /ˌdʒen(ə)rəl ˈmedɪk(ə)l ˌkaʊnsəl/ *noun* in the UK, the official body that licenses qualified doctors to practise medicine. Abbreviation **GMC**

General Optical Council /ˌdʒen(ə)rəl ˈɒptɪk(ə)l ˌkaʊnsəl/ *noun* in the UK, the official body that registers and supervises opticians

general practice /ˌdʒen(ə)rəl ˈpræktɪs/ *noun* a medical practice where doctors offer first-line medical care for all types of illness to people who live locally, refer them to hospital if necessary and encourage health promotion

general practitioner /ˌdʒen(ə)rəl prækˈtɪʃ(ə)nə/ *noun* a doctor who provides first-line medical care for all types of illness to people who live locally, refers them to hospital if necessary and encourages health promotion. Abbreviation **GP**

gene replacement therapy /ˌdʒiːn rɪˈpleɪsmənt ˌθerəpi/ *noun* the replacement of missing genes or damaging gene variations in cells by the insertion of appropriate genes to treat a genetic disorder. Also called **gene therapy**

COMMENT: Gene replacement therapy has been used successfully in animals, and is in the early stages of research in humans, but may be useful in the future treatment of cystic fibrosis, thalassaemia and other genetic disorders.

generic /dʒəˈnerɪk/ *adjective* **1.** referring to medicine which does not have a special trademark or brand name given to it by its manufacturer **2.** referring to a genus ○ *The generic name of this type of bacterium is Staphylococcus.*

-genesis /dʒenəsɪs/ *suffix* production or origin

gene therapy /ˈdʒiːn ˌθerəpi/ *noun* same as **gene replacement therapy**

genetic /dʒəˈnetɪk/ *adjective* referring to genes

genetic code /dʒəˌnetɪk ˈkəʊd/ *noun* the characteristics of the DNA of a cell which are passed on when the cell divides and so are inherited by a child from its parents

genetic counselling /dʒəˌnetɪk ˈkaʊnsəlɪŋ/ *noun* advice and support given to people if they or their children might be affected by inherited genetic disorders

genetic disorder /dʒəˌnetɪk dɪsˈɔːdə/ *noun* a disorder or disease caused by a damaging gene variation that may be inherited

genetic engineering /dʒəˌnetɪk endʒɪˈnɪərɪŋ/ *noun* same as **genetic modification** (*informal*)

genetic fingerprint /dʒəˌnetɪk ˈfɪŋgəprɪnt/ *noun* the pattern of sequences of genetic material unique to an individual. Also called **DNA fingerprint**

genetic fingerprinting /dʒəˌnetɪk ˈfɪŋgəˌprɪntɪŋ/ *noun* a method of revealing an individual's genetic profile, used in paternity queries and criminal investigations. Also called **DNA fingerprinting**

geneticist /dʒəˈnetɪsɪst/ *noun* a person who specialises in the study of the way in which characteristics and diseases are inherited through the genes

genetic modification /dʒəˌnetɪk ˌmɒdɪfɪˈkeɪʃ(ə)n/, **genetic manipulation** /dʒəˌnetɪk məˌnɪpjʊˈleɪʃ(ə)n/ *noun* the combination of genetic material from different sources to produce organisms with altered characteristics

genetics /dʒəˈnetɪks/ *noun* the study of genes, and of the way characteristics and diseases are inherited through the genes

genetic screening /dʒəˌnetɪk ˈskriːnɪŋ/ *noun* the process of testing large numbers of people to see if anyone has a particular genetic disorder

gene tracking /ˈdʒiːn ˌtrækɪŋ/ *noun* the method used to trace throughout a family the inheritance of a gene such as those causing cystic fibrosis or Huntington's Chorea, in order to diagnose and predict genetic disorders

-genic /dʒenɪk/ *suffix* referring to a product or something which produces

genicular /dʒeˈnɪkjʊlə/ *adjective* referring to the knee

genital /ˈdʒenɪt(ə)l/ *adjective* referring to the reproductive organs ■ *plural noun* **genitals** same as **genital organs**

genitalia /ˌdʒenɪˈteɪliə/ *noun* the genital organs

genital organs /ˌdʒenɪt(ə)l ˈɔːgənz/ *plural noun* the external organs for reproduction, i.e. the penis and testicles in males and the vulva in females. Also called **genitals, genitalia**

genital wart /ˌdʒenɪt(ə)l ˈwɔːt/ *noun* a wart in the genital or anal area, caused by a sexually transmitted virus

genito- /dʒenɪtəʊ/ *prefix* referring to the reproductive system

genitourinary /ˌdʒenɪtəʊˈjʊərɪnəri/ *adjective* referring to both the reproductive and urinary systems. Abbreviation **GU**

genitourinary system /ˌdʒenɪtəʊˈjʊərɪnəri ˌsɪstəm/ *noun* the organs of reproduction and urination, including the kidneys

genome /'dʒiːnəʊm/ *noun* the set of all the genes of an individual

genotype /'dʒenətaɪp/ *noun* the genetic makeup of an individual. Compare **phenotype**

gentamicin /ˌdʒentə'maɪsɪn/ *noun* an antibiotic that is effective against a variety of different disease-causing organisms. Patients usually receive it by injection and it can cause serious side effects.

gentian violet /ˌdʒenʃən 'vaɪələt/ *noun* an antiseptic blue dye, used to paint on skin infections and also to stain specimens. Also called **crystal violet**

genu /'dʒenjuː/ *noun* the knee

genual /'dʒenjuəl/ *adjective* referring to the knee

genucubital position /ˌdʒenjuː'kjuːbɪt(ə)l pəˌzɪʃ(ə)n/ *noun* the position of someone resting on their knees and elbows

genupectoral position /ˌdʒenjuː'pektər(ə)l pəˌzɪʃ(ə)n/ *noun* the position of someone resting on their knees and upper chest

genus /'dʒiːnəs/ *noun* a category of related living organisms ○ *A genus is divided into different species.* (NOTE: The plural is **genera**.)

genu valgum /ˌdʒenjuː 'vælgəm/ *noun* same as **knock-knee**

genu varum /ˌdʒenjuː 'veərəm/ *noun* same as **bow legs**

geri- /dʒeri/ *prefix* referring to old age

geriatric /ˌdʒeri'ætrɪk/ *adjective* **1.** referring to old people **2.** specialising in the treatment of old people ○ *geriatric unit*

geriatrician /ˌdʒeriə'trɪʃ(ə)n/ *noun* a doctor who specialises in the treatment or study of diseases of old people

geriatrics /ˌdʒeri'ætrɪks/ *noun* the study of the diseases and disorders of old people. Compare **paediatrics**

germ /dʒɜːm/ *noun* **1.** a microorganism which causes a disease, e.g. a virus or bacterium (*informal*) ○ *Germs are not visible to the naked eye.* **2.** a part of an organism capable of developing into a new organism

German measles /ˌdʒɜːmən 'miːz(ə)lz/ *noun* same as **rubella**

germ cell /'dʒɜːm sel/ *noun* a cell which is capable of developing into a spermatozoon or ovum. Also called **gonocyte**

germinal epithelium /ˌdʒɜːmɪn(ə)l ˌepɪ'θiːliəm/ *noun* the outer layer of the ovary

germ layer /'dʒɜːm ˌleɪə/ *noun* one of two or three layers of cells in animal embryos which form the organs of the body

gerontologist /ˌdʒerən'tɒlədʒɪst/ *noun* a specialist in gerontology

gerontology /ˌdʒerən'tɒlədʒi/ *noun* the study of the process of ageing and the diseases of old people

Gesell's developmental chart /gəˌzels dɪ ˌveləp'ment(ə)l tʃɑːt/ *noun* a chart showing the development of motor reactions and growth patterns in children

gestation /dʒe'steɪʃ(ə)n/ *noun* **1.** the process of development of a baby from conception to birth in the mother's womb **2.** same as **gestation period**

gestational age /dʒeˌsteɪʃ(ə)n(ə)l 'eɪdʒ/ *noun* the age of a fetus, calculated from the mother's last period to the date of birth

gestational diabetes /dʒeˌsteɪʃ(ə)n(ə)l ˌdaɪə'biːtiːz/ *noun* a form of diabetes mellitus which develops in a pregnant woman

gestation period /dʒe'steɪʃ(ə)n ˌpɪəriəd/ *noun* the period, usually of 266 days, from conception to birth, during which the baby develops in the mother's womb. Also called **pregnancy**

gestodene /'dʒestədiːn/ *noun* an oral contraceptive

get better /ˌget 'betə/ *verb* **1.** to become healthy again after being ill ○ *He was seriously ill, but seems to be getting better.* **2.** (*of an illness*) to stop or become less severe ○ *Her cold has got better.*

getting on /ˌgetɪŋ 'ɒn/ *adjective* becoming elderly ○ *Her parents are getting on.*

GFR *abbreviation* glomerular filtration rate

GH *abbreviation* growth hormone

Ghon's focus /ˌgɒnz 'fəʊkəs/ *noun* a spot on the lung produced by the tuberculosis bacillus [Described 1912. After Anton Ghon (1866–1936), Professor of Pathological Anatomy at Prague, Czech Republic.]

GI *abbreviation* gastrointestinal

Giardia /dʒiː'ɑːdiə/ *noun* a microscopic protozoan parasite which causes giardiasis

giardiasis /ˌdʒiːɑː'daɪəsɪs/ *noun* a disorder of the intestine caused by the parasite *Giardia lamblia*, usually with no symptoms, but in heavy infections the absorption of fat may be affected, causing diarrhoea. Also called **lambliasis**

giddiness /'gɪdinəs/ *noun* a condition in which someone has difficulty in standing up and keeping their balance because of a feeling that everything is turning around ○ *He began to experience attacks of giddiness.*

GIFT /gɪft/ *noun* a procedure in which a surgeon removes eggs from a woman's ovary, mixes them with sperm and places them in one of her Fallopian tubes to help her conceive a child. Full form **gamete intrafallopian transfer**

gigantism /dʒaɪ'gæntɪz(ə)m/ *noun* a condition in which someone grows very tall, caused by excessive production of growth hormone by the pituitary gland

Gilbert's syndrome /'gɪlbəts ˌsɪndrəʊm/ *noun* an inherited disorder where the liver does not deal with bilirubin correctly

Gilliam's operation /'gɪliəmz ɒpəˌreɪʃ(ə)n/ *noun* a surgical operation to correct retroversion of the uterus [After David Tod Gilliam (1844–1923), physician, Columbus, Ohio, USA.]

gingiv- /dʒɪndʒɪv/ *prefix* referring to the gums

gingiva /dʒɪn'dʒaɪvə/ *noun* same as **gum** (NOTE: The plural is **gingivae**.)

gingival /'dʒɪndʒɪv(ə)l/ *adjective* relating to the gums

gingivectomy /ˌdʒɪndʒɪ'vektəmi/ *noun* the surgical removal of excess gum tissue

gingivitis /ˌdʒɪndʒɪ'vaɪtɪs/ *noun* inflammation of the gums as a result of bacterial infection

ginglymus /'dʒɪŋglɪməs/ *noun* a joint which allows movement in two directions only, e.g. the knee or elbow. Also called **hinge joint**. Compare **ball and socket joint**

ginseng /'dʒɪnseŋ/ *noun* a plant root widely used as a tonic and a traditional Chinese herbal remedy

girdle /'gɜːd(ə)l/ *noun* a set of bones making a ring or arch

Girdlestone's operation /'gɜːdəlstəʊnz ɒpə ˌreɪʃ(ə)n/ *noun* a surgical operation to relieve osteoarthritis of the hip [After Gathorne Robert Girdlestone (1881–1950), Nuffield Professor of Orthopaedics at Oxford, UK]

glabella /glə'belə/ *noun* a flat area of bone in the forehead between the eyebrows

gladiolus /ˌglædi'əʊləs/ *noun* the middle section of the sternum

gland /glænd/ *noun* an organ in the body containing cells that secrete substances such as hormones, sweat or saliva which act elsewhere

glanders /'glændəz/ *noun* a bacterial disease of horses, which can be caught by humans, with symptoms of high fever and inflammation of the lymph nodes

glandular /'glændjʊlə/ *adjective* referring to glands

glandular fever /ˌglændjʊlə 'fiːvə/ *noun* same as **infectious mononucleosis**

glans /glænz/ *noun* a rounded part at the end of the penis or clitoris. See illustration at UROGENI-TAL SYSTEM (MALE) in Supplement

glare /gleə/ *noun* **1.** a long stare that expresses a negative emotion such as anger **2.** an uncomfortably or dazzlingly bright light **3.** scattered bright light when examining something with a microscope ■ *verb* **1.** to stare angrily **2.** to shine uncomfortably brightly **3.** to be very obvious or conspicuous

Glasgow coma scale /ˌglɑːsgəʊ 'kəʊmə ˌskeɪl/, **Glasgow scoring system** /ˌglɑːsgəʊ 'skɔːrɪŋ ˌsɪstəm/ *noun* a seven-point scale for evaluating someone's level of consciousness

glass eye /ˌglɑːs 'aɪ/ *noun* an artificial eye made of glass

glaucoma /glɔː'kəʊmə/ *noun* a condition of the eyes, caused by unusually high pressure of fluid inside the eyeball, resulting in disturbances of vision and blindness

gleet /gliːt/ *noun* a thin discharge from the vagina, penis, a wound or an ulcer

glenohumeral /ˌgliːnəʊ'hjuːmərəl/ *adjective* referring to both the glenoid cavity and the humerus

glenohumeral joint /ˌgliːnəʊ'hjuːmərəl dʒɔɪnt/ *noun* the shoulder joint

glenoid /'gliːnɔɪd/ *adjective* shaped like a small shallow cup or socket

glenoid cavity /ˌgliːnɔɪd 'kævɪti/, **glenoid fossa** /ˌgliːnɔɪd 'fɒsə/ *noun* a socket in the shoulder joint into which the head of the humerus fits

glia /'gliːə/ *noun* connective tissue of the central nervous system, surrounding cell bodies, axons and dendrites. Also called **neuroglia**

glial cell /'gliːəl sel/ *noun* a cell in the glia

glial tissue /ˌgliːəl 'tɪʃuː/ *noun* same as **glia**

glibenclamide /glɪ'beŋkləmaɪd/ *noun* a sulphonylurea drug used to treat Type II diabetes mellitus

gliclazide /'glɪkləzaɪd/ *noun* an antibacterial drug used to treat Type II diabetes mellitus

glio- /glaɪəʊ/ *prefix* referring to brain tissue

glioma /glaɪ'əʊmə/ *noun* any tumour of the glial tissue in the brain or spinal cord

gliomyoma /ˌglaɪəʊmaɪ'əʊmə/ *noun* a tumour of both the nerve and muscle tissue

glipizide /'glɪpɪzaɪd/ *noun* a drug used to reduce the glucose level in the blood

Glisson's capsule /ˌglɪs(ə)nz 'kæpsjuːl/ *noun* a tissue sheath in the liver containing the blood vessels [After Francis Glisson (1597–1677), philosopher, physician and anatomist at Cambridge and London, UK]

globin /'gləʊbɪn/ *noun* a protein which combines with other substances to form compounds such as haemoglobin and myoglobin

globule /'glɒbjuːl/ *noun* a round drop, especially of fat

globulin /'glɒbjʊlɪn/ *noun* a protein, present in blood, belonging to a group that includes antibodies

globus /'gləʊbəs/ *noun* any ball-shaped part of the body

globus hystericus /ˌgləʊbəs hɪ'sterɪkəs/ *noun* a feeling of not being able to swallow, caused by worry or embarrassment

glomerular /glɒ'merʊlə/ *adjective* referring to a glomerulus

glomerular capsule /glɒˌmerʊlə ˈkæpsjuːl/ *noun* same as **Bowman's capsule**

glomerular filtration rate /glɒˌmerʊlə fɪlˈtreɪʃ(ə)n ˌreɪt/ *noun* the rate at which the kidneys filter blood and remove waste matter

glomerular tuft /glɒˌmerʊlə ˈtʌft/ *noun* a group of blood vessels in the kidney which filter the blood

glomeruli plural of **glomerulus**

glomerulitis /glɒˌmerʊˈlaɪtɪs/ *noun* inflammation causing lesions of glomeruli in the kidney

glomerulonephritis /glɒˌmerʊləʊneˈfraɪtɪs/ *noun* same as **Bright's disease**

glomerulus /glɒˈmerʊləs/ *noun* a group of blood vessels which filter waste matter from the blood in a kidney (NOTE: The plural is **glomeruli**.)

gloss- /glɒs/ *prefix* same as **glosso-** (used before vowels)

glossa /ˈglɒsə/ *noun* same as **tongue**

glossal /ˈglɒs(ə)l/ *adjective* relating to the tongue

glossectomy /glɒˈsektəmi/ *noun* the surgical removal of the tongue

glossitis /glɒˈsaɪtɪs/ *noun* inflammation of the surface of the tongue

glosso- /glɒsəʊ/ *prefix* referring to the tongue

glossodynia /ˌglɒsəʊˈdɪniə/ *noun* pain in the tongue

glossopharyngeal /ˌglɒsəʊfærɪnˈdʒiːəl/ *adjective* relating to the tongue and pharynx

glossopharyngeal nerve /ˌglɒsəʊfærɪnˈdʒiːəl nɜːv/ *noun* the ninth cranial nerve which controls the pharynx, the salivary glands and part of the tongue

glossoplegia /ˌglɒsəʊˈpliːdʒə/ *noun* paralysis of the tongue

glossotomy /glɒˈsɒtəmi/ *noun* a surgical incision into the tongue

glottis /ˈglɒtɪs/ *noun* an opening in the larynx between the vocal cords, which forms the entrance to the main airway from the pharynx

gluc- /gluːk/ *prefix* referring to glucose

glucagon /ˈgluːkəgɒn/ *noun* a hormone secreted by the islets of Langerhans in the pancreas, which increases the level of blood sugar by stimulating the breakdown of glycogen

glucagonoma /ˌgluːkəgɒˈnəʊmə/ *noun* a tumour of the cells of the pancreas that produces glucagon

glucocorticoid /ˌgluːkəʊˈkɔːtɪkɔɪd/ *noun* any corticosteroid which breaks down carbohydrates and fats for use by the body, produced by the adrenal cortex

gluconeogenesis /ˌgluːkəʊˌniːəʊˈdʒenəsɪs/ *noun* the production of glucose in the liver from protein or fat reserves

glucose /ˈgluːkəʊz/ *noun* a simple sugar found in some fruit, but also broken down from white sugar or carbohydrate and absorbed into the body or secreted by the kidneys. Also called **dextrose**

glucose tolerance test /ˈgluːkəʊz ˌtɒlərəns test/ *noun* a test for diabetes mellitus, in which someone eats glucose and his or her urine and blood are tested at regular intervals. Abbreviation **GTT**

glue ear /ˈgluː ɪə/ *noun* a condition in which fluid forms behind the eardrum and causes deafness. Also called **secretory otitis media**

glue-sniffing /ˈgluː ˌsnɪfɪŋ/ *noun* ♦ **solvent abuse**

glutamic oxaloacetic transaminase /gluːˌtæmɪk ɒksələʊəˌsiːtɪk trænsˈæmɪneɪz/ *noun* an enzyme used to test for viral hepatitis

glutamic pyruvic transaminase /gluːˌtæmɪk paɪˌruːvɪk trænsˈæmɪneɪz/ *noun* an enzyme produced in the liver and released into the blood if the liver is damaged

gluteal /ˈgluːtiəl/ *adjective* referring to the buttocks

gluteal artery /ˈgluːtiəl ˌɑːtəri/ *noun* one of the two arteries supplying the buttocks, the **inferior gluteal artery** or the **superior gluteal artery**

gluteal muscle /ˈgluːtiəl ˌmʌs(ə)l/ *noun* a muscle in the buttock. ◊ **gluteus**

gluteal vein /ˈgluːtiəl veɪn/ *noun* one of two veins draining the buttocks, the **inferior gluteal vein** and the **superior gluteal vein**

gluten /ˈgluːt(ə)n/ *noun* a protein found in some cereals, which makes the grains form a sticky paste when water is added

gluten enteropathy /ˌgluːt(ə)n ˌentəˈrɒpəθi/ same as **gluten-induced enteropathy**

gluten-induced enteropathy /ˌgluːt(ə)n ɪn ˌdjuːst ˌentəˈrɒpəθi/ *noun* **1.** an allergic disease mainly affecting children, in which the lining of the intestine is sensitive to gluten, preventing the small intestine from digesting fat **2.** a condition in adults where the villi in the intestine become smaller and so reduce the surface which can absorb nutrients (NOTE: Symptoms include a swollen abdomen, pale diarrhoea, abdominal pains and anaemia.) ▶ also called **coeliac disease**

gluteus /ˈgluːtiəs/ *noun* one of three muscles in the buttocks, responsible for movements of the hip. The largest is the **gluteus maximus**, while the **gluteus medius** and **gluteus minimus** are smaller.

glyc- /glaɪk/ *prefix* same as **glyco-** (used before vowels)

glycaemia /glaɪˈsiːmiə/ *noun* the level of glucose found in the blood. ◊ **hypoglycaemia**, **hyperglycaemia**

glycerin /ˈglɪsərɪn/, **glycerine**, **glycerol** /ˈglɪsərɒl/ *noun* a colourless viscous sweet-tasting liquid present in all fats (NOTE: Synthetic glycerin is used in various medicinal preparations and also as a lubricant in items such as toothpaste and cough medicines.)

glyco- /glaɪkəʊ/ *prefix* referring to sugar

glycogen /ˈglaɪkədʒən/ *noun* a type of starch, converted from glucose by the action of insulin, and stored in the liver as a source of energy

glycogenesis /ˌglaɪkəʊˈdʒenəsɪs/ *noun* the process by which glucose is converted into glycogen in the liver

glycogenolysis /ˌglaɪkəʊdʒəˈnɒləsɪs/ *noun* the process by which glycogen is broken down to form glucose

glycolysis /glaɪˈkɒləsɪs/ *noun* the metabolic breakdown of glucose to release energy

glycoside /ˈglaɪkəʊsaɪd/ *noun* a chemical compound of a type which is formed from a simple sugar and another compound (NOTE: Many of the drugs produced from plants are glycosides.)

glycosuria /ˌglaɪkəʊˈsjʊəriə/ *noun* a high level of sugar in the urine, a symptom of diabetes mellitus

GMC *abbreviation* General Medical Council

gnathic /ˈnæθɪk/ *adjective* referring to the jaw

gnathoplasty /ˈnæθəʊˌplæsti/ *noun* surgery on the jaw

gnawing /ˈnɔːɪŋ/ *adjective* referring to a physical or emotional feeling that is persistent and uncomfortable ○ *a gnawing pain* ○ *gnawing anxiety*

goblet cell /ˈgɒblət sel/ *noun* a tube-shaped cell in the epithelium which secretes mucus

GOC *abbreviation* General Optical Council

goitre /ˈgɔɪtə/ *noun* an excessive enlargement of the thyroid gland, seen as a swelling round the neck, caused by a lack of iodine (NOTE: The US spelling is **goiter**.)

gold /gəʊld/ *noun* a soft yellow-coloured precious metal, used as a compound in various drugs, and sometimes as a filling for teeth (NOTE: The chemical symbol is **Au**.)

golden hour /ˌgəʊld(ə)n ˈaʊə/ *noun* the first hour after a serious injury when the most difference can be made to the patient's health

golfer's elbow /ˌgɒlfəz ˈelbəʊ/ *noun* inflammation of the tendons of the elbow

Golgi apparatus /ˈgɒldʒi æpəˌreɪtəs/ *noun* a folded membranous structure inside the cell cytoplasm which stores and transports enzymes and hormones [Described 1898. After Camillo Golgi (1843–1926), Professor of Histology and later Rector of the University of Pavia, Italy. In 1906 he shared the Nobel Prize with Santiago Ramón y Cajal for work on the nervous sytem.]

Golgi cell /ˈgɒldʒi ˌsel/ *noun* a type of nerve cell in the central nervous system, either with long axons (Golgi Type 1) or without axons (Golgi Type 2)

gomphosis /gɒmˈfəʊsɪs/ *noun* a joint which cannot move, like that between a tooth and the jaw

gonad /ˈgəʊnæd/ *noun* a sex gland which produces gametes and also sex hormones, e.g. a testicle in males or an ovary in females

gonadotrophic hormone /ˌgəʊnədəʊˌtrɒfɪk ˈhɔːməʊn/ *noun* one of two hormones, the follicle-stimulating hormone and the luteinising hormone, produced by the anterior pituitary gland which have an effect on the ovaries in females and on the testes in males

gonadotrophin /ˌgəʊnədəʊˈtrəʊfɪn/ *noun* any of a group of hormones produced by the pituitary gland which stimulates the sex glands at puberty. ◊ **human chorionic gonadotrophin**

goni- /gəʊni/ *prefix* same as **gonio-** (*used before a vowel*)

gonio- /gɒniəʊ/ *prefix* referring to an angle

gonion /ˈgəʊniɒn/ *noun* the outer point at which the lower jawbone angles upwards

goniopuncture /ˈgəʊniəʊˌpʌŋktʃə/ *noun* a surgical operation for draining fluid from the eyes of someone who has glaucoma

goniotomy /ˌgəʊniˈɒtəmi/ *noun* a surgical operation to treat glaucoma by cutting Schlemm's canal

gonococcal /ˌgɒnəˈkɒk(ə)l/ *adjective* referring to gonococcus

gonococcus /ˌgɒnəˈkɒkəs/ *noun* a type of bacterium, *Neisseria gonorrhoea,* which causes gonorrhoea (NOTE: The plural is **gonococci**.)

gonocyte /ˈgɒnəsaɪt/ *noun* same as **germ cell**

gonorrhoea /ˌgɒnəˈriːə/ *noun* a sexually transmitted disease which produces painful irritation of the mucous membrane and a watery discharge from the vagina or penis

goose bumps /ˈguːs bʌmps/, **goose flesh** /ˈguːs fleʃ/, **goose pimples** /ˈguːs ˌpɪmp(ə)lz/ *noun* a reaction of the skin when someone is cold or frightened, the skin being raised into many little bumps by the action of the arrector pili muscles. Also called **cutis anserina**

gorget /ˈgɔːdʒɪt/ *noun* a surgical instrument used to remove stones from the bladder

gouge /gaʊdʒ/ *noun* a surgical instrument like a chisel, used to cut bone

gout /gaʊt/ *noun* a disease in which unusual quantities of uric acid are produced and form crystals in the cartilage round joints. Also called **podagra**

GP *abbreviation* general practitioner

GP co-op /ˌdʒiː ˈpiː kəʊ ˌɒp/ *noun* a group of GPs who work together to provide out-of-hours care without making any profit

graft /ɡrɑːft/ *noun* the act of transplanting an organ or tissue to replace one which is not functioning or which is diseased ○ *a skin graft* ■ *verb* to take a healthy organ or tissue and transplant it in place of diseased or malfunctioning organ or tissue ○ *The surgeons grafted a new section of bone at the side of the skull.* ⟡ **autograft, homograft**

graft versus host disease /ˌɡrɑːft ˌvɜːsəs ˈhəʊst dɪˌziːz/ *noun* a condition which develops when cells from the grafted tissue react against the person's own tissue, causing skin disorders. Abbreviation **GVHD**

grain /ɡreɪn/ *noun* **1.** a very small piece of something hard such as salt **2.** a measure of weight equal to 0.0648 grams. Symbol **gr**

-gram /ɡræm/ *suffix* a record in the form of a picture

Gram-negative bacterium /ˌɡræm ˈneɡətɪv bækˌtɪəriəm/ *noun* a bacterium which takes up the red counterstain, after the alcohol has washed out the first violet dye

Gram-positive bacterium /ˌɡræm ˈpɒzɪtɪv bækˌtɪəriəm/ *noun* a bacterium which retains violet dye and appears blue-black when viewed under the microscope

Gram's stain /ˈɡræmz steɪn/ *noun* a method of staining bacteria so that they can be identified [Described 1884. After Hans Christian Joachim Gram (1853–1938), Professor of Medicine in Copenhagen, Denmark. He discovered the stain by accident as a student in Berlin, Germany.]

grand mal /ˌɡrɒn ˈmæl/ *noun* a type of epilepsy, in which someone becomes unconscious and falls down, while the muscles become stiff and twitch violently

grand multiparity /ˌɡræn mʌltiˈpærɪti/ *noun* the fact of having given birth to more than four children

granular /ˈɡrænjʊlə/ *adjective* made up of granules

granular cast /ˌɡrænjʊlə ˈkɑːst/ *noun* a cast composed of cells filled with protein and fatty granules

granular leucocyte /ˌɡrænjʊlə ˈluːkəsaɪt/ *noun* same as **granulocyte**

granulation /ˌɡrænjʊˈleɪʃ(ə)n/ *noun* the formation of rough red tissue on the surface of a wound or site of infection, the first stage in the healing process

granulation tissue /ˌɡrænjʊˈleɪʃ(ə)n ˌtɪʃuː/ *noun* soft tissue, consisting mainly of tiny blood vessels and fibres, which forms over a wound

granule /ˈɡrænjuːl/ *noun* a very small piece of something hard

granulocyte /ˈɡrænjʊləsaɪt/ *noun* a type of leucocyte or white blood cell which contains granules, e.g. a basophil, eosinophil or neutrophil

granulocytopenia /ˌɡrænjʊləʊˌsaɪtəʊˈpiːniə/ *noun* a usually fatal disease caused by the lowering of the number of granulocytes in the blood due to bone marrow malfunction

granuloma /ˌɡrænjʊˈləʊmə/ *noun* a mass of granulation tissue which forms at the site of bacterial infections (NOTE: The plural is **granulomata** or **granulomas**.)

granulomatosis /ˌɡrænjʊləʊməˈtəʊsɪs/ *noun* persistent inflammation leading to the formation of nodules

graph /ɡrɑːf/ *noun* a diagram which shows the relationship between quantities as a line

graph- /ɡræf/ *prefix* writing

-graph /ɡrɑːf/ *suffix* a machine which records something as pictures

-grapher /ɡrəfə/ *suffix* a technician who operates a machine which records

-graphy /ɡrəfi/ *suffix* the technique of study through pictures

grattage /ɡræˈtɑːʒ/ *noun* a procedure that involves scraping the surface of an ulcer which is healing slowly to make it heal more rapidly

gravel /ˈɡræv(ə)l/ *noun* small stones which pass from the kidney to the urinary system, causing pain in the ureter

Graves' disease /ˈɡreɪvz dɪˌziːz/ *noun* same as **exophthalmic goitre** [Described 1835. After Robert James Graves (1796–1853), Irish physician at the Meath Hospital, Dublin, Ireland, where he was responsible for introducing clinical ward work for medical students.]

gravid /ˈɡrævɪd/ *adjective* pregnant

gravides multiparae /ˌɡrævɪdiːz ˌmʌlti ˈpɑːriː/ *plural noun* women who have given birth to at least four live babies

gravity /ˈɡrævɪti/ *noun* the importance or potential danger of a disease or situation

Grawitz tumour /ˈɡrɑːvɪts ˌtjuːmə/ *noun* a malignant tumour in kidney cells [Described 1883. After Paul Albert Grawitz (1850–1932), Professor of Pathology at Greifswald, Germany.]

gray /ɡreɪ/ *noun* an SI unit of measurement of absorbed radiation equal to 100 rads. Symbol **Gy**. ⟡ **rad**

graze /ɡreɪz/ *noun* a scrape on the skin surface, making some blood flow ■ *verb* to scrape the skin surface accidentally

greater curvature /ˌɡreɪtə ˈkɜːvətʃə/ *noun* a convex line of the stomach

greater vestibular glands /ˌɡreɪtə ve ˈstɪbjʊlə ɡlændz/ *noun* same as **Bartholin's glands**

great toe /ˈgreɪt təʊ/ *noun* same as **big toe**

greenstick fracture /ˈgriːnstɪk ˌfræktʃə/ *noun* a type of fracture occurring in children, where a long bone bends, but is not completely broken

grey commissure /ˌgreɪ ˈkɒmɪsjʊə/ *noun* part of the grey matter nearest to the central canal of the spinal cord, where axons cross over each other

grey matter /ˈgreɪ ˌmætə/ *noun* nerve tissue which is of a dark grey colour and forms part of the central nervous system

COMMENT: In the brain, grey matter encloses the white matter, but in the spinal cord, white matter encloses the grey matter.

grief counsellor /ˈgriːf ˌkaʊns(ə)lə/ *noun* a person who helps someone to cope with the feelings they have when someone such as a close relative dies

gripe water /ˈgraɪp ˌwɔːtə/ *noun* a solution of glucose and alcohol, used to relieve abdominal pains in babies

groin /grɔɪn/ *noun* a junction at each side of the body where the lower abdomen joins the top of the thighs ○ *He had a dull pain in his groin.* (NOTE: For other terms referring to the groin, see **inguinal**.)

grommet /ˈgrɒmɪt/ *noun* a tube which can be passed from the external auditory meatus into the middle ear, usually to allow fluid to drain off, as in someone who has glue ear

ground substance /ˌgraʊnd ˈsʌbstəns/ *noun* same as **matrix**

group /gruːp/ *noun* several people, animals or things which are all close together ○ *A group of patients were waiting in the surgery.* ■ *verb* to bring things or people together in a group, or come together in a group ○ *The drugs are grouped under the heading 'antibiotics'.*

group practice /ˌgruːp ˈpræktɪs/ *noun* a medical practice where several doctors or dentists share the same office building and support services

group therapy /ˌgruːp ˈθerəpi/ *noun* a type of psychotherapy where a group of people with the same disorder meet together with a therapist to discuss their condition and try to help each other

growing pains /ˈgrəʊɪŋ peɪnz/ *plural noun* pains associated with adolescence, which can be a form of rheumatic fever

growth /grəʊθ/ *noun* **1.** the process of increasing in size ○ *the growth in the population since 1960* ○ *The disease stunts children's growth.* **2.** a cyst or tumour ○ *The doctor found a cancerous growth on the left breast.* ○ *He had an operation to remove a small growth from his chin.*

growth factor /ˈgrəʊθ ˌfæktə/ *noun* a chemical, especially a polypeptide, produced in the body which encourages particular cells to grow ○ *a nerve growth factor*

growth hormone /ˈgrəʊθ ˌhɔːməʊn/ *noun* a hormone secreted by the pituitary gland during deep sleep, which stimulates growth of the long bones and protein synthesis. Also called **somatropin**

grumbling appendix /ˌgrʌmblɪŋ əˈpendɪks/ *noun* a vermiform appendix that is always slightly inflamed (*informal*) ◊ **chronic appendicitis**

GU *abbreviation* **1.** gastric ulcer **2.** genitourinary

guanine /ˈgwɑːniːn/ *noun* one of the four basic chemicals in DNA

guardian ad litem /ˌgɑːdiən æd ˈliːtəm/ *noun* a person who acts on behalf of a minor who is a defendant in a court case

guardian Caldicott /ˌgɑːdiən ˈkɔːldɪkɒt/ *noun* in the UK, a person appointed by a hospital or Health Trust to make sure that information about patients is kept confidential, following the Caldicott Report of 1997

Guillain-Barré syndrome /ˌgiːjæn ˈbæreɪ ˌsɪndrəʊm/ *noun* a nervous disorder in which after a non-specific infection, demyelination of the spinal roots and peripheral nerves takes place leading to generalised weakness and sometimes respiratory paralysis. Also called **Landry's paralysis** [Described 1916. After Georges Guillain (1876–1961), Professor of Neurology in Paris, France, Jean Alexandre Barré (1880–1967), Professor of Neurology in Strasbourg France.]

guillotine /ˈgɪlətiːn/ *noun* a surgical instrument for cutting out tonsils

guinea worm /ˈgɪni wɜːm/ *noun* same as **Dracunculus**

Gulf War syndrome /ˌgʌlf ˈwɔː ˌsɪndrəʊm/ *noun* a collection of unexplained symptoms including fatigue, skin disorders, and muscle pains, affecting some soldiers who fought in the Gulf War in 1991

gullet /ˈgʌlɪt/ *noun* same as **oesophagus**

gum /gʌm/ *noun* the soft tissue covering the part of the jaw which surrounds the teeth ○ *Her gums are red and inflamed.* ○ *A build-up of tartar can lead to gum disease.* Also called **gingiva** (NOTE: For other terms referring to the gums, see words beginning with **gingiv-**.)

gumboil /ˈgʌmbɔɪl/ *noun* an abscess on the gum near a tooth

gustation /gʌˈsteɪʃ(ə)n/ *noun* the act of tasting

gustatory /ˈgʌstət(ə)ri/ *adjective* referring to the sense of taste

gut /gʌt/ *noun* **1.** the tubular organ for the digestion and absorption of food. Also called **intestine 2.** a type of thread, made from the intestines of sheep. It is used to sew up internal incisions and

dissolves slowly so does not need to be removed.
◊ **catgut**

Guthrie test /ˈgʌθri test/ *noun* a test used on babies to detect the presence of phenylketonuria [After R. Guthrie (1916–95), US paediatrician.]

gutta /ˈgʌtə/ *noun* a drop of liquid, as used in treatment of the eyes (NOTE: The plural is **guttae**.)

gutter splint /ˈgʌtə splɪnt/ *noun* a shaped container in which a broken limb can rest without being completely surrounded

GVHD *abbreviation* graft versus host disease

gyn- /gaɪn/ *prefix* same as **gynae-** (*used before a vowel*)

gynae- referring to women

gynaecological /ˌgaɪnɪkəˈlɒdʒɪk(ə)l/ *adjective* referring to the treatment of diseases of women

gynaecologist /ˌgaɪnɪˈkɒlədʒɪst/ *noun* a doctor who specialises in the treatment of diseases of women

gynaecology /ˌgaɪnɪˈkɒlədʒi/ *noun* the study of female sex organs and the treatment of diseases of women in general

gynaecomastia /ˌgaɪnɪkəˈmæstiə/ *noun* the unusual development of breasts in a male

gyne /ˈgaɪni/ same as **gynaecology, gynaecological** (*informal*) ○ *a gyne appointment*

gypsum /ˈdʒɪpsəm/ *noun* calcium sulphate, used as plaster of Paris

gyrus /ˈdʒaɪərəs/ *noun* a raised part of the cerebral cortex between the sulci

H

H2-receptor antagonist /ˌeɪtʃ tuː rɪˈseptər ænˌtægənɪst/ *noun* a drug that inhibits the production of stomach acid and so relieves indigestion and gastric ulcers

habit /ˈhæbɪt/ *noun* **1.** an action which is an automatic response to a stimulus **2.** a regular way of doing something ○ *He got into the habit of swimming every day before breakfast.* ○ *She's got out of the habit of taking any exercise.*

habit-forming drug /ˈhæbɪt ˌfɔːmɪŋ drʌg/ *noun* a drug which is addictive

habitual abortion /həˌbɪtʃuəl əˈbɔːʃ(ə)n/ *noun* a condition in which a woman has abortions with successive pregnancies

habituation /həˌbɪtʃuˈeɪʃ(ə)n/ *noun* the fact of being psychologically but not physically addicted to or dependent on a drug, alcohol or other substance

habitus /ˈhæbɪtəs/ *noun* the general physical appearance of a person, including build and posture

haem /hiːm/ *noun* a molecule containing iron which binds proteins to form haemoproteins such as haemoglobin and myoglobin

haem- /hiːm/ *prefix* same as **haemo-** (*used before vowels*)

haemagglutination /ˌhiːməgluːtɪˈneɪʃ(ə)n/ *noun* the clumping of red blood cells, often used to test for the presence of antibodies

haemangioma /ˌhiːmændʒiˈəʊmə/ *noun* a harmless tumour which forms in blood vessels and appears on the skin as a birthmark

haemarthrosis /ˌhiːmɑːˈθrəʊsɪs/ *noun* pain and swelling caused by blood leaking into a joint

haematemesis /ˌhiːməˈteməsɪs/ *noun* a condition in which someone vomits blood, usually because of internal bleeding

haematic /hiːˈmætɪk/ *adjective* referring to blood

haematin /ˈhiːmətɪn/ *noun* a substance which forms from haemoglobin when bleeding takes place

haematinic /ˌhiːməˈtɪnɪk/ *noun* a drug which increases haemoglobin in blood, used to treat anaemia, e.g. an iron compound

haemato- /hiːmətəʊ/ *prefix* referring to blood

haematocolpos /ˌhiːmətəʊˈkɒlpəs/ *noun* a condition in which the vagina is filled with blood at menstruation because the hymen has no opening

haematocrit /ˈhiːmətəʊkrɪt/ *noun* same as **packed cell volume**

haematocyst /ˈhiːmətəʊsɪst/ *noun* a cyst which contains blood

haematological /ˌhiːmətəʊˈlɒdʒɪk(ə)l/ *adjective* referring to haematology

haematologist /ˌhiːməˈtɒlədʒɪst/ *noun* a doctor who specialises in haematology

haematology /ˌhiːməˈtɒlədʒi/ *noun* the scientific study of blood, its formation and its diseases

haematoma /ˌhiːməˈtəʊmə/ *noun* a mass of blood under the skin caused by a blow or by the effects of an operation

haematometra /ˌhiːməˈtɒmɪtrə/ *noun* excessive bleeding in the uterus

haematomyelia /ˌhiːmətəʊmaɪˈiːliə/ *noun* a condition in which blood leaks into the spinal cord

haematopoiesis /ˌhiːmətəʊpɔɪˈiːsɪs/ *noun* same as **haemopoiesis**

haematosalpinx /ˌhiːmətəʊˈsælpɪŋks/ *noun* same as **haemosalpinx**

haematozoon /ˌhiːmətəʊˈzəʊɒn/ *noun* a parasite living in the blood (NOTE: The plural is **haematozoa.**)

haematuria /ˌhiːməˈtjʊəriə/ *noun* the unusual presence of blood in the urine, as a result of injury or disease of the kidney or bladder

haemin /ˈhiːmɪn/ *noun* a salt derived from haemoglobin, used in the treatment of porphyria

haemo- /hiːməʊ/ *prefix* referring to blood

haemochromatosis /ˌhiːməʊkrəʊməˈtəʊsɪs/ *noun* an inherited disease in which the body absorbs and stores too much iron, causing cirrhosis of the liver and giving the skin a dark colour. Also called **bronze diabetes**

haemoconcentration /ˌhiːməʊˌkɒnsənˈtreɪʃ(ə)n/ *noun* an increase in the percentage of red blood cells because the volume of plasma is reduced. Compare **haemodilution**

haemocytometer /ˌhiːməʊsaɪ'tɒmɪtə/ *noun* a glass jar in which a sample of blood is diluted and the blood cells counted

haemodialysed patient /ˌhiːməʊdaɪəlaɪzd 'peɪʃ(ə)nt/ *noun* someone who has undergone haemodialysis

haemodialysis /ˌhiːməʊdaɪ'æləsɪs/ *noun* same as **kidney dialysis**

haemodilution /ˌhiːməʊdaɪ'luːʃ(ə)n/ *noun* a decrease in the percentage of red blood cells because the volume of plasma has increased. Compare **haemoconcentration**

haemoglobin /ˌhiːmə'gləʊbɪn/ *noun* a red respiratory pigment formed of haem and globin in red blood cells which gives blood its red colour. It absorbs oxygen in the lungs and carries it in the blood to the tissues. Abbreviation **Hb**. ◊ **oxyhaemoglobin**, **carboxyhaemoglobin**

haemoglobinaemia /ˌhiːməʊgləʊbɪ'niːmiə/ *noun* a comdition in which haemoglobin is found in blood plasma

haemoglobinopathy /ˌhiːməʊgləʊbɪ'nɒpəθi/ *noun* an inherited disease of a group which result from damaging variations in the production of haemoglobin, e.g. sickle-cell anaemia

haemoglobinuria /ˌhiːməʊgləʊbɪ'njʊəriə/ *noun* a condition in which haemoglobin is found in the urine

haemogram /'hiːməʊgræm/ *noun* the printed result of a blood test

haemolysin /ˌhiːməʊ'laɪsɪn/ *noun* a protein which destroys red blood cells

haemolysis /hiː'mɒləsɪs/ *noun* the destruction of red blood cells

haemolytic /ˌhiːməʊ'lɪtɪk/ *adjective* destroying red blood cells ■ *noun* a substance which destroys red blood cells, e.g. snake venom

haemolytic anaemia /ˌhiːməlɪtɪk ə'niːmiə/ *noun* a condition in which the destruction of red blood cells is about six times the usual rate, and the supply of new cells from the bone marrow cannot meet the demand

haemolytic disease of the newborn /ˌhiːməʊlɪtɪk dɪˌziːz əv ðə 'njuːbɔːn/ *noun* a condition in which the red blood cells of the fetus are destroyed because antibodies in the mother's blood react against them

haemolytic jaundice /ˌhiːməʊlɪtɪk 'dʒɔːndɪs/ *noun* jaundice caused by haemolysis of the red blood cells. Also called **prehepatic jaundice**

haemolytic uraemic syndrome /ˌhiːməʊlɪtɪk jʊ'riːmɪk ˌsɪndrəʊm/ *noun* a condition in which haemolytic anaemia damages the kidneys

haemopericardium /ˌhiːməʊperɪ'kɑːdiəm/ *noun* a condition in which blood is found in the pericardium

haemoperitoneum /ˌhiːməʊperɪtə'niːəm/ *noun* a condition in which blood is found in the peritoneal cavity

haemophilia A /ˌhiːməʊfɪliə 'eɪ/ *noun* the most common type of haemophilia, in which the inability to synthesise Factor VIII, a protein that promotes blood clotting, means that the blood clots very slowly

haemophilia B /ˌhiːməfɪliə 'biː/ *noun* a less common type of haemophilia, in which the inability to synthesise Factor IX, a protein that promotes blood clotting, means that the blood clots very slowly. Also called **Christmas disease**

haemophiliac /ˌhiːmə'fɪliæk/ *noun* a person who has haemophilia

haemophilic /ˌhiːməʊ'fɪlɪk/ *adjective* referring to haemophilia

Haemophilus /hiː'mɒfɪləs/ *noun* a genus of bacteria which needs specific factors in the blood to grow

Haemophilus influenzae /hiːˌmɒfɪləs ˌɪnfluˈenzə/ *noun* a bacterium which lives in healthy throats, but which can cause pneumonia if a person's resistance is lowered by a bout of flu

Haemophilus influenzae type b /hiːˌmɒfɪləs ˌɪnfluˌenzə taɪp 'biː/ *noun* a bacterium which causes meningitis. Abbreviation **Hib**

haemophthalmia /ˌhiːmɒf'θælmiə/ *noun* a condition in which blood is found in the vitreous humour of the eye

haemopneumothorax /ˌhiːməʊˌnjuːməʊ 'θɔːræks/ *noun* same as **pneumohaemothorax**

haemopoiesis /ˌhiːməʊpɔɪ'iːsɪs/ *noun* the continual production of blood cells and blood platelets in the bone marrow. Also called **blood formation**

haemopoietic /ˌhiːməʊpɔɪ'etɪk/ *adjective* referring to the formation of blood in the bone marrow

haemoptysis /hiː'mɒptəsɪs/ *noun* a condition in which someone coughs blood from the lungs, caused by a serious illness such as anaemia, pneumonia, tuberculosis or cancer

haemorrhage /'hem(ə)rɪdʒ/ *noun* the loss of a large quantity of blood, especially from a burst blood vessel ○ *He died of a brain haemorrhage.* ■ *verb* to bleed heavily ○ *The injured man was haemorrhaging from the mouth.*

haemorrhagic /ˌhemə'rædʒɪk/ *adjective* referring to heavy bleeding

haemorrhagic disease of the newborn /ˌhemərædʒɪk dɪˌziːz əv ðə 'njuːbɔːn/ *noun* a disease of newly born babies, which makes them haemorrhage easily, caused by temporary lack of prothrombin

haemorrhagic disorder /ˌhemərædʒɪk dɪs'ɔːdə/ *noun* a disorder in which haemorrhages occur, e.g. haemophilia

haemorrhagic stroke /ˌhemərædʒɪk 'strəʊk/ *noun* a stroke caused by a burst blood vessel

haemorrhoidectomy /ˌhemərɔɪ'dektəmi/ *noun* the surgical removal of haemorrhoids

haemorrhoids /'hemərɔɪdz/ *plural noun* swollen veins in the anorectal passage. Also called **piles**

haemosalpinx /hiːməʊ'sælpɪŋks/ *noun* the accumulation of blood in the Fallopian tubes

haemosiderosis /ˌhiːməʊsɪdə'rəʊsɪs/ *noun* a disorder in which iron forms large deposits in the tissue, causing haemorrhaging and destruction of red blood cells

haemostasis /ˌhiːməʊ'steɪsɪs/ *noun* the process of stopping bleeding or slowing the movement of blood

haemostat /'hiːməʊstæt/ *noun* a device which stops bleeding, e.g. a clamp

haemostatic /ˌhiːməʊ'stætɪk/ *adjective* stopping bleeding ■ *noun* a drug which stops bleeding

haemothorax /ˌhiːməʊ'θɔːræks/ *noun* a condition in which blood is found in the pleural cavity

Hageman factor /'hɑːɡəmən ˌfæktə/ *noun* same as **Factor XII**

HAI *abbreviation* Hospital Acquired Infection

hair cell /'heə sel/ *noun* a receptor cell which converts fluid pressure changes into nerve impulses carried in the auditory nerve (NOTE: For other terms referring to hair, see words beginning with **pilo-, trich-, tricho-**.)

hair follicle /'heə ˌfɒlɪk(ə)l/ *noun* the cells and tissue that surround the root of a hair

hairline fracture /ˌheəlaɪn 'fræktʃə/ *noun* a very slight crack in a bone caused by injury

hair papilla /ˌheə pə'pɪlə/ *noun* a part of the skin containing capillaries which feed blood to the hair

half-life /'hɑːf laɪf/ *noun* **1.** a measurement of the period of time taken before the concentration of a drug has reached half of what it was when it was administered **2.** the time taken for half the atoms in a radioactive isotope to decay

halitosis /ˌhælɪ'təʊsɪs/ *noun* a condition in which a person has breath which smells unpleasant. Also called **bad breath**

hallucinate /hə'luːsɪneɪt/ *verb* to have hallucinations ○ *The patient was hallucinating.*

hallucination /həˌluːsɪ'neɪʃ(ə)n/ *noun* an experience of seeing an imaginary scene or hearing an imaginary sound as clearly as if it were really there

hallucinatory /hə'luːsɪnət(ə)ri/ *adjective* referring to a drug which causes hallucinations

hallucinogen /ˌhælu:'sɪnədʒən/ *noun* a drug which causes hallucinations, e.g. cannabis or LSD

hallucinogenic /həˌluːsɪnə'dʒenɪk/ *adjective* referring to a substance which produces hallucinations ○ *a hallucinogenic fungus*

hallux /'hæləks/ *noun* the big toe (NOTE: The plural is **halluces**.)

hallux valgus /ˌhæləks 'vælɡəs/ *noun* a condition of the foot, where the big toe turns towards the other toes and a bunion is formed

haloperidol /ˌhæləʊ'perɪdɒl/ *noun* a tranquilliser used in the treatment of schizophrenia, mania and psychoses

halo splint /'heɪləʊ splɪnt/ *noun* a device used to keep the head and neck still so that they can recover from injury or an operation

halothane /'hæləʊθeɪn/ *noun* a general anaesthetic that is given by inhalation

hamartoma /ˌhæmɑː'təʊmə/ *noun* a benign tumour containing tissue from any organ

hamate /'heɪmeɪt/, **hamate bone** /'heɪmeɪt bəʊn/ *noun* one of the eight small carpal bones in the wrist, shaped like a hook. Also called **unciform bone**. See illustration at HAND in Supplement

hammer /'hæmə/ *noun* same as **malleus**

hammer toe /'hæmə təʊ/ *noun* a toe which has the middle joint permanently bent downwards

hamstring /'hæmstrɪŋ/ *noun* one of a group of tendons behind the knee, which link the thigh muscles to the bones in the lower leg

hamstring muscles /'hæmstrɪŋ ˌmʌs(ə)lz/ *plural noun* a group of muscles at the back of the thigh, which flex the knee and extend the gluteus maximus

hand /hænd/ *noun* the part at the end of the arm, beyond the wrist, which is used for holding things ○ *He injured his hand with a saw.*

hand, foot and mouth disease /ˌhænd fʊt ən 'maʊθ dɪˌziːz/ *noun* a mild viral infection in children, causing small blisters

handicap /'hændikæp/ *noun* a physical or mental condition which prevents someone from doing some everyday activities ■ *verb* to prevent someone from doing an everyday activity (NOTE: The word 'handicap' is now usually avoided.)

handicapped /'hændikæpt/ *adjective* referring to a person who has a disability (NOTE: The word 'handicapped' is now usually avoided.)

hangnail /'hæŋneɪl/ *noun* a piece of torn skin at the side of a nail

hangover /'hæŋəʊvə/ *noun* a condition occurring after a person has drunk too much alcohol with dehydration caused by inhibition of the antidiuretic hormone in the kidneys. The symptoms include headache, inability to stand noise and trembling of the hands.

Hansen's disease /'hænsən dɪˌziːz/ *noun* same as **leprosy**

haploid /'hæplɔɪd/ *adjective* referring to a cell such as a gamete where each chromosome occurs only once. In humans the haploid number of chromosomes is 23.

hapt- /hæpt/ *prefix* relating to the sense of touch

hardening of the arteries /ˌhɑːd(ə)nɪŋ əv ðə 'ɑːtəriz/ *noun* same as **atherosclerosis**

harelip /'heəlɪp/ *noun* same as **cleft lip**

Harrison's sulcus /ˌhærɪsənz 'sʌlk(ə)s/, **Harrison's groove** /ˌhærɪs(ə)nz 'gruːv/ *noun* a hollow on either side of the chest which develops in children who have difficulty in breathing, seen especially in cases of rickets

Harris's operation /'hærɪsɪz ɒpəˌreɪʃ(ə)n/ *noun* the surgical removal of the prostate gland [After S.H. Harris (1880–1936), Australian surgeon.]

Hartmann's solution /'hɑːtmənz səˌluːʃ(ə)n/ *noun* a chemical solution used in drips to replace body fluids lost in dehydration, particularly as a result of infantile gastroenteritis [Described 1932. After Alexis Frank Hartmann (1898–1964), paediatrician, St Louis, Missouri, USA.]

Hartnup disease /'hɑːtnəp dɪˌziːz/ *noun* an inherited condition affecting amino acid metabolism and producing thick skin and impaired mental development [After the name of the family in which this hereditary disease was first recorded.]

harvest /'hɑːvɪst/ *verb* to take something for use elsewhere, e.g. a piece of skin for a graft or eggs for IVF

Hashimoto's disease /hæʃɪ'məʊtəz dɪˌziːz/ *noun* a type of goitre in middle-aged women, where the woman is sensitive to secretions from her own thyroid gland, and, in extreme cases, the face swells and the skin turns yellow [Described 1912. After Hakuru Hashimoto (1881–1934), Japanese surgeon.]

hashish /'hæʃɪʃ/ *noun* ♦ **cannabis**

haustrum /'hɔːstrəm/ *noun* a sac on the outside of the colon (NOTE: The plural is **haustra**.)

HAV *abbreviation* hepatitis A virus

Haversian canal /hə'vɜːʃ(ə)n kəˌnæl/ *noun* a fine canal which runs vertically through the Haversian systems in compact bone, containing blood vessels and lymph ducts [Described 1689. After Clopton Havers (1657–1702), English surgeon.]

Haversian system /hə'vɜːʃ(ə)n ˌsɪstəm/ *noun* a unit of compact bone built around a Haversian canal, made of a series of bony layers which form a cylinder. Also called **osteon**

hayfever /'heɪfiːvə/ *noun* inflammation in the nasal passage and eyes caused by an allergic reaction to plant pollen

Hb *abbreviation* haemoglobin

HBV *abbreviation* hepatitis B virus

hCG *abbreviation* human chorionic gonadotrophin

HCHS *abbreviation* Health and Community Health Services

HDL *abbreviation* high density lipoprotein

head /hed/ *noun* **1.** the round top part of the body, which contains the eyes, nose, mouth, brain, etc (NOTE: For other terms referring to the head, see words beginning with **cephal-**, **cephalo-**.) **2.** a rounded top part of a bone which fits into a socket ○ *head of humerus* ○ *head of femur*

headache /'hedeɪk/ *noun* a pain in the head, caused by changes in pressure in the blood vessels feeding the brain which act on the nerves. Also called **cephalalgia**

head cold /'hed kəʊld/ *noun* a minor illness, with inflammation of the nasal passages, excess mucus in the nose and sneezing

head louse /'hed laʊs/ *noun* a small insect of the *Pediculus* genus, which lives on the scalp and sucks blood. Also called **Pediculus capitis** (NOTE: The plural is **head lice**.)

Heaf test /'hiːf test/ *noun* a test in which tuberculin is injected into the skin to find out whether a person is immune to tuberculosis. ♦ **Mantoux test**

heal /hiːl/ *verb* **1.** (*of wound*) to return to a healthy state ○ *After six weeks, her wound had still not healed.* ○ *A minor cut will heal faster if it is left without a bandage.* **2.** to make someone or something get better

healing /'hiːlɪŋ/ *noun* the process of getting better ○ *a substance which will accelerate the healing process*

healing by first intention /ˌhiːlɪŋ baɪ ˌfɜːst ɪn'tenʃən/ *noun* the healing of a clean wound where the tissue reforms quickly

healing by second intention /ˌhiːlɪŋ baɪ ˌsekənd ɪn'tenʃən/ *noun* the healing of an infected wound or ulcer, which takes place slowly and may leave a permanent scar

health /helθ/ *noun* the general condition of the mind or body ○ *He's in good health.* ○ *She had suffered from bad health for some years.* ○ *The council said that fumes from the factory were a danger to public health.* ○ *All cigarette packets carry a government health warning.*

Health and Safety at Work Act /ˌhelθ ən ˌseɪfti ət 'wɜːk ˌækt/ *noun* in the UK, an Act of Parliament which rules how the health of workers should be protected by the companies they work for

Health and Safety Executive /ˌhelθ ən 'seɪfti ɪɡˌzekjʊtɪv/ *noun* in the UK, a government organisation responsible for overseeing the health and safety of workers

health authority /'helθ ɔ:ˌθɒrəti/ *noun* ♦ **Strategic Health Authority**

healthcare /'helθkeə/, **health care** *noun* the general treatment of people with medical disorders, especially the use of measures to stop a disease from occurring

healthcare assistant /'helθkeər əˌsɪstənt/ *noun* someone who assists health professionals in looking after a sick or dependent person

Healthcare Commission /'helθkeə kəˌmɪʃ(ə)n/ *noun* the independent inspection body for the NHS

healthcare delivery /'helθkeə dɪˌlɪv(ə)ri/ *noun* the provision of care and treatment by the health service

healthcare professional /'helθkeə prəˌfeʃ(ə)n(ə)l/ *noun* a qualified person who works in an occupation related to health care, e.g. a nurse

healthcare system /'helθkeə ˌsɪstəm/ *noun* any organised set of health services

health centre /'helθ ˌsentə/ *noun* a public building in which a group of doctors practise

health education /'helθ ˌedjʊkeɪʃ(ə)n/ *noun* the process of teaching people, both school children and adults, to do things to improve their health, e.g. to take more exercise

Health Education Authority /ˌhelθ ˌedjʊ ˈkeɪʃ(ə)n ɔ:ˌθɒriti/ *noun* a government health promotion agency in England designed to help people make aware of how they can improve their health. Abbreviation **HEA**

health food /'helθ fu:d/ *noun* food that is regarded as good for health, especially containing ingredients such as cereals, dried fruit and nuts and without additives

health inequality /'helθ ɪnɪˌkwɒləti/ *noun* the differences that exist in health across the social classes, with poorer people tending to experience poorer health

health information service /ˌhelθ ɪnfə ˈmeɪʃ(ə)n ˌsɜ:vɪs/ *noun* a nation-wide information service delivered via a free telephone helpline. Abbreviation **HIS**

health insurance /'helθ ɪnˌʃʊərəns/ *noun* insurance which pays the cost of treatment for illness

Health Ombudsman /'helθ ˌɒmbʊdzmən/ *noun* same as **Health Service Commissioner**

health promotion /'helθ prəˌməʊʃ(ə)n/ *noun* the act of improving the health of a particular community or of the public generally, e.g. using health education, immunisation and screening

Health Protection Agency /ˌhelθ prə ˈtekʃ(ə)n ˌeɪdʒənsi/ *noun* a national organisation for England and Wales, established in 2003, dedicated to the protection of people's health, especially by reducing the impact of infectious diseases, chemicals, poisons and radiation. It brings together existing sources of expertise in public health, communicable diseases, emergency planning, infection control, poisons and radiation hazards. Abbreviation **HPA**

health service /'helθ ˌsɜ:vɪs/ *noun* an organisation which is in charge of providing health care to a particular community

Health Service Commissioner /ˌhelθ ˌsɜ:vɪs kəˈmɪʃ(ə)nə/, **Health Service Ombudsman** /'helθ ˌsɜ:vɪs ˌɒmbʊdzmən/ *noun* in the UK, an official who investigates complaints from the public about the National Health Service

health service manager /ˌhelθ ˌsɜ:vɪs ˈmænɪdʒə/ *noun* someone who is responsible for the provision of local health care, through the management of hospital, GP, and community health services

health service planning /ˌhelθ ˌsɜ:vɪs ˈplænɪŋ/ *noun* the process of deciding what the health care needs of a community are, with the help of statistics, and what resources can be provided for that community

health service reforms /ˌhelθ ˌsɜ:vɪs rɪ ˈfɔ:mz/ *plural noun* any of several reforms to the NHS, the most recent package of reforms being that introduced in 2002

health visitor /'helθ ˌvɪzɪtə/ *noun* a registered nurse with qualifications in midwifery or obstetrics and preventive medicine, who visits mothers and babies and sick people in their homes and advises on treatment

hear /hɪə/ *verb* to sense sounds with the ears ○ *I can't hear what you're saying.* (NOTE: **hearing – heard**)

hearing /'hɪərɪŋ/ *noun* the ability to hear, or the function performed by the ear of sensing sounds and sending sound impulses to the brain ○ *His hearing is failing.* (NOTE: For other terms referring to hearing, see words beginning with **audio-**.)

hearing aid /'hɪərɪŋ eɪd/ *noun* a small electronic device fitted into or near the ear, to improve someone's hearing by making the sounds louder

hearing-impaired /ˌhɪərɪŋ ɪmˈpeəd/ *adjective* having a degree of hearing loss

hearing loss /'hɪərɪŋ lɒs/ *noun* partial or complete loss of the ability to hear

heart /hɑ:t/ *noun* the main organ in the body which maintains the circulation of the blood around the body by its pumping action ○ *The doctor listened to his heart.* ○ *She has heart trouble* (NOTE: For other terms referring to the heart, see also words beginning with **cardi-**,**cardio-**.)

heart attack /'hɑ:t əˌtæk/ *noun* a condition in which the heart has a reduced blood supply because one of the arteries becomes blocked by a blood clot, causing myocardial ischaemia and myocardial infarction (*informal*)

heartbeat /ˈhɑːtbiːt/ *noun* the regular noise made by the heart as it pumps blood

heart block /ˈhɑːt blɒk/ *noun* the slowing of the action of the heart because the impulses from the sinoatrial node to the ventricles are delayed or interrupted. There are either longer impulses (first degree block) or missing impulses (second degree block) or no impulses at all (complete heart block), in which case the ventricles continue to beat slowly and independently of the sinoatrial node.

heartburn /ˈhɑːtbɜːn/ *noun* indigestion which causes a burning feeling in the stomach and oesophagus, and a flow of acid saliva into the mouth (*informal*)

heart bypass /ˈhɑːt ˌbaɪpɑːs ɒpəˌreɪʃ(ə)n/, **heart bypass operation** *noun* same as **coronary artery bypass graft**

heart disease /ˈhɑːt dɪˌziːz/ *noun* any disease of the heart in general

heart failure /ˈhɑːt ˌfeɪljə/ *noun* the failure of the heart to maintain the output of blood to meet the demands of the body. It may affect the left or right sides of the heart, or both sides.

heart-lung machine /ˌhɑːt ˈlʌŋ məˌʃiːn/ *noun* a machine used to pump blood round the body and maintain the supply of oxygen to the blood during heart surgery

heart-lung transplant /ˌhɑːt ˈlʌŋ ˌtrænsplɑːnt/ *noun* an operation to transplant a new heart and lungs into someone

heart massage /ˈhɑːt ˌmæsɑːʒ/ *noun* a treatment which involves pressing on the chest to make a heart which has stopped beating start working again

heart murmur /ˈhɑːt ˌmɜːmə/ *noun* an unusual sound made by turbulent blood flow, sometimes as a result of valve disease

heart rate /ˈhɑːt reɪt/ *noun* the number of times the heart beats per minute

heart sounds /ˈhɑːt saʊndz/ *plural noun* two different sounds made by the heart as it beats. ◊ **lubb-dupp**

heart surgeon /ˈhɑːt ˌsɜːdʒən/ *noun* a surgeon who specialises in operations on the heart

heart surgery /ˈhɑːt ˌsɜːdʒəri/ *noun* a surgical operation to remedy a condition of the heart

heart tamponade /ˈhɑːt tæmpəˌneɪd/ *noun* same as **cardiac tamponade**

heart transplant /ˈhɑːt ˌtrænsplɑːnt/ *noun* a surgical operation to transplant a heart into someone

heat rash /ˈhiːt ræʃ/ *noun* same as **miliaria**

heat spots /ˈhiːt spɒts/ *plural noun* little red spots which develop on the face in very hot weather

heatstroke /ˈhiːtstrəʊk/ *noun* a condition in which someone becomes too hot and his or her body temperature rises abnormally, leading to headaches, stomach cramps and sometimes loss of consciousness

heat therapy /ˈhiːt ˌθerəpi/, **heat treatment** /ˈhiːt ˌtriːtmənt/ *noun* same as **thermotherapy**

heavy period /ˌhevi ˈpɪəriəd/ *noun* a monthly period during which a woman loses an unusually large amount of blood. It is often painful and sometimes indicates possible health problems, such as fibroids or hypothyroidism.

Heberden's node /ˌhiːbədənz ˈnəʊd/ *noun* a small bony lump which develops on the end joints of fingers in osteoarthritis [Described 1802. After William Heberden (1767–1845), British physician, specialist in rheumatic diseases.]

hebetude /ˈhebɪtjuːd/ *noun* dullness of the senses during acute fever, which makes the person uninterested in his or her surroundings and unable to respond to stimuli

hectic /ˈhektɪk/ *adjective* recurring regularly

hectic fever /ˌhektɪk ˈfiːvə/ *noun* an attack of fever which occurs each day in someone who has tuberculosis

heel /hiːl/ *noun* the back part of the foot

heel bone /ˈhiːl bəʊn/ *noun* the bone forming the heel, beneath the talus. Also called **calcaneus**

Hegar's sign /ˈheɪgəz ˌsaɪn/ *noun* a way of detecting pregnancy, by inserting the fingers into the uterus and pressing with the other hand on the pelvic cavity to feel if the neck of the uterus has become soft [After Alfred Hegar (1830–1914), Professor of Obstetrics and Gynaecology at Freiburg, Germany.]

Heimlich manoeuvre /ˈhaɪmlɪk məˌnuːvə/ *noun* an emergency treatment for choking, in which a strong upward push beneath the breastbone of a patient clasped from behind forces the blockage out of the windpipe

helco- /helkəʊ/ *prefix* relating to an ulcer

helcoplasty /ˈhelkəʊplæsti/ *noun* a skin graft to cover an ulcer to aid healing

Helicobacter pylori /ˌhelɪkəʊbæktə paɪ ˈlɔːriː/ *noun* a bacterium found in gastric secretions, strongly associated with duodenal ulcers and gastric carcinoma. Abbreviation **H pylori**

helicopter-based emergency medical services /ˌhelɪkɒptə beɪst ɪˌmɜːdʒənsi ˈmedɪk(ə)l ˌsɜːvɪsɪz/ *plural noun* full form of **HEMS**

helio- /hiːliəʊ/ *prefix* relating to the sun

heliotherapy /ˌhiːliəʊˈθerəpi/ *noun* treatment by sunlight or sunbathing

helium /ˈhiːliəm/ *noun* a very light gas used in combination with oxygen, especially to relieve asthma or sickness caused by decompression (NOTE: The chemical symbol is **He**.)

helix /'hi:lɪks/ *noun* the curved outer edge of the ear

Heller's operation /'helǝz ɒpǝ,reɪʃ(ǝ)n/ *noun* same as **cardiomyotomy** [After E. Heller (1877–1964), German surgeon.]

Heller's test /'helǝz test/ *noun* a test for protein in the urine [After Johann Florenz Heller (1813–71), Austrian physician.]

Hellin's law /,helɪnz 'lɔː/ *noun* a finding which states that twins should occur naturally once in 90 live births, triplets once in 8,100 live births, quadruplets once in 729, 000 live births, and quintuplets once in 65, 610, 000 live births (NOTE: Since the 1960s the numbers have changed due to fertility treatment. For example, twins now occur once in only 38 births.)

HELLP syndrome /'help ,sɪndrǝʊm/ *noun* a serious pre-eclamptic disorder which makes it necessary to terminate a pregnancy. Full form **haemolysis-elevated liver enzymes–low platelet count syndrome**

helminth /'helmɪnθ/ *noun* a parasitic worm, e.g. a tapeworm or fluke

helminthiasis /,helmɪn'θaɪǝsɪs/ *noun* infestation with parasitic worms

heloma /hɪ'lǝʊmǝ/ *noun* same as **corn**

helper T-cell /,helpǝ 'tiː sel/ *noun* a type of white blood cell that stimulates the production of cells that destroy antigens

hemeralopia /,hemǝrǝ'lǝʊpiǝ/ *noun* a usually congenital condition in which someone is able to see better in bad light than in ordinary daylight. Also called **day blindness**

hemi- /hemi/ *prefix* half

hemianopia /,hemiǝ'nǝʊpiǝ/ *noun* a state of partial blindness in which someone has only half the usual field of vision in each eye

hemiarthroplasty /,hemi'ɑːθrǝʊplæsti/ *noun* an operation to repair a joint which replaces one of its surfaces with an artificial substance, often metal

hemiballismus /,hemibǝ'lɪzmǝs/ *noun* a sudden movement of the limbs on one side of the body, caused by a disease of the basal ganglia

hemicolectomy /,hemikǝ'lektǝmi/ *noun* the surgical removal of part of the colon

hemimelia /,hemi'miːliǝ/ *noun* a congenital condition in which someone has absent or extremely short arms or legs

hemiparesis /,hemipǝ'riːsɪs/ *noun* slight paralysis of the muscles of one side of the body

hemiplegia /,hemi'pliːdʒǝ/ *noun* severe paralysis affecting one side of the body due to damage of the central nervous system. Compare **diplegia**

hemisphere /'hemɪsfɪǝ/ *noun* half of a sphere

HEMS /hemz/ *plural noun* a system of delivering a paramedic crew to the scene of an accident or medical emergency by helicopter and then transporting patients to the nearest major hospital or specialist unit. Full form **helicopter-based emergency medical services**

Henderson's model /'hendǝs(ǝ)nz ,mɒd(ǝ)l/ *noun* a model of nurse–patient relationships based on 14 basic principles of nursing. The main idea is that "the nurse does for others what they would do for themselves if they had the strength, the will, and the knowledge…but that the nurse makes the patient independent of him or her as soon as possible".

Henle's loop /,henliːz 'luːp/ *noun* same as **loop of Henle** [Described 1862. After Friedrich Gustav Jakob Henle (1809–85), Professor of Anatomy at Göttingen, Germany.]

Henoch-Schönlein purpura /,henǝk ,ʃɜːnlaɪn 'pɜːpjʊrǝ/, **Henoch's purpura** /,henǝks 'pɜːpjʊrǝ/ *noun* a condition in which blood vessels become inflamed and bleed into the skin, causing a rash called purpura and also pain in the stomach and the joints, vomiting and diarrhoea. It often occurs after an upper respiratory infection, mostly in children aged two to 11. [Described 1832 by Schönlein and 1865 by Henoch. Eduard Heinrich Henoch (1820–1910), Professor of Paediatrics at Berlin, Germany; Johannes Lukas Schönlein (1793–1864), physician and pathologist at Würzburg, Zürich and Berlin.]

heparin /'hepǝrɪn/ *noun* an anticoagulant substance found in the liver and lungs, and also produced artificially for use in the treatment of thrombosis

hepat- /hɪpæt/ *prefix* same as **hepato-** (used before vowels)

hepatectomy /,hepǝ'tektǝmi/ *noun* the surgical removal of part of the liver

hepatic /hɪ'pætɪk/ *adjective* referring to the liver

hepatic artery /hɪ,pætɪk 'ɑːtǝri/ *noun* an artery which takes the blood to the liver

hepatic cell /hɪ,pætɪk 'sel/ *noun* an epithelial cell of the liver acini

hepatic duct /hɪ,pætɪk 'dʌkt/ *noun* a duct which links the liver to the bile duct leading to the duodenum

hepatic flexure /hɪ,pætɪk 'flekʃǝ/ *noun* a bend in the colon, where the ascending and transverse colons join

hepaticostomy /hɪ,pætɪ'kɒstǝmi/ *noun* a surgical operation to make an opening in the hepatic duct taking bile from the liver

hepatic portal system /hɪ,pætɪk 'pɔːt(ǝ)l ,sɪstǝm/ *noun* a group of veins linking to form the portal vein, which brings blood from the pancreas, spleen, gall bladder and the abdominal part of the alimentary canal to the liver

hepatic vein /hɪˌpætɪk 'veɪn/ *noun* a vein which takes blood from the liver to the inferior vena cava

hepatitis /ˌhepə'taɪtɪs/ *noun* inflammation of the liver through disease or drugs

hepatitis A /ˌhepətaɪtɪs 'eɪ/ *noun* a relatively mild form of viral hepatitis that is transmitted through contaminated food and water

hepatitis A virus /ˌhepətaɪtɪs 'eɪ ˌvaɪrəs/ *noun* a virus which causes hepatitis A. Abbreviation **HAV**

hepatitis B /ˌhepətaɪtɪs 'biː/ *noun* a severe form of viral hepatitis that is transmitted by contact with infected blood or other body fluids

hepatitis B virus /ˌhepətaɪtɪs 'biː ˌvaɪrəs/ *noun* a virus which causes hepatitis B. Abbreviation **HBV**

hepatitis C /ˌhepətaɪtɪs 'siː/ *noun* a form of viral hepatitis that is transmitted by contact with infected blood or other body fluids but is often without symptoms (NOTE: It was formerly called non-A, non-B hepatitis.)

hepatitis C virus /ˌhepətaɪtɪs 'siː ˌvaɪrəs/ *noun* a virus which causes hepatitis C. Abbreviation **HCV**

hepato- /hepətəʊ/ *prefix* referring to the liver

hepatocellular /ˌhepətəʊ'seljʊlə/ *adjective* referring to liver cells

hepatocellular jaundice /ˌhepətəʊˌseljʊlə 'dʒɔːndɪs/ *noun* jaundice caused by injury to or disease of the liver cells

hepatocirrhosis /ˌhepətəʊsɪ'rəʊsɪs/ *noun* same as **cirrhosis**

hepatocyte /'hepətəʊsaɪt, hɪ'pætəsaɪt/ *noun* a liver cell which synthesises and stores substances, and produces bile

hepatogenous /ˌhepə'tɒdʒənəs/ *noun* referring to or originating in the liver ○ *hepatogenous jaundice*

hepatolenticular degeneration /ˌhepətəʊlen,tɪkjʊlə dɪ,dʒenə'reɪʃ(ə)n/ *noun* same as **Wilson's disease**

hepatoma /ˌhepə'təʊmə/ *noun* a malignant tumour of the liver formed of mature cells, especially found in people with cirrhosis

hepatomegaly /ˌhepətəʊ'megəli/ *noun* a condition in which the liver becomes very large

hepatosplenomegaly /ˌhepətəʊˌspliːnəʊ 'megəli/ *noun* enlargement of both the liver and the spleen, as occurs in leukaemia or lymphoma

hepatotoxic /ˌhepətəʊ'tɒksɪk/ *adjective* destroying the liver cells

herbalism /'hɜːbəlɪz(ə)m/ *noun* ♦ **herbal medicine**

herbalist /'hɜːbəlɪst/ *noun* a person who treats illnesses or disorders with substances extracted from plants

herbal medicine /ˌhɜːb(ə)l 'med(ə)sɪn/ *noun* a system of medical treatment involving the use of substances extracted from plants

herbal remedy /ˌhɜːb(ə)l 'remədi/ *noun* a medicine made from plants, e.g. an infusion made from dried leaves or flowers in hot water

herd immunity /'hɜːd ɪˌmjuːnɪti/ *noun* the fact of a group of people being resistant to a specific disease, because many individuals in the group are immune to or immunised against the microorganism which causes it

hereditary /hə'redɪt(ə)ri/ *adjective* passed as from parents to children through the genes

hereditary spherocytosis /hɪˌredɪt(ə)ri ˌsfɪərəʊsaɪ'təʊsɪs/ *noun* same as **acholuric jaundice**

heredity /hə'redɪti/ *noun* the process by which genetically controlled characteristics pass from parents to children

Hering-Breuer reflexes /ˌherɪŋ 'brɔɪə ˌriːfleksɪz/ *plural noun* the reflexes which maintain the usual rhythmic inflation and deflation of the lungs

hermaphrodite /hɜː'mæfrədaɪt/ *noun* a person with both male and female characteristics

hermaphroditism /hɜː'mæfrədaɪtɪz(ə)m/ *noun* a condition in which a person has both male and female characteristics

hernia /'hɜːniə/ *noun* a condition in which an organ bulges through a hole or weakness in the wall which surrounds it. Also called **rupture**

hernial /'hɜːniəl/ *adjective* referring to a hernia

hernial sac /ˌhɜːniəl 'sæk/ *noun* a sac formed where a membrane has pushed through a cavity in the body

herniated /'hɜːnieɪtɪd/ *adjective* referring to an organ which has developed a hernia

herniation /ˌhɜːni'eɪʃ(ə)n/ *noun* the development of a hernia

hernio- /hɜːniəʊ/ *prefix* relating to a hernia

hernioplasty /'hɜːniəʊˌplæsti/ *noun* a surgical operation to reduce a hernia

herniorrhaphy /ˌhɜːni'ɔːrəfi/ *noun* a surgical operation to remove a hernia and repair the organ through which it protruded

herniotomy /ˌhɜːni'ɒtəmi/ *noun* a surgical operation to remove a hernial sac

heroin /'herəʊɪn/ *noun* a narcotic drug in the form of a white powder derived from morphine

herpes /'hɜːpiːz/ *noun* inflammation of the skin or mucous membrane, caused by a virus, where small blisters are formed

herpes simplex /ˌhɜːpiːz 'sɪmpleks/ *noun* **1.** (*Type I*) a virus that produces a painful blister, called a cold sore, usually on the lips **2.** (*Type II*) a sexually transmitted disease which forms blisters in the genital region. Also called **genital herpes**

herpesvirus /'hɜːpiːz,vaɪrəs/ *noun* one of a group of viruses which cause herpes and chickenpox (herpesvirus Type I), and genital herpes (herpesvirus Type II)

herpes zoster /,hɜːpiːz 'zɒstə/ *noun* inflammation of a sensory nerve, characterised by pain along the nerve and causing a line of blisters to form on the skin, usually found mainly on the abdomen or back, or on the face. Also called **shingles**, **zona**

herpetic /hɜː'petɪk/ *adjective* referring to herpes

hetero- /hetərəʊ/ *prefix* different

heterochromia /,hetərəʊ'krəʊmiə/ *noun* a condition in which the irises of the eyes are different colours

heterogeneous /,hetərəʊ'dʒiːniəs/ *adjective* having different characteristics or qualities (NOTE: Do not confuse with **heterogenous**.)

heterogenous /,hetə'rɒdʒɪnəs/ *adjective* coming from a different source (NOTE: Do not confuse with **heterogeneous**.)

heterograft /'hetərəʊɡrɑːft/ *noun* tissue taken from one species and grafted onto an individual of another species. Compare **homograft**

heterologous /,hetə'rɒləɡəs/ *adjective* of a different type

heterophoria /,hetərəʊ'fɔːriə/ *noun* a condition in which if an eye is covered it tends to squint

heteroplasty /'hetərəʊplæsti/ *noun* same as **heterograft**

heteropsia /,hetə'rɒpsiə/ *noun* a condition in which the two eyes see differently

heterosexual /,hetərəʊ'sekʃuəl/ *adjective* attracted to people of the opposite sex or relating to relations between males and females ■ *noun* a person who is sexually attracted to people of the opposite sex. Compare **bisexual**, **homosexual**

heterosexuality /,hetərəʊsekʃu'ælɪti/ *noun* sexual attraction towards persons of the opposite sex

heterotopia /,hetərəʊ'təʊpiə/ *noun* **1.** a state where an organ is placed in a different position from usual or is malformed or deformed **2.** the development of tissue which is not natural to the part in which it is produced

heterotropia /,hetərəʊ'trəʊpiə/ *noun* same as **strabismus**

heterozygous /,hetərəʊ'zaɪɡəs/ *adjective* having two or more different versions of a specific gene. Compare **homozygous**

hex- /heks/ *prefix* same as **hexa-** (NOTE: used before vowels)

hexa- /heksə/ *prefix* six

HFEA *abbreviation* Human Fertilization and Embryology Authority

hGH *abbreviation* human growth hormone

HGPRT *abbreviation* hypoxanthine guanine phosphoribosyl transferase. ◊ **HPRT**

hiatus /haɪ'eɪtəs/ *noun* an opening or space

hiatus hernia /haɪ,eɪtəs 'hɜːniə/, **hiatal hernia** /haɪ,eɪt(ə)l 'hɜːniə/ *noun* a hernia where the stomach bulges through the opening in the diaphragm muscle through which the oesophagus passes

Hib /hɪb/ *abbreviation Haemophilus influenzae* type B

Hib vaccine /'hɪb ,væksiːn/ *noun* a vaccine used to inoculate against the bacterium *Haemophilius influenzae* that causes meningitis

hiccup /'hɪkʌp/, **hiccough** *noun* a spasm in the diaphragm which causes a sudden inhalation of breath followed by sudden closure of the glottis which makes a characteristic sound ○ *She had an attack of hiccups* or *had a hiccuping attack* or *got the hiccups.* Also called **singultus**

Hickman catheter /'hɪkmən ,kæθɪtə/, **Hickman line** /'hɪkmən laɪn/ *noun* a plastic tube which is put into the large vein above the heart so that drugs can be given and blood samples can be taken easily

hidr- /haɪdr/ *prefix* referring to sweat

hidradenitis /,haɪdrədə'naɪtɪs/ *noun* inflammation of the sweat glands

hidrosis /haɪ'drəʊsɪs/ *noun* sweating, especially when it is excessive

hidrotic /haɪ'drɒtɪk/ *adjective* referring to sweating ■ *noun* a substance which makes someone sweat

high-altitude sickness /,haɪ 'æltɪtjuːd ,sɪknəs/ *noun* same as **altitude sickness**

high blood pressure /,haɪ 'blʌd ,preʃə/ *noun* same as **hypertension**

high-calorie diet /haɪ ,kæləri 'daɪət/ *noun* a diet containing over 4000 calories per day

high-density lipoprotein /,haɪ ,densɪti 'lɪpəʊ,prəʊtiːn/ *noun* a lipoprotein with a low percentage of cholesterol. Abbreviation **HDL**

high-fibre diet /,haɪ ,faɪbə 'daɪət/ *noun* a diet which contains a high percentage of cereals, nuts, fruit and vegetables

high-protein diet /,haɪ ,prəʊtiːn 'daɪət/ *noun* a diet containing mostly foods high in protein and low in carbohydrates and saturated fat, adopted by people who are trying to lose weight

hilar /'haɪlə/ *adjective* referring to a hilum

hilum /'haɪləm/ *noun* a hollow where blood vessels or nerve fibres enter an organ such as a kidney or lung (NOTE: The plural is **hila**.)

hindbrain /'haɪndbreɪn/ *noun* the part of brain of an embryo from which the medulla oblongata, the pons and the cerebellum eventually develop

hindgut /'haɪndɡʌt/ *noun* part of an embryo which develops into the colon and rectum

hinge joint /'hɪndʒ dʒɔɪnt/ *noun* same as **ginglymus**

hip /hɪp/ *noun* a ball and socket joint where the thigh bone or femur joins the acetabulum of the hip bone

hip bone /'hɪp bəʊn/ *noun* a bone made of the ilium, the ischium and the pubis which are fused together, forming part of the pelvic girdle. Also called **innominate bone**

hip fracture /'hɪp ˌfræktʃə/ *noun* a fracture of the ball at the top of the femur

hip girdle /'hɪp ˌgɜːd(ə)l/ *noun* same as **pelvic girdle**

hip joint /'hɪp dʒɔɪnt/ *noun* the place where the hip is joined to the upper leg. See illustration at PELVIS in Supplement

Hippel-Lindau /ˌhɪpəl 'lɪndaʊ/ ♦ **von Hippel-Lindau syndrome**

hippocampus /ˌhɪpəʊ'kæmpəs/ *noun* a long rounded elevation projecting into the lateral ventricle in the brain

Hippocratic oath /ˌhɪpəkrætɪk 'əʊθ/ *noun* an ethical code observed by doctors, by which they will treat patients equally, put patients' welfare first and not discuss openly the details of a patient's case

hip replacement /'hɪp rɪˌpleɪsmənt/ *noun* a surgical operation to replace the whole ball and socket joint at the hip with an artificial one

Hirschsprung's disease /'hɪəʃsprʌŋz dɪ ˌziːz/ *noun* a congenital condition where parts of the lower colon lack nerve cells, making peristalsis impossible, so that food accumulates in the upper colon which becomes swollen [Described 1888. After Harald Hirschsprung (1830–1916), Professor of Paediatrics in Copenhagen, Denmark.]

hirsute /'hɜːsjuːt/ *adjective* with a lot of hair

hirsutism /'hɜːsjuːtɪz(ə)m/ *noun* the condition of having excessive hair, especially a condition in which a woman grows hair on the body in the same way as a man

hirudin /hɪ'ruːdɪn/ *noun* an anticoagulant substance produced by leeches, which is injected into the bloodstream while the leech is feeding on a body

HIS *abbreviation* Health Information Service

hist- /hɪst/ same as **histo-** (NOTE: used before vowels)

histamine /'hɪstəmiːn/ *noun* a substance released in response to allergens from mast cells throughout the body. Histamines dilate blood vessels, constrict the cells of smooth muscles and cause an increase in acid secretions in the stomach.

histamine test /'hɪstəmiːn test/ *noun* a test to determine the acidity of gastric juice

histaminic /ˌhɪstə'mɪnɪk/ *adjective* referring to histamines

histiocyte /'hɪstɪəʊsaɪt/ *noun* a macrophage of the connective tissue, involved in tissue defence

histiocytosis /ˌhɪstɪəʊsaɪ'təʊsɪs/ *noun* a condition in which histiocytes are present in the blood

histiocytosis X /ˌhɪstɪəʊsaɪˌtəʊsɪs 'eks/ *noun* any form of histiocytosis where the cause is not known, e.g. Hand-Schüller-Christian disease

histo- /hɪstəʊ/ *prefix* relating to the body's tissue ○ *histology*

histocompatible /ˌhɪstəʊkəm'pætɪb(ə)l/ *adjective* referring to tissues from two individuals which have compatible antigens

histogram /'hɪstəgræm/ *noun* a way of displaying frequency values as columns whose height is proportional to the corresponding frequency ○ *a histogram showing numbers of patients with the condition in each age group*

histological /ˌhɪstə'lɒdʒɪk(ə)l/ *adjective* referring to histology

histological grade /ˌhɪstəlɒdʒɪk(ə)l 'greɪd/ *noun* a system of classifying tumours according to how malignant they are

histology /hɪ'stɒlədʒi/ *noun* the study of the anatomy of tissue cells and minute cellular structure

histolysis /hɪ'stɒləsɪs/ *noun* the disintegration of tissue

histotoxic /ˌhɪstəʊ'tɒksɪk/ *adjective* referring to a substance which is poisonous to tissue

HIV *abbreviation* human immunodeficiency virus

hives /haɪvz/ *noun* same as **urticaria** (NOTE: Takes a singular verb.)

HIV-negative /ˌeɪtʃ aɪ ˌviː 'negətɪv/ *adjective* referring to someone who has been tested and shown not to have HIV

HIV-positive /ˌeɪtʃ aɪ ˌviː 'pɒzɪtɪv/ *adjective* referring to someone who has been tested and shown to have HIV

HLA *abbreviation* human leucocyte antigen

HLA system /ˌeɪtʃ el ˌeɪ ˌsɪstəm/ *noun* a system of HLA antigens on the surface of cells which need to be histocompatible to allow transplants to take place

HMO *abbreviation* US Health Maintenance Organization

hobnail liver /ˌhɒbneɪl 'lɪvə/ *noun* same as **atrophic cirrhosis**

Hodgkin's disease /'hɒdʒkɪnz dɪˌziːz/ *noun* a malignant disease in which the lymph glands are enlarged and there is an increase in the lymphoid tissues in the liver, spleen and bone marrow. It is frequently fatal if not treated early. [Described 1832. After Thomas Hodgkin (1798–1866), British physician.]

hoist /hɔɪst/ *noun* a device with pulleys and wires for raising a bed or a patient

hole in the heart /ˌhəʊl ɪn ðə ˈhɑːt/ *noun* same as **septal defect** (*informal*)

holism /ˈhəʊlɪz(ə)m/ *noun* the theory that all of a person's physical, mental and social conditions should be considered in the treatment of his or her illness

holistic /həʊˈlɪstɪk/ *adjective* referring to a method of treatment involving all of someone's mental and family circumstances rather than just dealing with the condition from which he or she is suffering

holistic care /həʊˌlɪstɪk ˈkeə/ *noun* the care and treatment of a whole person rather than just of his or her medical symptoms

holo- /hɒləʊ/ *prefix* entire, complete

holocrine /ˈhɒləkrɪn/ *adjective* referring to a gland where the secretions are made up of disintegrated cells of the gland itself

Homans' sign /ˈhəʊmənz saɪn/ *noun* pain in the calf when the foot is bent back, a sign of deep-vein thrombosis [Described 1941. After John Homans (1877–1954), Professor of Clinical Surgery at Harvard, USA.]

home help /ˌhəʊm ˈhelp/ *noun* **1.** a person who is paid to carry out ordinary domestic tasks such as cleaning and cooking for people who are unable to carry out these tasks for themselves **2.** same as **home help service**

home help service /ˌhəʊm ˈhelp ˌsɜːvɪs/ *noun* a publicly funded support service provided mainly for elderly and disabled people which offers help with ordinary household tasks of a non-nursing nature, such as cooking and washing to help people in their own homes

homeo- /həʊmiəʊ/ *prefix* like or similar

homeopathic /ˌhəʊmiəˈpæθɪk/, **homoeopathic** *adjective* **1.** referring to homeopathy ○ *a homeopathic clinic* ○ *She is having a course of homeopathic treatment.* **2.** referring to a drug which is given in very small quantities

homeopathist /ˌhəʊmiˈɒpəθɪst/, **homoeopathist** *noun* a person who practises homeopathy

homeopathy /ˌhəʊmiˈɒpəθi/, **homoeopathy** *noun* the treatment of a condition by giving the person very small quantities of a substance which, when given to a healthy person, would cause symptoms like those of the condition being treated. Compare **allopathy**

homeostasis /ˌhəʊmiəʊˈsteɪsɪs/ *noun* the process by which the functions and chemistry of a cell or internal organ are kept stable, even when external conditions vary greatly

homo- /həʊməʊ/ *prefix* the same

homoeo- /həʊmiəʊ/ *prefix* another spelling of **homeo-** (*used before vowels*)

homogenise /həˈmɒdʒənaɪz/, **homogenize** *verb* to give something a uniform nature

homograft /ˈhɒməɡrɑːft/ *noun* the graft of an organ or tissue from a donor to a recipient of the same species, e.g. from one person to another. Also called **allograft**. Compare **heterograft**

homolateral /ˌhɒməˈlæt(ə)rəl/ *adjective* same as **ipsilateral**

homologous /hɒˈmɒləɡəs/ *adjective* **1.** of the same type **2.** referring to chromosomes which form a pair

homonymous hemianopia /həˌmɒnɪməs ˌhemiəˈnəʊpiə/ *noun* a condition in which the same half of the field of vision is lost in each eye

homosexual /ˌhəʊməʊˈsekʃuəl/ *adjective* referring to homosexuality ■ *noun* a person who is sexually attracted to people of the same sex. Compare **bisexual**, **heterosexual** (NOTE: Although **homosexual** can apply to both males and females, it is commonly used for males only, and **lesbian** is used for females.)

homosexuality /ˌhəʊməʊsekʃuˈælɪti/ *noun* sexual attraction to people of the same sex or sexual relations with people of the same sex

homozygous /ˌhəʊməʊˈzaɪɡəs/ *adjective* having two identical versions of a specific gene. Compare **heterozygous**

hookworm /ˈhʊkwɜːm/ *noun* a parasitic worm

hookworm disease /ˈhʊkwɜːm dɪˌziːz/ *noun* ♦ **ancylostomiasis**

hordeolum /hɔːˈdiːələm/ *noun* an infection of the gland at the base of an eyelash. Also called **stye**

horizontal fissure /ˌhɒrɪzɒnt(ə)l ˈfɪʃə/ *noun* ANAT a horizontal groove between the superior and middle lobes of a lung. See illustration at LUNGS in Supplement

hormone /ˈhɔːməʊn/ *noun* a substance which is produced by one part of the body, especially the endocrine glands and is carried to another part of the body by the bloodstream where it has particular effects or functions

hormone replacement therapy /ˌhɔːməʊn rɪˈpleɪsmənt ˌθerəpi/, **hormone therapy** *noun* **1.** treatment for someone whose endocrine glands have been removed **2.** treatment to relieve the symptoms of the menopause by supplying oestrogen and reducing the risk of osteoporosis ▶ abbreviation **HRT**

Horner's syndrome /ˈhɔːnəz ˌsɪndrəʊm/ *noun* a condition caused by paralysis of the sympathetic nerve in one side of the neck, making the eyelids hang down and the pupils contract [Described 1869. After Johann Friedrich Horner (1831–86), Professor of Ophthalmology in Zürich, Switzerland.]

horny /ˈhɔːni/ *adjective* referring to skin which is very hard (NOTE: For terms referring to horny tissue, see words beginning with **kerat-**, **kerato-**.)

horseshoe kidney /ˌhɔːʃuː ˈkɪdni/ *noun* a congenital condition of the kidney, where sometimes the upper but usually the lower parts of both kidneys are joined together

Horton's syndrome /ˈhɔːt(ə)nz ˌsɪndrəʊm/ *noun* a severe headache, often with constant pain around one eye, which starts usually within a few hours of going to sleep. It is caused by the release of histamine in the body. [After Bayard Taylor Horton (1895–1980), US physician.]

hospice /ˈhɒspɪs/ *noun* a hospital which offers palliative care for terminally ill people

hospital /ˈhɒspɪt(ə)l/ *noun* a place where sick or injured people are looked after

hospital-acquired infection /ˌhɒspɪt(ə)l ə ˌkwaɪəd ɪnˈfekʃən/ *noun* a disease caught during a stay in hospital

Hospital Activity Analysis /ˌhɒspɪt(ə)l æk ˈtɪvɪti əˌnæləsɪs/ *noun* a regular detailed report on patients in hospitals, including information about treatment, length of stay and outcome

hospital care /ˈhɒspɪt(ə)l keə/ *noun* treatment in a hospital

hospital doctor /ˌhɒspɪt(ə)l ˈdɒktə/ *noun* a doctor who works only in a hospital and does not receive people in his or her own surgery

hospital gangrene /ˌhɒspɪt(ə)l ˈɡæŋɡriːn/ *noun* gangrene caused by insanitary hospital conditions

hospital infection /ˈhɒspɪt(ə)l ɪnˌfekʃən/ *noun* an infection which someone gets during a hospital visit, or one which develops among hospital staff

COMMENT: Hospital infection is an increasingly common problem due to growing antimicrobial resistance and inappropriate antibiotic use. Strains of bacteria such as MRSA have evolved which seem to be more easily transmitted between patients and are difficult to treat.

hospitalise /ˈhɒspɪt(ə)laɪz/, **hospitalize** *verb* to send someone to hospital ○ *He is so ill that he has had to be hospitalised.*

hospital trust /ˈhɒspɪt(ə)l trʌst/ *noun* same as **self-governing hospital**

host /həʊst/ *noun* a person or animal on which a parasite lives

hot /hɒt/ *adjective* very warm or having a high temperature

hot flush /ˌhɒt ˈflʌʃ/ *noun* a condition in menopausal women, in which the woman becomes hot and sweats, and which is often accompanied by redness of the skin

hotpack /ˈhɒtpæk/ *noun* a cloth bag or a pad filled with gel or grains which can be heated and applied to the skin to relieve pain or stiffness

hourglass contraction /ˈaʊəɡlɑːs kən ˌtrækʃən/ *noun* a condition in which an organ such as the stomach is constricted in the centre

hourglass stomach /ˈaʊəɡlɑːs ˌstʌmək/ *noun* a condition in which the wall of the stomach is pulled in so that it is divided into two cavities, cardiac and pyloric

houseman /ˈhaʊsmən/ *noun* same as **house officer**

house officer /ˈhaʊs ˌɒfɪsə/ *noun* a doctor who works in a hospital as a house surgeon or house physician during the final year of training before registration by the General Medical Council

HPA *abbreviation* Health Protection Agency

HPRT /ˌeɪtʃ piː ɑː ˈtiː/ *noun* an enzyme that is lacking in children, usually boys, who have Lesch-Nyhan disease. Full form **hypoxanthine phosphoribosyl transferase**. Also called **HGPRT (hypoxanthine guanine phosphoribosyl transferase)**

HPV *abbreviation* human papillomavirus

H pylori *abbreviation* Helicobacter pylori

HRT *abbreviation* hormone replacement therapy

human /ˈhjuːmən/ *adjective* referring to any man, woman or child ■ *noun* a person ○ *Most animals are afraid of humans.*

human anatomy /ˌhjuːmən əˈnætəmi/ *noun* the structure, shape and functions of the human body

human being /ˌhjuːmən ˈbiːɪŋ/ *noun* a person

human chorionic gonadotrophin /ˌhjuːmən kɔːriˌɒnɪk ˌɡəʊnədəˈtrəʊfɪn/ *noun* a hormone produced by the placenta, which suppresses the mother's usual menstrual cycle during pregnancy. It is found in the urine during pregnancy, and can be given by injection to encourage ovulation and help a woman to become pregnant. Abbreviation **hCG**

human crutch /ˌhjuːmən ˈkrʌtʃ/ *noun* a method of helping an injured person to walk, where they rest one arm over the shoulders of the person helping

human immunodeficiency virus /ˌhjuːmən ˌɪmjʊnəʊdɪˈfɪʃ(ə)nsi ˌvaɪrəs/ *noun* a virus which causes AIDS. Abbreviation **HIV**

human leucocyte antigen /ˌhjuːmən ˈluːkəsaɪt ˌæntɪdʒ(ə)n/ *noun* any of the system of antigens on the surface of cells which need to be histocompatible to allow transplants to take place. Abbreviation **HLA**. ◊ **HLA system**

human nature /ˌhjuːmən ˈneɪtʃə/ *noun* the general behavioural characteristics of human beings

human papillomavirus /ˌhjuːmən ˌpæpɪ ˈləʊmə ˌvaɪrəs/ *noun* a virus that causes genital warts in humans. Abbreviation **HPV**

humectant /hjuːˈmektənt/ *adjective* able to absorb or retain moisture ■ *noun* a substance that can absorb or retain moisture, e.g. a skin lotion

humeroulnar joint /ˌhjuːmərəʊˈʌlnə dʒɔɪnt/ *noun* part of the elbow joint, where the trochlea of the humerus and the trochlear notch of the ulna move next to each other

humerus /ˈhjuːmərəs/ *noun* the top bone in the arm, running from the shoulder to the elbow (NOTE: The plural is **humeri**.)

humoral /ˈhjuːmərəl/ *adjective* relating to human body fluids, in particular blood serum

humour /ˈhjuːmə/ *noun* a fluid in the body

hunchback /ˈhʌntʃbæk/ *noun* ♦ kyphosis

hunger /ˈhʌŋgə/ *noun* a need to eat

hunger pains /ˈhʌŋgə peɪnz/ *plural noun* pains in the abdomen when a person feels hungry, sometimes a sign of a duodenal ulcer

Hunter's syndrome /ˈhʌntəz ˌsɪndrəʊm/ *noun* an inherited disorder caused by an enzyme deficiency, which leads to learning difficulties

Huntington's chorea /ˌhʌntɪŋtənz kɔːˈriːə/ *noun* a progressive hereditary disease which affects adults, where the outer layer of the brain degenerates and the person makes involuntary jerky movements and develops progressive dementia [Described 1872. After George Sumner Huntington (1850–1916), US physician.]

Hurler's syndrome /ˈhɜːləz ˌsɪndrəʊm/ *noun* same as **gargoylism** [Described 1919. After Gertrud Hurler (1889–1965), German paediatrician.]

hurt /hɜːt/ *noun* **1.** emotional pain **2.** a painful area (*used by children*) ○ *She has a hurt on her knee.* ■ *verb* to have pain ○ *He's hurt his hand.* ■ *adjective* **1.** feeling physical pain ○ *He was slightly hurt in the car crash.* ○ *Two players got hurt in the football game.* **2.** feeling emotional pain ○ *Her parents' divorce hurt her deeply.*

Hutchinson's teeth /ˈhʌtʃɪnsənz ˌtiːθ/, **Hutchinson's tooth** /ˈhʌtʃɪnsənz ˌtuːθ/ *plural noun* incisor teeth which are narrower than usual and have a crescent-shaped notch at the biting edge. They are seen especially in children with congenital syphilis, but can also occur naturally. (NOTE: takes either a singular or a plural verb)

hyal- /haɪəl/ *prefix* like glass (*used before vowels*)

hyalin /ˈhaɪəlɪn/ *noun* a transparent substance produced from collagen and deposited around blood vessels and scars when some tissues degenerate

hyaline /ˈhaɪəlɪn/ *adjective* nearly transparent like glass

hyaline cartilage /ˌhaɪəlɪn ˈkɑːtɪlɪdʒ/ *noun* a type of cartilage found in the nose, larynx and joints. It forms most of the skeleton of the fetus. See illustration at CARTILAGINOUS JOINT in Supplement

hyaline membrane disease /ˌhaɪəlɪn ˈmembreɪn dɪˌziːz/ *noun* same as **respiratory distress syndrome**

hyalitis /ˌhaɪəˈlaɪtɪs/ *noun* inflammation of the vitreous humour or the hyaloid membrane in the eye. Also called **vitritis**

hyaloid membrane /ˈhaɪəlɔɪd ˌmembreɪn/ *noun* a transparent membrane round the vitreous humour in the eye

hybrid /ˈhaɪbrɪd/ *noun* an organism that is a result of a cross between individuals that are not genetically the same as each other

HYCOSY *abbreviation* hysterosalpingo-contrast sonography

hydatid /ˈhaɪdətɪd/ *noun* any cyst-like structure

hydatid cyst /ˌhaɪdətɪd ˈsɪst/ *noun* the larval form of the tapeworms of the genus *Echinococcus*

hydatid disease /ˈhaɪdətɪd dɪˌziːz/, **hydatidosis** /ˌhaɪdətɪˈdəʊsɪs/ *noun* an infection, usually in the lungs or liver, caused by expanding hydatid cysts that destroy the tissues of the infected organ

hydatid mole /ˌhaɪdətɪd ˈməʊl/ *noun* an abnormal pregnancy from a pathologic ovum, resulting in a mass of cysts shaped like a bunch of grapes

hydr- /haɪdr/ *prefix* same as **hydro-** (*used before vowels*)

hydraemia /haɪˈdriːmiə/ *noun* an excess of water in the blood

hydralazine /haɪˈdræləziːn/ *noun* a drug that lowers blood pressure. People usually receive it in combination with other drugs that increase the output of urine.

hydramnios /haɪˈdræmnɪɒs/ *noun* an unusually large amount of amniotic fluid surrounding the fetus

hydrarthrosis /ˌhaɪdrɑːˈθrəʊsɪs/ *noun* swelling caused by excess synovial liquid at a joint

hydrate /ˈhaɪdreɪt/ *verb* to give water to someone so as to re-establish or maintain fluid balance ■ *noun* a chemical compound containing water molecules that can usually be driven off by heat without altering the compound's structure

hydro- /haɪdrəʊ/ *prefix* referring to water

hydroa /haɪˈdrəʊə/ *noun* an eruption of small itchy blisters, e.g. those caused by sunlight

hydrocalycosis /ˌhaɪdrəʊˌkælɪˈkəʊsɪs/ *noun* same as **caliectasis**

hydrocele /ˈhaɪdrəʊsiːl/ *noun* the collection of watery liquid found in a cavity such as the scrotum

hydrocephalus /ˌhaɪdrəʊˈkefələs/ *noun* an excessive quantity of cerebrospinal fluid in the brain

hydrochloric acid /ˌhaɪdrəklɒrɪk ˈæsɪd/ *noun* an acid found in the gastric juices which helps to break apart the food

hydrocortisone /ˌhaɪdrəʊˈkɔːtɪzəʊn/ *noun* a steroid hormone secreted by the adrenal cortex or produced synthetically, used in the treatment of rheumatoid arthritis and inflammatory and allergic conditions

hydrogen /'haɪdrədʒən/ *noun* a chemical element, a gas which combines with oxygen to form water, and with other elements to form acids, and is present in all animal tissue (NOTE: The chemical symbol is **H**.)

hydrogen peroxide /ˌhaɪdrədʒən pə'rɒksaɪd/ *noun* a solution used as a disinfectant

hydrolysis /haɪ'drɒləsɪs/ *noun* the breaking down of a chemical compound when it reacts with water to produce two or more different compounds, as in the conversion of starch to glucose

hydroma /haɪ'drəʊmə/ *noun* same as **hygroma**

hydrometer /haɪ'drɒmɪtə/ *noun* an instrument which measures the density of a liquid

hydromyelia /ˌhaɪdrəʊmaɪ'iːliə/ *noun* a condition in which fluid swells the central canal of the spinal cord

hydronephrosis /ˌhaɪdrəʊne'frəʊsɪs/ *noun* swelling of the pelvis of a kidney caused by accumulation of water due to infection or a kidney stone blocking the ureter

hydropericarditis /ˌhaɪdrəʊˌperikɑː'daɪtɪs/, **hydropericardium** /ˌhaɪdrəʊˌperi'kɑːdiəm/ *noun* an accumulation of liquid round the heart

hydroperitoneum /ˌhaɪdrəʊˌperɪtə'niːəm/ *noun* a build-up of fluid in the peritoneal cavity (NOTE: The plural is **hydroperitoneums** or **hydroperitonea**.)

hydrophobia /ˌhaɪdrə'fəʊbiə/ *noun* same as **rabies**

hydropneumoperitoneum /ˌhaɪdrəʊ ˌnjuːməʊˌperɪtə'niːəm/ *noun* a condition in which watery fluid and gas collect in the peritoneal cavity

hydropneumothorax /ˌhaɪdrəʊˌnjuːməʊ 'θɔːræks/ *noun* a condition in which watery fluid and gas collect in the pleural cavity (NOTE: The plural is **hydropneumothoraxes** or **hydropneumothoraces**.)

hydrops /'haɪdrɒps/ *noun* same as **oedema** (NOTE: The plural is **hydropses**.)

hydrosalpinx /ˌhaɪdrəʊ'sælpɪŋks/ *noun* an occasion when watery fluid collects in one or both of the Fallopian tubes, causing swelling (NOTE: The plural is **hydrosalpinges**.)

hydrotherapy /ˌhaɪdrəʊ'θerəpi/ *noun* a type of physiotherapy involving treatment in water, where people are put in hot baths or are encouraged to swim

hydrothorax /ˌhaɪdrəʊ'θɔːræks/ *noun* the collection of liquid in the pleural cavity

hydrotubation /ˌhaɪdrəʊtjuː'beɪʃ(ə)n/ *noun* an act of putting a fluid through the neck of the uterus and the Fallopian tubes under pressure to check whether the tubes are blocked

hydroureter /ˌhaɪdrəʊjuː'riːtə/ *noun* a condition in which water or urine collect in the ureter because it is blocked

hygiene /'haɪdʒiːn/ *noun* the procedures and principles designed to keep things clean and to keep conditions healthy ○ *Nurses have to maintain a strict personal hygiene.*

hygienist /'haɪdʒiːnɪst/ *noun* a person who specialises in hygiene and its application

hygr- /haɪgr/ *prefix* same as **hygro-** (*used before vowels*)

hygro- /haɪgrəʊ/ *prefix* relating to moisture

hygroma /haɪ'grəʊmə/ *noun* a kind of cyst which contains a thin fluid

hymen /'haɪmen/ *noun* a membrane which partially covers the vaginal passage in a female who has never had sexual intercourse

hymenectomy /ˌhaɪmə'nektəmi/ *noun* **1.** the surgical removal of the hymen, or an operation to increase the size of the opening of the hymen **2.** the surgical removal of any membrane

hymenotomy /ˌhaɪmə'nɒtəmi/ *noun* an incision of the hymen during surgery

hyo- /haɪəʊ/ *prefix* relating to the hyoid bone

hyoglossus /ˌhaɪəʊ'glɒsəs/ *noun* a muscle which is attached to the hyoid bone and depresses the tongue

hyoid /'haɪɔɪd/ *adjective* relating to the hyoid bone

hyoid bone /'haɪɔɪd bəʊn/ *noun* a small U-shaped bone at the base of the tongue

hyoscine /'haɪəʊsiːn/ *noun* a drug used as a sedative, in particular for treatment of motion sickness

hyp- /haɪp/ *prefix* same as **hypo-** (*used before vowels*)

hypalgesia /ˌhaɪpəl'dʒiːziə/ *noun* low sensitivity to pain

hyper- /haɪpə/ *prefix* higher or too much. Opposite **hypo-**

hyperacidity /ˌhaɪpərə'sɪdɪti/ *noun* the production of more acid in the stomach than is usual. Also called **acidity**, **acid stomach**

hyperacousia /ˌhaɪpərə'kjuːziə/ *noun* same as **hyperacusis**

hyperactive /ˌhaɪpər'æktɪv/ *adjective* very or unusually active

hyperactivity /ˌhaɪpəræk'tɪvəti/ *noun* a condition in which something or someone, e.g. a gland or a child, is too active

hyperacusis /ˌhaɪpərə'kjuːsɪs/ *noun* a condition in which someone is very sensitive to sounds

hyperadrenalism /ˌhaɪpərə'driːn(ə)lɪz(ə)m/ *noun* a disorder in which too many adrenal hormones are produced, e.g. because of pituitary gland malfunction, a tumour of the adrenal gland or high doses of steroids

hyperaemia /ˌhaɪpərˈiːmiə/ *noun* excess blood in any part of the body

hyperaesthesia /ˌhaɪpəriːsˈθiːziə/ *noun* an extremely high sensitivity in the skin

hyperalgesia /ˌhaɪpərælˈdʒiːziə/ *noun* an increased sensitivity to pain

hyperalimentation /ˌhaɪpərˌælɪmenˈteɪʃ(ə)n/ *noun* the feeding of large amounts of nutrients by mouth or intravenously to someone with serious nutritional deficiency

hyperandrogenism /ˌhaɪpərænˈdrɒdʒənɪz(ə)m/ *noun* a condition in which a woman produces too many androgens, associated with many problems such as hirsutism, acne, infertility and polycystic ovarian disease

hyperbaric /ˌhaɪpəˈbærɪk/ *adjective* referring to a treatment in which someone is given oxygen at high pressure, used to treat carbon monoxide poisoning

hypercalcaemia /ˌhaɪpəkælˈsiːmiə/ *noun* an excess of calcium in the blood

hypercalcinuria /ˌhaɪpəkælsɪˈnjʊəriə/ *noun* a condition in which an unusually high amount of calcium occurs in the urine

hypercapnia /ˌhaɪpəˈkæpniə/ *noun* an unusually high concentration of carbon dioxide in the bloodstream

hypercatabolism /ˌhaɪpəkəˈtæbəlɪz(ə)m/ *noun* a condition in which the body breaks down its own tissues or a particular substance too much. It causes weight loss and wasting.

hyperchloraemia /ˌhaɪpəklɔːˈriːmiə/ *noun* a condition in which there is too much chloride in the blood

hyperchlorhydria /ˌhaɪpəklɔːˈhaɪdriə/ *noun* an excess of hydrochloric acid in the stomach

hyperdactylism /ˌhaɪpəˈdæktɪlɪz(ə)m/ *noun* the condition of having more than the usual number of fingers or toes. Also called **polydactylism**

hyperemesis /ˌhaɪpərˈemɪsɪs/ *noun* excessive vomiting (NOTE: The plural is **hyperemeses**.)

hyperemesis gravidarum /ˌhaɪpəremɪsɪs ˌɡrævɪˈdeərəm/ *noun* uncontrollable vomiting in pregnancy

hyperextension /ˌhaɪpərɪkˈstenʃən/ *noun* the act of stretching an arm or leg beyond its usual limits of movement

hyperflexion /ˌhaɪpəˈflekʃən/ *noun* the act of flexing a joint beyond the usual limit ○ *a hyperflexion injury*

hypergalactia /ˌhaɪpəɡəˈlæktiə/, **hypergalactosis** /ˌhaɪpəˌɡæləkˈtəʊsɪs/ *noun* a condition in which too much milk is secreted

hyperglycaemia /ˌhaɪpəɡlaɪˈsiːmiə/ *noun* an excess of glucose in the blood

hyperhidrosis /ˌhaɪpəhaɪˈdrəʊsɪs/ *noun* a condition in which too much sweat is produced

hyperinsulinism /ˌhaɪpərˈɪnsjʊlɪnɪz(ə)m/ *noun* the reaction of a diabetic to an excessive dose of insulin or to hypoglycaemia

hyperkalaemia /ˌhaɪpəkæˈliːmiə/ *noun* a condition in which too much potassium occurs in the blood, which can result in cardiac arrest. Various possible causes include kidney failure and chemotherapy.

hyperkeratosis /ˌhaɪpəkerəˈtəʊsɪs/ *noun* a condition in which the outer layer of the skin becomes unusually thickened

hyperkinesia /ˌhaɪpəkɪˈniːziə/ *noun* a condition in which there is unusually great strength or movement

hyperlipidaemia /ˌhaɪpəlɪpɪˈdiːmiə/ *noun* the pathological increase of the amount of lipids, or fat, in the blood

hypermetropia /ˌhaɪpəmɪˈtrəʊpiə/, **hyperopia** /ˌhaɪpəˈrəʊpiə/ *noun* a condition in which someone sees more clearly objects which are a long way away, but cannot see objects which are close. Also called **longsightedness**, **hyperopia**

hypernatraemia /ˌhaɪpənæˈtriːmiə/ *noun* a serious condition occurring most often in babies or elderly people, in which too much sodium is present in the blood as a result of loss of water and electrolytes through diarrhoea, excessive sweating, not drinking enough or excessive salt intake

hypernephroma /ˌhaɪpənəˈfrəʊmə/ *noun* same as **Grawitz tumour**

hyperopia /ˌhaɪpəˈrəʊpiə/ *noun* same as **hypermetropia**

hyperostosis /haɪpərɒˈstəʊsɪs/ *noun* excessive overgrowth on the outside surface of a bone, especially the frontal bone

hyperparathyroidism /ˌhaɪpəˌpærəˈθaɪrɔɪdɪz(ə)m/ *noun* an unusually high concentration of parathyroid hormone in the body. It causes various medical problems including damage to the kidneys.

hyperphagia /ˌhaɪpəˈfeɪdʒiə/ *noun* long-term compulsive overeating

hyperpiesia /ˌhaɪpəpaɪˈiːziə/ *noun* same as **hypertension**

hyperpituitarism /ˌhaɪpəˈpɪtjuːɪtərɪz(ə)m/ *noun* a condition in which the pituitary gland is overactive

hyperplasia /ˌhaɪpəˈpleɪziə/ *noun* a condition in which there is an increase in the number of cells in an organ

hyperpyrexia /ˌhaɪpəpaɪˈreksiə/ *noun* a body temperature of above 41.1°C

hypersecretion /ˌhaɪpəsɪˈkriːʃ(ə)n/ *noun* a condition in which too much of a substance is secreted

hypersensitive /ˌhaɪpəˈsensɪtɪv/ *adjective* referring to a person who reacts more strongly than usual to an antigen

hypersensitivity /ˌhaɪpəsensɪˈtɪvɪti/ *noun* a condition in which someone reacts very strongly to something such as an allergic substance ○ *her hypersensitivity to dust* ○ *Anaphylactic shock shows hypersensitivity to an injection.*

hypersplenism /ˌhaɪpəˈspliːnɪz(ə)m/ *noun* a condition in which too many red blood cells are destroyed by the spleen, which is often enlarged

hypertelorism /ˌhaɪpəˈtelərɪz(ə)m/ *noun* a condition in which there is too much space between two organs or parts of the body

hypertension /ˌhaɪpəˈtenʃən/ *noun* arterial blood pressure that is higher than the usual range for gender and age. Also called **high blood pressure**, **hyperpiesia**. Compare **hypotension**

hypertensive /ˌhaɪpəˈtensɪv/ *adjective* referring to high blood pressure

hypertensive headache /ˌhaɪpətensɪv ˈhedeɪk/ *noun* a headache caused by high blood pressure

hyperthermia /ˌhaɪpəˈθɜːmiə/ *noun* a very high body temperature

hyperthyroidism /ˌhaɪpəˈθaɪrɔɪdɪz(ə)m/ *noun* a condition in which the thyroid gland is too active and releases unusual amounts of thyroid hormones into the blood, giving rise to a rapid heartbeat, sweating and trembling. It can be treated with carbimazole. Also called **thyrotoxicosis**

hypertonia /ˌhaɪpəˈtəʊniə/ *noun* an increased rigidity and spasticity of the muscles

hypertonic /ˌhaɪpəˈtɒnɪk/ *adjective* **1.** referring to a solution which has a higher osmotic pressure than another specified solution **2.** referring to a muscle which is under unusually high tension

hypertrichosis /ˌhaɪpətrɪˈkəʊsɪs/ *noun* a condition in which someone has excessive growth of hair on the body or on part of the body

hypertrophic /ˌhaɪpəˈtrɒfɪk/ *adjective* associated with hypertrophy

hypertrophy /haɪˈpɜːtrəfi/ *noun* an increase in the number or size of cells in a tissue

hyperventilation /ˌhaɪpəventɪˈleɪʃ(ə)n/ *noun* very fast breathing which can be accompanied by dizziness or tetany

hypervitaminosis /ˌhaɪpəˌvɪtəmɪˈnəʊsɪs/ *noun* a condition caused by taking too many synthetic vitamins, especially Vitamins A and D

hypervolaemia /ˌhaɪpəvɒˈliːmiə/ *noun* a condition in which there is too much plasma in the blood

hyphaema /haɪˈfiːmiə/ *noun* bleeding into the front chamber of the eye

hypn- /hɪpn/ *prefix* referring to sleep

hypnosis /hɪpˈnəʊsɪs/ *noun* a state like sleep, but caused artificially, where a person can remem-

ber forgotten events in the past and will do whatever the hypnotist tells him or her to do

hypnotherapy /ˌhɪpnəʊˈθerəpi/ *noun* treatment by hypnosis, used in treating some addictions

hypnotic /hɪpˈnɒtɪk/ *adjective* **1.** relating to hypnosis and hypnotism **2.** referring to a state which is like sleep but which is caused artificially **3.** referring to a drug which causes sleep

hypnotism /ˈhɪpnətɪz(ə)m/ *noun* the techniques used to induce hypnosis

hypo /ˈhaɪpəʊ/ *noun* (*informal*) **1.** same as **hypodermic syringe 2.** an attack of hypoglycaemia, experienced, e.g., by people who are diabetic

hypo- /haɪpəʊ/ *prefix* less, too little or beneath

hypoaesthesia /ˌhaɪpəʊiːsˈθiːziə/ *noun* a condition in which someone has a diminished sense of touch

hypocalcaemia /ˌhaɪpəʊkælˈsiːmiə/ *noun* an unusually low amount of calcium in the blood, which can cause tetany

hypocapnia /ˌhaɪpəʊˈkæpniə/ *noun* a condition in which there is not enough carbon dioxide in the blood

hypochloraemia /ˌhaɪpəʊklɔːˈriːmiə/ *noun* a condition in which there are not enough chlorine ions in the blood

hypochlorhydria /ˌhaɪpəʊklɔːˈhaɪdriə/ *noun* a condition in which there is not enough hydrochloric acid in the stomach

hypochondria /ˌhaɪpəʊˈkɒndriə/ *noun* a condition in which a person is too worried about his or her own health and believes he or she is ill

hypochondriac /ˌhaɪpəʊˈkɒndriæk/ *noun* a person who worries about his or her health too much

hypochondriac region /ˌhaɪpəʊˈkɒndriæk ˌriːdʒən/ *noun* one of two parts of the upper abdomen, on either side of the epigastrium below the floating ribs

hypochondrium /ˌhaɪpəʊˈkɒndriəm/ *noun* one of the two hypochondriac regions in the upper part of the abdomen

hypochromic /ˌhaɪpəʊˈkrəʊmɪk/ *adjective* referring to blood cells or body tissue which do not have the usual amount of pigmentation ○ *hypochromic scars*

hypodermic /ˌhaɪpəˈdɜːmɪk/ *adjective* beneath the skin ■ *noun* a hypodermic syringe, needle or injection (*informal*)

hypodermic injection /ˌhaɪpədɜːmɪk ɪnˈdʒekʃən/ *noun* an injection of a liquid, e.g. a painkilling drug, beneath the skin. Also called **subcutaneous injection**

hypodermic needle /ˌhaɪpədɜːmɪk ˈniːd(ə)l/ *noun* a needle for injecting liquid under the skin

hypodermic syringe /ˌhaɪpədɜːmɪk sɪ
ˈrɪndʒ/ *noun* a syringe fitted with a hypodermic
needle for injecting liquid under the skin

hypofibrinogenaemia /ˌhaɪpəʊˌfɪbrɪnəʊdʒə
ˈniːmiə/ *noun* a condition in which there is not
enough fibrinogen in the blood, e.g. because of
several blood transfusions or as an inherited condition

hypogammaglobulinaemia /ˌhaɪpəʊgæmə
ˌglɒbjʊlɪnˈiːmiə/ *noun* an unusually low concentration of gamma globulin in the blood that causes
an immune deficiency. It may be present from
birth or acquired later in life.

hypogastrium /ˌhaɪpəˈgæstriəm/ *noun* the
part of the abdomen beneath the stomach

hypoglossal /ˌhaɪpəʊˈglɒsəl/ *adjective* **1.**
underneath or on the lower side of the tongue **2.**
relating to the hypoglossal nerve

hypoglossal nerve /haɪpəˌglɒs(ə)l ˈnɜːv/
noun the twelfth cranial nerve which governs the
muscles of the tongue

hypoglycaemia /ˌhaɪpəʊglaɪˈsiːmiə/ *noun* a
low concentration of glucose in the blood

hypoglycaemic /ˌhaɪpəʊglaɪˈsiːmɪk/ *adjective* having hypoglycaemia

hypoglycaemic coma /ˌhaɪpəʊglaɪˌsiːmɪk
ˈkəʊmə/ *noun* a state of unconsciousness affecting diabetics after taking an overdose of insulin

hypohidrosis /ˌhaɪpəʊhaɪˈdrəʊsɪs/, **hypoid-
rosis** /ˌhaɪpəʊɪˈdrəʊsɪs/ *noun* a condition in
which someone produces too little sweat

hypoinsulinism /ˌhaɪpəʊˈɪnsjʊlɪnɪz(ə)m/
noun a condition in which the body does not have
enough insulin, often because of a problem with
the pancreas

hypokalaemia /ˌhaɪpəʊkæˈliːmiə/ *noun* a
deficiency of potassium in the blood

hypomania /ˌhaɪpəʊˈmeɪniə/ *noun* a state of
mild mania or overexcitement, especially when
part of a manic-depressive cycle

hypometropia /ˌhaɪpəʊmɪˈtrəʊpiə/ *noun*
same as **myopia**

hyponatraemia /ˌhaɪpəʊnæˈtriːmiə/ *noun* a
lack of sodium in the body

hypoparathyroidism /ˌhaɪpəʊˌpærə
ˈθaɪrɔɪdɪz(ə)m/ *noun* a condition in which the
parathyroid glands do not secrete enough parathyroid hormone, leading to low blood calcium and
muscle spasms

hypopharynx /ˌhaɪpəʊˈfærɪŋks/ *noun* the part
of the pharynx between the hyoid bone and the
bottom of the cricoid cartilage (NOTE: The plural
is **hypopharynxes** or **hypopharynges**.)

hypophyseal /ˌhaɪpəˈfɪziəl/ *adjective* referring to the pituitary gland

hypophysectomy /haɪˌpɒfɪˈsektəmi/ *noun*
the surgical removal of the pituitary gland

hypophysis cerebri /haɪˌpɒfəsɪs ˈserəbri/
noun same as **pituitary gland**

hypopiesis /ˌhaɪpəʊpaɪˈiːsɪs/ *noun* a condition in which the blood pressure is too low

hypopituitarism /ˌhaɪpəʊpɪˈtjuːɪtərɪz(ə)m/
noun a condition in which the pituitary gland is
underactive

hypoplasia /ˌhaɪpəʊˈpleɪziə/ *noun* a lack of
development or incorrect formation of a body tissue or an organ

hypoplastic left heart /haɪpəʊˌplæstɪk left
ˈhɑːt/ *noun* a serious heart disorder in which the
left side of the heart does not develop properly,
leading to death within six weeks of birth unless
surgery is performed

hypoproteinaemia /ˌhaɪpəʊprəʊtiˈniːmiə/
noun a condition in which there is not enough
protein in the blood

hypoprothrombinaemia /ˌhaɪpəʊprəʊ
ˌθrɒmbɪˈniːmiə/ *noun* a condition in which there
is not enough prothrombin in the blood, so that
the person bleeds and bruises easily

hypopyon /ˌhaɪpəˈpaɪən/ *noun* an accumulation of pus in the aqueous humour in the front
chamber of the eye

hyposensitive /ˌhaɪpəʊˈsensɪtɪv/ *adjective*
being less sensitive than usual

hypospadias /ˌhaɪpəˈspeɪdiəs/ *noun* a congenital condition of the wall of the male urethra or
the vagina, so that the opening occurs on the
under side of the penis or in the vagina. Compare
epispadias

hypostasis /haɪˈpɒstəsɪs/ *noun* a condition in
which fluid accumulates in part of the body
because of poor circulation

hypostatic /ˌhaɪpəʊˈstætɪk/ *adjective* referring to hypostasis

hypostatic eczema /ˌhaɪpəʊstætɪk ˈeksɪmə/
noun same as **varicose eczema**

hypostatic pneumonia /haɪpəʊstætɪk njuː
ˈməʊniə/ *noun* pneumonia caused by fluid accumulating in the lungs of a bedridden person with
a weak heart

hyposthenia /ˌhaɪpɒsˈθiːniə/ *noun* a condition
of unusual bodily weakness

hypotension /ˌhaɪpəʊˈtenʃən/ *noun* a condition in which the pressure of the blood is unusually low. Also called **low blood pressure**. Compare **hypertension**

hypotensive /ˌhaɪpəˈtensɪv/ *adjective* having
low blood pressure

hypothalamic /ˌhaɪpəʊθəˈlæmɪk/ *adjective*
referring to the hypothalamus

hypothalamic hormone /ˌhaɪpəʊθəˌlæmɪk
ˈhɔːməʊn/ *noun* same as **releasing hormone**

hypothalamus /ˌhaɪpəʊˈθæləməs/ *noun* the
part of the brain above the pituitary gland, which
controls the production of hormones by the pitui-

tary gland and regulates important bodily functions such as hunger, thirst and sleep. See illustration at BRAIN in Supplement

hypothalmus /ˌhaɪpəʊˈθælməs/ *noun* same as **hypothalamus** (NOTE: The plural is **hypothalmuses** or **hypothalmi**.)

hypothenar /haɪˈpɒθɪnə/ *adjective* referring to the soft fat part of the palm beneath the little finger

hypothenar eminence /haɪˌpɒθɪnə ˈemɪnəns/ *noun* a lump on the palm beneath the little finger. Compare **thenar**

hypothermia /ˌhaɪpəʊˈθɜːmiə/ *noun* a reduction in body temperature below normal, for medical purposes taken to be below 35°C

hypothesis /haɪˈpɒθəsɪs/ *noun* a suggested explanation for an observation or experimental result, which is then refined or disproved by further investigation

hypothyroidism /ˌhaɪpəʊˈθaɪrɔɪdɪz(ə)m/ *noun* underactivity of the thyroid gland

hypotonia /ˌhaɪpəʊˈtəʊniə/ *noun* reduced tone of the skeletal muscles

hypotonic /ˌhaɪpəʊˈtɒnɪk/ *adjective* **1.** showing hypotonia **2.** referring to a solution with a lower osmotic pressure than plasma

hypotrichosis /ˌhaɪpəʊtrɪˈkəʊsɪs/ *noun* a condition in which less hair develops than usual. Compare **alopecia** (NOTE: The plural is **hypotrichoses**.)

hypotropia /ˌhaɪpəʊˈtrəʊpiə/ *noun* a form of squint where one eye looks downwards

hypoventilation /ˌhaɪpəʊventɪˈleɪʃ(ə)n/ *noun* very slow breathing

hypovitaminosis /ˌhaɪpəʊˌvɪtəmɪˈnəʊsɪs/ *noun* a lack of vitamins

hypoxaemia /ˌhaɪpɒkˈsiːmiə/ *noun* an inadequate supply of oxygen in the arterial blood

hypoxanthine phosphoribosyl transferase /ˌhaɪpəʊzænθiːn ˌfɒsfəˈrɪbəsɪl ˌtrænsfəreɪs/ *noun* full form of **HPRT**

hypoxia /haɪˈpɒksiə/ *noun* **1.** an inadequate supply of oxygen to tissue as a result of a lack of oxygen in the arterial blood **2.** same as **hypoxaemia**

hyster- /hɪstə/ *prefix* same as **hystero-** (*used before vowels*)

hysteralgia /ˌhɪstərˈældʒə/ *noun* pain in the uterus

hysterectomy /ˌhɪstəˈrektəmi/ *noun* the surgical removal of the uterus, often either to treat cancer or because of the presence of fibroids

hysteria /hɪˈstɪəriə/ *noun* a term formerly used in psychiatry, but now informally used for a condition in which the person appears unstable, and may scream and wave their arms about, but also is repressed, and may be slow to react to outside stimuli (*dated*)

hysterical /hɪˈsterɪk(ə)l/ *adjective* referring to a reaction showing hysteria (*informal*)

hysterics /hɪˈsterɪks/ *noun* an attack of hysteria (*dated*)

hystero- /hɪstərəʊ/ *prefix* referring to the uterus

hystero-oöphorectomy /ˌhɪstərəʊ ˌəʊəfəˈrektəmi/ *noun* the surgical removal of the uterus, the uterine tubes and the ovaries

hysteroptosis /ˌhɪstərɒpˈtəʊsɪs/ *noun* prolapse of the uterus

hysterosalpingo-contrast sonography /ˌhɪstərəʊˌsælpɪŋgəʊ ˌkɒntrɑːst sɒnˈɒgrəfi/ *noun* examination of the uterus and Fallopian tubes by ultrasound. Abbreviation **HYCOSY**

hysterosalpingography /ˌhɪstərəʊˌsælpɪŋˈɡɒgrəfi/ *noun* an X-ray examination of the uterus and Fallopian tubes following injection of radio-opaque material. Also called **uterosalpingography**

hysterosalpingosonography /ˌhɪstərəʊˌsælpɪŋgəʊsəˈnɒgrəfi/ *noun* examination of the uterus and Fallopian tubes by ultrasound

hysterosalpingostomy /ˌhɪstərəʊˌsælpɪŋˈɡɒstəmi/ *noun* an operation to remake an opening between the uterine tube and the uterus, to help with infertility problems

hysteroscope /ˈhɪstərəskəʊp/ *noun* a tube for inspecting the inside of the uterus

hysteroscopy /ˌhɪstəˈrɒskəpi/ *noun* an examination of the uterine cavity using a hysteroscope or fibrescope

hysterotomy /ˌhɪstəˈrɒtəmi/ *noun* a surgical incision into the uterus, as in caesarean section or for some types of abortion

hysterotrachelorrhaphy /ˌhɪstərəʊˌtrækɪəˈlɒrəfi/ *noun* an operation to repair a tear in the cervix

I

-iasis /aɪəsɪs/ *suffix* disease caused by something ○ *amoebiasis*

iatro- /aɪætrəʊ/ *prefix* relating to medicine or doctors

iatrogenesis /aɪˌætrəʊˈdʒenəsɪs/ *noun* any condition caused by the actions of doctors or other healthcare professionals

iatrogenic /aɪˌætrəˈdʒenɪk/ *adjective* referring to a condition which is caused by a doctor's treatment for another disease or condition ○ *an iatrogenic infection*

IBS *abbreviation* irritable bowel syndrome

ibuprofen /ˌaɪbjuːˈprəʊfən/ *noun* a nonsteroidal anti-inflammatory drug that relieves pain and swelling, especially in arthritis and rheumatism. It is also widely used as a household painkiller.

ice pack /ˈaɪs pæk/ *noun* a cold compress made of lumps of ice wrapped in a cloth, and pressed on a swelling or bruise to reduce the pain

ichthamol /ˈɪkˈθæmɒl/ *noun* a thick dark red liquid which is a mild antiseptic and analgesic, used in the treatment of skin diseases

ichthyosis /ˌɪkθɪˈəʊsɪs/ *noun* a hereditary condition in which the skin does not form properly, resulting in a dry, non-inflammatory and scaly appearance

ICM *abbreviation* International Confederation of Midwives

ICN *abbreviation* **1.** International Council of Nurses **2.** infection control nurse

ICP *abbreviation* intracranial pressure

ICRC *abbreviation* International Committee of the Red Cross

ICSH *abbreviation* interstitial cell stimulating hormone

icteric /ɪkˈterɪk/ *adjective* referring to someone with jaundice

icterus /ˈɪktərəs/ *noun* same as **jaundice**

icterus gravis neonatorum /ˌɪktərəs ˌɡrævɪs ˌniːəʊnəˈtɔːrəm/ *noun* jaundice associated with erythroblastosis fetalis

ictus /ˈɪktəs/ *noun* a stroke or fit

ICU *abbreviation* intensive care unit

id /ɪd/ *noun* (*in Freudian psychology*) the basic unconscious drives which exist in hidden forms in a person

ideation /ˌaɪdiˈeɪʃ(ə)n/ *noun* the act or process of imagining or forming thoughts and ideas

identical twins /aɪˌdentɪk(ə)l ˈtwɪnz/ *plural noun* twins who are exactly the same in appearance because they developed from the same ovum. Also called **monozygotic twins, uniovular twins**

identification /aɪˌdentɪfɪˈkeɪʃ(ə)n/ *noun* the act of discovering or stating who someone is or what something is

ideo- /aɪdiəʊ/ *prefix* involving ideas

idio- /ɪdiəʊ/ *prefix* referring to one particular person

idiopathic /ˌɪdiəˈpæθɪk/ *adjective* referring to idiopathy

idiopathic epilepsy /ˌɪdiəpæθɪk ˈepɪˌlepsi/ *noun* epilepsy not caused by a brain disorder, beginning during childhood or adolescence

idiopathy /ˌɪdiˈɒpəθi/ *noun* a condition which develops without any known cause

idiosyncrasy /ˌɪdiəʊˈsɪŋkrəsi/ *noun* a way of behaving which is particular to one person

idiot savant /ˌɪdiəʊ ˈsævɒŋ/ *noun* a person with learning difficulties who also possesses a single particular mental ability, such as the ability to play music by ear, to draw remembered objects or to do mental calculations, which is very highly developed

idioventricular /ˌɪdiəʊvenˈtrɪkjʊlə/ *adjective* relating to the ventricles of the heart

idioventricular rhythm /ˌɪdiəʊvenˌtrɪkjʊlə ˈrɪð(ə)m/ *noun* a slow natural rhythm in the ventricles of the heart, but not in the atria

IDK *abbreviation* internal derangement of the knee

Ig *abbreviation* immunoglobulin

Ig A antiendomysial antibody /ˌaɪ dʒiː eɪ ˌæntiendəʊˌmaɪsiəl ˈæntɪbɒdi/ *noun* a serological screening test for coeliac disease

IHD *abbreviation* ischaemic heart disease

IL-1 *abbreviation* interleukin-1

IL-2 *abbreviation* interleukin-2

ile- /ɪli/ *prefix* same as **ileo-** (*used before vowels*)

ileal /ˈɪlɪəl/ *adjective* referring to the ileum

ileal bladder /ˌɪlɪəl ˈblædə/, **ileal conduit** /ˌɪlɪəl ˈkɒndjuɪt/ *noun* an artificial tube formed when the ureters are linked to part of the ileum, and that part is linked to an opening in the abdominal wall

ileal pouch /ˌɪlɪəl ˈpaʊtʃ/ *noun* a part of the small intestine which is made into a new rectum in a surgical operation, freeing someone from the need for an ileostomy after their colon is removed

ileectomy /ˌɪliˈektəmi/ *noun* the surgical removal of all or part of the ileum

ileitis /ˌɪliˈaɪtɪs/ *noun* inflammation of the ileum

ileo- /ɪlɪəʊ/ *prefix* relating to the ileum

ileocaecal /ˌɪlɪəʊˈsiːk(ə)l/ *adjective* referring to the ileum and the caecum

ileocaecal orifice /ˌɪliəʊsiːk(ə)l ˈɒrɪfɪs/ *noun* an opening where the small intestine joins the large intestine

ileocaecal valve /ˌɪliːəʊsiːk(ə)l ˈvælv/ *noun* a valve at the end of the ileum, which allows food to pass from the ileum into the caecum

ileocaecocystoplasty /ˌɪlɪəʊˌsiːkəʊˈsaɪtəʊplæsti/ *noun* an operation to reconstruct the bladder using a piece of the combined ileum and caecum

ileocolic /ˌɪlɪəʊˈkɒlɪk/ *adjective* referring to both the ileum and the colon

ileocolic artery /ˌɪliːəʊkɒlɪk ˈɑːtəri/ *noun* a branch of the superior mesenteric artery

ileocolitis /ˌɪlɪəʊkəˈlaɪtɪs/ *noun* inflammation of both the ileum and the colon

ileocolostomy /ˌɪlɪəʊkəˈlɒstəmi/ *noun* a surgical operation to make a link directly between the ileum and the colon

ileoproctostomy /ˌɪlɪəʊprɒkˈtɒstəmi/ *noun* a surgical operation to create a link between the ileum and the rectum

ileorectal /ˌɪlɪəʊˈrekt(ə)l/ *adjective* referring to both the ileum and the rectum

ileosigmoidostomy /ˌɪlɪəʊsɪgmɔɪˈdɒstəmi/ *noun* a surgical operation to create a link between the ileum and the sigmoid colon

ileostomy /ˌɪliˈɒstəmi/ *noun* a surgical operation to make an opening between the ileum and the abdominal wall to act as an artificial opening for excretion of faeces

ileostomy bag /ˌɪliˈɒstəmi bæg/ *noun* a bag attached to the opening made by an ileostomy, to collect faeces as they are passed out of the body

ileum /ˈɪlɪəm/ *noun* the lower part of the small intestine, between the jejunum and the caecum. Compare **ilium**. See illustration at **DIGESTIVE SYSTEM** in Supplement (NOTE: The plural is **ilea**.)

ileus /ˈɪlɪəs/ *noun* obstruction of the intestine, usually distension caused by loss of muscular action in the bowel. ◊ **paralytic ileus**

ili- /ɪli/ *prefix* same as **ilio-** (*used before vowels*)

iliac /ˈɪlɪæk/ *adjective* referring to the ilium

iliac crest /ˌɪliæk ˈkrest/ *noun* a curved top edge of the ilium. See illustration at **PELVIS** in Supplement

iliac fossa /ˌɪliæk ˈfɒsə/ *noun* a depression on the inner side of the hip bone

iliac region /ˈɪlɪæk ˌriːdʒən/ *noun* one of two regions of the lower abdomen, on either side of the hypogastrium

iliac spine /ˈɪlɪæk spaɪn/ *noun* a projection at the posterior end of the iliac crest

ilio- /ɪlɪəʊ/ *prefix* relating to the ilium

iliococcygeal /ˌɪliəʊkɒkˈsɪdʒɪəl/ *adjective* referring to both the ilium and the coccyx

iliolumbar /ˌɪliəʊˈlʌmbə/ *adjective* referring to the iliac and lumbar regions

iliopectineal /ˌɪliəʊpekˈtɪnɪəl/ *adjective* referring to both the ilium and the pubis

iliopectineal eminence /ˌɪliəʊpektɪnɪəl ˈemɪnəns/ *noun* a raised area on the inner surface of the innominate bone

iliopubic /ˌɪliəʊˈpjuːbɪk/ *adjective* same as **iliopectineal**

iliopubic eminence /ˌɪliəʊˌpjuːbɪk ˈemɪnəns/ *noun* same as **iliopectineal eminence**

ilium /ˈɪlɪəm/ *noun* the top part of each of the hip bones, which form the pelvis. Compare **ileum**. See illustration at **PELVIS** in Supplement (NOTE: The plural is **ilia**.)

ill /ɪl/ *adjective* not well ○ *If you feel very ill you ought to see a doctor.*

illness /ˈɪlnəs/ *noun* **1.** a state of not being well ○ *Most of the children stayed away from school because of illness.* **2.** a type of disease ○ *Scarlet fever is no longer considered to be a very serious illness.* ○ *He is in hospital with an infectious tropical illness.*

illusion /ɪˈluːʒ(ə)n/ *noun* a condition in which a person has a wrong perception of external objects

i.m., IM *abbreviation* intramuscular

image /ˈɪmɪdʒ/ *noun* a sensation, e.g. a smell, sight or taste, which is remembered clearly

imagery /ˈɪmɪdʒəri/ *noun* visual sensations clearly produced in the mind

imaginary /ɪˈmædʒɪn(ə)ri/ *adjective* referring to something which does not exist but is imagined

imagination /ɪˌmædʒɪˈneɪʃ(ə)n/ *noun* the ability to see or invent things in your mind ○ *In her imagination she saw herself sitting on a beach in the sun.*

imagine /ɪˈmædʒɪn/ *verb* to see, hear or feel something in your mind ○ *Imagine yourself sitting on the beach in the sun.* ○ *I thought I heard someone shout, but I must have imagined it because there is no one there.*

imaging /'ɪmɪdʒɪŋ/ *noun* a technique for creating pictures of sections of the body, using scanners attached to computers

imbalance /ɪm'bæləns/ *noun* a situation in which things are unequal or in the wrong proportions to one another, e.g. in the diet

imipramine /ɪ'mɪprəmiːn/ *noun* a drug that is used as a treatment for depression

immature /ˌɪmə'tʃʊə/ *adjective* not mature, lacking insight and emotional stability

immature cell /ˌɪmətʃʊə 'sel/ *noun* a cell which is still developing

immaturity /ˌɪmə'tʃʊərɪti/ *noun* behaviour which is lacking in maturity

immobilisation /ɪˌməʊbɪlaɪ'zeɪʃ(ə)n/, **immobilization** *noun* the act of preventing somebody or something from being able to move

immobilise /ɪ'məʊbɪlaɪz/, **immobilize** *verb* **1.** to keep someone from moving **2.** to attach a splint to a joint or fractured limb to prevent the bones from moving

immune /ɪ'mjuːn/ *adjective* protected against an infection or allergic disease ○ *She seems to be immune to colds.* ○ *The injection should make you immune to yellow fever.*

immune deficiency /ɪˌmjuːn dɪ'fɪʃ(ə)nsi/ *noun* a lack of immunity to a disease. ◊ **AIDS**

immune reaction /ɪ'mjuːn ri,ækʃən/, **immune response** /ɪ'mjuːn rɪ,spɒns/ *noun* a reaction of a body to an antigen

immune system /ɪ'mjuːn ,sɪstəm/ *noun* a complex network of cells and cell products, which protects the body from disease. It includes the thymus, spleen, lymph nodes, white blood cells and antibodies.

immunisation /ˌɪmjʊnaɪ'zeɪʃ(ə)n/, **immunization** *noun* the process of making a person immune to an infection, either by injecting an antiserum, passive immunisation or by inoculation

immunise /'ɪmjʊnaɪz/, **immunize** *verb* to give someone immunity from an infection. ◊ **vaccinate** (NOTE: You immunise someone **against** a disease.)

immunity /ɪ'mjuːnɪti/ *noun* the ability to resist attacks of a disease because antibodies are produced ○ *The vaccine gives immunity to tuberculosis.*

immuno- /ɪmjʊnəʊ, ɪmjuː'nəʊ/ *prefix* immune, immunity

immunoassay /ˌɪmjʊnəʊ'æseɪ/ *noun* a test for the presence and strength of antibodies

immunocompetence /ˌɪmjʊnəʊ'kɒmpɪtəns/ *noun* the ability to develop an immune response following exposure to an antigen

immunocompromised /ˌɪmjʊnəʊ'kɒmprəmaɪzd/ *adjective* not able to offer resistance to infection

immunodeficiency /ˌɪmjʊnəʊdɪ'fɪʃ(ə)nsi/ *noun* a lack of immunity to a disease

immunodeficiency virus /ˌɪmjʊnəʊdɪ'fɪʃ(ə)nsi ,vaɪrəs/ *noun* a retrovirus which attacks the immune system

immunodeficient /ˌɪmjʊnəʊdɪ'fɪʃ(ə)nt/ *adjective* lacking immunity to a disease ○ *This form of meningitis occurs in persons who are immunodeficient.*

immunogenic /ˌɪmjʊnəʊ'dʒenɪk/ *adjective* producing an immune response

immunogenicity /ˌɪmjʊnəʊdʒə'nɪsɪti/ *noun* the property which makes a substance able to produce an immune response in an organism

immunoglobulin /ˌɪmjʊnəʊ'glɒbjʊlɪn/ *noun* an antibody, a protein produced in blood plasma as protection against infection, the commonest being gamma globulin. Abbreviation **Ig** (NOTE: The five main classes are called: **immunoglobulin G, A, D, E and M** or **IgG, IgA, IgD, IgE and IgM**.)

immunological /ˌɪmjʊnə'lɒdʒɪk(ə)l/ *adjective* referring to immunology

immunologist /ˌɪmjʊ'nɒlədʒɪst/ *noun* a specialist in immunology

immunology /ˌɪmjʊ'nɒlədʒi/ *noun* the study of immunity and immunisation

immunosuppressant /ˌɪmjʊnəʊsə'pres(ə)nt/ *noun* a drug used to act against the response of the immune system to reject a transplanted organ

immunosuppression /ˌɪmjʊnəʊsə'preʃ(ə)n/ *noun* the suppression of the body's natural immune system so that it will not reject a transplanted organ

immunosuppressive /ˌɪmjʊnəʊsə'presɪv/ *noun* a drug used to counteract the response of the immune system to reject a transplanted organ ■ *adjective* counteracting the immune system

immunotherapy /ˌɪmjʊnəʊ'θerəpi/ *noun* ◆ **adoptive immunotherapy**

immunotransfusion /ˌɪmjʊnəʊtræns'fjuːʒ(ə)n/ *noun* a transfusion of blood, serum or plasma containing immune bodies

Imodium /ɪ'məʊdiəm/ a trade name for loperamide hydrochloride

impacted /ɪm'pæktɪd/ *adjective* tightly pressed or firmly lodged against something

impacted faeces /ɪm,pæktɪd 'fiːsiːz/ *plural noun* extremely hard dry faeces which cannot pass through the anus and have to be surgically removed

impacted fracture /ɪm,pæktɪd 'fræktʃə/ *noun* a fracture where the broken parts of the bones are pushed into each other

impacted tooth /ɪmˌpæktɪd 'tuːθ/ *noun* a tooth which is held against another tooth and so cannot grow normally

impacted ureteric calculus /ɪmˌpæktɪd ˌjʊərɪterɪk 'kælkjʊləs/ *noun* a small hard mass of mineral salts which is lodged in a ureter

impaction /ɪm'pækʃən/ *noun* a condition in which things are closely pressed together and cannot develop or move normally

impair /ɪm'peə/ *verb* to harm a sense or function so that it does not work properly

impaired hearing /ɪmˌpeəd 'hɪərɪŋ/ *noun* hearing which is not clear and sharp

impaired vision /ɪmˌpeəd 'vɪʒ(ə)n/ *noun* eyesight which is not fully clear

impairment /ɪm'peəmənt/ *noun* a condition in which a sense or function is harmed so that it does not work properly ○ *His hearing impairment does not affect his work.* ○ *The impairment was progressive, but she did not notice that her eyesight was getting worse.*

impalpable /ɪm'pælpəb(ə)l/ *adjective* not able to be felt when touched

impediment /ɪm'pedɪmənt/ *noun* an obstruction

imperforate /ɪm'pɜːf(ə)rət/ *adjective* without an opening

imperforate anus /ɪmˌpɜːf(ə)rət 'eɪnəs/ *noun* same as **proctatresia**

imperforate hymen /ɪmˌpɜːf(ə)rət 'haɪmen/ *noun* a membrane in the vagina which is missing the opening for the menstrual flow

impermeable /ɪm'pɜːmiəb(ə)l/ *adjective* not allowing liquids or gases to pass through

impetigo /ˌɪmpɪ'taɪgəʊ/ *noun* an irritating and very contagious skin disease caused by staphylococci, which spreads rapidly and is easily passed from one child to another, but can be treated with antibiotics

implant *noun* /'ɪmplɑːnt/ something grafted or inserted into a person, e.g. tissue, a drug, inert material or a device such as a pacemaker ■ *verb* /ɪm'plɑːnt/ **1.** to fix into something ○ *The ovum implants in the wall of the uterus.* **2.** to graft or insert tissue, a drug, inert material or a device ○ *The site was implanted with the biomaterial.*

implantation /ˌɪmplɑːn'teɪʃ(ə)n/ *noun* **1.** the act of grafting or inserting tissue, a drug, inert material or a device into a person, or the introduction of one tissue into another surgically **2.** a place in or on the body where an implant is positioned **3.** same as **nidation**

implant site /'ɪmplɑːnt saɪt/ *noun* a place in or on the body where the implant is positioned

implosion /ɪm'pləʊʒ(ə)n/ *noun* the violent inward collapse of a hollow structure. It happens when the pressure outside the structure is greater than the pressure inside it.

impotence /'ɪmpət(ə)ns/ *noun* the inability in a male to have an erection or to ejaculate, and so have sexual intercourse

impotent /'ɪmpət(ə)nt/ *adjective* (*of a man*) unable to have sexual intercourse

impregnate /'ɪmpregneɪt/ *verb* **1.** to make a female pregnant **2.** to soak a cloth with a liquid ○ *a cloth impregnated with antiseptic*

impregnation /ˌɪmpreg'neɪʃ(ə)n/ *noun* the action of impregnating

impression /ɪm'preʃ(ə)n/ *noun* **1.** a mould of a person's jaw made by a dentist before making a denture **2.** a depression on an organ or structure into which another organ or structure fits

impulse /'ɪmpʌls/ *noun* **1.** a message transmitted by a nerve **2.** a sudden feeling of wanting to act in a specific way

in- /ɪn/ *prefix* **1.** in, into, towards **2.** not

inaccessible /ˌɪnək'sesɪb(ə)l/ *adjective* **1.** physically difficult or impossible to reach **2.** very technical and difficult to understand

inanition /ˌɪnə'nɪʃ(ə)n/ *noun* a state of exhaustion caused by starvation

inarticulate /ˌɪnɑː'tɪkjʊlət/ *adjective* **1.** without joints or segments, as in the bones of the skull **2.** unable to speak fluently or intelligibly **3.** not understandable as speech or language

in articulo mortis /ɪn ɑːˌtɪkjʊləʊ 'mɔːtɪs/ *adverb* a Latin phrase meaning 'at the onset of death'

inborn /ɪn'bɔːn/ *adjective* congenital, which is in the body from birth ○ *A body has an inborn tendency to reject transplanted organs.*

inbreeding /'ɪnbriːdɪŋ/ *noun* a situation where closely related males and females, or those with very similar genetic make-up, have children together, so allowing congenital conditions to be passed on

incapacitated /ˌɪnkə'pæsɪteɪtɪd/ *adjective* not able to act or work ○ *He was incapacitated for three weeks by his accident.*

incarcerated /ɪn'kɑːsəreɪtɪd/ *adjective* referring to a hernia which cannot be corrected by physical manipulation

inception rate /ɪn'sepʃən reɪt/ *noun* the number of new cases of a disease during a period of time, per thousand of population

incest /'ɪnsest/ *noun* an act of sexual intercourse or other sexual activity with so close a relative, that it is illegal or culturally not allowed

incidence /'ɪnsɪd(ə)ns/ *noun* the number of times something happens in a specific population over a period of time ○ *the incidence of drug-related deaths* ○ *Men have a higher incidence of strokes than women.*

incidence rate /'ɪnsɪd(ə)ns reɪt/ *noun* the number of new cases of a disease during a given period, per thousand of population

incipient /ɪnˈsɪpiənt/ *adjective* just beginning or in its early stages ○ *He has an incipient appendicitis.* ○ *The tests detected incipient diabetes mellitus.*

incision /ɪnˈsɪʒ(ə)n/ *noun* a cut in a person's body made by a surgeon using a scalpel, or any cut made with a sharp knife or razor ○ *The first incision is made two millimetres below the second rib.* Compare **excision**

incisional /ɪnˈsɪʒ(ə)n(ə)l/ *adjective* referring to an incision

incisional hernia /ɪnˌsɪʒ(ə)n(ə)l ˈhɜːniə/ *noun* a hernia which breaks through the abdominal wall at a place where a surgical incision was made during an operation

incisor /ɪnˈsaɪzə/, **incisor tooth** /ɪnˈsaɪzə tuːθ/ *noun* one of the front teeth, of which there are four each in the upper and lower jaws, which are used to cut off pieces of food. See illustration at TEETH in Supplement

inclusion /ɪnˈkluːʒ(ə)n/ *noun* something enclosed inside something else

inclusion bodies /ɪnˈkluːʒ(ə)n ˌbɒdiz/ *plural noun* very small particles found in cells infected by a virus

inclusive /ɪnˈkluːsɪv/ *adjective* (*of health services*) provided whether or not someone has a disability or special needs

incompatibility /ˌɪnkəmpætɪˈbɪlɪti/ *noun* the fact of being incompatible ○ *the incompatibility of the donor's blood with that of the patient*

incompatible /ˌɪnkəmˈpætɪb(ə)l/ *adjective* **1.** referring to something which does not go together with something else **2.** referring to drugs which must not be used together because they undergo chemical change and the therapeutic effect is lost or changed to something undesirable **3.** referring to tissue which is genetically different from other tissue, making it impossible to transplant into that tissue

incompatible blood /ˌɪnkəmpætəb(ə)l ˈblʌd/ *noun* blood from a donor that does not match the blood of the person receiving the transfusion

incompetence /ɪnˈkɒmpɪt(ə)ns/ *noun* the inability to do a particular act, especially a lack of knowledge or skill which makes a person unable to do particular job

incompetent cervix /ɪnˌkɒmpɪt(ə)nt ˈsɜːvɪks/ *noun* a dysfunctional cervix of the uterus which is often the cause of spontaneous abortions and premature births and can be remedied by purse-string stitching

incomplete abortion /ˌɪnkəmpliːt əˈbɔːʃ(ə)n/ *noun* an abortion where part of the contents of the uterus is not expelled

incontinence /ɪnˈkɒntɪnəns/ *noun* the inability to control the discharge of urine or faeces (NOTE: Single incontinence is the inability to control the bladder. Double incontinence is the inability to control both the bladder and the bowels.)

incontinence pad /ɪnˈkɒntɪnəns pæd/ *noun* a pad of material to absorb urine

incontinent /ɪnˈkɒntɪnənt/ *adjective* unable to control the discharge of urine or faeces

incoordination /ˌɪnkəʊɔːdɪˈneɪʃ(ə)n/ *noun* a situation in which the muscles in various parts of the body do not act together, making it impossible to carry out some actions

incubation /ˌɪŋkjʊˈbeɪʃ(ə)n/ *noun* **1.** the development of an infection inside the body before the symptoms of the disease appear **2.** the keeping of an ill or premature baby in a controlled environment in an incubator **3.** the process of culturing cells or microorganisms under controlled conditions

incubation period /ˌɪŋkjʊˈbeɪʃ(ə)n ˌpɪəriəd/ *noun* the time during which a virus or bacterium develops in the body after contamination or infection, before the appearance of the symptoms of the disease. Also called **stadium invasioni**

incubator /ˈɪŋkjʊbeɪtə/ *noun* **1.** an apparatus for growing bacterial cultures **2.** an enclosed container in which a premature baby can be kept, within which conditions such as temperature and oxygen levels can be controlled

incurable /ɪnˈkjʊərəb(ə)l/ *adjective* who or which cannot be cured ○ *He is suffering from an incurable disease of the blood.* ■ *noun* a patient who will never be cured ○ *She has been admitted to a hospital for incurables.*

incus /ˈɪŋkəs/ *noun* one of the three ossicles in the middle ear, shaped like an anvil. See illustration at EAR in Supplement

independent /ˌɪndɪˈpendənt/ *adjective* not controlled by someone or something else

independent nursing function /ˌɪndɪpendənt ˈnɜːsɪŋ ˌfʌŋkʃən/ *noun* any part of the nurse's job for which the nurse takes full responsibility

Inderal /ˈɪndəræl/ a trade name for propranolol

index finger /ˈɪndeks ˌfɪŋɡə/ *noun* the first finger next to the thumb

indication /ˌɪndɪˈkeɪʃ(ə)n/ *noun* a situation or sign which suggests that a specific treatment should be given or that a condition has a particular cause ○ *Sulpha drugs have been replaced by antibiotics in many indications.* ◊ **contraindication**

indicator /ˈɪndɪkeɪtə/ *noun* **1.** a substance which shows something, e.g. a substance secreted in body fluids which shows which blood group a person belongs to **2.** something that serves as a warning or guide

indigenous /ɪnˈdɪdʒɪnəs/ *adjective* **1.** natural or inborn **2.** native to or representative of a country or region

indigestion /ˌɪndɪˈdʒestʃən/ *noun* a disturbance of the normal process of digestion, where the person experiences pain or discomfort in the stomach ○ *He is taking tablets to relieve his indigestion* or *He is taking indigestion tablets.* ◊ **dyspepsia**

indigo carmine /ˌɪndɪgəʊ ˈkɑːmaɪn/ *noun* a blue dye which is injected into a person to test how well their kidneys are working

indirect contact /ˌɪndaɪrekt ˈkɒntækt/ *noun* the fact of catching a disease by inhaling germs or by being in contact with a vector

individualise /ˌɪndɪˈvɪdʒuəˌlaɪz/, **individualize** *verb* to provide something that matches the needs of a specific person or situation ○ *individualised care*

individualised nursing care /ˌɪndɪvɪdʒuəlaɪzd ˈnɜːsɪŋ ˌkeə/ *noun* care which is designed to provide exactly what one particular patient needs ○ *The home's staff are specially trained to provide individualised nursing care.*

Indocid /ˈɪndəsɪd/ a trade name for indomethacin

indolent /ˈɪndələnt/ *adjective* **1.** causing little pain **2.** referring to an ulcer which develops slowly and does not heal

indomethacin /ˌɪndəʊˈmeθəsɪn/ *noun* a drug that reduces pain, fever and inflammation, especially that caused by arthritis

indrawn /ɪnˈdrɔːn/ *adjective* pulled inside

induce /ɪnˈdjuːs/ *verb* to make something happen

induced abortion /ɪnˌdjuːst əˈbɔːʃ(ə)n/ *noun* an abortion which is deliberately caused by drugs or by surgery

induction /ɪnˈdʌkʃən/ *noun* **1.** the process of starting or speeding up the birth of a baby **2.** the stimulation of an enzyme's production when the substance on which it acts increases in concentration **3.** a process by which one part of an embryo influences another part's development **4.** information and support given to new employees in an organisation

induction of labour /ɪnˌdʌkʃən əv ˈleɪbə/ *noun* the action of starting childbirth artificially

induration /ˌɪndjʊəˈreɪʃ(ə)n/ *noun* the hardening of tissue or of an artery because of pathological change

industrial disease /ɪnˈdʌstriəl dɪˌziːz/ *noun* a disease which is caused by the type of work done by a worker or by the conditions in which he or she works, e.g. by dust produced or chemicals used in the factory

inebriation /ɪˌniːbriˈeɪʃ(ə)n/ *noun* a state where a person is drunk, especially habitually drunk

inertia /ɪˈnɜːʃə/ *noun* a lack of activity in the body or mind

in extremis /ɪn ɪksˈtriːmɪs/ *adverb* at the moment of death

infant /ˈɪnfənt/ *noun* a child under two years of age

infanticide /ɪnˈfæntɪsaɪd/ *noun* **1.** the act of killing an infant **2.** a person who kills an infant

infantile /ˈɪnfəntaɪl/ *adjective* referring to small children

infantile convulsions /ˌɪnfəntaɪl kənˈvʌlʃənz/, **infantile spasms** *plural noun* convulsions or minor epileptic fits in small children

infantile paralysis /ˌɪnfəntaɪl pəˈræləsɪs/ *noun* a former name for poliomyelitis

infantilism /ɪnˈfæntɪlɪz(ə)m/ *noun* a condition in which a person keeps some characteristics of an infant when he or she becomes an adult

infant mortality rate /ˌɪnfənt mɔːˈtælɪti ˌreɪt/ *noun* the number of infants who die per thousand births

infarct /ˈɪnfɑːkt/ *noun* an area of tissue which is killed when the blood supply is cut off by the blockage of an artery

infarction /ɪnˈfɑːkʃ(ə)n/ *noun* a condition in which tissue is killed by the cutting off of the blood supply

infect /ɪnˈfekt/ *verb* to contaminate someone or something with microorganisms that cause disease or toxins ○ *The disease infected her liver.* ○ *The whole arm soon became infected.*

infected wound /ɪnˌfektɪd ˈwuːnd/ *noun* a wound into which bacteria have entered

infection /ɪnˈfekʃən/ *noun* **1.** the entry or introduction into the body of microorganisms, which then multiply ○ *As a carrier he was spreading infection to other people in the office.* **2.** an illness which is caused by the entry of microbes into the body ○ *She is susceptible to minor infections.*

infectious /ɪnˈfekʃəs/ *adjective* referring to a disease which is caused by microorganisms and can be transmitted to other persons by direct means ○ *This strain of flu is highly infectious.* ○ *Her measles is at the infectious stage.*

infectious disease /ɪnˌfekʃəs dɪˈziːz/ *noun* a disease caused by microorganisms such as bacteria, viruses or fungi. ◊ **communicable disease**, **contagious disease**

infectious mononucleosis /ɪnˌfekʃəs ˌmɒnəʊˌnjuːkliˈəʊsɪs/ *noun* an infectious disease where the body has an excessive number of white blood cells. Also called **glandular fever**

infectious parotitis /ɪnˌfekʃəs ˌpærəˈtaɪtɪs/ *noun* same as **mumps**

infective /ɪnˈfektɪv/ *adjective* referring to a disease caused by a microorganism, which can be caught from another person but which may not always be directly transmitted

inferior /ɪnˈfɪəriə/ *adjective* referring to a lower part of the body. Opposite **superior**

inferior aspect /ɪnˌfɪəriər ˈæspekt/ *noun* a view of the body from below

inferiority /ɪn,fɪəri'ɒrɪti/ *noun* the fact of being lower in value or quality, substandard

inferiority complex /ɪn,fɪəri'ɒrɪti ,kɒmpleks/ *noun* a mental disorder arising from a combination of wanting to be noticed and fear of humiliation. The resulting behaviour may either be aggression or withdrawal from the external world.

inferior mesenteric artery /ɪn,fɪəriə mesen ,terɪk 'ɑːtəri/ *noun* one of the arteries which supply the transverse colon and rectum

inferior vena cava /ɪn,fɪəriə ,viːnə 'kɑːvə/ *noun* the main vein carrying blood from the lower part of the body to the heart. See illustration at **HEART** in Supplement, **KIDNEY** in Supplement

infertility /,ɪnfə'tɪlɪti/ *noun* the fact of not being fertile, not able to reproduce

infestation /,ɪnfe'steɪʃ(ə)n/ *noun* the fact of having large numbers of parasites, or an invasion of the body by parasites ○ *The condition is caused by infestation of the hair with lice.*

infiltrate /'ɪnfɪltreɪt/ *verb* (*of liquid or waste*) to pass from one part of the body to another through a wall or membrane and be deposited in the other part ■ *noun* a substance which has infiltrated a part of the body

infiltration /,ɪnfɪl'treɪʃ(ə)n/ *noun* **1.** the process where a liquid passes through the walls of one part of the body into another part **2.** a condition in which waste is brought to and deposited around cells

infirm /ɪn'fɜːm/ *adjective* old and weak

infirmary /ɪn'fɜːməri/ *noun* **1.** a room in a school or workplace where people can go if they are ill **2.** a former name for a hospital (NOTE: **Infirmary** is still used in the names of some hospitals: **the Glasgow Royal Infirmary.**)

infirmity /ɪn'fɜːmɪti/ *noun* a lack of strength and energy because of illness or age (*formal*)

inflamed /ɪn'fleɪmd/ *adjective* sore, red and swollen ○ *The skin has become inflamed around the sore.*

inflammation /,ɪnflə'meɪʃ(ə)n/ *noun* the fact of having become sore, red and swollen as a reaction to an infection, an irritation or a blow ○ *She has an inflammation of the bladder* or *a bladder inflammation.* ○ *The body's reaction to infection took the form of an inflammation of the eyelid.*

inflammatory /ɪn'flæmət(ə)ri/ *adjective* causing an organ or a tissue to become sore, red and swollen

inflammatory bowel disease /ɪn ,flæmət(ə)ri 'baʊəl dɪ,ziːz/ *noun* any condition, e.g. Crohn's disease, colitis or ileitis, in which the bowel becomes inflamed

inflammatory response /ɪn,flæmət(ə)ri rɪ 'spɒns/, **inflammatory reaction** /ɪn ,flæmət(ə)ri rɪ'ækʃən/ *noun* any condition where an organ or a tissue reacts to an external stimulus by becoming inflamed ○ *She showed an inflammatory response to the ointment.*

influenza /,ɪnflu'enzə/ *noun* an infectious disease of the upper respiratory tract with fever and muscular aches, which is transmitted by a virus and can occur in epidemics. Also called **flu**

informed /ɪn'fɔːmd/ *adjective* having the latest information

informed consent /ɪn,fɔːmd kən'sent/ *noun* an agreement to allow a procedure to be carried out, given by a patient, or the guardian of a patient, who has been provided with all the necessary information

infra- /'ɪnfrə/ *prefix* below

infrared /,ɪnfrə'red/ *adjective* relating to infrared radiation ■ *noun* invisible electromagnetic radiation between light and radio waves

infrared rays /,ɪnfrəred 'reɪz/ *plural noun* long invisible rays, below the visible red end of the colour spectrum, used to produce heat in body tissues in the treatment of traumatic and inflammatory conditions. ◊ **light therapy**

infundibulum /,ɪnfʌn'dɪbjʊləm/ *noun* any part of the body shaped like a funnel, especially the stem which attaches the pituitary gland to the hypothalamus

infusion /ɪn'fjuːʒ(ə)n/ *noun* **1.** a drink made by pouring boiling water on a dry substance such as herb tea or a powdered drug **2.** the process of putting of liquid into someone's body, using a drip

ingesta /ɪn'dʒestə/ *plural noun* food or liquid that enters the body via the mouth

ingestion /ɪn'dʒestʃən/ *noun* the act of taking in food, drink or medicine by the mouth

ingrowing toenail /,ɪngrəʊɪŋ 'təʊneɪl/, **ingrowing nail** /,ɪngrəʊɪŋ 'neɪl/, **ingrown toenail** /,ɪngrəʊn 'təʊneɪl/ *noun* a toenail which is growing into the skin at the side of the nail, causing pain and swelling. The toenail cuts into the tissue on either side of it, creating inflammation and sometimes sepsis and ulceration.

inguinal /'ɪŋgwɪn(ə)l/ *adjective* referring to the groin

inguinal canal /,ɪŋgwɪn(ə)l kə'næl/ *noun* a passage in the lower abdominal wall, carrying the spermatic cord in the male and the round ligament of the uterus in the female

inguinal hernia /,ɪŋgwɪn(ə)l 'hɜːniə/ *noun* a hernia where the intestine bulges through the muscles in the groin

inguinal ligament /,ɪŋgwɪn(ə)l 'lɪgəmənt/ *noun* a ligament in the groin, running from the spine to the pubis. Also called **Poupart's ligament**

inguinal region /,ɪŋgwɪn(ə)l 'riːdʒən/ *noun* the part of the body where the lower abdomen joins the top of the thigh. ◊ **groin**

inhalation /ˌɪnhəˈleɪʃ(ə)n/ *noun* **1.** the act of breathing in. Opposite **exhalation 2.** the action of breathing in a medicinal substance as part of a treatment **3.** a medicinal substance which is breathed in

inhale /ɪnˈheɪl/ *verb* **1.** to breathe in, or breathe something in ○ *She inhaled some toxic gas fumes and was rushed to hospital.* **2.** to breathe in a medicinal substance as part of a treatment. Opposite **exhale**

inhaler /ɪnˈheɪlə/ *noun* a small device for administering medicinal substances into the mouth or nose so that they can be breathed in

inherent /ɪnˈhɪərənt/ *adjective* referring to a thing which is part of the essential character of a person or a permanent characteristic of an organism

inherit /ɪnˈherɪt/ *verb* to receive genetically controlled characteristics from a parent ○ *She inherited her father's red hair.* ○ *Haemophilia is a condition which is inherited through the mother's genes.*

inheritance /ɪnˈherɪt(ə)ns/ *noun* **1.** the process by which genetically controlled characteristics pass from parents to offspring ○ *the inheritance of chronic inflammatory bowel disease* **2.** all of the qualities and characteristics which are passed down from parents ○ *an unfortunate part of our genetic inheritance*

inherited /ɪnˈherɪtɪd/ *adjective* passed on from a parent through the genes ○ *an inherited disorder of the lungs*

inhibit /ɪnˈhɪbɪt/ *verb* to prevent an action happening, or stop a functional process ○ *Aspirin inhibits the clotting of blood.*

inhibition /ˌɪnhɪˈbɪʃ(ə)n/ *noun* **1.** the action of blocking or preventing something happening, especially of preventing a muscle or organ from functioning properly **2.** (*in psychology*) the suppression of a thought which is associated with a sense of guilt **3.** (*in psychology*) the blocking of a spontaneous action by some mental influence

inhibitor /ɪnˈhɪbɪtə/ *noun* a substance which inhibits

inject /ɪnˈdʒekt/ *verb* to put a liquid into someone's body under pressure, by using a hollow needle inserted into the tissues ○ *He was injected with morphine.* ○ *She injected herself with a drug.*

injected /ɪnˈdʒektɪd/ *adjective* **1.** referring to a liquid or substance introduced into the body **2.** referring to surface blood vessels which are swollen

injection /ɪnˈdʒekʃən/ *noun* **1.** the act of injecting a liquid into the body ○ *He had a penicillin injection.* **2.** a liquid introduced into the body

injury /ˈɪndʒəri/ *noun* damage or a wound caused to a person's body ○ *His injuries required*

hospital treatment. ○ *He received severe facial injuries in the accident.*

injury scoring system /ˌɪndʒəri ˈskɔːrɪŋ ˌsɪstəm/ *noun* any system used for deciding how severe an injury is ○ *a standard lung injury scoring system* Abbreviation **ISS**

inlay /ˈɪnleɪ/ *noun* (*in dentistry*) a type of filling for teeth

inlet /ˈɪnlet/ *noun* a passage or opening through which a cavity can be entered

innate /ɪˈneɪt/ *adjective* inherited, which is present in a body from birth

inner pleura /ˌɪnə ˈplʊərə/ *noun* same as **visceral pleura**

innervation /ˌɪnɜːˈveɪʃ(ə)n/ *noun* the nerve supply to an organ, including both motor nerves and sensory nerves

innocent /ˈɪnəs(ə)nt/ *adjective* referring to a growth which is benign, not malignant

innominate /ɪˈnɒmɪnət/ *adjective* with no name

innominate artery /ɪˌnɒmɪnət ˈɑːtəri/ *noun* the largest branch of the arch of the aorta, which continues as the right common carotid and right subclavian arteries

innominate bone /ɪˌnɒmɪnət ˈbəʊn/ *noun* same as **hip bone**

innominate vein /ɪˌnɒmɪnət ˈveɪn/ *noun* same as **brachiocephalic vein**

inoculate /ɪˈnɒkjʊleɪt/ *verb* to introduce vaccine into a person's body in order to make the body create its own antibodies, so making the person immune to the disease ○ *The baby was inoculated against diphtheria.* (NOTE: You inoculate someone **with** or **against** a disease.)

inoculation /ɪˌnɒkjʊˈleɪʃ(ə)n/ *noun* the action of inoculating someone ○ *Has the baby had a diphtheria inoculation?*

inoculum /ɪˈnɒkjʊləm/ *noun* a substance used for inoculation, e.g. a vaccine (NOTE: The plural is **inocula.**)

inoperable /ɪnˈɒpər(ə)b(ə)l/ *adjective* referring to a condition which cannot be operated on ○ *The surgeon decided that the cancer was inoperable.*

inorganic /ˌɪnɔːˈɡænɪk/ *adjective* referring to a substance which is not made from animal or vegetable sources

inorganic acid /ˌɪnɔːɡænɪk ˈæsɪd/ *noun* an acid which comes from minerals, used in dilute form to help indigestion

inotropic /ˌɪnəʊˈtrɒpɪk/ *adjective* affecting the way muscles contract, especially those of the heart

inpatient /ˈɪnˌpeɪʃ(ə)nt/ *noun* someone who stays overnight or for some time in a hospital for treatment or observation. Compare **outpatient**

inquest /'ɪŋkwest/ noun an inquiry by a coroner into the cause of a death

insanitary /ɪn'sænɪt(ə)ri/ adjective not hygienic ○ *Cholera spread rapidly because of the insanitary conditions in the town.*

insanity /ɪn'sænɪti/ noun a psychotic mental disorder or illness

insect /'ɪnsekt/ noun a small animal with six legs and a body in three parts

insect bite /'ɪnsekt baɪt/ noun a sting caused by an insect which punctures the skin to suck blood, and in so doing introduces irritants

COMMENT: Most insect bites are simply irritating. Others can be more serious, as insects can carry the organisms which produce typhus, sleeping sickness, malaria, filariasis and many other diseases.

insecticide /ɪn'sektɪsaɪd/ noun a substance which kills insects

insemination /ɪn,semɪ'neɪʃ(ə)n/ noun the fertilisation of an ovum by a sperm

insensible /ɪn'sensɪb(ə)l/ adjective **1.** lacking feeling or consciousness **2.** not aware of or responding to a stimulus **3.** too slight to be perceived by the senses

insertion /ɪn'sɜːʃ(ə)n/ noun the point of attachment of a muscle to a bone

insidious /ɪn'sɪdiəs/ adjective causing harm without showing any obvious signs

insidious disease /ɪn,sɪdiəs dɪ'ziːz/ noun a disease which causes damage before being detected

insight /'ɪnsaɪt/ noun the ability of a person to realise that he or she is ill or has particular problems or characteristics

in situ /,ɪn 'sɪtjuː/ adverb in place

insoluble /ɪn'sɒljʊb(ə)l/ adjective not able to be dissolved in liquid

insoluble fibre /ɪn,sɒljʊb(ə)l 'faɪbə/ noun the fibre in bread and cereals, which is not digested but which swells inside the intestine

insomnia /ɪn'sɒmniə/ noun the inability to sleep ○ *She experiences insomnia.* ○ *What does the doctor give you for your insomnia?* Also called **sleeplessness**

insomniac /ɪn'sɒmniæk/ noun a person who has insomnia

inspiration /,ɪnspɪ'reɪʃ(ə)n/ noun the act of taking air into the lungs. Opposite **expiration**

instep /'ɪnstep/ noun an arched top part of the foot

instillation /,ɪnstɪ'leɪʃ(ə)n/ noun **1.** the process of putting a liquid in drop by drop **2.** a liquid put in drop by drop

instinct /'ɪnstɪŋkt/ noun a tendency or ability which the body has from birth and does not need to learn ○ *The body has a natural instinct to protect itself from danger.*

institution /,ɪnstɪ'tjuːʃ(ə)n/ noun a place where people are cared for, e.g. a hospital or clinic, especially a psychiatric hospital or children's home

institutionalisation /,ɪnstɪ,tjuːʃ(ə)nəlaɪ'zeɪʃ(ə)n/, **institutionalization**, **institutional neurosis** /,ɪnstɪtjuːʃən(ə)l njʊ'rəʊsɪs/ noun a condition in which someone has become so adapted to life in an institution that it is impossible for him or her to live outside it

instrument /'ɪnstrʊmənt/ noun a piece of equipment or a tool ○ *The doctor had a box of surgical instruments.*

instrumental delivery /,ɪnstrʊmənt(ə)l dɪ'lɪv(ə)ri/ noun childbirth where the doctor uses forceps to help the baby out of the mother's uterus

insufficiency /,ɪnsə'fɪʃ(ə)nsi/ noun the fact of not being strong or large enough to perform usual functions ○ *The patient is suffering from a renal insufficiency.*

insufflation /,ɪnsə'fleɪʃ(ə)n/ noun the act of blowing gas, vapour or powder into the lungs or another body cavity as a treatment

insulin /'ɪnsjʊlɪn/ noun a hormone produced by the islets of Langerhans in the pancreas

insulinase /'ɪnsjʊlɪneɪz/ noun an enzyme which breaks down insulin

insulin dependence /,ɪnsjʊlɪn dɪ'pendəns/ noun the fact of being dependent on insulin injections

insulin-dependent diabetes /,ɪnsjʊlɪn dɪ,pendənt ,daɪə'biːtiz/ noun same as **Type I diabetes mellitus**

insulinoma /,ɪnsjʊlɪ'nəʊmə/ noun a tumour in the islets of Langerhans

insulin-resistant /,ɪnsjʊlɪn rɪ'zɪst(ə)nt/ adjective referring to a condition in which the muscle and other tissue cells respond inadequately to insulin, as in Type II diabetes

insuloma /,ɪnsjʊ'ləʊmə/ noun same as **insulinoma**

insult /'ɪnsʌlt/ noun **1.** a physical injury or trauma **2.** something that causes a physical injury or trauma

Intal /'ɪntæl/ a trade name for a preparation of cromolyn sodium

integrated service /,ɪntɪgreɪtɪd 'sɜːvɪs/ noun a broad care service provided by health and social agencies acting together

integrative medicine /,ɪntɪgreɪtɪv 'med(ə)s(ə)n/ noun the combination of mainstream therapies and those complementary or alternative therapies for which there is scientific evidence of efficacy and safety

integument /ɪn'tegjʊmənt/ noun a covering layer, e.g. the skin

intellect /'ɪntɪlekt/ noun a person's ability to think, reason and understand

intelligence /ɪnˈtelɪdʒəns/ *noun* the ability to learn and understand quickly

intelligence quotient /ɪnˈtelɪdʒəns ˌkwəʊʃ(ə)nt/ *noun* the ratio of the mental age, as given by an intelligence test, to the chronological age of the person. Abbreviation **IQ**

intensity /ɪnˈtensɪti/ *noun* the strength of e.g. pain

intensive care /ɪnˌtensɪv ˈkeə/ *noun* **1.** the continual supervision and treatment of an extremely ill person in a special section of a hospital ○ *The patient was put in intensive care.* ◊ **residential care 2.** same as **intensive care unit**

intensive care unit /ɪnˌtensɪv ˈkeə ˌjuːnɪt/ *noun* a section of a hospital equipped with life-saving and life-support equipment in which seriously ill people who need constant medical attention are cared for. Abbreviation **ICU**

intention /ɪnˈtenʃən/ *noun* **1.** the healing process **2.** a plan to do something

intention tremor /ɪnˈtenʃən ˌtremə/ *noun* a trembling of the hands seen when people suffering from particular brain diseases make voluntary movements to try to touch something

inter- /ɪntə/ *prefix* between

interaction /ˌɪntərˈækʃən/ *noun* an effect which two or more substances such as drugs have on each other

interatrial septum /ˌɪntərˈeɪtriəl ˌseptəm/ *noun* a membrane between the right and left atria in the heart

intercalated /ɪnˈtɜːkəleɪtɪd/ *adjective* inserted between other tissues

intercalated disc /ɪnˌtɜːkəleɪtɪd ˈdɪsk/ *noun* closely applied cell membranes at the end of adjacent cells in cardiac muscle, seen as transverse lines

intercellular /ˌɪntəˈseljʊlə/ *adjective* between the cells in tissue

intercostal /ˌɪntəˈkɒst(ə)l/ *adjective* between the ribs ■ *noun* same as **intercostal muscle**

intercostal muscle /ɪntəˌkɒst(ə)l ˈmʌs(ə)l/ *noun* one of the muscles between the ribs

COMMENT: The intercostal muscles expand and contract the thorax, so changing the pressure in the thorax and making the person breathe in or out. There are three layers of intercostal muscle: external, internal and innermost or intercostalis intimis.

intercurrent disease /ˌɪntəkʌrənt dɪˈziːz/, **intercurrent infection** /ˌɪntəkʌrənt ɪnˈfekʃən/ *noun* a disease or infection which affects someone who has another disease

interdigital /ˌɪntəˈdɪdʒɪt(ə)l/ *adjective* referring to the space between the fingers or toes

interdisciplinary /ˌɪntəˌdɪsɪˈplɪnəri/ *adjective* combining two or more different areas of medical or scientific study

interferon /ˌɪntəˈfɪərɒn/ *noun* a protein produced by cells, usually in response to a virus, and which then reduces the spread of viruses

interior /ɪnˈtɪəriə/ *noun* a part which is inside ■ *adjective* inside

interleukin /ˌɪntəˈluːkɪn/ *noun* a protein produced by the body's immune system

interleukin-1 /ˌɪntəluːkɪn ˈwʌn/ *noun* a protein which causes high temperature. Abbreviation **IL-1**

interleukin-2 /ˌɪntəluːkɪn ˈtuː/ *noun* a protein which stimulates T-cell production, used in the treatment of cancer. Abbreviation **IL-2**

interlobar /ˌɪntəˈləʊbə/ *adjective* between lobes

interlobar artery /ˌɪntələʊbər ˈɑːtəri/ *noun* an artery running towards the cortex on each side of a renal pyramid

interlobular /ˌɪntəˈlɒbjʊlə/ *adjective* between lobules

interlobular artery /ɪntəˈlɒbjʊlə ˌɑːtəri/ *noun* one of the arteries running to the glomeruli of the kidneys

intermediate care /ˌɪntəmiːdiət ˈkeə/ *noun* care following surgery or illness that can be delivered in special units attached to a hospital or in the person's home by a special multidisciplinary team

intermittent /ˌɪntəˈmɪt(ə)nt/ *adjective* occurring at intervals

intermittent claudication /ˌɪntəmɪt(ə)nt ˌklɔːdɪˈkeɪʃ(ə)n/ *noun* a condition of the arteries causing severe pain in the legs which makes the person limp after having walked a short distance (NOTE: The symptoms increase with walking, stop after a short rest and recur when the person walks again.)

intermittent fever /ˌɪntəmɪt(ə)nt ˈfiːvə/ *noun* fever which rises and falls regularly, as in malaria

intermittent self-catheterisation /ˌɪntəmɪt(ə)nt self ˌkæθɪtəraɪˈzeɪʃ(ə)n/ *noun* a procedure in which someone puts a catheter through the urethra into their own bladder from time to time to empty out the urine. Abbreviation **ISC**

internal /ɪnˈtɜːn(ə)l/ *adjective* inside the body or a body part

internal auditory meatus /ɪnˌtɜːn(ə)l ˌɔːdɪt(ə)ri miˈeɪtəs/ *noun* a channel which takes the auditory nerve through the temporal bone

internal cardiac massage /ɪnˌtɜːn(ə)l ˌkɑːdiæk ˈmæsɑːʒ/ *noun* a method of making the heart start beating again by pressing on the heart itself

internal carotid /ɪnˌtɜːn(ə)l kæˈrɒtɪd/ *noun* an artery in the neck, behind the external carotid, which gives off the ophthalmic artery and ends by dividing into the anterior and middle cerebral arteries

internal derangement of the knee /ɪn
ˌtɜːn(ə)l dɪ'reɪnʒmənt əv ðə 'niː/ *noun* a condition in which the knee cannot function properly because of a torn meniscus. Abbreviation **IDK**

internal ear /ɪnˌtɜːn(ə)l 'ɪə/ *noun* the part of the ear inside the head, behind the eardrum, containing the semicircular canals, the vestibule and the cochlea

internal haemorrhage /ɪnˌtɜːn(ə)l 'hem(ə)rɪdʒ/ *noun* a haemorrhage which takes place inside the body

internal haemorrhoids /ɪnˌtɜːn(ə)l 'hemərɔɪdz/ *plural noun* swollen veins inside the anus

internal iliac artery /ɪnˌtɜːn(ə)l 'ɪliæk ˌɑːtəri/ *noun* an artery which branches from the aorta in the abdomen and leads to the pelvis

internal injury /ɪnˌtɜːn(ə)l 'ɪndʒəri/ *noun* damage to one of the internal organs

internal jugular /ɪnˌtɜːn(ə)l 'dʒʌɡjʊlə/ *noun* the largest jugular vein in the neck, leading to the brachiocephalic veins

internal nares /ɪnˌtɜːn(ə)l 'neəriːz/ *plural noun* the two openings shaped like funnels leading from the nasal cavity to the pharynx. Also called **posterior nares**

internal oblique /ɪnˌtɜːn(ə)l ə'bliːk/ *noun* the middle layer of muscle covering the abdomen, beneath the external oblique

internal respiration /ɪnˌtɜːn(ə)l ˌrespɪ'reɪʃ(ə)n/ *noun* the part of respiration concerned with the passage of oxygen from the blood to the tissues, and the passage of carbon dioxide from the tissues to the blood

International Committee of the Red Cross /ɪntəˌnæʃ(ə)n(ə)l kəˌmɪti əv ðə ˌred 'krɒs/ *noun* an international organisation which provides mainly emergency medical help, but also relief to victims of earthquakes, floods and other disasters, or to prisoners of war. Abbreviation **ICRC**

International Council of Nurses /ˌɪntənæʃ(ə)n(ə)l ˌkaʊnsəl əv 'nɜːsɪz/ *noun* an organisation founded in 1899 which now represents nurses in more than 120 countries. Its aims are to bring nurses together, to advance nursing worldwide and to influence health policies. Abbreviation **ICN**

international unit /ˌɪntənæʃ(ə)nəl 'juːnɪt/ *noun* an internationally agreed standard used in pharmacy as a measure of a substance such as a drug or hormone. Abbreviation **IU**

internodal /ˌɪntə'nəʊd(ə)l/ *adjective* between two nodes

interosseous /ˌɪntər'ɒsiəs/ *adjective* between bones

interparietal /ˌɪntəpə'raɪət(ə)l/ *adjective* between parietal parts, especially between the parietal bones ■ *noun* same as **interparietal bone**

interparietal bone /ˌɪntəpə'raɪət(ə)l ˌbəʊn/ *noun* a triangular bone in the back of the skull, rarely present in humans

interphalangeal joint /ˌɪntəfə'lændʒiəl ˌdʒɔɪnt/ *noun* a joint between the phalanges. Also called **IP joint**

interphase /'ɪntəfeɪz/ *noun* a stage of a cell between divisions

interpubic joint /ˌɪntəpjuːbɪk 'dʒɔɪnt/ *noun* a piece of cartilage which joins the two sections of the pubic bone. Also called **pubic symphysis**

intersex /'ɪntəseks/ *noun* an organism that has both male and female characteristics

intersexuality /ˌɪntəsekʃu'ælɪti/ *noun* a condition in which a baby has both male and female characteristics, as in Klinefelter's syndrome and Turner's syndrome

interstice /ɪn'tɜːstɪs/ *noun* a small space between body parts or within a tissue

interstitial /ˌɪntə'stɪʃ(ə)l/ *adjective* referring to tissue located in the spaces between parts of something, especially between the active tissues in an organ

interstitial cell /ˌɪntə'stɪʃ(ə)l ˌsel/ *noun* a testosterone-producing cell between the tubules in the testes. Also called **Leydig cell**

interstitial cell stimulating hormone /ˌɪntəˌstɪʃ(ə)l sel 'stɪmjʊleɪtɪŋ ˌhɔːməʊn/ *noun* a hormone produced by the pituitary gland which stimulates the formation of corpus luteum in females and testosterone in males. Abbreviation **ICSH**. Also called **luteinising hormone**

interstitial cystitis /ˌɪntəstɪʃ(ə)l sɪ'staɪtɪs/ *noun* a persistent nonbacterial condition in which someone has bladder pain and wants to pass urine frequently. It is often associated with Hunner's ulcer.

intertrigo /ˌɪntə'traɪgəʊ/ *noun* an irritation which occurs when two skin surfaces rub against each other, as in the armpit or between the buttocks

intertubercular plane /ˌɪntətjuːˌbɜːkjʊlə 'pleɪn/ *noun* same as **transtubercular plane**

intervention /ˌɪntə'venʃən/ *noun* a treatment

interventional radiology /ˌɪntəvenʃən(ə)l ˌreɪdi'ɒlədʒi/ *noun* the area of medicine which uses X-rays, ultrasound and CAT to guide small instruments into the body for procedures such as biopsies, draining fluids or widening narrow vessels

interventricular /ˌɪntəven'trɪkjʊlə/ *adjective* between ventricles in the heart or brain

interventricular foramen /ˌɪntəvenˌtrɪkjʊlə fə'reɪmən/ *noun* an opening in the brain between the lateral ventricle and the third ventricle, through which the cerebrospinal fluid passes

interventricular septum /ˌɪntəvenˌtrɪkjʊlə 'septəm/ *noun* a membrane between the right and left ventricles in the heart

intervertebral /ˌɪntə'vɜːtɪbr(ə)l/ *adjective* between vertebrae

intervertebral disc /ˌɪntə,vɜːtɪbrəl 'dɪsk/ *noun* a round plate of cartilage which separates two vertebrae in the spinal column. See illustration at **CARTILAGINOUS JOINT** in Supplement. Also called **vertebral disc**

intervertebral foramen /ˌɪntə,vɜːtɪbrəl fə 'reɪmən/ *noun* a space between two vertebrae

intestinal /ɪn'testɪn(ə)l/ *adjective* referring to the intestine

intestinal anastomosis /ɪn,testɪn(ə)l ə ˌnæstə'məʊsɪs/ *noun* a surgical operation to join one part of the intestine to another, after a section has been removed

intestinal flora /ɪn,testɪn(ə)l 'flɔːrə/ *plural noun* beneficial bacteria which are always present in the intestine

intestinal glands /ɪn'testɪn(ə)l glændz/ *plural noun* tubular glands found in the mucous membrane of the small and large intestine, especially those between the bases of the villi in the small intestine. Also called **Lieberkühn's glands, crypts of Lieberkühn**

intestinal obstruction /ɪn,testɪn(ə)l əb 'strʌkʃən/ *noun* a blocking of the intestine

intestinal villi /ɪn,testɪn(ə)l 'vɪlaɪ/ *plural noun* projections on the walls of the intestine which help in the digestion of food

intestinal wall /ɪn,testɪn(ə)l 'wɔːl/ *noun* the layers of tissue which form the intestine

intestine /ɪn'testɪn/ *noun* the part of the digestive system between the stomach and the anus that digests and absorbs food. ◊ **large intestine, small intestine** (NOTE: For other terms referring to the intestines, see words beginning with **entero-**.)

intima /'ɪntɪmə/ ♦ **tunica intima**

intolerance /ɪn'tɒlərəns/ *noun* the fact of being unable to endure something such as pain or to take a medicine without an adverse reaction ○ *He developed an intolerance to penicillin.*

intoxication /ɪn,tɒksɪ'keɪʃ(ə)n/ *noun* a condition which results from the absorption and diffusion in the body of a substance such as alcohol ○ *She was driving in a state of intoxication.*

intra- /ɪntrə/ *prefix* inside

intra-abdominal /ˌɪntrə æb'dɒmɪn(ə)l/ *adjective* inside the abdomen

intra-articular /ˌɪntrə ɑː'tɪkjʊlə/ *adjective* inside a joint

intracellular /ˌɪntrə'seljʊlə/ *adjective* inside a cell

intracerebral haematoma /ˌɪntrə,serəbrəl ˌhiːmə'təʊmə/ *noun* a blood clot inside a cerebral hemisphere

intracranial /ˌɪntrə'kreɪniəl/ *adjective* inside the skull

intracranial pressure /ˌɪntrəkreɪniəl 'preʃə/ *noun* the pressure of the subarachnoidal fluid, which fills the space between the skull and the brain. Abbreviation **ICP**

intractable /ɪn'træktəb(ə)l/ *adjective* not able to be controlled ○ *an operation to relieve intractable pain*

intracutaneous /ˌɪntrəkjuː'teɪniəs/ *adjective* inside layers of skin tissue

intracutaneous injection /ˌɪntrəkjuː ˌteɪniəs ɪn'dʒekʃən/ *noun* an injection of a liquid between the layers of skin, as for a test for an allergy

intradermal test /ˌɪntrə'dɜːm(ə)l ˌtest/ *noun* a test requiring an injection into the thickness of the skin, e.g. a Mantoux test or an allergy test

intradural /ˌɪntrə'djʊərəl/ *adjective* inside the dura mater

intramedullary /ˌɪntrəme'dʌləri/ *adjective* inside the bone marrow or spinal cord

intramural /ˌɪntrə'mjʊərəl/ *adjective* inside the wall of an organ

intramuscular /ˌɪntrə'mʌskjʊlə/ *adjective* inside a muscle

intramuscular injection /ˌɪntrə,mʌskjʊlə ɪn 'dʒekʃən/ *noun* an injection of liquid into a muscle, e.g. for a slow release of a drug

intranasal /ˌɪntrə'neɪz(ə)l/ *adjective* inside or into the nose

intraocular /ˌɪntrə'ɒkjʊlə/ *adjective* inside the eye

intraocular lens /ˌɪntrə,ɒkjʊlə 'lenz/ *noun* an artificial lens implanted inside the eye. Abbreviation **IOL**

intraocular pressure /ˌɪntrə,ɒkjʊlə 'preʃə/ *noun* the pressure inside the eyeball (NOTE: If the pressure is too high, it causes glaucoma.)

intraoperative ultrasound /ˌɪntrəɒpərətɪv 'ʌltrəsaʊnd/ *noun* high-resolution imaging used in surgery. Abbreviation **IOUS**

intraorbital /ˌɪntrə'ɔːbɪt(ə)l/ *adjective* within the orbit of the eye

intraosseous /ˌɪntrə'ɒsiəs/ *adjective* within a bone

intrathecal /ˌɪntrə'θiːk(ə)l/ *adjective* inside a sheath, especially inside the intradural or subarachnoid space

intratracheal /ˌɪntrətrə'kiəl/ *adjective* within the trachea. Also called **endotracheal**

intrauterine /ˌɪntrə'juːtəraɪn/ *adjective* inside the uterus

intrauterine contraceptive device /ˌɪntrə juːtəraɪn ˌkɒntrə'septɪv dɪ,vaɪs/, **intrauterine**

device /ˌɪntrəjuːtəraɪn dɪˈvaɪs/ *noun* a plastic coil placed inside the uterus to prevent pregnancy. Abbreviation **IUCD, IUD**

intravascular /ˌɪntrəˈvæskjʊlə/ *adjective* inside the blood vessels

intravenous /ˌɪntrəˈviːnəs/ *adjective* into a vein. Abbreviation **IV**

intravenous drip /ˌɪntrəviːnəs ˈdrɪp/ *noun* a thin tube that is inserted into a vein and is used to very gradually give a person fluids, either for rehydration, feeding or medication purposes

intravenous feeding /ˌɪntrəviːnəs ˈfiːdɪŋ/ *noun* the procedure of giving someone liquid food by means of a tube inserted into a vein

intravenous injection /ˌɪntrəviːnəs ɪnˈdʒekʃən/ *noun* an injection of liquid into a vein, e.g. for the fast release of a drug

intravenously /ˌɪntrəˈviːnəsli/ *adverb* into a vein ○ *a fluid given intravenously*

intravenous pyelogram /ˌɪntrəviːnəs ˈpaɪələɡræm/, **intravenous urogram** /ˌɪntrəviːnəs ˈjʊərəɡræm/ *noun* a series of X-ray photographs of the kidneys using pyelography. Abbreviation **IVP**

intravenous pyelography /ˌɪntrəviːnəs ˌpaɪəˈlɒɡrəfi/, **intravenous urography** /ˌɪntrəviːnəs jʊˈrɒɡrəfi/ *noun* an X-ray examination of the urinary tract after opaque liquid has been injected intravenously into the body and taken by the blood into the kidneys

intraventricular /ˌɪntrəvenˈtrɪkjʊlə/ *adjective* inside or placed into a ventricle in the heart or the brain

intrinsic /ɪnˈtrɪnsɪk/ *adjective* belonging to the essential nature of an organism, or entirely within an organ or part

intrinsic factor /ɪnˌtrɪnsɪk ˈfæktə/ *noun* a protein produced in the gastric glands which reacts with the extrinsic factor, and which, if lacking, causes pernicious anaemia

intrinsic ligament /ɪnˌtrɪnsɪk ˈlɪɡəmənt/ *noun* a ligament which forms part of the capsule surrounding a joint

intrinsic muscle /ɪnˌtrɪnsɪk ˈmʌs(ə)l/ *noun* a muscle lying completely inside the part or segment, especially of a limb, which it moves

intro- /ɪntrəʊ/ *prefix* inward

introitus /ɪnˈtrəʊɪtəs/ *noun* an opening into any hollow organ or canal

introjection /ˌɪntrəʊˈdʒekʃən/ *noun* a person's unconscious adoption of the attitudes or values of another person whom he or she wants to impress

introspection /ˌɪntrəˈspekʃən/ *noun* a detailed and sometimes obsessive mental self-examination of feelings, thoughts and motives

introversion /ˌɪntrəˈvɜːʃ(ə)n/ *noun* a condition in which a person is excessively interested in

himself or herself and his or her own mental state. Compare **extroversion**

introvert /ˈɪntrəvɜːt/ *noun* a person who thinks only about himself or herself and his or her own mental state. Compare **extrovert**

intubate /ˈɪntjuːbeɪt/ *verb* to insert a tube into any organ or part of the body. Also called **catheterise**

intubation /ˌɪntjuːˈbeɪʃ(ə)n/ *noun* the therapeutic insertion of a tube into the larynx through the glottis to allow the passage of air. Also called **catheterisation**

intumescence /ˌɪntjuːˈmes(ə)ns/ *noun* the swelling of an organ

intussusception /ˌɪntəsəˈsepʃən/ *noun* a condition in which part of the gastrointestinal tract becomes folded down inside the part beneath it, causing an obstruction and strangulation of the folded part

inunction /ɪnˈʌŋkʃən/ *noun* **1.** the act of rubbing an ointment into the skin so that the medicine in it is absorbed **2.** an ointment which is rubbed into the skin

invagination /ɪnˌvædʒɪˈneɪʃ(ə)n/ *noun* same as **intussusception**

invalid /ˈɪnvəlɪd/ (*dated*) *noun* someone who has had an illness and has not fully recovered from it or who has been permanently disabled ■ *adjective* weak or disabled

invasion /ɪnˈveɪʒ(ə)n/ *noun* the entry of bacteria into a body, or the first attack of a disease

invasive /ɪnˈveɪsɪv/ *adjective* **1.** referring to cancer which tends to spread throughout the body **2.** referring to an inspection or treatment which involves entering the body by making an incision. ◊ **non-invasive**

inverse care law /ˌɪnvɜːs ˈkeə ˌlɔː/ *noun* the idea that the people who most need care and services are least likely or able to access them

inversion /ɪnˈvɜːʃ(ə)n/ *noun* the fact of being turned towards the inside ○ *inversion of the foot* See illustration at **ANATOMICAL TERMS** in Supplement

investigative surgery /ɪnˌvestɪɡətɪv ˈsɜːdʒəri/ *noun* surgery to investigate the cause of a condition

in vitro /ˌɪn ˈviːtrəʊ/ *adjective, adverb* a Latin phrase meaning 'in a glass', i.e. in a test tube or similar container used in a laboratory

in vitro fertilisation /ˌɪn ˌviːtrəʊ ˌfɜːtəlaɪˈzeɪʃ(ə)n/ *noun* the fertilisation of an ovum in the laboratory. ◊ **test-tube baby**. Abbreviation **IVF**

in vivo *adjective, adverb* a Latin phrase meaning 'in living tissue', i.e. referring to an experiment which takes place on the living body

in vivo experiment /ɪn ˌviːvəʊ ɪkˈsperɪmənt/ *noun* an experiment on a living body, e.g. that of an animal

involucrum /ˌɪnvəˈluːkrəm/ *noun* a covering of new bone which forms over diseased bone

involuntary /ɪnˈvɒlənt(ə)ri/ *adjective* done automatically, without any conscious thought or decision-making being involved ○ *Patients are advised not to eat or drink, to reduce the risk of involuntary vomiting while on the operating table.*

involuntary action /ɪn ˌvɒlənt(ə)ri ˈækʃən/ *noun* an action which someone does without thinking or making a conscious decision

involuntary muscle /ɪn ˌvɒlənt(ə)ri ˈmʌs(ə)l/ *noun* a muscle supplied by the autonomic nervous system, and therefore not under voluntary control, e.g. the muscle which activates a vital organ such as the heart

involution /ˌɪnvəˈluːʃ(ə)n/ *noun* **1.** the return of an organ to its usual size, e.g. the shrinking of the uterus after childbirth **2.** a period of decline of organs which sets in after middle age

involutional /ˌɪnvəˈluːʃ(ə)n(ə)l/ *adjective* referring to involution

involutional melancholia /ɪnvəˌluːʃ(ə)n(ə)l ˌmelənˈkəʊliə/ *noun* a depression which occurs in people, mainly women, after middle age, probably caused by a change of endocrine secretions

iodine /ˈaɪədiːn/ *noun* a chemical element which is essential to the body, especially to the functioning of the thyroid gland (NOTE: Lack of iodine in the diet can cause goitre. The chemical symbol is I.)

IOL *abbreviation* intraocular lens

ion /ˈaɪən/ *noun* an atom that has an electric charge (NOTE: Ions with a positive charge are called cations and those with a negative charge are called anions.)

ionise /ˈaɪənaɪz/, **ionize** *verb* to give an atom an electric charge

ioniser /ˈaɪənaɪzə/, **ionizer** *noun* a machine that increases the amount of negative ions in the atmosphere of a room, so counteracting the effect of positive ions

iontophoresis /aɪˌɒntəʊfəˈriːsɪs/ *noun* the movement of ions through a biological material when an electric current passes through it

IOUS *abbreviation* intraoperative ultrasound

IPAV *abbreviation* intermittent positive airway ventilation. ◊ **positive pressure ventilation**

ipecacuanha /ˌɪpɪkækjʊˈænə/ *noun* a drug made from the root of an American plant, used as a treatment for coughs, and also as an emetic

IP joint /ˌaɪ ˈpiː ˌdʒɔɪnt/ *noun* same as **interphalangeal joint**

IPPV *abbreviation* intermittent positive pressure ventilation. ◊ **positive pressure ventilation**

ipratropium /ˌaɪprəˈtrəʊpiəm/, **ipratropium bromide** /ˌaɪprəˌtrəʊpiəm ˈbrəʊmaɪd/ *noun* a drug which helps to relax muscles in the airways,

used in the treatment of conditions such as asthma, bronchitis and emphysema

ipsilateral /ˌɪpsɪˈlætərəl/ *adjective* located on or affecting the same side of the body. Also called **homolateral**. Opposite **contralateral**

IQ *abbreviation* intelligence quotient

IRDS *abbreviation* infant respiratory distress syndrome

irid- /ɪrɪd/ *prefix* referring to the iris

iridectomy /ˌɪrɪˈdektəmi/ *noun* the surgical removal of part of the iris

iridocyclitis /ˌɪrɪdəʊsɪˈklaɪtɪs/ *noun* inflammation of the iris and the tissues which surround it

iridodialysis /ˌɪrɪdəʊdaɪˈæləsɪs/ *noun* the separation of the iris from its insertion

iridoplegia /ˌɪrɪdəʊˈpliːdʒə/ *noun* paralysis of the iris

iridoptosis /ˌɪrɪdəʊˈtəʊsɪs/ *noun* the pushing forward of the iris through a wound in the cornea

iridotomy /ˌɪrɪˈdɒtəmi/ *noun* a surgical incision into the iris

iris /ˈaɪrɪs/ *noun* a coloured ring in the eye, with the pupil at its centre. See illustration at EYE in Supplement

COMMENT: The iris acts like the aperture in a camera shutter, opening and closing to allow more or less light through the pupil into the eye.

iritis /aɪˈraɪtɪs/ *noun* inflammation of the iris

iron /ˈaɪən/ *noun* **1.** a chemical element essential to the body, present in foods such as liver and eggs **2.** a common grey metal (NOTE: The chemical symbol is Fe.)

iron-deficiency anaemia /ˌaɪən dɪˈfɪʃ(ə)nsi əˌniːmiə/ *noun* anaemia caused by a lack of iron in red blood cells

iron lung /ˌaɪən ˈlʌŋ/ *noun* same as **Drinker respirator**

irradiation /ɪˌreɪdiˈeɪʃ(ə)n/ *noun* **1.** the process of spreading from a centre, as e.g., nerve impulses do **2.** the use of radiation to treat people or to kill bacteria in food

irreducible hernia /ɪrɪˌdjuːsəb(ə)l ˈhɜːniə/ *noun* a hernia where the organ cannot be returned to its usual position

irrigation /ˌɪrɪˈgeɪʃ(ə)n/ *noun* the washing out of a cavity in the body

irritability /ˌɪrɪtəˈbɪlɪti/ *noun* the state of being irritable

irritable /ˈɪrɪtəb(ə)l/ *adjective* **1.** easily able to become inflamed and painful **2.** feeling annoyed and impatient

irritable bowel syndrome /ˌɪrɪtəb(ə)l ˈbaʊəl ˌsɪndrəʊm/ *noun* ♦ **mucous colitis**. Abbreviation **IBS**

irritable hip /ˌɪrɪtəb(ə)l ˈhɪp/ *noun* a condition of pain in the hip which is caused by swelling of the synovium. Treatment involves bed rest, traction and anti-inflammatory drugs.

irritant /'ɪrɪt(ə)nt/ *noun* a substance which can irritate

irritant dermatitis /ˌɪrɪt(ə)nt ˌdɜːməˈtaɪtɪs/ *noun* same as **contact dermatitis**

irritate /'ɪrɪteɪt/ *verb* to cause a painful reaction in part of the body, especially to make it inflamed ○ *Some types of wool can irritate the skin.*

irritation /ˌɪrɪˈteɪʃ(ə)n/ *noun* a feeling of being irritated ○ *an irritation caused by the ointment*

ISC *abbreviation* intermittent self-catheterisation

isch- /ɪsk/ *prefix* too little

ischaemia /ɪˈskiːmiə/ *noun* a deficient blood supply to a part of the body

ischaemic /ɪˈskiːmɪk/ *adjective* lacking in blood

ischi- /ɪski/ *prefix* same as **ischio-** (*used before vowels*)

ischia /'ɪskiə/ plural of **ischium**

ischial /'ɪskiəl/ *adjective* referring to the ischium or hip joint

ischial tuberosity /ˌɪskiəl ˌtjuːbəˈrɒsɪti/ *noun* a lump of bone forming the ring of the ischium

ischio- /ɪskiəʊ/ *prefix* referring to the ischium

ischiorectal /ˌɪskiəʊˈrekt(ə)l/ *adjective* referring to both the ischium and the rectum

ischiorectal abscess /ˌɪskiəʊˌrekt(ə)l ˈæbses/ *noun* an abscess which forms in fat cells between the anus and the ischium

ischiorectal fossa /ˌɪskiəʊˌrekt(ə)l ˈfɒsə/ *noun* a space on either side of the lower end of the rectum and anal canal

ischium /'ɪskiəm/ *noun* the lower part of the hip bone in the pelvis. See illustration at **PELVIS** in Supplement (NOTE: The plural is **ischia**.)

Ishihara colour charts /ˌɪʃɪhɑːrə ˈkʌlə ˌtʃɑːts/ *plural noun* charts used in a test for colour vision in which numbers or letters are shown in dots of primary colours with dots of other colours around them. People with normal colour vision can see them, but people who are colour-blind cannot.

islets of Langerhans /ˌaɪləts əv ˈlæŋəhæns/, **islands of Langerhans** /ˌaɪləndz əv ˈlæŋəhænz/, **islet cells** /'aɪlət selz/ *plural noun* groups of cells in the pancreas which secrete the hormones glucagon, insulin and gastrin [Described 1869. After Paul Langerhans (1847–88), Professor of Pathological Anatomy at Freiburg, Germany.]

iso- /aɪsəʊ/ *prefix* equal

isograft /'aɪsəʊɡrɑːft/ *noun* a graft of tissue from an identical twin. Also called **syngraft**

isoimmunisation /ˌaɪsəʊˌɪmjuːnaɪˈzeɪʃ(ə)n/, **isoimmunization** *noun* immunisation of a person with antigens derived from another person

isolation /ˌaɪsəˈleɪʃ(ə)n/ *noun* the separation of a person, especially one with an infectious disease, from others

isolation ward /ˌaɪsəˈleɪʃ(ə)n wɔːd/ *noun* a special ward where people who have dangerous infectious diseases can be kept isolated from others

isolator /'aɪsəleɪtə/ *noun* **1.** a large clear plastic bag in which a person can be nursed, or operated on, in a sterile environment **2.** a room or piece of equipment which keeps people or substances separated from others which may contaminate them ○ *an isolator stretcher* ○ *an isolator cabinet*

isoleucine /ˌaɪsəʊˈluːsiːn/ *noun* an essential amino acid

isometric /ˌaɪsəʊˈmetrɪk/ *adjective* **1.** involving equal measurement ○ *an isometric view of the system* **2.** referring to muscle contraction in which tension occurs with very little shortening of muscle fibres **3.** referring to exercises in which the muscles are put under tension but not contracted

isometrics /ˌaɪsəʊˈmetrɪks/ *plural noun* exercises to strengthen the muscles, in which the muscles contract but do not shorten

isoprenaline /ˌaɪsəʊˈprenəliːn/, **isoproterenol** /ˌaɪsəʊprəʊˈterənɒl/ *noun* a drug that relieves asthma by widening the bronchial tubes in the lungs

isosorbide dinitrate /ˌaɪsəˌsɔːbaɪd daɪˈnaɪtreɪt/ *noun* a compound which causes widening or relaxation of the blood vessels, used in the treatment of angina pectoris

isotonic /ˌaɪsəʊˈtɒnɪk/ *adjective* referring to a solution, e.g. a saline drip, which has the same osmotic pressure as blood serum and which can therefore be passed directly into the body. Compare **hypertonic**, **hypotonic**

isotonic solution /ˌaɪsəʊtɒnɪk səˈluːʃ(ə)n/ *noun* a solution which has the same osmotic pressure as blood serum, or as another liquid it is compared with

isotope /'aɪsətəʊp/ *noun* a form of a chemical element which has the same chemical properties as other forms but a different atomic mass

isotretinoin /ˌaɪsəʊtreˈtɪnɔɪn/ *noun* a drug used in the treatment of severe acne and several other skin diseases

ispaghula /ˌɪspəˈɡuːlə/, **ispaghula husk** /ˌɪspəˈɡuːlə hʌsk/ *noun* a natural dietary fibre used to treat constipation, diverticulitis and irritable bowel syndrome

ISS *abbreviation* injury scoring system

isthmus /'ɪsməs/ *noun* a short narrow canal or cavity

itch /ɪtʃ/ *noun* an irritated place on the skin which makes a person want to scratch ■ *verb* to produce an irritating sensation, making someone want to scratch

itching /ˈɪtʃɪŋ/ *noun* same as **pruritus**

itchy /ˈɪtʃi/ *adjective* making a person want to scratch ○ *The main symptom of the disease is an itchy red rash.*

-itis /aɪtɪs/ *suffix* inflammation

ITU *abbreviation* intensive therapy unit

IU *abbreviation* international unit

IUCD *abbreviation* intrauterine contraceptive device

IUD *abbreviation* **1.** intrauterine death **2.** intrauterine device

IV *abbreviation* intravenous

IVF *abbreviation* in vitro fertilisation

IVP *abbreviation* intravenous pyelogram

IVU *abbreviation* intravenous urography

J

J /dʒeɪ/ *abbreviation* joule

jab /dʒæb/ *noun* an injection or inoculation (*informal*) ○ *a tetanus jab*

Jacksonian epilepsy /dʒæk,səʊniən 'epɪlepsi/ *noun* a form of epilepsy in which the jerking movements start in one part of the body before spreading to others [Described 1863. After John Hughlings Jackson (1835–1911), British neurologist.]

Jacquemier's sign /'dʒækəmiəz ,saɪn/ *noun* a sign of early pregnancy in which the vaginal mucosa becomes slightly blue due to an increased amount of blood in the arteries [After Jean Marie Jacquemier (1806–79), French obstetrician.]

jactitation /,dʒæktɪ'teɪʃ(ə)n/ *noun* the action of constantly moving the body around in a restless way, especially because of mental illness

jag /dʒæg/ *noun* in Scotland, an injection or inoculation (*informal*)

jargon /'dʒɑːgən/ *noun* **1.** the words used by people who have a particular area of knowledge, which are usually only understood by those people ○ *medical jargon* **2.** a stream of words that makes no sense, produced by someone with aphasia or a severe mental disorder

jaundice /'dʒɔːndɪs/ *noun* a condition in which there is an excess of bile pigment in the blood, and in which the pigment is deposited in the skin and the whites of the eyes, which have a yellow colour. Also called **icterus**

jaw /dʒɔː/ *noun* the bones in the face which hold the teeth and form the mouth ○ *He fell down and broke his jaw.* ○ *The punch on his mouth broke his jaw.*

COMMENT: The jaw has two parts, the upper (the maxillae) being fixed parts of the skull, and the lower (the mandible) being attached to the skull with a hinge so that it can move up and down.

jawbone /'dʒɔːbəʊn/ *noun* one of the bones which form the jaw, especially the lower jaw or mandible

jejun- /dʒɪdʒuːn/ *prefix* same as **jejuno-** (*used before vowels*)

jejunal /dʒɪ'dʒuːn(ə)l/ *adjective* referring to the jejunum

jejunal ulcer /dʒɪ,dʒuːn(ə)l 'ʌlsə/ *noun* an ulcer in the jejunum

jejunectomy /,dʒɪdʒuː'nektəmi/ *noun* a surgical operation to remove all or part of the jejunum (NOTE: The plural is **jejunectomies**.)

jejuno- /dʒiːdʒuːnəʊ/ *prefix* referring to the jejunum

jejunoileostomy /dʒɪ,dʒuːnəʊ,ɪli'ɒstəmi/ *noun* a surgical operation to make an artificial link between the jejunum and the ileum (NOTE: The plural is **jejunoileostomies**.)

jejunostomy /,dʒɪdʒu'nɒstəmi/ *noun* a surgical operation to make an artificial passage to the jejunum through the wall of the abdomen (NOTE: The plural is **jejunostomies**.)

jejunotomy /,dʒɪdʒu'nɒtəmi/ *noun* a surgical operation to cut into the jejunum (NOTE: The plural is **jejunotomies**.)

jejunum /dʒɪ'dʒuːnəm/ *noun* the part of the small intestine between the duodenum and the ileum, about 2 metres long. See illustration at **DIGESTIVE SYSTEM** in Supplement

jerk /dʒɜːk/ *noun* a sudden movement of part of the body which indicates that the local reflex arc is intact ■ *verb* to make sudden movements, or cause something to make sudden movements ○ *In some forms of epilepsy the limbs jerk.*

jet lag /'dʒet læg/ *noun* a condition suffered by people who travel long distances in planes, caused by rapid changes in time zones which affect sleep patterns and meal times and thus interfere with the body's metabolism ○ *We had jet lag when we flew from Australia.*

jet-lagged /'dʒet lægd/ *adjective* experiencing jet lag ○ *jet-lagged travellers* ○ *We were jet-lagged for a week.*

joint /dʒɔɪnt/ *noun* a structure at a point where two or more bones join, especially one which allows movement of the bones ○ *The elbow is a joint in the arm.* ○ *Arthritis is accompanied by stiffness in the joints.* ◊ **Charcot's joint** (NOTE: For other terms referring to joints, see words beginning with **arthr-, arthro-**.)

joint capsule /'dʒɔɪnt ,kæpsjuːl/ *noun* white fibrous tissue which surrounds and holds a joint together. See illustration at **SYNOVIAL JOINT** in Supplement

joint investment plan /ˌdʒɔɪnt ɪnˈvestmənt plæn/ *noun* a plan that health and social services draw up together for specific areas of care

joint mouse /ˈdʒɔɪnt maʊs/ *plural noun* a loose piece of bone or cartilage in the knee joint, making the joint lock

joule /dʒuːl/ *noun* the SI unit of measurement of work or energy. 4.184 joules equals one calorie. Symbol **J**

jugular /ˈdʒʌɡjʊlə/ *adjective* referring to the throat or neck ■ *noun* same as **jugular vein**

jugular nerve /ˈdʒʌɡjʊlə nɜːv/ *noun* one of the nerves in the neck

jugular trunk /ˈdʒʌɡjʊlə trʌŋk/ *noun* a terminal lymph vessel in the neck, draining into the subclavian vein

jugular vein /ˈdʒʌɡjʊlə veɪn/ *noun* one of the veins which pass down either side of the neck. Also called **jugular**

jumper's knee /ˌdʒʌmpəz ˈniː/ *noun* a painful condition suffered by athletes and dancers in which inflammation develops in the knee joint

junction /ˈdʒʌŋkʃən/ *noun* a joining point

junior doctor /ˌdʒuːniə ˈdɒktə/ *noun* a doctor who is completing his or her training in hospital

junk food /ˈdʒʌŋk fuːd/ *noun* food of little nutritional value, e.g. high-fat processed snacks, eaten between or instead of meals

juvenile /ˈdʒuːvənaɪl/ *adjective* relating to or affecting children or adolescents

juxta- /dʒʌkstə/ *prefix* beside or near

juxta-articular /ˌdʒʌkstə ɑːˈtɪkjʊlə/ *adjective* occurring near a joint

juxtaposition /ˌdʒʌkstəpəˈzɪʃ(ə)n/ *noun* the placing of two or more things side by side so as to make their similarities or differences more obvious

K

k *symbol* kilo-

kala-azar /ˌkɑːlə əˈzɑː/ *noun* an often fatal form of leishmaniasis caused by the infection of the intestines and internal organs by a parasite, *Leishmania*, spread by flies. Symptoms are fever, anaemia, general wasting of the body and swelling of the spleen and liver.

kaolin /ˈkeɪəlɪn/ *noun* a fine soft clay used in the making of medical preparations, especially for the treatment of diarrhoea

Kaposi's sarcoma /kəˌpəʊziz sɑːˈkəʊmə/ *noun* a cancer which takes the form of many haemorrhagic nodes affecting the skin, especially on the extremities [Described 1872. After Moritz Kohn Karposi (1837–1902), Professor of Dermatology at Vienna, Austria.]

Kartagener's syndrome /ˌkɑːtəˈdʒiːnəz ˌsɪndrəʊm/ *noun* a hereditary condition in which all the organs in the chest and abdomen are positioned on the opposite side from the usual one, i.e. the heart and stomach are on the right

karyo- /kæriəʊ/ *prefix* relating to a cell nucleus

karyotype /ˈkæriəʊtaɪp/ *noun* the chromosome complement of a cell, shown as a diagram or as a set of letters and numbers

Kawasaki disease /ˌkɑːwəˈsɑːkiz dɪˌziːz/ *noun* a retrovirus infection that often occurs in small children and causes a high temperature, rash, reddened eyes, peeling skin and swollen lymph nodes

Kayser-Fleischer ring /ˌkaɪzə ˈflaɪʃə ˌrɪŋ/ *noun* a brown ring on the outer edge of the cornea, which is a diagnostic sign of hepatolenticular degeneration [Described 1902 by Kayser, 1903 by Fleischer. Bernard Kayser (1869–1954), German ophthalmologist; Bruno Richard Fleischer (1848–1904), German physician.]

kcal *abbreviation* kilocalorie

Kegel exercises /ˈkeɪɡ(ə)l ˌeksəsaɪzɪz/ *plural noun* exercises which strengthen the muscles of the pelvic floor in women and help to prevent any accidental leakage of urine when they cough, sneeze or lift things

Keller's operation /ˈkeləz ɒpəˌreɪʃ(ə)n/ *noun* a surgical operation on the big toe to remove a bunion or to correct an ankylosed joint [Described 1904. After William Lordan Keller (1874–1959), US surgeon.]

keloid /ˈkiːlɔɪd/ *noun* an excessive amount of scar tissue at the site of a skin injury

kerat- /kerət/ *prefix* same as **kerato-** (*used before vowels*)

keratectasia /ˌkerətekˈteɪziə/ *noun* a condition in which the cornea bulges

keratectomy /ˌkerəˈtektəmi/ *noun* a surgical operation to remove the whole or part of the cornea (NOTE: The plural is **keratectomies**.)

keratic /kəˈrætɪk/ *adjective* **1.** relating to horny tissue or to keratin **2.** relating to the cornea

keratin /ˈkerətɪn/ *noun* a protein found in horny tissue such as fingernails, hair or the outer surface of the skin

keratinisation /ˌkerətɪnaɪˈzeɪʃ(ə)n/, **keratinization** *noun* the appearance of horny characteristics in tissue. Also called **cornification**

keratinise /ˈkerətɪnaɪz, kəˈrætɪnaɪz/, **keratinize** *verb* to convert something into keratin or into horny tissue (NOTE: **keratinising – keratinised**)

keratinocyte /ˌkerəˈtɪnəʊsaɪt/ *noun* a cell which produces keratin

keratitis /ˌkerəˈtaɪtɪs/ *noun* inflammation of the cornea

kerato- /kerətəʊ/ *prefix* referring to horn, horny tissue or the cornea

keratoconjunctivitis /ˌkerətəʊkənˌdʒʌŋktɪˈvaɪtɪs/ *noun* inflammation of the cornea with conjunctivitis

keratoma /ˌkerəˈtəʊmə/ *noun* a hard thickened growth due to hypertrophy of the horny zone of the skin (NOTE: The plural is **keratomas** or **keratomata**.)

keratomalacia /ˌkerətəʊməˈleɪʃə/ *noun* a softening of the cornea frequently caused by Vitamin A deficiency

keratome /ˈkerətəʊm/ *noun* a surgical knife used for operations on the cornea

keratometer /ˌkerəˈtɒmɪtə/ *noun* an instrument for measuring the curvature of the cornea

keratopathy /ˌkerəˈtɒpəθi/ *noun* any non-inflammatory disorder of the cornea (NOTE: The plural is **keratopathies**.)

keratoplasty /ˈkerətəplæsti/ *noun* a surgical operation to graft corneal tissue from a donor in place of diseased tissue (NOTE: The plural is **keratoplasties**.)

keratoprosthesis /ˌkerətəʊprɒsˈθiːsɪs/ *noun* **1.** a surgical operation to replace the central area of a cornea with clear plastic, when it has become opaque **2.** a piece of clear plastic put into the cornea (NOTE: The plural is **keratoprostheses**.)

keratoscope /ˈkerətəskəʊp/ *noun* an instrument for examining the cornea to see if it has an unusual curvature. Also called **Placido's disc**

keratosis /ˌkerəˈtəʊsɪs/ *noun* a lesion of the skin (NOTE: The plural is **keratoses**.)

keratotomy /ˌkerəˈtɒtəmi/ *noun* a surgical operation to make a cut in the cornea, the first step in many intraocular operations (NOTE: The plural is **keratotomies**.)

kerion /ˈkɪəriɒn/ *noun* a painful soft mass, usually on the scalp, caused by ringworm

kernicterus /kəˈnɪktərəs/ *noun* yellow pigmentation of the basal ganglia and other nerve cells in the spinal cord and brain, found in children with icterus

Kernig's sign /ˈkɜːnɪgz saɪn/ *noun* a symptom of meningitis in which the knee cannot be straightened if the person is lying down with the thigh brought up against the abdomen [Described 1882. After Vladimir Mikhailovich Kernig (1840–1917), Russian neurologist.]

ketamine /ˈketəmiːn/ *noun* a white crystalline powder used as a general anaesthetic, used in human and veterinary medicine

ketoacidosis /ˌkiːtəʊˌæsɪˈdəʊsɪs/ *noun* an accumulation of ketone bodies in tissue in diabetes, causing acidosis

ketoconazole /ˌkiːtəʊˈkɒnəzəʊl/ *noun* a drug which is effective against a wide range of fungal infections such as cryptococcosis and thrush

ketogenesis /ˌkiːtəʊˈdʒenəsɪs/ *noun* the production of ketone bodies

ketogenic /ˌkiːtəʊˈdʒenɪk/ *adjective* forming ketone bodies

ketogenic diet /ˌkiːtəʊdʒenɪk ˈdaɪət/ *noun* a diet with a high fat content, producing ketosis

ketonaemia /ˌkiːtəʊˈniːmiə/ *noun* a morbid state in which ketone bodies exist in the blood

ketone /ˈkiːtəʊn/ *noun* a chemical compound produced when glucose is unavailable for use as energy, as in untreated diabetes, and fats are used instead, leading to ketosis

ketone bodies /ˈkiːtəʊn ˌbɒdiz/ *plural noun* ketone compounds formed from fatty acids

ketone group /ˈkiːtəʊn gruːp/ *noun* a chemical group characteristic of ketones, with carbon atoms doubly bonded to an oxygen atom and to the carbon atoms of two other organic groups

ketonuria /ˌkiːtəʊˈnjʊəriə/ *noun* a state in which ketone bodies are excreted in the urine

ketoprofen /ˌkiːtəʊˈprəʊfən/ *noun* an anti-inflammatory drug used in the treatment of rheumatoid arthritis and osteoarthritis

ketosis /kiːˈtəʊsɪs/ *noun* a state in which ketone bodies such as acetone and acetic acid accumulate in the tissues, a late complication of Type I diabetes mellitus

ketosteroid /ˌkiːtəʊˈstɪərɔɪd/ *noun* a steroid such as cortisone which contains a ketone group

keyhole surgery /ˈkiːhəʊl ˌsɜːdʒəri/ *noun* surgery carried out by inserting tiny surgical instruments through an endoscope (*informal*) Also called **laparoscopic surgery**

kg *abbreviation* kilogram

kidney /ˈkɪdni/ *noun* either of two organs situated in the lower part of the back on either side of the spine behind the abdomen, whose function is to maintain the usual concentrations of the main constituents of blood, passing the waste matter into the urine. See illustration at **KIDNEY** in Supplement

kidney dialysis /ˈkɪdni daɪˌæləsɪs/ *noun* the process of removing waste matter from blood by passing it through a kidney machine. Also called **haemodialysis**

kidney donor /ˈkɪdni ˌdəʊnə/ *noun* a person who gives one of his or her kidneys as a transplant

kidney failure /ˈkɪdni ˌfeɪljə/ *noun* a situation in which the kidneys do not function properly

kidney machine /ˈkɪdni məˌʃiːn/ *noun* an apparatus through which blood is passed to be cleaned by dialysis if the person's kidneys have failed

kidney stone /ˈkɪdni stəʊn/ *noun* a hard mass of calcium like a little piece of stone which forms in the kidney

kidney transplant /ˈkɪdni ˌtrænsplɑːnt/ *noun* a surgical operation to give someone with a diseased or damaged kidney a kidney from another person

killer cell /ˈkɪlə sel/, **killer T cell** /ˌkɪlə ˈtiː ˌsel/ *noun* a type of immune cell that recognises and destroys cells that have specific antigens on their surface, e.g. virus-infected or cancerous cells

kilo- /ˈkɪləʊ/ *prefix* one thousand (10^3). Symbol **k**

kilogram /ˈkɪləgræm/ *noun* an SI unit of measurement of weight equal to 1000 grams ○ *She weighs 62 kilos (62 kg).* Symbol **kg**

kilojoule /ˈkɪləʊdʒuːl/ *noun* an SI unit of measurement of energy or heat equal to 1000 joules. Symbol **kJ**

kilopascal /ˈkɪləʊpæskəl/ *noun* an SI unit of measurement of pressure equal to 1000 pascals. Symbol **kPa**

Kimmelstiel-Wilson disease /ˌkɪməlstiːl ˈwɪlsən dɪˌziːz/, **Kimmelstiel-Wilson syn-**

drome /ˌkɪməlstiːl ˈwɪlsən ˌsɪndrəʊm/ *noun* a form of nephrosclerosis found in people with diabetes [Described 1936. After Paul Kimmelstiel (1900–70), US pathologist; Clifford Wilson (1906–98), Professor of Medicine, London University, UK]

kin /kɪn/ *noun* relatives or close members of the family

kin- /kɪn/ *prefix* same as **kine-** (*used before vowels*)

kinaesthesia /ˌkɪniːsˈθiːziə/ *noun* the fact of being aware of the movement and position of parts of the body (NOTE: The US spelling is **kinesthesia**.)

kinanaesthesia /ˌkɪnænɪːsˈθiːziə/ *noun* the fact of not being able to sense the movement and position of parts of the body (NOTE: The US spelling is **kinanesthesia**.)

kinase /ˈkaɪneɪz/ *noun* an enzyme belonging to a large family of related substances that bind to the energy-providing molecule ATP and regulate functions such as cell division and signalling between cells

kine- /kɪni/ *prefix* movement

kinematics /ˌkɪnɪˈmætɪks/ *noun* the science of movement, especially of body movements (NOTE: Also spelled **cinematics**.)

kineplasty /ˈkɪnɪplæsti/ *noun* an amputation in which the muscles of the stump of the amputated limb are used to operate an artificial limb (NOTE: Also spelled **cineplasty**. The plural is **kineplasties**.)

kinesi- /kaɪniːsi/ *prefix* movement (NOTE: used before vowels)

kinesiology /ˌkaɪniːsiˈɒlədʒi/ *noun* the study of human movements, particularly with regard to their use in treatment

kinesis /kɪˈniːsɪs/ *noun* the movement of a cell in response to a stimulus. Compare **taxis**

-kinesis /kɪniːsɪs/ *suffix* **1.** activity or motion **2.** a change in the movement of a cell, though not in any particular direction. Examples are a change in its speed or in its turning behaviour.

kinesitherapy /ˌkaɪniːsiˈθerəpi/ *noun* therapy involving movement of parts of the body

kinetic /kɪˈnetɪk, kaɪˈnetɪk/ *adjective* relating to movement

King's Fund /ˈkɪŋz fʌnd/ *noun* a major independent health charity in London

King's model /ˈkɪŋz ˌmɒd(ə)l/ *noun* a model of nurse–patient relationships based on ten principles: interaction, perception, communication, transaction, role, stress, growth and development, time, self and space. Through an exchange of information nurses and patients work together to help individuals and groups attain, maintain and restore health.

kinin /ˈkaɪnɪn/ *noun* a polypeptide that makes blood vessels widen and smooth muscles contract

Kirschner wire /ˌkɜːʃ(ə)nə ˈwaɪə/, **Kirschner's wire** *noun* a wire attached to a bone and tightened to provide traction to a fracture [Described 1909. After Martin Kirschner (1879–1942), Professor of Surgery at Heidelberg, Germany.]

kiss of life /ˌkɪs əv ˈlaɪf/ *noun* same as **cardiopulmonary resuscitation** (*informal*)

kJ *abbreviation* kilojoule

Klebsiella /ˌklebsiˈelə/ *noun* a Gram-negative bacterium, one form of which, *Klebsiella pneumoniae*, can cause pneumonia

Klebs-Loeffler bacillus /ˌklebz ˈleflə bə ˌsɪləs/ *noun* the bacterium which causes diphtheria, *Corynebacterium diphtheriae* [After Theodor Albrecht Klebs (1834–1913), bacteriologist in Zürich, Switzerland, and Chicago, USA; Friedrich August Loeffler (1852–1915), bacteriologist in Berlin, Germany.]

Kleihauer test /ˈklaɪhaʊə test/, **Kleihauer-Betke test** *noun* a test used to check whether there has been any blood loss from a fetus to the mother across the placenta. It is usually done immediately after delivery.

klepto- /kleptəʊ/ *prefix* stealing or theft

kleptomania /ˌkleptəʊˈmeɪniə/ *noun* a form of mental disorder in which someone has a compulsive desire to steal things, even things of little value

kleptomaniac /ˌkleptəʊˈmeɪniæk/ *noun* a person who has a compulsive desire to steal

Klinefelter's syndrome /ˈklaɪnfeltəz ˌsɪndrəʊm/ *noun* a genetic disorder in which a male has an extra female chromosome, making an XXY set, giving sterility and partial female characteristics [Described 1942. After Harry Fitch Klinefelter Jr. (b. 1912), Associate Professor of Medicine, Johns Hopkins Medical School, Baltimore, USA.]

Klumpke's paralysis /ˌkluːmpkəz pə ˈræləsɪs/ *noun* a form of paralysis due to an injury during birth, affecting the forearm and hand. Also called **Déjerine-Klumpke's syndrome** [Described 1885. After Augusta Klumpke (Madame Déjerine-Klumpke) (1859–1937), French neurologist, one of the first women to qualify in Paris in 1888.]

knee /niː/ *noun* a joint in the middle of the leg, joining the femur and the tibia (NOTE: For other terms referring to the knee, see **genu**.)

kneecap /ˈniːkæp/ *noun* same as **patella**

knee jerk /ˈniː dʒɜːk/ *noun* same as **patellar reflex**

knee joint /ˈniː dʒɔɪnt/ *noun* a joint where the femur and the tibia are joined, covered by the kneecap

knock-knee /ˌnɒk ˈniː/ *noun* a state in which the knees touch and the ankles are apart when a person is standing straight. Also called **genu valgum**

knock-kneed /ˌnɒk 'niːd/ *adjective* referring to a person whose knees touch when he or she stands straight with feet slightly apart

knock out /ˌnɒk 'aʊt/ *verb* to hit someone so hard that he or she is no longer conscious ○ *He was knocked out by a blow on the head.*

knowledge and skills framework /ˌnɒlɪdʒ ən 'skɪlz ˌfreɪmwɜːk/ *noun* full form of **KSF**

knuckle /'nʌk(ə)l/ *noun* the back of each joint on a person's hand

Kocher manoeuvre /'kɒkə məˌnuːvə/ *noun* a method for realigning a dislocated shoulder in which the arm is raised and a sudden change is made between inward and outward rotation of the head of the joint

Koch's bacillus /ˌkəʊks bə'sɪləs/ *noun* the bacterium which causes tuberculosis, *Mycobacterium tuberculosis* [Described 1882. After Robert Koch (1843–1910), Professor of Hygiene in Berlin, Germany, later Director of the Institute for Infectious Diseases. (Nobel Prize 1905).]

Köhler's disease /'kɜːləz dɪˌsiːz/ *noun* a degeneration of the navicular bone in children. Also called **scaphoiditis** [Described 1908 and 1926. After Alban Köhler (1874–1947), German radiologist.]

koilonychia /ˌkɔɪləʊ'nɪkiə/ *noun* a condition in which the fingernails are brittle and concave, caused by iron-deficiency anaemia

Koplik's spots /'kɒplɪks spɒts/ *plural noun* small white spots with a blue tinge surrounded by a red areola, found in the mouth in the early stages of measles [Described 1896. After Henry Koplik (1858–1927), US paediatrician.]

Korotkoff's method /'kɒrətkɒfs ˌmeθəd/ *noun* a method of finding a person's blood pressure by inflating a cuff around his or her upper arm to a pressure well above the systolic blood pressure and then gradually decreasing it

Korsakoff's syndrome /'kɔːsəkɒfs ˌsɪndrəʊm/ *noun* a condition, caused usually by chronic alcoholism or disorders in which there is a deficiency of vitamin B, in which a person's memory fails and he or she invents things which have not happened and is confused [Described 1887. After Sergei Sergeyevich Korsakoff (1854–1900), Russian psychiatrist.]

kraurosis penis /krɔːˌrəʊsɪs 'piːnɪs/ *noun* a condition in which the foreskin becomes dry and shrivelled

kraurosis vulvae /krɔːˌrəʊsɪs 'vʌlvə/ *noun* a condition in which the vulva becomes thin and dry due to lack of oestrogen, found usually in elderly women

Krause corpuscles /'kraʊzə ˌkɔːpʌs(ə)lz/ *plural noun* encapsulated nerve endings in the mucous membrane of the mouth, nose, eyes and genitals [Described 1860. After Wilhelm Johann Friedrich Krause (1833–1910), German anatomist.]

Krebs cycle /'krebz ˌsaɪk(ə)l/ *noun* same as **citric acid cycle** [Described 1937. After Sir Hans Adolf Krebs (1900–81), German biochemist who emigrated to England in 1934. Shared the Nobel prize for Medicine 1953 with F.A. Lipmann.]

KSF /ˌkeɪ es 'ef/ *noun* a document setting out the knowledge and skills required in a particular healthcare post, giving guidance on professional development, and setting out the pay progression. Full form **knowledge and skills framework**

Kuntscher nail /'kʌntʃə neɪl/, **Küntscher nail** *noun* a long steel nail used in operations to pin fractures of long bones, especially the femur, through the bone marrow [Described 1940. After Gerhard Küntscher (1900–72), German surgeon.]

Kupffer's cells /'kʊpfəz selz/, **Kupffer cells** /'kʊpfə selz/ *plural noun* large specialised liver cells which break down haemoglobin into bile [Described 1876. After Karl Wilhelm von Kupffer (1829–1902), German anatomist.]

Kveim test /'kvaɪm test/ *noun* a skin test to confirm the presence of sarcoidosis [After Morten Ansgar Kveim (1892–1966), Swedish physician.]

kwashiorkor /ˌkwɒʃi'ɔːkɔː/ *noun* malnutrition of small children, mostly in tropical countries, causing anaemia, wasting of the body and swollen liver

kypho- /kaɪfəʊ/ *prefix* a hump

kyphoscoliosis /ˌkaɪfəʊˌskɒli'əʊsɪs/ *noun* a condition in which someone has both backward and lateral curvature of the spine

kyphosis /kaɪ'fəʊsɪs/ *noun* an excessive backward curvature of the top part of the spine (NOTE: The plural is **kyphoses**.)

kyphotic /kaɪ'fɒtɪk/ *adjective* referring to kyphosis

L

l, L symbol **litre**

lab- /leɪb/ *prefix* same as **labio-** (*used before vowels*)

labia /ˈleɪbiə/ plural of **labium**

labial /ˈleɪbiəl/ *adjective* referring to the lips or to labia

labia majora /ˌleɪbiə məˈdʒɔːrə/ *plural noun* two large fleshy folds at the outside edge of the vulva. See illustration at **UROGENITAL SYSTEM (FEMALE)** in Supplement

labia minora /ˌleɪbiə mɪˈnɔːrə/ *plural noun* two small fleshy folds on the inside edge of the vulva. See illustration at **UROGENITAL SYSTEM (FEMALE)** in Supplement. Also called **nymphae**

labile /ˈleɪbaɪl/ *adjective* referring to a drug which is unstable and likely to change if heated or cooled

lability of mood /ləˌbɪlɪti əv ˈmuːd/ *noun* a tendency for a person's mood to change suddenly

labio- /leɪbiəʊ/ *prefix* referring to the lips or to labia

labioplasty /ˈleɪbiəʊˌplæsti/ *noun* a surgical operation to repair damaged or deformed lips (NOTE: The plural is **labioplasties**.)

labium /ˈleɪbiəm/ *noun* any of the four fleshy folds which surround the female genital organs

laboratory technician /ləˌbɒrət(ə)ri tekˈnɪʃ(ə)n/ *noun* a person who does practical work in a laboratory and has particular care of equipment

laboratory techniques /ləˈbɒrət(ə)ri tekˌniːkz/ *plural noun* the methods or skills needed to perform experiments in a laboratory

laboratory test /ləˈbɒrət(ə)ri test/ *noun* a test carried out in a laboratory

labour /ˈleɪbə/ *noun* childbirth, especially the contractions in the uterus which take place during childbirth

laboured breathing /ˌleɪbəd ˈbriːðɪŋ/ *noun* difficult breathing, which can be due to various causes such as asthma

labour pains /ˈleɪbə peɪnz/ *plural noun* the pains felt at regular intervals by a woman as the muscles of the uterus contract during childbirth

labrum /ˈleɪbrəm/ *noun* a ring of cartilage around the rim of a joint (NOTE: The plural is **labra**.)

labyrinth /ˈlæbərɪnθ/ *noun* a series of interconnecting tubes, especially those in the inside of the ear

labyrinthectomy /ˌlæbərɪnˈθektəmi/ *noun* a surgical operation to remove the labyrinth of the inner ear (NOTE: The plural is **labyrinthectomies**.)

labyrinthitis /ˌlæbərɪnˈθaɪtɪs/ *noun* same as **otitis interna**

laceration /ˌlæsəˈreɪʃ(ə)n/ *noun* **1.** a wound which has been cut or torn with rough edges, and is not the result of stabbing or pricking **2.** the act of tearing tissue

lachrymal /ˈlækrɪm(ə)l/ *adjective* same as **lacrimal**

lacrimal /ˈlækrɪm(ə)l/ *adjective* referring to tears, the tear ducts or the tear glands. ◊ **nasolacrimal**

lacrimal apparatus /ˌlækrɪm(ə)l ˌæpəˈreɪtəs/ *noun* the arrangement of glands and ducts which produce and drain tears. Also called **lacrimal system**

lacrimal bone /ˈlækrɪm(ə)l bəʊn/ *noun* one of two little bones which join with others to form the orbits

lacrimal canaliculus /ˌlækrɪm(ə)l ˌkænəˈlɪkjʊləs/ *noun* a small canal draining tears into the lacrimal sac

lacrimal caruncle /ˌlækrɪm(ə)l kəˈrʌŋk(ə)l/ *noun* a small red point at the inner corner of each eye

lacrimal duct /ˈlækrɪm(ə)l dʌkt/ *noun* a small duct leading from the lacrimal gland. Also called **tear duct**

lacrimal gland /ˈlækrɪm(ə)l glænd/ *noun* a gland beneath the upper eyelid which secretes tears. Also called **tear gland**

lacrimal puncta /ˌlækrɪm(ə)l ˈpʌŋktə/ *plural noun* small openings of the lacrimal canaliculus at the corners of the eyes through which tears drain into the nose

lacrimal sac /ˌlækrɪm(ə)l 'sæk/ *noun* a sac at the upper end of the nasolacrimal duct, linking it with the lacrimal canaliculus

lacrimal system /'lækrɪm(ə)l ˌsɪstəm/ *noun* same as **lacrimal apparatus**

lacrimation /ˌlækrɪ'meɪʃ(ə)n/ *noun* the production of tears

lacrimator /'lækrɪmeɪtə/ *noun* a substance which irritates the eyes and makes tears flow

lacrymal /'lækrɪm(ə)l/, **lachrymal** /'lækrɪm(ə)l/ *adjective* same as **lacrimal**

lact- /lækt/ *prefix* same as **lacto-** (*used before vowels*)

lactase /'lækteɪz/ *noun* an enzyme, secreted in the small intestine, which converts milk sugar into glucose and galactose

lactate /læk'teɪt/ *verb* to produce milk in the body (NOTE: **lactating – lactated**)

lactation /læk'teɪʃ(ə)n/ *noun* the production of milk in the body

lacteal /'læktiəl/ *adjective* referring to milk ■ *noun* a lymph vessel in a villus which helps the digestive process in the small intestine by absorbing fat

lactic /'læktɪk/ *adjective* relating to milk

lactic acid /ˌlæktɪk 'æsɪd/ *noun* a sugar which forms in cells and tissue, and also in sour milk, cheese and yoghurt

lactiferous /læk'tɪfərəs/ *adjective* producing, secreting or carrying milk

lactiferous duct /lækˌtɪfərəs 'dʌkt/ *noun* a duct in the breast which carries milk

lactiferous sinus /lækˌtɪfərəs 'saɪnəs/ *noun* a dilatation of the lactiferous duct at the base of the nipple

lacto- /læktəʊ/ *prefix* referring to milk

Lactobacillus /ˌlæktəʊbə'sɪləs/ *noun* a genus of Gram-positive bacteria which produces lactic acid from glucose and may be found in the digestive tract and the vagina

lactogenic hormone /ˌlæktəʊˌdʒenɪk 'hɔːməʊn/ *noun* same as **prolactin**

lactose /'læktəʊs/ *noun* a type of sugar found in milk

lactose intolerance /'læktəʊs ɪnˌtɒlərəns/ *noun* a condition in which a person cannot digest lactose because lactase is absent in the intestine or because of an allergy to milk, causing diarrhoea

lactosuria /ˌlæktəʊ'sjʊəriə/ *noun* the excretion of lactose in the urine

lactulose /'læktjʊləʊs/ *noun* an artificially produced sugar used as a laxative

lacuna /læ'kjuːnə/ *noun* a small hollow or cavity (NOTE: The plural is **lacunae**.)

Laënnec's cirrhosis /ˌleɪəneks sə'rəʊsɪs/ *noun* the commonest form of alcoholic cirrhosis of the liver [Described 1819. After René

Théophile Hyacinthe Laennec (1781–1826), Professor of medicine at the Collège de France, and inventor of the stethoscope.]

-lalia /leɪliə/ *suffix* speech or a speech disorder

lambda /'læmdə/ *noun* **1.** the 11th letter of the Greek alphabet **2.** the point at the back of the skull where the sagittal suture and lambdoidal suture meet

lambdoid /'læmdɔɪd/ *adjective* shaped like the capital Greek letter lambda, like an upside down V or y

lambdoid suture /'læmdɔɪd ˌsuːtʃə/, **lambdoidal suture** /'læmdɔɪd(ə)l ˌsuːtʃə/ *noun* a horizontal joint across the back of the skull between the parietal and occipital bones

lambliasis /læm'blaɪəsɪs/ *noun* same as **giardiasis**

lame /leɪm/ *adjective* not able to walk easily because of pain, stiffness or damage in a leg or foot (NOTE: This term is regarded as offensive.)

lamella /lə'melə/ *noun* a thin sheet of tissue (NOTE: The plural is **lamellae**.)

lamina /'læmɪnə/ *noun* a thin membrane

lamina propria /ˌlæmɪnə 'prəʊpriə/ *noun* the connective tissue of mucous membranes containing, e.g., blood vessels and lymphatic tissues

laminectomy /ˌlæmɪ'nektəmi/ *noun* a surgical operation to cut through the lamina of a vertebra in the spine to get to the spinal cord. Also called **rachiotomy** (NOTE: The plural is **laminectomies**.)

lamotrigine /lə'mɒtrɪdʒiːn/ *noun* a drug that helps to control petit mal epilepsy

lance /lɑːns/ *verb* to make a cut in a boil or abscess to remove the pus

lancet /'lɑːnsɪt/ *noun* **1.** a sharp two-edged pointed knife formerly used in surgery **2.** a small pointed implement used to take a small capillary blood sample, e.g. to measure blood glucose levels

lancinate /'lɑːnsɪneɪt/ *verb* to lacerate or cut something (NOTE: **lancinating – lancinated**)

lancinating /'lɑːnsɪneɪtɪŋ/ *adjective* referring to pain which's sharp and cutting

Landsteiner's classification /'lændstaɪnəz klæsɪfɪˌkeɪʃ(ə)n/ *noun* same as **ABO system**

Langerhans' cells /'læŋəhæns selz/ *plural noun* cells on the outer layers of the skin

Langer's lines /'læŋəz laɪnz/ *plural noun* the arrangement of collagen protein fibres which causes the usual skin creases. Cuts made along these lines sever fewer fibres and heal better than other cuts. Also called **cleavage lines**

lanolin /'lænəlɪn/ *noun* grease from sheep's wool which absorbs water and is used to rub on dried skin, or in the preparation of cosmetics

lanugo /lə'njuːgəʊ/ *noun* **1.** soft hair on the body of a fetus or newborn baby **2.** soft hair on the body of an adult, except on the palms of the hands, the soles of the feet and the parts where long hair grows

laparo- /ˈlæpərəʊ/ *prefix* the lower abdomen

laparoscope /ˈlæpərəskəʊp/ *noun* a surgical instrument which is inserted through a hole in the abdominal wall to allow a surgeon to examine the inside of the abdominal cavity. Also called **peritoneoscope**

laparoscopic surgery /ˌlæpərəˌskɒpɪk ˈsɜːdʒəri/ *noun* same as **keyhole surgery**

laparoscopy /ˌlæpəˈrɒskəpi/ *noun* a procedure in which a laparoscope is used to examine the inside of the abdominal cavity. Also called **peritoneoscopy** (NOTE: The plural is **laparoscopies**.)

laparotomy /ˌlæpəˈrɒtəmi/ *noun* a surgical operation to cut open the abdominal cavity (NOTE: The plural is **laparotomies**.)

large intestine /ˌlɑːdʒ ɪnˈtestɪn/ *noun* the section of the digestive system from the caecum to the rectum

Lariam /ˈlæriəm/ a trade name for mefloquine hydrochloride

laryng- /lərɪndʒ/ *prefix* same as **laryngo-** (*used before vowels*)

laryngeal /ləˈrɪndʒiəl/ *adjective* referring to the larynx

laryngeal inlet /ləˌrɪndʒiəl ˈɪnlət/ *noun* the entrance from the laryngopharynx leading through the vocal cords to the trachea

laryngeal prominence /ləˌrɪndʒiəl ˈprɒmɪnəns/ *noun* same as **Adam's apple**

laryngeal reflex /ləˌrɪndʒiəl ˈriːfleks/ *noun* the reflex that makes a person cough

laryngectomy /ˌlærɪnˈdʒektəmi/ *noun* a surgical operation to remove the larynx, usually as treatment for throat cancer (NOTE: The plural is **laryngectomies**.)

laryngismus /ˌlærɪnˈdʒɪzməs/, **laryngismus stridulus** /lærɪnˌdʒɪzməs ˈstrɪdjʊləs/ *noun* a spasm of the throat muscles with a sharp intake of breath which occurs when the larynx is irritated, as in children who have croup

laryngitis /ˌlærɪnˈdʒaɪtɪs/ *noun* inflammation of the larynx

laryngo- /ləˈrɪŋgəʊ/ *prefix* larynx

laryngology /ˌlærɪnˈgɒlədʒi/ *noun* the study of diseases of the larynx, throat and vocal cords

laryngomalacia /ləˌrɪŋgəʊməˈleɪʃə/ *noun* a condition in which breathing is made difficult by softness of the larynx, occurring mainly in children under the age of two

laryngopharyngeal /ləˌrɪŋgəʊfəˈrɪndʒiæl/ *adjective* referring to both the larynx and the pharynx

laryngopharynx /ləˌrɪŋgəʊˈfærɪŋks/ *noun* the part of the pharynx below the hyoid bone

laryngoscope /ləˈrɪŋgəskəʊp/ *noun* an instrument for examining the inside of the larynx using a light and mirrors

laryngoscopy /ˌlærɪnˈgɒskəpi/ *noun* an examination of the larynx with a laryngoscope (NOTE: The plural is **laryngoscopies**.)

laryngospasm /ləˈrɪŋgəspæzm/ *noun* a muscular spasm which suddenly closes the larynx

laryngostenosis /ləˌrɪŋgəʊstəˈnəʊsɪs/ *noun* narrowing of the lumen of the larynx

laryngostomy /ˌlærɪnˈgɒstəmi/ *noun* a surgical operation to make a permanent opening from the neck into the larynx (NOTE: The plural is **laryngostomies**.)

laryngotomy /ˌlærɪnˈgɒtəmi/ *noun* a surgical operation to make an opening in the larynx through the membrane, especially in an emergency, when the throat is blocked (NOTE: The plural is **laryngotomies**.)

laryngotracheal /ləˌrɪŋgəʊˈtreɪkiəl/ *adjective* relating to both the larynx and the trachea ○ *laryngotracheal stenosis*

laryngotracheobronchitis /ləˌrɪŋgəʊˌtreɪkiəʊbrɒŋˈkaɪtɪs/ *noun* inflammation of the larynx, trachea and bronchi, as in croup

larynx /ˈlærɪŋks/ *noun* the organ in the throat which produces sounds. Also called **voice box** (NOTE: The plural is **larynges** or **larynxes**.)

laser /ˈleɪzə/ *noun* an instrument which produces a highly concentrated beam of light which can be used to cut or attach tissue, as in operations for a detached retina

laser laparoscopy /ˌleɪzə læpəˈrɒskəpi/ *noun* surgery performed through a laparoscope using a laser

laser probe /ˈleɪzə prəʊb/ *noun* a metal probe which is inserted into the body and through which a laser beam can be passed to remove a blockage in an artery

laser surgery /ˈleɪzə ˌsɜːdʒəri/ *noun* surgery using lasers, e.g. for the removal of tumours, sealing blood vessels, or the correction of shortsightedness

Lasix /ˈleɪzɪks/ a trade name for frusemide

Lassa fever /ˈlæsə ˌfiːvə/ *noun* a highly infectious and often fatal virus disease found in Central and West Africa, causing high fever, pains, and ulcers in the mouth [After a village in northern Nigeria where the fever was first reported.]

lassitude /ˈlæsɪtjuːd/ *noun* a state where a person does not want to do anything, sometimes because he or she is depressed

latent /ˈleɪt(ə)nt/ *adjective* referring to a disease which is present in the body but does not show any signs ○ *The children were tested for latent viral infection.*

lateral /ˈlæt(ə)rəl/ *adjective* further away from the midline of the body

lateral aspect /ˌlæt(ə)rəl ˈæspekt/ *noun* a view of the side of part of the body. Also called **lateral view**. See illustration at ANATOMICAL TERMS in Supplement

lateral epicondyle /ˌlæt(ə)rəl ˌepɪˈkɒndaɪl/, **lateral epicondyle of the humerus** /ˌlæt(ə)rəl epɪˌkɒndaɪl əv ðə ˈhjuːmərəs/ *noun* a lateral projection on the rounded end of the humerus at the elbow jointc

lateral epicondylitis /ˌlæt(ə)rəl ˌepɪkɒndɪ ˈlaɪtɪs/ *noun* same as **tennis elbow**

laterally /ˈlætrəli/ *adverb* towards or on the side of the body. See illustration at ANATOMICAL TERMS in Supplement

lateral malleolus /ˌlæt(ə)rəl məˈliːələs/ *noun* the part of the end of the fibula which protrudes on the outside of the ankle

lateral view /ˌlæt(ə)rəl ˈvjuː/ *noun* same as **lateral aspect**

lateroversion /ˌlæt(ə)rəʊˈvɜːʃ(ə)n/ *noun* a condition in which an organ is turned to one side

latissimus dorsi /ləˌtɪsɪməs ˈdɔːsi/ *noun* a large flat triangular muscle covering the lumbar region and the lower part of the chest

laudanum /ˈlɔːd(ə)nəm/ *noun* a solution of opium in alcohol that was formerly in widespread use for pain relief

laughing gas /ˈlɑːfɪŋ ɡæs/ *noun* same as **nitrous oxide** (*informal*)

lavage /ˈlævɪdʒ, læˈvɑːʒ/ *noun* the act of washing out or irrigating an organ such as the stomach

laxative /ˈlæksətɪv/ *adjective* causing a bowel movement ■ *noun* a medicine which causes a bowel movement, e.g. bisacodyl, which stimulates intestinal motility, or lactulose which alters fluid retention in the bowel ▶ also called (all senses) **purgative**

lazy eye /ˌleɪzi ˈaɪ/ *noun* an eye which does not focus properly without an obvious cause (*informal*) ◊ **amblyopia**

LD *abbreviation* lethal dose

LDL *abbreviation* low-density lipoprotein

L-dopa /ˌel ˈdəʊpə/ *noun* same as **levodopa**

LE *abbreviation* lupus erythematosus

lead /led/ *noun* a very heavy soft metallic element, which is poisonous in compounds (NOTE: The chemical symbol is **Pb**.)

lead poisoning /ˌled ˈpɔɪz(ə)nɪŋ/ *noun* poisoning caused by taking in lead salts. Also called **plumbism**, **saturnism**

learning /ˈlɜːnɪŋ/ *noun* the act of gaining knowledge of something or of how to do something

learning disability /ˈlɜːnɪŋ dɪsəˌbɪlɪti/, **learning difficulty** /ˈlɜːnɪŋ ˌdɪfɪk(ə)lti/ *noun* a condition that results in someone finding it difficult to learn skills or information at the same rate

as others of similar age ○ *children with learning disabilities*

LE cells /ˌel ˈiː ˌselz/ *plural noun* white blood cells which show that someone has lupus erythematosus

lecithin /ˈlesɪθɪn/ *noun* a chemical which is a constituent of all animal and plant cells and is involved in the transport and absorption of fats

leech /liːtʃ/ *noun* a blood-sucking parasitic worm which lives in water, occasionally used in specialist procedures

leg /leɡ/ *noun* a part of the body with which a person or animal walks and stands

Legg-Calvé disease /ˌleɡ ˈkælveɪ dɪˌziːz/, **Legg-Calvé-Perthes disease** /ˌleɡ ˌkælveɪ ˈpɜːtiz dɪˌziːz/ *noun* degeneration of the upper end of the thighbone in young boys, which prevents the bone growing properly and can result in a permanent limp [Described 1910 separately by all three workers. Arthur Thornton Legg (1874–1939), American orthopaedic surgeon; Jacques Calvé (1875–1954), French orthopaedic surgeon; Georg Clemens Perthes (1869–1927), German surgeon.]

Legionnaires' disease /ˌliːdʒəˈneəz dɪˌziːz/ *noun* a bacterial disease similar to pneumonia

leio- /ˈleɪəʊ/ *prefix* smooth or smoothness

leiomyoma /ˌlaɪəʊmaɪˈəʊmə/ *noun* a tumour of smooth muscle, especially the smooth muscle coating the uterus (NOTE: The plural is **leiomyomas** or **leiomyomata**.)

leiomyosarcoma /ˌlaɪəʊˌmaɪəʊsɑːˈkəʊmə/ *noun* a sarcoma in which large bundles of smooth muscle are found (NOTE: The plural is **leiomyosarcomas** or **leiomyosarcomata**.)

leishmaniasis /ˌliːʃməˈnaɪəsɪs/ *noun* a disease caused by the parasite *Leishmania*, one form of which causes disfiguring ulcers, while another attacks the liver and bone marrow

Lembert's suture /ˈlɑːmbeəz ˌsuːtʃə/ *noun* a suture used to close a wound in the intestine which includes all the coats of the intestine [Described 1826. After Antoine Lembert (1802–51), French surgeon.]

lens /lenz/ *noun* **1.** the part of the eye behind the iris and pupil, which focuses light coming from the cornea onto the retina. See illustration at EYE in Supplement **2.** a piece of shaped glass or plastic which forms part of a pair of spectacles or microscope **3.** same as **contact lens**

lens implant /ˈlenz ˌɪmplɑːnt/ *noun* an artificial lens implanted in the eye when the natural lens is removed, as in the case of cataract

lenticular /lenˈtɪkjʊlə/ *adjective* referring to or like a lens

lentigo /lenˈtaɪɡəʊ/ *noun* a small brown spot on the skin often caused by exposure to sunlight. Also called **freckle** (NOTE: The plural is **lentigines**.)

leontiasis /ˌliːɒnˈtaɪəsɪs/ *noun* a rare disorder in which the skull bones become enlarged and may give the appearance of a lion's head. It occurs if Paget's disease is not treated.

leprosy /ˈleprəsi/ *noun* an infectious bacterial disease of skin and peripheral nerves caused by *Mycobacterium leprae*, which destroys the tissues and causes severe disfigurement if left untreated. Also called **Hansen's disease**

leptin /ˈleptɪn/ *noun* a hormone produced by fat cells that signals the body's level of hunger to the hypothalamus of the brain

lepto- /leptəʊ/ *prefix* thin

leptocyte /ˈleptəsaɪt/ *noun* a thin red blood cell found in anaemia

leptomeninges /ˌleptəʊmeˈnɪndʒiːz/ *plural noun* the two inner meninges, the pia mater and arachnoid

leptomeningitis /ˌleptəʊmenɪnˈdʒaɪtɪs/ *noun* inflammation of the leptomeninges

Leptospira /ˌleptəʊˈspaɪrə/ *noun* a genus of bacteria excreted continuously in the urine of rats and many domestic animals. It can infect humans, causing leptospirosis or Weil's disease.

leptospirosis /ˌleptəʊspaɪˈrəʊsɪs/ *noun* an infectious disease caused by the spirochaete *Leptospira*, transmitted to humans from rat urine, causing jaundice and kidney damage. Also called **Weil's disease**

lesbianism /ˈlezbiənɪz(ə)m/ *noun* sexual attraction in one woman for another. Compare **homosexuality**

Lesch-Nyhan disease /ˌleʃ ˈnaɪhən dɪˌziːz/, **Lesch-Nyhan syndrome** /ˌleʃ ˈnaɪhən ˌsɪndrəʊm/ *noun* a rare genetic disorder in boys caused by a lack of the enzyme HPRT. Symptoms include uncontrolled muscle movements and learning disabilities, and life expectancy is 20 – 25.

lesion /ˈliːʒ(ə)n/ *noun* a wound, sore or damage to the body (NOTE: **Lesion** is used to refer to any damage to the body, from the fracture of a bone to a cut on the skin.)

lesser /ˈlesə/ *adjective* smaller

lesser circulation /ˌlesə ˌsɜːkjʊˈleɪʃ(ə)n/ *noun* same as **pulmonary circulation**

lesser trochanter /ˌlesə trəˈkæntə/ *noun* a projection on the femur which is the insertion of the psoas major muscle

lesser vestibular gland /ˌlesə veˈstɪbjʊlə glænd/ *noun* the more anterior of the vestibular glands

lethal /ˈliːθ(ə)l/ *adjective* killing or able to kill ○ *These fumes are lethal if inhaled.*

lethal dose /ˈliːθ(ə)l ˈdəʊs/ *noun* the amount of a drug or other substance which will kill the person who takes it ○ *She took a lethal dose of aspirin.* Abbreviation **LD**

lethal gene /ˈliːθ(ə)l ˈdʒiːn/, **lethal mutation** /ˈliːθ(ə)l mjuːˈteɪʃ(ə)n/ *noun* a gene, usually recessive, that results in the premature death of an individual who inherits it, e.g. the gene controlling sickle-cell anaemia

lethargic /lɪˈθɑːdʒɪk/ *adjective* showing lethargy

lethargy /ˈleθədʒi/ *noun* a state in which someone is not mentally alert, has slow movements and is almost inactive

Letterer-Siwe disease /ˌletərə ˈsiːweɪ dɪˌziːz/ *noun* a usually fatal disease, most common in infants, caused by the overproduction of a specialised type of immune cell

leucine /ˈluːsiːn/ *noun* an essential amino acid

leuco- /luːkəʊ/, **leuko-** *prefix* white

leucocyte /ˈluːkəsaɪt/, **leukocyte** *noun* a white blood cell which contains a nucleus but has no haemoglobin

leucocytolysis /ˌluːkəsaɪˈtɒləsɪs/, **leukocytolysis** /ˌluːkəsaɪˈtɒləsɪs/ *noun* destruction of leucocytes

leucocytosis /ˌluːkəsaɪˈtəʊsɪs/, **leukocytosis** /ˌluːkəsaɪˈtəʊsɪs/ *noun* an increase in the numbers of leucocytes in the blood above the usual upper limit, in order to fight an infection

leucoderma /ˌluːkəʊˈdɜːmə/, **leukoderma** *noun* same as **vitiligo**

leucolysin /ˌluːkəʊˈlaɪsɪn/, **leukolysin** *noun* a protein which destroys white blood cells

leuconychia /ˌluːkəʊˈnɪkiə/, **leukonychia** *noun* a condition in which white marks appear on the fingernails

leucopenia /ˌluːkəˈpiːniə/, **leukopenia** *noun* a reduction in the number of leucocytes in the blood, usually as the result of a disease

leucoplakia /ˌluːkəʊˈplækiə/, **leukoplakia** *noun* a condition in which white patches form on mucous membranes, e.g. on the tongue or inside of the mouth

leucopoiesis /ˌluːkəʊpɔɪˈiːsɪs/, **leukopoiesis** *noun* the production of leucocytes

leucorrhoea /ˌluːkəˈriːə/, **leukorrhoea** *noun* an excessive discharge of white mucus from the vagina. Also called **whites** (NOTE: The US spelling is **leukorrhea**.)

leukaemia /luːˈkiːmiə/ *noun* any of several malignant diseases where an unusual number of leucocytes form in the blood (NOTE: The US spelling is **leukemia**.)

leuko- /luːkəʊ/ *prefix* same as **leuco-**

levator /ləˈveɪtə/ *noun* **1.** a surgical instrument for lifting pieces of fractured bone **2.** a muscle which lifts a limb or a part of the body

level of care /ˌlev(ə)l əv ˈkeə/ *noun* any of the planned divisions within the system of health care which is offered by a particular organisation ○

Our care homes offer six different levels of care to allow the greatest independence possible.

level one bed /ˌlev(ə)l ˈwʌn ˌbed/ *noun* a bed occupied by a patient whose needs can be managed in a ward but who has an increased requirement for nursing support, e.g. a post-operative patient with fluctuating vital signs

level three bed /ˌlev(ə)l ˈθriː ˌbed/ *noun* a bed occupied by a patient whose needs should not be managed in a ward, e.g. a patient intubated following a cardiac arrest

level two bed /ˌlev(ə)l ˈtuː ˌbed/ *noun* a bed occupied by a patient whose needs would not normally be managed in a ward, e.g. a patient with a deteriorating condition awaiting transfer to a high-dependency unit

levodopa /ˌliːvəˈdəʊpə/ *noun* a natural chemical that stimulates the production of dopamine in the brain and is used to treat Parkinson's disease

levonorgestrel /ˌliːvəʊnɔːˈdʒestrəl/ *noun* an artificially produced female sex hormone, used mostly in birth control pills or capsules

Leydig cells /ˈlaɪdɪg selz/ *plural noun* testosterone-producing cells between the tubules in the testes. Also called **interstitial cells** [Described 1850. After Franz von Leydig (1821–1908), Professor of Histology at Würzburg, Tübingen and then Bonn, Germany.]

Leydig tumour /ˈlaɪdɪg ˌtjuːmə/ *noun* a tumour of the Leydig cells of the testis. It often releases testosterone, which makes young boys show early signs of maturing.

l.g.v. *abbreviation* lymphogranuloma venereum

LH *abbreviation* luteinising hormone

libido /lɪˈbiːdəʊ/ *noun* **1.** the sexual urge **2.** (*in psychology*) a force which drives the unconscious mind

Librium /ˈlɪbriəm/ *noun* a trade name for chlordiazepoxide

lice /laɪs/ *plural of* **louse**

lichen /ˈlaɪken/ *noun* a type of skin disease with thick skin and small lesions

lichenification /laɪˌkenɪfɪˈkeɪʃ(ə)n/ *noun* a thickening of the skin at the site of a lesion

lichen planus /ˌlaɪken ˈpleɪnəs/ *noun* a skin disease where itchy purple spots appear on the arms and thighs

lid /lɪd/ *noun* the top which covers a container ○ *a medicine bottle with a child-proof lid*

lidocaine /ˈlaɪdəkeɪn/ *noun* US a drug used as a local anaesthetic. Also called **lignocaine**

lie /laɪ/ *noun* same as **lie of fetus** ■ *verb* to be in a flat position ○ *The accident victim was lying on the pavement.* ○ *Make sure the patient lies still and does not move.* (NOTE: **lying – lay – lain**)

Lieberkühn's glands /ˈliːbəkuːnz glændz/ *plural noun* same as **crypts of Lieberkühn**

lien- /laɪən/ *prefix* spleen

lienal /ˈlaɪən(ə)l/ *adjective* relating to or affecting the spleen ○ *the lienal artery*

lienculus /laɪˈeŋkjʊləs/ *noun* a small secondary spleen sometimes found in the body (NOTE: The plural is **lienculi**.)

lienorenal /ˌlaɪənəʊˈriːn(ə)l/ *adjective* relating to or affecting both the spleen and the kidneys

lie of fetus /ˌlaɪ əv ˈfiːtəs/ *noun* the position of the fetus in the uterus ○ *Cause of rupture: abnormal lie of fetus.*

life /laɪf/ *noun* the quality that makes a person or thing alive and not dead or inorganic ○ *The surgeons saved the patient's life.* ○ *Her life is in danger because the drugs are not available.* ○ *The victim showed no sign of life.*

life event /ˈlaɪf ɪˌvent/ *noun* a significant event which alters a person's status as regards taxation, insurance or employment benefits, e.g. the birth of a child or the onset of a disability

life expectancy /ˈlaɪf ɪkˌspektənsi/ *noun* the number of years a person of a particular age is likely to live

life-support system /ˌlaɪf səˈpɔːt ˌsɪstəm/ *noun* a machine that takes over one or more vital functions such as breathing when someone is unable to survive unaided because of a disease or injury

lift /lɪft/ *noun* **1.** a particular way of carrying an injured or unconscious person ○ *a four-handed lift* ○ *a shoulder lift* **2.** a cosmetic operation to remove signs of age or to change a body feature ○ *a face lift*

ligament /ˈlɪgəmənt/ *noun* a thick band of fibrous tissue which connects the bones at a joint and forms the joint capsule

ligate /ˈlaɪgeɪt/ *verb* to tie something with a ligature, e.g. to tie a blood vessel to stop bleeding or to tie the Fallopian tubes as a sterilisation procedure (NOTE: **ligating – ligated**)

ligation /laɪˈgeɪʃ(ə)n/ *noun* a surgical operation to tie up a blood vessel

ligature /ˈlɪgətʃə/ *noun* a thread used to tie vessels or a lumen, e.g. to tie a blood vessel to stop bleeding ■ *verb* same as **ligate** (NOTE: **ligaturing – ligatured**)

light /laɪt/ *adjective* **1.** bright so that a person can see ○ *At six o'clock in the morning it was just getting light.* **2.** referring to hair or skin which is very pale ○ *She has a very light complexion.* ○ *He has light-coloured hair.* **3.** weighing a comparatively small amount ■ *noun* the energy that makes things bright and helps a person to see ○ *There's not enough light in here to take a photo.*

light adaptation /ˈlaɪt ædæpˌteɪʃ(ə)n/ *noun* changes in the eye to adapt to an unusually bright or dim light or to adapt to light after being in darkness

lightening /'laɪtənɪŋ/ *noun* a late stage in pregnancy where the fetus goes down into the pelvic cavity

lightning pains /'laɪtnɪŋ peɪnz/ *plural noun* sharp pains in the legs in someone who has tabes dorsalis

light reflex /'laɪt ˌriːfleks/ *noun* same as **pupillary reaction**

light therapy /'laɪt ˌθerəpi/, **light treatment** /'laɪt ˌtriːtmənt/ *noun* the treatment of a disorder by exposing the person to light such as sunlight or infrared light

lignocaine /'lɪgnəkeɪn/ *noun* same as **lidocaine**

limb /lɪm/ *noun* one of the legs or arms

limbic system /'lɪmbɪk ˌsɪstəm/ *noun* a system of nerves in the brain, including the hippocampus, the amygdala and the hypothalamus, which are associated with emotions such as fear and anger

limb lead /'lɪm liːd/ *noun* an electrode attached to an arm or leg when taking an electrocardiogram

limb lengthening /'lɪm ˌleŋθənɪŋ/ *noun* a procedure in which an arm or a leg is made longer. Its bone is divided in two and new bone forms in the gap between the ends.

limbus /'lɪmbəs/ *noun* an edge, especially the edge of the cornea where it joins the sclera (NOTE: The plural is **limbi**.)

liminal /'lɪmɪn(ə)l/ *adjective* referring to a stimulus at the lowest level which can be sensed

limp /lɪmp/ *noun* a way of walking awkwardly because of pain, stiffness or malformation of a leg or foot ○ *She walks with a limp.* ■ *verb* to walk awkwardly because of pain, stiffness or malformation of a leg or foot ○ *He was still limping three weeks after the accident.*

linctus /'lɪŋktəs/ *noun* a sweet cough medicine

linea nigra /ˌlɪniə 'naɪgrə/ *noun* a dark line on the skin from the navel to the pubis which appears during the later months of pregnancy (NOTE: The plural is **lineae nigrae**.)

linear /'lɪniə/ *adjective* 1. long and narrow in shape 2. able to be represented by a straight line

lingual /'lɪŋgwəl/ *adjective* referring to the tongue

lingual tonsil /ˌlɪŋgwəl 'tɒns(ə)l/ *noun* a mass of lymphoid tissue on the top surface of the back of the tongue

lingula /'lɪŋgjʊlə/ *noun* a long thin piece of bone or other tissue ○ *the lingula of the left lung* (NOTE: The plural is **lingulae**.)

lingular /'lɪŋgjʊlə/ *adjective* relating to a lingula

liniment /'lɪnɪmənt/ *noun* an oily liquid rubbed on the skin to ease the pain or stiffness of a sprain or bruise by acting as a vasodilator or counterirritant. Also called **embrocation**

lining /'laɪnɪŋ/ *noun* a substance or tissue on the inside of an organ ○ *the thick lining of the aorta*

link /lɪŋk/ *verb* 1. to join things together ○ *The ankle bone links the bones of the lower leg to the calcaneus.* 2. to be related to or associated with something ○ *Health is linked to diet.*

linkage /'lɪŋkɪdʒ/ *noun* (*of genes*) the fact of being close together on a chromosome, and therefore likely to be inherited together

linoleic acid /ˌlɪnəʊliːɪk 'æsɪd/ *noun* one of the essential fatty acids, found in grains and seeds

linolenic acid /lɪnəʊˌlenɪk 'æsɪd/ *noun* one of the essential fatty acids, found in linseed and other natural oils

lint /lɪnt/ *noun* thick flat cotton wadding, used as part of a surgical dressing

lip /lɪp/ *noun* 1. each of two fleshy muscular parts round the edge of the mouth ○ *Her lips were dry and cracked.* 2. same as **labium**

lipaemia /lɪ'piːmiə/ *noun* an excessive amount of fat in the blood (NOTE: The US spelling is **lipemia**.)

lipase /'lɪpeɪz/ *noun* an enzyme which breaks down fats in the intestine. Also called **lipolytic enzyme**

lipid /'lɪpɪd/ *noun* an organic compound which is insoluble in water, e.g. a fat, oil or wax

lipid metabolism /ˌlɪpɪd mə'tæbəlɪz(ə)m/ *noun* the series of chemical changes by which lipids are broken down into fatty acids

lipidosis /ˌlɪpɪ'dəʊsɪs/ *noun* a disorder of lipid metabolism in which subcutaneous fat is not present in some parts of the body

lipochondrodystrophy /ˌlɪpəʊˌkɒndrəʊ'dɪstrəfi/ *noun* a congenital disorder affecting lipid metabolism, the bones and the main organs, causing learning difficulties and physical deformity

lipodystrophy /ˌlɪpəʊ'dɪstrəfi/ *noun* a disorder of lipid metabolism

lipogenesis /ˌlɪpəʊ'dʒenəsɪs/ *noun* the production or making of deposits of fat

lipoid /'lɪpɔɪd/ *noun* a compound lipid, or a fatty substance such as cholesterol which is like a lipid ■ *adjective* like a lipid

lipoidosis /ˌlɪpɔɪ'dəʊsɪs/ *noun* a group of diseases with reticuloendothelial hyperplasia and unusual deposits of lipoids in the cells

lipolysis /lɪ'pɒlɪsɪs/ *noun* the process of breaking down fat by lipase

lipolytic enzyme /ˌlɪpəlɪtɪk 'enzaɪm/ *noun* same as **lipase**

lipoma /lɪ'pəʊmə/ *noun* a benign tumour formed of fatty tissue (NOTE: The plural is **lipomas** or **lipomata**.)

lipoprotein /ˌlɪpəʊˈprəʊtiːn/ *noun* a protein which combines with lipids and carries them in the bloodstream and lymph system (NOTE: Lipoproteins are classified according to the percentage of protein which they carry.)

liposuction /ˈlɪpəʊˌsʌkʃ(ə)n/ *noun* the surgical removal of fatty tissue for cosmetic reasons

lipping /ˈlɪpɪŋ/ *noun* a condition in which bone tissue grows over other bones

lip salve /ˈlɪp sælv/ *noun* an ointment, usually sold as a soft stick, used to rub on lips to prevent them cracking

liquid diet /ˌlɪkwɪd ˈdaɪət/ *noun* a diet consisting only of liquids ○ *The clear liquid diet is a temporary diet used in preparation for surgery.*

liquid paraffin /ˌlɪkwɪd ˈpærəfɪn/ *noun* an oil used as a laxative

liquor /ˈlɪkə/ *noun* (*in pharmacy*) a solution, usually aqueous, of a pure substance

lisp /lɪsp/ *noun* a speech condition in which someone replaces 's' sounds with 'th' ■ *verb* to talk with a lisp

Listeria /lɪˈstɪəriə/ *noun* a genus of bacteria found in domestic animals and in unpasteurised milk products which can cause uterine infection or meningitis

listeriosis /lɪˌstɪəriˈəʊsɪs/ *noun* an infectious disease transmitted from animals to humans by the bacterium *Listeria*

listlessness /ˈlɪstləsnəs/ *noun* the fact of being generally weak and tired

liter /ˈliːtə/ *noun* US spelling of **litre**

lith- /lɪθ/ *prefix* same as **litho-** (*used before vowels*)

lithagogue /ˈlɪθəɡɒɡ/ *noun* a drug which helps to remove stones from the urine

lithiasis /lɪˈθaɪəsɪs/ *noun* the formation of stones in an organ

lithium /ˈlɪθiəm/ *noun* a soft silver-white metallic element that forms compounds, used as a medical treatment for bipolar disorder

litho- /lɪθəʊ/ *prefix* referring to a calculus

litholapaxy /lɪˈθɒləpæksi/ *noun* the evacuation of pieces of a stone in the bladder after crushing it with a lithotrite. Also called **lithotrity**

lithonephrotomy /ˌlɪθəʊnəˈfrɒtəmi/ *noun* a surgical operation to remove a stone in the kidney (NOTE: The plural is **lithonephrotomies**.)

lithotomy /lɪˈθɒtəmi/ *noun* a surgical operation to remove a stone from the bladder (NOTE: The plural is **lithotomies**.)

lithotomy position /lɪˈθɒtəmi pəˌzɪʃ(ə)n/ *noun* a position for some medical examinations in which the person lies on his or her back with the legs flexed and the thighs against the abdomen

lithotripsy /ˈlɪθətrɪpsi/ *noun* the process of breaking up kidney or gall bladder stones into small fragments that the body can eliminate them unaided

lithotrite /ˈlɪθətraɪt/ *noun* a surgical instrument which crushes a stone in the bladder

lithotrity /lɪˈθɒtrɪti/ *noun* same as **litholapaxy**

lithuresis /ˌlɪθjʊˈriːsɪs/ *noun* the passage of small stones from the bladder during urination

litmus /ˈlɪtməs/ *noun* a substance which turns red in acid and blue in alkali

litmus paper /ˈlɪtməs ˌpeɪpə/ *noun* a small piece of paper impregnated with litmus, used to test for acidity or alkalinity

litre /ˈliːtə/ *noun* a unit of measurement of liquids equal to 1.76 pints. Abbreviation **l**, **L** (NOTE: With figures, usually written **l** or **L**: *2.5l*, but it can be written in full to avoid confusion with the numeral **1**. The US spelling is **liter**.)

Little's area /ˈlɪt(ə)lz ˌeəriə/ *noun* an area of blood vessels in the nasal septum

Little's disease /ˈlɪt(ə)lz dɪˌziːz/ *noun* same as **spastic diplegia** [Described 1843. After William John Little (1810–94), physician at the London Hospital, UK]

liver /ˈlɪvə/ *noun* a large gland in the upper part of the abdomen. See illustration at **DIGESTIVE SYSTEM** in Supplement (NOTE: For other terms referring to the liver, see words beginning with **hepat-, hepato-**.)

liver fluke /ˈlɪvə fluːk/ *noun* a parasitic flatworm which can infest the liver

liver spot /ˈlɪvə spɒt/ *noun* a little brown patch on the skin of the backs of the hands, attributed to sun damage (NOTE: Liver spots are unconnected with any liver disorder.)

liver transplant /ˈlɪvə ˌtrænsplɑːnt/ *noun* a surgical operation to give a person the liver of another person who has died

livid /ˈlɪvɪd/ *adjective* referring to skin with a blue colour because of being bruised or because of asphyxiation

living will /ˌlɪvɪŋ ˈwɪl/ *noun* a document signed by a person while in good health to specify the decisions he or she wishes to be taken about medical treatment if he or she becomes incapable of making or communicating them

LMC *abbreviation* local medical committee

lobar /ˈləʊbə/ *adjective* referring to a lobe

lobar bronchi /ˌləʊbə ˈbrɒŋkiː/ *plural noun* air passages supplying a lobe of a lung. Also called **secondary bronchi**

lobar pneumonia /ˌləʊbə njuːˈməʊniə/ *noun* pneumonia which affects one or more lobes of the lung

lobe /ləʊb/ *noun* a rounded section of an organ such as the brain, lung or liver. See illustration at **LUNGS** in Supplement

lobectomy /ləʊˈbektəmi/ *noun* a surgical operation to remove one of the lobes of an organ such as the lung ○ *The plural is lobectomies.*

lobotomy /ləʊˈbɒtəmi/ *noun* a surgical operation formerly used to treat mental illness by cutting into a lobe of the brain to cut the nerve fibres (NOTE: The plural is **lobotomies**.)

lobular /ˈlɒbjʊlə/ *adjective* relating to a lobule ○ *lobular carcinoma*

lobule /ˈlɒbjuːl/ *noun* a small section of a lobe in the lung, formed of acini

local /ˈləʊk(ə)l/ *adjective* **1.** referring to a separate place **2.** confined to one part ■ *noun* same as **local anaesthetic**

local anaesthesia /ˌləʊk(ə)l ænəsˈθiːziə/ *noun* loss of feeling in a single part of the body

local anaesthetic /ˌləʊk(ə)l ænəsˈθetɪk/ *noun* an anaesthetic such as lignocaine which removes the feeling in a single part of the body only ○ *The surgeon removed the growth under local anaesthetic.*

localise /ˈləʊkəlaɪz/, **localize** *verb* **1.** to restrict the spread of something to a specific area **2.** to find where something is **3.** to transfer power from a central authority to local organisations (NOTE: **localising – localised**)

localised /ˈləʊkəlaɪzd/, **localized** *adjective* referring to an infection which occurs in one part of the body only. Opposite **generalised**

local supervising authority /ˌləʊk(ə)l ˈsuːpəvaɪzɪŋ ɔːˌθɒrɪti/ *noun* an organisation which controls midwife services within its area

lochia /ˈlɒkiə/ *noun* a discharge from the vagina after childbirth or abortion

lochiometra /ˌlɒkiəmiːtrə/ *noun* a condition in which lochia remains in the uterus after a baby is born, making it swollen

lock /lɒk/ *verb* to fix something in a position

locked-in syndrome /ˌlɒkt ˈɪn ˌsɪndrəʊm/ *noun* a condition in which only the eyes and eyelids can move although the person is fully alert and conscious. It results from severe damage to the brain stem.

locked knee /ˌlɒkt ˈniː/ *noun* a condition in which a piece of the cartilage in the knee slips out of position. The symptom is a sharp pain, and the knee remains permanently bent.

locking joint /ˌlɒkɪŋ ˈdʒɔɪnt/ *noun* a joint which can be locked in an extended position, e.g. the knee or elbow

lockjaw /ˈlɒkdʒɔː/ *noun* same as **tetanus** (*dated informal*)

locomotion /ˌləʊkəˈməʊʃ(ə)n/ *noun* the fact of being able to move

locomotor /ˌləʊkəˈməʊtə/ *adjective* relating to locomotion

locomotor ataxia /ˌləʊkəˌməʊtər əˈtæksiə/ *noun* same as **tabes dorsalis**

loculated /ˈlɒkjʊleɪtɪd/ *adjective* referring to an organ or a growth which is divided into many compartments ○ *a loculated renal abscess*

locule /ˈlɒkjuːl/ *noun* same as **loculus**

loculus /ˈlɒkjʊləs/ *noun* a small space in an organ (NOTE: The plural is **loculi**.)

locum /ˈləʊkəm/ *noun* a healthcare professional such as a doctor or pharmacist who takes the place of another for a time. Also called **locum tenens**

locum tenens /ˌləʊkəm ˈtenənz/ *noun* same as **locum** (NOTE: The plural is **locum tenentes**.)

locus /ˈləʊkəs/ *noun* **1.** an area or point where an infection or disease is to be found **2.** a position on a chromosome occupied by a gene (NOTE: The plural is **loci**.)

lofepramine /lɒˈfeprəmiːn/ *noun* an antidepressant drug

log roll /ˈlɒg rəʊl/ *noun* a method of turning people in bed onto their side by putting them into a straight position and pulling on the sheet under them

logrolling /ˈlɒgrəʊlɪŋ/ *noun* the process of moving a person who is lying down into another position using the log roll method

-logy /lədʒi/ *suffix* **1.** science or study ○ *psychology* ○ *embryology* **2.** speech or expression

loin /lɔɪn/ *noun* the lower back part of the body above the buttocks

Lomotil /ləʊˈməʊtɪl/ a trade name for a preparation containing diphenoxalate

longitudinal /ˌlɒŋgɪˈtjuːdɪn(ə)l/ *adjective* **1.** positioned lengthwise **2.** in the direction of the long axis of the body

longitudinal arch /ˌlɒŋgɪtjuːdɪn(ə)l ˈɑːtʃ/ *noun* same as **plantar arch**

longitudinal lie /ˌlɒŋgɪtjuːdɪn(ə)l ˈlaɪ/ *noun* the usual position of a fetus, lying along the axis of the mother's body

longitudinal study /ˌlɒŋgɪtjuːdɪn(ə)l ˈstʌdi/ *noun* a study of individuals or groups of people and of how some aspect such as their health or education changes over a long time

longsighted /ˌlɒŋˈsaɪtɪd/ *adjective* able to see clearly things which are far away but not things which are close

longsightedness /ˌlɒŋˈsaɪtɪdnəs/ *noun* the condition of being longsighted. Also called **hypermetropia**

loo /luː/ *noun* a toilet, or a room containing a toilet (*informal*) □ **to go to the loo** to urinate or defecate

loop /luːp/ *noun* **1.** a curve or bend in a line, especially one of the particular curves in a fingerprint **2.** a curved piece of wire placed in the uterus to prevent contraception

loop of Henle /ˌluːp əv ˈhenli/ *noun* a curved tube which forms the main part of a nephron in the kidney

loperamide /ləʊˈperəmaɪd/, **loperamide hydrochloride** /ləʊˌperəmaɪd ˌhaɪdrəʊˈklɔːraɪd/ *noun* a drug that relieves severe diarrhoea by slowing down the movements of the intestine

loratidine /lɒrˈætɪdiːn/ *noun* an antihistamine drug

lorazepam /lɔːˈræzɪpæm/ *noun* a mild tranquilliser that people often receive before surgery to lessen anxiety

lordosis /lɔːˈdəʊsɪs/ *noun* excessive forward curvature of the lower part of the spine. ◊ **kyphosis**

lordotic /lɔːˈdɒtɪk/ *adjective* referring to lordosis

lotion /ˈləʊʃ(ə)n/ *noun* a medicinal liquid used to rub on the skin ○ *a mild antiseptic lotion*

louse /laʊs/ *noun* a small insect of the *Pediculus* genus, which sucks blood and lives on the skin as a parasite on animals and humans (NOTE: The plural is **lice**.)

low-density lipoprotein /ˌləʊ ˌdensɪti ˈlɪpəʊprəʊtiːn/ *noun* a lipoprotein with a large percentage of cholesterol which deposits fats in muscles and arteries. Abbreviation **LDL**

lower motor neurones /ˌləʊə ˈməʊtə ˌnjʊərəʊnz/ *plural noun* linked neurones which carry motor impulses from the spinal cord to the muscles

lozenge /ˈlɒzɪndʒ/ *noun* a sweet medicinal tablet ○ *She was sucking a cough lozenge.*

LRCP *abbreviation* licentiate of the Royal College of Physicians

LSA *abbreviation* local supervising authority

LSD *abbreviation* lysergic acid diethylamide

lubb-dupp /ˌlʌb ˈdʌb/ *noun* two sounds made by the heart, which represent each cardiac cycle when heard through a stethoscope

lubricant /ˈluːbrɪkənt/ *noun* a fluid which lubricates

lubricate /ˈluːbrɪkeɪt/ *verb* to cover something with a fluid to reduce friction (NOTE: **lubricating – lubricated**)

lucid /ˈluːsɪd/ *adjective* with a clearly working mind ○ *In spite of the pain, he was still lucid.*

lucid interval /ˌluːsɪd ˈɪntəv(ə)l/ *noun* a period of clear thinking which occurs between two periods of unconsciousness or of mental illness

lumbago /lʌmˈbeɪgəʊ/ *noun* pain in the lower back (*informal*) ○ *She has been suffering from lumbago for years.* ○ *He has had an attack of lumbago.*

lumbar /ˈlʌmbə/ *adjective* referring to the lower part of the back

lumbar puncture /ˈlʌmbə ˌpʌŋktʃə/ *noun* a surgical operation to remove a sample of cerebrospinal fluid by inserting a hollow needle into the

lower part of the spinal canal. Also called **spinal puncture**

lumbar region /ˈlʌmbə ˌriːdʒən/ *noun* the two parts of the abdomen on each side of the umbilical region

lumbar vertebra /ˌlʌmbə ˈvɜːtɪbrə/ *plural noun* each of the five vertebrae between the thoracic vertebrae and the sacrum

lumbo- /lʌmbəʊ/ *prefix* the lumbar region

lumbosacral /ˌlʌmbəʊˈseɪkrəl/ *adjective* referring to both the lumbar vertebrae and the sacrum

lumbosacral joint /ˌlʌmbəʊˈseɪkrəl ˌdʒɔɪnt/ *noun* a joint at the bottom of the back between the lumbar vertebrae and the sacrum

lumen /ˈluːmɪn/ *noun* **1.** an SI unit of light emitted per second **2.** the inside width of a passage in the body or of an instrument such as an endoscope

lump /lʌmp/ *noun* a mass of hard tissue which rises on the surface or under the surface of the skin ○ *He has a lump where he hit his head on the low door.* ○ *She noticed a lump in her right breast and went to see the doctor.*

lumpectomy /lʌmˈpektəmi/ *noun* a surgical operation to remove a hard mass of tissue such as a breast tumour, leaving the surrounding tissue intact (NOTE: The plural is **lumpectomies**.)

lunate /ˈluːneɪt bəʊn/, **lunate bone** *noun* one of the eight small carpal bones in the wrist. See illustration at HAND in Supplement

Lund and Browder chart /ˌlʌnd ən ˈbraʊdə ˌtʃɑːt/ *noun* a chart for calculating the surface area of a burn

lung /lʌŋ/ *noun* one of two organs of respiration in the body into which air is sucked when a person breathes (NOTE: For other terms referring to the lungs, see words beginning with **bronch-, broncho-, pneum-, pneumo-, pneumon-, pneumono-, pulmo-**.)

lunula /ˈluːnjʊlə/ *noun* a curved white mark at the base of a fingernail (NOTE: The plural is **lunulae**.)

lupus /ˈluːpəs/ *noun* a persistent skin disease, of which there are several unrelated types

lupus erythematosus /ˌluːpəs ˌerɪθiːmə ˈtəʊsəs/ *noun* an inflammatory disease of connective tissue of which the more serious, systemic, form affects the heart, joints and blood vessels. Abbreviation **LE**

lupus vulgaris /ˌluːpəs vʌlˈgeərɪs/ *noun* a form of tuberculosis of the skin in which red spots appear on the face and become infected

lutein /ˈluːtiɪn/ *noun* a yellow pigment in the corpus luteum

luteinising hormone /ˈluːtiɪnaɪzɪŋ ˌhɔːməʊn/, **luteinizing hormone** *noun* a hormone produced by the pituitary gland, which stimulates the formation of the corpus luteum in females and of testosterone in males. Abbreviation **LH**. Also called **interstitial cell stimulating hormone**

luteo- /luːtiəʊ/ *prefix* **1.** yellow **2.** corpus luteum

luxation /lʌkˈseɪʃ(ə)n/ *noun* same as **dislocation**

Lyme disease /ˈlaɪm dɪˌziːz/ *noun* a viral disease caused by *Borrelia burgdorferi* transmitted by bites from deer ticks. It causes rashes, nervous pains, paralysis and, in extreme cases, death.

lymph /lɪmf/ *noun* a colourless liquid containing white blood cells which circulates in the lymph system from all body tissues, carrying waste matter away from tissues to the veins. Also called **lymph fluid**

COMMENT: Lymph drains from the tissues through capillaries into lymph vessels. It is formed of water, protein and white blood cells (lymphocytes). Waste matter such as infection in the lymph is filtered out and destroyed as it passes through the lymph nodes, which then add further lymphocytes to the lymph before it continues in the system. It eventually drains into the brachiocephalic (innominate) veins, and joins the venous bloodstream. Lymph is not pumped round the body like blood but moves by muscle pressure on the lymph vessels and by the negative pressure of the large veins into which the vessels empty. Lymph is an essential part of the body's defence against infection.

lymph- /lɪmf/ *prefix meaning* same as **lympho-** (*used before vowels*)

lymphaden- /lɪmfædən/ *prefix* relating to the lymph nodes

lymphadenectomy /ˌlɪmfædəˈnektəmi/ *noun* the surgical removal of a lymph node (NOTE: The plural is **lymphadenectomies**.)

lymphadenitis /ˌlɪmfædəˈnaɪtɪs/ *noun* inflammation of the lymph nodes

lymphadenoma /ˌlɪmfædəˈnəʊmə/ *noun* same as **lymphoma**

lymphadenopathy /ˌlɪmfædəˈnɒpəθi/ *noun* any unusual condition of the lymph nodes (NOTE: The plural is **lymphadenopathies**.)

lymphangi- /lɪmfændʒi/ *prefix* lymphatic vessel

lymphangiectasis /ˌlɪmfændʒiˈektəsɪs/ *noun* swelling of the smaller lymph vessels as a result of obstructions in larger vessels

lymphangiography /ˌlɪmfændʒiˈɒɡrəfi/ *noun* an X-ray examination of the lymph vessels following introduction of radio-opaque material (NOTE: The plural is **lymphangiographies**.)

lymphangioma /ˌlɪmfændʒiˈəʊmə/ *noun* a benign tumour formed of lymph tissues (NOTE: The plural is **lymphangiomas** or **lymphangiomata**.)

lymphangioplasty /lɪmfˈændʒiəplæsti/ *noun* a surgical operation to make artificial lymph channels (NOTE: The plural is **lymphangioplasties**.)

lymphangitis /ˌlɪmfænˈdʒaɪtɪs/ *noun* inflammation of the lymph vessels

lymphatic /lɪmˈfætɪk/ *adjective* referring to lymph

lymphatic capillary /lɪmˌfætɪk kəˈpɪləri/ *plural noun* any of the capillaries which lead from tissue and join lymphatic vessels

lymphatic duct /lɪmˈfætɪk dʌkt/ *noun* the main channel for carrying lymph

lymphatic node /lɪmˈfætɪk nəʊd/ *noun* same as **lymph gland**

lymphatic nodule /lɪmˌfætɪk ˈnɒdjuːl/ *noun* a small lymph node found in clusters in tissues

lymphatics /lɪmˈfætɪks/ *plural noun* lymph vessels

lymphatic system /lɪmˈfætɪk ˌsɪstəm/ *noun* a series of vessels which transport lymph from the tissues through the lymph nodes and into the bloodstream

lymphatic vessel /lɪmˈfætɪk ˌves(ə)l/ *noun* a tube which carries lymph round the body from the tissues to the veins

lymph duct /ˈlɪmf dʌkt/ *noun* any channel carrying lymph

lymph gland /ˈlɪmf ɡlænd/, **lymph node** /ˈlɪmf nəʊd/ *noun* a mass of lymphoid tissue situated in various points of the lymphatic system, especially under the armpits and in the groin, through which lymph passes and in which lymphocytes are produced. Also called **lymphatic node**

lympho- /lɪmfəʊ/ *prefix meaning* lymph

lymphoblast /ˈlɪmfəʊblæst/ *noun* an unusual cell which forms in acute lymphoblastic leukaemia as a result of the change which takes place in a lymphocyte on contact with an antigen

lymphoblastic /ˌlɪmfəʊˈblæstɪk/ *adjective* referring to lymphoblasts, or forming lymphocytes

lymphocele /ˈlɪmfəsiːl/ *noun* a cyst containing lymph from injured or diseased lymph nodes or ducts

lymphocyte /ˈlɪmfəsaɪt/ *noun* a type of mature leucocyte or white blood cell formed by the lymph nodes and concerned with the production of antibodies

lymphocytopenia /ˌlɪmfəʊˌsaɪtəʊˈpiːniə/ *noun* same as **lymphopenia**

lymphocytosis /ˌlɪmfəʊsaɪˈtəʊsɪs/ *noun* an increased number of lymphocytes in the blood

lymphoedema /ˌlɪmfəʊɪˈdiːmə/ *noun* a swelling caused by obstruction of the lymph vessels or unusual development of lymph vessels (NOTE: The US spelling is **lymphedema**.)

lymphogranuloma venereum /ˌlɪmfəʊ ˌɡrænjʊˌləʊmə vəˈnɪərəm/ *noun* a sexually transmitted bacterial infection that causes swelling of the genital lymph nodes and, especially in men, a genital ulcer. Abbreviation **l.g.v.**

lymphoid tissue /ˈlɪmfɔɪd ˌtɪʃuː/ *noun* tissue in the lymph nodes, the tonsils and the spleen where masses of lymphocytes are supported by a network of reticular fibres and cells

lymphokine /ˈlɪmfəʊkaɪn/ *noun* a protein produced by lymphocytes that has an effect on other cells in the immune system. ◊ **cytokine**

lymphoma /lɪmˈfəʊmə/ *noun* a malignant tumour arising from lymphoid tissue. Also called **lymphadenoma** (NOTE: The plural is **lymphomas** or **lymphomata**.)

lymphopenia /ˌlɪmfəʊˈpiːniə/ *noun* a reduction in the number of lymphocytes in the blood. Also called **lymphocytopenia**

lymphopoiesis /ˌlɪmfəʊpɔɪˈiːsɪs/ *noun* the production of lymphocytes or lymphoid tissue

lymph vessel /ˈlɪmf ˌves(ə)l/ *noun* one of the tubes which carry lymph round the body from the tissues to the veins

lyophilisation /laɪˌɒfɪlaɪˈzeɪʃ(ə)n/, **lyophilization** *noun* the act of preserving tissue, plasma or serum by freeze-drying it in a vacuum

lysergic acid diethylamide /laɪˌsɜːdʒɪk ˌæsɪd daɪˈeθɪləmaɪd/ *noun* a powerful hallucinogenic drug which can cause psychosis. Abbreviation **LSD**

lysin /ˈlaɪsɪn/ *noun* **1.** a protein in the blood which destroys the cell against which it is directed **2.** a toxin which causes the lysis of cells

lysine /ˈlaɪsiːn/ *noun* an essential amino acid

lysis /ˈlaɪsɪs/ *noun* **1.** the destruction of a cell by a lysin, in which the membrane of the cell is destroyed **2.** a reduction in a fever or disease slowly over a period of time

-lysis /lɪsɪs/ *suffix* referring to processes which involve breaking up or decaying, or to objects which are doing this ○ *haemolysis*

lysosome /ˈlaɪsəsəʊm/ *noun* a particle in a cell which contains enzymes which break down substances such as bacteria which enter the cell

lysozyme /ˈlaɪsəzaɪm/ *noun* an enzyme found in the whites of eggs and in tears, which destroys specific bacteria

M

m *symbol* **1.** metre **2.** milli-

M *symbol* mega-

MAAG *abbreviation* medical audit advisory group

maceration /ˌmæsəˈreɪʃ(ə)n/ *noun* the process of softening a solid by letting it lie in a liquid so that the soluble matter dissolves

Mackenrodt's ligaments /ˈmækənrəʊdz ˌlɪgəmənts/ *plural noun* same as **cardinal ligaments**

Macmillan nurse /məkˈmɪlən nɜːs/ *noun* a nurse who specialises in cancer care and is employed by the organisation Macmillan Cancer Relief

macro- /mækrəʊ/ *prefix* large. Opposite **micro-**

macrobiotic /ˌmækrəʊbaɪˈɒtɪk/ *adjective* referring to food which has been produced naturally without artificial additives or preservatives

macrocephaly /ˌmækrəʊˈkefəli/ *noun* the condition of having an unusually large head

macrocheilia /ˌmækrəʊˈkaɪliə/ *noun* the condition of having large lips

macrocyte /ˈmækrəʊsaɪt/ *noun* an unusually large red blood cell found in people who have pernicious anaemia

macrocythaemia /mækrəʊsaɪˈθiːmiə/ *noun* same as **macrocytosis**

macrocytic /ˌmækrəʊˈsɪtɪk/ *adjective* referring to macrocytes

macrocytic anaemia /ˌmækrəʊsɪtɪk əˈniːmiə/ *noun* anaemia in which someone has unusually large red blood cells

macrocytosis /ˌmækrəʊsaɪˈtəʊsɪs/ *noun* the condition of having macrocytes in the blood. Also called **macrocythaemia**

macrodactyly /ˌmækrəʊˈdæktɪli/ *noun* a condition in which a person has unusually large or long fingers or toes

macroglobulin /ˌmækrəʊˈglɒbjʊlɪn/ *noun* a class of immunoglobulin, a globulin protein of high molecular weight, which serves as an antibody

macroglossia /ˌmækrəʊˈglɒsiə/ *noun* the condition of having an unusually large tongue

macrognathia /ˌmækrəʊˈneɪθiə/ *noun* a condition in which the jaw is larger than usual

macromastia /ˌmækrəʊˈmæstiə/ *noun* overdevelopment of the breasts

macronutrient /ˈmækrəʊˌnjuːtriənt/ *noun* a substance which an organism needs in large amounts for normal growth and development, e.g. nitrogen, carbon or potassium. Compare **micronutrient**

macrophage /ˈmækrəʊfeɪdʒ/ *noun* any of several large cells which destroy inflammatory tissue, found in connective tissue, wounds, lymph nodes and other parts

macroscopic /ˌmækrəʊˈskɒpɪk/ *adjective* able to be seen with the naked eye

macrosomia /ˌmækrəʊˈsəʊmiə/ *noun* a condition in which the body grows too much

macrostomia /ˌmækrəʊˈstəʊmiə/ *noun* a condition in which the mouth is too wide because the bones of the upper and lower jaw have not fused, either on one or on both sides

macula /ˈmækjʊlə/ *noun* **1.** same as **macule 2.** a small coloured area, e.g. a macula lutea

macula lutea /ˌmækjʊlə ˈluːtiə/ *noun* a yellow spot on the retina, surrounding the fovea, the part of the eye which sees most clearly. Also called **yellow spot**

macular /ˈmækjʊlə/ *adjective* referring to a macula

macular degeneration /ˌmækjʊlə dɪˌdʒenə ˈreɪʃ(ə)n/ *noun* an eye disorder in elderly people in which fluid leaks into the retina and destroys cones and rods, reducing central vision

macule /ˈmækjuːl/ *noun* a small flat coloured spot on the skin. Compare **papule**

maculopapular /ˌmækjʊləʊˈpæpjʊlə/ *adjective* made up of both macules and papules ○ *maculopapular rash*

mad cow disease /ˌmæd ˈkaʊ dɪˌziːz/ *noun* same as **bovine spongiform encephalopathy** (*informal*)

Magendie's foramen /məˌdʒendɪz fə ˈreɪmen/ *noun* an opening in the fourth ventricle of the brain which allows cerebrospinal fluid to flow [Described 1828. After François Magendie

(1783–1855), French physician and physiologist.]

magnesium /mæg'niːziəm/ *noun* a chemical element found in green vegetables, which is essential especially for the correct functioning of muscles (NOTE: The chemical symbol is **Mg**.)

magnesium sulphate /mæg,niːziəm 'sʌlfeɪt/ *noun* a magnesium salt used as a laxative. Also called **Epsom salts**

magnesium trisilicate /mæg,niːziəm traɪ 'sɪlɪkət/ *noun* a magnesium compound used to treat peptic ulcers

magnetic /mæg'netɪk/ *adjective* able to attract objects, like a magnet

magnetic field /mæg,netɪk 'fiːld/ *noun* an area round an object which is under the influence of the magnetic force exerted by the object

magnetic resonance imaging /mæg,netɪk 'rezənəns ,ɪmɪdʒɪŋ/ *noun* a scanning technique which exposes the body to a strong magnetic field and uses the electromagnetic signals emitted by the body to form an image of soft tissue and cells. Abbreviation **MRI**

magnum /'mægnəm/ ♦ **foramen magnum**

main bronchi /,meɪn 'brɒŋkiː/ *plural noun* the two main air passages which branch from the trachea outside the lung. Also called **primary bronchi**

major surgery /,meɪdʒə 'sɜːdʒəri/ *noun* surgical operations involving important organs in the body

mal /mæl/ *noun* an illness or disease

mal- /mæl/ *prefix* bad or unusual

malabsorption /,mæləb'sɔːpʃən/ *noun* a situation where the intestines are unable to absorb the fluids and nutrients in food properly

malabsorption syndrome /,mæləb'sɔːpʃən ,sɪndrəʊm/ *noun* a group of symptoms and signs, including malnutrition, anaemia, oedema and dermatitis, which results from steatorrhoea and malabsorption of vitamins, protein, carbohydrates and water

malacia /mə'leɪʃə/ *noun* the pathological softening of an organ or tissue

malaise /mə'leɪz/ *noun* a feeling of discomfort

malaligned /,mælə'laɪnd/ *adjective* not in the correct position relative to other parts of the body

malalignment /,mælə'laɪnmənt/ *noun* a condition in which something is malaligned, especially in which a tooth is not in its correct position in the mouth

malar /'meɪlə/ *adjective* referring to the cheek

malar bone /'meɪlə bəʊn/ *noun* same as **cheekbone**

malaria /mə'leəriə/ *noun* a mainly tropical disease caused by a parasite *Plasmodium*, which enters the body after a bite from the female anopheles mosquito

malarial /mə'leəriəl/ *adjective* referring to malaria

malarial parasite /mə,leəriəl 'pærəsaɪt/ *noun* a parasite transmitted into the human bloodstream by the bite of the female anopheles mosquito

malarial therapy /mə'leəriə ,θerəpi/ *noun* a treatment in which a person is given a form of malaria in the belief that the high fevers they experience can stimulate the immune system to fight off serious diseases such as syphilis and HIV

male menopause /,meɪl 'menəpɔːz/ *noun* a period in middle age when a man may feel insecure and anxious about the fact that his physical powers are declining (*informal*)

malformation /,mælfɔː'meɪʃ(ə)n/ *noun* an unusual variation in the shape, structure or development of something

malfunction /mæl'fʌŋkʃən/ *noun* a situation in which a particular organ does not work in the usual way ○ *Her loss of consciousness was due to a malfunction of the kidneys* or *to a kidney malfunction.*

malignancy /mə'lɪgnənsi/ *noun* **1.** the state of being malignant ○ *The tests confirmed the malignancy of the growth.* **2.** a cancerous growth (NOTE: The plural is **malignancies**.)

malignant /mə'lɪgnənt/ *adjective* likely to cause death or serious disablement if not properly treated

malignant hypertension /mə,lɪgnənt ,haɪpə'tenʃən/ *noun* dangerously high blood pressure

malignant melanoma /mə,lɪgnənt ,melə 'nəʊmə/ *noun* a dark tumour which develops on the skin from a mole, caused by exposure to strong sunlight

malignant pustule /mə,lɪgnənt 'pʌstjuːl/ *noun* a pus-filled swelling that results from infection of the skin with anthrax

malignant tumour /mə,lɪgnənt 'tjuːmə/ *noun* a tumour which is cancerous and can grow again or spread into other parts of the body, even if removed surgically. Opposite **benign tumour**

malingerer /mə'lɪŋgərə/ *noun* a person who pretends to be ill

malingering /mə'lɪŋgərɪŋ/ *adjective* the act of pretending to be ill

malleolar /mə'liːələ/ *adjective* referring to a malleolus

malleolus /mə'liːələs/ *noun* one of two bony prominences at each side of the ankle (NOTE: The plural is **malleoli**.)

mallet finger /,mælɪt 'fɪŋgə/ *noun* a finger which cannot be straightened because the tendon attaching the top joint has been torn

malleus /'mæliəs/ *noun* the largest of the three ossicles in the middle ear, shaped like a hammer. See illustration at **EAR** in Supplement

Mallory bodies /'mæləri ˌbɒdiz/ *plural noun* large irregular masses which occur in the cytoplasm of damaged liver cells, often a sign of an alcohol-related disease

Mallory-Weiss syndrome /ˌmæləri 'vais ˌsindrəʊm/, **Mallory-Weiss tear** /ˌmæləri 'vais ˌteə/ *noun* a condition in which there is a tearing in the mucous membrane where the stomach and oesophagus join, e.g. because of strain on them due to vomiting [Described 1929. After G. Kenneth Mallory (1900–86), Professor of Pathology, Boston University, USA; Konrad Weiss (1898–1942) US physician.]

malnourished /mæl'nʌrɪʃt/ *adjective* not having enough to eat or having only poor-quality food, leading to ill-health

malnutrition /ˌmælnjʊ'trɪʃ(ə)n/ *noun* a lack of food or of good-quality food, leading to ill-health

malocclusion /ˌmælə'kluːʒ(ə)n/ *noun* a condition in which the teeth in the upper and lower jaws do not meet properly when the person's mouth is closed

malodorous /mæl'əʊdərəs/ *adjective* with a strong unpleasant smell

Malpighian body /mæl'pɪgiən ˌbɒdi/, **Malpighian corpuscle** /mæl'pɪgiən ˌkɔːpʌs(ə)l/ *noun* same as **renal corpuscle** [Described 1666. After Marcello Malpighi (1628–94), anatomist and physiologist in Rome and Bologna, Italy.]

Malpighian glomerulus /mæl,pɪgiən glɒ'merʊləs/ *noun* same as **Bowman's capsule**

Malpighian layer /mæl'pɪgiən ˌleiə/ *noun* the deepest layer of the epidermis

malposition /ˌmælpə'zɪʃ(ə)n/ *noun* an unusual or unexpected position of something such as a fetus in the uterus or fractured bones

malpractice /mæl'præktɪs/ *noun* illegal, unethical, negligent or immoral behaviour by a professional person, especially a healthcare professional ○ *The surgeon was found guilty of malpractice.*

malpresentation /ˌmælprez(ə)n'teɪʃ(ə)n/ *noun* an unusual position of a fetus in the uterus just before it is ready to be born

Malta fever /'mɔːltə ˌfiːvə/ *noun* same as **brucellosis**

maltase /'mɔːlteɪz/ *noun* an enzyme in the small intestine which converts maltose into glucose

maltose /'mɔːltəʊs/ *noun* a sugar formed by digesting starch or glycogen

malunion /mæl'juːnjən/ *noun* a bad join of the pieces of a broken bone

mamilla /mə'mɪlə/ *noun* another spelling of **mammilla**

mamillary /'mæmɪl(ə)ri/ *adjective* another spelling of **mammillary**

mamm- /mæm/ *prefix* same as **mammo-** (used before vowels)

mamma /'mæmə/ *noun* same as **breast** (NOTE: The plural is **mammae**.)

mammary /'mæməri/ *adjective* referring to the breast

mammary gland /'mæməri glænd/ *noun* a gland in female mammals which produces milk

mammilla /mə'mɪlə/, **mamilla** *noun* the protruding part in the centre of the breast, containing the milk ducts through which the milk flows. Also called **nipple**

mammillary /'mæmɪl(ə)ri/, **mamillary** *adjective* referring to the nipple

mammo- /mæməʊ/ *prefix* referring to breasts

mammogram /'mæməgræm/ *noun* a picture of a breast made using a special X-ray technique

mammography /mæ'mɒgrəfi/ *noun* examination of the breast using a special X-ray technique

mammoplasty /'mæməplæsti/ *noun* plastic surgery to alter the shape or size of the breasts

Manchester operation /'mæntʃistər ɒpə ˌreɪʃ(ə)n/ *noun* a surgical operation to correct downward movement of the uterus, involving removal of the cervix

mandible /'mændɪb(ə)l/ *noun* the lower bone in the jaw. Also called **lower jaw**

mandibular /mæn'dɪbjʊlə/ *adjective* referring to the lower jaw

mane /'meɪni/ *adverb* (used on prescriptions) during the daytime. Opposite **nocte**

manganese /'mæŋgəniːz/ *noun* a metallic trace element (NOTE: The chemical symbol is **Mn**.)

mania /'meɪniə/ *noun* a state of bipolar disorder in which the person is excited, very sure of his or her own abilities and has increased energy

-mania /meɪniə/ *suffix* obsession with something

maniac /'meɪniæk/ *noun* a person who behaves in an uncontrolled way or is considered to have an obsession (NOTE: This term is regarded as offensive.)

manic /'mænɪk/ *adjective* referring to mania

manic depression /ˌmænɪk dɪ'preʃ(ə)n/ *noun* same as **bipolar disorder**

manic-depressive /ˌmænɪk dɪ'presɪv/ *adjective* relating to bipolar disorder ■ *noun* a person with bipolar disorder

manic-depressive illness /ˌmænɪk dɪ'presɪv ˌɪlnəs/, **manic-depressive psychosis** /ˌmænɪk dɪˌpresɪv saɪ'kəʊsɪs/ *noun* same as **bipolar disorder**

manifestation /ˌmænɪfe'steɪʃ(ə)n/ *noun* a sign, indication or symptom of a disease

manipulation /mə,nɪpjʊ'leɪʃ(ə)n/ *noun* a form of treatment that involves moving or rubbing parts of the body with the hands, e.g. to treat a disorder of a joint

manometer /məˈnɒmɪtə/ *noun* an instrument for comparing pressures

manometry /məˈnɒmɪtri/ *noun* the measurement of pressures within organs of the body which contain gases or liquids, e.g. the oesophagus or parts of the brain

Mantoux test /ˈmæntuː test/ *noun* a test for tuberculosis, in which a person is given an intracutaneous injection of tuberculin. ◊ **Heaf test** [Described 1908. After Charles Mantoux (1877–1947), French physician.]

manual /ˈmænjuəl/ *adjective* done by hand

manubrium sterni /məˌnuːbriəm ˈstɜːnaɪ/ *noun* the upper part of the sternum

MAO *abbreviation* monoamine oxidase

MAOI *abbreviation* monoamine oxidase inhibitor

MAO inhibitor /ˌem eɪ ˈəʊ ɪnˌhɪbɪtə/ *noun* same as **monoamine oxidase inhibitor**

maple syrup urine disease /ˌmeɪp(ə)l ˌsɪrəp ˈjʊərɪn dɪˌziːz/ *noun* an inherited condition caused by not having enough of a particular enzyme which helps the body to deal with amino acid. The urine smells like maple syrup. It can be fatal if not treated.

marasmus /məˈræzməs/ *noun* a wasting disease which affects small children who have difficulty in absorbing nutrients or who are malnourished. Also called **failure to thrive**

marble bone disease /ˌmɑːb(ə)l ˈbəʊn dɪˌziːz/ *noun* same as **osteopetrosis**

march fracture /ˈmɑːtʃ ˌfræktʃə/ *noun* a fracture of one of the metatarsal bones in the foot, caused by excessive exercise to which the body is not accustomed

Marfan's syndrome /ˈmɑːfɑːnz ˌsɪndrəʊm/, **Marfan syndrome** /ˈmɑːfɑːn ˌsɪndrəʊm/ *noun* a hereditary condition in which a person has extremely long fingers and toes, with disorders of the heart, aorta and eyes [Described 1896. After Bernard Jean Antonin Marfan (1858–1942), French paediatrician.]

marijuana /ˌmærɪˈwɑːnə/ *noun* same as **cannabis**

marker /ˈmɑːkə/ *noun* 1. something which acts an indicator of something else 2. a substance introduced into the body to make internal structures clearer to X-rays

marrow /ˈmærəʊ/ *noun* soft tissue in cancellous bone. In young animals red marrow is concerned with blood formation while in adults it becomes progressively replaced with fat and is known as yellow marrow. Also called **bone marrow**. See illustration at BONE STRUCTURE in Supplement

marsupialisation /mɑːˌsuːpiəlaɪˈzeɪʃ(ə)n/, **marsupialization** *noun* a surgical procedure in which the inside of a cyst is opened up so that the cyst can be allowed to shrink gradually, because it cannot be cut out

masculinisation /ˌmæskjʊlɪnaɪˈzeɪʃ(ə)n/, **masculinization** *noun* the development of male characteristics such as body hair and a deep voice in a woman, caused by hormone deficiency or by treatment with male hormones

Maslow's hierarchy of human needs /ˌmæzləʊz ˌhaɪrɑːki əv ˌhjuːmən ˈniːdz/ *noun* a system which explains human behaviour by organising human needs in order of priority, from basic ones such as finding food to complex ones such as finding self-fulfilment, a higher level of motivation not being activated until the lesser needs have been satisfied

masochism /ˈmæsəkɪz(ə)m/ *noun* a sexual condition in which a person takes pleasure in being hurt or badly treated

masochistic /ˌmæsəˈkɪstɪk/ *adjective* referring to masochism

mass /mæs/ *noun* 1. a large quantity, e.g. a large number of people ○ *The patient's back was covered with a mass of red spots.* 2. a body of matter with no clear shape

massage /ˈmæsɑːʒ/ *noun* a treatment for muscular conditions which involves rubbing, stroking or pressing the body with the hands ▪ *verb* to rub, stroke or press the body with the hands

masseter /mæˈsiːtə/, **masseter muscle** /mæˈsiːtə ˌmʌs(ə)l/ *noun* a muscle in the cheek which clenches the lower jaw making it move up, to allow chewing

mast- /mæst/ *prefix* same as **masto-** (*used before vowels*)

mast cell /ˈmæst sel/ *noun* a large cell in connective tissue, which carries histamine and reacts to allergens

mastectomy /mæˈstektəmi/ *noun* the surgical removal of a breast

mastication /ˌmæstɪˈkeɪʃ(ə)n/ *noun* the act of chewing food

mastitis /mæˈstaɪtɪs/ *noun* inflammation of the breast

masto- /mæstəʊ/ *prefix* referring to a breast

mastoid /ˈmæstɔɪd/ *adjective* shaped like a nipple ▪ *noun* same as **mastoid process**

mastoid air cell /ˌmæstɔɪd ˈeə ˌsel/, **mastoid cell** /ˈmæstɔɪd sel/ *noun* an air cell in the mastoid process

mastoid antrum /ˌmæstɔɪd ˈæntrəm/ *noun* a cavity linking the air cells of the mastoid process with the middle ear

mastoidectomy /ˌmæstɔɪˈdektəmi/ *noun* a surgical operation to remove part of the mastoid process, as a treatment for mastoiditis

mastoiditis /ˌmæstɔɪˈdaɪtɪs/ *noun* inflammation of the mastoid process and air cells. The symptoms are fever and pain in the ears.

mastoid process /ˌmæstɔɪd ˈprəʊses/ *noun* part of the temporal bone which protrudes at the side of the head behind the ear

masturbation /ˌmæstəˈbeɪʃ(ə)n/ *noun* stimulation of one's own genitals to produce an orgasm. Also called **onanism**

mater /ˈmeɪtə/ ♦ **dura mater**

materia medica /məˌtɪəriə ˈmedɪkə/ *noun* the study of drugs or dosages as used in treatment (NOTE: It comes from a Latin term meaning 'medical substance'.)

maternal /məˈtɜːn(ə)l/ *adjective* referring to a mother

maternal death /məˌtɜːn(ə)l ˈdeθ/ *noun* the death of a mother during pregnancy, childbirth or up to twelve months after childbirth

maternal deprivation /məˌtɜːn(ə)l ˌdeprɪˈveɪʃ(ə)n/ *noun* a psychological condition caused when a child does not have a proper relationship with a mother

maternal dystocia /məˌtɜːn(ə)l dɪsˈtəʊsiə/ *noun* difficult childbirth caused by a physical problem in the mother

maternal instincts /məˌtɜːn(ə)l ˈɪnstɪŋkts/ *plural noun* instinctive feelings in a woman to look after and protect her child

maternity /məˈtɜːnɪti/ *noun* childbirth, the fact of becoming a mother

maternity clinic /məˈtɜːnɪti ˌklɪnɪk/ *noun* same as **antenatal clinic**

maternity hospital /məˈtɜːnɪti ˌhɒspɪt(ə)l/, **maternity ward** /məˈtɜːnɪti wɔːd/, **maternity unit** /məˈtɜːnɪti ˌjuːnɪt/ *noun* a hospital, ward or unit which deals only with women giving birth

matrix /ˈmeɪtrɪks/ *noun* an amorphous mass of cells forming the basis of connective tissue. Also called **ground substance**

matron /ˈmeɪtrən/ *noun* a title formerly given to a woman in charge of the nurses in a hospital. ◊ **modern matron**

mattress suture /ˈmætrəs ˌsuːtʃə/ *noun* a suture made with a loop on each side of the incision

maturation /ˌmætʃʊˈreɪʃ(ə)n/ *noun* the process of becoming mature or fully developed

mature /məˈtʃʊə/ *adjective* fully developed

mature follicle /məˌtʃʊə ˈfɒlɪk(ə)l/ *noun* a Graafian follicle just before ovulation

maturing /məˈtʃʊərɪŋ/ *adjective* becoming mature

maxilla /mækˈsɪlə/, **maxilla bone** /mækˈsɪlə bəʊn/ *noun* the upper jaw bone (NOTE: The plural is **maxillae**. It is more correct to refer to the upper jaw as the **maxillae**, as it is in fact formed of two bones which are fused together.)

maxillary /mækˈsɪləri/ *adjective* referring to the maxilla

maxillary antrum /mækˌsɪləri ˈæntrəm/, **maxillary air sinus** /mækˌsɪləri ˈeə ˌsaɪnəs/ *noun* one of two sinuses behind the cheekbones in the upper jaw. Also called **antrum of Highmore**

maxillo-facial /mækˌsɪləʊˈfeɪʃ(ə)l/ *adjective* referring to the maxillary bone and the face ○ *maxillo-facial surgery*

MB *abbreviation* bachelor of medicine

McBurney's point /məkˌbɜːniz ˈpɔɪnt/ *noun* a point which indicates the usual position of the appendix on the right side of the abdomen, between the hip bone and the navel, which is extremely painful if pressed when the person has appendicitis [Described 1899. After Charles McBurney (1845–1913), US surgeon.]

McNaghten's Rules on Insanity at Law /məkˌnɔːtənz ˌruːlz ɒn ɪnˌsænɪti ət ˈlɔː/, **McNaghten's Rules** /məkˈnɔːtənz ˌruːlz/ *plural noun* a set of principles which explain how people can defend themselves in law by claiming that they committed a murder because they were mentally ill, and therefore not responsible for any of their actions. In 1957 it was adapted to include the idea of knowing that an action is wrong but being unable to stop yourself from committing it because of your mental condition.

MCP joint /ˌem siː ˈpiː ˌdʒɔɪnt/ *noun* same as **metacarpophalangeal joint**

MCU, MCUG *abbreviation* micturating cysto(-urethro)gram

MD *abbreviation* doctor of medicine

ME *abbreviation* myalgic encephalomyelitis

measles /ˈmiːz(ə)lz/ *noun* an infectious disease of children, where the body is covered with a red rash ○ *She's in bed with measles.* ○ *He's got measles.* ○ *They caught measles from their friend at school.* ○ *Have you had the measles?* Also called **morbilli, rubeola** (NOTE: Takes a singular or plural verb.)

meat- /miːt/ *prefix* relating to a meatus

meatus /miˈeɪtəs/ *noun* an opening leading to an internal passage in the body, e.g. the urethra or the nasal cavity (NOTE: The plural is **meatuses** or **meatus**.)

mechanism /ˈmekənɪz(ə)m/ *noun* **1.** a physical or chemical change by which a function is carried out **2.** a system in the body which carries out or controls a particular function ○ *The inner ear is the body's mechanism for the sense of balance.*

mechanism of labour /ˌmekənɪz(ə)m əv ˈleɪbə/ *noun* all the forces and processes which combine to push a foetus out of the uterus during its birth, together with the ones which oppose it

mechanotherapy /ˌmekənəʊˈθerəpi/ *noun* the treatment of injuries through mechanical means, such as massage and exercise machines

meconism /ˈmekəʊnɪz(ə)m/ *noun* poisoning by opium or morphine

meconium /mɪˈkəʊniəm/ *noun* the first dark green faeces produced by a newborn baby

media /ˈmiːdiə/ *noun* same as **tunica media**

medial /ˈmiːdiəl/ *adjective* nearer to the central midline of the body or to the centre of an organ. Compare **lateral**

medially /ˈmiːdiəli/ *adverb* towards or on the sagittal plane of the body. See illustration at **ANATOMICAL TERMS** in Supplement

medial malleolus /ˌmiːdiəl məˈliːələs/ *noun* a bone at the end of the tibia which protrudes at the inside of the ankle

median /ˈmiːdiən/ *adjective* towards the central midline of the body, or placed in the middle

median nerve /ˈmiːdiən nɜːv/ *noun* one of the main nerves of the forearm and hand

median plane /ˈmiːdiən pleɪn/ *noun* an imaginary flat surface on the midline and at right angles to the coronal plane, which divides the body into right and left halves. See illustration at **ANATOMICAL TERMS** in Supplement

mediastinal /miːdiəˈstaɪn(ə)l/ *adjective* referring to the mediastinum ○ *the mediastinal surface of pleura* or *of the lungs*

mediastinitis /ˌmiːdiəstɪˈnaɪtɪs/ *noun* inflammation of the mediastinum

mediastinoscopy /ˌmiːdiəstɪˈnɒskəpi/ *noun* an operation in which a tube is put into the mediastinum so that its organs can be examined

mediastinum /miːdiəˈstaɪnəm/ *noun* the section of the chest between the lungs, where the heart, oesophagus and phrenic and vagus nerves are situated

medic /ˈmedɪk/ *noun* a doctor or medical student (*informal*)

medical /ˈmedɪk(ə)l/ *adjective* referring to the study of diseases ○ *a medical student* ■ *noun* an official examination of a person by a doctor ○ *He wanted to join the army, but failed his medical.* ○ *You will have to have a medical if you take out an insurance policy.*

medical alert bracelet /ˌmedɪk(ə)l əˈlɜːt ˌbreɪslət/ *noun* a band or chain worn around the wrist giving information about the wearer's medical needs, allergies or condition

medical assistant /ˈmedɪk(ə)l əˌsɪst(ə)nt/ *noun* someone who performs routine administrative and clinical tasks to help in the offices and clinics of doctors and other medical practitioners

medical audit /ˌmedɪk(ə)l ˈɔːdɪt/ *noun* a systematic critical analysis of the quality of medical care provided to a person, which examines the procedures used for diagnosis and treatment, the use of resources and the resulting outcome and quality of life for the person

medical audit advisory group /ˌmedɪk(ə)l ˌɔːdɪt ədˈvaɪz(ə)ri ˌgruːp/ *noun* a body with the responsibility of advising on medical audit in primary care. Abbreviation **MAAG**

medical certificate /ˈmedɪk(ə)l səˌtɪfɪkət/ *noun* an official document signed by a doctor, giving someone permission to be away from work or not to do specific types of work

medical committee /ˈmedɪk(ə)l kəˌmɪti/ *noun* a committee of doctors in a hospital who advise the management on medical matters

medical doctor /ˈmedɪk(ə)l ˌdɒktə/ *noun* a doctor who practises medicine, but is not usually a surgeon

medical ethics /ˌmedɪk(ə)l ˈeθɪks/ *plural noun* the moral and professional principles which govern how doctors and nurses should work, and, in particular, what type of relationship they should have with their patients

medical examination /ˌmedɪk(ə)l ɪgˌzæmɪˈneɪʃ(ə)n/ *noun* an examination of a person by a doctor

medical history /ˌmedɪk(ə)l ˈhɪst(ə)ri/ *noun* the details of a person's medical condition and treatment over a period of time

medical intervention /ˌmedɪk(ə)l ˌɪntəˈvenʃən/ *noun* the treatment of illness by drugs

medicalisation /ˌmedɪkəlaɪˈzeɪʃ(ə)n/, **medicalization** *noun* the act of looking at something as a medical issue or problem

medical jurisprudence /ˌmedɪk(ə)l ˌdʒʊərɪsˈpruːd(ə)ns/ *noun* the use of the principles of law as they relate to the practice of medicine and the relationship of doctors with each other, their patients and society. ◊ **forensic medicine**

Medical Officer of Health /ˌmedɪk(ə)l ˌɒfɪsər əv ˈhelθ/ *noun* formerly, a local government official in charge of the health services in an area. Abbreviation **MOH**

medical practitioner /ˌmedɪk(ə)l prækˈtɪʃ(ə)nə/ *noun* a person qualified in medicine, i.e. a doctor or surgeon

medical profession /ˈmedɪk(ə)l prəˌfeʃ(ə)n/ *noun* all doctors

Medical Register /ˌmedɪk(ə)l ˈredʒɪstə/ *noun* a list of doctors approved by the General Medical Council ○ *The committee ordered his name to be struck off the Medical Register.*

Medical Research Council /ˌmedɪk(ə)l rɪˈsɜːtʃ ˌkaʊnsəl/ *noun* a government body which organises and pays for medical research. Abbreviation **MRC**

medical school /ˈmedɪk(ə)l skuːl/ *noun* a section of a university which teaches medicine ○ *He is at medical school.*

medical secretary /ˌmedɪk(ə)l ˈsekrɪt(ə)ri/ *noun* a qualified secretary who specialises in medical documentation, either in a hospital or in a doctor's surgery

medical social worker /ˌmedɪk(ə)l ˈsəʊʃ(ə)l ˌwɜːkə/ *noun* someone who helps people with family problems or problems related to their work which may have an effect on their response to treatment

medical ward /'medɪk(ə)l wɔːd/ *noun* a ward for people who do not have to undergo surgical operations

Medicare /'medɪkeə/ *noun* a system of public health insurance in the US

medicated /'medɪkeɪtɪd/ *adjective* containing a medicinal drug ○ *medicated cough sweet*

medicated shampoo /ˌmedɪkeɪtɪd ʃæm 'puː/ *noun* a shampoo containing a chemical which is supposed to prevent dandruff

medication /ˌmedɪ'keɪʃ(ə)n/ *noun* **1.** the treatment of illnesses by giving people drugs. ◊ **premedication 2.** a drug used to treat a particular illness ○ *What sort of medication has she been taking?* ○ *80% of elderly patients admitted to geriatric units are on medication.*

medicinal /mə'dɪs(ə)n(ə)l/ *adjective* which has healing properties or a beneficial effect on someone's health ○ *He has a drink of whisky before he goes to bed for medicinal purposes.*

medicinal leech /mə,dɪs(ə)n(ə)l 'liːtʃ/ *noun* a leech which is raised specially for use in medicine

medicine /'med(ə)s(ə)n/ *noun* **1.** a preparation taken to treat a disease or condition, especially one in liquid form ○ *Take some cough medicine if your cough is bad.* ○ *You should take the medicine three times a day.* **2.** the study of diseases and how to cure or prevent them ○ *She is studying medicine because she wants to be a doctor.*

medicine cabinet /'med(ə)s(ə)n ,kæbɪnət/, **medicine chest** /'med(ə)s(ə)n tʃest/ *noun* a cupboard where medicines, bandages, thermometers and other pieces of medical equipment can be left locked up, but ready for use in an emergency

medico /medɪkəʊ/ *noun* a doctor (*informal*) ○ *The medico said I was perfectly fit.*

medico- /medɪkəʊ/ *prefix* referring to medicine or to doctors

medicochirurgical /ˌmedɪkəʊkaɪ 'rɜːdʒɪk(ə)l/ *adjective* referring to both medicine and surgery

medicolegal /ˌmedɪkəʊ'liːg(ə)l/ *adjective* referring to both medicine and the law

medicosocial /ˌmedɪkəʊ'səʊʃ(ə)l/ *adjective* involving both medical and social factors

medium /'miːdiəm/ *adjective* average, in the middle or at the halfway point ■ *noun* a substance through which something acts

medroxyprogesterone /mə,drɒksɪprəʊ 'dʒestərəʊn/ *noun* a synthetic hormone used to treat menstrual disorders, in oestrogen replacement therapy and as a contraceptive

medulla /me'dʌlə/ *noun* the soft inner part of an organ, as opposed to the outer cortex. See illustration at **KIDNEY** in Supplement

medulla oblongata /me,dʌlə ,ɒblɒŋ'geɪtə/ *noun* a continuation of the spinal cord going through the foramen magnum into the brain

medullary /me'dʌləri/ *adjective* similar to marrow

medullary cavity /me,dʌləri 'kævɪti/ *noun* a hollow centre of a long bone, containing bone marrow. See illustration at **BONE STRUCTURE** in Supplement

medullated nerve /'medəleɪtɪd nɜːv/ *noun* a nerve surrounded by a myelin sheath

mefenamic acid /ˌmefənæmɪk 'æsɪd/ *noun* a drug which reduces inflammation and pain, used in the treatment of rheumatoid arthritis and menstrual problems

mefloquine /'mefləkwiːn/, **mefloquine hydrochloride** /ˌmefləkwiːn ,haɪdrəʊ 'klɔːraɪd/ *noun* a drug used in the prevention and treatment of malaria

mega- /megə/ *prefix* **1.** large. Opposite **micro- 2.** one million, or 10^6

megacolon /ˌmegə'kəʊlən/ *noun* a condition in which the lower colon is very much larger than normal, because part of the colon above is constricted, making bowel movements impossible

megajoule /'megədʒuːl/ *noun* a unit of measurement of energy equal to one million joules. Symbol **Mj**

megakaryocyte /ˌmegə'kæriəsaɪt/ *noun* a bone marrow cell which produces blood platelets

megalo- /megaləʊ/ *prefix* large

megaloblast /'megələʊblæst/ *noun* an unusually large blood cell found in the bone marrow of people who have some types of anaemia caused by Vitamin B_{12} deficiency

megaloblastic anaemia /ˌmegələʊ,blæstɪk ə'niːmiə/ *noun* anaemia caused by Vitamin B_{12} deficiency

megalocyte /'megələʊsaɪt/ *noun* an unusually large red blood cell, found in pernicious anaemia

megalomania /ˌmegələʊ'meɪniə/ *noun* a psychiatric disorder in which a person believes they are very powerful and important

megalomaniac /ˌmegələʊ'meɪniæk/ *noun* someone who has megalomania ■ *adjective* having megalomania

-megaly /megəli/ *suffix* enlargement

megaureter /ˌmegəjʊ'riːtə/ *noun* a condition in which a part of the ureter becomes very wide, above the site of a blockage

meibomian cyst /maɪ,bəʊmiən 'sɪst/ *noun* the swelling of a sebaceous gland in the eyelid. Also called **chalazion**

meibomian gland /maɪ'bəʊmiən ,glænd/ *noun* a sebaceous gland on the edge of the eyelid which secretes a liquid to lubricate the eyelid. Also called **tarsal gland**

meibomianitis /maɪˌbəʊmiəˈnaɪtɪs/ *noun* a condition in which the meibomian glands become swollen

Meigs' syndrome /ˈmeɡz ˌsɪndrəʊm/ *noun* a condition in which liquid collects in the chest and abdominal cavities. It is associated with pelvic tumours.

meiosis /maɪˈəʊsɪs/ *noun* the process of cell division which results in two pairs of haploid cells, i.e. cells with only one set of chromosomes. Compare **mitosis**

Meissner's corpuscle /ˌmaɪsnəz ˈkɔːpʌs(ə)l/ *noun* a receptor cell in the skin which is thought to be sensitive to touch

Meissner's plexus /ˌmaɪsnəz ˈpleksəs/ *noun* a network of nerve fibres in the wall of the alimentary canal [Described 1853. After Georg Meissner (1829–1905), German anatomist and physiologist.]

melaena /məˈliːnə/ *noun* black faeces where the colour is caused by bleeding in the intestine

melan- /melən/ *prefix* same as **melano-** (*used before vowels*)

melancholia /ˌmelənˈkəʊliə/ *noun* a severe depressive illness occurring usually between the ages of 45 and 65

melanin /ˈmelənɪn/ *noun* a dark pigment which gives colour to skin and hair, also found in the choroid of the eye and in some tumours

melano- /melənəʊ/ *prefix* black or dark

melanocyte /ˈmelənəʊsaɪt/ *noun* any cell which carries pigment

melanocyte-stimulating hormone /ˌmelənəʊsaɪt ˈstɪmjʊleɪtɪŋ ˌhɔːməʊm/ *noun* a hormone produced by the pituitary gland which causes darkening in the colour of the skin. Abbreviation **MSH**

melanoma /ˌmeləˈnəʊmə/ *noun* a tumour formed of dark pigmented cells

melatonin /ˌmeləˈtəʊnɪn/ *noun* a hormone produced by the pineal gland during the hours of darkness, which makes animals sleep during the winter months. It is thought to control the body's rhythms.

melena /məˈliːnə/ *noun* same as **melaena**

mellitus /ˈmelɪtəs/ ♦ **diabetes mellitus**

membrane /ˈmembreɪn/ *noun* a thin layer of tissue which lines or covers an organ

membranous /ˈmembrənəs/ *adjective* referring to membranes, or like a membrane

membranous labyrinth /ˌmembrənəs ˈlæbərɪnθ/ *noun* a series of ducts and canals formed of membrane inside the osseous labyrinth

menarche /məˈnɑːki/ *noun* the start of menstrual periods

Mendel's laws /ˈmendəlz lɔːz/ *plural noun* the laws of heredity, that are the basis of the science of genetics [Described 1865. After Gregor

Johann Mendel (1822–84), Austrian Augustinian monk and naturalist of Brno, whose work was rediscovered by de Vries in 1900.]

Ménière's disease /meniˈeəz dɪˌziːz/, **Ménière's syndrome** /ˈsɪndrəʊm/ *noun* a disease of the middle ear, in which someone becomes dizzy, hears ringing in the ears and may vomit, and becomes progressively deaf. The causes may include infections or allergies, which increase the fluid contents of the labyrinth in the middle ear. [Described 1861. After Prosper Ménière (1799–1862) and his son, Emile Antoine Ménière (1839–1905), French physicians.]

mening- /menɪndʒ/ *prefix* same as **meningo-** (*used before vowels*)

meningeal /meˈnɪndʒiəl/ *adjective* referring to the meninges

meninges /meˈnɪndʒiːz/ *plural noun* the membranes which surround the brain and spinal cord (NOTE: The singular is **meninx**.)

meningioma /ˌmenɪndʒiˈəʊmə/ *noun* a benign tumour in the meninges

meningism /meˈnɪndʒɪz(ə)m/ *noun* a condition in which there are signs of meningeal irritation suggesting meningitis, but where there is no pathological change in the cerebrospinal fluid

meningitis /ˌmenɪnˈdʒaɪtɪs/ *noun* inflammation of the meninges, causing someone to have violent headaches, fever, and stiff neck muscles, and sometimes to become delirious

meningo- /mənɪŋgəʊ/ *prefix* referring to the meninges

meningocele /məˈnɪŋgəʊsiːl/ *noun* a condition in which the meninges protrude through the vertebral column or skull

meningococcal /məˌnɪŋgəʊˈkɒk(ə)l/ *adjective* referring to meningococci

meningococcal meningitis /məˌnɪŋgəʊ ˌkɒk(ə)l ˌmenɪnˈdʒaɪtɪs/ *noun* the commonest epidemic form of meningitis, caused by a bacterium *Neisseria meningitidis*, where the meninges become inflamed causing headaches and fever

meningococcus /məˌnɪŋgəʊˈkɒkəs/ *noun* the bacterium *Neisseria meningitidis* which causes meningococcal meningitis (NOTE: The plural is **meningococci**.)

meningoencephalitis /məˌnɪŋgəʊen,kefə ˈlaɪtɪs/ *noun* inflammation of the meninges and the brain

meningoencephalocele /məˌnɪŋgəʊen ˈkefələʊsiːl/ *noun* a condition in which part of the meninges and the brain push through a gap in the skull

meningomyelocele /məˌnɪŋgəʊ ˈmaɪələʊsiːl/ *noun* the pushing forward of part of the meninges and spinal cord through a gap in the spine. Also called **myelomeningocele**, **myelocele**

meninx /ˈmenɪŋks/ *noun* ♦ **meninges**

meniscectomy /ˌmenɪˈsektəmi/ *noun* the surgical removal of a cartilage from the knee

meniscus /məˈnɪskəs/ *noun* one of two pads of cartilage, the lateral meniscus and medial meniscus, between the femur and tibia in a knee joint. Also called **semilunar cartilage** (NOTE: The plural is **menisci**.)

meno- /menəʊ/ *prefix* referring to menstruation

menopause /ˈmenəpɔːz/ *noun* a period, usually between 45 and 55 years of age, when a woman stops menstruating and can no longer bear children. Also called **climacteric**, **change of life**

menorrhagia /ˌmenəˈreɪdʒiə/ *noun* very heavy bleeding during menstruation. Also called **flooding**

menses /ˈmensiːz/ *plural noun* same as **menstruation**

menstrual /ˈmenstruəl/ *adjective* referring to menstruation

menstrual cramp /ˌmenstruəl ˈkræmp/ *noun* a cramp in the muscles round the uterus during menstruation

menstrual cycle /ˈmenstruəl ˌsaɪk(ə)l/ *noun* a period, usually of 28 days, during which a woman ovulates, the walls of the uterus swell and bleeding takes place if the ovum has not been fertilised

menstrual flow /ˈmenstruəl fləʊ/ *noun* the discharge of blood from the uterus during menstruation

menstruate /ˈmenstrueɪt/ *verb* to bleed from the uterus during menstruation

menstruation /ˌmenstruˈeɪʃ(ə)n/ *noun* bleeding from the uterus which occurs in a woman each month when the lining of the uterus is shed because no fertilised egg is present

mental /ˈment(ə)l/ *adjective* **1.** referring to the mind **2.** referring to the chin

mental aberration /ˌment(ə)l ˌæbəˈreɪʃ(ə)n/ *noun* slight forgetfulness or confusion (*often humorous*) ○ *I thought the meeting was at 11 – I must have had a mental aberration.*

mental age /ˌment(ə)l ˈeɪdʒ/ *noun* a measurement based on intelligence tests that shows a person's intellectual development, usually compared to standardised data for a chronological age □ **he's nine, but he has a mental age of five** although he is nine years old, his level of intellectual development is the same as that of an average child of five

mental block /ˌment(ə)l ˈblɒk/ *noun* a temporary inability to remember something, caused by the effect of nervous stress on the mental processes

Mental Capacity Act /ˌment(ə)l kəˈpæsɪti ˌækt/ *noun* a piece of UK legislation, introduced in 2007, that establishes five principles in relation to mental capacity and medical treatment, namely that patients should be assumed to be capable of making their own decisions, that they should be given support in decision-making, that it is patients' capacity to make decisions that should be judged, not the decisions themselves, that treatment must be in patients' best interests, and that treatment should restrict rights and freedoms as little as possible

mental deficiency /ˌment(ə)l dɪˈfɪʃ(ə)nsi/ *noun* a former term for learning disability (NOTE: This term is regarded as offensive.)

mental development /ˌment(ə)l dɪˈveləpmənt/ *noun* the development of the mind ○ *Her mental development is higher than usual for her age.*

mental disorder /ˌment(ə)l dɪsˈɔːdə/ *noun* a temporary or permanent change in a person's mental state which makes them function less effectively than they would usually, or than the average person would be expected to function

mental faculties /ˌment(ə)l ˈfækəltiːz/ *plural noun* abilities such as thinking and decision-making ○ *There has been no impairment of the mental faculties.*

mental handicap /ˌment(ə)l ˈhændikæp/ *noun* a former term for learning disability (NOTE: This term is regarded as offensive.)

mental health /ˈment(ə)l helθ/ *noun* the condition of someone's mind

Mental Health Acts /ˌment(ə)l ˈhelθ ækts/ *plural noun* laws made by a parliament which lay down rules for the care of people with mental illness

Mental Health Review Tribunal /ˌment(ə)l helθ rɪˈvjuː traɪˌbjuːn(ə)l/ *noun* a committee which makes decisions about whether people who have been detained under the Mental Health Acts should be released. It consists of medical members, legal experts and lay members, who include people with experience in social services. Abbreviation **MHRT**

mental hospital /ˈment(ə)l ˌhɒspɪt(ə)l/ *noun* a psychiatric hospital (NOTE: This term is regarded as offensive.)

mental illness /ˌment(ə)l ˈɪlnəs/ *noun* any disorder which affects the mind

mental impairment /ˌment(ə)l ɪmˈpeəmənt/ *noun* a temporary or permanent condition which affects a person's mental state, making them function less effectively than they would usually, or than the average person would be expected to function

mentally /ˈment(ə)li/ *adverb* in the mind ○ *Mentally, she is very advanced for her age.*

mentally handicapped /ˌment(ə)li ˈhændikæpt/ *adjective* a former term for someone with learning disability (NOTE: This term is usually regarded as offensive.)

mentally ill /ˌment(ə)li ˈɪl/ *adjective* experiencing mental illness

mental nerve /'ment(ə)l nɜːv/ *noun* a nerve which supplies the chin

mental patient /'ment(ə)l ˌpeɪʃ(ə)nt/ *noun* a former term of a patient who has mental illness (NOTE: This term is regarded as offensive.)

mental retardation /ˌment(ə)l ˌriːtɑː'deɪʃ(ə)n/ *noun* a former term for learning disability, a condition that results in someone finding it difficult to learn skills or information at the same rate as others of a similar age (NOTE: This term is regarded as offensive.)

mental subnormality /ˌment(ə)l ˌsʌbnɔː'mælɪti/ *noun* a former term for mental impairment (NOTE: This term is usually regarded as offensive.)

menthol /'menθɒl/ *noun* a strongly scented compound, produced from peppermint oil, used in cough medicines and in the treatment of neuralgia

mentholated /'menθəleɪtɪd/ *adjective* impregnated with menthol

mento- /mentəʊ/ *prefix* relating to the chin

mentor /'mentɔː/ *noun* somebody who advises and guides a younger, less experienced person ■ *verb* to act as a mentor to somebody

mentum /'mentəm/ *noun* the chin

mercury /'mɜːkjʊri/ *noun* a poisonous liquid metal, used in thermometers (NOTE: The chemical symbol is **Hg**.)

mercury poisoning /'mɜːkjʊri ˌpɔɪz(ə)nɪŋ/ *noun* poisoning by drinking mercury or mercury compounds or by inhaling mercury vapour

mercy killing /'mɜːsi ˌkɪlɪŋ/ *noun* same as **euthanasia**

meridian /mə'rɪdiən/ *noun* in acupuncture and Chinese medicine, one of the pathways in the body along which its energy is believed to flow

mes- /mes/ *prefix* same as **meso-** (*used before vowels*)

mesencephalon /mesen'kefəlɒn/ *noun* same as **midbrain**

mesenteric /ˌmesen'terɪk/ *adjective* referring to the mesentery

mesentery /'mesent(ə)ri/ *noun* a double-layer peritoneum which attaches the small intestine and other abdominal organs to the abdominal wall

mesial /'miːsiəl/ *adjective* **1.** in dentistry, relating to the middle of the front of the jaw, or occurring in a place near this **2.** relating to or located in the middle part of something

meso- /mesəʊ/ *prefix* middle

mesometrium /ˌmesəʊ'miːtriəm/ *noun* a muscle layer of the uterus

mesothelioma /ˌmesəʊtiːli'əʊmə/ *noun* a tumour of the serous membrane, which can be benign or malignant

mesothelium /ˌmesəʊ'θiːliəm/ *noun* a layer of cells lining a serous membrane. Compare **epithelium, endothelium**

messenger RNA /ˌmes(ə)ndʒə ˌɑːr en 'eɪ/ *noun* a type of ribonucleic acid which transmits the genetic code from the DNA to the ribosomes which form the proteins coded on the DNA. Abbreviation **mRNA**

mestranol /'miːstrənɒl/ *noun* a synthetically produced oestrogen used in birth control pills

meta- /metə/ *prefix* referring to change

metabolic /ˌmetə'bɒlɪk/ *adjective* referring to metabolism

metabolic acidosis /ˌmetəbɒlɪk ˌæsɪ'dəʊsɪs/ *noun* acidosis caused by a malfunction of the body's metabolism

metabolic alkalosis /ˌmetəbɒlɪk ælkə'ləʊsɪs/ *noun* alkalosis caused by a malfunction of the body's metabolism

metabolise /mə'tæbəlaɪz/, **metabolize** *verb* to change the nature of something by metabolism ○ *The liver metabolises proteins and carbohydrates.*

metabolism /mə'tæbəlɪz(ə)m/ *noun* the chemical processes which are continually taking place in the human body and which are essential to life, especially the processes that convert food into energy

metabolite /mə'tæbəlaɪt/ *noun* a substance produced by metabolism, or a substance taken into the body in food and then metabolised

metacarpal bone /ˌmetə'kɑːp(ə)l bəʊn/, **metacarpal** /ˌmetə'kɑːp(ə)l/ *noun* one of the five bones in the metacarpus

metacarpophalangeal /ˌmetəˌkɑːpəʊfə'lændʒiəl/ *adjective* relating to the part of the hand between the wrist and the fingers

metacarpophalangeal joint /ˌmetəˌkɑːpəʊfə'lændʒiəl ˌdʒɔɪnt/ *noun* a joint between a metacarpal bone and a finger. Also called **MCP joint, MP joint**

metacarpus /ˌmetə'kɑːpəs/ *noun* the five bones in the hand between the fingers and the wrist. See illustration at **HAND** in Supplement

metaphase /'metəfeɪz/ *noun* one of the stages in mitosis or meiosis

metaphysis /me'tæfəsɪs/ *noun* the end of the central section of a long bone, where the bone grows and where it joins the epiphysis

metaplasia /ˌmetə'pleɪziə/ *noun* a change of one tissue to another

metastasis /me'tæstəsɪs/ *noun* the spreading of a malignant disease from one part of the body to another through the bloodstream or the lymph system. Also called **secondary growth** (NOTE: The plural is **metastases**.)

metastasise /me'tæstəsaɪz/, **metastasize** *verb* to spread by metastasis

metastatic /ˌmetəˈstætɪk/ *adjective* relating to, or produced by, metastasis ○ *Metastatic growths developed in the liver.*

metatarsal /ˌmetəˈtɑːs(ə)l/ *noun* one of the five bones in the metatarsus ■ *adjective* relating to the metatarsus

metatarsal arch /ˌmetəˈtɑːs(ə)l ɑːtʃ/ *noun* an arched part of the sole of the foot, running across the sole of the foot from side to side. Also called **transverse arch**

metatarsalgia /ˌmetətɑːˈsældʒə/ *noun* pain in the heads of the metatarsal bones

metatarsophalangeal joint /metəˌtɑːsəʊfəˈlændʒɪəl ˌdʒɔɪnt/ *noun* a joint between a metatarsal bone and a toe

metatarsus /ˌmetəˈtɑːsəs/ *noun* the five long bones in the foot between the toes and the tarsus. See illustration at **FOOT** in Supplement (NOTE: The plural is **metatarsi**.)

meteorism /ˈmiːtiərɪz(ə)m/ *noun* same as **tympanites**

meter /ˈmiːtə/ *noun* US same as **metre**

-meter /miːtə, mɪtə/ *suffix* measuring instrument

metformin /metˈfɔːmɪn/ *noun* a drug which reduces the level of the blood sugar levels, used to treat non-insulin dependent diabetes which does not respond to dietary measures

methadone /ˈmeθədəʊn/ *noun* a synthetically produced narcotic drug, used to reduce pain and as a substitute for heroin in the treatment of addiction

methaemoglobin /metˌhiːməʊˈgləʊbɪn/ *noun* a dark brown substance formed from haemoglobin which develops during illness, following treatment with some drugs. Methaemoglobin cannot transport oxygen round the body, and so causes cyanosis.

methaemoglobinaemia /metˌhiːməʊˌgləʊbɪˈniːmiə/ *noun* the presence of methaemoglobin in the blood

methane /ˈmiːθeɪn, ˈmeθeɪn/ *noun* a colourless flammable gas with no smell

methanol /ˈmeθənɒl/ *noun* a colourless poisonous liquid, used as a solvent and a fuel. It changes easily into a gas. Also called **methyl alcohol**

methicillin /ˌmeθɪˈsɪlɪn/ *noun* a synthetically produced antibiotic, used in the treatment of infections which are resistant to penicillin

methicillin-resistant Staphylococcus aureus /meθɪˌsɪlɪn rɪˌzɪstənt stæfɪləˌkɒkəs ˈɔːriəs/ *noun* a bacterium resistant to almost all antibiotics and which can cause life-threatening infection in people recovering from surgery. Abbreviation **MRSA**

methionine /meˈθaɪəniːn/ *noun* an essential amino acid

methotrexate /ˌmeθəˈtrekseɪt/ *noun* a drug which helps to prevent cells reproducing, used in the treatment of cancer

methyl alcohol /ˌmiːθaɪl ˈælkəhɒl/ *noun* same as **methanol**

methylated spirits /ˌmeθəleɪtɪd ˈspɪrɪts/ *plural noun* almost pure alcohol, with wood alcohol and colouring added

methylphenidate /ˌmiːθaɪlˈfenɪdeɪt/ *noun* a drug which stimulates the central nervous system, used in the treatment of narcolepsy and attention deficit disorder

methylprednisolone /ˌmiːθaɪlpred ˈnɪsələʊn/ *noun* a corticosteroid drug which reduces inflammation, used in the treatment of arthritis, allergies and asthma

metoclopramide /ˌmetəʊˈkləʊprəmaɪd/ *noun* a drug used to treat nausea, vomiting and indigestion

metoprolol /mɪˈtɒprəlɒl/ *noun* a drug which controls the activity of the heart, used to treat angina and high blood pressure

metr- /metr/ *prefix* same as **metro-** (*used before vowels*)

metra /ˈmetrə/ *noun* the uterus

metralgia /meˈtrældʒə/ *noun* pain in the uterus

metre /ˈmiːtə/ *noun* an SI unit of length ○ *The room is four metres by three.* Symbol **m**

metritis /meˈtraɪtɪs/ *noun* same as **myometritis**

metro- /metrəʊ/ *prefix* referring to the uterus

metrocolpocele /ˌmetrəˈkɒlpəʊsiːl/ *noun* a condition in which the uterus protrudes into the vagina

metronidazole /ˌmetrəˈnɪdəzəʊl/ *noun* a yellow antibiotic compound, used especially in the treatment of vaginal infections

metroptosis /ˌmetrəˈtəʊsɪs/ *noun* a condition in which the uterus has moved downwards out of its usual position. Also called **prolapse of the uterus**

metrorrhagia /ˌmiːtrəʊˈreɪdʒɪə/ *noun* unusual bleeding from the vagina between the menstrual periods

-metry /mətri/ *suffix* relating to the process of measuring, or to instruments which are used for measuring

mg *abbreviation* milligram

MI *abbreviation* **1.** mitral incompetence **2.** myocardial infarction

Michel's clips /miˌʃelz ˈklɪps/ *plural noun* metal clips used to suture a wound [After Gaston Michel (1874–1937), Professor of Clinical Surgery at Nancy, France.]

miconazole /maɪˈkɒnəzəʊl/ *noun* a drug used to treat fungal infections of the skin and nails

micro- /maɪkrəʊ/ *prefix* **1.** very small. Opposite **macro-**, **mega-**, **megalo- 2.** one millionth (10^{-6})

microangiopathy /ˌmaɪkrəʊˌændʒiˈɒpəθi/ *noun* any disease of the capillaries

microbe /ˈmaɪkrəʊb/ *noun* a microorganism which may cause disease and which can only be seen with a microscope, e.g. a bacterium

microbiologist /ˌmaɪkrəʊbaɪˈɒlədʒɪst/ *noun* a scientist who specialises in the study of microorganisms

microbiology /ˌmaɪkrəʊbaɪˈɒlədʒi/ *noun* the scientific study of microorganisms

microcephalic /ˌmaɪkrəʊkeˈfælɪk/ *adjective* having microcephaly

microcephaly /ˌmaɪkrəʊˈkefəli/ *noun* a condition in which a person has an unusually small head, sometimes caused by the mother having had a rubella infection during pregnancy

microcyte /ˈmaɪkrəʊsaɪt/ *noun* an unusually small red blood cell

microcythaemia /maɪkrəʊsaɪˈθiːmiə/ *noun* same as **microcytosis**

microcytic /ˌmaɪkrəˈsɪtɪk/ *adjective* referring to microcytes

microcytosis /ˌmaɪkrəʊsaɪˈtəʊsɪs/ *noun* the presence of excess microcytes in the blood

microdactylia /ˌmaɪkrəʊdækˈtɪliə/, **microdactyly** /ˌmaɪkrəʊˈdæktɪli/ *noun* a condition in which a person has unusually small or short fingers or toes

microdiscectomy /ˌmaɪkrəʊdɪskˈektəmi/ *noun* a surgical operation to remove all or part of a disc in the spine which is pressing on a nerve

microglossia /ˌmaɪkrəʊˈɡlɒsiə/ *noun* a condition in which a person has an unusually small tongue

micrognathia /ˌmaɪkrəʊˈneɪθiə/ *noun* a condition in which one jaw is unusually smaller than the other

microgram /ˈmaɪkrəgræm/ *noun* a unit of measurement of weight equal to one millionth of a gram

micromastia /ˌmaɪkrəʊˈmæstiə/ *noun* a condition in which a person has unusually small breasts

micromelia /ˌmaɪkrəʊˈmiːliə/ *noun* a condition in which a person has unusually small arms or legs

micromole /ˈmaɪkrəʊˌməʊl/ *noun* a unit of measurement of the amount of substance equal to one millionth of a mole. Symbol **μ**

micronutrient /ˈmaɪkrəʊˌnjuːtriənt/ *noun* a substance which an organism needs for normal growth and development, but only in very small quantities, e.g. a vitamin or mineral. Compare **macronutrient**

microorganism /ˌmaɪkrəʊˈɔːɡənɪz(ə)m/ *noun* an organism which can only be seen under a microscope and which may cause disease.

Viruses, bacteria and protozoa are microorganisms.

microphthalmia /ˌmaɪkrɒfˈθælmiə/ *noun* a condition in which the eyes are unusually small

microscope /ˈmaɪkrəskəʊp/ *noun* a scientific instrument with lenses, which makes very small objects appear larger ○ *The tissue was examined under the microscope.* ○ *Under the microscope it was possible to see the cancer cells.*

microscopic /ˌmaɪkrəˈskɒpɪk/ *adjective* so small that it can only be seen through a microscope

microscopy /maɪˈkrɒskəpi/ *noun* the science of the use of microscopes

Microsporum /ˈmaɪkrəʊspɔːrəm/ *noun* a type of fungus which causes ringworm of the hair, skin and sometimes nails

microsurgery /ˈmaɪkrəʊˌsɜːdʒəri/ *noun* surgery using tiny instruments and a microscope. Microsurgery is used in operations on eyes and ears, and also to connect severed nerves and blood vessels.

microvillus /ˌmaɪkrəʊˈvɪləs/ *noun* a very small process found on the surface of many cells, especially the epithelial cells in the intestine (NOTE: The plural is **microvilli**.)

microwave therapy /ˈmaɪkrəʊweɪv ˌθerəpi/ *noun* treatment using high-frequency radiation

micturate /ˈmɪktjʊreɪt/ *verb* same as **urinate**

micturating cystogram /ˌmɪktjʊreɪtɪŋ ˈsɪstəʊɡræm/, **micturating cysto-urethrogram** /ˌmɪktjʊreɪtɪŋ ˌsɪstəʊ jʊˈriːθrəɡræm/ *noun* an X-ray of the bladder and urethra taken while the bladder is being filled and then emptied. Abbreviation **MCU**, **MCUG**

micturition /ˌmɪktjʊˈrɪʃ(ə)n/ *noun* same as **urination**

mid- /mɪd/ *prefix* middle

midazolam /mɪˈdæzəlæm/ *noun* a drug used to produce sleepiness and to reduce anxiety before surgery or other procedures

midbrain /ˈmɪdbreɪn/ *noun* the small middle section of the brain stem above the pons and between the cerebrum and the hindbrain. Also called **mesencephalon**

midcarpal /mɪdˈkɑːp(ə)l/ *adjective* between the two rows of carpal bones

middle colic /ˌmɪd(ə)l ˈkɒlɪk/ *noun* an artery which leads from the superior mesenteric artery

middle ear /ˌmɪd(ə)l ˈɪə/ *noun* a section of the ear between the eardrum and the inner ear

middle ear infection /ˌmɪd(ə)l ˈɪər ɪn ˌfekʃən/ *noun* same as **otitis media**

midgut /ˈmɪdɡʌt/ *noun* the middle part of the gut in an embryo, which develops into the small intestine

mid-life crisis /ˌmɪd laɪf ˈkraɪsɪs/ *noun* a period in early middle age when some people experience feelings of anxiety, insecurity and self-doubt

midline /'mɪdlaɪn/ *noun* an imaginary line drawn down the middle of the body from the head through the navel to the point between the feet

midstream specimen /'mɪdstriːm ˌspesɪmɪn/, **midstream specimen of urine** /ˌmɪdstriːm ˌspesɪmɪn əv 'jʊərɪn/ *noun* a sample of urine collected in a sterile bottle in the middle of a flow of urine, because the first part of the flow may be contaminated with bacteria from the skin. Abbreviation **MSU**

midtarsal /mɪd'tɑːs(ə)l/ *adjective* between the tarsal bones

midwife /'mɪdwaɪf/ *noun* a professional person who helps a woman give birth to a child, often at home

midwifery /mɪd'wɪfəri/ *noun* the profession of a midwife

midwifery course /mɪd'wɪfəri kɔːs/ *noun* a training course to teach nurses the techniques of being a midwife

Midwives Rules /'mɪdwaɪvz ruːlz/ *plural noun* laws relating to midwifery

migraine /'miːɡreɪn, 'maɪɡreɪn/ *noun* a sharp severe recurrent headache, often associated with vomiting and visual disturbances ○ *He had an attack of migraine and could not come to work.* ○ *Her migraine attacks seem to be worse in the summer.*

miliaria /ˌmɪli'eəriə/ *noun* itchy red spots which develop on the chest, under the armpits and between the thighs in hot countries, caused by blocked sweat glands. Also called **prickly heat, heat rash**

miliary /'mɪliəri/ *adjective* small in size, like a seed

miliary tuberculosis /ˌmɪliəri tjuːˌbɜːkjʊ 'ləʊsɪs/ *noun* a form of tuberculosis which occurs as little nodes in many parts of the body, including the meninges of the brain and spinal cord

milk /mɪlk/ *noun* **1.** a white liquid produced by female mammals to feed their young. Cow's milk and other dairy products are important parts of most diets, especially children's. ○ *The patient can only drink warm milk.* (NOTE: No plural: *some milk, a bottle of milk* or *a glass of milk.*) **2.** the breast milk produced by a woman ○ *The milk will start to flow a few days after childbirth.* (NOTE: For other terms referring to milk, see words beginning with **galact-, galacto-, lact-, lacto-**.)

milk dentition /'mɪlk denˌtɪʃ(ə)n/ *noun* same as **deciduous dentition**

milk leg /'mɪlk leg/ *noun* acute oedema of the leg, a condition which affects women after childbirth, where a leg becomes pale and inflamed as a result of lymphatic obstruction. Also called **white leg, phlegmasia alba dolens**

milk rash /'mɪlk ræʃ/ *noun* a temporary blotchiness of the skin seen in young babies

milk sugar /ˌmɪlk 'ʃʊɡə/ *noun* same as **lactose**

milk tooth /'mɪlk tuːθ/ *noun* same as **primary tooth**

Miller-Abbott tube /ˌmɪlər 'æbət ˌtjuːb/ *noun* a tube with a balloon at the end, used to clear the small intestine. The balloon is inflated after the tip of the tube reaches an obstruction.

milli- /mɪlɪ/ *prefix* one thousandth (10^{-3}). Symbol **m**

milligram /'mɪlɪɡræm/ *noun* a unit of measurement of weight equal to one thousandth of a gram. Symbol **mg**

millilitre /'mɪliliːtə/ *noun* a unit of measurement of liquid equal to one thousandth of a litre. Abbreviation **ml**

millimetre /'mɪlimiːtə/ *noun* a unit of measurement of length equal to one thousandth of a metre. Abbreviation **mm**

millimole /'mɪliməʊl/ *noun* a unit of measurement of the amount of a substance equal to one thousandth of a mole. Abbreviation **mmol**

millisievert /'mɪlisiːvət/ *noun* a unit of measurement of radiation

Milwaukee brace /mɪlˌwɔːki 'breɪs/ *noun* a support for people with unusually curved spines, consisting of a leather or metal pelvic girdle with two bars at the back and one at the front, which connect into a neck ring

mind /maɪnd/ *noun* the part of the brain which controls memory, consciousness or reasoning

minimally invasive surgery /ˌmɪnɪm(ə)l ɪn ˌveɪsɪv 'sɜːdʒəri/ *noun* surgery which involves the least possible disturbance to the body. It often uses lasers and other high-tech devices.

mini mental state examination /ˌmɪni 'ment(ə)l ˌsteɪt ɪɡzæmɪˌneɪʃ(ə)n/ *noun* a test performed mainly by psychiatrists to determine someone's mental ability, used in the diagnosis of dementia

minimum lethal dose /ˌmɪnɪməm ˌliːθ(ə)l 'dəʊs/ *noun* the smallest amount of a substance required to kill someone or something. Abbreviation **MLD**

ministroke /'mɪnistrəʊk/ *noun* same as **transient ischaemic attack**

minitracheostomy /ˌmɪnitreɪki'ɒstəmi/ *noun* a temporary tracheostomy

minor injuries unit /ˌmaɪnər 'ɪndʒəriz ˌjuːnɪt/ *noun* a hospital department which treats most accidents and emergencies. Abbreviation **MIU**

mio- /maɪəʊ/ *prefix* less

miosis /maɪ'əʊsɪs/ *noun* **1.** the contraction of the pupil of the eye, as in bright light **2.** *US* same as **meiosis**

miotic /maɪˈɒtɪk/ *noun* a drug which makes the pupil of the eye become smaller ∎ *adjective* causing the pupil of the eye to become smaller

mis- /mɪs/ *prefix* wrong

miscarriage /ˈmɪskærɪdʒ/ *noun* a situation in which an unborn baby leaves the uterus before the end of the pregnancy, especially during the first seven months of pregnancy ○ *She had two miscarriages before having her first child.* Also called **spontaneous abortion**

mismatch /ˈmɪsmætʃ/ *verb* to match tissues wrongly

missed case /ˌmɪst ˈkeɪs/ *noun* someone with an infection or disease which is not identified by a doctor

mist. /mɪst/, **mistura** /mɪsˈtjʊərə/ ♦ re. mist.

Misuse of Drugs Act 1971 /mɪsˌjuːs əv ˈdrʌɡz ˌækt/ *noun* a law relating to all aspects of the supply and possession of dangerous drugs such as morphine, anabolic steroids, LSD and cannabis. In 2002 many new benzodiazepines were added.

mite /maɪt/ *noun* a very small parasite, which causes dermatitis

mitochondrial /ˌmaɪtəˈkɒndriəl/ *adjective* referring to mitochondria

mitochondrion /ˌmaɪtəˈkɒndriən/ *noun* a tiny rod-shaped part of a cell's cytoplasm responsible for cell respiration (NOTE: The plural is **mitochondria**.)

mitomycin C /ˌmaɪtəʊmaɪsɪn ˈsiː/ *noun* an antibiotic which helps to prevent cancer cells from growing, used especially in the chemotherapy treatment of bladder and rectal cancers

mitosis /maɪˈtəʊsɪs/ *noun* the process of cell division, where the mother cell divides into two identical daughter cells. Compare **meiosis**

mitral /ˈmaɪtrəl/ *adjective* referring to the mitral valve

mitral incompetence /ˌmaɪtrəl ɪnˈkɒmpɪt(ə)ns/ *noun* abbreviation **MI**. Now called **mitral regurgitation**

mitral regurgitation /ˌmaɪtrəl rɪˌɡɜːdʒɪˈteɪʃ(ə)n/ *noun* a situation in which the mitral valve does not close completely so that blood goes back into the atrium

mitral stenosis /ˌmaɪtrəl steˈnəʊsɪs/ *noun* a condition in which the opening in the mitral valve becomes smaller because the cusps have fused (NOTE: This condition is almost always the result of rheumatic endocarditis.)

mitral valve /ˈmaɪtrəl vælv/ *noun* a valve in the heart which allows blood to flow from the left atrium to the left ventricle but not in the opposite direction. Also called **bicuspid valve**

mitral valvotomy /ˌmaɪtrəl vælˈvɒtəmi/ *noun* a surgical operation to separate the cusps of the mitral valve in mitral stenosis

mittelschmerz /ˈmɪt(ə)lˌʃmeəts/ *noun* a pain felt by women in the lower abdomen at ovulation

MIU *abbreviation* minor injuries unit

ml *abbreviation* millilitre

MLD *abbreviation* minimum lethal dose

MLSO *abbreviation* medical laboratory scientific officer

mm *abbreviation* millimetre

mmol *abbreviation* millimole

MMR /ˌem em ˈɑː/, **MMR vaccine** /ˌem em ˈɑː ˌvæksiːn/ *noun* a single vaccine given to small children to protect them against measles, mumps and rubella

MND *abbreviation* motor neurone disease

MO *abbreviation* medical officer

mobilisation /ˌməʊbɪlaɪˈzeɪʃ(ə)n/, **mobilization** *noun* the act of making something mobile

modality /məʊˈdælɪti/ *noun* a method used in the treatment of a disorder, e.g. surgery or chemotherapy

modernisation agenda /ˌmɒdənaɪˈzeɪʃ(ə)n əˌdʒendə/ *noun* same as **Agenda for Change**

modern matron /ˌmɒd(ə)n ˈmeɪtrən/ *noun* a nursing post which supports the ward sister in ensuring that basic care of patients, including cleanliness of the ward and infection control, is carried out to a high standard

MODS *abbreviation* multiple organ dysfunction syndrome

MOF *abbreviation* 1. male or female 2. multi-organ failure

Mogadon /ˈmɒɡədɒn/ a trade name for nitrazepam

MOH *abbreviation* Medical Officer of Health

mol *symbol* mole 2

molar /ˈməʊlə/ *adjective* 1. referring to the large back teeth 2. referring to the mole, the SI unit of amount of a substance ∎ *noun* one of the large back teeth, used for grinding food. In milk teeth there are eight molars and in permanent teeth there are twelve. See illustration at TEETH in Supplement

molarity /məʊˈlærɪti/ *noun* the strength of a solution shown as the number of moles of a substance per litre of solution

mole /məʊl/ *noun* 1. a dark raised spot on the skin ○ *She has a large mole on her chin.* ◊ **melanoma** 2. an SI unit of measurement of the amount of a substance. Symbol **mol**

molecular /məˈlekjʊlə/ *adjective* referring to a molecule

molecular biology /məˌlekjʊlə baɪˈɒlədʒi/ *noun* the study of the molecules of living matter

molecular weight /məˌlekjʊlə ˈweɪt/ *noun* the weight of one molecule of a substance

molecule /ˈmɒlɪkjuːl/ *noun* the smallest independent mass of a substance

molluscum contagiosum /məˌlʌskəm kənˌteɪdʒiˈəʊsəm/ *noun* a contagious viral skin infection which gives a small soft sore

molluscum fibrosum /məˌlʌskəm ˌfaɪˈbrəʊsəm/ *noun* same as **neurofibromatosis**

monaural /mɒnˈɔːrəl/ *adjective* referring to the use of one ear only

mongolism /ˈmɒŋɡəlɪz(ə)m/ *noun* a former name for Down's syndrome (NOTE: This term is regarded as offensive.)

monitor /ˈmɒnɪtə/ *noun* a screen on a computer ■ *verb* **1.** to check something **2.** to examine how someone is progressing

monitoring /ˈmɒnɪt(ə)rɪŋ/ *noun* the regular examination and recording of a person's temperature, weight, blood pressure and other essential indicators

mono- /mɒnəʊ/ *prefix* single or one

monoamine oxidase /ˌmɒnəʊˌæmiːn ˈɒksɪdeɪz/ *noun* an enzyme which breaks down the catecholamines to their inactive forms. Abbreviation **MAO**

monoamine oxidase inhibitor /ˌmɒnəʊ ˌæmiːn ˌɒksɪdeɪz ɪnˈhɪbɪtə/ *noun* a drug which inhibits monoamine oxidase and is used to treat depression, e.g. phenelzine. Its use is limited, because of the potential for drug and dietary interactions and the necessity for slow withdrawal. It can also cause high blood pressure. Abbreviation **MAOI**. Also called **MAO inhibitor**

monoblast /ˈmɒnəʊblæst/ *noun* a cell which produces a monocyte

monochromatism /ˌmɒnəʊˈkrəʊmætɪʒ(ə)m/ *noun* colour blindness in which all colours appear to be black, grey or white. Compare **dichromatism**, **trichromatism**

monoclonal /ˌmɒnəʊˈkləʊn(ə)l/ *adjective* referring to cells or products of cells which are formed or derived from a single clone

monoclonal antibody /ˌmɒnəʊkləʊn(ə)l ˈæntɪbɒdi/ *noun* an antibody which can be easily made in the laboratory by a single clone of cells. It may be useful in the treatment of cancer.

monocular /mɒˈnɒkjʊlə/ *adjective* referring to one eye. Compare **binocular**

monocular vision /məˌnɒkjʊlə ˈvɪʒ(ə)n/ *noun* the ability to see with one eye only, so that the sense of distance is impaired

monocyte /ˈmɒnəʊsaɪt/ *noun* a white blood cell with a nucleus shaped like a kidney, which destroys bacterial cells

monocytosis /ˌmɒnəʊsaɪˈtəʊsɪs/ *noun* a condition in which there is an unusually high number of monocytes in the blood. Symptoms include sore throat, swelling of the lymph nodes and fever. It is probably caused by the Epstein–Barr virus. Also called **glandular fever**

mononucleosis /ˌmɒnəʊˌnjuːkliˈəʊsɪs/ *noun* same as **monocytosis**

monoplegia /ˌmɒnəʊˈpliːdʒə/ *noun* the paralysis of one part of the body only, i.e. one muscle or one limb

monosaccharide /ˌmɒnəʊˈsækraɪd/ *noun* a simple sugar which cannot be broken down any further, such as glucose or fructose

monosodium glutamate /ˌmɒnəʊsəʊdiəm ˈɡluːtəmeɪt/ *noun* a sodium salt of glutamic acid, often used to make food taste better. ◊ **Chinese restaurant syndrome**

monosomy /ˈmɒnəʊsəʊmi/ *noun* a condition in which a person has a chromosome missing from one or more pairs

monoxide /məˈnɒksaɪd/ ◆ **carbon**

monozygotic twins /ˌmɒnəʊzaɪˌɡɒtɪk ˈtwɪnz/ *plural noun* same as **identical twins**

mons /mɒnz/ *noun* a fleshy body part which sticks out, especially the one formed by the pad of flesh where the pubic bones join (NOTE: The plural is **montes**.)

mons pubis /ˌmɒnz ˈpjuːbɪs/ *noun* a cushion of fat covering the pubis

mons veneris /ˌmɒnz ˈvenərɪs/ *noun* same as **mons pubis**

Montgomery's glands /məntˈɡʌməriz ɡlændz/ *plural noun* sebaceous glands around the nipple which become more marked in pregnancy [After William Fetherstone Montgomery (1797–1859), Dublin gynaecologist.]

mood /muːd/ *noun* a person's mental state at a particular time ○ *a mood of excitement* □ **in a bad mood** feeling angry or irritable □ **in a good mood** feeling happy

moon face /ˈmuːn feɪs/ *noun* a condition in which someone has a round red face, occurring in Cushing's syndrome and when there are too many steroid hormones in the body

Mooren's ulcer /ˈmɔːrənz ˌʌlsə/ *noun* a persistent ulcer of the cornea, found in elderly people [After Albert Mooren (1828–99), ophthalmologist in Düsseldorf, Germany.]

morbid /ˈmɔːbɪd/ *adjective* showing symptoms of being diseased ○ *The X-ray showed a morbid condition of the kidneys.*

morbid anatomy /ˌmɔːbɪd əˈnætəmi/ *noun* same as **pathology**

morbidity /mɔːˈbɪdɪti/ *noun* the condition of being diseased or sick

morbidity rate /mɔːˈbɪdɪti reɪt/ *noun* the number of cases of a disease per hundred thousand of population

morbilli /mɔːˈbɪli/ *noun* same as **measles**

morbilliform /mɔːˈbɪlifɔːm/ *adjective* referring to a rash which is similar to measles

morbus /ˈmɔːbəs/ *noun* disease

moribund /ˈmɒrɪbʌnd/ *adjective* dying ■ *noun* a dying person

morning-after pill /ˌmɔːnɪŋ ˈɑːftə pɪl/ *noun* a contraceptive pill taken after intercourse. Also called **next-day pill**

morning sickness /ˈmɔːnɪŋ ˌsɪknəs/ *noun* nausea and vomiting experienced by women in the early stages of pregnancy when they get up in the morning

Moro reflex /ˈmɔːrəʊ ˌriːfleks/ *noun* a reflex of a newborn baby when it hears a loud noise (NOTE: The baby is laid on a table and observed to see if it raises its arms when the table is struck.) [After Ernst Moro (1874–1951), paediatrician in Heidelberg, Germany.]

morphea /mɔːˈfiə/ *noun* a form of scleroderma, a disease where the skin is replaced by thick connective tissue

morpho- /mɔːfəʊ/ *prefix* relating to form, shape or structure

morphoea /mɔːˈfiə/ *noun* same as **morphea**

morphology /mɔːˈfɒlədʒi/ *noun* the study of the structure and shape of living organisms

-morphous /mɔːfəs/ *suffix* relating to form or structure of a particular type

mortality rate /mɔːˈtæləti reɪt/ *noun* the number of deaths per year, shown per hundred thousand of population

mortification /ˌmɔːtɪfɪˈkeɪʃ(ə)n/ *noun* ♦ **necrosis**

mortis /ˈmɔːtɪs/ ♦ **rigor**

mortuary /ˈmɔːtjuəri/ *noun* a room in a hospital where dead bodies are kept until removed by an undertaker for burial

mosquito /mɒˈskiːtəʊ/ *noun* an insect which sucks human blood, some species of which can pass viruses or parasites into the bloodstream

mother /ˈmʌðə/ *noun* a biological or adoptive female parent

mother-fixation /ˈmʌðə fɪkˌseɪʃ(ə)n/ *noun* a condition in which a person's development has been stopped at a stage where he or she remains like a child, dependent on his or her mother

motile /ˈməʊtaɪl/ *adjective* referring to a cell or microorganism which can move spontaneously ○ *Sperm cells are extremely motile.*

motility /məʊˈtɪlɪti/ *noun* **1.** (*of cells or microbes*) the fact of being able to move about **2.** (*of the gut*) the action of peristalsis

motion /ˈməʊʃ(ə)n/ *noun* **1.** movement **2.** same as **bowel movement**

motion sickness /ˌməʊʃ(ə)n ˈsɪknəs/ *noun* illness and nausea felt when travelling. It is caused by the movement of liquid inside the labyrinth of the middle ear and is particularly noticeable in vehicles which are closed, such as planes, coaches or hovercraft. (*informal*)

COMMENT: The movement of liquid inside the labyrinth of the middle ear causes motion sickness, which is particularly noticeable in

vehicles which are closed, such as planes, coaches, hovercraft.

motor /ˈməʊtə/ *adjective* referring to movement, which produces movement

motor area /ˈməʊtər ˌeəriə/, **motor cortex** /ˌməʊtə ˈkɔːteks/ *noun* the part of the cortex in the brain which controls voluntary muscle movement by sending impulses to the motor nerves

motor disorder /ˈməʊtə dɪsˌɔːdə/ *noun* impairment of the nerves or neurons that cause muscles to contract to produce movement

motor end plate /ˌməʊtər ˈend pleɪt/ *noun* the end of a motor nerve where it joins muscle fibre

motor nerve /ˈməʊtə nɜːv/ *noun* a nerve which carries impulses from the brain and spinal cord to muscles and causes movements. Also called **efferent nerve**

motor neurone /ˌməʊtə ˈnjʊərəʊn/ *noun* a neurone which is part of a nerve pathway transmitting impulses from the brain to a muscle or gland

motor neurone disease /ˌməʊtə ˈnjʊərəʊn dɪˌziːz/ *noun* a disease of the nerve cells which control the movement of the muscles. Abbreviation **MND**

COMMENT: Motor neurone disease has three forms: progressive muscular atrophy (PMA), which affects movements of the hands, lateral sclerosis, and bulbar palsy, which affects the mouth and throat.

motor pathway /ˌməʊtə ˈpɑːθweɪ/ *noun* a series of motor neurones leading from the motor cortex to a muscle

mottled /ˈmɒt(ə)ld/ *adjective* with patches of different colours

mountain fever /ˈmaʊntɪn ˌfiːvə/ *noun* same as **brucellosis**

mountain sickness /ˈmaʊntɪn ˌsɪknəs/ *noun* same as **altitude sickness**

mouth /maʊθ/ *noun* an opening at the head of the alimentary canal, through which food and drink are taken in, and through which a person speaks and can breathe ○ *She was sleeping with her mouth open.* (NOTE: For other terms referring to the mouth, see **oral** and words beginning with **stomat-, stomato-**.)

mouth-to-mouth /ˌmaʊθ tə ˈmaʊθ/, **mouth-to-mouth resuscitation** /ˌmaʊθ tə ˌmaʊθ rɪˌsʌsɪˈteɪʃ(ə)n/, **mouth-to-mouth ventilation** /ˌmaʊθ tə ˌmaʊθ ˌventɪˈleɪʃ(ə)n/ *noun* same as **cardiopulmonary resuscitation** (*informal*)

mouthwash /ˈmaʊθwɒʃ/ *noun* an antiseptic solution used to treat infection in the mouth

movement /ˈmuːvmənt/ *noun* the act of changing position or the fact of not being still

MP joint /ˌem ˈpiː ˌdʒɔɪnt/ *noun* same as **metacarpophalangeal joint**

MRC *abbreviation* Medical Research Council

MRCGP *abbreviation* Member of the Royal College of General Practitioners

MRCP *abbreviation* Member of the Royal College of Physicians

MRCS *abbreviation* Member of the Royal College of Surgeons

MRI *abbreviation* magnetic resonance imaging

mRNA *abbreviation* messenger RNA

MRSA *abbreviation* methicillin-resistant Staphylococcus aureus

MS *abbreviation* 1. mitral stenosis 2. multiple sclerosis

MSH *abbreviation* melanocyte-stimulating hormone

MSU *abbreviation* midstream specimen of urine

mSv *abbreviation* millisievert

mucin /'mjuːsɪn/ *noun* a compound of sugars and protein which is the main substance in mucus

muco- /mjuːkəʊ/ *prefix* referring to mucus

mucocele /'mjuːkəʊsiːl/ *noun* a cavity containing an accumulation of mucus

mucociliary transport /ˌmjuːkəʊˌsɪliəri 'trænspɔːt/ *noun* the process in which the cilia, the microscopic structures within the nose, move mucus towards the oesophagus, cleansing the nose of dust and bacteria

mucocoele /'mjuːkəʊsiːl/ *noun* 1. a condition in which a cavity or organ becomes swollen because there is too much mucus in it 2. the swelling produced by this condition

mucocutaneous /ˌmjuːkəʊkjuː'teɪniəs/ *adjective* referring to both mucous membrane and the skin

mucoid /'mjuːkɔɪd/ *adjective* similar to mucus

mucolytic /ˌmjuːkəʊ'lɪtɪk/ *noun* a substance which dissolves mucus

mucopurulent /ˌmjuːkəʊ'pjʊərʊlənt/ *adjective* consisting of a mixture of mucus and pus

mucopus /ˌmjuːkəʊ'pʌs/ *noun* a mixture of mucus and pus

mucosa /mjuː'kəʊzə/ *noun* same as **mucous membrane** (NOTE: The plural is **mucosae**.)

mucosal /mjuː'kəʊz(ə)l/ *adjective* referring to a mucous membrane

mucous /'mjuːkəs/ *adjective* referring to mucus, covered in mucus

mucous colitis /ˌmjuːkəs kə'laɪtɪs/ *noun* an inflammation of the mucous membrane in the intestine, in which the person experiences pain caused by spasms in the muscles of the walls of the colon, accompanied by constipation or diarrhoea or alternating attacks of both. Also called **irritable bowel syndrome**

mucous membrane /ˌmjuːkəs 'membreɪn/ *noun* a wet membrane which lines internal passages in the body, e.g. the nose, mouth, stomach and throat, and secretes mucus. Also called **mucosa**

mucous plug /'mjuːkəs plʌg/ *noun* a plug of mucus which blocks the cervical canal during pregnancy

mucoviscidosis /mjuːkəʊvɪsi'dəʊsɪs/ *noun* same as **cystic fibrosis**

mucus /'mjuːkəs/ *noun* a slippery liquid secreted by mucous membranes inside the body, which protects those membranes (NOTE: For other terms referring to mucus, see words beginning with **blenno-**.)

multi- /mʌlti/ *prefix* many

multidisciplinary /ˌmʌlti'dɪsɪplɪnəri/ *adjective* using or involving several specialised subjects or skills ○ *a multidisciplinary team*

multifactorial /ˌmʌltifæk'tɔːriəl/ *adjective* 1. involving several different factors or elements 2. referring to inheritance which depends on more than one gene. Height and weight are examples of characteristics determined by multifactorial inheritance.

multifocal lens /ˌmʌltiˌfəʊk(ə)l 'lenz/ *noun* a lens in spectacles whose focus changes from top to bottom so that the person wearing the spectacles can see objects clearly at different distances

multiforme /'mʌltifɔːm/ ♦ **erythema multiforme**

multigravida /ˌmʌlti'grævɪdə/ *noun* a pregnant woman who has been pregnant two or more times before

multi-infarct dementia /ˌmʌlti 'ɪnfɑːkt dɪ ˌmenʃə/ *noun* dementia caused by a number of small strokes, when the dementia is not progressive as in Alzheimer's disease but increases in steps as new strokes occur

multilocular /ˌmʌlti'lɒkjʊlə/ *adjective* referring to a body part or growth which has a lot of separate compartments or locules

multi-organ failure /ˌmʌlti 'ɔːgən ˌfeɪljə/ *noun* an extremely serious condition in which several of the body's organs stop functioning at the same time. The person may survive, depending on how many organs fail and the length of time that the failure lasts. Abbreviation **MOF**

multipara /mʌl'tɪpərə/ *noun* a woman who has given birth to two or more live children

multiple /'mʌltɪp(ə)l/ *adjective* occurring several times or in several places

multiple birth /ˌmʌltɪp(ə)l 'bɜːθ/ *noun* a birth where more than one child is born at the same time

multiple fracture /ˌmʌltɪp(ə)l 'fræktʃə/ *noun* a condition in which a bone is broken in several places

multiple organ dysfunction syndrome /ˌmʌltɪp(ə)l ˌɔːgən dɪs'fʌŋkʃ(ə)n ˌsɪndrəʊm/ *noun* a state of continuous disturbances and abnormalities in organ systems, rather than true failure, e.g. following trauma and sepsis. It is often fatal. Abbreviation **MODS**

multiple pregnancy /ˌmʌltɪp(ə)l 'pregnənsi/ *noun* a pregnancy where the mother is going to give birth to more than one child

multiple sclerosis /ˌmʌltɪp(ə)l sklə'rəʊsɪs/ *noun* a nervous disease which gets progressively worse, where patches of the fibres of the central nervous system lose their myelin, causing numbness in the limbs and progressive weakness and paralysis. Abbreviation **MS**. Also called **disseminated sclerosis**. ◊ **arteriosclerosis**, **atherosclerosis**

multipolar neurone /ˌmʌltɪˌpəʊlə 'njʊərəʊn/ *noun* a neurone with several processes. See illustration at **NEURONE** in Supplement. Compare **bipolar neurone**, **unipolar neurone**

multiresistant /ˌmʌltɪrɪ'zɪstənt/ *adjective* resistant to several types of antibiotic

multivitamin /ˈmʌltiˌvɪtəmɪn/ *noun* a preparation containing several vitamins and sometimes minerals, used as a dietary supplement ■ *adjective* referring to a preparation containing several vitamins, and sometimes minerals ○ *multivitamin pills* ○ *multivitamin supplement*

mumps /mʌmps/ *noun* an infectious disease of children, with fever and swellings in the salivary glands, caused by a paramyxovirus ○ *He caught mumps from the children next door.* Also called **infectious parotitis** (NOTE: Takes a singular or a plural verb.)

Münchausen's syndrome /ˈmʌntʃaʊz(ə)nz ˌsɪndrəʊm/ *noun* a mental disorder in which someone tries to get hospital treatment by claiming symptoms of an illness which he or she does not have. Many people will undergo very painful procedures which they do not need. [Described by Richard Asher in 1951, and named after Baron von Münchhausen, a 16th century traveller and inveterate liar.]

Münchausen's syndrome by proxy /ˌmʌntʃaʊz(ə)nz ˌsɪndrəʊm baɪ 'prɒksi/ *noun* a mental disorder in which someone tries to get hospital treatment for someone else such as their child or an elderly relative. It is regarded as a form of child abuse, as the person may cause a child to be ill in order to receive attention.

murmur /ˈmɜːmə/ *noun* a sound, usually the sound of the heart, heard through a stethoscope

muscae volitantes /ˌmʌskaɪ ˌvɒlɪ'tænteɪz/ *plural noun* pieces of cellular or blood debris present in the vitreous of the eye, common in old age but, if a sudden event, can be a symptom of retinal haemorrhage. Also called **floaters**

muscarine /ˈmʌskəriːn/ *noun* a poison found in fungi

muscarinic /ˌmʌskə'rɪnɪk/ *adjective* referring to a neurone or receptor stimulated by acetylcholine and muscarine

muscle /ˈmʌs(ə)l/ *noun* **1.** an organ in the body, which contracts to make part of the body move ○ *If you do a lot of exercises you develop strong muscles.* ○ *The muscles in his legs were still weak after he had spent two months in bed.* ○ *She had muscle cramp after going into the cold water.* See illustration at **EYE** in Supplement. **2.** same as **muscle tissue**

muscle fatigue /ˈmʌs(ə)l fə,tiːɡ/, **muscular fatigue** /ˌmʌskjʊlə fə'tiːɡ/ *noun* tiredness in the muscles after strenuous exercise

muscle fibre /ˈmʌs(ə)l ,faɪbə/ *noun* a component fibre of muscles (NOTE: There are two types of fibre which form striated and smooth muscles.)

muscle relaxant /ˈmʌs(ə)l rɪ,læksənt/ *noun* a drug which reduces contractions in the muscles, e.g. baclofen

muscle spasm /ˈmʌs(ə)l ,spæz(ə)m/ *noun* a sudden contraction of a muscle

muscle tissue /ˈmʌs(ə)l ,tɪʃuː/, **muscular tissue** /ˌmʌskjʊlə 'tɪʃuː/ *noun* the specialised type of tissue which forms the muscles and which can contract and expand

muscle wasting /ˈmʌs(ə)l ,weɪstɪŋ/ *noun* a condition in which the muscles lose weight and become thin

muscular /ˈmʌskjʊlə/ *adjective* referring to muscle

muscular dystrophy /ˌmʌskjʊlə 'dɪstrəfi/ *noun* a type of muscle disease where some muscles become weak and are replaced with fatty tissue. ◊ **Duchenne muscular dystrophy**

muscular fatigue /ˌmʌskjʊlə fə'tiːɡ/ *noun* same as **muscle fatigue**

muscular tissue /ˌmʌskjʊlə 'tɪʃuː/ *noun* same as **muscle tissue**

musculo- /mʌskjʊləʊ/ *prefix* relating to or affecting muscle

musculocutaneous /ˌmʌskjʊləʊkjuː'teɪniəs/ *adjective* referring to muscle and skin

musculoskeletal /ˌmʌskjʊləʊ'skelɪt(ə)l/ *adjective* referring to muscles and bone

mutant /ˈmjuːt(ə)nt/ *adjective* in which mutation has occurred

mutant gene /ˌmjuːt(ə)nt 'dʒiːn/ *noun* a gene which has undergone mutation

mutation /mjuː'teɪʃ(ə)n/ *noun* a change in DNA which changes the physiological effect of the DNA on the cell

mute /mjuːt/ *adjective* **1.** unwilling or unable to speak **2.** felt or expressed without speech ■ *noun* somebody who is unable or unwilling to speak (NOTE: This term is sometimes considered offensive.)

mutism /ˈmjuːtɪz(ə)m/ *noun* the condition of being unable to speak. Also called **dumbness**

my- /maɪ/ *prefix* same as **myo-** (*used before vowels*)

myalgia /maɪˈældʒə/ *noun* a muscle pain

myalgic encephalomyelitis /maɪˌældʒɪk en ˌkefələumaɪəˈlaɪtɪs/ *noun* a long-term condition affecting the nervous system, in which someone feels tired and depressed and has pain and weakness in the muscles. Abbreviation **ME**. Also called **chronic fatigue syndrome**, **postviral fatigue syndrome**

myasthenia /ˌmaɪəsˈθiːniə/, **myasthenia gravis** /ˌmaɪəsˌθiːniə ˈɡrɑːvɪs/ *noun* a general weakness and dysfunction of the muscles, caused by poor conduction at the motor end plates

myc- /maɪk, maɪs/ *prefix* same as **myco-** (*used before vowels*)

myco- /maɪkəʊ/ *prefix* referring to fungus

Mycobacterium /ˌmaɪkəʊbæk'tiːəriəm/ *noun* one of a group of bacteria including those which cause leprosy and tuberculosis

Mycoplasma /ˈmaɪkəʊˌplæzmə/ *noun* a type of microorganism, similar to a bacterium, associated with diseases such as pneumonia and urethritis

mycosis /maɪˈkəʊsɪs/ *noun* any disease caused by a fungus, e.g. athlete's foot

mydriasis /maɪˈdraɪəsɪs/ *noun* an enlargement of the pupil of the eye

mydriatic /ˌmɪdriˈætɪk/ *noun* a drug which makes the pupil of the eye become larger

myelin /ˈmaɪəlɪn/ *noun* the substance of the cell membrane of Schwann cells that coils into a protective covering around nerve fibres called a myelin sheath

myelinated /ˈmaɪəlɪneɪtɪd/ *adjective* referring to nerve fibre covered by a myelin sheath

myelination /ˌmaɪəlɪˈneɪʃ(ə)n/ *noun* the process by which a myelin sheath forms around nerve fibres

myelin sheath /ˈmaɪəlɪn ʃiːθ/ *noun* a layer of myelin that insulates some nerve cells and speeds the conduction of nerve impulses. See illustration at **NEURONE** in Supplement

myelocele /ˈmaɪələsiːl/ *noun* same as **meningomyelocele**

myelography /ˌmaɪəˈlɒɡrəfi/ *noun* an X-ray examination of the spinal cord and subarachnoid space after a radio-opaque substance has been injected

myeloid /ˈmaɪəlɔɪd/ *adjective* **1.** referring to bone marrow, or produced by bone marrow **2.** referring to the spinal cord

myeloid leukaemia /ˌmaɪəlɔɪd luːˈkiːmiə/ *noun* an acute form of leukaemia in adults

myeloid tissue /ˈmaɪəlɔɪd ˌtɪʃuː/ *noun* red bone marrow

myeloma /ˌmaɪəˈləʊmə/ *noun* a malignant tumour in bone marrow, at the ends of long bones or in the jaw

myelomeningocele /ˌmaɪələʊmə ˈnɪŋɡəʊsiːl/ *noun* same as **meningomyelocele**

myelopathy /ˌmaɪəˈlɒpəθi/ *noun* any disorder of the spinal cord or bone marrow

myelosuppression /ˌmaɪələʊsəˈpreʃ(ə)n/ *noun* a condition in which the bone marrow does not produce enough blood cells, often occurring after chemotherapy

myo- /maɪəʊ/ *prefix* referring to muscle

myocardial /ˌmaɪəʊˈkɑːdiəl/ *adjective* referring to the myocardium

myocardial infarction /ˌmaɪəʊˌkɑːdiəl ɪnˈfɑːkʃən/ *noun* the death of part of the heart muscle after coronary thrombosis. Abbreviation **MI**

myocarditis /ˌmaɪəʊkɑːˈdaɪtɪs/ *noun* inflammation of the heart muscle

myocardium /ˌmaɪəʊˈkɑːdiəm/ *noun* the middle layer of the wall of the heart, formed of heart muscle. See illustration at **HEART** in Supplement

myocele /ˈmaɪəsiːl/ *noun* a condition in which a muscle pushes through a gap in the surrounding membrane

myoclonic /ˌmaɪəʊˈklɒnɪk/ *adjective* referring to myoclonus

myoclonic epilepsy /ˌmaɪəʊklɒnɪk ˈepɪlepsi/ *noun* a form of epilepsy where the limbs jerk frequently

myoclonus /maɪˈɒklənəs/ *noun* a muscle spasm which makes a limb give an involuntary jerk

myocyte /ˈmaɪəʊsaɪt/ *noun* a muscle cell

myofibril /ˌmaɪəʊˈfaɪbrɪl/ *noun* a long thread of striated muscle fibre

myofibrosis /ˌmaɪəʊfaɪˈbrəʊsɪs/ *noun* a condition in which muscle tissue is replaced by fibrous tissue

myoma /maɪˈəʊmə/ *noun* a benign tumour in a smooth muscle

myomectomy /ˌmaɪəʊˈmektəmi/ *noun* the surgical removal of a benign growth from a muscle, especially removal of a fibroid from the uterus

myometritis /ˌmaɪəʊməˈtraɪtɪs/ *noun* inflammation of the myometrium. Also called **metritis**

myometrium /ˌmaɪəʊˈmiːtriəm/ *noun* the muscular tissue in the uterus

myoneural /ˌmaɪəʊˈnjʊərəl/ *adjective* relating to or involving both the muscles and the nerves

myoneural junction /ˌmaɪəʊnjʊərəl ˈdʒʌŋkʃ(ə)n/ *noun* same as **neuromuscular junction**

myopathy /maɪˈɒpəθi/ *noun* a disease of a muscle, especially one in which the muscle wastes away

myopia /maɪˈəʊpiə/ *noun* a condition in which someone can see clearly objects which are close, but not ones which are further away. Also called **shortsightedness**. Opposite **longsightedness**

myopic /maɪˈɒpɪk/ *adjective* able to see close objects clearly, but not objects which are further away. Also called **shortsighted, nearsighted**

myoplasty /ˈmaɪəʊplæsti/ *noun* a form of plastic surgery to repair a muscle

myosarcoma /ˌmaɪəʊsɑːˈkəʊmə/ *noun* a malignant tumour containing unstriated muscle

myosis /maɪˈəʊsɪs/ *noun* another spelling of **miosis 1**

myositis /ˌmaɪəʊˈsaɪtɪs/ *noun* inflammation and degeneration of a muscle

myotic /maɪˈɒtɪk/ *noun* a drug which causes the pupil of the eye to contract

myotomy /maɪˈɒtəmi/ *noun* a surgical operation to cut a muscle

myotonia /ˌmaɪəʊˈtəʊniə/ *noun* difficulty in relaxing a muscle after exercise

myotonic /ˌmaɪəʊˈtɒnɪk/ *adjective* referring to tone in a muscle

myringa /mɪˈrɪŋgə/ *noun* same as **eardrum**

myringitis /ˌmɪrɪnˈdʒaɪtɪs/ *noun* inflammation of the eardrum

myringoplasty /mɪˈrɪŋgəʊplæsti/ *noun* the surgical repair of a perforated eardrum. Also called **tympanoplasty**

myringotome /mɪˈrɪŋgəʊtəʊm/ *noun* a sharp knife used in myringotomy

myringotomy /ˌmɪrɪŋˈgɒtəmi/ *noun* a surgical operation to make an opening in the eardrum to allow fluid to escape. Also called **tympanotomy**

myx- /mɪks/, **myxo-** /mɪksəʊ/ *prefix* referring to mucus

myxoedema /ˌmɪksəˈdiːmə/ *noun* a condition caused when the thyroid gland does not produce enough thyroid hormone. The person, often a middle-aged woman, becomes overweight, moves slowly and develops coarse skin. It can be treated with thyroxine.

myxoedematous /ˌmɪksəˈdemətəs/ *adjective* referring to myxoedema

myxoid cyst /ˌmɪksɔɪd ˈsɪst/ *noun* a cyst which develops at the base of a fingernail or toenail

myxovirus /ˌmɪksəʊˈvaɪrəs/ *noun* any virus which has an affinity for the mucoprotein receptors in red blood cells. One of these viruses causes influenza.

N

n *symbol* nano-

nabothian cyst /nəˌbəʊθiən ˈsɪst/, **nabothian follicle** /nəˌbəʊθiən ˈfɒlɪk(ə)l/, **nabothian gland** /nəˌbəʊθiən ˈglænd/ *noun* a cyst which forms in the cervix of the uterus when the ducts in the cervical glands are blocked

Naegele rule /ˈneɪɡələ ruːl/ *noun* a method used to determine when a pregnant woman is likely to go into labour, in which nine months and seven days are added to the date on which her last period started. If the woman does not have a 28-day menstrual cycle, an adjustment is made: e.g., if she has a 26-day cycle you would subtract 2 days from the Naegele's estimated due date.

naevus /ˈniːvəs/ *noun* same as **birthmark** (NOTE: The plural is **naevi**.)

NAI *abbreviation* non-accidental injury

nail /neɪl/ *noun* a hard growth, made of keratin, which forms on the top surface at the end of each finger and toe. Also called **unguis** (NOTE: For terms referring to nail, see words beginning with **onych-, onycho-**.)

nail avulsion /ˈneɪl əˌvʌlʃən/ *noun* the act of pulling away an ingrowing toenail

nail bed /ˈneɪl bed/ *noun* the part of the finger which is just under the nail and on which the nail rests

nail matrix /ˈneɪl ˌmeɪtrɪks/ *noun* the internal structure of the nail, the part of the finger from which the nail grows

naloxone /nəˈlɒksəʊn/ *noun* a drug resembling morphine, used in the diagnosis of narcotics addiction and to reverse the effects of narcotics poisoning

named nurse /ˌneɪmd ˈnɜːs/ *noun* a nurse, midwife or health visitor who is responsible for communicating with a particular person and ensuring that his or her needs for care and information are met

nandrolone /ˈnændrələʊn/ *noun* an anabolic steroid which builds muscle. Its use is banned by the International Amateur Athletics Federation.

nano- /nænəʊ/ *prefix* one thousand millionth (10^{-9}). Symbol **n**

nanometre /ˈnænəʊmitə/ *noun* a unit of measurement of length equal to one thousand millionth of a metre. Symbol **nm**

nanomole /ˈnænəʊməʊl/ *noun* a unit of measurement of the amount of a substance equal to one thousand millionth of a mole. Symbol **nmol**

nanosecond /ˈnænəʊˌsekənd/ *noun* a unit of measurement of time equal to one thousand millionth of a second. Symbol **ns**

nape /neɪp/ *noun* the back of the neck. Also called **nucha**

nappy /ˈnæpi/ *noun* a cloth used to wrap round a baby's bottom and groin, to keep clothing clean and dry

nappy rash /ˈnæpi ræʃ/ *noun* sore red skin on a baby's buttocks and groin, caused by long contact with ammonia in a wet nappy

naproxen /næˈprɒksen/ *noun* a drug which reduces inflammation and pain, used in the treatment of arthritis

narcissism /ˈnɑːsɪsɪz(ə)m/ *noun* in psychiatry, a personality disorder in which someone has a very confident opinion about their own appearance and abilities, and a great need to be admired by other people. It sometimes involves sexual interest in their own body.

narco- /nɑːkəʊ/ *prefix* referring to sleep or stupor

narcolepsy /ˈnɑːkəlepsi/ *noun* a condition in which someone has an uncontrollable tendency to fall asleep at any time

narcoleptic /ˌnɑːkəˈleptɪk/ *adjective* **1.** causing narcolepsy **2.** having narcolepsy ■ *noun* **1.** a substance which causes narcolepsy **2.** someone who has narcolepsy

narcosis /nɑːˈkəʊsɪs/ *noun* a state of lowered consciousness induced by a drug

narcotic /nɑːˈkɒtɪk/ *noun* a pain-relieving drug which makes someone sleep or become unconscious ○ *The doctor put her to sleep with a powerful narcotic.* ■ *adjective* causing sleep or unconsciousness ○ *the narcotic side-effects of an antihistamine*

nares /ˈneəriːz/ *plural noun* the nostrils (NOTE: The singular is **naris**.)

nasal /ˈneɪz(ə)l/ *adjective* referring to the nose

nasal apertures /ˌneɪz(ə)l ˈæpətʃəs/ *plural noun* the two openings shaped like funnels leading from the nasal cavity to the pharynx. ◊ **choana**

nasal cavity /ˌneɪz(ə)l ˈkævɪti/ *noun* the cavity behind the nose between the cribriform plates above and the hard palate below, divided in two by the nasal septum and leading to the nasopharynx

nasal conchae /ˌneɪz(ə)l ˈkɒŋkiː/ *plural noun* the three ridges of bone, called the superior, middle and inferior conchae, which project into the nasal cavity from the side walls. Also called **turbinate bones**

nasal congestion /ˌneɪz(ə)l kənˈdʒestʃ(ə)n/ *noun* the blocking of the nose by inflammation as a response to a cold or other infection

nasal drops /ˈneɪz(ə)l drɒps/ *plural noun* drops of liquid inserted into the nose

nasal septum /ˌneɪz(ə)l ˈseptəm/ *noun* a wall of cartilage between the two nostrils and the two parts of the nasal cavity

nasal spray /ˈneɪz(ə)l spreɪ/ *noun* a spray of liquid into the nose

nascent /ˈnæs(ə)nt, ˈneɪs(ə)nt/ *adjective* **1.** in the process of coming into existence and starting to develop **2.** referring to a substance, especially hydrogen, in the process of being created. At this stage it is often in a highly active form.

Naseptin /næˈseptɪn/ a trade name for a mixture containing chlorhexidine and neomycin, used to treat nasal infection by organisms such as staphylococci

naso- /neɪzəʊ/ *prefix* referring to the nose

nasogastric /ˌneɪzəʊˈgæstrɪk/ *adjective* referring to the nose and stomach

nasogastric tube /ˌneɪzəʊˌgæstrɪk ˈtjuːb/ *noun* a tube passed through the nose into the stomach

nasolacrimal /ˌneɪzəʊˈlækrɪm(ə)l/ *adjective* referring to the nose and the tear glands

nasolacrimal duct /ˌneɪzəʊˌlækrɪm(ə)l ˈdʌkt/ *noun* a duct which drains tears from the lacrimal sac into the nose

nasopharyngeal /ˌneɪzəʊˌfærɪnˈdʒiːəl/ *adjective* referring to the nasopharynx

nasopharyngitis /ˌneɪzəʊˌfærɪnˈdʒaɪtɪs/ *noun* inflammation of the mucous membrane of the nasal part of the pharynx

nasopharynx /ˌneɪzəʊˈfærɪŋks/ *noun* the top part of the pharynx which connects with the nose

nasosinusitis /ˌneɪzəʊˌsaɪnəˈsaɪtɪs/ *noun* a condition in which the nose and sinuses swell up

nates /ˈneɪtiːz/ *noun* same as **buttock**

National Boards /ˌnæʃ(ə)nəl ˈbɔːrdz/ *plural noun* the National Boards for Nursing, Midwifery, and Health Visiting, which were formerly responsible for the education of professionals in these fields in England, Wales, Scotland and Northern Ireland

National Council for Vocational Qualifications /ˌnæʃ(ə)nəl ˌkaʊns(ə)l fə vəʊˌkeɪʃ(ə)nəl ˌkwɒlɪfɪˈkeɪʃ(ə)nz/ *noun* full form of **NCVQ**

National Health Service /ˌnæʃ(ə)nəl ˈhelθ ˌsɜːvɪs/ *noun* a government service in the UK which provides medical services free of charge at the point of delivery, or at reduced cost, to the whole population. The service is paid for out of tax revenue. Abbreviation **NHS**

National Institute for Clinical Excellence /ˌnæʃ(ə)n(ə)l ˌɪnstɪtjuːt fə ˌklɪnɪk(ə)l ˈeksələns/ *noun* an organisation in the UK which produces recommendations for treatments based on clinical evidence and cost-effectiveness. Abbreviation **NICE**

National Service Framework /ˌnæʃ(ə)nəl ˈsɜːvɪs ˌfreɪmwɜːk/ *noun* full form of **NSF**

natriuretic /ˌneɪtrijʊˈretɪk/ *noun* something which helps sodium to be excreted in the urine

natural childbirth /ˌnætʃ(ə)rəl ˈtʃaɪldbɜːθ/ *noun* childbirth where the mother is not given any pain-killing drugs or anaesthetic but is encouraged to give birth after having prepared herself through relaxation and breathing exercises and a new psychological outlook

natural immunity /ˌnætʃ(ə)rəl ɪˈmjuːnɪti/ *noun* the immunity from disease which a newborn baby has from birth and which is inherited or acquired in the uterus or from the mother's milk

natural killer cell /ˌnætʃ(ə)rəl ˈkɪlə ˌsel/ *noun* a white blood cell which can recognise microorganisms and tumour cells as foreign without any previous exposure to them, and destroy them

natural mother /ˌnætʃ(ə)rəl ˈmʌðə/, **natural parent** /ˌnætʃ(ə)rəl ˈpeərənt/ *noun* same as **birth mother**, **birth parent**

nature nurture debate /ˌneɪtʃə ˈnɜːtʃə dɪ ˌbeɪt/ *noun* the arguments put forward about whether human beings behave in the way they do because of their genetic make-up and instincts or because of the way they are educated and the influences they are exposed to when they are young

naturopathy /ˌneɪtʃəˈrɒpəθi/ *noun* a method of treatment of diseases and disorders which does not use medical or surgical means, but natural forces such as light, heat, massage, eating natural foods and using herbal remedies

nausea /ˈnɔːziə/ *noun* a feeling that you want to vomit ○ *She suffered from nausea in the morning.* ○ *He felt slight nausea after getting onto the boat.*

nauseated /ˈnɔːzieɪtɪd/ *adjective* feeling as if you are about to vomit ○ *The casualty may feel nauseated.*

navel /ˈneɪv(ə)l/ *noun* the scar with a depression in the middle of the abdomen where the umbilical cord was detached after birth. Also called **umbilicus** (NOTE: For other terms referring to the navel, see words beginning with **omphal-, omphalo-**.)

navicular /nə'vɪkjʊlə/ *adjective* relating to a navicular bone ∎ *noun* same as **navicular bone**

navicular bone /nə'vɪkjʊlə bəʊn/ *noun* one of the tarsal bones in the foot. See illustration at FOOT in Supplement

NCVQ /,en si: vi: 'kju:/ *noun* a government body in the UK responsible for setting standards of qualification for specific jobs. Full form **National Council for Vocational Qualifications**

NDU *abbreviation* Nursing Development Unit

nearsighted /nɪə'saɪtɪd/ *adjective* same as **myopic**

nebula /'nebjʊlə/ *noun* a slightly cloudy spot on the cornea

nebuliser /'nebjʊlaɪzə/, **nebulizer** *noun* same as **atomiser**

neck /nek/ *noun* **1.** the part of the body which joins the head to the body ○ *He is suffering from pains in the neck.* ○ *The front of the neck is swollen with goitre.* ○ *The jugular veins run down the side of the neck.* **2.** a narrow part of a bone or organ

neck collar /'nek ,kɒlə/ *noun* a strong high collar to support the head of a person with neck injuries or a condition such as cervical spondylosis

necro- /nekrəʊ/ *prefix* referring to death

necrology /ne'krɒlədʒi/ *noun* the scientific study of mortality statistics

necrophilia /,nekrəʊ'fɪliə/, **necrophilism** /ne'krɒfɪlɪz(ə)m/ *noun* unusual pleasure in corpses

necropsy /'nekrɒpsi/ *noun* same as **post mortem**

necrosis /ne'krəʊsɪs/ *noun* the death of a part of the body such as a bone, tissue or an organ as a result of disease or injury ○ *Gangrene is a form of necrosis.*

necrotic /ne'krɒtɪk/ *adjective* referring to, or affected with, necrosis ○ *necrotic tissue*

necrotising enterocolitis /,nekrətaɪzɪŋ ,entərəʊkə'laɪtɪs/ *noun* a disorder in which patches of dead tissue are found in the small or large intestine as a result of severe bacterial infection. It occurs in babies, especially premature ones.

necrotomy /ne'krɒtəmi/ *noun* the dissection of a dead body (NOTE: The plural is **necrotomies**.)

needle /'ni:d(ə)l/ *noun* **1.** a thin metal instrument with a sharp point at one end and a hole at the other for attaching a thread, used for sewing up surgical incisions **2.** the hollow pointed end of a hypodermic syringe, or the syringe itself

needlestick /'ni:d(ə)lstɪk/ *noun* an accidental pricking of your own skin by a needle, as by a nurse picking up a used syringe

needlestick injury /'ni:d(ə)lstɪk ,ɪndʒəri/ *noun* the real or potential harm resulting from a prick with a needle previously used to take blood or give an injection. The main concern is the risk of HIV or hepatitis B infection.

needling /'ni:d(ə)lɪŋ/ *noun* the puncture of a cataract with a needle

needs assessment /'ni:dz ə,sesmənt/ *noun* the investigation of what a particular group of people need in terms of health and social care, so that services can be matched to their needs

needs deprivation /'ni:dz deprɪ,veɪʃ(ə)n/ *noun* a state in which someone does not have the opportunity or capacity to fulfil his or her basic needs

negative /'negətɪv/ *adjective* **1.** meaning or showing 'no' **2.** indicating that something being tested for is not present ○ *The test results were negative.* Opposite **positive**

negative feedback /,negətɪv 'fi:dbæk/ *noun* a situation in which the result of a process represses the process which caused it

negligence /'neglɪdʒəns/ *noun* the act of causing injury or harm to another person or to property as the result of doing something wrongly or failing to provide a proper level of care

Neisseria /naɪ'sɪəriə/ *noun* a genus of bacteria which includes gonococcus, which causes gonorrhoea, and meningococcus, which causes meningitis

nematode /'nemətəʊd/ *noun* a type of parasitic roundworm, e.g. a hookworm, pinworm or roundworm

neo- /ni:əʊ/ *prefix* new

neoadjuvant chemotherapy /,ni:əʊ ,ædʒʊvənt ,ki:məʊ'θerəpi/ *noun* chemotherapy given to people with tumours instead of immediate surgery or radiotherapy, in the hope of reducing the need for these later

neomycin /,ni:əʊ'maɪsɪn/ *noun* a drug used externally to treat bacterial infections

neonatal /,ni:əʊ'neɪt(ə)l/ *adjective* referring to the first few weeks after birth

neonatal death rate /,ni:əʊneɪt(ə)l 'deθ ,reɪt/ *noun* the number of babies who die soon after birth, shown per thousand babies born

neonatal screening /,ni:əʊ,neɪt(ə)l 'skri:nɪŋ/ *noun* a set of tests performed on babies soon after birth so that any problems can be treated immediately (NOTE: Tests for certain diseases such as hypothyroidism and phenylketonuria are a legal duty.)

neonate /'ni:əʊneɪt/ *noun* a baby which is less than four weeks old

neonatologist /,ni:ənə'tɒlədʒɪst/ *noun* a specialist who looks after babies during the first few weeks of life, or premature babies and babies with some congenital disorders

neonatology /ˌniːəʊnəˈtɒlədʒi/ *noun* the branch of medicine dealing with babies in the first few weeks of life

neoplasm /ˈniːəʊplæz(ə)m/ *noun* any new and morbid formation of tissue

neoplasty /ˈniːəʊplæsti/ *noun* the surgical repair or replacement of damaged tissue

neostigmine /ˌniːəʊˈstɪgmiːn/ *noun* a white crystalline compound used in the treatment of muscle fatigue myasthenia and to reverse the effects of muscle relaxant drugs

nephr- /nefr/ *prefix* kidney

nephralgia /neˈfrældʒə/ *noun* pain in the kidney

nephralgic /neˈfrældʒɪk/ *adjective* relating to pain in the kidney

nephrectomy /neˈfrektɒmi/ *noun* a surgical operation to remove the whole kidney (NOTE: The plural is **nephrectomies**.)

nephritis /neˈfraɪtɪs/ *noun* inflammation of the kidney

nephroblastoma /ˌnefrəʊblæˈstəʊmə/ *noun* a malignant tumour in the kidneys in young children, usually under the age of 10, leading to swelling of the abdomen. It is treated by removal of the affected kidney. Also called **Wilms' tumour** (NOTE: The plural is **nephroblastomas** or **nephrobrastomata**.)

nephrocalcinosis /ˌnefrəʊˌkælsɪˈnəʊsɪs/ *noun* a condition in which calcium deposits are found in the kidney

nephrocapsulectomy /ˌnefrəʊˌkæpsjʊˈlektəmi/ *noun* a surgical operation to remove the capsule round a kidney (NOTE: The plural is **nephrocapsulectomies**.)

nephrogram /ˈnefrəgræm/ *noun* a radiographic examination of the kidney

nephrolith /ˈnefrəlɪθ/ *noun* a stone in the kidney

nephrolithiasis /ˌnefrəʊlɪˈθaɪəsɪs/ *noun* a condition in which stones form in the kidney

nephrolithotomy /ˌnefrəʊlɪˈθɒtəmi/ *noun* a surgical operation to remove a stone in the kidney (NOTE: The plural is **nephrolithotomies**.)

nephrologist /neˈfrɒlədʒɪst/ *noun* a doctor who specialises in the study of the kidney and its diseases

nephrology /neˈfrɒlədʒi/ *noun* the study of the kidney and its diseases

nephroma /neˈfrəʊmə/ *noun* a tumour in the kidney, or a tumour derived from renal substances (NOTE: The plural is **nephromas** or **nephromata**.)

nephron /ˈnefrɒn/ *noun* a tiny structure in the kidney through which fluid is filtered

nephropathy /neˈfrɒpəθi/ *noun* a disease or medical disorder of the kidney (NOTE: The plural is **nephropathies**.)

nephropexy /ˈnefrəʊpeksi/ *noun* a surgical operation to attach a mobile kidney (NOTE: The plural is **nephropexies**.)

nephroptosis /ˌnefrɒpˈtəʊsɪs/ *noun* a condition in which a kidney is mobile. Also called **floating kidney**

nephrosclerosis /ˌnefrəʊskləˈrəʊsɪs/ *noun* a kidney disease due to vascular change

nephroscope /ˈnefrəskəʊp/ *noun* a type of endoscope used to examine the kidneys

nephrosis /neˈfrəʊsɪs/ *noun* degeneration of the tissue of a kidney

nephrostomy /neˈfrɒstəmi/ *noun* a surgical operation to make a permanent opening into the pelvis of the kidney from the surface (NOTE: The plural is **nephrostomies**.)

nephrotic /neˈfrɒtɪk/ *adjective* relating to or caused by nephrosis

nephrotic syndrome /neˌfrɒtɪk ˈsɪndrəʊm/ *noun* increasing oedema, albuminuria and raised blood pressure resulting from nephrosis

nephrotomy /neˈfrɒtəmi/ *noun* a surgical operation to cut into a kidney (NOTE: The plural is **nephrotomies**.)

nephrotoxic /ˌnefrəʊˈtɒksɪk/ *adjective* poisonous or damaging to kidney cells

nephroureterectomy /ˌnefrəʊˌjʊərɪtəˈrektəmi/ *noun* a surgical operation to remove all or part of a kidney and the ureter attached to it. Also called **ureteronephrectomy** (NOTE: The plural is **nephroureterectomies**.)

nerve /nɜːv/ *noun* **1.** a bundle of fibres that can transmit electrochemical impulses and that forms part of the network that connects the brain and spinal cord to the body's organs **2.** the sensitive tissue in the root of a tooth (NOTE: For other terms referring to nerves, see words beginning with **neur-, neuro-**.)

nerve block /ˈnɜːv blɒk/ *noun* the act of stopping the function of a nerve by injecting an anaesthetic

nerve centre /ˈnɜːv ˌsentə/ *noun* the point at which nerves come together

nerve ending /ˈnɜːv ˌendɪŋ/ *noun* same as **sensory receptor**

nerve entrapment syndrome /ˌnɜːv ɪn ˈtræpmənt ˌsɪndrəʊm/ *noun* pain caused by pressure on a nerve, especially where nerves occur in narrow passages such as the wrist

nerve fibre /ˈnɜːv ˌfaɪbə/ *noun* a thin structure leading from a nerve cell and carrying nerve impulses, e.g. an axon

nerve gas /ˈnɜːv gæs/ *noun* a gas which attacks the nervous system

nerve impulse /'nɜːv ˌɪmpʌls/ *noun* an electrochemical impulse which is transmitted by nerve cells

nerve regeneration /'nɜːv rɪˌdʒenəreɪʃ(ə)n/ *noun* the growth of new nerve tissue after damage has occurred

nerve root /'nɜːv ruːt/ *noun* the first part of a nerve as it leaves or joins the spinal column (NOTE: The dorsal nerve root is the entry for a sensory nerve, and the ventral nerve root is the exit for a motor nerve.)

nerve tissue /'nɜːv ˌtɪʃuː/ *noun* tissue which forms nerves, and which is able to transmit the nerve impulses

nervosa /nə'vəʊsə/ ♦ **anorexia nervosa**

nervous /'nɜːvəs/ *adjective* **1.** referring to nerves **2.** very easily worried ○ *Don't be nervous – the operation is a very simple one.*

nervous breakdown /ˌnɜːvəs 'breɪkdaʊn/ *noun* any sudden mental illness (*informal*)

nervous complaint /ˌnɜːvəs kəm'pleɪnt/, **nervous disorder** /ˌnɜːvəs dɪs'ɔːdə/ *noun* an emotional or mental illness (*informal*)

nervousness /'nɜːvəsnəs/ *noun* the state of being nervous

nervous system /'nɜːvəs ˌsɪstəm/ *noun* the nervous tissues of the body, including the peripheral nerves, spinal cord, ganglia and nerve centres

nether parts /'neðə pɑːts/, **nether regions** /'neðə ˌriːdʒ(ə)nz/ *plural noun* the lower part of the body, especially the buttocks or genital area (*informal*)

nettle rash /'net(ə)l ræʃ/ *noun* same as **urticaria**

network /'netwɜːk/ *noun* any of various computer-based systems designed to allow fast communication of information between NHS agencies, e.g. communication of X-ray results from a hospital to a GP surgery ○ *a network of fine blood vessels*

Neuman's model /'nɔɪmənz ˌmɒd(ə)l/ *noun* a modern model for nursing in which prevention is the primary nursing aim (NOTE: Prevention focuses on keeping both the things which cause stress and the patient's response to stress from having a damaging effect on the body.)

neur- /njʊər/ *prefix* same as **neuro-** (*used before vowels*)

neural /'njʊərəl/ *adjective* referring to a nerve or the nervous system

neural arch /ˌnjʊərəl 'ɑːtʃ/ *noun* a curved part of a vertebra, which forms the space through which the spinal cord passes

neuralgia /njʊ'rældʒə/ *noun* a spasm of pain which runs along a nerve

neural tube /'njʊərəl tjuːb/ *noun* a tube lined with ectodermal cells running the length of an embryo, which develops into the brain and spinal cord

neural tube defect /ˌnjʊərəl 'tjuːb dɪˌfekt/ *noun* a congenital anomaly which occurs when the edges of the neural tube do not close up properly while the fetus develops in the uterus, e.g. spina bifida (NOTE: There is less risk of a neural tube defect if the mother takes folic acid during her pregnancy.)

neurapraxia /ˌnjʊərə'præksiə/ *noun* a lesion of a nerve which leads to paralysis for a very short time, giving a tingling feeling and loss of function

neurectomy /njʊ'rektəmi/ *noun* a surgical operation to remove all or part of a nerve (NOTE: The plural is **neurectomies**.)

neurilemma /ˌnjʊərɪ'lemə/ *noun* the outer sheath, formed of Schwann cells, which covers the myelin sheath around a nerve fibre. Also called **neurolemma**. See illustration at NEURONE in Supplement

neuritis /njʊ'raɪtɪs/ *noun* inflammation of a nerve, giving a constant pain

neuro- /njʊərəʊ/ *prefix* nerve or nervous system

neuroendocrine system /ˌnjʊərəʊ 'endəkrɪn ˌsɪstəm/ *noun* a system in which the central nervous system and hormonal systems interact to control the function of organs and tissues

neuroepithelial /ˌnjʊərəʊepɪ'θiːliəl/ *adjective* referring to the neuroepithelium

neuroepithelium /ˌnjʊərəʊepɪ'θiːliəm/ *noun* the layer of epithelial cells forming part of the lining of the mucous membrane of the nose and the labyrinth of the middle ear

neurofibril /ˌnjʊərəʊ'faɪbrɪl/ *noun* a fine thread in the cytoplasm of a neurone

neurofibrilla /ˌnjʊərəʊ'fɪbrɪlə/ *noun* same as **neurofibril**. See illustration at NEURONE in Supplement (NOTE: The plural is **neurofibrillae**.)

neurofibroma /ˌnjʊərəʊfaɪ'brəʊmə/ *noun* a benign tumour of a nerve, formed from the neurilemma (NOTE: The plural is **neurofibromas** or **neurofibromata**.)

neurofibromatosis /ˌnjʊərəʊˌfaɪbrəʊmə 'təʊsɪs/ *noun* a hereditary condition in which a person has neurofibromata on the nerve trunks, limb plexuses or spinal roots, and pale brown spots appear on the skin. Abbreviation **NF**. Also called **molluscum fibrosum**, **von Recklinghausen's disease**

neurogenic /ˌnjʊərəʊ'dʒenɪk/ *adjective* coming from the nervous system

neurogenic bladder /ˌnjʊərəʊdʒenɪk 'blædə/ *noun* a disturbance of the bladder function caused by lesions in the nerve supply to the bladder

neurogenic shock /ˌnjʊərəʊdʒenɪk 'ʃɒk/ *noun* a state of shock caused by bad news or an unpleasant surprise

neuroglandular junction /ˌnjʊərəʊ ˌɡlændjʊlə 'dʒʌŋkʃən/ *noun* the point where a nerve joins the gland which it controls

neurohormone /ˌnjʊərəʊ'hɔːməʊn/ *noun* a hormone produced in some nerve cells and secreted from the nerve endings

neurohypophysis /ˌnjʊərəʊhaɪ'pɒfəsɪs/ *noun* the lobe at the back of the pituitary gland, which secretes oxytocin and vasopressin (NOTE: The plural is **neurohypophyses**.)

neurolemma /ˌnjʊərəʊ'lemə/ *noun* same as **neurilemma**

neuroleptic /ˌnjʊərəʊ'leptɪk/ *noun* an antipsychotic drug which calms a person and stops him or her from worrying, e.g. chlorpromazine hydrochloride

neurological /ˌnjʊərə'lɒdʒɪk(ə)l/ *adjective* referring to neurology

neurological assessment /ˌnjʊərəlɒdʒɪk(ə)l ə'sesmənt/ *noun* an evaluation of the health of a person with a disorder of the nervous system, using interviews, a physical examination, and specific diagnostic tests, sometimes with the help of a family member or close friend

neurologist /njʊ'rɒlədʒɪst/ *noun* a doctor who specialises in the study of the nervous system and the treatment of its diseases

neurology /njʊ'rɒlədʒi/ *noun* the scientific study of the nervous system and its diseases

neuroma /njʊ'rəʊmə/ *noun* a benign tumour formed of nerve cells and nerve fibres (NOTE: The plural is **neuromas** or **neuromata**.)

neuromuscular /ˌnjʊərəʊ'mʌskjʊlə/ *adjective* referring to both nerves and muscles

neuromuscular junction /ˌnjʊərəʊmʌskjʊlə 'dʒʌŋkʃən/ *noun* the point where a motor nerve joins muscle fibre. Also called **myoneural junction**

neuron /'njʊərəʊn/, **neurone** /'njʊərɒn/ *noun* a cell in the nervous system which transmits nerve impulses. Also called **nerve cell**

neuropathic bladder /ˌnjʊərəʊpæθɪk 'blædə/ *noun* a condition in which the bladder does not function properly because its nerve supply is damaged, e.g. due to an injury to the spinal cord

neuropathology /ˌnjʊərəʊpə'θɒlədʒi/ *noun* the study of diseases of the nervous system

neuropathy /njʊə'rɒpəθi/ *noun* a disease involving destruction of the tissues of the nervous system (NOTE: The plural is **neuropathies**.)

neurophysiology /ˌnjʊərəʊfɪzi'ɒlədʒi/ *noun* the study of the physiology of nerves

neuroplasty /'njʊərəʊplæsti/ *noun* surgery to repair damaged nerves

neuropsychiatry /ˌnjʊərəʊsaɪ'kaɪətri/ *noun* the study of mental and nervous disorders

neurorrhaphy /njʊ'rɔːrəfi/ *noun* a surgical operation to join by suture a nerve which has been cut (NOTE: The plural is **neurorraphies**.)

neurosecretion /ˌnjʊərəʊsɪ'kriːʃ(ə)n/ *noun* a substance secreted by a nerve cell

neurosis /njʊ'rəʊsɪs/ *noun* a disorder of the personality in which a person experiences obsessive negative emotions towards someone or something, e.g. fear of empty spaces or jealousy of a sibling. ◊ **psychoneurosis** (NOTE: The plural is **neuroses**.)

neurosurgeon /'njʊərəʊˌsɜːdʒən/ *noun* a surgeon who operates on the nervous system, including the brain and spinal cord

neurosurgery /'njʊərəʊˌsɜːdʒəri/ *noun* surgery on the nervous system, including the brain and spinal cord

neurotic /njʊ'rɒtɪk/ *adjective* relating to or having neurosis

neurotomy /njʊ'rɒtəmi/ *noun* a surgical operation to cut a nerve (NOTE: The plural is **neurotomies**.)

neurotoxic /ˌnjʊərəʊ'tɒksɪk/ *adjective* harmful or poisonous to nerve cells

neurotransmitter /ˌnjʊərəʊtræns'mɪtə/ *noun* a chemical substance which transmits nerve impulses from one neurone to another

neurotripsy /'njʊərəʊtrɪpsi/ *noun* surgical bruising or crushing of a nerve

neurotrophic /ˌnjʊərəʊ'trəʊfɪk/ *adjective* relating to the nutrition and maintenance of tissue of the nervous system

neurotropic /ˌnjʊərəʊ'trɒpɪk/ *adjective* referring to a bacterium which is attracted to and attacks nerves

neuter /'njuːtə/ *adjective* neither male nor female

neutral /'njuːtrəl/ *adjective* (of a substance) neither acid nor alkali ○ *A pH factor of 7 is neutral.*

neutralise /'njuːtrəlaɪz/, **neutralize** *verb* **1.** to counteract the effect of something ○ *Alkali poisoning can be neutralised by applying acid solution.* (NOTE: **neutralising – neutralised**) **2.** to form a salt from an acid

neutropenia /ˌnjuːtrə'piːniə/ *noun* a condition in which there are fewer neutrophils than usual in the blood

neutrophil /'njuːtrəfɪl/ *noun* a type of white blood cell with an irregular nucleus, which can attack and destroy bacteria. Also called **polymorph**

newton /'njuːt(ə)n/ *noun* an SI unit of measurement of force. Symbol **N**

new variant CJD /ˌnjuː ˌveəriənt ˌsiː dʒeɪ 'diː/ *noun* ♦ **variant CJD**

next-day pill /ˌnekst deɪ 'pɪl/ *noun* same as **morning-after pill**

next of kin /ˌnekst əv 'kɪn/ *noun* the person or persons who are most closely related to someone ○ *The hospital has notified the next of kin of the death of the accident victim.* (NOTE: Takes a singular or plural verb.)

nexus /'neksəs/ *noun* a point where two organs or tissues join

NHS *abbreviation* National Health Service

NHS Direct /ˌen eɪtʃ es dɪ'rekt/ *noun* in the UK, a national telephone helpline run by nurses to provide information about health and health services for the public

NHS targets /ˌen eɪtʃ es 'tɑːgɪts/ *plural noun* performance targets set by the government for individual NHS primary care trusts

niacin /'naɪəsɪn/ *noun* a vitamin of the vitamin B complex found in milk, meat, liver, kidney, yeast, beans, peas and bread, lack of which can cause mental disorders and pellagra. Also called **nicotinic acid**

nicardipine /nɪ'kɑːdɪpiːn/ *noun* a drug which slows down the movement of calcium ions into smooth muscle cells, used especially to treat angina

NICE /naɪs/ *abbreviation* National Institute for Clinical Excellence

niclosamide /nɪ'kləʊsəmaɪd/ *noun* a drug used for removing tapeworms

nicotine /'nɪkətiːn/ *noun* the main alkaloid substance found in tobacco

nicotine addiction /'nɪkətiːn əˌdɪkʃən/ *noun* an addiction to nicotine, derived from smoking tobacco

nicotine patch /'nɪkətiːn pætʃ/ *noun* a patch containing nicotine which is released slowly into the bloodstream, applied to the skin as a method of curing nicotine addiction

nicotine replacement /'nɪkətiːn rɪˌpleɪsmənt/ *noun* the use of nicotine patches or other products to help during an attempt to give up smoking

nicotinic acid /ˌnɪkətɪnɪk 'æsɪd/ same as **niacin**

nictation /nɪk'teɪʃ(ə)n/, **nictitation** /nɪktɪ'teɪʃ(ə)n/ *noun* the act of winking

nidation /naɪ'deɪʃ(ə)n/ *noun* 1. the process of building the endometrial layers of the uterus between menstrual periods 2. the point in the development of an embryo at which the fertilised ovum reaches the uterus and implants in the wall of the uterus. Also called **implantation**

nidus /'naɪdəs/ *noun* a site where bacteria can settle and breed, which becomes a centre of infection (NOTE: The plural is **niduses** or **nidi**.)

Niemann-Pick disease /ˌniːmən 'pɪk dɪˌziːz/ *noun* a rare inherited disease of a group which affect metabolism. Signs in babies include feeding difficulties, a large abdomen within 3 to 6 months, and progressive loss of early motor skills.

nifedipine /nɪ'fedɪpiːn/ *noun* a drug which stops the heart muscles from taking up calcium, used in the treatment of high blood pressure and angina pectoris

night nurse /'naɪt nɜːs/ *noun* a nurse who is on duty at night

night sweat /'naɪt swet/ *noun* heavy sweating when a person is asleep at night

night terror /'naɪt ˌterə/ *noun* a period of disturbed sleep, which a child does not remember afterwards

nigra /'naɪgrə/ ♦ **linea nigra**

nihilism /'naɪhɪlɪz(ə)m/ *noun* the rejection of all the usual social conventions and beliefs, especially of morality and religion

nihilistic /ˌnaɪhɪ'lɪstɪk/ *adj* relating to or showing a belief in nihilism

nipple /'nɪp(ə)l/ *noun* 1. same as **mammilla** 2. *US* a rubber teat on a baby's feeding bottle

Nissl granule /'nɪs(ə)l ˌgrænjuːl/, **Nissl body** /'nɪs(ə)l ˌbɒdi/ *noun* one of the coarse granules surrounding the nucleus in the cytoplasm of nerve cells. See illustration at **NEURONE** in Supplement [Described 1894. After Franz Nissl (1860–1919), German psychiatrist.]

nit /nɪt/ *noun* an egg or larva of a louse

nitrate /'naɪtreɪt/ *noun* a drug such as glyceryl trinitrate which dilates the vessels leading to the heart muscle and lowers cardiac work by reducing venous return to the heart, for rapid relief of angina and in heart failure (NOTE: Patients can develop tolerance to these drugs.)

-nitrate /naɪtreɪt/ *suffix* used in names of nitrate drugs

nitrazepam /naɪ'træzɪpæm/ *noun* a tranquilliser used in some sleeping pills

nitrofurantoin /ˌnaɪtrəʊfjʊ'ræntəʊɪn/ *noun* a drug which helps to prevent the growth of bacteria, used in the treatment of urinary infections

nitrogen /'naɪtrədʒən/ *noun* a chemical element, which is a gas that is the main component of air and is an essential part of protein (NOTE: The chemical symbol is **N**.)

nitroglycerin /ˌnaɪtrəʊ'glɪsərɪn/ *noun* a drug which helps the veins and coronary arteries to become wider

nitrous oxide /ˌnaɪtrəs 'ɒksaɪd/ *noun* a colourless gas with a sweet smell, used in combination with other gases as an anaesthetic in dentistry and surgery. Also called **laughing gas**

nm *abbreviation* nanometre

NMC *abbreviation* Nursing and Midwifery Council

nmol *abbreviation* nanomole

NMR *abbreviation* nuclear magnetic resonance

noci- /nəʊsi/ *prefix* pain or injury

nociassociation /ˌnəʊsiəˌsəʊsiˈeɪʃ(ə)n/ *noun* an unconscious release of nervous energy, e.g. as a result of shock

nociceptive /ˌnəʊsiˈseptɪv/ *adjective* referring to nerves which carry pain to the brain

nociceptor /ˈnəʊsiˌseptə/ *noun* a sensory nerve which carries pain to the brain

noct- /nɒkt/ *prefix* same as **nocti-**

nocte /ˈnɒkti/ *adverb* at night. Opposite **mane** (NOTE: used on prescriptions)

nocti- /nɒkti/ *prefix* referring to night

nocturia /nɒkˈtjʊəriə/ *noun* the fact of passing an unusually large quantity of urine during the night

nocturnal /nɒkˈtɜːn(ə)l/ *adjective* referring to or taking place at night

nocturnal emission /nɒkˌtɜːn(ə)l ɪˈmɪʃ(ə)n/ *noun* the production of semen from the penis while a man is asleep

nocturnal enuresis /nɒkˌtɜːn(ə)l ˌenjʊ ˈriːsɪs/ *noun* the act of passing urine when asleep in bed at night. Also called **bedwetting**

nodal /ˈnəʊd(ə)l/ *adjective* referring to nodes

nodal tachycardia /ˌnəʊd(ə)l ˌtæki'kɑːdiə/ *noun* a sudden attack of rapid heartbeats. Also called **paroxysmal tachycardia**

node /nəʊd/ *noun* a small mass of tissue

node of Ranvier /ˌnəʊd əv ˈrænviə/ *noun* one of a series of gaps in the myelin sheath surrounding a nerve fibre. See illustration at **NEURONE** in Supplement

nod off /ˌnɒd ˈɒf/ *verb* to fall asleep (*informal*)

nodosum /nəʊˈdəʊsəm/ ♦ **erythema nodosum**

nodular /ˈnɒdjʊlə/ *adjective* formed of nodules

nodule /ˈnɒdjuːl/ *noun* **1.** a small node or group of cells. ◊ **Bohn's nodules 2.** the anterior part of the inferior vermis

nomen proprium /ˌnəʊmən ˈprəʊpriəm/ *noun* full form of **n.p.**

non- /nɒn/ *prefix* not

non-absorbable suture /ˌnɒn əbˌzɔːbəb(ə)l ˈsuːtʃə/ *noun* a suture made of a substance which cannot be absorbed into the body and which eventually has to be removed

non-accidental injury /ˌnɒn æksɪˌdent(ə)l ˈɪndʒəri/ *noun* an injury which is not caused accidentally

non-allergenic /ˌnɒn ælə'dʒenɪk/ *adjective* not aggravating an allergy

non-compliance /ˌnɒn kəmˈplaɪəns/ *noun* the failure to take drugs at the correct times and in the dosages prescribed, or to take them at all

non compos mentis /ˌnɒn ˌkɒmpəs ˈmentɪs/ *adjective* referring to a person who is mentally incapable of managing his or her own affairs (NOTE: From a Latin phrase meaning 'not of sound mind'.)

non-contagious /ˌnɒn kənˈteɪdʒəs/ *adjective* not contagious

non-emergency surgery /ˌnɒn ɪˌmɜːdʒənsi ˈsɜːdʒəri/ *noun* a surgical operation which does not need to be performed immediately because it is for a condition which is not life-threatening, e.g. joint replacement. Also called **non-urgent surgery**

non-Hodgkins lymphoma /ˌnɒn ˌhɒdʒkɪnz lɪmˈfəʊmə/ *noun* a cancer of the lymph nodes which differs from Hodgkin's disease by the absence of a particular type of cell with double nuclei

non-insulin-dependent diabetes /ˌnɒn ˌɪnsjʊlɪn dɪˌpendənt ˌdaɪəˈbiːtiːz/ *noun* same as **Type II diabetes mellitus**

non-invasive /ˌnɒn ɪnˈveɪzɪv/ *adjective* referring to treatment which does not involve entering the body by making an incision. ◊ **invasive**

non-maleficence /ˌnɒn məˈlefɪs(ə)ns/ *noun* the concept that professionals in the health service have a duty to protect the patient from harm

non-medical prescriber /ˌnɒn ˌmedɪk(ə)l prɪˈskraɪbə/ *noun* a professional healthcare worker who prescribes medicine but is not a registered doctor or dentist

non-official drug /ˌnɒn əˌfɪʃ(ə)l ˈdrʌg/ *noun* a drug that is not listed in the national pharmacopoeia. Compare **official drug**

non-palpable /ˌnɒn ˈpælpəb(ə)l/ *adjective* not able to be felt when touched

non-secretor /ˌnɒn sɪˈkriːtə/ *noun* a person who does not secrete substances indicating ABO blood group into mucous fluids such as semen or saliva

non-smoker /ˌnɒn ˈsməʊkə/ *noun* a person who does not smoke

non-specific /ˌnɒn spəˈsɪfɪk/ *adjective* not caused by any single identifiable cause

non-specific urethritis /ˌnɒn spəˌsɪfɪk ˌjʊərɪˈθraɪtɪs/ *noun* any sexually transmitted inflammation of the urethra not caused by gonorrhoea (*dated*) Abbreviation **NSU**

non-steroidal /ˌnɒn steˈrɔɪd(ə)l/ *adjective* not containing steroids

non-steroidal anti-inflammatory drug /ˌnɒn steˌrɔɪd(ə)l ˌænti ɪnˈflæmət(ə)ri drʌg/ *noun* a drug used in the treatment of pain associated with inflammation, including rheumatic disease, post-operative analgesia and dysmenorrhoea, by inhibiting the release of prostaglandins. Abbreviation **NSAID** (NOTE: Non-steroidal anti-inflammatory drugs have names ending in **-fen:** **ibuprofen.**)

non-union /ˌnɒn ˈjuːnjən/ *noun* a condition in which the two parts of a fractured bone do not join together and do not heal

non-urgent surgery /ˌnɒn ˈɜːdʒənt ˈsɜːdʒəri/ same as **non-emergency surgery**

noradrenaline /ˌnɔːrəˈdrenəlɪn/ *noun* a hormone secreted by the medulla of the adrenal glands which acts as a vasoconstrictor and is used to maintain blood pressure in shock, haemorrhage or hypotension

normal /ˈnɔːm(ə)l/ *adjective* usual, ordinary or conforming to a standard ○ *After he took the tablets, his blood pressure went back to normal.* ○ *Her temperature is two degrees above normal.* ○ *He had an above-normal pulse rate.* ○ *Is it normal for a person with myopia to suffer from headaches?*

normo- /nɔːməʊ/ *prefix* normal, usual or expected

normoblast /ˈnɔːməʊblæst/ *noun* an early form of a red blood cell, usually found only in bone marrow but occurring in the blood in some types of leukaemia and anaemia

normocyte /ˈnɔːməʊsaɪt/ *noun* a red blood cell

normotension /ˌnɔːməʊˈtenʃən/ *noun* blood pressure at the usual level

normotensive /ˌnɔːməʊˈtensɪv/ *adjective* referring to blood pressure at the usual level

Norton score /ˈnɔːt(ə)n skɔː/ *noun* a scale for deciding how likely it is that pressure sores will develop, used mostly in assessing elderly patients

nortriptyline /nɔːˈtrɪptəliːn/ *noun* a drug used to reduce pain and as an antidepressant and tranquilliser

nose /nəʊz/ *noun* an organ through which a person breathes and smells

nosebleed /ˈnəʊzbliːd/ *noun* an incident of bleeding from the nose, usually caused by a blow or by sneezing, by blowing the nose hard or by high blood pressure (*informal*) ○ *She had a headache, followed by a violent nosebleed.* Also called **epistaxis**

noso- /nɒsəʊ/ *prefix* disease

nosocomial /ˌnɒsəʊˈkəʊmiəl/ *adjective* referring to hospitals

nosocomial infection /ˌnɒsəʊˌkəʊmiəl ɪnˈfekʃən/ *noun* an infection which is passed on to a person being treated in a hospital

nosology /nɒˈsɒlədʒi/ *noun* the classification of diseases

nostril /ˈnɒstrɪl/ *noun* one of the two passages in the nose through which air is breathed in or out ○ *His right nostril is blocked.* (NOTE: The nostrils are also referred to as the **nares**.)

notch /nɒtʃ/ *noun* a depression on a surface, usually on a bone, but sometimes on an organ. ◊ **cardiac notch**

notifiable /ˈnəʊtɪfaɪəb(ə)l/ *adjective* referring to an infectious disease which must be reported to the appropriate authorities when it occurs, so that they can attempt to control its spread

notifiable disease /ˌnəʊtɪfaɪəb(ə)l dɪˈziːz/ *noun* a serious infectious disease which, in the UK, has to be reported by a doctor to the Department of Health so that steps can be taken to stop it spreading

noxious /ˈnɒkʃəs/ *adjective* harmful ○ *a noxious gas*

n.p. *noun* the name of the drug written on the label of its container. Full form **nomen proprium**

NPO *abbreviation* used to refer to patients being kept without food ○ *The patient should be kept NPO for five hours before the operation.* Full form **ne per oris**

NSAID *abbreviation* non-steroidal anti-inflammatory drug

NSF /ˌen es ˈef/ *noun* a long-term strategy for improving a specific area of healthcare across the UK. Full form **National Service Framework**

NSU *abbreviation* non-specific urethritis

nucha /ˈnjuːkə/ *noun* same as **nape** (NOTE: The plural is **nuchae**.)

nuchal /ˈnjuːk(ə)l/ *adjective* referring to the back of the neck

nucle- /njuːkli/ *prefix* same as **nucleo-** (*used before vowels*)

nuclear /ˈnjuːkliə/ *adjective* referring to nuclei, e.g. of a cell or an atom

nuclear magnetic resonance /ˌnjuːkliə mægˌnetɪk ˈrezənəns/ *noun* a scanning technique using magnetic fields and radio waves which reveals abnormalities in soft tissue and body fluids. ◊ **magnetic resonance imaging**. Abbreviation **NMR**

nuclear medicine /ˌnjuːkliə ˈmed(ə)s(ə)n/ *noun* the use of radioactive substances for detecting and treating disorders

nuclease /ˈnjuːklieɪz/ *noun* an enzyme which breaks down nucleic acids

nucleic acid /njuːˌkliːɪk ˈæsɪd/ *noun* an organic acid of a type found in all living cells, which consists of complex nucleotide chains which pass on genetic information, e.g. DNA or RNA

nucleo- /njuːkliəʊ/ *prefix* referring to a cell or atomic nucleus

nucleus /ˈnjuːkliəs/ *noun* **1.** the central body in a cell, which contains DNA and RNA and controls the function and characteristics of the cell. See illustration at **NEURONE** in Supplement **2.** a group of nerve cells in the brain or spinal cord (NOTE: The plural is **nuclei**.)

nullipara /nʌˈlɪpərə/ *noun* a woman who has never had a child (NOTE: The plural is **nulliparas** or **nulliparae**.) ■ *adjective* referring to a woman who has never had a child

nurse /nɜːs/ *noun* a person who looks after sick people in a hospital or helps a doctor in a local surgery. Some nurses may be trained to diagnose and treat patients. ○ *She works as a nurse in the local hospital.* ○ *He's training to be a nurse.* ◊ **nurse practitioner** ■ *verb* to look after a sick person, or to be employed as a nurse ○ *When he was ill his mother nursed him until he was better.*

nurse executive director /ˌnɜːs ɪgˌzekjʊtɪv daɪˈrektə/ *noun* in the UK, a senior nurse who sits on the Board of an NHS Trust and has corporate as well as professional responsibilities in the organisation for nursing and sometimes other aspects such as quality or human resources

nurse practitioner /ˌnɜːs prækˈtɪʃ(ə)nə/ *noun* a nurse with additional clinical training at degree level who often works independently, assessing, diagnosing and treating patients, particularly in primary care

nurse prescriber /ˈnɜːs prɪˌskraɪbə/ *noun* a nurse who is qualified and entitled to prescribe medicines for patients

nurse station /ˈnɜːs ˌsteɪʃ(ə)n/, **nurses' station** /ˈnɜːsɪz ˌsteɪʃ(ə)n/ *noun* an area in or near a ward from which nurses work, keep records and control the activities of the ward

nursing /ˈnɜːsɪŋ/ *noun* **1.** the work or profession of being a nurse ○ *He has chosen nursing as his career.* **2.** care for sick people provided by a nurse ■ *adjective* providing care as a nurse

Nursing and Midwifery Council /ˌnɜːsɪŋ ən mɪdˈwɪfəri ˌkaʊnsəl/ *noun* in the UK, an organisation that sets standards for the education, practice and conduct of nurses, midwives and health visitors. Abbreviation **NMC**

nursing audit /ˈnɜːsɪŋ ˌɔːdɪt/ *noun* a formal detailed review of records or observation of nursing actions so that judgments can be made about the quality of nursing care being given

nursing dependency /ˈnɜːsɪŋ dɪˌpendənsi/ *noun* the extent to which a patient requires nursing care

nursing development unit /ˌnɜːsɪŋ dɪˈveləpmənt ˌjuːnɪt/ *noun* a nurse-led ward or unit that sets out to demonstrate by example innovative high-quality care, to reflect on practice and draw lessons from this experience, and to provide learning opportunities for other nurses. Abbreviation **NDU**

nursing diagnosis /ˈnɜːsɪŋ daɪəˌgnəʊsɪs/ *noun* an assessment of the nursing needs of a patient, which forms the basis of a subsequent care plan

nursing home /ˈnɜːsɪŋ həʊm/ *noun* a house where convalescents or dependent elderly people can live under medical supervision by a qualified nurse

nursing intervention /ˌnɜːsɪŋ ˌɪntəˈvenʃən/ *noun* the treatment of illness by nursing care, without surgery

nursing language /ˈnɜːsɪŋ ˌlæŋgwɪdʒ/ *noun* the standard terminology used in nursing

nursing model /ˈnɜːsɪŋ ˌmɒd(ə)l/ *noun* a set of stated principles about nursing which gives professionals a way of formulating a plan of care, assessing its success and addressing any problems which arise from it

nursing mother /ˌnɜːsɪŋ ˈmʌðə/ *noun* a mother who breast-feeds her baby

Nursing Officer /ˈnɜːsɪŋ ˌɒfɪsə/ *noun* in the UK, a nurse employed by the Department of Health to assist the Chief Nursing Officer in providing professional advice to Ministers and policy-makers

nursing practice /ˈnɜːsɪŋ ˌpræktɪs/ *noun* treatment given by nurses

nursing process /ˌnɜːsɪŋ ˈprəʊses/ *noun* a standard method of treatment and documentation of treatment carried out by nurses

nursing standard /ˈnɜːsɪŋ ˌstændəd/ *noun* an accepted level of achievement by which nursing care can be assessed or compared

nutation /njuːˈteɪʃ(ə)n/ *noun* involuntary nodding of the head

nutrient /ˈnjuːtriənt/ *noun* a substance in food which is necessary to provide energy or to help the body grow, e.g. protein, fat or a vitamin

nutrition /njuːˈtrɪʃ(ə)n/ *noun* the study of the supply of nutrients to the body from digesting food

nutritional /njuːˈtrɪʃ(ə)n(ə)l/ *adjective* referring to nutrition

nyct- /nɪkt/ *prefix* night or darkness

nyctalopia /ˌnɪktəˈləʊpiə/ *noun* the condition of being unable to see in bad light. Also called **night blindness**

nyctophobia /ˌnɪktəˈfəʊbiə/ *noun* fear of the dark

nymphae /ˈnɪmfiː/ *plural noun* same as **labia minora**

nympho- /nɪmfəʊ/ *prefix* **1.** female sexuality **2.** nymphae

nymphomania /ˌnɪmfəˈmeɪniə/ *noun* an obsessive sexual urge in a woman (NOTE: A similar condition in a man is called **satyriasis**.)

nymphomaniac /ˌnɪmfəˈmeɪniæk/ *noun* a woman who has an unusually obsessive sexual urge (NOTE: This term is regarded as offensive.)

nystagmus /nɪˈstægməs/ *noun* a rapid, involuntary movement of the eyes up and down or from side to side

nystatin /naɪˈstætɪn/ *noun* an anti-microbial drug used in the treatment of fungal infections, especially thrush

O

oat cell carcinoma /'əʊt sel kɑːsɪ,nəʊmə/ *noun* a type of cancer of the bronchi, with distinctive small cells

OB *abbreviation* obstetrics

obese /əʊ'biːs/ *adjective* so overweight as to be at risk of several serious illnesses, including diabetes and heart disease

obesity /əʊ'biːsɪti/ *noun* the condition of being seriously overweight

objective /əb'dʒektɪv/ *noun* an aim or goal ■ *adjective* **1.** existing independently of any individual person's mind **2.** not influenced by any bias or prejudice caused by personal feelings **3.** referring to symptoms of illness which can be observed by somebody other than the person who is ill. Compare **subjective**

obligate /'ɒblɪgeɪt/ *adjective* referring to an organism which exists and develops in only one way, e.g. a virus which is a parasite only inside cells

oblique /ə'bliːk/ *adjective* lying at an angle

oblique fissure /ə,bliːk 'fɪʃə/ *noun* a groove between the superior and inferior lobes of a lung. See illustration at LUNGS in Supplement

oblique fracture /ə,bliːk 'fræktʃə/ *noun* a fracture in which the bone is broken diagonally

oblique muscle /ə,bliːk 'mʌs(ə)l/ *noun* **1.** each of two muscles in the wall of the abdomen **2.** each of two muscles which control the movement of the eyeball

obliterans /ə'blɪtərænz/ ♦ **endarteritis obliterans**

oblongata /,ɒblɒŋ'geɪtə/ ♦ **medulla oblongata**

observable /əb'zɜːvəb(ə)l/ *adjective* which can be seen or measured

observation /,ɒbzə'veɪʃ(ə)n/ *noun* the process of watching and examining a person or thing over a period of time ○ *She was admitted to hospital for observation.*

observation register /,ɒbzə'veɪʃ(ə)n ,redʒɪstə/ *noun* a record of children who have had problems at birth, or soon after their birth, and so need particular follow-up care from a health visitor, general practitioner or social worker

observe /əb'zɜːv/ *verb* **1.** to see something ○ *The nurses observed signs of improvement in the patient's condition.* ○ *The girl's mother observed symptoms of anorexia.* **2.** to watch a person or thing carefully in order to discover something ○ *Observe the way in which the patient is lying.* **3.** to take something into account ○ *You're expected to observe the rules of conduct.*

obsession /əb'seʃ(ə)n/ *noun* a mental disorder in which a person has a fixed idea or emotion which he or she cannot get rid of, even if he or she knows it is wrong or unpleasant ○ *She has an obsession about cats.*

obsessional /əb'seʃ(ə)n(ə)l/ *adjective* referring to or having an obsession ○ *He is suffering from an obsessional disorder.*

obsessive /əb'sesɪv/ *adjective* having or showing an obsession ○ *He has an obsessive desire to steal little objects.*

obsessive action /əb,sesɪv 'ækʃən/ *noun* an action such as washing which is repeated over and over again and indicates a mental disorder

obsessive–compulsive disorder /əb,sesɪv kəm'pʌlsɪv dɪs,ɔːdə/ *noun* a mental disorder characterised by the need to perform repeated ritual acts such as checking or cleaning, which can be treated with psychotherapy and antidepressants. Abbreviation **OCD**

obstetrical forceps /əb,stetrɪk(ə)l 'fɔːseps/ *plural noun* a type of large forceps used to hold a baby's head during childbirth

obstetrician /,ɒbstə'trɪʃ(ə)n/ *noun* a doctor who specialises in obstetrics

obstetrics /əb'stetrɪks/ *noun* a branch of medicine and surgery dealing with pregnancy, childbirth and the period immediately after childbirth. Abbreviation **OB**

obstipation /,ɒbstɪ'peɪʃ(ə)n/ *noun* severe constipation, often caused by a blockage in the intestines

obstruction /əb'strʌkʃən/ *noun* something which blocks a passage or a blood vessel

obstructive /əb'strʌktɪv/ *adjective* caused by an obstruction

obstructive jaundice /əb,strʌktɪv 'dʒɔːndɪs/ *noun* jaundice caused by an obstruction of the bile ducts. Also called **posthepatic jaundice**. ◊ **acholuric jaundice**, **icterus gravis neonatorum**

obstructive lung disease /əb,strʌktɪv 'lʌŋ dɪ,ziːz/ *noun* bronchitis and emphysema

obstructive sleep apnoea /əb,strʌktɪv 'sliːp ,æpniə/ *noun* the stopping of breathing, or difficulty in breathing, during sleep, resulting in loud snoring

obturation /,ɒbtjʊ'reɪʃ(ə)n/ *noun* the act of obstructing a body passage, or the state of a body passage when it is obstructed, e.g. by hard faeces

obturator /'ɒbtjʊreɪtə/ *noun* one of two muscles in the pelvis which govern the movement of the hip and thigh

obturator foramen /,ɒbtjʊreɪtə fə'reɪmən/ *noun* an opening in the hip bone near the acetabulum. See illustration at **PELVIS** in Supplement (NOTE: The plural is **obturator foramina**.)

obtusion /əb'tjuːʒ(ə)n/ *noun* a condition in which perception and feelings become dulled

OC *abbreviation* oral contraceptive

occipital /ɒk'sɪpɪt(ə)l/ *adjective* referring to the back of the head ■ *noun* same as **occipital bone**

occipital bone /ɒk'sɪpɪt(ə)l bəʊn/, **occipital** *noun* the bone at the back of the head

occipital condyle /ɒk,sɪpɪt(ə)l 'kɒndaɪl/ *noun* a round part of the occipital bone which joins it to the atlas

occipito-anterior /ɒk,sɪpɪtəʊ æn'tɪəriə/ *adjective* referring to a position of a baby during birth, in which the baby faces the mother's back

occipito-posterior /ɒk,sɪpɪtəʊ pɒ'stɪəriə/ *adjective* referring to a position of a baby during birth in which the baby faces the front

occiput /'ɒksɪpʌt/ *noun* the lower part of the back of the head or skull (NOTE: The plural is **occiputs** or **occipita**.)

occlusion /ə'kluːʒ(ə)n/ *noun* **1.** a thing which blocks a passage or which closes an opening **2.** the way in which the teeth in the upper and lower jaws fit together when the jaws are closed (NOTE: A bad fit between the teeth is a **malocclusion**.)

occlusive /ə'kluːsɪv/ *adjective* referring to occlusion or blocking

occlusive stroke /ə,kluːsɪv 'strəʊk/ *noun* a stroke caused by a blood clot

occlusive therapy /ə,kluːsɪv 'θerəpi/ *noun* a treatment for a squint in which the good eye is covered up in order to encourage the squinting eye to become straight

occult /ə'kʌlt/ *adjective* not easy to see with the naked eye. Opposite **overt**

occult blood /ə,kʌlt 'blʌd/ *noun* very small quantities of blood in the faeces, which can only be detected by tests

occupancy rate /'ɒkjʊpənsi reɪt/ *noun* the number of beds occupied in a hospital, shown as a percentage of all the beds

occupational /,ɒkjʊ'peɪʃ(ə)nəl/ *adjective* referring to work

occupational asthma /,ɒkjʊpeɪʃ(ə)n(ə)l 'æsmə/ *noun* asthma caused by materials with which people come into contact at work

occupational dermatitis /,ɒkjʊpeɪʃ(ə)n(ə)l ,dɜːmə'taɪtɪs/ *noun* dermatitis caused by materials touched at work

occupational disease /,ɒkjʊpeɪʃ(ə)nəl dɪ'ziːz/ *noun* a disease which is caused by the type of work a person does or the conditions in which a person works, e.g. a disease caused by dust or chemicals in a factory

occupational hazard /,ɒkjʊpeɪʃ(ə)n(ə)l 'hæzəd/ *noun* a dangerous situation related to the working environment

occupational health nurse /,ɒkjʊpeɪʃ(ə)n(ə)l 'helθ ,nɜːs/ *noun* a nurse who deals with health problems of people at work. Abbreviation **OH nurse**

occupational medicine /,ɒkjʊpeɪʃ(ə)n(ə)l 'med(ə)sɪn/ *noun* the branch of medicine concerned with accidents and diseases connected with work

occupational therapist /,ɒkjʊpeɪʃ(ə)n(ə)l 'θerəpɪst/ *noun* a qualified health professional who offers patients occupational therapy

occupational therapy /,ɒkjʊpeɪʃ(ə)n(ə)l 'θerəpi/ *noun* light work or hobbies used as a means of treatment, especially for physically challenged or mentally ill people, to promote independence during the recovery period after an illness or operation

OCD *abbreviation* obsessive-compulsive disorder

oct- /ɒkt/ *prefix* same as **octo-** (*used before vowels*)

octo- /ɒktəʊ/, **octa-** /ɒktə/ *prefix* eight

ocular /'ɒkjʊlə/ *adjective* referring to the eye ○ *Opticians are trained to detect all kinds of ocular imbalance.*

ocular dominance /,ɒkjʊlə 'dɒmɪnəns/ *noun* a condition in which a person uses one eye more than the other

ocular prosthesis /,ɒkjʊlə prɒs'θiːsɪs/ *noun* a false eye

oculist /'ɒkjʊlɪst/ *noun* a qualified physician or surgeon who specialises in the treatment of eye disorders

oculo- /ɒkjʊləʊ/ *prefix* eye

oculomotor /,ɒkjʊləʊ'məʊtə/ *adjective* referring to movements of the eyeball

oculomotor nerve /,ɒkjʊləʊ'məʊtə ,nɜːv/ *noun* the third cranial nerve which controls the eyeballs and eyelids

oculonasal /ˌɒkjʊləʊˈneɪz(ə)l/ *adjective* referring to both the eye and the nose

oculoplethysmography /ˌɒkjʊləʊˌpleˈθɪz ˈmɒɡrəfi/ *noun* measurement of the pressure inside the eyeball

OD /əʊ ˈdiː/ *abbreviation* overdose

o.d. *adverb* (*written on a prescription*) every day. Full form **omni die** ■ *abbreviation* overdose

ODA *abbreviation* operating department assistant

odont- /ɒdɒnt/ *prefix* same as **odonto-** (*used before vowels*)

odonto- /ɒdɒntəʊ/ *prefix* tooth

odontoid /ɒˈdɒntɔɪd/ *adjective* similar to a tooth, especially in shape

odontoid process /ɒˌdɒntɔɪd ˈprəʊses/ *noun* a projecting part of a vertebra, shaped like a tooth

odontology /ˌɒdɒnˈtɒlədʒi/ *noun* the study of teeth and associated structures, and their disorders

odyn- /ɒdɪn/ *prefix* same as **odyno-** (*used before vowels*)

-odynia /ədɪniə/ *suffix* pain

odyno- /ɒdɪnəʊ/ *prefix* pain

odynophagia /ɒˌdɪnəˈfeɪdʒə/ *noun* a condition in which pain occurs when food is swallowed

oedema /ɪˈdiːmə/ *noun* the swelling of part of the body caused by accumulation of fluid in the intercellular tissue spaces ○ *Her main problem is oedema of the feet.* Also called **dropsy.** ◊ **tumescence**

oedematous /ɪˈdemətəs/ *adjective* referring to oedema (NOTE: The US spelling is **edematous**.)

Oedipus complex /ˈiːdɪpəs ˌkɒmpleks/ *noun* (*in Freudian psychology*) a condition in which a boy feels sexually attracted to his mother and sees his father as an obstacle

oesophag- /iːsɒfədʒ/ *prefix* same as **oesophago-** (*used before vowels*)

oesophageal /iːˌsɒfəˈdʒiːəl/ *adjective* referring to the oesophagus (NOTE: The US spelling is **esophageal**.)

oesophageal hiatus /iːˌsɒfəˌdʒiːəl haɪ ˈeɪtəs/ *noun* the opening in the diaphragm through which the oesophagus passes

oesophageal spasm /iːˌsɒfəˌdʒiːəl ˈspæz(ə)m/ *noun* a spasm in the oesophagus

oesophageal ulcer /iːˌsɒfəˌdʒiːəl ˈʌlsə/ *noun* an ulcer in the oesophagus

oesophageal varices /iːˌsɒfəˌdʒiːəl ˈværɪsiːz/ *plural noun* varicose veins in the oesophagus

oesophagectomy /iːˌsɒfəˈdʒektəmi/ *noun* a surgical operation to remove part of the oesophagus (NOTE: The plural is **oesophagectomies**.)

oesophagi /iːˈsɒfəgi/ *plural of* **oesophagus**

oesophagitis /iːˌsɒfəˈdʒaɪtɪs/ *noun* inflammation of the oesophagus, caused by acid juices from the stomach or by infection

oesophago- /iːsɒfəgəʊ/ *prefix* oesophagus (NOTE: The US spelling is **esophago-**.)

oesophagogastroduodenoscopy /ɪː ˌsɒfəgəʊˌɡæstrəʊˌdjuːəʊdəˈnɒskəpi/ *noun* a surgical operation in which a tube is put down into the oesophagus so that the doctor can examine it, the stomach and the duodenum. Abbreviation **OGD** (NOTE: The plural is **oesophagogastroduodenoscopies**.)

oesophagojejunostomy /iːˌsɒfəgəʊdʒɪ ˌdʒuːˈnɒstəmi/ *noun* a surgical operation to create a junction between the jejunum and the oesophagus after the stomach has been removed (NOTE: The plural is **oesophagojejunostomies**.)

oesophagoscope /iːˈsɒfəgəʊskəʊp/ *noun* a thin tube with a light at the end, which is passed down the oesophagus to examine it

oesophagoscopy /iːˌsɒfəˈgɒskəpi/ *noun* an examination of the oesophagus with an oesophagoscope (NOTE: The plural is **oesophagoscopies**.)

oesophagostomy /iːˌsɒfəˈgɒstəmi/ *noun* a surgical operation to make an opening in the oesophagus to allow the person to be fed, usually after an operation on the pharynx (NOTE: The plural is **oesophagostomies**.)

oesophagus /iːˈsɒfəgəs/ *noun* a tube down which food passes from the pharynx to the stomach

oestradiol /ˌiːstrəˈdaɪɒl/ *noun* a type of oestrogen secreted by an ovarian follicle, which stimulates the development of secondary sexual characteristics in females at puberty (NOTE: A synthetic form of oestradiol is given as treatment for oestrogen deficiency. The US spelling is **estradiol**.)

oestriol /ˈiːstrɪɒl/ *noun* a placental hormone with oestrogenic properties, found in the urine of pregnant women (NOTE: The US spelling is **estriol**.)

oestrogen /ˈiːstrədʒən/ *noun* any steroid hormone which stimulates the development of secondary sexual characteristics in females at puberty (NOTE: The US spelling is **estrogen**.)

oestrogenic hormone /ˌiːstrədʒenɪk ˈhɔːməʊn/ *noun* synthetic oestrogen used to treat conditions which develop during menopause (NOTE: The US spelling is **estrogenic hormone**.)

official drug /əˌfɪʃ(ə)l ˈdrʌg/ *noun* any drug listed in the national pharmacopoiea. Compare **non-official drug**

OGD *abbreviation* oesophagogastroduodenoscopy

OH nurse /ˌəʊ 'eɪtʃ ˌnɜːs/ *abbreviation* occupational health nurse

-oid /ɔɪd/ *suffix* like or related to

ointment /'ɔɪntmənt/ *noun* a smooth oily medicinal preparation which can be spread on the skin to soothe or to protect

old age /ˌəʊld 'eɪdʒ/ *noun* a period in a person's life, usually taken to be after the age of sixty-five

olecranon /əʊ'lekrənɒn/, **olecranon process** /əʊ'lekrənɒn ˌprəʊsəs/ *noun* a curved projecting part at the end of the ulna at the elbow, which gives rise to a painful tingling sensation if hit by accident. Also called **funny bone**

oleic /əʊ'liːɪk/ *adjective* referring to oil

oleic acid /əʊˌliːɪk 'æsɪd/ *noun* a fatty acid which is present in most oils

oleo- /əʊliəʊ/ *prefix* oil

oleum /'əʊliəm/ *noun* oil (*used in pharmacy*)

olfaction /ɒl'fækʃən/ *noun* **1.** the sense of smell **2.** the way in which a person's sensory organs detect smells

olfactory /ɒl'fækt(ə)ri/ *adjective* referring to the sense of smell

olfactory cortex /ɒlˌfækt(ə)ri 'kɔːteks/ *noun* the parts of the cerebral cortex which receive information about smell

olfactory nerve /ɒl'fækt(ə)ri nɜːv/ *noun* the first cranial nerve which controls the sense of smell

olig- /ɒlɪg/ *prefix* same as **oligo-** (*used before vowels*)

oligaemia /ˌɒlɪ'giːmiə/ *noun* a condition in which a person has too little blood in his or her circulatory system (NOTE: The US spelling is **oligemia.**)

oligo- /ɒlɪgəʊ/ *prefix* few or little

oligodactylism /ˌɒlɪgəʊ'dæktɪlɪz(ə)m/ *noun* a congenital condition in which a baby is born without some fingers or toes

oligodipsia /ˌɒlɪgəʊ'dɪpsiə/ *noun* a condition in which a person does not want to drink

oligodontia /ˌɒlɪgəʊ'dɒnʃə/ *noun* a state in which most of the teeth are lacking

oligohydramnios /ˌɒlɪgəʊhaɪ'dræmniəs/ *noun* a condition in which the amnion surrounding the fetus contains too little amniotic fluid

oligomenorrhoea /ˌɒlɪgəʊmenə'riːə/ *noun* a condition in which a person menstruates infrequently (NOTE: The US spelling is **oligomenorrhea.**)

oligo-ovulation /ˌɒlɪgəʊ ˌɒvjʊ'leɪʃ(ə)n/ *noun* ovulation which does not occur as often as is usual

oligospermia /ˌɒlɪgəʊ'spɜːmiə/ *noun* a condition in which there are too few spermatozoa in the semen

oliguria /ˌɒlɪ'gjʊəriə/ *noun* a condition in which a person does not produce enough urine

-ology /ɒlədʒi/ *suffix* area of study

-olol /əlɒl/ *suffix* beta blocker ○ *atenolol* ○ *propranolol hydrochloride*

o.m. *adverb* (*written on a prescription*) every morning. Full form **omni mane**

om- /ɒm/ *prefix* relating to the shoulder

-oma /əʊmə/ *suffix* tumour

oment- /əʊment/ *prefix* omentum

omenta plural of **omentum**

omental /əʊ'ment(ə)l/ *adjective* referring to the omentum

omentum /əʊ'mentəm/ *noun* a double fold of peritoneum hanging down over the intestines. Also called **epiploon** (NOTE: The plural is **omenta.** For other terms referring to the omentum see words beginning with **epiplo-.**)

omeprazole /əʊ'meprəzəʊl/ *noun* a drug which reduces the amount of acid released in the stomach, used in the treatment of ulcers and heartburn

omphal- /ɒmfəl/ *prefix* same as **omphalo-** (*used before vowels*)

omphalitis /ˌɒmfə'laɪtɪs/ *noun* inflammation of the navel

omphalo- /ɒmfələʊ/ *prefix* navel

omphalocele /'ɒmfələsiːl/ *noun* a hernia in which part of the intestine protrudes through the abdominal wall near the navel

omphalus /'ɒmfələs/ *noun* a scar with a depression in the middle of the abdomen where the umbilical cord was detached after birth. Also called **navel**, **umbilicus** (NOTE: The plural is **omphali.**)

-omycin /əʊmaɪsɪn/ *suffix* macrolide drug ○ *erythromycin*

o.n. *adverb* (*written on a prescription*) every night. Full form **omni nocte**

onco- /ɒŋkəʊ/ *prefix* tumour

oncogene /'ɒŋkədʒiːn/ *noun* a part of the genetic system which causes malignant tumours to develop

oncogenesis /ˌɒŋkə'dʒenəsɪs/ *noun* the origin and development of a tumour

oncogenic /ˌɒŋkə'dʒenɪk/ *adjective* causing tumours to develop ○ *an oncogenic virus*

oncologist /ɒŋ'kɒlədʒɪst/ *noun* a doctor who specialises in oncology, especially cancer

oncology /ɒŋ'kɒlədʒi/ *noun* the scientific study of new growths, especially cancers

oncometer /ɒŋ'kɒmɪtə/ *noun* **1.** an instrument for measuring swelling in an arm or leg using changes in their blood pressure **2.** an instrument for measuring the variations in size of the kidney and other organs of the body

ondansetron /ɒnˈdænsɪtrɒn/ *noun* a drug which helps to prevent the production of serotonin, used to control nausea and vomiting caused by drug treatment and radiotherapy for cancer

onych- /ɒnɪk/ *prefix* same as **onycho-** (*used before vowels*)

onycho- /ɒnɪkəʊ/ *prefix* nails

onycholysis /ˌɒnɪˈkɒləsɪs/ *noun* a condition in which a nail becomes separated from its bed, without falling out

onychomadesis /ˌɒnɪkəʊməˈdiːsɪs/ *noun* a condition in which the nails fall out

onychomycosis /ˌɒnɪkəʊmaɪˈkəʊsɪs/ *noun* an infection of a nail with a fungus

oo- /əʊə/ *prefix* ovum or embryo

oocyte /ˈəʊəsaɪt/ *noun* a cell which forms from an oogonium and becomes an ovum by meiosis

oocyte donation /ˌəʊəsaɪt dəʊˈneɪʃ(ə)n/ *noun* the transfer of oocytes from one woman to another who cannot produce her own, so that she can have a baby. The oocytes are removed in a laparoscopy and fertilised in vitro.

oogenesis /ˌəʊəˈdʒenəsɪs/ *noun* the formation and development of ova

COMMENT: In oogenesis, an oogonium produces an oocyte, which develops through several stages to produce a mature ovum. Polar bodies are also formed which do not develop into ova.

oophor- /əʊəfɔːr/ *prefix* same as **oophoro-** (*used before vowels*)

oophore /ˈəʊəfɔː/ *noun* same as **ovary**

oophorectomy /ˌəʊəfəˈrektəmi/ *noun* a surgical operation to remove an ovary. Also called **ovariectomy** (NOTE: The plural is **oophorectomies**.)

oophoritis /ˌəʊəfəˈraɪtɪs/ *noun* inflammation in an ovary, which can be caused by mumps. Also called **ovaritis**

oophoro- /əʊɒfərəʊ/ *prefix* ovary

oophorocystectomy /əʊˌɒfərəʊsɪˈstektəmi/ *noun* a surgical operation to remove an ovarian cyst (NOTE: The plural is **oophorocystectomies**.)

oophorocystosis /əʊˌɒfərəʊsɪˈstəʊsɪs/ *noun* the development of one or more ovarian cysts

oophoron /əʊˈɒfərɒn/ *noun* same as **ovary** (*technical*) (NOTE: The plural is **oophora**.)

oophoropexy /əʊˈɒfərəpeksi/ *noun* a surgical operation to attach an ovary (NOTE: The plural is **oophoropexies**.)

oophorosalpingectomy /əʊˌɒfərəˌsælpɪnˈdʒektəmi/ *noun* a surgical operation to remove an ovary and the Fallopian tube attached to it (NOTE: The plural is **oophorosalpingectomies**.)

op /ɒp/ *noun* an operation (*informal*)

OP *abbreviation* outpatient

opacification /əʊˌpæsɪfɪˈkeɪʃ(ə)n/ *noun* the fact of becoming opaque, as the lens does in a case of cataract

opacity /əʊˈpæsɪti/ *noun* the fact of not allowing light to pass through

opaque /əʊˈpeɪk/ *adjective* not allowing light to pass through

operant conditioning /ˈɒpərənt kənˌdɪʃ(ə)nɪŋ/ *noun* a form of learning which takes place when a piece of spontaneous behaviour is either reinforced by a reward or discouraged by punishment

operating department assistant /ˌɒpəreɪtɪŋ dɪˌpɑːtmənt əˈsɪstənt/ *noun* a person who works in an operating department. Abbreviation **ODA**

operating microscope /ˈɒpəreɪtɪŋ ˌmaɪkrəskəʊp/ *noun* a special microscope with two eyepieces and a light, used in very delicate surgery

operating table /ˈɒpəreɪtɪŋ ˌteɪb(ə)l/ *noun* a special table on which the patient is placed to undergo a surgical operation

operating theatre /ˈɒpəreɪtɪŋ ˌθɪətə/ *noun* a special room in a hospital, where surgical operations are carried out (NOTE: The US term is **operating room**.)

operation /ˌɒpəˈreɪʃ(ə)n/ *noun* **1.** a surgical procedure carried out to repair or remove a damaged body part ○ *She's had an operation on her foot.* (NOTE: A surgeon **performs** or **carries out** an operation **on** a patient.) **2.** the way in which a drug acts

ophth- /ɒfθ, ɒpθ/ *prefix* eye

ophthalm- /ɒfθælm, ɒpθælm/ *prefix* same as **ophthalmo-** (*used before vowels*)

ophthalmectomy /ˌɒfθælˈmektəmi/ *noun* a surgical operation to remove an eye (NOTE: The plural is **ophthalmectomies**.)

ophthalmia /ɒfˈθælmiə/ *noun* inflammation of the eye

ophthalmia neonatorum /ɒfˌθælmiə ˌniːəʊneɪˈtɔːrəm/ *noun* conjunctivitis of a newborn baby, beginning 21 days after birth, caused by infection in the birth canal

ophthalmic /ɒfˈθælmɪk/ *adjective* referring to the eye

ophthalmic nerve /ɒfˈθælmɪk nɜːv/ *noun* a branch of the trigeminal nerve, supplying the eyeball, the upper eyelid, the brow and one side of the scalp

ophthalmic optician /ɒfˌθælmɪk ɒpˈtɪʃ(ə)n/, **ophthalmic practitioner** /ɒfˌθælmɪk prækˈtɪʃ(ə)nə/ *noun* same as **optician**

ophthalmic surgeon /ɒfˌθælmɪk ˈsɜːdʒən/ *noun* a surgeon who specialises in surgery to treat eye disorders

ophthalmitis /ˌɒfθæl'maɪtɪs/ *noun* inflammation of the eye

ophthalmo- /ɒfθælməʊ, ɒpθælməʊ/ *prefix* eye or eyeball

ophthalmological /ɒfˌθælmə'lɒdʒɪk(ə)l/ *adjective* referring to ophthalmology

ophthalmologist /ˌɒfθæl'mɒlədʒɪst/ *noun* a doctor who specialises in the study of the eye and its diseases. Also called **eye specialist**

ophthalmology /ˌɒfθæl'mɒlədʒi/ *noun* the study of the eye and its diseases

ophthalmoplegia /ˌɒfθælmə'pliːdʒə/ *noun* paralysis of the muscles of the eye

ophthalmoscope /ɒf'θælməskəʊp/ *noun* an instrument containing a bright light and small lenses, used by a doctor to examine the inside of an eye

ophthalmoscopy /ˌɒfθæl'mɒskəpi/ *noun* an examination of the inside of an eye using an ophthalmoscope (NOTE: The plural is **ophthalmoscopies**.)

ophthalmotomy /ˌɒfθæl'mɒtəmi/ *noun* a surgical operation to make a cut in the eyeball (NOTE: The plural is **ophthalmotomies**.)

ophthalmotonometer /ˌɒfθælmətə'nɒmɪtə/ *noun* an instrument which measures pressure inside the eye

-opia /əʊpiə/ *suffix* eye condition

opiate /'əʊpiət/ *noun* a sedative which is prepared from opium, e.g. morphine or codeine

opistho- /ɒpɪsθəʊ/ *prefix* backbone

opisthotonos /ˌɒpɪs'θɒtənəs/ *noun* a spasm of the body in which the spine is arched backwards, occurring, e.g., in people with tetanus

opium /'əʊpiəm/ *noun* a substance made from poppies which is used in the preparation of codeine and heroin

opponens /ə'pəʊnənz/ *noun* one of a group of muscles which control the movements of the fingers, especially one which allows the thumb and little finger to come together

opportunist /ˌɒpə'tjuːnɪst/, **opportunistic** /ˌɒpətjuː'nɪstɪk/ *adjective* referring to a parasite or microorganism which takes advantage of the host's weakened state to cause infection

opsonic index /ɒpˌsɒnɪk 'ɪndeks/ *noun* a number which gives the strength of an individual's serum reaction to bacteria

opsonin /'ɒpsənɪn/ *noun* a substance, usually an antibody, in blood which sticks to the surface of bacteria and helps to destroy them

optic /'ɒptɪk/ *adjective* referring to the eye or to sight ·

optical /'ɒptɪk(ə)l/ *adjective* **1.** same as **optic 2.** relating to the visible light spectrum

optical fibre /ˌɒptɪk(ə)l 'faɪbə/ *noun* an artificial fibre which can carry light or images

optical illusion /ˌɒptɪk(ə)l ɪ'luːʒ(ə)n/ *noun* something which is seen wrongly so that it appears to be something else

optic chiasma /ˌɒptɪk kaɪ'æzmə/ *noun* a structure where some of the optic nerves from each eye partially cross each other in the hypothalamus

optic disc /'ɒptɪk dɪsk/ *noun* the point on the retina where the optic nerve starts. Also called **optic papilla**

optic fundus /ˌɒptɪk 'fʌndəs/ *noun* the back part of the inside of the eye, opposite the lens

optician /ɒp'tɪʃ(ə)n/ *noun* a qualified person who specialises in making glasses and in testing eyes and prescribing lenses. Also called **ophthalmic optician**

optic nerve /'ɒptɪk nɜːv/ *noun* the second cranial nerve which transmits the sensation of sight from the eye to the brain. See illustration at EYE in Supplement

optic neuritis /ˌɒptɪk njʊ'raɪtɪs/ *noun* same as **retrobulbar neuritis**

optic papilla /ˌɒptɪk pə'pɪlə/ *noun* same as **optic disc**

optics /'ɒptɪks/ *noun* the study of the visible light spectrum and sight

opto- /ɒptəʊ/ *prefix* sight

optometrist /ɒp'tɒmətrɪst/ *noun* mainly US a person who specialises in testing eyes and prescribing lenses

optometry /ɒp'tɒmətri/ *noun* the testing of eyes and prescribing of lenses to correct sight

-oquine /əkwɪn/ *suffix* antimalarial drug ○ *chloroquine*

OR *abbreviation US* operating room

ora /'ɔːrə/ *plural noun* plural of **os 2**

oral /'ɔːrəl/ *adjective* **1.** referring to the mouth **2.** referring to medication that is swallowed ○ *an oral contraceptive* Compare **enteral**, **parenteral**

oral cavity /ˌɔːrəl 'kævɪti/ *noun* the mouth

oral contraceptive /ˌɔːrəl ˌkɒntrə'septɪv/ *noun* a contraceptive pill which is swallowed

oral hygiene /ˌɔːrəl 'haɪdʒiːn/ *noun* the practice of keeping the mouth clean by gargling and mouthwashes

orally /'ɔːrəli/ *adverb* by swallowing ○ *not to be taken orally*

oral medication /ˌɔːrəl ˌmedɪ'keɪʃ(ə)n/ *noun* medication which is taken by swallowing

oral rehydration therapy /ˌɔːrəl ˌriːhaɪ'dreɪʃ(ə)n ˌθerəpi/ *noun* the administration of a simple glucose and electrolyte solution to treat acute diarrhoea, particularly in children, which has greatly reduced the number of deaths from dehydration. Abbreviation **ORT**

oral thermometer /ˌɔːrəl θə'mɒmɪtə/ *noun* a thermometer which is put into the mouth to take someone's temperature

orbicularis /ɔːˌbɪkjʊˈleərɪs/ *noun* a circular muscle in the face

orbicularis oculi /ɔːˌbɪkjʊˌleərɪs ˈɒkjʊlaɪ/ *noun* a muscle which opens and closes the eye

orbicularis oris /ɔːˌbɪkjʊˌleərɪs ˈɔːrɪs/ *noun* a muscle which closes the lips tight

orbit /ˈɔːbɪt/ *noun* the hollow bony depression in the front of the skull in which each eye and lacrimal gland are situated. Also called **eye socket**

orbital /ˈɔːbɪt(ə)l/ *adjective* referring to the orbit

orchi- /ɔːki/ *prefix* testiss

orchidalgia /ˌɔːkɪˈdældʒə/ *noun* a neuralgic-type pain in a testis

orchidectomy /ˌɔːkɪˈdektəmi/ *noun* a surgical operation to remove a testis (NOTE: The plural is **orchidectomies**.)

orchidopexy /ˈɔːkɪdəʊˌpeksi/ *noun* a surgical operation to place an undescended testis in the scrotum. Also called **orchiopexy** (NOTE: The plural is **orchidopexies**.)

orchiepididymitis /ˌɔːkiˌepɪdɪdɪˈmaɪtɪs/ *noun* a condition in which a testicle and its epididymis become swollen

orchiopexy /ˈɔːkiəʊˌpeksi/ *noun* same as **orchidopexy** (NOTE: The plural is **orchiopexies**.)

orchis /ˈɔːkɪs/ *noun* a testis

orchitis /ɔːˈkaɪtɪs/ *noun* inflammation of the testes, characterised by hypertrophy, pain and a sensation of weight

Orem's model /ˈɔːrəmz ˌmɒd(ə)l/ *noun* a modern model for nursing which focuses on a person's ability to perform self-care, defined as activities which individuals initiate and perform on their own behalf to maintain life, health and well-being. The goal of nursing is to help people meet their own self-care demands.

organ /ˈɔːgən/ *noun* a part of the body which is distinct from other parts and has a particular function, e.g. the liver, an eye or ovaries

organic /ɔːˈgænɪk/ *adjective* **1.** referring to organs in the body **2.** coming from an animal, plant or other organism

organic disease /ɔːˌgænɪk dɪˈziːz/, **organic disorder** /ɔːˌgænɪk dɪsˈɔːdə/ *noun* a disease or disorder associated with physical changes in one or more organs of the body

organisation /ˌɔːgənaɪˈzeɪʃ(ə)n/, **organization** *noun* **1.** a group of people set up for a particular purpose **2.** the planning or arranging of something ○ *the organisation of the rota* **3.** the way in which the component parts of something are arranged

organism /ˈɔːgənɪz(ə)m/ *noun* any single plant, animal, bacterium, fungus or other living thing

organo- /ɔːgənəʊ, ɔːgænəʊ/ *prefix* organ

organ of Corti /ˌɔːgən əv ˈkɔːti/ *noun* a membrane in the cochlea which takes sounds and converts them into impulses sent to the brain along the auditory nerve. Also called **spiral organ** [Described 1851. After Marquis Alfonso Corti (1822–88), Italian anatomist and histologist.]

organ transplant /ˈɔːgən ˌtrænsplɑːnt/ *noun* a surgical operation to transplant an organ from one person to another

orgasm /ˈɔːgæz(ə)m/ *noun* the climax of the sexual act, when a person experiences a moment of great excitement

orifice /ˈɒrɪfɪs/ *noun* an opening in the body, e.g. the mouth or anus

origin /ˈɒrɪdʒɪn/ *noun* **1.** the source or beginning of something **2.** a place where a muscle is attached, or where the branch of a nerve or blood vessel begins

oris /ˈɔːrɪs/ ♦ **cancrum oris, orbicularis oris**

ornithosis /ˌɔːnɪˈθəʊsɪs/ *noun* a disease of birds which can be passed to humans as a form of pneumonia

oro- /ɔːrəʊ/ *prefix* mouth

orogenital /ˌɔːrəʊˈdʒenɪt(ə)l/ *adjective* relating to both the mouth and the genitals

oropharynx /ˌɔːrəʊˈfærɪŋks/ *noun* a part of the pharynx below the soft palate at the back of the mouth (NOTE: The plural is **oropharynxes** or **oropharynges**.)

ORT *abbreviation* oral rehydration therapy

ortho- /ɔːθəʊ/ *prefix* correct or straight

orthodontics /ˌɔːθəʊˈdɒntɪks/ *noun* a branch of dentistry which deals with correcting badly placed teeth

orthopaedic /ˌɔːθəˈpiːdɪk/ *adjective* **1.** referring to treatment which corrects badly formed bones or joints **2.** referring to or used in orthopaedics (NOTE: The US spelling is **orthopedic**.)

orthopaedic collar /ˌɔːθəpiːdɪk ˈkɒlə/ *noun* a special strong collar to support the head of a person with neck injuries or a condition such as cervical spondylosis

orthopaedic hospital /ˌɔːθəpiːdɪk ˈhɒspɪt(ə)l/ *noun* a hospital which specialises in operations to correct badly formed joints or bones

orthopaedics /ˌɔːθəˈpiːdɪks/ *noun* a branch of surgery dealing with irregularities, diseases and injuries of the locomotor system (NOTE: The US spelling is **orthopedics**.)

orthopaedic surgeon /ˌɔːθəpiːdɪk ˈsɜːdʒən/ *noun* a surgeon who specialises in orthopaedics

orthopnoea /ˌɔːθɒpˈniːə/ *noun* a condition in which a person has great difficulty in breathing while lying down. ◊ **dyspnoea** (NOTE: The US spelling is **orthopnea**.)

orthopnoeic /ˌɔːθəpˈniːɪk/ *adjective* referring to orthopnoea (NOTE: The US spelling is **orthopneic**.)

orthoptics /ɔːˈθɒptɪks/ *noun* the study of methods used to treat squints

orthoptist /ɔːˈθɒptɪst/ *noun* an eye specialist, working in an eye hospital, who treats squints and other disorders of eye movement

orthoptoscope /ɔːˈθɒptəskəʊp/ *noun* same as **amblyoscope**

orthosis /ɔːˈθəʊsɪs/ *noun* a device which is fitted to the outside of the body to support a weakness or correct a malformation, e.g. a surgical collar or leg brace (NOTE: The plural is **orthoses**.)

orthostatic /ˌɔːθəˈstætɪk/ *adjective* referring to the position of the body when standing up straight

orthostatic hypotension /ˌɔːθəstætɪk ˌhaɪpəʊˈtenʃən/ *noun* a common condition where the blood pressure drops when a person stands up suddenly, causing dizziness

orthotics /ɔːˈθɒtɪks/ *plural noun* the branch of medical engineering which deals with the design and fitting of devices such as braces in the treatment of orthopaedic disorders (NOTE: Takes a singular verb.)

orthotist /ˈɔːθətɪst/ *noun* a qualified person who fits orthoses

Ortolani's sign /ˌɔːtəˈlɑːniz saɪn/, **Ortolani manoeuvre** /ˌɔːtəˈlɑːni məˌnuːvə/, **Ortolani's test** /ˌɔːtəˈlɑːniz test/ *noun* a test for congenital dislocation of the hip in babies aged 6–12, in which the hip makes sharp sounds if the joint is rotated [Described 1937. After Marino Ortolani (1904–83), Italian orthopaedic surgeon.]

os /ɒs/ *noun* (*technical*) **1.** a bone (NOTE: The plural is **ossa**.) **2.** the mouth (NOTE: The plural is **ora**.)

OSA *abbreviation* obstructive sleep apnoea

osche- /ˈɒski/ *prefix* relating to the scrotum

oscillation /ˌɒsɪˈleɪʃ(ə)n/ *noun* **1.** the action of moving backwards and forwards between two points at a regular speed **2.** a single movement between two points

oscilloscope /ɒˈsɪləskəʊp/ *noun* a device which produces a visual record of an electrical current on a screen using a cathode ray tube. It is used in the testing of electronic equipment and in measuring electrical impulses of the heart or the brain.

osculum /ˈɒskjʊləm/ *noun* a small opening or pore (NOTE: The plural is **oscula**.)

-osis /əʊsɪs/ *suffix* disease

Osler's nodes /ˈɒsləz nəʊdz/ *plural noun* tender swellings at the ends of fingers and toes in people who have subacute bacterial endocarditis [Described 1885. After Sir William Osler (1849–1919), Professor of Medicine in Montreal, Philadelphia, Baltimore and then Oxford.]

osm- /ɒzm/ *prefix* **1.** smell **2.** osmosis

osmoreceptor /ˌɒzməʊrɪˈseptə/ *noun* a cell in the hypothalamus which checks the level of osmotic pressure in the blood by altering the secretion of ADH and regulates the amount of water in the blood

osmosis /ɒzˈməʊsɪs/ *noun* the movement of a solvent from one part of the body through a semipermeable membrane to another part where there is a higher concentration of molecules

osmotic pressure /ɒzˌmɒtɪk ˈpreʃə/ *noun* the pressure required to stop the flow of a solvent through a membrane

osseous /ˈɒsiəs/ *adjective* referring to or resembling bone

osseous labyrinth /ˌɒsiəs ˈlæbərɪnθ/ *noun* same as **bony labyrinth**

ossicle /ˈɒsɪk(ə)l/ *noun* a small bone

ossification /ˌɒsɪfɪˈkeɪʃ(ə)n/ *noun* the formation of bone. Also called **osteogenesis**

ossium /ˈɒsiəm/ ♦ **fragilitas ossium**

ost- /ɒst/ *prefix* same as **osteo-** (*used before vowels*)

ostectomy /ɒˈstektəmi/ *noun* a surgical operation in which a bone, or a piece of bone, is removed (NOTE: The plural is **ostectomies**.)

osteitis /ˌɒstiˈaɪtɪs/ *noun* inflammation of a bone due to injury or infection

osteitis deformans /ˌɒstiˌaɪtɪs diːˈfɔːmənz/ *noun* a disease which gradually softens bones in the spine, legs and skull, so that they become curved. Also called **Paget's disease**

osteitis fibrosis cystica /ˌɒstiaɪtɪs faɪ ˌbrəʊsɪs ˈsɪstɪkə/ *noun* a generalised weakness of bones, caused by excessive activity of the thyroid gland and associated with formation of cysts, in which bone tissue is replaced by fibrous tissue. Also called **von Recklinghausen's disease** (NOTE: The localised form is **osteitis fibrosis localista**.)

osteo- /ɒstiəʊ/ *prefix* bone

osteoarthritis /ˌɒstiəʊɑːˈθraɪtɪs/ *noun* a degenerative disease of middle-aged and elderly people characterised by inflamed joints which become stiff and painful. Also called **osteoarthrosis**

osteoarthropathy /ˌɒstiəʊɑːˈθrɒpəθi/ *noun* a disease of the bone and cartilage at a joint, particularly the ankles, knees or wrists, associated with carcinoma of the bronchi

osteoarthrosis /ˌɒstiəʊɑːˈθrəʊsɪs/ *noun* same as **osteoarthritis**

osteoarthrotomy /ˌɒstiəʊɑːˈθrɒtəmi/ *noun* a surgical operation to remove the articular end of a bone (NOTE: The plural is **osteoarthrotomies**.)

osteochondritis /ˌɒstiəʊkənˈdraɪtɪs/ *noun* degeneration of the epiphyses

osteochondritis dissecans /ˌɒstiəʊkəndraɪtɪs ˈdɪsəkænz/ *noun* a painful condition where pieces of articular cartilage become detached from the joint surface

osteochondrosis /ˌɒstiəʊkɒnˈdrəʊsɪs/ *noun* a disorder of cartilage and bone formation which affects the joints in children, causing pain and a limp, probably due to circulation disturbances to that part of the bone

osteoclast /ˈɒstiəʊklæst/ *noun* a cell which destroys bone

osteocyte /ˈɒstiəʊsaɪt/ *noun* a bone cell

osteogenesis /ˌɒstiəʊˈdʒenəsɪs/ *noun* same as **ossification**

osteogenesis imperfecta /ˌɒstiəʊˌdʒenəsɪs ɪmpəˈfektə/ *noun* a congenital condition in which bones are brittle and break easily due to unusual bone formation. Also called **brittle bone disease**

osteology /ˌɒstiˈɒlədʒi/ *noun* the study of bones and their structure

osteolysis /ˌɒstiˈɒləsɪs/ *noun* destruction of bone tissue by osteoclasts

osteolytic /ˌɒstiəʊˈlɪtɪk/ *adjective* referring to osteolysis

osteoma /ˌɒstiˈəʊmə/ *noun* a benign tumour in a bone (NOTE: The plural is **osteomas** or **osteomata**.)

osteomalacia /ˌɒstiəʊməˈleɪʃə/ *noun* a condition in adults in which the bones become soft because of lack of calcium and Vitamin D, or limited exposure to sunlight

osteomyelitis /ˌɒstiəʊmaɪəˈlaɪtɪs/ *noun* inflammation of the interior of bone, especially the marrow spaces

osteon /ˈɒstiɒn/ *noun* same as **Haversian system**

osteopath /ˈɒstiəʊˌpæθ/ *noun* a person who practises osteopathy

osteopathy /ˌɒstiˈɒpəθi/ *noun* **1.** the treatment of disorders by massage and manipulation of joints **2.** any disease of bone (NOTE: The plural is **osteopathies**.)

osteopetrosis /ˌɒstiəʊpəˈtrəʊsɪs/ *noun* a disease of a group in which bones increase in density. Also called **marble bone disease**

osteophyte /ˈɒstiəʊfaɪt/ *noun* a bony growth

osteoplasty /ˈɒstiəʊplæsti/ *noun* plastic surgery on bones

osteoporosis /ˌɒstiəʊpɔːˈrəʊsɪs/ *noun* a condition in which the bones become thin, porous and brittle, due to low levels of oestrogen, lack of calcium and lack of physical exercise. Also called **brittle bone disease**

osteosarcoma /ˌɒstiəʊsɑːˈkəʊmə/ *noun* a malignant tumour of bone cells (NOTE: The plural is **osteosarcomas** or **osteosarcomata**.)

osteosclerosis /ˌɒstiəʊskləˈrəʊsɪs/ *noun* a condition in which the bony spaces become hardened as a result of persistent inflammation

osteotome /ˈɒstiəʊtəʊm/ *noun* a type of chisel used by surgeons to cut bone

osteotomy /ˌɒstiˈɒtəmi/ *noun* a surgical operation to cut a bone, especially to relieve pain in a joint (NOTE: The plural is **osteotomies**.)

ostium /ˈɒstiəm/ *noun* an opening into a passage (NOTE: The plural is **ostia**.)

-ostomy /ɒstəmi/ *suffix* operation to make an opening

OT *abbreviation* occupational therapist

ot- /əʊt/ *prefix* same as **oto-** (*used before vowels*)

otalgia /əʊˈtældʒə/ *noun* same as **earache**

OTC *abbreviation* referring to medication which can be bought freely at a chemist's shop, and does not need a prescription. Full form **over the counter**

OTC drug /ˌəʊ tiː ˈsiː drʌg/ *noun* same as **over-the-counter drug**

otic /ˈəʊtɪk/ *adjective* referring to the ear

otitis /əʊˈtaɪtɪs/ *noun* inflammation of the ear

otitis externa /əʊˌtaɪtɪs ɪkˈstɜːnə/ *noun* inflammation of the external auditory meatus to the eardrum

otitis interna /əʊˌtaɪtɪs ɪnˈtɜːnə/ *noun* inflammation of the inner ear. Also called **labyrinthitis**

otitis media /əʊˌtaɪtɪs ˈmiːdiə/ *noun* an infection of the middle ear, usually accompanied by headaches and fever. Also called **middle ear infection**, **tympanitis**

oto- /əʊtəʊ/ *prefix* ear

otolaryngologist /ˌəʊtəʊlærɪŋˈgɒlədʒɪst/ *noun* a doctor who specialises in treatment of diseases of the ear and throat

otolaryngology /ˌəʊtəʊlærɪŋˈgɒlədʒi/ *noun* the study of diseases of the ear and throat

otolith /ˈəʊtəlɪθ/ *noun* a stone which forms in the inner ear

otolith organ /ˌəʊtəlɪθ ˈɔːgən/ *noun* one of two pairs of sensory organs in the inner ear, the saccule and the utricle, which pass information to the brain about the position of the head

otologist /əʊˈtɒlədʒɪst/ *noun* a doctor who specialises in the study of the ear

otology /əʊˈtɒlədʒi/ *noun* the scientific study of the ear and its diseases

-otomy /ɒtəmi/ *suffix* an act of cutting into an organ or part of the body in a surgical operation

otoplasty /ˈəʊtəplæsti/ *noun* plastic surgery of the external ear to repair damage or deformity

otorhinolaryngologist /ˌəʊtəʊˌraɪnəʊˌlærɪŋˈgɒlədʒɪst/ *noun* a doctor who specialises in the study of the ear, nose and throat

otorhinolaryngology /ˌəʊtəʊˌraɪnəʊˌlærɪŋˈgɒlədʒi/ *noun* the study of the ear, nose and throat. Also called **ENT**

otorrhagia /ˌəʊtəˈreɪdʒə/ *noun* bleeding from the external ear

otorrhoea /ˌəʊtəˈriːə/ *noun* the discharge of pus from the ear (NOTE: The US spelling is **otorrhea**.)

otosclerosis /ˌəʊtəʊskləˈrəʊsɪs/ *noun* a condition in which the ossicles in the middle ear become thicker and the stapes becomes fixed to the oval window leading to deafness

otoscope /ˈəʊtəskəʊp/ *noun* same as **auriscope**

otospongiosis /ˌəʊtəˌspʌndʒiˈəʊsɪs/ *noun* the formation of spongy bone in the labyrinth of the ear which occurs in otosclerosis

Otosporin /ˈəʊtəspɒrɪn/ a trade name for ear drops containing hydrocortisone, neomycin and polymyxin

ototoxic /ˌəʊtəˈtɒksɪk/ *adjective* referring to a drug or an effect which is damaging to organs or nerves involved in hearing or balance

outcome /ˈaʊtkʌm/ *noun* a measure of the result of an intervention or treatment, e.g. the mortality rate following different methods of surgery ○ *medical outcomes*

outer /ˈaʊtə/ *adjective* outside or external

outer ear /ˌaʊtə ˈɪə/ *noun* the part of the ear which is on the outside of the head, together with the passage leading to the eardrum. Also called **external ear**

outer pleura /ˌaʊtə ˈplʊərə/ *noun* same as **parietal pleura**

out-of-body experience /ˌaʊt əv ˈbɒdi ɪk ˌspɪəriəns/ *noun* an occasion when a person feels as though they have left their body and, often, travelled along a tunnel towards a bright light

outpatient /ˈaʊtpeɪʃ(ə)nt/ *noun* someone who comes to a hospital for treatment but does not stay overnight ○ *She goes for treatment as an outpatient.* Abbreviation **OP**. Compare **inpatient**

outpatient department /ˈaʊtpeɪʃ(ə)nt dɪ ˌpɑːtmənt/, **outpatients' department** /ˈaʊtpeɪʃ(ə)nts dɪˌpɑːtmənt/, **outpatients' clinic** /ˈaʊtpeɪʃ(ə)nts ˌklɪnɪk/ *noun* a department of a hospital which deals with outpatients

outreach /ˈaʊtriːtʃ/ *noun* services provided for patients or the public in general, outside a hospital or clinic

ova /ˈəʊvə/ plural of **ovum**

oval window /ˈəʊv(ə)l ˌwɪndəʊ/ *noun* an oval opening between the middle ear and the inner ear. Also called **fenestra ovalis**. See illustration at **EAR** in Supplement

ovar- /ˈəʊvər/ *prefix* same as **ovari-** (*used before vowels*)

ovari- /ˈəʊvəri/ *prefix* ovaries

ovarian /əʊˈveəriən/ *adjective* referring to the ovaries

ovarian cancer /əʊˌveəriən ˈkænsə/ *noun* a malignant tumour of the ovary, which occurs especially after the menopause

ovarian cycle /əʊˌveəriən ˈsaɪk(ə)l/ *noun* the regular changes in the ovary during a woman's reproductive life

ovarian cyst /əʊˌveəriən ˈsɪst/ *noun* a cyst which develops in the ovaries

ovarian follicle /əʊˌveəriən ˈfɒlɪk(ə)l/ *noun* a cell which contains an ovum. Also called **Graafian follicle**

ovariectomy /ˌəʊvəriˈektəmi/ *noun* same as **oophorectomy** (NOTE: The plural is **ovariectomies**.)

ovariotomy /ˌəʊvəriˈɒtəmi/ *noun* a surgical operation to remove an ovary or a tumour in an ovary (NOTE: The plural is **ovariotomies**.)

ovaritis /ˌəʊvəˈraɪtɪs/ *noun* same as **oophoritis**

ovary /ˈəʊv(ə)ri/ *noun* one of two organs in a woman which produce ova or egg cells and secrete the female hormone oestrogen. Also called **oophoron**. See illustration at **UROGENITAL SYSTEM (FEMALE)** in Supplement (NOTE: The plural is **ovaries**. For other terms referring to ovaries, see words beginning with **oophor-, oophoro-**.)

over- /ˈəʊvə/ *prefix* too much

overbite /ˈəʊvəbaɪt/ *noun* the usual formation of the teeth, in which the top incisors come down over and in front of the bottom incisors when the jaws are closed

overcompensation /ˌəʊvəkɒmpənˈseɪʃ(ə)n/ *noun* an attempt by a person to remove the bad effects of a mistake or a fault in their character in which they make too much effort, and so cause some other problem

overflow incontinence /ˌəʊvəfləʊ ɪn ˈkɒntɪnəns/ *noun* a leakage of urine because the bladder is too full

overjet /ˈəʊvədʒet/ *noun* a space which separates the top incisors from the bottom incisors when the jaws are closed

oversew /ˈəʊvəsəʊ/ *verb* to sew a patch of tissue over a perforation (NOTE: **oversewing – oversewed – oversewn**)

overt /əʊˈvɜːt/ *adjective* easily seen with the naked eye. Opposite **occult**

over-the-counter drug /ˌəʊvə ðə ˈkaʊntə ˌdrʌg/ *noun* a drug which you can buy from a pharmacy without a doctor's prescription. Also called **OTC drug**

ovi- /ˈəʊvi/ *prefix* eggs or ova

oviduct /ˈəʊvɪdʌkt/ *noun* same as **Fallopian tube**

ovulate /ˈɒvjʊleɪt/ *verb* to release a mature ovum into a Fallopian tube (NOTE: **ovulating – ovulated**)

ovulation /ˌɒvjʊˈleɪʃ(ə)n/ *noun* the release of an ovum from the mature ovarian follicle into the Fallopian tube

ovum /ˈəʊvəm/ *noun* a female egg cell which, when fertilised by a spermatazoon, begins to develop into an embryo (NOTE: The plural is **ova**. For other terms referring to ova, see words beginning with **oo-**.)

-oxacin /ɒksəsɪn/ *suffix* quinolone drug ○ *ciprofloxacin*

oxidase /ˈɒksɪdeɪz/ *noun* an enzyme which encourages oxidation by removing hydrogen. ◊ **monoamine oxidase**

oxidation /ˌɒksɪˈdeɪʃ(ə)n/ *noun* the action of making oxides by combining with oxygen or removing hydrogen

oximeter /ɒkˈsɪmɪtə/ *noun* an instrument which measures the amount of oxygen in something, especially in blood

oxybutynin /ˌɒksiˈbjuːtənɪn/, **oxybutinin** *noun* a drug which reduces the need to pass urine

oxycephalic /ˌɒksikəˈfælɪk/ *adjective* referring to oxycephaly

oxycephaly /ˌɒksɪˈkefəli/ *noun* a condition in which the skull is shaped into a point, with exophthalmos and poor sight. Also called **turricephaly**

oxygen /ˈɒksɪdʒən/ *noun* a chemical element that is a common colourless gas which is present in the air and essential to human life (NOTE: The chemical symbol is **O**.)

oxygenate /ˈɒksɪdʒəneɪt/ *verb* to combine blood with oxygen (NOTE: **oxygenating – oxygenated**)

oxygenated blood /ˌɒksɪdʒəneɪtɪd ˈblʌd/ *noun* blood which has received oxygen in the lungs and is being carried to the tissues along the arteries. Also called **arterial blood**. Compare **deoxygenated blood** (NOTE: Oxygenated blood is brighter red than venous deoxygenated blood.)

oxygenation /ˌɒksɪdʒəˈneɪʃ(ə)n/ *noun* the fact of becoming combined or filled with oxygen ○ *Blood is carried along the pulmonary artery to the lungs for oxygenation.*

oxygenator /ˈɒksɪdʒəˌneɪtə/ *noun* a machine which puts oxygen into the blood, used as an artificial lung in surgery

oxygen cylinder /ˈɒksɪdʒən ˌsɪlɪndə/ *noun* a heavy metal tube which contains oxygen and is connected to a patient's oxygen mask

oxygen mask /ˈɒksɪdʒən mɑːsk/ *noun* a mask connected to a supply of oxygen, which can be put over the face to help someone with breathing difficulties

oxygen tent /ˈɒksɪdʒən tent/ *noun* a type of cover put over a person so that he or she can breathe in oxygen

oxygen therapy /ˈɒksɪdʒən ˌθerəpi/ *noun* any treatment involving the administering of oxygen, e.g. in an oxygen tent or in emergency treatment for heart failure

oxyhaemoglobin /ˌɒksiˌhiːməˈɡləʊbɪn/ *noun* a compound of haemoglobin and oxygen, which is the way oxygen is carried in arterial blood from the lungs to the tissues. ◊ **haemoglobin** (NOTE: The US spelling is **oxyhemoglobin**.)

oxyntic /ɒkˈsɪntɪk/ *adjective* referring to glands and cells in the stomach which produce acid

oxyntic cell /ɒkˈsɪntɪk sel/ *noun* a cell in the gastric gland which secretes hydrochloric acid. Also called **parietal cell**

oxytetracycline /ˌɒksiˌtetrəˈsaɪkliːn/ *noun* an antibiotic which is effective against a wide range of organisms

oxytocic /ˌɒksiˈtəʊsɪk/ *noun* a drug which helps to start the process of childbirth, or speeds it up ■ *adjective* starting or speeding up childbirth by causing contractions in the muscles of the uterus

oxytocin /ˌɒksiˈtəʊsɪn/ *noun* a hormone secreted by the posterior pituitary gland, which controls the contractions of the uterus and encourages the flow of milk

ozone /ˈəʊzəʊn/ *noun* a gas present in the atmosphere in small quantities, which is harmful at high levels of concentration

ozone sickness /ˈəʊzəʊn ˌsɪknəs/ *noun* a condition experienced by jet travellers, due to levels of ozone in aircraft

P

Pa *abbreviation* pascal

pacemaker /'peɪsmeɪkə/ *noun* **1.** a node in the heart which regulates the heartbeat. Also called **sinoatrial node, SA node 2.** ♦ **cardiac pacemaker, epicardial pacemaker**

pachy- /pæki/ *prefix* thickening

pachydactyly /ˌpæki'dæktɪli/ *noun* a condition in which the fingers and toes become thicker than usual

pachydermia /ˌpæki'dɜːmiə/, **pachyderma** /ˌpæki'dɜːmə/ *noun* a condition in which the skin becomes thicker than normal

pachymeningitis /ˌpæki,menɪn'dʒaɪtɪs/ *noun* inflammation of the dura mater

pachyonychia /ˌpækiə'nɪkiə/ *noun* unusual thickness of the nails

pachysomia /ˌpæki'səʊmiə/ *noun* a condition in which soft tissues of the body become unusually thick

pacing /'peɪsɪŋ/ *noun* a surgical operation to implant or attach a cardiac pacemaker

Pacinian corpuscle /pə,sɪniən 'kɔːpʌs(ə)l/ *noun* a sensory nerve ending in the skin which is sensitive to touch and vibrations

pack /pæk/ *noun* a tampon of gauze or cotton wool, used to fill an orifice such as the nose or vagina ■ *verb* to fill an orifice with a tampon ○ *The ear was packed with cotton wool to absorb the discharge.*

packed cell volume /ˌpækt 'sel ,vɒljuːm/ *noun* the volume of red blood cells in a person's blood shown against the total volume of blood. Also called **haematocrit**

PACT /pækt/ *abbreviation* prescribing analyses and cost

pad /pæd/ *noun* a piece or mass of soft absorbent material, placed on part of the body to protect it ○ *She wrapped a pad of soft cotton wool round the sore.*

paed- /piːd/ *prefix* same as **paedo-** (*used before vowels*)

paediatric /ˌpiːdi'ætrɪk/ *adjective* referring to the treatment of the diseases of children ○ *A new paediatric hospital has been opened.* ○ *Parents can visit children in the paediatric wards at any time.*

paediatrician /ˌpiːdiə'trɪʃ(ə)n/ *noun* a doctor who specialises in the treatment of diseases of children

paediatrics /ˌpiːdi'ætrɪks/ *noun* the study of children, their development and diseases. Compare **geriatrics**

paedo- /piːdəʊ/ *prefix* referring to children

paedodontia /ˌpiːdə'dɒnʃə/ *noun* another spelling of **pedodontia**

Paget's disease /'pædʒəts dɪ,ziːz/ *noun* **1.** same as **osteitis deformans 2.** a form of breast cancer which starts as an itchy rash round the nipple [Described 1877. After Sir James Paget (1814–99), British surgeon.]

pain /peɪn/ *noun* the feeling of severe discomfort which a person has when hurt ○ *The doctor gave him an injection to relieve the pain.* ○ *She is suffering from back pain.* (NOTE: Pain can be used in the plural to show that it recurs: **She has pains in her left leg.**)

pain clinic /'peɪn ,klɪnɪk/ *noun* a centre which looks after people with severe persistent pain and whose staff include professionals from many specialist areas of medicine

painkiller /'peɪn,kɪlə/ *noun* a drug that reduces pain

pain pathway /'peɪn ,pɑːθweɪ/ *noun* a series of linking nerve fibres and neurones which carry impulses of pain from the site to the sensory cortex

pain receptor /'peɪn rɪ,septə/ *noun* a nerve ending which is sensitive to pain

pain relief /'peɪn rɪ,liːf/ *noun* the act of easing pain by using analgesics

paint /peɪnt/ *noun* a coloured antiseptic, analgesic or astringent liquid which is put on the surface of the body ■ *verb* to cover a wound with an antiseptic, analgesic or astringent liquid or lotion ○ *She painted the rash with calamine.*

pain threshold /'peɪn ,θreʃhəʊld/ *noun* the point at which a person finds it impossible to bear pain without crying

palate /'pælət/ *noun* the roof of the mouth and floor of the nasal cavity, formed of the hard and soft palates

palate bone /ˈpælət bəʊn/ *noun* one of two bones which form part of the hard palate, the orbits of the eyes and the cavity behind the nose. Also called **palatine bone**

palatine /ˈpælətaɪn/ *adjective* referring to the palate

palatine bone /ˈpælətaɪn bəʊn/ *noun* same as **palate bone**

palatine tonsil /ˌpælətaɪn ˈtɒns(ə)l/ *noun* same as **tonsil**

palato- /pælətəʊ/ *prefix* the palate

palatoplasty /ˈpælətəplæsti/ *noun* plastic surgery of the roof of the mouth, e.g. to repair a cleft palate

palatoplegia /ˌpælətəˈpliːdʒə/ *noun* paralysis of the soft palate

palatorrhaphy /ˌpæləˈtɔːrəfi/ *noun* a surgical operation to suture and close a cleft palate. Also called **staphylorrhaphy**, **uraniscorrhaphy**

pali- /pæli/ *prefix* same as **palin-**

palin- /ˈpælɪn/ *prefix* repeating

palindromic /ˌpælɪnˈdrəʊmɪk/ *adjective* recurring ○ *a palindromic disease*

palliative /ˈpæliətɪv/ *noun* a treatment or drug which relieves symptoms but does nothing to cure the disease which causes the symptoms. For example, a painkiller can reduce the pain in a tooth, but will not cure the caries which causes the pain. ■ *adjective* providing relief

palliative care /ˈpæliətɪv ˌkeə/, **palliative treatment** /ˈpæliətɪv ˌtriːtmənt/ *noun* treatment which helps to reduce the symptoms of a disease, especially a terminal or chronic condition, but does not cure it

COMMENT: Palliative care may involve giving antibiotics, transfusions, pain-killing drugs, low-dose chemotherapy and psychological and social support to help the person and their family adjust to the illness. The treatment is often provided in a hospice.

pallidotomy /ˌpælɪˈdɒtəmi/ *noun* an operation on the brain which can reduce many of the symptoms of Parkinson's disease, such as tremor, bradykinesia and stooped posture

pallor /ˈpælə/ *noun* the condition of being pale

palm /pɑːm/ *noun* the inner surface of the hand, extending from the bases of the fingers to the wrist

palmar /ˈpælmə/ *adjective* referring to the palm of the hand

palmar arch /ˈpælmər ɑːtʃ/ *noun* one of two arches or joins within the palm formed by two arteries which link together

palmar fascia /ˌpælmə ˈfeɪʃə/ *noun* the tendons in the palm of the hand

palpate /pælˈpeɪt/ *verb* to examine part of the body by feeling it with the hand

palpation /pælˈpeɪʃ(ə)n/ *noun* an examination of part of the body by feeling it with the hand

palpebra /ˈpælpɪbrə/ *noun* same as **eyelid** (NOTE: The plural is **palpebrae**.)

palpebral /ˈpælpɪbrəl/ *adjective* referring to the eyelids

palpitation /ˌpælpɪˈteɪʃ(ə)n/ *noun* awareness that the heart is beating rapidly or irregularly, possibly caused by stress or by a disease

pan- /pæn/ *prefix* referring to everything

panacea /ˌpænəˈsiːə/ *noun* a medicine which is supposed to cure everything

panarthritis /ˌpænɑːˈθraɪtɪs/ *noun* inflammation of all the tissues of a joint or of all the joints in the body

pancarditis /ˌpænkɑːˈdaɪtɪs/ *noun* inflammation of all the tissues in the heart, i.e. the heart muscle, the endocardium and the pericardium

pancreas /ˈpæŋkriəs/ *noun* a gland which lies across the back of the body between the kidneys. See illustration at DIGESTIVE SYSTEM in Supplement

pancreatectomy /ˌpæŋkriəˈtektəmi/ *noun* the surgical removal of all or part of the pancreas

pancreatic /ˌpæŋkriˈætɪk/ *adjective* referring to the pancreas

pancreatic duct /ˌpæŋkriˈætɪk dʌkt/ *noun* a duct leading through the pancreas to the duodenum

pancreatic juice /ˌpæŋkriætɪk ˈdʒuːs/, **pancreatic secretion** /ˌpæŋkriætɪk sɪˈkriːʃ(ə)n/ *noun* a digestive juice, formed of enzymes produced by the pancreas, which digests fats and carbohydrates

pancreatin /ˈpæŋkriətɪn/ *noun* a substance made from enzymes secreted by the pancreas, used to treat someone whose pancreas does not produce pancreatic enzymes

pancreatitis /ˌpæŋkriəˈtaɪtɪs/ *noun* inflammation of the pancreas

pancreatomy /ˌpæŋkriˈætəmi/, **pancreatotomy** /ˌpæŋkriəˈtɒtəmi/ *noun* a surgical operation to open the pancreatic duct

pancytopenia /ˌpænsaɪtəˈpiːniə/ *noun* a condition in which there are too few red and white blood cells and blood platelets

pandemic /pænˈdemɪk/ *noun* an epidemic disease which affects many parts of the world. Compare **endemic**, **epidemic** ■ *adjective* widespread

panhysterectomy /ˌpænhɪstəˈrektmi/ *noun* the surgical removal of all the uterus and the cervix

panic /ˈpænɪk/ *noun* a feeling of great fear which cannot be stopped and which sometimes results in irrational behaviour ○ *He was in a panic as he sat in the consultant's waiting room.* ■ *verb* to be suddenly afraid ○ *She panicked* *when the surgeon told her she might need to have an operation.*

panic attack /'pænɪk ə,tæk/ *noun* a sudden onset of panic

panic disorder /'pænɪk dɪs,ɔːdə/ *noun* a condition in which somebody has frequent panic attacks

panniculitis /pə,nɪkjʊ'laɪtɪs/ *noun* inflammation of the panniculus adiposus, producing tender swellings on the thighs and breasts

panniculus /pə'nɪkjʊləs/ *noun* a layer of membranous tissue

panniculus adiposus /pə'nɪkjʊləs ædɪ,pəʊsəs/ *noun* a layer of fat underneath the skin

pannus /'pænəs/ *noun* a growth on the cornea containing tiny blood vessels

panophthalmia /,pænɒf'θælmiə/, **panophthalmitis** /,pænɒfθæl'maɪtɪs/ *noun* inflammation of the whole of the eye

panosteitis /,pænɒsti'aɪtɪs/, **panostitis** /,pænɒ'staɪtɪs/ *noun* inflammation of the whole of a bone

panotitis /,pænəʊ'taɪtɪs/ *noun* inflammation affecting all of the ear, but especially the middle ear

panproctocolectomy /,pænprɒktəkə'lektəmi/ *noun* the surgical removal of the whole of the rectum and the colon

pant- /pænt/ *prefix* same as **pan-**

panto- /pæntəʊ/ *prefix* same as **pan-**

pantothenic acid /,pæntəθenɪk 'æsɪd/ *noun* a vitamin of the vitamin B complex, found in liver, yeast and eggs

Papanicolaou test /,pæpənɪkə'leɪu: test/ *noun* a method of staining samples from various body secretions to test for malignancy, e.g. testing a cervical smear sample to see if cancer is present. Also called **Pap test** [Described 1933. After George Nicholas Papanicolaou (1883–1962), Greek anatomist and physician who worked in the USA.]

papaveretum /pə,pævə'riːtəm/ *noun* a preparation of opium used to reduce pain

papilla /pə'pɪlə/ *noun* a small swelling which sticks up above the usual surface level ○ *The upper surface of the tongue is covered with papillae.* (NOTE: The plural is **papillae**.)

papillary /pə'pɪləri/ *adjective* referring to papillae

papillitis /,pæpɪ'laɪtɪs/ *noun* inflammation of the optic disc at the back of the eye

papilloedema /,pæpɪləʊ'diːmə/ *noun* an accumulation of fluid in the optic disc at the back of the eye

papilloma /,pæpɪ'ləʊmə/ *noun* a benign tumour on the skin or mucous membrane (NOTE: The plural is **papillomas** or **papillomata**.)

papillomatosis /,pæpɪləʊmə'təʊsɪs/ *noun* being affected with papillomata

papillotomy /,pæpɪ'lɒtəmi/ *noun* the operation of cutting into the body at the point where the common bile duct and pancreatic duct meet to go into the duodenum, in order to improve bile drainage and allow any stones to pass out

papovavirus /pə'pəʊvəvaɪrəs/ *noun* a family of viruses which start tumours, some of which are malignant, and some of which, such as warts, are benign

Pap test /'pæp test/, **Pap smear** /'pæp smɪə/ *noun* same as **Papanicolaou test**

papular /'pæpjʊlə/ *adjective* referring to a papule

papule /'pæpjuːl/ *noun* a small coloured spot raised above the surface of the skin as part of a rash (NOTE: A flat spot is a **macule**.)

papulo- /pæpjʊləʊ/ *prefix* relating to a papule

papulopustular /,pæpjʊləʊ'pʌstjʊlə/ *adjective* referring to a rash with both papules and pustules

papulosquamous /,pæpjʊləʊ'skweɪməs/ *adjective* referring to a rash with papules and a scaly skin

para- /pærə/ *prefix* **1.** similar to or near **2.** changed or beyond

paracentesis /,pærəsen'tiːsɪs/ *noun* the procedure of draining fluid from a cavity inside the body using a hollow needle, either for diagnostic purposes or because the fluid is harmful. Also called **tapping**

paracetamol /,pærə'siːtəmɒl/ *noun* a common drug used to relieve mild to moderate pain and reduce fever (NOTE: The US name is **acetaminophen**.)

paracusis /,pærə'kjuːsɪs/, **paracousia** /,pærə'kuːsiə/ *noun* a disorder of hearing

paradoxical breathing /,pærədɒksɪk(ə)l 'briːðɪŋ/, **paradoxical respiration** /,pærədɒksɪk(ə)l ,respɪ'reɪʃ(ə)n/ *noun* a condition affecting someone with broken ribs, where the chest appears to move in when he or she breathes in, and appears to move out when he or she breathes out

paradoxus /,pærə'dɒksəs/ ♦ **pulsus paradoxus**

paraesthesia /,pæriːs'θiːziə/ *noun* an unexplained tingling sensation. ◊ **pins and needles** (NOTE: The plural is **paraesthesiae**.)

paraffin /'pærəfɪn/ *noun* an oil produced from petroleum, forming the base of some ointments, and also used for heating and light

paraffin gauze /'pærəfɪn gɔːz/ *noun* gauze covered with solid paraffin, used as a dressing

parageusia /,pærə'gjuːsiə/ *noun* a disorder of the sense of taste

paralyse /ˈpærəlaɪz/ *verb* to make a part of the body unable to carry out voluntary movements by weakening or damaging muscles or nerves so that they cannot function, or by using a drug ○ *His arm was paralysed after the stroke.* ○ *She is paralysed from the waist down.*

paralysis /pəˈræləsɪs/ *noun* a condition in which part of the body cannot be moved because the motor nerves have been damaged or the muscles have been weakened ○ *The condition causes paralysis of the lower limbs.* ○ *He suffered temporary paralysis of the right arm.*

paralytic /ˌpærəˈlɪtɪk/ *adjective* 1. referring to paralysis 2. referring to a person who is paralysed

paralytic ileus /ˌpærəlɪtɪk ˈɪliəs/ *noun* an obstruction in the ileum caused by paralysis of the muscles of the intestine. Also called **adynamic ileus**

paramedian /ˌpærəˈmiːdiən/ *adjective* near the midline of the body

paramedian plane /ˌpærəˈmiːdiən ˌpleɪn/ *noun* a plane near the midline of the body, parallel to the sagittal plane and at right angles to the coronal plane. See illustration at **ANATOMICAL TERMS** in Supplement

paramedic /ˌpærəˈmedɪk/ *noun* a person whose work involves the restoration of health and normal functioning

parameter /pəˈræmɪtə/ *noun* a measurement of something such as blood pressure which may be an important consideration in treating the condition which the person has

parametritis /ˌpærəmɪˈtraɪtɪs/ *noun* inflammation of the parametrium

parametrium /ˌpærəˈmiːtriəm/ *noun* the connective tissue around the uterus

paranasal /ˌpærəˈneɪz(ə)l/ *adjective* by the side of the nose

paranasal sinus /ˌpærəneɪz(ə)l ˈsaɪnəs/, **paranasal air sinus** /ˌpærəneɪz(ə)l ˈeə ˌsaɪnəs/ *noun* one of the four pairs of sinuses in the skull near the nose, which open into the nasal cavity and are lined with sticky mucus (NOTE: They are the frontal, maxillary, ethmoidal and sphenoidal sinuses.)

paranoia /ˌpærəˈnɔɪə/ *noun* a behaviour characterised by mistaken ideas or delusions of persecution or self-importance

paranoiac /ˌpærəˈnɔɪæk/ *noun* a person affected by paranoia

paranoid /ˈpærənɔɪd/ *adjective* having a fixed delusion

paranoid disorder /ˌpærənɔɪd dɪsˈɔːdə/ *noun* a mental disorder which causes someone experiencing it to believe strongly that something is not right with them, with someone else or with the world generally and to maintain the belief even when given evidence against it

paranoid schizophrenia /ˌpærənɔɪd ˌskɪtsəʊˈfriːniə/ *noun* a form of schizophrenia in which the person believes he or she is being persecuted

paraparesis /ˌpærəpəˈriːsɪs/ *noun* incomplete paralysis of the legs

paraphimosis /ˌpærəfaɪˈməʊsɪs/ *noun* a condition in which the foreskin around the penis is tight and may have to be removed by circumcision

paraplegia /ˌpærəˈpliːdʒə/ *noun* paralysis which affects the lower part of the body and the legs, usually caused by an injury to the spinal cord

paraplegic /ˌpærəˈpliːdʒɪk/ *noun* someone who has paraplegia ■ *adjective* paralysed in the lower part of the body and legs

paraprofessional /ˌpærəprəˈfeʃ(ə)n(ə)l/ *noun* somebody with training who acts as an assistant to a professional person

parapsychology /ˌpærəsaɪˈkɒlədʒi/ *noun* the study of effects of the mind which appear not to be explained by known psychological or scientific principles, e.g. extrasensory perception and telepathy

Paraquat /ˈpærəkwɒt/ a trade name for dimethyl dupyridilium used as a weedkiller

parasagittal /ˌpærəˈsædʒɪt(ə)l/ *adjective* near the midline of the body

parasagittal plane /ˌpærəˈsædʒɪt(ə)l ˌpleɪn/ *noun* a plane near the midline of the body, parallel to the sagittal plane and at right angles to the coronal plane. Also called **paramedian plane**. See illustration at **ANATOMICAL TERMS** in Supplement

parasite /ˈpærəsaɪt/ *noun* a plant or animal which lives on or inside another organism and draws nourishment from that organism

parasitic /ˌpærəˈsɪtɪk/ *adjective* referring to parasites

parasitic cyst /ˌpærəsɪtɪk ˈsɪst/ *noun* a cyst caused by the growing larvae of a parasite in the body

parasiticide /ˌpærəˈsaɪtɪsaɪd/ *noun* a substance which kills parasites ■ *adjective* killing parasites

parasuicide /ˌpærəˈsuːɪsaɪd/ *noun* an act where someone tries to kill himself or herself, but without really intending to do so, rather as a way of drawing attention to his or her psychological condition

parasympathetic nervous system /ˌpærəsɪmpəˌθetɪk ˈnɜːvəs ˌsɪstəm/, **parasympathetic system** /ˌpærəsɪmpəˈθetɪk ˌsɪstəm/ *noun* one of two parts of the autonomic nervous system. Its messages reach the organs of the body through the cranial and sacral nerves to the eyes, the gastrointestinal system and other organs. ◊ **sympathetic nervous system**

parasympatholytic /ˌpærəsɪmˌpæθəˈlɪtɪk/ *noun* a drug which reduces the effects of the parasympathetic nervous system by relaxing smooth muscle, reducing the amount of sweat and saliva produced and widening the pupil of the eye. An example is atropine. ■ *adjective* relating to a par-asympatholytic drug

parasympathomimetic   /ˌpærəsɪmˌpæθəʊmɪˈmetɪk/ *noun* a drug which stimulates the parasympathetic nervous system by making smooth muscle more tense, widening the blood vessels, slowing the heart rate, increasing the amount of sweat and saliva produced and contracting the pupil of the eye ■ *adjective* producing effects similar to those of a parasympathomimetic drug

parathormone /ˌpærəˈθɔːməʊn/ *noun* the hormone secreted by the parathyroid glands which regulates the level of calcium in blood plasma. Also called **parathyroid hormone**

parathyroid /ˌpærəˈθaɪrɔɪd/ *noun* same as **parathyroid gland** ■ *adjective* **1.** relating to a parathyroid gland **2.** located close to the thyroid gland

parathyroidectomy /ˌpærəˌθaɪrɔɪˈdektəmi/ *noun* the surgical removal of a parathyroid gland

parathyroid gland /ˌpærəˈθaɪrɔɪd ˌɡlænd/ *noun* one of four small glands which are situated in or near the wall of the thyroid gland and secrete a hormone which controls the way in which calcium and phosphorus are deposited in bones

parathyroid   hormone   /ˌpærəˈθaɪrɔɪd ˌhɔːməʊn/ *noun* same as **parathormone**

paratyphoid /ˌpærəˈtaɪfɔɪd/, **paratyphoid fever** /ˌpærəˈtaɪfɔɪd ˌfiːvə/ *noun* an infectious disease which has similar symptoms to typhoid and is caused by bacteria transmitted by humans or animals

COMMENT: There are three forms of paratyphoid fever, known by the letters A, B, and C, caused by three types of bacterium, *Salmonella paratyphi* A, B, and C. TAB injections give immunity against paratyphoid A and B, but not against C.

paravertebral /ˌpærəˈvɜːtɪbrəl/ *adjective* near the vertebrae, beside the spinal column

paravertebral injection /ˌpærəvɜːtɪbrəl ɪnˈdʒekʃən/ *noun* an injection of local anaesthetic into the back near the vertebrae

parenchyma /pəˈreŋkɪmə/ *noun* tissues which contain the working cells of an organ

parenchymal /pəˈreŋkɪməl/ *adjective* relating to parenchyma

parenteral /pæˈrentərəl/ *adjective* referring to medication which is not given by mouth but in the form of injections or suppositories. Compare **enteral**, **oral**

parenteral   nutrition   /pæˌrentərəl njuːˈtrɪʃ(ə)n/, **parenteral feeding** /pæˌrentərəl ˈfiːdɪŋ/ *noun* the process of feeding someone by means other than the digestive tract, especially by

giving injections of glucose to someone critically ill

parenting /ˈpeərəntɪŋ/ *noun* the activities involved in bringing up children □ **parenting skills** the abilities and experience that make someone a good parent

paresis /pəˈriːsɪs/ *noun* partial paralysis

parietal /pəˈraɪət(ə)l/ *adjective* referring to the wall of a cavity or any organ

parietal bone /pəˈraɪət(ə)l bəʊn/, **parietal** /pəˈraɪət(ə)l/ *noun* one of two bones which form the sides of the skull

parietal cell /pəˈraɪət(ə)l sel/ *noun* same as **oxyntic cell**

parietal lobe /pəˈraɪət(ə)l ləʊb/ *noun* the middle lobe of the cerebral hemisphere, which is associated with language and other mental processes, and also contains the postcentral gyrus

parietal pleura /pəˈraɪət(ə)l ˈplʊərə/ *noun* a membrane attached to the diaphragm and covering the chest cavity. Also called **outer pleura**. See illustration at LUNGS in Supplement

-parin /pərɪn/ *suffix* used for anticoagulants ○ *heparin*

Paris /ˈpærɪs/ ♦ **plaster of Paris**

parity /ˈpærɪti/ *noun* **1.** equality of status or position, especially in terms of pay or rank **2.** the number of children that a woman has given birth to

Parkinsonism /ˈpɑːkɪnsənɪz(ə)m/ *noun* a progressive nervous disorder, which may be an effect of some drugs, repeated head injuries or brain tumours. The main symptoms are trembling hands and a slow shuffling walk. Also called **paralysis agitans**

Parkinson's disease /ˈpɑːkɪnsənz dɪˌziːz/ *noun* a progressive nervous disorder without a known cause which is a type of Parkinsonism, the main symptoms of which are trembling hands, a slow shuffling walk and difficulty in speaking [Described 1817. After James Parkinson (1755–1824), English physician.]

paronychia /ˌpærəˈnɪkiə/ *noun* inflammation near the nail which forms pus, caused by an infection in the fleshy part of the tip of a finger. ◊ **whitlow**

parosmia /pəˈrɒzmiə/ *noun* a disorder of the sense of smell

parotid /pəˈrɒtɪd/ *adjective* near the ear

parotid gland /pəˈrɒtɪd ɡlænd/, **parotid** /pəˈrɒtɪd/ *noun* one of the glands which produces saliva, situated in the neck behind the joint of the jaw and ear

parotitis /ˌpærəˈtaɪtɪs/ *noun* inflammation of the parotid glands

parous /ˈpeərəs/ *adjective* referring to a woman who has given birth to one or more children

paroxetine /pə'rɒksɪtiːn/ *noun* an antidepressant drug which prolongs the effects of serotonin in the brain

paroxysm /'pærəksɪz(ə)m/ *noun* a sudden movement of the muscles ○ *She suffered paroxysms of coughing during the night.*

paroxysmal /ˌpærək'sɪzm(ə)l/ *adjective* referring to a paroxysm, or similar to a paroxysm

paroxysmal dyspnoea /pærəkˌsɪzm(ə)l dɪsp'niːə/ *noun* an attack of breathlessness at night, usually caused by congestive heart failure

paroxysmal tachycardia /pærəkˌsɪzm(ə)l tæki'kɑːdiə/ *noun* same as **nodal tachycardia**

pars /pɑːz/ *noun* the Latin word for part

partially /'pɑːʃ(ə)li/ *adverb* not completely ○ *He is partially paralysed in his right side.* □ **partially sighted** having only partial vision ○ *Large print books are available for people who are partially sighted.*

partially sighted register /ˌpɑːʃ(ə)li 'saɪtɪd ˌredʒɪstə/ *noun* a list of people who have poor sight but are not blind, and may require some special services

partial mastectomy /ˌpɑːʃ(ə)l mæ'stektəmi/ *noun* an operation to remove part of a breast

partial thickness burn /ˌpɑːʃ(ə)l 'θɪknəs ˌbɜːn/ *noun* a burn which leaves enough tissue for the skin to grow again. Also called **superficial thickness burn**

particle /'pɑːtɪk(ə)l/ *noun* a very small piece of matter

particulate /pɑː'tɪkjʊlət/ *adjective* referring to or composed of particles

particulate matter /pɑː'tɪkjʊlət ˌmætə/ *noun* particles of less than a specified size, usually of carbon, which are used as a measure of air pollution and can affect asthma

parturient /pɑː'tjʊəriənt/ *adjective* referring to childbirth

parturition /ˌpɑːtjʊ'rɪʃ(ə)n/ *noun* same as **childbirth**

parv- /pɑːv/, **parvo-** *prefix* small

pass /pɑːs/ *verb* to allow faeces, urine or any other body product to come out of the body ○ *Have you passed anything this morning?* ○ *He passed a small stone in his urine.* □ **to pass blood** to produce faeces or urine that contain blood □ **to pass water** to urinate (*informal*)

passage /'pæsɪdʒ/ *noun* **1.** a long narrow channel inside the body **2.** the introduction of an instrument into a cavity

pass away /ˌpɑːs ə'weɪ/ *verb* used to avoid saying 'die' (*informal*) ○ *Mother passed away during the night.*

passive /'pæsɪv/ *adjective* receiving rather than initiating an action

passive immunity /ˌpæsɪv ɪ'mjuːnɪti/ *noun* immunity which is acquired by a baby in the uterus or by a person through an injection with an antitoxin

passive movement /ˌpæsɪv 'muːvmənt/ *noun* movement of a limb or other body part by a doctor or therapist, not by the person

passive smoking /ˌpæsɪv 'sməʊkɪŋ/ *noun* the act of breathing in smoke from other people's cigarettes when you do not smoke yourself

pass on /ˌpɑːs 'ɒn/ *verb* **1.** to give a disease to someone ○ *Haemophilia is passed on by a woman to her sons.* ○ *The disease was quickly passed on by carriers to the rest of the population.* **2.** used to avoid saying 'die' ○ *My father passed on two years ago.*

pass out /ˌpɑːs 'aʊt/ *verb* to faint (*informal*) ○ *When we told her that her father was ill, she passed out.*

pasteurisation /ˌpɑːstʃəraɪ'zeɪʃ(ə)n/, **pasteurization** *noun* the process of heating food or food products to destroy bacteria [After Louis Pasteur (1822–95), French chemist and bacteriologist.]

pasteurise /'pɑːstʃəraɪz/, **pasteurize** *verb* to kill bacteria in food by heating it ○ *The government is telling people to drink only pasteurised milk.*

pastille /'pæst(ə)l/ *noun* a sweet jelly with medication in it, which can be sucked to relieve a sore throat

patch /pætʃ/ *noun* a piece of sticking plaster with a substance on it, which is stuck to the skin to allow the substance to be gradually absorbed into the system through the skin, e.g. in HRT

patch test /'pætʃ test/ *noun* a test for allergies or tuberculosis, where a piece of sticking plaster containing an allergic substance or tuberculin is stuck to the skin to see if there is a reaction

patella /pə'telə/ *noun* the small bone in front of the knee joint. Also called **kneecap**

patellar /pə'telə/ *adjective* referring to the kneecap

patellar reflex /pəˌtelə 'riːfleks/ *noun* the jerk made as a reflex action by the knee, when the legs are crossed and the patellar tendon is tapped sharply. Also called **knee jerk**

patellar tendon /pəˌtelə 'tendən/ *noun* a tendon just below the kneecap

patellectomy /ˌpætə'lektəmi/ *noun* a surgical operation to remove the kneecap

patent /'peɪtənt, 'pætənt/ *adjective* open, exposed ○ *The presence of a pulse shows that the main blood vessels from the heart to the site of the pulse are patent.*

patent ductus arteriosus /ˌpeɪtənt ˌdʌktəs ɑːˌtɪəri'əʊsəs/ *noun* a congenital condition in which the ductus arteriosus does not close, allowing blood into the circulation without having passed through the lungs

patent medicine /ˌpeɪtənt ˈmed(ə)sɪn/ *noun* a medicinal preparation which is made and sold under a trade name and is protected by law from being copied or sold by other manufacturers for a certain length of time after its invention. ◊ **proprietary medicine**

paternity /pəˈtɜːnɪti/ *noun* the fact of being or becoming a father ○ *paternity leave* Compare **maternity**

paternity test /pəˈtɜːnɪti test/ *noun* a test such as blood grouping which makes it possible to determine the identity of the father of a child

COMMENT: DNA fingerprinting may be required in order to identify a man who might be the father according to his blood group and that of the child, but is not in fact the father.

path- /pæθ/, **patho-** /pæθəʊ/ *prefix* referring to disease

pathogen /ˈpæθədʒən/ *noun* a microorganism which causes a disease

pathogenesis /ˌpæθəˈdʒenəsɪs/ *noun* the origin, production and development of a morbid or diseased condition

pathogenic /ˌpæθəˈdʒenɪk/ *adjective* causing or producing a disease

pathogenicity /ˌpæθədʒəˈnɪsɪti/ *noun* the ability of a pathogen to cause a disease

pathognomonic /ˌpæθəgnəʊˈmɒnɪk/ *adjective* referring to a symptom which is typical and characteristic, and which indicates that someone has a particular disease

pathological /ˌpæθəˈlɒdʒɪk(ə)l/, **pathologic** /ˌpæθəˈlɒdʒɪk/ *adjective* 1. referring to a disease, or caused by a disease 2. indicating a disease

pathological depression /ˌpæθəlɒdʒɪk(ə)l dɪˈpreʃ(ə)n/ *noun* an unusually severe state of depression, possibly leading to suicide

pathological dislocation /ˌpæθəlɒdʒɪk(ə)l ˌdɪsləˈkeɪʃ(ə)n/ *noun* the dislocation of a diseased joint

pathological fracture /ˌpæθəlɒdʒɪk(ə)l ˈfræktʃə/ *noun* a fracture of a diseased bone

pathologist /pəˈθɒlədʒɪst/ *noun* 1. a doctor who specialises in the study of diseases and the changes in the body caused by disease, examining tissue specimens from patients and reporting on the presence or absence of disease in them 2. a doctor who examines dead bodies in order to find out the cause of death

pathology /pəˈθɒlədʒi/ *noun* the study of diseases and the changes in structure and function which diseases cause in the body. Also called **morbid anatomy**

pathology report /pəˈθɒlədʒi rɪˌpɔːt/ *noun* a report on tests carried out to find the cause of a disease

pathophysiology /ˌpæθəʊfɪziˈɒlədʒi/ *noun* the study of unusual or diseased organs

-pathy /pəθi/ *suffix* disease

patient /ˈpeɪʃ(ə)nt/ *noun* a person who is in hospital or who is being treated by a doctor ○ *The patients are all asleep in their beds.* ○ *The doctor is taking the patient's temperature.*

patient allocation /ˌpeɪʃ(ə)nt ˌæləˈkeɪʃ(ə)n/ *noun* a system of assigning each patient to a particular nurse for all their care needs

patient-group direction /ˈpeɪʃ(ə)nt gruːp daɪˌrekʃ(ə)n/ *noun* full form of **PGD**

patient identifier /ˌpeɪʃ(ə)nt aɪˈdentɪfaɪə/ *noun* a code of letters and numbers attached to the patient's medical records by which all information concerning the patient can be tracked, e.g. cause of death

Paul–Bunnell reaction /ˌpɔːl ˈbʌn(ə)l rɪˌækʃən/, **Paul–Bunnell test** /ˌpɔːl ˈbʌn(ə)l ˌtest/ *noun* a blood test to see if someone has glandular fever, where the person's blood is tested against a solution containing glandular fever bacilli [Described 1932. After John Rodman Paul (1893–1971), US physician; Walls Willard Bunnell (1902–66), US physician.]

pavement epithelium /ˈpeɪvmənt epɪˌθiːliəm/ *noun* same as **squamous epithelium**

Pavlov's method /ˈpævlɒvz ˌmeθəd/ *noun* a set of procedures for the study or production of conditioned reflexes

PBI test /ˌpiː biː ˈaɪ test/ *noun* same as **protein-bound iodine test**

p.c. /ˌpiː ˈsiː/ *adverb* (*used on prescriptions*) after food. Full form **post cibum**

PCC *abbreviation* Professional Conduct Committee

PCG *abbreviation* primary care group

PCOD *abbreviation* polycystic ovary disease

PCOS *abbreviation* polycystic ovary syndrome

PCP *abbreviation* pneumocystis carinii pneumonia

PCT *abbreviation* primary care trust

p.d. *adverb* (*used on prescriptions*) per day. Full form **per diem**

PDA /ˌpiː diː ˈeɪ/ *noun* a handheld computer with various functions, e.g. information storage and digital notetaking. Full form **personal digital assistant**

PE *abbreviation* pulmonary embolism

peak expiratory flow rate /ˌpiːk ɪk ˌspaɪərət(ə)ri ˈfləʊ ˌreɪt/ *noun* the rate at which someone can expel air from their lungs when they are full and with no time limit. Abbreviation **PEFR**

Pearson bed /ˈpɪəs(ə)n bed/ *noun* a type of bed with a Balkan frame, a rectangular frame attached to and overhanging the bed, used mainly for people with splints

peau d'orange /ˌpəʊ dɒˈrɑːnʒ/ *noun* thickened skin with many little depressions caused by lymphoedema which forms over a breast tumour or in elephantiasis (NOTE: From the French phrase meaning 'orange peel'.)

PEC /ˌpiː iː ˈsiː/ *noun* the committee responsible for the day-to-day management of a Primary Care Trust and for developing service policies and investment plans. Full form **Professional Executive Committee**

pecten /ˈpektən/ *noun* **1.** the middle section of the wall of the anal passage **2.** a hard ridge on the pubis

pectineal /pekˈtɪniəl/ *adjective* referring to the pecten of the pubis

pectoral /ˈpekt(ə)rəl/ *noun* **1.** a therapeutic substance which has a good effect on respiratory disease **2.** same as **pectoral muscle** ■ *adjective* referring to the chest

pectoral girdle /ˌpekt(ə)rəl ˈɡɜːd(ə)l/ *noun* the shoulder bones, the scapulae and clavicles, to which the upper arm bones are attached. Also called **shoulder girdle**

pectoralis /ˌpektəˈreɪlɪs/ *noun* a chest muscle

pectoralis major /pektəˌreɪlɪs ˈmeɪdʒə/ *noun* a large chest muscle which pulls the arm forward or rotates it

pectoralis minor /pektəˌreɪlɪs ˈmaɪnə/ *noun* a small chest muscle which allows the shoulder to be depressed

pectoral muscle /ˈpekt(ə)rəl ˌmʌs(ə)l/ *noun* one of two muscles which lie across the chest and control movements of the shoulder and arm. Also called **chest muscle**

pectus /ˈpektəs/ *noun* the anterior part of the chest

pectus carinatum /ˌpektəs ˌkærɪˈnɑːtəm/ *noun* a condition in which the sternum is unusually prominent. Also called **pigeon breast**

pectus excavatum /ˌpektəs ˌekskəˈveɪtəm/ *noun* a congenital condition, in which the chest is depressed in the centre because the lower part of the breastbone is curved backwards. Also called **funnel chest**

pedicle /ˈpedɪk(ə)l/ *noun* a long thin piece of skin which attaches a skin graft to the place where it was growing originally

pediculosis /pɪˌdɪkjʊˈləʊsɪs/ *noun* a skin disease caused by being infested with lice

Pediculus /pɪˈdɪkjʊləs/ *noun* same as **louse** (NOTE: The plural is **Pediculi**.)

Pediculus capitis /pɪˌdɪkjʊləs kəˈpaɪtɪs/ *noun* same as **head louse**

pedo- /piːd/ *prefix* same as **paedo-**

pedodontia /ˌpiːdəˈdɒnʃə/ *noun* the study of children's teeth

pedodontist /ˌpiːdəˈdɒntɪst/ *noun* a dentist who specialises in the treatment of children's teeth

peduncle /pɪˈdʌŋkəl/ *noun* a stem or stalk

pee /piː/ *verb* same as **urinate** (*informal*)

peel /piːl/ *verb* **1.** to take the skin off a fruit or vegetable **2.** (*of skin*) to come off in pieces ○ *After getting sunburnt, his skin began to peel.*

PEEP *abbreviation* positive end-expiratory pressure

peer review /ˈpɪə rɪˌvjuː/ *noun* an assessment of a piece of someone's work by people who are experts on the subject

PEFR *abbreviation* peak expiratory flow rate

Pel–Ebstein fever /ˌpel ˈebstaɪn ˌfiːvə/ *noun* a fever associated with Hodgkin's disease which recurs regularly [Described 1885. After Pieter Klaases Pel (1852–1919), Professor of Medicine in Amsterdam, Netherlands; Wilhelm Ebstein (1836–1912), Professor of Medicine at Göttingen, Germany.]

pellagra /pəˈlæɡrə/ *noun* a disease caused by a deficiency of nicotinic acid, riboflavine and pyridoxine from the vitamin B complex, where patches of skin become inflamed, and the person has anorexia, nausea and diarrhoea

pellet /ˈpelɪt/ *noun* a small rod- or oval-shaped pill of steroid hormone, usually either oestrogen or testosterone, that is implanted under the skin for slow absorption

pelvic /ˈpelvɪk/ *adjective* referring to the pelvis

pelvic brim /ˌpelvɪk ˈbrɪm/ *noun* a line on the ilium which separates the false pelvis from the true pelvis

pelvic cavity /ˌpelvɪk ˈkævɪti/ *noun* a space below the abdominal cavity, above the pelvis

pelvic colon /ˌpelvɪk ˈkəʊlɒn/ *noun* same as **sigmoid colon**

pelvic diaphragm /ˌpelvɪk ˈdaɪəfræm/ *noun* a sheet of muscle between the pelvic cavity and the peritoneum

pelvic floor /ˌpelvɪk ˈflɔː/ *noun* the lower part of the space beneath the pelvic girdle, formed of muscle

pelvic fracture /ˌpelvɪk ˈfræktʃə/ *noun* a fracture of the pelvis

pelvic girdle /ˌpelvɪk ˈɡɜːd(ə)l/ *noun* the ring formed by the two hip bones to which the thigh bones are attached. Also called **hip girdle**

pelvic inflammatory disease /ˌpelvɪk ɪn ˈflæmət(ə)ri dɪˌziːz/ *noun* an inflammation of a woman's reproductive organs in the pelvic area, which can cause infertility

pelvic outlet /ˌpelvɪk ˈaʊtlet/ *noun* an opening at the base of the pelvis

pelvimeter /pelˈvɪmɪtə/ *noun* an instrument to measure the diameter and capacity of the pelvis

pelvimetry /pelˈvɪmɪtri/ *noun* the act of measuring the pelvis, especially to see if the internal ring is wide enough for a baby to pass through in childbirth

pelvis /'pelvɪs/ *noun* **1.** the strong basin-shaped ring of bone near the bottom of the spine, formed of the hip bones at the front and sides and the sacrum and coccyx at the back **2.** the internal space inside the pelvic girdle (NOTE: [all senses] The plural is **pelvises** or **pelves**.)

pelvis of the kidney /,pelvɪs əv ðə 'kɪdni/ *noun* see illustration at **KIDNEY** in Supplement (NOTE: For other terms referring to the pelvis of the kidney, see words beginning with **pyel-**, **pyelo-**.)

pemphigoid /'pemfɪgɔɪd/ *noun* a skin disease which is similar to pemphigus ■ *adjective* referring to a skin disease similar to pemphigus

pemphigus /'pemfɪgəs/ *noun* a rare disease where large blisters form inside the skin

pendulous /'pendjʊləs/ *adjective* referring to an object or body part which hangs loosely or swings freely

-penia /piːniə/ *suffix* meaning a deficiency or not enough of something

penicillamine /,penɪ'sɪləmiːn/ *noun* a chelating agent which is used to help the body get rid of toxic metals

penicillin /,penɪ'sɪlɪn/ *noun* a common antibiotic originally produced from a fungus (NOTE: Penicillin drugs have names ending in **-cillin**: **amoxicillin**.)

penicillin resistance /,penɪsɪlɪn rɪ'zɪstəns/ *noun* the ability of bacteria to resist penicillin

Penicillium /,penɪ'sɪliəm/ *noun* the fungus from which penicillin is derived

penile /'piːnaɪl/ *adjective* referring to the penis

penis /'piːnɪs/ *noun* the male genital organ, which also passes urine. See illustration at **URO-GENITAL SYSTEM (MALE)** in Supplement. ◊ **kraurosis penis**

pentamidine /pen'tæmɪdiːn/ *noun* an antibiotic used in the treatment of African sleeping sickness and of pneumonia in people with AIDS

pentazocine /pen'tæzəsiːn/ *noun* an artificially produced narcotic drug used to reduce pain

Pentothal /'pentəθæl/ a trade name for thiopentone

PEP *abbreviation* post-exposure prophylaxis

Peplau's model /'peplaʊz ,mɒd(ə)l/ *noun* a model for nursing which describes the individual as a system with physiological, psychological and social components. The nurse and patient work together to define the patient's problems and to understand their reactions to one another, and the nurse takes on different roles in each phase of the relationship, such as a teacher, counsellor, leader, and technical expert, until the patient no longer needs their care.

pepsin /'pepsɪn/ *noun* an enzyme in the stomach which breaks down the proteins in food into peptones

pepsinogen /pep'sɪnədʒən/ *noun* a secretion from the gastric gland which is the inactive form of pepsin

peptic /'peptɪk/ *adjective* referring to digestion or to the digestive system

peptic ulcer /,peptɪk 'ʌlsə/ *noun* a benign ulcer in the duodenum or in the stomach

peptidase /'peptɪdeɪz/ *noun* an enzyme which breaks down proteins in the intestine into amino acids

peptide /'peptaɪd/ *noun* a compound formed of two or more amino acids

per /pɜː, pə/ *preposition* **1.** out of each ○ *ten per thousand* **2.** by or through ○ *per rectum*

perception /pə'sepʃən/ *noun* an impression formed in the brain as a result of information about the outside world which is passed back by the senses

perceptive deafness /pe,septɪv 'defnəs/ *noun* same as **sensorineural deafness**

percussion /pə'kʌʃ(ə)n/ *noun* a test, usually on the heart and lungs, in which the doctor taps part of the person's body and listens to the sound produced

percutaneous /,pɜːkjuː'teɪniəs/ *adjective* through the skin

percutaneous absorption /,pɜːkjuː,teɪniəs əb'zɔːpʃən/ *noun* the process of absorbing a substance through the skin

percutaneous angioplasty /,pɜːkjuː ,teɪniəs 'ændʒɪəplæsti/ *noun* the repair of a narrowed artery by passing a balloon into the artery through a catheter and then inflating it. Also called **balloon angioplasty**

percutaneous epididymal sperm aspiration /,pɜːkjuːteɪniəs ,epɪdɪdɪm(ə)l 'spɜːm ,æspɪreɪʃ(ə)n/ *noun* the removal of sperm from the epididymis by withdrawing it through the skin, usually as part of fertility treatment. Abbreviation **PESA**

per diem /,pɜː 'diːem/ *adverb* (*written on prescriptions*) per day

perforated eardrum /,pɜːfəreɪtɪd 'ɪədrʌm/ *noun* an eardrum with a hole in it

perforation /,pɜːfə'reɪʃ(ə)n/ *noun* a hole through the whole thickness of a tissue or membrane such as the intestine or eardrum

performance indicators /pə'fɔːməns ,ɪndɪkeɪtəz/ *plural noun* statistical information needed for analysis of how effectively health organisations are meeting their objectives, produced by health authorities and sent to the government. Abbreviation **PIs**

perfusion /pə'fjuːʒ(ə)n/ *noun* the process of passing a liquid through vessels, an organ or tissue, e.g. the flow of blood into lung tissue

perfusion scan /pə'fjuːʒ(ə)n skæn/ *noun* a procedure in which radioactive or radiopaque substances are introduced into the body so that the blood supply of an organ can be traced

peri- /peri/ *prefix* near, around or enclosing

periadenitis /ˌperiədɪ'naɪtɪs/ *noun* inflammation of tissue around a gland

perianal /ˌperi'eɪn(ə)l/ *adjective* around the anus

periarteritis /ˌperiɑːtə'raɪtɪs/ *noun* inflammation of the outer coat of an artery and the tissue round it

periarteritis nodosa /ˌperiɑːtəˌraɪtɪs nəʊ'dəʊsə/ *noun* same as **polyarteritis nodosa**

periarthritis /ˌperiɑː'θraɪtɪs/ *noun* inflammation of the tissue round a joint

pericard- /perikɑːd/ *prefix* referring to the pericardium

pericardectomy /ˌperikɑː'dektəmi/ *noun* the surgical removal of the pericardium

pericardial /ˌperi'kɑːdiəl/ *adjective* referring to the pericardium

pericardial effusion /ˌperikɑːdiəl ɪ'fjuːʒ(ə)n/ *noun* an excess of fluid which forms in the pericardial sac

pericardial sac /ˌperikɑːdiəl 'sæk/ *noun* the inner part of the pericardium forming a bag-like structure or sac which contains fluid to prevent the two parts of the pericardium rubbing together

pericardiectomy /ˌperikɑːdi'ektəmi/ *noun* same as **pericardectomy**

pericardiocentesis /ˌperiˌkɑːdiəʊsen'tiːsɪs/ *noun* the puncture of the pericardium to remove fluid

pericardiorrhaphy /ˌperikɑːdi'ɔːrəfi/ *noun* a surgical operation to repair a wound in the pericardium

pericardiostomy /ˌperikɑːdi'ɒstəmi/ *noun* a surgical operation to open the pericardium through the thoracic wall to drain off fluid

pericardiotomy /ˌperikɑːdi'ɒtəmi/ *noun* same as **pericardotomy**

pericarditis /ˌperikɑː'daɪtɪs/ *noun* inflammation of the pericardium

pericardium /ˌperi'kɑːdiəm/ *noun* a membrane which surrounds and supports the heart

pericardotomy /ˌperikɑː'dɒtəmi/ *noun* a surgical operation to open the pericardium

perichondritis /ˌperikɒn'draɪtɪs/ *noun* inflammation of cartilage, especially in the outer ear

perichondrium /ˌperi'kɒndriəm/ *noun* the fibrous connective tissue which covers cartilage

pericranium /ˌperi'kreɪniəm/ *noun* connective tissue which covers the surface of the skull

perilymph /'perilɪmf/ *noun* a fluid found in the labyrinth of the inner ear

perimenopause /ˌperi'menəpɔːz/ *noun* the few years before the menopause, in which oestrogen levels start to fall

perimeter /pə'rɪmɪtə/ *noun* **1.** an instrument to measure the field of vision **2.** the length of the outside line around an enclosed area

perimetritis /ˌperimə'traɪtɪs/ *noun* inflammation of the perimetrium

perimetrium /ˌperi'miːtriəm/ *noun* a membrane round the uterus

perimetry /pə'rɪmɪtri/ *noun* a measurement of the field of vision

perimysium /ˌperi'maɪsiəm/ *noun* a sheath which surrounds a bundle of muscle fibres

perinatal /ˌperi'neɪt(ə)l/ *adjective* referring to the period just before and after childbirth

perinatal mortality rate /ˌperineɪt(ə)l mɔː'tælɪti reɪt/ *noun* the number of babies born dead or who die during the period immediately after childbirth, shown per thousand babies born

perinatal period /ˌperi'neɪt(ə)l ˌpɪəriəd/ *noun* the period of time before and after childbirth, from the 28th week after conception to the first week after delivery

perinatologist /ˌperinə'tɒlədʒɪst/ *noun* an obstetrician who is a specialist in perinatology

perinatology /ˌperinə'tɒlədʒi/ *noun* a branch of medicine which studies and treats physiological and pathological conditions affecting the mother and/or infant just before and just after the birth of a baby

perineal /ˌperi'niːəl/ *adjective* referring to the perineum

perineoplasty /ˌperi'niːəplæsti/ *noun* a surgical operation to repair the perineum by grafting tissue

perineorrhaphy /ˌperini'ɔːrəfi/ *noun* a surgical operation to stitch up a perineum which has torn during childbirth

perinephric /ˌperi'nefrɪk/ *adjective* around the kidney

perinephritis /ˌperini'fraɪtɪs/ *noun* inflammation of tissue round the kidney, which spreads from an infected kidney

perineum /ˌperi'niːəm/ *noun* the skin and tissue between the opening of the urethra and the anus

perineurium /ˌperi'njʊəriəm/ *noun* connective tissue which surrounds bundles of nerve fibres

periocular /ˌperi'ɒkjʊlə/ *adjective* around the eyeball

periodic /ˌpɪəri'ɒdɪk/ *adjective* occurring from time to time ○ *He has periodic attacks of migraine.* ○ *She has to go to the clinic for periodic checkups.*

periodic fever /ˌpɪərɪɒdɪk ˈfiːvə/ *noun* a disease of the kidneys, common in Mediterranean countries

periodic paralysis /ˌpɪərɪɒdɪk pəˈræləsɪs/ *noun* recurrent attacks of weakness where the level of potassium in the blood is low

periodontal /ˌperiəʊˈdɒnt(ə)l/, **periodontic** /ˌperiəʊˈdɒntɪk/ *adjective* referring to the area around the teeth

periodontal membrane /ˌperiəʊdɒnt(ə)l ˈmembreɪn/, **periodontal ligament** /ˌperiəʊdɒnt(ə)l ˈlɪɡəmənt/ *noun* a ligament which attaches a tooth to the bone of the jaw

periodontics /ˌperiəʊˈdɒntɪks/, **periodontia** /ˌperiəʊˈdɒnʃə/ *noun* the study of diseases of the periodontal membrane

periodontist /ˌperiəʊˈdɒntɪst/ *noun* a dentist who specialises in the treatment of gum diseases

periodontitis /ˌperiəʊdɒnˈtaɪtɪs/ *noun* an infection of the periodontal membrane leading to pyorrhoea, and resulting in the teeth falling out if untreated

periodontium /ˌperiəʊˈdɒnʃiəm/ *noun* **1.** the gums, bone and periodontal membrane around a tooth **2.** same as **periodontal membrane**

perionychia /ˌperiəʊˈnɪkiə/, **perionyxis** /ˌperiəʊˈnɪksɪs/ *noun* a painful swelling round a fingernail

perioperative /ˌperiˈɒp(ə)rətɪv/ *adjective* before and after a surgical operation

periorbital /ˌperiəʊˈɔːbɪt(ə)l/ *adjective* around the eye socket

periosteal /ˌperiˈɒstiəl/ *adjective* referring to, or attached to, the periosteum

periosteotome /ˌperiˈɒstiəʊtəʊm/ *noun* a surgical instrument used to cut the periosteum

periosteum /ˌperiˈɒstiəm/ *noun* a dense layer of connective tissue around a bone. See illustration at **BONE STRUCTURE** in Supplement

periosteum elevator /ˌperiɒstiəm ˈeləveɪtə/ *noun* a surgical instrument used to remove the periosteum from a bone

periostitis /ˌperiəˈstaɪtɪs/ *noun* inflammation of the periosteum

peripheral /pəˈrɪf(ə)rəl/ *adjective* at the edge

peripheral nerves /pəˈrɪf(ə)rəl nɜːvz/ *plural noun* the parts of motor and sensory nerves which branch from the brain and spinal cord

peripheral nervous system /pəˌrɪf(ə)rəl ˈnɜːvəs ˌsɪstəm/ *noun* all the nerves in different parts of the body which are linked and governed by the central nervous system. Abbreviation **PNS**

peripheral resistance /pəˌrɪf(ə)rəl rɪˈzɪstəns/ *noun* the ability of the peripheral blood vessels to slow down the flow of blood inside them

peripheral vascular disease /pəˌrɪf(ə)rəl ˈvæskjʊlə dɪˌziːz/ *noun* a disease affecting the blood vessels which supply the arms and legs

peripheral vasodilator /pəˌrɪf(ə)rəl ˌveɪzəʊdaɪˈleɪtə/ *noun* a chemical substance which acts to widen the blood vessels in the arms and legs and so improves bad circulation

periphery /pəˈrɪf(ə)ri/ *noun* **1.** the regions of the body where the nerves end, such as the sense organs or the muscles **2.** the surface of something

periproctitis /ˌperiprɒkˈtaɪtɪs/ *noun* swelling of the tissues around the rectum

peristalsis /ˌperiˈstælsɪs/ *noun* the movement, like waves, produced by alternate contraction and relaxation of muscles along an organ such as the intestine or oesophagus, which pushes the contents of the organ along it. Compare **antiperistalsis**

peristaltic /ˌperiˈstæltɪk/ *adjective* occurring in waves, as in peristalsis

peritendinitis /ˌperitendiˈnaɪtɪs/ *noun* same as **tenosynovitis**

peritoneal /ˌperitəˈniːəl/ *adjective* referring to, or belonging to, the peritoneum

peritoneal cavity /ˌperitəniːəl ˈkævɪti/ *noun* a space between the layers of the peritoneum, containing the major organs of the abdomen

peritoneal dialysis /ˌperitəniːəl daɪˈæləsɪs/ *noun* removing waste matter from someone's blood by introducing fluid into the peritoneum which then acts as a filter, as opposed to haemodialysis

peritoneoscope /ˌperiˈtəʊniəskəʊp/ *noun* same as **laparoscope**

peritoneoscopy /ˌperitəʊniˈɒskəpi/ *noun* same as **laparoscopy**

peritoneum /ˌperitəˈniːəm/ *noun* a membrane which lines the abdominal cavity and covers the organs in it

peritonitis /ˌperitəˈnaɪtɪs/ *noun* inflammation of the peritoneum as a result of bacterial infection

peritonsillar /ˌperiˈtɒnsɪlə/ *adjective* around the tonsils

peritonsillar abscess /ˌperitɒnsɪlə ˈæbses/ *noun* same as **quinsy**

perityphlitis /ˌperitɪˈflaɪtɪs/ *noun* swelling of the tissues around the caecum

PERLA *abbreviation* Pupils Equal and Reactive to Light and Accommodation

perle /pɜːl/ *noun* a soft capsule of medicine

perleche /pɜːˈleʃ/ *noun* inflammation, with small cracks, at the corners of the mouth, caused by infection, poor diet, or producing too much saliva

permeability /ˌpɜːmiəˈbɪlɪti/ *noun* (*of a membrane*) the ability to allow some substances to pass through

permeable membrane /ˌpɜːmiəb(ə)l ˈmembreɪn/ *noun* a membrane which allows some substances to pass through it

pernicious /pəˈnɪʃəs/ *adjective* harmful or dangerous, or unusually severe and likely to end in death

pernicious anaemia /pəˌnɪʃəs əˈniːmiə/ *noun* a disease where an inability to absorb vitamin B₁₂ prevents the production of red blood cells and damages the spinal cord. Also called **Addison's anaemia**

perniosis /ˌpɜːniˈəʊsɪs/ *noun* any condition caused by cold which affects blood vessels in the skin

pero- /perəʊ/ *prefix* malformed or impaired

peroneal /ˌperəʊˈniːəl/ *adjective* referring to the outside of the leg

peroneal muscle /ˌperəʊˈniːəl ˌmʌs(ə)l/, **peroneus** /ˌperəʊˈniːəs/ *noun* one of three muscles, the peroneus brevis, longus and tertius, on the outside of the lower leg which make the leg turn outwards

peroperative /pəˈrɒp(ə)rətɪv/ *adjective* taking place during a surgical operation

peroral /pəˈrɔːrəl/ *adjective* through the mouth

per os /pər ˈɒs/ *adverb* referring to a drug or other substance to be taken through the mouth

persistent vegetative state /pəˌsɪstənt ˈvedʒɪtətɪv steɪt/ *noun* a condition in which someone is alive and breathes, but shows no brain activity, and will never recover consciousness. Abbreviation **PVS**

personal care /ˈpɜːs(ə)nəl keə/ *noun* the act of washing, toileting and dressing someone who cannot do these things for themselves

personal digital assistant /ˌpɜːs(ə)n(ə)l ˌdɪdʒɪt(ə)l əˈsɪstənt/ *noun* full form of **PDA**

personal hygiene /ˌpɜːs(ə)n(ə)l ˈhaɪdʒiːn/ *noun* the standards someone has of looking after parts of their body such as hair, skin, teeth and breath, hands and nails, and keeping them clean

personality /ˌpɜːsəˈnælɪti/ *noun* all the characteristics which are typical of one particular person and the way he or she thinks and behaves, and which make him or her different from other people

personality disorder /ˌpɜːsəˈnælɪti dɪsˌɔːdə/ *noun* a disorder which affects the way a person behaves, especially in relation to other people

perspiration /ˌpɜːspəˈreɪʃ(ə)n/ *noun* sweat or the action of sweating ○ *Perspiration broke out on her forehead.*

Perthes' disease /ˈpɜːtiːz dɪˌziːz/, **Perthes' hip** /ˈpɜːtiːz ˈhɪp/ *noun* a disease found in young boys, in which the upper end of the femur degenerates and does not develop as expected, sometimes resulting in a permanent limp

pertussis /pəˈtʌsɪs/ *noun* same as **whooping cough**

perversion /pəˈvɜːʃ(ə)n/ *noun* a form of behaviour which is thought to be unnatural, dangerous or disgusting ○ *He is suffering from a form of sexual perversion.*

pes /pes/ *noun* a foot

PESA *abbreviation* percutaneous epididymal sperm aspiration

pes cavus /ˌpes ˈkeɪvəs/ *noun* same as **claw foot**

pes planus /ˌpes ˈpleɪnəs/ *noun* same as **flat foot**

pessary /ˈpesəri/ *noun* **1.** a drug in soluble material which is pushed into the vagina and absorbed into the blood there. Also called **vaginal suppository 2.** a contraceptive device worn inside the vagina to prevent spermatozoa entering **3.** a device like a ring, which is put into the vagina as treatment for prolapse of the uterus

pesticide /ˈpestɪsaɪd/ *noun* a substance which kills pests

PET *abbreviation* positron-emission tomography

petechia /peˈtiːkiə/ *noun* a small red spot which does not go white when pressed, caused by bleeding under the skin (NOTE: The plural is **petechiae**.)

pethidine /ˈpeθɪdiːn/ *noun* a synthetically produced narcotic drug, used to reduce pain and as a sedative

petit mal /ˌpeti ˈmæl/ *noun* a less severe form of epilepsy, where loss of consciousness attacks last only a few seconds and the person appears simply to be thinking deeply. Compare **grand mal**

Petri dish /ˈpiːtri dɪʃ/ *noun* a small glass or plastic dish with a lid, in which a culture is grown

petrissage /ˌpetrɪˈsɑːʒ/ *noun* an action used in massaging the muscles

petrositis /ˌpetrəʊˈsaɪtɪs/ *noun* inflammation of the petrous part of the temporal bone

petrous /ˈpetrəs/ *adjective* like stone

petrous bone /ˈpetrəs bəʊn/ *noun* the part of the temporal bone which forms the base of the skull and the inner and middle ears

-pexy /peksi/ *suffix* referring to fixation of an organ by surgery

Peyer's patches /ˌpaɪəz ˈpætʃɪz/ *plural noun* patches of lymphoid tissue on the mucous membrane of the small intestine [Described 1677. After Johann Conrad Peyer (1653–1712), Swiss anatomist.]

Peyronie's disease /ˈperəniːz dɪˌziːz/ *noun* a condition associated with Dupuytren's contracture in which hard fibre develops in the penis which becomes painful when erect [Described 1743. After François de la Peyronie (1678–1747), Surgeon to Louis XV in Paris, France.]

PGD /ˌpiː dʒiː ˈdiː/ *noun* a document that allows the supply of prescription-only drugs to a group of patients without individual prescriptions. Full form **patient-group direction**

pH /ˌpi: ˈeɪt ʃ/ *noun* the concentration of hydrogen ions in a solution, which determines its acidity

phaco- /fækəʊ/ *prefix* referring to the lens of the eye

phacoemulsification /ˌfækəʊɪˌmʌlsɪfɪ ˈkeɪʃ(ə)n/ *noun* an ultrasonic technique which turns a cataract in the eye into liquid. It is then removed by suction and a plastic lens is put into the eye.

phaeochromocytoma /ˌfiːəʊˌkrəʊməʊsaɪ ˈtəʊmə/ *noun* a tumour of the adrenal glands which affects the secretion of hormones such as adrenaline, which in turn results in hypertension and hyperglycaemia

phag- /fæg/ *prefix* same as **phago-** (*used before vowels*)

phage /feɪdʒ/ *noun* same as **bacteriophage**

-phage /feɪdʒ/ *suffix* referring to something which eats

-phagia /feɪdʒə/ *suffix* referring to eating

phago- /fægəʊ/ *prefix* referring to eating

phagocyte /ˈfægəʊsaɪt/ *noun* a cell, especially a white blood cell, which can surround and destroy other cells such as bacteria cells

phagocytic /ˌfægəˈsɪtɪk/ *adjective* referring to phagocytes ○ *Monocytes become phagocytic during infection.*

phagocytosis /ˌfægəʊsaɪˈtəʊsɪs/ *noun* destruction of bacteria cells and foreign bodies by phagocytes

phakic /ˈfækɪk/ *adjective* referring to an eye which has its natural lens

phako- /fækəʊ/ *prefix* same as **phaco-**

phalangeal /fəˈlændʒiəl/ *adjective* referring to the phalanges

phalanges /fəˈlændʒiːz/ plural of **phalanx**

phalanx /ˈfælæŋks/ *noun* a bone in a finger or toe. See illustration at HAND in Supplement, FOOT in Supplement

phalloplasty /ˈfæləʊplæsti/ *noun* a surgical operation to repair a deformed or deformed penis

phantom limb /ˌfæntəm ˈlɪm/ *noun* a condition in which someone seems to feel sensations in a limb which has been amputated

phantom pregnancy /ˌfæntəm ˈpregnənsi/ *noun* same as **pseudocyesis**

phantom tumour /ˌfæntəm ˈtjuːmə/ *noun* a condition in which a swelling occurs which imitates a swelling caused by a tumour

pharmaceutical /ˌfɑːməˈsjuːtɪk(ə)l/ *adjective* referring to pharmacy or drugs

pharmaceuticals /ˌfɑːməˈsjuːtɪk(ə)lz/ *plural noun* drugs prescribed as medicines

Pharmaceutical Society /ˌfɑːməˈsjuːtɪk(ə)l səˌsaɪəti/ *noun* a professional association for pharmacists

pharmacist /ˈfɑːməsɪst/ *noun* a trained person who is qualified to prepare medicines according to the instructions on a doctor's prescription

pharmaco- /fɑːməkəʊ/ *prefix* referring to drugs

pharmacodynamic /ˌfɑːməkəʊdaɪˈnæmɪk/ *adjective* referring to a property of a drug which affects the part where it is applied

pharmacodynamics /ˌfɑːməkəʊdaɪ ˈnæmɪks/ *plural noun* the study of the effects of drugs on living organisms, and especially of how much the body's response changes when you increase the dose of a drug. Compare **pharmacokinetics** (NOTE: Takes a singular verb.)

pharmacokinetic /ˌfɑːməkəʊkaɪˈnetɪk/ *adjective* referring to a property of a drug which has an effect over a period of time

pharmacokinetics /ˌfɑːməkəʊkaɪˈnetɪks/ *plural noun* **1.** the study of how the body reacts to drugs over a period of time. Compare **pharmacodynamics** (NOTE: Takes a singular verb.) **2.** the way in which a drug interacts with the body

pharmacological /ˌfɑːməkəˈlɒdʒɪk(ə)l/ *adjective* referring to pharmacology

pharmacologist /ˌfɑːməˈkɒlədʒɪst/ *noun* a scientist who specialises in the study of drugs

pharmacology /ˌfɑːməˈkɒlədʒi/ *noun* the study of drugs or medicines, and their actions, properties and characteristics

pharmacopoeia /ˌfɑːməkəˈpiːə/ *noun* an official list of drugs, their methods of preparation, dosages and the ways in which they should be used

pharmacy /ˈfɑːməsi/ *noun* **1.** the study of the making and dispensing of drugs ○ *He has a qualification in pharmacy.* **2.** a shop or department in a hospital where drugs are prepared

Pharmacy Act /ˈfɑːməsi ækt/ *noun* in the UK, one of several Acts of Parliament which regulate the making, prescribing and selling of drugs, e.g. the Pharmacy and Poisons Act 1933, the Misuse of Drugs Act 1971 and the Poisons Act 1972

pharyng- /færɪndʒ/ *prefix* same as **pharyngo-** (*used before vowels*)

pharyngeal /ˌfærɪnˈdʒiːəl/ *adjective* referring to the pharynx

pharyngeal pouch /ˌfærɪndʒiːəl ˈpaʊtʃ/ *noun* one of the pouches on each side of the throat of an embryo. Also called **visceral pouch**

pharyngeal tonsils /ˌfærɪndʒiːəl ˈtɒns(ə)lz/ *plural noun* same as **adenoids**

pharyngectomy /ˌfærɪnˈdʒektəmi/ *noun* the surgical removal of part of the pharynx, especially in cases of cancer of the pharynx

pharyngismus /ˌfærɪnˈdʒɪzməs/, **pharyngism** /ˈfærɪndʒɪz(ə)m/ *noun* a spasm which contracts the muscles of the pharynx

pharyngitis /ˌfærɪnˈdʒaɪtɪs/ *noun* inflammation of the pharynx

pharyngo- /fərɪŋgəʊ/ *prefix* referring to the pharynx

pharyngolaryngeal /fəˌrɪŋgəʊləˈrɪndʒiəl/ *adjective* referring to the pharynx and the larynx

pharyngoscope /fəˈrɪŋgəʊskəʊp/ *noun* an instrument with a light attached, used by a doctor to examine the pharynx

pharyngotympanic tube /fəˌrɪŋgəʊtɪm ˌpænɪk ˈtjuːb/ *noun* one of two tubes which connect the back of the throat to the middle ear. Also called **eustachian tube**

pharynx /ˈfærɪŋks/ *noun* a muscular passage leading from the back of the mouth to the oesophagus (NOTE: The plural is **pharynges** or **pharynxes**.)

phenazopyridine /fəˌnæzəʊˈpɪrɪdiːn/ *noun* a drug used to reduce pain in conditions of the urinary tract, such as cystitis

phenobarbitone /ˌfiːnəʊˈbɑːbɪtəʊn/ *noun* a barbiturate drug which is used as a sedative, a hypnotic and an anticonvulsant

phenol /ˈfiːnɒl/ *noun* a strong disinfectant used for external use. Also called **carbolic acid**

phenomenon /fəˈnɒmɪnən/ *noun* 1. a fact or situation which can be observed 2. someone or something that is considered to be extraordinary and marvellous

phenotype /ˈfiːnətaɪp/ *noun* the particular characteristics of an organism. Compare **genotype**

phenylalanine /ˌfiːnaɪlˈæləniːn/ *noun* an essential amino acid

phenylketonuria /ˌfiːnaɪlˌkiːtəʊˈnjʊəriə/ *noun* a hereditary condition which affects the way in which the body breaks down phenylalanine, which in turn concentrates toxic metabolites in the nervous system causing brain damage

phenytoin /ˈfenɪtɔɪn/ *noun* a drug which helps to prevent convulsions, used in the treatment of epilepsy

phial /ˈfaɪəl/ *noun* a small medicine bottle

-philia /fɪliə/ *suffix* attraction to or liking for something

philtrum /ˈfɪltrəm/ *noun* a groove in the centre of the top lip

phimosis /faɪˈməʊsɪs/ *noun* a condition in which the foreskin is tight and has to be removed by circumcision

phleb- /fleb/ *prefix* same as **phlebo-** (used before vowels)

phlebectomy /flɪˈbektəmi/ *noun* the surgical removal of a vein or part of a vein

phlebitis /flɪˈbaɪtɪs/ *noun* inflammation of a vein

phlebo- /flebəʊ/ *prefix* referring to a vein

phlebogram /ˈflebəgræm/ *noun* an X-ray picture of a vein or system of veins. Also called **venogram**

phlebography /flɪˈbɒgrəfi/ *noun* an X-ray examination of a vein using a radio-opaque dye so that the vein will show up on the film. Also called **venography**

phlebolith /ˈflebəlɪθ/ *noun* a stone which forms in a vein as a result of an old thrombus becoming calcified

phlebothrombosis /ˌflebəʊθrɒmˈbəʊsɪs/ *noun* a blood clot in a deep vein in the legs or pelvis, which can easily detach and form an embolus in a lung

phlebotomy /flɪˈbɒtəmi/ *noun* an operation where a vein or an artery is cut so that blood can be removed, as when taking blood from a donor

phlegm /flem/ *noun* same as **sputum** ○ *She was coughing up phlegm into her handkerchief.*

phlegmasia alba dolens /flegˌmeɪziə ˌælbə ˈdəʊləns/ *noun* same as **milk leg**

phlyctena /flɪkˈtiːnə/, **phlycten** /ˈflɪktən/ *noun* 1. a small blister caused by a burn 2. a small vesicle on the conjunctiva

phlyctenule /flɪkˈtenjuːl/ *noun* a tiny blister on the cornea or conjunctiva

phobia /ˈfəʊbiə/ *noun* an unusually strong and irrational fear ○ *She has a phobia about* or *of dogs.* ○ *Fear of snakes is one of the commonest phobias.*

-phobia /fəʊbiə/ *suffix* neurotic fear of something ○ *agoraphobia* ○ *claustrophobia*

phobic /ˈfəʊbɪk/ *adjective* referring to a phobia

-phobic /fəʊbɪk/ *suffix* a person who has a phobia of something

phocomelia /ˌfəʊkəˈmiːliə/, **phocomely** /fəʊ ˈkɒməli/ *noun* a congenital condition in which the upper parts of the limbs are missing or poorly developed, leaving the hands or feet directly attached to the body

phon- /fəʊn/ *prefix* same as **phono-** (used before vowels)

phonation /fəʊˈneɪʃ(ə)n/ *noun* the production of vocal sounds, especially speech

phoniatrics /ˌfəʊniˈætrɪks/ *noun* the study of speech and disorders related to it

phono- /fəʊnəʊ/ *prefix* referring to sound or voice

phonocardiogram /ˌfəʊnəʊˈkɑːdiəgræm/ *noun* a chart of the sounds made by the heart

phonocardiography /ˌfəʊnəʊˌkɑːdiˈɒgrəfi/ *noun* the process of recording the sounds made by the heart

phonology /fəˈnɒlədʒi/ *noun* the study of the system of speech sounds used in a particular language or in human speech generally

phonosurgery /ˈfəʊnəʊˌsɜːdʒəri/ *noun* surgery performed to alter the quality of the voice

phosphatase /ˈfɒsfəteɪz/ *noun* a group of enzymes which are important in the cycle of muscle contraction and in the calcification of bones

phosphate /ˈfɒsfeɪt/ *noun* a salt of phosphoric acid

phosphaturia /ˌfɒsfəˈtjʊəriə/ *noun* the presence of excess phosphates in the urine

phospholipid /ˌfɒsfəʊˈlɪpɪd/ *noun* a compound with fatty acids, which is one of the main components of membranous tissue

phosphorescent /ˌfɒsfəˈres(ə)nt/ *adjective* shining without producing heat

phosphoric acid /fɒsˌfɒrɪk ˈæsɪd/ *noun* an acid which is very soluble in water and gives rise to acid, neutral and alkali salts

phosphorus /ˈfɒsf(ə)rəs/ *noun* a toxic chemical element which is present in very small quantities in bones and nerve tissue. It causes burns if it touches the skin, and can poison if swallowed. (NOTE: The chemical symbol is **P**.)

phosphorylase /fɒsˈfɒrɪleɪz/ *noun* an enzyme that aids the process of carbohydrate metabolism

phot- /fɒt, fəʊt/ *prefix* same as **photo-** (*used before vowels*)

photalgia /fəʊˈtældʒə/ *noun* pain in the eye caused by bright light

photo- /fəʊtəʊ/ *prefix* referring to light

photoablation /ˌfəʊtəʊəˈbleɪʃ(ə)n/ *noun* the removal of tissue using lasers

photocoagulation /ˌfəʊtəʊkəʊˌægjʊˈleɪʃ(ə)n/ *noun* the process in which tissue coagulates from the heat caused by light, used to treat a detached retina

photodermatosis /ˌfəʊtəʊˌdɜːməˈtəʊsɪs/ *noun* a lesion of the skin after exposure to bright light

photogenic /ˌfəʊtəˈdʒenɪk/ *adjective* 1. produced by the action of light 2. producing light

photophobia /ˌfəʊtəʊˈfəʊbiə/ *noun* a condition in which the eyes become sensitive to light and conjunctivitis may be caused (NOTE: It can be associated with measles and some other infectious diseases.)

photophthalmia /ˌfəʊtɒfˈθælmiə/ *noun* inflammation of the eye caused by bright light, as in snow blindness

photopic vision /fəʊˌtɒpɪk ˈvɪʒ(ə)n/ *noun* vision which is adapted to bright light such as daylight, using the cones in the retina instead of the rods, which are used in scotopic vision. ◊ **light adaptation**

photopsia /fəʊˈtɒpsiə/ *noun* a condition of the eye in which someone sees flashes of light

photoreceptor neurone /ˌfəʊtəʊrɪˌseptə ˈnjʊərəʊn/ *noun* a rod or cone in the retina, which is sensitive to light or colour

photoretinitis /ˌfəʊtəʊretɪˈnaɪtɪs/ *noun* damage to a retina caused by looking directly at the sun. Also called **sun blindness**

photosensitive /ˌfəʊtəʊˈsensɪtɪv/ *adjective* sensitive to light, or stimulated by light

photosensitivity /ˌfəʊtəʊsensɪˈtɪvɪti/ *noun* the fact of being sensitive to light

phototherapy /ˌfəʊtəʊˈθerəpi/ *noun* a treatment for jaundice and vitamin D deficiency, which involves exposing the person to ultraviolet rays

phren- /fren/ *prefix* same as **phreno-** (*used before vowels*)

-phrenia /friːniə/ *suffix* disorder of the mind

phrenic /ˈfrenɪk/ *adjective* referring to the diaphragm

phrenic nerve /ˈfrenɪk nɜːv/ *noun* a pair of nerves which controls the muscles in the diaphragm

phreno- /frenəʊ/ *prefix* 1. referring to the brain 2. referring to the phrenic nerve

pH test /ˌpiː ˈeɪtʃ test/ *noun* a test to see how acid or alkaline a solution is

phthiriasis /θɪˈraɪəsɪs/ *noun* infestation with the crab louse

Phthirius pubis /ˌθaɪəriəs ˈpjuːbɪs/ *noun* a louse which infests the pubic region. Also called **pubic louse**, **crab**

physi- /fɪzi/ *prefix* same as **physio-** (*used before vowels*)

physical /ˈfɪzɪk(ə)l/ *adjective* referring to the body, as opposed to the mind ■ *noun* a physical examination ○ *He has to pass a physical before being accepted by the police force.*

physical drug dependence /ˌfɪzɪk(ə)l ˈdrʌg dɪˌpendəns/ *noun* a state where a person is addicted to a drug such as heroin and suffers physical effects if he or she stops or reduces the drug

physical education /ˌfɪzɪk(ə)l ˌedjʊˈkeɪʃ(ə)n/ *noun* the teaching of sports and exercises in school

physical examination /ˌfɪzɪk(ə)l ɪgˌzæmɪˈneɪʃ(ə)n/ *noun* an examination of someone's body to see if he or she is healthy

physical genetic trait /ˌfɪzɪk(ə)l dʒəˈnetɪk treɪt/ *noun* a characteristic of the body of a person, e.g. red hair or big feet, which is inherited

physical medicine /ˌfɪzɪk(ə)l ˈmed(ə)sɪn/ *noun* a branch of medicine which deals with physical disabilities or with treatment of disorders after they have been diagnosed

physical sign /ˌfɪzɪk(ə)l ˈsaɪn/ *noun* a symptom which can be seen on someone's body or which can be produced by percussion and palpitation

physical therapy /ˌfɪzɪk(ə)l ˈθerəpi/ *noun* the treatment of disorders by heat, by massage, by exercise and other physical means

physician /fɪˈzɪʃ(ə)n/ *noun* a registered doctor who is not a surgeon

physio /ˈfɪziəʊ/ *noun* (*informal*) **1.** a session of physiotherapy treatment **2.** a physiotherapist

physio- /fɪziəʊ/ *prefix* **1.** referring to physiology **2.** physical

physiological /ˌfɪziəˈlɒdʒɪk(ə)l/ *adjective* referring to physiology and the regular functions of the body

physiological saline /ˌfɪziəlɒdʒɪk(ə)l ˈseɪlaɪn/, **physiological solution** /ˌfɪziə lɒdʒɪk(ə)l səˈluːʃ(ə)n/ *noun* any solution used to keep cells or tissue alive

physiological tremor /ˌfɪziəlɒdʒɪk(ə)l ˈtremə/ *noun* a small movement of the limbs which takes place when a person tries to remain still

physiologist /ˌfɪziˈɒlədʒɪst/ *noun* a scientist who specialises in the study of the functions of living organisms

physiology /ˌfɪziˈɒlədʒi/ *noun* the study of regular body functions

physiotherapist /ˌfɪziəʊˈθerəpɪst/ *noun* a trained specialist who gives physiotherapy

physiotherapy /ˌfɪziəʊˈθerəpi/ *noun* the treatment of a disorder or condition by exercise, massage, heat treatment, infrared lamps or other external means, e.g. to restore strength or function after a disease or injury

physiotherapy clinic /ˌfɪziəʊˈθerəpi ˌklɪnɪk/ *noun* a clinic where people can have physiotherapy

physique /fɪˈziːk/ *noun* the shape and size of a person's body

physo- /faɪsəʊ/ *prefix* **1.** tending to swell **2.** relating to air or gas

phyt- /faɪt/, **phyto-** /faɪtəʊ/ *prefix* referring to plants or coming from plants

PI *abbreviation* pressure index

pia /ˈpaɪə/, **pia mater** /ˌpaɪə ˈmeɪtə/ *noun* the delicate innermost membrane of the three which cover the brain. ◊ **arachnoid**, **dura mater**

pica /ˈpaɪkə/ *noun* a desire to eat things which are not food, e.g. wood or paper, often found in pregnant women and small children

Pick's disease /ˈpɪks dɪˌziːz/ *noun* a rare form of presenile dementia, in which a disorder of the lipoid metabolism causes mental impairment, anaemia, loss of weight and swelling of the spleen and liver

pico- /piːkəʊ/ *prefix* one million millionth (10⁻¹²). Symbol **p**

picomole /ˈpiːkəʊməʊl/ *noun* a unit of measurement of the amount of substance equal to one million millionth of a mole. Symbol **pmol**

Pierre Robin syndrome /ˌpjeə rɒˈbæn ˌsɪndrəʊm/ *noun* a combination of facial features including a small lower jaw and a cleft palate that exist at birth, causing breathing and feeding problems early in a child's life

pigeon breast /ˈpɪdʒɪn brest/, **pigeon chest** /ˈpɪdʒɪn tʃest/ *noun* same as **pectus carinatum**

pigeon toes /ˈpɪdʒən təʊz/ *plural noun* a condition in which the feet turn towards the inside when a person is standing upright

pigment /ˈpɪgmənt/ *noun* a substance which gives colour to part of the body such as blood, the skin or hair

pigmentation /ˌpɪgmenˈteɪʃ(ə)n/ *noun* the colouring of the body, especially that produced by deposits of pigment

PIH *abbreviation* pregnancy-induced hypertension

piles /paɪlz/ *plural noun* same as **haemorrhoids**

pili /ˈpaɪlaɪ/ ◆ **arrector pili**

pill /pɪl/ *noun* a small hard round ball of medication that is taken by swallowing ○ *He has to take the pills twice a day.* □ **the pill** an oral contraceptive. ◊ **morning-after pill** □ **on the pill** taking a regular course of contraceptive pills

pillar /ˈpɪlə/ *noun* a part that is long and thin

pilo- /paɪləʊ/ *prefix* referring to hair

pilocarpine /ˌpaɪləʊˈkɑːpiːn/ *noun* an organic compound of plant origin which is used in eye drops to treat glaucoma

pilomotor /ˌpaɪləʊˈməʊtə/ *adjective* referring to something that moves the hairs of the skin

pilomotor nerve /ˌpaɪləʊˈməʊtə ˌnɜːv/ *noun* a nerve which supplies the arrector pili muscles attached to hair follicles

pilomotor reflex /ˌpaɪləʊˈməʊtə ˌriːfleks/ *noun* a reaction of the dermal papillae of the skin to cold and fear which causes the hairs on the skin to become erect

pilonidal /ˌpaɪləˈnaɪd(ə)l/ *adjective* relating to a cyst or cavity which has a growth of hair

pilonidal cyst /ˌpaɪlənaɪd(ə)l ˈsɪst/ *noun* a cyst containing hair, usually found at the bottom of the spine near the buttocks

pilonidal sinus /ˌpaɪlənaɪd(ə)l ˈsaɪnəs/ *noun* a small depression with hairs at the base of the spine

pilosis /paɪˈləʊsɪs/, **pilosism** /ˈpaɪləsɪz(ə)m/ *noun* a condition in which someone has an unusual amount of hair or where hair is present in an unusual place

pilot study /ˈpaɪlət ˌstʌdi/ *noun* a small version of a project which is carried out first, in order to discover how well it works and to solve any problems, before going ahead with the full version

pilus /'paɪləs/ *noun* one hair (NOTE: The plural is **pili**.)

pimple /'pɪmpəl/ *noun* a small swelling on the skin, containing pus ○ *He had pimples on his neck.*

pineal /'pɪniəl/ *adjective* relating to or released by the pineal gland

pineal body /'pɪniəl ˌbɒdi/, **pineal gland** /'pɪniəl glænd/ *noun* a small cone-shaped gland situated below the corpus callosum in the brain, which produces melatonin and is believed to be associated with the circadian rhythm. See illustration at BRAIN in Supplement

pinguecula /pɪŋ'gwekjʊlə/, **pinguicula** /pɪŋ'gwɪkjʊlə/ *noun* a condition affecting elderly people, in which the conjunctiva in the eyes has small yellow growths near the edge of the cornea, usually on the nasal side

pinna /'pɪnə/ *noun* the outer ear, the part of the ear which is outside the head, connected by a passage to the eardrum. See illustration at EAR in Supplement

pinnaplasty /'pɪnəplæsti/ *noun* a cosmetic surgical procedure to correct the shape of the ear

pinocytosis /ˌpiːnəʊsaɪ'təʊsɪs/ *noun* the process by which a cell surrounds and takes in fluid

pins and needles /ˌpɪnz ən 'niːd(ə)lz/ *noun* an unpleasant tingling sensation, usually occurring after a temporarily restricted blood supply returns to an arm or leg (*informal*) ◊ **paraesthesia**

PIP *abbreviation* proximal interphalangeal joint

piriform fossae /ˌpɪrifɔːm 'fɒsiː/ *plural noun* the two hollows at the sides of the upper end of the larynx

Piriton /'pɪrɪtɒn/ a trade name for chlorpheniramine

piroxicam /pɪ'rɒksɪkæm/ *noun* a non-steroidal anti-inflammatory drug used in the treatment of rheumatoid arthritis and osteoarthritis

PIs *abbreviation* performance indicators

pisiform /'pɪsifɔːm/, **pisiform bone** /'pɪsifɔːm bəʊn/ *noun* one of the eight small carpal bones in the wrist. See illustration at HAND in Supplement

pit /pɪt/ *noun* a hollow place on a surface

pitting /'pɪtɪŋ/ *noun* the formation of hollows in the skin

pituitary /pɪ'tjuːɪt(ə)ri/ *adjective* **1.** relating to or produced by the pituitary gland **2.** caused by a disturbance of the pituitary gland ■ *noun* same as **pituitary gland**

pituitary body /pɪ'tjuːɪt(ə)ri ˌbɒdi/ *noun* same as **pituitary gland**

pituitary fossa /pɪˌtjuːɪt(ə)ri 'fɒsə/ *noun* same as **sella turcica**

pituitary gland /pɪ'tjuːɪt(ə)ri glænd/ *noun* the main endocrine gland in the body which secretes hormones that stimulate other glands. Also called **pituitary body**, **hypophysis cerebri**. See illustration at BRAIN in Supplement

COMMENT: The pituitary gland is about the size of a pea and hangs down from the base of the brain, inside the sphenoid bone, on a stalk which attaches it to the hypothalamus. The front lobe of the gland (the adenohypophysis) secretes several hormones (TSH, ACTH) which stimulate the adrenal and thyroid glands, or which stimulate the production of sex hormones, melanin and milk. The posterior lobe of the pituitary gland (the neurohypophysis) secretes the antidiuretic hormone (ADH) and oxytocin.

pituitrin /pɪ'tjuːɪtrɪn/ *noun* a hormone secreted by the pituitary gland

pityriasis /ˌpɪtɪ'raɪəsɪs/ *noun* any skin disease in which the skin develops thin scales

pityriasis alba /pɪtɪˌraɪəsɪs 'ælbə/ *noun* a disease affecting children which results in flat white patches on the cheeks that usually heal naturally

pityriasis capitis /pɪtɪˌraɪəsɪs kə'paɪtɪs/ *noun* ♦ **dandruff**

pityriasis rosea /pɪtɪˌraɪəsɪs 'rəʊziə/ *noun* a mild irritating rash affecting young people, which appears especially in the early part of the year and has no known cause

pityriasis rubra /pɪtɪˌraɪəsɪs 'ruːbrə/ *noun* a serious, sometimes fatal, skin disease, a type of exfoliative dermatitis in which the skin turns dark red and is covered with white scales

pivot /'pɪvət/ *noun* a stem used to attach an artificial crown to the root of a tooth ■ *verb* to rest and turn on a point ○ *The atlas bone pivots on the second vertebra.*

pivot joint /'pɪvət dʒɔɪnt/ *noun* same as **trochoid joint**

PKD *abbreviation* polycystic kidney disease

PKU *abbreviation* phenylketonuria

placebo /plə'siːbəʊ/ *noun* a tablet which appears to be a drug, but has no medicinal substance in it

placebo effect /plə'siːbəʊ ɪˌfekt/ *noun* the apparently beneficial effect of telling someone that he or she is having a treatment, even if this is not true, caused by the hope that the treatment will be effective

placenta /plə'sentə/ *noun* the tissue which grows inside the uterus during pregnancy and links the baby to the mother

placental /plə'sent(ə)l/ *adjective* referring to the placenta

placental barrier /pləˌsent(ə)l 'bæriə/ *noun* a barrier which prevents the blood of a fetus and that of the mother from mixing, but allows water, oxygen and hormones to pass from mother to fetus

placental insufficiency /plə,sent(ə)l ,insə 'fɪʃ(ə)nsi/ *noun* a condition in which the placenta does not provide the fetus with the necessary oxygen and nutrients

placenta praevia /plə,sentə 'pri:viə/ *noun* a condition in which the fertilised egg becomes implanted in the lower part of the uterus, which means that the placenta lies across the cervix and may become detached during childbirth and cause brain damage to the baby

plagiocephaly /,pleɪdʒɪə'kefəli/ *noun* a condition in which a person has a distorted head shape, from irregular closure of the cranial sutures

plague /pleɪg/ *noun* an infectious disease which occurs in epidemics where many people are killed

plane /pleɪn/ *noun* a flat surface, especially that of the body seen from a specific angle

planning /'plænɪŋ/ *noun* the work of deciding and arranging how something should be done

planta /'plæntə/ *noun* the sole of the foot

plantar /'plæntə/ *adjective* referring to the sole of the foot

plantar arch /,plæntər 'ɑːtʃ/ *noun* the curved part of the sole of the foot running along the length of the foot. Also called **longitudinal arch**

plantar flexion /,plæntə 'flekʃən/ *noun* the bending of the toes downwards

plantar reflex /,plæntə 'ri:fleks/**, plantar response** /,plæntə rɪ'spɒns/ *noun* the usual downward movement of the toes when the sole of the foot is stroked in the Babinski test

plantar region /'plæntə ,ri:dʒən/ *noun* the sole of the foot

plantar surface /'plæntə ,sɜ:fɪs/ *noun* the skin of the sole of the foot

planus /'pleɪnəs/ ♦ **lichen planus**

plaque /plæk, plɑ:k/ *noun* **1.** a flat area **2.** a film of saliva, mucus, bacteria and food residues that builds up on the surface of teeth and can cause gum damage

-plasia /pleɪzɪə/ *suffix* referring to something which develops or grows

plasm- /plæz(ə)m/ *prefix* same as **plasmo-** (used before vowels)

plasma /'plæzmə/ *noun* a yellow watery liquid which makes up the main part of blood

plasma cell /'plæzmə sel/ *noun* a lymphocyte which produces a particular type of antibody

plasmapheresis /,plæzməfə'ri:sɪs/ *noun* an operation to take blood from someone, then to separate the red blood cells from the plasma, and to return the red blood cells suspended in a saline solution to the patient through a transfusion

plasma protein /'plæzmə ,prəʊti:n/ *noun* a protein in plasma, e.g. albumin, gamma globulin or fibrinogen

plasmin /'plæzmɪn/ *noun* same as **fibrinolysin**

plasminogen /plæz'mɪnədʒən/ *noun* a substance in blood plasma which becomes activated and forms plasmin

plasmo- /plæzməʊ/ *prefix* referring to blood plasma

Plasmodium /plæz'məʊdiəm/ *noun* a type of parasite which infests red blood cells and causes malaria

plaster /'plɑ:stə/ *noun* a white powder which is mixed with water and used to make a solid support to cover a broken limb ○ *After his accident he had his leg in plaster for two months.*

plaster cast /'plɑ:stə kɑ:st/ *noun* a hard support made of bandage soaked in liquid plaster of Paris, which is allowed to harden after being wrapped round a broken limb and which prevents the limb moving while the bone heals

plaster of Paris /,plɑ:stər əv 'pærɪs/ *noun* a fine white plaster used to make plaster casts

plastic /'plæstɪk/ *noun* an artificial material made from petroleum, and used to make many objects, including replacement organs ■ *adjective* able to change shape or develop in different shapes

plastic lymph /'plæstɪk lɪmf/ *noun* a yellow liquid produced by an inflamed wound which helps the healing process

plastic surgeon /,plæstɪk 'sɜ:dʒən/ *noun* a surgeon who specialises in plastic surgery

plastic surgery /,plæstɪk 'sɜ:dʒəri/ *noun* surgery to repair damaged or malformed parts of the body (*informal*)

COMMENT: Plastic surgery is especially important in treating accident victims or people who have suffered burns. It is also used to correct congenital disorders such as a cleft palate. When the aim is simply to improve the patient's appearance, it is usually referred to as 'cosmetic surgery'.

plastin /'plæstɪn/ *noun* same as **fibrinolysin**

-plasty /plæsti/ *suffix* referring to plastic surgery

plate /pleɪt/ *noun* a flat sheet of metal or bone ○ *The surgeon inserted a plate in her skull.*

platelet /'pleɪtlət/ *noun* a small blood cell which releases thromboplastin and which multiplies rapidly after an injury, encouraging the coagulation of blood. Also called **thrombocyte**

platelet count /'pleɪtlət kaʊnt/ *noun* a test to count the number of platelets in a specific quantity of blood

platy- /plæti/ *prefix* flat

pledget /'pledʒɪt/ *noun* a small piece of gauze or cotton wool used to protect or apply medication to a small enclosed space, such as the ear passage

-plegia /pliːdʒə/ *suffix* paralysis

pleio- /plaɪəʊ/ *prefix* same as **pleo-**

pleo- /pliːəʊ/ *prefix* too many

pleocytosis /ˌpliːəʊsaɪˈtəʊsɪs/ *noun* a condition in which there are an unusual number of leucocytes in the cerebrospinal fluid

pleoptics /pliːˈɒptɪks/ *noun* treatment to help the partially sighted

plessor /ˈplesə/ *noun* a little hammer with a rubber tip, used by doctors to tap tendons to test for reflexes or for percussion of the chest. Also called **plexor**

plethysmography /ˌpleθɪzˈmɒɡrəfi/ *noun* a method of recording the changes in the volume of organs, mainly used to measure blood flow in the limbs

pleur- /plʊər/ *prefix* same as **pleuro-** (*used before vowels*)

pleura /ˈplʊərə/ *noun* one of two membranes lining the chest cavity and covering each lung (NOTE: The plural is **pleuras** or **pleurae**.)

pleuracentesis /ˌplʊərəsenˈtiːsɪs/ *noun* same as **pleurocentesis**

pleural /ˈplʊərəl/ *adjective* referring to the pleura

pleural cavity /ˌplʊərəl ˈkævɪti/ *noun* a space between the inner and outer pleura of the chest. See illustration at LUNGS in Supplement

pleural effusion /ˌplʊərəl ɪˈfjuːʒ(ə)n/ *noun* an excess of fluid formed in the pleural sac

pleural fluid /ˌplʊərəl ˈfluːɪd/ *noun* a fluid which forms between the layers of the pleura in pleurisy

pleural membrane /ˌplʊərəl ˈmembreɪn/ *noun* same as **pleura**

pleurectomy /plʊəˈrektəmi/ *noun* the surgical removal of part of the pleura which has been thickened or made stiff by chronic empyema

pleurisy /ˈplʊərɪsi/ *noun* inflammation of the pleura, usually caused by pneumonia

pleuritis /plʊəˈraɪtɪs/ *noun* same as **pleurisy**

pleuro- /plʊərəʊ/ *prefix* referring to the pleura

pleurocentesis /ˌplʊərəʊsenˈtiːsɪs/ *noun* an operation in which a hollow needle is put into the pleura to drain liquid. Also called **pleuracentesis**

pleurodesis /ˌplʊərəʊˈdiːsɪs/ *noun* treatment for a collapsed lung, in which the inner and outer pleura are stuck together

pleurodynia /ˌplʊərəʊˈdɪniə/ *noun* pain in the muscles between the ribs, due to rheumatic inflammation

pleuropneumonia /ˌplʊərəʊnjʊˈməʊniə/ *noun* acute lobar pneumonia, the classic type of pneumonia

plexor /ˈpleksə/ *noun* same as **plessor**

plexus /ˈpleksəs/ *noun* a network of nerves, blood vessels or lymphatics

plica /ˈplaɪkə/ *noun* a fold

plicate /ˈplaɪkeɪt/ *adjective* folded

plication /plaɪˈkeɪʃ(ə)n/ *noun* a surgical operation to reduce the size of a muscle or a hollow organ by making folds in its walls and attaching them

ploidy /ˈplɔɪdi/ *noun* the number of sets of chromosomes within a cell

plumbing /ˈplʌmɪŋ/ *noun* any system of tubes or vessels in the body, but especially the urinary system (*informal humorous*)

Plummer–Vinson syndrome /ˌplʌmə ˈvɪnsən ˌsɪndrəʊm/ *noun* a type of iron-deficiency anaemia, in which the tongue and mouth become inflamed and the person cannot swallow [Described 1912 by Plummer, 1919 by Vinson (also described in 1919 by Patterson and Brown Kelly, whose names are frequently associated with the syndrome). Henry Stanley Plummer (1874–1937), US physician; Porter Paisley Vinson (1890–1959), physician at the Mayo Clinic, Minnesota, USA.]

pluri- /plʊəri/ *prefix* indicating more than one of something

PM *abbreviation* post mortem

PMA *abbreviation* progressive muscular atrophy

pmol *symbol* picomole

PMR *abbreviation* polymyalgia rheumatica

PMS *abbreviation* premenstrual syndrome

PMT *abbreviation* premenstrual tension

-pnea /pniːə/ *suffix* same as **-pnoea**

pneo- /niːəʊ/ *prefix* relating to breathing

pneum- /njuːm/ *prefix* same as **pneumo-** (*used before vowels*)

pneumat- /njuːmət/ *prefix* same as **pneumato-** (*used before vowels*)

pneumato- /njuːmətəʊ/ *prefix* relating to air, gas or breath

pneumatocele /njuːˈmætəʊsiːl/ *noun* a sac or tumour filled with gas

pneumatonometer /ˌnjuːmətəˈnɒmɪtə/ *noun* an instrument which measures the air pressure in the eye, used in testing for glaucoma. It blows a puff of air onto the cornea.

pneumatosis /ˌnjuːməˈtəʊsɪs/ *noun* the occurrence of gas in an unusual place in the body

pneumaturia /ˌnjuːməˈtjʊəriə/ *noun* the act of passing air or gas in the urine

pneumo- /njuːməʊ/ *prefix* referring to air, to the lungs or to breathing

pneumococcal /ˌnjuːməʊˈkɒk(ə)l/ *adjective* referring to pneumococci

pneumococcus /ˌnjuːməʊˈkɒkəs/ *noun* a bacterium which causes respiratory tract infections including pneumonia (NOTE: The plural is **pneumococci**.)

pneumoconiosis /ˌnjuːməʊkəʊniˈəʊsɪs/ *noun* a lung disease in which fibrous tissue forms in the lungs because the person has inhaled particles of stone or dust over a long period of time

pneumocystis carinii pneumonia /ˌnjuːməʊsɪstɪs kəˌriːniː njuːˈməʊniə/ *noun* a form of pneumonia found in people with impaired immune systems after radiotherapy or with AIDS. Abbreviation **PCP**

pneumocyte /ˈnjuːməʊsaɪt/ *noun* a cell of the walls between the air sacs in the lung

pneumoencephalography /ˌnjuːməʊenˌkefəˈlɒgrəfi/ *noun* same as **encephalogram**

pneumogastric /ˌnjuːməʊˈgæstrɪk/ *adjective* referring to the lungs and the stomach

pneumograph /ˈnjuːməgrɑːf/ *noun* an instrument which records chest movements during breathing

pneumohaemothorax /ˌnjuːməʊˌhiːməʊˈθɔːræks/ *noun* blood or air in the pleural cavity. Also called **haemopneumothorax**

pneumomycosis /ˌnjuːməʊmaɪˈkəʊsɪs/ *noun* an infection of the lungs caused by a fungus

pneumon- /njuːmən/ *prefix* same as **pneumono-** (*used before vowels*)

pneumonectomy /ˌnjuːməˈnektəmi/ *noun* the surgical removal of all or part of a lung. Also called **pulmonectomy**

pneumonia /njuːˈməʊniə/ *noun* inflammation of a lung, where the tiny alveoli of the lung become filled with fluid ○ *He developed pneumonia and had to be hospitalised.* ○ *She died of pneumonia.*

pneumonitis /ˌnjuːməʊˈnaɪtɪs/ *noun* inflammation of the lungs

pneumono- /njuːmənəʊ/ *prefix* referring to the lungs

pneumoperitoneum /ˌnjuːməʊperɪtəˈniːəm/ *noun* air in the peritoneal cavity

pneumoradiography /ˌnjuːməʊˌreɪdiˈɒgrəfi/ *noun* an X-ray examination of part of the body after air or a gas has been inserted to make the organs show more clearly

pneumothorax /ˌnjuːməʊˈθɔːræks/ *noun* a condition in which air or gas is in the thorax. Also called **collapsed lung**

-pnoea /pniːə/ *suffix* referring to breathing

PNS *abbreviation* peripheral nervous system

pock /pɒk/ *noun* a localised lesion on the skin, due to smallpox or chickenpox

pod- /pɒd/ *prefix* referring to the foot

podagra /pɒˈdægrə/ same as **gout**

podalic /pəʊˈdælɪk/ *adjective* relating to the feet

podalic version /pəʊˌdælɪk ˈvɜːʃ(ə)n/ *noun* the procedure of turning a fetus in the uterus by its feet

podarthritis /ˌpɒdɑːˈθraɪtɪs/ *noun* the swelling of one or more joints of the foot

podiatrist /pəʊˈdaɪətrɪst/ *noun* US a person who specialises in the care of the foot and its diseases

podiatry /pəʊˈdaɪətri/ *noun* US the study of minor diseases and disorders of the feet

-poiesis /pɔiːsɪs/ *suffix* referring to something which forms

poikilo- /pɔɪkɪləʊ/ *prefix* irregular or varied

poison /ˈpɔɪz(ə)n/ *noun* a substance which can kill or harm body tissues if eaten or drunk ■ *verb* to harm or kill someone with a poison

poisoning /ˈpɔɪz(ə)nɪŋ/ *noun* a condition in which a person is made ill or is killed by a poisonous substance

poison ivy /ˌpɔɪz(ə)n ˈaɪvi/, **poison oak** /ˌpɔɪz(ə)n ˈəʊk/ *noun* American plants whose leaves can cause a painful rash if touched

Poisons Act /ˈpɔɪz(ə)nz ækt/ *noun* in the UK, one of several Acts of Parliament which regulate the making, prescribing and selling of drugs, e.g. the Pharmacy and Poisons Act 1933, Misuse of Drugs Act 1971, or Poisons Act 1972

polar /ˈpəʊlə/ *adjective* with a pole

polar body /ˌpəʊlə ˈbɒdi/ *noun* a small cell which is produced from an oocyte but does not develop into an ovum

pole /pəʊl/ *noun* the end of an axis

poli- /pɒli/ *prefix* same as **polio-** (*used before vowels*)

polio /ˈpəʊliəʊ/ *noun* same as **poliomyelitis** (*informal*)

polio- /pəʊliəʊ/ *prefix* grey matter in the nervous system

polioencephalitis /ˌpəʊliəʊenˌkefəˈlaɪtɪs/ *noun* a type of viral encephalitis, an inflammation of the grey matter in the brain caused by the same virus as poliomyelitis

polioencephalomyelitis /ˌpəʊliəʊenˌkefələʊˌmaɪəˈlaɪtɪs/ *noun* polioencephalitis which also affects the spinal cord

poliomyelitis /ˌpəʊliəʊˌmaɪəˈlaɪtɪs/ *noun* an infection of the anterior horn cells of the spinal cord caused by a virus which attacks the motor neurones and can lead to paralysis. Also called **polio, infantile paralysis**

poliovirus /ˈpəʊliəʊˌvaɪrəs/ *noun* a virus which causes poliomyelitis

Politzer bag /ˈpɒlɪtsə bæg/ *noun* a rubber bag which is used to blow air into the middle ear to unblock a Eustachian tube [Described 1863. After Adam Politzer (1835–1920), Professor of Otology in Vienna, Austria.]

pollex /ˈpɒleks/ *noun* the thumb (*technical*) (NOTE: The plural is **pollices**.)

pollution /pəˈluːʃ(ə)n/ *noun* the act of making dirty, or substances which make e.g. air or water impure

poly- /ˈpɒli/ *prefix* **1.** many or much **2.** touching many organs

polyarteritis /ˌpɒliɑːtəˈraɪtɪs/ *noun* a condition in which a lot of arteries swell up at the same time

polyarteritis nodosa /ˌpɒliɑːtəˌraɪtɪs nəˈdəʊsə/ *noun* a collagen disease in which the walls of the arteries in various parts of the body become inflamed, leading to asthma, high blood pressure and kidney failure. Also called **periarteritis nodosa**

polyarthritis /ˌpɒliɑːˈθraɪtɪs/ *noun* inflammation of several joints, as in rheumatoid arthritis

polycystic /ˌpɒliˈsɪstɪk/ *adjective* referring to an organ which has developed more than one cyst, or to a disease caused by the development of cysts

polycystic kidney disease /ˌpɒlisɪstɪk ˈkɪdni dɪˌziːz/ *noun* a condition in which there are multiple cysts on each kidney which grow and multiply over time. Abbreviation **PKD**

> COMMENT: The diseased kidney finally shuts down in over 60% of cases, and dialysis and transplantation are the only forms of treatment.

polycystic ovary disease /ˌpɒlisɪstɪk ˈəʊvəri dɪˌziːz/ *noun* same as **polycystic ovary syndrome**. Abbreviation **PCOD**

polycystic ovary syndrome /ˌpɒlisɪstɪk ˈəʊvəri ˌsɪndrəʊm/, **polycystic ovarian syndrome** /ˌpɒlisɪstɪk əʊˈveəriən ˌsɪndrəʊm/ *noun* a hormonal disorder in which a woman's ovaries are enlarged and contain many small painless cysts, hair growth is excessive, acne develops and infertility may occur. Also called **Stein Leventhal syndrome**. Abbreviation **PCOS**

polycystitis /ˌpɒlisɪˈstaɪtɪs/ *noun* a congenital disease in which several cysts form in the kidney at the same time

polycythaemia /ˌpɒlisaɪˈθiːmiə/ *noun* a condition in which the number of red blood cells increases (NOTE: The US spelling is **polycythemia**.)

polydactylism /ˌpɒliˈdæktɪlɪz(ə)m/ *noun* same as **hyperdactylism**

polydipsia /ˌpɒliˈdɪpsiə/ *noun* a condition, often caused by diabetes insipidus, in which a person is unusually thirsty

polymyalgia rheumatica /ˌpɒlimaɪˌældʒə ruːˈmætɪkə/ *noun* a disease of elderly people characterised by pain and stiffness in the shoulder and hip muscles making them weak and sensitive

polymyositis /ˌpɒlimaɪəʊˈsaɪtɪs/ *noun* a condition in which a lot of muscles swell up at the same time, especially the ones in the trunk of the

body, causing weakness. It is treated with steroid drugs or immunosuppressants, and also exercise.

polyneuritis /ˌpɒlinjʊˈraɪtɪs/ *noun* inflammation of many nerves

polyneuropathy /ˌpɒlinjʊˈrɒpəθi/ *noun* any disease which affects several nerves (NOTE: The plural is **polyneuropathies**.)

polyopia /ˌpɒliˈəʊpiə/, **polyopsia** /ˌpɒliˈɒpsiə/, **polyopy** /ˈpɒliəʊpi/ *noun* a condition in which a person sees several images of one object at the same time. Compare **diplopia**

polyp /ˈpɒlɪp/ *noun* a tumour growing on a stalk in mucous membrane, which can be cauterised. Polyps are often found in the nose, mouth or throat. Also called **polypus**

polypectomy /ˌpɒlɪˈpektəmi/ *noun* a surgical operation to remove a polyp (NOTE: The plural is **polypectomies**.)

polypeptide /ˌpɒliˈpeptaɪd/ *noun* a type of protein formed of linked amino acids

polypi /ˈpɒlɪpi/ plural of **polypus**

polyploid /ˈpɒlɪplɔɪd/ *adjective* referring to a cell where there are more than two copies of each chromosome, which is not viable in humans

polypoid /ˈpɒlɪpɔɪd/ *adjective* looking like a polyp

polyposis /ˌpɒlɪˈpəʊsɪs/ *noun* a condition in which many polyps form in the mucous membrane of the colon. ◊ **familial adenomatous polyposis**

polypus /ˈpɒlɪpəs/ *noun* same as **polyp** (NOTE: The plural is **polypi**.)

polysaccharide /ˌpɒliˈsækəraɪd/ *noun* a type of carbohydrate made up of a lot of monosaccharides joined together in chains. They include starch and cellulose, are insoluble in water and do not form crystals.

polysomnograph /ˌpɒliˈsɒmnəgrɑːf/ *noun* a record of bodily activity during sleep to identify possible causes of sleep disorders

polyspermia /ˌpɒliˈspɜːmiə/, **polyspermism** /ˌpɒliˈspɜːmɪz(ə)m/, **polyspermy** /ˌpɒliˈspɜːmi/ *noun* excessive seminal secretion

polyuria /ˌpɒliˈjʊəriə/ *noun* a condition in which a person passes a large quantity of urine, usually as a result of diabetes insipidus

pompholyx /ˈpɒmfɒlɪks/ *noun* a type of eczema with many irritating little blisters on the hands and feet

pons /pɒnz/ *noun* a bridge of tissue joining parts of an organ. See illustration at **BRAIN** in Supplement (NOTE: The plural is **pontes**.)

pons Varolii /ˌpɒnz vəˈrəʊliaɪ/ *noun* part of the hindbrain, formed of fibres which continue the medulla oblongata. See illustration at **BRAIN** in Supplement (NOTE: The plural is **pontes Varolii**.) [After Constanzo Varolius (1543–75),

Italian physician and anatomist, doctor to Pope Gregory XIII.]

pontine /'pɒntaɪn/ *adjective* referring to a pons

POP /pɒp/ *abbreviation* progesterone only pill

popliteal /ˌpɒplɪ'tiːəl/ *adjective* referring to the back of the knee

popliteal artery /ˌpɒplɪtiəl 'ɑːtəri/ *noun* an artery which branches from the femoral artery behind the knee and leads into the tibial arteries

popliteal fossa /ˌpɒplɪtiəl 'fɒsə/ *noun* a space behind the knee between the hamstring and the calf muscle. Also called **popliteal space**

popliteal muscle /ˌpɒplɪ'tiːəl ˌmʌs(ə)l/ *noun* same as **popliteus**

popliteal space /ˌpɒplɪtiːəl 'speɪs/ *noun* same as **popliteal fossa**

popliteus /pɒ'plɪtiəs/ *noun* a muscle at the back of the knee. Also called **popliteal muscle**

population /ˌpɒpjʊ'leɪʃ(ə)n/ *noun* **1.** the number of people living in a country or town ○ *Population statistics show that the birth rate is slowing down.* ○ *The government has decided to screen the whole population of the area.* **2.** the number of patients in hospital ○ *The hospital population in the area has fallen below 10,000.*

pore /pɔː/ *noun* a tiny hole in the skin through which the sweat passes

porphyria /pɔː'fɪriə/ *noun* a hereditary disease affecting the metabolism of porphyrin pigments

COMMENT: Porphyria causes abdominal pains and attacks of mental confusion. The skin becomes sensitive to light and the urine becomes coloured and turns dark brown when exposed to the light.

porphyrin /'pɔːfərɪn/ *noun* a member of a family of metal-containing biological pigments, the commonest of which is protoporphyrin IX

porphyrinuria /ˌpɔːfɪrɪ'njʊəriə/ *noun* the presence of excess porphyrins in the urine, a sign of porphyria or of metal poisoning

porta /'pɔːtə/ *noun* an opening which allows blood vessels to pass into an organ (NOTE: The plural is **portae**.)

Portacath /'pɔːtəkæθ/ *noun* a type of catheter put in place under a person's skin to make it easier to have chemotherapy, transfusions and blood tests. It is accessed by the use of a special needle and flushed regularly with sterile saline.

portacaval /ˌpɔːtə'keɪv(ə)l/ *adjective* another spelling of **portocaval**

portae /'pɔːti/ *plural of* **porta**

porta hepatis /ˌpɔːtə 'hepatɪs/ *noun* an opening in the liver through which the hepatic artery, hepatic duct and portal vein pass (NOTE: The plural is **portae hepatitis**.)

portal /'pɔːt(ə)l/ *adjective* referring to a porta, especially the portal system or the portal vein

portal hypertension /ˌpɔːt(ə)l ˌhaɪpə'tenʃən/ *noun* high pressure in the portal vein, caused by cirrhosis of the liver or a clot in the vein and causing internal bleeding

portal system /'pɔːt(ə)l ˌsɪstəm/ *noun* a group of veins which have capillaries at both ends and do not go to the heart

portal vein /'pɔːt(ə)l veɪn/ *noun* a vein which takes blood from the stomach, pancreas, gall bladder, intestines and spleen to the liver (NOTE: For other terms referring to the portal vein, see words beginning with **pyl-, pyle-**.)

portocaval /ˌpɔːtəʊ'keɪv(ə)l/ *adjective* linking the portal vein to the inferior vena cava

portocaval anastomosis /ˌpɔːtəʊkeɪv(ə)l ən,æstə'məʊsɪs/ *noun* a surgical operation to join the portal vein to the inferior vena cava and divert blood past the liver

portocaval shunt /ˌpɔːtəʊkeɪv(ə)l 'ʃʌnt/ *noun* an artificial passage made between the portal vein and the inferior vena cava to relieve portal hypertension

port wine stain /ˌpɔːt 'waɪn ˌsteɪn/ *noun* a purple birthmark

position /pə'zɪʃ(ə)n/ *noun* **1.** the place where something is ○ *The exact position of the tumour is located by an X-ray.* **2.** the way a person's body is arranged ○ *in a sitting position* ○ *The accident victim had been placed in the recovery position.* ■ *verb* to place something in a particular position ○ *The fetus is correctly positioned in the uterus.*

positive /'pɒzɪtɪv/ *adjective* **1.** indicating the answer 'yes' **2.** indicating the presence of something being tested for ○ *Her cervical smear was positive.* Opposite **negative**

positive end-expiratory pressure /ˌpɒzɪtɪv ˌend ɪk,spaɪrət(ə)ri 'preʃə/ *noun* the procedure of forcing a person to breathe through a mask in cases where fluid has collected in the lungs. Abbreviation **PEEP**

positive feedback /ˌpɒzɪtɪv 'fiːdbæk/ *noun* a situation in which the result of a process stimulates the process which caused it

positive pressure respirator /ˌpɒzɪtɪv 'preʃə ˌrespɪreɪtə/ *noun* a machine which forces air into the lungs through a tube inserted in the mouth

positive pressure ventilation /ˌpɒzɪtɪv 'preʃə ventɪˌleɪʃ(ə)n/ *noun* the act of forcing air into the lungs to encourage the lungs to expand. Abbreviation **PPV**

positron-emission tomography /ˌpɒzɪtrɒn ɪ'mɪʃ(ə)n tə,mɒgrəfi/ *noun* a method of scanning the tissues of the brain, chest and abdomen for unusual metabolic activity after injecting a radioactive substance into the body. Abbreviation **PET**

posology /pə'sɒlədʒi/ *noun* the study of doses of medicine

posseting /'pɒsɪtɪŋ/ *noun* (*in babies*) the act of bringing up small quantities of curdled milk into the mouth after feeding

Possum /'pɒsəm/ *noun* a device using electronic switches which helps a person who is severely paralysed to work a machine such as a telephone (NOTE: The name is derived from the first letters of **patient-operated selector mechanism**.)

post- /pəʊst/ *prefix* after or later

post-cibal /ˌpəʊst 'saɪb(ə)l/ *adjective* after having eaten food

post cibum /ˌpəʊst 'kɪbəm/ *adverb* full form of **p.c.**

post-coital /ˌpəʊst 'kɔɪt(ə)l/ *adjective* taking place after sexual intercourse

postconcussional syndrome /ˌpəʊstkən'kʌʃ(ə)n(ə)l ˌsɪndrəʊm/ *noun* a set of symptoms which sometimes follow a head injury in which a person lost consciousness, including headache, loss of concentration, memory loss, depression and irritability

post-epileptic /ˌpəʊst epɪ'leptɪk/ *adjective* taking place after an epileptic fit

posterior /pɒ'stɪəriə/ *adjective* at the back. Opposite **anterior** □ **posterior to** behind ○ *The cerebellum is posterior to the medulla oblongata.* ■ *noun* same as **buttock** (*informal*)

posterior approach /pɒ'stɪəriər əˌprəʊtʃ/ *noun* an operation carried out from the back

posterior aspect /pɒ'stɪəriər ˌæspekt/ *noun* a view of the back of the body, or of the back of part of the body. See illustration at ANATOMICAL TERMS in Supplement

posterior chamber /pɒˌstɪəriə 'tʃeɪmbə/ *noun* a part of the aqueous chamber which is behind the iris

posterior fontanelle /pɒˌstɪəriə ˌfɒntə'nel/ *noun* a cartilage at the back of the head where the parietal bones join the occipital. ◊ **bregma**

posterior nares /pɒˌstɪəriə 'neəriːz/ *plural noun* same as **internal nares**

postero- /'pɒstərəʊ/ *prefix* back or behind

posteroanterior /ˌpɒstərəʊæn'tɪəriə/ *adjective* lying from the back to the front

post-exposure prophylaxis /ˌpəʊst ɪk ˌspəʊʒə ˌprɒfə'læksɪs/ *noun* a treatment given to a person who has been exposed to a harmful agent, in an effort to prevent or reduce injury or infection. Abbreviation PEP

postganglionic neurone /ˌpəʊstgæŋgli ˌɒnɪk 'njʊərəʊn/ *noun* a neurone which starts in a ganglion and ends in a gland or unstriated muscle

postgastrectomy syndrome /ˌpəʊst gæ 'strektəmi ˌsɪndrəʊm/ *noun* a group of symptoms which can occur after eating in people who have had stomach operations. It is caused by a lot of food passing into the small intestine too fast and can cause dizziness, nausea, sweating and weakness. Also called **dumping syndrome**

posthepatic jaundice /ˌpəʊsthɪˌpætɪk 'dʒɔːndɪs/ *noun* same as **obstructive jaundice**

post herpetic neuralgia /ˌpəʊst həˌpetɪk njuː'rældʒə/ *noun* pains felt after an attack of shingles

posthitis /pɒs'θaɪtɪs/ *noun* inflammation of the foreskin

posthumous /'pɒstjʊməs/ *adjective* occurring after death

postmature /ˌpəʊstmə't ʃʊə/ *adjective* referring to a baby born after the usual gestation period of 42 weeks

postmature baby /ˌpəʊstmətʃʊə 'beɪbi/ *noun* a baby born more than nine months after conception

postmaturity /ˌpəʊstmə'tʃʊərɪti/ *noun* a pregnancy which lasts longer than the usual gestation period of 42 weeks

postmenopausal /ˌpəʊstmenəʊ'pɔːz(ə)l/ *adjective* happening or existing after the menopause ○ *She experienced some postmenopausal bleeding.*

post mortem /ˌpəʊst 'mɔːtəm/, **post mortem examination** /ˌpəʊst 'mɔːtəm ɪgˌzæmɪ ˌneɪʃ(ə)n/ *noun* an examination of a dead body by a pathologist to find out the cause of death ○ *The post mortem showed that he had been poisoned.* Abbreviation PM. Also called **autopsy**

postnasal /ˌpəʊst'neɪz(ə)l/ *adjective* situated or happening behind the nose

postnasal drip /ˌpəʊst neɪz(ə)l 'drɪp/ *noun* a condition in which mucus from the nose runs down into the throat and is swallowed

postnatal /ˌpəʊst'neɪt(ə)l/ *adjective* referring to the period after the birth of a child

postnatal care /ˌpəʊst neɪt(ə)l 'keə/ *noun* the care given to a woman after the birth of her child

postnatal depression /ˌpəʊst neɪt(ə)l dɪ 'preʃ(ə)n/ *noun* depression which sometimes affects a woman after childbirth

postnecrotic cirrhosis /ˌpəʊstnekrɒtɪk sɪ 'rəʊsɪs/ *noun* cirrhosis of the liver caused by viral hepatitis

post-op /ˌpəʊst 'ɒp/ *adjective* same as **postoperative** (*informal*)

postoperative /ˌpəʊst'ɒp(ə)rətɪv/ *adjective* referring to the period after a surgical operation ○ *The patient has suffered postoperative nausea and vomiting.* ○ *Occlusion may appear as postoperative angina pectoris.*

postoperative pain /ˌpəʊstˌɒp(ə)rətɪv 'peɪn/ *noun* pain felt after a surgical operation

postpartum /ˌpəʊst'pɑːtəm/ *adjective* referring to the period after the birth of a child

postpartum fever /pəʊst,pɑːtəm 'fiːvə/ noun same as **puerperal infection**

postpartum haemorrhage /pəʊst,pɑːtəm 'hem(ə)rɪdʒ/ noun heavy bleeding after childbirth. Abbreviation **PPH**

post-primary tuberculosis /pəʊst ,praɪməri tjuː,bɜːkjʊ'ləʊsɪs/ noun the reappearance of tuberculosis in a person who has been infected with it before

post-registration education and practice /,pəʊst redʒɪ,streɪʃ(ə)n edjʊ,keɪʃ(ə)n ənd 'præktɪs/ noun in the UK, the requirement for all registered nurses and midwives to undertake educational activities and keep up with contemporary practice, and also for their employers to address the learning needs of staff. It was started by the UKCC in 1993. Abbreviation **PREP**

post-traumatic /,pəʊst trɔː'mætɪk/ adjective appearing after a trauma, e.g. after an accident, rape or fire

post-traumatic amnesia /,pəʊst trɔː,mætɪk æm'niːziə/ noun amnesia which follows a trauma

post-traumatic stress disorder /,pəʊst trɔː,mætɪk 'stres dɪs,ɔːdə/ noun a psychological condition affecting people who have suffered severe emotional trauma, e.g. occasioned by war or natural disaster. Its symptoms include chest pain, dizziness, sleep disturbances, flashbacks, anxiety, tiredness, and depression. Abbreviation **PTSD**

postural /'pɒstʃərəl/ adjective referring to posture ○ a study of postural disorders

postural drainage /,pɒstʃərəl 'dreɪnɪdʒ/ noun a a procedure for removing matter from infected lungs by making the person lie down with the head lower than the feet, so that he or she can cough more easily

postural hypotension /,pɒstʃərəl ,haɪpəʊ 'tenʃən/ noun low blood pressure when standing up suddenly, causing dizziness

posture /'pɒstʃə/ noun the position in which a body is arranged, or the way a person usually holds his or her body when standing ○ Bad posture can cause pain in the back. ○ She has to do exercises to correct her bad posture.

postviral /pəʊst'vaɪrəl/ adjective occurring after a viral infection

postviral fatigue syndrome /pəʊst,vaɪrəl fə'tiːg ,sɪndrəʊm/ noun same as **myalgic encephalomyelitis**

potassium /pə'tæsiəm/ noun a metallic element (NOTE: The chemical symbol is **K**.)

potassium permanganate /pə,tæsiəm pə 'mæŋgənət/ noun a purple-coloured poisonous salt, used as a disinfectant

Pott's fracture /'pɒts ,fræktʃə/ noun a fracture of the lower end of the fibula together with displacement of the ankle and foot outwards

[Described 1765. After Sir Percivall Pott (1714–88), London surgeon.]

pouch /paʊtʃ/ noun a small sac or pocket attached to an organ

poultice /'pəʊltɪs/ noun a compress made of hot water and flour paste or other substances which is pressed onto an infected part to draw out pus, to relieve pain or to encourage the circulation. Also called **fomentation**

Poupart's ligament /'puːpɑːts ,lɪgəmənt/ noun same as **inguinal ligament** [Described 1705. After François Poupart (1616–1708), French surgeon and anatomist.]

powder /'paʊdə/ noun a medicine in the form of a fine dry dust made from particles of drugs ○ He took a powder to help his indigestion or He took an indigestion powder.

pox /pɒks/ noun same as **syphilis** (old)

poxvirus /'pɒks,vaɪrəs/ noun any of a group of viruses which cause cowpox, smallpox and related diseases

p.p. abbreviation after a meal. Full form **post prandium**

PPH abbreviation postpartum haemorrhage

PPV abbreviation positive pressure ventilation

PQRST complex noun the set of deflections on an electrocardiogram, labelled P to T, which show ventricular contraction

p.r. adverb (of an examination) by the rectum. Full form **per rectum**

practice /'præktɪs/ noun 1. the business, or the premises occupied by, a doctor, dentist, or a group of doctors or dentists working together ○ After qualifying she joined her father's practice. □ **in practice** doing the work of a doctor or dentist ○ He has been in practice for six years. 2. the fact of doing something, as opposed to thinking or talking about it ○ theory and practice 3. a usual way of doing something ○ Such practices are now regarded as unsafe.

practice nurse /'præktɪs nɜːs/ noun a nurse employed by a GP or primary care trust to work in a GP's practice providing treatment, health promotion, screening and other services to patients of the practice

practitioner /præk'tɪʃ(ə)nə/ noun a qualified person who works in the medical profession

praevia /'priːviə/ noun ♦ **placenta praevia**

pravastatin /,prævə'stætɪn/ noun a drug used to reduce unusually high levels of blood cholesterol

prazosin /'præzəsɪn/ noun a drug which relaxes or widens the blood vessels, used to treat hypertension

pre- /priː/ prefix before or in front of

preadmission information /,priːəd'mɪʃ(ə)n ɪnfə,meɪʃ(ə)n/ noun information given to a person before he or she is admitted to hospital

pre-anaesthetic round /ˌpriː ˌænəsˈθetɪk ˌraʊnd/ *noun* an examination of patients by the surgeon before they are anaesthetised

precancerous /priːˈkænsərəs/ *adjective* referring to a growth which is not malignant now, but which can become cancerous later

preceptor /prɪˈseptə/ *noun* a specialist who gives practical training to a student

preceptorship /prɪˈseptəʃɪp/ *noun* a period of time during which a recently trained nurse, midwife or health visitor can gain practical experience working with a specialist who advises and guides them

precipitate /prɪˈsɪpɪtət/ *noun* a substance which is precipitated during a chemical reaction ■ *verb* **1.** to make a substance separate from a chemical compound and fall to the bottom of a liquid during a chemical reaction ○ *Casein is precipitated when milk comes into contact with an acid.* **2.** to make something start suddenly (NOTE: [all verb senses] **precipitating – precipitated**)

precipitate labour /prɪˌsɪpɪtət ˈleɪbə/ *noun* unusually fast labour, lasting two hours or less. It can be dangerous both to the mother and to the child.

precipitin /prɪˈsɪpɪtɪn/ *noun* an antibody which reacts to an antigen and forms a precipitate, used in many diagnostic tests

precocious /prɪˈkəʊʃəs/ *adjective* more physically or mentally developed than is usual for a specific age

precocious puberty /prɪˌkəʊʃəs ˈpjuːbəti/ *noun* the development of signs of puberty in girls before the age of seven, and in boys before the age of nine. If untreated, affected boys typically grow no taller than 1.6 metres and girls rarely reach 1.5 metres.

precocity /prɪˈkɒsɪti/ *noun* the state or fact of being precocious

precordia /priːˈkɔːdiə/ *plural noun* plural of **precordium**

precordial /priːˈkɔːdiəl/ *adjective* referring to the precordium

precordium /priːˈkɔːdiəm/ *noun* the part of the thorax over the heart (NOTE: The plural is **precordia**.)

precursor /prɪˈkɜːsə/ *noun* a substance or cell from which another substance or cell is developed, e.g. dopa, the precursor for dopamine, which is converted to dopamine by the enzyme dopa decarboxylase

predisposing factor /ˌpriːdɪspəʊzɪŋ ˈfæktə/ *noun* a factor which will increase the risk of disease

prednisolone /predˈnɪsələʊn/ *noun* a synthetically produced steroid hormone, similar to cortisone, used especially to control inflammatory diseases such as rheumatoid arthritis

prednisone /predˈnɪsəʊn/ *noun* a synthetically produced steroid hormone produced from cortisone, used to treat allergies and rheumatoid arthritis

pre-eclampsia /ˌpriː ɪˈklæmpsiə/ *noun* a condition in pregnant women towards the end of the pregnancy which may lead to eclampsia. Symptoms are high blood pressure, oedema and protein in the urine. Also called **pregnancy-induced hypertension**

pre-eclamptic /ˌpriː ɪˈklæmptɪk/ *adjective* referring to pre-eclampsia

prefrontal leucotomy /priːˌfrʌnt(ə)l luːˈkɒtəmi/ *noun* a surgical operation to divide some of the white matter in the prefrontal lobe, formerly used as a treatment for schizophrenia

prefrontal lobe /priːˈfrʌnt(ə)l ləʊb/ *noun* an area of the brain in the front part of each hemisphere, in front of the frontal lobe, which is concerned with memory and learning

preganglionic neurone /ˌpriːgæŋgliˌɒnɪk ˈnjʊərəʊn/ *noun* a neurone which ends in a ganglion

pregnancy /ˈpregnənsi/ *noun* **1.** same as **gestation period 2.** the condition of being pregnant. Also called **cyesis**

pregnancy-induced hypertension /ˌpregnənsi ɪnˈdjuːst ˌhaɪpəˈtenʃən/ *noun* same as **pre-eclampsia**

pregnancy test /ˈpregnənsi test/ *noun* a test to see if a woman is pregnant or not

pregnant /ˈpregnənt/ *adjective* with an unborn child in the uterus ○ *She is six months pregnant.*

prehepatic jaundice /ˌpriːhɪˌpætɪk ˈdʒɔːndɪs/ *noun* same as **haemolytic jaundice**

prem /prem/ (*informal*) *adjective* same as **premature** ■ *noun* a premature baby

premature /ˈpremətʃə/ *adjective* before the expected or desirable time ○ *The baby was five weeks premature.*

COMMENT: Babies can survive even if born several weeks premature. Even babies weighing less than one kilo at birth can survive in an incubator, and develop healthily.

premature baby /ˌpremətʃə ˈbeɪbi/ *noun* a baby born earlier than 37 weeks from conception, or weighing less than 2.5 kg, but capable of independent life

premature birth /ˌpremətʃə ˈbɜːθ/ *noun* the birth of a baby earlier than 37 weeks from conception

premature ejaculation /ˌpremətʃə ɪˌdʒækjʊˈleɪʃ(ə)n/ *noun* a situation in which a man ejaculates too early during sexual intercourse

premature labour /ˌpremətʃə ˈleɪbə/ *noun* the condition of starting to give birth earlier than 37 weeks from conception ○ *After the accident she went into premature labour.*

premed /ˈpriːmed/ noun a stage of being given premedication (*informal*) ○ *The patient is in premed.*

premedication /ˌpriːmedɪˈkeɪʃ(ə)n/, **premedicant drug** /priːˌmedɪkənt ˈdrʌg/ noun a drug given before an operation in order to block the parasympathetic nervous system and prevent vomiting during the operation, e.g. a sedative

premenstrual /priːˈmenstruəl/ adjective happening before menstruation

premenstrual syndrome /priːˌmenstruəl ˈsɪndrəʊm/, **premenstrual tension** /priː ˌmenstruəl ˈtenʃən/ noun nervous stress experienced by a woman for one or two weeks before a menstrual period starts. Abbreviation **PMS**, **PMT**

premolar /priːˈməʊlə/ noun a tooth with two points, situated between the canines and the first proper molar. See illustration at TEETH in Supplement

prenatal /priːˈneɪt(ə)l/ adjective during the period between conception and childbirth

prenatal diagnosis /priːˌneɪt(ə)l ˌdaɪəg ˈnəʊsɪs/ noun same as **antenatal diagnosis**

pre-op /ˌpriː ˈɒp/ adjective same as **preoperative** (*informal*)

preoperative /priːˈɒp(ə)rətɪv/ adjective during the period before a surgical operation

preoperative medication /priːˌɒp(ə)rətɪv ˌmedɪˈkeɪʃən/ noun a drug given before an operation, e.g. a sedative

PREP /prep/ abbreviation post-registration education and practice

prepatellar bursitis /ˌpriːpəˌtelə bɜːˈsaɪtɪs/ noun a condition in which the fluid sac at the knee becomes inflamed, caused by kneeling on hard surfaces. Also called **housemaid's knee**

prepubertal /priːˈpjuːbət(ə)l/ adjective referring to the period before puberty

prepuce /ˈpriːpjuːs/ noun same as **foreskin**

presby- /prezbi/ prefix same as **presbyo-** (*used before vowels*)

presbyacusis /ˌprezbiəˈkuːsɪs/ noun a condition in which an elderly person's hearing fails gradually, through to degeneration of the internal ear

presbyo- /prezbiəʊ/ prefix referring to the last stages of the natural life span

presbyopia /ˌprezbiˈəʊpiə/ noun a condition in which an elderly person's sight fails gradually, through hardening of the lens

prescribed disease /prɪˌskraɪbd dɪˈziːz/ noun an illness caused by the type of work a person does which is on an annually reviewed official list, entitling the person to claim benefit. Examples are deafness, pneumoconiosis and RSI.

prescribing analyses and cost /prɪ ˌskraɪbɪŋ əˌnælɪsiːz ənd ˈkɒst/ plural noun data

on the prescribing of drugs in primary care. Abbreviation **PACT**

prescription /prɪˈskrɪpʃən/ noun an order written by a doctor to a pharmacist asking for a drug to be prepared and given or sold to a person

presenile /priːˈsiːnaɪl/ adjective prematurely showing the effects of advanced age

presenile dementia /priːˌsiːnaɪl dɪˈmenʃə/ noun mental degeneration affecting adults of around 40–60 years of age (*dated*)

COMMENT: Patients used to be diagnosed with presenile dementia if they showed symptoms of dementia and were under the age of 65, and senile dementia if over 65. However, the terms are no longer often used and instead the type of dementia is used for diagnostic purposes, e.g. Alzheimer's disease, multi-infarct or vascular.

present /ˈprez(ə)nt/ verb /prɪˈzent/ **1.** (*of a patient*) to show particular symptoms ○ *The patient presented with severe chest pains.* **2.** (*of a symptom*) to be present ○ *The doctors' first task is to relieve the presenting symptoms.* ○ *The condition may also present in a baby.* **3.** (*of a baby*) to appear in the vaginal channel ■ adjective currently existing in a place ○ *All the symptoms of the disease are present.*

presentation /ˌprez(ə)nˈteɪʃ(ə)n/ noun the way in which a baby will be born, in respect of the part of the baby's body which will appear first in the vaginal channel

presenting part /prɪˈzentɪŋ pɑːt/ noun the part of a baby which appears first during birth

pressor /ˈpresə/ adjective **1.** referring to a nerve which increases the action of part of the body **2.** raising blood pressure

pressure /ˈpreʃə/ noun the action of squeezing or forcing something

pressure area /ˈpreʃər ˌeəriə/ noun an area of the body where a bone is near the surface of the skin, so that if the skin is pressed the circulation will be cut off

pressure bandage /ˈpreʃə ˌbændɪdʒ/ noun a bandage which presses on a part of the body

pressure index /ˈpreʃər ˌɪndeks/ noun a method for determining the extent of obstruction to the artery in the leg by measuring the blood pressure in the arms and legs and then dividing the systolic pressure in the leg by that in the arm. Abbreviation **PI**

pressure point /ˈpreʃə pɔɪnt/ noun a place where an artery crosses over a bone, so that the blood can be cut off by pressing with the finger

presystole /priːˈsɪstəli/ noun the period before systole in the cycle of heartbeats

preterm /priːˈtɜːm/ adjective referring to the birth of a child which takes place before the expected time

preterm birth /priː'tɜːm ˌbɜːθ/ *noun* the birth of a baby before 37 completed weeks of pregnancy, which presents a greater risk of serious health problems (NOTE: About 12 per cent of births in the UK are preterm births.)

preventative /prɪ'ventətɪv/ *adjective* same as **preventive**

preventive /prɪ'ventɪv/ *adjective* referring to an action taken to stop something happening, especially to stop a disease or infection from spreading ○ *preventive treatment* ○ *preventive action*

preventive medicine /prɪˌventɪv 'med(ə)s(ə)n/ *noun* action carried out to stop disease from occurring, e.g. by education in health-related issues, immunisation and screening for known diseases

Priadel /'praɪədel/ a trade name for lithium

priapism /'praɪəpɪz(ə)m/ *noun* an erection of the penis without sexual stimulus, caused by a blood clot in the tissue of the penis, injury to the spinal cord or stone in the urinary bladder

prickly heat /'prɪkli hiːt/ *noun* same as **miliaria**

-pril /prɪl/ *suffix* used for ACE inhibitors ○ *Captopril*

prilocaine /'praɪləkeɪn/ *noun* a local anaesthetic used especially in dentistry

primaquine /'praɪməkwiːn/ *noun* a synthetically produced drug used in the treatment of malaria

primary /'praɪməri/ *adjective* **1.** happening first, and leading to something else **2.** most important

primary amenorrhoea /ˌpraɪməri ˌeɪmenə'riːə/ *noun* a condition in which a woman has never had menstrual periods

primary bronchi /ˌpraɪməri 'brɒŋkiː/ *plural noun* same as **main bronchi**

primary care /ˌpraɪməri 'keə/ *noun* in the UK, health services offered directly to individuals by GPs, dentists, opticians and other health professionals who may also refer a patient on to specialists for further treatment. Also called **primary health care**, **primary medical care**. Compare **secondary care**, **tertiary care**

primary care group /ˌpraɪməri 'keə ˌgruːp/ *noun* an organisation responsible for overseeing the provision of primary healthcare and the commissioning of secondary care in a district. Key members include GPs, community nurses, social services and lay members. Abbreviation **PCG**

primary care team /ˌpraɪməri 'keə ˌtiːm/ *noun* same as **primary health care team**

primary care trust /ˌpraɪməri 'keə ˌtrʌst/ *noun* in the UK, the top level of the primary care group with extra responsibilities such as direct employment of community staff. Abbreviation **PCT**

primary haemorrhage /ˌpraɪməri 'hem(ə)rɪdʒ/ *noun* bleeding which occurs immediately after an injury has taken place

primary health care /ˌpraɪməri 'helθ ˌkeə/ *noun* same as **primary care**

primary health care team /ˌpraɪməri 'helθ keə ˌtiːm/ *noun* a group of professional medical workers who have first contact with someone needing medical attention and are responsible for delivering a range of health care services. Abbreviation **PHCT**

primary medical care /ˌpraɪməri 'medɪk(ə)l ˌkeə/ *noun* same as **primary care**

primary nurse /ˌpraɪməri 'nɜːs/ *noun* a nurse who is responsible for planning a person's nursing care in consultation with that person and his or her family. In the absence of the primary nurse, associate nurses provide care based on the plan designed by the primary nurse.

primary nursing /ˌpraɪməri 'nɜːsɪŋ/ *noun* a model of nursing that involves the delivery of comprehensive, continuous, co-ordinated and individualised patient care through a primary nurse, who has autonomy, accountability and authority in relation to his or her patient's care

primary tooth /'praɪməri tuːθ/ *noun* any one of the first twenty teeth which develop in children between about six months and two-and-a-half years of age, and are replaced by the permanent teeth at around the age of six. Also called **milk tooth**, **deciduous tooth**

primary tuberculosis /ˌpraɪməri tjuːˌbɜːkjʊ'ləʊsɪs/ *noun* a person's first infection with tuberculosis

primary tumour /ˌpraɪməri 'tjuːmə/ *noun* a site of the original malignant growth from which cancer spreads

prime /praɪm/ *adjective* **1.** of the greatest importance or the highest rank **2.** of the highest quality ■ *noun* the best state or period of something, especially the most active and enjoyable period in adult life ■ *verb* to make something ready for use, or to become ready for use (NOTE: **priming – primed**)

prime mover /ˌpraɪm 'muːvə/ *noun* **1.** same as **agonist 2.** somebody or something which has the most influence over the starting of a process or activity

primigravida /ˌpraɪmɪ'grævɪdə/, **primigravid patient** /ˌpraɪmɪ'grævɪd ˌpeɪʃ(ə)nt/ *noun* a woman who is pregnant for the first time (NOTE: The plural is **primigravidas** or **primigravidae**.)

primipara /praɪ'mɪpərə/ *noun* a woman who has given birth to one child. Also called **unipara** (NOTE: The plural is **primiparas** or **primiparae**.)

primordial /praɪ'mɔːdiəl/ *adjective* in the very first stage of development

primordial follicle /praɪˌmɔːdiəl ˈfɒlɪk(ə)l/ noun the first stage of development of an ovarian follicle

P-R interval /ˌpiː ˈɑːr ˌɪntəv(ə)l/ noun the time recorded on an electrocardiogram between the start of atrial activity and ventricular activity

prion /ˈpriːɒn/ noun a particle of protein which contains no nucleic acid, does not trigger an immune response and is not destroyed by extreme heat or cold. Prions are considered to be the agents responsible for scrapie, BSE, and Creutzfeldt-Jakob disease.

priority despatch /praɪˈɒrɪti dɪˌspætʃ/ noun the process of talking to people who need medical help on the telephone in order to make sure that ambulances are sent to the most urgent cases first

priority matrix /praɪˈɒrɪti ˌmeɪtrɪks/ noun a way of trying to make sure that each community has a fair number of services for its particular health needs

private hospital /ˌpraɪvət ˈhɒspɪt(ə)l/ noun a hospital which takes only paying patients

private parts /ˈpraɪvət pɑːts/ plural noun the genital area (informal) Also called **privates**

private patient /ˌpraɪvət ˈpeɪʃ(ə)nt/ noun a patient who is paying for treatment and who is not being treated under the National Health Service

privates /ˈpraɪvəts/ plural noun same as **private parts** (informal)

p.r.n. adverb (written on a prescription) as and when required. Full form **pro re nata**

pro- /prəʊ/ prefix before or in front of

probe /prəʊb/ noun an instrument used to explore inside a cavity or wound ■ verb to investigate the inside of something ○ The surgeon probed the wound with a scalpel. (NOTE: **probing – probed**)

problem /ˈprɒbləm/ noun 1. something which is difficult to find an answer to ○ Scientists are trying to find a solution to the problem of drug-related disease. 2. a medical disorder ○ heart problems □ he has an alcohol problem or a drugs problem he is addicted to alcohol or drugs 3. an addiction to something ○ has a drug problem

problem child /ˈprɒbləm tʃaɪld/ noun a child who is difficult to control

problem drinking /ˌprɒbləm ˈdrɪŋkɪŋ/ noun alcoholism or heavy drinking which has a bad effect on a person's behaviour or work

problem-oriented record /ˌprɒbləm ˌɔːrientɪd ˈrekɔːd/ noun a record of patient care which links patients' clinical data with their problems, so that all aspects of the care process are focused on resolving those problems

problem-solving approach /ˈprɒbləm ˌsɒlvɪŋ əˌprəʊtʃ/ noun the provision of nursing care based on assessment, problem identification

(nursing diagnosis), planning implementation (nursing intervention) and evaluation

process /ˈprəʊses/ noun 1. a technical or scientific action ○ A new process for testing serum samples has been developed in the research laboratory. 2. a projecting part of the body ■ verb 1. to deal with a person or thing according to a standard procedure 2. to examine or test samples ○ The blood samples are being processed by the laboratory.

prochlorperazine /ˌprəʊklɔːˈperəziːn/ noun a drug used to control nausea and vomiting, and to reduce the symptoms of Ménière's disease, migraine and anxiety

procidentia /ˌprəʊsɪˈdenʃə/ noun movement of an organ downwards

proct- /prɒkt/ prefix same as **procto-** (used before vowels)

proctalgia /prɒkˈtældʒə/ noun pain in the lower rectum or anus, caused by neuralgia

proctalgia fugax /prɒkˌtældʒə ˈfjuːgæks/ noun a condition in which a person has sudden pains in the rectum during the night, usually relieved by eating or drinking

proctatresia /ˌprɒktəˈtriːziə/ noun a condition in which the anus does not have an opening. Also called **imperforate anus**

proctectasia /ˌprɒktekˈteɪziə/ noun a condition in which the rectum or anus is dilated because of continued constipation

proctectomy /prɒkˈtektəmi/ noun a surgical operation to remove the rectum (NOTE: The plural is **proctectomies**.)

proctitis /prɒkˈtaɪtɪs/ noun inflammation of the rectum

procto- /prɒktəʊ/ prefix the anus or rectum

proctocele /ˈprɒktəsiːl/ noun same as **rectocele**

proctocolectomy /ˌprɒktəʊkɒˈlektəmi/ noun a surgical operation to remove the rectum and the colon (NOTE: The plural is **proctocolectomies**.)

proctocolitis /ˌprɒktəkəˈlaɪtɪs/ noun inflammation of the rectum and part of the colon

proctodynia /ˌprɒktəˈdɪniə/ noun a sensation of pain in the anus

proctogram /ˈprɒktəgræm/ noun an X-ray photograph of the rectum taken after a contrast agent is introduced

proctologist /prɒkˈtɒlədʒɪst/ noun a specialist in proctology

proctology /prɒkˈtɒlədʒi/ noun the scientific study of the rectum and anus and their associated diseases

proctorrhaphy /prɒkˈtɔːrəfi/ noun a surgical operation to stitch up a tear in the rectum or anus (NOTE: The plural is **proctorrhaphies**.)

proctoscope /ˈprɒktəskəʊp/ *noun* a surgical instrument consisting of a long tube with a light in the end, used to examine the rectum

proctoscopy /prɒkˈtɒskəpi/ *noun* an examination of the rectum using a proctoscope (NOTE: The plural is **proctoscopies**.)

proctosigmoiditis /ˌprɒktəʊˌsɪgmɔɪˈdaɪtɪs/ *noun* inflammation of the rectum and the sigmoid colon

proctotomy /prɒkˈtɒtəmi/ *noun* a surgical operation to divide a structure of the rectum or anus (NOTE: The plural is **proctotomies**.)

prodromal /prəʊˈdrəʊm(ə)l/ *adjective* occurring between the appearance of the first symptoms of a disease and the major effect, e.g. a fever or rash

prodromal rash /prəʊˌdrəʊm(ə)l ˈræʃ/ *noun* a rash which appears as a symptom of a disease before the major rash

prodrome /ˈprəʊdrəʊm/, **prodroma** /prəʊˈdrəʊmə/ *noun* an early symptom of an attack of a disease

productive cough /prəˌdʌktɪv ˈkɒf/ *noun* a cough where phlegm is produced

profession /prəˈfeʃ(ə)n/ *noun* a type of job for which special training is needed

professional /prəˈfeʃ(ə)nəl/ *adjective* referring to a profession

professional body /prəˌfeʃ(ə)nəl ˈbɒdi/ *noun* an organisation which acts for all the members of a profession

Professional Conduct Committee /prəˌfeʃ(ə)n(ə)l ˈkɒndʌkt kəˌmɪti/ *noun* a committee of the General Medical Council which decides on cases of professional misconduct. Abbreviation **PCC**

Professional Executive Committee /prəˌfeʃ(ə)nəl ɪgˈzekjʊtɪv kəˌmɪti/ *noun* full form of **PEC**

profile /ˈprəʊfaɪl/ *noun* **1.** a brief description of the characteristics of a person or thing **2.** a set of data, usually in graph or table form, which indicates to what extent something has the same characteristics as a group tested or considered standard **3.** the amount that other people notice somebody or something ■ *verb* to give a short description or assessment of somebody or something (NOTE: **profiling – profiled**)

profunda /prəˈfʌndə/ *adjective* referring to blood vessels which lie deep in tissues

profundaplasty /prəˈfʌndəplæsti/ *noun* a surgical operation to widen a junction of the femoral artery, in order to relieve narrowing by atherosclerosis (NOTE: The plural is **profundaplasties**.)

progeny /ˈprɒdʒəni/ *noun* a person's child or children (NOTE: Takes a singular or plural verb.)

progeria /prəʊˈdʒɪəriə/ *noun* a condition of premature ageing. Also called **Hutchinson-Gilford syndrome**

progesterone /prəʊˈdʒestərəʊn/ *noun* a hormone which is produced in the second part of the menstrual cycle by the corpus luteum and which stimulates the formation of the placenta if an ovum is fertilised (NOTE: Progesterone is also produced by the placenta itself.)

progestogen /prəˈdʒestədʒən/ *noun* any substance which has the same effect as progesterone

prognathic jaw /prɒgˌnæθɪk ˈdʒɔː/ *noun* a jaw which protrudes further than the other

prognathism /ˈprɒgnəθɪz(ə)m/ *noun* a condition in which one jaw, especially the lower jaw, or both jaws protrude

prognosis /prɒgˈnəʊsɪs/ *noun* an opinion of how a disease or disorder will develop ○ *This cancer has a prognosis of about two years.* ○ *The prognosis is not good.* (NOTE: The plural is **prognoses**.)

progressive /prəˈgresɪv/ *adjective* developing all the time ○ *Alzheimer's disease is a progressive disorder which sees a gradual decline in intellectual functioning.*

progressive deafness /prəˌgresɪv ˈdefnəs/ *noun* a condition, common in people as they get older, in which a person gradually becomes more and more deaf

progressive muscular atrophy /prəˌgresɪv ˌmʌskjʊlə ˈætrəfi/ *noun* muscular dystrophy, with progressive weakening of the muscles, particularly in the pelvic and shoulder girdles

proguanil /prəʊˈgwænɪl/ *noun* a drug used in the prevention and treatment of malaria

project /prəˈdʒekt/ *verb* to protrude or stick out

Project 2000 /ˌprɒdʒekt tuː ˈθaʊz(ə)nd/ *noun* a revision of nursing education introduced by the UKCC in 1989. It included new courses which prepare individuals to work in all settings, both in hospitals and in the community, and gave a student the ability to qualify as a midwife without first qualifying as a nurse and the chance to gain specialist qualifications in all areas of practice.

projection /prəˈdʒekʃən/ *noun* **1.** a part of the body which sticks out or stands out. Also called **prominence**. Compare **promontory 2.** (*in psychology*) mental action in which a person blames another person for his or her own faults

prolactin /prəʊˈlæktɪn/ *noun* a hormone secreted by the pituitary gland which stimulates the production of milk. Also called **lactogenic hormone**

prolapse /ˈprəʊlæps/ *noun* a condition in which an organ has moved downwards out of its usual position ■ *verb* to move downwards out of the usual position (NOTE: **prolapsing – prolapsed**)

prolapsed intervertebral disc /prəʊ‚læpst ɪntə‚vɜːtəbrəl 'dɪsk/ *noun* a condition in which an intervertebral disc becomes displaced or where the soft centre of a disc passes through the hard cartilage of the exterior and presses onto a nerve. Abbreviation **PID**. Also called **slipped disc**

prolapse of the rectum /‚prəʊlæps əv ðə 'rektəm/ *noun* a condition in which mucous membrane of the rectum moves downwards and passes through the anus

prolapse of the uterus /‚prəʊlæps əv ðə 'juːtərəs/, **prolapse of the womb** /‚prəʊlæps əv ðə 'wuːm/ *noun* a movement of the uterus downwards due to weakening of the structures of the pelvic floor, e.g. because of age or a difficult childbirth. Also called **metroptosis**, **prolapsed uterus**, **uterine prolapse**

proliferate /prə'lɪfəreɪt/ *verb* to produce many similar cells or parts, and so grow (NOTE: **proliferating – proliferated**)

proliferation /prə‚lɪfə'reɪʃ(ə)n/ *noun* the process of proliferating

promethazine /prəʊ'meθəziːn/ *noun* an antihistamine drug used in the treatment of allergies and motion sickness

prominence /'prɒmɪnəns/ *noun* a part of the body which sticks out or stands out. Also called **projection**. Compare **promontory**

promontory /'prɒmənt(ə)ri/ *noun* a section of an organ, especially the middle ear and sacrum which stands out above the rest. Compare **projection**, **prominence**

pronation /prəʊ'neɪʃ(ə)n/ *noun* the act of turning the hand round so that the palm faces downwards. Opposite **supination**. See illustration at ANATOMICAL TERMS in Supplement

pronator /prəʊ'neɪtə/ *noun* a muscle which makes the hand turn face downwards

prone /prəʊn/ *adjective* lying face downwards. Opposite **supine**

prophase /'prəʊfeɪz/ *noun* the first stage of mitosis when the chromosomes are visible as long thin double threads

prophylactic /‚prɒfə'læktɪk/ *noun* a substance which helps to prevent the development of a disease ■ *adjective* preventive

prophylaxis /‚prɒfə'læksɪs/ *noun* the prevention of disease (NOTE: The plural is **prophylaxes**.)

propranolol /prəʊ'pænəlɒl/ *noun* a drug that slows heart rate and heart output, used in the treatment of angina pectoris, irregular heart rhythms, migraine and high blood pressure

proprietary /prə'praɪət(ə)ri/ *adjective* belonging to a commercial company

proprietary medicine /prə‚praɪət(ə)ri 'med(ə)s(ə)n/, **proprietary drug** /prə ‚praɪət(ə)ri 'drʌg/ *noun* a drug which is sold under a trade name. ◊ **patent medicine**

proprietary name /prə‚praɪət(ə)ri 'neɪm/ *noun* a trade name for a drug

proprioception /‚prəʊpriə'sepʃən/ *noun* the reaction of nerves to body movements and the relaying of information about movements to the brain

proprioceptor /‚prəʊpriə'septə/ *noun* the end of a sensory nerve which reacts to stimuli from muscles and tendons as they move

proptosis /prɒp'təʊsɪs/ *noun* forward displacement of the eyeball

prosop- /prɒsəp/, **prosopo-** /prɒsəpəʊ/ *prefix* referring to the face

prostaglandin /‚prɒstə'glændɪn/ *noun* any of a class of unsaturated fatty acids found in all mammals which control smooth muscle contraction, inflammation and body temperature, are associated with the sensation of pain and have an effect on the nervous system, blood pressure and in particular the uterus at menstruation

prostate /'prɒsteɪt/ *noun* same as **prostate gland** (NOTE: Do not confuse with **prostrate**.) □ **prostate trouble** inflammation or enlargement of the prostate gland (*informal*)

prostate cancer /'prɒsteɪt ‚kænsə/ *noun* a malignant tumour of the prostate gland, found especially in men over 55

prostatectomy /‚prɒstə'tektəmi/ *noun* a surgical operation to remove all or part of the prostate gland (NOTE: The plural is **prostatectomies**.)

prostate gland /'prɒsteɪt glænd/ *noun* an O-shaped gland in males which surrounds the urethra below the bladder and secretes a fluid containing enzymes into the sperm. See illustration at UROGENITAL SYSTEM (MALE) in Supplement. Also called **prostate**

COMMENT: As a man grows older, the prostate gland tends to enlarge and constrict the point at which the urethra leaves the bladder, making it difficult to pass urine.

prostatic /prɒ'stætɪk/ *adjective* referring to or belonging to the prostate gland

prostatic hypertrophy /prɒ‚stætɪk haɪ 'pɜːtrəfi/ *noun* an enlargement of the prostate gland

prostatitis /‚prɒstə'taɪtɪs/ *noun* inflammation of the prostate gland

prostatorrhoea /‚prɒstətə'riːə/ *noun* discharge of fluid from the prostate gland (NOTE: The US spelling is **prostatorrhea**.)

prosthesis /prɒs'θiːsɪs/ *noun* a device which is attached to the body to take the place of a part which is missing, e.g. an artificial leg or glass eye (NOTE: The plural is **prostheses**.)

prosthetic /prɒs'θetɪk/ *adjective* replacing a part of the body which has been amputated or removed ○ *He was fitted with a prosthetic hand.*

prosthetic dentistry /prɒsˌθetɪk 'dentɪstri/ *noun* the branch of dentistry which deals with replacing missing teeth parts of the jaw, and fitting dentures, bridges and crowns. Also called **prosthodontics**

prosthodontics /ˌprɒsθə'dɒntɪks/ *noun* same as **prosthetic dentistry** (NOTE: Takes a singular verb.)

prostrate /'prɒstreɪt/ *adjective* lying face down (NOTE: Do not confuse with **prostate**.)

prostration /prɒ'streɪʃ(ə)n/ *noun* extreme tiredness of body or mind

protamine /'prəʊtəmiːn/ *noun* a simple protein found in fish, used with insulin to slow down the insulin absorption rate

protanopia /ˌprəʊtə'nəʊpiə/ *noun* same as **Daltonism**

protease /'prəʊtieɪz/ *noun* a digestive enzyme which breaks down protein in food by splitting the peptide link. Also called **proteolytic enzyme**

Protection of Children Act 1999 /prəˌtekʃən əv 'tʃɪldrən ˌækt/ *noun* in the UK, an Act of Parliament to protect children by restricting the employment of certain nurses, teachers or other workers whose jobs bring them into contact with children, on grounds such as misconduct or health

protective isolation /prəˌtektɪv ˌaɪsə'leɪʃ(ə)n/ *noun* a set of procedures used to protect people who have impaired resistance to infectious disease, e.g. those with leukemia and lymphoma, Aids and graft patients. Also called **reverse isolation**

protein /'prəʊtiːn/ *noun* a nitrogen compound which is present in and is an essential part of all living cells in the body, formed by the linking of amino acids

protein balance /'prəʊtiːn ˌbæləns/ *noun* a situation when the nitrogen intake in protein is equal to the excretion rate in the urine

protein-bound iodine /ˌprəʊtiːn baʊnd 'aɪədiːn/ *noun* a compound of thyroxine and iodine

protein-bound iodine test /ˌprəʊtiːn baʊnd 'aɪədiːn test/ *noun* a test to measure if the thyroid gland is producing adequate quantities of thyroxine. Abbreviation **PBI test**

protein deficiency /'prəʊtiːn dɪˌfɪʃ(ə)nsi/ *noun* a lack of enough proteins in the diet

proteinuria /ˌprəʊtiˈnjʊəriə/ *noun* a condition in which there are proteins in the urine

proteose /'prəʊtiəʊs/ *noun* a water-soluble compound formed during hydrolytic processes such as digestion

Proteus /'prəʊtiəs/ *noun* a genus of bacteria commonly found in the intestines

prothrombin /prəʊ'θrɒmbɪn/ *noun* a protein in blood which helps blood to coagulate and which needs Vitamin K to be effective. Also called **Factor II**

prothrombin time /prəʊ'θrɒmbɪn taɪm/ *noun* the time taken in Quick test for clotting to take place

proto- /prəʊtəʊ/ *prefix* first or at the beginning

proton pump /'prəʊtɒn pʌmp/ *noun* an enzyme system within the gastric mucosa that secretes gastric acids ○ *The drug acts on the proton pump mechanism.*

proton-pump inhibitor /'prəʊtɒn pʌmp ɪnˌhɪbɪtə/ *noun* a drug which suppresses the final stage of gastric acid secretion by the proton pump in the gastric mucosa

protoplasm /'prəʊtəʊˌplæz(ə)m/ *noun* a substance like a jelly which makes up the largest part of each cell

protozoa /ˌprəʊtə'zəʊə/ plural of **protozoon**

protozoan /ˌprəʊtə'zəʊən/ *adjective* referring to protozoa

protozoon /ˌprəʊtə'zəʊɒn/ *noun* a tiny simple organism with a single cell (NOTE: The plural is **protozoa** or **protozoons**.)

COMMENT: Parasitic protozoa can cause several diseases, including amoebiasis, malaria and other tropical diseases.

protuberance /prə'tjuːb(ə)rəns/ *noun* a rounded part of the body which projects above the rest

proud flesh /ˌpraʊd 'fleʃ/ *noun* new vessels and young fibrous tissue which form when a wound, incision or lesion is healing

provider /prə'vaɪdə/ *noun* a hospital which provides secondary care which is paid for by another body such as a PCG or social services. ◊ **purchaser**

provitamin /prəʊ'vɪtəmɪn/ *noun* a chemical compound which is converted to a vitamin during usual biochemical processes, e.g. the amino acid tryptophan, which is converted to niacin, and beta carotene, which is converted into vitamin A

proximal /'prɒksɪm(ə)l/ *adjective* near the midline, the central part of the body

proximal convoluted tubule /ˌprɒksɪm(ə)l ˌkɒnvəluːtɪd 'tjuːbjuːl/ *noun* a part of the kidney filtering system between the loop of Henle and the glomerulus

proximal interphalangeal joint /ˌprɒksɪm(ə)l ˌɪntəfə'lændʒiəl ˌdʒɔɪnt/ *noun* a joint nearest the point of attachment of a finger or toe. Abbreviation **PIP**

proximally /'prɒksɪmli/ *adverb* further towards the centre or point of attachment. Opposite **distally**. See illustration at **ANATOMICAL TERMS** in Supplement

Prozac /'prəʊzæk/ a trade name for fluoxetine

prurigo /pruə'raɪgəʊ/ *noun* an itchy eruption of papules

pruritus /pruəˈraɪtəs/ *noun* an irritation of the skin which makes a person want to scratch. Also called **itching**

pruritus ani /pruə,raɪtɪs 'eɪnaɪ/ *noun* itching round the anal orifice

pruritus vulvae /pruə,raɪtɪs 'vʌlviː/ *noun* itching round the vulva

pseud- /sjuːd/ *prefix* same as **pseudo-** (*used before vowels*)

pseudarthrosis /,sjuːdɑːˈθrəʊsɪs/ *noun* a false joint, as when the two broken ends of a fractured bone do not bind together but heal separately (NOTE: The plural is **pseudarthroses**.)

pseudo- /sjuːdəʊ/ *prefix* similar to something but not the same

pseudoangina /,sjuːdəʊænˈdʒaɪnə/ *noun* pain in the chest, caused by worry but not indicating heart disease

pseudocrisis /ˈsjuːdəʊ,kraɪsɪs/ *noun* a sudden fall in the temperature of a person with fever which does not mark the end of the fever

pseudocroup /,sjuːdəʊˈkruːp/ *noun* same as **laryngismus**

pseudocyesis /,sjuːdəʊsaɪˈiːsɪs/ *noun* a condition in which a woman has the physical symptoms of pregnancy but is not pregnant. Also called **phantom pregnancy**, **pseudopregnancy**

pseudocyst /ˈsjuːdəʊsɪst/ *noun* a false cyst

pseudogynaecomastia /,sjuːdəʊ,gaɪnɪkəʊ'mæstiə/ *noun* enlargement of the male breast because of extra fatty tissue (NOTE: The US spelling is **pseudogynecomastia**.)

pseudohermaphroditism /,sjuːdəʊhɜː'mæfrədaɪtɪz(ə)m/ *noun* a condition in which a person has either ovaries or testes but external genitalia that are not clearly of either sex

pseudohypertrophy /,sjuːdəʊhaɪ'pɜːtrəfi/ *noun* an overgrowth of fatty or fibrous tissue in a part or organ, which results in the part or organ being enlarged

pseudomonad /,sjuːdəʊ'məʊnəd/ *noun* a rod-shaped bacterium which lives in soil or decomposing organic material and can cause disease in plants and sometimes in humans

Pseudomonas /,suːdəʊ'məʊnəs/ *noun* ♦ **pseudomonad**

pseudo-obstruction /,sjuːdəʊ əb'strʌkʃən/ *noun* a condition in which symptoms such as stomach cramps, nausea and bloating indicate a blockage in the intestines although no blockage exists

pseudoplegia /,sjuːdəʊ'pliːdʒə/, **pseudoparalysis** /,sjuːdəʊpə'ræləsɪs/ *noun* loss of muscular power in the limbs without true paralysis

pseudopolyposis /,sjuːdəʊpɒli'pəʊsɪs/ *noun* a condition in which polyps are found in many places in the intestine, usually resulting from an earlier infection

psilosis /saɪ'ləʊsɪs/ *noun* a disease of the small intestine which prevents a person from absorbing food properly. Also called **sprue**

psoas major /,səʊæs 'meɪdʒə/ *noun* a muscle in the groin which flexes the hip

psoas minor /,səʊæs 'maɪnə/ *noun* a small muscle similar to the psoas major but not always present

psoriasis /sə'raɪəsɪs/ *noun* a common inflammatory skin disease where red patches of skin are covered with white scales

psoriatic /,sɔːri'ætɪk/ *adjective* referring to psoriasis

psoriatic arthritis /,sɔːriætɪk ɑː'θraɪtɪs/ *noun* a form of psoriasis which is associated with arthritis

psych- /saɪk/ *prefix* same as **psycho-** (*used before vowels*)

psyche /ˈsaɪki/ *noun* the mind

psychedelic /,saɪkə'delɪk/ *adjective* referring to drugs such as LSD which expand a person's consciousness

psychiatric /,saɪki'ætrɪk/ *adjective* referring to psychiatry ○ *He is undergoing psychiatric treatment.*

psychiatric hospital /,saɪki'ætrɪk ,hɒspɪt(ə)l/ *noun* a hospital which specialises in the treatment of patients with mental disorders

psychiatrist /saɪ'kaɪətrɪst/ *noun* a doctor who specialises in the diagnosis and treatment of mental and behavioural disorders

psychiatry /saɪ'kaɪətri/ *noun* a branch of medicine concerned with the diagnosis and treatment of mental and behavioural disorders

psychic /ˈsaɪkɪk/, **psychical** /ˈsaɪkɪk(ə)l/ *adjective* **1.** referring to a person who is supposedly able to guess thoughts which people have not expressed, or to foresee the future **2.** relating to or originating in the human mind

psycho- /saɪkəʊ/ *prefix* referring to the mind

psychoanalysis /,saɪkəʊə'næləsɪs/ *noun* a form of treatment for mental disorders in which a specialist and patient talk and together analyse the patient's condition and past events which may have contributed to it

psychoanalyst /,saɪkəʊ'æn(ə)lɪst/ *noun* a person who is trained in psychoanalysis

psychodrama /ˈsaɪkəʊ,drɑːmə/ *noun* a type of psychotherapy in which patients act out roles in dramas illustrating their emotional problems, in front of other patients

psychodynamics /,saɪkəʊdaɪ'næmɪks/ *noun* the study of how the forces which affect human behaviour and mental states work, especially on a subconscious level

psychogenic /,saɪkə'dʒenɪk/, **psychogenetic** /,saɪkəʊdʒə'netɪk/, **psychogenous** /saɪ'kɒdʒənəs/ *adjective* referring to an illness which starts in the mind, rather than in a physical state

psychogeriatrics /ˌsaɪkəʊdʒeriˈætrɪks/ *noun* the study of the mental disorders of the late stages of the natural life span

psychological /ˌsaɪkəˈlɒdʒɪk(ə)l/ *adjective* referring to psychology, or caused by a mental state

psychological dependence /ˌsaɪkə ˌlɒdʒɪk(ə)l dɪˈpendəns/, **psychological drug dependence** /ˌsaɪkəˌlɒdʒɪk(ə)l ˈdrʌg dɪ ˌpendəns/ *noun* a state in which a person is addicted to a drug such as cannabis or alcohol but does not suffer physical effects if he or she stops taking it

psychologist /saɪˈkɒlədʒɪst/ *noun* a person who specialises in the study of the mind and mental processes

psychology /saɪˈkɒlədʒi/ *noun* the study of the mind and mental processes

psychometrics /ˌsaɪkəˈmetrɪks/ *noun* a way of measuring intelligence and personality in which the result is shown as a number on a scale

psychomotor /ˌsaɪkəˈməʊtə/ *adjective* referring to muscle movements caused by mental activity

psychoneuroimmunology /ˌsaɪkəʊ ˌnjʊərəʊˌɪmjʊˈnɒlədʒi/ *noun* a branch of medicine which deals with how emotions affect the immune system

psychoneurosis /ˌsaɪkəʊnjʊˈrəʊsɪs/ *noun* any of a group of mental disorders in which a person has a faulty response to the stresses of life. ◊ **neurosis** (NOTE: The plural is **psychoneuroses.**)

psychopath /ˈsaɪkəpæθ/ *noun* a person with a long-term mental disorder characterised by anti-social and often violent behaviour

psychopathic /ˌsaɪkəˈpæθɪk/ *adjective* referring to psychopaths or psychopathy

psychopathological /ˌsaɪkəʊpæθə ˈlɒdʒɪk(ə)l/ *adjective* referring to psychopathology

psychopathology /ˌsaɪkəpəˈθɒlədʒi/ *noun* a branch of medicine concerned with the pathology of mental disorders and diseases

psychopathy /saɪˈkɒpəθi/ *noun* any disease of the mind (NOTE: The plural is **psychopathies.**)

psychopharmacology /ˌsaɪkəʊˌfɑːmə ˈkɒlədʒi/ *noun* the study of the actions and applications of drugs which have a powerful effect on the mind and behaviour

psychophysiological /ˌsaɪkəʊˌfɪziə ˈlɒdʒɪk(ə)l/ *adjective* referring to psychophysiology

psychophysiology /ˌsaɪkəʊˌfɪziˈɒlədʒi/ *noun* the physiology of the mind and its functions

psychoses /saɪˈkəʊsiːz/ plural of **psychosis**

psychosexual /ˌsaɪkəʊˈsekʃuəl/ *adjective* relating to the mental and emotional aspects of sexuality and sexual development

psychosexual development /ˌsaɪkəʊ ˌsekʃuəl dɪˈveləpmənt/ *noun* the development of human personality in stages based upon the ability to experience sexual pleasure, and the way in which sexuality plays a role in a person's life

psychosis /saɪˈkəʊsɪs/ *noun* any serious mental disorder in which a person has a distorted perception of reality (NOTE: The plural is **psychoses.**)

psychosocial /ˌsaɪkəʊˈsəʊʃ(ə)l/ *adjective* relating to the interaction of psychological and social factors

psychosomatic /ˌsaɪkəʊsəˈmætɪk/ *adjective* referring to the relationship between body and mind

psychosurgery /ˌsaɪkəʊˈsɜːdʒəri/ *noun* brain surgery, used as a treatment for psychological disorders

psychosurgical /ˌsaɪkəʊˈsɜːdʒɪk(ə)l/ *adjective* referring to psychosurgery

psychotherapeutic /ˌsaɪkəʊθerəˈpjuːtɪk/ *adjective* referring to psychotherapy

psychotherapist /ˌsaɪkəʊˈθerəpɪst/ *noun* a person trained to give psychotherapy

psychotherapy /ˌsaɪkəʊˈθerəpi/ *noun* the treatment of mental disorders by psychological methods, as when a psychotherapist encourages a person to talk about his or her problems. ◊ **therapy**

psychotic /saɪˈkɒtɪk/ *adjective* referring to psychosis

psychotropic /ˌsaɪkəˈtrɒpɪk/ *adjective* referring to a drug such as a stimulant or sedative which affects a person's mood

pterion /ˈtɪəriɒn/ *noun* the point on the side of the skull where the frontal, temporal parietal and sphenoid bones meet

pteroylglutamic acid /ˌterəʊaɪlgluːˌtæmɪk ˈæsɪd/ *noun* same as **folic acid**

pterygium /təˈrɪdʒiəm/ *noun* a degenerative condition in which a triangular growth of conjunctiva covers part of the cornea, with its apex towards the pupil

pterygo- /ˈterɪgəʊ/ *suffix* the pterygoid process

pterygoid process /ˈterɪgɔɪd ˌprəʊses/ *noun* one of two projecting parts on the sphenoid bone

ptosis /ˈtəʊsɪs/ *noun* prolapse of an organ

-ptosis /ˈtəʊsɪs/ *suffix* prolapse

PTSD *abbreviation* post-traumatic stress disorder

ptyal- /taɪəl/ *prefix* same as **ptyalo-** (*used before vowels*)

ptyalin /ˈtaɪəlɪn/ *noun* an enzyme in saliva which cleanses the mouth and converts starch into sugar

ptyalism /'taɪəlɪz(ə)m/ *noun* the production of an excessive amount of saliva

ptyalith /'taɪəlɪθ/ *noun* same as **sialolith**

ptyalo- /'taɪələʊ/ *prefix* referring to saliva

pubertal /'pjuːbət(ə)l/, **puberal** /'pjuːbərəl/ *adjective* referring to puberty

puberty /'pjuːbəti/ *noun* **1.** the physical and psychological changes which take place when childhood ends and adolescence and sexual maturity begin and the sex glands become active **2.** the time when these changes take place

pubes[1] /'pjuːbiːz/ *noun* the part of the body just above the groin, where the pubic bones are found

pubes[2] /'pjuːbiːz/ plural of **pubis**

pubic /'pjuːbɪk/ *adjective* referring to the area near the genitals

pubic bone /'pjuːbɪk bəʊn/ *noun* the bone in front of the pelvis. Also called **pubis**. See illustration at UROGENITAL SYSTEM (MALE) in Supplement

pubic hair /ˌpjuːbɪk 'heə/ *noun* tough hair growing in the genital region

pubic louse /ˌpjuːbɪk 'laʊs/ *noun* also called **Pediculus pubis**

pubic symphysis /ˌpjuːbɪk 'sɪmfəsɪs/ *noun* a piece of cartilage which joins the two sections of the pubic bone. Also called **symphysis pubis**

COMMENT: In a pregnant woman, the pubic symphysis stretches to allow the pelvic girdle to expand so that there is room for the baby to pass through.

pubiotomy /ˌpjuːbiˈɒtəmi/ *noun* a surgical operation to divide the pubic bone during labour, in order to make the pelvis wide enough for the child to be born safely (NOTE: The plural is **pubiotomies**.)

pubis /'pjuːbɪs/ *noun* a bone forming the front part of the pelvis. See illustration at PELVIS in Supplement (NOTE: The plural is **pubes**.)

public health /ˌpʌblɪk 'helθ/ *noun* the study of illness, health and disease in the community

public health laboratory service /ˌpʌblɪk ˌhelθ ləˈbɒrət(ə)ri ˌsɜːvɪs/ *noun* in the UK, a former service of the NHS which detected, diagnosed and monitored suspected cases of infectious disease in a countrywide network of laboratories. Abbreviation **PHLS**

public health medicine /ˌpʌblɪk ˌhelθ 'med(ə)s(ə)n/ *noun* the branch of medicine concerned with health and disease in populations, with the responsibilities of monitoring health, identification of health needs, development of policies which promote health and evaluation of health services

public health nurse /ˌpʌblɪk ˌhelθ 'nɜːs/ *noun* a nurse such as a school nurse, health visitor or other community nurse who monitors health and works to prevent illness in community situations

public health physician /ˌpʌblɪk ˌhelθ fɪ'zɪʃ(ə)n/ *noun* a consultant who has special training in public health medicine

pudenda /pjuː'dendə/ plural of **pudendum**

pudendal /pjuː'dend(ə)l/ *adjective* referring to the pudendum

pudendal block /pjuːˌdend(ə)l 'blɒk/ *noun* an operation to anaesthetise the pudendum during childbirth

pudendum /pjuː'dendəm/ *noun* an external genital organ of a woman (NOTE: The plural is **pudenda**.)

puerpera /pjuːˈɜːp(ə)rə/ *noun* a woman who has recently given birth, or is giving birth, and whose uterus is still distended (NOTE: The plural is **puerperae**.)

puerperal /pjuːˈɜːp(ə)rəl/ *adjective* referring to the puerperium

puerperal infection /pjuːˌɜːp(ə)rəl ɪnˈfekʃən/, **puerperal fever** /pjuːˌɜːp(ə)rəl 'fiːvə/ *noun* an infection of the uterus and genital tract after the birth of a baby, which is more common in women who have had a caesarean section. It causes a high fever, and occasionally sepsis, which can be fatal and was commonly so in the past. Also called **postpartum fever**

puerperalism /pjuːˈɜːp(ə)rəlɪz(ə)m/ *noun* an illness of a baby or its mother resulting from or associated with childbirth

puerperium /ˌpjuːəˈpɪəriəm/ *noun* a period of about six weeks which follows immediately after the birth of a child, during which the mother's sexual organs recover from childbirth

puerperous /pjuːˈɜːprəs/ *adjective* same as **puerperal**

puke /pjuːk/ *verb* same as **vomit** (*informal*)

pull /pʊl/ *verb* to make a muscle move in a wrong direction ○ *He pulled a muscle in his back.* □ **to pull the plug** to switch off life support (*informal*) ■ □ **to pull yourself together** to become calmer ○ *Although he was very angry he soon pulled himself together.*

pull through /ˌpʊl 'θruː/ *verb* to recover from a serious illness (*informal*) ○ *The doctor says she is strong and should pull through.*

pulmo- /pʌlməʊ/, **pulmon-** /pʌlmən/ *prefix* referring to the lungs

pulmonary /'pʌlmən(ə)ri/ *adjective* referring to the lungs

pulmonary artery /ˌpʌlmən(ə)ri 'ɑːtəri/ *noun* one of the two arteries which take deoxygenated blood from the heart to the lungs for oxygenation. See illustration at HEART in Supplement

pulmonary circulation /ˌpʌlmən(ə)ri ˌsɜːkjʊ'leɪʃ(ə)n/ *noun* the circulation of blood from the heart through the pulmonary arteries to the lungs for oxygenation and back to the heart through the pulmonary veins. Also called **lesser circulation**

pulmonary embolism /ˌpʌlmən(ə)ri 'embəlɪz(ə)m/ *noun* a blockage of a pulmonary artery by a blood clot. Abbreviation **PE**

pulmonary hypertension /ˌpʌlmən(ə)ri ˌhaɪpə'tenʃən/ *noun* high blood pressure in the blood vessels supplying blood to the lungs

pulmonary insufficiency /ˌpʌlmən(ə)ri ˌɪnsə'fɪʃ(ə)nsi/, **pulmonary incompetence** /ˌpʌlmən(ə)ri ɪn'kɒmpɪt(ə)ns/ *noun* a condition characterised by dilatation of the main pulmonary artery and stretching of the valve ring, due to pulmonary hypertension

pulmonary oedema /ˌpʌlmən(ə)ri ɪ'diːmə/ *noun* the collection of fluid in the lungs, as occurs in left-sided heart failure

pulmonary stenosis /ˌpʌlmən(ə)ri ste 'nəʊsɪs/ *noun* a condition in which the opening to the pulmonary artery in the right ventricle becomes narrow

pulmonary tuberculosis /ˌpʌlmən(ə)ri tjuː ˌbɜːkjʊ'ləʊsɪs/ *noun* tuberculosis in the lungs, which makes the person lose weight, cough blood and have a fever

pulmonary valve /'pʌlmən(ə)ri vælv/ *noun* a valve at the opening of the pulmonary artery

pulmonary vein /'pʌlmən(ə)ri veɪn/ *noun* one of the four veins which carry oxygenated blood from the lungs back to the left atrium of the heart. See illustration at **HEART** in Supplement (NOTE: The pulmonary veins are the only veins which carry oxygenated blood.)

pulmonectomy /ˌpʌlmə'nektəmi/ *noun* same as **pneumonectomy** (NOTE: The plural is **pulmonectomies**.)

pulp /pʌlp/ *noun* soft tissue, especially when surrounded by hard tissue as in the inside of a tooth

pulp cavity /'pʌlp ˌkævɪti/ *noun* the central part of a tooth containing soft tissue

pulsation /pʌl'seɪʃ(ə)n/ *noun* the action of beating regularly, e.g. the visible pulse which can be seen under the skin in some parts of the body

pulse /pʌls/ *noun* the regular expansion and contraction of an artery caused by the heart pumping blood through the body, which can be felt with the fingers especially where an artery is near the surface of the body, as in the wrist or neck ○ *Her pulse is very irregular.* □ **to take** *or* **feel a person's pulse** to measure a person's pulse rate by pressing on the skin above an artery with the fingers ○ *Has the patient's pulse been taken?*

pulseless /'pʌlsləs/ *adjective* referring to a person who has no pulse because the heart is beating very weakly

pulse oximetry /ˌpʌls ɒk'sɪmətri/ *noun* a method of measuring the oxygen content of arterial blood

pulse point /'pʌls pɔɪnt/ *noun* a place on the body where the pulse can be taken

pulse pressure /'pʌls ˌpreʃə/ *noun* the difference between the diastolic and systolic pressure. ◊ **Corrigan's pulse**

pulse rate /'pʌls reɪt/ *noun* the number of times the pulse beats per minute

pulsus /'pʌlsəs/ *noun* same as **pulse**

pulsus alternans /ˌpʌlsəs 'ɔːltənænz/ *noun* a pulse with a beat which is alternately strong and weak

pulsus bigeminus /ˌpʌlsəs baɪ'gemɪnəs/ *noun* a double pulse, with an extra ectopic beat

pulsus paradoxus /ˌpʌlsəs ˌpærə'dɒksəs/ *noun* a condition in which there is a sharp fall in the pulse when the person breathes in

pulvis /'pʌlvɪs/ *noun* powder

punch drunk syndrome /ˌpʌntʃ 'drʌŋk ˌsɪndrəʊm/ *noun* a condition affecting a person, usually a boxer, who has been hit on the head many times and develops impaired mental faculties, trembling limbs and speech disorders

puncta /'pʌŋktə/ *plural of* **punctum**

puncta lacrimalia /ˌpʌŋktə ˌlækrɪ'meɪliə/ *plural noun* small openings at the corners of the eyes through which tears drain into the nose

punctate /'pʌŋkteɪt/ *adjective* referring to tissue or a surface which has tiny spots, holes or dents in it

punctum /'pʌŋktəm/ *noun* a point (NOTE: The plural is **puncta**.)

puncture /'pʌŋktʃə/ *noun* a neat hole made by a sharp instrument ■ *verb* to make a hole in tissue with a sharp instrument (NOTE: **puncturing – punctured**)

puncture wound /'pʌŋktʃə wuːnd/ *noun* a wound made by a sharp instrument which makes a hole in the tissue

pupil /'pjuːp(ə)l/ *noun* the central opening in the iris of the eye, through which light enters the eye. See illustration at **EYE** in Supplement

pupillary /'pjuːpɪləri/ *adjective* referring to the pupil

pupillary reaction /ˌpjuːpɪləri ri'ækʃən/ *noun* a reflex of the pupil of the eye which contracts when exposed to bright light. Also called **light reflex**

purchaser /'pɜːtʃɪsə/ *noun* a body, usually a PCG, which commissions health care and manages the budget to pay for the service. ◊ **provider**

purgation /pɜː'geɪʃ(ə)n/ *noun* the use of a drug to cause a bowel movement

purgative /'pɜːgətɪv/ *noun* a drug used to empty the bowels. ◊ **laxative**

purine /'pjʊəriːn/ *noun* **1.** a nitrogen-containing substance derived from uric acid which is the parent compound of several biologically important substances **2.** a derivative of purine, especially either of the bases adenine and guanine, which are found in RNA and DNA

Purkinje cells /pə'kɪndʒi selz/ *plural noun* neurones in the cerebellar cortex [Described 1837. After Johannes Evangelista Purkinje (1787–1869), Professor of Physiology at Breslau, now in Poland, and then Prague, Czech Republic.]

Purkinje fibres /pə'kɪndʒi ˌfaɪbəz/ *plural noun* a bundle of fibres which form the atrioventricular bundle and pass from the atrioventricular node to the septum [Described 1839. After Johannes Evangelista Purkinje (1787–1869), Professor of Physiology at Breslau, now in Poland, and then Prague, Czech Republic.]

Purkinje shift /pə'kɪndʒi ʃɪft/ *noun* the change in colour sensitivity which takes place in the eye in low light when the eye starts using the rods in the retina because the light is too weak to stimulate the cones

purpura /'pɜːpjʊrə/ *noun* a purple colouring on the skin, similar to a bruise, caused by blood disease and not by trauma

pursestring operation /ˌpɜːsstrɪŋ ˌɒpə'reɪʃ(ə)n/ same as **Shirodkar's operation**

pursestring stitch /'pɜːsstrɪŋ stɪtʃ/ *noun* same as **Shirodkar suture**

purulent /'pjʊərʊlənt/ *adjective* containing or producing pus

pus /pʌs/ *noun* a yellow liquid composed of blood serum, pieces of dead tissue, white blood cells and the remains of bacteria, formed by the body in reaction to infection (NOTE: For other terms referring to pus, see words beginning with **py-** or **pyo-**.)

pustule /'pʌstjuːl/ *noun* a small pimple filled with pus

putrefaction /ˌpjuːtrɪ'fækʃən/ *noun* the decomposition of organic substances by bacteria, making an unpleasant smell

p.v. *adverb* by way of the vagina. Full form **per vaginam**

PVS *abbreviation* persistent vegetative state

py- /paɪ/, **pyo-** /paɪəʊ/ *prefix* same as **pyo-** (*used before vowels*)

pyaemia /paɪ'iːmiə/ *noun* invasion of blood with bacteria which then multiply and form many little abscesses in various parts of the body (NOTE: The US spelling is **pyemia**.)

pyarthrosis /ˌpaɪɑː'θrəʊsɪs/ *noun* a condition in which a joint becomes infected with pyogenic organisms and fills with pus. Also called **acute suppurative arthritis**

pyel- /paɪəl/ *prefix* same as **pyelo-** (*used before vowels*)

pyelitis /ˌpaɪə'laɪtɪs/ *noun* inflammation of the central part of the kidney

pyelo- /paɪələʊ/ *prefix* referring to the pelvis of the kidney

pyelocystitis /ˌpaɪələʊsɪ'staɪtɪs/ *noun* inflammation of the pelvis of the kidney and the urinary bladder

pyelogram /'paɪələgræm/ *noun* an X-ray photograph of a kidney and the urinary tract

pyelography /ˌpaɪə'lɒgrəfi/ *noun* X-ray examination of a kidney after introduction of a contrast medium

pyelolithotomy /ˌpaɪələʊlɪ'θɒtəmi/ *noun* a surgical operation to remove a stone from the pelvis of the kidney (NOTE: The plural is **pyelolithotomies**.)

pyelonephritis /ˌpaɪələʊnɪ'fraɪtɪs/ *noun* inflammation of the kidney and the pelvis of the kidney

pyeloplasty /'paɪələplæsti/ *noun* any surgical operation on the pelvis of the kidney (NOTE: The plural is **pyeloplasties**.)

pyelotomy /ˌpaɪə'lɒtəmi/ *noun* a surgical operation to make an opening in the pelvis of the kidney (NOTE: The plural is **pyelotomies**.)

pyg- /pɪdʒ/, **pygo-** *prefix* relating to the buttocks

pykno- /pɪknəʊ/ *prefix* indicating thickness or density

pyl- /paɪl/, **pyle-** /paɪli/ *prefix* referring to the portal vein

pylephlebitis /ˌpaɪlɪflə'baɪtɪs/ *noun* thrombosis of the portal vein

pylethrombosis /ˌpaɪliθrɒm'bəʊsɪs/ *noun* a condition in which blood clots are present in the portal vein or any of its branches

pylor- /paɪlɔːr/ *prefix* same as **pyloro-** (*used before vowels*)

pylorectomy /ˌpaɪlə'rektəmi/ *noun* a surgical operation to remove the pylorus and the antrum of the stomach (NOTE: The plural is **pylorectomies**.)

pylori /paɪ'lɔːri/ *plural of* **pylorus**

pyloric /paɪ'lɒrɪk/ *adjective* referring to the pylorus

pyloric antrum /paɪˌlɒrɪk 'æntrəm/ *noun* a space at the bottom of the stomach, before the pyloric sphincter

pyloric orifice /paɪˌlɒrɪk 'ɒrɪfɪs/ *noun* an opening where the stomach joins the duodenum

pyloric sphincter /paɪˌlɒrɪk 'sfɪŋktə/ *noun* a muscle which surrounds the pylorus, makes it contract and separates it from the duodenum

pyloric stenosis /paɪˌlɒrɪk ste'nəʊsɪs/ *noun* a blockage of the pylorus, which prevents food from passing from the stomach into the duodenum

pyloro- /paɪ'lɔːrəʊ/ *prefix* the pylorus

pyloroplasty /paɪ'lɔːrəplæsti/ *noun* a surgical operation to make the pylorus larger, sometimes combined with treatment for peptic ulcers (NOTE: The plural is **pyloroplasties**.)

pylorospasm /paɪˈlɔːrəspæz(ə)m/ *noun* a muscle spasm which closes the pylorus so that food cannot pass through into the duodenum

pylorotomy /ˌpaɪləˈrɒtəmi/ *noun* a surgical operation to cut into the muscle surrounding the pylorus to relieve pyloric stenosis. Also called **Ramstedt's operation** (NOTE: The plural is **pylorotomies**.)

pylorus /paɪˈlɔːrəs/ *noun* an opening at the bottom of the stomach leading into the duodenum (NOTE: The plural is **pylori**.)

pyo- /paɪəʊ/ *prefix* referring to pus

pyocolpos /ˌpaɪəˈkɒlpəs/ *noun* an accumulation of pus in the vagina

pyoderma /ˌpaɪəˈdɜːmə/ *noun* an eruption of pus in the skin

pyoderma gangrenosum /ˌpaɪədɜːmə ˌgæŋgrɪˈnəʊsəm/ *noun* a serious ulcerating disease of the skin, especially the legs, usually treated with steroid drugs

pyogenic /ˌpaɪəˈdʒenɪk/ *adjective* producing or forming pus

pyometra /ˌpaɪəˈmiːtrə/ *noun* an accumulation of pus in the uterus

pyomyositis /ˌpaɪəʊmaɪəˈsaɪtɪs/ *noun* inflammation of a muscle caused by staphylococci or streptococci

pyonephrosis /ˌpaɪəʊnɪˈfrəʊsɪs/ *noun* the distension of the kidney with pus

pyopericarditis /ˌpaɪəʊperikɑːˈdaɪtɪs/ *noun* an inflammation of the pericardium due to infection with staphylococci, streptococci or pneumococci

pyopneumothorax /ˌpaɪəʊˌnjuːməʊˈθɔːræks/ *noun* an accumulation of pus and gas or air in the pleural cavity

pyorrhoea /ˌpaɪəˈriə/ *noun* discharge of pus (NOTE: The US spelling is **pyorrhea**.)

pyosalpinx /ˌpaɪəˈsælpɪŋks/ *noun* inflammation and formation of pus in a Fallopian tube

pyothorax /ˌpaɪəˈθɔːræks/ *noun* same as **empyema**

pyr- /paɪr/ *prefix* same as **pyro-** (*used before vowels*)

pyramid /ˈpɪrəmɪd/ *noun* a cone-shaped part of the body, especially a cone-shaped projection on the surface of the medulla oblongata or in the medulla of the kidney. See illustration at **KIDNEY** in Supplement

pyramidal /pɪˈræmɪd(ə)l/ *adjective* referring to a pyramid

pyramidal cell /pɪˈræmɪd(ə)l sel/ *noun* a cone-shaped cell in the cerebral cortex

pyramidal system /pɪˈræmɪd(ə)l ˈsɪstəm/, **pyramidal tract** /pɪˈræmɪd(ə)l trækt/ *noun* a group of nerve fibres within the pyramid of the medulla oblongata in the brain. It is thought to be vital in controlling movement and speech.

pyret- /paɪret/, **pyreto-** *prefix* relating to heat or fever

pyrexia /paɪˈreksiə/ *noun* same as **fever**

pyridostigmine /ˌpɪrɪdəʊˈstɪgmiːn/ *noun* a drug which stops or delays the action of the enzyme cholinesterase, used to treat myasthenia gravis

pyridoxine /ˌpɪrɪˈdɒksɪn/ *noun* same as **Vitamin B_6**

pyrimidine /pɪˈrɪmɪdiːn/ *noun* **1.** a strong-smelling nitrogenous based compound with a six-sided ring structure that is the parent compound of several biologically important substances **2.** a derivative of pyrimidine, especially any of the bases cytosine, thymine, and uracil which are found in RNA and DNA

pyro- /paɪrəʊ/ *prefix* burning or fever

pyrogen /ˈpaɪrədʒen/ *noun* a substance which causes a fever

pyrogenic /ˌpaɪrəˈdʒenɪk/ *adjective* causing a fever

pyromania /ˌpaɪrəʊˈmeɪniə/ *noun* an uncontrollable desire to start fires

pyruvic acid /paɪˌruːvɪk ˈæsɪd/ *noun* a substance formed from glycogen in the muscles when it is broken down to release energy

pyuria /paɪˈjʊəriə/ *noun* pus in the urine

Q

q.d.s. *adverb* (*written on prescriptions*) to be taken four times a day. Full form **quater in die sumendus**

Q fever /ˈkjuː ˌfiːvə/ *noun* an infectious rickettsial disease of sheep and cows caused by *Coxiella burnetti* transmitted to humans

QRS complex /ˌkjuː ɑːr ˈes ˌkɒmpleks/ *noun* the deflections on an electrocardiogram, labelled Q, R, and S, which show ventricular contraction. ◊ **PQRST complex**

q.s. *adverb* (*written on prescriptions*) as much as necessary. Full form **quantum sufficiat**

Q-T interval /ˌkjuː ˈtiː ˌɪntəv(ə)l/, **Q-S2 interval** /ˌkjuː es ˈtuː ˌɪntəv(ə)l/ *noun* the length of the QRS complex in an electrocardiogram. ◊ **PQRST complex**

quad /kwɒd/ *noun* same as **quadruplet** (*informal*)

quadrant /ˈkwɒdrənt/ *noun* one of four sectors of the body thought of as being divided by the sagittal plane and the intertubercular plane ○ *tenderness in the right lower quadrant*

quadratus femoris /kwɒˌdreɪtəs ˈfemərɪs/ *noun* a muscle at the top of the femur which rotates the thigh

quadri- /kwɒdri/ *prefix* four

quadriceps /ˈkwɒdrɪseps/, **quadriceps femoris** /ˌkwɒdrɪseps ˈfemərɪs/ *noun* a large muscle in the front of the thigh, which extends to the leg

quadriplegia /ˌkwɒdrɪˈpliːdʒə/ *noun* paralysis of all four limbs, both arms and both legs

quadriplegic /ˌkwɒdrɪˈpliːdʒɪk/ *adjective* paralysed in both arms and both legs ■ *noun* a person paralysed in both arms and both legs

quadruple /ˈkwɒdrʊp(ə)l/ *adjective* **1.** consisting of four times as much **2.** having four parts

quadruplet /ˈkwɒdrʊplət/ *noun* one of four babies born to a mother at the same time. Also called **quad**

quadruple vaccine /ˌkwɒdrʊp(ə)l ˈvæksiːn/ *noun* a vaccine which immunises against four diseases, diphtheria, whooping cough, poliomyelitis and tetanus

qualitative /ˈkwɒlɪtətɪv/ *adjective* referring to a study in which descriptive information is collected. Compare **quantitative**

quality /ˈkwɒlɪti/ *noun* **1.** a characteristic of somebody or something **2.** the general standard or grade of something **3.** the highest or finest standard

quality assurance /ˈkwɒlɪti əˌʃʊərəns/ *noun* a set of criteria which are designed to check that people in an organisation maintain a high standard in the products or services they supply

quality circle /ˈkwɒləti ˌsɜːk(ə)l/ *noun* a group of employees from different levels of an organisation who meet regularly to discuss ways of improving the quality of its products or services

Qualpacs /ˈkwɒlpæks/, **Quality Patient Care Scale** /ˌkwɒlɪti ˌpeɪʃ(ə)nt ˈkeə ˌskeɪl/ *noun* a method which guides nurses to evaluate their activity in terms of efficiency of cost, time, use of skill level and workload

quantitative /ˈkwɒntɪtətɪv/ *adjective* referring to a study in which numerical information is collected. Compare **qualitative**

quantitative digital radiography /ˌkwɒntɪtətɪv ˌdɪdʒɪt(ə)l ˌreɪdiˈɒɡrəfi/ *noun* the use of digital X-ray scans to find out whether a person has a bone disease such as osteoporosis. The levels of calcium in the bones are measured, usually in the spine and hip.

quarantine /ˈkwɒrəntiːn/ *noun* **1.** the situation in which a person, animal or ship just arrived in a country is kept isolated in case it carries a serious disease, to allow the disease time to develop and be detected **2.** the period of such isolation to prevent the spread of disease ○ *six months' quarantine* ■ *verb* to put a person or animal in quarantine (NOTE: **quarantining – quarantined**)

quartan fever /ˈkwɔːt(ə)n ˌfiːvə/ *noun* a form of malaria caused by *Plasmodium malariae* in which the fever returns every four days. ◊ **tertian fever**

queasiness /ˈkwiːzɪnəs/ *noun* the feeling of being about to vomit

queasy /ˈkwiːzi/ *adjective* feeling as though about to vomit

Queckenstedt test /ˈkwekənsted test/ *noun* a test done during a lumbar puncture in which pressure is applied to the jugular veins to see if the cerebrospinal fluid is flowing correctly [Described 1916. After Hans Heinrich George Queckenstedt (1876–1918), German physician.]

quickening /ˈkwɪknɪŋ/ *noun* the first sign of life in an unborn baby, usually after about four months of pregnancy, when the mother can feel it moving in her uterus

quiescent /kwiˈes(ə)nt/ *adjective* referring to a disease with symptoms reduced either by treatment or in the usual course of the disease

quin /kwɪn/ *noun* same as **quintuplet** (*informal*) (NOTE: The US term is **quint**.)

quinine /kwɪˈniːn/ *noun* an alkaloid drug made from the bark of cinchona, a South American tree

quinolone /ˈkwɪnələʊn/ *noun* a drug used to treat Gram-negative and Gram-positive bacterial infections of the respiratory and urinary tracts and of the gastro-intestinal system (NOTE: Quinolone

drugs have names ending in **-oxacin: ciprofloxacin**)

quinsy /ˈkwɪnzi/ *noun* acute throat inflammation with an abscess round a tonsil. Also called **peritonsillar abscess**

quint /kwɪnt/ *noun US* same as **quintuplet**

quintuplet /ˈkwɪntjʊplət/ *noun* one of five babies born to a mother at the same time. Also called **quin, quint**

quotidian /kwəʊˈtɪdiən/ *adjective* recurring daily

quotidian fever /kwəʊˌtɪdiən ˈfiːvə/ *noun* a violent form of malaria in which the fever returns at daily or even shorter intervals

quotient /ˈkwəʊʃ(ə)nt/ *noun* the result when one number is divided by another

Q wave /ˈkjuː weɪv/ *noun* a negative deflection at the start of the QRS complex on an electrocardiogram, going downwards

R

R *symbol* roentgen

R/ *abbreviation* prescription. Full form **recipe**

rabid /'ræbɪd/ *adjective* referring to rabies, or affected by rabies ○ *She was bitten by a rabid dog.*

rabid encephalitis /,ræbɪd en,kefə'laɪtɪs/ *noun* a fatal form of encephalitis resulting from the bite of a rabid animal

rabies /'reɪbiːz/ *noun* a frequently fatal viral disease transmitted to humans by infected animals ○ *The hospital ordered a batch of rabies vaccine.* Also called **hydrophobia**

racemose /'ræsɪməʊs/ *adjective* referring to glands which look like a bunch of grapes

rachi- /reɪki/ *prefix* same as **rachio-** (*used before vowels*)

rachides /'reɪkɪdiːz/ plural of **rachis**

rachio- /reɪkiəʊ/ *prefix* referring to the spine

rachis /'reɪkɪs/ *noun* same as **backbone** (NOTE: The plural is **rachises** or **rachides**.)

rachischisis /reɪ'kɪskɪsɪs/ *noun* same as **spina bifida**

rachitic /rə'kɪtɪk/ *adjective* referring to rickets

rachitis /rə'kaɪtɪs/ *noun* same as **rickets**

rad /ræd/ *noun* a unit of measurement of absorbed radiation dose. ◊ **becquerel**, **gray** (NOTE: **Gray** is now used to mean one hundred rads.)

radial /'reɪdiəl/ *adjective* **1.** referring to something which branches **2.** referring to the radius bone in the arm

radial artery /'reɪdiəl ,ɑːtəri/ *noun* an artery which branches from the brachial artery, running near the radius, from the elbow to the palm of the hand

radial nerve /'reɪdiəl nɜːv/ *noun* the main motor nerve in the arm, running down the back of the upper arm and the outer side of the forearm

radial pulse /'reɪdiəl pʌls/ *noun* the main pulse in the wrist, taken near the outer edge of the forearm just above the wrist

radial recurrent /,reɪdiəl rɪ'kʌrənt/ *noun* an artery in the arm which forms a loop beside the brachial artery

radial reflex /,reɪdiəl 'riːfleks/ *noun* a jerk made by the forearm when the insertion in the radius of one of the muscles, the brachioradialis, is hit

radiant /'reɪdiənt/ *adjective* **1.** lit with a bright or glowing light **2.** referring to light, heat or other energy sent out in the form of rays or waves **3.** sending out light, heat or other energy in the form of rays or waves

radiation /,reɪdi'eɪʃ(ə)n/ *noun* waves of energy which are given off by some substances, especially radioactive substances

radiation burn /,reɪdi'eɪʃ(ə)n bɜːn/ *noun* a burn on the skin caused by exposure to large amounts of radiation

radiation sickness /,reɪdi'eɪʃ(ə)n ,sɪknəs/ *noun* an illness caused by exposure to radiation from radioactive substances

radiation treatment /,reɪdi'eɪʃ(ə)n ,triːtmənt/ *noun* same as **radiotherapy**

radical /'rædɪk(ə)l/ *adjective* aiming to deal with the root of a problem, taking thorough action to remove the source of a disease rather than treat its symptoms

radical mastectomy /,rædɪk(ə)l mæ'stektəmi/ *noun* a surgical operation to remove a breast and the lymph nodes and muscles associated with it

radical mastoidectomy /,rædɪk(ə)l ,mæstɔɪ'dektəmi/ *noun* a surgical operation to remove all of the mastoid process

radical treatment /,rædɪk(ə)l 'triːtmənt/ *noun* treatment which aims at complete eradication of a disease

radicle /'rædɪk(ə)l/ *noun* a small root or vein

radicular /rə'dɪkjʊlə/ *adjective* referring to a radicle

radiculitis /rə,dɪkjʊ'laɪtɪs/ *noun* inflammation of a radicle of a cranial or spinal nerve

radio- /reɪdiəʊ/ *prefix* **1.** referring to radiation **2.** referring to radioactive substances **3.** referring to the radius in the arm

radioactive /,reɪdiəʊ'æktɪv/ *adjective* with a nucleus which disintegrates and gives off energy in the form of radiation which can pass through other substances

radioactive isotope /ˌreɪdiəʊæktɪv ˈaɪsətəʊp/ *noun* an isotope which sends out radiation, used in radiotherapy and scanning

radioactivity /ˌreɪdiəʊækˈtɪvɪti/ *noun* energy in the form of radiation emitted by a radioactive substance

radiobiologist /ˌreɪdiəʊbaɪˈɒlədʒɪst/ *noun* a doctor who specialises in radiobiology

radiobiology /ˌreɪdiəʊbaɪˈɒlədʒi/ *noun* the scientific study of radiation and its effects on living things

radiocarpal joint /ˌreɪdiəʊˈkɑːp(ə)l ˌdʒɔɪnt/ *noun* the joint where the radius articulates with the scaphoid, one of the carpal bones. Also called **wrist joint**

radiodermatitis /ˌreɪdiəʊˌdɜːməˈtaɪtɪs/ *noun* inflammation of the skin caused by exposure to radiation

radiograph /ˈreɪdiəɡrɑːf/ *noun* an image produced on film or another sensitive surface when radiation such as X-rays or gamma rays passes through an object ■ *verb* to make a radiograph of something, especially a part of the body

radiographer /ˌreɪdiˈɒɡrəfə/ *noun* **1.** a person specially trained to operate a machine to take X-ray photographs or radiographs. Also called **diagnostic radiographer 2.** a person specially trained to use X-rays or radioactive isotopes in the treatment of patients. Also called **therapeutic radiographer**

radiography /ˌreɪdiˈɒɡrəfi/ *noun* the work of examining the internal parts of the body by taking X-ray photographs

radioimmunoassay /ˌreɪdiəʊˌɪmjʊnəʊˈæseɪ/ *noun* the use of radioactive tracers to investigate the presence of antibodies in blood samples, in order to measure the antibodies themselves or the amount of particular substances, such as hormones, in the blood

radioisotope /ˌreɪdiəʊˈaɪsətəʊp/ *noun* an isotope of a chemical element which is radioactive

radiologist /ˌreɪdiˈɒlədʒɪst/ *noun* a doctor who specialises in radiology

radiology /ˌreɪdiˈɒlədʒi/ *noun* the use of radiation to diagnose disorders, e.g. through the use of X-rays or radioactive tracers, or to treat diseases such as cancer

radiomimetic /ˌreɪdiəʊmɪˈmetɪk/ *adjective* referring to a drug or chemical which produces similar effects to those of radiation, e.g. the nitrogen mustard group of chemicals used in chemotherapy

radionuclide /ˌreɪdiəʊˈnjuːklaɪd/ *noun* an element which gives out radiation

radionuclide scan /ˌreɪdiəʊˈnjuːklaɪd ˌskæn/ *noun* a scan, especially of the brain, where radionuclides are put in compounds which are concentrated in particular parts of the body

radio-opaque /ˌreɪdiəʊ əʊˈpeɪk/ *adjective* absorbing and blocking radiant energy, e.g. X-rays

radio-opaque dye /ˌreɪdiəʊ əʊˌpeɪk ˈdaɪ/ *noun* a liquid which appears on an X-ray, and which is introduced into soft organs such as the kidney so that they show up clearly on an X-ray photograph

radiopaque /ˌreɪdiəʊˈpeɪk/ *adjective* same as **radio-opaque**

radioscopy /ˌreɪdiˈɒskəpi/ *noun* an examination of an X-ray photograph on a fluorescent screen

radiosensitive /ˌreɪdiəʊˈsensɪtɪv/ *adjective* referring to a cancer cell which is sensitive to radiation and can be treated by radiotherapy

radiotherapist /ˌreɪdiəʊˈθerəpɪst/ *noun* a doctor who specialises in radiotherapy

radiotherapy /ˌreɪdiəʊˈθerəpi/ *noun* the treatment of diseases by exposing the affected part to radioactive rays such as X-rays or gamma rays

radium /ˈreɪdiəm/ *noun* a radioactive metallic element (NOTE: The chemical symbol is **Ra**.)

radius /ˈreɪdiəs/ *noun* the shorter and outer of the two bones in the forearm between the elbow and the wrist. See illustration at **HAND** in Supplement (NOTE: The plural is **radii**. The other bone in the forearm is the **ulna**.)

radix /ˈreɪdɪks/ *noun* same as **root** (NOTE: The plural is **radices** or **radixes**.)

radon /ˈreɪdɒn/ *noun* a radioactive gas, formed from the radioactive decay of radium, and used in capsules called radon seeds to treat cancers inside the body (NOTE: The chemical symbol is **Rn**.)

rale /rɑːl/ *noun* same as **crepitation**

Ramstedt's operation /ˈrɑːmstets ɒpəˌreɪʃ(ə)n/ *noun* same as **pylorotomy** [Described 1912. After Wilhelm Conrad Ramstedt (1867–1963), German surgeon.]

ramus /ˈreɪməs/ *noun* **1.** a branch of a nerve, artery or vein **2.** the ascending part on each side of the mandible (NOTE: The plural is **rami**.)

R & D *abbreviation* research and development

randomised /ˈrændəmaɪzd/, **randomized** *adjective* involving subjects which have been selected without a prearranged plan and in no particular pattern or order

ranitidine /ræˈnɪtɪdiːn/ *noun* a drug which reduces the amount of acid released by the stomach. It is used to treat peptic ulcers and gastritis.

ranula /ˈrænjʊlə/ *noun* a small cyst under the tongue, on the floor of the mouth, which forms when a salivary duct is blocked

Ranvier /ˈrɑːnvɪˌeɪ/ ♦ **node of Ranvier**

rape /reɪp/ *noun* the crime of forcing somebody to have sexual intercourse ■ *verb* to force somebody to have sexual intercourse

raphe /ˈreɪfi/ *noun* a long thin fold which looks like a seam, along a midline such as on the dorsal face of the tongue

rapid eye movement sleep /ˌræpɪd ˈaɪ ˌmuːvmənt ˌsliːp/ *noun* same as **REM sleep**

rapport /ræˈpɔː/ *noun* an emotional bond or friendly relationship between people ○ *a psychiatrist who quickly establishes a rapport with his patients*

rarefaction /ˌreərɪˈfækʃən/ *noun* a condition in which bone tissue becomes more porous and less dense because of a lack of calcium

rash /ræʃ/ *noun* a mass of small spots which stays on the skin for a period of time, and then disappears

raspatory /ˈræspət(ə)ri/ *noun* a surgical instrument like a file, which is used to scrape the surface of a bone

rate /reɪt/ *noun* **1.** the amount or proportion of something compared with something else **2.** the number of times something happens in a set time ○ *The heart was beating at a rate of only 59 per minute.*

ratio /ˈreɪʃiəʊ/ *noun* a number which shows a proportion or which is the result of one number divided by another ○ *An IQ is the ratio of the person's mental age to his or her chronological age.*

Raynaud's disease /ˈreɪnəʊz dɪˌziːz/, **Raynaud's phenomenon** /ˈreɪnəʊz fɪˌnɒmɪnən/ *noun* a condition with various possible causes in which the blood supply to the fingers and toes is restricted and they become cold, white and numb. Also called **dead man's fingers**, **vasospasm** [Described 1862. After Maurice Raynaud (1834–81), French physician.]

RBC *abbreviation* red blood cell

RCGP *abbreviation* Royal College of General Practitioners

RCN *abbreviation* Royal College of Nursing

RCOG *abbreviation* Royal College of Obstetricians and Gynaecologists

RCP *abbreviation* Royal College of Physicians

RCPsych /ˌɑː siː ˈsaɪk/ *abbreviation* Royal College of Psychiatrists

RCS *abbreviation* Royal College of Surgeons

RCT *abbreviation* randomised controlled trial

reaction /riˈækʃən/ *noun* **1.** an action which takes place as a direct result of something which has happened earlier ○ *A rash appeared as a reaction to the penicillin injection.* **2.** the particular response of someone to a test

reactionary /riˈækʃən(ə)ri/ *adjective* same as **reactive**

reactionary haemorrhage /riˌækʃən(ə)ri ˈhem(ə)rɪdʒ/ *noun* bleeding which follows an operation

reactivate /riˈæktɪveɪt/ *verb* to make something active again ○ *His general physical weakness has reactivated the dormant virus.*

reactive /riˈæktɪv/ *adjective* taking place as a reaction to something else

reagent /riˈeɪdʒ(ə)nt/ *noun* a chemical substance which reacts with another substance, especially one which is used to detect the presence of the second substance

real-time imaging /ˌrɪəl taɪm ˈɪmɪdʒɪŋ/ *noun* the use of ultrasound information to produce a series of images of a process or changing object almost instantly

rear /rɪə/, **rear end** /rɪə end/ *noun* same as **buttock** (*informal*)

recalcitrant /rɪˈkælsɪtrənt/ *adjective* not responding to treatment ○ *a recalcitrant condition*

recall /rɪˈkɔːl/ *noun* the act of remembering something from the past ■ *verb* /rɪˈkɔːl/ to remember something which happened in the past

receptor /rɪˈseptə/, **receptor cell** /rɪˈseptə sel/ *noun* a nerve ending or cell which senses a change such as cold or heat in the surrounding environment or in the body and reacts to it by sending an impulse to the central nervous system

recess /rɪˈses/ *noun* a hollow part in an organ

recessive /rɪˈsesɪv/ *adjective* (*of an allele*) having the characteristic that leads to the trait which it controls being suppressed by the presence of the corresponding dominant allele. Compare **dominant**

recipient /rɪˈsɪpiənt/ *noun* a person who receives something such as a transplant or a blood transfusion from a donor

recombinant DNA /rɪˌkɒmbɪnənt diː en ˈeɪ/ *noun* DNA extracted from two or more different sources and joined together to form a single molecule or fragment. This technology is used to produce molecules and organisms with new properties.

recover /rɪˈkʌvə/ *verb* to get better after an illness, operation or accident ○ *She recovered from her concussion in a few days.* ○ *It will take him weeks to recover from the accident.* (NOTE: You recover **from** an illness.)

recovery /rɪˈkʌv(ə)ri/ *noun* the process of returning to health after being ill or injured

recovery position /rɪˈkʌv(ə)ri pəˌzɪʃ(ə)n/ *noun* a position in which someone is lying face downwards, with one knee and one arm bent forwards and the face turned to one side

recovery room /rɪˈkʌv(ə)ri ruːm/ *noun* a room in a hospital where patients are cared for after they have had a surgical operation and are recovering from the effects of the anaesthetic. Abbreviation **RR**

recreational drug /ˌrekriˈeɪʃ(ə)n(ə)l drʌg/ noun a drug that is taken for pleasure rather than because of medical need

recrudescence /ˌriːkruːˈdes(ə)ns/ noun the reappearance of symptoms of a disease which seemed to have got better

rect- /rekt/ prefix same as **recto-** (used before vowels)

rectal /ˈrekt(ə)l/ adjective referring to the rectum

rectal fissure /ˌrekt(ə)l ˈfɪʃə/ noun a crack in the wall of the anal canal

rectal prolapse /ˌrekt(ə)l ˈprəʊlæps/ noun a condition in which part of the rectum moves downwards and passes through the anus

recto- /rektəʊ/ prefix referring to the rectum

rectocele /ˈrektəʊsiːl/ noun a condition associated with prolapse of the uterus, in which the rectum protrudes into the vagina. Also called **proctocele**

rectopexy /ˈrektəʊpeksi/ noun a surgical operation to attach a rectum which has prolapsed

rectoscope /ˈrektəskəʊp/ noun an instrument for looking into the rectum

rectosigmoid /ˌrektəʊˈsɪgmɔɪd/ noun the part of the large intestine where the sigmoid colon joins the rectum

rectosigmoidectomy /ˌrektəʊˌsɪgmɔɪˈdektəmi/ noun the surgical removal of the sigmoid colon and the rectum

rectovaginal /ˌrektəʊvəˈdʒaɪn(ə)l/ adjective relating to both the rectum and the vagina

rectovaginal examination /ˌrektəʊvə ˌdʒaɪn(ə)l ɪgˌzæmɪˈneɪʃ(ə)n/ noun an examination of the rectum and vagina

rectovesical /ˌrektəʊˈvesɪk(ə)l/ adjective referring to both the rectum and the bladder

rectum /ˈrektəm/ noun the end part of the large intestine leading from the sigmoid colon to the anus. See illustration at DIGESTIVE SYSTEM in Supplement, UROGENITAL SYSTEM (MALE) in Supplement (NOTE: For other terms referring to the rectum, see words beginning with **proct-, procto-**.)

rectus /ˈrektəs/ noun a straight muscle (NOTE: The plural is **recti**.)

rectus abdominis /ˌrektəs æbˈdɒmɪnɪs/ noun a long straight muscle which runs down the front of the abdomen

rectus femoris /ˌrektəs ˈfemɒrɪs/ noun a flexor muscle in the front of the thigh, one of the four parts of the quadriceps femoris. ◊ **medial**

recumbent /rɪˈkʌmbənt/ adjective lying down

recuperation /rɪˌkuːpəˈreɪʃ(ə)n/ noun the process of getting better after an illness ○ His recuperation will take several months.

recurrent /rɪˈkʌrənt/ adjective **1.** occurring in the same way many times **2.** referring to a vein, artery or nerve which forms a loop

recurrent abortion /rɪˌkʌrənt əˈbɔːʃ(ə)n/ noun a condition in which a woman has abortions with one pregnancy after another

recurrent fever /rɪˌkʌrənt ˈfiːvə/ noun a fever like malaria which returns at regular intervals

red blood cell /ˌred ˈblʌd ˌsel/ noun a blood cell which contains haemoglobin and carries oxygen to the tissues and takes carbon dioxide from them. Abbreviation **RBC**. Also called **erythrocyte**

Red Crescent /ˌred ˈkrez(ə)nt/ noun in Islamic countries, an international organisation dedicated to the medical care of the sick and wounded in wars and natural disasters (NOTE: It is known as the Red Cross elsewhere.)

Red Cross /ˌred ˈkrɒs/ noun an international organisation dedicated to the medical care of the sick and wounded in wars and natural disasters (NOTE: It is known as the Red Crescent in Islamic countries.)

Redivac drain /ˈredɪvæk dreɪn/, **Redivac drainage tube** /ˌredɪvæk ˈdreɪnɪdʒ ˌtjuːb/ trademark a tube which drains fluid away from the inside of a wound into a bottle, used mainly after operations on the abdomen

reducible /rɪˈdjuːsɪb(ə)l/ adjective capable of being reduced

reducible hernia /rɪˌdjuːsɪb(ə)l ˈhɜːniə/ noun a hernia where the organ can be pushed back into place without an operation

reduction /rɪˈdʌkʃən/ noun the action of putting a hernia, a dislocated joint or a broken bone back into the correct position

reduction division /rɪˈdʌkʃən dɪˌvɪʒ(ə)n/ noun same as **meiosis**

refer /rɪˈfɜː/ verb **1.** to mention or to talk about something ○ The doctor referred to the patient's history of sinus problems. **2.** to pass on information about a patient to someone else ○ They referred her case to a gynaecologist. **3.** to send someone to another doctor, usually a specialist, for advice or treatment ○ She was referred to a cardiologist.

referral /rɪˈfɜːrəl/ noun the act of sending someone to a specialist ○ She asked for a referral to a gynaecologist.

referred pain /rɪˌfɜːd ˈpeɪn/ noun same as **synalgia**

reflection /rɪˈflekʃən/ noun **1.** the image of somebody or something which is seen in a mirror or still water **2.** the process of reflecting something, especially light, sound or heat **3.** careful thought **4.** a situation in which an anatomical structure bends back upon itself

reflective practice /rɪˌflektɪv ˈpræktɪs/ noun the process of improving professional skills by monitoring your own actions while they are being carried out, and by then later evaluating them by talking or writing about them and asking other professionals to give their assessments of you

reflex /'ri:fleks/, **reflex action** /'ri:fleks ˌækʃən/ *noun* a physiological reaction without any conscious thought involved, e.g. a knee jerk or a sneeze, which happens in response to a particular stimulus

reflex arc /'ri:fleks ɑːk/ *noun* the basic system of a reflex action, where a receptor is linked to a motor neurone which in turn is linked to an effector muscle

reflexologist /ˌri:flək'sɒlədʒɪst/ *noun* a person specialising in reflexology

reflexology /ˌri:flek'sɒlədʒi/ *noun* a treatment to relieve tension by massaging the soles of the feet and thereby stimulating the nerves and increasing the blood supply

reflux /'ri:flʌks/ *noun* a situation where a fluid flows in the opposite direction to its usual flow ○ *The valves in the veins prevent blood reflux.* ◊ **vesicoureteric reflux**

reflux oesophagitis /ˌri:flʌks iːˌsɒfə'dʒaɪtɪs/ *noun* inflammation of the oesophagus caused by regurgitation of acid juices from the stomach

refraction /rɪ'frækʃən/ *noun* a change of direction of light rays as they enter a medium such as the eye

refractory /rɪ'fræktəri/ *adjective* difficult or impossible to treat, or not responding to treatment

refractory period /rɪˌfræktəri 'pɪəriəd/ *noun* a short space of time after the ventricles of the heart have contracted, when they cannot contract again

refrigeration /rɪˌfrɪdʒə'reɪʃ(ə)n/ *noun* the process of making something cold

regeneration /rɪˌdʒenə'reɪʃ(ə)n/ *noun* the process where tissue that has been destroyed grows again

regimen /'redʒɪmən/ *noun* a fixed course of treatment, e.g. a course of drugs or a special diet

regional /'ri:dʒ(ə)nəl/ *adjective* in a particular region, referring to a particular region

register /'redʒɪstə/ *noun* an official list ■ *verb* to write a name on an official list, especially the official list of patients treated by a GP or dentist, or the list of people with a particular disease ○ *He is a registered heroin addict.* ○ *They went to register the birth with the Registrar of Births, Marriages and Deaths.* □ **to register with someone** to put your name on someone's official list, especially the list of patients treated by a GP or dentist ○ *Before registering with the GP, she asked if she could visit him.* ○ *All practising doctors are registered with the General Medical Council.*

registered midwife /ˌredʒɪstəd 'mɪdwaɪf/ *noun* a qualified midwife who is registered to practise

Registered Nurse /ˌredʒɪstəd 'nɜːs/, **Registered General Nurse** /ˌredʒɪstəd 'dʒen(ə)rəl ˌnɜːs/, **Registered Theatre Nurse** /ˌredʒɪstəd 'θɪətə ˌnɜːs/ *noun* a nurse who has been registered by the UKCC. Abbreviation **RN, RGN, RTN**

registrar /ˌredʒɪ'strɑː/ *noun* **1.** a qualified doctor or surgeon in a hospital who supervises house officers **2.** a person who registers something officially

registration /ˌredʒɪ'streɪʃ(ə)n/ *noun* the act of registering ○ *A doctor cannot practise without registration by the General Medical Council.*

regression /rɪ'greʃ(ə)n/ *noun* a stage where symptoms of a disease are disappearing and the person is getting better

regurgitation /rɪˌɡɜːdʒɪ'teɪʃ(ə)n/ *noun* the process of flowing back in the opposite direction to the usual flow, especially of bringing up partly digested food from the stomach into the mouth

rehabilitation /ˌri:əbɪlɪ'teɪʃ(ə)n/ *noun* the process of making someone fit to work or to lead an ordinary life again

rehydration /ˌri:haɪ'dreɪʃ(ə)n/ *noun* the act of giving water or liquid to someone who has dehydration

Reiter's syndrome /'raɪtəz ˌsɪndrəʊm/, **Reiter's disease** /'raɪtəz dɪˌziːz/ *noun* an illness which may be sexually transmitted and affects mainly men, causing arthritis, urethritis and conjunctivitis at the same time [Described 1916. After Hans Conrad Reiter (1881–1969), German bacteriologist and hygienist.]

reject /rɪ'dʒekt/ *verb* **1.** to refuse to accept something **2.** to be unable to tolerate tissue or an organ transplanted from another body because it is immunologically incompatible ○ *The new heart was rejected by the body.* ○ *They gave the patient drugs to prevent the transplant being rejected.* **3.** to be unable to keep food down and vomit it up again

rejection /rɪ'dʒekʃən/ *noun* the act of rejecting tissue ○ *The patient was given drugs to reduce the possibility of tissue rejection.*

relapse /'ri:læps, rɪ'læps/ *noun* a situation in which someone gets worse after seeming to be getting better, or where a disease appears again after seeming to be cured ■ *verb* to return to an earlier and worse state, especially to get ill again after getting better ○ *She relapsed into a coma.*

relapsing fever /rɪ'læpsɪŋ ˌfiːvə/ *noun* a disease caused by a bacterium, where attacks of fever recur from time to time

relative density /ˌrelətɪv 'densɪti/ *noun* the ratio of the density of a substance to the density of a standard substance at the same temperature and pressure. For liquids and solids the standard substance is usually water, and for gases, it is air.

relative risk /ˌrelətɪv 'rɪsk/ *noun* a measure of the likelihood of developing a disease for people who are exposed to a particular risk, relative to people who are not exposed to the same risk. For example, the relative risk of myocardial infarction for oral contraceptive users is 1.6 times that of non-users. Abbreviation **RR**

relaxant /rɪˈlæksənt/ *noun* a substance which relieves strain ■ *adjective* relieving strain

relaxation /ˌriːlækˈseɪʃ(ə)n/ *noun* the process of reducing strain in a muscle

relaxation therapy /ˌriːlækˈseɪʃ(ə)n ˌθerəpi/ *noun* a treatment in which people are encouraged to relax their muscles to reduce stress

relaxin /rɪˈlæksɪn/ *noun* a hormone which is secreted by the placenta to make the cervix relax and open fully in the final stages of pregnancy before childbirth

release /rɪˈliːs/ *noun* the process of allowing something to go out ○ *the slow release of the drug into the bloodstream* ■ *verb* to let something out ○ *Hormones are released into the body by glands.*

releasing factor /rɪˈliːsɪŋ ˌfæktə/ *noun* a substance produced in the hypothalamus which encourages the release of hormones

releasing hormone /rɪˈliːsɪŋ ˌhɔːməʊn/ *noun* a hormone secreted by the hypothalamus which makes the pituitary gland release particular hormones. Also called **hypothalamic hormone**

rem /rem/ *noun* a unit for measuring amounts of radiation, equal to the effect that one roentgen of X-rays or gamma-rays would produce in a human being. It is used in radiation protection and monitoring.

REM /rem/ *abbreviation* rapid eye movement. ⟡ **REM sleep**

remission /rɪˈmɪʃ(ə)n/ *noun* a period when an illness or fever is less severe

re. mist. /ˌriː ˈmɪst/ *adverb* (*on a prescription*) repeat the same mixture. Full form **repetatur mistura**

REM sleep /ˈrem sliːp/ *noun* a stage of sleep which happens several times each night and is characterised by dreaming, rapid eye movement and increased pulse rate and brain activity. Also called **rapid eye movement sleep**

COMMENT: During REM sleep, a person dreams, breathes lightly and has a raised blood pressure and an increased rate of heartbeat. The eyes may be half-open, and the sleeper may make facial movements.

ren- /riːn/ *prefix* same as **reno-** (*used before vowels*)

renal /ˈriːn(ə)l/ *adjective* referring to the kidneys

renal artery /ˌriːn(ə)l 'ɑːtəri/ *noun* one of two arteries running from the abdominal aorta to the kidneys

renal calculus /ˌriːn(ə)l 'kælkjʊləs/ *noun* a small hard mineral mass called a stone in the kidney

renal capsule /ˌriːn(ə)l 'kæpsjuːl/ *noun* same as **fibrous capsule**

renal colic /ˌriːn(ə)l 'kɒlɪk/ *noun* a sudden pain caused by a kidney stone or stones in the ureter

renal corpuscle /ˌriːn(ə)l 'kɔːpʌs(ə)l/ *noun* part of a nephron in the cortex of a kidney. Also called **Malpighian body**

renal cortex /ˌriːn(ə)l 'kɔːteks/ *noun* the outer covering of the kidney, immediately beneath the capsule. See illustration at **KIDNEY** in Supplement

renal dialysis /ˌriːn(ə)l daɪˈæləsɪs/ *noun* a method of artificially maintaining the chemical balance of the blood when the kidneys have failed, or the process of using this method. Also called **dialysis**

renal hypertension /ˌriːn(ə)l ˌhaɪpəˈtenʃən/ *noun* high blood pressure linked to kidney disease

renal medulla /ˌriːn(ə)l meˈdʌlə/ *noun* the inner part of a kidney containing no glomeruli. See illustration at **KIDNEY** in Supplement

renal pelvis /ˌriːn(ə)l 'pelvɪs/ *noun* the upper and wider part of the ureter leading from the kidney where urine is collected before passing down the ureter into the bladder. Also called **pelvis of the kidney**. See illustration at **KIDNEY** in Supplement

renal transplant /ˌriːn(ə)l 'trænsplɑːnt/ *noun* a kidney transplant

renal tubule /ˌriːn(ə)l 'tjuːbjuːl/ *noun* a tiny tube which is part of a nephron. Also called **uriniferous tubule**

reni- /riːni/ *prefix* referring to the kidneys

renin /ˈriːnɪn/ *noun* an enzyme secreted by the kidney to prevent loss of sodium, and which also affects blood pressure

rennin /ˈrenɪn/ *noun* an enzyme which makes milk coagulate in the stomach, so as to slow down the passage of the milk through the digestive system

reno- /riːnəʊ/ *prefix* referring to the kidneys

renovascular system /ˌriːnəʊˈvæskjʊlə ˌsɪstəm/ *noun* the blood vessels associated with the kidney

reorganisation /riːˌɔːɡənaɪˈzeɪʃ(ə)n/, **reorganization** *noun* 1. a change in the way something is organised or done 2. the process of changing the way something is organised or done 3. an occasion when a business or organisation is given a completely new structure

reovirus /ˈriːəʊˌvaɪrəs/ *noun* a virus which affects both the intestine and the respiratory system, but does not cause serious illness. Compare **echovirus**

rep /rep/ *adverb* (*written on a prescription*) repeat. Full form **repetatur**

repetitive strain injury /rɪ,petɪtɪv 'streɪn ,ɪndʒəri/, **repetitive stress injury** /rɪ,petɪtɪv 'stres ,ɪndʒəri/ *noun* pain, usually in a limb, felt by someone who performs the same movement many times over a period, e.g. when operating a computer terminal or playing a musical instrument. Abbreviation **RSI**

replantation /,riːplɑːnˈteɪʃ(ə)n/ *noun* a surgical technique which reattaches parts of the body which have been accidentally cut or torn off

replication /,replɪˈkeɪʃ(ə)n/ *noun* the process in the division of a cell, where the DNA makes copies of itself

repolarisation /riː,pəʊləraɪˈzeɪʃ(ə)n/, **repolarization** *noun* the restoration of the usual electrical polarity of a nerve or muscle cell membrane after reversal of its polarity while a nerve impulse or muscle contraction travelled along it

reportable diseases /rɪ,pɔːtəb(ə)l dɪˈziːzɪz/ *plural noun* diseases such as asbestosis, hepatitis or anthrax which may be caused by working conditions or may infect other workers and must be reported to the District Health Authority

repositor /rɪˈpɒzɪtə/ *noun* a surgical instrument used to push a prolapsed organ back into its usual position

repression /rɪˈpreʃ(ə)n/ *noun* (*in psychiatry*) the act of ignoring or forgetting feelings or thoughts which might be unpleasant

reproduction /,riːprəˈdʌkʃ(ə)n/ *noun* the process of making new living beings by existing ones, e.g. producing children or derived other descendants

reproductive /,riːprəˈdʌktɪv/ *adjective* referring to reproduction

reproductive organs /,riːprəˈdʌktɪv ,ɔːgənz/ *plural noun* parts of the bodies of men and women which are involved in the conception and development of a fetus

reproductive system /,riːprəˈdʌktɪv ,sɪstəm/ *noun* the arrangement of organs and ducts in the bodies of men and women which produce spermatozoa or ova

COMMENT: In the human male, the testes produce the spermatozoa which pass through the vasa efferentia and the vasa deferentia where they receive liquid from the seminal vesicles, then out of the body through the urethra and penis on ejaculation. In the female, an ovum, produced by one of the two ovaries, passes through the Fallopian tube where it is fertilised by a spermatozoon from the male. The fertilised ovum moves down into the uterus where it develops into an embryo.

RES *abbreviation* reticuloendothelial system

research and development /rɪ,sɜːtʃ ən dɪ'veləpmənt/ *noun* the process by which pharmaceutical companies find new drugs and test their suitability. Abbreviation **R & D**

resection /rɪˈsekʃən/ *noun* the surgical removal of any part of the body

resection of the prostate /rɪ,sekʃən əv ðə 'prɒsteɪt/ *noun* same as **transurethral prostatectomy**

resectoscope /rɪˈsektəskəʊp/ *noun* a surgical instrument used to carry out a transurethral resection

reservoir /'rezəvwɑː/ *noun* **1.** a cavity in an organ or group of tissues in which fluids collect and are stored **2.** an organism in which a parasite lives and develops without damaging it, but from which the parasite then passes to another species which is damaged by it **3.** a part of a machine or piece of equipment where liquid is stored for it to use

resident /'rezɪd(ə)nt/ *adjective* living in a place

residential /,rezɪˈdenʃəl/ *adjective* **1.** living in a hospital **2.** living at home

residential care /,rezɪˈdenʃəl ,keə/ *noun* the care of patients either in a hospital or at home, but not as outpatients

residual /rɪˈzɪdjuəl/ *adjective* remaining, which is left behind

residual air /rɪ,zɪdjuəl 'eə/, **residual volume** /rɪ,zɪdjuəl 'vɒljuːm/ *noun* air left in the lungs after a person has breathed out as much air as possible

residual urine /rɪ,zɪdjuəl 'jʊərɪn/ *noun* urine left in the bladder after a person has passed as much urine as possible

resistance /rɪˈzɪstəns/ *noun* **1.** the ability of a person not to get a disease **2.** the ability of bacteria or a virus to remain unaffected by a drug ○ *The bacteria have developed a resistance to certain antibiotics.* **3.** opposition to a force

resolution /,rezəˈluːʃ(ə)n/ *noun* the amount of detail which can be seen in a microscope or on a computer monitor

resonance /'rez(ə)nəns/ *noun* a sound made by a hollow part of the body when hit. ◊ **magnetic**

resorption /rɪˈsɔːpʃən/ *noun* the process of absorbing a substance produced by the body back into the body

respiration /,respəˈreɪʃ(ə)n/ *noun* the act of taking air into the lungs and blowing it out again through the mouth or nose. Also called **breathing**

respiration rate /,respəˈreɪʃ(ə)n ,reɪt/ *noun* the number of times a person breathes per minute

respirator /'respəreɪtə/ *noun* **1.** same as **ventilator 2.** a mask worn to prevent someone breathing harmful gas or fumes

respiratory /rɪˈspɪrət(ə)ri/ *adjective* referring to breathing

respiratory centre /rɪ,spɪrət(ə)ri 'sentə/ *noun* a nerve centre in the brain which regulates the breathing

respiratory distress syndrome /rɪ
ˌspɪrət(ə)ri dɪˈstres ˌsɪndrəʊm/ *noun* a condition of newborn babies, and especially common in premature babies, in which the lungs do not expand properly, due to lack of surfactant. Also called **hyaline membrane disease**

respiratory failure /rɪˌspɪrət(ə)ri ˈfeɪljə/ *noun* failure of the lungs to oxygenate the blood correctly

respiratory quotient /rɪˌspɪrət(ə)ri ˈkwəʊʃ(ə)nt/ *noun* the ratio of the amount of carbon dioxide taken into the alveoli of the lungs from the blood to the amount of oxygen which the alveoli take from the air. Abbreviation **RQ**

respiratory syncytial virus /rɪˌspɪrət(ə)ri sɪnˈsɪtiəl ˌvaɪrəs/ *noun* a virus which causes infections of the nose and throat in adults, but serious bronchiolitis in children. Abbreviation **RSV**

respiratory system /rɪˈspɪrət(ə)ri ˌsɪstəm/, **respiratory tract** /rɪˈspɪrət(ə)ri trækt/ *noun* the series of organs and passages which take air into the lungs, and exchange oxygen for carbon dioxide

respite care /ˈrespaɪt keə/ *noun* temporary care provided to people with disabilities, serious conditions or terminal illness, so that their families can have a rest from the daily routine

response /rɪˈspɒns/ *noun* a reaction by an organ, tissue or a person to an external stimulus

responsibility /rɪˌspɒnsɪˈbɪlɪti/ *noun* **1.** somebody or something which a person or organisation has a duty to take care of ○ *Checking the drip is your responsibility.* **2.** the blame for something bad which has happened ○ *She has taken full responsibility for the mix-up.* **3.** the position of having to explain to somebody why something was done ○ *Whose responsibility is it to talk to the family?*

rest /rest/ *noun* a period of time spent relaxing or sleeping ○ *What you need is a good night's rest.* ■ *verb* **1.** to spend time relaxing or sleeping **2.** to use a body part less for a period of time ○ *Rest your arm for a week.*

restenosis /ˌriːstəˈnəʊsɪs/ *noun* an occasion when something becomes narrow again, e.g. a coronary artery which has previously been widened by balloon angioplasty (NOTE: The plural is **restenoses.**)

resuscitation /rɪˌsʌsɪˈteɪʃ(ə)n/ *noun* the act of reviving someone who seems to be dead, by making him or her breathe again and restarting the heart

retardation /ˌriːtɑːˈdeɪʃ(ə)n/ *noun* the process of making something slower

retching /ˈretʃɪŋ/ *noun* the fact of attempting to vomit without being able to do so

rete /ˈriːtiː/ *noun* a network of veins, arteries or nerve fibres in the body. ◊ **reticular** (NOTE: The plural is **retia.**)

retention /rɪˈtenʃ(ə)n/ *noun* the act of not letting out something, especially a fluid, which is usually released from the body, e.g. holding back urine in the bladder

retention cyst /rɪˈtenʃən sɪst/ *noun* a cyst which is formed when a duct from a gland is blocked

retention of urine /rɪˌtenʃ(ə)n əv ˈjʊərɪn/ *noun* a condition in which passing urine is difficult or impossible because the urethra is blocked or because the prostate gland is enlarged

rete testis /ˌriːtiː ˈtestɪs/ *noun* a network of channels in the testis which take the sperm to the epididymis

retia /ˈriːʃiə/ plural of **rete**

reticular /rɪˈtɪkjʊlə/ *adjective* relating to or in the form of a network

reticular fibres /rɪˌtɪkjʊlə ˈfaɪbəs/ *plural noun* fibres in connective tissue which support, e.g., organs or blood vessels

reticulocyte /rɪˈtɪkjʊləʊsaɪt/ *noun* a red blood cell which has not yet fully developed

reticulocytosis /rɪˌtɪkjʊləʊsaɪˈtəʊsɪs/ *noun* a condition in which the number of reticulocytes in the blood increases unusually

reticuloendothelial cell /rɪˌtɪkjʊləʊˌendəʊ ˈθiːliəl sel/ *noun* a phagocytic cell in the reticuloendothelial system

reticuloendothelial system /rɪˌtɪkjʊləʊ ˌendəʊˈθiːliəl ˌsɪstəm/ *noun* a series of phagocytic cells in the body, found especially in bone marrow, lymph nodes, liver and spleen, which attack and destroy bacteria and form antibodies. Abbreviation **RES**

retin- /retɪn/ *prefix* same as **retino-** (*used before vowels*)

retina /ˈretɪnə/ *noun* the inside layer of the eye which is sensitive to light. ◊ **detached retina.** See illustration at **EYE** in Supplement (NOTE: The plural is **retinae.**)

retinal /ˈretɪn(ə)l/ *adjective* referring to the retina

retinal artery /ˈretɪn(ə)l ˌɑːtəri/ *noun* the only artery of the retina, which accompanies the optic nerve

retinal detachment /ˌretɪn(ə)l dɪˈtætʃmənt/ *noun* a condition in which the retina is partly detached from the choroid

retinitis /ˌretɪˈnaɪtɪs/ *noun* inflammation of the retina

retinitis pigmentosa /ˌretɪˌnaɪtɪs ˌpɪgmen ˈtəʊsə/ *noun* a hereditary condition in which inflammation of the retina can result in blindness

retino- /retɪnəʊ/ *prefix* referring to the retina

retinol /ˈretɪnɒl/ *noun* a vitamin found in liver, vegetables, eggs and cod liver oil which is essential for good vision. Also called **Vitamin A**

retinopathy /ˌretɪˈnɒpəθi/ *noun* any disease of the retina

retinoscope /ˈretɪnəskəʊp/ *noun* an instrument with various lenses, used to measure the refraction of the eye

retraction /rɪˈtrækʃən/ *noun* the fact of moving backwards or becoming shorter ○ *There is retraction of the overlying skin.*

retraction ring /rɪˈtrækʃən rɪŋ/ *noun* a groove round the uterus, separating its upper and lower parts, which, in obstructed labour, prevents the baby from moving forward as expected into the cervical canal. Also called **Bandl's ring**

retractor /rɪˈtræktə/ *noun* a surgical instrument which pulls and holds back the edge of the incision in an operation

retro- /retrəʊ/ *prefix* at the back, behind

retrobulbar /ˌretrəʊˈbʌlbə/ *adjective* behind the eyeball

retrobulbar neuritis /ˌretrəʊbʌlbə njuːˈraɪtɪs/ *noun* inflammation of the optic nerve which makes objects appear blurred. Also called **optic neuritis**

retroflexion /ˌretrəʊˈflekʃ(ə)n/ *noun* the fact of being bent backwards

retrograde /ˈretrəʊɡreɪd/ *adjective* going backwards or deteriorating, getting worse

retrograde pyelography /ˌretrəʊɡreɪd ˌpaɪəˈlɒɡrəfi/ *noun* an X-ray examination of the kidney where a catheter is passed into the kidney and an opaque liquid is injected directly into it

retrolental fibroplasia /ˌretrəʊlent(ə)l ˌfaɪbrəʊˈpleɪziə/ *noun* a condition in which fibrous tissue develops behind the lens of the eye, resulting in blindness

retro-ocular /ˌretrəʊ ˈɒkjʊlə/ *adjective* at the back of the eye

retroperitoneal /ˌretrəʊˌperɪtəˈniːəl/ *adjective* at the back of the peritoneum

retroperitoneal space /ˌretrəʊperɪtəʊˌniːəl ˈspeɪs/ *noun* the area between the posterior parietal peritoneum and the posterior abdominal wall, containing the kidneys, adrenal glands, duodenum, ureters and pancreas

retropharyngeal /ˌretrəʊˌfærɪnˈdʒiːəl/ *adjective* at the back of the pharynx

retropubic /ˌretrəʊˈpjuːbɪk/ *adjective* at the back of the pubis

retrospection /ˌretrəʊˈspekʃən/ *noun* the act of recalling what happened in the past

retrospective /ˌretrəʊˈspektɪv/ *adjective* applying to the past, tracing what has happened already to selected people

retroversion /ˌretrəʊˈvɜːʃ(ə)n/ *noun* the fact of sloping backwards □ **retroversion of the uterus** Same as **retroverted uterus**

retroverted uterus /ˌretrəʊvɜːtɪd ˈjuːtərəs/ *noun* a condition in which the uterus slopes backwards away from its usual position. Also called **retroversion of the uterus, tipped womb**

retrovirus /ˈretrəʊvaɪrəs/ *noun* a virus whose genetic material contains RNA from which DNA is synthesised (NOTE: The AIDS virus and many carcinogenic viruses are retroviruses.)

revascularisation /riːˌvæskjʊləraɪˈzeɪʃ(ə)n/, **revascularization** *noun* **1.** the act of restoring an adequate blood supply to an organ or tissue, especially in a surgical operation using a blood vessel graft **2.** the condition of having an adequate blood supply restored

reverse isolation /rɪˌvɜːs ˌaɪsəˈleɪʃ(ə)n/ *noun* same as **protective isolation**

revision /rɪˈvɪʒ(ə)n/ *noun* an examination of a surgical operation after it has been carried out ○ *a revision of a radical mastoidectomy*

Reye's syndrome /ˈraɪz ˌsɪndrəʊm/ *noun* a form of brain disease affecting young children, which is possibly due to viral infection and has a suspected link with aspirin

RGN *abbreviation* Registered General Nurse

Rh *abbreviation* rhesus

rhabdomyosarcoma /ˌræbdəʊˌmaɪəʊsɑːˈkəʊmə/ *noun* a malignant tumour of striated muscle tissue. It occurs mostly in children.

rhabdovirus /ˈræbdəʊvaɪrəs/ *noun* any of a group of viruses containing RNA, one of which causes rabies

rhachio- /reɪkiəʊ/ *prefix* referring to the spine

Rh disease /ˌɑːr ˈeɪtʃ dɪˌziːz/ *noun* same as **rhesus factor disease**

rheo- /riːəʊ/ *prefix* **1.** relating to the flow of liquids **2.** relating to the flow of electrical current

rhesus baby /ˈriːsəs ˌbeɪbi/ *noun* a baby with erythroblastosis fetalis

rhesus factor /ˈriːsəs ˌfæktə/ *noun* an antigen in red blood cells, which is an element in blood grouping. Also called **Rh factor**

rhesus factor disease /ˈriːsəs ˌfæktə dɪˌziːz/ *noun* a disease which occurs when the blood of a fetus has a different rhesus factor from that of the mother. Also called **Rh disease**

rheumatic /ruːˈmætɪk/ *adjective* referring to rheumatism

rheumatic fever /ruːˌmætɪk ˈfiːvə/ *noun* a collagen disease of young people and children, caused by haemolytic streptococci, where the joints and also the valves and lining of the heart become inflamed. Also called **acute rheumatism**

COMMENT: Rheumatic fever often follows another streptococcal infection such as a strep throat or tonsillitis. Symptoms are high fever, pains in the joints, which become red, formation of nodules on the ends of bones and difficulty in breathing. Although recovery can be complete, rheumatic fever can recur and damage the heart permanently.

rheumatism /'ru:mətɪz(ə)m/ *noun* pains and stiffness in the joints and muscles (*informal*) ○ *She has rheumatism in her hips.* ○ *He complained of rheumatism in the knees.*

rheumatoid /'ru:mətɔɪd/ *adjective* relating to rheumatism

rheumatoid arthritis /,ru:mətɔɪd ɑː'θraɪtɪs/ *noun* a general painful disabling collagen disease affecting any joint, but especially the hands, feet and hips, making them swollen and inflamed. ◊ **osteoarthritis**

rheumatologist /,ru:mə'tɒlədʒɪst/ *noun* a doctor who specialises in rheumatology

rheumatology /,ru:mə'tɒlədʒi/ *noun* a branch of medicine dealing with rheumatic disease of muscles and joints

Rh factor /,ɑːr eɪtʃ ,fæktə/ *noun* same as **rhesus factor**

rhin- /raɪn/ *prefix* same as **rhino-** (*used before vowels*)

rhinitis /raɪ'naɪtɪs/ *noun* inflammation of the mucous membrane in the nose, which makes the nose run, caused, e.g., by a virus infection or an allergic reaction to dust or flowers

rhino- /raɪnəʊ/ *prefix* referring to the nose

rhinology /raɪ'nɒlədʒi/ *noun* a branch of medicine dealing with diseases of the nose and the nasal passages

rhinophyma /,raɪnəʊ'faɪmə/ *noun* a condition caused by rosacea, in which the nose becomes permanently red and swollen

rhinoplasty /'raɪnəʊplæsti/ *noun* plastic surgery to correct the appearance of the nose

rhinorrhoea /,raɪnəʊ'rɪə/ *noun* a watery discharge from the nose

rhinoscope /'raɪnəskəʊp/ *noun* an instrument for examining the inside of the nose

rhinoscopy /raɪ'nɒskəpi/ *noun* an examination of the inside of the nose

rhinosinusitis /,raɪnəʊ,saɪnə'saɪtɪs/ *noun* swelling of the lining of the nose and paranasal sinuses, as a result of either a viral infection or allergic rhinitis. It is usually treated with antibiotics, antihistamines or steroids.

rhinovirus /'raɪnəʊ,vaɪrəs/ *noun* a group of viruses containing RNA, which cause infection of the nose and include the virus which causes the common cold

rhiz- /raɪz/, **rhizo-** /raɪzəʊ/ *prefix* referring to a root

rhizotomy /raɪ'zɒtəmi/ *noun* a surgical operation to cut or divide the roots of a nerve to relieve severe pain

Rh-negative /,ɑː eɪtʃ 'negətɪv/ *adjective* who does not have the rhesus factor in his or her blood

rhodopsin /rəʊ'dɒpsɪn/ *noun* a light-sensitive purple pigment in the rods of the retina, which makes it possible to see in dim light. Also called **visual purple**

rhomboid /'rɒmbɔɪd/ *noun* one of two muscles in the top part of the back which move the shoulder blades

rhonchus /'rɒŋkəs/ *noun* an unusual sound in the chest, heard through a stethoscope, caused by a partial blockage in the bronchi (NOTE: The plural is **rhonchi**.)

Rh-positive /,ɑː eɪtʃ 'pɒzɪtɪv/ *adjective* who has the rhesus factor in his or her blood

rhythm method /'rɪð(ə)m ,meθəd/ *noun* a method of birth control where sexual intercourse should take place only during the safe periods when conception is least likely to occur, i.e. at the beginning and at the end of the menstrual cycle

COMMENT: This method is not as safe or reliable as other methods of contraception because the time when ovulation takes place cannot be accurately calculated if a woman does not have regular periods.

rib /rɪb/ *noun* one of twenty-four curved bones which protect the chest (NOTE: For other terms referring to the ribs, see words beginning with **cost-, costo-**.)

ribavirin /'raɪbə,vaɪrɪn/ *noun* a synthetic drug which helps to prevent the synthesis of viral DNA and RNA, used in the treatment of viral diseases

rib cage /'rɪb keɪdʒ/ *noun* the ribs and the space enclosed by them

riboflavine /,raɪbəʊ'fleɪvɪn/ same as **Vitamin B$_2$**

ribonuclease /,raɪbəʊ'nju:klieɪz/ *noun* an enzyme which breaks down RNA

ribonucleic acid /,raɪbəʊnjuː,kliːɪk 'æsɪd/ *noun* one of the nucleic acids in the nucleus of all living cells, which takes coded information from DNA and translates it into specific enzymes and proteins. ◊ **DNA**. Abbreviation **RNA**

ribosome /'raɪbəsəʊm/ *noun* a tiny particle in a cell, containing RNA and protein, where protein is synthesised

ricewater stools /'raɪswɔːtə stuːlz/ *plural noun* watery faeces that are typically passed by people who have cholera

ricin /'raɪsɪn/ *noun* a highly toxic albumin found in the seeds of the castor oil plant

rickets /'rɪkɪts/ *noun* a disease of children, where the bones are soft and do not develop properly due to lack of Vitamin D. Also called **rachitis**

ridge /rɪdʒ/ *noun* a long raised part on the surface of a bone or organ

rifampicin /rɪfˈæmpɪsɪn/ *noun* an antibiotic which works by interfering with RNA synthesis in the infecting bacteria, used in the treatment of tuberculosis, leprosy and other bacterial infections

right-left shunt /ˌraɪt left ˈʃʌnt/ *noun* a malformation in the heart, allowing blood to flow from the pulmonary artery to the aorta

rigidity /rɪˈdʒɪdɪti/ *noun* the fact of being rigid, bent or not able to be moved. ◊ **spasticity**

rigor /ˈrɪgə/ *noun* an attack of shivering, often with fever

rigor mortis /ˌrɪgə ˈmɔːtɪs/ *noun* a condition in which the muscles of a dead body become stiff after death and then become relaxed again

COMMENT: Rigor mortis starts about eight hours after death, and begins to disappear several hours later. Environment and temperature play a large part in the timing.

rima /ˈraɪmə/ *noun* a narrow crack or cleft

rima glottidis /ˌriːmə ˈglɒtɪdɪs/ *noun* a space between the vocal cords

ring /rɪŋ/ *noun* a circle of tissue, or tissue or muscle shaped like a circle

ring block /ˈrɪŋ blɒk/ *noun* the process of inserting local anaesthetic all the way round a digit, e.g a finger, in order to perform a procedure distal to the block.

Ringer's solution /ˈrɪŋəz səˌluːʃ(ə)n/ *noun* a solution of inorganic salts which is used both to treat burns and cuts and to keep cells, tissues or organs alive outside the body

ring finger /ˈrɪŋ ˌfɪŋgə/ *noun* the third finger, the finger between the little finger and the middle finger

ringworm /ˈrɪŋwɜːm/ *noun* any of various infections of the skin by a fungus, in which the infection spreads out in a circle from a central point. It is very contagious and difficult to get rid of. Also called **tinea**

Rinne's test /ˈrɪniz test/ *noun* a hearing test in which a tuning fork is hit and its handle placed near the ear, to test for air conduction, and then on the mastoid process, to test for bone conduction. It is then possible to determine the type of lesion which exists by finding if the sound is heard for a longer period by air or by bone conduction. [Described 1855. After Friedrich Heinrich Rinne (1819–68), otologist at Göttingen, Germany.]

ripple bed /ˈrɪp(ə)l bed/ *noun* a type of bed with an air-filled mattress divided into sections, in which the pressure is continuously being changed so that the body can be massaged and bedsores can be avoided

risk /rɪsk/ *noun* the possibility of something harmful happening ○ *There is a risk of a cholera epidemic.* ○ *There is no risk of the disease* spreading to other members of the family.* □ **at risk** in danger of being harmed ○ *Businessmen are particularly at risk of having a heart attack.* ■ *verb* to do something which may possibly cause harm or have bad results ○ *If the patient is not moved to an isolation ward, all the patients and staff in the hospital risk catching the disease.*

risk factor /ˈrɪsk ˌfæktə/ *noun* a characteristic that increases a person's likelihood of getting a particular disease ○ *Smoking is a risk factor for lung cancer.* ○ *Obesity is a risk factor for diabetes.*

risus sardonicus /ˌraɪsəs sɑːˈdɒnɪkəs/ *noun* a twisted smile which is a symptom of tetanus

rite of passage /ˌraɪt əv ˈpæsɪdʒ/ *noun* a ceremony which shows that somebody is moving from one stage of their life to another, e.g. from childhood to puberty or from unmarried to married life

RM *abbreviation* Registered Midwife

RMN *abbreviation* Registered Mental Nurse

RN *abbreviation* Registered Nurse

RNA *abbreviation* ribonucleic acid

RNMH *abbreviation* Registered Nurse for the Mentally Handicapped

Rocky Mountain spotted fever /ˌrɒki ˌmaʊntɪn ˌspɒtɪd ˈfiːvə/ *noun* a type of typhus caused by *Rickettsia rickettsii,* transmitted to humans by ticks

rod /rɒd/ *noun* **1.** a stick shape with rounded ends ○ *Some bacteria are shaped like rods* or *are rod-shaped.* **2.** one of two types of light-sensitive cell in the retina of the eye. Rods are sensitive to dim light, but not to colour. ◊ **cone**

rodent ulcer /ˌrəʊd(ə)nt ˈʌlsə/ *noun* a malignant tumour on the face

roentgen /ˈrɒntgən/ *noun* a unit of radiation used to measure the exposure of someone or something to X-rays or gamma rays. Symbol **R** [After Wilhelm Konrad von Röntgen (1845–1923), physicist at Strasbourg, Geissen, Würzburg and Munich, and then Director of the physics laboratory at Würzburg where he discovered X-rays in 1895. Nobel prize for Physics 1901.]

role /rəʊl/ *noun* **1.** the usual or expected function of somebody or something in a particular process or event ○ *the role of haemoglobin in blood clotting* **2.** the characteristic or expected pattern of behaviour of a particular member of a social group ○ *the eldest child's role in the family*

role playing /ˈrəʊl ˌpleɪɪŋ/ *noun* the act of pretending to be somebody else in a situation, so that you have to imagine how that person feels and thinks. It usually involves several people. It is used in many training exercises and psychiatric evaluations.

rolled bandage /ˌrəʊld ˈbændɪdʒ/, **roller bandage** /ˈrəʊlə ˌbændɪdʒ/ *noun* a bandage in the form of a long strip of cloth which is rolled up from one or both ends

Romberg's sign /'rɒmbɜːgz saɪn/ *noun* a swaying of the body or falling when standing with the feet close together and the eyes closed, the result of loss of the joint position sense [Described 1846. After Moritz Heinrich Romberg (1795–1873), German physician and pioneer neurologist.]

rongeur /rɒŋ'gɜː/ *noun* a strong surgical instrument like a pair of pliers, used for cutting bone

root /ruːt/ *noun* **1.** a point from which a part of the body grows ○ *root of hair* or *hair root* ○ *root of nerve* or *nerve root* **2.** part of a tooth which is connected to a socket in the jaw ▶ also called **radix**

root canal /'ruːt kə,næl/ *noun* a canal in the root of a tooth through which the nerves and blood vessels pass

rooting reflex /'ruːtɪŋ ,riːfleks/ *noun* the instinct in new babies to turn their heads towards a touch on the cheek or mouth, which is important for breastfeeding

Roper, Logan and Tierney model /,rəʊpə ,ləʊgən ən 'tɪəni ,mɒd(ə)l/ *noun* an important model of nursing developed in the UK in 1980. Various factors such as necessary daily tasks, lifespan and health status are used to assess the relative independence of an individual, which the nurse will help them to increase.

Rorschach test /'rɔːʃɑːk test/ *noun* the ink blot test, used in psychological diagnosis, where someone is shown a series of blots of ink on paper and is asked to say what each blot reminds him or her of. The answers give information about the person's psychological state. [Described 1921. After Hermann Rorschach (1884–1922), German-born psychiatrist who worked in Bern, Switzerland.]

rosacea /rəʊ'zeɪʃə/ *noun* a common skin disease seen from middle age affecting the face, and especially the nose, which becomes red because of enlarged blood vessels. The cause is not known. Also called **acne rosacea** (NOTE: Despite its alternative name, rosacea is not a type of acne.)

rosea /'rəʊziə/ ♦ **pityriasis**

rostrum /'rɒstrəm/ *noun* a projecting part of a bone or structure shaped like a beak (NOTE: The plural is **rostra**.)

rotation /rəʊ'teɪʃ(ə)n/ *noun* the act of moving in a circle. See illustration at **ANATOMICAL TERMS** in Supplement

rotator /rəʊ'teɪtə/ *noun* a muscle which makes a limb rotate

Rothera's test /'rɒðərəz test/ *noun* a test to see if acetone is present in urine, a sign of ketosis which is a complication of diabetes mellitus [After

Arthur Cecil Hamel Rothera (1880–1915), biochemist in Melbourne, Australia.]

Roth spot /'rəʊt spɒt/ *noun* a pale spot which sometimes occurs on the retina of a person who has leukaemia or some other diseases [After Moritz Roth (1839–1915), Swiss pathologist and physician.]

rotunda /rəʊ'tʌndə/ ♦ **fenestra**

roughage /'rʌfɪdʒ/ *noun* same as **dietary fibre**

round /raʊnd/ *adjective* shaped like a circle ■ *noun* a regular visit

round ligament /'raʊnd ,lɪgəmənt/ *noun* a band of muscle which stretches from the uterus to the labia

round window /'raʊnd ,wɪndəʊ/ *noun* a round opening between the middle ear and the cochlea, and closed by a membrane. Also called **fenestra rotunda**. See illustration at **EAR** in Supplement

Rovsing's sign /'rɒvsɪŋz saɪn/ *noun* pain in the right iliac fossa when the left iliac fossa is pressed, which is a sign of acute appendicitis [Described 1907. After Nils Thorkild Rovsing (1862–1927), Professor of Surgery at Copenhagen, Denmark.]

Royal College of General Practitioners /,rɔɪəl ,kɒlɪdʒ əv 'dʒen(ə)rəl/ *noun* a professional association which represents family doctors. Abbreviation **RCGP**

Royal College of Nursing /,rɔɪəl ,kɒlɪdʒ əv 'nɜːsɪŋ/ *noun* a professional association which represents nurses. Abbreviation **RCN**

Roy's model /'rɔɪz ,mɒd(ə)l/ *noun* a model for nursing developed in the US in the 1970s. It describes a person's health as being a state of successful positive adaptation to all those stimuli from the environment which could interfere with their basic need satisfaction. Illness results from an inability to adapt to such stimuli, so nurses should help patients to overcome this.

RQ *abbreviation* respiratory quotient

RR *abbreviation* **1.** recovery room **2.** relative risk

-rrhage /rɪdʒ/, **-rrhagia** /'reɪdʒə/ *suffix* referring to an unusual flow or discharge of blood

-rrhaphy /rəfi/ *suffix* referring to surgical sewing or suturing

-rrhexis /reksɪs/ *suffix* referring to splitting or rupture

-rrhoea /rɪə/ *suffix* referring to an unusual flow or discharge of fluid from an organ

RSCN *abbreviation* Registered Sick Children's Nurse

RSI *abbreviation* repetitive strain injury

RSV *abbreviation* respiratory syncytial virus

RTN *abbreviation* Registered Theatre Nurse

rubefacient /,ruːbɪ'feɪʃ(ə)nt/ *noun* a substance which makes the skin warm, and pink or red ■ *adjective* causing the skin to become red

rubella /ruːˈbelə/ *noun* a common infectious viral disease of children with mild fever, swollen lymph nodes and rash. Also called **German measles**

COMMENT: Rubella can cause stillbirth or malformation of an unborn baby if the mother catches the disease while pregnant. One component of the MMR vaccine immunises against rubella.

rubeola /ruːˈbiːələ/ *noun* same as **measles**

rubor /ˈruːbə/ *noun* redness of the skin or tissue

Ruffini corpuscles /ruːˈfiːni ˌkɔːpʌs(ə)lz/, **Ruffini nerve endings** /ruːˈfiːni nɜːv ˌendɪŋz/ *plural noun* branching nerve endings in the skin, which are thought to be sensitive to heat

ruga /ˈruːgə/ *noun* a fold or ridge, especially in a mucous membrane such as the lining of the stomach (NOTE: The plural is **rugae**.)

rumination /ˌruːmɪˈneɪʃ(ə)n/ *noun* **1.** a condition in which someone has constant irrational thoughts which they cannot control **2.** the regurgitation of food from the stomach which is then swallowed again

run-down /ˌrʌn ˈdaʊn/ *adjective* exhausted and unwell

running /ˈrʌnɪŋ/ *adjective* from which liquid is flowing ○ *running eyes*

running sore /ˌrʌnɪŋ ˈsɔː/ *noun* a sore which is discharging pus

runs /rʌnz/ *noun* **the runs** same as **diarrhoea** (*informal*) ○ *I've got the runs again.* (NOTE: Takes a singular or plural verb.)

rupture /ˈrʌptʃə/ *noun* **1.** the breaking or tearing of an organ such as the appendix **2.** same as **hernia** ■ *verb* to break or tear something

ruptured spleen /ˌrʌptʃəd ˈspliːn/ *noun* a spleen which has been torn by piercing or by a blow

Russell traction /ˈrʌs(ə)l ˌtrækʃ(ə)n/ *noun* a type of traction with weights and slings used to straighten a femur which has been fractured [Described 1924. After R. Hamilton Russell (1860–1933), Australian surgeon.]

Ryle's tube /ˈraɪlz ˌtjuːb/ *noun* a thin tube which is passed into the stomach through either the nose or mouth, used to pump out the contents of the stomach or to introduce a barium meal in the stomach [Described 1921. After John Alfred Ryle (1882–1950), physician at London, Cambridge and Oxford, UK]

S

Sabin vaccine /ˈseɪbɪn ˌvæksiːn/ *noun* an oral vaccine against poliomyelitis, consisting of weak live polio virus. Compare **Salk vaccine** (NOTE: This is the vaccine used in the UK) [Developed 1955. After Albert Bruce Sabin (1906–93), Russian-born New York bacteriologist.]

sac /sæk/ *noun* a part of the body shaped like a bag

saccades /sæˈkeɪdz/ *plural noun* controlled rapid movements of the eyes made when a person is changing the direction in which they are focusing, e.g. when they are reading

racchar- /ˈsækə/ *prefix* same as **saccharo-** (*used before vowels*)

saccharide /ˈsækəraɪd/ *noun* a form of carbohydrate

saccharin /ˈsækərɪn/ *noun* a white crystalline substance, used in place of sugar because, although it is nearly 500 times sweeter than sugar, it contains no carbohydrates

saccharine /ˈsækəraɪn/ *adjective* relating to, resembling or containing sugar

saccharo- /sækərəʊ/ *prefix* referring to sugar

saccule /ˈsækjuːl/, **sacculus** /ˈsækjʊləs/ *noun* the smaller of two sacs in the vestibule of the inner ear which is part of the mechanism which relates information about the position of the head in space

sacral /ˈseɪkrəl/ *adjective* referring to the sacrum

sacral foramen /ˌseɪkrəl fəˈreɪmən/ *noun* one of the openings in the sacrum through which the sacral nerves pass. See illustration at **PELVIS** in Supplement (NOTE: The plural is **sacral foramina**.)

sacral nerve /ˈseɪkrəl nɜːv/ *noun* one of the nerves which branch from the spinal cord in the sacrum and govern the legs, the arms and the genital area

sacral plexus /ˌseɪkrəl ˈpleksəs/ *noun* a group of nerves inside the pelvis near the sacrum which lead to nerves in the buttocks, back of the thigh and lower leg and foot

sacral vertebrae /ˌseɪkrəl ˈvɜːtɪbriː/ *plural noun* the five vertebrae in the lower part of the spine which are fused together to form the sacrum

sacro- /seɪkrəʊ/ *prefix* referring to the sacrum

sacrococcygeal /ˌseɪkrəʊkɒkˈsiːdʒiəl/ *adjective* referring to the sacrum and the coccyx

sacroiliac /ˌseɪkrəʊˈɪliæk/ *adjective* referring to the sacrum and the ilium

sacroiliac joint /ˌseɪkrəʊˈɪliæk ˌdʒɔɪnt/ *noun* a joint where the sacrum joins the ilium

sacroiliitis /ˌseɪkrəʊɪliˈaɪtɪs/ *noun* inflammation of the sacroiliac joint

sacrum /ˈseɪkrəm/ *noun* a flat triangular bone, formed of five sacral vertebrae fused together, located between the lumbar vertebrae and the coccyx. It articulates with the coccyx and also with the hip bones. See illustration at **PELVIS** in Supplement (NOTE: The plural is **sacra**.)

SAD *abbreviation* seasonal affective disorder

saddle joint /ˈsæd(ə)l dʒɔɪnt/ *noun* a synovial joint where one element is concave and the other convex, like the joint between the thumb and the wrist

sadism /ˈseɪdɪz(ə)m/ *noun* a sexual condition in which a person finds sexual pleasure in hurting others

sadist /ˈseɪdɪst/ *noun* a person whose sexual urge is linked to sadism

sadistic /səˈdɪstɪk/ *adjective* referring to sadism. Compare **masochism**

SADS *abbreviation* seasonal affective disorder syndrome

safe /seɪf/ *adjective* **1.** not likely to cause harm ○ *Is it safe to use this drug on someone who is diabetic?* **2.** in a protected place or situation and not likely to be harmed or lost ○ *Keep the drugs in a safe place.* ○ *He's safe in hospital being looked after by the doctors and nurses.* (NOTE: **safer – safest**)

safe dose /ˈseɪf dəʊs/ *noun* the amount of a drug which can be given without being harmful

safe sex /ˌseɪf ˈseks/ *noun* the use of measures such as a contraceptive sheath and having only one sexual partner to reduce the possibility of catching a sexually transmitted disease

sagittal /ˈsædʒɪt(ə)l/ *adjective* going from the front of the body to the back, dividing it into right and left

sagittal plane /ˌsædʒɪt(ə)l 'pleɪn/ *noun* the division of the body along the midline, at right angles to the coronal plane, dividing the body into right and left parts. Also called **median plane**. See illustration at **ANATOMICAL TERMS** in Supplement

sagittal section /ˌsædʒɪt(ə)l 'sekʃən/ *noun* any section or cut through the body, going from the front to the back along the length of the body

sagittal suture /ˌsædʒɪt(ə)l 'suːtʃə/ *noun* a joint along the top of the head where the two parietal bones are fused

St Vitus's dance /sənt 'vaɪtəsɪz ˌdɑːns/ *noun* a former name for Sydenham's chorea

salbutamol /sæl'bjuːtəmɒl/ *noun* a drug which relaxes and dilates the bronchi, used in the relief of asthma, emphysema and chronic bronchitis

salicylate /sə'lɪsɪleɪt/ *noun* one of various pain-killing substances derived from salicylic acid, e.g. aspirin

salicylic acid /ˌsælɪsɪlɪk 'æsɪd/ *noun* a white antiseptic substance which destroys bacteria and fungi and which is used in ointments to treat corns, warts and other skin disorders

salicylism /'sælɪsɪlɪz(ə)m/ *noun* the effects of poisoning due to too much salicylic acid. Symptoms include headache, tinnitus, faintness and vomiting.

saline /'seɪlaɪn/ *adjective* referring to or containing salt ○ *The patient was given a saline transfusion.* ■ *noun* same as saline solution

saline drip /ˌseɪlaɪn 'drɪp/ *noun* a drip containing a saline solution

saline solution /'seɪlaɪn sə,luːʃ(ə)n/ *noun* a solution made of distilled water and sodium chloride, which is introduced into the body intravenously through a drip

saliva /sə'laɪvə/ *noun* a fluid in the mouth, secreted by the salivary glands, which starts the process of digesting food (NOTE: For terms referring to saliva, see words beginning with ptyal-, ptyalo- or sial-, sialo-.)

salivary /sə'laɪv(ə)ri/ *adjective* referring to saliva

salivary calculus /sə,laɪv(ə)ri 'kælkjʊləs/ *noun* a stone which forms in a salivary gland

salivary gland /sə'laɪv(ə)ri glænd/ *noun* a gland which secretes saliva, situated under the tongue (the **sublingual gland**), beneath the lower jaw (the **submandibular gland**) and in the neck at the back of the lower jaw joint (the **parotid gland**)

salivation /ˌsælɪ'veɪʃ(ə)n/ *noun* the production of saliva

Salk vaccine /'sɔːk ˌvæksiːn/ *noun* an injected vaccine against poliomyelitis, consisting of inactivated polio virus. Compare **Sabin vaccine**

[Developed 1954. After Jonas Edward Salk (1914–95), virologist in Pittsburgh, USA.]

salmeterol /sæl'metərɒl/ *noun* a drug which relaxes and widens the airways, used to treat severe asthma

Salmonella /ˌsælmə'nelə/ *noun* a genus of pathogenic bacteria which live in the intestines and are usually acquired by eating contaminated food, responsible for many cases of gastroenteritis and for typhoid or paratyphoid fever (NOTE: The plural is **Salmonellae**.)

Salmonella poisoning /ˌsælmə'nelə ˌpɔɪz(ə)nɪŋ/ *noun* poisoning caused by Salmonellae which develop in the intestines ○ *Five people were taken to hospital with Salmonella poisoning.*

salmonellosis /ˌsælmənə'ləʊsɪs/ *noun* food poisoning caused by *Salmonella* in the digestive system

salping- /sælpɪndʒ/ *prefix* same as **salpingo-** (*used before vowels*)

salpingectomy /ˌsælpɪn'dʒektəmi/ *noun* a surgical operation to remove or cut a Fallopian tube, used as a method of contraception

salpingitis /ˌsælpɪn'dʒaɪtɪs/ *noun* inflammation, usually of a Fallopian tube

salpingo- /sælpɪŋgəʊ/ *prefix* **1.** referring to the Fallopian tubes **2.** referring to the auditory meatus

salpingography /ˌsælpɪŋ'gɒgrəfi/ *noun* an X-ray examination of the Fallopian tubes

salpingolysis /ˌsælpɪŋ'gɒlɪsɪs/ *noun* a surgical operation to open up blocked Fallopian tubes by removing any adhesions near the ovaries

salpingo-oophorectomy /sæl,pɪŋgəʊ ˌəʊəfə'rektəmi/ *noun* a surgical operation to remove a Fallopian tube and ovary

salpingo-oophoritis /sæl,pɪŋgəʊ ˌəʊəfə 'raɪtɪs/, **salpingo-oothecitis** /sæl,pɪŋgəʊ ˌəʊəθɪ'saɪtɪs/ *noun* inflammation of a Fallopian tube and the ovary connected to it

salpingo-oophorocele /sæl,pɪŋgəʊ əʊ 'ɒfərəʊsiːl/, **salpingo-oothecocele** /sæl ,pɪŋgəʊ ˌəʊə'θiːkəʊsiːl/ *noun* a hernia where a Fallopian tube and its ovary pass through a weak point in the surrounding tissue

salpingostomy /ˌsælpɪŋ'gɒstəmi/ *noun* a surgical operation to open up a blocked Fallopian tube

salpinx /'sælpɪŋks/ *noun* same as **Fallopian tube** (NOTE: The plural is **salpinges**.)

salt /sɔːlt/ *noun* **1.** small white crystals mainly of sodium chloride used to flavour and preserve food **2.** a crystalline compound, usually containing a metal, formed when an acid is neutralised by an alkali

salt-free diet /ˌsɔːlt friː 'daɪət/ *noun* a diet in which no salt is allowed

salve /sælv/ *noun* an ointment

sample /ˈsɑːmpəl/ *noun* a small quantity of something used for testing ○ *Blood samples were taken from all the staff in the hospital.* ○ *The doctor asked her to provide a urine sample.*

sanatorium /ˌsænəˈtɔːriəm/ *noun* an institution, similar to a hospital, which treats particular types of disorder such as tuberculosis, or offers special treatment such as hot baths or massage (NOTE: The plural is **sanatoria** or **sanatoriums**.)

sandfly fever /ˈsændflaɪ ˌfiːvə/ *noun* a virus infection like influenza, which is transmitted by the bite of the sandfly *Phlebotomus papatasii* and is common in the Middle East

sandwich therapy /ˈsænwɪdʒ ˌθerəpi/ *noun* a system in which one type of treatment is used between exposures to a different treatment, e.g., chemotherapy given before and after radiation, or radiation given before and after surgery

sangui- /ˈsæŋgwɪ/ *prefix* relating to blood

sanguineous /sæŋˈgwɪniəs/ *adjective* referring to blood, containing blood

sanies /ˈseɪniiːz/ *noun* a discharge from a sore or wound which has an unpleasant smell

sanitary towel /ˈsænɪt(ə)ri ˌtaʊəl/ *noun* a disposable unit of absorbent material worn by women to absorb the blood flow during menstruation

SA node /ˌes ˈeɪ ˌnəʊd/, **S-A node** /ˌes ˈeɪ ˌnəʊd/ *noun* same as **sinoatrial node**

saphena /səˈfiːnə/ *noun* same as **saphenous vein** (NOTE: The plural is **saphenae**.)

saphenous /səˈfiːnəs/ *adjective* relating to the saphenous veins

saphenous nerve /səˈfiːnəs nɜːv/ *noun* a branch of the femoral nerve which connects with the sensory nerves in the skin of the lower leg

saphenous vein /səˈfiːnəs veɪn/ *noun* one of two veins which take blood from the foot up the leg. Also called **saphena**

> COMMENT: The long (internal) saphenous vein, the longest vein in the body, runs from the foot up the inside of the leg and joins the femoral vein. The short (posterior) saphenous vein runs up the back of the lower leg and joins the popliteal vein.

sapphism /ˈsæfɪz(ə)m/ *noun* same as **lesbianism**

sarc- /sɑːk/, **sarco-** /sɑːkəʊ/ *prefix* 1. referring to flesh 2. referring to muscle

sarcoid /ˈsɑːkɔɪd/ *noun* a tumour which is like a sarcoma ■ *adjective* like a sarcoma

sarcoidosis /ˌsɑːkɔɪˈdəʊsɪs/ *noun* a disease causing enlargement of the lymph nodes, where small nodules or granulomas form in certain tissues, especially in the lungs or liver and other parts of the body. Also called **Boeck's disease**, **Boeck's sarcoid** (NOTE: The Kveim test confirms the presence of sarcoidosis.)

sarcolemma /ˌsɑːkəʊˈlemə/ *noun* a membrane surrounding a muscle fibre

sarcoma /sɑːˈkəʊmə/ *noun* a cancer of connective tissue such as bone, muscle or cartilage

sarcomatosis /sɑːˌkəʊməˈtəʊsɪs/ *noun* a condition in which a sarcoma has spread through the bloodstream to many parts of the body

sarcoptes /sɑːˈkɒptiːz/ *noun* a type of mite which causes scabies

SARS /sɑːz/ *noun* a serious, sometimes fatal, infection affecting the respiratory system, first seen in China. Suspected cases of SARS must be isolated with full barrier nursing precautions. Full form **severe acute respiratory syndrome**

sartorius /sɑːˈtɔːriəs/ *noun* a very long muscle, the longest muscle in the body, which runs from the anterior iliac spine, across the thigh down to the tibia

saturated fat /ˌsætʃəreɪtɪd ˈfæt/ *noun* a fat which has the largest amount of hydrogen possible

satyriasis /ˌsætəˈraɪəsɪs/ *noun* an obsessive sexual urge in a man (NOTE: A similar condition in a woman is called **nymphomania**.)

saucerisation /ˌsɔːsəraɪˈzeɪʃ(ə)n/, **saucerization** *noun* 1. a surgical operation in which tissue is cut out in the form of a saucer-like depression, usually in order to help material drain away from infected areas of bone 2. the shallow saucer-like appearance of the upper surface of a vertebra after a compression fracture

s.c. *abbreviation* subcutaneous

scab /skæb/ *noun* a crust of dry blood which forms over a wound and protects it

scabicide /ˈskeɪbəsaɪd/ *noun* a solution which kills mites ■ *adjective* killing mites

scabies /ˈskeɪbiːz/ *noun* a very irritating infection of the skin caused by a mite which lives under the skin

scala /ˈskɑːlə/ *noun* a spiral canal in the cochlea

scald /skɔːld/ *noun* an injury to the skin caused by touching a very hot liquid or steam. Also called **wet burn** ■ *verb* to injure the skin with a very hot liquid or steam

scale /skeɪl/ *noun* 1. a thin flat piece of something such as dead skin 2. same as **tartar** 3. a system of measurement or valuation based on a series of marks or levels with regular intervals between them ○ *a pay scale* 4. same as **scales** ■ *verb* to remove the calcium deposits from teeth

scalenus /skeɪˈliːnəs/, **scalene** /ˈskeɪliːn/ *noun* one of a group of muscles in the neck which bend the neck forwards and sideways, and also help expand the lungs in deep breathing

scalenus syndrome /skeɪˈliːnəs ˌsɪndrəʊm/ *noun* a pain in an arm, caused by the scalenus anterior muscle pressing the subclavian artery and the brachial plexus against the vertebrae. Also called **thoracic outlet syndrome**

scaler /'skeɪlə/ *noun* a surgical instrument for scaling teeth

scales /skeɪlz/ *noun* a machine for weighing ○ *The nurses weighed the baby on the scales.*

scalp /skælp/ *noun* the thick skin and muscle, with the hair, which covers the skull

scalpel /'skælpəl/ *noun* a small sharp-pointed knife used in surgery

scan /skæn/ *noun* an examination of part of the body using computer-interpreted X-rays to create a picture of the part on a screen ■ *verb* to examine part of the body using computer-interpreted X-rays to create a picture of the part on a screen

scanning /'skænɪŋ/ *noun* **1.** the act of examining an area with the eyes **2.** the act of examining internal organs of the body with a piece of electronic equipment

scaphocephalic /,skæfəʊsə'fælɪk/ *adjective* having a long narrow skull

scaphocephaly /,skæfəʊ'kefəli, ,skæfəʊ 'sefəli/ *noun* a condition in which the skull is unusually long and narrow

scaphoid /'skæfɔɪd/, **scaphoid bone** /'skæfɔɪd bəʊn/ *noun* one of the carpal bones in the wrist. See illustration in **HAND** in Supplement

scapula /'skæpjʊlə/ *noun* one of two large flat bones covering the top part of the back. Also called **shoulder blade** (NOTE: The plural is **scapulae**.)

scapular /'skæpjʊlə/ *adjective* referring to the shoulder blade

scapulo- /skæpjʊləʊ/ *prefix* relating to the scapula

scapulohumeral /,skæpjʊləʊ'hjuːmərəl/ *adjective* referring to the scapula and humerus

scar /skɑː/ *noun* the mark left on the skin after a wound or surgical incision has healed ○ *He still has the scar of his appendicectomy.* Also called **cicatrix** ■ *verb* to leave a scar on the skin ○ *The burns have scarred him for life.* ○ *Plastic surgeons have tried to repair the scarred arm.* ○ *Patients were given special clothes to reduce hypertrophic scarring.*

scarlatina /,skɑːlə'tiːnə/, **scarlet fever** /,skɑːlət 'fiːvə/ *noun* an infectious disease with a fever, sore throat and a red rash. It is caused by a haemolytic streptococcus and can sometimes have serious complications if the kidneys are infected.

scar tissue /'skɑː ,tɪʃuː/ *noun* fibrous tissue which forms a scar

scat- /skæt/, **scato-** /skætəʊ/ *prefix* referring to the faeces

scatole /'skætəʊl/ *noun* a substance in faeces, formed in the intestine, which causes a strong smell (NOTE: Also spelled **skatole**.)

SCC *abbreviation* squamous cell carcinoma

Scheuermann's disease /'ʃɔɪəmənz dɪ ,ziːz/ *noun* inflammation of the bones and cartilage in the spine, usually affecting adolescents [Described 1920. After Holger Werfel Scheuermann (1877–1960), Danish orthopaedic surgeon and radiologist.]

Schick test /'ʃɪk test/ *noun* a test to see if a person is immune to diphtheria [Described 1908. After Bela Schick (1877–1967), paediatrician in Vienna, Austria, and New York, USA.]

Schilling test /'ʃɪlɪŋ test/ *noun* a test to see if someone can absorb Vitamin B_{12} through the intestines, to determine cases of pernicious anaemia [After Robert Frederick Schilling (b. 1919), US physician.]

-schisis /skaɪsɪs/ *suffix* referring to a fissure or split

schisto- /ʃɪstəʊ/ *prefix* referring to something which is split

Schistosoma /,ʃɪstə'səʊmə/, **schistosome** /'ʃɪstəsəʊm/ same as **bilharzia**

schistosomiasis /,ʃɪstəsəʊ'maɪəsɪs/ *noun* same as **bilharziasis**

schiz- /skɪts/, **schizo-** /skɪtsəʊ/ *prefix* referring to something which is split

schizoid /'skɪtsɔɪd/ *adjective* referring to schizophrenia ■ *noun* a person who has a less severe form of schizophrenia

schizoid personality /,skɪtsɔɪd ,pɜːsə 'nælɪti/ *noun* a disorder in which someone is cold towards other people, thinks mainly about himself or herself and behaves in an odd way. Also called **split personality**

schizophrenia /,skɪtsəʊ'friːniə/ *noun* a mental disorder in which someone withdraws from contact with other people, has delusions and seems to lose contact with the real world

schizophrenic /,skɪtsəʊ'frenɪk/ *noun* someone who has schizophrenia ■ *adjective* having schizophrenia

Schlemm's canal /'ʃlemz kə,næl/ *noun* a circular canal in the sclera of the eye, which drains the aqueous humour [Described 1830. After Friedrich Schlemm (1795–1858), Professor of Anatomy in Berlin, Germany.]

Schönlein–Henoch purpura /,ʃɜːnlaɪn 'henɒk ,pɜːpjʊrə/, **Schönlein's purpura** /'ʃɜːnlaɪnz ,pɜːpjʊrə/ *noun* a blood disorder of children, in which the skin becomes purple on the buttocks and lower legs, the joints are swollen and painful and there are gastrointestinal problems

school health service /sku:l 'helθ ,sɜːvɪs/ *noun* a special service, part of the local health authority, which looks after the health of children in school

school nurse /'sku:l nɜːs/ *noun* a nurse who works in a school, treating health problems and promoting health and safety

Schwann cells /'ʃvɒn selz/ *plural noun* the cells which form the myelin sheath around a nerve fibre. See illustration at **NEURONE** in Supplement [Described 1839. After Friedrich Theodor Schwann (1810–82), German anatomist.]

sciatic /saɪ'ætɪk/ *adjective* **1.** referring to the hip **2.** referring to the sciatic nerve

sciatica /saɪ'ætɪkə/ *noun* pain along the sciatic nerve, usually at the back of the thighs and legs

sciatic nerve /saɪ'ætɪk nɜːv/ *noun* one of two main nerves which run from the sacral plexus into each of the thighs, dividing into a series of nerves in the lower legs and feet. They are the largest nerves in the body.

scintigram /'sɪntɪɡræm/ *noun* an image recording radiation from radioactive isotopes injected into the body

scirrhous /'sɪrəs/ *adjective* hard ○ *a scirrhous tumour*

scirrhus /'sɪrəs/ *noun* a hard malignant tumour, especially in the breast

scissor leg /'sɪzə leɡ/ *noun* a condition in which someone walks with one leg crossing over the other, usually as a result of spasticity of the leg's adductor muscles

scissor legs /'sɪzə leɡz/ *plural noun* malformed legs, where one leg is permanently crossed over in front of the other

scissura /'sɪʃʊrə/ *noun* an opening in something or a splitting of something

scler- /sklɪə/ *prefix* same as **sclero-** (*used before vowels*)

sclera /'sklɪərə/ *noun* the hard white outer covering of the eyeball. See illustration at **EYE** in Supplement. Also called **sclerotic, sclerotic coat, albuginea oculi**

scleral /'sklɪərəl/ *adjective* referring to the sclera

scleritis /sklə'raɪtɪs/ *noun* inflammation of the sclera

sclero- /sklɪərəʊ/ *prefix* **1.** hard, thick **2.** referring to the sclera

scleroderma /ˌsklɪərə'dɜːmə/ *noun* a collagen disease which thickens connective tissue and produces a hard thick skin

scleromalacia /ˌsklɪərəʊmə,leɪʃɪə pə 'fɔːrəns/, **scleromalacia perforans** /ˌsklɪərəʊmə'leɪʃɪə/ *noun* a condition of the sclera in which holes appear in it

sclerosant agent /sklə'rəʊs(ə)nt ˌeɪdʒənt/ *noun* an irritating liquid injected into tissue to harden it

sclerosing /sklə'rəʊsɪŋ/ *adjective* becoming hard, or making tissue hard

sclerosing agent /sklə'rəʊsɪŋ ˌeɪdʒ(ə)nt/, **sclerosing solution** /sklə'rəʊsɪŋ sə,luːʃ(ə)n/ *noun* same as **sclerosant agent**

sclerosis /sklə'rəʊsɪs/ *noun* a condition in which tissue becomes hard

sclerotherapy /ˌsklɪərəʊ'θerəpi/ *noun* the treatment of a varicose vein by injecting a sclerosant agent into the vein, and so encouraging the blood in the vein to clot

sclerotic /sklə'rɒtɪk/ *adjective* referring to sclerosis, or having sclerosis ■ *noun* same as **sclera**

sclerotic coat /skləˌrɒtɪk 'kəʊt/ *noun* same as **sclera**

sclerotome /'sklɪərətəʊm/ *noun* a sharp knife used in sclerotomy

sclerotomy /sklə'rɒtəmi/ *noun* a surgical operation to cut into the sclera

scolex /'skəʊleks/ *noun* the head of a tapeworm, with hooks which attach it to the wall of the intestine (NOTE: The plural is **scolices** or **scolexes**.)

scoliosis /ˌskəʊli'əʊsɪs/ *noun* a condition in which the spine curves sideways

scoliotic /ˌskəʊli'ɒtɪk/ *adjective* referring to a spine which curves sideways

SCOPE /skəʊp/ *noun* a UK organisation that offers support and services to people with cerebral palsy

-scope /skəʊp/ *suffix* referring to an instrument for examining by sight

scopolamine /skə'pɒləmiːn/ *noun* a colourless thick liquid poisonous alkaloid found in some plants of the nightshade family. It is used especially to prevent motion sickness and as a sedative.

scorbutic /skɔː'bjuːtɪk/ *adjective* referring to scurvy

scorbutus /skɔː'bjuːtəs/ *noun* same as **scurvy**

scoto- /skəʊtə/ *prefix* dark

scotoma /skɒ'təʊmə/ *noun* a small area in the field of vision where someone cannot see

scotometer /skəʊ'tɒmɪtə/ *noun* an instrument used to measure areas of impaired vision

scotopia /skəʊ'təʊpiə/ *noun* the power of the eye to adapt to poor lighting conditions and darkness

scotopic /skəʊ'tɒpɪk/ *adjective* referring to scotopia

scotopic vision /skəʊˌtɒpɪk 'vɪʒ(ə)n/ *noun* vision in the dark and in dim light, where the rods of the retina are used instead of the cones, which are used for photopic vision. ◊ **dark adaptation**

screen /skriːn/ *noun* **1.** a light wall, sometimes with a curtain, which can be moved about and put round a bed to shield a person **2.** same as **screening** ■ *verb* to examine large numbers of people to test them for a disease ○ *The population of the village was screened for meningitis.*

screening /'skri:nɪŋ/ *noun* the process of testing large numbers of people to see if any of them have a particular type of disease. ◊ **genetic screening**

screening test /'skri:nɪŋ test/ *noun* a test for a particular disease which is given to people who have no symptoms in order to identify how many of them have that disease or are showing early signs of it

scrotal /'skrəʊt(ə)l/ *adjective* referring to the scrotum

scrototomy /skrəʊ'tɒtəmi/ *noun* a surgical operation to open up and examine the scrotum (NOTE: The plural is **scrototomies**.)

scrotum /'skrəʊtəm/ *noun* a bag of skin hanging from behind the penis, containing the testes, epididymides and part of the spermatic cord. See illustration at UROGENITAL SYSTEM (MALE) in Supplement (NOTE: The plural is **scrotums** or **scrota**.)

scrub up /ˌskrʌb 'ʌp/ *verb* (*of a surgeon or theatre nurse*) to clean the hands and arms thoroughly before performing surgery (NOTE: **scrubbing up – scrubbed up**)

scrumpox /'skrʌmpɒks/ *noun* a form of herpes simplex found especially in male sports players, passed on easily due to the presence of small cuts in the skin combined with the abrasive effects of facial stubble

scurf /skɜːf/ *noun* same as **dandruff**

scurvy /'skɜːvi/ *noun* a disease caused by lack of vitamin C or ascorbic acid which is found in fruit and vegetables. Also called **scorbutus**

scybalum /'sɪbələm/ *noun* very hard faeces

seasickness /'siːsɪknəs/ *noun* illness, with nausea, vomiting and sometimes headache, caused by the movement of a ship ○ *Take some seasickness tablets if you are going on a long journey.*

seasonal affective disorder /ˌsiːz(ə)n(ə)l ə 'fektɪv dɪsˌɔːdə/, **seasonal affective disorder syndrome** /ˌsiːz(ə)n(ə)l ə'fektɪv dɪsˌɔːdə ˌsɪndrəʊm/ *noun* a condition in which a person becomes depressed and anxious during the winter when there are fewer hours of daylight. Its precise cause is not known, but it is thought that the shortage of daylight may provoke a reaction between various hormones and neurotransmitters in the brain. Abbreviation **SAD, SADS**

seat /siːt/ *noun* same as **buttock** (*informal*)

seat-belt syndrome /'siːt belt ˌsɪndrəʊm/ *noun* a group of injuries between the neck and the abdomen which occur in a car accident when a person is using either a lap belt or a shoulder belt incorrectly, not over the strongest part of the chest

sebaceous /sə'beɪʃəs/ *adjective* referring to sebum

sebaceous cyst /səˌbeɪʃəs 'sɪst/ *noun* a cyst which forms when a sebaceous gland is blocked. ◊ **steatoma**

sebaceous gland /səˌbeɪʃəs 'glænd/ *noun* a gland in the skin which secretes sebum at the base of each hair follicle

seborrhoea /ˌsebə'riːə/ *noun* an excessive secretion of sebum by the sebaceous glands, common in young people at puberty, and sometimes linked to seborrhoeic dermatitis (NOTE: The US spelling is **seborrhea**.)

seborrhoeic /ˌsebə'riːɪk/ *adjective* caused by seborrhoea (NOTE: The US spelling is **seborrheic**.)

seborrhoeic dermatitis /ˌsebəriːɪk ˌdɜːmə 'taɪtɪs/, **seborrhoeic eczema** /ˌsebəriːɪk 'eksɪmə/ *noun* a type of eczema where scales form on the skin

sebum /'siːbəm/ *noun* an oily substance secreted by a sebaceous gland, which makes the skin smooth. It also protects the skin against bacteria and the body against rapid evaporation of water.

secondary /'sekənd(ə)ri/ *adjective* **1.** occurring after the first stage **2.** less important than something else ■ *noun* a malignant tumour which has developed and spread from another malignant tumour. ◊ **primary** (NOTE: The plural is **secondaries**.)

secondary amenorrhoea /ˌsekənd(ə)ri eɪ ˌmenə'riːə/ *noun* a situation in which a premenopausal woman's menstrual periods have stopped

secondary biliary cirrhosis /ˌsekənd(ə)ri ˌbɪliəri sə'rəʊsɪs/ *noun* cirrhosis of the liver caused by an obstruction of the bile ducts

secondary care /ˌsekənd(ə)ri 'keə/ *noun* treatment provided by the professional team in a hospital, rather than by a GP or other primary care provider and the primary health care team. Compare **primary care**, **tertiary care**. Also called **secondary health care**

secondary growth /ˌsekənd(ə)ri 'grəʊθ/ *noun* same as **metastasis**

secondary haemorrhage /ˌsekənd(ə)ri 'hem(ə)rɪdʒ/ *noun* a haemorrhage which occurs some time after an injury, usually due to infection of the wound

secondary health care /ˌsekənd(ə)ri 'helθ ˌkeə/ *noun* same as **secondary care**

secondary infection /ˌsekənd(ə)ri ɪn 'fekʃən/ *noun* an infection which affects a person while he or she is weakened through having another infection

secondary medical care /ˌsekənd(ə)ri 'medɪk(ə)l ˌkeə/ *noun* specialised treatment provided by a hospital

secondary peritonitis /ˌsekənd(ə)ri ˌperɪtə 'naɪtɪs/ *noun* peritonitis caused by infection from an adjoining tissue, e.g. from the rupturing of the appendix

secondary prevention /ˌsekənd(ə)ri prɪ'venʃən/ *noun* the use of methods such as screening tests which avoid a serious disease by detecting it early

secondary sexual characteristic /ˌsekənd(ə)ri ˌsekʃuəl ˌkærɪktə'rɪstɪk/ *noun* a sexual characteristic which develops after puberty, e.g. pubic hair or breasts

second-degree burn /ˌsekənd dɪˌgriː 'bɜːn/ *noun* a burn where the skin becomes very red and blisters

second-level nurse /ˌsekənd ˌlev(ə)l 'nɜːs/, **second-level registered nurse** /ˌsekənd ˌlev(ə)l ˌredʒɪstəd 'nɜːs/ *noun* a trained person who delivers nursing care under the direction and supervision of a first-level nurse. Compare **first-level nurse**

secretin /sɪ'kriːtɪn/ *noun* a hormone secreted by the duodenum which encourages the production of pancreatic juice

secretion /sɪ'kriːʃ(ə)n/ *noun* **1.** the process by which a substance is produced by a gland ○ *The pituitary gland stimulates the secretion of hormones by the adrenal gland.* **2.** a substance produced by a gland ○ *Sex hormones are bodily secretions.*

secretor /sɪ'kriːtə/ *noun* a person who secretes substances indicating ABO blood group into mucous fluids such as semen or saliva

secretory otitis media /sɪˌkriːtəri əʊˌtaɪtɪs 'miːdiə/ *noun* same as **glue ear**

section /'sekʃən/ *noun* **1.** a part of something ○ *the middle section of the aorta* **2.** the action of cutting tissue **3.** a slice of tissue cut for examination under a microscope **4.** a part of a document such as an Act of Parliament ○ *She was admitted under section 5 of the Mental Health Act.*

Section 47 /ˌsekʃən ˌfɔːti 'sev(ə)n/ *noun* a UK law under which a local authority has the power to seek an order from a magistrate's court authorising the removal of a person at severe risk from their home. The authority must have a doctor's certificate that the person is either suffering from a grave and chronic disease or is unable to look after himself or herself and is not receiving proper care and attention from other people.

security blanket /sɪ'kjʊərəti ˌblæŋkɪt/ *noun* a familiar blanket, toy or other object which a child carries around because it makes him or her feel safe

sedation /sɪ'deɪʃ(ə)n/ *noun* the act of calming someone using a sedative

sedative /'sedətɪv/ *noun* an anxiolytic or hypnotic drug such as benzodiazepine, which acts on the nervous system to help a person sleep or to relieve stress (*dated*) ○ *She was prescribed seda-*

tives by the doctor. ■ *adjective* acting to help a person sleep or to relieve stress

sedentary /'sed(ə)nt(ə)ri/ *adjective* involving a lot of sitting and little exercise

sedentary occupation /ˌsed(ə)nt(ə)ri ˌɒkjʊ'peɪʃ(ə)n/ *noun* a job where the workers sit down for most of the time

sedimentation /ˌsedɪmen'teɪʃ(ə)n/ *noun* the action of solid particles falling to the bottom of a liquid

sedimentation rate /ˌsedɪmen'teɪʃ(ə)n ˌreɪt/ *noun* the rate at which solid particles are deposited from a solution, measured especially in a centrifuge

segment /'segmənt/ *noun* a part of an organ or piece of tissue which is clearly separate from other parts

segmental /seg'ment(ə)l/ *adjective* formed of segments

segmental ablation /segˌment(ə)l æ'bleɪʃ(ə)n/ *noun* a surgical operation to remove part of a nail, e.g. treatment for an ingrowing toenail

segregation /ˌsegrɪ'geɪʃ(ə)n/ *noun* **1.** the act of separating one person, group or thing from others, or of dividing people or things into separate groups which are kept apart from each other **2.** the separation of the alleles of each gene and their distribution to separate sex cells during the formation of these cells in organisms with paired chromosomes

seizure /'siːʒə/ *noun* a fit, convulsion or sudden contraction of the muscles, especially in a heart attack, stroke or epileptic fit

selective /sɪ'lektɪv/ *adjective* choosing only one person, thing or group, and not others

selective serotonin re-uptake inhibitor /sɪˌlektɪv serəˌtəʊnin riː'ʌpteɪk ɪnˌhɪbɪtə/ *noun* a drug which causes a selective accumulation of serotonin in the central nervous system, and is used in the treatment of depression, e.g. fluoxetine. Abbreviation **SSRI**

COMMENT: The drug should not be started immediately after stopping an MAOI and should be withdrawn slowly.

selenium /sə'liːniəm/ *noun* a non-metallic trace element (NOTE: The chemical symbol is **Se**.)

self- /self/ *prefix* yourself

self-abuse /ˌself ə'bjuːs/ *noun* same as **self-harm**

self-actualisation /self ˌæktjuəlaɪ'zeɪʃ(ə)n/, **self-actualization** *noun* the successful development and use of personal talents and abilities

self-care /ˌself 'keə/ *noun* the act of looking after yourself properly, so that you remain healthy

self-catheterisation /ˌself ˌkæθɪtəraɪ'zeɪʃ(ə)n/, **self-catheterization** *noun* a procedure in which a person puts a catheter through the urethra into his or her own bladder to empty out the urine

self-governing hospital /,self ˌgʌvənɪŋ 'hɒspɪt(ə)l/ *noun* in the UK, a hospital which earns its revenue from services provided to the District Health Authorities and family doctors. Also called **hospital trust**

self-harm /,self 'hɑːm/ *noun* a deliberate act by which someone injures part of their body as the result of a personal trauma. Cutting and burning are two of the most common forms of self-harm. Also called **self-abuse**, **self-injury**, **self-mutilation**, **self-wounding**

self-image /,self 'ɪmɪdʒ/ *noun* the opinion which a person has about how worthwhile, attractive, or intelligent he or she is

self-injury /,self 'ɪndʒəri/, **self-mutilation** /,self ˌmjuːtɪ'leɪʃ(ə)n/ *noun* same as **self-harm**

self-retaining catheter /,self rɪˌteɪnɪŋ 'kæθɪtə/ *noun* a catheter which remains in place until it is deliberately removed

self-wounding /,self 'wuːndɪŋ/ *noun* same as **self-harm**

sella turcica /,selə 'tɜːsɪkə/ *noun* a hollow in the upper surface of the sphenoid bone in which the pituitary gland sits. Also called **pituitary fossa**

semeiology /,siːmaɪ'ɒlədʒi/ *noun* same as **symptomatology**

semen /'siːmən/ *noun* a thick pale fluid containing spermatozoa, produced by the testes and seminal vesicles and ejaculated from the penis

semi- /semi/ *prefix* half

semicircular /,semi'sɜːkjʊlə/ *adjective* shaped like half a circle

semicircular canal /,semisɜːkjʊlə kə'næl/ *noun* any one of three tubes in the inner ear which are partly filled with fluid and help to maintain balance. See illustration at **EAR** in Supplement

COMMENT: The three semicircular canals are on different planes. When a person's head moves, as when he or she bends down, the fluid in the canals moves and this movement is communicated to the brain through the vestibular section of the auditory nerve.

semicomatose /,semi'kəʊmətəʊs/ *adjective* almost unconscious or half asleep, but capable of being woken up

semilunar /,semi'luːnə/ *adjective* shaped like half a moon

semilunar cartilage /,semiluːnə 'kɑːtəlɪdʒ/ *noun* same as **meniscus**

semilunar valve /,semiluːnə 'vælv/ *noun* either of two valves in the heart, the pulmonary valve and the aortic valve, through which blood flows out of the ventricles

seminal /'semɪn(ə)l/ *adjective* referring to semen

seminal fluid /'semɪn(ə)l ˌfluːɪd/ *noun* the fluid part of semen, formed in the epididymis and seminal vesicles

seminal vesicle /,semɪn(ə)l 'vesɪk(ə)l/ *noun* one of two glands at the end of the vas deferens which secrete the fluid part of semen. See illustration at **urogenital system (male)** in Supplement

seminiferous tubule /semiˌnɪfərəs 'tjuːbjuːl/ *noun* a tubule in the testis which carries semen

seminoma /,semɪ'nəʊmə/ *noun* a malignant tumour in the testis (NOTE: The plural is **seminomas** or **seminomata**.)

semipermeable /,semi'pɜːmiəb(ə)l/ *adjective* allowing some types of particle to pass through but not others

semipermeable membrane /,semi ˌpɜːmiəb(ə)l 'membreɪn/ *noun* a membrane which allows some substances in liquid solution to pass through but not others

semiprone /,semi'prəʊn/ *adjective* referring to a position in which someone lies face downwards, with one knee and one arm bent forwards and the face turned to one side

SEN *abbreviation* State Enrolled Nurse

senescence /sɪ'nesəns/ *noun* the ageing process

senescent /sɪ'nesənt/ *adjective* approaching the last stages of the natural life span

Sengstaken tube /'seŋzteɪkən tjuːb/ *noun* a tube with a balloon, which is passed through the mouth into the oesophagus to stop oesophageal bleeding [After Robert William Sengstaken (b. 1923), US surgeon.]

senile /'siːnaɪl/ *adjective* referring to the last stages of the natural life span or to the medical conditions associated with it

senile dementia /,siːnaɪl dɪ'menʃə/ *noun* mental degeneration affecting elderly people (*dated*)

senilis /sə'naɪlɪs/ ♦ **arcus senilis**

senility /sə'nɪlɪti/ *noun* the deterioration of mental activity associated with the last stages of the natural life span

senna /'senə/ *noun* a laxative made from the dried fruit and leaves of a tropical tree

sensation /sen'seɪʃ(ə)n/ *noun* a feeling or information about something which has been sensed by a sensory nerve and is passed to the brain

sense /sens/ *noun* **1.** one of the five faculties by which a person notices things in the outside world: sight, hearing, smell, taste and touch ○ *When she had a cold, she lost her sense of smell.* **2.** the ability to discern or judge something ■ *verb* to notice something by means other than sight ○ *Teeth can sense changes in temperature.*

sense organ /ˈsens ˌɔːɡən/ *noun* an organ in which there are various sensory nerves which can detect environmental stimuli such as scent, heat or pain, and transmit information about them to the central nervous system, e.g. the nose or the skin

sensibility /ˌsensɪˈbɪlɪti/ *noun* the ability to detect and interpret sensations

sensible /ˈsensɪb(ə)l/ *adjective* **1.** showing common sense or good judgment **2.** able to be detected by the senses

sensible perspiration /ˌsensəb(ə)l ˌpɜːspə ˈreɪʃ(ə)n/ *noun* drops of sweat which can be seen on the skin, secreted by the sweat glands

sensitisation /ˌsensɪtaɪˈzeɪʃ(ə)n/, **sensitization** *noun* **1.** the process of making a person sensitive to something **2.** an unexpected reaction to an allergen or to a drug, caused by the presence of antibodies which were created when the person was exposed to the drug or allergen in the past

sensitive /ˈsensɪtɪv/ *adjective* **1.** able to detect and respond to an outside stimulus **2.** having an unexpected reaction to an allergen or to a drug, caused by the presence of antibodies which were created when the person was exposed to the drug or allergen in the past

sensitivity /ˌsensɪˈtɪvɪti/ *noun* **1.** the fact of being able to detect and respond to an outside stimulus **2.** the rate of positive responses in a test from persons with a specific disease. A high rate of sensitivity means a low rate of people being incorrectly classed as negative. Compare **specificity**

sensorineural deafness /ˌsensəriˌnjʊərəl ˈdefnəs/, **sensorineural hearing loss** /ˌsensəri ˌnjʊərəl ˈhɪərɪŋ ˌlɒs/ *noun* deafness caused by a disorder in the auditory nerves or the brain centres which receive impulses from the nerves. Also called **perceptive deafness**

sensory /ˈsensəri/ *adjective* referring to the detection of sensations by nerve cells

sensory cortex /ˌsensəri ˈkɔːteks/ *noun* the area of the cerebral cortex which receives information from nerves in all parts of the body (*dated*)

sensory deprivation /ˈsensəri ˌdeprɪveɪʃ(ə)n/ *noun* a condition in which a person becomes confused because they lack sensations

sensory nerve /ˈsensəri nɜːv/ *noun* a nerve which registers a sensation such as heat, taste or smell and carries impulses to the brain and spinal cord. Also called **afferent nerve**

sensory neurone /ˈsensəri ˌnjʊərəʊn/ *noun* a nerve cell which transmits impulses relating to sensations from the receptor to the central nervous system

sensory receptor /ˈsensəri rɪˌseptə/ *noun* a cell which senses a change in the surrounding environment, e.g. cold or pressure, and reacts to it by sending out an impulse through the nervous system. Also called **nerve ending**

sepsis /ˈsepsɪs/ *noun* the presence of bacteria and their toxins in the body, which kill tissue and produce pus, usually following the infection of a wound

sept- /sept/ *prefix* same as **septi-** (*used before vowels*)

septa /ˈseptə/ plural of **septum**

septal /ˈsept(ə)l/ *adjective* referring to a septum

septal defect /ˌsept(ə)l ˈdiːfekt/ *noun* a congenital condition in which a hole exists in the wall between the left and right sides of the heart allowing an excessive amount of blood to flow through the lungs, leading in severe cases to pulmonary hypertension and sometimes heart failure

septate /ˈsepteɪt/ *adjective* divided by a septum

septi- /septɪ/ *prefix* referring to sepsis

septic /ˈseptɪk/ *adjective* referring to or produced by sepsis

septicaemia /ˌseptɪˈsiːmiə/ *noun* a condition in which bacteria or their toxins are present in the blood, multiply rapidly and destroy tissue (NOTE: The US spelling is **septicemia**.)

septic shock /ˌseptɪk ˈʃɒk/ *noun* shock caused by bacterial toxins in the blood as a result of infection. There is a dramatic drop in blood pressure, preventing the delivery of blood to the organs. Toxic shock syndrome is one type of septic shock.

septo- /septəʊ/ *prefix* referring to a septum

septoplasty /ˈseptəʊplæsti/ *noun* a surgical operation to straighten the cartilage in the septum (NOTE: The plural is **septoplasties**.)

Septrin /ˈseptrɪn/ a trade name for co-trimoxazole

septum /ˈseptəm/ *noun* a wall between two parts of an organ, e.g. between two parts of the heart or between the two nostrils in the nose. See illustration at HEART in Supplement (NOTE: The plural is **septa**.)

sequela /sɪˈkwiːlə/ *noun* a disease or disorder that is caused by a disease or injury which the person had previously ○ *a case of osteomyelitis as a sequela of multiple fractures of the mandible* ○ *biochemical and hormonal sequelae of the eating disorders* ○ *Kaposi's sarcoma can be a sequela of Aids.* (NOTE: The plural is **sequelae**.)

sequestra /sɪˈkwestrə/ *plural noun* plural of **sequestrum**

sequestration /ˌsiːkweˈstreɪʃ(ə)n/ *noun* **1.** the act of putting someone in an isolated place **2.** the loss of blood into spaces in the body, reducing the circulating volume. It can occur naturally or can be produced artificially by applying tourniquets. ○ *pulmonary sequestration* ○ *A dry hacking cough can cause sequestration of the perito-*

neum in the upper abdomen. **3.** the formation of a sequestrum

sequestrectomy /ˌsiːkwɪˈstrektəmi/ *noun* a surgical operation to remove a sequestrum (NOTE: The plural is **sequestrectomies**.)

sequestrum /sɪˈkwestrəm/ *noun* a piece of dead bone which is separated from whole bone (NOTE: The plural is **sequestra**.)

ser- /sɪər/ *prefix* same as **sero-** (*used before vowels*)

sera /ˈsɪərə/ *plural noun* plural of **serum**

SERM *abbreviation* selective (o)estrogen receptor modulator

sero- /sɪərəʊ/ *prefix* **1.** referring to blood serum **2.** referring to the serous membrane

seroconvert /ˌsɪərəʊkənˈvɜːt/ *verb* to produce specific antibodies in response to the presence of an antigen such as a bacterium or virus

serological /ˌsɪərəˈlɒdʒɪk(ə)l/ *adjective* referring to serology

serological type /ˌsɪərəlɒdʒɪk(ə)l ˈtaɪp/ *noun* same as **serotype**

serology /sɪəˈrɒlədʒi/ *noun* the scientific study of serum and the antibodies contained in it

seropus /ˈsɪərəʊˌpʌs/ *noun* a mixture of serum and pus

serosa /sɪˈrəʊsə/ *noun* same as **serous membrane** (NOTE: The plural is **serosas** or **serosae**.)

serositis /ˌsɪərəʊˈsaɪtɪs/ *noun* inflammation of a serous membrane

serotherapy /ˌsɪərəʊˈθerəpi/ *noun* treatment of a disease using serum from immune people or immunised animals

serotonin /ˌsɪərəˈtəʊnɪn/ *noun* a compound which is a neurotransmitter and exists mainly in blood platelets. It is released after tissue is injured and is important in sleep, mood and vasoconstriction.

serotype /ˈsɪərəʊtaɪp/ *noun* a group of closely related microorganisms which all have the same type of antigens

serous /ˈsɪərəs/ *adjective* referring to, producing, or like serum

serous membrane /ˌsɪərəs ˈmembreɪn/ *noun* a membrane which both lines an internal cavity and covers the organs in the cavity, e.g. the peritoneum lining the abdominal cavity or pleura lining the chest cavity. Also called **serosa**

serpiginous /səˈpɪdʒɪnəs/ *adjective* referring to an ulcer or eruption which creeps across the skin

serrated /səˈreɪtɪd/ *adjective* with a zigzag or saw-like edge

serration /səˈreɪʃ(ə)n/ *noun* one of the points in a zigzag or serrated edge

Sertoli cells /səˈtəʊli selz/ *plural noun* cells which support the seminiferous tubules in the tes-

tis [Described 1865. After Enrico Sertoli (1842–1910), Italian histologist, Professor of Experimental Physiology at Milan, Italy.]

sertraline /ˈsɜːtrəliːn/ *noun* an antidepressant drug which extends the action of the neurotransmitter serotonin. It is also used in the treatment of obsessive-compulsive disorder and post-traumatic stress disorder.

serum /ˈsɪərəm/ *noun* **1.** a fluid which separates from clotted blood and is similar to plasma except that it has no clotting agents. Also called **blood serum 2.** blood serum taken from an animal which has developed antibodies to bacteria, used to give humans temporary immunity to a disease. Also called **antiserum 3.** any clear watery body fluid, especially a fluid that comes from a serous membrane (NOTE: The plural is **serums** or **sera**.)

serum albumin /ˌsɪərəm ˈælbjʊmɪn/ *noun* a major protein in blood plasma

serum bilirubin /ˌsɪərəm ˌbɪlɪˈruːbɪn/ *noun* bilirubin in serum, converted from haemoglobin as red blood cells are destroyed

serum globulin /ˌsɪərəm ˈglɒbjʊlɪn/ *noun* a major protein in blood serum that is an antibody

serum glutamic–oxalacetic transaminase /ˌsɪərəm gluːˌtæmɪk ˌɒksæləsiːtɪk trænsˈæmɪneɪz/ *noun* an enzyme excreted by damaged heart muscle, which appears in the blood of people who have had a heart attack. Abbreviation **SGOT**

serum glutamic–pyruvic transaminase /ˌsɪərəm gluːˌtæmɪk paɪˌruːvɪk trænsˈæmɪneɪz/ *noun* an enzyme secreted by the parenchymal cells of the liver, occurring in increased amounts in the blood of people with infectious hepatitis. Abbreviation **SGPT**

serum hepatitis /ˌsɪərəm ˌhepəˈtaɪtɪs/ *noun* a serious form of hepatitis transmitted by infected blood, unsterilised surgical instruments, shared needles or sexual intercourse. Also called **hepatitis B**, **viral hepatitis**

serum sickness /ˈsɪərəm ˌsɪknəs/ *noun* an allergic reaction to serum therapy which was formerly used as a way of boosting passive immunity

serum therapy /ˈsɪərəm ˌθerəpi/ *noun* the administration of treated serum, often from horses, formerly used as a way of boosting passive immunity

serve /sɜːv/ *verb* **1.** to give a person food or drink ○ *Lunch is served in the ward at 12:30.* **2.** to be useful or helpful to a person or group ○ *The clinic serves the local community well.* **3.** to have a particular effect or result ○ *The letter serves to remind you of your outpatients' appointment.* (NOTE: [all senses] **serves – serving – served**)

sesamoid /ˈsesəmɔɪd/, **sesamoid bone** /ˈsesəmɔɪd bəʊn/ *noun* any small bony nodule in a tendon, the largest being the kneecap

severe acute respiratory disorder /sɪ,vɪə ə,kjuːt rɪ'spɪrət(ə)ri dɪs,ɔːdə/ *noun* full form of **SARS**

sex /seks/ *noun* one of two groups, male and female, into which animals and plants can be divided ○ *The sex of a baby can be identified before birth.*

sexarche /'seksɑːki/ *noun* the age when a person first has sexual intercourse

sex chromosome /'seks ,krəʊməsəʊm/ *noun* a chromosome which determines if a person is male or female

sex determination /'seks dɪtɜːmɪ,neɪʃ(ə)n/ *noun* the way in which the sex of an individual organism is fixed by the number of chromosomes which make up its cell structure

sex hormone /'seks ,hɔːməʊn/ *noun* an oestrogen or androgen which promotes the growth of secondary sexual characteristics

sex-linked /'seks lɪŋkt/ *adjective* referring to genes which are linked to X chromosomes

sexology /sek'sɒlədʒi/ *noun* the study of sex and sexual behaviour

sextuplet /'sekstjʊplət/ *noun* one of six babies born to a mother at the same time

sexual /'sekʃuəl/ *adjective* referring to sex

sexual act /'sekʃuəl ækt/ *noun* an act of sexual intercourse

sexual deviation /,sekʃuəl diːvi'eɪʃ(ə)n/ *noun* any sexual behaviour which is not accepted as usual in the society in which you live. Examples in Western society are sadism and voyeurism.

sexually transmitted disease /,sekʃuəli træns,mɪtɪd dɪ'ziːz/, **sexually transmitted infection** /,sekʃuəli træns,mɪtɪd ɪn'fekʃ(ə)n/ *noun* a disease or infection transmitted from an infected person to another person during sexual intercourse. Abbreviation **STD**, **STI**

sexual reproduction /,sekʃuəl ,riːprə'dʌkʃən/ *noun* reproduction in which gametes from two individuals fuse together

SFD *abbreviation* small for dates

SGOT *abbreviation* serum glutamic-oxalacetic transaminase

SGPT *abbreviation* serum glutamic-pyruvic transaminase

SHA *abbreviation* Strategic Health Authority

shaft /ʃɑːft/ *noun* the long central section of a long bone

shaken baby syndrome /,ʃeɪkən 'beɪbi ,sɪndrəʊm/, **shaken infant syndrome** /,ʃeɪkən 'ɪnfənt ,sɪndrəʊm/ *noun* a series of internal head injuries in a very young child, caused by being shaken violently. It can result in brain damage leading to speech and learning disabilities, paralysis, seizures and hearing loss, and may be life-threatening.

shaky /'ʃeɪki/ *adjective* feeling weak and unsteady

share /ʃeə/ *verb* **1.** to use or do something together with others **2.** to divide something and give parts of it to different people or groups (NOTE: [all verb senses] **shares – sharing – shared**) ■ *noun* a single part of something divided among different people or groups

shared care /,ʃeəd 'keə/ *noun* antenatal care given jointly by an obstetrician in a hospital together with a general practitioner or a midwife working in the community

sharps /ʃɑːps/ *plural noun* objects with points, e.g. syringes (*informal*)

sheath /ʃiːθ/ *noun* **1.** a layer of tissue which surrounds a muscle or a bundle of nerve fibres **2.** same as **condom**

shiatsu /ʃi'ætsuː/ *noun* a form of healing massage in which the hands are used to apply pressure at acupuncture points on the body in order to stimulate and redistribute energy

Shigella /ʃɪ'gelə/ *noun* a genus of bacteria which causes dysentery

shigellosis /,ʃɪge'ləʊsɪs/ *noun* infestation of the digestive tract with *Shigella*, causing bacillary dysentery

shin /ʃɪn/ *noun* the front part of the lower leg

shinbone /'ʃɪnbəʊn/ *noun* same as **tibia**

shiner /'ʃaɪnə/ *noun* same as **black eye** (*informal*)

shingles /'ʃɪŋɡəlz/ *noun* same as **herpes zoster**

shin splints /'ʃɪn splɪnts/ *plural noun* extremely sharp pains in the front of the lower leg, felt by athletes

Shirodkar's operation /ʃɪ'rɒdkɑːz ɒpə,reɪʃ(ə)n/, **Shirodkar pursestring** /ʃɪ,rɒdkɑː 'pɜːsstrɪŋ/ *noun* a surgical operation to narrow the cervix of the uterus in a woman who experiences habitual abortion in order to prevent another miscarriage, the suture being removed before labour starts. Also called **pursestring operation** [After N. V. Shirodkar (1900–71), Indian obstetrician.]

Shirodkar suture /ʃɪ'rɒdkɑː ,suːtʃə/ *noun* a type of suture which is placed around a cervix to tighten it during pregnancy and prevent miscarriage. Also called **pursestring stitch**

shivery /'ʃɪvəri/ *adjective* trembling from cold, fear or a medical condition

shock /ʃɒk/ *noun* a state of weakness caused by illness or injury that suddenly reduces the blood pressure ○ *The patient went into shock.* ○ *Several of the passengers were treated for shock.* ■ *verb* to give someone an unpleasant surprise, and so put him or her in a state of shock ○ *She was still shocked several hours after the accident.* (NOTE: You say that someone is **in shock**, **in a state of shock** or that they **went into shock.**)

shock lung /'ʃɒk lʌŋ/ *noun* a serious condition in which a person's lungs fail to work following a trauma

shock syndrome /'ʃɒk ˌsɪndrəʊm/ *noun* a group of symptoms, a pale face, cold skin, low blood pressure and rapid and irregular pulse, which show that someone is in a state of shock. ◊ **anaphylactic shock**

shock therapy /'ʃɒk ˌθerəpi/, **shock treatment** /'ʃɒk ˌtriːtmənt/ *noun* a method of treating some mental disorders by giving an anaesthetised patient an electric shock to induce an epileptic convulsion

shoot /ʃuːt/ *verb* (*of pain*) to seem to move suddenly through the body with a piercing feeling ○ *The pain shot down his arm.*

shooting /'ʃuːtɪŋ/ *adjective* (*of pain*) sudden and intense

short of breath /ˌʃɔːt əv 'breθ/ *adjective* unable to breathe quickly enough to supply the oxygen needed ○ *After running up the stairs he was short of breath.*

shortsighted /ʃɔːt'saɪtɪd/ *adjective* same as **myopic**

shortsightedness /ʃɔːt'saɪtɪdnəs/ *noun* same as **myopia**

shot /ʃɒt/ *noun* same as **injection** (*informal*) ○ *The doctor gave her a tetanus shot.* ○ *He needed a shot of morphine to relieve the pain.*

shoulder /'ʃəʊldə/ *noun* a joint where the top of the arm joins the main part of the body ○ *He dislocated his shoulder.* ○ *She was complaining of pains in her shoulder or of shoulder pains.*

shoulder blade /'ʃəʊldə bleɪd/ *noun* same as **scapula**

shoulder girdle /'ʃəʊldə ˌɡɜːd(ə)l/ *noun* same as **pectoral girdle**

shoulder joint /'ʃəʊldə dʒɔɪnt/ *noun* a ball and socket joint which allows the arm to rotate and move in any direction

shoulder presentation /'ʃəʊldə ˌprez(ə)nˌteɪʃ(ə)n/ *noun* a position of a baby in the uterus, in which the shoulder will first appear

show /ʃəʊ/ *noun* the first discharge of blood at the beginning of childbirth ■ *verb* **1.** to cause or allow something to be visible **2.** to provide convincing evidence of something

shunt /ʃʌnt/ *noun* the passing of fluid through a channel which is not the usual one ■ *verb* (*of blood*) to pass through a channel which is not the usual one ○ *As much as 5% of venous blood can be shunted unoxygenated back to the arteries.*

shunting /'ʃʌntɪŋ/ *noun* a condition in which some of the deoxygenated blood in the lungs does not come into contact with air, and full gas exchange does not take place

SI *abbreviation* the international system of metric measurements. Full form **Système International**

sial- /saɪəl/ *prefix* same as **sialo-** (*used before vowels*)

sialadenitis /ˌsaɪəlˌædɪ'naɪtɪs/ *noun* inflammation of a salivary gland. Also called **sialoadenitis**, **sialitis**

sialitis /ˌsaɪə'laɪtɪs/ *noun* same as **sialadenitis**

sialo- /saɪələʊ/ *prefix* **1.** referring to saliva **2.** referring to a salivary gland

sialoadenitis /ˌsaɪələʊˌædɪ'naɪtɪs/ *noun* same as **sialadenitis**

sialography /ˌsaɪə'lɒɡrəfi/ *noun* X-ray examination of a salivary gland. Also called **ptyalography**

sialolith /saɪ'æləʊlɪθ/ *noun* a stone in a salivary gland. Also called **ptyalith**

sialorrhoea /ˌsaɪələʊ'riːə/ *noun* the production of an excessive amount of saliva (NOTE: The US spelling is **sialorrhea**.)

Siamese twins /ˌsaɪəmiːz 'twɪnz/ *plural noun* same as **conjoined twins**

sib /sɪb/ *noun* same as **sibling** (*informal*)

sibling /'sɪblɪŋ/ *noun* a brother or sister

sick /sɪk/ *adjective* **1.** having an illness ○ *He was sick for two weeks.* □ **to report** *or* **call in sick** to say officially that you are unwell and cannot work **2.** about to vomit ○ *The patient got up this morning and felt sick.* □ **to be sick** to vomit ○ *The child was sick all over the floor.* □ **to make someone sick** to cause someone to vomit ○ *He was given something to make him sick.*

sick building syndrome /ˌsɪk 'bɪldɪŋ ˌsɪndrəʊm/ *noun* a condition in which many people working in a building feel ill or have headaches, caused by blocked air-conditioning ducts in which stale air is recycled round the building, often carrying allergenic substances or bacteria (*informal*)

sickle cell /'sɪk(ə)l sel/ *noun* a red blood cell shaped like a sickle, formed as a result of the presence of an unusual form of haemoglobin. Also called **drepanocyte**

sickle-cell anaemia /'sɪk(ə)l sel əˌniːmiə/ *noun* an inherited condition in which someone develops sickle cells which block the circulation, causing anaemia and pains in the joints and abdomen. Also called **drepanocytosis**, **sickle cell disease**

COMMENT: Sickle-cell anaemia is a hereditary condition which is mainly found in people from Africa and the West Indies.

sickle-cell chest syndrome /ˌsɪk(ə)l sel 'tʃest ˌsɪndrəʊm/ *noun* a common complication of sickle-cell disease, with chest pain, fever and leucocytosis

sickle-cell disease /'sɪk(ə)l sel dɪˌziːz/ *noun* abbreviation **SCD**. Same as **sickle-cell anaemia**

sickle-cell trait /'sɪk(ə)l sel ˌtreɪt/ *noun* a hereditary condition of the blood in which some red cells become sickle-shaped, but there are not enough affected cells to cause anaemia

side-effect /'saɪd ɪ,fekt/ *noun* an effect produced by a drug or treatment which is not the main effect intended ○ *One of the side-effects of chemotherapy is that the patient's hair falls out.*

sidero- /saɪdərəʊ/ *prefix* referring to iron

sideropenia /,saɪdərəʊ'piːniə/ *noun* a lack of iron in the blood usually caused by insufficient iron in the diet

siderophilin /,saɪdə'rɒfəlɪn/ *noun* same as **transferrin**

siderosis /,saɪdə'rəʊsɪs/ *noun* a condition in which iron deposits form in tissue

SIDS *abbreviation* sudden infant death syndrome

sigmoid /'sɪgmɔɪd/ *adjective* **1.** shaped like the letter S **2.** referring to the sigmoid colon ■ *noun* same as **sigmoid colon**

sigmoid colon /,sɪgmɔɪd 'kəʊlɒn/ *noun* the fourth section of the colon which continues as the rectum. See illustration at **DIGESTIVE SYSTEM** in Supplement. Also called **pelvic colon, sigmoid, sigmoid flexure**

sigmoidectomy /,sɪgmɔɪ'dektəmi/ *noun* a surgical operation to remove the sigmoid colon (NOTE: The plural is **sigmoidectomies**.)

sigmoid flexure /,sɪgmɔɪd 'flekʃə/ *noun* same as **sigmoid colon**

sigmoidoscope /sɪg'mɔɪdəskəʊp/ *noun* a surgical instrument with a light at the end which can be passed into the rectum so that the sigmoid colon can be examined

sigmoidoscopy /,sɪgmɔɪ'dɒskəpi/ *noun* a procedure in which the rectum and sigmoid colon are examined with a sigmoidoscope

sigmoidostomy /,sɪgmɔɪ'dɒstəmi/ *noun* a surgical operation to bring the sigmoid colon out through a hole in the abdominal wall (NOTE: The plural is **sigmoidostomies**.)

sign /saɪn/ *noun* a movement, mark, colouring or change which has a meaning and can be recognised by a doctor as indicating a condition (NOTE: A change in function which is also noticed by the patient is a **symptom**.)

sign language /'saɪn ,læŋgwɪdʒ/ *noun* a set of agreed signs made with the fingers and hands, used to indicate words by or for people who cannot hear or speak

sildenafil citrate /,sɪldənəfɪl 'saɪtreɪt/ *noun* an enzyme-inhibiting drug used in the treatment of male impotence

silicon /'sɪlɪkən/ *noun* a non-metallic chemical element (NOTE: The chemical symbol is **Si**.)

silicosis /,sɪlɪ'kəʊsɪs/ *noun* a disease of the lungs caused by inhaling silica dust from mining or stone-crushing operations

silver nitrate /,sɪlvə 'naɪtreɪt/ *noun* a salt of silver that is mixed with a cream or solution and used, e.g., to disinfect burns or to kill warts

Simmonds' disease /'sɪməndz dɪ,ziːz/ *noun* a condition of women due to postpartum haemorrhage, in which there is lack of activity in the pituitary gland, resulting in wasting of tissue, brittle bones and premature senility [Described 1914. After Morris Simmonds (1855–1925), German physician and pathologist.]

simple fracture /,sɪmpəl 'fræktʃə/ *noun* a fracture where the skin surface around the damaged bone has not been broken and the broken ends of the bone are close together. Also called **closed fracture**

simple tachycardia /,sɪmpəl ,tæki'kɑːdiə/ *noun* same as **sinus tachycardia**

simplex /'sɪmpleks/ ♦ **herpes simplex**

Sims' position /'sɪmz pə,zɪʃ(ə)n/ *noun* a position of the body in which the person lies on his or her left side with their left arm behind their back and their right knee and thigh flexed. It is used to allow the anal or vaginal area to be examined easily.

simvastatin /sɪm'væstɪn/ *noun* a drug which lowers lipid levels in the blood, used in the treatment of high cholesterol

sinew /'sɪnjuː/ *noun* same as **tendon**

singer's nodule /,sɪŋəz 'nɒdjuːl/ *noun* a small white polyp which can develop in the larynx of people who use their voice too much or too loudly

singultus /sɪŋ'gʌltəs/ *noun* same as **hiccup**

sino- /saɪnəʊ/ *prefix* referring to a sinus

sinoatrial /,saɪnəʊ'eɪtriəl/ *adjective* relating to the sinus venosus and the right atrium of the heart

sinoatrial node /,saɪnəʊ'eɪtriəl nəʊd/ *noun* a node in the heart at the junction of the superior vena cava and the right atrium, which regulates the heartbeat. Also called **SA node, sinus node**

sinogram /'saɪnəʊgræm/ *noun* an X-ray photograph of a sinus

sinography /saɪ'nɒgrəfi/ *noun* examination of a sinus by taking an X-ray photograph

sinu- /saɪnə/ *prefix* same as **sino-**

sinuatrial /,saɪnə'eɪtriəl/ *adjective* same as **sinoatrial**

sinus /'saɪnəs/ *noun* a cavity inside the body, including the cavities inside the head behind the cheekbone, forehead and nose ○ *The doctor diagnosed a sinus infection.*

sinusitis /,saɪnə'saɪtɪs/ *noun* inflammation of the mucous membrane in the sinuses, especially the maxillary sinuses

sinusoid /'saɪnəsɔɪd/ *noun* a specially shaped small blood vessel in the liver, adrenal glands and other organs

sinus tachycardia /ˌsaɪnəs ˌtæki'kɑːdiə/ *noun* rapid beating of the heart caused by stimulation of the sinoatrial node. Also called **simple tachycardia**

sinus trouble /'saɪnəs ˌtrʌb(ə)l/ *noun* same as **sinusitis** (*informal*)

sinus venosus /ˌsaɪnəs və'nəʊsɪs/ *noun* a cavity in the heart of an embryo, part of which develops into the coronary sinus and part of which is absorbed into the right atrium

siphonage /'saɪfənɪdʒ/ *noun* the removal of liquid from one place to another with a tube, as used to empty the stomach of its contents

sit /sɪt/ *verb* **1.** to rest with your weight largely supported by the buttocks **2.** to cause a person to sit somewhere (NOTE: [all senses] **sitting – sat**)

situs inversus /ˌsaɪtəs ɪn'vɜːsəs/, **situs inversus viscerum** /ˌsaɪtəs ɪn,vɜːsəs 'vɪsərəm/ *noun* a congenital condition, in which the organs are not on the usual side of the body, i.e. where the heart is on the right side and not the left

sitz bath /'sɪts bɑːθ/ *noun* a small low bath where someone can sit, but not lie down

SI units /ˌes 'aɪ ˌjuːnɪts/ *plural noun* the units used in an international system of units for measuring physical properties such as weight, speed and light

skatole /'skætəʊl/ *noun* another spelling of **scatole**

skeletal /'skelɪt(ə)l/ *adjective* referring to the skeleton

skeletal muscle /'skelɪt(ə)l ˌmʌs(ə)l/ *noun* a muscle attached to a bone, which makes a limb move

skeleton /'skelɪt(ə)n/ *noun* all the bones which make up a body

skia- /skaɪə/ *prefix* referring to shadow

skier's thumb /ˌskiːəz 'θʌm/ *noun* an injury to the thumb caused by falling directly onto it when it is outstretched, resulting in tearing or stretching of the ligaments of the main thumb joint

skill /skɪl/ *noun* an ability to do difficult work, which is acquired by training ○ *You need special skills to become a doctor.*

skill mix /'skɪl mɪks/ *noun* the range of different skills possessed by the members of a group or required for a particular job

skin /skɪn/ *noun* the tissue which forms the outside surface of the body ○ *His skin turned brown in the sun.* ○ *Skin problems in adolescents may be caused by diet.* (NOTE: For other terms referring to skin, see words beginning with **cut-**, **derm-**, **derma-**, **dermato-**, **dermo-**.)

skin graft /'skɪn grɑːft/ *noun* a layer of skin transplanted from one part of the body to cover an area where the skin has been destroyed ○ *After the operation she had to have a skin graft.*

skull /skʌl/ *noun* the eight bones which are fused or connected together to form the head, along with the fourteen bones which form the face. Also called **cranium**

SLE *abbreviation* systemic lupus erythematosus

sleep /sliːp/ *noun* the state or a period of resting, usually at night, when the eyes are closed and you are not conscious of what is happening ○ *You need to get a good night's sleep if you have a lot of work to do tomorrow.* ○ *He had a short sleep in the middle of the afternoon.*

sleep apnoea /'sliːp æp,niːə/ *noun* a condition related to heavy snoring, with prolonged respiratory pauses leading to cerebral hypoxia and subsequent daytime drowsiness

sleeping sickness /'sliːpɪŋ ˌsɪknəs/ *noun* an African disease, spread by the tsetse fly, where trypanosomes infest the blood. Also called **African trypanosomiasis**

sleeping tablet /'sliːpɪŋ ˌtæblət/ *noun* a tablet containing a drug, usually a barbiturate, which makes a person sleep

sleepwalker /'sliːpwɔːkə/ *noun* same as **somnambulist**

sleepwalking /'sliːpwɔːkɪŋ/ *noun* same as **somnambulism**

sliding sheet /ˌslaɪdɪŋ 'ʃiːt/ *noun* a silicon-coated nylon sheet used for transferring and repositioning patients

sling /slɪŋ/ *noun* a triangular bandage attached round the neck, used to support an injured arm and prevent it from moving ○ *She had her left arm in a sling.*

slipped disc /ˌslɪpt 'dɪsk/ *noun* same as **prolapsed intervertebral disc**

slit lamp /'slɪt læmp/ *noun* a piece of equipment which provides a narrow beam of light and is connected to a special microscope, used to examine the eye

slough /slaʊ/ *noun* dead tissue, especially dead skin, which has separated from healthy tissue ■ *verb* to lose dead skin which falls off

slow-release vitamin tablet /ˌsləʊ rɪ,liːs 'vɪtəmɪn ˌtæblət/ *noun* a vitamin tablet which will dissolve slowly in the body and give a longer and more constant effect

small for dates /ˌsmɔːl fə 'deɪts/ *adjective* referring to an unborn baby which is small in comparison to the average size for that number of weeks. Abbreviation **SFD**

small intestine /ˌsmɔːl ɪn'testɪn/ *noun* a section of the intestine from the stomach to the caecum, consisting of the duodenum, the jejunum and the ileum

small of the back /ˌsmɔːl əv ðə 'bæk/ *noun* the middle part of the back between and below the shoulder blades

smallpox /'smɔːlpɒks/ *noun* a very serious, usually fatal, contagious disease caused by the pox virus, with a severe rash, leaving masses of small scars on the skin. Also called **variola**

smear /smɪə/ *noun* a sample of soft tissue, e.g. blood or mucus, taken from a person and spread over a glass slide to be examined under a microscope

smear test /'smɪə test/ *noun* same as **Papanicolaou test**

smegma /'smegmə/ *noun* an oily secretion with an unpleasant smell which collects on and under the foreskin of the penis

Smith-Petersen nail /,smɪθ 'piːtəs(ə)n neɪl/ *noun* a metal nail used to attach the fractured neck of a femur [Described 1931. After Marius Nygaard Smith-Petersen (1886–1953), Norwegian-born Boston orthopaedic surgeon.]

Smith's fracture /'smɪθs ,fræktʃə/ *noun* a fracture of the radius just above the wrist

smoke inhalation /'sməʊk ɪnhə,leɪʃ(ə)n/ *noun* the breathing in of smoke, as in a fire

smoking /'sməʊkɪŋ/ *noun* the action of smoking a cigarette, pipe or cigar ○ *Smoking can injure your health.*

smooth /smuːð/ *adjective* flat, not rough ■ *verb* to make something smooth ○ *She smoothed down the sheets on the bed.*

smooth muscle /'smuːð ,mʌs(ə)l/ *noun* a type of muscle found in involuntary muscles. Also called **unstriated muscle**

SMR *abbreviation* submucous resection

snare /sneə/ *noun* a surgical instrument made of a loop of wire, used to remove growths without the need of an incision

sneeze /sniːz/ *noun* a reflex action to blow air suddenly out of the nose and mouth because of irritation in the nasal passages ○ *She gave a loud sneeze.* ■ *verb* to blow air suddenly out of the nose and mouth because of irritation in the nasal passages ○ *The smell of flowers makes her sneeze.* ○ *He was coughing and sneezing and decided to stay in bed.* (NOTE: **sneezing – sneezed**)

Snellen chart /'snelən tʃɑːt/ *noun* a chart commonly used by opticians to test eyesight [Described 1862. After Hermann Snellen (1834–1908), Dutch ophthalmologist.]

sniffles /'snɪf(ə)lz/ *plural noun* a slight head cold, or an allergy that causes a running nose (*informal; used to children*) ○ *Don't go out into the cold when you have the sniffles.*

snoring /'snɔːrɪŋ/ *noun* noisy breathing while asleep

snow blindness /'snəʊ ,blaɪndnəs/ *noun* temporary painful blindness caused by bright sunlight shining on snow

snuffles /'snʌf(ə)lz/ *plural noun* the condition of breathing noisily through a nose which is blocked with mucus, which is usually a symptom

of the common cold, but can sometimes be a sign of congenital syphilis (*informal; used to children*)

social /'səʊʃ(ə)l/ *adjective* referring to society or to groups of people

socialisation /,səʊʃ(ə)laɪ'zeɪʃ(ə)n/, **socialization** *noun* the process involved when young children are becoming aware of society and learning how they are expected to behave

social services /,səʊʃ(ə)l 'sɜːvɪsɪz/ *plural noun* the special facilities which the government or local authorities provide to people in the community who need help, such as the elderly, children whose parents have died or the unemployed

social worker /'səʊʃ(ə)l ,wɜːkə/ *noun* a government employee who works to provide social services to people in need and improve their living standards

society /sə'saɪəti/ *noun* **1.** the community of people who live in a particular country and share its institutions and customs **2.** an organisation of people who have a shared interest

sociology /,səʊsi'ɒlədʒi/ *noun* **1.** the study of the origin, development and structure of human societies and the behaviour of individual people and groups in society **2.** the study of a particular social institution and the part it plays in society

sociopath /'səʊsiəpæθ/ *noun* same as **psychopath**

socket /'sɒkɪt/ *noun* a hollow part in a bone, into which another bone or organ fits ○ *The tip of the femur fits into a socket in the pelvis.*

sodium /'səʊdiəm/ *noun* a chemical element which is the basic substance in salt (NOTE: The chemical symbol is **Na**.)

sodium balance /'səʊdiəm ,bæləns/ *noun* the balance maintained in the body between salt lost in sweat and urine and salt taken in from food. The balance is regulated by aldosterone.

sodium bicarbonate /,səʊdiəm baɪ'kɑːbənət/ *noun* sodium salt used in cooking, and also as a relief for indigestion and acidity. Also called **bicarbonate of soda**

sodium fusidate /,səʊdiəm 'fjuːsɪdeɪt/ *noun* an antibiotic used mainly to treat penicillin-resistant staphylococcal infections

sodium pump /'səʊdiəm pʌmp/ *noun* a cellular process in which sodium is immediately excreted from any cell which it enters and potassium is brought in

sodium valproate /,səʊdiəm væl'prəʊeɪt/ *noun* an anticonvulsant drug used especially to treat migraines, seizures and epilepsy

soft /sɒft/ *adjective* not hard or not resistant to pressure

soft chancre /,sɒft 'ʃæŋkə/ *noun* same as **soft sore**

soft palate /,sɒft 'pælət/ *noun* the back part of the palate leading to the uvula. ◊ **cleft palate**

soft sore /ˌsɒft ˈsɔː/ *noun* a venereal sore with a soft base, situated in the groin or on the genitals and caused by the bacterium *Haemophilus ducreyi*. Also called **chancroid**, **soft chancre**

soft tissue /ˌsɒft ˈtɪʃuː/ *noun* skin, muscles, ligaments or tendons

solar plexus /ˌsəʊlə ˈpleksəs/ *noun* a nerve network situated at the back of the abdomen between the adrenal glands

solar retinopathy /ˌsəʊlə retɪˈnɒpəθi/ *noun* irreparable damage to the most sensitive part of the retina, the macula, caused by looking at the sun with no protection or inadequate protection, as when looking at an eclipse of the sun

soleus /ˈsəʊliəs/ *noun* a flat muscle which goes down the calf of the leg (NOTE: The plural is **solei**.)

solids /ˈsɒlɪdz/ *noun* solid food

soluble /ˈsɒljʊb(ə)l/ *adjective* able to dissolve ○ *a tablet of soluble aspirin*

soluble fibre /ˌsɒljʊb(ə)l ˈfaɪbə/ *noun* a fibre in vegetables, fruit and pulses and porridge oats which is partly digested in the intestine and reduces the absorption of fats and sugar into the body, so lowering the level of cholesterol

solute /ˈsɒljuːt/ *noun* a solid substance which is dissolved in a solvent to make a solution

solution /səˈluːʃ(ə)n/ *noun* a mixture of a solid substance dissolved in a liquid

solvent /ˈsɒlv(ə)nt/ *noun* a liquid in which a solid substance can be dissolved

solvent abuse /ˈsɒlvənt əˌbjuːs/, **solvent inhalation** /ˌsɒlvənt ˌɪnhəˈleɪʃ(ə)n/ *noun* a type of drug abuse in which someone inhales the toxic fumes given off by particular types of volatile chemical. Also called **glue-sniffing**

soma /ˈsəʊmə/ *noun* the body, as opposed to the mind (NOTE: The plural is **somata** or **somas**.)

somat- /ˈsəʊmət/ *prefix* same as **somato-** (*used before vowels*)

somata /ˈsəʊmətə/ *plural noun* plural of **soma**

somatic /səʊˈmætɪk/ *adjective* referring to the body, either as opposed to the mind, or as opposed to the intestines and inner organs. Compare **psychosomatic**

somato- /ˈsəʊmətəʊ/ *prefix* referring to the body

somatostatin /ˌsəʊmətəʊˈstætɪn/ *noun* a hormone produced in the hypothalamus which helps to prevent the release of the growth hormone

somatotrophic hormone /ˌsəʊmətəˌtrɒfɪk ˈhɔːməʊn/, **somatotrophin** /ˌsəʊmətəˈtrəʊfɪn/ *noun* a growth hormone, secreted by the pituitary gland, which stimulates the growth of long bones

somatropin /ˌsəʊməˈtrəʊpɪn/ *noun* same as **growth hormone**

-some /səʊm/ *suffix* tiny cell bodies

somnambulism /sɒmˈnæmbjʊlɪz(ə)m/ *noun* a condition especially affecting children where the person gets up and walks about while still asleep. Also called **sleepwalking**

somnambulist /sɒmˈnæmbjʊlɪst/ *noun* a person who walks in his or her sleep. Also called **sleepwalker**

somnolent /ˈsɒmnələnt/ *adjective* sleepy

somnolism /ˈsɒmnəlɪz(ə)m/ *noun* a trance which is induced by hypnotism

Somogyi effect /ˈʃɒmɒdʒi ɪˌfekt/, **Somogyi phenomenon** /ˈʃɒmɒdʒi fɪˌnɒmənən/ *noun* in diabetes mellitus, a swing to a high level of glucose in the blood from an extremely low level, usually occurring after an untreated insulin reaction during the night. It is caused by the release of stress hormones to counter low glucose levels.

-somy /səʊmi/ *suffix* the presence of chromosomes

son /sʌn/ *noun* a male child of a parent ○ *They have two sons and one daughter.*

Sonne dysentery /ˈsɒnə ˌdɪsəntri/ *noun* a common form of mild dysentery in the UK, caused by *Shigella sonnei* [Described 1915. After Carl Olaf Sonne (1882–1948), Danish bacteriologist and physician.]

sonogram /ˈsəʊnəgræm/ *noun* a chart produced using ultrasound waves to find where something is situated in the body

sonography /səˈnɒgrəfi/ *noun* same as **ultrasonography**

sonotopography /ˌsəʊnətəˈpɒgrəfi/ *noun* the use of ultrasound waves to produce a sonogram

soporific /ˌsɒpəˈrɪfɪk/ *noun* a drug which makes a person go to sleep ■ *adjective* causing sleep

sorbitol /ˈsɔːbɪtɒl/ *noun* a white crystalline sweet alcohol which is used as a sweetener and a moisturiser, and in the manufacture of Vitamin C

sordes /ˈsɔːdiːz/ *plural noun* dry deposits round the lips of someone who has a fever

sore /sɔː/ *noun* a small wound on any part of the skin, usually with a discharge of pus ■ *adjective* **1.** rough and inflamed ○ *a sore patch on the skin* **2.** painful ○ *My ankle still feels very sore.*

sore throat /ˌsɔː ˈθrəʊt/ *noun* a condition in which the mucous membrane in the throat is inflamed, sometimes because the person has been talking too much, but usually because of an infection (*informal*)

s.o.s. *adverb* (*on prescriptions*) if necessary. Full form **si opus sit** (NOTE: It means that the dose should be taken once.)

sotalol /ˈsɒtəlɒl/ *noun* a drug used to treat an irregular heartbeat and high blood pressure

souffle /ˈsuːf(ə)l/ *noun* a soft breathing sound, heard through a stethoscope

sound /saʊnd/ *noun* **1.** something which can be heard ○ *The doctor listened to the sounds of the patient's lungs.* ○ *His breathing made a whistling sound.* **2.** a long rod, used to examine or to dilate the inside of a cavity in the body ■ *verb* to examine the inside of a cavity using a rod

spansule /'spænsjuːl/ *noun* a drug in the form of a capsule which is specially designed to release its contents slowly in the stomach

spasm /'spæz(ə)m/ *noun* a sudden, usually painful, involuntary contraction of a muscle, as in cramp ○ *The muscles in his leg went into spasm.* ○ *She had painful spasms in her stomach.*

spasmo- /spæzməʊ/ *prefix* referring to a spasm

spasmodic /spæz'mɒdɪk/ *adjective* occurring in spasms

spasmolytic /ˌspæzmə'lɪtɪk/ *noun* a drug which relieves muscle spasms

spasmus nutans /ˌspæzməs 'njuːtənz/ *noun* a condition in which someone nods his or her head and at the same time has spasms in the neck muscles and rapid movements of the eyes

spastic /'spæstɪk/ *adjective* with spasms or sudden contractions of muscles ■ *noun* a person affected with cerebral palsy (NOTE: The noun sense is now considered to be offensive.)

spastic colon /ˌspæstɪk 'kəʊlɒn/ *noun* same as **mucous colitis**

spastic diplegia /ˌspæstɪk daɪ'pliːdʒə/ *noun* a congenital form of cerebral palsy which affects mainly the legs. Also called **Little's disease**

spastic gait /ˌspæstɪk 'geɪt/ *noun* a way of walking where the legs are stiff and the feet not lifted off the ground

spasticity /spæ'stɪsti/ *noun* a condition in which a limb resists passive movement. ◊ **rigidity**

spastic paralysis /ˌspæstɪk pə'ræləsɪs/ *noun* same as **cerebral palsy**

spastic paraplegia /ˌspæstɪk ˌpærə'pliːdʒə/ *noun* paralysis of one side of the body after a stroke

spatula /'spætjʊlə/ *noun* **1.** a flat flexible tool with a handle, used to scoop, lift, spread or mix things **2.** a flat wooden stick used to press the tongue down when the mouth or throat is being examined

special care baby unit /ˌspeʃ(ə)l keə 'beɪbi ˌjuːnɪt/ *noun* a unit in a hospital which deals with premature babies or babies with serious disorders

special health authority /ˌspeʃ(ə)l 'helθ ɔːˌθɒrɪti/ *noun* a health authority which has unique national functions, or covers various regions. An example is UK Transplant, which manages the National Transplant Database and provides a 24-hour service for the matching and allocation of donor organs.

special hospital /ˌspeʃ(ə)l 'hɒspɪt(ə)l/ *noun* a hospital for people whose mental condition

makes them a potential danger to themselves and/or others

specialise /'speʃəlaɪz/, **specialize** *verb* **1.** to concentrate on a specific subject or activity **2.** to be an expert in a specific subject or area of knowledge (NOTE: **specialising – specialised**)

specialised /'speʃəlaɪzd/, **specialized** *adjective* **1.** designed for a particular purpose **2.** concentrating on a particular activity or subject ○ *specialised skills*

specialist registrar /ˌspeʃ(ə)lɪst 'redʒɪ ˌstrɑː/ *noun* a junior doctor in a hospital who is doing further specialist training

speciality /ˌspeʃi'æləti/ *noun* a particular activity or type of work which someone is specially trained for or very interested in. Also called **specialism, specialty**

special school /'speʃ(ə)l skuːl/ *noun* a school for children with disabilities

specialty /'speʃ(ə)lti/ *noun US* same as **speciality**

species /'spiːʃiːz/ *noun* a group of living things with the same characteristics and which can interbreed (NOTE: The plural is **species**.)

specific /spə'sɪfɪk/ *adjective* referring to a disease caused by one type of microorganism only. Opposite **non-specific** ■ *noun* a drug which is only used to treat one disease

specific gravity /spəˌsɪfɪk 'grævɪti/ *noun* same as **relative density**

specificity /ˌspesɪ'fɪsəti/ *noun* the rate of negative responses in a test from persons free from a disease. A high specificity means a low rate of false positives. Compare **sensitivity**

specific urethritis /spəˌsɪfɪk jʊərɪ'θraɪtɪs/ *noun* inflammation of the urethra caused by gonorrhoea

specimen /'spesɪmɪn/ *noun* a small quantity of something given for testing ○ *He was asked to bring a urine specimen.*

spectacles /'spektək(ə)lz/ *plural noun* glasses which are worn in front of the eyes to help correct problems in vision

spectrography /spek'trɒgrəfi/ *noun* the recording of a spectrum on photographic film

spectroscope /'spektrəskəʊp/ *noun* an instrument used to analyse a spectrum

spectrum /'spektrəm/ *noun* **1.** the range of colours, from red to violet, into which white light can be split when it is passed through something (NOTE: Different substances in solution have different spectra.) **2.** the range of organisms that an antibiotic or chemical can kill (NOTE: The plural is **spectra** or **spectrums**.) □ **broad-spectrum antibiotic** an antibiotic which kills a large number of different organisms □ **narrow-spectrum antibiotic** an antibiotic which is targeted at a few particular organisms

speculum /'spekjʊləm/ *noun* a surgical instrument which is inserted into an opening in the body such as a nostril or the vagina to keep it open in order to allow a doctor to examine the inside (NOTE: The plural is **specula** or **speculums**.)

speech /spiːtʃ/ *noun* **1.** the ability to make intelligible sounds with the vocal cords **2.** a talk given to an audience

speech block /'spiːtʃ blɒk/ *noun* a temporary inability to speak, caused by the effect of nervous stress on the mental processes

speech impediment /'spiːtʃ ɪm,pedɪmənt/ *noun* an inability to speak easily or in the usual way because of the physical structure of the mouth or other disorders

speech therapist /'spiːtʃ ,θerəpɪst/ *noun* a qualified person who practises speech therapy

speech therapy /'spiːtʃ ,θerəpi/ *noun* treatment for a speech disorder such as stammering or one which results from a stroke or physical malformation

sperm /spɜːm/ *noun* same as **spermatozoon** (NOTE: The plural is **sperm**.)

spermat- /spɜːmət/ *prefix* same as **spermato-** (*used before vowels*)

spermatic /spɜːˈmætɪk/ *adjective* referring to sperm

spermatic artery /spɜː,mætɪk 'ɑːtəri/ *noun* an artery which leads into the testes. Also called **testicular artery**

spermatic cord /spɜː,mætɪk 'kɔːd/ *noun* a cord running from the testis to the abdomen carrying the vas deferens, the blood vessels, nerves and lymphatics of the testis

spermatid /'spɜːmətɪd/ *noun* an immature male sex cell that develops into a spermatozoon

spermato- /spɜːmətəʊ/ *prefix* **1.** referring to sperm **2.** referring to the male reproductive system

spermatocele /'spɜːmətəsiːl/ *noun* a cyst which forms in the scrotum

spermatogenesis /,spɜːmətəˈdʒenəsɪs/ *noun* the formation and development of spermatozoa in the testes

spermatorrhoea /,spɜːmətəˈrɪə/ *noun* the discharge of a large amount of semen frequently and without an orgasm (NOTE: The US spelling is **spermatorrhea**.)

spermatozoon /,spɜːmətəˈzəʊɒn/ *noun* a mature male sex cell, which is ejaculated from the penis and is capable of fertilising an ovum. Also called **sperm** (NOTE: The plural is **spermatozoa**.)

spermaturia /,spɜːməˈtjʊəriə/ *noun* sperm in the urine

sperm bank /'spɜːm bæŋk/ *noun* a place where sperm can be stored for use in artificial insemination

sperm count /'spɜːm kaʊnt/ *noun* a calculation of the number of sperm in a quantity of semen

sperm donor /'spɜːm ,dəʊnə/ *noun* a male who gives sperm, for a fee, to allow a childless woman to bear a child

spermi- /spɜːmi/ *prefix* referring to sperm and semen

spermicidal /,spɜːmɪˈsaɪd(ə)l/ *adjective* killing or able to kill sperm

spermicidal jelly /,spɜːmɪsaɪd(ə)l 'dʒeli/ *noun* a jelly-like product which acts as a contraceptive

spermicide /'spɜːmɪsaɪd/ *noun* a substance which kills sperm

spermio- /spɜːmiəʊ/ *prefix* same as **spermi-**

spermiogenesis /,spɜːmiəʊˈdʒenəsɪs/ *noun* the stage of spermatogenesis during which a spermatid changes into a spermatozoon

spheno- /sfiːnəʊ/ *prefix* referring to the sphenoid bone

sphenoid /'sfiːnɔɪd/ *adjective* **1.** relating to the sphenoid bone **2.** shaped like a wedge ■ *noun* same as **sphenoid bone**

sphenoid bone /'sfiːnɔɪd bəʊn/ *noun* one of two bones in the skull which form the side of the socket of the eye. Also called **sphenoid**

sphenoid sinus /,sfiːnɔɪd 'saɪnəs/ *noun* one of the sinuses in the skull behind the nasal passage

spherocyte /'sfɪərəʊsaɪt/ *noun* a red blood cell that is round rather than than the usual disc shape

spherocytosis /,sfɪərəʊsaɪˈtəʊsɪs/ *noun* a condition in which someone has spherocytes in the blood, causing anaemia, enlarged spleen and gallstones, as in acholuric jaundice

sphincter /'sfɪŋktə/, **sphincter muscle** /'sfɪŋktə ,mʌs(ə)l/ *noun* a circular band of muscle which surrounds an opening or passage in the body, especially the anus, and can narrow or close the opening or passage by contracting

sphincterectomy /,sfɪŋktəˈrektəmi/ *noun* **1.** a surgical operation to remove a sphincter **2.** a surgical operation to remove part of the edge of the iris in the eye (NOTE: The plural is **sphincterectomies**.)

sphincteroplasty /'sfɪŋktərə,plæsti/ *noun* a surgical operation to relieve a tightened sphincter (NOTE: The plural is **sphincteroplasties**.)

sphincterotomy /,sfɪŋktəˈrɒtəmi/ *noun* a surgical operation to make an incision into a sphincter (NOTE: The plural is **sphincterotomies**.)

sphyg /sfɪg/ *noun* same as **sphygmomanometer** (*informal*)

sphygmo- /sfɪgməʊ/ *prefix* referring to the pulse

sphygmocardiograph /ˌsfɪgməʊ
'kɑːdiəʊgrɑːf/ *noun* a device which records
heartbeats and pulse rate

sphygmograph /'sfɪgməgrɑːf/ *noun* a device
which records the pulse

sphygmomanometer /ˌsfɪgməʊmə'nɒmɪtə/
noun an instrument which measures blood pressure in the arteries

spica /'spaɪkə/ *noun* a way of bandaging a joint
where the bandage crosses over itself like the fig-
ure 8 on the inside of the bend of the joint (NOTE:
The plural is **spicae** or **spicas**.)

spicule /'spɪkjuːl/ *noun* a small splinter of bone

spigot /'spɪgət/ *noun* the end of a pipe which is
joined by insertion into the enlarged end of
another pipe

spina /'spaɪnə/ *noun* **1.** a thin sharp piece of
bone **2.** the vertebral column

spina bifida /ˌspaɪnə 'bɪfɪdə/ *noun* a serious
condition in which part of the spinal cord protrudes through the spinal column. Also called
rachischisis

spinal /'spaɪn(ə)l/ *adjective* referring to the
spine ○ *She suffered spinal injuries in the crash.*

spinal accessory nerve /ˌspaɪn(ə)l ək
'sesəri nɜːv/ *noun* the eleventh cranial nerve
which supplies the muscles in the neck and shoulders

spinal anaesthesia /ˌspaɪn(ə)l ˌænəs'θiːziə/
noun local anaesthesia in which an anaesthetic is
injected into the cerebrospinal fluid

spinal anaesthetic /ˌspaɪn(ə)l ˌænəs'θetɪk/
noun an anaesthetic given by injection into the
spine, which results in large parts of the body losing the sense of feeling

spinal block /ˌspaɪn(ə)l 'blɒk/ *noun* analgesia
produced by injecting the spinal cord with an
anaesthetic

spinal canal /ˌspaɪn(ə)l kə'næl/ *noun* the hollow channel running down the back of the vertebrae, containing the spinal cord. Also called **vertebral canal**

spinal column /'spaɪn(ə)l ˌkɒləm/ *noun* same
as **spine**

spinal cord /'spaɪn(ə)l kɔːd/ *noun* part of the
central nervous system, running from the medulla
oblongata to the filum terminale, in the vertebral
canal of the spine (NOTE: For other terms referring to the spinal cord, see words beginning with
myel-, myelo-.)

spinal curvature /ˌspaɪn(ə)l 'kɜːvətʃə/ *noun*
unusual bending of the spinal column

spinal fusion /ˌspaɪn(ə)l 'fjuːʒ(ə)n/ *noun* a
surgical operation to join two vertebrae together
to make the spine more rigid. Also called **spondylosyndesis**

spinal ganglion /ˌspaɪn(ə)l 'gæŋgliən/ *noun*
a cone-shaped mass of cells on the posterior root,

the main axons of which form the posterior root
of the spinal nerve

spinal nerve /'spaɪn(ə)l nɜːv/ *noun* one of the
31 pairs of nerves which lead from the spinal cord
and govern mainly the trunk and limbs

spinal puncture /ˌspaɪn(ə)l 'pʌŋktʃə/ *noun*
same as **lumbar puncture**

spinal shock /'spaɪn(ə)l 'ʃɒk/ *noun* a loss of
feeling in the lower part of the body below a point
at which the spine has been injured

spindle /'spɪnd(ə)l/ *noun* **1.** a long thin structure **2.** a structure formed in cells during division
to which the chromosomes are attached by their
centromeres

spine /spaɪn/ *noun* the series of bones, the vertebrae, linked together to form a flexible supporting column running from the pelvis to the skull ○
She injured her spine in the crash. Also called
backbone, spinal column, vertebral column

Spinhaler /spɪn'heɪlə/ a trade name for a
device from which a person with breathing problems can inhale a preset dose of a drug

spinnbarkeit /'spɪnbɑːkaɪt/ *noun* a thread of
mucus formed in the cervix which is used in
determining the time of ovulation. At this time it
can be drawn out on a glass slide to its maximum
length.

spino- /spaɪnəʊ/ *prefix* **1.** referring to the spine
2. referring to the spinal cord

spiral /'spaɪrəl/ *adjective* running in a continuous circle upwards

spiral bandage /ˌspaɪrəl 'bændɪdʒ/ *noun* a
bandage which is wrapped round a limb, each
turn overlapping the one before

spiral organ /ˌspaɪrəl 'ɔːgən/ *noun* same as
organ of Corti

spiro- /spaɪrəʊ/ *prefix* **1.** referring to a spiral **2.**
referring to respiration

spirogram /'spaɪrəʊgræm/ *noun* a record of
someone's breathing made by a spirograph

spirograph /'spaɪrəʊgrɑːf/ *noun* a device
which records depth and rapidity of breathing

spirography /spaɪ'rɒgrəfi/ *noun* the recording
of a someone's breathing by use of a spirograph

spirometer /spaɪ'rɒmɪtə/ *noun* an instrument
which measures the amount of air a person
inhales or exhales

spirometry /spaɪ'rɒmətri/ *noun* a measurement of the vital capacity of the lungs by use of a
spirometer

spironolactone /ˌspaɪrənə'læktəʊn/ *noun* a
steroid which helps the body produce urine, used
in the treatment of oedema and hypertension

Spitz-Holter valve /ˌspɪts 'hɒltə ˌvælv/ *noun*
a valve with a one-way system, surgically placed
in the skull and used to drain excess fluid from the
brain in hydrocephalus

splanchnic /'splæŋknɪk/ *adjective* referring to viscera

splanchnic nerve /'splæŋknɪk nɜːv/ *noun* any sympathetic nerve which supplies organs in the abdomen

spleen /spliːn/ *noun* an organ in the top part of the abdominal cavity behind the stomach and below the diaphragm, which helps to destroy old red blood cells, form lymphocytes and store blood. See illustration at **DIGESTIVE SYSTEM** in Supplement

splen- /splen/ *prefix* same as **spleno-** (*used before vowels*)

splenectomy /spleˈnektəmi/ *noun* a surgical operation to remove the spleen (NOTE: The plural is **splenectomies**.)

splenic /'splenɪk/ *adjective* referring to the spleen

splenic anaemia /ˌsplenɪk əˈniːmiə/ *noun* a type of anaemia, caused by cirrhosis of the liver, in which the person has portal hypertension, an enlarged spleen and haemorrhages. Also called **Banti's syndrome**

splenic flexure /ˌsplenɪk 'flekʃə/ *noun* a bend in the colon where the transverse colon joins the descending colon

splenitis /spləˈnaɪtɪs/ *noun* inflammation of the spleen

spleno- /spliːnəʊ/ *prefix* referring to the spleen

splenomegaly /ˌspliːnəʊˈmegəli/ *noun* a condition in which the spleen is unusually large, associated with several disorders including malaria and some cancers

splenorenal /ˌspliːnəʊˈriːn(ə)l/ *adjective* relating to both the spleen and the kidneys

splenorenal anastomosis /ˌspliːnəʊ ˌriːn(ə)l əˌnæstəˈməʊsɪs/ *noun* a surgical operation to join the splenic vein to a renal vein, as a treatment for portal hypertension

splenovenography /ˌspliːnəʊvəˈnɒɡrəfi/ *noun* X-ray examination of the spleen and the veins which are connected to it

splint /splɪnt/ *noun* a stiff support attached to a limb to prevent a broken bone from moving ○ *He had to keep his arm in a splint for several weeks.* ◊ **shin splints**

splinter haemorrhage /'splɪntə ˌhem(ə)rɪdʒ/ *noun* a tiny line of haemorrhaging under the nails or in the eyeball

split personality /ˌsplɪt ˌpɜːsəˈnæləti/ *noun* same as **schizoid personality**

split-skin graft /ˌsplɪt ˌskɪn 'ɡrɑːft/ *noun* a type of skin graft in which thin layers of skin are grafted over a wound. Also called **Thiersch graft**

spondyl /'spɒndɪl/ *noun* same as **vertebra**

spondyl- /spɒndɪl/ *prefix* same as **spondylo-** (*used before vowels*)

spondylitis /ˌspɒndɪˈlaɪtɪs/ *noun* inflammation of the vertebrae

spondylo- /spɒndɪləʊ/ *prefix* referring to the vertebrae

spondylolisthesis /ˌspɒndɪləʊˈlɪsθəsɪs/ *noun* a condition in which one of the lumbar vertebrae moves forwards over the one beneath

spondylosis /ˌspɒndɪˈləʊsɪs/ *noun* stiffness in the spine and degenerative changes in the intervertebral discs, with osteoarthritis. This condition is common in older people.

spondylosyndesis /ˌspɒndɪləʊsɪnˈdiːsɪs/ *noun* same as **spinal fusion**

sponge bath /'spʌndʒ bɑːθ/ *noun* the act of washing someone in bed, using a sponge or damp cloth ○ *The nurse gave the elderly lady a sponge bath.*

spongiform encephalopathy /ˌspʌndʒɪfɔːm enˌkefəˈlɒpəθi/ *noun* a brain disease in humans and animals in which areas of the brain slowly develop holes in their cells and begin to look like a sponge

spontaneous /spɒnˈteɪniəs/ *adjective* happening without any particular outside cause

spontaneous delivery /spɒnˌteɪniəs dɪˈlɪv(ə)ri/ *noun* a delivery of a baby which takes places naturally, without any medical or surgical help

spontaneous pneumothorax /spɒnˌteɪniəs ˌnjuːməʊˈθɔːræks/ *noun* a condition occurring when an opening is created on the surface of the lung allowing air to leak into the pleural cavity

spontaneous version /spɒnˌteɪniəs 'vɜːʃ(ə)n/ *noun* a movement of a fetus to take up another position in the uterus, caused by the contractions of the uterus during childbirth or by the movements of the baby itself before birth

sporadic /spəˈrædɪk/ *adjective* referring to outbreaks of disease that occur as separate cases, not in epidemics

spore /spɔː/ *noun* a reproductive body of particular bacteria and fungi which can survive in extremely hot or cold conditions for a long time

sporicidal /ˌspɔːrɪˈsaɪd(ə)l/ *adjective* killing spores

sporicide /'spɔːrɪsaɪd/ *noun* a substance which kills bacterial spores

Sporozoa /ˌspɔːrəˈzəʊə/ *noun* a type of parasitic Protozoa which includes Plasmodium, the cause of malaria

sports injury /'spɔːts ˌɪndʒəri/ *noun* an injury caused by playing a sport, e.g. a sprained ankle or tennis elbow

sports medicine /'spɔːts ˌmed(ə)sɪn/ *noun* the study of the treatment of sports injuries

spotted fever /ˌspɒtɪd 'fiːvə/ *noun* same as **meningococcal meningitis**

sprain /spreɪn/ *noun* a condition in which the ligaments in a joint are stretched or torn because of a sudden movement ■ *verb* to tear the ligaments in a joint with a sudden movement ○ *She sprained her wrist when she fell.*

Sprengel's deformity /'spreŋgəlz dɪ,fɔːmɪti/, **Sprengel's shoulder** /,spreŋgəlz 'ʃəʊldə/ *noun* a congenitally malformed shoulder, in which one scapula is smaller and higher than the other [Described 1891. After Otto Gerhard Karl Sprengel (1852–1915), German surgeon.]

sprue /spruː/ *noun* same as **psilosis**

spud /spʌd/ *noun* a needle used to get a piece of dust or other foreign body out of the eye

spur /spɜː/ *noun* a sharp projecting part of a bone

sputum /'spjuːtəm/ *noun* mucus which is formed in the inflamed nose, throat or lungs and is coughed up ○ *She was coughing up blood-stained sputum.* Also called **phlegm**

squama /'skweɪmə/ *noun* a thin piece of hard tissue, e.g. a thin flake of bone or scale on the skin (NOTE: The plural is **squamae**.)

squamo- /skweɪməʊ/ *prefix* **1.** relating to the squamous part of the temporal bone **2.** scaly

squamous /'skweɪməs/ *adjective* thin and hard like a scale

squamous bone /'skweɪməs bəʊn/ *noun* a part of the temporal bone which forms the side of the skull

squamous cell carcinoma /,skweɪməs sel ,kɑːsɪ'nəʊmə/ *noun* a common type of cancer which usually develops in the outer layer of the skin, on the lips, or inside the mouth or oesophagus. Abbreviation **SCC**

squamous epithelium /,skweɪməs ,epɪ'θiːliəm/ *noun* epithelium with flat cells like scales, which forms the lining of the pericardium, the peritoneum and the pleura. Also called **pavement epithelium**

squint /skwɪnt/ *noun* a condition in which the eyes focus on different points. Also called **strabismus** ■ *verb* to have one eye or both eyes looking towards the nose ○ *Babies often appear to squint, but it is corrected as they grow older.*

SRN *abbreviation* State Registered Nurse

SSRI *abbreviation* selective serotonin re-uptake inhibitor

stabbing pain /'stæbɪŋ peɪn/ *noun* pain which comes in a series of short sharp bursts ○ *He had stabbing pains in his chest.*

staccato speech /stə,kɑːtəʊ 'spiːtʃ/ *noun* an unusual way of speaking with short pauses between each word

Stacke's operation /'stækiz ɒpə,reɪʃ(ə)n/ *noun* a surgical operation to remove the posterior and superior wall of the auditory meatus [After Ludwig Stacke (1859–1918), German otologist.]

stadium /'steɪdiəm/ *noun* a particular stage of a disease (NOTE: The plural is **stadia**.)

stadium invasioni /,steɪdiəm ɪn,veɪʃi'əʊni/ *noun* same as **incubation period**

staff nurse /'stɑːf nɜːs/ *noun* a nurse who is on the permanent staff of a hospital

stage /steɪdʒ/ *noun* a point in the development of a disease at which a decision can be taken about the treatment which should be given or at which distinctive developments take place ○ *The disease has reached a critical stage.* ○ *This is a symptom of the second stage of syphilis.*

staging /'steɪdʒɪŋ/ *noun* the process of performing tests to learn the extent of a disease within the body, in order to decide the best treatment for someone

stain /steɪn/ *noun* a substance used to give colour to tissues which are going to be examined under the microscope ■ *verb* to treat a piece of tissue with a dye to increase contrast before it is examined under the microscope

Stamey procedure /'steɪmi prə,siːdʒə/ *noun* a surgical operation to cure stress incontinence in women. A minor abdominal incision is made as well as a vaginal incision, and the neck of the bladder is stitched to the abdominal wall.

stammer /'stæmə/ *noun* a speech difficulty in which someone repeats parts of a word or the whole word several times or stops to try to pronounce a word ○ *He has a bad stammer.* ■ *verb* to speak with a stammer

stammerer /'stæmərə/ *noun* a person who stammers

stammering /'stæmərɪŋ/ *noun* difficulty in speaking, in which the person repeats parts of a word or the whole word several times or stops to try to pronounce a word. Also called **dysphemia**

stand /stænd/ *verb* **1.** to be in an upright position with your bodyweight resting on your feet, or to put a person in this position **2.** to get to your feet from a sitting position (NOTE: **stood**)

standard /'stændəd/ *adjective* usual, recommended or established ○ *It is standard practice to take the patient's temperature twice a day.* ■ *noun* **1.** something which has been agreed upon and is used to measure other things by **2.** a level of quality achieved by someone or something ○ *The standard of care in hospitals has increased over the last years.* ○ *The report criticised the standards of hygiene in the clinic.*

standardise /'stændədaɪz/, **standardize** *verb* to make all things of the same type follow the same standard

Standard Precautions /,stændəd prɪ'kɔːʃ(ə)nz/ *plural noun* the most recent set of guidelines for health care workers on dealing with blood, all body fluids, secretions and excretions (except sweat), non-intact skin and mucous membranes. They are designed to reduce the risk of transmission of microorganisms. The Standard Precautions are implemented automatically for everyone, as all patients are presumed to be potentially infectious.

stapedectomy /ˌsteɪpɪ'dektəmi/ *noun* a surgical operation to remove the stapes (NOTE: The plural is **stapedectomies**.)

stapedial mobilisation /stəˌpiː'diəl ˌməʊbɪlaɪ'zeɪʃ(ə)n/, **stapediolysis** /stəˌpiː'dɪ'ɒləsɪs/ *noun* a surgical operation to relieve deafness by detaching the stapes from the fenestra ovalis (NOTE: The plural of **stapediolysis** is **stapediolyses**.)

stapes /'steɪpiːz/ *noun* one of the three ossicles in the middle ear, shaped like a stirrup. See illustration at **EAR** in Supplement

staphylectomy /ˌstæfɪ'lektəmi/ *noun* a surgical operation to remove the uvula (NOTE: The plural is **staphylectomies**.)

staphylococcal /ˌstæfɪlə'kɒk(ə)l/ *adjective* referring to Staphylococci

Staphylococcus /ˌstæfɪlə'kɒkəs/ *noun* a bacterium which grows in a bunch like a bunch of grapes, and causes boils and food poisoning (NOTE: The plural is **Staphylococci**.)

staphyloma /ˌstæfɪ'ləʊmə/ *noun* a swelling of the cornea or the white of the eye (NOTE: The plural is **staphylomas** or **staphylomata**.)

staphylorrhaphy /ˌstæfɪ'lɔːrəfi/ *noun* same as **palatorrhaphy** (NOTE: The plural is **staphylorrhaphies**.)

staple /'steɪp(ə)l/ *noun* a small piece of bent metal, used to attach tissues together ■ *verb* to attach tissues with staples

stapler /'steɪplə/ *noun* a device used in surgery to attach tissues with staples, instead of suturing

starch /stɑːtʃ/ *noun* the usual form in which carbohydrates exist in food, especially in bread, rice and potatoes. It is broken down by the digestive process into forms of sugar.

startle reflex /'stɑːt(ə)l ˌriːfleks/ *noun* the usual response of a young baby to a sudden loud noise or a sudden fall through the air, by contracting the limb and neck muscles

starvation /stɑː'veɪʃ(ə)n/ *noun* the fact of having had very little or no food

stasis /'steɪsɪs/ *noun* a stoppage or slowing in the flow of a liquid, such as blood in veins, or food in the intestine

-stasis /steɪsɪs/ *suffix* referring to stoppage in the flow of a liquid

stat. /stæt/ *adverb* (*written on prescriptions*) immediately. Full form **statim**

State Enrolled Nurse /ˌsteɪt ɪnˌrəʊld 'nɜːs/ *noun* abbreviation **SEN**. Now called **second-level nurse**

State Registered Nurse /ˌsteɪt ˌredʒɪstəd 'nɜːs/ *noun* abbreviation **SRN**. Now called **first-level nurse**

-statin /stætɪn/ *suffix* used in generic names of lipid-lowering drugs ○ *pravastatin*

statistics /stə'tɪstɪks/ *plural noun* official figures which show facts ○ *Population statistics show that the birth rate is slowing down.*

status /'steɪtəs/ *noun* a state or condition

status asthmaticus /ˌsteɪtəs æs'mætɪkəs/ *noun* an attack of bronchial asthma which lasts for a long time and results in exhaustion and collapse

status epilepticus /ˌsteɪtəs epɪ'leptɪkəs/ *noun* repeated and prolonged epileptic seizures without recovery of consciousness between them

status lymphaticus /ˌsteɪtəs lɪm'fætɪkəs/ *noun* a condition in which the glands in the lymphatic system are enlarged

statutory bodies /ˌstætjʊt(ə)ri 'bɒdiz/ *plural noun* organisations set up by Acts of Parliament to carry out specific functions, e.g. the Nursing and Midwifery Council, set up to regulate the nursing and midwifery professions

STD *abbreviation* sexually transmitted disease

steam inhalation /ˌstiːm ɪnhə'leɪʃ(ə)n/ *noun* a treatment for respiratory disease in which someone breathes in steam with medicinal substances in it

steat- /stiːət/, **steato-** /stiːətəʊ/ *prefix* referring to fat

steatoma /ˌstiːə'təʊmə/ *noun* a cyst in a blocked sebaceous gland. ◊ **sebaceous cyst** (NOTE: The plural is **steatomata**.)

steatopygia /ˌstiːətə'pɪdʒiə/ *noun* excessive fat on the buttocks

steatorrhoea /ˌstiːətə'rɪə/ *noun* a condition in which fat is passed in the faeces

Stein-Leventhal syndrome /ˌstaɪn 'levəntɑːl ˌsɪndrəʊm/ *noun* ♦ **polycystic ovary syndrome** [Described 1935. After Irving F. Stein (1887–1976), US gynaecologist; Michael Leo Leventhal (1901–71), US obstetrician and gynaecologist.]

Steinmann's pin /ˌstaɪnmænz 'pɪn/ *noun* a pin for attaching traction wires to a fractured bone [Described 1907. After Fritz Steinmann (1872–1932), Swiss surgeon.]

stellate /'steleɪt/ *adjective* shaped like a star

stellate fracture /ˌsteleɪt 'fræktʃə/ *noun* a fracture of the kneecap shaped like a star

stellate ganglion /ˌsteleɪt 'gæŋgliən/ *noun* a group of nerve cells in the neck, shaped like a star

Stellwag's sign /'stelvɑːgz saɪn/ *noun* a symptom of exophthalmic goitre, where someone does not blink often, because the eyeball is protruding [After Carl Stellwag von Carion (1823–1904), ophthalmologist in Vienna, Austria.]

stem /stem/ *noun* a thin piece of tissue which attaches an organ or growth to the main tissue

steno- /stenəʊ/ *prefix* narrow or constricted

stenosed valve /steˌnəʊst ˈvælv/ *noun* a valve which has become narrow or constricted

stenosis /steˈnəʊsɪs/ *noun* a condition in which a passage becomes narrow

stenostomia /ˌstenəʊˈstəʊmiə/, **stenostomy** /steˈnɒstəmi/ *noun* the narrowing of an opening

Stensen's duct /ˌstensənz ˈdʌkt/ *noun* a duct which carries saliva from the parotid glands [Described 1661. After Niels Stensen (1638–86), Danish physician and priest, anatomist, physiologist and theologian.]

stent /stent/ *noun* a support of artificial material often inserted in a tube or vessel which has been sutured

sterco- /stɜːkəʊ/ *prefix* referring to faeces

stercobilin /ˌstɜːkəˈbaɪlɪn/ *noun* a brown pigment which colours the faeces

stercolith /ˈstɜːkəlɪθ/ *noun* a hard ball of dried faeces in the bowel

stereognosis /ˌsterɪɒɡˈnəʊsɪs/ *noun* the ability to tell the shape of an object in three dimensions by means of touch

stereoscopic vision /ˌsterɪəskɒpɪk ˈvɪʒ(ə)n/ *noun* the ability to judge the distance and depth of an object by binocular vision

stereotactic /ˌsterɪəʊˈtæktɪk/ *adjective* referring to procedures which use coordinates put into a computer or scanner in order to locate and operate upon tumours precisely. Examples are biopsies, surgery or radiation therapy.

stereotaxy /ˌsterɪəʊˈtæksi/, **stereotaxic surgery** /ˌsterɪəʊtæksɪk ˈsɜːdʒəri/ *noun* a surgical procedure to identify a point in the interior of the brain, before an operation can begin, to locate exactly the area to be operated on

Sterets /ˈsterəts/ a trademark for a type of swab used for cleaning the skin before an injection

sterile /ˈsteraɪl/ *adjective* **1.** with no harmful microorganisms present ○ *a sterile environment* **2.** not able to produce children

sterile dressing /ˌsteraɪl ˈdresɪŋ/ *noun* a dressing which is sold in a sterile pack, ready for use

sterilisation /ˌsterɪlaɪˈzeɪʃ(ə)n/, **sterilization** *noun* **1.** the action of making instruments or areas completely free from microorganisms which might cause infection **2.** a procedure that makes someone unable to have children

sterilise /ˈsterɪlaɪz/, **sterilize** *verb* **1.** to make something completely free from microorganisms which might cause infection **2.** to make someone unable to have children

sterilising /ˈsterɪlaɪzɪŋ/ *adjective* able to kill microorganisms ○ *Wipe the surface with sterilising fluid.*

sterility /stəˈrɪlɪti/ *noun* **1.** the state of being free from microorganisms **2.** the state of being unable to have children

Steri-Strips /ˈsteri strɪps/ a trademark for thin paper strips which are placed over an incision in the skin. They help its edges to come together and form a scar.

sternal /ˈstɜːn(ə)l/ *adjective* referring to the breastbone

sternal angle /ˌstɜːn(ə)l ˈæŋɡ(ə)l/ *noun* the ridge of bone where the manubrium articulates with the body of the sternum

sterno- /stɜːnəʊ/ *prefix* relating to the breastbone

sternocleidomastoid muscle /ˌstɜːnəʊˌklaɪdəʊˈmæstɔɪd ˌmʌs(ə)l/ *noun* a muscle in the neck, running from the breastbone to the mastoid process

sternocostal joint /ˌstɜːnəʊˈkɒst(ə)l ˌdʒɔɪnt/ *noun* a joint where the breastbone joins a rib

sternohyoid /ˌstɜːnəʊˈhaɪɔɪd/ *adjective* relating to the sternum and the hyoid bone

sternohyoid muscle /ˌstɜːnəʊˈhaɪɔɪd ˌmʌs(ə)l/ *noun* a muscle in the neck which runs from the breastbone into the hyoid bone

sternomastoid /ˌstɜːnəʊˈmæstɔɪd/ *adjective* referring to the breastbone and the mastoid

sternomastoid tumour /ˌstɜːnəʊˌmæstɔɪd ˈtjuːmə/ *noun* a benign tumour which appears in the sternomastoid muscle in newborn babies

sternotomy /stɜːˈnɒtəmi/ *noun* a surgical operation to cut through the breastbone, so as to be able to operate on the heart

sternum /ˈstɜːnəm/ *noun* same as **breastbone**

steroid /ˈstɪərɔɪd/ *noun* any of several chemical compounds, including the sex hormones, which have characteristic ring systems and which affect the body and its functions

stertor /ˈstɜːtə/ *noun* noisy breathing sounds in someone unconscious

stertorous /ˈstɜːt(ə)rəs/ *adjective* characterised by heavy snoring

steth- /steθ/, **stetho-** /steθə/ *prefix* referring to the chest

stethoscope /ˈsteθəskəʊp/ *noun* a surgical instrument with two earpieces connected to a tube and a metal disc, used by doctors to listen to sounds made inside the body, e.g. the sounds of the heart or lungs

Stevens-Johnson syndrome /ˌstiːvənz ˈdʒɒnsən ˌsɪndrəʊm/ *noun* a severe form of erythema multiforme affecting the face and genitals, caused by an allergic reaction to drugs [Described 1922. After Albert Mason Stevens (1884–1945); Frank Chambliss Johnson (1894–1934), physicians in New York, USA.]

sthenia /'sθiːniə/ *noun* a condition of great strength or vitality

STI *abbreviation* sexually transmitted infection

sticking plaster /'stɪkɪŋ ˌplɑːstə/ *noun* an adhesive plaster or tape used to cover a small wound or to attach a pad of dressing to the skin

stiff neck /ˌstɪf 'nek/ *noun* a condition in which moving the neck is painful, usually caused by a strained muscle or by sitting in a cold wind

stigma /'stɪgmə/ *noun* a visible symptom which shows that someone has a particular disease (NOTE: The plural is **stigmas** or **stigmata**.)

stilet /staɪ'let/ *noun* **1.** a fine wire used as a probe in surgery **2.** a wire inserted in a catheter to give it rigidity

stillbirth /'stɪlbɜːθ/ *noun* the birth of a dead fetus, more than 28 weeks after conception (*informal*)

Still's disease /'stɪlz dɪˌziːz/ *noun* arthritis affecting children, similar to rheumatoid arthritis in adults [Described 1896. After Sir George Frederic Still (1868–1941), British paediatrician and physician to the king.]

stimulant /'stɪmjʊlənt/ *noun* a substance which makes part of the body function faster ○ *Caffeine is a stimulant.* ■ *adjective* increasing body function

stimulate /'stɪmjʊleɪt/ *verb* to make a person or organ react, respond or function ○ *The therapy should stimulate the patient into attempting to walk unaided.* ○ *The drug stimulates the heart.*

stimulus /'stɪmjʊləs/ *noun* something which has an effect on a person or a part of the body and makes them react (NOTE: The plural is **stimuli**.)

stinging /'stɪŋɪŋ/ *adjective* referring to a sharp unpleasant feeling of pricking or burning ○ *a sudden stinging sensation in the back of her leg*

stirrup /'stɪrəp/ *noun* same as **stapes**

stitch /stɪtʃ/ *noun* **1.** same as **suture** noun 2 ○ *He had three stitches in his head.* ○ *The doctor told her to come back in ten days' time to have the stitches taken out.* **2.** pain caused by cramp in the side of the body after running ○ *He had to stop running because he developed a stitch.* ■ *verb* same as **suture** ○ *They tried to stitch back the finger which had been cut off in an accident.*

stitch abscess /'stɪtʃ ˌæbses/ *noun* an abscess which forms at the site of a stitch or suture

Stokes–Adams syndrome /ˌstəʊks 'ædəmz ˌsɪndrəʊm/ *noun* a loss of consciousness due to the stopping of the action of the heart because of asystole or fibrillation [After William Stokes (1804–78), Irish physician; Robert Adams (1791–1875), Irish surgeon.]

stoma /'stəʊmə/ *noun* any opening into a cavity in the body (NOTE: The plural is **stomata**.)

stomach /'stʌmək/ *noun* **1.** the part of the body shaped like a bag, into which food passes after being swallowed and where the process of digestion continues ○ *She complained of pains in the stomach or of stomach pains.* ○ *He has had stomach trouble for some time.* See illustration at **DIGESTIVE SYSTEM** in Supplement **2.** the abdomen (*informal*) ○ *He had been kicked in the stomach.* (NOTE: For other terms referring to the stomach, see words beginning with **gastr-, gastro-**.)

stomach ache /'stʌmək eɪk/ *noun* pain in the abdomen or stomach, caused by eating too much food or by an infection

stomach cramp /'stʌmək kræmp/ *noun* a sharp spasm of the stomach muscles

stomach hernia /'stʌmək ˌhɜːniə/ *noun* same as **gastrocele**

stomach pump /'stʌmək pʌmp/ *noun* an instrument for sucking out the contents of the stomach, e.g. to extract a poison that has been swallowed

stomach upset /'stʌmək ˌʌpset/ *noun* a slight infection of the stomach ○ *She is in bed with a stomach upset.* Also called **upset stomach**

stomach washout /ˌstʌmək 'wɒʃaʊt/ *noun* same as **gastric lavage**

stomal /'stəʊm(ə)l/ *adjective* referring to a stoma

stomat- /stəʊmət/ *prefix* same as **stomato-** (used before vowels)

stomatitis /ˌstəʊmə'taɪtɪs/ *noun* inflammation of the inside of the mouth

stomato- /stəʊmətə/ *prefix* referring to the mouth

stomatology /ˌstəʊmə'tɒlədʒi/ *noun* a branch of medicine which studies diseases of the mouth

-stomy /stəmi/ *suffix* meaning an operation to make an opening

stone /stəʊn/ *noun* **1.** same as **calculus** (*informal*) (NOTE: For other terms referring to stones, see words beginning with **lith-, litho-**, or ending with **-lith**.) **2.** a measure of weight equal to 14 pounds or 6.35 kilograms ○ *He tried to lose weight and lost three stone.* ○ *She weighs eight stone ten (i.e. 8 stone 10 pounds).*

stool /stuːl/ *noun* **1.** an act of emptying the bowels **2.** a piece of solid waste matter which is passed out of the bowels ○ *an abnormal stool* ○ *loose stools* ○ *a stool test* (NOTE: Often used in the plural.) ■ *verb* to pass a piece of solid matter out of the bowels

strabismal /strə'bɪzm(ə)l/ *adjective* with the eyes focusing on different points

strabismus /strə'bɪzməs/ *noun* a condition in which the eyes focus on different points. Also called **squint, heterotropia**

strabotomy /strə'bɒtəmi/ *noun* a surgical operation to divide the muscles of the eye in order to correct a squint

strain /streɪn/ *noun* **1.** a condition in which a muscle has been stretched or torn by a strong or sudden movement **2.** a group of microorganisms which are different from others of the same type ○ *a new strain of influenza virus* **3.** nervous tension and stress ○ *Her work is causing her a lot of strain.* ○ *He is suffering from nervous strain and needs to relax.* ■ *verb* to stretch a muscle too far ○ *He strained his back lifting the table.* ○ *She had to leave the game with a strained calf muscle.* ○ *The effort of running upstairs strained his heart.*

strangulated /ˈstræŋɡjʊleɪtɪd/ *adjective* referring to part of the body which is caught in an opening in such a way that the circulation of blood is stopped

strangulated hernia /ˌstræŋɡjʊleɪtɪd ˈhɜːniə/ *noun* a condition in which part of the intestine is squeezed in a hernia and the supply of blood to it is cut off

strangulation /ˌstræŋɡjʊˈleɪʃ(ə)n/ *noun* the act of squeezing a passage in the body

strangury /ˈstræŋɡjʊri/ *noun* a condition in which very little urine is passed, although the person wants to urinate, caused by a bladder disorder or by a stone in the urethra

Strategic Health Authority /strəˌtiːdʒɪk ˈhelθ ɔːˌθɒrɪti/ *noun* in the UK, an organisation, accountable to government, that assesses the health needs of local people and ensures that local health services are commissioned and provided to meet those needs. Abbreviation **SHA**

stratified /ˈstrætɪfaɪd/ *adjective* made of several layers

stratified epithelium /ˌstrætɪfaɪd epɪ ˈθiːliəm/ *noun* epithelium formed of several layers of cells

strawberry mark /ˈstrɔːb(ə)ri mɑːk/ *noun* a red birthmark in children, which will often disappear in later life

streak /striːk/ *noun* a long thin line of a different colour

strepto- /streptə/ *prefix* referring to organisms which grow in chains

streptococcal /ˌstreptəˈkɒk(ə)l/ *adjective* caused by a streptococcus

streptococcus /ˌstreptəˈkɒkəs/ *noun* a genus of bacteria which grows in long chains, and causes fevers such as scarlet fever, tonsillitis and rheumatic fever (NOTE: The plural is **streptococci.**)

streptokinase /ˌstreptəˈkaɪneɪz/ *noun* an enzyme formed by streptococci which can break down blood clots and is therefore used in the treatment of myocardial infarction

streptolysin /strepˈtɒləsɪn/ *noun* a toxin produced by streptococci in rheumatic fever, which acts to destroy red blood cells

stress /stres/ *noun* **1.** physical pressure on an object or part of the body **2.** a factor or combination of factors in a person's life which make him or her feel tired and anxious **3.** a condition in which an outside influence such as overwork or a mental or emotional state such as anxiety changes the working of the body and can affect the hormone balance

stress disorder /ˈstres dɪsˌɔːdə/ *noun* a disorder caused by stress

stress fracture /ˈstres ˌfræktʃə/ *noun* a fracture of a bone caused by excessive force, as in some types of sport. Also called **fatigue fracture**

stress incontinence /ˈstres ɪnˌkɒntɪnəns/ *noun* a condition in women in which the muscles in the floor of the pelvis become incapable of retaining urine when the intra-abdominal pressure is raised by coughing or laughing

stress reaction /ˈstres riˌækʃən/ *noun* a response to an outside stimulus which disturbs the usual physiological balance of the body

stress-related illness /ˌstres rɪˌleɪtɪd ˈɪlnəs/ *noun* an illness which is due in part or completely to stress

stretch /stretʃ/ *verb* to pull something out, or make something longer

stretch mark /ˈstretʃ mɑːk/ *noun* a mark on the skin of the abdomen of a pregnant woman or of a woman who has recently given birth. ◊ **striae gravidarum**

stretch reflex /ˈstretʃ ˌriːfleks/ *noun* a reflex reaction of a muscle which contracts after being stretched

stria /ˈstraɪə/ *noun* a pale line on skin which is stretched, as in obese people (NOTE: The plural is **striae.**)

striae gravidarum /ˌstraɪiː ˌɡrævɪˈdeərəm/ *plural noun* the lines on the skin of the abdomen of a pregnant woman or of a woman who has recently given birth

striated /straɪˈeɪtɪd/ *adjective* marked with pale lines

striated muscle /straɪˈeɪtɪd ˌmʌs(ə)l/ *noun* a type of muscle found in skeletal muscles whose movements are controlled by the central nervous system. Also called **striped muscle**

stricture /ˈstrɪktʃə/ *noun* the narrowing of a passage in the body

stricturoplasty /ˈstrɪktʃərəʊˌplæsti/ *noun* a surgical operation in which a part of the intestine is widened

stridor /ˈstraɪdɔː/, **stridulus** /ˈstraɪdjʊləs/ *noun* a sharp high sound made when air passes an obstruction in the larynx. ◊ **laryngismus**

striped muscle /ˈstraɪpt ˌmʌs(ə)l/ *noun* same as **striated muscle**

stroke /strəʊk/ *noun* same as **cerebrovascular accident** ○ *He had a stroke and died.* ○ *She was* *paralysed after a stroke.* ■ *verb* to touch something or someone softly with the fingers

stroke patient /'strəʊk ˌpeɪʃ(ə)nt/ *noun* a person who has had a stroke

stroke volume /'strəʊk ˌvɒljuːm/ *noun* the amount of blood pumped out of the ventricle at each heartbeat

stroma /'strəʊmə/ *noun* tissue which supports an organ, as opposed to the parenchyma or functioning tissues in the organ

strontium /'strɒntiəm/ *noun* a metallic element (NOTE: The chemical symbol is **Sr**.)

strontium-90 /ˌstrɒntiəm 'naɪnti/ *noun* an isotope of strontium which is formed in the fallout of nuclear reactions and, because it is part of the fallout of nuclear explosions, can enter the food chain, attacking in particular the bones of humans and animals

strychnine /'strɪkniːn/ *noun* a poisonous alkaloid drug, made from the seeds of a tropical tree, and formerly used in small doses as a tonic

Stryker frame /'straɪkə freɪm/ *noun* a special piece of equipment on which a patient can easily be rotated by a nurse, used for patients with spinal injuries

ST segment /ˌes 'tiː ˌsegmənt/, **S-T segment** *noun* the part of an electrocardiogram, between the points labelled S and T, immediately before the last phase of the cardiac cycle. ◊ **PQRST complex**

study /'stʌdi/ *noun* the act of examining something to learn about it ○ *She's making a study of diseases of small children.* ○ *They have finished their study of the effects of the drug on pregnant women.* ■ *verb* to examine something to learn about it ○ *He's studying pharmacy.* ○ *Doctors are studying the results of the screening programme.*

stupe /stjuːp/ *noun* a wet medicated dressing used as a compress

stupor /'stjuːpə/ *noun* a state of being semiconscious ○ *After the party several people were found lying on the floor in a stupor.*

Sturge-Weber syndrome /ˌstɜːdʒ 'webə ˌsɪndrəʊm/ *noun* a dark red mark on the skin above the eye, together with similar marks inside the brain, possibly causing epileptic fits

stuttering /'stʌtərɪŋ/ *noun* same as **stammering**

stye /staɪ/ *noun* same as **hordeolum**

stylet /'staɪlət/ *noun* **1.** a very thin piece of wire which is put into a catheter or hollow needle so that it will not become blocked when it is not being used **2.** any long thin pointed instrument

stylo- /staɪləʊ/ *prefix* referring to the styloid process

styloid /'staɪlɔɪd/ *adjective* pointed

styloid process /'staɪlɔɪd ˌprəʊses/ *noun* a piece of bone which projects from the bottom of the temporal bone

stylus /'staɪləs/ *noun* a long thin instrument used for applying antiseptics or ointments to the skin

styptic /'stɪptɪk/ *noun* a substance which stops bleeding ■ *adjective* used to stop bleeding

styptic pencil /ˌstɪptɪk 'pens(ə)l/ *noun* a stick of alum, used to stop bleeding from small cuts

sub- /sʌb/ *prefix* underneath or below

subacute /ˌsʌbə'kjuːt/ *adjective* referring to a condition which is not acute but may become chronic

subacute bacterial endocarditis /ˌsʌbəkjuːt bæk,tɪəriəl ˌendəʊkɑː'daɪtɪs/, **subacute infective endocarditis** /ˌsʌbəkjuːt ɪn,fektɪv ˌendəʊkɑː'daɪtɪs/ *noun* an infection of the membrane covering the inner surfaces of the heart caused by bacteria

subacute combined degeneration of the spinal cord /ˌsʌbəkjuːt kəm,baɪnd dɪ ˌdʒenəreɪʃ(ə)n əv ðə 'spaɪn(ə)l kɔːd/ *noun* a condition, caused by Vitamin B_{12} deficiency, in which the sensory and motor nerves in the spinal cord become damaged and the person has difficulty in moving

subacute sclerosing panencephalitis /ˌsʌbə,kjuːt sklə,rəʊsɪŋ ˌpænenkefə'laɪtɪs/ *noun* a rare inflammatory disease of the brain, mostly affecting children. It is linked to having measles at a very young age, and is usually fatal.

subarachnoid /ˌsʌbə'ræknɔɪd/ *adjective* beneath the arachnoid membrane

subarachnoid haemorrhage /ˌsʌbə,ræknɔɪd 'hem(ə)rɪdʒ/ *noun* bleeding into the cerebrospinal fluid of the subarachnoid space

subarachnoid space /ˌsʌbə,ræknɔɪd 'speɪs/ *noun* a space between the arachnoid membrane and the pia mater in the brain, containing cerebrospinal fluid

subclavian /sʌb'kleɪviən/ *adjective* underneath the clavicle

subclavian artery /sʌb,kleɪviən 'ɑːtəri/ *noun* one of two arteries branching from the aorta on the left and from the innominate artery on the right, continuing into the brachial arteries and supplying blood to each arm

subclavian vein /sʌb,kleɪviən 'veɪn/ *noun* one of the veins which continue the axillary veins into the brachiocephalic vein

subclinical /sʌb'klɪnɪk(ə)l/ *adjective* referring to a disease which is present in the body, but which has not yet developed any symptoms

subconscious /sʌb'kɒnʃəs/ *noun* the part of a person's mental processes which he or she is not aware of most of the time, but which can affect his or her actions ■ *adjective* present in the mind although a person is not aware of it

subcostal plane /sʌb,kɒst(ə)l 'pleɪn/ *noun* an imaginary horizontal line drawn across the front of the abdomen below the ribs

subcutaneous /,sʌbkjuːˈteɪniəs/ *adjective* under the skin. Abbreviation **s.c.**

subcutaneous injection /,sʌbkjuː,teɪniəs ɪnˈdʒekʃən/ *noun* same as **hypodermic injection**

subcutaneous oedema /,sʌbkjuː,teɪniəs ɪˈdiːmə/ *noun* a fluid collecting under the skin, usually at the ankles

subcutaneous tissue /,sʌbkjuː,teɪniəs ˈtɪʃuː/ *noun* fatty tissue under the skin

subdural /sʌbˈdjʊərəl/ *adjective* between the dura mater and the arachnoid

subdural haematoma /sʌb,djʊərəl ,hiːmə ˈtəʊmə/ *noun* a haematoma between the dura mater and the arachnoid which displaces the brain, caused by a blow on the head

subglottis /sʌbˈɡlɒtɪs/ *noun* the lowest part of the laryngeal cavity, below the vocal folds

subinvolution /,sʌbɪnvəˈluːʃ(ə)n/ *noun* a condition in which a part of the body does not go back to its former size and shape after having swollen or stretched, as in the case of the uterus after childbirth

subjective /səbˈdʒektɪv/ *adjective* representing the views or feelings of the person concerned and not impartial ○ *The psychiatrist gave a subjective opinion on the patient's problem.* Compare **objective**

sublimate /ˈsʌblɪmeɪt/ *noun* a deposit left when a vapour condenses ■ *verb* to convert violent emotion into action which is not antisocial

sublimation /,sʌblɪˈmeɪʃ(ə)n/ *noun* a psychological process in which violent emotions which would otherwise be expressed in antisocial behaviour are directed into actions which are socially acceptable

subliminal /sʌbˈlɪmɪn(ə)l/ *adjective* too slight to be noticed by the senses

sublingual /sʌbˈlɪŋwəl/ *adjective* under the tongue

sublingual gland /sʌbˈlɪŋwəl ɡlænd/ *noun* a salivary gland under the tongue

subluxation /,sʌblʌkˈseɪʃ(ə)n/ *noun* a condition in which a joint is partially dislocated

submandibular gland /,sʌbmænˈdɪbjʊlə ,ɡlænd/, **submaxillary gland** /sʌbˈmæksɪləri ,ɡlænd/ *noun* a salivary gland on each side of the lower jaw

submental /sʌbˈment(ə)l/ *adjective* under the chin

submucosa /,sʌbmjuːˈkəʊsə/ *noun* tissue under a mucous membrane

submucous /sʌbˈmjuːkəs/ *adjective* under a mucous membrane

submucous resection /sʌb,mjuːkəs rɪ ˈsekʃən/ *noun* the removal of a bent cartilage from the septum in the nose. Abbreviation **SMR**

subnormal /sʌbˈnɔːm(ə)l/ *adjective* with a mind which has not developed fully (NOTE: This term is regarded as offensive.)

subphrenic /sʌbˈfrenɪk/ *adjective* under the diaphragm

subphrenic abscess /sʌb,frenɪk ˈæbses/ *noun* an abscess which forms between the diaphragm and the liver

substance /ˈsʌbstəns/ *noun* a chemical material, e.g. a drug ○ *toxic substances released into the bloodstream* ○ *He became addicted to certain substances.*

substance abuse /ˈsʌbstəns ə,bjuːs/, **substance misuse** /ˈsʌbstəns mɪs,juːz/ *noun* the misuse or excessive use of drugs, alcohol or other substances for pleasure or to satisfy addiction, which often causes health, emotional or social problems for the user

substitution /,sʌbstɪˈtjuːʃ(ə)n/ *noun* the act of replacing one thing with another

substitution therapy /,sʌbstɪˈtjuːʃ(ə)n ,θerəpi/ *noun* a way of treating a condition by using a different drug from the one used before

substrate /ˈsʌbstreɪt/ *noun* a substance which is acted on by an enzyme

subsultus /sʌbˈsʌltəs/ *noun* a twitching of the muscles and tendons, caused by fever

subtertian fever /sʌb,tɜːʃ(ə)n ˈfiːvə/ *noun* a type of malaria, where the fever is present most of the time

subtotal gastrectomy /,sʌbtəʊt(ə)l ɡæ ˈstrektəmi/ *noun* the surgical removal of all but the top part of the stomach in contact with the diaphragm

subtotal hysterectomy /,sʌbtəʊt(ə)l ,hɪstə ˈrektəmi/ *noun* the surgical removal of the uterus, but not the cervix

subtotal pancreatectomy /,sʌbtəʊt(ə)l ,pæŋkriəˈtektəmi/ *noun* the surgical removal of most of the pancreas

subungual /sʌbˈʌŋwəl/ *adjective* under a nail

succus /ˈsʌkəs/ *noun* juice secreted by an organ

succus entericus /,sʌkəs enˈterɪkəs/ *noun* juice formed of enzymes, produced in the intestine to help the digestive process

succussion /səˈkʌʃ(ə)n/ *noun* a splashing sound made when there is a large amount of liquid inside a cavity in the body, e.g. the stomach

sucrose /ˈsuːkrəʊs/ *noun* a sugar, formed of glucose and fructose, found in plants, especially in sugar cane, beet and maple syrup

suction /ˈsʌkʃən/ *noun* a force created by the action of sucking ○ *The dentist hooked a suction tube into the patient's mouth.*

sudden /ˈsʌd(ə)n/ *adjective* happening quickly

sudden death /ˌsʌd(ə)n 'deθ/ *noun* death without any identifiable cause, not preceded by an illness

sudden infant death syndrome /ˌsʌd(ə)n ˌɪnfənt 'deθ ˌsɪndrəʊm/ *noun* the sudden death of a baby under the age of about twelve months in bed, without any identifiable cause. Abbreviation **SIDS**. Also called **cot death**

sudor /'suːdɔː/ *noun* sweat

sudorific /ˌsuːdə'rɪfɪk/ *noun* a drug which makes someone sweat

suffer /'sʌfə/ *verb* **1.** to have an illness for a long period of time ○ *I suffer from headaches.* **2.** to feel pain ○ *I didn't suffer much.* **3.** to receive an injury ○ *He suffered multiple injuries in the accident.*

suffering /'sʌf(ə)rɪŋ/ *noun* the experiencing of pain over a long period of time

suffocation /ˌsʌfə'keɪʃ(ə)n/ *noun* the act of making someone become unconscious by cutting off his or her supply of air

suffusion /sə'fjuːʒ(ə)n/ *noun* the spreading of a red flush over the skin

sugar /'ʃʊɡə/ *noun* any of several sweet carbohydrates (NOTE: For other terms referring to sugar, see words beginning with **glyc-, glyco-**.)

sugar intolerance /'ʃʊɡər ɪn,tɒlərəns/ *noun* diarrhoea caused by sugar which has not been absorbed

suggestibility /sə,dʒestɪ'bɪlɪti/ *noun* a mental state in which somebody just accepts other people's ideas, attitudes or instructions, without questioning them. It is usually increased under hypnosis.

suggestible /sə'dʒestɪb(ə)l/ *adjective* easily influenced by other people

suggestion /sə'dʒestʃən/ *noun* **1.** an idea which has been mentioned ○ *The doctor didn't agree with the suggestion that the disease had been caught in the hospital.* **2.** (*in psychiatry*) the process of making a person's ideas change, by suggesting different ideas which the person can accept, such as that he or she is in fact cured

suicide /'suːɪsaɪd/ *noun* the act of killing oneself

sulcus /'sʌlkəs/ *noun* a groove or fold, especially between the gyri in the brain

sulfa drug /'sʌlfə drʌɡ/, **sulfa compound** /'sʌlfə ˌkɒmpaʊnd/ *noun* same as **sulfonamide**

sulfasalazine /ˌsʌlfə'sæləziːn/ *noun* a drug belonging to the sulfonamide group of antibacterial drugs. It is used in the treatment of ulcerative colitis and Crohn's disease, and also of severe rheumatoid arthritis.

sulfonamide /sʌl'fɒnəmaɪd/ *noun* a bacteriostatic drug, e.g. trimethoprim, used to treat bacterial infection, especially in the intestine and urinary system, but now less important due to increasing bacterial resistance

sulfonylurea /ˌsʌlfənaɪljʊ'riːə/ *noun* any of a group of drugs which lower blood sugar, used in the treatment of diabetes

sulfur /'sʌlfə/ *noun* another spelling of **sulphur**

sulphur /'sʌlfə/ *noun* a yellow non-metallic chemical element which is contained in some amino acids and is used in creams to treat some skin disorders (NOTE: The chemical symbol is **S**.)

sulphuric acid /sʌl,fjʊərɪk 'æsɪd/ *noun* a strong colourless oily corrosive acid which has many uses

sumatriptan /ˌsuːmə'trɪptæn/ *noun* a drug which helps to narrow the blood vessels, used in the treatment of acute migraine

sun blindness /'sʌn ˌblaɪndnəs/ *noun* same as **photoretinitis**

sunburn /'sʌnbɜːn/ *noun* damage to the skin by excessive exposure to sunlight

sunstroke /'sʌnstrəʊk/ *noun* a serious condition caused by excessive exposure to the sun or to hot conditions, in which the person becomes dizzy and has a high body temperature but does not perspire

super- /suːpə/ *prefix* **1.** above **2.** extremely

superciliary /ˌsuːpə'sɪliəri/ *adjective* referring to the eyebrows

superego /ˌsuːpər'iːɡəʊ/ *noun* (*in psychology*) the part of the mind which is a person's conscience, which is concerned with right and wrong

superfecundation /ˌsuːpəfiːkən'deɪʃ(ə)n/ *noun* a condition in which two or more ova produced at the same time are fertilised by different males

superfetation /ˌsuːpəfiː'teɪʃ(ə)n/ *noun* a condition in which an ovum is fertilised in a woman who is already pregnant

superficial /ˌsuːpə'fɪʃ(ə)l/ *adjective* on the surface, close to the surface or on the skin

superficial thickness burn /ˌsuːpəfɪʃ(ə)l 'θɪknəs ˌbɜːn/ *noun* same as **partial thickness burn**

superinfection /'suːpərɪn,fekʃən/ *noun* a second infection which affects the treatment of the first infection, because it is resistant to the drug used to treat the first

superior /sʊ'pɪəriə/ *adjective* (*of part of the body*) higher up than another part

superior aspect /sʊ,pɪəriə 'æspekt/ *noun* a view of the body from above

superiority complex /sʊ,pɪəri'ɒrɪti ˌkɒmpleks/ *noun* a condition in which a person feels he or she is better and more important than others and pays little attention to them

superior mesenteric artery /sʊ,pɪəriə mes(e)n,terɪk 'ɑːtəri/ *noun* one of the arteries which supply the small intestine

superior vena cava /sʊ,pɪəriə ˌviːnə 'keɪvə/ *noun* a branch of the large vein into the heart, carrying blood from the head and the top part of the body. See illustration at **HEART** in Supplement

supernumerary /ˌsuːpəˈnjuːmərəri/ *adjective* extra, more than the usual number

superovulation /ˌsuːpərˌɒvjʊˈleɪʃ(ə)n/ *noun* an increased frequency of ovulation, or production of a large number of ova at one time. It is often caused by giving a woman with infertility problems gonadotrophin hormones to stimulate ovulation.

supination /ˌsuːpɪˈneɪʃ(ə)n/ *noun* the act of turning the hand so that the palm faces upwards. Opposite **pronation**. See illustration at **ANATOMICAL TERMS** in Supplement

supinator /ˈsuːpɪneɪtə/ *noun* a muscle which turns the hand so that the palm faces upwards

supine /ˈsuːpaɪn/ *adjective* lying on the back. Opposite **prone**

supplement /ˈsʌplɪmənt/ *noun* **1.** any extra nutrients that are taken to help a specific condition when someone is not getting all they need from their food ○ *vitamin and folic acid supplements* **2.** a pill or product regarded as helpful in improving health that can be bought without a prescription. Supplements are not tested in the same way as prescription drugs. ○ *dietary or food supplements* ■ *verb* to add on or increase above what is taken usually ○ *She supplemented her diet with folic acid when she was planning a pregnancy.*

supplementary prescriber /ˌsʌplɪˈment(ə)ri prɪˌskraɪbə/ *noun* a healthcare professional who, in agreement with a patient's doctor, implements an agreed course of treatment

support hose /səˈpɔːt həʊz/ *plural noun* stockings that fit tightly to the legs, worn to help the flow of blood

supportive /səˈpɔːtɪv/ *adjective* helping or comforting someone in trouble ○ *Her family was very supportive when she was in hospital.* ○ *The local health authority has been very supportive of the hospital management.*

support worker /səˈpɔːt ˌwɜːkə/ *noun* someone who assists registered health service professionals as part of a team, e.g. as a nursing auxiliary or assistant, or in specialist areas such as mental health, speech therapy or physiotherapy

suppository /səˈpɒzɪt(ə)ri/ *noun* a piece of a soluble material such as glycerine jelly containing a drug, which is placed in the rectum to act as lubricant, or in the vagina, to treat disorders such as vaginitis, and is dissolved by the body's fluids

suppress /səˈpres/ *verb* to reduce the action of something completely, e.g. to remove a symptom or to stop the release of a hormone ○ *a course of treatment which suppresses the painful irritation* ○ *The drug suppresses the body's natural instinct to reject the transplanted tissue.* ○ *The release of adrenaline from the adrenal cortex is suppressed.*

suppression /səˈpreʃ(ə)n/ *noun* the act of suppressing something ○ *the suppression of allergic responses* ○ *the suppression of a hormone*

suppressor T-cell /səˌpresə ˈtiː ˌsel/ *noun* a T-cell which stops or reduces the immune response to an antigen of B-cells and other T-cells

suppuration /ˌsʌpjʊˈreɪʃ(ə)n/ *noun* the formation and discharge of pus

supra- /suːprə/ *prefix* above or over

supraglottis /ˌsuːprəˈɡlɒtɪs/ *noun* the part of the larynx above the vocal folds, including the epiglottis

supraorbital /ˌsuːprəˈɔːbɪt(ə)l/ *adjective* above the orbit of the eye

supraorbital ridge /ˌsuːprəˌɔːbɪt(ə)l ˈrɪdʒ/ *noun* the ridge of bone above the eye, covered by the eyebrow

suprapubic /ˌsuːprəˈpjuːbɪk/ *adjective* above the pubic bone or pubic area

suprarenal /ˌsuːprəˈriːn(ə)l/ *adjective* above the kidneys ■ *noun* same as **suprarenal gland**

suprarenal gland /ˌsuːprəˈriːn(ə)l ɡlænd/, **suprarenal** /ˌsuːprəˈriːn(ə)l/ *noun* one of two endocrine glands at the top of the kidneys, which secrete adrenaline and other hormones

suprarenal medulla /ˌsuːprəriːn(ə)l meˈdʌlə/ *noun* same as **adrenal medulla**

suprasternal /ˌsuːprəˈstɜːn(ə)l/ *adjective* above the sternum

supraventricular tachycardia /ˌsʌbven ˌtrɪkjʊlə ˌtækɪˈkɑːdiə/ *noun* tachycardia coming from the upper chambers of the heart

surfactant /sɜːˈfæktənt/ *noun* a substance in the alveoli of the lungs which keeps the surfaces of the lungs wet and prevents lung collapse

surgeon /ˈsɜːdʒən/ *noun* a doctor who specialises in surgery (NOTE: Although surgeons are doctors, in the UK they are traditionally called 'Mr' and not 'Dr', so 'Dr Smith' may be a GP, but 'Mr Smith' is a surgeon.)

surgeon general /ˌsɜːdʒən ˈdʒen(ə)rəl/ *noun* US a government official responsible for all aspects of public health

surgery /ˈsɜːdʒəri/ *noun* **1.** the treatment of diseases or disorders by procedures which require an operation to cut into, to remove or to manipulate tissue, organs or parts ○ *The patient will need plastic surgery to remove the scars he received in the accident.* ○ *The surgical ward is for patients waiting for surgery.* ○ *Two of our patients had to have surgery.* ○ *She will have to undergo surgery.* **2.** a room where a doctor or dentist sees and examines patients ○ *There are ten patients waiting in the surgery.* ○ *Surgery hours are from 8.30 in the morning to 6.00 at night.*

surgical /ˈsɜːdʒɪk(ə)l/ *adjective* referring to surgery ○ *All surgical instruments must be sterilised.*

surgical diathermy /ˌsɜːdʒɪk(ə)l ˌdaɪə'θɜːmi/ *noun* a procedure which uses a knife or electrode which is heated by a strong electric current until it coagulates tissue

surgical fixation /ˌsɜːdʒɪk(ə)l fɪk'seɪʃ(ə)n/ *noun* a method of immobilising something such as a bone either externally by the use of a splint or internally by a metal plate and screws

surgical gloves /'sɜːdʒɪk(ə)l glʌvz/ *plural noun* thin plastic gloves worn by surgeons

surgical intervention /ˌsɜːdʒɪk(ə)l ˌɪntə'venʃən/ *noun* the treatment of disease or other condition by surgery

surgical neck /ˌsɜːdʒɪk(ə)l 'nek/ *noun* the narrow part at the top of the humerus, where the arm can easily be broken

surgical ward /'sɜːdʒɪk(ə)l wɔːd/ *noun* a ward for patients who have undergone surgery

surgical wound /'sɜːdʒɪk(ə)l wuːnd/ *noun* an incision made during a surgical operation

surrogate /'sʌrəgət/ *adjective* taking the place of ■ *noun* someone or something that takes the place of another person or thing

surrogate mother a woman who has a child by artificial insemination for a woman who cannot become pregnant, with the intention of handing the child over to her when it is born

susceptibility /səˌseptɪ'bɪlɪti/ *noun* lack of resistance to a disease

suspension /sə'spenʃən/ *noun* a liquid with solid particles in it

suspensory /sə'spensəri/ *adjective* hanging down

suspensory bandage /səˌspensəri 'bændɪdʒ/ *noun* a bandage to hold a part of the body which hangs

suspensory ligament /səˌspensəri 'lɪgəmənt/ *noun* a ligament which holds a part of the body in position. See illustration at EYE in Supplement

sustentacular /ˌsʌstən'tækjʊlə/ *adjective* referring to a sustentaculum

sustentaculum /ˌsʌstən'tækjʊləm/ *noun* a part of the body which supports another part

suture /'suːtʃə/ *noun* **1.** a fixed joint where two bones are fused together, especially the bones in the skull **2.** a procedure for attaching the sides of an incision or wound with thread, so that healing can take place. Also called **stitch 3.** a thread used for attaching the sides of a wound so that they can heal ■ *verb* to attach the sides of a wound or incision together with thread so that healing can take place. Also called **stitch**

suxamethonium /ˌsʌksəmɪ'θəʊniəm/ *noun* a drug similar to acetylcholine in structure, used as a muscle relaxant during surgery

swab /swɒb/ *noun* **1.** a cotton wool pad, often attached to a small stick, used, e.g., to clean a wound, to apply ointment or to take a specimen **2.** a specimen taken with a swab ○ *a cervical swab*

swallowing /'swɒləʊɪŋ/ *noun* same as **deglutition**

Swan-Ganz catheter /ˌswɒn 'gæntz ˌkæθɪtə/ *noun* a special catheter which can be floated through the right chamber of the heart into the pulmonary artery. The balloon at its tip is then inflated to measure arterial pressure.

sweat /swet/ *noun* a salty liquid produced by the sweat glands to cool the body as the liquid evaporates from the skin ○ *Sweat was running off the end of his nose.* ○ *Her hands were covered with sweat.* Also called **perspiration** ■ *verb* to produce moisture through the sweat glands and onto the skin ○ *After working in the fields she was sweating.*

sweat duct /'swet dʌkt/ *noun* a thin tube connecting the sweat gland with the surface of the skin

sweat gland /'swet glænd/ *noun* a gland which produces sweat, situated beneath the dermis and connected to the skin surface by a sweat duct

sweat pore /'swet pɔː/ *noun* a hole in the skin through which the sweat comes out

swell /swel/ *verb* to become larger, or cause something to become larger ○ *The disease affects the lymph glands, making them swell.* ○ *The doctor noticed that the patient had swollen glands in his neck.* ○ *She finds her swollen ankles painful.* (NOTE: **swelling – swelled – swollen**)

swelling /'swelɪŋ/ *noun* a condition in which fluid accumulates in tissue, making the tissue become large ○ *They applied a cold compress to try to reduce the swelling.*

sycosis /saɪ'kəʊsɪs/ *noun* a bacterial infection of hair follicles

sycosis barbae /saɪˌkəʊsɪs 'bɑːbi/ *noun* an infection of hair follicles on the sides of the face and chin. Also called **barber's itch**, **barber's rash**

Sydenham's chorea /ˌsɪdnəmz kɒ'riːə/ *noun* temporary chorea affecting children, frequently associated with endocarditis and rheumatism [Described 1686. After Thomas Sydenham (1624–89), English physician.]

symbiosis /ˌsɪmbaɪ'əʊsɪs/ *noun* a condition in which two organisms exist together and help each other to survive

symblepharon /sɪm'blefərɒn/ *noun* a condition in which the eyelid sticks to the eyeball

symbol /'sɪmbəl/ *noun* a sign or letter which means something

Syme's amputation /ˌsaɪmz æmpjʊ'teɪʃ(ə)n/ *noun* a surgical operation to amputate the foot above the ankle [Described 1842. After James Syme (1799–1870), Edinburgh surgeon and teacher; one of the first to adopt antisepsis

(Joseph Lister was his son-in-law), and also among the early users of anaesthesia.]

symmetry /ˈsɪmətri/ *noun* the regularity of structure and distribution of parts of the body, each side of the body being structurally similar to the other

sympathectomy /ˌsɪmpəˈθektəmi/ *noun* a surgical operation to cut part of the sympathetic nervous system, as a treatment of high blood pressure

sympathetic /ˌsɪmpəˈθetɪk/ *adjective* **1.** feeling or showing shared feelings, pity or compassion **2.** relating to or belonging to the sympathetic nervous system, or to one of its parts

sympathetic nervous system /ˌsɪmpəθetɪk ˈnɜːvəs ˌsɪstəm/, **sympathetic system** /ˌsɪmpəθetɪk ˈsɪstəm/ *noun* part of the autonomic nervous system, which leaves the spinal cord from the thoracic and lumbar regions to go to various important organs such as the heart, the lungs and the sweat glands, and which prepares the body for emergencies and vigorous muscular activity. ◊ **parasympathetic nervous system**

sympatholytic /ˌsɪmpəθəʊˈlɪtɪk/ *noun* a drug which stops the sympathetic nervous system working

sympathomimetic /ˌsɪmpəθəʊmɪˈmetɪk/ *adjective* referring to a drug such as dopamine hydrochloride which stimulates the activity of the sympathetic nervous system and is used in cardiac shock following myocardial infarction and in cardiac surgery

sympathy /ˈsɪmpəθi/ *noun* **1.** the feeling or expression of pity or sorrow for the pain or distress of somebody else **2.** the relationship between people which causes one of them to provoke a similar condition to their own in the other one. For example, when the first person yawns, the second feels an urge to yawn too. **3.** the influence produced on any part of the body by disease or change in another part

symphysis /ˈsɪmfəsɪs/ *noun* the point where two bones are joined by cartilage which makes the joint rigid

symphysis pubis /ˌsɪmfəsɪs ˈpjuːbɪs/ *noun* same as **pubic symphysis**

symptom /ˈsɪmptəm/ *noun* a change in the way the body works or a change in the body's appearance, which shows that a disease or disorder is present and which the person is aware of ○ *The symptoms of hay fever are a running nose and eyes.* ○ *A doctor must study the symptoms before making his diagnosis.* ○ *The patient presented all the symptoms of rheumatic fever.* (NOTE: If a symptom is noticed only by the doctor, it is a **sign**.)

symptomatic /ˌsɪmptəˈmætɪk/ *adjective* being a symptom of something ○ *The rash is symptomatic of measles.*

symptomatology /ˌsɪmptəməˈtɒlədʒi/ *noun* a branch of medicine concerned with the study of symptoms. Also called **semeiology**

syn- /sɪn/ *prefix* joint, or fused

synalgia /sɪˈnældʒə/ *noun* a pain which is felt in one part of the body, but is caused by a condition in another part, e.g. pain in the groin which can be a symptom of a kidney stone or pain in the right shoulder which can indicate gall bladder infection. Also called **referred pain**

synapse /ˈsaɪnæps/ *noun* a point in the nervous system where the axons of neurones are in contact with the dendrites of other neurones ■ *verb* to link something with a neurone

synaptic /sɪˈnæptɪk/ *adjective* referring to a synapse

synarthrosis /ˌsɪnɑːˈθrəʊsɪs/ *noun* a joint, e.g. in the skull, where the bones have fused together

synchondrosis /ˌsɪnkɒnˈdrəʊsɪs/ *noun* a joint, as in children, where the bones are linked by cartilage, before the cartilage has changed to bone

synchysis /ˈsɪŋkɪsɪs/ *noun* a condition in which the vitreous humour in the eye becomes soft

syncope /ˈsɪŋkəpi/ *noun* a condition in which someone becomes unconscious for a short time because of reduced flow of blood to the brain. Also called **fainting fit**

syndactyly /sɪnˈdæktɪli/, **syndactylism** /sɪnˈdæktɪlɪz(ə)m/ *noun* a condition in which two toes or fingers are joined together with tissue

syndesm- /sɪndesm/, **syndesmo-** /sɪndesməʊ/ *prefix* referring to ligaments

syndesmology /ˌsɪndesˈmɒlədʒi/ *noun* a branch of medicine which studies joints

syndesmosis /ˌsɪndesˈməʊsɪs/ *noun* a joint where the bones are tightly linked by ligaments

syndrome /ˈsɪndrəʊm/ *noun* a group of symptoms and other changes in the body's functions which, when taken together, show that a particular disease is present

synechia /sɪˈnekiə/ *noun* a condition in which the iris sticks to another part of the eye

synergism /ˈsɪnədʒɪz(ə)m/ *noun* a situation where two or more things are acting together in such a way that both are more effective. Also called **synergy**

synergist /ˈsɪnədʒɪst/ *noun* a muscle or drug which acts with another and increases the effectiveness of both

synergy /ˈsɪnədʒi/ *noun* same as **synergism**

syngeneic /ˌsɪndʒəˈniːɪk/ *adjective* referring to individuals or tissues that have an identical or closely similar genetic make-up, especially one that will allow the transplanting of tissue without provoking an immune response

synostosed /ˈsɪnɒˌstəʊzd/ *adjective* (of bones) fused together with new bone tissue

synostosis /ˌsɪnɒ'stəʊsɪs/ *noun* the fusing of two bones together by the formation of new bone tissue

synovectomy /ˌsɪnəʊ'vektəmi/ *noun* a surgical operation to remove the synovial membrane of a joint

synovia /saɪ'nəʊviə/ *noun* same as **synovial fluid**

synovial /saɪ'nəʊviəl/ *adjective* referring to the synovium

synovial fluid /saɪˌnəʊviəl 'fluːɪd/ *noun* a fluid secreted by a synovial membrane to lubricate a joint. See illustration at **SYNOVIAL JOINT** in Supplement

synovial joint /saɪˌnəʊviəl 'dʒɔɪnt/ *noun* a joint where the two bones are separated by a space filled with synovial fluid which nourishes and lubricates the surfaces of the bones. Also called **diarthrosis**

synovial membrane /saɪˌnəʊviəl 'membreɪn/, **synovium** *noun* a smooth membrane which forms the inner lining of the capsule covering a joint and secretes the fluid which lubricates the joint. See illustration at **SYNOVIAL JOINT** in Supplement

synovitis /ˌsaɪnə'vaɪtɪs/ *noun* inflammation of the synovial membrane

synthesis /'sɪnθəsɪs/ *noun* **1.** the process of combining different ideas or objects into a new whole **2.** a new unified whole resulting from the combination of different ideas or objects **3.** the formation of compounds through chemical reactions involving simpler compounds or elements **4.** in psychiatry, the fusing together of all the various elements of the personality (NOTE: The plural is **syntheses**.)

synthesise /'sɪnθəsaɪz/, **synthesize** *verb* to make a chemical compound from its separate components ○ *Essential amino acids cannot be synthesised.* ○ *The body cannot synthesise essential fatty acids and has to absorb them from food.*

synthetic /sɪn'θetɪk/ *adjective* made by humans, made artificially

syphilis /'sɪfəlɪs/ *noun* a sexually transmitted disease caused by a spirochaete *Treponema pallidum*

syring- /sɪrɪndʒ/ *prefix* same as **syringo-** (*used before vowels*)

syringe /sɪ'rɪndʒ/ *noun* a medical instrument made of a tube with a plunger which either slides down inside the tube, forcing the contents out through a needle as in an injection, or slides up the tube, allowing a liquid to be sucked into it ■ *verb* to wash out the ears using a syringe

syringo- /sɪrɪŋgəʊ/ *prefix* referring to tubes, especially the central canal of the spinal cord

syringomyelia /sɪˌrɪŋgəʊmaɪ'iːliə/ *noun* a disease which forms cavities in the neck section of the spinal cord, affecting the nerves so that the person loses the sense of touch and pain

syringomyelitis /sɪˌrɪŋgəʊmaɪə'laɪtɪs/ *noun* a swelling of the spinal cord, which results in the formation of cavities in it

syringomyelocele /sɪˌrɪŋgəʊ'maɪələʊsiːl/ *noun* a severe form of spina bifida where the spinal cord pushes through a hole in the spine

system /'sɪstəm/ *noun* **1.** the body as a whole ○ *Amputation of a limb gives a serious shock to the system.* **2.** the arrangement of particular parts of the body so that they work together ○ *the lymphatic system*

systemic /sɪ'stiːmɪk/ *adjective* referring to or affecting the whole body ○ *Septicaemia is a systemic infection.*

systemic circulation /sɪˌstiːmɪk ˌsɜːkjʊ'leɪʃ(ə)n/ *noun* the circulation of blood around the whole body, except the lungs, starting with the aorta and returning through the venae cavae

systemic lupus erythematosus /sɪˌstiːmɪk ˌluːpəs ˌerɪθiːmə'təʊsəs/ *noun* one of several collagen diseases which are forms of lupus, where red patches form on the skin and spread throughout the body. Abbreviation **SLE**

systole /'sɪstəli/ *noun* a phase in the beating of the heart when it contracts as it pumps blood out

systolic /sɪ'stɒlɪk/ *adjective* referring to the systole

systolic murmur /sɪˌstɒlɪk 'mɜːmə/ *noun* a sound produced during systole which indicates an unusual condition of a heart valve

systolic pressure /sɪˌstɒlɪk 'preʃə/ *noun* the high point of blood pressure which occurs during the systole. Systolic pressure is always higher than diastolic pressure.

T

TAB *abbreviation* typhoid-paratyphoid A and B ○ *He was given a TAB injection.* ○ *TAB injections give only temporary immunity against paratyphoid.* ◊ **TAB vaccine**

tabes /'teɪbiːz/ *noun* a condition in which someone is wasting away

tabes dorsalis /ˌteɪbiːz dɔː'seɪlɪs/ *noun* a disease of the nervous system, caused by advanced syphilis, in which the person loses the sense of feeling, control of the bladder and the ability to coordinate movements of the legs, and has severe pains. Also called **locomotor ataxia**

tablet /'tæblət/ *noun* **1.** a small flat round object containing medicine that is taken by swallowing ○ *a bottle of aspirin tablets* ○ *Take two tablets three times a day.* **2.** any tablet, pill or capsule taken by swallowing (*informal*)

taboparesis /ˌteɪbəupə'riːsɪs/ *noun* the final stage of syphilis in which the person has locomotor ataxia, general paralysis and mental deterioration

TAB vaccine /ˌtiː eɪ 'biː ˌvæksiːn/ *noun* a vaccine which immunises against typhoid fever and paratyphoid A and B

tachy- /tæki/ *prefix* fast

tachycardia /ˌtæki'kɑːdiə/ *noun* a rapid beating of the heart

tachyphrasia /ˌtæki'freɪziə/, **tachyphasia** /ˌtæki'feɪziə/ *noun* a particularly rapid way of speaking, as occurs with some people with mental disorders

tachypnoea /ˌtækɪp'niːə/ *noun* very fast breathing

tacrolimus /ˌtækrə'liːməs/ *noun* a powerful immunosuppressant drug used to reduce the risk of organ transplant rejection

tactile /'tæktaɪl/ *adjective* able to be sensed by touch

taeniasis /tiː'naɪəsɪs/ *noun* infestation of the intestines with tapeworms

Tagamet /'tægəmet/ a trade name for a preparation of cimetidine

tai chi /ˌtaɪ 'tʃiː/, **t'ai chi** *noun* an ancient Chinese system of exercises designed for health, self-defence and spiritual development

talc /tælk/ *noun* a soft white powder used to dust on irritated skin

talipes /'tælɪpiːz/ *noun* a foot with a shape that does not allow usual walking, a congenital condition. Also called **cleft foot**, **club foot**

talo- /teɪləu/ *prefix* referring to the ankle bone

talus /'teɪləs/ *noun* the top bone in the tarsus which articulates with the tibia and fibula in the leg, and with the calcaneus in the heel. Also called **anklebone**. See illustration at FOOT in Supplement (NOTE: The plural is **tali**.)

tamoxifen /tə'mɒksɪfen/ *noun* a drug which helps to prevent the actions of oestrogen, used especially in the treatment of breast cancer and some types of infertility

tampon /'tæmpɒn/ *noun* **1.** a wad of absorbent material put into a wound to soak up blood during an operation **2.** a cylindrical plug of soft material put into the vagina to absorb blood during menstruation

tamponade /ˌtæmpə'neɪd/ *noun* the action of putting a tampon into a wound

tan /tæn/ *verb* (*of skin*) to become brown in sunlight ○ *He tans easily.* ○ *She is using a tanning lotion.*

tantalum /'tæntələm/ *noun* a rare metal, used to repair damaged bones (NOTE: The chemical symbol is **Ta**.)

tantalum mesh /'tæntələm meʃ/ *noun* a type of net made of tantalum wire, used to repair cranial conditions

tantrum /'tæntrəm/ *noun* a sudden episode of bad behaviour, usually in a child, where the child throws things or lies on the floor and screams

tap /tæp/ *noun* a surgical procedure to drain off body fluid with a hollow needle or a tube ■ *verb* to remove or drain liquid from part of the body. ◊ **spinal**

tapeworm /'teɪpwɜːm/ *noun* a parasitic worm with a small head and long body like a ribbon. Tapeworms enter the intestine when a person eats raw meat or fish. The worms attach themselves with hooks to the side of the intestine and grow longer by adding sections to their bodies.

tapotement /təˈpəʊtmənt/ *noun* a type of massage where the therapist taps the person with his or her hands

tapping /ˈtæpɪŋ/ *noun* same as **paracentesis**

tarry stool /ˌtɑːri ˈstuːl/ *noun* dark and sticky solid matter which is passed out of the bowels

tars- /tɑːs/ *prefix* same as **tarso-** (*used before vowels*)

tarsal /ˈtɑːs(ə)l/ *adjective* referring to the tarsus ■ *noun* same as **tarsal bone**

tarsal bone /ˈtɑːs(ə)l bəʊn/ *noun* one of seven small bones in the ankle, including the talus and calcaneus. Also called **tarsal**

tarsalgia /tɑːˈsældʒə/ *noun* a pain in the ankle

tarsal gland /ˈtɑːs(ə)l glænd/ *noun* same as **meibomian gland**

tarsectomy /tɑːˈsektəmi/ *noun* **1.** a surgical operation to remove one of the tarsal bones in the ankle **2.** a surgical operation to remove the tarsus of the eyelid

tarsitis /tɑːˈsaɪtɪs/ *noun* an inflammation of the edge of the eyelid

tarso- /tɑːsəʊ/ *prefix* **1.** relating to the ankle **2.** relating to the edge of the eyelid

tarsorrhaphy /tɑːˈsɒrəfi/ *noun* an operation to join the two eyelids together to protect the eye after an operation

tarsus /ˈtɑːsəs/ *noun* **1.** the seven small bones of the ankle. See illustration at FOOT in Supplement **2.** a connective tissue which supports an eyelid (NOTE: The plural is **tarsi**.)

tartar /ˈtɑːtə/ *noun* a hard deposit of calcium which forms on teeth, and has to be removed by scaling. Also called **scale**

task allocation /ˈtɑːsk æləˌkeɪʃ(ə)n/ *noun* a system in which patient care is divided into tasks which are given to different nurses with specific skills

taste /teɪst/ *noun* one of the five senses, where food or substances in the mouth are noticed through the tongue ○ *She doesn't like the taste of onions.* ○ *He has a cold, so food seems to have lost all taste* or *seems to have no taste.* ■ *verb* to notice the taste of something with the tongue ○ *I have a cold so I can't taste anything* ○ *You can taste the salt in this butter.*

taste bud /ˈteɪst bʌd/ *noun* a tiny sensory receptor in the vallate and fungiform papillae of the tongue and in part of the back of the mouth

COMMENT: The taste buds can tell the difference between salt, sour, bitter and sweet tastes. The buds on the tip of the tongue identify salt and sweet tastes, those on the sides of the tongue identify sour, and those at the back of the mouth the bitter tastes. Note that most of what we think of as taste is in fact smell, and this is why when someone has a cold and a blocked nose, food seems to lose its taste. The impulses from the taste buds are received by the taste cortex in the temporal lobe of the cerebral hemisphere.

taxis /ˈtæksɪs/ *noun* the procedure of pushing or massaging dislocated bones or hernias to make them return to their usual position

-taxis /tæksɪs/ *suffix* manipulation

taxonomy /tækˈsɒnəmi/ *noun* **1.** the practice or principles of classification generally ○ *Any diagnostic task can be aided by a taxonomy of symptoms and a taxonomy of causes together with connections between them.* **2.** the science of classifying plants, animals and microorganisms into increasingly broader categories based on shared features. Traditionally, organisms were grouped by physical resemblances, but recently other criteria such as genetic matching have also been used.

Tay-Sachs disease /ˌteɪ ˈsæks dɪˌziːz/ *noun* an inherited condition affecting the metabolism, characterised by progressive paralysis of the legs, blindness and learning disabilities [Described 1881. After Warren Tay (1843–1927), British ophthalmologist; Bernard Sachs (1858–1944), US neurologist.]

TB *abbreviation* tuberculosis ○ *He is suffering from TB.* ○ *She has been admitted to a TB sanatorium.*

TBI *abbreviation* total body irradiation

T-cell /ˈtiː sel/ *noun* same as **T-lymphocyte**

TCP /ˌtiː siː ˈpiː/ a trade name for various mild antiseptic liquids

t.d.s. /ˌtiː diː ˈes/, **TDS** *adverb* (*written on prescriptions*) three times a day. Full form **ter in diem sumendus**

teaching hospital /ˈtiːtʃɪŋ ˌhɒspɪt(ə)l/ *noun* a hospital attached to a medical school where student doctors work and study as part of their training

team nursing /ˈtiːm ˌnɜːsɪŋ/ *noun* a system in which the care of a group of patients is assigned to a team of four or five health workers, led by a professional nurse who assigns them various tasks. They meet at the beginning and end of each shift to exchange information.

tear /tɪə/ *noun* a drop of the salty fluid which forms in the lacrimal gland. The fluid keeps the eyeball moist and clean and is produced in large quantities when a person cries. ○ *Tears ran down her face.* (NOTE: For other terms referring to tears, see words beginning with **dacryo-** or **lacrimal**.)

tear duct /ˈtɪə dʌkt/ *noun* same as **lacrimal duct**

tear gland /ˈtɪə glænd/ *noun* same as **lacrimal gland**

teat /tiːt/ *noun* a rubber nipple on the end of a baby's feeding bottle

TED *abbreviation* thrombo-embolic deterrent stocking

teeth /tiːθ/ plural of **tooth**

Teflon /'teflɒn/ *trademark* a synthetic polymer injected into the joints of the larynx to increase movement and help hoarseness of voice

tegmen /'tegmən/ *noun* the covering for an organ (NOTE: The plural is **tegmina**.)

tegument /'tegjʊmənt/ *noun* a covering, especially the protective outer covering of an organism

tel- /tel/ *prefix* same as **tele-** (*used before vowels*)

tela /'tiːlə/ *noun* a delicate part or tissue in the body with a fine or intricate pattern like a web

telangiectasis /teˌlændʒiˈektəsɪs/, **telangiectasia** /teˌlændʒiekˈteɪsiə/ *noun* small dark red spots on the skin, formed by swollen capillaries

telangioma /teˌlændʒiˈəʊmə/ *noun* a tumour or haematoma of the blood capillaries

tele- /teli/ *prefix* referring to distance

teleceptor /'telɪseptə/ *noun* a sensory receptor which receives sensations from a distance. These occur in the eyes, ears and nose. Also called **telereceptor**

telemedicine /'telimed(ə)sɪn/ *noun* the provision of diagnosis and health care from a distance using media such as interactive computer programs or off-site advisers

telencephalon /ˌtelenˈkefəlɒn/ *noun* same as **cerebrum**

telepathy /təˈlepəθi/ *noun* the apparent communication directly from one person's mind to another person's, without the use of speech, writing or other signs or symbols

teleradiology /ˌtelireɪdiˈɒlədʒi/ *noun* the process of transmitting scans and other images electronically so that they can be viewed by surgeons or other health care workers in different locations at the same time

telereceptor /'teliriˌseptə/ *noun* same as **teleceptor**

telophase /'teləʊfeɪz/ *noun* the final stage of mitosis, the stage in cell division after anaphase

temazepam /təˈmæzɪpæm/ *noun* a hypnotic drug used in the short-term treatment of insomnia

temperature /'temprɪtʃə/ *noun* the heat of the body or of the surrounding air, measured in degrees ○ *The doctor asked the nurse what the patient's temperature was.* ○ *His temperature was slightly above normal.* ○ *The thermometer showed a temperature of 99°F.*

temperature chart /'temprɪtʃə tʃɑːt/ *noun* a chart showing changes in a person's temperature over a period of time

temple /'tempəl/ *noun* the flat part of the side of the head between the top of the ear and the eye

temporal /'temp(ə)rəl/ *adjective* referring to the temple

temporal arteritis /ˌtemp(ə)rəl ˌɑːtəˈraɪtɪs/ *noun* a headache caused by inflammation of the region over the temporal artery, usually occurring in older people

temporal bone /'tempərəl bəʊn/ *noun* one of the bones which form the sides and base of the cranium. See illustration at EAR in Supplement

temporalis /ˌtempəˈreɪlɪs/, **temporalis muscle** /ˌtempəˈreɪlɪs ˌmʌs(ə)l/ *noun* a flat muscle running down the side of the head from the temporal bone to the coronoid process, which makes the jaw move up

temporal lobe /'temp(ə)rəl ləʊb/ *noun* the lobe above the ear in each cerebral hemisphere

temporal lobe epilepsy /ˌtemp(ə)rəl ləʊb 'epɪlepsi/ *noun* epilepsy due to a disorder of the temporal lobe and causing impaired memory, hallucinations and automatism

temporo- /tempərəʊ/ *prefix* **1.** referring to the temple **2.** referring to the temporal lobe

temporomandibular /ˌtempərəʊmænˈdɪbjʊlə/ *adjective* relating to the temporal bone and the mandible

temporomandibular joint /ˌtempərəʊmænˈdɪbjʊlə ˌdʒɔɪnt/ *noun* a joint between the jaw and the skull, in front of the ear

tenacious /tɪˈneɪʃəs/ *adjective* sticking or clinging to something else, especially a surface

tenaculum /təˈnækjʊləm/ *noun* a surgical instrument shaped like a hook, used to pick up small pieces of tissue during an operation

tender /'tendə/ *adjective* referring to skin or a body part which is painful when touched ○ *The bruise is still tender.* ○ *Her shoulders are still tender where she got sunburnt.* ○ *A tender spot on the abdomen indicates that an organ is inflamed.*

tendinitis /ˌtendɪˈnaɪtɪs/ *noun* an inflammation of a tendon, especially after playing sport, and often associated with tenosynovitis

tendinous /'tendɪnəs/ *adjective* referring to a tendon

tendon /'tendən/ *noun* a strip of connective tissue which attaches a muscle to a bone. Also called **sinew** (NOTE: For other terms referring to a tendon, see words beginning with **teno-**.)

tendonitis /ˌtendəˈnaɪtɪs/ *noun* same as **tendinitis**

tendon sheath /'tendən ʃiːθ/ *noun* a tube of membrane which covers and protects a tendon

tendovaginitis /ˌtendəʊvædʒɪˈnaɪtɪs/ *noun* an inflammation of a tendon sheath, especially in the thumb

tenens /'tenənz/ ♦ **locum**

tenesmus /təˈnezməs/ *noun* a condition in which someone feels the need to pass faeces, or sometimes urine, but is unable to do so and experiences pain

tennis elbow /ˌtenɪs 'elbəʊ/ *noun* an inflammation of the tendons of the extensor muscles in the hand which are attached to the bone near the elbow. Also called **lateral epicondylitis**

teno- /tenəʊ/ *prefix* referring to a tendon

tenonitis /ˌtenəʊ'naɪtɪs/ *noun* the inflammation of a tendon

Tenon's capsule /'tiːnɒns ˌkæpsjuːl/ *noun* a tissue which lines the orbit of the eye [After Jacques René Tenon (1724–1816), French surgeon.]

tenoplasty /'tenəplæsti/ *noun* a surgical operation to repair a torn tendon

tenorrhaphy /te'nɒrəfi/ *noun* a surgical operation to stitch pieces of a torn tendon together

tenosynovitis /ˌtenəʊˌsaɪnə'vaɪtɪs/ *noun* a painful inflammation of the tendon sheath and the tendon inside. Also called **peritendinitis**

tenotomy /tə'nɒtəmi/ *noun* a surgical operation to cut through a tendon

tenovaginitis /ˌtenəʊˌvædʒɪ'naɪtɪs/ *noun* inflammation of the tendon sheath, especially in the thumb

TENS /tens/ *abbreviation* a method of treating pain by applying electrodes to the skin. Small electric currents are passed through sensory nerves and the spinal cord. This suppresses the transmission of pain signals. ○ *a TENS unit or machine* Full form **transcutaneous electrical nerve stimulation**

tension /'tenʃən/ *noun* 1. the act of stretching or the state of being stretched 2. an emotional strain or stress

tension headache /'tenʃən ˌhedeɪk/ *noun* a headache all over the head, caused by worry and stress

tension pneumothorax /'tenʃən njuːməʊ ˌθɔːræks/ *noun* a condition of the pneumothorax in which rupture of the pleura forms an opening like a valve, through which air is forced during coughing but cannot escape

tensor /'tensə/ *noun* a muscle which makes a joint stretch out

tent /tent/ *noun* a small shelter put over and around someone's bed so that gas or vapour can be passed inside

tera- /terə/ *prefix* 10^{12}. Symbol **T**

terat- /terət/, **terato-** /terətəʊ/ *prefix* congenitally unusual

teratogen /tə'rætədʒen/ *noun* a substance which causes the usual development of an embryo or fetus to be disrupted, e.g. the German measles virus

teratogenesis /ˌterətə'dʒenəsɪs/ *noun* an unusual pattern of development in an embryo and fetus

teratogenic /ˌterətə'dʒenɪk/ *adjective* 1. having the tendency to produce physical disorders in an embryo or fetus 2. relating to the production of physical disorders in an embryo or fetus

teratology /ˌterə'tɒlədʒi/ *noun* the study of the unhealthy development of embryos and fetuses

teratoma /ˌterə'təʊmə/ *noun* a tumour, especially in an ovary or testis, which is formed of tissue not usually found in that part of the body

terbutaline /tɜː'bjuːtəliːn/ *noun* a drug which relaxes muscles, used in the treatment of respiratory disorders and to control premature labour

teres /'tɪəriːz/ *noun* one of two shoulder muscles running from the shoulder blade to the top of the humerus. The larger of the two muscles, the teres major, makes the arm turn towards the inside, and the smaller, the teres minor, makes it turn towards the outside.

terfenadine /tɜː'fenədiːn/ *noun* an antihistamine used in the treatment of hay fever and urticaria

terminal branch /'tɜːmɪn(ə)l brɑːntʃ/ *noun* the end part of a neurone which is linked to a muscle. See illustration at **NEURONE** in Supplement

terminal illness /ˌtɜːmɪn(ə)l 'ɪlnəs/ *noun* an illness from which someone will soon die

terminally ill /ˌtɜːmɪnəli 'ɪl/ *adjective* very ill and about to die ○ *She was admitted to a hospice for terminally ill patients* or *for the terminally ill.*

-terol /terɒl/ *suffix* used in names of bronchodilators

tertian /'tɜːʃ(ə)n/ *adjective* referring to a fever with symptoms which appear every other day ■ *noun* a tertian fever or set of symptoms

tertian fever /'tɜːʃ(ə)n ˌfiːvə/ *noun* a type of malaria where the fever returns every two days. ◊ **quartan fever**

tertiary /'tɜːʃəri/ *adjective* third, coming after secondary and primary

tertiary bronchi /ˌtɜːʃəri 'brɒnkiː/ *plural noun* ♦ **syphilis**

tertiary care /ˌtɜːʃəri 'keə/, **tertiary health care** /ˌtɜːʃəri 'helθ ˌkeə/ *noun* highly specialised treatment given in a health care centre, often using very advanced technology. Compare **primary care**, **secondary care**

test /test/ *noun* a short examination to see if a sample is healthy or if part of the body is working well ○ *He had an eye test this morning.* ○ *Laboratory tests showed that she was a meningitis carrier.* ○ *Tests are being carried out on swabs taken from the operating theatre.*

testicle /'testɪk(ə)l/ *noun* same as **testis**

testicular /te'stɪkjʊlə/ *adjective* referring to the testes ○ *Testicular cancer comprises only 1% of all malignant neoplasms in the male.*

testicular artery /teˌstɪkjʊlə 'ɑːtəri/ *noun* same as **spermatic artery**

testis /'testɪs/ *noun* one of two male sex glands in the scrotum. See illustration at **UROGENITAL**

SYSTEM (MALE) in Supplement. Also called **testicle** (NOTE: The plural is **testes**. For other terms referring to the testes, see words beginning with **orchi-**.)

COMMENT: The testes produce both spermatozoa and the sex hormone, testosterone. Spermatozoa are formed in the testes, and passed into the epididymis to be stored. From the epididymis they pass along the vas deferens through the prostate gland which secretes the seminal fluid, and are ejaculated through the penis.

test meal /'test miːl/ *noun* a test to check the secretion of gastric juices, no longer much used

testosterone /teˈstɒstərəʊn/ *noun* a male sex hormone, secreted by the Leydig cells in the testes, which causes physical changes, e.g. the development of body hair and a deep voice, to take place in males as they become sexually mature

test tube /'test tjuːb/ *noun* a small glass tube with a rounded bottom, used in laboratories to hold samples of liquids

test-tube baby /'test tjuːb ˌbeɪbi/ *noun* a baby conceived through in vitro fertilisation in which the mother's ova are removed from the ovaries, fertilised with a man's spermatozoa in a laboratory, and returned to the mother's uterus to continue developing in the usual way

tetanic /teˈtænɪk/ *adjective* referring to tetanus

tetano- /tetənəʊ/ *prefix* **1.** relating to tetanus **2.** relating to tetany

tetanus /'tet(ə)nəs/ *noun* **1.** the continuous contraction of a muscle, under repeated stimuli from a motor nerve **2.** an infection caused by *Clostridium tetani* in the soil, which affects the spinal cord and causes spasms in the muscles which occur first in the jaw. Also called **lockjaw**

tetany /'tetəni/ *noun* spasms of the muscles in the feet and hands, caused by a reduction in the level of calcium in the blood or by lack of carbon dioxide

tetra- /tetrə/ *prefix* four

tetracycline /ˌtetrəˈsaɪkliːn/ *noun* an antibiotic of a group used to treat a wide range of bacterial diseases such as chlamydia. However, they are deposited in bones and teeth and cause a permanent yellow stain in teeth if given to children.

tetralogy of Fallot /teˌtrælədʒi əv ˈfæləʊ/ *noun* a disorder of the heart which makes a child's skin blue. Also called **Fallot's tetralogy**. ◊ **Blalock's operation, Waterston's operation** [Described 1888. After Etienne-Louis Arthur Fallot (1850–1911), Professor of Hygiene and Legal Medicine at Marseilles, France.]

tetraplegia /ˌtetrəˈpliːdʒə/ same as **quadriplegia**

thalam- /θæləm/ *prefix* same as **thalamo-** (*used before vowels*)

thalamo- /θæləməʊ/ *prefix* referring to the thalamus

thalamus /'θæləməs/ *noun* one of two masses of grey matter situated beneath the cerebrum where impulses from the sensory neurones are transmitted to the cerebral cortex. See illustration at BRAIN in Supplement (NOTE: The plural is **thalami**.)

thalassaemia /ˌθæləˈsiːmiə/ *noun* a hereditary disorder of which there are several forms caused by an anomalies in the protein component of the haemoglobin, leading to severe anaemia. It is found especially in people from Mediterranean countries, the Middle East and East Asia. Also called **Cooley's anaemia**

thalidomide /θəˈlɪdəmaɪd/ *noun* a synthetic drug given to pregnant women for morning sickness in the 1960s which caused babies to be born with stunted limbs. It is now used in the treatment of leprosy.

thallium scan /'θæliəm skæn/ *noun* a method of finding out about the blood supply to the heart muscle by scanning to see how the radioactive element thallium moves when injected into the bloodstream and where it attaches itself to the heart wall

thanatology /ˌθænəˈtɒlədʒi/ *noun* the study of the medical, psychological and sociological aspects of death and the ways in which people deal with it

theatre nurse /'θɪətə nɜːs/ *noun* a nurse who is specially trained to assist a surgeon during an operation

theca /'θiːkə/ *noun* tissue shaped like a sheath

thelarche /'θelɑːki/ *noun* the beginning of the process of breast development in young women

thenar /'θiːnə/ *adjective* referring to the palm of the hand ■ *noun* the palm of the hand. Compare **hypothenar**

thenar eminence /ˌθiːnər ˈemɪnəns/ *noun* the ball of the thumb, the lump of flesh in the palm of the hand below the thumb

theophylline /θiˈɒfɪliːn/ *noun* a compound made synthetically or extracted from tea leaves which helps to widen blood vessels and airways, and to stimulate the central nervous system and heart. It is used in the treatment of breathing disorders.

therapeutic /ˌθerəˈpjuːtɪk/ *adjective* given in order to cure a disorder or disease

therapeutic abortion /ˌθerəpjuːtɪk əˈbɔːʃ(ə)n/ *noun* an abortion which is carried out because the health of the mother is in danger

therapeutic index /ˌθerəpjuːtɪk ˈɪndeks/ *noun* the ratio of the dose of a drug which causes cell damage to the dose of that drug which is typically needed to effect a cure, by which the safety of the drug is decided

therapeutic radiographer /ˌθerəˌpjuːtɪk ˌreɪdiˈɒɡrəfə/ *noun* someone specially trained to use X-rays or radioactive isotopes in the treatment of patients

therapeutics /ˌθerəˈpjuːtɪks/ *noun* the study of various types of treatment and their effect on patients

therapist /ˈθerəpɪst/ *noun* a person specially trained to give therapy ○ *an occupational therapist* ◊ **psychotherapist**

therapy /ˈθerəpi/ *noun* the treatment of a person to help cure a disease or disorder

therm /θɜːm/ *noun* a unit of heat equal to 100,000 British thermal units or 1.055×10^8 joules

thermal /ˈθɜːm(ə)l/ *adjective* referring to heat

thermo- /θɜːməʊ/ *prefix* referring to heat or temperature

thermoanaesthesia /ˌθɜːməʊˌænəsˈθiːziə/ *noun* a condition in which someone cannot tell the difference between hot and cold

thermocautery /ˌθɜːməʊˈkɔːtəri/ *noun* the procedure of removing dead tissue by heat

thermogram /ˈθɜːməɡræm/ *noun* an infrared photograph of part of the body

thermography /θɜːˈmɒɡrəfi/ *noun* a technique, used especially in screening for breast cancer, where part of the body is photographed using infrared rays which record the heat given off by the skin and show variations in the blood circulating beneath the skin

thermolysis /θɜːˈmɒləsɪs/ *noun* a loss of body temperature, e.g. by sweating

thermometer /θəˈmɒmɪtə/ *noun* an instrument for measuring temperature

thermoreceptor /ˌθɜːməʊrɪˈseptə/ *noun* a sensory nerve which registers heat

thermotaxis /ˌθɜːməʊˈtæksɪs/ *noun* an automatic regulation of the body's temperature

thermotherapy /ˌθɜːməʊˈθerəpi/ *noun* treatment using heat, e.g. from hot water or infrared lamps, to treat conditions such as arthritis and bad circulation. Also called **heat therapy**

thiamine /ˈθaɪəmiːn/, **thiamin** /ˈθaɪəmɪn/ *noun* same as **Vitamin B₁**

Thiersch graft /ˈtɪəʃ ɡrɑːft/, **Thiersch's graft** /ˈtɪəʃɪz ɡrɑːft/ *noun* same as **split-skin graft**

thigh /θaɪ/ *noun* the top part of the leg from the knee to the groin

thiopental sodium /ˌθaɪəʊpent(ə)l ˈsəʊdiəm/ *noun* a barbiturate drug used as a rapid-acting intravenous general anaesthetic. Also called **thiopentone**

thiopentone /ˌθaɪəʊˈpentəʊn/, **thiopentone sodium** /ˌθaɪəʊpentəʊn ˈsəʊdiəm/ *noun* same as **thiopental sodium** (NOTE: Its chemical formula is $C_{11}H_{17}N_2O2SNa$.)

thioridazine /ˌθaɪəʊˈrɪdəziːn/ *noun* a synthetic compound used as a tranquilliser for people who are suffering from a psychosis

third-degree haemorrhoids /ˌθɜːd dɪˌɡriː ˈhemərɔɪdz/ *plural noun* haemorrhoids which protrude into the anus permanently

third molar /ˌθɜːd ˈməʊlə/ *noun* one of the four molars at the back of the jaw, which only appears at about the age of 20 and sometimes does not appear at all. Same as **wisdom tooth**

thirst /θɜːst/ *noun* a feeling of wanting to drink ○ *He had a fever and a violent thirst.*

Thomas's splint /ˈtɒməsɪz splɪnt/, **Thomas splint** /ˈtɒməs splɪnt/ *noun* a metal splint used to keep a fractured leg still. It has a padded ring at the hip attached to rods to which bandages are bound and a bar under the foot at the lower end. [Described 1875. After Hugh Owen Thomas (1834–91), British surgeon and bonesetter.]

thorac- /θɔːrəs/ *prefix* same as **thoraco-** (*used before vowels*)

thoracectomy /ˌθɔːrəˈsektəmi/ *noun* a surgical operation to remove one or more ribs

thoracentesis /ˌθɔːrəsenˈtiːsɪs/ *noun* same as **thoracocentesis**

thoracic /θɔːˈræsɪk/ *adjective* referring to the chest or thorax

thoracic cavity /θɔːˌræsɪk ˈkævɪti/ *noun* the chest cavity, containing the diaphragm, heart and lungs

thoracic duct /θɔːˈræsɪk dʌkt/ *noun* one of the main terminal ducts carrying lymph, on the left side of the neck

thoracic vertebrae /θɔːˌræsɪk ˈvɜːtɪbriː/ *plural noun* the twelve vertebrae in the spine behind the chest, to which the ribs are attached

thoraco- /θɔːrəkəʊ/ *prefix* relating to the thorax

thoracocentesis /ˌθɔːrəkəʊsenˈtiːsɪs/ *noun* an operation in which a hollow needle is inserted into the pleura to drain fluid

thoracoscope /ˈθɔːrəkəskəʊp/ *noun* a surgical instrument, like a tube with a light at the end, used to examine the inside of the chest

thoracoscopy /ˌθɔːrəˈkɒskəpi/ *noun* an examination of the inside of the chest, using a thoracoscope

thoracotomy /ˌθɔːrəˈkɒtəmi/ *noun* a surgical operation to make a hole in the wall of the chest

thorax /ˈθɔːræks/ *noun* the cavity in the top part of the front of the body above the abdomen, containing the diaphragm, heart and lungs, and surrounded by the ribcage

threadworm /ˈθredwɜːm/ *noun* a thin parasitic worm, *Enterobius vernicularis*, which infests the large intestine and causes itching round the anus. ◊ **Enterobius**. Also called **pinworm**

thready pulse /ˌθredi ˈpʌls/ *noun* a very weak pulse which is hard to detect

threatened abortion /ˌθret(ə)nd əˈbɔːʃ(ə)n/ *noun* a possible abortion in the early stages of pregnancy, indicated by bleeding

threshold /ˈθreʃhəʊld/ *noun* the point at which something starts, e.g. where something can be perceived by the body or where a drug starts to have an effect ○ *She has a low hearing threshold.*

thrill /θrɪl/ *noun* a vibration which can be felt with the hands

-thrix /θrɪks/ *suffix* relating to a hair

throat /θrəʊt/ *noun* the top part of the tube which goes down from the mouth to the stomach

throbbing pain /ˌθrɒbɪŋ ˈpeɪn/ *noun* pain which continues in repeated short attacks

thrombectomy /θrɒmˈbektəmi/ *noun* a surgical operation to remove a blood clot

thrombin /ˈθrɒmbɪn/ *noun* a substance which converts fibrinogen to fibrin and so coagulates blood

thrombo- /θrɒmbəʊ/ *prefix* **1.** referring to a blood clot **2.** referring to thrombosis

thromboangiitis /ˌθrɒmbəʊˌændʒiˈaɪtɪs/ *noun* a condition in which the blood vessels swell and develop blood clots along their walls

thromboangiitis obliterans /ˌθrɒmbəʊændʒiˌaɪtɪs əbˈlɪtərənz/ *noun* a disease of the arteries in which the blood vessels in a limb, usually the leg, become narrow, causing gangrene. Also called **Buerger's disease**

thromboarteritis /ˌθrɒmbəʊˌɑːtəˈraɪtɪs/ *noun* inflammation of an artery caused by thrombosis

thrombocyte /ˈθrɒmbəʊsaɪt/ *noun* same as **platelet**

thrombocythaemia /ˌθrɒmbəʊsaɪˈθiːmiə/ *noun* a disease in which someone has an unusually high number of platelets in the blood

thrombocytopenia /ˌθrɒmbəʊˌsaɪtəʊˈpiːniə/ *noun* a condition in which someone has an unusually low number of platelets in the blood

thrombocytopenic /ˌθrɒmbəʊˌsaɪtəʊˈpenɪk/ *adjective* referring to thrombocytopenia

thrombocytosis /ˌθrɒmbəʊsaɪˈtəʊsɪs/ *noun* an increase in the number of platelets in someone's blood

thrombo-embolic deterrent stocking /ˌθrɒmbəʊ emˌbɒlɪk dɪˈterənt ˌstɒkɪŋ/ *noun* a support stocking to prevent thrombus formation following surgery. Abbreviation **TED**

thromboembolism /ˌθrɒmbəʊˈembəlɪz(ə)m/ *noun* a condition in which a blood clot forms in one part of the body and moves through the blood vessels to block another, usually smaller, part

thromboendarterectomy /ˌθrɒmbəʊ ˌendɑːtəˈrektəmi/ *noun* a surgical operation to open an artery to remove a blood clot which is blocking it

thromboendarteritis /ˌθrɒmbəʊˌendɑːtəˈraɪtɪs/ *noun* inflammation of the inside of an artery, caused by thrombosis

thrombokinase /ˌθrɒmbəʊˈkaɪneɪz/ *noun* an enzyme which converts prothrombin into thrombin, so starting the sequence for coagulation of blood. Also called **thromboplastin**

thrombolysis /θrɒmˈbɒləsɪs/ *noun* same as **fibrinolysis**

thrombolytic /ˌθrɒmbəʊˈlɪtɪk/ *adjective* same as **fibrinolytic**

thrombophlebitis /ˌθrɒmbəʊflɪˈbaɪtɪs/ *noun* the blocking of a vein by a blood clot, sometimes causing inflammation

thromboplastin /ˌθrɒmbəʊˈplæstɪn/ *noun* same as **thrombokinase**

thrombosis /θrɒmˈbəʊsɪs/ *noun* the blocking of an artery or vein by a mass of coagulated blood

thrombus /ˈθrɒmbəs/ *noun* same as **blood clot**

throw up /ˌθrəʊ ˈʌp/ *verb* same as **vomit** (*informal*)

thrush /θrʌʃ/ *noun* an infection of the mouth or the vagina with the bacterium *Candida albicans*

thumb /θʌm/ *noun* the short thick finger, with only two bones, which is separated from the other four fingers on the hand

thym- /θaɪm/ *prefix* referring to the thymus gland

thymectomy /θaɪˈmektəmi/ *noun* a surgical operation to remove the thymus gland

-thymia /θaɪmiə/ *suffix* referring to a state of mind

thymic /ˈθaɪmɪk/ *adjective* referring to the thymus gland

thymine /ˈθaɪmiːn/ *noun* one of the four basic chemicals in DNA

thymol /ˈθaɪmɒl/ *noun* a colourless compound which is made synthetically or extracted from thyme oil, used as an antiseptic

thymus /ˈθaɪməs/, **thymus gland** /ˈθaɪməs glænd/ *noun* an endocrine gland in the front part of the top of the thorax, behind the breastbone

thyro- /θaɪrəʊ/ *prefix* referring to the thyroid gland

thyrocalcitonin /ˌθaɪrəʊkælsiˈtəʊnɪn/ *noun* same as **calcitonin**

thyroglossal /ˌθaɪrəʊˈglɒs(ə)l/ *adjective* referring to the thyroid gland and the throat

thyroglossal cyst /ˌθaɪrəʊglɒs(ə)l ˈsɪst/ *noun* a cyst in the front of the neck

thyroid /ˈθaɪrɔɪd/, **thyroid gland** *noun* /ˈθaɪrɔɪd glænd/ an endocrine gland in the neck, which is activated by the pituitary gland and secretes a hormone which regulates the body's metabolism ■ *adjective* referring to the thyroid gland

thyroid cartilage /ˌθaɪrɔɪd 'kɑːtəlɪdʒ/ *noun* a large cartilage in the larynx, part of which forms the Adam's apple. See illustration at **LUNGS** in Supplement

thyroidectomy /ˌθaɪrɔɪ'dektəmi/ *noun* a surgical operation to remove all or part of the thyroid gland

thyroid gland /'θaɪrɔɪd glænd/ *noun* same as **thyroid**

thyroid hormone /'θaɪrɔɪd ˌhɔːməʊn/ *noun* a hormone produced by the thyroid gland

thyroiditis /ˌθaɪrɔɪ'daɪtɪs/ *noun* inflammation of the thyroid gland

thyroid-stimulating hormone /'θaɪrɔɪd ˌstɪmjʊleɪtɪŋ ˌhɔːməʊn/ *noun* a hormone secreted by the pituitary gland which stimulates the thyroid gland. Abbreviation **TSH**. Also called **thyrotrophin**

thyroparathyroidectomy /ˌθaɪrəʊˌpærə ˌθaɪrɔɪ'dektəmi/ *noun* a surgical operation to remove the thyroid and parathyroid glands

thyroplasty /'θaɪrəʊplæsti/ *noun* a surgical procedure performed on the cartilages of the larynx to improve the quality of the voice

thyrotoxic /ˌθaɪrəʊ'tɒksɪk/ *adjective* referring to severe hyperthyroidism

thyrotoxic crisis /ˌθaɪrəʊˌtɒksɪk 'kraɪsɪs/ *noun* a sudden illness caused by hyperthyroidism

thyrotoxic goitre /ˌθaɪrəʊˌtɒksɪk 'ɡɔɪtə/ *noun* overactivity of the thyroid gland, as in hyperthyroidism

thyrotoxicosis /ˌθaɪrəʊtɒksɪ'kəʊsɪs/ *noun* same as **hyperthyroidism**

thyrotrophin /ˌθaɪrəʊ'trəʊfɪn/ *noun* same as **thyroid-stimulating hormone**

thyrotrophin-releasing hormone /ˌθaɪrəʊ ˌtrəʊfɪn rɪ'liːsɪŋ ˌhɔːməʊn/ *noun* a hormone secreted by the hypothalamus, which makes the pituitary gland release thyrotrophin, which in turn stimulates the thyroid gland. Abbreviation **TRH**

thyroxine /θaɪ'rɒksiːn/ *noun* a hormone produced by the thyroid gland which regulates the body's metabolism and the conversion of food into heat, used in treatment of hypothyroidism

TIA *abbreviation* transient ischaemic attack

tibia /'tɪbiə/ *noun* the larger of the two long bones in the lower leg between the knee and the ankle. Also called **shinbone**. Compare **fibula**

tibial /'tɪbiəl/ *adjective* referring to the tibia

tibialis /ˌtɪbi'eɪlɪs/ *noun* one of two muscles in the lower leg running from the tibia to the foot

tibial torsion /ˌtɪbiəl 'tɔːʃ(ə)n/ *noun* a persistent slight twist in the tibia, caused by a cramped position in the uterus. It makes the feet of young children point inwards for up to a year after they begin to walk on their own, but it corrects itself as the leg grows.

tibio- /tɪbiəʊ/ *prefix* referring to the tibia

tibiofibular /ˌtɪbiəʊ'fɪbjʊlə/ *adjective* referring to both the tibia and the fibula

tic /tɪk/ *noun* an involuntary twitch of the muscles usually in the face (*informal*)

tic douloureux /ˌtɪk ˌduːlə'ruː/ *noun* same as **trigeminal neuralgia**

tick /tɪk/ *noun* a tiny parasite which sucks blood from the skin

t.i.d. /ˌtiː aɪ 'diː/, **TID** *adverb* (*used on prescriptions*) three times a day. Full form **ter in die**

tidal air /'taɪd(ə)l ˌeə/, **tidal volume** /ˌtaɪd(ə)l 'vɒljuːm/ *noun* the amount of air that passes in and out of the body in breathing

-tidine /tɪdiːn/ *suffix* used for antihistamine drugs

timolol /'tɪməlɒl/ *noun* a beta-blocker used in the treatment of migraine, high blood pressure and glaucoma

tincture /'tɪŋktʃə/ *noun* a medicinal substance dissolved in alcohol

tincture of iodine /ˌtɪŋktʃər əv 'aɪədiːn/ *noun* a weak solution of iodine in alcohol, used as an antiseptic

tinea /'tɪniə/ *noun* ♦ **ringworm**

tinea barbae /ˌtɪniə 'bɑːbiː/ *noun* a fungal infection in the beard

tinea capitis /ˌtɪniə kə'paɪtɪs/ *noun* a fungal infection on the scalp

tinea pedis /ˌtɪniə 'pedɪs/ *noun* same as **athlete's foot**

tingle /'tɪŋɡəl/ *verb* to have a pricking or stinging sensation in a body part

tingling /'tɪŋɡlɪŋ/ *noun* a feeling of pricking or stinging in a body part ○ *an unpleasant tingling down her arm* ■ *adjective* pricking or stinging ○ *a tingling sensation*

tinnitus /'tɪnɪtəs/ *noun* a condition in which someone hears a ringing sound in the ears

tissue /'tɪʃuː/ *noun* a group of cells that carries out a specific function (NOTE: For other terms referring to tissue, see words beginning with **hist-**, **histo-**.)

COMMENT: Most of the body is made up of soft tissue, with the exception of the bones and cartilage. The main types of body tissue are connective, epithelial, muscular and nerve tissue.

tissue culture /'tɪʃuː ˌkʌltʃə/ *noun* tissue grown in a culture medium in a laboratory

tissue plasminogen activator /ˌtɪʃuː plæz 'mɪnədʒən ˌæktɪveɪtə/ *noun* an agent given to cause fibrinolysis in blood clots. Abbreviation **TPA**

tissue typing /'tɪʃuː ˌtaɪpɪŋ/ *noun* the process of identifying various elements in tissue from a donor and comparing them to those of the recipient to see if a transplant is likely to be rejected

titanium /taɪˈteɪniəm/ *noun* a light metallic element which does not corrode (NOTE: The chemical symbol is **Ti**.)

titration /taɪˈtreɪʃ(ə)n/ *noun* the process of measuring the strength of a solution

titre /ˈtiːtə/ *noun* a measurement of the quantity of antibodies in a serum

T-lymphocyte /ˈtiː ˌlɪmfəsaɪt/ *noun* a lymphocyte formed in the thymus gland. Also called **T-cell**

TNM classification /ˌtiː en ˈem klæsɪfɪ ˌkeɪʃ(ə)n/ *noun* an internationally agreed standard which is the most widely used means for classifying the extent of cancer. T refers to the size of the tumour, N to the lymph node involvement and M to the presence or absence of metastasis.

toco- /təʊkəʊ/ *prefix* referring to childbirth

tocography /tɒˈkɒɡrəfi/ *noun* the process of recording the contractions of the uterus during childbirth

tocopherol /tɒˈkɒfərɒl/ *noun* one of a group of fat-soluble compounds which make up vitamin E, found in vegetable oils and leafy green vegetables

toddler's diarrhoea /ˌtɒdləz daɪəˈriːə/ *noun* a condition in which recurrent loose stools are produced, often containing partially digested food. It usually occurs in children between the ages of one and three years.

toileting /ˈtɔɪlətɪŋ/ *noun* the act of helping someone to perform the actions of urinating or opening their bowels, including helping them to do so if they are unable to get out of bed or are incontinent

tolbutamide /tɒlˈbjuːtəmaɪd/ *noun* a drug which lowers blood-glucose levels by stimulating the pancreas to produce more insulin. It is used in the treatment of Type II diabetes.

tolerance /ˈtɒlərəns/ *noun* the ability of the body to tolerate a substance or an action ○ *He has been taking the drug for so long that he has developed a tolerance to it.*

tolerate /ˈtɒləreɪt/ *verb* **1.** not to be affected by the unpleasant effects of something, especially not to experience bad effects from being exposed to something harmful **2.** not to react to a drug through having developed a resistance to it

-tome /təʊm/ *suffix* **1.** a cutting instrument **2.** a segment ○ *a dermatome*

tomo- /təʊməʊ/ *prefix* referring to cutting or a section

tomogram /ˈtəʊməɡræm/ *noun* a picture of part of the body taken by tomography

tomography /təˈmɒɡrəfi/ *noun* the scanning of a particular part of the body using X-rays or ultrasound

-tomy /təmi/ *suffix* referring to a surgical operation

tone /təʊn/ *noun* the slightly tense state of a healthy muscle when it is not fully relaxed. Also called **tonicity, tonus**

tongue /tʌŋ/ *noun* the long muscular organ inside the mouth which can move and is used for tasting, swallowing and speaking. The top surface is covered with papillae, some of which contain taste buds. ○ *The doctor told him to stick out his tongue and say 'Ah'.* Also called **glossa** (NOTE: For other terms referring to the tongue, see **lingual** and words beginning with **gloss-, glosso-**.)

tongue depressor /ˈtʌŋ dɪˌpresə/ *noun* an instrument, usually a thin piece of wood, used by a doctor to hold someone's tongue down while the throat is being examined

tongue-tie /ˈtʌŋ taɪ/ *noun* the condition of being unable to move your tongue with the usual amount of freedom, because the small membrane which attaches the tongue to the floor of the mouth is unusually short

tonic /ˈtɒnɪk/ *adjective* referring to a muscle which is contracted ■ *noun* a substance which improves the someone's general health or which makes a tired person more energetic ○ *He is taking a course of iron tonic tablets.* ○ *She asked the doctor to prescribe a tonic for her anaemia.*

tonicity /təʊˈnɪsɪti/ *noun* same as tone

tono- /təʊnəʊ/ *prefix* referring to pressure

tonography /təʊˈnɒɡrəfi/ *noun* a measurement of the pressure inside an eyeball

tonometer /təʊˈnɒmɪtə/ *noun* an instrument which measures the pressure inside an organ, especially the eye

tonometry /təʊˈnɒmətri/ *noun* a measurement of pressure inside an organ, especially the eye

tonsil /ˈtɒns(ə)l/ *noun* an area of lymphoid tissue at the back of the throat in which lymph circulates and protects the body against germs entering through the mouth. Also called **palatine tonsil**

tonsillar /ˈtɒnsɪlə/ *adjective* referring to the tonsils

tonsillectomy /ˌtɒnsɪˈlektəmi/ *noun* a surgical operation to remove the tonsils

tonsillitis /ˌtɒnsɪˈlaɪtɪs/ *noun* inflammation of the tonsils

tonsillotomy /ˌtɒnsɪˈlɒtəmi/ *noun* a surgical operation to make a cut into the tonsils

tonus /ˈtəʊnəs/ *noun* same as tone

tooth /tuːθ/ *noun* one of a set of bones in the mouth which are used to chew food (NOTE: The plural is **teeth**. For other terms relating to the teeth, see words beginning with **dent-**.)

tophus /ˈtəʊfəs/ *noun* a deposit of solid crystals in the skin or in the joints, especially in someone with gout (NOTE: The plural is **tophi**.)

topical /'tɒpɪk(ə)l/ *adjective* referring to a specific area of the external surface of the body ○ *suitable for topical application*

topical drug /'tɒpɪk(ə)l drʌg/ *noun* a drug which is applied to a specific external part of the body only

topically /'tɒpɪkli/ *adverb* by putting on a specific external part of the body only ○ *The cream is applied topically.*

topo- /tɒpə/ *prefix* a place or region

topographical /ˌtɒpə'græfɪk(ə)l/ *adjective* referring to topography

topography /tə'pɒgrəfi/ *noun* the description of each particular part of the body

torpor /'tɔːpə/ *noun* a condition in which someone seems sleepy or slow to react

torsion /'tɔːʃ(ə)n/ *noun* **1.** the twisting of something, or a twisted state **2.** the stress placed on an object which has been twisted

torso /'tɔːsəʊ/ *noun* the main part of the body, not including the arms, legs and head. Also called **trunk**

torticollis /ˌtɔːtɪ'kɒlɪs/ *noun* a condition of the neck, where the head is twisted to one side by contraction of the sternocleidomastoid muscle. Also called **wry neck**

total recall /ˌtəʊt(ə)l rɪ'kɔːl/ *noun* the fact of being able to remember something in complete detail

Tourette's syndrome /tuː'rets ˌsɪndrəʊm/, **Tourette syndrome** /tuː'ret ˌsɪndrəʊm/ *noun* a condition which includes involuntary movements, tics, use of foul language and respiratory disorders. Also called **Gilles de la Tourette Syndrome**

tourniquet /'tɔːnɪkeɪ/ *noun* an instrument or tight bandage wrapped round a limb to constrict an artery, so reducing the flow of blood and stopping bleeding from a wound

tox- /tɒks/ *prefix* same as **toxo-** (*used before vowels*)

toxaemia /tɒk'siːmiə/ *noun* the presence of poisonous substances in the blood

toxaemia of pregnancy /tɒkˌsiːmiə əv 'pregnənsi/ *noun* a condition which can affect women towards the end of pregnancy, in which they develop high blood pressure and pass protein in the urine

toxic /'tɒksɪk/ *adjective* poisonous

toxicity /tɒk'sɪsɪti/ *noun* **1.** the degree to which a substance is poisonous or harmful **2.** the amount of poisonous or harmful material in a substance

toxico- /tɒksɪkəʊ/ *prefix* referring to poison

toxicologist /ˌtɒksɪ'kɒlədʒɪst/ *noun* a scientist who specialises in the study of poisons

toxicology /ˌtɒksɪ'kɒlədʒi/ *noun* the scientific study of poisons and their effects on the human body

toxicosis /ˌtɒksɪ'kəʊsɪs/ *noun* poisoning

toxic shock syndrome /ˌtɒksɪk 'ʃɒk ˌsɪndrəʊm/ *noun* a serious condition caused by a staphylococcus infection of the skin or soft tissue. Its symptoms include vomiting, high fever, faintness, muscle aches, a rash and confusion. Abbreviation **TSS**

toxin /'tɒksɪn/ *noun* a poisonous substance produced in the body by microorganisms, and which, if injected into an animal, stimulates the production of antitoxins

toxo- /tɒksəʊ/ *prefix* referring to poison

toxocariasis /ˌtɒksəkə'raɪəsɪs/ *noun* the infestation of the intestine with worms from a dog or cat. Also called **visceral larva migrans**

toxoid /'tɒksɔɪd/ *noun* a toxin which has been treated and is no longer poisonous, but which can still provoke the formation of antibodies. Toxoids are used as vaccines, and are injected into a patient to give immunity against specific diseases.

toxoplasmosis /ˌtɒksəʊplæz'məʊsɪs/ *noun* a disease caused by the parasite *Toxoplasma* which is carried by animals. Toxoplasmosis can cause encephalitis or hydrocephalus and can be fatal.

TPA *abbreviation* tissue plasminogen activator

trabecula /trə'bekjʊlə/ *noun* a thin strip of stiff tissue which divides an organ or bone tissue into sections (NOTE: The plural is **trabeculae**.)

trabeculectomy /trəˌbekjʊ'lektəmi/ *noun* a surgical operation to treat glaucoma by cutting a channel through trabeculae to link with Schlemm's canal

trace /treɪs/ *noun* a very small amount ○ *There are traces of the drug in the blood sample.* ○ *The doctor found traces of alcohol in the patient's urine.* ■ *verb* to find someone or something that you are looking for

trace element /'treɪs ˌelɪmənt/ *noun* a substance which is essential to the human body, but only in very small quantities

COMMENT: The trace elements are cobalt, chromium, copper, magnesium, manganese, molybdenum, selenium and zinc.

tracer /'treɪsə/ *noun* a substance, often a radioactive one, injected into a substance in the body, so that doctors can follow its passage round the body

trache- /treɪki/ *prefix* same as **tracheo-** (NOTE: used before vowels)

trachea /trə'kiːə/ *noun* the main air passage which runs from the larynx to the lungs, where it divides into the two main bronchi. It is about 10 cm long, and is formed of rings of cartilage and connective tissue. See illustration at LUNGS in Supplement. Also called **windpipe**

tracheal /trə'kiːəl/ *adjective* referring to the trachea

tracheal tugging /trəˌkiːəl 'tʌgɪŋ/ *noun* the feeling that something is pulling on the windpipe when the person breathes in, a symptom of aneurysm

tracheitis /ˌtreɪkiˈaɪtɪs/ *noun* inflammation of the trachea due to an infection

trachelorrhaphy /ˌtreɪkiˈlɒrəfi/ *noun* a surgical operation to repair tears in the cervix of the uterus

tracheo- /treɪkiəʊ/ *prefix* relating to the trachea

tracheobronchitis /ˌtreɪkiəʊbrɒŋˈkaɪtɪs/ *noun* inflammation of both the trachea and the bronchi

tracheostomy /ˌtræki'ɒstəmi/, **tracheotomy** /ˌtræki'ɒtəmi/ *noun* a surgical operation to make a hole through the throat into the windpipe, so as to allow air to get to the lungs in cases where the trachea is blocked, as in pneumonia, poliomyelitis or diphtheria

tract /trækt/ *noun* a series of organs or tubes which allow something to pass from one part of the body to another

traction /ˈtrækʃən/ *noun* a procedure that consists of using a pulling force to straighten a broken or deformed limb ○ *The patient was in traction for two weeks.*

tragus /ˈtreɪgəs/ *noun* a piece of cartilage in the outer ear which projects forward over the entrance to the auditory canal

trait /treɪt/ *noun* 1. a typical characteristic of someone 2. a genetically controlled characteristic

trance /trɑːns/ *noun* a condition in which a person is in a dream, but not asleep, and seems not to be aware of what is happening round him or her ○ *a hypnotic trance*

tranexamic acid /ˌtrænekˌsæmɪk ˈæsɪd/ *noun* a drug used to control severe bleeding

tranquilliser /ˈtræŋkwɪlaɪzə/, **tranquillizer**, **tranquillising drug** /ˈtræŋkwɪlaɪzɪŋ drʌg/ *noun* an antipsychotic, anxiolytic or hypnotic drug which relieves someone's anxiety and calms him or her down (*informal*) ○ *She's taking tranquillisers to calm her nerves.* ○ *He's been on tranquillisers ever since he started his new job.*

trans- /trænz/ *prefix* through or across

transaminase /trænˈsæmɪneɪz/ *noun* an enzyme involved in the transamination of amino acids

transcendental meditation /ˌtrænsendent(ə)l ˌmedɪˈteɪʃ(ə)n/ *noun* a type of meditation in which the same words or sounds are repeated silently

transcription /trænˈskrɪpʃən/ *noun* 1. the act of copying something written, or of putting something spoken into written form 2. the first step in carrying out genetic instructions in living cells, in which the genetic code is transferred from DNA to molecules of messenger RNA, which then direct protein manufacture

transcutaneous electrical nerve stimulation /ˌtrænskjuːˌteɪniəs ɪˌlektrɪk(ə)l ˈnɜːv stɪmjuˌleɪʃ(ə)n/ *noun* full form of **TENS**

transdermal /trænzˈdɜːm(ə)l/ *adjective* referring to a drug which is released through the skin

transference /ˈtrænsf(ə)rəns/ *noun* (*in psychiatry*) a condition in which someone transfers to the psychoanalyst the characteristics belonging to a strong character from his or her past such as a parent, and reacts as if the analyst were that person

transferrin /trænsˈferɪn/ *noun* a substance found in the blood, which carries iron in the bloodstream. Also called **siderophilin**

transfer RNA /ˌtrænsfɜː ˌɑːr en ˈeɪ/ *noun* RNA which attaches amino acids to protein chains being made at ribosomes

transfusion /trænsˈfjuːʒ(ə)n/ *noun* the procedure of transferring blood or saline fluids from a container into a someone's bloodstream

transient /ˈtrænziənt/ *adjective* not lasting long

transient ischaemic attack /ˌtrænziənt ɪ ˈskiːmɪk əˌtæk/ *noun* a mild stroke caused by a brief stoppage of blood supply to the brain. Abbreviation **TIA**

transillumination /ˌtrænsɪˌluːmɪˈneɪʃ(ə)n/ *noun* an examination of an organ by shining a bright light through it

transitional epithelium /trænˌzɪʃ(ə)nəl epɪ ˈθiːliəm/ *noun* a type of epithelium found in the urethra

translation /trænsˈleɪʃ(ə)n/ *noun* 1. the act of putting something written or spoken in one language into words of a different language 2. the process by which information in messenger RNA controls the sequence of amino acids assembled by a ribosome during protein synthesis

translocation /ˌtrænsləʊˈkeɪʃ(ə)n/ *noun* the movement of part of a chromosome to another part of the same chromosome or to a different chromosome pair, leading to genetic disorders

translucent /trænsˈluːs(ə)nt/ *adjective* allowing light to pass through, but not enough to allow objects on the other side to be clearly distinguished

transmission-based precautions /træns ˌmɪʃ(ə)n beɪst prɪˈkɔːʃ(ə)nz/ *plural noun* the most recent set of guidelines for health care workers on dealing with highly infectious diseases, to be used in addition to the Standard Precautions. There are three categories: Airborne Precautions, Droplet Precautions and Contact Precautions, sometimes used in combination for diseases which can be transmitted in various ways.

transplacental /ˌtrænspləˈsent(ə)l/ *adjective* through the placenta

transplant *noun* /ˈtrænsplɑːnt/ 1. a procedure which involves taking an organ such as the heart or kidney, or tissue such as skin, and grafting it into someone to replace an organ or tissue which is diseased or not functioning properly ○ *She had a heart-lung transplant.* **2.** the organ or tissue which is grafted ○ *The kidney transplant was rejected.* ■ *verb* /træns'plɑːnt/ to graft an organ or tissue onto or into someone to replace an organ or tissue which is diseased or not functioning correctly

transplantation /ˌtrænsplɑːn'teɪʃ(ə)n/ *noun* the act of transplanting something

transposition /ˌtrænspə'zɪʃ(ə)n/ *noun* a congenital condition where the aorta and pulmonary artery are placed on the opposite side of the body to their usual position

transpyloric plane /ˌtrænspaɪlɒrɪk 'pleɪn/ *noun* a plane at right angles to the sagittal plane, passing midway between the suprasternal notch and the symphysis pubis. See illustration at **ANATOMICAL TERMS** in Supplement

transsexual /trænz'sekʃuəl/ *adjective* feeling uncomfortable with the birth gender ■ *noun* a person, especially a man, who feels uncomfortable with their birth gender

transsexualism /trænz'sekʃuəlɪz(ə)m/ *noun* a condition in which a person, especially a man, feels uncomfortable with their birth gender

transtubercular plane /ˌtrænstjuːˌbɜːkjʊlə 'pleɪn/ *noun* an imaginary horizontal line drawn across the lower abdomen at the level of the projecting parts of the iliac bones. See illustration at **ANATOMICAL TERMS** in Supplement. Also called **intertubercular plane**

transudate /'trænsjuːdeɪt/ *noun* a fluid which passes through the pores of a membrane. It contains less protein or solid material than an exudate.

transudation /ˌtrænsjuː'deɪʃ(ə)n/ *noun* the process of passing a fluid from the body's cells through the pores of a membrane

transuretero-ureterostomy /ˌtræns juːrɪtərəʊ juːriːtə'rɒstəmi/ *noun* a surgical operation in which both ureters are brought to the same side in the abdomen, because one is damaged or obstructed

transurethral /ˌtrænsjʊ'riːθrəl/ *adjective* through the urethra

transurethral prostatectomy /ˌtrænsjʊriːθrəl ˌprɒstə'tektəmi/, **transurethral resection** /ˌtrænsjʊriːθrəl rɪ'sekʃən/ *noun* a surgical operation to remove the prostate gland, where the operation is carried out through the urethra. Abbreviation **TUR**. Also called **resection of the prostate**

transvaginal /ˌtrænsvə'dʒaɪn(ə)l/ *adjective* across or through the vagina

transverse /trænz'vɜːs/ *adjective* across, at right angles to an organ

transverse arch /ˌtrænz'vɜːs ɑːtʃ/ *noun* same as **metatarsal arch**

transverse colon /ˌtrænzvɜːs 'kəʊlɒn/ *noun* the second section of the colon which crosses the body below the stomach. See illustration at **DIGESTIVE SYSTEM** in Supplement

transverse fracture /ˌtrænzvɜːs 'fræktʃə/ *noun* a fracture where the bone is broken straight across

transverse lie /ˌtrænzvɜːs 'laɪ/ *noun* the position of a fetus across the body of the mother

transverse plane /ˌtrænzvɜːs 'pleɪn/ *noun* a plane at right angles to the sagittal plane, running horizontally across the body. See illustration at **ANATOMICAL TERMS** in Supplement

transverse presentation /ˌtrænzvɜːs ˌprez(ə)n'teɪʃ(ə)n/ *noun* a position of the baby in the uterus, where the baby's side will appear first, usually requiring urgent manipulation or caesarean section to prevent complications

transverse process /ˌtrænzvɜːs 'prəʊses/ *noun* the part of a vertebra which protrudes at the side

transvesical prostatectomy /træns ˌvesɪk(ə)l ˌprɒstə'tektəmi/ *noun* an operation to remove the prostate gland, carried out through the bladder

transvestism /trænz'vestɪz(ə)m/ *noun* the condition of liking to dress and behave as a member of the opposite sex

transvestite /trænz'vestaɪt/ *noun* a person who dresses and behaves as a member of the opposite sex

trapezium /trə'piːziəm/ *noun* one of the eight small carpal bones in the wrist, below the thumb. See illustration at **HAND** in Supplement (NOTE: The plural is **trapeziums** or **trapezia**.)

trapezius /trə'piːziəs/ *noun* a triangular muscle in the upper part of the back and the neck, which moves the shoulder blade and pulls the head back

trapezoid /'træpɪzɔɪd/, **trapezoid bone** /'træpɪzɔɪd bəʊn/ *noun* one of the eight small carpal bones in the wrist, below the first finger. See illustration at **HAND** in Supplement

trauma /'trɔːmə/ *noun* a wound or injury

traumatic /trɔː'mætɪk/ *adjective* **1.** caused by an injury **2.** extremely frightening, distressing or shocking

traumatic fever /trɔːˌmætɪk 'fiːvə/ *noun* a fever caused by an injury

traumatic pneumothorax /trɔːˌmætɪk ˌnjuːməʊ'θɔːræks/ *noun* pneumothorax which results from damage to the lung surface or to the wall of the chest, allowing air to leak into the space between the pleurae

traveller's diarrhoea /ˌtræv(ə)ləz ˌdaɪə'riːə/ *noun* diarrhoea that affects people who travel to foreign countries and which is due to contact with a different type of *E. coli* from the one they are used to. (*informal*)

travel sickness /'træv(ə)l ˌsɪknəs/ *noun* same as **motion sickness**

trazodone /'træzədəʊn/ *noun* an antidepressant drug which has a strong sedative effect, used in the treatment of depressive disorders accompanied by insomnia

Treacher Collins syndrome /ˌtriːtʃə 'kɒlɪnz ˌsɪndrəʊm/ *noun* a hereditary disorder in which the lower jaw, the cheek bones, and the ear are not fully developed

treat /triːt/ *verb* to use medical methods to cure a disease or help a sick or injured person to recover ○ *She has been treated with a new antibiotic.* ○ *She's being treated by a specialist for heart disease.*

treatment /'triːtmənt/ *noun* **1.** actions taken to look after sick or injured people or to cure disease ○ *He is receiving treatment for a slipped disc.* **2.** a particular way of looking after a sick or injured person or trying to cure a disease ○ *cortisone treatment* ○ *This is a new treatment for heart disease.*

tremens /'triːmenz/ ♦ **delirium tremens**

tremor /'tremə/ *noun* slight involuntary movements of a limb or muscle

trench foot /ˌtrentʃ 'fʊt/ *noun* a condition, caused by exposure to cold and damp, in which the skin of the foot becomes red and blistered and in severe cases turns black when gangrene sets in. Also called **immersion foot** (NOTE: Trench foot was common among soldiers serving in the trenches during the First World War.)

Trendelenburg's operation /tren 'delənbɜːgz ɒpəˌreɪʃ(ə)n/ *noun* an operation to tie a saphenous vein in the groin before removing varicose veins [After Friedrich Trendelburg (1844–1924), German surgeon.]

Trendelenburg's position /tren'delənbɜːgz pəˌzɪʃ(ə)n/, **Trendelenburg position** /tren 'delənbɜːg pəˌzɪʃ(ə)n/ *noun* a position in which someone lies on a sloping bed, with the head lower than the feet, and the knees bent. It is used in surgical operations to the pelvis and for people who have shock.

Trendelenburg's sign /tren'delənbɜːgz saɪn/ *noun* a symptom of congenital dislocation of the hip, where the person's pelvis is lower on the opposite side to the dislocation

trephine /trɪ'fiːn/ *noun* a surgical instrument for making a round hole in the skull or for removing a round piece of tissue

TRH *abbreviation* thyrotrophin-releasing hormone

triage /'triːɑːʒ/ *noun* the system in which a doctor or nurse sees patients briefly in order to decide who should be treated first

trial /'traɪəl/ *noun* a process of testing something such as a drug or treatment to see how effective it is, especially before allowing it to be used generally ○ *clinical trials* ○ *a six-month trial period* ○ *We're supplying it on a trial basis.* ■ *verb* to test something as part of a trial

triamcinolone /ˌtraɪæm'sɪnələʊn/ *noun* a synthetic corticosteroid drug used in the treatment of skin, mouth and joint inflammations

triangular bandage /traɪˌæŋɡjʊlə 'bændɪdʒ/ *noun* a bandage made of a triangle of cloth, used to make a sling for the arm

triceps /'traɪseps/ *noun* a muscle formed of three parts, which are joined to form one tendon

trich- /trɪk/ *prefix* same as **tricho-** (*used before vowels*)

trichiasis /trɪ'kaɪəsɪs/ *noun* a painful condition in which the eyelashes grow in towards the eye and scratch the eyeball

trichinosis /ˌtrɪkɪ'nəʊsɪs/, **trichiniasis** /ˌtrɪkɪ 'naɪəsɪs/ *noun* a disease caused by infestation of the intestine by larvae of roundworms or nematodes, which pass round the body in the bloodstream and settle in muscles

tricho- /trɪkəʊ/ *prefix* referring to hair

trichology /trɪ'kɒlədʒi/ *noun* the study of hair and the diseases which affect it

Trichomonas /ˌtrɪkə'məʊnəs/ *noun* a species of long thin parasite which infests the intestines

Trichomonas vaginalis /trɪkəˌməʊnəs vædʒɪ'neɪlɪs/ *noun* a parasite which infests the vagina and causes an irritating discharge

trichomoniasis /ˌtrɪkəʊmə'naɪəsɪs/ *noun* infestation of the intestine or vagina with Trichomonas

Trichophyton /traɪ'kɒfɪtɒn/ *noun* a fungus which affects the skin, hair and nails

trichophytosis /ˌtrɪkəʊfaɪ'təʊsɪs/ *noun* an infection caused by Trichophyton

trichosis /traɪ'kəʊsɪs/ *noun* any unusual condition of the hair

trichromatism /traɪ'krəʊmətɪz(ə)m/ *noun* vision which allows the difference between the three primary colours to be seen. Compare **dichromatism**, **monochromatism**

tricuspid /traɪ'kʌspɪd/ *noun* something which has three cusps, e.g. a tooth or leaf ■ *adjective* **1.** having three cusps or points **2.** referring to a tricuspid valve or tooth

tricuspid valve /traɪ'kʌspɪd vælv/ *noun* an inlet valve with three cusps between the right atrium and the right ventricle in the heart. See illustration at HEART in Supplement

tricyclic antidepressant /traɪˌsaɪklɪk ˌæntɪdɪ'pres(ə)nt/, **tricyclic antidepressant drug** /traɪˌsaɪklɪk ˌæntɪdɪ'pres(ə)nt ˌdrʌg/ *noun* a drug used to treat depression and panic disorder, e.g. amitriptyline and nortriptyline

tridactyly /traɪˈdæktɪli/ *noun* the condition of having only three fingers or toes

trifocal lenses /traɪˌfəʊk(ə)l ˈlenzɪz/, **trifocal glasses** /traɪˌfəʊk(ə)l ˈglɑːsɪz/, **trifocals** /traɪ ˈfəʊk(ə)lz/ *plural noun* spectacles which have three lenses combined in one piece of glass to give clear vision over different distances. ◊ **bifocal**

trigeminal /traɪˈdʒemɪn(ə)l/ *adjective* in three parts

trigeminal nerve /traɪˈdʒemɪn(ə)l nɜːv/ *noun* the fifth cranial nerve, formed of the ophthalmic nerve, the maxillary nerve and the mandibular nerve, which controls the sensory nerves in the forehead, face and chin, and the muscles in the jaw

trigeminal neuralgia /traɪˌdʒemɪn(ə)l njʊ ˈrældʒə/ *noun* a disorder of the trigeminal nerve, which sends intense pains shooting across the face. Also called **tic douloureux**

trigeminy /traɪˈdʒemɪni/ *noun* an irregular heartbeat, where a regular beat is followed by two ectopic beats

trigger finger /ˈtrɪgə ˌfɪŋgə/ *noun* a condition in which a finger can bend but is difficult to straighten, probably because of a nodule on the flexor tendon

triglyceride /traɪˈglɪsəraɪd/ *noun* a substance such as fat which contains three fatty acids

trigonitis /ˌtrɪgəˈnaɪtɪs/ *noun* inflammation of the bottom part of the wall of the bladder

trigonocephalic /traɪˌgɒnəkəˈfælɪk/ *adjective* referring to a skull which shows signs of trigonocephaly

trigonocephaly /traɪˌgɒnəˈkef(ə)li/ *noun* a condition in which the skull is in the shape of a triangle, with points on either side of the face in front of the ears

triiodothyronine /traɪˌaɪədəʊˈθaɪrəniːn/ *noun* a hormone synthesised in the body from thyroxine secreted by the thyroid gland

trimeprazine /traɪˈmeprəziːn/ *noun* an antihistamine used to relieve the itching caused by eczema and various skin rashes, including allergic skin rashes caused by poison ivy

trimester /traɪˈmestə/ *noun* one of the three 3-month periods of a pregnancy

trimethoprim /traɪˈmiːθəprɪm/ *noun* a synthetic drug used in the treatment of malaria

triple marker test /ˌtrɪp(ə)l ˈmɑːkə test/ *noun* a blood test performed on pregnant women which can detect Down's syndrome in a fetus by analysing the relative levels of substances produced by the mother's placenta and the fetus itself

triplet /ˈtrɪplət/ *noun* one of three babies born to a mother at the same time

triple vaccine /ˌtrɪp(ə)l ˈvæksiːn/ *noun* a vaccine which induces protection against three dis-

eases e.g. diphtheria, tetanus and whooping cough

triquetrum /traɪˈkwetrəm/, **triquetral** /traɪ ˈkwetr(ə)l/, **triquetral bone** /traɪˈkwetr(ə)l bəʊn/ *noun* one of the eight small carpal bones in the wrist. See illustration at **HAND** in Supplement

trismus /ˈtrɪzməs/ *noun* a spasm in the lower jaw, which makes it difficult to open the mouth, a symptom of tetanus

trisomy /ˈtraɪsəʊmi/ *noun* a condition in which someone has three chromosomes instead of a pair

trisomy 21 /ˌtraɪsəʊmi ˌtwenti ˈwʌn/ *noun* same as **Down's syndrome**

trocar /ˈtrəʊkɑː/ *noun* a surgical instrument or pointed rod which slides inside a cannula to make a hole in tissue to drain off fluid

trochanter /trəˈkæntə/ *noun* two bony lumps on either side of the top end of the femur where muscles are attached

trochlea /ˈtrɒkliə/ *noun* any part of the body shaped like a pulley, especially part of the lower end of the humerus, which articulates with the ulna, or a curved bone in the frontal bone through which one of the eye muscles passes (NOTE: The plural is **trochleae**.)

trochlear /ˈtrɒkliə/ *adjective* referring to a ring in a bone

trochlear nerve /ˈtrɒkliə nɜːv/ *noun* the fourth cranial nerve which controls the muscles of the eyeball

trochoid joint /ˈtrəʊkɔɪd dʒɔɪnt/ *noun* a joint where a bone can rotate freely about a central axis as in the neck, where the atlas articulates with the axis. Also called **pivot joint**

troph- /trɒf/ *prefix* same as **tropho-** (*used before vowels*)

trophic /ˈtrɒfɪk/ *adjective* relating to food and nutrition

trophic ulcer /ˌtrɒfɪk ˈʌlsə/ *noun* an ulcer caused by lack of blood, e.g. a bedsore

tropho- /trɒfəʊ/ *prefix* referring to food or nutrition

-trophy /trəfi/ *suffix* **1.** nourishment **2.** referring to the development of an organ

tropia /ˈtrəʊpiə/ *noun* same as **squint**

-tropic /trɒpɪk/ *suffix* **1.** turning towards **2.** referring to something which influences

tropical /ˈtrɒpɪk(ə)l/ *adjective* located in or coming from areas around the equator where the climate is generally very hot and humid

tropical disease /ˌtrɒpɪk(ə)l dɪˈziːz/ *noun* a disease which is found in tropical countries, e.g. malaria, dengue or Lassa fever

tropical medicine /ˌtrɒpɪk(ə)l ˈmed(ə)sɪn/ *noun* a branch of medicine which deals with tropical diseases

tropical ulcer /ˌtrɒpɪk(ə)l ˈʌlsə/ *noun* a large area of infection which forms around a wound, found especially in tropical countries. Also called **Naga sore**

trots /trɒts/ □ **the trots** an attack of diarrhoea (*informal*)

trouble /'trʌb(ə)l/ *noun* a disorder or condition (*informal*) ○ *treatment for back trouble* ○ *She has kidney trouble.*

Trousseau's sign /'truːsəʊz saɪn/ *noun* a spasm in the muscles in the forearm when a tourniquet is applied to the upper arm, which causes the index and middle fingers to extend. It is a sign of latent tetany, showing that the blood contains too little calcium. [After Armand Trousseau (1801–67), French physician.]

true vocal cords /ˌtruː 'vəʊk(ə)l ˌkɔːdz/ *plural noun* the cords in the larynx which can be brought together to make sounds as air passes between them

trunk /trʌŋk/ *noun* same as **torso**

truss /trʌs/ *noun* a belt worn round the waist, with pads, to hold a hernia in place

trust status /'trʌst ˌsteɪtəs/ *noun* the position of a hospital which is a self-governing trust

trypanosome /'trɪpənəʊsəʊm/ *noun* a microscopic organism which lives as a parasite in human blood. It is transmitted by the bite of insects such as the tsetse fly and causes sleeping sickness and other serious illnesses.

trypsin /'trɪpsɪn/ *noun* an enzyme converted from trypsinogen by the duodenum and secreted into the digestive system where it absorbs protein

trypsinogen /trɪp'sɪnədʒən/ *noun* an enzyme secreted by the pancreas into the duodenum

tryptophan /'trɪptəfæn/ *noun* an essential amino acid

tsetse fly /'tetsi flaɪ, 'setsi flaɪ/ *noun* an African insect which passes trypanosomes into the human bloodstream, causing sleeping sickness

TSH *abbreviation* thyroid-stimulating hormone

TSS *abbreviation* toxic shock syndrome

tubal /'tjuːb(ə)l/ *adjective* referring to a tube

tubal ligation /ˌtjuːb(ə)l laɪ'geɪʃ(ə)n/ *noun* a surgical operation to tie up the Fallopian tubes as a sterilisation procedure

tubal occlusion /ˌtjuːb(ə)l ə'kluːʒ(ə)n/ *noun* a condition in which the Fallopian tubes are blocked, either as a result of disease or surgery

tubal pregnancy /ˌtjuːb(ə)l 'pregnənsi/ *noun* the most common form of ectopic pregnancy, in which the fetus develops in a Fallopian tube instead of the uterus

tube /tjuːb/ *noun* **1.** a long hollow passage in the body **2.** a soft flexible pipe for carrying liquid or gas **3.** a soft plastic or metal pipe, sealed at one end and with a lid at the other, used to dispense a paste or gel

tube feeding /'tjuːb ˌfiːdɪŋ/ *noun* the process of giving someone nutrients through a tube directly into their stomach or small intestine

tuber /'tjuːbə/ *noun* a swollen or raised area

tubercle /'tjuːbək(ə)l/ *noun* **1.** a small bony projection, e.g. on a rib **2.** a small infected lump characteristic of tuberculosis, where tissue is destroyed and pus forms

tubercular /tjʊ'bɜːkjʊlə/ *adjective* causing or referring to tuberculosis

tuberculin /tjʊ'bɜːkjʊlɪn/ *noun* a substance which is derived from the culture of the tuberculosis bacillus and is used to test people for the presence of tuberculosis

tuberculin test /tjʊ'bɜːkjʊlɪn test/ *noun* a test to see if someone has tuberculosis, in which someone is exposed to tuberculin and the reaction of the skin is noted

tuberculosis /tjʊˌbɜːkjʊ'ləʊsɪs/ *noun* an infectious disease caused by the tuberculosis bacillus, where infected lumps form in the tissue. Abbreviation **TB**

tuberculous /tjʊ'bɜːkjʊləs/ *adjective* referring to tuberculosis

tuberose sclerosis /ˌtjuːbərəʊs sklə'rəʊsɪs/ *noun* same as **epiloia**

tuberosity /ˌtjuːbə'rɒsɪti/ *noun* a large lump on a bone

tuberous /'tjuːbərəs/ *adjective* with lumps or nodules

tubo- /tjuːbəʊ/ *prefix* referring to a Fallopian tube or to the internal or external auditory meatus

tuboabdominal /ˌtjuːbəʊæb'dɒmɪn(ə)l/ *adjective* referring to a Fallopian tube and the abdomen

tubocurarine /ˌtjuːbəʊ'kjʊərəriːn/ *noun* a toxic alkaloid which is the active constituent of curare, used as a muscle relaxant

tubo-ovarian /ˌtjuːbəʊ əʊ'veəriən/ *adjective* referring to a Fallopian tube and an ovary

tubotympanal /ˌtjuːbəʊ'tɪmpən(ə)l/ *adjective* referring to the Eustachian tube and the tympanum

tubular /'tjuːbjʊlə/ *adjective* shaped like a tube

tubular bandage /ˌtjuːbjʊlə 'bændɪdʒ/ *noun* a bandage made of a tube of elastic cloth

tubular reabsorption /ˌtjuːbjʊlə ˌriːəb'sɔːpʃən/ *noun* the process by which some of the substances filtered into the kidney are absorbed back into the bloodstream by the tubules

tubule /'tjuːbjuːl/ *noun* a small tube in the body. ◊ **renal tubule**

tumefaction /ˌtjuːmɪ'fækʃən/ *noun* swelling within body tissue, usually caused a build-up of blood or water

tumescence /tjuː'mes(ə)ns/ *noun* swollen tissue where liquid has accumulated underneath. ◊ **oedema**

tumid /'tjuːmɪd/ *adjective* swollen

tummy /'tʌmi/ *noun* stomach or abdomen (*informal*)

tummy ache /'tʌmi eɪk/ *noun* stomach pain (*informal*)

tumoral /'tjuːmərəl/, **tumorous** /'tjuːmərəs/ *adjective* referring to a tumour

tumour /'tjuːmə/ *noun* an unusual swelling or growth of new cells ○ *The X-ray showed a tumour in the breast.* ○ *a brain tumour.* (NOTE: For other terms referring to tumours, see words beginning with **onco-**.)

tunica /'tjuːnɪkə/ *noun* a layer of tissue which covers an organ

tunica albuginea testis /ˌtjuːnɪkə ælbjʊ ˌdʒɪniə 'testɪs/ *noun* a white fibrous membrane covering the testes and the ovaries

tunica intima /ˌtjuːnɪkə 'ɪntɪmə/ *noun* the inner layer of the wall of an artery or vein. Also called **intima**

tunica media /ˌtjuːnɪkə 'miːdiə/ *noun* the middle layer of the wall of an artery or vein. Also called **media**

tunica vaginalis /ˌtjuːnɪkə ˌvædʒɪ'neɪlɪs/ *noun* a membrane covering the testes and epididymis

tuning fork /'tjuːnɪŋ fɔːk/ *noun* a metal fork which, if hit, gives out a perfect note, used in hearing tests such as Rinne's test

tunnel /'tʌn(ə)l/ *noun* a passage or channel through or under something ○ *the carpal tunnel* ■ *verb* **1.** to make a tunnel under or through something **2.** to produce or dig something which is shaped like a tunnel

tunnel vision /ˌtʌn(ə)l 'vɪʒ(ə)n/ *noun* vision which is restricted to the area directly in front of the eye

turbinate /'tɜːbɪnət/ *adjective* **1.** having a shape like a spiral or an inverted cone **2.** referring to any of the three bones found on the walls of the nasal passages of mammals

turbinate bone /'tɜːbɪnət bəʊn/ *noun* ♦ **nasal conchae**

turbinectomy /ˌtɜːbɪ'nektəmi/ *noun* a surgical operation to remove a turbinate bone

turgescence /tɜː'dʒes(ə)ns/ *noun* a swelling in body tissue caused by the accumulation of fluid

turgid /'tɜːdʒɪd/ *adjective* swollen with blood

turgor /'tɜːgə/ *noun* the condition of being swollen

Turner's syndrome /'tɜːnəz ˌsɪndrəʊm/ *noun* a congenital condition in females, caused by the absence of one of the pair of X chromosomes, in which sexual development is retarded and no ovaries develop [Described 1938. After Henry Hubert Turner (1892–1970), US endocrinologist, Clinical professor of Medicine, Oklahoma University, USA.]

turricephaly /ˌtʌrɪ'sefəli/ same as **oxycephaly**

tussis /'tʌsɪs/ *noun* coughing

twenty-twenty vision /ˌtwenti ˌtwenti 'vɪʒ(ə)n/ *noun* perfect vision

twilight sleep /'twaɪlaɪt ˌsliːp/ *noun* a type of anaesthetic sleep, in which the patient is semiconscious but cannot feel any pain

twilight state /'twaɪlaɪt steɪt/ *noun* a condition of epileptics and alcoholics in which the person can do some automatic actions, but is not conscious of what he or she is doing

COMMENT: Twilight state is induced at childbirth, by introducing anaesthetics into the rectum.

twin /twɪn/ *noun* one of two babies born to a mother at the same time

tylosis /taɪ'ləʊsɪs/ *noun* the development of a callus

tympan- /tɪmpən/ *prefix* same as **tympano-** (NOTE: used before vowels)

tympanectomy /ˌtɪmpə'nektəmi/ *noun* a surgical operation to remove the tympanic membrane

tympanic /tɪm'pænɪk/ *adjective* referring to the eardrum

tympanic membrane /tɪmˌpænɪk 'membreɪn/ *noun* the membrane at the inner end of the external auditory meatus leading from the outer ear, which vibrates with sound and passes the vibrations on to the ossicles in the middle ear. Also called **tympanum**, **eardrum**. See illustration at EAR in Supplement

tympanites /ˌtɪmpə'naɪtiːz/ *noun* the expansion of the stomach with gas. Also called **meteorism**

tympanitis /ˌtɪmpə'naɪtɪs/ *noun* same as **otitis media**

tympano- /tɪmpənəʊ/ *prefix* referring to the eardrum

tympanoplasty /'tɪmpənəʊplæsti/ *noun* same as **myringoplasty**

tympanosclerosis /ˌtɪmpənəʊsklə'rəʊsɪs/ *noun* irreversible damage to the tympanic membrane and middle ear, starting with the replacement of tissues or fibrin by collagen and hyalin. Then calcification occurs, leading to deafness.

tympanotomy /ˌtɪmpə'nɒtəmi/ *noun* same as **myringotomy**

tympanum /'tɪmpənəm/ *noun* same as **tympanic membrane**

type A behaviour /ˌtaɪp 'eɪ bɪˌheɪvjə/ *noun* a behaviour pattern which may contribute to coronary heart disease, in which an individual is aggressive and over-competitive, and usually lives at a stressful pace. Compare **type B behaviour**

type B behaviour /ˌtaɪp ˈbiː bɪˌheɪvjə/ *noun* a behaviour pattern which is unlikely to contribute to coronary heart disease, in which an individual is patient, tolerant, not very competitive and lives at a more relaxed pace. Compare **type A behaviour**

Type I diabetes mellitus /ˌtaɪp ˌwʌn daɪə ˌbiːtiːz məˈlaɪtəs/ *noun* the type of diabetes mellitus in which the beta cells of the pancreas produce little or no insulin, and the person is completely dependent on injections of insulin for survival. It is more likely to develop in people under 30. Symptoms are usually severe and occur suddenly. Also called **insulin-dependent diabetes**

Type II diabetes mellitus /ˌtaɪp ˌtuː daɪə ˌbiːtiːz məˈlaɪtəs/ *noun* the type of diabetes mellitus in which cells throughout the body lose some or most of their ability to use insulin. It is more likely to develop in people who are over 40, who are overweight or obese, and who do not exercise regularly. It can be controlled in some cases with diet and exercise, but more severe cases may need oral medication which reduces glucose concentrations in the blood, or insulin injections, so that even cells with a poor uptake will capture enough insulin. Also called **non-insulin-dependent diabetes**

typho- /taɪfəʊ/ *prefix* **1.** relating to typhoid fever **2.** relating to typhus

typhoid /ˈtaɪfɔɪd/, **typhoid fever** /ˌtaɪfɔɪd ˈfiːvə/ *noun* an infection of the intestine caused by *Salmonella typhi* in food and water

typhus /ˈtaɪfəs/ *noun* one of several fevers caused by the Rickettsia bacterium, transmitted by fleas and lice, producing a fever, extreme weakness and a dark rash on the skin. The test for typhus is the Weil-Felix reaction.

tyramine /ˈtaɪrəmiːn/ *noun* an enzyme found in cheese, beans, tinned fish, red wine and yeast extract, which can cause high blood pressure if found in excessive quantities in the brain. ◊ **monoamine oxidase**

tyrosine /ˈtaɪrəsiːn/ *noun* an amino acid in protein which is a component of thyroxine, and is a precursor to the catecholamines dopamine, noradrenaline and adrenaline

U

UKCC *abbreviation* United Kingdom Central Council for Nursing, Midwifery and Health Visiting

ulcer /'ʌlsə/ *noun* an open sore in the skin or in a mucous membrane, which is inflamed and difficult to heal ○ *stomach ulcer*

ulcerative /'ʌls(ə)rətɪv/ *adjective* referring to ulcers, or characterised by ulcers

ulcerative colitis /ˌʌls(ə)rətɪv kə'laɪtɪs/ *noun* severe pain in the colon, with diarrhoea and ulcers in the rectum, often with a psychosomatic cause

ulceromembranous gingivitis /ˌʌlsərəʊˌmembrənəs ˌdʒɪndʒɪ'vaɪtɪs/ *noun* inflammation of the gums, which can also affect the mucous membrane in the mouth

ule- *prefix* relating to a scar, or to scar tissue

ulna /'ʌlnə/ *noun* the longer and inner of the two bones in the forearm between the elbow and the wrist. See illustration at HAND in Supplement. Compare **radius**

ulnar /'ʌlnə/ *adjective* referring to the ulna

ulnar artery /'ʌlnər ˌɑːtəri/ *noun* an artery which branches from the brachial artery at the elbow and runs down the inside of the forearm to join the radial artery in the palm of the hand

ulnar nerve /'ʌlnə nɜːv/ *noun* a nerve which runs from the neck to the elbow and controls the muscles in the forearm and some of the fingers

COMMENT: The ulnar nerve passes near the surface of the skin at the elbow, where it can easily be hit, giving the effect of the 'funny bone'.

ultra- *prefix* **1.** further than **2.** extremely

ultrafiltration /ˌʌltrəfɪl'treɪʃ(ə)n/ *noun* the process of filtering the blood to remove tiny particles, e.g. when the blood is filtered by the kidney

ultrasonic /ˌʌltrə'sɒnɪk/ *adjective* referring to ultrasound

ultrasonic probe /ˌʌltrəsɒnɪk 'prəʊb/ *noun* an instrument which locates organs or tissues inside the body using ultrasound

ultrasonics /ˌʌltrə'sɒnɪks/ *noun* the study of ultrasound and its use in medical treatments

ultrasonic waves /ˌʌltrəsɒnɪk 'weɪvz/ *plural noun* same as **ultrasound**

ultrasonogram /ˌʌltrə'sɒnəgræm/ *noun* a picture made with ultrasound for the purpose of medical examination or diagnosis

ultrasonograph /ˌʌltrə'sɒnəgrɑːf/ *noun* a machine which takes pictures of internal organs, using ultrasound

ultrasonography /ˌʌltrəsə'nɒgrəfi/ *noun* the procedure of passing ultrasound waves through the body and recording echoes which show details of internal organs. Also called **echography**

ultrasound /'ʌltrəsaʊnd/ *noun* very high frequency sound waves which can be reflected off internal body parts or off a fetus in the womb to create images for medical examination (NOTE: No plural for **ultrasound**.)

ultrasound marker /'ʌltrəsaʊnd ˌmɑːkə/ *noun* an unusual physical characteristic seen in an ultrasound examination of a fetus which is an indication of the existence of a genetic or developmental disorder

ultrasound probe /'ʌltrəsaʊnd prəʊb/ *noun* same as **ultrasonic probe**

ultrasound scanning /'ʌltrəsaʊnd ˌskænɪŋ/, **ultrasound screening** /'ʌltrəsaʊnd ˌskriːnɪŋ/ *noun* a method of gathering information about the body by taking images using high-frequency sound waves

ultrasound treatment /'ʌltrəsaʊnd ˌtriːtmənt/ *noun* the treatment of soft tissue inflammation using ultrasound waves

ultraviolet /ˌʌltrə'vaɪələt/ *adjective* referring to the short invisible rays beyond the violet end of the spectrum, which form the element in sunlight which tans the skin, helps the skin produce Vitamin D and kills bacteria. Abbreviation **UV**

ultraviolet lamp /ˌʌltrəvaɪələt 'læmp/ *noun* a lamp which gives off ultraviolet rays

ultraviolet radiation /ˌʌltrəvaɪələt ˌreɪdi'eɪʃ(ə)n/, **ultraviolet rays** /ˌʌltrə'vaɪələt reɪs/ *noun* short invisible rays of ultraviolet light. Abbreviation **UVR**

umbilical /ʌm'bɪlɪk(ə)l/ *adjective* referring to the navel

umbilical cord /ʌm'bɪlɪk(ə)l kɔːd/ *noun* a cord containing two arteries and one vein which links the fetus inside the uterus to the placenta

umbilical hernia /ˌʌmˌbɪlɪk(ə)l ˈhɜːniə/ *noun* a hernia which bulges at the navel, usually in young children. Also called **exomphalos**

umbilicated /ˌʌmˈbɪlɪkeɪtɪd/ *adjective* with a small depression, like a navel, in the centre

umbilicus /ˌʌmˈbɪlɪkəs/ *noun* same as **navel**

umbo /ˈʌmbəʊ/ *noun* a projecting part in the middle of the outer side of the eardrum

un- /ʌn/ *prefix* not

unciform bone /ˈʌnsɪfɔːm bəʊn/ *noun* one of the eight small carpal bones in the wrist, shaped like a hook. Also called **hamate bone**

uncinate /ˈʌnsɪnət/ *adjective* shaped like a hook

unconditioned response /ˌʌnkəndɪʃ(ə)nd rɪˈspɒns/ *noun* a response to a stimulus which occurs automatically, by instinct, and has not been learned

unconscious /ʌnˈkɒnʃəs/ *adjective* not aware of what is happening ○ *She was unconscious for two days after the accident.* ■ *noun* □ **the unconscious** (*in psychology*) the part of the mind which stores feelings, memories or desires that someone cannot consciously call up. ◊ **subconscious**

unconsciousness /ʌnˈkɒnʃəsnəs/ *noun* the state of being unconscious, e.g. as a result of lack of oxygen or from some other external cause such as a blow on the head

undecenoic acid /ˌʌnˌdesɪnəʊɪk ˈæsɪd/, **undecylenic acid** /ˌʌnˌdɪsɪlenɪk ˈæsɪd/ *noun* a substance made from castor bean oil, used in the treatment of fungal infections such as thrush

undine /ˈʌndiːn/ *noun* a glass container for a solution to bathe the eyes

undulant fever /ˈʌndjʊlənt ˌfiːvə/ same as **brucellosis**

ungual /ˈʌŋgwəl/ *adjective* referring to the fingernails or toenails

unguentum /ʌŋˈgwentəm/ *noun* (*in pharmacy*) an ointment

unguis /ˈʌŋgwɪs/ same as **nail**

uni- /juːni/ *prefix* one

unicellular /ˌjuːnɪˈseljʊlə/ *adjective* referring to an organism formed of one cell

unigravida /ˌjuːniˈgrævɪdə/ *noun* same as **primigravida**

unilateral /ˌjuːnɪˈlæt(ə)rəl/ *adjective* affecting one side of the body only

unilateral oophorectomy /ˌjuːnɪlæt(ə)rəl ˌəʊəfəˈrektəmi/ *noun* the surgical removal of one ovary

union /ˈjuːnjən/ *noun* the joining together of two parts of a fractured bone. Opposite **non-union**. ◊ **malunion**

uniovular /ˌjuːniˈɒvjʊlə/ *noun* consisting of, or coming from, one ovum

uniovular twins /ˌjuːniɒvjʊlə ˈtwɪnz/ *plural noun* same as **identical twins**

unipara /juːˈnɪpərə/ *noun* same as **primipara**

unipolar neurone /juːnɪˌpəʊlə ˈnjʊərəʊn/ *noun* a neurone with a single process. Compare **multipolar neurone**, **bipolar neurone**. See illustration at **NEURONE** in Supplement

unit /ˈjuːnɪt/ *noun* **1.** a single part of a larger whole **2.** a part of a hospital that has a specialised function ○ *a burns unit* **3.** a named and agreed standard amount used for measuring something ○ *A gram is an SI unit of weight.* **4.** a quantity of a drug, enzyme, hormone or of blood, taken as a standard for measurement and producing a given effect ○ *three units of blood* ○ *a unit of insulin* **5.** a machine or device ○ *a waste-disposal unit*

United Kingdom Central Council for Nursing, Midwifery, and Health Visiting /juːˌnaɪtɪd ˌkɪŋdəm ˌsentrəl ˌkaʊnsəl fə ˌnɜːsɪŋ mɪdˌwɪfəri ənd ˈhelθ ˌvɪzɪtɪŋ/ *noun* in the UK from 1979 until April 2002, an organisation which regulated nurses, midwives, and health visitors. The UKCC and the four National Boards have now been replaced by the Nursing and Midwifery Council. Abbreviation **UKCC**

universal donor /ˌjuːnɪvɜːs(ə)l ˈdəʊnə/ *noun* a person with blood group O, whose blood may be given to anyone

Universal Precautions /ˌjuːnɪvɜːs(ə)l prɪ ˈkɔːʃ(ə)nz/ *abbreviation* UP. ◊ **Standard Precautions**

universal recipient /ˌjuːnɪvɜːs(ə)l rɪ ˈsɪpiənt/ *noun* a person with blood group AB who can receive blood from all the other blood groups

unsaturated fat /ʌnˌsætʃəreɪtɪd ˈfæt/ *noun* fat which does not have a large amount of hydrogen, and so can be broken down more easily

unstable angina /ʌnˌsteɪb(ə)l ænˈdʒaɪnə/ *noun* angina which has suddenly become worse

unstriated muscle /ˌʌnstraɪˌeɪtɪd ˈmʌs(ə)l/ *noun* same as **smooth muscle**

upper respiratory infection /ˌʌpə rɪ ˈspɪrət(ə)ri ɪnˌfekʃən/ *noun* an infection in the upper part of the respiratory system

UPPP *abbreviation* uvulopalatopharyngoplasty

upset stomach /ʌpˌset ˈstʌmək/ *noun* same as **stomach upset**

uracil /ˈjʊərəsɪl/ *noun* a pyrimidine base, one of the four bases in RNA in which it pairs with thymine

uraemia /jʊˈriːmiə/ *noun* a disorder caused by kidney failure, where urea is retained in the blood, and the person develops nausea, convulsions and in severe cases goes into a coma

uraemic /jʊˈriːmɪk/ *adjective* referring to uraemia, or having uraemia

uran- /jʊərən/ *prefix* referring to the palate

urate /ˈjʊəreɪt/ *noun* a salt of uric acid found in urine

uraturia /ˌjʊərəˈtjʊəriə/ *noun* the presence of excessive amounts of urates in the urine, e.g. in gout

urea /jʊˈriːə/ *noun* a substance produced in the liver from excess amino acids, and excreted by the kidneys into the urine

uresis /jʊˈriːsɪs/ *noun* the act of passing urine

ureter /jʊˈriːtə, ˈjʊərɪtə/ *noun* one of the two tubes which take urine from the kidneys to the urinary bladder. See illustration at **KIDNEY** in Supplement. Also called **urinary duct**

ureter- /jʊriːtə/ *prefix* same as **uretero-** (*used before vowels*)

ureteral /jʊˈriːtərəl/ *adjective* referring to the ureters

ureterectomy /ˌjʊərɪtəˈrektəmi/ *noun* the surgical removal of a ureter

ureteric /ˌjʊərɪˈterɪk/ *adjective* same as **ureteral**

ureteric calculus /ˌjʊərɪterɪk ˈkælkjʊləs/ *noun* a kidney stone in the ureter

ureteric catheter /ˌjʊərɪterɪk ˈkæθɪtə/ *noun* a catheter passed through the ureter to the kidney, to inject an opaque solution into the kidney before taking an X-ray

ureteritis /ˌjʊərɪtəˈraɪtɪs/ *noun* inflammation of a ureter

uretero- /jʊriːtərəʊ/ *prefix* referring to the ureter

ureterocele /jʊˈriːtərəʊsiːl/ *noun* swelling in a ureter caused by narrowing of the opening where the ureter enters the bladder

ureterocolostomy /jʊˌriːtərəʊkɒˈlɒstəmi/ *noun* a surgical operation to implant the ureter into the sigmoid colon, so as to bypass the bladder

ureteroenterostomy /jʊˌriːtərəʊˌentəˈrɒstəmi/ *noun* an artificially formed passage between the ureter and the intestine

ureterolith /jʊˈriːtərəʊlɪθ/ *noun* a stone in a ureter

ureterolithotomy /jʊˌriːtərəʊlɪˈθɒtəmi/ *noun* the surgical removal of a stone from the ureter

ureterolysis /ˌjʊərɪtəˈrɒləsɪs/ *noun* a surgical operation to free one or both ureters from adhesions or surrounding tissue

ureteroneocystostomy /jʊˌriːtərəʊˌniːəʊsaɪˈstɒstəmi/ *noun* a surgical operation to transplant a ureter to a different location in the bladder

ureteronephrectomy /jʊˌriːtərəʊnɪˈfrektəmi/ *noun* same as **nephroureterectomy**

ureteroplasty /jʊˈriːtərəʊplæsti/ *noun* a surgical operation to repair a ureter

ureteropyelonephritis /jʊˌriːtərəʊˌpaɪələʊnɪˈfraɪtɪs/ *noun* inflammation of the ureter and the pelvis of the kidney to which it is attached

ureteroscope /jʊˈriːtərəʊskəʊp/ *noun* an instrument which is passed into the ureter and up into the kidneys, usually used to locate or remove a stone

ureteroscopy /ˌjʊərɪtəˈrɒskəpi/ *noun* an examination of the ureter with a ureteroscope

ureterosigmoidostomy /jʊˌriːtərəʊsɪgmɔɪˈdɒstəmi/ same as **ureterocolostomy**

ureterostomy /ˌjʊərɪtəˈrɒstəmi/ *noun* a surgical operation to make an artificial opening for the ureter into the abdominal wall, so that urine can be passed directly out of the body

ureterotomy /ˌjʊərɪtəˈrɒtəmi/ *noun* a surgical operation to make an incision into the ureter, mainly to remove a stone

ureterovaginal /jʊˌriːtərəʊvəˈdʒaɪn(ə)l/ *adjective* referring to the ureter and the vagina

urethra /jʊˈriːθrə/ *noun* a tube which takes urine from the bladder to be passed out of the body. See illustration at **UROGENITAL SYSTEM** in Supplement

urethral /jʊˈriːθr(ə)l/ *adjective* referring to the urethra

urethral catheter /jʊˌriːθr(ə)l ˈkæθɪtə/ *noun* a catheter passed up the urethra to allow urine to flow out of the bladder, used to empty the bladder before an abdominal operation. Also called **urinary catheter**

urethral stricture /jʊˌriːθrəl ˈstrɪktʃə/ *noun* a condition in which the urethra is narrowed or blocked by a growth. Also called **urethrostenosis**

urethritis /ˌjʊərəˈθraɪtɪs/ *noun* inflammation of the urethra

urethro- /jʊriːθrəʊ/ *prefix* referring to the urethra

urethrocele /jʊˈriːθrəsiːl/ *noun* a swelling formed in a weak part of the wall of the urethra

urethrogram /jʊˈriːθrəgræm/ *noun* an X-ray photograph of the urethra

urethrography /ˌjʊərɪˈθrɒgrəfi/ *noun* X-ray examination of the urethra

urethroplasty /jʊˈriːθrəplæsti/ *noun* a surgical operation to repair a urethra

urethrorrhaphy /ˌjʊərɪˈθrɒrəfi/ *noun* a surgical operation to repair a torn urethra

urethrorrhoea /jʊˌriːθrəˈriːə/ *noun* the discharge of fluid from the urethra, usually associated with urethritis

urethroscope /jʊˈriːθrəskəʊp/ *noun* a surgical instrument, used to examine the interior of a man's urethra

urethroscopy /ˌjʊərɪˈθrɒskəpi/ *noun* an examination of the inside of a man's urethra with a urethroscope

urethrostenosis /juˌriːθrəʊstəˈnəʊsɪs/ *noun* same as **urethral stricture**

urethrostomy /ˌjʊərɪˈθrɒstəmi/ *noun* a surgical operation to make an opening for a man's urethra between the scrotum and the anus

urethrotomy /ˌjʊərɪˈθrɒtəmi/ *noun* a surgical operation to open a blocked or narrowed urethra. Also called **Wheelhouse's operation**

urge incontinence /ˈɜːdʒ ɪnˌkɒntɪnəns/ *noun* a condition in which someone feels a very strong need to urinate and cannot retain their urine

-uria /jʊəriə/ *suffix* **1.** a condition of the urine **2.** a disease characterised by a condition of the urine

uric acid /ˌjʊərɪk ˈæsɪd/ *noun* a chemical compound which is formed from nitrogen in waste products from the body and which also forms crystals in the joints of people who have gout

urin- /jʊərɪn/ *prefix* same as **urino-** (*used before vowels*)

urinalysis /ˌjʊərɪˈnæləsɪs/ *noun* the analysis of urine, to detect diseases such as diabetes mellitus

urinary /ˈjʊərɪn(ə)ri/ *adjective* referring to urine

urinary bladder /ˌjʊərɪn(ə)ri ˈblædə/ *noun* a sac where the urine collects after passing from the kidneys through the ureters, before being passed out of the body through the urethra. See illustration at **KIDNEY, UROGENITAL SYSTEM (MALE)** in Supplement

urinary catheter /ˌjʊərɪn(ə)ri ˈkæθɪtə/ *noun* same as **urethral catheter**

urinary duct /ˈjʊərɪn(ə)ri dʌkt/ *noun* same as **ureter**

urinary incontinence /ˌjʊərɪn(ə)ri ɪnˈkɒntɪnəns/ *noun* the involuntary emission of urine

urinary obstruction /ˌjʊərɪn(ə)ri əbˈstrʌkʃən/ *noun* a blockage of the urethra, which prevents urine being passed

urinary retention /ˌjʊərɪn(ə)ri rɪˈtenʃən/ *noun* the inability to pass urine, usually because the urethra is blocked or because the prostate gland is enlarged. Also called **urine retention**

urinary system /ˌjʊərɪn(ə)ri ˈsɪstəm/ *noun* a system of organs and ducts which separate waste liquids from the blood and excrete them as urine, including the kidneys, bladder, ureters and urethra

urinary tract /ˈjʊərɪn(ə)ri trækt/ *noun* the set of tubes down which the urine passes from the kidneys to the bladder and from the bladder out of the body

urinary tract infection /ˈjʊərɪn(ə)ri trækt ɪnˌfekʃən/ *noun* a bacterial infection of any part of the urinary system. Symptoms are usually a need to urinate frequently and pain on urination. Abbreviation **UTI**

urinate /ˈjʊərɪneɪt/ *verb* to pass urine from the body

urination /ˌjʊərɪˈneɪʃ(ə)n/ *noun* the passing of urine out of the body. Also called **micturition**

urine /ˈjʊərɪn/ *noun* a yellowish liquid, containing water and waste products, mainly salt and urea, which is excreted by the kidneys and passed out of the body through the ureters, bladder and urethra

urine retention /ˈjʊərɪn rɪˌtenʃ(ə)n/ *noun* same as **urinary retention**

uriniferous tubule /ˌjʊərɪˌnɪf(ə)rəs ˈtjuːbjuːl/ *noun* same as **renal tubule**

urino- /jʊərɪnəʊ/ *prefix* referring to urine

urinogenital /ˌjʊərɪnəʊˈdʒenɪt(ə)l/ *adjective* same as **urogenital**

urinometer /ˌjʊərɪˈnɒmɪtə/ *noun* an instrument which measures the specific gravity of urine

urobilin /ˌjʊərəʊˈbaɪlɪn/ *noun* a yellow pigment formed when urobilinogen comes into contact with air

urobilinogen /ˌjʊərəʊbaɪˈlɪnədʒən/ *noun* a colourless pigment formed when bilirubin is reduced to stercobilinogen in the intestines

urochrome /ˈjʊərəkrəʊm/ *noun* the pigment which colours the urine yellow

urodynamics /ˌjʊərəʊdaɪˈnæmɪks/ *plural noun* the active changes which occur during the function of the bladder, urethral sphincter and pelvic floor muscles

urogenital /ˌjʊərəʊˈdʒenɪt(ə)l/ *adjective* referring to the urinary and genital systems. Also called **urinogenital**

urogenital system /ˌjʊərəʊˈdʒenɪt(ə)l ˌsɪstəm/ *noun* the whole of the urinary tract and reproductive system

urogram /ˈjʊərəgræm/ *noun* an X-ray picture of the urinary tract, or of a part of it

urography /jʊˈrɒgrəfi/ *noun* an X-ray examination of part of the urinary system after injection of radio-opaque dye

urokinase /ˌjʊərəʊˈkaɪneɪz/ *noun* an enzyme formed in the kidneys, which begins the process of breaking down blood clots

urolith /ˈjʊərəlɪθ/ *noun* a stone in the urinary system

urological /ˌjʊərəˈlɒdʒɪk(ə)l/ *adjective* referring to urology

urologist /jʊˈrɒlədʒɪst/ *noun* a doctor who specialises in urology

urology /jʊˈrɒlədʒi/ *noun* the scientific study of the urinary system and its diseases

urostomy /jʊˈrɒstəmi/ *noun* the surgical creation of an artificial urethra

urticaria /ˌɜːtɪˈkeəriə/ *noun* an allergic reaction to injections, particular foods or plants where the skin forms irritating reddish patches. Also called **hives, nettle rash**

usual /'juːʒuəl/ *adjective* expected or typical

uter- /juːtə/ *prefix* same as **utero-** (*used before vowels*)

uterine /'juːtəraɪn/ *adjective* referring to the uterus

uterine cavity /ˌjuːtəraɪn 'kævɪti/ *noun* the inside of the uterus

uterine procidentia /ˌjuːtəraɪn ˌprəʊsɪ'denʃə/, **uterine prolapse** /ˌjuːtəraɪn 'prəʊlæps/ *noun* a condition in which part of the uterus has passed through the vagina, usually after childbirth

COMMENT: Uterine procidentia has three stages of severity: in the first the cervix descends into the vagina, in the second the cervix is outside the vagina, but part of the uterus is still inside, and in the third stage, the whole uterus passes outside the vagina.

uterine retroflexion /ˌjuːtəraɪn ˌretrəʊ'flekʃ(ə)n/ *noun* a condition in which the uterus bends backwards away from its usual position

uterine retroversion /ˌjuːtəraɪn retrəʊ'vɜːʃ(ə)n/ *noun* a condition in which the uterus slopes backwards away from its usual position

utero- /juːtərəʊ/ *prefix* referring to the uterus

uterography /ˌjuːtə'rɒgrəfi/ *noun* an X-ray examination of the uterus

uterosalpingography /ˌjuːtərəʊsælpɪŋ'gɒgrəfi/ *noun* same as **hysterosalpingography**

uterovesical /ˌjuːtərəʊ'vesɪk(ə)l/ *adjective* referring to the uterus and the bladder

uterus /'juːt(ə)rəs/ *noun* the hollow organ in a woman's pelvic cavity, behind the bladder and in front of the rectum in which the embryo develops before birth. Also called **womb**. See illustration at UROGENITAL SYSTEM (FEMALE) in Supplement (NOTE: For other terms referring to the uterus, see words beginning with **hyster-, hystero-, metr-, metro-**.)

uterus didelphys /ˌjuːt(ə)rəs daɪ'delfɪs/ *noun* same as **double uterus**

utricle /'juːtrɪk(ə)l/, **utriculus** /jʊ'trɪkjʊləs/ *noun* a large sac inside the vestibule of the ear, which relates information about the upright position of the head to the brain

UV *abbreviation* ultraviolet

uvea /'juːviə/ *noun* a layer of organs in the eye beneath the sclera, formed of the iris, the ciliary body and the choroid. Also called **uveal tract**

uveal /'juːviəl/ *adjective* referring to the uvea

uveal tract /'juːviəl trækt/ *noun* same as **uvea**

uveitis /ˌjuːvi'aɪtɪs/ *noun* inflammation of any part of the uvea

UVR *abbreviation* ultraviolet radiation

uvula /'juːvjʊlə/ *noun* a piece of soft tissue which hangs down from the back of the soft palate

uvular /'juːvjʊlə/ *adjective* referring to the uvula

uvulectomy /ˌjuːvjʊ'lektəmi/ *noun* the surgical removal of the uvula

uvulitis /ˌjuːvjʊ'laɪtɪs/ *noun* inflammation of the uvula

uvulopalatopharyngoplasty /ˌjuːvjʊləʊˌpælətəʊfə'rɪŋgəʊplæsti/ *noun* a surgical operation to remove the uvula and other soft tissue in the palate, in order to widen the airways and treat the problem of snoring. Abbreviation **UPPP**

V

vaccinate /'væksɪneɪt/ *verb* to introduce vaccine into a person's body in order to make the body create its own antibodies, so making the person immune to the disease (NOTE: You vaccinate someone **against** a disease.)

vaccination /ˌvæksɪ'neɪʃ(ə)n/ *noun* the action of vaccinating someone

COMMENT: Originally the words **vaccination** and **vaccine** applied only to smallpox immunisation, but they are now used for immunisation against any disease. Vaccination is mainly given against cholera, diphtheria, rabies, smallpox, tuberculosis, and typhoid.

vaccine /'væksiːn/ *noun* a substance which contains antigens to a disease or a weak form of a disease, used to protect people against it

vacuum /'vækjuːm/ *noun* a space which is completely empty of all matter, including air

vacuum extraction /'vækjuəm ɪkˌstrækʃ(ə)n/ *noun* the procedure of pulling on the head of the baby with a suction instrument to aid birth

vacuum extractor /'vækjuəm ɪkˌstræktə/ *noun* a surgical instrument formed of a rubber suction cup which is used in vacuum extraction during childbirth

vacuum suction /'vækjuəm ˌsʌkʃən/ *noun* a method used to achieve an abortion, after dilatation of the cervix. Also called **aspiration**

vagal /'veɪg(ə)l/ *adjective* referring to the vagus nerve

vagal tone /ˌveɪg(ə)l 'təʊn/ *noun* the action of the vagus nerve to slow the beat of the sinoatrial node

vagin- /vədʒaɪn/ *prefix* referring to the vagina

vagina /və'dʒaɪnə/ *noun* a passage in a woman's reproductive tract between the entrance to the uterus, the cervix, and the vulva, able to stretch enough to allow a baby to pass through during childbirth. See illustration at **UROGENITAL SYSTEM (FEMALE)** in Supplement (NOTE: For other terms referring to the vagina, see words beginning with **colp-, colpo-**.)

vaginal bleeding /vəˌdʒaɪn(ə)l 'bliːdɪŋ/ *noun* bleeding from the vagina

vaginal delivery /vəˌdʒaɪn(ə)l dɪ'lɪv(ə)ri/ *noun* the birth of a baby through the mother's vagina, without surgical intervention

vaginal diaphragm /vəˌdʒaɪn(ə)l 'daɪəfræm/ *noun* a circular contraceptive device for women, which is inserted into the vagina and placed over the neck of the uterus before sexual intercourse

vaginal discharge /vəˌdʒaɪn(ə)l 'dɪstʃɑːdʒ/ *noun* the flow of liquid from the vagina

vaginal douche /vəˌdʒaɪn(ə)l 'duːʃ/ *noun* **1.** the process of washing out the vagina **2.** a device or liquid for washing out the vagina

vaginal examination /vəˌdʒaɪn(ə)l ɪgˌzæmɪ'neɪʃ(ə)n/ *noun* the act of checking the vagina for signs of disease or growth

vaginal suppository /ˌvædʒɪn(ə)l sə'pɒzɪt(ə)ri/ *noun* same as **pessary 1**

vaginismus /ˌvædʒɪ'nɪzməs/ *noun* a painful contraction of the vagina which prevents sexual intercourse

vaginitis /ˌvædʒɪ'naɪtɪs/ *noun* inflammation of the vagina which is mainly caused by the bacterium *Trichomonas vaginalis* or by a fungus *Candida albicans*

vaginoplasty /və'dʒaɪnəplæsti/ *noun* a surgical operation to graft tissue on to the vagina

vaginoscope /'vædʒɪnəʊskəʊp/ *noun* same as **colposcope**

vago- /veɪgʊ/ *prefix* referring to the vagus nerve

vagotomy /veɪ'gɒtəmi/ *noun* a surgical operation to cut through the vagus nerve which controls the nerves in the stomach, as a treatment for peptic ulcers

vagus /'veɪgəs/, **vagus nerve** /'veɪgəs nɜːv/ *noun* either of the tenth pair of cranial nerves which carry sensory and motor neurons serving the heart, lungs, stomach, and various other organs and control swallowing. Also called **pneumogastric nerve**

valgus /'vælgəs/, **valgum** /'vælgəm/, **valga** /'vælgə/ *adjective* turning outwards. ◊ **hallux valgus**. Compare **varus**

validity /və'lɪdɪti/ *noun* (*of a study*) the fact of being based on sound research and methods which exclude alternative explanations of a result

valine /'veɪliːn/ *noun* an essential amino acid

Valium /'væliəm/ a trade name for diazepam

vallate papillae /,væleɪt pə'piliː/ *plural noun* large papillae which form a line towards the back of the tongue and contain taste buds

Valsalva's manoeuvre /væl'sælvəz mə ,nuːvə/ *noun* the process of breathing out while holding the nostrils closed and keeping the mouth shut, used in order to test the functioning of the Eustachian tubes or to adjust the pressure in the middle ear

valve /vælv/ *noun* a flap which opens and closes to allow liquid to pass in one direction only, e.g. in the heart, blood vessels or lymphatic vessels

valvotomy /væl'vɒtəmi/ *noun* a surgical operation to cut into a valve to make it open wider

valvula /'vælvjʊlə/ *noun* a small valve (NOTE: The plural is **valvulae**.)

valvulitis /,vælvjʊ'laɪtɪs/ *noun* inflammation of a valve in the heart

valvuloplasty /'vælvjʊləʊplæsti/ *noun* surgery to repair valves in the heart without opening the heart

valvulotomy /,vælvjʊ'lɒtəmi/ *noun* same as **valvotomy**

vancomycin /,væŋkəʊ'maɪsɪn/ *noun* an antibiotic which is effective against some bacteria which are resistant to other antibiotics. Strains of bacteria resistant to vancomycin have now developed.

van den Bergh test /,væn den 'bɜːg ,test/ *noun* a test of blood serum to see if a case of jaundice is caused by an obstruction in the liver or by haemolysis of red blood cells [After A.A. Hijmans van den Bergh (1869–1943), Dutch physician.]

vaporiser /'veɪpəraɪzə/, **vaporizer** *noun* a device which warms a liquid to which medicinal oil has been added, so that it provides a vapour which someone can inhale

vapour /'veɪpə/ *noun* 1. a substance in the form of a gas 2. steam from a mixture of a liquid and a medicinal oil

vara /'veərə/ *adjective* same as **varus**

variant CJD /,veəriənt ,siːdʒeɪ 'diː/ *noun* a form of Creutzfeldt-Jakob disease which was observed first in the 1980s, especially affecting younger people. Abbreviation **vCJD**

varicectomy /,væri'sektəmi/ *noun* a surgical operation to remove a vein or part of a vein

varicella /,væri'selə/ *noun* same as **chickenpox**

varices /'værɪsiːz/ plural of **varix**

varicose /'værɪkəʊs/ *adjective* 1. affected with or having varicose veins 2. designed for the treatment of varicose veins 3. relating to or producing swelling

varicose eczema /,værɪkəʊs 'eksɪmə/ *noun* eczema which develops on the legs, caused by bad circulation. Also called **hypostatic eczema**

varicose ulcer /,værɪkəʊs 'ʌlsə/ *noun* an ulcer in the leg as a result of bad circulation and varicose veins

varicose vein /,værɪkəʊs 'veɪn/ *noun* a vein, usually in the legs, which becomes twisted and swollen

varicosity /,væri'kɒsɪti/ *noun* (of veins) the condition of being swollen and twisted

varicotomy /,væri'kɒtəmi/ *noun* a surgical operation to make a cut into a varicose vein

varifocals /'veəri,fəʊk(ə)lz/ *plural noun* spectacles with lenses which have varying focal lengths from top to bottom, for looking at things at different distances from the wearer

variola /və'raɪələ/ *noun* same as **smallpox**

varix /'veərɪks/ *noun* a swollen blood vessel, especially a swollen vein in the leg (NOTE: The plural is **varices**.)

varus /'veərəs/, **varum** /'veərəm/, **vara** /'veərə/ *adjective* turning inwards. ◊ **coxa vara**. Compare **valgus**

vas /væs/ *noun* a tube in the body (NOTE: The plural is **vasa**.)

vas- /væs/ *prefix* same as **vaso-**

vasa efferentia /,veɪsə ,efə'rentɪə/ *plural noun* the group of small tubes which sperm travel down from the testis to the epididymis

vasa vasorum /,veɪsə veɪ'sɔːrəm/ *plural noun* tiny blood vessels in the walls of larger blood vessels

vascular /'væskjʊlə/ *adjective* referring to blood vessels

vascularisation /,væskjʊləraɪ'zeɪʃ(ə)n/, **vascularization** *noun* the development of new blood vessels

vascular lesion /,væskjʊlə 'liːʒ(ə)n/ *noun* damage to a blood vessel

vascular system /'væskjʊlə ,sɪstəm/ *noun* the series of vessels such as veins, arteries and capillaries, carrying blood around the body

vasculitis /,væskjʊ'laɪtɪs/ *noun* inflammation of a blood vessel

vas deferens /,væs 'defərənz/ *noun* see illustration at UROGENITAL SYSTEM (MALE) in Supplement. Also called **ductus deferens**, **sperm duct** (NOTE: The plural is **vasa deferentia**.)

vasectomy /və'sektəmi/ *noun* a surgical operation to cut a vas deferens, in order to prevent sperm travelling from the epididymis up the duct

vas efferens /,væs 'efərenz/ *noun* one of many tiny tubes which take the spermatozoa from the testis to the epididymis (NOTE: The plural is **vasa efferentia**.)

vaso- /veɪzəʊ/ *prefix* 1. referring to a blood vessel 2. referring to the vas deferens

vasoactive /,veɪzəʊ'æktɪv/ *adjective* having an effect on the blood vessels, especially constricting the arteries

vasoconstriction /ˌveɪzəʊkən'strɪkʃən/ *noun* a contraction of blood vessels which makes them narrower

vasoconstrictor /ˌveɪzəʊkən'strɪktə/ *noun* a chemical substance which makes blood vessels become narrower, so that blood pressure rises, e.g. ephedrine hydrochloride

vasodilatation /ˌveɪzəʊˌdaɪlə'teɪʃ(ə)n/, **vasodilation** /ˌveɪzəʊdaɪ'leɪʃ(ə)n/ *noun* the relaxation of blood vessels, especially the arteries, making them wider and leading to increased blood flow or reduced blood pressure

vasodilator /ˌveɪzəʊdaɪ'leɪtə/ *noun* a chemical substance which makes blood vessels become wider, so that blood flows more easily and blood pressure falls, e.g. hydralazine hydrochloride

vaso-epididymostomy /ˌveɪzəʊ ˌepɪdɪdɪ'mɒstəmi/ *noun* a surgical operation to reverse a vasectomy in which the cut end of the vas deferens is joined to a tubule within the epididymis above a blockage in it

vasomotion /veɪzə'məʊʃ(ə)n/ *noun* the control of the diameter of blood vessels and thus of blood flow. ◊ **vasoconstriction, vasodilatation**

vasomotor /ˌveɪzəʊ'məʊtə/ *adjective* referring to the control of the diameter of blood vessels

vasomotor centre /ˌveɪzə'məʊtə ˌsentə/ *noun* a nerve centre in the brain which changes the rate of heartbeat and the diameter of blood vessels and so regulates blood pressure

vasomotor nerve /ˌveɪzəʊ'məʊtə ˌnɜːv/ *noun* a nerve in the wall of a blood vessel which affects the diameter of the vessel

vasopressor /ˌveɪzəʊ'presə/ *noun* a substance which increases blood pressure by narrowing the blood vessels

vasospasm /'veɪzəʊspæzm/ *noun* a muscle spasm causing the fingers to become cold, white and numb. ◊ **Raynaud's disease**

vasovagal /ˌveɪzəʊ'veɪg(ə)l/ *adjective* referring to the vagus nerve and its effect on the heartbeat and blood circulation

vasovagal attack /ˌveɪzəʊ'veɪg(ə)l ə,tæk/ *noun* a fainting fit as a result of a slowing down of the heartbeats caused by excessive activity of the vagus nerve

vasovasostomy /ˌveɪzəʊvə'sɒstəmi/ *noun* a surgical operation to reverse a vasectomy

vasovesiculitis /ˌveɪzəʊvesɪkju'laɪtɪs/ *noun* inflammation of the seminal vesicles and a vas deferens

VBAC *abbreviation* vaginal birth after Caesarean section

vCJD *abbreviation* variant CJD

VD *abbreviation* venereal disease

VD clinic /ˌviː 'diː ˌklɪnɪk/ *noun* a clinic specialising in the diagnosis and treatment of venereal diseases

vector /'vektə/ *noun* an insect or animal which carries a disease and can pass it to humans ○ *The tsetse fly is a vector of sleeping sickness.*

vegan /'viːgən/ *noun* someone who does not eat meat, dairy produce, eggs or fish and eats only vegetables and fruit ■ *adjective* involving a diet of only vegetables and fruit

vegetarian /ˌvedʒɪ'teəriən/ *noun* someone who does not eat meat, but eats mainly vegetables and fruit and sometimes dairy produce, eggs or fish ■ *adjective* involving a diet without meat

vegetation /ˌvedʒɪ'teɪʃ(ə)n/ *noun* a growth on a membrane, e.g. on the cusps of valves in the heart

vegetative /'vedʒɪtətɪv/ *adjective* referring to growth of tissue or organs

vehicle /'viːɪk(ə)l/ *noun* a liquid in which a dose of a drug is put

vein /veɪn/ *noun* a blood vessel which takes deoxygenated blood containing waste carbon dioxide from the tissues back to the heart (NOTE: For other terms referring to veins see words beginning **phleb-, phlebo-** or **vene-, veno-**.)

vena cava /ˌviːnə 'keɪvə/ *noun* one of two large veins which take deoxygenated blood from all the other veins into the right atrium of the heart. See illustration at **HEART** in Supplement, **KIDNEY** in Supplement (NOTE: The plural is **venae cavae**.)

vene- /venɪ/ *prefix* referring to veins

venepuncture /'venɪpʌŋktʃə/ *noun* the act of puncturing a vein either to inject a drug or to take a blood sample

venereal /və'nɪəriəl/ *adjective* **1.** relating to sex acts or sexual desire **2.** relating to the genitals **3.** referring to an infection or disease which is transmitted through sexual intercourse ○ *venereal warts*

venereal disease /və'nɪəriəl dɪ,ziːz/ *noun* a disease which is passed from one person to another during sexual intercourse. Abbreviation **VD** (NOTE: Now usually called a **sexually transmitted infection (STI)**.)

venereal wart /və,nɪəriəl 'wɔːt/ *noun* a wart on the genitals or in the urogenital area

venereology /və,nɪəri'ɒlədʒi/ *noun* the scientific study of venereal diseases

venesection /,venɪ'sekʃən/ *noun* an operation where a vein is cut so that blood can be removed, e.g. when taking blood from a donor

venipuncture /'venɪpʌŋktʃə/ *noun* same as **venepuncture**

veno- /viːnəʊ/ *prefix* referring to veins

venoclysis /və'nɒkləsɪs/ *noun* the procedure of slowly introducing a saline or other solution into a vein

venogram /'viːnəgræm/ *noun* same as **phlebogram**

venography /vɪ'nɒɡrəfi/ *noun* same as **phle-bography**

venom /'venəm/ *noun* a poison in the bite of a snake or insect

venous /'viːnəs/ *adjective* referring to the veins

venous blood /'viːnəs blʌd/ *noun* same as **deoxygenated blood**

venous system /'viːnəs ˌsɪstəm/ *noun* a system of veins which brings blood back to the heart from the tissues

venous thrombosis /ˌviːnəs θrɒm'bəʊsɪs/ *noun* the blocking of a vein by a blood clot

venous ulcer /ˌviːnəs 'ʌlsə/ *noun* an ulcer in the leg, caused by varicose veins or by a blood clot

ventilation /ˌventɪ'leɪʃ(ə)n/ *noun* the act of breathing air in or out of the lungs, so removing waste products from the blood in exchange for oxygen. ◊ **dead space**

ventilator /'ventɪleɪtə/ *noun* a machine which pumps air into and out of the lungs of someone who has difficulty in breathing ○ *The newborn baby was put on a ventilator.* Also called **respirator**

Ventimask /'ventimɑːsk/ a trademark for a type of oxygen mask

Ventolin /'ventəlɪn/ a trade name for salbutamol

ventouse /'ventuːs/ *noun* a cup-like vacuum device attached to the top of an unborn baby's head in the process of delivery, used to enable a distressed baby to be born quickly

ventral /'ventr(ə)l/ *adjective* **1.** referring to the abdomen **2.** referring to the front of the body. Opposite **dorsal**

ventricle /'ventrɪk(ə)l/ *noun* a cavity in an organ, especially in the heart or brain. See illustration at **HEART** in Supplement

ventricul- /ventrɪkjʊl/ *prefix* referring to a ventricle in the brain or heart

ventricular /ven'trɪkjʊlə/ *adjective* referring to the ventricles

ventricular fibrillation /ven,trɪkjʊlə ˌfaɪbrɪ'leɪʃ(ə)n/ *noun* a serious heart condition where the ventricular muscles flutter and the heart no longer beats. Abbreviation **VF**

ventricular folds /ven'trɪkjʊlə fəʊldz/ *plural noun* same as **vocal cords**

ventricular septal defect /ven,trɪkjʊlə 'sept(ə)l dɪˌfekt/ *noun* a condition in which blood can flow between the two ventricles of the heart, because the intraventricular septum has not developed properly. Abbreviation **VSD**

ventriculoatriostomy /ven,trɪkjʊləʊ,eɪtri 'ɒstəmi/ *noun* an operation to relieve pressure caused by excessive quantities of cerebrospinal fluid in the brain ventricles

ventriculo-peritoneal shunt /ven,trɪkjʊləʊ ˌperɪtə,niːəl 'ʃʌnt/ *noun* an artificial drain used in hydrocephalus to drain cerebrospinal fluid from the ventricles

ventriculoscopy /ven,trɪkjʊ'lɒskəpi/ *noun* an examination of the brain using an endoscope

ventriculostomy /ven,trɪkjʊ'lɒstəmi/ *noun* a surgical operation to pass a hollow needle into a ventricle of the brain so as to reduce pressure, take a sample of fluid or enlarge the ventricular opening to prevent the need for a shunt

ventro- /ventrəʊ/ *prefix* ventral

ventrofixation /ˌventrəʊfɪk'seɪʃ(ə)n/ *noun* a surgical operation to treat retroversion of the uterus by attaching the uterus to the wall of the abdomen

ventrosuspension /ˌventrəʊsə'spenʃən/ *noun* a surgical operation to treat retroversion of the uterus

Venturi mask /ven'tjʊəri mɑːsk/ *noun* a type of disposable mask which gives the person a controlled mixture of oxygen and air

Venturi nebuliser /ven'tjʊəri ˌnebjʊlaɪzə/ *noun* a type of nebuliser which is used in aerosol therapy

venule /'venjuːl/ *noun* a small vein or vessel leading from tissue to a larger vein

vera /'vɪərə/ ♦ **decidua**

verapamil /və'ræpəmɪl/ *noun* a synthetic compound which helps to prevent the movement of calcium ions across membranes. It is used in the treatment of angina pectoris, hypertension and irregular heartbeat.

vermiform appendix /ˌvɜːmɪfɔːm ə'pendɪks/ *noun* same as **appendix 1**

vermillion border /vəˌmɪliən 'bɔːdə/ *noun* the external red parts of the lips

vermix /'vɜːmɪks/ *noun* a vermiform appendix

vernix caseosa /ˌvɜːnɪks keɪsi'əʊsə/ *noun* an oily substance which covers a baby's skin at birth

verruca /və'ruːkə/ *noun* a small hard harmless growth on the sole of the foot, caused by a virus (NOTE: Verrucas are a type of wart. The plural is **verrucas** or **verrucae**.)

version /'vɜːʃ(ə)n/ *noun* the procedure of turning a fetus in a uterus so as to put it in a better position for birth

vertebra /'vɜːtɪbrə/ *noun* one of twenty-four ring-shaped bones which link together to form the backbone. See illustration at **CARTILAGINOUS JOINT** in Supplement (NOTE: The plural is **vertebrae**.)

vertebral /'vɜːtɪbrəl/ *adjective* referring to the vertebrae

vertebral artery /ˌvɜːtɪbrəl 'ɑːtəri/ *noun* one of two arteries which go up the back of the neck into the brain

vertebral canal /ˌvɜːtɪbrəl kəˈnæl/ *noun* same as **spinal canal**

vertebral column /ˈvɜːtɪbrəl ˌkɒləm/ *noun* the series of bones and discs linked together to form a flexible column running from the base of the skull to the pelvis. Also called **backbone**, **spinal column**. See illustration at PELVIS in Supplement

vertebral disc /ˌvɜːtɪbrəl ˈdɪsk/ *noun* same as **intervertebral disc**

vertebral foramen /ˌvɜːtɪbrəl fəˈreɪmən/ *noun* a hole in the centre of a vertebra which links with others to form the vertebral canal through which the spinal cord passes

vertex /ˈvɜːteks/ *noun* the top of the skull

vertex delivery /ˈvɜːteks dɪˌlɪv(ə)ri/ *noun* a normal birth, where the baby's head appears first

vertigo /ˈvɜːtɪɡəʊ/ *noun* 1. feelings of dizziness or giddiness caused by a malfunction of the sense of balance 2. a fear of heights, as a result of a sensation of dizziness which is felt when high up, especially on a tall building ○ *She won't sit near the window – she suffers from vertigo.*

vesical /ˈvesɪk(ə)l/ *adjective* referring to the bladder

vesicle /ˈvesɪk(ə)l/ *noun* 1. a small blister on the skin, e.g. caused by eczema 2. a sac which contains liquid

vesico- /vesɪkəʊ/ *prefix* referring to the urinary bladder

vesicostomy /ˌvesɪˈkɒstəmi/, **vesicotomy** /ˌvesɪˈkɒtəmi/ *noun* same as **cystostomy**

vesicoureteric reflux /ˌvesɪkəʊjʊəriˌterɪk ˈriːflʌks/ *noun* the flowing of urine back from the bladder up the ureters during urination, which may carry infection from the bladder to the kidneys. Also called **vesicouretic reflux**

vesicouretic /ˌvesɪkəʊjʊˈretɪk/ *adjective* relating to the urinary bladder and the ureters

vesicouretic reflux /ˌvesɪkəʊjʊˌretɪk ˈriːflʌks/ *noun* same as **vesicoureteric reflux**

vesicovaginal /ˌvesɪkəʊvəˈdʒaɪn(ə)l/ *adjective* referring to the bladder and the vagina

vesicovaginal fistula /ˌvesɪkəʊvəˌdʒaɪn(ə)l ˈfɪstjʊlə/ *noun* an unusual opening between the bladder and the vagina

vesicular /vəˈsɪkjʊlə/ *adjective* referring to a vesicle

vesicular breathing /vəˌsɪkjʊlə ˈbriːðɪŋ/, **vesicular breath sound** /vəˌsɪkjʊlə ˈbreθ saʊnd/ *plural noun* the sound made during the normal breathing process

vesiculation /vəˌsɪkjʊˈleɪʃ(ə)n/ *noun* the formation of blisters on the skin

vesiculitis /vəˌsɪkjʊˈlaɪtɪs/ *noun* inflammation of the seminal vesicles

vesiculography /vəˌsɪkjʊˈlɒɡrəfi/ *noun* an X-ray examination of the seminal vesicles

vesiculopapular /vəˌsɪkjʊləʊˈpæpjʊlə/ *adjective* referring to a skin disorder which has both blisters and papules

vesiculopustular /vəˌsɪkjʊləʊˈpʌstjʊlə/ *adjective* referring to a skin disorder which has both blisters and pustules

vessel /ˈves(ə)l/ *noun* 1. a tube in the body along which liquid flows, especially a blood vessel 2. a container for fluids

vestibular /veˈstɪbjʊlə/ *adjective* referring to a vestibule, especially the vestibule of the inner ear

vestibular glands /veˈstɪbjʊlə ɡlændz/ *plural noun* the glands at the point where the vagina and vulva join, which secrete a lubricating substance

vestibular nerve /veˈstɪbjʊlə nɜːv/ *noun* the part of the auditory nerve which carries information about balance to the brain

vestibule /ˈvestɪbjuːl/ *noun* a cavity in the body at the entrance to an organ, especially the first cavity in the inner ear or the space in the larynx above the vocal cords or a nostril. See illustration at EAR in Supplement

vestibulocochlear nerve /veˌstɪbjʊləʊ ˈkɒkliə ˌnɜːv/ *noun* the eighth cranial nerve which governs hearing and balance. Also called **acoustic nerve**, **auditory nerve**

vestigial /veˈstɪdʒiəl/ *adjective* existing in a rudimentary form ○ *The coccyx is a vestigial tail.*

VF *abbreviation* ventricular fibrillation

viable /ˈvaɪəb(ə)l/ *adjective* referring to a fetus which can survive if born ○ *A fetus is viable by about the 28th week of pregnancy.*

Viagra /vaɪˈæɡrə/ a trade name for sildenafil citrate

vial /ˈvaɪəl/ *noun* same as **phial**

Vibramycin /ˌvaɪbrəˈmaɪsɪn/ a trade name for doxycycline

vibrate /vaɪˈbreɪt/ *verb* to move rapidly and continuously

vibration /vaɪˈbreɪʃ(ə)n/ *noun* rapid and continuous movement ○ *Speech is formed by the vibrations of the vocal cords.*

Vibrio /ˈvɪbriəʊ/ *noun* a genus of Gram-negative bacteria which are found in water and cause cholera

vibrissae /vaɪˈbrɪsiː/ *plural noun* hairs in the nostrils or ears

vicarious /vɪˈkeəriəs/ *adjective* done by one organ or agent in place of another

vicarious menstruation /vɪˌkeəriəs ˌmenstruˈeɪʃ(ə)n/ *noun* the discharge of blood other than by the vagina during menstrual periods

victim /ˈvɪktɪm/ *noun* a person who is injured in an accident or who has caught a disease ○ *The victims of the rail crash were taken to the local hospital.* □ **to fall victim to something** to become a victim of or to experience bad effects from something ○ *Half the people eating at the restaurant fell victim to salmonella poisoning.*

vigour /ˈvɪgə/ *noun* a combination of positive attributes expressed in rapid growth, large size, high fertility and long life in an organism

villous /ˈvɪləs/ *adjective* shaped like a villus, or formed of villi

villus /ˈvɪləs/ *noun* a tiny projection like a finger on the surface of a mucous membrane (NOTE: The plural is **villi**.)

vinblastine /vɪnˈblæstiːn/ *noun* an alkaloid drug used in the treatment of cancer

vincristine /vɪnˈkrɪstiːn/ *noun* an alkaloid drug similar to vinblastine, also used in the treatment of cancer. It works by blocking cell division and is highly toxic.

viraemia /vaɪˈriːmiə/ *noun* a virus in the blood

viral hepatitis /ˌvaɪrəl ˌhepəˈtaɪtɪs/ *noun* same as **serum hepatitis**

viral infection /ˈvaɪrəl ɪnˌfekʃən/ *noun* an infection caused by a virus

viral pneumonia /ˌvaɪrəl njuːˈməʊniə/ *noun* a type of inflammation of the lungs caused by a virus. Also called **virus pneumonia**

virilisation /ˌvɪrɪlaɪˈzeɪʃ(ə)n/, **virilization** *noun* the development of male characteristics in a woman, caused by a hormone imbalance or therapy

virilism /ˈvɪrɪlɪz(ə)m/ *noun* male characteristics such as body hair and a deep voice in a woman

virology /vaɪˈrɒlədʒi/ *noun* the scientific study of viruses

virulence /ˈvɪrʊləns/ *noun* **1.** the ability of a microorganism to cause a disease **2.** the degree of effect of a disease

virulent /ˈvɪrʊlənt/ *adjective* **1.** referring to the ability of a microorganism to cause a disease ○ *an unusually virulent strain of the virus* **2.** referring to a disease which develops rapidly and has strong effects

virus /ˈvaɪrəs/ *noun* a parasite consisting of a nucleic acid surrounded by a protein coat that can only develop in other cells. Viruses cause many diseases including the common cold, AIDS, herpes and polio. (NOTE: Antibiotics have no effect on viruses, but effective vaccines have been developed for some viral diseases.)

virus pneumonia /ˌvaɪrəs njuːˈməʊniə/ *noun* same as **viral pneumonia**

viscera /ˈvɪsərə/ *plural noun* the internal organs, e.g. the heart, lungs, stomach and intestines

visceral /ˈvɪsərəl/ *adjective* referring to the internal organs

visceral larva migrans /ˌvɪsərəl ˌlɑːvə ˈmaɪgrænz/ *noun* same as **toxocariasis**

visceral pleura /ˌvɪsərəl ˈplʊərə/ *noun* a membrane attached to the surface of a lung. See illustration at LUNGS in Supplement

visceral pouch /ˈvɪsərəl paʊtʃ/ *noun* same as **pharyngeal pouch**

viscero- /vɪsərəʊ/ *prefix* relating to the viscera

viscid /ˈvɪsɪd/ *adjective* referring to a liquid which is sticky and slow-moving

viscosity /vɪˈskɒsɪti/ *noun* the state of a liquid which moves slowly

viscous /ˈvɪskəs/ *adjective* referring to a liquid which is thick and slow-moving

viscus /ˈvɪskəs/ ♦ **viscera**

vision /ˈvɪʒ(ə)n/ *noun* the ability to see, eyesight ○ *After the age of 50, many people's vision begins to fail.*

visual /ˈvɪʒʊəl/ *adjective* referring to sight or vision

visual acuity /ˌvɪʒʊəl əˈkjuːɪti/ *noun* the ability to see objects clearly

visual cortex /ˌvɪʒʊəl ˈkɔːteks/ *noun* the part of the cerebral cortex which receives information about sight

visual field /ˈvɪʒʊəl fiːld/ *noun* the area which can be seen without moving the eye. Also called **field of vision**

visualisation /ˌvɪʒʊəlaɪˈzeɪʃ(ə)n/, **visualization** *noun* **1.** a technique in which an image of an internal organ or other part of the body is produced by using X-rays or other means such as magnetic resonance imaging **2.** a technique in which someone creates a strongly positive mental picture of something such as the way in which they would like to solve a problem, in order to help them cope with it

visually impaired person /ˌvɪʒʊəli ɪmˌpeəd ˈpɜːs(ə)n/ *noun* a person whose eyesight is not clear

visual purple /ˌvɪʒʊəl ˈpɜːp(ə)l/ *noun* same as **rhodopsin**

vital /ˈvaɪt(ə)l/ *adjective* very important or necessary for life ○ *If circulation is stopped, vital nerve cells begin to die in a few minutes.* ○ *Oxygen is vital to the human system.*

vital capacity /ˌvaɪt(ə)l kəˈpæsɪti/ *noun* the largest amount of air which a person can exhale at one time

vital organs /ˌvaɪt(ə)l ˈɔːgənz/ *plural noun* the most important organs in the body, without which a human being cannot live, e.g. the heart, lungs and brain

vital signs /ˌvaɪt(ə)l ˈsaɪnz/ *plural noun* measurements of pulse, breathing and temperature

vital statistics /ˌvaɪt(ə)l stəˈtɪstɪks/ *plural noun* a set of official statistics relating to the population of a place, such as the percentage of live births per thousand, the incidence of particular diseases and the numbers of births and deaths

vitamin /'vɪtəmɪn/ *noun* an essential substance not synthesised in the body, but found in most foods, and needed for good health

Vitamin A /ˌvɪtəmɪn 'eɪ/ *noun* a vitamin which is soluble in fat and can be formed in the body from precursors but is mainly found in food such as liver, vegetables, eggs and cod liver oil. Also called **retinol**

Vitamin B₁ /ˌvɪtəmɪn biː 'wʌn/ *noun* a vitamin found in yeast, liver, cereals and pork. Also called **thiamine**

Vitamin B₂ /ˌvɪtəmɪn biː 'tuː/ *noun* a vitamin found in eggs, liver, green vegetables, milk and yeast. Also called **riboflavine**

Vitamin B₆ /ˌvɪtəmɪn biː 'sɪks/ *noun* a vitamin found in meat, cereals and molasses. Also called **pyridoxine**

Vitamin B₁₂ /ˌvɪtəmɪn biː 'twelv/ *noun* a vitamin found in liver and kidney, but not present in vegetables. Also called **cyanocobalamin**

Vitamin B complex /ˌvɪtəmɪn biː 'kɒmpleks/ *noun* a group of vitamins such as folic acid, riboflavine and thiamine

Vitamin C /ˌvɪtəmɪn 'siː/ *noun* a vitamin which is soluble in water and is found in fresh fruit, especially oranges and lemons, raw vegetables and liver. Also called **ascorbic acid**

Vitamin D /ˌvɪtəmɪn 'diː/ *noun* a vitamin which is soluble in fat and is found in butter, eggs and fish. It is also produced by the skin when exposed to sunlight. It helps in the formation of bones, and lack of it causes rickets in children.

vitamin deficiency /'vɪtəmɪn dɪˌfɪʃ(ə)nsi/ *noun* a lack of necessary vitamins ○ *He is suffering from Vitamin A deficiency.* ○ *Vitamin C deficiency causes scurvy.*

Vitamin E /ˌvɪtəmɪn 'iː/ *noun* a vitamin found in vegetables, vegetable oils, eggs and wholemeal bread

Vitamin K /ˌvɪtəmɪn 'keɪ/ *noun* a vitamin found in green vegetables such as spinach and cabbage, and which helps the clotting of blood and is needed to activate prothrombin

vitiligo /ˌvɪti'laɪɡəʊ/ *noun* a condition in which white patches appear on the skin. Also called **leucoderma**

vitrectomy /vɪ'trektəmi/ *noun* a surgical operation to remove some or all of the vitreous humour of the eye

vitreous /'vɪtriəs/ *adjective* **1.** having the characteristics of glass **2.** relating to the vitreous humour of the eye

vitreous body /'vɪtriəs ˌbɒdi/ *noun* same as **vitreous humour**

vitreous detachment /ˌvɪtriəs dɪ'tætʃmənt/ *noun* the separation of the vitreous humour from the retina, often due to natural ageing when the vitreous humour thins, but also occurring in other conditions such as diabetes

vitreous humour /ˌvɪtriəs 'hjuːmə/ *noun* a transparent jelly which fills the main cavity behind the lens in the eye. See illustration at **EYE** in Supplement

vitritis /vɪ'traɪtɪs/ *noun* same as **hyalitis**

vitro /'viːtriəʊ/ ♦ **in vitro**

Vitus /'vaɪtəs/ ♦ **St Vitus's dance**

vivisection /ˌvɪvɪ'sekʃən/ *noun* the act of dissecting a living animal as an experiment

vocal /'vəʊk(ə)l/ *adjective* referring to the voice

vocal cords /'vəʊk(ə)l kɔːdz/ *plural noun* a pair of fibrous sheets of tissue which span the cavity of the voice box (**larynx**) and produce sounds by vibrating. Also called **ventricular folds**

vocal folds /'vəʊk(ə)l fəʊldz/ *plural noun* same as **vocal cords**

vocal folds abducted /ˌvəʊk(ə)l fəʊldz əb 'dʌktɪd/ *noun* the usual condition of the vocal cords in quiet breathing

vocal folds adducted /ˌvəʊk(ə)l fəʊldz ə 'dʌktɪd/ *noun* the position of the vocal cords for speaking

vocal fremitus /ˌvəʊk(ə)l 'fremɪtəs/ *noun* a vibration of the chest when a person speaks or coughs

vocal resonance /ˌvəʊk(ə)l 'rezənəns/ *noun* a sound heard by a doctor when he or she listens through a stethoscope to the chest while a person is speaking

volar /'vəʊlə/ *adjective* referring to the palm of the hand or sole of the foot

volatile /'vɒlətaɪl/ *adjective* referring to a liquid which turns into gas at room temperature

volitantes /ˌvɒlɪ'tænti:z/ ♦ **muscae volitantes**

volition /və'lɪʃ(ə)n/ *noun* the ability to use the will

Volkmann's contracture /'fɒlkmɑːnz kən ˌtræktʃə/ *noun* a fibrosis and tightening of the muscles of the forearm because blood supply has been restricted, leading to contraction of the fingers

volsella /vɒl'selə/ *noun* a type of surgical forceps with claw-like hooks at the end of each arm. Also called **vulsella**

volume /'vɒljuːm/ *noun* an amount of a substance

voluntary /'vɒlənt(ə)ri/ *adjective* done because one wishes to do it

voluntary admission /ˌvɒlənt(ə)ri əd 'mɪʃ(ə)n/ *noun* the process of taking someone into a psychiatric hospital with the person's consent

voluntary movement /ˌvɒlənt(ə)ri 'muːvmənt/ *noun* a movement directed by the person's willpower, using voluntary muscles, e.g. walking or speaking

voluntary muscle /ˈvɒlənt(ə)ri ˌmʌs(ə)l/ *noun* a muscle which is consciously controlled. It is usually made up of striated fibres.

COMMENT: Voluntary muscles work in pairs, where one contracts and pulls, while the other relaxes to allow the bone to move.

volvulus /ˈvɒlvjʊləs/ *noun* a condition in which a loop of intestine is twisted and blocked, so cutting off its blood supply

vomer /ˈvəʊmə/ *noun* a thin flat vertical bone in the septum of the nose

vomica /ˈvɒmɪkə/ *noun* 1. a cavity in the lungs containing pus 2. the act of vomiting pus from the throat or lungs

vomit /ˈvɒmɪt/ *noun* partly digested food which has been brought up from the stomach into the mouth ○ *His bed was covered with vomit.* ○ *She died after choking on her own vomit.* Also called **vomitus** ■ *verb* to bring up partly digested food from the stomach into the mouth ○ *He had a fever, and then started to vomit.* ○ *She vomited her breakfast.*

vomiting /ˈvɒmɪtɪŋ/ *noun* the act of bringing up vomit into the mouth. Also called **emesis**

vomitus /ˈvɒmɪtəs/ *noun* same as **vomit**

von Hippel-Lindau syndrome /vɒn ˌhɪp(ə)l ˈlɪndaʊ ˌsɪndrəʊm/ *noun* a disease in which angiomas of the brain are related to angiomas and cysts in other parts of the body

von Recklinghausen's disease /ˌvɒn ˈreklɪŋhaʊz(ə)nz dɪˌziːz/ *noun* 1. same as **neurofibromatosis** 2. same as **osteitis fibrosis**

cystica [Described 1882. After Friedrich Daniel von Recklinghausen (1833–1910), Professor of Pathology at Strasbourg, France.]

von Willebrand's disease /ˌvɒn ˈvɪlɪbrændz dɪˌziːz/ *noun* a hereditary blood disease, occurring in both sexes, in which the mucous membrane starts to bleed without any apparent reason. It is caused by a deficiency of a clotting factor in the blood, called von Willebrand's factor. [Described 1926. After E. A. von Willebrand (1870–1949), Finnish physician.]

von Willebrand's factor /ˌvɒn ˈvɪlɪbrændz ˌfæktə/ *noun* a protein substance in plasma involved in platelet aggregation

VSD *abbreviation* ventricular septal defect

vulgaris /vʌlˈgeərɪs/ ♦ **lupus vulgaris**

vulsella /vʌlˈselə/, **vulsellum** /vʌlˈseləm/ *noun* same as **volsella**

vulv- /vʌlv/ *prefix* referring to the vulva (*used before vowels*)

vulva /ˈvʌlvə/ *noun* a woman's external sexual organs, at the opening leading to the vagina. ◊ **kraurosis vulvae** (NOTE: For other terms referring to the vulva, see words beginning with **episi-**.)

vulvectomy /vʌlˈvektəmi/ *noun* a surgical operation to remove the vulva

vulvitis /vʌlˈvaɪtɪs/ *noun* inflammation of the vulva, causing intense irritation

vulvovaginitis /ˌvʌlvəʊvædʒɪˈnaɪtɪs/ *noun* inflammation of the vulva and vagina

W

waiting list /'weɪtɪŋ lɪst/ *noun* a list of people waiting for admission to hospital usually for treatment of non-urgent disorders ○ *The length of waiting lists for non-emergency surgery varies enormously from one region to another.* ○ *It is hoped that hospital waiting lists will get shorter.*

walking distance /'wɔːkɪŋ ˌdɪstəns/ *noun* the distance which someone can walk before they experience pain in their muscles, which shows the effectiveness of the blood supply to their legs

walking frame /'wɔːkɪŋ freɪm/ *noun* a metal frame used by people who have difficulty in walking. ◊ **Zimmer frame**

Wangensteen tube /'wæŋgənstiːn tjuːb/ *noun* a tube which is passed into the stomach to remove the stomach's contents by suction [Described 1832. After Owen Harding Wangensteen (1898–1980), US surgeon.]

ward /wɔːd/ *noun* a room or set of rooms in a hospital, with beds for the patients ○ *He is in Ward 8B.* ○ *The children's ward is at the end of the corridor.*

ward manager /'wɔːd ˌmænɪdʒə/ *noun* a nurse in charge of a ward

ward nurse /'wɔːd nɜːs/ *noun* a nurse who works in a hospital ward

ward sister /'wɔːd ˌsɪstə/ *noun* a senior nurse in charge of a ward

warfarin /'wɔːf(ə)rɪn/ *noun* a colourless crystalline compound used to help prevent the blood clotting

wart /wɔːt/ *noun* a small hard harmless growth on the skin, usually on the hands, feet or face, caused by a virus (NOTE: Warts on the feet are called **verrucas**.)

wasting disease /'weɪstɪŋ dɪˌziːz/ *noun* a disease which causes severe loss of weight or reduction in size of an organ

water /'wɔːtə/ *noun* **1.** the liquid essential to life which makes up a large part of the body ○ *Can I have a glass of water please?* ○ *They suffered dehydration from lack of water.* □ **water on the knee** fluid in the knee joint under the kneecap, caused by a blow on the knee **2.** urine (*informal*) ○ *He passed a lot of water during the night.* ○ *She noticed blood streaks in her water.* ○ *The nurse asked him to give a sample of his water.* ■ *plural noun* **waters** the fluid in the amnion in which a fetus floats (*informal*) Also called **amniotic fluid**

water bed /'wɔːtə bed/ *noun* a mattress made of a large heavy plastic bag filled with water, used to prevent bedsores

waterbrash /'wɔːtəbræʃ/ *noun* a condition caused by dyspepsia, in which there is a burning feeling in the stomach and the mouth suddenly fills with acid saliva

water-hammer pulse /'wɔːtə ˌhæmə pʌls/ *noun* same as **Corrigan's pulse**

Waterhouse-Friderichsen syndrome /ˌwɔːtəhaʊs 'friːdərɪksən ˌsɪndrəʊm/ *noun* a condition caused by blood poisoning with meningococci, in which the tissues of the adrenal glands die and haemorrhage [Described 1911 by Rupert Waterhouse (1873–1958), physician at Bath, UK; described 1918 by Carl Friderichsen (1886–1979), Danish physician.]

Waterston's operation /'wɔːtəstənz ˌɒpəreɪʃ(ə)n/ *noun* a surgical operation to treat Fallot's tetralogy, in which the right pulmonary artery is joined to the ascending aorta [After David James Waterston (1910–85), paediatric surgeon in London, UK]

waterworks /'wɔːtəwɜːks/ *plural noun* same as **urinary system** (*informal*)

Watson-Crick helix /ˌwɒts(ə)n 'krɪk ˌhiːlɪks/ *noun* a molecular model for DNA in which the organic base pairs are linked by hydrogen bonds which form the rungs of a ladder spiralling in the form of a helix

WBC *abbreviation* white blood cell

weal /wiːl/ *noun* a small area of skin which swells because of a sharp blow or an insect bite

wean /wiːn/ *verb* to make a baby stop breastfeeding and take other liquid or solid food, or to make a baby start to eat solid food after having only had liquids to drink ○ *The baby was breastfed for two months and then was gradually weaned onto the bottle.*

webbing /'webɪŋ/ *noun* the condition of having an extra membrane of skin joining two structures in the body together

Weber-Christian disease /ˌveɪbə ˈkrɪstʃən dɪˌziːz/ *noun* a type of panniculitis where the liver and spleen become enlarged [After Frederick Parkes Weber (1863–1962), British physician; Henry Asbury Christian (1876–1951), US physician.]

Weber's test /ˈveɪbəz test/ *noun* a test to see if both ears hear correctly, where a tuning fork is struck and the end placed on the head [After Friedrich Eugen Weber-Liel (1832–91), German otologist.]

web space /ˈweb speɪs/ *noun* the soft tissue between the bases of the fingers and toes

Wechsler scales /ˈvekslə skeɪlz/ *plural noun* a set of standardised scales for measuring someone's IQ. There are three separate versions developed for different age groups.

wee /wiː/ *verb* same as **urinate** (*informal*)

weep /wiːp/ *verb* 1. to cry 2. (*of a wound*) to ooze fluid

Wegener's granulomatosis /ˌvegənəz ˌɡrænjʊləʊməˈtəʊsɪs/ *noun* a disease of connective tissue, where the nasal passages, lungs and kidneys are inflamed and ulcerated, with formation of granulomas. It is usually fatal.

Weil-Felix reaction /ˌvaɪl ˈfeɪlɪks rɪˌækʃən/, **Weil-Felix test** /ˌvaɪl ˈfeɪlɪks test/ *noun* a test to see if someone has typhus, in which the person's serum is tested for antibodies against *Proteus vulgaris* [Described 1916. After Edmund Weil (1880–1922) Austrian physician and bacteriologist; Arthur Felix (1887–1956), British bacteriologist.]

Weil's disease /ˈweɪlz dɪˌziːz/ *noun* same as **leptospirosis** [Described 1886. After Adolf Weil (1848–1916), physician in Estonia who also practised in Wiesbaden, Germany.]

well /wel/ *adjective* healthy ○ *He's not a well man.* ○ *You're looking very well after your holiday.* ○ *He's quite well again after his flu.* ○ *She's not very well, and has had to stay in bed.*

well-baby clinic /ˌwel ˈbeɪbi ˌklɪnɪk/ *noun* a clinic where parents can ask a doctor or nurse any questions they have about their child's growth and development. Their babies can be weighed and measured and their development monitored.

wellbeing /ˈwel ˌbiːɪŋ/ *noun* the state of being in good health and having good living conditions ○ *She is responsible for the wellbeing of the patients under her care.*

well-man clinic /ˌwel ˈmæn ˌklɪnɪk/ *noun* a clinic just for men where they can get check-ups, advice and health information

well-woman clinic /ˌwel ˈwʊmən ˌklɪnɪk/ *noun* a clinic which specialises in preventive medicine for women, e.g. breast screening and cervical smear tests, and gives advice on pregnancy, contraception and the menopause

wen /wen/ *noun* a cyst which forms in a sebaceous gland

Werdnig-Hoffmann disease /ˌvɜːdnɪɡ ˈhɒfmən dɪˌziːz/ *noun* a disease in which the spinal muscles atrophy, making the muscles of the shoulders, arms and legs weak. In its most severe form, infants are born floppy, have feeding and breathing problems and rarely live more than two or three years.

Werner's syndrome /ˈvɜːnəz ˌsɪndrəʊm/ *noun* an inherited disorder involving premature ageing, persistent hardening of the skin, underdevelopment of the sex organs and cataracts

Wernicke's encephalopathy /ˌvɜːnɪkəz en ˌkefəˈlɒpəθi/ *noun* a condition caused by lack of Vitamin B, which often affects alcoholics and in which the person is delirious, moves the eyes about rapidly, walks unsteadily and is subject to constant vomiting [Described 1875. After Karl Wernicke (1848–1905), Breslau psychiatrist and neurologist.]

Wertheim's operation /ˈvɜːthaɪmz ɒpə ˌreɪʃ(ə)n/ *noun* a surgical operation to remove the uterus, the lymph nodes which are next to it and most of the vagina, the ovaries and the Fallopian tubes, as treatment for cancer of the uterus [Described 1900. After Ernst Wertheim (1864–1920), Austrian gynaecologist.]

wet burn /ˈwet bɜːn/ *noun* same as **scald**

Wharton's duct /ˌwɔːt(ə)nz ˈdʌkt/ *noun* a duct which takes saliva into the mouth from the salivary glands under the lower jaw [After Thomas Wharton (1614–73), English physician and anatomist at St Thomas's Hospital, London, UK]

Wharton's jelly /ˌwɔːt(ə)nz ˈdʒeli/ *noun* a jelly-like tissue in the umbilical cord

wheal /wiːl/ same as **weal**

wheeze /wiːz/ *noun* a whistling noise in the bronchi ○ *The doctor listened to his wheezes.* ■ *verb* to make a whistling sound when breathing ○ *When she has an attack of asthma, she wheezes and has difficulty in breathing.*

wheezing /ˈwiːzɪŋ/ *noun* whistling noises in the bronchi when breathing. Wheezing is often found in people with asthma and is also associated with bronchitis and heart disease.

whiplash injury /ˈwɪplæʃ ˌɪndʒəri/ *noun* an injury to the vertebrae in the neck, caused when the head jerks backwards, often occurring in a car that is struck from behind

whiplash shake syndrome /ˌwɪplæʃ ˈʃeɪk ˌsɪndrəʊm/ *noun* in young babies, a series of internal head injuries caused by being shaken violently. They can result in brain damage leading to speech and learning disabilities, paralysis, seizures, blindness and hearing loss. They are often life-threatening.

Whipple's disease /ˈwɪp(ə)lz dɪˌziːz/ *noun* a disease in which someone has difficulty in absorbing nutrients and passes fat in the faeces, the joints are inflamed and the lymph glands enlarged [Described 1907. After George Hoyt Whipple (1878–1976), US pathologist. Nobel prize for Pathology and Medicine 1934.]

Whipple's operation /'wɪp(ə)lz ɒpə ˌreɪʃ(ə)n/ *noun* same as **pancreatectomy**

white /waɪt/ *adjective* of a colour like snow or milk ○ *White patches developed on his skin.* ○ *Her hair has turned quite white.* (NOTE: **whiter – whitest**) ■ *noun* the main part of the eye which is white ○ *The whites of his eyes turned yellow when he developed jaundice.*

white blood cell /ˌwaɪt 'blʌd ˌsel/ *noun* a colourless blood cell which contains a nucleus but has no haemoglobin, is formed in bone marrow and creates antibodies. Abbreviation **WBC**. Also called **leucocyte**

white finger /'waɪt ˌfɪŋɡə/ *noun* a condition in which a finger has a mottled discoloured appearance because its blood vessels are damaged. The thumb is usually not affected. Very severe cases can result in finger loss. It occurs most commonly in Raynaud's disease.

white leg /'waɪt leɡ/ *noun* a condition which affects women after childbirth, in which a leg becomes pale and inflamed as a result of lymphatic obstruction. Also called **milk leg, phlegmasia alba dolens**

white matter /'waɪt ˌmætə/ *noun* nerve tissue in the central nervous system which contains more myelin than grey matter

white noise instrument /ˌwaɪt 'nɔɪz ˌɪnstrʊmənt/ *noun* a small electronic device worn in the ear. It combines sounds of many different frequencies. It is used to mask internal noise in the ear due to tinnitus.

whites /waɪts/ *plural noun* same as **leucorrhoea** (*informal*)

whitlow /'wɪtləʊ/ *noun* an inflammation caused by infection near the nail in the fleshy part of the tip of a finger. Also called **felon**

WHO *abbreviation* World Health Organization

whoop /wuːp, huːp/ *noun* a loud noise made when inhaling by a person who has whooping cough

whooping cough /'huːpɪŋ kɒf/ *noun* an infectious disease caused by *Bordetella pertussis* affecting the bronchial tubes, common in children, and sometimes very serious. Also called **pertussis**

Widal reaction /viː'dɑːl rɪˌækʃən/, **Widal test** /viː'dɑːl test/ *noun* a test to detect typhoid fever. A sample of the person's blood is put into a solution containing typhoid bacilli, or anti-typhoid serum is added to a sample of bacilli from the person's faeces. If the bacilli agglutinate, i.e. form into groups, this indicates that the person has typhoid fever. [Described 1896. After Georges

Fernand Isidore Widal (1862–1929), French physician and teacher.]

Willis /'wɪlɪs/ ♦ **circle of Willis**

Wilms' tumour /'vɪlmz ˌtjuːmə/ *noun* same as **nephroblastoma** [Described 1899. After Max Wilms (1867–1918), Professor of Surgery at Leipzig, Basle and Heidelberg.]

Wilson's disease /'wɪlsənz dɪˌziːz/ *noun* a hereditary disease where copper deposits accumulate in the liver and the brain, causing cirrhosis. Also called **hepatolenticular degeneration** [Described 1912. After Samuel Alexander Kinnier Wilson (1878–1937), British neurologist.]

windpipe /'wɪndpaɪp/ *noun* same as **trachea**

wiring /'waɪərɪŋ/ *noun* **1.** a network of wires **2.** a neurological or physiological structure or process which controls a function in the body **3.** the act of fixing a piece of bone in place using wires

wisdom tooth /'wɪzdəm tuːθ/ *noun* one of the four teeth in the back of the jaw which only appear at about the age of 20 and sometimes do not appear at all. Also called **third molar**

witch hazel /'wɪtʃ ˌheɪz(ə)l/ *noun* a lotion made from the bark of a tree, used to check bleeding and harden inflamed tissue and bruises. Also called **hamamelis**

withdrawal /wɪð'drɔːəl/ *noun* **1.** a loss of interest in having contact with other people, which leads to a person becoming isolated **2.** a period during which a person who has been addicted to a drug stops taking it and experiences unpleasant symptoms

withdrawal symptom /wɪð'drɔːəl ˌsɪmptəm/ *noun* an unpleasant physical condition, e.g. vomiting, headaches or fever, which occurs when someone stops taking an addictive drug

Wolff-Parkinson-White syndrome /wʊlf ˌpɑːkɪns(ə)n 'waɪt ˌsɪndrəʊm/ *noun* a condition within the heart's conducting tissue which makes the heart beat dangerously fast. It can be fatal.

womb /wuːm/ *noun* same as **uterus** (NOTE: For other terms referring to the womb, see words beginning with **hyster-, hystero-, metr-, metro-, uter-, utero-.**)

Wood's lamp /'wʊdz læmp/ *noun* an ultraviolet lamp which allows a doctor to see fluorescence, e.g. in the hair of someone who has a fungal infection [After Robert Williams Wood (1868–1955), US physicist.]

word blindness /'wɜːd ˌblaɪndnəs/ *noun* same as **alexia**

work-related upper limb disorder /ˌwɜːk rɪˌleɪtɪd ˌʌpə 'lɪm dɪsˌɔːdə/ same as **repetitive strain injury**. Abbreviation **WRULD**.

World Health Organization /ˌwɜːld 'helθ ɔːɡənaɪˌzeɪʃ(ə)n/ *noun* an organisation, part of the United Nations, which aims to improve health in the world. Abbreviation **WHO**

worm /wɜːm/ *noun* a long thin animal with no legs or backbone, which can infest the human body, especially the intestines

wound /wuːnd/ *noun* damage to external tissue which allows blood to escape ○ *He had a knife wound in his leg.* ○ *The doctors sutured the wound in his chest.* ■ *verb* to harm someone by making a hole in the tissue of the body ○ *She was wounded three times in the head.*

wound dehiscence /ˈwuːnd dɪˌhɪs(ə)ns/ *noun* the splitting open of a surgical incision

wound healing /ˈwuːnd ˌhiːlɪŋ/ *noun* the replacement of dead tissue with new tissue

wrist /rɪst/ *noun* a joint between the hand and forearm ○ *He sprained his wrist and can't play tennis tomorrow.* See illustration at **HAND** in Supplement (NOTE: For other terms referring to the wrist, see words beginning with **carp-, carpo-**.)

wrist drop /ˈrɪst drɒp/ *noun* paralysis of the wrist muscles, caused by damage to the radial nerve in the upper arm, which causes the hand to hang limp

writer's cramp /ˌraɪtəz ˈkræmp/ *noun* a painful spasm of the muscles in the forearm and hand which comes from writing too much

WRULD *abbreviation* work-related upper limb disorder

wry neck /ˈraɪ nek/, **wryneck** /ˈraɪnek/ *noun* same as **torticollis**

XYZ

xanth- /zænθ/ *prefix* same as **xantho-** (*used before vowels*)

xanthaemia /zæn'θi:miə/ *noun* same as **carotenaemia**

xanthelasma /ˌzænθə'læzmə/ *noun* the formation of little yellow fatty tumours on the eyelids

xanthine /'zænθiːn/ *noun* **1.** an intermediate product in the breakdown of nucleic acids to uric acid, found in blood, body tissue and urine **2.** a derivative of xanthine, e.g. caffeine or theophylline

xantho- /zænθəʊ/ *prefix* yellow

xanthochromia /ˌzænθə'krəʊmiə/ *noun* yellow colour of the skin as in jaundice

xanthoma /zæn'θəʊmə/ *noun* a yellow fatty mass, often on the eyelids and hands, found in people with a high level of cholesterol in the blood (NOTE: The plural is **xanthomata**.)

xanthomatosis /ˌzænθəmə'təʊsɪs/ *noun* a condition in which several small masses of yellow fatty substance appear in the skin or some internal organs, caused by an excess of fat in the body

xanthopsia /zæn'θɒpsiə/ *noun* a disorder of the eyes, making everything appear yellow

xanthosis /zæn'θəʊsɪs/ *noun* yellow colouring of the skin, caused by eating too much food containing carotene

X chromosome /'eks ˌkrəʊməsəʊm/ *noun* a chromosome that determines sex. Compare **Y chromosome**. ◊ **sex chromosome**

xeno- /zenəʊ/ *prefix* different

xenotransplantation /ˌzenəʊtrænspluː'teɪʃ(ə)n/ *noun* the process of transplanting organs from one species to another, especially from animals to humans

xero- /zɪərəʊ/ *prefix* dry

xeroderma /ˌzɪərə'dɜːmə/ *noun* a skin disorder where dry scales form on the skin

xerophthalmia /ˌzɪərɒf'θælmiə/ *noun* a condition of the eye, in which the cornea and conjunctiva become dry because of a lack of Vitamin A

xerosis /zɪ'rəʊsɪs/ *noun* extreme dryness of skin or mucous membrane

xerostomia /ˌzɪərə'stəʊmiə/ *noun* dryness of the mouth, caused by lack of a saliva

xiphi- /zɪfɪ/ *prefix* relating to the xiphoid process

xiphisternal plane /ˌzɪfɪstɜːn(ə)l 'pleɪn/ *noun* an imaginary horizontal line across the middle of the chest at the point where the xiphoid process starts

xiphisternum /ˌzɪfɪ'stɜːnəm/ *noun* same as **xiphoid process**

xiphoid process /'zɪfɔɪd ˌprəʊses/, **xiphoid cartilage** /'zɪfɔɪd ˌkɑːtɪlɪdʒ/ *noun* the bottom part of the breastbone which is cartilage in young people but becomes bone by middle age. Also called **ensiform cartilage**, **xiphisternum**

X-linked /'eks ˌlɪŋkt/ *adjective* relating to the genes situated on the X chromosome

X-linked disease /'eks ˌlɪŋkt dɪˌziːz/ *noun* a genetic disorder caused by a mutation on the X chromosome which only appears in males, e.g. one form of haemophilia

X-ray /'eks ˌreɪ/, **x-ray** *noun* **1.** a ray with a very short wavelength, which is invisible, but can go through soft tissue and register as a photograph on a film. X-rays are used in diagnosis in radiography, and in treating disease by radiotherapy. ○ *The X-ray examination showed the presence of a tumour in the colon.* **2.** a photograph taken using X-rays ○ *The dentist took some X-rays of the patient's teeth.* ○ *He pinned the X-rays to the light screen.* **3.** an examination in which X-ray photographs are taken ○ *All the staff had to have chest X-rays.* ■ *verb* to take an X-ray photograph of a patient ○ *There are six patients waiting to be X-rayed.*

X-ray imaging /'eks reɪ ˌɪmɪdʒɪŋ/ *noun* the process of showing X-ray pictures of the inside of part of the body on a screen

X-ray screening /'eks reɪ ˌskriːnɪŋ/ *noun* a method of gathering information about the body by taking images using X-rays. It is carried out by a radiographer or radiologist.

Xylocaine /'zaɪləkeɪn/ a trade name for a preparation of lignocaine

xylometazoline hydrochloride /ˌzaɪləʊmə ˌtæzəliːn ˌhaɪdrə'klɔːraɪd/, **xylometazoline** /ˌzaɪləʊmə'tæzəliːn/ *noun* a drug which helps to narrow blood vessels, used in the treatment of colds and sinusitis

XYY syndrome /ˌeks waɪ 'waɪ ˌsɪndrəʊm/ *noun* an extremely rare condition in males in which they have two Y chromosomes instead of one. They grow faster than normal, and their final height is approximately 7cm above average. Many experience severe acne during adolescence.

yawn /jɔːn/ *noun* a reflex action when tired or sleepy, in which the mouth is opened wide and after a deep intake of air, the breath exhaled slowly ○ *His yawns made everyone feel sleepy.* ■ *verb* to open the mouth wide and breathe in deeply and then breathe out slowly

yawning /'jɔːnɪŋ/ *noun* the act of opening the mouth wide without conscious control and slowly releasing a deep breath, usually a sign of tiredness or boredom

Y chromosome /'waɪ ˌkrəʊməsəʊm/ *noun* a chromosome that determines sex, it is carried by males and is shorter than an X chromosome. Compare **X chromosome**. ◊ **sex chromosome**

yeast /jiːst/ *noun* a fungus which is used in the fermentation of alcohol and in making bread. It is a good source of Vitamin B.

yellow /'jeləʊ/ *adjective* of a colour like that of the sun or of gold ○ *His skin turned yellow when he had hepatitis.* ○ *The whites of the eyes become yellow as a symptom of jaundice.* ■ *noun* a colour like that of the sun or of gold

yellow fever /'jeləʊ ˌfiːvə/ *noun* an infectious disease, occurring especially in Africa and South America, caused by an arbovirus carried by the mosquito *Aedes aegypti*. It affects the liver and causes jaundice. There is no known cure and it can be fatal, but vaccination can prevent it.

yellow marrow /ˌjeləʊ 'mærəʊ/ *noun* ♦ **marrow**

yellow spot /'jeləʊ spɒt/ *noun* same as **macula lutea**

yin and yang /ˌjɪn ənd 'jæŋ/ *noun* the two opposite and complementary principles of Chinese philosophy which are thought to exist in varying proportions in all things. They are sometimes thought of as femininity and masculinity.

yoga /'jəʊgə/ *noun* **1.** a Hindu discipline which promotes spiritual unity with a Supreme Being through a system of postures and rituals **2.** any one of dozens of systems and methods derived from or based on Hindu yoga. Many include breathing exercises and postures which are thought to aid health.

Zadik's operation /'zeɪdɪks ɒpəˌreɪʃ(ə)n/ *noun* a surgical operation to remove the whole of an ingrowing toenail

Zantac /'zæntæk/ a trade name for ranitidine

zidovudine /zɪ'dəʊvjʊdiːn/ *noun* azidothymidine or AZT, a drug used in the treatment of

AIDS, which helps to slow the progress of the disease

Zimmer frame /'zɪmə freɪm/ a trademark for a metal frame used by people who have difficulty in walking ○ *She managed to walk some steps with a Zimmer frame.* ◊ **walking frame**

zinc /zɪŋk/ *noun* a white metallic trace element (NOTE: The chemical symbol is **Zn**.)

zinc ointment /'zɪŋk ˌɔɪntmənt/ *noun* a soothing ointment made of zinc oxide and oil

zinc oxide /ˌzɪŋk 'ɒksaɪd/ *noun* a compound of zinc and oxygen, which forms a soft white soothing powder used in creams and lotions (NOTE: Its chemical formula is **ZnO**.)

Zollinger-Ellison syndrome /ˌzɒlɪndʒər 'elɪs(ə)n ˌsɪndrəʊm/ *noun* a condition in which tumours are formed in the islet cells of the pancreas together with peptic ulcers [Described 1955. After Robert Milton Zollinger (1903–92), Professor of Surgery at Ohio State University, USA; Edwin H. Ellison (1918–70), Associate Professor of Surgery at Ohio State University, USA.]

zona /'zəʊnə/ *noun* a zone or area

zone /zəʊn/ *noun* an area of the body

zonula /'zɒnjʊlə/, **zonule** /'zɒnjuːl/ *noun* a small area of the body

zoo- /zəʊə, zuːə/ *prefix* relating to animals

zoonosis /ˌzəʊə'nəʊsɪs/ *noun* a disease which a human can catch from an animal (NOTE: The plural is **zoonoses**.)

zoster /'zɒstə/ ♦ **herpes zoster**

Z-plasty /'zed ˌplæsti/ *noun* a technique used in plastic surgery. A deep Z-shaped incision is made to relieve tension in the area of a scar, or to change the direction of a scar.

zygoma /zaɪ'gəʊmə/ *noun* same as **zygomatic arch** (NOTE: The plural is **zygomata**.)

zygomatic /ˌzaɪgə'mætɪk/ *adjective* referring to the zygomatic arch

zygomatic arch /ˌzaɪgəmætɪk 'ɑːtʃ/ *noun* the ridge of bone across the temporal bone, running between the ear and the bottom of the eye socket. Also called **zygoma**

zygomatic bone /ˌzaɪgəmætɪk 'bəʊn/ *noun* a bone which forms the prominent part of the cheek and the lower part of the eye socket. Also called **cheekbone**, **malar bone**

zygomatic process /ˌzaɪgəmætɪk 'prəʊses/ *noun* one of the bony projections which form the zygomatic arch

zygote /'zaɪgəʊt/ *noun* a fertilised ovum, the first stage of development of an embryo

zym- /zaɪm/ *prefix* (used before vowels) **1.** enzymes **2.** fermentation

Supplement

Anatomical Terms

The body is always described as if standing upright with the palms of the hands facing forward. There is only one central vertical plane, termed the *median* or *sagittal* plane, and this passes through the body from front to back. Planes parallel to this on either side are *parasagittal* or *paramedian* planes. Vertical planes at right angles to the median are called *coronal* planes. The term *horizontal* (or *transverse*) plane speaks for itself. Two specific horizontal planes are (a) the *transpyloric,* midway between the suprasternal notch and the symphysis pubis, and (b) the *transtubercular* or *intertubercular* plane, which passes through the tubercles of the iliac crests. Many other planes are named from the structures they pass through.

Views of the body from some different points are shown on the diagram; a view of the body from above is called the *superior aspect,* and that from below is the *inferior aspect.*

Cephalic means toward the head; *caudal* refers to positions (or in a direction) towards the tail. *Proximal* and *distal* refer to positions respectively closer to and further from the centre of the body in any direction, while *lateral* and *medial* relate more specifically to relative sideways positions, and also refer to movements. *Ventral* refers to the abdomen, front or anterior, while *dorsal* relates to the back of a part or organ. The hand has a *dorsal* and a *palmar* surface, and the foot a *dorsal* and a *plantar* surface.

Note that *flexion of the thigh* moves it forward while *flexion of the leg* moves it backwards; the movements of *extension* are similarly reversed. Movement and rotation of limbs can be *medial,* which is with the front moving towards the centre line, or *lateral,* which is in the opposite direction. Specific terms for limb movements are *adduction,* towards the centre line, and *abduction,* which is away from the centre line. Other specific terms are *supination* and *pronation* for the hand, and *inversion* and *eversion* for the foot.

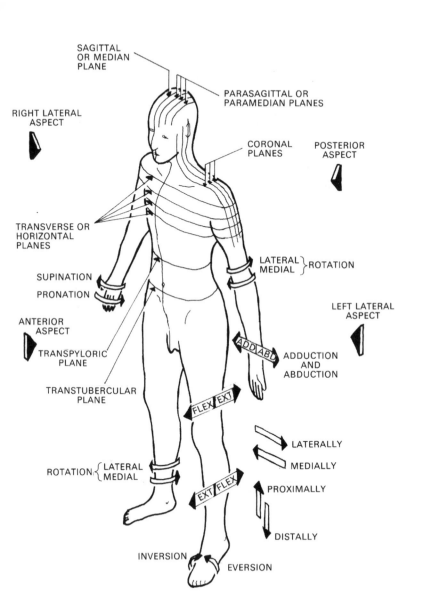

SAGITTAL
OR MEDIAN
PLANE

PARASAGITTAL OR
PARAMEDIAN PLANES

RIGHT LATERAL
ASPECT

CORONAL
PLANES

POSTERIOR
ASPECT

TRANSVERSE OR
HORIZONTAL
PLANES

LATERAL
MEDIAL } ROTATION

SUPINATION

PRONATION

LEFT LATERAL
ASPECT

ANTERIOR
ASPECT

ADD ABD

ADDUCTION
AND
ABDUCTION

TRANSPYLORIC
PLANE

TRANSTUBERCULAR
PLANE

FLEX EXT

LATERALLY

MEDIALLY

PROXIMALLY

ROTATION { LATERAL
MEDIAL

EXT FLEX

DISTALLY

INVERSION

EVERSION

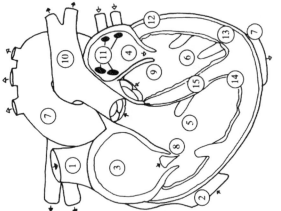

HEART

1. superior vena cava
2. inferior vena cava
3. right atrium
4. left atrium
5. right ventricle
6. left ventricle
7. aorta
8. tricuspid valve
9. bicuspid valve
10. pulmonary artery
11. pulmonary veins
12. epicardium
13. myocardium
14. endocardium
15. septum

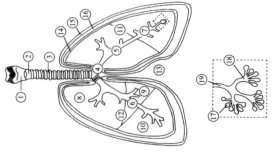

LUNGS

1. thyroid cartridge
2. cricoid cartridge
3. trachea
4. main bronchus
5. superior lobe bronchus
6. middle lobe bronchus
7. inferior lobe bronchus
8. superior lobe
9. middle lobe
10. inferior lobe
11. oblique fissure
12. horizontal fissure
13. cardiac notch
14. visceral pleura
15. parietal pleura
16. pleural cavity
17. alveolus
18. alveolar duct
19. bronchiole

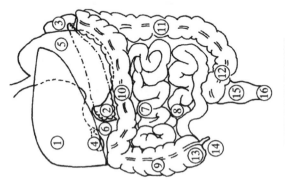

KIDNEY

1. kidney
2. calyx
3. pyramid
4. cortex
5. medulla
6. renal pelvis
7. adrenal gland
8. abdominal aorta
9. inferior vena cava
10. ureter
11. urinary bladder

DIGESTIVE SYSTEM

1. liver
2. pancreas
3. spleen
4. gall bladder
5. stomach
6. duodenum
7. jejunum
8. ileum
9. ascending colon
10. transverse colon
11. descending colon
12. sigmoid colon
13. caecum
14. appendix
15. rectum
16. anus

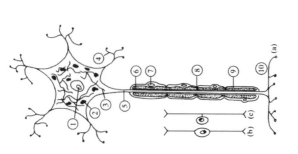

BRAIN

1. corpus callosum
2. thalamus
3. hypothalamus
4. pineal body
5. pituitary gland
6. superior colliculi

7. inferior colliculi
8. cerebellum
9. cerebral peduncle
10. fornix
11. pons

NEURONE

(a) multipolar   (b) bipolar   (c) unipolar

1. nucleus
2. Nissl granules
3. neurofibrilla
4. dendrite
5. axon

6. myelin sheath
7. Schwann cell nucleus
8. node of Ranvier
9. neurilemma
10. terminal branch

EAR

1. pinna
2. temporal bone
3. external auditory meatus
4. ceruminous glands
5. semicircular canals
6. cochlea
7. Eustachian tube
8. malleus
9. incus
10. stapes
11. tympanic membrane (eardrum)
12. round window
13. auditory nerve
14. vestibule
15. oval window

EYE

1. optic nerve
2. vitreous humour
3. sclera
4. choroid
5. retina
6. conjunctiva
7. aqueous humour
8. lens
9. iris
10. cornea
11. ciliary body
12. suspensory ligament
13. fovea
14. muscle
15. ciliary muscle
16. pupil

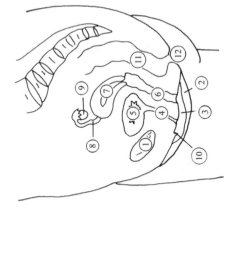

UROGENITAL SYSTEM (male)

1. penis
2. scrotum
3. testis
4. epididymis
5. ductus deferens
6. seminal vesicle
7. ejaculatory duct
8. prostate gland

9. glans
10. urinary bladder
11. urethra
12. rectum
13. anus
14. corpus cavernosum
15. corpus spongiosum
16. pubic bone

UROGENITAL SYSTEM (female)

1. pubic bone
2. labia majora
3. labia minora
4. urethra
5. urinary bladder
6. vagina

7. uterus
8. fallopian tube
9. ovary
10. clitoris
11. rectum
12. anus

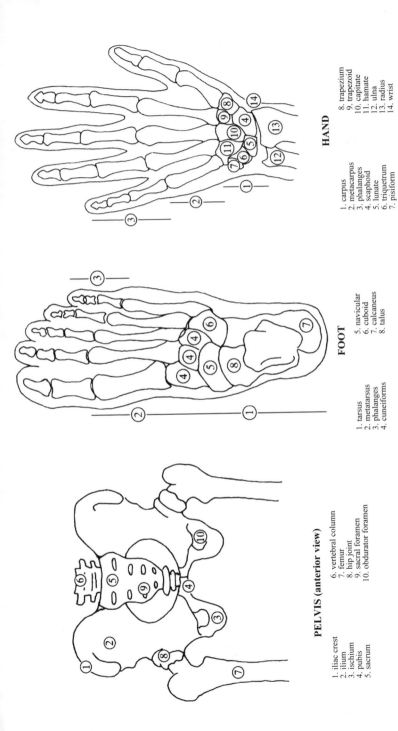

PELVIS (anterior view)

1. iliac crest
2. ilium
3. ischium
4. pubis
5. sacrum
6. vertebral column
7. femur
8. hip joint
9. sacral foramen
10. obdurator foramen

FOOT

1. tarsus
2. metatarsus
3. phalanges
4. cuneiforms
5. navicular
6. cuboid
7. calcaneus
8. talus

HAND

1. carpus
2. metacarpus
3. phalanges
4. scaphoid
5. lunate
6. triquetrum
7. pisiform
8. trapezium
9. trapezoid
10. capitate
11. hamate
12. ulna
13. radius
14. wrist

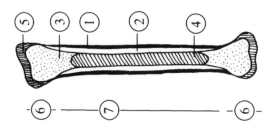

BONE STRUCTURE

1. periosteum
2. compact bone
3. cancellous (spongy) bone (red marrow)
4. medullary cavity (yellow marrow)
5. articular cartilage
6. epiphysis
7. diaphysis

TEETH

1. incisors
2. canines
3. premolars
4. molars

CARTILAGINOUS JOINT

1. intervertebral disc
2. vertebra
3. hyaline cartridge

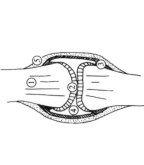

SYNOVIAL JOINT

1. bone
2. articular membrane
3. synovial membrane
4. synovial cavity and fluid
5. joint capsule